Foreign & Commonwealth Office

The Diplomatic Service List 2006

FORTY-FIRST EDITION

London: TSO

Published by The Stationery Office and available from:

Online
www.tsoshop.co.uk

Mail, Telephone, Fax & E-mail
TSO
PO Box 29. Norwich NR3 IGN
Telephone orders/General enquiries: 0870 600 5522
Fax orders: 0870 600 5533
E-mail: book.orders@tso.co.uk
Textphone: 0870 240 3701

TSO Shops
123 Kingsway. London WC2B 6PQ
020 7242 6393 Fax 020 7242 6394
68 69 Bull Street, Birmingham B4 6AD
0121 236 9696 Fax 0121 236 9699
9-21 Princess Street, Manchester M60 8AS
0161834 7201 Fax 0161 833 0634
16 Arthur Street Belfast BT 1 4GD
028 9023 8451 Fax 028 9023 5401
18 19 High Street, Cardiff CF1 2BZ
029 2039 5548 Fax 029 2038 4347
71 Lothian Road, Edinburgh EH3 9AZ
0870 606 5566 Fax 0870 606 5588

TSO Accredited Agents
(see Yellow Pages)

and through good booksellers

Published with the permission of the Foreign and Commonwealth Office on behalf of the Controller of Her Majesty's Stationery Office.

ISBN 0 11 591784 5

Preface

Her Majesty's Diplomatic Service provides the staffs of British Diplomatic and Consular posts overseas in Commonwealth and Foreign countries, as well as in the Foreign & Commonwealth Office in London.

The organisation of the Service and the careers of its members are described in this List, which will be published each year. It is based on information available in August 2005 but includes details of some later changes.

The Diplomatic Service was established on 1 January, 1965, by the merger of the former Foreign, Commonwealth and Trade Commissioner Services. Subsequently, it incorporated the staffs of the Colonial Office in London, which merged with the Commonwealth Relations Office on 1 August, 1966, to form the Commonwealth Office.

The Foreign Office and Commonwealth Office continued as separate Departments of State responsible to separate Secretaries of State until 17 October, 1968. On that day they combined to form the Foreign and Commonwealth Office responsible to one Secretary of State. The Permanent Under-Secretary of the Office and the Head of the Diplomatic Service is Sir Michael Jay, KCMG.

Representatives of Commonwealth countries and foreign states serving in London are shown in a separate publication, the London Diplomatic List, published by The Stationery Office every six months.

Every effort has been made to ensure that the information given in this edition is correct at the time of going to press. Human Resources Directorate will continue to provide the Editor with information on staff movements for Part IV. However, it will be the officer's responsibility to provide information about changes in personal family details such as new marriages, births, dissolved marriages etc. Please refer to re-issued circular 127-03 dated 25th June 2003 for further details.

New Diplomatic Service staff who wish to have an entry will need to complete a DSL entry form, which can be found on FCONet (under Doing my Job > Forms > Miscellaneous).

Amendments and new entries for the 2007 edition of the Diplomatic Service List should be sent to the Editor to arrive no later than Friday, 25th August 2006:-

Lisa T Gamandi (Editor)
Foreign and Commonwealth Office
Publications Section, Information Strategy Team,
IT Strategy Unit,
Room WH. MZ. 23,
King Charles St,
LONDON SW1A 2AH.

November 2005.

Table of Contents

Part I

Page

HOME DEPARTMENTS

List of Ministers, Senior Officers and Home Departments in the Foreign and Commonwealth Office. 4
Senior Officers in the Foreign and Commonwealth Office 4
Departments in the Foreign and Commonwealth Office 5

Part II

BRITISH REPRESENTATION OVERSEAS (AUTUMN 2005)

British Representatives in the Commonwealth, Foreign Countries and Ireland 17
British Missions and Delegations 113
Governors and Commanders-in-Chief of the Overseas Territories 118
Small Posts and Annex 121
Index of place names 123

Part III

CHRONOLOGICAL LISTS FROM 1985 of SECRETARIES OF STATE, MINISTERS OF STATE, PERMANENT UNDER-SECRETARIES, AMBASSADORS, HIGH COMMISSIONERS, PERMANENT REPRESENTATIVES TO INTERNATIONAL ORGANISATIONS AND GOVERNORS AND COMMANDERS-IN-CHIEF OF OVERSEAS TERRITORIES

Secretaries of State for Foreign and Commonwealth Affairs 129
Ministers of State for Foreign and Commonwealth Affairs 129
Permanent Under-Secretaries of State for Foreign and Commonwealth Affairs and Heads of HM Diplomatic Service 129
List of British Representatives in Commonwealth Countries, to foreign states and in Ireland 130
British Representatives to international organisations 147
Governors and Commanders-in-Chief of Overseas Territories 148
Annex 149

Part IV

BIOGRAPHICAL NOTES AND LISTS OF STAFF

Biographical Notes of SMS to Band A2 of the Diplomatic Service, officers of the Secretarial Branch, officers of the Security Officer Branch and officers of the Executive Assistant Branch 153

Part I

Home Departments

List of Ministers, Senior Officers and Home Departments in the Foreign Commonwealth Office

Part I: Home Departments

ACCOMMODATION

Ministers, Senior Officers and most geographical departments are accommodated in the Main Building, Downing Street, London SW1. Departments are also accommodated in other buildings.

Foreign and Commonwealth Office, Downing Street (West) SW1A 2AL	020 7008 1500
Foreign and Commonwealth Office, Downing Street (East) SW1A 2AL	020 7008 1500
Foreign and Commonwealth Office, Whitehall SW1A 2AP	020 7008 1500
Foreign and Commonwealth Office, King Charles St SW1A 2AH	020 7008 1500
Old Admiralty Building, Whitehall, London SW1A 2PA	020 7008 1500
UKVisas, 89 Albert Embankment, London SE1 7TP	020 7008 8438
Vauxhall Cross, 85 Albert Embankment, London SE1 7TP	020 7008 4440
Apollo House, 36 Wellesley Road, Croydon CR0 9YA	020 8686 5622
Hanslope Park, Hanslope, Milton Keynes MK19 7BH	01908 510444
UK Trade & Investment, Kingsgate House, 66-74 Victoria Street. London SW1E 6SW	020 7215 5000

TELEPHONE ENQUIRIES
If the number, department or building is not known, callers should ring 020 7270 3000 and ask to be connected to the Central Enquiry point.

TELEGRAPHIC ADDRESS
PRODROME LONDON

TELEX 297711 (a/b PRODROME G)

Internet World Wide Web Address: www.fco.gov.uk

The Foreign and Commonwealth Office provides, through its staff in the UK and through its diplomatic missions abroad, the means of communication between the British Government and other governments and international governmental organisations on all matters falling within the field of international relations. It is responsible for alerting the British Government to the implications of developments overseas; for promoting British interests overseas; for protecting British citizens abroad; for explaining British policies to, and cultivating relationships with, governments overseas; for the discharge of British responsibilities to the overseas territories; for entry clearance (through UK Visas, with the Home Office); and for promoting British business overseas (jointly with the Department of Trade and Industry through UK Trade and Investment).

MINISTERS AND THEIR STAFFS

Secretary of State for Foreign & Commonwealth Affairs
The Rt Hon Jack Straw MP
Parliamentary Private Secretary: Paddy Tipping MP
Principal Private Secretary: Peter Hayes
Telephone: 020 7008 2059
GTN: 7008 2059
Private Secretaries: Caroline Wilson, Irfan Siddiq
Telephone: 020 7008 2069
Telephone: 020 7008 2070
GTN: 7008 2069
GTN: 7008 2070
Enquiries: 020 7008 2079 *(Diary Enquiries)*
GTN: 7008 2079
Enquiries: 020 7008 2057 *(Clerical Enquiries)*
GTN: 7008 2057
Special Advisers:
Sir Brian Donnelly KBE, CMG, Mark Davies
Telephone: 020 7008 2112
Telephone: 020 7008 2117
GTN: 7008 2112
GTN: 7008 2117

Minister of State for Europe
Douglas Alexander MP
Parliamentary Private Secretary: Bob Blizzard MP
Private Secretary: Sophie Honey
Assistant Private Secretaries: Sara Hunt, Stuart Templar
Telephone: 020 7008 2128
Telephone: 020 7008 8032
GTN: 7008 2128
GTN: 7008 8032

Minister of State for the Middle East
Dr Kim Howells MP
Parliamentary Private Secretary:
John Robertson MP
Private Secretary: Emma Wade
Telephone: 020 7008 2090
GTN: 7008 2090
Assistant Private Secretaries: Stephanie Al-Qaq, Sarah Fellous
Telephone: 020 7008 2091
Telephone: 020 7008 2092
GTN: 020 7008 2091
GTN: 020 7008 2092

Minister of State for Trade, Investment and Foreign Affairs
Ian Pearson MP
Parliamentary Private Secretary: Siôn Simon MP
Private Secretary: Nick Leake
Telephone: 020 7008 2129
GTN: 7008 2129
Assistant Private Secretaries: Darren James, Derek Turner
Telephone: 020 7008 3371
Telephone: 020 7008 1889
GTN: 7008 3371
GTN: 7008 1889
Diary Manager: Nicola Powell
Telephone: 020 7008 2127
GTN: 7008 2127

Parliamentary Under-Secretary of State
Lord Triesman
Private Secretary: Bharat Joshi
Telephone: 020 7008 2173
GTN: 7008 2173
Assistant Private Secretaries: Caron Röhsler, Nicky Wilbrey, Richard Cowin
Telephone: 020 7008 2172
Telephone: 020 7008 3363
Telephone: 020 7008 2520
GTN: 7008 2172
GTN: 7008 3363
GTN: 7008 2520
Diary Co-ordinator/Office Manager: Carmen Gray
Telephone: 020 7008 3983
GTN: 7008 3983
Parliamentary Clerk: Gery Juleff
Telephone: 020 7008 4005
GTN: 7008 4005

SENIOR OFFICERS AND THEIR STAFFS

Permanent Under-Secretary of State and Head of the Diplomatic Service
Sir Michael Jay KCMG
Private Secretary: Matthew Lodge
Assistant Private Secretaries: Nicola Friel, Andrea McGlone, James Dunlop (G8PT Implant)
Diary Secretaries/PA: Carla Williams, Claire Ledward, Martin Naughton
Telephone: 020 7008 2145
Telephone: 020 7008 2143
Telephone: 020 7008 3232
GTN: 7008 2145
GTN: 7008 2143
GTN: 7008 3232

Group Chief Executive UK Trade and Investment
Sir Stephen Brown KCVO
Telephone: 020 7215 4643
GTN: 7215 4643
Private Secretary:
Simon Cooper
Telephone: 020 7215 4300
GTN: 215 4300

DIRECTORS GENERAL
Dickie Stagg CMG *(Corporate Affairs)*
John Sawers CMG *(Political)*
Nicola Brewer CMG *(EU Policy)*
David Richmond CMG *(Defence/Intelligence)*
Martin Donnelly CMG *(Economic)*
Sir Michael Wood KCMG *(Legal Adviser)*

DIRECTORS
James Bevan *(Africa)*
Robert Culshaw MVO *(Americas/Overseas Territories)*
Edward Oakden *(Defence and Strategic Threats)*
Stephen Pattison *(International Security)*
Dominick Chilcott *(Mediterranean Europe, Bilateral, Resources)*
Paul Sizeland *(Consular Services)*
Robin Barnett *(UK Visas)*
Denise Holt *(Migration)*

Stephen Sage *(Chief Executive, FCO Services)*
Philippa Drew *(Global Issues)*
Peter Gooderham *(Middle East/North Africa)*
Dominic Asquith CMG *(Iraq)*
Anne Pringle CMG *(Strategy and Information)*
John Williams *(Communications)*
Sebastian Wood *(Asia Pacific)*
Tom Phillips CMG *(South Asia and Afghanistan)*
Darren Warren *(Human Resources)*
Ric Todd *(Finance)*
Creon Butler *(Chief Economist) (Economic Policy)*

SPECIAL REPRESENTATIVES

Tom Phillips CMG *(UK Special Representative for Afghanistan)*
Sir Brian Fall KCMG *(UK Special Representative for South Caucasus)*
Alastair McPhail OBE *(UK Special Representative for Sudan)*

DEPARTMENTS IN THE FOREIGN AND COMMONWEALTH OFFICE

Afghanistan Group

The Mission of the Afghanistan Group is to help Afghanistan achieve stability, security and prosperity, to the benefit of the Afghan people, the United Kingdom and the world community.

Whitehall,
LONDON SW1A 2AH
Enquiries: 020 7008 2866
Enquiries: 020 7008 2995
GTN: 7008 2866
GTN: 7008 2995
UK Special Representative: Tom Phillips CMG
Head of Group: Richard Codrington
Deputy Head of Group: David Ellis

Africa Department (Equatorial)

Political and economic relations with Benin, Burkina Faso, Cameroon, Cape Verde, Central African Republic, Chad, Djibouti, Equatorial Guinea, Eritrea, Ethiopia, Gabon, Ghana, Guinea, Guinea Bissau, Ivory Coast (Cote d'Ivoire), Kenya, Liberia, Mali, Niger, Nigeria, Senegal, Sierra Leone, Somalia, Tanzania, The Gambia, Togo, Uganda, Economic Community of West African States (ECOWAS) and East African Community (EAC), Africa Union, Inter-Governmental Authority for Development (IGAD).

King Charles Street,
LONDON SW1A 2AH
Enquiries: 020 7008 2903
GTN: 7008 2903
Superintending Director: James Bevan
Head of Department: Vacant
Deputy Head of Department: Patrick Moody

Africa Department (Southern)

Political and economic relations with Angola, Botswana, Burundi, The Comoros, Congo, Democratic Republic of Congo, Lesotho, Madagascar, Malawi, Mauritius, Mozambique, Namibia, Rwanda, Sao Tomé and Principe, Seychelles, South Africa, Swaziland, Zambia and Zimbabwe; Southern African Development Community (SADC).

King Charles Street,
LONDON SW1A 2AH
Enquiries: 020 7008 2552
GTN: 7008 2552
Superintending Director: James Bevan
Head of Department: Andrew Lloyd
Deputy Head of Department: Nicholas Cannon

Association of South East Asian Nations and Oceania Group

Political and economic relations with Australia, Brunei, Burma, Cambodia, East Timor, Indonesia, Laos, Malaysia, New Zealand, Philippines, Singapore, South Pacific, Thailand and Vietnam; ASEAN, ASEM, ARF and COASI.

FCO,
Whitehall,
LONDON SW1A 2AH
Enquiries: 020 7008 2600
GTN: 7008 2600
Superintending Director: Sebastian Wood
Head of Group: Paul Speller
Deputy Head of Group: Valerie Brownridge

Climate Change and Energy Group

Delivery of HMG international Energy and Climate Change objectives; International energy policy and collaboration; multilateral and bilateral producer-consumer dialogue; promotion of international action and policies and measures to combat Climate Change; nuclear power (including reprocessing and shipments); physical security of energy infrastructure; energy sector investment and governance; oil, gas, coal, renewables, and new energy technologies; energy efficiency, sustainable energy and low carbon energy solutions; carbon sequestration; electricity; pipelines and interconnectors.

King Charles Street,
LONDON SW1A 2AH
Enquiries: 020 7008 2621
GTN: 7008 2621
Superintending Director: Philippa Drew
Head of Group: Valerie Caton
Deputy Head of Group: Simon Banks

Consular Directorate

Consular Directorate comprises five Groups: Assistance; Crisis; Passports and Documentary Services; Policy, Communications and Training; Resources. Correspondence and enquiries should be directed to the relevant Group, and copies to the Director.
Director of Consular Services: Paul Sizeland

CONSULAR ASSISTANCE GROUP:
Help given to individual cases of Britons in distress overseas; policy related to the human rights of Britons in distress overseas.

Old Admiralty Building,
LONDON SW1A 2PA
Enquiries: 020 7008 0223

GTN: 7008 0223
Head of Group: Janet Douglas

CONSULAR CRISIS GROUP:
Provides consular assistance to British nationals affected by major incidents overseas. Publishes FCO Travel Advice (www.fco.gov.uk/travel) for British nationals travelling overseas. Undertakes consular emergency and contingency planning, including management of Rapid Deployment Teams.

Old Admiralty Building,
LONDON SW1A 2PA
Enquiries: 020 7008 0225
GTN: 7008 0225
Head of Group: David Fitton

PASSPORTS & DOCUMENTARY SERVICES GROUP:
FCO passport policy and co-ordination of Posts' passport operations; birth and death registration and marriages abroad; advise on nationality and passport matters; overseas document searches. Civil matters; coroners requests; notarial acts; claims for compensation from other Governments in respect of loss, injury or damage suffered overseas by individuals or companies; legalisation of documents in the UK and overseas. Modernisation of Consular work using latest IT advancements; projects include GenIE secure digital passports and biometric passports.

Downing Street (East),
King Charles Street,
LONDON SW1A 2AH
Enquiries: 020 7008 1967
GTN: 7008 1967
Head of Group: David Clegg MVO

POLICY, COMMUNICATIONS AND TRAINING GROUP:
Consular cross cutting policy (customer satisfaction), the Consular Strategy 2004-07, information handling, including access requests under the Data Protection Act and Freedom of Information Act. Manages the "Know Before You Go" travel safety campaign (www.fco.gov.uk/travel) and consular publications. Responsible for training within the global consular operation.

Old Admiralty Building,
LONDON SW1A 2PA
Enquiries: 020 7008 0083
GTN: 7008 0083
Head of Group: Nic Hailey

CONSULAR RESOURCES GROUP:
Resource management of worldwide consular operations. Funding, planning, deployment and monitoring of staff and resources to achieve best value. Forecasting and monitoring of consular income, costs and expenditure. Measurement of performance against Public Service Agreement targets. Information management and staffing reviews

Old Admiralty Building,
LONDON SW1A 2PA
Enquiries: 020 7008 0078
GTN: 7008 0078
Head of Group: David Popplestone

Counter-Proliferation Department
Nuclear non-proliferation issues, including the Nuclear Non-Proliferation Treaty, CTBT, IAEA and Nuclear Suppliers Group. Missile proliferation issues and MTCR. Chemical and Biological Weapons Conventions, Australia Group and CW/BW proliferation issues. Policy on conventional arms sales, MANPADS and exports of Dual-Use Goods. UN Arms Register. Wassenaar Arrangement. Arms Control and Disarmament Research Unit.

King Charles Street,
LONDON SW1A 2AH
Enquiries: 020 7008 2261
Enquiries: 020 7008 2751
GTN: 7008 2261
GTN: 7008 2751
Superintending Director: Edward Oakden
Head of Department: David Landsman
Deputy Heads of Department: Sarah Price, Trevor Moore

Counter Terrorism Policy Department
Counter-terrorism policy, bilaterally and in international fora. Crisis management.

King Charles Street,
LONDON SW1A 2AH
Enquiries: 020 7008 2583
GTN: 7008 2583
Superintending Director: Edward Oakden
Head of Department: Philip Parham
Deputy Heads of Department: Martyn Warr OBE, Carl Newns

Diplomatic Service Families Association
Works with the Administration for "best practice family-friendly policy". Informs, assists and campaigns on behalf of all UK diplomatic families, spouses and partners, at home and abroad, on matters including: career development, child education, special needs, disabilities, and welfare and social issues.

FCO,
Old Admiralty Building,
LONDON SW1A 2PA
Enquiries: 020 7008 0286
GTN: 7008 0286
E-mail: dsfa.enquiries@fco.gov.uk
DSFA Chairwoman: Tina Attwood
Vice-Chairwoman: Jane Chilcott
Education Adviser: Anne-Marie Cole
Employment/Training Adviser:
Geraldine McKendrick
Executive Secretary: Alex Hennessy

Drugs and International Crime Department
International aspects of UK activity against drug trafficking, human trafficking, money laundering and other international organised crime.

King Charles Street,
LONDON SW1A 2AH
Enquiries: 020 7008 1833
Enquiries: 020 7008 1808
GTN: 7008 1833
GTN: 7008 1808
Superintending Director: Edward Oakden
Head of Department: Lesley Pallett
Deputy Head of Department: Rowan Laxton

Eastern Adriatic Department
Relations with Croatia, Serbia and Montenegro (including Kosovo), Bosnia and Herzegovina, Macedonia and Albania.

Downing Street West,
LONDON SW1A 2AL
Enquiries: 020 7008 2756
Enquiries: 020 7008 2372
Enquiries: 020 7008 3433
Enquiries: 020 7008 3459
GTN: 7008 2756
GTN: 7008 2372
GTN: 7008 3433
GTN: 7008 3459
Superintending Director: Dominick Chilcott
Head of Department: Karen Pierce CVO
Deputy Head of Department: Angus Lapsley

Eastern Department
Policy on Russia, the Caucasus (Armenia, Azerbaijan, Georgia), Central Asia (Kazakhstan, Kyrgyzstan, Tajikistan, Turkmenistan, Uzbekistan) and Caspian energy issues.

Downing Street West,
LONDON SW1A 2AL
Enquiries: 020 7008 2427
Enquiries: 020 7008 2423
Enquiries: 020 7008 3831
GTN: 7008 2427
GTN: 7008 2423
GTN: 7008 3831
Director General: John Sawer
Head of Department: Simon Smith
Deputy Head of Department: Andrew Page

Economic Policy Directorate
Economic Policy Directorate's principal task is the pursuit of FCO Strategic Priority No 5: Promotion of UK economic interests in an open and expanding global economy. The Directorate's work also makes a strong contribution in support of other Strategic Priorities, particularly No 6 (Sustainable Development).

FCO,
Whitehall,
LONDON SW1A 2AH
Enquiries: 020 7008 2732
GTN: 7008 2732
Director General: Martin Donnelly CMG
Director and Chief Economist: Creon Butler

GLOBAL ECONOMY GROUP:
The performance of the UK economy increasingly relies on a stable and prosperous international economic environment. The Global Economy Group (GEG), and its network of economic officers, will support this through promoting the economic development and stability of other nations, and engaging with key multilateral institutions. There are three main areas where GEG will support Strategic Priority 5: Working with multilateral institutions to promote global stability and prosperity; Promotion of UK economic interests, Promotion of good economic governance and reform in key countries (excluding EU) through our network of economic officers overseas.
Head of Group: Vacant

GLOBAL BUSINESS GROUP:
Against a background of rapid globalisation, partnership with business is crucial to meeting foreign policy goals. Global Business Group is the FCO's link department to business, using its unique worldwide network to build favourable conditions for sustainable global prosperity. Its main goals are to protect the UK's overseas investments; to secure international maritime and aviation arrangements that benefit the global economy; to encourage responsible behaviour by business overseas, especially in the extractives sector; to combat bribery and corruption; and to certify transactions of the UK diamond trade.
Head of Group: David Roberts

G8 PRESIDENCY TEAM:
This team led within Whitehall on the UK Presidency of the G8 in 2005 and co-ordinated the UK's participation in the G8 processes.
Head of Team: Charles Hay

SCIENCE AND INNOVATION GROUP:
Co-ordination of global Science and Technology Network and advising of issues within the Foreign and Commonwealth Office.
Head of Group: Fiona Clouder Richards

Estate Strategy Unit
Formulation and implementation of strategy for the FCO's estate in the UK and overseas.

Apollo House,
36 Wellesley Road,
CROYDON CR0 9YA
Enquiries: 020 8253 6380
Enquiries: 020 8253 6353
GTN: 3822 6380
GTN: 3822 6353
Director General: Dickie Stagg CMG
Head of Unit: Geoff Gillham
Deputy Head of Unit: Jeremy Neate

European Union (External) Assistant Directorate
Comprises of three teams: EU Northern Europe and International Team; Common Foreign and Security Policy Team; EU Enlargement and Wider Europe Team.

Downing Street East,
LONDON SW1A 2AL
Enquiries: 020 7008 3812

Enquiries: 020 7008 4266
GTN: 7008 3812
GTN: 7008 4266
Director General: Nicola Brewer CMG
Assistant Director EU-External:
Tim Barrow LVO MBE

COMMON FOREIGN AND SECURITY POLICY TEAM:
Co-ordination of foreign policy among EU member states and implementation of Common Foreign and Security Policy.

Downing Street (East),
LONDON SW1A 2AH
Enquiries: 020 7008 2807
GTN: 7008 2807
Team Leader: Dominic Schroeder

EU NORTHERN EUROPE AND INTERNATIONAL TEAM:
Relations between the European Union, Accession States, Third countries, Ukraine, Belarus and Moldova; international trade and development matters.

Downing Street (East),
LONDON SW1A 2AH
Enquiries: 020 7008 3018
GTN: 7008 3018
Team Leader: Andrew Key

ENLARGEMENT TEAM:
Relations between the European Union and third countries; international trade and development matters; enlargement of the Union.

Downing Street (East),
LONDON SW1A 2AH
Enquiries: 020 7008 3018
GTN: 7008 3018
Team Leader: Martin Reynolds

European Union (Internal)
The internal economic and institutional policies of the European Union. Comprised of four teams: Economic/Ireland/Central Europe Team; JHA/Global Migration Team; Future of Europe Team and Western Mediterranean Team.

Downing Street (East)/(West),
LONDON SW1A 2AH
Enquiries: 020 7008 3388
GTN: 7008 3388
Director General: Nicola Brewer CMG
Assistant Director: David Frost
Team Leaders: Simon Manley *(Economic/Ireland/Central Europe Team) (including Hungary, Slovenia, Czech Republic, Ireland, Poland and Slovakia),*
Mara Goldstein/Georgina Simpson *(JHA/Global Migration Team) (including Austria and Germany)*, James Bryce *(Future of Europe Team)*, Richard Crowder *(Western Mediterranean Team) (Italy, Holy See, Malta, Spain, Portugal, Andorra and Gibraltar)*.

Far East Group
Relations between the United Kingdom and China, including the Hong Kong Special Administrative Region, Japan, Democratic People's Republic of Korea, Republic of Korea and Mongolia.

FCO,
Whitehall,
LONDON SW1A 2AP
Enquiries: 020 7008 3074
GTN: 7008 3074
Superintending Director: Sebastian Wood
Head of Group: Denis Keefe
Deputy Heads of Group: Geoff Cole, Julia Sutherland

Financial Planning and Performance Department
Resource planning, budgeting and allocation, expenditure monitoring and performance measurement, fees and charging.

Old Admiralty Building,
LONDON SW1A 2PA
Enquiries: 020 7008 1085
GTN: 7008 1085
Superintending Director: Ric Todd
Head of Department: Tristan Price
Deputy Heads of Department: Matthew Owen, Noel Langley, James Tansley

FCO Association
Old Admiralty Building,
LONDON SW1A 2PA
Enquiries: 020 7008 0967
GTN: 7008 0967
Chairman: Roger Westbrook CMG
Hon Secretary: Maureen Howley MBE

FCO Services
FCO Services provides the main support services for the FCO at home and overseas. FCO Services is based at the locations below.

King Charles Street,
LONDON SW1A 2AH

Old Admiralty Building,
Whitehall,
LONDON SW1A 2PA

Apollo House,
Wellesley Road,
CROYDON CR0 9YA

Hanslope Park,
Hanslope,
MILTON KEYNES MK19 7BH

Enquiries: 01908 852222 (FCO Services Support Centre)
GTN: 3905 2222
Chief Executive: Stephen Sage

CLIENT SERVICES:
The first point of contact for all customers. Accounts managers, sales and marketing, strategic planning.

Enquiries: 01908 852222 (FCO Services Support Centre)
GTN: 3905 2222
Group Director: Vacant

Estates and Security Service Delivery Group:
Property and estate management services for the diplomatic estate at home and overseas. Technical and protective security measures.
Enquiries: 01908 852222 (FCO Services Support Centre)
GTN: 3905 2222
Group Director: Nigel Morris

ICT Service Delivery Group:
Installation and support of the FCO's ICT infrastructure.

Enquiries: 01908 852222 (FCO Services Support Centre)
GTN: 3905 2222
Group Directors: Patrick Cullen, Michael Blake

People and Best Practice Service Delivery Group:
Provides the following services: IT and technical training; language training; language testing and examinations; security clearance.

Enquiries: 01908 852222 (FCO Services Support Centre)
GTN: 3905 2222
Group Director: Sarah Squire

Positive Image UK Service Delivery Group:
Organisation of conference visits, production of publications and films, printing services and management of fine rooms.

Enquiries: 01908 852222 (FCO Services Support Centre)
GTN: 3905 2222
Group Director: Sarah Squire

Supply Chain Service Delivery Group:
Services cover purchasing, supply and delivery of stationery, office equipment and furniture at home and overseas, Also covers worldwide delivery of mail and personnel travel arrangements.

Enquiries: 01908 852222 (FCO Services Support Centre)
GTN: 3905 2222
Group Director: Rod Peters

Finance Group:
Financial management.

Enquiries: 01908 852222 (FCO Services Support Centre)
GTN: 3905 2222
Group Director: Kerry Simmonds

Human Resources Group:
Personnel management and developmental training.

Enquiries: 01908 852222 (FCO Services Support Centre)
GTN: 3905 2222
Group Director: Elaine Kennedy

Grant-Aided Public Bodies and Scholarships Team, Public Diplomacy Group
Administration of the grants-in-aid to, and policy on, the BBC World Service and the British Council. Responsibility for the Wilton Park Executive Agency. Bilateral and multilateral cultural relations, other than EU; FCO Chevening and Commonwealth scholarship programmes for overseas students. Aspects of international education and international sport.

King Charles Street,
LONDON SW1A 2AH
Enquiries: 020 7008 1618
GTN: 7008 1618
Superintending Director: Anne Pringle CMG
Assistant Director: Timothy Livesey
Head of Team: Lyn Bennett

Human Resources Directorate
The purpose of the Human Resource Directorate is to recruit, develop, deploy, motivate and support FCO staff to meet the FCO's objectives.

Old Admiralty Building,
LONDON SW1A 2PA
Superintending Director and Head of HR Directorate: David Warren

HR Direct:
A one stop shop service for HR enquiries from staff throughout the FCO.
Assistant Director (Operations): Greg Dorey

Health and Welfare Policy Team:
Health, safety and welfare of staff at home and overseas.
Assistant Director: Andrew George

Employment Policy Team:
Human resource policy and management questions including implementation of employment legislation and relations with the trade union side, organisation and structure of the FCO's personnel, conduct and discipline, diplomatic status, diversity and equal opportunities.
Assistant Director: Carole Sweeney

Pay and Benefits Policy Team:
Pay, pensions, allowances, conditions of service.
Head of Team: David Powell

Professional Development:
All aspects of staff performance management and development, including training, learning and development, mentoring, core competences, staff appraisal and assessment, promotion competitions and Assessment and Development Centres.
Assistant Director: Gerry Reffo

Workforce Planning Team:
Human resource planning, personnel statistics; individual personnel movements, appointments, probation, promotions, sick absence, recruitment; transfers, secondments and loans to and from other services.
Assistant Director: Simon Pease

Human Rights Democracy and Governance Group
The FCO point of advice on human rights policy questions in all international organisations, including obligations and commitments at the UN, Council of Europe, OSCE and Commonwealth. Responsible, in co-operation with geographical departments, for: developing and co-ordinating HMG's human rights policy and ensuring consistency of application in the UK's overseas bilateral relations; liaison with Department for International Development on human rights aspects of bilateral and multilateral development policy; liaison with Whitehall departments, ensuring that the development of domestic policy takes account of HMG's international human rights obligations and objectives; supervision of UK and Overseas Territory periodic reports under international treaty obligations; FCO point of contact and liaison for NGOs and other bodies on general (i.e. non-country specific) human rights matters. Manages FCO's Human Rights Project Fund and produces the Human Rights Annual Report.

King Charles Street,
LONDON SW1A 2AH
Enquiries: 020 7008 3616
GTN: 7008 3616
Superintending Director: Philippa Drew
Head of Group: Alexandra Hall Hall
Deputy Head of Group: Charles Lonsdale

Information Management Group
Information Rights: Freedom of Information, Data Protection, EIRs; Records Management: registry, records custody, e-archiving, review and release; Treaty information and publication; Historical advice; publication of Documents on British Policy Overseas; Library and Information Services.

Old Admiralty Building,
LONDON SW1A 2PA
Enquiries: 020 7008 1128
GTN: 7008 1128
Superintending Director: Anne Pringle CMG
Head of Group: Heather Yasamee
Information Rights Team: Richard Barr
Records Management: Penny Prior
Treaty: Paul Barnett
Historians: Patrick Salmon

Internal Audit Department
King Charles Street,
LONDON SW1A 2AH
Enquiries: 020 7008 8010
GTN: 7008 8010
Superintending Director: Ric Todd
Head of Department: Jon Hews
Deputy Head of Department: Trevor Jarvis
Head of Financial Compliance Unit: Jon Heath
Audit Manager: Richard Clark

International Organisations Department
Policy towards the United Nations, particularly Security Council, General Assembly; Counter-Terrorism Committee; United Nations peace-keeping operations; International Policing Unit; sanctions; conflict prevention; International humanitarian law (including Geneva Conventions); Red Cross/Crescent issues; War Crimes; International Criminal Tribunals for former Yugoslavia and Rwanda; International Criminal Court; humanitarian mine action; migration/refugee policy; UN finance, development and reform; general aspects of policy towards the UN specialised agencies.

King Charles Street,
LONDON SW1A 2AH
Enquiries: 020 7008 2558
Enquiries: 020 7008 2487
GTN: 7008 2558
GTN: 7008 2487
Superintending Director: Stephen Pattison
Head of Department: Tim Morris
Head of Conflict Issues Group: Joan Link
Deputy Head of Department: Martyn Roper

IT Strategy Unit
Responsible for ICT investment policy and budgets and co-ordination with central government Departments on ICT issues.

Old Admiralty Building,
Whitehall,
LONDON SW1A 2PA
Enquiries: 020 7008 0524
GTN: 7008 0524
Director General: Dickie Stagg CMG
Head of Unit: Nick Westcott
Deputy Head of Unit: Nick Clouting
Head of Information Strategy: Carryl Allardice

Latin America and Caribbean Department
Relations with all the independent countries of Latin America and the Caribbean, and with the OAS, Caricom and other regional organisations.

FCO,
King Charles Street,
LONDON SW1A 2AH
Enquiries: 020 7008 2481
GTN: 7008 2481
E-mail: latin.america.caribbean@fco.gov.uk
Superintending Director: Robert Culshaw MVO
Head of Department: Steve Williams
Deputy Head of Department: Andrew Allen

Legal Advisers
Advice on international, EU and UK law and practice in connection with HMG's foreign relations, including treaties and international litigation, and with the work of the FCO generally. Legal advice concerning the governance of UK overseas territories.

King Charles Street,
LONDON SW1A 2AH
Enquiries: 020 7008 3080
Enquiries: 020 7008 3081
GTN: 7008 3080
GTN:7008 3081
Legal Adviser: Sir Michael Wood KCMG
Deputy Legal Advisers: Ian Hendry CMG, Christopher Whomersley, John Grainger CMG

Middle East and North Africa Directorate
Comprises four groups: Engaging with the Islamic World Group; Arab/Israel and North Africa Group; Arabian Peninsula Group; Iran Coordination Group.

King Charles Street,
LONDON SW1A 2AH
Enquiries: 020 7008 2982
GTN: 7008 2982
Director General: John Sawers CMG
Director: Peter Gooderham
Deputy Director: Mark Sedwill

ENGAGING WITH THE ISLAMIC WORLD GROUP:
The group is working to build a better understanding of Western and Muslim government and society motivations and how they impact on each other, in order to strengthen common values in the shared pursuit of a more just world. It promotes a better and closer relationship with British Muslims on foreign policy and works in support of confidence-building measures towards the negotiated settlement of disputes. The group also works to promote regionally led political, economic and social reform in the Arab world.

King Charles Street,
LONDON SW1A 2AH
Enquiries: 020 7008 2982
GTN: 7008 2982
Head of Group: Frances Guy

ARAB/ISRAEL AND NORTH AFRICA GROUP:
Responsible for relations with the countries of North Africa (Morocco, Algeria, Tunisia, Libya, Mauritania) and the Near East (Syria, Lebanon, Israel, Jordan, the Palestinian Authority, as well as Egypt); also responsible for UK policy on and input to resolution of Arab/Israeli issues.

King Charles Street,
LONDON SW1A 2AH
Enquiries: 020 7008 2982
GTN: 7008 2982
Head of Group: Nick Banner

ARABIAN PENINSULA GROUP:
Responsible for policy on and relations with Bahrain, Kuwait, Oman, Qatar, Saudi Arabia, United Arab Emirates and Yemen.

King Charles Street,
LONDON SW1A 2AH
Enquiries: 020 7008 2982
GTN: 7008 2982
Head of Group: Jolyon Welsh

IRAN COORDINATION GROUP:
Responsible for policy on and relations with Iran.

King Charles Street,
LONDON SW1A 2AH
Enquiries: 020 7008 2997
GTN: 7008 2997
Iran Coordinator: Neil Crompton

North America Team
Relations with Canada and the United States (including the US Virgin Islands and Puerto Rico).

FCO,
Whitehall,
LONDON SW1A 2AP
Enquiries: 020 7008 2663
GTN: 7008 2663
Superintending Director: Robert Culshaw MVO
Team Leaders: Nigel Pooley, Rupert Potter

Overseas Territories Department
Management of HMG's responsibilities for the Overseas Territories of Anguilla, Bermuda, the British Antarctic Territory, the British Indian Ocean Territory, the British Virgin Islands, the Cayman Islands, the Falkland Islands, Montserrat, Pitcairn, South Georgia and the South Sandwich Islands, St Helena and Ascension and Tristan da Cunha and the Turks and Caicos Islands. Co-ordination of UK policy on the Overseas Territories and organisation of the annual Overseas Territories Consultative Council; liaison on South Atlantic matters. Also includes Polar Regions Unit, which leads on HMG's responsibilities under the Antarctic Treaty and represents the UK at Arctic Council.

King Charles Street,
LONDON SW1A 2AH
Enquiries: 020 7008 2643
GTN: 7008 2643
Superintending Director: Robert Culshaw MVO
Head of Department: Tony Crombie OBE
Deputy Heads of Department: Fraser Wilson, Hugh Philpott
Head of Polar Regions Unit: Dr Mike Richardson

Parliamentary Relations and Devolution Team
Advice and guidance to FCO Ministers and officials on parliamentary practice and procedure. Monitoring of all parliamentary business of interest to the FCO. Contact with Select Committees of both Houses of Parliament. Liaison with the British Group of the Inter-Parliamentary Union. Liaison with the Parliamentary Commissioner for Administration. Responsibility for FCO relations with the devolved administrations and legislatures in Scotland, Wales and Northern Ireland.

King Charles Street,
LONDON SW1A 2AH
Enquiries: 020 7008 2236
Enquiries: 020 7008 2235
Enquiries: 020 7008 2234
GTN: 7008 2236
GTN: 7008 2235
GTN: 7008 2234
Superintending Director: Anne Pringle CMG
Head of Team: Chris Stanton
Deputy Head of Team: Steve Collier
Parliamentary Clerk: Gery Juleff
Head, Select Committees and Devolution: Mark Turner

Press Office
Advises the Secretary of State, Foreign Office Ministers and departments of the FCO on questions of presentation relating to the British Government's foreign policy. It is the authorised contact between the FCO and the British media.

Downing Street West,
LONDON SW1A 2AH
Enquiries: 020 7008 3100
GTN: 7008 3100
Superintending Director and Press Secretary: John Williams
Head of Newsroom and Deputy Head of Department: Peter Reid

Prism Programme
Prism is a business change management programme. Prism will provide the FCO with a global on-line management information system (covering personnel, pay, finance and procurement), which will enable better decision making.

Old Admiralty Building,Whitehall,
LONDON SW1A 2PA
Superintending Director: Ric Todd
Programme Manager (FCO): Andy Tucker

Procurement Policy Department
Advice and guidance to FCO departments and posts overseas on best practice in the purchase of goods and services; sponsorship and selling into wider markets; operational environmental issues; Programme and project management best practice.

Old Admiralty Building,
LONDON SW1A 2PA
Enquiries: 020 7008 0924
GTN: 7008 0924
Superintending Director: Ric Todd
Head of Department: Roger Seager
Deputy Head of Department: Ken Price

Protocol Division
Diplomatic Missions: Policy on handling of appointments, privileges, immunities and security of the Diplomatic Corps and International Organisations in Britain. Diplomatic and International Organisations lists. Organisation of ceremonial events, and policy and advice on protocol and precedence. Honours Secretariat: FCO aspects of honours policy. Diplomatic Service and Overseas Honours Lists, British honorary awards, Foreign and Commonwealth honours for British citizens. Investitures, presentation of insignia. Royal Households Secretariat: Co-ordination between the FCO and Royal Households, especially on overseas visits by the Royal Family. Royal Visits Committee.

Old Admiralty Building,
Whitehall,
LONDON SW1A 2PA
Head of Division and Vice Marshal of the Diplomatic Corps: Charles de Chassiron CVO
Deputy Head of Division and Assistant Marshal of the Diplomatic Corps: Jackie A Barson MBE
Director General: Dickie Stagg CMG

Public Diplomacy Team, Public Diplomacy Group
Strategic guidance on public diplomacy to Foreign and Commonwealth Office Directorates and Posts overseas. Co-ordination of major public diplomacy campaigns. Advice on research and evaluation of public diplomacy projects and campaigns.

King Charles Street,
LONDON SW1A 2AH
Enquiries: 020 7008 1618
GTN: 7008 1618
Superintending Director: Anne Pringle CMG
Assistant Director, Public Diplomacy Group: Timothy Livesey

Research Analysts
Contributes to the formulation of foreign policy through objective, policy relevant research and analysis based on specialist expertise.

King Charles Street,
Whitehall,
LONDON SW1A 2AH
Enquiries: 020 7008 1901
GTN: 7008 1901
Director: Anne Pringle
Head of Research Analysts: Robin Hoggard
Heads of Research Groups:
Dr Lillian Wong *(Africa Research Group)*
Patrick Holdich *(Americas Research Group)*
Duncan Allan *(Eastern Research Group)*
Anne McNess *(Europe Research Group)*
Paul Bentall *(International Security and Global Issues Research Group)*
Greg Shapland *(Middle East and North Africa Research Group)*
Peter Clark *(North Asia and Pacific Research Group)*
David Howlett *(South and South East Asia Research Group)*

Resource Accounting Department
Preparation of Resource Accounts. Accounting Policy and advice. Payment of invoices. Debtor control, maintenance and development of Fixed Asset Register and Management Accounts. Funding of FCO posts overseas. Accounting systems and financial training.

Old Admiralty Building,
LONDON SW1A 2PA
Enquiries: 020 7008 1063
GTN: 7008 1063

Hanslope Park,
MILTON KEYNES MK19 7BH
Enquiries: 01908 515531
GTN: 3905 5531
Finance Director: Ric Todd
Head of Department and Chief Accountant: Iain Morgan

Security Policy Group
NATO and EU security and defence policy issues; the foreign policy implications of British defence

policy as regards Transatlantic and European defence, including nuclear weapons issues; nuclear and conventional arms control and disarmament; missile defence issues; UN disarmament fora; armaments policy and defence equipment procurement including collaborative projects; conflict prevention; UK defence attachés.

Downing Street East,
LONDON SW1A 2AH
Enquiries: 020 7008 3131
GTN: 7008 3131
Superintending Directors: Stephen Pattison *(NATO/EU issues)* / Edward Oakden *(other)*
Head of Group: Hugh Powell
Deputy Heads of Group: Jon Wilks, Ajay Sharma

Security Strategy Unit
Formulation of FCO security policy and co-ordination of physical, technical and personnel counter measures, and security education training.

Old Admiralty Building,
LONDON SW1A 2PA
Enquiries: 020 7008 1153
GTN: 7008 1153
Director General: Dickie Stagg CMG
Head of Unit: Andrew Noble
Deputy Head of Unit: Julian Chandler

South Asian Group
Relations with India, Pakistan, Bangladesh, Sri Lanka, Nepal, Bhutan, the Maldives.

Whitehall,
LONDON SW1A 2AL
Enquiries: 020 7008 2388
GTN: 7008 2388
Superintending Director: Tom Phillips
Head of Group: Antony Stokes
Deputy Head of Group: John Yapp

Strategy Group
Support for FCO Board and corporate governance, lead responsibility for the FCO Strategy, promotion of strategic policy thinking. Internal communication.

King Charles Street,
LONDON SW1A 2AH
Enquiries: 020 7008 2911
GTN: 7008 2911
Superintending Director: Anne Pringle CMG
Head of Strategic Policy: Peter Hill
Head of Internal Communications Teams: Jane Clarke

Sudan Unit
Joint FCO/DFID Unit set up in April 2002 to work on the peace process, humanitarian aid and development projects in Sudan.

King Charles Street,
LONDON SW1A 2AH
Telephone: 020 7008 3947
GTN: 7008 3947
UK Special Representative for Sudan: Dr Alastair McPhail
Head of Unit: Anna Bewes

Sustainable Development and Commonwealth Group
International sustainable development policy; EU environment policy; natural resource management; environmental governance and PP10; biodiversity; environmental security. Details at www.fco.gov.uk/environment.

FCO,
King Charles Street,
LONDON SW1A 2AH
Enquiries: 020 7008 4075
Enquiries: 020 7008 4112
GTN: 7008 4075
GTN: 7008 4112
Superintending Director: Philippa Drew
Head of Group: Andrew Soper
Deputy Head of Group: John Marshall

Trade Union Side (of the Diplomatic Service Whitley Council)
Collective Bargaining (pay, terms and conditions of service) on behalf of approximately 5,800 Diplomatic Service and Home Civil Service FCO staff.

Trade Union Side,
FCO,
King Charles Street,
LONDON SW1A 2AH
Enquiries: 020 7008 1708
GTN: 7008 1708
TUS Chair: Stephen Watson
TUS Deputy Chair: Robert Streeton
TUS Vice-Chairs: Michael Carbine, Mary Catlin, Martin Couch, Sandra Davis ,Patrick Holdich, Colin Moss, Winston Murray
TUS Secretary: Pam Chapman
TUS Assistant Secretary: Christopher Sattaur

UK Outreach Team
Widening and deepening the FCO's engagement with key organisations and communities in strategic policy areas: improving the projection of the FCO to its key audiences.

King Charles Street,
LONDON SW1A 2AH
Telephone: 020 7008 6063
GTN: 7008 6063
Web: http://www.pndu.net
Superintending Director: Anne Pringle CMG
Head of Team: Graeme Thomas

UK Trade and Investment
The Foreign and Commonwealth Office and Department of Trade and Industry trade support services are operated by UK Trade and Investment.

Kingsgate House,
66-74 Victoria Street,
LONDON SW1E 6SW
Enquiries: 020 7215 8000
Joint Board Chairman: Douglas Alexander MP
Group Chief Executive: Sir Stephen Brown KCVO

Deputy Chief Executive & Group Director (Corporate Planning Group): Susan Haird
Group Director (International Sectors & E-Transformation Group): Paul Madden
Group Director (International Trade Development Group): Ian Fletcher
Group Director (Inward Investment Group): William Pedder

UK Visas (Joint FCO/Home Office Directorate)
Management of the visa operation at British missions overseas in accordance with UK Immigration Rules. Liaison with other FCO and Home Office departments on policy and matters arising from the visa operation overseas. Replies to letters from MPs and members of the public on individual visa cases.

King Charles Street,
LONDON SW1 2AH
Enquiries: 020 7008 8438
GTN: 7008 8438
Web: http://www.ukvisas.gov.uk/enquiries
Superintending Directors: Dickie Stagg CMG
Director General Corporate Affairs: Lin Homer

Director General Immigration and Nationality Directorate (Home Office).
Director UK Visas: Robin Barnett
Head of Directorate: Mandie Campbell
Deputy Heads of Directorate: Sue Davidson, Simon Lovett, Lorraine Fussey (IT and Business Change)
Biometrics Programme Director: Tony Mercer

Whitehall Liaison Department
General co-ordination duties and responsibility for liaison with the Cabinet Office and other government departments.

Downing Street West,
LONDON SW1A 2AH
Enquiries: 020 7008 2350
GTN: 7008 2350
Vauxhall Cross,
85 Albert Embankment,
LONDON SE1 7TP
Director General: David Richmond CMG
Head of Department: Claire Smith
Deputy Head of Department: Iain Kelly

Wilton Park
Wilton Park Conferences, lasting up to a maximum of three and a half days, examine current international challenges, especially EU issues, security policy, European and Atlantic relations; Russia, Central Europe, the Caspian, South Asia, North East and Central Asia; and Africa; areas of conflict in the developing world and global economic policies. Conference participants are experts on the conference topic drawn from different professions and from all over the world. Wiston House is also available for conferences organised by other institutions.

Wilton Park,
Wiston House,
STEYNING,
West Sussex BN44 3DZ
Telephone: 01903 817772
Fax: 01903 816373
Email: lorraine.jones@wiltonpark.org.uk
Web: http://www.wiltonpark.org.uk
Chief Executive: Colin Jennings

Part II

Lists of British Representatives in Commonwealth and Foreign Countries and in Ireland

British Missions Overseas (addresses and contact Numbers of Missions and Consulates etc.)

PART II. Embassies, High Commissions, Deputy High Commissions and Consular Posts.

AFGHANISTAN

Kabul
British Embassy
15th Street Roundabout
Wazir Akbar Khan
P.O. Box 334
Kabul
FTN Code – 8404 followed by 4 digit extn number
Telephone: (00) (93) 70 102 000 (Switchboard)
Facsimile: (00) (93) 70 102 274 (Political Section)
250 (Management)
Office Hours (GMT): Sun-Thurs: 05 00 – 13 00
Ambassador: Dr Rosalind M Marsden, DCMG
Deputy Head of Mission: Mr Simon Buckle
Counsellor (Political):
Mr Martin M H Clements, OBE
Counsellor (Political): Mr Chris Jones
Counsellor (Political): Mr Mike Seaman
Defence Attaché: Colonel Charles Darell
First Secretary (Political): Ms Rebecca Sagar
First Secretary (British Council Director):
Mr Richard Weyers
First Secretary (Political): Mr Tony Regan
First Secretary (Political): Mr Martin Duffy
First Secretary (Management): Mr David Gardner
First Secretary (Political): Mr Michael Bispham
First Secretary (Political): (Vacant)
First Secretary (Political): Mr Richard Ivers
First Secretary (Development): Mr Damon Bristow
First Secretary (DLO): Mr Martin Smale
Second Secretary (DLO): Mr Andrew Stevenson
Second Secretary (Political): Mr Nicholas Conway
Second Secretary (Political):
Mr Nicholas Hutchings
Second Secretary (Political): Mr Anthony Ellis
Second Secretary (Press and Public Affairs):
Mr George Hodgson
Second Secretary (Political): (Vacant)
Second Secretary (Repatriation Liaison):
Mr Neil Roberts
Third Secretary (Management): Ms Layla Slatter
Third Secretary (Estate Management): (Vacant)
Third Secretary (OSM): Mr Trevor McKie
Third Secretary (Political):
Mr Matthew Halksworth
Attaché: Ms Tarah McCabe
Attaché: Mr Russell Pheasey
Attaché: Mr Keith I Rowland, MVO
Attaché: Mr Jim Ponsonby

Mazar-e-Sharif
UK Provincial Reconstruction Team
First Secretary and FCO Representative:
Ms Jacqueline Lawson-Smith, OBE

ALBANIA

Tirana (SP - see page 121)
British Embassy
Rruga Skenderbeg 12
Tirana
FTN Code – 8503 followed by 4 digit extn number
Telephone: (00) (355) (42) 34973/4/5
Facsimile: (00) (355) (42) 47697
Airtech: (00) (355) (42) 25455
Office Hours (GMT):
Winter: Mon-Thurs: 07 30 – 16 00
Fri: 07 30 – 13 30
Summer: Mon-Thurs: 06 30 – 15 00
Fri: 06 30 – 12 30
Ambassador: Mr Richard Jones
Deputy Head of Mission: Mr Joe Preston
Defence Attaché:
Lieutenant Colonel Philip G Cox, OBE
First Secretary (Cultural) (British Council Director): Ms Joan Barry
First Secretary (Political): Mr Nicholas Turnbull
First Secretary (resides in Budapest):
Ms Sandra Agnew
Second Secretary (Management Officer and Consul): Mr Julian Pearson
Second Secretary: Mr Ben Swanson
Second Secretary (resides in Rome):
Mr Dennis Norman
Second Secretary (resides in Rome):
Mr Graham Dempsey
Second Secretary (resides in Budapest):
Mr Steve Brown
Second Secretary (resides in Athens):
Mr Nigel Willmer
Third Secretary (Political/PPA): Ms Louise Taylor
Third Secretary (Political): Mrs Sandra Preston
Third Secretary (Immigration): Mrs Julie Beard
Third Secretary (Immigration): Mr Mark Griffith
Staff Assistant to *Defence Attaché:*
Staff Sergeant Karl Brooks
Attaché: Ms Teresa McDonough
Attaché: Mrs Wendy Pitchford
Attaché (Cultural): Mr Paul Wilson

ALGERIA

Algiers (SP - see page 121)
British Embassy
7th Floor
Hotel Hilton International
Palais des Expositions
Pins Maritimes
El Mohammadia
Algiers
FTN Code – 8388 + extn number
Telephone: (00) (213) 021 23 00 68 (Switchboard)
Facsimile: (00) (213) 021 23 00 67
021 23 07 51 (Commercial Section)
Airtech (00) (213) 021 23 00 69
e-mail: BritishEmbassy.Algiers@fco.gov.uk
VisaEnquiries.Algiers@fco.gov.uk (Visa Section)
Website: http://www.britishembassy.gov.uk/algeria
Office Hours (GMT):
Summer: Sun – Thurs 08 00 – 15 00
Winter: Sun – Thurs 07 00 – 14 00
Ambassador (3212): Mr Andrew Tesoriere
Deputy Head of Mission (3308):
Mr Nicholas D Low
Counsellor (Political) (3310): Mr Ian Lancaster
Defence Attaché (resides in London):
Commander Matt P Briers, RN
British Council Director (resides in Tunis):
Mr Peter Skelton
Second Secretary (Management/Consul) (3214):
Ms Susan Hewer
Second Secretary (Commercial) (3207):
Ms Shikha Tiwari
Third Secretary (Immigration) (3218):
Mr Anthony Mesarowicz
Attaché (3204): Ms Samantha Daniells

ANDORRA

British Embassy
Ambassador (resides at Madrid):
Mr Stephen John L Wright, CMG
Consul-General (resides at Barcelona):
Mr Geoffrey S Cowling
N.B Consular and Commercial Enquiries should be addressed to Barcelona
British Honorary Consulate
Avinguda Sant Antoni, 23
Cal Sastre Vell, 1°
La Massana AD 400
Principality of Andorra
Telephone/Facsimile: (00) (376) 839 840
e-mail: britconsul@andorra.ad
Office Hours (GMT): Mon-Fri: 08 30 – 10 30
Honorary Consul: Mr Hugh Garner

ANGOLA

Luanda
British Embassy
Rua Diogo Cao, 4
Caixa Postal 1244, Luanda
FTN Code – 8501 + extn number
Telephone: (00) (244) (2) 334582, 334583,
392991, 387681
Facsimile: (00) (244) (2) 333331 (U/C)
Satellite Fax: 00 871 144 5140 (Airtech)
e-mail: postmaster@luanda.fco.gov.uk
Office Hours (GMT): Mon and Fri 07 00 – 13 00
Tue-Thur 07 00 – 11 30 and 13 00 – 16 00
Ambassador: Mr Ralph Publicover
Deputy Head of Mission and Consul:
Mr Ross Denny
Defence Attaché:
Lieutenant Colonel The Lord Crofton
Head of DFID Angola: Mr Russell Phillips
Second Secretary (Political/PPA): Mr Adrian Lee
Second Secretary (Trade): Mr Stewart Gorman
Second Secretary (Management) and Vice-Consul:
Mr Peter Ford
Registrar and PA to HMA: Ms Pauline Shodeke
Defence Attaché's Assistant:
Staff Sergeant Dean Sprouting

ANTIGUA AND BARBUDA

St. John's
British High Commission
P.O. Box 483, Price Waterhouse Centre,
11, Old Parham Road, St. John's
FTN Code – 8481 + extn number
Telephone: (00) (1) (268) 462 0008/9, 463 0010
Facsimile: (00) (1) (268) 562 2124
Airtech: (00) (1) (268) 462 2806
e-mail: britishc@candw.ag
Office Hours (GMT): Mon – Thurs: 12 00 – 20 00
and Fri: 12 00 – 17 00 (only)
Open to the Public: Mon – Fri: 12 00 – 16 30
**High Commissioner:* Mr Duncan Taylor, CBE
Resident British Commissioner:
Miss Jean Sharpe, OBE
**Deputy Resident British Commissioner:*
Mr Paul Lawrence
Deputy High Commissioner: Mr Alan Drury
**Defence Adviser:* Captain Steve G Wilson, RN
**First Secretary:* Mr Eamon Kearney
**First Secretary (Management):* Mrs Ros Day, MBE
**Second Secretary (Chancery):* Mr Rick Gomez
**Second Secretary (Chancery/Information):*
Mr Nick J Pyle, MBE
**Third Secretary (Immigration):* Mr Mark Harrison
**Resides at Bridgetown*

ARGENTINA

Buenos Aires
British Embassy
Dr. Luis Agote 2412/52, 1425 Capital Federal,
Buenos Aires
FTN Code – 8502 + extn number
Telephone: (00) (54) (11) 4808 2200 Switchboard
4808 + Direct Extension Access
Facsimile: (00) (54) (11) 4808 2274 Management
4808 2283 Commercial
4808 2228 Political and Public Diplomacy
4808 2316 Chancery
4808 2221 Defence Section
4808 2235 Consular
Airtech: (00) (54) (11) 4808 2211 Chancery
Office Hours (GMT): Mon-Thurs: 11 45 – 16 00
and 17 00 – 20 30 (Mar-Dec)
Fri: 11 45 – 17 00

Mon-Fri: 11 45 – 17 30 (Jan, Feb)
Ambassador (2202): Dr John Hughes
Minister and Deputy Head of Mission (2204):
Mrs Catherine Royle
Counsellor: (2209): Mr John Lewis
Defence, Naval and Military Attaché (2218):
Captain Chris J Hyldon, RN
Air Attaché (2218):
Group Captain Ian Capewell, RAF
First Secretary (Head of Political/Economic Section) (2205): Mr Owen Jenkins
First Secretary (Commercial) (2251):
Mr Dave Prodger
Cultural Attaché (British Council Director) (tel: 4311 9814 extn 140): Mr Martin Fryer
First Secretary (Management) (2255):
Miss Christine E McEwen
First Secretary (Technical Works Officer) (2291):
Mr Ronnie Clarke
Second Secretary (Political) (2207): Mr Mal Green
Second Secretary (Political) (2275): Mr Lill Shield
Second Secretary (Political) (2268): Mr Ian Duddy
Second Secretary (Political) (2312):
Ms Amy Harland
Second Secretary (Technical) (2215):
Mr Stuart Moss
Second Secretary (Consul) (2294):
Mr Jim Edwards
Assistant Cultural Attaché (Deputy Director British Council) (tel: 4311 9814 extn 142):
Ms Lena Milosevic
Third Secretary (Management) (2210):
Mr Matthew Withers

Mendoza
Honorary Consulate
Emilio Civit 778
Telephone: (00) (54) (261) 4238529/4238514
Facsimile: (00) (54) (261) 4238565
Office Hours: Mon-Fri 08 30 – 13 00 and 17 00 – 20 30
Honorary Consul: Mr Carlos Alberto Pulenta

Córdoba
Honorary Consulate
Chacabuco 716
Córdoba
Telephone: (00) (54) (351) 4208293
Facsimile: (00) (54) (351) 4208201/4208259
Office Hours: Mon-Fri 09 00 – 13 00 and 16.30 – 20 30
Honorary Consul: Mr Fulvio Pagani

Santa Fe
Honorary Consulate
Av Pte J D Perón 8101
Rosario
Telephone/Fax: (00) (54) (341) 4590206
Office Hours: Mon-Fri 09 00 – 13 00 and 14 30 – 17 30
Honorary Consul: Mr Alberto C Gollan

ARMENIA

Yerevan (SP - see page 121)
British Embassy
34 Baghramyan Ave, Yerevan 375019
FTN Code – 8339 + 4 digit extn number
Telephone: (00) 3741 264301
Facsimile: (00) 3741 264318 (Unclassified)
070 9238 3796 (Efax)
Airtech (00) 3741 264327
e-mail: britemb@arminco.com
Commercial/General/Other Enquiries
dfidhead@netsys.am DFID
dfidassist@netsys.am DFID
Officer's:- firstname.lastname@fco.gov.uk
Office Hours (GMT): 05 00 – 09 00 and 10 00 – 13 00
Ambassador: Miss Thorda Abbott-Watt
(Mr Anthony Cantor w.e.f Jan 06)
Deputy Head of Mission: Mr Richard Hyde
Third Secretary (Management and Vice-Consul):
Mr Ian Cramman
Third Secretary (Political/PPAS):
Ms Sarah L Murrell
Defence Attaché (resides at Tbilisi):
Lieutenant Colonel Chris J Nunn, OBE, RM
TMO's (resides at HP): Mr Bob Fletcher
Cultural Attaché: Mr Nigel Townson
Attaché: Mr Gary Walker

AUSTRALIA

Canberra
British High Commission
Commonwealth Avenue, Yarralumla
Canberra, ACT 2600
FTN Code – 8471 + extn number
Telephone: (00) (61) (2) 6270 6666
Facsimile: (00) (61) (2) 6273 3236 General
6273 4360 Economic
6270 6653 Chancery
e-mail: bhc.canberra@uk.emb.gov.au
Consular Section:
39 Brindabella Crt, Brindabella Business Park, Canberra Airport, ACT 2609
Telephone: (00) (61) (2) 1902 941 555 Passports/ Entry Clearances
1300 367 066 Passports/Entry Clearances – Credit Cards Only
e-mail: bhc.consular@uk.emb.gov.au
Office Hours (GMT): Apr-Oct 22 45 – 02 30 and 03 30 – 07 00, Nov-Mar 21 45 – 01 30 and 02 30 – 06 00
High Commissioner (3680): Mrs Helen Liddell
Deputy High Commissioner (3656):
Mrs Jean Harrod, MBE
Counsellor (Multilateral) (3685):
Dr Patrick Topping
Defence and Naval Adviser and Head BDLS (3650): Commodore Bob J Love, RN, CBE
Counsellor (Police Liaison) (3684):
Mr Nicholas O.Brien
Military and Air Adviser (3677):
Group Captain Steven Duffill, RAF
First Secretary (Global Issues) (3668):
Mr Peter Elder
First Secretary (Foreign and Security Policy) (3695): Mr Jeff Harrod
First Secretary (Management) (3617):
Mr Malcolm Surman

First Secretary (Defence/Research) Head of the British Defence Research and Supply Staff: Dr David Watson
First Secretary (Defence Equipment Cooperation) (3686): Ms Lindsey Pratt
First Secretary: Mr Bill McCarthy
First Secretary: Mrs Susan Morris
First Secretary (Technical Management) (3638): Mr Larry King
First Secretary (Technical Security): Mr Liam Brennan
First Secretary (TWO) (3634): Mr David Holmes
Second Secretary (Consular) (3742): Ms Julie Johnson
Second Secretary (Technical Management) (3676): Mr Colin Avery
Second Secretary: Miss Janice Black
Third Secretary (External Affairs) (3675): Miss Jacqui Richards
Third Secretary (Political) (3673): Mrs Nina MacKenzie
Attaché (Passports) (3728): Mr Darren Cogger

Adelaide
British Consulate
Level 22, 25 Grenfell Street
Adelaide SA 5000
Telephone: (00) (61) (8) 8212 7280
Facsimile: (00) (61) (8) 8212 7282
Airtech: (00) (61) (8) 8212 7283
e-mail: bc.adelaide@mail.uk.emb.gov.au
Consul: Mr Vic S Warrington

Brisbane
British Consulate-General
Level 26, Waterfront Place
1 Eagle Street, Brisbane, Queensland, 4000
Telephone: (00) (61) (7) 3223 3200 General/Consular 3223 3206/7 Commercial Section
Facsimile: (00) (61) (7) 3236 2576
Airtech: (00) (61) (7) 3236 1668
e-mail: bcgbris1@mail.uk.emb.gov.au
(All information, visa and routine passport work is centralised in Canberra).
Office Hours (GMT): 00 00 – 08 00 Public Service Hours (GMT): 00 30 – 06 00
Consul-General: Miss Helen M Horn, MBE
Vice-Consul: Mrs Megan M Hunt, MBE

Melbourne
British Consulate-General
17th Floor, 90 Collins Street
Melbourne, Victoria 3000
Telephone: (00) (61) (3) 9652 1670 Commercial
1600 Consular
Facsimile: (00) (61) (3) 9650 2990
Airtech: (00) (61) (3) 9650 2716
e-mail: bcgmelb1@mail.uk.emb.gov.au
Office Hours (GMT): Apr-Oct 23 00 – 07 30
Nov-Mar 22 00 – 06 30
Consul-General: Mr Peter West
Deputy Consul-General: Mr David Seddon
Vice-Consul: Mr Philip J Mudie

Perth
British Consulate-General
Level 26, Allendale Square
77 St. George's Terrace
Perth, Western Australia 6000
Telephone: (00) (61) (8) 9224 4700
Facsimile: (00) (61) (8) 9224 4720
Consular and Management
(00) (61) 9224 4719 Commercial
Airtech (00) (61) 9224 4718
e-mail: bcgperth@mail.uk.emb.gov.au
Issue of all general information about the UK, UK visas/entry clearances, and passports, centralised at Canberra
Office Hours (GMT): 01 00 – 05 00, 06 00 – 09 00 (Public counter 01 00 – 06 00)
Consul-General: Mr Stuart Gregson
Deputy Consul-General: Mr John Makin

Sydney
British Consulate-General and Directorate of Trade and Investment Promotion
Level 16, The Gateway
1 Macquarie Place, Sydney NSW, 2000
Telephone: (00) (61) (2) 9247 7521 (8 lines)
Facsimile: (00) (61) (2) 9233 1826 Commercial
(00) (61) 9251 6201 Consular, Management
e-mail: bcgsyd2@mail.uk.emb.gov.au
(Commercial)
bcgsyd1@mail.uk.emb.gov.au
(Press and Public Affairs/Consular)
Offices Hours (GMT): Apr-Oct 23 00 – 02 30 and 03 30 – 07 00
Nov-Mar 22 00 – 01 30 and 02 30 – 06 00
Consul-General: Mr Timothy Holmes
Director of Trade Promotion and Deputy Consul-General: Mr Chris Glynn
Director of Investment and Consul: Mr Jamie Banks
British Council Director: Mr Simon Gammell, OBE
Vice-Consul (Commercial): Mr Chris Henderson
Management Officer: Mrs Heather Halliwell
Consular/Admin Officer: Mr Les Tod
Press and Public Affairs Manager: Mr Robert Swift

Tasmania
British Honorary Consulate
1a Brisbane St
Hobart TAS 7000
Telephone: (00) (61) (3) 6213 3310
Facsimile: (00) (61) (3) 6231 1139
e-mail: djmotors@onaustralia.com.au
Office Hours (GMT): Apr – Oct: 23 00 – 07 30
Nov – Mar: 22 00 – 06 30
Honorary Consul: Mr Michael Johns

AUSTRIA

Vienna
British Embassy
Jaurèsgasse 12, 1030 Vienna
FTN Code – 8310 + extn number
Telephone: (00) (43) (1) 716 130
Facsimile: (00) (43) (1) 71613 2999 Chancery
71613 6900 Commercial
71613 2900 Management
Airtech: (00) (43) (1) 71613 2310

e-mail: press@britishembassy.at (Press and Public Affairs Section)
commerce@britishembassy.at (Commercial Section)
chancery@britishembassy.at (Chancery)
visa-consular@britishembassy.at (Consular Section)
Website: www.britishembassy.at
Consular Section
Jaurèsgasse 10, 1030 Vienna
FTN Code – 8310 + extn number
Telephone: (00) (43) (1) 71613 5151 or 00 43 1 71613 followed by individual extn number
Facsimile: (00) (43) (1) 71613 5900
(All mail should be addressed to the British Embassy)
Office Hours (GMT): Winter: Mon – Fri 08 00 – 12 00 and 13 00 – 16 00
Summer: Mon – Fri 07 00 – 11 00 and 12 00 – 15 00
Ambassador (2202): Mr John Macgregor, CVO
Counsellor, Consul-General, Dep. Head of Mission (2204): Dr Piers Baker
Counsellor (Chancery) (2211): Mr Adrian M Gamble
Counsellor (Labour) (resides at Berlin): Miss Elaine Trewartha
Defence Attaché (2216): Lieutenant Colonel Len W Chapman, RE
First Secretary (Management) and Consul (2261): Mr Eric M Jones
First Secretary (Technical Works) (2264): Mr John Darlington
First Secretary (Commercial) (6148): Mr Tony Lamb
First Secretary (FLO) (2318): Mr Nicholas Hamill
British Council Director and Regional Director South East Europe: Mr Martin Davidson
Second Secretary (2219): Mr Thomas Young
Second Secretary (EU Affairs) (2343): Mr Andrew Ayre
Second Secretary (Chancery) (2220): Mr William Gatward
Second Secretary (Chancery) (2224): (Vacant)
Second Secretary (2210): Mr Rod Parker
Second Secretary (2225): Mr Martin J Reeve
Attaché and Vice-Consul (ECO) (5330): Mr Adam Radcliffe
Third Secretary (Management) (2260): Miss Jan H Richardson
Third Secretary (2272): Mr Gordon J Winter
Vice-Consul (5332): Mr Harald De Soye

Vienna United Kingdom Mission to the United Nations in Vienna, see page 114

Vienna United Kingdom Delegation to the Organisation for Security and Cooperation in Europe (OSCE), see page 114

Bregenz
British Consulate
Bundesstrasse 110
A-6923 Lauterach/Bregenz
Telephone: (00) (43) (5574) 696507
Facsimile: (00) (43) (5574) 696340
Office Hours (GMT): Mon-Fri 08 00 – 11 00
Honorary Consul: Dipl-Ing P Senger-Weiss

Graz
British Consulate
Schmiedgasse 12, A-8010 Graz
Telephone: (00) (43) (316) 821616 / 21 / 27
Facsimile: (00) (43) (316) 821616 / 45
Office Hours (GMT): Mon-Thurs 08 30 – 11 00 and 13 30 – 15 00 Fri 08 30 – 11 00
Honorary Consul: Mr K D Bruhl, CBE
Honorary Vice-Consul: Mrs Eva Bruhl
Secretary: Ms C Casati / Ms C Nietzsche

Innsbruck
British Consulate
Kaiserjagerstrasse 1/Top B9
A-6020 Innsbruck
Telephone: (00) (43) (512) 579973 / 15 / 35
Facsimile: (00) (43) (512) 5799738
Office Hours (GMT): Mon-Fri 08 00 – 11 00
Honorary Consul: Ing Hellmut Buchroithner
Honorary Vice-Consul: Dr Ivo Rungg
Secretary: Ms Stefanie Gapp / Ms M Siebert

Salzburg
British Consulate
Alter Markt 4, A-5020 Salzburg
Telephone: (00) (43) (662) 848133
Facsimile: (00) (43) (662) 845563
Office Hours (GMT): Mon-Fri 08 00 – 11 00
Honorary Consul: Mr M M Kaindl, OBE
Honorary Pro-Consul: Mrs Helga Danmayr

AZERBAIJAN

Baku (SP - see page 121)
British Embassy
45, Khagani Street
Baku AZ1000
FTN Code – 8483 + extn number
Telephone: (00) (99 412) 497 5188/89/90
Facsimile: (00) (99 412) 492 2739, 497 2474 (Commercial Section)
Airtech: (00) (99 412) 497 5893
e-mail: office@britemb.baku.az
office@ukemb.baku.az (Commercial Section)
Website: www.britishembassy.gov.uk/azerbaijan
Office Hours (GMT): Mon – Fri: 05 00 – 09 00 and 10 00 – 13 00
Ambassador: Dr Lawrence S C Bristow
Deputy Head of Mission: Mr Colin Wells
Defence Attaché (resides at Tbilisi): Lieutenant Colonel Christopher J Nunn, OBE, RM
Cultural Attaché (British Council): Mr Andy Williams
First Secretary (Political): (Vacant)
Second Secretary (Commercial): Mr Chris Gotch
Second Secretary (Political): Mr Sean Melbourne
Second Secretary (Political): Mr David Proudfoot
Vice-Consul: Mr Derek Lavery
Third Secretary (Management): Mr Mark Dawson
Attaché: Mr Jamal Williams

BAHAMAS, THE

Nassau (SP - see page 121)
British High Commission – (Closed)

BAHRAIN

Bahrain
British Embassy
21 Government Avenue, Manama 306
P.O. Box 114
FTN Code – 8484 + extn number
Telephone: (00) (973) (17) 574100
574167 Information
Facsimile: (00) (973) (17) 574161 Chancery
574138 Consular/Management
574101 Commercial
574121 Visa
574140 Registry (Comms)
574135 Airtech
e-mail: britemb@batelco.com.bh
Website: www.ukembassy.gov.bh
Office Hours (GMT): Sat – Wed 04 30 – 11 30
Ambassador and Consul-General:
Mr Robin D Lamb
Deputy Head of Mission and Head of Political Section: Mr Steve Harrison
Defence Attaché: Commander Nigel P Smith, RN
First Secretary (Political): Mr Simon Page
First Secretary (Regional Expert, Engaging with the Arab World): Mrs Jacky Perkins
British Council Director: Ms Sandra Hamrouni
Second Secretary (Consul/ECM/MO):
Mr Iain Kingston
Airline Liaison Officer: Mr Mark Casali
Third Secretary (Political, Press and Public Affairs): Mrs Karen Williams
Third Secretary (ECO): Mrs Jane Allan

BANGLADESH

Dhaka
British High Commission
United Nations Road, Baridhara Dhaka 1212
Postal address: P.O. Box 6079, Dhaka-1212
FTN Code – 8211 + extn number
Telephone: (00) (880) (2) 8822705 (5 lines) followed by individual extension number
8821273 DHC Direct line
Facsimile: (00) (880) (2) 8826181 High Commissioner's Office
8816135 Chancery
8823437 Management
8823666 Immigration
9882819 Consular
e-mail: Dhaka.Commercial@fco.gov.uk (Commercial Section)
Dhaka.Consular@fco.gov.uk (Consular)
Dhaka.Immigration@fco.gov.uk (Immigration)
Dhaka.Management@fco.gov.uk (Management)
Dhaka.Press@fco.gov.uk (Press and Public Affairs)
Clodhaka@fco.gov.uk (Community Liaison Officer)
Website: www.ukinbangladesh.org
Office Hours (GMT): Sun to Wed: 02 00 – 10 00 and Thur 02 00 – 08 00
High Commissioner (2201): Mr Anwar Choudhury
Deputy High Commissioner and Commercial Counsellor (2203): Mr Stephen Bridges
Counsellor (2211): Mr Ian Simmons
Defence Adviser (resides in New Delhi):
Brigadier Ian D O Rees
First Secretary (Medical Officer):
Dr Jacqueline Howell
First Secretary (Senior Management Officer) (2230): Mr Mike Stevenson
Director of Visa Services (Immigration) (2302):
Mr Lawson Ross
First Secretary (Immigration) (2301):
Mr Jon Verney
First Secretary (Drug Liaison) (resides in Mumbai): Mr Simon Sutcliffe
British Council Director: Ms June Rollinson
Second Secretary (Airline Liaison Officer) (2212):
Mr Paul Kramer
Second Secretary (Press and Public Affairs) (2209): Ms Millie Sen-Gupta
Second Secretary (Commercial) (2313):
Mr Clifford Bebb
Second Secretary (Immigration) (2453):
Mr Mark Date
Second Secretary (Immigration) (2300):
Ms Sheilani Nandy
Second Secretary (Immigration) (2309):
Mr Derek Jones
Second Secretary (Management): (Vacant)
Second Secretary (Political) (2210):
Mr Jason Grimes
Second Secretary (Consul) (2354): Mr Toff Wahab
Vice-Consul (2305): Ms Amanda Cooper
Third Secretary (AMO-Resources) (2236):
Mr Derek Griffiths
Third Secretary (AMO-Estates) (2231):
Ms Liz Sands
International Pensions Service Officer (IPSO) (2317): Mr Campbell Wallace
Registrar (2217): Mr Nicholas Marmion

Department for International Development (DFID) Bangladesh
United House, 10 Gulshan Avenue
Gulshan, Dhaka 1212
FTN Code – 8775 + extn number
Telephone: (00) (880) (2) 881 0800 (hunting number)
Facsimile: (00) (880) (2) 882 4661 / 882 3181
Head of DFID Bangladesh (3113):
Mr David Wood
Deputy Head (2137): Dr Mehtab Currey
Head of Management Services (3112):
Mr Bo Sundstrom
Estate and Facilities Manager (1052):
Ms Marina Negri
Senior Economic Adviser (2012): (Vacant)
Economic Adviser (3007): Mr Jason Hayman
Enterprise Adviser (2057): Mr Frank Matsaert
Social and Political Governance Adviser (2126):
Mr Peter Evans
Senior Infrastructure and Livelihoods Adviser (2001): Mr Michael Scott
Infrastructure Adviser (2019): Mr Asufta Alam
Senior Programme Manager (2064):
Mr Martin Leach
Environment and Livelihoods Adviser (2105):
Mrs Yolande Wright

Rural Livelihoods Programme Adviser (2053):
Mr Duncan King
International Specialist (APSU) (3032):
Mr Guy Howard
Governance Adviser (2129): Mr David Gray
Senior Programme Manager (Health) (3066):
Mr Gareth Aickin
Senior Education Adviser (3064):
Ms Barbara Payne
Health Adviser (3018): Mr Dinesh Nair
Senior Social Development Adviser (2130):
Mr Eric Hanley
Deputy Programme Manager (3024):
Mr Chris Allen
Deputy Programme Manager (2029):
Mr Mick McGill
Programme Manager (3093): Mrs Sue McGill
Programme Manager (3080): Mr Jim Brady
Deputy Programme Manager (2085):
Mr Daniel Shimmin
Deputy Programme Manager (2086):
Mr Jeremy Orton
Deputy Programme Manager (3049):
Mrs Riffat Young

BARBADOS

Bridgetown
British High Commission
Lower Collymore Rock (P.O. Box 676),
Bridgetown
FTN Code – 8389 + extn number
Telephone: (00) (1) (246) 430 7800
Facsimile: (00) (1) (246) 430 7851 Chancery
430 7860 Management/Consular
430 7826 Commercial/Information
Airtech: (00) (1) (246) 430 7845
e-mail: britishhc@sunbeach.net
Office Hours (GMT): 12 00 – 20 00 Monday to Thursday 12 00 – 17 00 Friday
High Commissioner: Mr Duncan Taylor, CBE
Also High Commissioner (Non Resident) To Antigua and Barbuda, Commonwealth of Dominica, Grenada, St Kitts and Nevis, St Lucia and St Vincent and the Grenadines.
Deputy High Commissioner: Mr Alan Drury
Defence Adviser: Captain Steve G Wilson, RN
First Secretary: Mr Eamon Kearney
First Secretary (Management): Ms Ros Day, MBE
Second Secretary (Chancery/Information):
Mr Nick J Pyle, MBE
Second Secretary (Chancery): Mr Andy Danton
Second Secretary (Chancery): Mr Rick Gomez
Third Secretary (Management/ Consular):
Mr Jim Collins
Third Secretary (Technical Works): Mr Phil Barker
Third Secretary (Immigration): Mr Mark Harrison
Head of Commercial Section:
Mr Hadford S Howell, MBE
Overseas Territories Advisers
First Secretary (Financial Services Adviser):
Mr Kevin Mann

Department for International Development (DFID) Caribbean
Chelsea House, Chelsea Road
(P.O. Box 167), St Michael
Telephone: (00) (1) (246) 430 7900
Facsimile: (00) (1) (246) 430 7959
Office Hours (GMT): 12 00 – 20 00
Head of DFID (C): Ms Sandra Pepera
Senior Policy and Private Sector Adviser:
Ms Sarah Dunn
Senior Social Development Adviser: Ms Pat Holden
Senior Governance Adviser: Ms Kathy Higgins
Economic Adviser: Mr Paul Mullard
Economic Assistant: Ms Lindsey Block
Human Resources/Finance Manager:
Mr Robert Bateson
Regional IS Manager: Ms Denise Niles
Head of Regional Unit: Ms Jane Armstrong
Programme Officer: Ms Cherianne Clarke
Executive Support and Programme Officer:
Mrs Sandee Layne-Waterman

BELARUS

Minsk (SP - see page 121)
British Embassy
37 Karl Marx Street, 220030 Minsk
Telephone: (00) (375) (172) 105920 (Switchboard)
Facsimile: (00) (375) (172) 292306 (General)
292311 (Visa Section)
Airtech: 292315
e-mail: britinfo@nsys.by
Website: www.britishembassy.gov.uk/belarus
Office Hours (GMT): Summer: Mon-Thur 06 00 – 10 00 and 11 00 – 14 30; Fri 06 00 – 12 00
Winter: Mon-Thur 07 00 – 11 00 and 12 00 – 15 30; Fri 07 00 – 13 00
Ambassador and Consul-General:
Mr Brian Bennett
Deputy Head of Mission: Mr Greg Quinn
Defence Attaché (resides at Moscow):
Colonel Colin A Bulleid
Assistant Defence Attaché (resides at Moscow):
Squadron Leader Sean T O'Brien, RAF
First Secretary (Technical Works) (resides in Vienna): Mr Ian Sweeney
Second Secretary (ILO) (resides in Kiev):
Mr Chris Lain
Second Secretary (Technical. Management) (resides in Warsaw): Mr Simon Lochmuller
Third Secretary (Immigration) and Vice-Consul:
Miss Melanie Tankard
Attaché: Miss Julia Windle

BELGIUM

Brussels
British Embassy
Rue D'Arlon/Aarlenstraat 85
B-1040 Brussels
Telephone: (00) (32) (2) 287 6211
Facsimile: (00) (32) (2) 287 6250 HMA's and DHM's Offices
6355 Political
6270 Consular
6240 Trade and Investment
6360 Economic and Public Diplomacy
Airtech: 6380
e-mail: firstname.surname@fco.gov.uk

Website: www.britishembassy.gov.uk/belgium
Office Hours (GMT): Mon-Fri 09 00 – 17 30
Ambassador: Mr Richard Kinchen, MVO
Deputy Head of Mission and Consul-General: Mr Nigel Bowie
Counsellor (Global and Regional Affairs): Ms Christine A MacQueen
Defence Attaché (Resides in The Hague): Captain A Robin Davies, RN
Cultural Counsellor (British Council): Mr Stephan Roman
First Secretary (Global and Regional Affairs): Mr Paul S R Norman
First Secretary (Political): Mr Jules Irens
First Secretary (Trade and Investment): Mr Guy A Harrison
First Secretary (Technical): Mr Stephen Roseblade
First Secretary (Economic/Public Diplomacy): Ms Elisabeth Boyles
Second Secretary (Consul): Mrs Salud Murphy
Second Secretary (Technical): Mr Peter Bryan
Second Secretary (Technical): Mr Neil Sturgess
Third Secretary (Political): Mr Mark Kelly
Third Secretary (Global and Regional Affairs): Mrs Rebecca Murray

Brussels
British Embassy
Joint Management Office
Rue d'Arlon/Aarlenstraat 85
1040 Brussels
Telephone: (00) (32) (2) 287 6211
Facsimile: (00) (32) (2) 287 6320
Counsellor (Head of Joint Management Office): Mr Roger A Cambridge, MVO
First Secretary: Mrs Sharon Campbell
Second Secretary: Mr Allan Cook

Brussels United Kingdom Delegation to NATO, see page 115

Brussels Office of the United Kingdom Permanent Representative to the European Union, see page 116

Antwerp
British Honorary Consulate-General
Postbox 580
Groenplaats
2000 Antwerp 1
Telephone: (00) (32) (3) 213 2125
Facsimile: (00) (32) (3) 213 2991
e-mail: cgantwerp@unicall.be
Office Hours: Callers are advised to telephone for an appointment.
Honorary Consul-General: Baron Paul Buysse, CBE
Pro-Consul: Mrs Mary Ann Marinus

Ghent
British Honorary-Consulate
c/o Meyvaert Glass Engineering NV
Dok Noord 3
9000 Ghent
Telephone: (00) (32) (9) 235 7221 / 225 5427
Facsimile: (00) (32) (9) 222 8127
e-mail: british.consul@meyvaert.be
Office Hours: Callers are advised to telephone for an appointment.
Honorary Consul: Mr Paul Meyvaert

BELIZE

Belmopan (SP - see page 121)
British High Commission
P. O. Box 91 Belmopan or B.F.P.O 12
FTN Code – 8494 + 1000 for switchboard
Telephone: (00) (501) 822 2146
Facsimile: (00) (501) 822 2761
Airtech: (00) (501) 822 3694
e-mail: brithicom@btl.net
Website: www.britishhighbze.com
Office Hours (GMT): Mon-Thurs: 14 00 – 18 00 and 19 00 – 22 00 Fri: 14 00 – 20 00
High Commissioner (2001): Mr Alan Jones
Deputy High Commissioner (2003): Mr David Spires
Defence Adviser (resides in Kingston): Colonel Charles G Le Brun
First Secretary (Technical Works) (resides in Mexico): Mr Steve Collick
First Secretary (resides in Panama): Mr Alan Pamplin
Second Secretary (Consular/Management) (2008): Mr Carl Mackerras
Second Secretary (resides in Mexico): Mr Ian Taylor
Third Secretary (Chancery) (2004): Ms Catherine Kell

BENIN

Cotonou
British Embassy (all staff resident in Nigeria)
Ambassador: Mr Richard Gozney, CMG
Consul: Mr Maurice Harper
Second Secretary (Commercial): Ms Deborah Fern

BOLIVIA

La Paz (SP - see page 121)
British Embassy
Avenida Arce No.2732
Casilla (PO Box) 694
FTN Code – 8504+ extn number
Telephone: (00) (591) (2) 2433424 (connects to 9 lines)
Facsimile: (00) (591) (2) 2431073
Airtech: (00) (591) (2) 2432301
Duty Officer: (00) (591) 772 92311
e-mail: ppa@megalink.com (Embassy)
Website: www.britishembassy.gov.uk/bolivia
Office Hours (GMT): Monday – Thursday 12:30 – 16:30 and 17:30 to 21:00 Friday 12:30 – 17:30
Ambassador: Mr Peter Bateman
Deputy Head of Mission and HM Consul: Mr Chris Poole
Defence Attaché (resides in Santiago): Colonel Iain S Campbell
Second Secretary and Vice-Consul (Management): Mr Peter Cartwright
Third Secretary (Technical Management) (resides in Brasilia): Mr Alan Barnes
Commercial Officer: Mr Eduardo Suarez

Department for International Development (DFID) Bolivia
Av. Arce No. 2799,
Esquina Cordero,
Edificio Fortaleza,
Piso 14
Telephone: (00) (591) (2) 243 5000
Facsimile: (00) (591) (2) 243 4306
Head of Development Co-operation:
Ms Jennie Richmond
Social Inclusion Adviser / Human Rights and Health Adviser: Ms Emma Donlan

BOSNIA AND HERZEGOVINA

Sarajevo
British Embassy
Tina Ujevica 8, Sarajevo
Telephone: (00 387 33) (28) 2200
Main switchboard
(28) 2235 Consular/Visa
Facsimile: (00 387 33) (28) 2203
Chancery; Management
(20) 4780 Commercial; DFID; Consular/Visa
Airtech: (28) 2223
e-mail: PoliticalEnquiries.Sarajevo@fco.gov.uk
CommercialEnquiries.Sarajevo@fco.gov.uk
DFIDEnquiries.Sarajevo@fco.gov.uk
ConsularEnquiries.Sarajevo@fco.gov.uk
VisaEnquiries.Sarajevo@fco.gov.uk
britemb@bih.net.ba
Website: www.britishembassy.ba
Office Hours (GMT): April-October: Mon-Thurs 06 30 – 15 00; Fri 06 30 – 13 30 November-March: Mon-Thurs 07 30 – 16 00; Fri 07 30 – 14 30
Ambassador (2214): Mr Matthew Rycroft, CBE
Deputy Head of Mission (2211):
Ms Catherine Knight-Sands
First Secretary (Political) (2216):
Ms Geraldine McCooey
First Secretary (British Council Director):
Mr Chris Rawlings
First Secretary (Director of Commercial and Economic Affairs) (2233): Mr Richard Salt
First Secretary (Management and HM Consul) (2232): Mr John Ellis
Second Secretary (DFID) (2248):
Ms Mary Shockledge
Second Secretary (Political/PPA) (2244):
Ms Alex Cole
Second Secretary (Political) (2215):
Mr Alistair Bridgwood
Third Secretary (Political):
Miss Philippa Chatterton
Vice-Consul (2245): Mr James Hudson
Attaché: Ms Kerry Day

Banja Luka
British Embassy Office
Simeuna Dzaka 8, Banja Luka
Tel/Fax: (00 387 51) 212 395/216 842
Mobile: (00 387 65) 512 698
e-mail: BLOffice.Sarajevo@fco.gov.uk
Head of Office: Mr Robert Contractor

BOTSWANA

Gaborone (SP - see page 121)
British High Commission
Private Bag 0023, Gaborone
FTN Code – 8515 + extn number
Telephone: (00) (267) 395 2841
Facsimile: (00) (267) 395 6105
Airtech: (00) (267) 395 2650
e-mail: bhc@botsnet.bw
Website:
www.britishhighcommission.gov.uk/botswana
Office Hours (GMT): Mon – Thurs: 06 00 – 10 30 and 11 30 – 14 30 Fri: 06 00 – 11 00
High Commissioner: Mr Francis Martin
Deputy High Commissioner: Mr John L Smith
Defence Adviser (resides at Harare):
Colonel Bob J Griffiths, MBE
British Council Director: Ms Honor Flanagan
Second Secretary (Development/Regional Affairs):
Mr John L Riley
Third Secretary (Consular and Management):
Mr Michael J Redden

BRAZIL

Brasilia
British Embassy
Setor de Embaixadas Sul, Quadra 801, Conjunto K, CEP 70.408-900, Brasilia – DF
FTN Code – 8455 + extn number
Telephone: (00) (55) (61) 3329 2300
Facsimile: (00) (55) (61) 3329 2369
Airtech: (00) (55) (61) 3329 2343
e-mail: contact@uk.org.br
Website: www.uk.org.br
Office Hours (GMT): Mon – Thurs: 11 30 – 20 30 Fri: 11 30 – 15 30
Ambassador (2353): Dr Peter Collecott, CMG
Deputy Head of Mission (2305): Mr Hugo Shorter
Defence, Military and Air Attaché (2351):
Group Captain Ralph Ashenhurst, RAF
Naval Attaché (2324):
Commander R A Harry Harrison, RN
First Secretary (Economic and Commercial/Trade Policy) (2337): Mr Matthew Lownds
First Secretary (Management) and Consul (2319):
Mr Neil Storey
First Secretary (2356): Mr Ray Tyler
British Council Director and Regional Director Latin America Caribbean: Mr Alan Curry
DFID Director: Mrs Miranda Munro
Second Secretary (Economic) (2333):
Mr Paul Rennie
Second Secretary (Political) (2309):
Mr Richard Barlow
Second Secretary (Political) (2336):
Mr Robert Luke
Second Secretary (Technical Management) (2345):
Mr Alan Barnes
Third Secretary (Management) and Vice-Consul (2314): Ms Aileen Carrick

Department for International Development (DFID) Brazil
Ed. Centro Empresarial Varig Scn,
Quadra 4, Bloco B,

2o Andar, Sala 202
CEP 70.710-926, Brasilia – DF
Telephone: (00) (55) (61) 3327 7230
Facsimile: (00) (55) (61) 3326 8918
Head of Office: Ms Miranda Munro
Environmental and Sustainable Livelihoods: Mr Marcel Viergever
Governance Adviser: Mr Ernesto Jeger
Accounts Manager: Ms Magda Lambert
Accounts Assistant: Ms Claudia Maria
Programme Officer: Ms Karla Skeff
Project Officer: Ms Ana Cristina Cortes
Programme Assistant: Ms Ana Carla Nascimento
Administrative Assistant: Mrs Michele Martins
Trade and Markets Adviser: Mr Siegfried Hirsch

British Council (Brazil)
Ed. Centro Empresarial Varig Scn,
Quadra 4, Bloco B,
Torre Ouest, Conjunto 202
CEP 70.710-926, Brasilia – DF
Telephone: (00) (55) (61) 2106 7500
Facsimile: (00) (55) (61) 2106 7599
e-mail: brasilia@britishcouncil.org.br
Website: www.britishcouncil.org.br

Belém
British Consulate
Av. Governador Malcher, 815 Ed Palladium Center
Conj. 410/411
Belém – Para
CEP 66.035-900
Caixa Postal 98
Telephone: (00) (55) (91) 222 5074, 223 0990
Facsimile: (00) (55) (91) 212 0274
Honorary Consul: Dr A M dos Santos

Manáus
British Consulate
Swedish Match da Amazonia S.A
Rua Poraque 240
Distrito Industrial
Manáus – Am
CEP 69075 –180
Telephone: (00) (55) (92) 613 1819
Facsimile: (00) (55) (92) 613 1420
Honorary Consul: Mr V J Brown

Rio de Janeiro
British Consulate-General
Praia do Flamengo, 284/2 andar,
Rio de Janeiro – RJ, CEP 22210-030
FTN Code – 8456 + 1000 (Switchboard)
Telephone: (00) (55) (21) 2555 9600 (Switchboard) (FTN 8456 2600) 9640 (Consular Section) (FTN 8456 2640)
Facsimile: (00) (55) (21) 2555 9672 (Management) (FTN 8456 2672) 9604 (Chancery) (FTN 8456 2604) 9670 (Commercial) (FTN 8456 2670) 9671 (Consular) (FTN 8456 2671)
Airtech: (00) (55) (21) 2555 9608 (FTN 8456 2608)
e-mail: britishconsulaterio@terra.com.br (General) consular.rio@fco.gov.uk (Consular Section)
Office Hours (GMT): Mon – Fri: 11 30 – 20 00
Consul-General: Mr Paul Yaghmourian
Deputy Consul-General and Consul (Commercial): Mr Tim Dearden
British Council Director: Mr Sital Dhillon
Vice-Consul (Management): Ms Susan McKenzie
Vice-Consul (Consular/Immigration): Mr Andy Cole
Pro-Consul: Mr Murilo Veiga
Pro-Consul: Ms Marina Zelenoy

Belo Horizonte
British Consulate
Rua dos Inconfidentes, 1075, Sala 1302
Belo Horizonte – MG – 30140 120
Savassi
Telephone: (00) (31) 3261 2072
Facsimile: (00) (31) 3261 0226
e-mail: belohorizonte@gra-bretanha.org.br
Honorary Consul: Mr Roger A Gough, MBE
Commercial Officer: Mr Rogerio Pacheco, MBE

Fortaleza
British Consulate
c/o Grupo Edson Queiroz, Praca da Imprensa s/n, Aldeota, Fortaleza – CE, CEP 60135-900
Telephone: (00) (55) (85) 466 8580/8582
Facsimile: (00) (55) (85) 261 8763
e-mail: annette@edsonqueiroz.com.br
Honorary Consul: Mrs Annette T Reeves de Castro

Recife
Av. Conselheiro Aguiar, 2941/3°
Boa Viagem
Recife-PE, CEP 51020-020
Telephone: (00) (55) (81) 3465 0230
Facsimile: (00) (55) (81) 3465 0247
e-mail: recife@gra-bretanha.org.br
Honorary Consul: Mr Alan E Fiore
Commercial Officer: Mr Chris Cobb

Salvador
British Consulate
Av. Estados Unidos, No 18-B
8 Andar-Comercio, Ed-Estados Unidos
CEP 40010 – 020, Salvador – BA
Telephone: (00) (55) (71) 243 7399
Facsimile: (00) (55) (71) 242 7293/243 7856
e-mail: adcos@allways.com.br
Honorary Consul: Mr Nigel Lee

São Paulo
British Consulate-General
Centro Brasileiro Britanico
Rua Ferreira de Araujo, 741-2 Andar
Pinheiros
05428-002-São Paulo-SP
FTN Code – 8463 + extn number
Telephone: (00) (55) (11) 3094 2700
Facsimile: (00) (55) (11) 3094 2717 (Commercial) 3094 2750 (Management)
Airtech: (00) (55) (11) 3816 4887
e-mail: saopaulo@gra-bretanha.org.br
Website: www.gra-bretanha.org.br
Office Hours (GMT): Mon – Thurs: 11 30 – 19 45, Fri 11 30 – 19 30 (UK Summer)
Mon – Thurs: 10 30 – 18 45, Fri 10 30 – 18 30 (UK Winter)

Consul-General and Director of Trade and Investment Brazil (2707, PA's 2710): Mr Andy Henderson
Deputy Consul-General and Deputy Director of Trade and Investment (2713): Mr Pat Ashworth
British Council Director: Mr Mike Winter
Vice-Consul (Consular/Management) (2714): Mr David Paginton
Vice-Consul (Commercial) (2735): Mr Andy Burch
Vice-Consul (Customs) (2701): Mr Nick Freeman
Pro-Consul (Consular/Management) (2727): Ms Melanie Capelin
Pro-Consul (Consular/Management) (2756): Ms Ana Armond

Curitiba
British Trade Office and British Consulate
Rua Presidente Faria, 51, 2 andar,
CJ.204 – Curitiba, PR CEP 80020-918
Telephone/ Facsimile: (00) (55) (41) 322 1202
e-mail: curitiba@gra-bretanha.org.br
Commercial Officer and Honorary Consul: Mr Peter ter Poorten

Porto Alegre
British Consulate and British Commercial Office
Rua Antenor Lemos 57 Cj 303,
Bairro Menino Deus, 90850-100,
Porto Alegre -RS
Telephone: (00) (55) (51) 3232 1414
Facsimile: (00) (55) (51) 3231 6094
e-mail: portoalegre@gra-bretanha.org.br
Honorary Consul/Commercial Officer: Mrs Denise Pellin

Rio Grande
British Consulate
Wilson Sons, Rua Riachuelo, 201 terreo,
CEP 96200-390, Rio Grande – RS
Porto Alegre – RS
Telephone: (00) (55) (53) 233 7700
Facsimile: (00) (55) (53) 233 7701
(00) (55) (53) 231 1530
e-mail: rjg@wilsonsons.com.br
Honorary Consul: Mr Richard Grantham

Santos
British Consulate
Rua Tuiuti 58, 2 andar, Caixa Postal 204,
11010-220, Santos
Telephone: (00)(55) (13) 3211 2300, Direct: (55) (13) 3219 4659
Mobile: (55) (13) 9135 0206
Facsimile: (00) (55) (13) 3219 3840
e-mail: daw@wilsonsons.com.br
Honorary Consul (2310): Mr David A Walton

BRUNEI

Bandar Seri Begawan
British High Commission
PO Box 2197
Bandar Seri Begawan 8674
FTN Code – 8359 + extn number or 1000 for switchboard
Telephone: (00) (673) (2)222231/223121 (switchboard)
226001 Consular/Visa (FTN: 8359 2500)
Facsimile: (00) (673) (2) 234315 (FTN: 8359 2245)
Airtech: (00) (673) (2) 234316 (FTN: 8359 2231)
e-mail: brithc@brunet.bn
Website: www.britishhighcommission.gov.uk/brunei
Office Hours (GMT): Mon to Thurs 00 30 – 04 45 and 06 00 – 09 00. Fri 00 30 – 04 30
High Commissioner (2211): Mr John D W Saville
Deputy High Commissioner (2213): Mr Martin Walley
Defence Adviser (2230 + direct 2219): Captain Paddy H Watson, RN
First Secretary (Defence Cooperation) (2214): Mr Colin Britteon
Third Secretary (Trade and Investment) (2226): Mr Brian Price
Third Secretary (Management/Consular) (2220): Mrs Lisa Jennians
Attaché (2212): Miss Tina Nickels
Attaché (2217): Mr Samuel Hayes

BULGARIA

Sofia
British Embassy
9 Moskovska Street, Sofia
FTN Code – 8477 + extn number
Telephone: (00) (359) (2) 933 9222
Facsimile: 933 9219 (Chancery)
9250 (Management)
9289 (Defence)
9279 (Commercial)
9263 (Visa/Consular)
9233 (DFID)
9265 (Airtech)
942 4344 (British Council)
e-mail: Officer's firstname.surname@fco.gov.uk
Website: www.british-embassy.bg
Office Hours (GMT): Mon – Thurs 06 30 – 15 30, Fri 06 30 – 11 00
Ambassador (2203): Mr Jeremy Hill
Deputy Head of Mission (2204): Mr Laurence Broyd
Counsellor (2206): Mr Ian Woods
Defence Attaché (2214): Colonel John R C Saville
Cultural Attaché (British Council Director): Mr Ian Stewart
First Secretary (Commercial) (2228): Mrs Christine McNeil
Deputy Defence Attaché (2212): Lieutenant Commander Ken M Smith, RN
Second Secretary (Management) (2238): Ms Sheila Towe
Second Secretary (Political/Press) (2207): Mr Iain Stewart
Second Secretary (EU/Economic) (2299): Mr Richard Shackleton
Second Secretary (Political) (2301): Mr Rob Finley
Second Secretary (2282): Mr Lee Williams
Second Secretary (2303): Mr Adrian Barnard
Second Secretary (Consul and ECM) (2260): Miss Hilary Arthur

Assistant Cultural Attaché (British Council Deputy Director): Ms Lisa McManus
Head of DFID Section (2226):
Mrs Toni Grancharova
Third Secretary (Political) (2223):
Mr Karl Tluczek
Attaché (Immigration and Vice-Consul) (2262):
Mr Ramesh Jogiya
Attaché (Immigration and Vice-Consul) (2287):
Mr Ian Hollis
Attaché (Immigration) (2261): Mr Cris Ashworth
Chaplain: Rev James Ramsay

Varna
British Consulate
40 Graf Igantiev Street
PO Box 229
Varna
Telephone: (00) (359) (52) 6655 555
Facsimile: 6655 755
e-mail: nikolai.bozhilov@unimasters.com
Honorary Consul: Mr Nikolai Bozhilov

BURKINA

Ouagadougou
British Embassy (all staff reside at Accra)
Ambassador: Mr Gordon Wetherell
Deputy Head of Mission: Mr Robin Gwynn
Defence Attaché:
Lieutenant Colonel Jonathan A F Howard
First Secretary (Management): Mr David S Jones
First Secretary (Trade and Investment):
Ms Sarah Stevenson
First Secretary (Immigration): Mr Andy Holden
Second Secretary (Political): Ms Farida Shaikh
Second Secretary (Political): Mr Gary Nicholls
Second Secretary (Consular): Ms Caroline Cross

British Honorary Consulate
Hotel Yibi
10 BP 13593
Ouagadougou
Telephone: (00) (226) 30 73 23
Facsimile: (00) (226) 30 59 00
e-mail: ypi@cenatrin.bf
Honorary Consul: Mr Y Pichot

BURMA (SP - see page 121)

Rangoon (Yangon)
British Embassy
80 Strand Road (P.O. Box 638), Rangoon
FTN Code – 8412 + extn number
Telephone: (00) (95) (1) 256918, 380322, 370863-5, 370867, 371852-3, 256438
Facsimile: (00) (95) (1) 370866
Airtech: (00) (95) (1) 380321
Office Hours (GMT): 01 30 – 10 00.
Except Wed: 01 30 – 06 30
Ambassador: Ms Victoria J Bowman
Deputy Head of Mission and HM Consul:
Mrs Catherine Firth
Cultural Attaché, British Council Director (Tel: 256290 ext:312): Mr Marcus Milton
First Secretary (Technical) (resides at Bangkok):
Miss Teresa Hyman
First Secretary (DFID): Mr Rurik Marsden
Second Secretary (Political):
Miss Angela M E Macro
Second Secretary (Management) and Vice-Consul:
Mr Nick J Enescott
Third Secretary (Technical) (resides at Bangkok):
Mr David Ellis
Third Secretary (Political): Mr Nigel P Blackwood
Attaché: Mrs Karen D H Sowerby

BURUNDI

Bujumbura
British Embassy (all staff resident in Kigali)
Ambassador: Mr J J Macadie
Deputy Head of Mission: Mr C W Frean
Defence Attaché (resides at Kampala):
Lieutenant Colonel C J A Wilton
Third Secretary (Political): Ms C Vaudrey

British Embassy Liaison Office
Bujumbura
Burundi
Telephone: (00) (257) 827 602
Facsimile: (00) (257) 246 479
e-mail: BELO@cbinf.com
Liaison Officer: Mr M Nzigamasabo

CAMBODIA

Phnom Penh (SP - see page 121)
British Embassy
27-29 Street 75, Phnom Penh
FTN Code – 8393 + extn number
Telephone: (00) (855 23) 427124, 428295
Facsimile: (00) (855 23) 427125
Airtech: (00) (855 23) 427390
e-mail: BRITEMB@bigpond.com.kh
Consular@phnompenh.mail.fco.gov.uk
Website: www.britishembassy.gov.uk/cambodia
Office Hours (GMT): Mon – Thurs: 01 00 – 10 00.
Fri: 01 00 – 06 00
Ambassador (2202): Mr David G Reader
Deputy Head of Mission and HM Consul (2204):
Mr John Mitchell
Second Secretary (Technical Management Officer) (resides at Bangkok): Ms Teresa Hyman
Second Secretary (Technical Works Officer) (resides at Singapore): Mr Andrew Lelliott
Third Secretary (Vice-Consul and Management Officer) (2214): Mr Gary Benham
Attaché (2203): Ms Siân Martin

Department for International Development (Cambodia)
34 Monivong Boulevard
Phnom Penh
Telephone: (00) (855 23) 430240
Facsimile: (00) (855 23) 430254
e-mail: c-khieu@dfid.gov.uk
First Secretary (Head of Office and Health Adviser): Ms Elizabeth (Lizzie) Smith
Second Secretary (Governance Adviser):
Mr Nigel Coulson
Second Secretary (Rural Livelihoods Adviser):
Mr Chris Price

Second Secretary (Deputy Programme Manager):
Mr Graham MacKenzie
Second Secretary (Social Development Adviser):
Ms Helen Appleton
Attaché (Programme Support Officer – HIV/AIDS):
Ms Nicolette Hutter
Attaché (Associate Professional Officer – Health):
Ms Joanna Nicholls

CAMEROON

Yaoundé
British High Commission
Avenue Winston Churchill
BP 547, Yaoundé
FTN Code – 8394 + extn number
Telephone: (00) (237) 2 22 05 45/2 22 07 96
Facsimile: (00) (237) 2 22 01 48
Airtech: (00) (237) 2 22 91 55
Duty Officer Mobile: (00) (237) 7 713 053
e-mail: BHC.yaounde@fco.gov.uk
Office Hours (GMT): Mon- Thu: 06 45 – 14 45.
Fri: 06 45 – 12 45
High Commissioner: Mr Syd Maddicott
Deputy High Commissioner: Mr Steve Crossman
British Council Director: Ms Jenny Scott
British Council Deputy Director: Mr Tom Hinton
Second Secretary: Mr Nick Baker
Third Secretary (MO/Vice-Consul): Mr Steve Auld
Third Secretary (Entry Clearance): Ms Jo Parry
Attaché: Ms Brenda Thurston

CANADA

Ottawa
British High Commission
80 Elgin Street, Ottawa, Ontario K1P 5K7
FTN Code – 8421 + extn number
Telephone: (00) (1) (613) 237 1530
Voicemail and Direct Lines: (00) (1) (613) 364 + key in extension shown by name
Facsimile: (00) (1) (613) 237 7980
232 0738 Management
232 2533 Visa
237 5211 Economic
237 6537 Passport
567 8045 Political
e-mail: passportenquiries@fco.gov.uk
visaenquiries@fco.gov.uk
Website: www.britainincanada.org
Office Hours (GMT): 13 00 – 21 00
High Commissioner:
Mr David N Reddaway, CMG, MBE
Deputy High Commissioner (6102):
Mr Julian A Evans
Counsellor (Trade/Economic) (6144):
Mr Neil R Chrimes
Counsellor (Political) (6105): Mr Clive Newell
Counsellor (Cultural Affairs) (British Council Director) (6234): Mr Peter Chenery
Defence and Military Adviser (6249):
Brigadier Simon Young
Naval and Air Adviser (6242):
Group Captain Tim P Brewer, OBE, RAF
First Secretary (Head of Political/Information Section) (6120): Mr Andrew Staunton
First Secretary (Science and Technology) (6146):
Ms Julia Hinde
First Secretary (Management) (6160):
Mr Richard Sharp
First Secretary (Political) (6114): Mr Dave Masson
First Secretary (Political) (00 1 613 991 7239):
Ms Janis Sleep
Second Secretary (Economic) (6147):
Mr George Norris
Assistant Naval Adviser B.D.L.S. (6245):
Lieutenant Commander John R Cunane, RN
Second Secretary (Consular) (6200):
Mr Chris Smart
Third Secretary (Political) (6111):
Mrs Katherine Hickey

Montreal
British Consulate-General
Suite 4200, 1000 De La Gauchetiere West
Montreal, Quebec
H3B 4W5
Telephone: (00) (1) (514) 866-5863
Direct Line – see individual officers
Facsimile: (00) (1) (514) 866 0202
Airtech: (00) (1) (514) 866 4867
Office Hours (GMT): 14 00 – 22 00
Consul-General (230): Ms Anne Jarrett
Deputy Consul-General (225): Mr Barry Davidson

Montreal United Kingdom Representative on the Council of the International Civil Aviation Organisation, see page 118

Toronto
British Consulate-General
British Trade and Investment Office
777 Bay Street, Suite 2800, College Park
Toronto, Ontario M5G 2G2
FTN Code – 8423 + extn number
Telephone: (00) (1) 416 593 1290
Facsimile: (00) (1) 416 593 1229
Airtech: (00) (1) 416 593 1425
e-mail: britcon.toronto@fco.gov.uk
Website: http://www.uktradeinvestcanada.org
Office Hours (GMT): 12 30 – 21 00
Consul-General and Director, Trade and Investment: Mr Nicholas Armour
Deputy Consul-General and Deputy Director Trade (2236): Mr Mike Upton
Consul (Investment) (2234): Mr Mike Moon
Management Officer (2227): Mr Gareth Jones
Political and Public Affairs Officer:
Mrs Elizabeth Young
Consular Officer: Mr Jamil Malik

Vancouver
British Consulate-General
1111 Melville Street, Suite 800
Vancouver, British Colombia, V6E 3V6
FTN Code – 8422 + extn number
Telephone: (00) (1) (604) 683 4421
Direct Lines – see individual officers
Facsimile: (00) (1) (604) 681 0693
Airtech: (00) (1) (604) 683 7768
Office Hours (GMT): 16 30 – 00 30
Consul-General (1-2205): Mr James Rawlinson

Deputy Consul-General (1-2208):
Mr Andy Newlands

Calgary
British Trade Office
Suite 1500, Bow Valley Square IV
250-6th Avenue S.W.
Calgary, Alberta T2P 3H7
Telephone: (00) (1) (403) 705 1755
Facsimile: (00) (1) (403) 264 1262
Office Hours (GMT): 15 30 – 23 30
Director: Mr Rob Elgie
Commercial Assistant: Ms Tara Meinhardt

Halifax/Dartmouth
British Consulate
1, Canal Street, P.O. Box 605
Dartmouth, Nova Scotia B2Y 3Y9
Telephone: (00) (1) (902) 461 1381
Facsimile: (00) (1) (902) 465 2578
Honorary Consul: Mr A A Smithers

St. John's
British Consulate
113 Topsail Road, St. John's
Newfoundland A1E 2A9
Telephone: (00) (1) (709) 579 2002
Facsimile: (00) (1) (709) 579 0475
Honorary Consul: Mr F D Smith

Winnipeg
British Consulate
229, Athlone Drive, Winnipeg,
Manitoba, R3J 3L6
Telephone: (00) (1) (204) 896 1380
Facsimile: (00) (1) (204) 269 3025
Honorary Consul: Mr R M Hill

Quebec City
British Consulate
Le Complexe St-Amable
700 – 1150 Claire-Fontaine, Quebec City
Quebec, G1R 5G4
Telephone: (00) (1) (418) 521 3000
Facsimile: (00) (1) (418) 521 3099
Honorary Consul: Mr R Drouin

CAPE VERDE

Praia
British Embassy (all staff resident at Dakar)
Ambassador: Mr Peter Newall
Deputy Head of Mission and Consul:
Mr Derek Levoir
Vice-Consul/ECO: Mrs Elizabeth Changai
Management Officer: Mr Nick Faulkner

São Vincente
British Honorary Consulate
CP423
Mindelo, São Vincente
Telephone: (00) (238) 232 28 30
991 6168 (Mobile)
Facsimile: (00) (238) 232 66 29
e-mail: canutoantoniorc@yahoo.com
Honorary Consul: Mr Antonio Canuto (Hon) MBE

CENTRAL AFRICAN REPUBLIC

Bangui
British Embassy (all staff reside at Yaoundé)
Ambassador and Consul-General:
Mr Syd Maddicott
First Secretary and Consul: Mr Steve Crossman

CHAD

Ndjamena
British Embassy (all staff reside at Yaoundé)
Ambassador: Mr Syd Maddicott
First Secretary and Consul: Mr Steve Crossman

Ndjamena
British Consulate
BP1060
Ndjamena
Tel/Fax: (00) (235) 52 39 70
Mobile: (00) (235) 841 11 02
e-mail: econsit@hotmail.com
Honorary Consul: Mrs Ermanna Delacroix

CHILE

Santiago
British Embassy
Av. El Bosque Norte 0125, Casilla 72-D
Santiago
FTN Code – 8317+ extn number
Telephone: (00) (56) (2) 370 4100
Facsimile: (00) (56) (2) 370 4180 Commercial
4170 Consulate
4160 Management
4140 Chancery
5988 Information
235 7375 British Council
e-mail: chancery.santiago@fco.gov.uk
commercial.santiago@fco.gov.uk
consular.santiago@fco.gov.uk
defence.santiago@fco.gov.uk
Website: www.britemb.cl
Office Hours (GMT): (October – March): Mon-Thurs: 12 00 – 20 30 Fri: 12 00 – 16 00.
(March – October): Mon-Thurs: 13 00 – 21.30.
Fri: 13 00 – 17 00
Ambassador: Mr Howard Drake, OBE
Deputy Head of Mission (4112): Mr James de Waal
Defence Attaché (4120): Colonel Iain S Campbell
Counsellor – Defence Export Services (4149):
Mrs Jackie Callcut
Counsellor (Political) (4123): Mr Ian Anderson
First Secretary (Commercial) (4174):
Mr Duncan Hill
Second Secretary (Management) and Consul (4138): Mr Kevin Brind
Second Secretary (4114): Miss Sarah Anderson
Third Secretary (4124): Miss Imogen Firmstone

British Council
Av. Eliodoro Yañez 831
Providencia – Santiago
Telephone: (00) (56) (2) 410 6900
Facsimile: (00) (56) (2) 410 6929
Cultural Attaché (British Council Director) (6955):
Mr John Knagg, OBE

Valparaíso
British Consulate
Blanco 1199 Piso 5
Casilla 68 – V
Valparaíso
Telephone / Facsimile: (00) (56) (32) 213063
e-mail: con.britanico@entelchile.net
Honorary Consul: Mr Iain Hardy

Punta Arenas
British Consulate
Cataratas del Niagara 01325, Punta Arenas
Casilla 22-D
Telephone: (00) (56) (61) 211535
Facsimile: (00) (56) (61) 239880
e-mail: reesking@tie.cl
Honorary Consul: Mr John Rees

CHINA

Beijing
British Embassy
Main Building
11 Guang Hua Lu, Jian Guo Men Wai, Beijing 100600
FTN Code – 8403 + and individuals extn number
Telephone: (00) (86) (10) 5192 4000 (extension numbers given)
Facsimile: (00) (86) (10) 6532 1937
6532 7989 (Management)
e-mail: commercialmail.beijing@fco.gov.uk (UK Trade and Investment Section)
info@britishcentre.org.cn (UK Trade and Investment Information Resources)
s.t.beijing@fco.gov.uk (Science and Technology)
Office Hours (GMT): 00 30 – 04 00 and 05 30 – 09 00

Consular/Visa Section:
Kerry Centre, 21st Floor, 1 Guang Hua Lu, Beijing 100600
FTN Code – 8465 + extn number
Telephone: (00) (86) (10) 8529 6600 (extension numbers given)
6532 1961, 6750 (Out of Hours)
8529 6600 (24hr Recorded Information Service)
Facsimile: (00) (86) (10) 8529 6081 (Consular)
8529 6080 (Visa Section)
e-mail: visamail@beijing.mail.fco.gov.uk (Visa Enquiries)
consularmail@beijing.mail.fco.gov.uk (Consular Enquiries)
Office Hours (GMT): 00 30 – 04 00 and 05 00 – 08 30

Cultural and Education Section:
4th Floor Landmark Building, Tower 1, 8 North Dongsanhuan Road,
Chaoyang District, Beijing 100004
Telephone: (00) (86) (10) 6590 6903 (extension numbers given)
Facsimile: (00) (86) (10) 6590 0977
e-mail: enquiry@britishcouncil.org.cn
Office Hours (GMT): 00 30 – 04 00 and 05 30 – 09 00

Ambassador (PA 4231): Sir Christopher Hum, KCMG (Mr William G Ehrman, CMG w.e.f Jan 06)
Minister, Consul-General and Deputy Head of Mission (PA 4254): Mr John Dennis
Counsellor (Director of Trade and Investment) (4256): Mr Neil Blakeman
Counsellor (Political/Economic) (4253): Ms Barbara Woodward
Counsellor (Global Affairs) (4368): Mr Peter Wood
Counsellor (British Council Director and Regional Director China / HK) (219): Mr Michael O'Sullivan
Defence, Military and Air Attaché (PA 4258): Brigadier Archie J Miller-Bakewell, OBE, QGM
Naval and Air Attaché (4246): Group Captain Keith J Parkes, MBE, RAF
First Secretary (Political) (4309): Mr John Fox
First Secretary (Political) (4441): Mr David McFarlane
First Secretary (Political) (4381): Mr Denis Pygall
First Secretary (Economic) (4322): Mr Ananda Guha
First Secretary (Economic) (4227): Ms Nicola Willey
First Secretary (Economic) (4217): Mr Simon Goya-Brown
First Secretary (Trade and Investment) (4205): Ms Carol Hinchley
First Secretary (Trade and Investment) (4339): Mr Nick Whittingham
First Secretary (Trade and Investment) (4320): Mr Dennis Leith
First Secretary (Management) (4228): Ms Louise Foxworth
First Secretary (Technical Management) (4223): Mr John Thornton
First Secretary (Regional Technical Works) (4435): Mr Carl Gray
First Secretary (Clinical Nursing Officer) (4424): Ms Jayne Senior, MBE
First Secretary (HM Consul) (3301): Ms Nicole Davison
First Secretary (Science and Technology) (4384): Mr David Concar
First Secretary (Visa) (3392): Mr Paul Sherar
First Secretary (British Council Deputy Director) (237): Mr Robin Rickard
First Secretary (Education) (British Council) (238): Mr Andrew Disbury
First Secretary (Cultural) (British Council) (221): Mr Alex Thompson
First Secretary (Education) (British Council) (266): Ms Nicole de Lalouviere
First Secretary (Examination) (British Council) (227): Mr Brendan McSharry
First Secretary (Examination) (British Council) (314): Ms Sarah Deverall
Second Secretary (Economic) (4437): Mr Ian McKendrick
Second Secretary (Political) (4216): Ms Claire Filshie
Second Secretary (Political) (4315): Ms Jennifer Grange
Second Secretary (Political/Information) (4233): Ms Alexandra Louizos

Second Secretary (Trade and Investment) (4308): Mrs Kirstie Cranshaw
Second Secretary (Trade and Investment) (4311): Mr Ian Cranshaw
Second Secretary (Trade and Investment) (4285): Mr Bikash Dawahoo
Second Secretary (Trade and Investment) (4274): Ms Jane Baxter
Second Secretary (Inward Investment) (4439): Ms Corin Wilson
Second Secretary (Management) (4219): Mr Steve Mitchell
Second Secretary (Management) (4259): Mr Kevin Dillow
Second Secretary (Technical Management) (4234): Mr Simon Moseley
Second Secretary (Security) (4270): Mr Stuart Smith
Second Secretary (Immigration) (3340): Mr Malcolm Whatley
Second Secretary (Immigration) (3315): Mr David Rolls
Second Secretary (Airport Liaison Officer) (3304): Mr Seamus Casserley
Second Secretary (Arts and Science) (British Council) (220): Mr Neil Webb
Second Secretary (Governance) (British Council) (232): Mr Gary Hallsworth
Second Secretary (Governance) (British Council) (228): Mr Ian Robinson
Second Secretary (EU – China Project) (British Council) (tel. 8527 5155 extn.33): Mr Stephen Forbes
Third Secretary (Vice-Consul) (3303): Mrs Gail Johnson
Third Secretary (Immigration) (3381): Mr Yatin Madlani
Third Secretary (Immigration) (3317): Miss Helen Askew
Third Secretary (Immigration) (3318): Mrs Sam Schinkel
Third Secretary (Immigration) (3380): Mrs Lindy Beach
Third Secretary (Immigration) (3345): Mr Andrew Davies
Third Secretary (Immigration) (3319): Mr Mike Berry
Third Secretary (Immigration) (3346): Mr Ian Findlay
Third Secretary (Immigration) (3338): Mrs Mary Whatley
Third Secretary (Immigration) (3347): Mrs Liz Moriarty
Third Secretary (Immigration) (3382): Mr Joseph Horbacki
Third Secretary (Technical Works) (4266): Mr Malcolm Roberts
Defence Attaché (4215): Captain Brian Joyce
Defence Attaché (4226): Sergeant Dave Bell
Attaché (PA to Ambassador) (4231): Mrs Avril Chassels
Attaché (PA to Minister and Deputy Head of Mission) (4254): Ms Julie O'Brien
Attaché (PA to Political Counsellor) (4244): Mrs Roisin Hayes
Attaché (Head of Registry, Political) (4319): Ms Chimene Deane
Attaché (Political) (4236): Mrs Tanya Robinson
Attaché (Political) (4241): Mr John Moriarty
Attaché (Political) (4229): Mr John Randall
Attaché (Trade and Investment) (4257): Ms Katrina McCreadie
Attaché (Head of Visa Registry) (3350): Ms Nicola Smith
Defence Attaché (4215): Mr Ian Knapp

Department for International Development (DFID) China
30th Floor, South Tower, Beijing Kerry Centre, 1 Guang Hua Lu, Beijing 100020
Telephone: (00) (86) (10) 8529 6882 (extension numbers given)
Facsimile: (00) (86) (10) 8529 6002/3/4/5
e-mail: dfid@beijing.mail.fco.gov.uk
Office Hours (GMT): 00 30 – 04 00 and 05 30 – 09 00
Counsellor (Development, Head DFID China) (2002): Mr Adrian Davis
First Secretary (Development, Deputy Head DFID China) (2023): Mr Chris Athayde
First Secretary (Development, Programme Manager) (2044): Mr Pete Shelley
First Secretary (Development, Economics) (2043): Mr Mark George
First Secretary (Development, Education) (2006): Ms Christine Wallace
First Secretary (Development, Environment) (2024): Mr John Warburton
First Secretary (Development, Pro-poor Growth) (2015): Mr Holger Grundel
First Secretary (Development, Health) (2022): Mr Martin Taylor
First Secretary (Development, Social Development) (2011): Mr Rahul Malhotra
First Secretary (Development, Sustainable Livelihoods) (2033): Ms Jane Jamieson
Second Secretary (Development, Deputy Programme Manager) (2010): Mr Matthew Perkins
Second Secretary (Development, Deputy Programme Manager) (2034): Mr Kevin Leitch
Second Secretary (Development, Administration) (2017): Mr Graeme Dixon
Third Secretary (Development, Programme Officer) (2045): Mr Kebur Azbaha
Third Secretary (Development, Programme Officer) (2037): Ms Teresa Kondratowicz

Shanghai
British Consulate-General
Suite 301, Shanghai Centre
1376 Nan Jing Xi Lu
Shanghai 200040
Telephone: (00) (86) (21) 6279 7650
Facsimile: (00) (86) (21) 6279 7651 (General)
6279 7388 (Commercial)
e-mail: britishconsulate@shanghai.mail.fco.gov.uk
firstname.lastname@fco.gov.uk
Website: www.britishconsulate.sh.cn
Office Hours (GMT): 00 30 – 09 00 (Mon – Thu). 00 30 – 07 30 (Fri)

Visa Section
Suite 751, Shanghai Centre
1376 Nan Jing Xi Lu
Shanghai 200040
Telephone: (00) (86) (21) 6279 8130
Facsimile: (00) (86) (21) 6279 8254
e-mail: visa@shanghai.mail.fco.gov.uk
Office Hours (GMT): 00 30 – 09 00 (Mon – Thu).
00 30 – 07 30 (Fri)

British Council
1 Floor Pidemco Tower
318 Fu Zhou Lu
Shanghai 200001
Telephone: (00) (86) (21) 6391 2626
Facsimile: (00) (86) (21) 6391 2121
e-mail: bc.shanghai@britishcouncil.org.cn
firstname.lastname@britishcouncil.org.cn
Website: www.britishcouncil.org.cn
Office Hours (GMT): 00 30 – 09 00
Consul-General: Ms Sue Bishop
Deputy Consul-General: Mr Philip Mani
Head of Commercial: Mr Douglas Barrett
Head of Science and Technology: Mr Nick Khosla
Consul (Commercial): Mr Bob Shead
Consul (Commercial): Mr Barry Nicholson
Consul (Commercial): Mr Tim Standbrook
Consul (Economic/Press and Public Affairs):
Mr Mark Gooding
Consul – British Council Director (Cultural and Education): Mr Jeff Streeter
Consul – British Council Deputy Director (Cultural): Mr Jim Hollington
Consul – British Council Assistant Director (Education): Mr Richard Everitt
Consul – Examinations Services Manager (Education): Ms Sarah Deverall
Consul (Entry Clearance Manager):
Mr Ian Sargeant
Consul (Management/Consular):
Mrs Angela Morgan
Vice-Consul (Visa): Miss Emily Graham
Vice-Consul (Visa): Miss Norah Finlay
Vice-Consul (Visa): Mr Nigel Rennison
Pro-Consul (Consular): Mrs Emma Nicholson

Guangzhou
British Consulate-General
2nd Floor Guangdong International Hotel
(Visa/Consular/Management Sections)
7th Floor Guangdong International Hotel
(Commercial/Political/Economic Sections)
339 Huanshi Dong Lu
Guangzhou 510098
Telephone: (00) (86) (20) 8314 3000 General
8335 1316 British Council
Facsimile: (00) (86) (20) 8331 2799
Management/Consular
8333 6485 Trade and Investment
8332 7509 Visa
8335 1321 British Council
e-mail: guangzhou.commercial@fco.gov.uk (Commercial)
guangzhou.consular@fco.gov.uk (Consular)
guangzhou.visas@fco.gov.uk (Visas)
bc.guangzhou@britishcouncil.org.cn (British Council)
Office Hours (GMT): Mon-Fri: 01 00 – 04 30 and 05 30 – 09 00
Consul-General: Mr Christopher Wood
Deputy Consul-General / Head of Trade and Investment: Mr David Lusher
Consul (Political/Economic):
Miss Claire Lawrence
(Mr Matthew Moody w.e.f Feb 06)
Consul (Science and Innovation): Mr Nigel Birch
Consul (Trade and Investment):
Mr Tom Marchbanks
Consul (Trade and Investment): Mr Paul Wills
Consul (Trade and Investment): Mr John Christie
Consul (Trade and Investment): Mr Brian Price
Consul (Consular/Management): Ms Claire Lawley
Consul (Cultural and Education):
Ms Christine Skinner
Consul (Visas): Mr Richard Burns
Vice-Consul (Visa): Mr Andrew Bartholomeou
Vice-Consul (Visa): Miss Justine Elder
Vice-Consul (Visa): Miss Huma Allahwala
Vice-Consul (Visa): Miss Roslyn McCourty
Vice-Consul (Visa): Miss Kausar Bibi
Vice-Consul (Visa): Mr Mark Aarons
Vice-Consul (Visa): Mr Andy Dallas
Attaché: Mr Andy Sharp

Chongqing
British Consulate-General
Suite 2801, Metropolitan Tower
68 Zourong Road
Chongqing 40010
Telephone: (00) (86) (23) 6381 0321
Facsimile: (00) (86) (23) 6381 0322
Airtech: (00) (86) (23) 6381 0320
e-mail: bcgchq@public.cta.cq.cn
Office Hours (GMT): Mon – Fri 01 00 – 04 00 and 05 00 – 09 00
Consul-General: Miss Carma Elliot
Consul: Mr Scott Strain
British Council Director: Ms Joanne Speakman

Hong Kong Special Administrative Region
British Consulate-General
No. 1 Supreme Court Road
Central, Hong Kong
PO Box 528
FTN Code – 8440 +extn number
Telephone: (00) (852) 2901 3000
Facsimile: (00) (852) 2901 3066 Commercial
3007 Management
3008 Press and Public Affairs
3204 Consular
3347 Visa
3420 Fiscal and Drugs Liaison Office
3143 BC Passport
3195 Passport
3034 Airport Liaison Office
e-mail: political@britishconsulate.org.hk (Political and Economic)
commercial@britishconsulate.org.hk (Commercial)
management@britishconsulate.org.hk (Management)

press@britishconsulate.org.hk (Press and Public Affairs)
consular@britishconsulate.org.hk (Consular)
visa@britishconsulate.org.hk (Visa)
passport@britishconsulate.org.hk (Passport)
Website: www.britishconsulate.org.hk
Office Hours (GMT): Mon – Fri: 00 30 – 09 15
Consul-General (PA 3021): Mr Stephen Bradley
Deputy Head of Mission (PA 3141): Mr Adam Noble
Deputy Consul-General and Director of Trade and Investment (3030): Mr Bob Rayner
Deputy Consul-General (Regional Affairs) (3345): Mr Christopher Sykes
Consul (Management) (3388): Mr Peter Phelan, OBE
Consul (Trade Commissioner) (3408): Mr Philip Tissot
HM Consul and Director of Public Services (3210): Mr Bill Ridout
Consul (Fiscal and Drugs Liaison) (3350): Mr Andy Lawson
Consul (Senior Passports Officer) (3425): Mr John Geoghegan
Consul (Immigration Services) (3126): Mrs Jane F Lacey-Smith
Consul (Deputy Trade Commissioner) (3355): Mr Timothy Hanson
Consul (Regional Airline Liaison Officer) (3032): Ms Sandie Blandford
Vice-Consul (Airline Liaison) (3037): Mr Andrew Gray
Vice-Consul (Airline Liaison) (3036): Mr Philip Boyle
British Council Director (PA: 00 852 2913 5195): Ms Ruth Gee
Vice-Consul (Political/Economic) (3374): Mrs Sarah Robinson
Vice-Consul (Management) (3173): Mr Simon Drew
Vice-Consul (IT and Technical Management) (3158): Mr Glyn Griffiths
Vice-Consul (Security Management) (3430): Mr John Vowles, MBE
Vice-Consul (Political/Economic) (3061): Mr Brian Simpson
Vice-Consul (Political/Economic) (3027): Mr Nicholas Dean
Vice-Consul (Political/Economic) (3239): Miss Clare Jackson
Vice-Consul (Regional Affairs) (3212): Mr Martin Lerigo
Vice-Consul (Visas) (3228): Mr Craig Hiden
Vice-Consul (Passports) (3213): Mrs Sarah Taylor
Vice-Consul (Consular) (3433): Mr Alan Morrison
Vice-Consul (Technical Management) (3168): Mr Matthew Hasker
Attaché (Passports): Ms Shubina Pasha
Vice-Consul (Executive Assistant to Consul-General) (3021): Miss Alyson Garden
Attaché (PA to Consul-General) (3224): Ms Julie Donaldson
Attaché (Political/Economic) (3141): Miss Catriona Souter
Attaché (Political/Economic) (3386): Mr Chris Naylor
Attaché (Chancery) (3310): Mr Gary Davies
Attaché (Chancery) (3369): Ms Claire Scarratt

UK Trade and Investment – Inward Investment Regional Office
British Consulate-General, No 1 Supreme Court Road,
Central, Hong Kong
Telephone: (00) (852) 2901 3367
Facsimile: (00) (852) 2901 3155
e-mail: ukinvestmentap@fco.gov.uk
Website: www.uktradeinvest.gov.uk
Consul (Regional Director Invest UK) (3265): Mr Paul Grey

FCO Supply Solutions Hong Kong
7/F, 3 Supreme Court Road, Hong Kong
Telephone: (00) (852) 2901 3488
Facsimile: (00) (852) 2901 3477
e-mail: sales@fco.gov.uk
Office Hours (GMT): Mon-Fri 00 15 – 09 30
Consul (Regional Manager FCO Services Supply Solutions HK) (3480): Mr Robert Thursfield

Macao
British Consulate-General
No. 1 Supreme Court Rd, Central, Hong Kong
FTN Code – 8440 +extn number
Telephone: (00) (852) 2901 3000
Facsimile: (00) (852) 2901 3066
Consul-General (Resides at Hong Kong) (PA 3021): Mr Stephen Bradley
Deputy Head of Mission (Resides at Hong Kong) (PA 3141): Mr Adam Noble
Deputy Consul-General and Director of Trade and Investment (Resides at Hong Kong) (3030): Mr Bob Rayner
HM Consul (Resides at Hong Kong) (3210): Mr Bill Ridout
Consul (Commercial) (Resides at Hong Kong) (3408): Mr Philip Tissot
Vice-Consul (Resides at Hong Kong) (3433): Mr Alan Morrison
Vice-Consul (Political/Economic) (Resides at Hong Kong) (3239): Miss Clare Jackson

Macao
PO Box 1148
Macao SAR
Telephone: (00) (853) 6850886
Facsimile: (00) (853) 810222
e-mail: honbcmo@yahoo.co.uk
Honorary Consul: Mr Glenn McCartney

COLOMBIA

Bogotá
British Embassy
Edificio ING Barings
Carrera 9 No 76-49 Piso 9
Bogotá
FTN Code – 8448 + extn or 1000 for switchboard
Telephone: (00) (57) (1) 326 8300
Facsimile: 326 8302 (Management)
326 8305 (Commercial)
326 8298 (Political)
326 5303 (Visa/Consular)
326 8280 (Airtech)

e-mail: britain@cable.net.co or
firstname.surname@fco.gov.uk
Office Hours (GMT): Mon-Thur: 13 30 – 17 30 and 18 30 – 21 30. Fri: 13 30 – 18 30
Ambassador (5202): Mr Haydon Warren-Gash
Counsellor and Deputy Head of Mission (5203): Mr James Darius
Counsellor (5214): (Vacant)
Counsellor (Cultural – British Council Director): Mr Charles Nuttall
Defence Attaché (5210): Colonel Mark Ridley
First Secretary (5218): Mr Andrew Gay
First Secretary (Works) (resides at Buenos Aires): Mr Ronnie Clarke
First Secretary (Management) (5212): Mr Alan Marshall
First Secretary (5208): Mr Steve Reynolds
First Secretary (Trade and Investment) (5262): Mr Gary Soper
Second Secretary (5240): Mr Steve Morgan
Second Secretary (5316): Mr Philip Sheriff
Second Secretary (Immigration/Consular) (5221): Mr Nicholas Miller
Second Secretary (Technical Management) (5200): Mr Nick Moss-Norbury
Second Secretary (5209): Mr Chris Marshall
Second Secretary (5207): Ms Rebecca Brown
Second Secretary (Cultural – British Council): Mr Richard Everitt
Second Secretary (Cultural – British Council): Mr Carl Rhymer
Second Secretary (Regional Security): Mr Andy Davis
Second Secretary (5206): Mr Andy Bonsey
Second Secretary (5336): Mr Brendan Gill
Second Secretary (5211): Mr Andy Bridges
Second Secretary (5204/5213): Mr Iain McLennan
Second Secretary (5310): Mr Jack Dodds
Second Secretary (5207): Mr Peter West
Third Secretary (Management) (5247): Mr Ralph Jones
Third Secretary (5217): Mr Kevan Reeves
Third Secretary (Immigration) (5270): Miss Caroline Wise
Third Secretary (Immigration) (5285): Mrs Julie Clarke Soper
Third Secretary (Immigration) (5265): Mr Micheal Saunders
Third Secretary (5333): Mr Pete Brough
Third Secretary (5206): Mr Richard Austin
Assistant Defence Attaché: Mr Allan Dawson
Assistant Defence Attaché: Mr Jamie Lucas
Assistant Defence Attaché: Mr Wayne Arden
Assistant Defence Attaché: Mr Kenny Wonnacott
Assistant Defence Attaché: Mr Roger Moscrop
Assistant Defence Attaché: Mr Tom Palmer
Attaché (Security): Mr Andy Stainton
Attaché (PA/Ambassador) (5202): Ms Pauline Langridge
Attaché: Mr Jo Simon

Cali
British Consulate
Av 4N No 5N – 20
Airmail Box 1326, Cali
Telephone/Facsimile: (00) (57) (2) 653 6089/666 6888
e-mail: britishcali@uniweb.net.co
Honorary Consul: Mr Peter Lawrence
Consular Assistant: Ms Constanza Diez

Medellín
British Consulate
Carrera 42 No 53-26
Itagui, Medellín
Telephone: (00) (57) (4) 377 9966/0952
Facsimile: (00) (57) (4) 377 2212
e-mail consuladobritanico@emp.net.co
Honorary Consul: Mr Fernando Osorio, MBE
Consular Assistant: Ms Maria Mercedes Botero

COMOROS

Moroni
British Embassy (all staff resident in Madagascar)
Ambassador: Mr Anthony Godson
Deputy Head of Mission: Ms R M Owens

Moroni
British Consulate: vacant

CONGO (DEMOCRATIC REPUBLIC)

Kinshasa (SP - see page 121)
British Embassy
83 Avenue du Roi Baudouin,
Kinshasa
FTN Code – 8706 + extn number
Telephone: (00) (243) 98169100, 98169111, 98169200
Facsimile: (00) (243) 8846102
Duty Officer: (00) (243) 9906129
DHM: (00) (243) 9951429
e-mail: ambrit@ic.cd
Office Hours (GMT): Mon -Thurs 06 30 – 13 30; Fri 06 30 – 13 00
Ambassador: Mr Andrew Sparkes
Consul and Deputy Head of Mission: Mr Mark Bensberg
Defence Attaché: Lieutenant Colonel James R Charlesworth
Second Secretary: Ms Josephine Gauld
Third Secretary (Consular/Management): Mr Francis Kayada
Attaché (Immigration): Mr Kevin Brady

CONGO

Brazzaville
British Embassy (all staff reside in Kinshasa)
Ambassador: Mr Andrew Sparkes
Consul and Deputy Head of Mission: Mr Mark Bensberg
Defence Attaché: Lieutenant Colonel James R Charlesworth
Head of DFID Congo: Ms Bronte Flecker

Brazzaville
Ets LISA (à côté de DHL)
Avenue Fosch, Brazzaville
Telephone: (00) (242) 620893
Facsimile: (00) (242) 838543
e-mail: yorick@congonet.cg

Honorary Consul: Mr Dominique Picard, MBE

COSTA RICA

San José (SP - see page 121)
British Embassy
Apartado 815, Edificio Centro Colon
(11th Floor), San José 1007
FTN Code – 8399 + extn number
Telephone: (00) (506) 258 2025
Facsimile: (00) (506) 233 9938
Airtech: (00) (506) 258 5537
e-mail: britemb@racsa.co.cr
Website: www.britishembassycr.com
Office Hours (GMT) Mon-Thurs 14 00 – 22 00.
Fri 14 00 – 19 00
Ambassador and Consul-General:
Ms Georgina Susan Butler
Deputy Head of Mission: Mr Oriel Willock
First Secretary (resides at Panama City):
Mr Alan David Pamplin
Second Secretary (resides at Panama City):
Mr Gary Foster
Second Secretary (Management) (resides at Bogotá): Mr Nick Moss-Norbury

CÔTE D'IVOIRE SEE IVORY COAST

CROATIA

Zagreb
British Embassy
Ul Ivana Lucica 4, 10000 Zagreb
FTN Code – 8384 + extn number
Telephone: (00) (385) (1) 600 9100 (Switchboard)
600 9122 (Visa and Consular)
Facsimile: (00) (385) (1) 600 9111
600 9298 (Visa and Consular)
600 9256 (EU Section)
600 9260 (Commercial)
600 9305 (Press and Public Affairs Section)
600 9245 (Management Section)
Airtech: 600 9210
e-mail: british.embassyzagreb@fco.gov.uk
commercial.section@zg.htnet.hr
Office Hours (GMT): Mon-Thurs: 07 30 – 16 00.
Fri: 07 30 – 13 00
Ambassador: Sir John Ramsden
Deputy Head of Mission: Mr David Hunt
Defence Attaché:
Lieutenant Colonel Michael S Rees
First Secretary (Commercial): Mr Jim T Fraser
British Council Director: Mr Adrian Chadwick
Second Secretary (Immigration/Consular):
Mr Bob Hunter
Second Secretary (EU): Mr Richard A O Jones
Second Secretary (Management): Mr John Burran
Second Secretary (Immigration Liaison):
Mr Tom Attwood
Third Secretary (Political): Ms Elizabeth Ryan
Third Secretary (Vice-Consul): Mr Spencer O'Neil
Third Secretary (Immigration):
Mr Richard Mindang
Assistant Defence Attaché: Sergeant Mark Teasdale

Split
British Consulate
Obala Hrvatskog Narodnog Preporoda 10/III
21000 Split
Telephone: (00) (385) (21) 346 007
Facsimile: (00) (385) (21) 362 905
e-mail: british-consulat-st@st.tel.hr
Office Hours (GMT): Summer: Mon, Wed, Thurs
06 00 – 13 30. Tues 06 00 – 17 00.
Fri 06 00 – 12 00.
Winter: Mon, Wed, Thurs 07 00 – 14 30.
Tues 07 00 – 18 00. Fri 07 00 – 13 00
Honorary Consul: Captain Ante Roje
Pro Consul: Mrs Sarina Kalebota

Dubrovnik
British Consulate
Buniceva Poljana 3/1, 20000 Dubrovnik
Telephone/Facsimile: (00) (385) (20) 324 597
e-mail: honcons.dubrovnik@inet.hr
Office Hours (GMT): Mon, Tue, Thurs and
Fri: 08 00 – 11 00
Honorary Consul: Mrs Sara Marojica, MBE

CUBA

Havana
British Embassy
Calle 34 No. 702/4 entre 7ma Avenida y 17
Miramar, Havana
FTN Code – 8533+ extn number
Telephone: (00) (53) (7) 204 1771 Switchboard
Facsimile: (00) (53) (7) 204 8104
Management/Consular/Immigration
204 1049 Commercial/Information
204 9214 Chancery
e-mail: embrit@ceniai.inf.cu (Embassy)
britcoun@ip.etecsa.cu (British Council)
Office Hours (GMT): Summer: 12 00 – 19 30.
Winter: 13 00 – 20 30
Ambassador: Mr John Dew
First Secretary and Deputy Head of Mission:
Mr Nigel Baker
Defence Attaché (resides at Caracas):
Group Captain Willie G S Dobson, RAF
First Secretary (Management) and Consul:
Mr John Farrand
First Secretary (Science/Culture, British Council Director): Mr William Edmundson
First Secretary (resides at Kingston): Mr Jim Day
Second Secretary (Commercial/Economic):
Ms Janet Sullivan
Second Secretary (Political/Information): Miss
Melanie Hopkins
Second Secretary (resides at Kingston):
Mr Keith Wiggins
Second Secretary (resides at Mexico City):
Mr Ian Taylor
Third Secretary (Commercial/Immigration):
Mr Alan Dacey
Attaché (Chief Security Officer): Mr Fred Belcher
Attaché: Miss Rebecca Jones
Attaché: Miss Melanie Cook
Attaché (Technical Works): Mr Patrick O'Driscoll

CYPRUS

Nicosia

British High Commission
Alexander Pallis Street (PO Box 21978), 1587 Nicosia or BFPO 567
FTN Code – 8534 + extn number
Telephone: (00) (357) (22) 861100
Facsimile: (00) (357) (22) 861125 Information
861315 Chancery
861175 Management
861200 Consular
861150 Commercial
Airtech: 861287
e-mail: infobhc@cylink.com.cy
Office Hours (GMT): Mon – Fri 05 30 – 12 30
High Commissioner: Mr Peter Millett
Counsellor and Deputy High Commissioner: Mr Rob Fenn
Defence Adviser: Colonel Thomas M Fitzalan Howard, CBE
Counsellor (Political): Mr Charles Parton
British Council Director: Mr Richard Walker
First Secretary (Consular) (tel: 22861360): Mr Gordon MacLeod
First Secretary (Commercial) (tel: 22861340): Mr David Brown
Second Secretary (Management) (tel: 22861350): Mr Bob Jackson
Second Secretary (Political) (tel: 22861230): Mr Andrew O'Henley
Second Secretary (Economic) (tel: 22861231): Ms Johanna Liddle
Second Secretary (EU/Economic) (tel: 22861339): Ms Kristina Hill
Second Secretary (Chancery/Information) (tel: 22862380): Mr Nigel Bond
Second Secretary (resides in Tel Aviv): Mr John Walker
Attaché (Consular) (tel: 22861362): Mr Daniel Barker
Attaché (Consular) (tel: 22861363): Ms Claire Dorrian
Attaché (Consular) (tel: 22861361): Ms Emma Pavey
Attaché (Chancery) (tel: 22861331): Ms Heidi Gundersen
Attaché (Chancery): Mr Tim Hingston

Zygi

British East Mediterranean Relay Station
PO Box 54912, Limassol
Telephone: (00) (357) (24) 332511, 332341
Facsimile: (00) (357) (24) 332595, 332180
Office Hours (GMT): Mon – Fri 05 50 – 12 40
Second Secretary (Management) (Resides in Nicosia): Mr Bob Jackson

CZECH REPUBLIC

Prague

British Embassy
Thunovska 14
118 00 Prague 1
FTN Code – 8334 + extn number
Telephone: (00) (420) 2 5740 2111
Facsimile: (00) (420) 2 5740 2296
Airtech: (00) (420) 2 5740 2249
e-mail: info@britain.cz

Trade and Investment Section
Palac Myslbek
Na Prikope 21
117 19 Prague 1
FTN Code – 8363 + extn number
Telephone: (00) (420) 2 2224 0021/2/3
Facsimile: (00) (420) 2 2224 3625
e-mail: tradeinvest.PRAGC@fco.gov.uk

British Council
Bredovsky dvůr, Politickych vězňu 13
110 00 Prague 1
Telephone: (00) (420) 2 2199 1162
Facsimile: (00) (420) 2 2493 3847
Telex: 122097 (a/b BCCZ C)
e-mail: Forename.Surname@britishcouncil.cz
Office Hours (GMT): end Mar – end Oct: 06 30 – 15 00 (local 08.30 – 17 00)
Ambassador: Linda J Duffield, CMG
Counsellor and Deputy Head of Mission (2253): Mr Simon Martin
Defence Attaché (2261): Colonel Simon C Newton
Cultural Attaché (British Council Director): Mrs Mandy Johnson
First Secretary (Commercial): Mrs Karen Stanton
First Secretary (EU/Economic) (2315): Ms Jill Parkinson
First Secretary (Management/Consul) (2226): Mr Gavin Scott
First Secretary (Political/External) (2258): Mr Alexander Martin
First Secretary (TWO) (resides in Vienna): Mr Ian Sweeney
First Secretary/FLO (resides in Vienna): Mr Nicholas Hamill
British Council Assistant Director: Mr Matt Burney
Assistant Defence Attaché (2240): Squadron Leader Euan C Alexander, RAF
Second Secretary (Political/Press and Public Affairs) (2245): Mr Peter Wickenden
Second Secretary (Political/EU) (2237): Mr Stuart Summers
Second Secretary (Commercial): Mr Andrew Wells
Second Secretary: Mr Steven Hemsley
Second Secretary/TMO (resides in Vienna): Mr Rod Parker
Second Secretary/ALO (resides in Budapest): Mr Steve Brown
Third Secretary and Vice-Consul (2205): Mrs Maggie Yarunina
Third Secretary (Political) (2259): Mr Peter Culyer
Third Secretary (Management) (2223): Mrs Julie B Jackson

DENMARK

Copenhagen

British Embassy
Kastelsvej 36/38/40, DK-2100 Copenhagen Ø
FTN Code – 8320 + extn number
Telephone: (00) (45) 35 44 52 00
Facsimile: (00) (45) 35 44 52 93 Information Section

52 14 Political Section
52 46 Commercial Department
52 53 Consular
52 59 Management
e-mail: info@britishembassy.dk
Website: www.britishembassy.dk
Office Hours (GMT): end Mar – end Oct 07 00 – 15 00 and end Oct – end Mar 08 00 – 16 00
Consular/Visa Section:
Consular: end Mar – end Oct 07 00 – 10 30 and 11 30 – 13 00
end Oct – end Mar 08 00 – 11 30 and 12 30 – 14 00
Visa: end Mar – end Oct 07 00 – 09 00
end Oct – end Mar 08 00 – 10 00
Commercial: end Mar – end Oct 06 30 – 10 30 and 11 30 – 14 30
end Oct – end Mar 07 30 – 11 30 and 12 30 – 15 30
British Council (Cultural Section) – Director: Dr Michael Sorensen-Jones
Gammel Mønt 12. 3. 1117 Copenhagen K
Telephone: (00) (45) 33 36 94 00
(Tel. Hours: 09 00 – 12 00, 13 00 – 15 30)
Educational Enquiries:
Telephone: (00) (45) 33 36 94 04
(Tel. Hours: 12 30 – 15 30)
e-mail: british.council@britishcouncil.dk
Ambassador: Sir Nicholas W Browne, KBE, CMG
Counsellor (5223): Mr Tarquin S A Folliss
Defence Attaché (5209): Commander Charlie D Wilson, OBE, RN
First Secretary (Political) (5207): Ms Wendy Wyver
First Secretary (Management) and Consul (5263): Mr Stuart Puryer
First Secretary (Commercial) (5283): Ms Pam Balkin
Second Secretary (Political) (5229): Mr Alan Campbell
Second Secretary (Political) (5216): Ms Karen Brooking
Second Secretary (Technical/Management) (5215): Mr Jim Preston
Second Secretary (Commercial) (5291): Mr Stephen Metti
Third Secretary (Political) (5205): Mr Gavin Crockard
Attaché (AMO/Vice-Consul) (5264): Mr Neale Jones
Vice-Consul (5249): Mrs Jeanie T P Christoffersen

Aabenraa
British Consulate
Turistchef
c/o Turistbureauet
H.P. Hanssens Gade 5
6200 Aabenraa
Telephone: (00) (45) 74 62 35 00
Facsimile: (00) (45) 74 63 07 44
e-mail: wk@visitaabenraa.dk
Office Hours (GMT): 06 30 – 14 30
Honorary Consul: Mr William Klinker (Danish)

Aalborg
British Consulate
Hasserisvej 112
Postboks 23
9100 Aalborg
Telephone: (00) (45) 98 11 34 99
Facsimile: (00) (45) 98 11 56 99
e-mail: jbh.as@mail.dk
Office Hours (GMT): 05 30 – 13 30
Honorary Consul: Mr Jørgen Bladt, MBE (Danish)

Aarhus
British Consulate
c/o Scanad Udviklingsbureau A/S
Skolegade 19B, 8100 Aarhus C
Telephone: (00) (45) 86 27 33 38
Mobile: (00) (45) 70 28 67 00
e-mail: claus.herluf@mail.dk
Office Hours (GMT): 06 30 – 14 30
Honorary Consul: Mr Claus R Herluf (Danish)

Esbjerg
British Consulate
Kraven Projekter Aps
Østervangsvej 2-6
6715 Esbjerg N
Telephone: (00) (45) 75 18 14 76
Facsimile: (00) (45) 75 45 38 52
e-mail: gk@kravin.dk
Office Hours (GMT): 06 30 – 14 00
Honorary Consul: Mr Gert Kragelund (Danish)

Fredericia
British Consulate
Vesthavnen, P O Box 235
7000 Fredericia
Telephone: (00) (45) 75 92 20 00
Facsimile: (00) (45) 76 20 29 65
e-mail: pia raun rasmussen@rahbek.dk
Office Hours (GMT): 06 00 – 14 30
Honorary Consul: Mr Morten Rahbek Hansen (Danish)

Herning
British Consulate
Aage Damgaard ApS
Lundvej 8, 7400 Herning
Telephone: (00) (45) 96 27 73 00
Facsimile: (00) (45) 97 12 48 58
e-mail: lars@aage-damgaard.dk
Office Hours (GMT): 06 30 – 14 30
Honorary Consul: Mr Lars Damgaard (Danish)

Odense
British Consulate
Albanitorv 4, Postboks 308
5100 Odense C
Telephone: (00) (45) 66 14 47 14
Facsimile: (00) (45) 66 14 61 30
Office Hours (GMT): 06 00 – 14 00
Honorary Consul: Mr Frits Niegel, MBE, OBE (Danish)

Tórshavn, Faroe Islands
British Consulate
P/F Damfar, P O Box 1154
Niels Finsensgøta 5
FR-110 Tórshavn
Faroe Islands
Telephone: (00) (298) 35 99 77

Facsimile: (00) (298) 35 99 80
e-mail: thd@damfar.fo
Office Hours (GMT): 09 00 – 17 00
Honorary Consul: Mr Tummas H Dam

DJIBOUTI

British Embassy (All staff resident at Addis Ababa)
Ambassador: Mr R Dewar
First Secretary (Management and Consul): Miss A Marriott, MBE
Second Secretary: Mr O Richards

British Consulate
PO Box 169, Rue de Djibouti
Djibouti
Telephone (00) (253) 25 09 17
Facsimile: (00) (253) 35 78 15
e-mail: british.consulate@intnet.dj
Honorary Consul (Resident in Djibouti): Mr A Martinet

DOMINICA

Roseau
British High Commission
Lower Collymore Rock (PO Box 676)
Bridgetown, Barbados
Telephone: (00) (1) (246) 430 7800
Facsimile: (00) (1) (246) 430 7851 Chancery
(246) 430 7860 Management/Consular
(246) 430 7826 Commercial/Information
e-mail: britishhc@sunbeach.net
Office Hours (GMT) 12 00 – 16 30 and 17 30 – 20 00
(All staff reside at Bridgetown)
High Commissioner: Mr Duncan Taylor, CBE
Deputy High Commissioner: Mr Alan Drury
Defence Adviser: Captain Steve G Wilson, RN
First Secretary: Mr Eamon Kearney
First Secretary (Management): Ms Ros Day, MBE
High Commissioner's Special Representative: Mr Nick J Pyle, MBE
Second Secretary (Chancery): Mr Rick Gomez
Third Secretary (Immigration): Mr Mark Harrison

Roseau
British Consulate
Office of the Honorary British Consul
c/o Courts (Dominica) Ltd
PO Box 2269, Roseau
Telephone: Office: (1 767) 448 7655 or 448 0166
Facsimile: (1 767) 448 7817
e-mail: smaynard@courts.co.dm
Honorary Consul: Mr Simon Maynard

DOMINICAN REPUBLIC

Santo Domingo (SP - see page 121)
British Embassy
Ave 27 de Febrero No 233
Edificio Corominas Pepín
Santo Domingo
Telephone: (00) (1) (809) 472 7111
472 7905 (Commercial)
472 7373/7671 (Consular)
Facsimile: (00) (1) (809) 472 7190
(Chancery/Commerial)
472 7574 (Consular/Management)
e-mail: brit.emb.sadom@codetel.net.do
Office Hours (GMT): Mon-Thurs 12 00 – 20 30. Fri 12 00 – 17:00
Ambassador: Mr Andy Ashcroft
Deputy Head of Mission: Mr Kevin Shaughnessy
Defence Attaché (Resides at Caracas): Group Captain Willie G S Dobson, RAF

Puerto Plata
British Consulate
Calle Beller No.51
Puerto Plata, R.D.
Telephone: (00) (1) (809) 586-4244 / 8464
Facsimile: (00) (1) (809) 586-3096
Honorary Consul: Mrs Cindy Salem
Consular Agent: Mr Genny Mendez

EAST TIMOR

Dili (SP - see page 121)
British Embassy
Pantai Kelapa (Avenida de Portugal)
Dili
(Postal Address: PO Box 194, The Post Office, Dili)
FTN Code – 8445 + extn
Telephone: (00) (670) 332 2838
(00) (670) 723 1600 (HM Ambassador)
(00) (670) 723 1601 (DHM)
Facsimile: (00) (670) 331 2652
Airtech: (00) (670) 332 2837
e-mail: britishembassydili@fco.gov.uk
Office Hours (GMT): Mon-Fri 00 30 – 08 00
Ambassador: Ms Tina S Redshaw
Deputy Head of Mission: Mr Lee Jackson
Defence Attaché (resides at Jakarta): Colonel Stuart Jarvis
First Secretary (Technical) (resides at Singapore): Mr Richard Hardy
Second Secretary (Technical) (resides at Singapore): Mr Dave Guy

ECUADOR

Quito (SP - see page 121)
British Embassy
Citiplaza Building
Naciones Unidas Ave and República de El Salvador
14th Floor
(Consular Section 12th Floor) Quito
FTN Code – 8279 + extn number
Telephone: (00) (593) (2) 2 970 800 / 970 801
Facsimile: (00) (593) (2) 2 970 807 Consular
2 970 809 Commercial
2 970 810 Management
2 970 811 Chancery
Airtech: 2 970 812
P.O. Box: 17 – 17 – 830
e-mail: britembq@interactive.net.ec
Office Hours (GMT): Mon – Thur 13 30 – 17 30 and 18 30 – 22 00. Fri 13 30 – 18 30
Ambassador (2204): Mr Richard Lewington
Consul and Deputy Head of Mission (2217): Mr Peter Evans

Defence Attaché (resides at Caracas):
Group Captain William G S Dobson, RAF
Second Secretary (2215): Ms Theresa Lee
Second Secretary (Management) (resides at Bogotá): Mr Nick Moss-Norbury
Third Secretary (Management) (2205):
Miss Suzanne Manley
Third Secretary (Vice-Consul) (2221):
Miss Sofie Deeks
Vice-Consul (2236): Miss Verónica Ruiz

Guayaquil
British Consulate
c/o Agripac
General Córdova 623 y Padre Solano
PO Box 09-10-8598, Guayaquil
Telephone: (00) (593) (4) 2 560400, extn 318
Facsimile: (00) (593) (4) 2 562641
e-mail: carmstrong@agripac.com.ec or rtorres@agripac.com.ec
Office Hours (GMT): 14 30 – 18 00 and 20 00 – 23 00
Honorary Consul: Mr Colin R Armstrong, OBE
Honorary Vice-Consul: Mrs Rocio Torres

Guayaquil
British Embassy – Trade Office
Torres del Norte Building,
Torre A, 5th Floor, Office 503
Kennedy Norte, Av. Miguel H. Alcivar, Manzana 506
Telephone: (00) (593) (4) 2 687112
Facsimile: (00) (593) (4) 2 687113
e-mail: gye_ukti@telconet.net
Office Hours (GMT): Mon-Thurs: 13 30 – 17 30 and 18 30 – 22 00. Fri: 13 30 – 18 30
Commercial Officer: Miss Irene Lertora
Commercial Assistant: Miss Monica Ingarévalo

Galápagos
British Consulate
c/o Etica Office, Barrio Estrada,
Puerto Ayora, Isla Santa Cruz, Galápagos
Telephone: (00) (593) (5) 526157 / 526159
Facsimile: (00) (593) (5) 526591
e-mail: dbalfour@eticapa.com.ec
Office Hours (GMT): 13 00 – 17 00 and 19 00 – 23 00
Honorary Consul: Mr David Balfour, MBE

EGYPT

Cairo
British Embassy
7, Ahmed Ragheb Street, Garden City, Cairo
FTN Code – 8538 + extn number
Telephone: (00) (20) (2) 794 0850, 794 0852/8
Facsimile: 796 1458 Political,
794 3065 Consular and Information
794 0859 Commercial
796 3222 Management
795 1235 Visa
Airtech: 8538 2215
e-mail: info@britishembassy.org.eg
Website: www.britishembassy.org.eg
Office Hours (GMT): Sunday – Wednesday:
Chancery, Commercial sections work: 06 30 – 14 00
Defence: 06 00 – 14 00 (including lunch)
Consular, Visa, Management: 06 00 – 13 30
Office Hours (GMT): Thursday:
Chancery, Commercial: 06 30 – 12 30
Defence: 06 00 – 12 30
Consular, Visa, Managament: 06 00 – 12 00
Ambassador: Sir Derek Plumbly, KCMG
Counsellor and Deputy of Mission:
Mr Michael Davenport
Defence Attaché: Captain Philip W Holihead, RN
Cultural Counsellor (British Council Director):
Mr Paul Smith
Counsellor (Regional Affairs):
Mr Christopher Breeze
First Secretary (Commercial): Mr Simon Fisher
First Secretary and Head of Political and Economic Section: Mr Tim Stew, MBE
First Secretary (Political): Mr David Kilby
First Secretary (Cultural) and British Council Deputy Director: Ms Sally Goggin
First Secretary and Consul: Mr Mark Rakestraw
First Secretary (Cultural): Mr Steven Murrell
First Secretary (Technical Works Officer):
Mr John Warrener
First Secretary (Management): Mr Shaun Flaherty
First Secretary (Regional Expert, Arab World Projects): Mr Nicholas Abbott
Second Secretary (Aid): Mr Ian Ruff
Second Secretary (Commercial):
Mr Stephen Townsend
Second Secretary (Technical Management):
Mr Andrew Higham
Second Secretary (Immigration):
Mr Rupert Montgomery
Second Secretary (Press and Public Affairs):
Ms Caroline Alcock
Second Secretary (Cultural):
Miss Samantha Harvey
Deputy Management Officer: Mr Gordon Horne
Attaché and Vice-Consul: Mr Jason Lambert
Attaché and Vice-Consul: Mr Richard Postill
Attaché and Vice-Consul: Mrs Debbie Hare
Attaché: Mr Roger Williams
Attaché: Mrs Jacqui Glen
Attaché: Ms Caroline Begley
Attaché: Mr Adam Harris
Attaché: Mrs Ruth Whelan
Attaché: Ms Aurea Marshall
Attaché: Mr Paul Hyde

Alexandria (SP)
British Consulate-General
3 Mina Street, Kafr Abdou, Roushdi,
Ramley Alexandria, 21529
Telephone: (00) (20) (3) 5467001, 5467002, 5223717, 5220507
Facsimile: (00) (20) (3) 5467177
Office Hours (GMT): Sun – Wed: 06 00 – 13 30
Thurs: 06 00 – 13 00
Consul-General: Mr Alan Cobden

Suez
British Consulate
HS Supply Co.

9 El-Galaa Street, Suez
Telephone: (00) (20) (62) 334102 (Consulate), (00) (20) (62) 313872 (Office), 314055 (Home)
Telex: 66112 DRHSS UN
Facsimile: (00) (20) (62) 320729
Mobile: 012 210 1343
Honorary Consul: Dr Hussein Samir

Luxor
British Honorary Consular Agent
Gaddis Hotel
Khaled Ibn El Walid St.
Luxor
Telephone: (00) (20) (95) 382838 (Consulate and Office), 374814 (Home)
Facsimile: (00) (20) (95) 380814, 382837
Mobile: 012 210 5456
Honorary Consular Agent: Mr Ehab Gaddis

EL SALVADOR

San Salvador (SP - see page 121)
British Embassy (except where shown all staff reside at Guatemala City)
Ambassador: Mr Richard D Lavers
(Mr Ian Hughes w.e.f March 06)
First Secretary and Deputy Head of Mission:
Mr Kevin A Garvey
Defence Attaché: Colonel Ian Blair-Pilling, OBE
First Secretary (DLO) (resides at Panama City):
Mr Alan Pamplin
Second Secretary (Management) and Consul:
Mr Colin Gracey
Second Secretary (Chancery): Mrs Susie Kitchens
Assistant Defence Attaché:
W.O. Eugene J McCran, RAF
Second Secretary (DLO) (resides at Panama City):
Mr Gary Foster
Third Secretary: Mr Amar Shazad

San Salvador
British Consulate
PO Box 242
San Salvador
Telephone: (00) (503) 281 5555 or 271 1050
Telefax: (00) (503) 271 1026
Honorary Consul: Mr George Chippendale, MBE

EQUATORIAL GUINEA

Malabo
British Embassy (all staff reside at Yaoundé)
Ambassador and Consul-General:
Mr Syd Maddicott
First Secretary and Consul: Mr Steve Crossman

Malabo
British Consulate
Telephone: (00) 240 256 482 (Office)
Facsimile: (00) 1 713 328 1249
e-mail: GMcCullough@terra.es
GMcCullough@MarathonOil.com
Honorary Consul: Mr Gerard McCullough
Commercial Attaché (tel. (00) 240 275 948):
Ms Colette Jones
(e-mail: nahsang@yahoo.com)

ERITREA

Asmara
British Embassy
66-68 Mariam Ghimbi Street
PO Box 5584 Asmara
FTN Code – 8309 + extn number
Telephone: (00) (291) 1 12 01 45
Facsimile: (00) (291) 1 12 01 04
1 18 80 31
Airtech: (00) (291) 1 20 28 39
e-mail: Asmara.Enquiries@fco.gov.uk
Office Hours (GMT): Mon-Thurs 05 00 – 10 30 and 11 30 – 13 30. Fri 05 00 – 10 30
Ambassador (2200): Mr Nick Astbury
Defence Attaché (Resides in Nairobi):
Colonel A D K Inkster
Third Secretary (Management/Immigration/Vice-Consul and Deputy Head of Mission) (2230):
Miss K Gould

ESTONIA (SP - see page 121)

Tallinn
British Embassy
Wismari 6
10136 Tallinn
FTN Code – 8321 + extn number
Telephone: (00) (372) 667 4700 (Switchboard)
Facsimile: (00) (372) 667 4755
(Political/HMA/DHM)
4724 (Commercial)
4756 (Management/Defence)
4725 (Consular/Visa)
e-mail: information@britishembassy.ee
Website: www.britishembassy.ee
Office Hours (GMT): Summer: 06 00 – 14 00
Winter: 07 00 – 15 00
Ambassador (4703): Mr Nigel R Haywood
Deputy Head of Mission (4713):
Mr William Elliott
Defence Attaché (resides at Riga):
Lieutenant Colonel Glen A B Grant
First Secretary (British Council Director):
Ms Kyllike Tohver
First Secretary (Political) (4704):
Ms Sarah Bewley
Second Secretary (Technical Management) (resides at Helsinki): Mr Tim Goode
Third Secretary (Management) and Consul (4728):
Miss Tiiu Morris
Third Secretary (Political) (4722): Mr Stuart Peters
Third Secretary (Regional Affairs) (4744):
Mr Christopher Rowswell
UKTI Officer (4736): Miss Ketevan Moseshvili
Vice-Consul and ECO (4706): Mr Paul Jordan
Political Attaché (4715): Mr Daniel Garlick
Press Officer (4719): Miss Kaire Kroos

ETHIOPIA

Addis Ababa
British Embassy
Comoros Street
PO Box 858
Addis Ababa
FTN Code – 8539 + 1000 for switchboard

Telephone: (00) (251) 1 61 23 54
Facsimile: (00) (251) 1 61 05 88
(00) (251) 1 61 41 54
(Visa/Consular Section)
e-mail: BritishEmbassy.AddisAbaba@fco.gov.uk
Office Hours (GMT): Mon-Thurs: 05 00 – 13 30
Fri: 05 00 – 10 00
Consular/Visa Section Public Opening Hours: Mon – Fri: 05 30 – 09 00
Ambassador: Mr Robert Dewar
Deputy Head of Mission: Ms Deborah Fisher
Defence Attaché: Colonel David S Charters
First Secretary (Conflict Prevention): Mr Jeremy Astill Brown
First Secretary (British Council Director): Mr Michael Moore
First Secretary (Management/Consul): Mr Doug Winter
First Secretary (British Council): Mr Simon Mills
Second Secretary (Political): Mr Daniel Drake
Second Secretary (Political/Economic/ Information): Miss Holly Tett
Second Secretary (Technical Management Officer): Mr Peter Waterhouse
Third Secretary (Immigration/Vice-Consul): Ms Carole Jarvie
Third Secretary (Management/Security): Mr Glyn Cartmell

Department for International Development (DFID) Ethiopia
British Embassy Compound
PO Box.858
Addis Ababa
Telephone: (00) (251) 1 61 23 54
Facsimile: (00) (251) 1 62 24 32
Head of Office: Mr Paul Ackroyd
Deputy Head of Office (Programme): Mr Anthony Way
Deputy Head of Office (Management): Mr Toby Weaver
Social Development Adviser: Ms Claudia Fumo
Education Adviser: Ms Laure Beaufils
Food Security Adviser: Mr Tim Robertson
Food Security Adviser: Ms Melkamnesh Alemu
Governance Adviser: Mr Rupert Bladon
HIV/AIDS Adviser: Ms Marion Kelly
Peace and Security Adviser: Ms Lu Ecclestone
Economic Adviser: Ms Vanessa Head
Food Security Adviser (EU): Mr Tim Waites
Rural Development Adviser (WB): Ms Michelle Philips
Deputy Programme Manager: Ms Carol Norman
Deputy Programme Manager: Ms Helen Winterton
Office Manager: Mr John Hawkes
IT Manager: Ms Sara Green
Programme Officer: Ms Helen Ireton

FIJI

Suva (SP - see page 121)
British High Commission
Victoria House
Gladstone Road
Suva (PO Box 1355)
FTN Code – 8443 + extn number
Telephone: (00) (679) 3229100
Facsimile: (00) (679) 3229132 (General)
3229140 (Chancery)
3307118 (Visa)
Airtech: (00) (679) 3229139
e-mail: Public Affairs:
publicdiplomacysuva@fco.gov.uk
Commercial Office:
tradeinvestmentsuva@fco.gov.uk
e-mail for individual officers – insert:
firstname.surname + @fco.gov.uk
Website:
http://www.britishhighcommission.gov.uk/fiji
Office Hours (GMT): Sun -Wed 20 15 – 01 00 and 02 00 – 05 00. Thurs 20 15 – 01 00
High Commissioner, also Alternate Representative for Pitcairn; South Pacific Commission; non-resident High Commissioner to Nauru, Kiribati and Tuvalu: Mr Charles F Mochan (ext 2120)
Deputy High Commissioner. Also non-resident Ambassador to Micronesia, Marshall Islands and Palau; Deputy High Commissioner to Nauru, Kiribati and Tuvalu: Mr Ian Powell (ext 2122)
Defence Adviser (resides at Wellington): Colonel Nigel Lloyd
Second Secretary (Political, Press and Public Affairs); Deputy Head of Mission and Consul to Micronesia, Marshall Islands and Palau: Mr Stephen Tarry (ext 2110):
Third Secretary (Management/Consular/ Immigration): Mr Andrew Osborn (ext 2105)

FINLAND

Helsinki
British Embassy
Itainen Puistotie 17, 00140
Helsinki
FTN Code – 8322 + 1000 for switchboard
Telephone: (00) (358) (9) 2286 5100
Telefax: Political Section (00) (358) (9) 2286 5284
All other Sections (00) (358) (9) 2286 5262, 5272
Airtech: (00) (358) (9) 8322 5237
e-mail: info@britishembassy.fi
Website: www.britishembassy.fi
Office Hours (GMT): Sep-June: 07 00 – 15 00
June-Aug: 06 30 – 13 00
Ambassador (5222): Mr Matthew Kirk
Counsellor and Deputy Head of Mission (5234): Mr Richard Powell
Counsellor (Political/PPAS) (5264): Mr Brian Olley
Counsellor (Regional Affairs) (5207): Mr Keith Malin
Defence Attaché (5246): Lieutenant Colonel Rick M Andrews
Head of UK Trade and Investment Services (5219): Mr John Slate
Regional Director of Inward Investment Services (Resident in Stockholm): Mr Adrian Pinder
HM Consul and First Secretary (Management) (5221): Mr Roger Woodward
British Council Director: Ms Tuija Talvitie
Deputy Head of UK Trade and Investment Services (5229): Mr Stephen Conlon

Second Secretary (Political/EU) (5240):
Mr Andy Pryce
Second Secretary (Management/Technical) (5244):
Mr Tim Goode
Vice-Consul/Deputy Management Officer (5238):
Ms Anne Gill
Chaplain: Rev. Rupert Moreton

Jyväskylä
British Consulate
Telephone: (00) (358) (14) 446 9211
Telefax: (00) (358) (14) 446 9216
Honorary Consul: Mr Risto Jamsen (Finnish)

Kotka
British Consulate
Telephone: (00) (358) (5) 234 4281
Telefax: (00) (358) (5) 218 1375
Honorary Consul: Mr K Näski (Finnish)

Kuopio
British Consulate
70100 Kuopio
Telephone: (00) (358) (17) 265 7777
Telefax: (00) (358) (17) 261 1085
Honorary Consul: Mr H A Palsola (Finnish)

Åland Islands
British Consulate
Telephone: (00) (358) (18) 27600
Telefax: (00) (358) (18) 27699
Honorary Consul: Mr B S Sjölund (Finnish)

Oulu
British Consulate
Telephone: (00) (358) (83) 310 7117
Telefax: (00) (358) (83) 310 7133
Honorary Consul: Mr P Koskela (Finnish)

Rovaniemi
British Consulate
Telephone: (00) (358) (16) 317 831
Honorary Consul: Mr L Pitkanen (Finnish)

Tampere
British Consulate
Telephone: (00) (358) (3) 256 5701
Telefax: (00) (358) (3) 256 5739
Honorary Consul: Mrs R K Varpe (Finnish)

Turku
British Consulate
Telephone: (00) (358) (2) 274 3410
Telefax: (00) (358) (2) 274 3440
Honorary Consul: Mr Jari Lähteenmäki (Finnish)

Vaasa
British Consulate
Telephone: (00) (358) (6) 2822 000
Telefax: (00) (358) (6) 2822 055
Honorary Consul: Mr R Grönblom (Finnish)

FRANCE

Paris
British Embassy
35 rue du Faubourg St. Honoré
75383 Paris Cedex 08
FTN Code – 8330 + extn number
Telephone: (00) (33) (1) 44 51 31 00
Facsimile: (00) (33) (1) 44 51 34 83
Ambassador's Office/Chancery
32 88 Management
34 01 Commercial
34 85 Political/Economic
32 34 Press and Public Affairs
34 40 Defence/Global Issues
31 27 Consular
31 28 Visa
Telephone: (00) (33) (1) 49 55 73 00
British Council
Facsimile: (00) (33) (1) 47 05 77 02
British Council
Website: http://www.amb-grandebretagne.fr
Office Hours (GMT): Summer 08 30 – 12 00 and 13 30 – 17 00. Winter 09 30 – 13 00 and 14 30 – 18 00
Ambassador: Sir John Holmes, GCVO, KBE, CMG
Minister: Mr Giles Paxman, LVO
Defence/Air Attaché:
Air Commodore Christopher J Blencowe, RAF
Naval Attaché: Captain Didier Lombard, RN
Military Attaché: Brigadier Timothy J Gregson, MBE
Counsellor (Trade, Development and Investment):
Mr John Duncan, OBE
Counsellor (Global Issues): Mr Hugh Elliott
Counsellor (EU/Economic): Mr Nicholas Hopton
Counsellor (Political): Mr Peter McQuibban
Counsellor (Cultural) (British Council Director):
Mr Paul de Quincey
Counsellor (Management): Mr Richard White, MBE
First Secretary (Press and Public Affairs):
Mr Nicholas Allan
First Secretary and Consul-General:
Mr Jeffrey Thomas
First Secretary (Global Issues):
Dr Helen Dickinson
First Secretary (Global Issues):
Mr Ken O'Flaherty
First Secretary (EU/Economic):
Mr Andrew Gregory
First Secretary (EU/Economic): Ms Shona Riach
First Secretary (EU/Economic):
Mr Damian Nussbaum
First Secretary (EU/Economic): Mrs Helen Pennant
First Secretary (Political): Mr Angus Lapsley
First Secretary (Political): Mr Jonathan Luff
First Secretary (Political): Dr Stephen Brain
First Secretary (Political): Mr Thomas Fletcher
First Secretary (Political): Ms Cathy Ward, LVO
First Secretary (Defence Procurement):
Mrs Jennifer Grogan
First Secretary (Commercial): Mr Ulrich Marthaler
First Secretary (Management): Mr Peter Duffy
First Secretary (Estate Manager):
Mr John Darlington
First Secretary (Technical): Mr John Ward
First Secretary (Commercial): Mr Russell Baker
First Secretary (Commercial):
Mr John Greengrass, MBE
Cultural Attaché (British Council Deputy Director): Mr David Kirwan
First Secretary and Consul: Mr Brian West
Assistant Air Attaché:
Wing Commander Graham August, RAF

Second Secretary (Global Issues): Miss Kirsteen Hall
Second Secretary (EU/Economic): Dr Kay Williams
Second Secretary (EU/Economic): Ms Frances Hooper
Second Secretary (Political): Mr Michael Botly
Second Secretary (Political): Ms Cecily Newby
Second Secretary (Global Issues): Ms Stephanie Smith
Second Secretary (Political): Miss Lucy Joyce
Second Secretary (Immigration): Mr Kevin Chaplin
Second Secretary (Technical): Mr Martin Price
Second Secretary (Press and Public Affairs): Mr Sujeevan Satheesan
Private Secretary: Miss Joanna Samuels-Watson
Third Secretary (Management): Mr Christopher Daltrey
Third Secretary (Passports): Miss Lucy Foster
Third Secretary (Immigration): Mr Michael Kearney
Third Secretary (Political) Visits Officer: Mrs Marina Pettigrew, MVO
Third Secretary (Commercial): Mr Kevin Brant

Paris British Consulate-General (see entry under Paris below)
Paris United Kingdom Delegation to OECD, see page 115
Paris United Kingdom Delegation to UNESCO, see page 114
Strasbourg United Kingdom Delegation to Council of Europe, see page 117

Bordeaux
British Consulate-General
353 Boulevard du President Wilson
33073 Bordeaux Cedex
Telephone: (00) (33) (5) 57 22 21 10
Facsimile: (00) (33) (5) 56 08 33 12
Office Hours (GMT): Summer 07 00 – 10 30 and 12 00 – 15 30. Winter 08 00 – 11 30 and 13 00 – 16 30
Consul-General: Mr Thomas Kennedy, LVO
Consul (Commercial): Mr Alastair Roberts
Vice-Consul: Mr Paul Dixon, MBE

Toulouse
British Consulate
Telephone/Facsimile: (00) (33) (5) 61 30 37 91
Honorary Consul: Mr Roger Virnuls, MBE

Biarritz
Honorary British Consulate – Vacant

Cahors
Mas d'Aspech
46230 Belmont Sainte Foi
Consular Correspondent: Mr Norman Thompson

La Rochelle
10 rue Charles Lemanissier
17000 La Rochelle
Telephone: (00) (33) (5) 46 67 25 52
Consular Correspondent: Mr John Paul

Périgueux
31 rue Lagrange Chancel
24000 Périgueux
Telephone: (00) (33) (5) 53 09 26 28
Facsimile: (00) (33) (5) 53 53 03 42
Consular Correspondent: Mrs Sheila Douglas, MBE

Poitiers
48 rue Jean-Jaurès
86000 Poitiers
Telephone: (00) (33) (5) 05 49 88 19 03
Consular Correspondent: Mrs Gillian Piget

Lille
British Consulate-General
11 Square Dutilleul
59000 Lille
Telephone: (00) (33) (3) 20 12 82 72
Facsmilie: (00) (33) (3) 20 54 88 16
Airtech: (00) (33) (3) 20 54 46 15
Office Hours (GMT): Summer 07 30 – 10 30 and 12 00 – 15 00. Winter 08 30 – 11 30 and 13 00 – 16 00
Consul-General: Mr Clive Alderton
Vice-Consul (Commercial): Mr David Hinchliffe
Vice-Consul (Commercial): Mr John Gleave
Vice-Consul: Mrs Carol Vorobieff, MBE

Amiens
British Consulate
Telephone: (00) (33) (3) 22 72 08 48
Facsimile: (00) (33) (3) 22 82 23 01
Office Hours (GMT): Summer 06 30 – 10 30 and 12 00 – 16 00. Winter 07 30 – 11 30 and 13 00 – 17 00
Honorary British Consul: Mr Roger Davis

Boulogne-sur-Mer
British Consulate
Telephone: (00) (33) (3) 21 87 16 80
Facsimile: (00) (33) (3) 21 91 30 30
Office Hours (GMT): Summer 06 00 – 10 00 and 12 00 – 16 00. Winter 07 00 – 11 00 and 13 00 – 17 00
Honorary Consul: Mr Gerard Barron, MBE

Calais
British Consulate
Telephone: (00) (33) (3) 21 96 33 76
Facsimile: (00) (33) (3) 21 19 43 69
Office Hours (GMT): Summer 06 30 – 16 00. Winter 07 30 – 17 00
Honorary Consul: Mr Jean-Michel Inglis, MBE

Dunkirk
British Consulate
Telephone: (00) (33) (3) 28 66 11 98
Facsimile: (00) (33) (3) 28 59 09 99
Office Hours (GMT): Summer 06 30 – 10 00 and 12 00 – 16 00. Winter 07 30 – 11 00 and 13 00 – 17 00
Honorary Consul: Mr Christopher R Baker, MBE

Lyon
British Consulate-General
24 rue Childebert, 69002 Lyon
Telephone: (00) (33) (4) 72 77 81 70
Facsimile: (00) (33) (4) 72 77 81 79
Airtech: (00) (33) (4) 78 38 27 77

Office Hours (GMT): Summer 07 00 – 10 30 and 12 00 – 15 30. Winter 08 00 – 11 30 and 13 00 – 16 30
Consul-General: Mr Colin Bright
Vice-Consul: Mrs Jeanie Labaye
Vice-Consul (Commercial): Mr Tim Suggitt

Marseille
British Consulate-General
24 Avenue de Prado, 13006 Marseilles
Telephone: (00) (33) (4) 91 15 72 10
Facsimile: (00) (33) (4) 91 37 47 06
Office Hours (GMT): Summer 07 00 – 10 00 and 12 00 – 15 00. Winter 08 00 – 11 00 and 13 00 – 16 00
Consul-General (resides in Lyon): Mr Colin Bright
Vice-Consul: Ms Donna Faure
Management Officer: Ms Mireille Brown

Nice
By appointment only, please contact British Consulate-General Marseille
Honorary Consul: Mrs Simone Paissoni

Montpellier
British Consulate
Telephone/Facsimile: (00) (33) (4) 67 15 52 07
Honorary Consul: Mr Norman J Paget

Paris
British Consulate-General
18bis rue d'Anjou 75008 Paris
(All mail should be sent to the British Embassy, Paris)
Telephone: (00) (33) (1) 44 51 31 00
Facsimile: (00) (33) (1) 44 51 31 27
(00) (33) (1) 44 51 31 28 (Visas)
Office Hours (GMT): Summer 07 30 – 11 00 and 12 30 – 16 00. Winter 08 30 – 12 00 and 13 30 – 17 00
Consul-General: Mr Jeffrey Thomas
Consul: Mr Brian West
Vice-Consul: Mr Stephen J Donnelly, MBE
Vice-Consul (Passport Officer): Miss Lucy Foster
Vice-Consul (Immigration): Mr Michael Kearney
Vice-Consul (Immigration): Mrs Suzanne Groves
Vice-Consul (Immigration):
Mr Frederick Cracknell
Vice-Consul: Mr Simon M Taylor
Vice-Consul: Mr Mark Pettigrew

Cherbourg
British Consulate
Telephone: (00) (33) (2) 33 88 65 60
Facsimile: (00) (33) (2) 33 88 67 07
Honorary Consul: Mr Gérard R Caron, MBE

French Guiana (Cayenne)
British Consulate
Telephone: (00) (594) 31 10 34
Facsimile: (00) (594) 30 40 94
Honorary Consul: Mr Joseph G Nouh-Chaia MBE

French Polynesia (Papeete)
British Consulate
Telephone: (00) (689) 70 63 82
Facsimile: (00) (689) 42 00 50
Honorary Consul: Mr Marc Allain

Nantes
British Consulate
B P 22026
44020 Nantes
Telephone: (00) (33) (2) 51 72 72 60
Facsimile: (00) (33) (2) 40 47 36 92
Office Hours (GMT): 07 00 – 10 15 and 12 00 – 15 00
Honorary Consul: Mrs Angela M Stokes

Le Havre
British Consulate
B.P. 10515
76058 Le Havre
Telephone: (00) (33) (2) 35 19 78 88
Facsimile: (00) (33) (2) 35 19 78 98
Honorary Consul: Mme Nadine H Corbel

Lorient
British Consulate
Telephone: (00) (33) (2) 97 87 36 20
Facsimile: (00) (33) (2) 97 87 36 49
Honorary Consul: Mr Anthony M Le Saffre

Fort de France, Martinique
British Consulate
Telephone: (00) (596) 61 88 92
Facsimile: (00) (596) 61 33 89
Honorary Consul: Mme Alison J Ernoult

Guadeloupe
British Consulate
Telephone: (00) (590) 82 57 57
Facsimile: (00) (590) 82 89 33
Honorary Consul: Mr David A Wood

La Réunion
British Consulate
Telephone: (00) (33) (2) 62 34 75 76
Honorary Consul: Mr Gordon Smith

New Caledonia
British Consulate
Telephone: (00) (687) 27 36 27 or 28 21 53
Facsimile: (00) (687) 28 51 44
Honorary Consul: Mr Maxwell Shekleton

Saumur
British Consulate
Telephone: (00) (33) (2) 41 52 90 54
Facsimile: (00) (33) (2) 41 52 99 92
Consular Agent: Mr Khrisna C Lester

St Malo-Dinard
British Consulate
Telephone: (00) (33) (2) 23 18 30 30
Facsimile: (00) (33) (2) 99 40 64 42
Honorary Consul: Mrs Veronique Rondel

Tours
British Consulate
Telephone/Facsimile: (00) (33) (2) 47 43 50 58
Honorary Consul: Mr Brian J Cordery, OBE

GABON

Libreville
British Embassy (except where shown all staff reside at Yaoundé)

Ambassador and Consul-General:
Mr Syd Maddicott
First Secretary and Consul: Mr Steve Crossman
Defence Attaché (resides at Kinshasa):
Lieutenant Colonel James R Charlesworth

British Consulate
c/o Brossette, BP 486,
Libreville
Telephone: (00) (241) 76 22 00/74 20 41
Facsimile: (00) (241) 76 57 89
Mobile: (00) (241) 75 86 36
Honorary Consul: Mr David Harwood, MBE

GAMBIA, THE

Banjul (SP - see page 121)
British High Commission
48 Atlantic Road, Fajara (PO Box 507), Banjul
FTN Code – 8540 + extn number
Telephone: (00) (220) 4495133, 4495134
Facsimile: (00) (220) 4496134
Airtech: (00) (220) 4494505
e-mail: bhcbanjul@gamtel.gm
Office Hours (GMT): Mon-Thurs 08 00 – 15 00 and Fri 08 00 – 13 00
High Commissioner: Mr Eric Jenkinson, OBE
Deputy High Commissioner: Ms Jennifer Fenton
Defence Adviser (resides at Rabat):
Lieutenant Colonel Simon J A Lloyd, MBE
Third Secretary (Management/Consular):
Mr Stephen Farrow
Third Secretary (Immigration):
Mrs Caroline Dogan
Third Secretary (Immigration):
Mr Nicholas Hackett

Department for International Development (DFID) Gambia
c/o British High Commission
Banjul
Telephone: (00) (220) 4497537, 4495578
Facsimile: (00) (220) 4494127
e-mail: r-watt.dfid@qanet.gm
Head of DFID Office: Mr Robert Watt

GEORGIA

Tbilisi (SP - see page 121)
British Embassy
GMT Plaza, 4 Freedom Square
0105 Tbilisi
FTN Code – 8319 + extn number or 1000 for Operator
Telephone: (00) (995) (32) 274747
Facsimile: (00) (995) (32) 274792
274779 (Visa)
274724 (Political)
e-mail: British.Embassy.Tbilisi@fco.gov.uk
Office Hours (GMT): Mon-Fri 06 00 – 14 00
Ambassador (2201): The MacLaren of MacLaren
Deputy Head of Mission (2204): Mr Roy Wilson
Defence Attaché (2210): Lieutenant Colonel Christopher J Nunn, OBE, RM
Second Secretary (Political): Mr Iain Lunt
Second Secretary (Technical Management) (based at Ankara): Mr Paul Holmes
Third Secretary (Management) (2240):
Ms Kate Beggs
Third Secretary (Political) (2280):
Mr William Robinson
Third Secretary (Political) (2214):
Mr Darren Woodcock
Vice-Consul (2271): Ms Amanda Lissenden
Attaché (Management/Immigration) (2220):
Ms Karen Hennessy
Assistant Defence Attaché (2212):
Mr Rob Hamling

GERMANY

Berlin
British Embassy
Wilhelmstrasse 70
10117 Berlin
FTN Code – 8340 + extn number
Telephone: (00) (49) (30) 20457 0
Facsimile: (00) (49) (30) 20457 571 (Ambassador)
20457 572 (DHM's Office)
20457 573 (Political)
20457 574 (Media)
20457 594 (Public Relations)
20457 575 (EU and Economics)
20457 576 (Labour, Social Affairs and Environment)
20457 577 (Commercial)
20457 578 (Management)
20457 579 (Consular)
20457 581 (Defence)
20457 582 (Defence Supply)
20457 347 (Agriculture)
20457 346 (Science andTechnology)
Website: http://www.britischebotschaft.de
Office Hours (GMT): 08 00 – 12 00 and 13 00 – 16 30
Ambassador (101): Sir Peter Torry, GCVO, KCMG
Deputy Head of Mission and Head of Political, Media and Public Affairs (151):
Mr Hugh Mortimer, LVO
Counsellor (Research and Technology) (resides at Munich): Mr Steve Plater
Counsellor and Head of EU and Economic Section (301): Ms Pamela Major
Defence Attaché (401):
Brigadier Robert Pridham, OBE
Counsellor (Labour) (310): Miss Elaine Trewartha
Political Counsellor (451): Mr David Woods
First Secretary (Political External) (223):
Mr Nick Alexander
First Secretary and Head of Media (251):
Mr Jonathan Brenton
First Secretary (Technical Management) (521):
Mr Colin Buswell
First Secretary (Political External) (336):
Mr Paul Carwithen
First Secretary (Economic) (321): Mr Steve Cook
First Secretary (Agriculture) (335):
Mr Craig Egner
Naval Attaché (403):
Captain Stephen R Gosden, RN
First Secretary (European Union) (331):
Mr Paul Heardman

First Secretary (Political External):
Mr Neil Holland
First Secretary (Political Internal) (211):
Mr John Kraus
First Secretary (Political External) (222):
Andrew Macmillan
First Secretary (Political External):
Ms Michaela Miller
Air Attaché (405):
Group Captain John P Moloney, RAF
First Secretary and Head of Public Relations (223): Mr Paul O'Connor
Military Attaché (407): Colonel Mike C Parish, OBE
First Secretary (Technical Works Officer) (559):
Mr Steve Pink
First Secretary (Science and Innovation) (338):
Ms Alison Pring
First Secretary and Head of Management (501):
Mr Mike Purves
First Secretary (Environment and Energy) (341):
Ms Lynn Sheppard
First Secretary (Fiscal Liaison Officer) (241):
Mr Mike Stevens
First Secretary (Political External) (221):
Mr Paul Williams
First Secretary and Head of Trade and Investment (451): Mr Ian Worthington OBE
Second Secretary (PS/Ambassador) (102):
Mr Simon Ferrand
Second Secretary (Political) (227):
Mr Philip Owen
Second Secretary (Technical Management) (522):
Mr Denis Price
Second Secretary (European Union) (332):
Ms Helen Walters
Third Secretary (Consular/Management) (541):
Mr Ed Noble

Leipzig
British Trade Office
Gohliser Str 7
0-04105 Leipzig
Telephone: (00) (49) 0341 564 9672, 564 9674
Facsimile: (00) (49) 0341 564 9673
Commercial Officer: Frau K Rath
Commercial Assistant: Frau Pia Mann

Düsseldorf
British Consulate-General
Yorckstrasse 19, 40476 Düsseldorf
(Mail from United Kingdom only can be sent to Box 2002, BFPO 105)
FTN Code – 8344 + extn number (When dialling from the UK dial 8344 2 +extn number – e.g 203)
Telephone: (00) (49) (211) 94 48-0 or 94 48 + (extn – see entries)
Direct Lines: 94 48 170 (Passport Section)
0190 700 661 (Passport Section call centre)
0190 700 611 (Visa Section call centre)
94 48 222 (Commercial Section)
94 48 245 (Press and Public Affairs)
Facsimile: (00) (49) (211) 48 63 59 (Commercial and Investment Sections,Press, PR)
48 81 90 (Passport, Consular and Management)
48 86 03 (Visa Section)
Airtech: 94 48 225
e-mail:
Consular.Section@duesseldorf.mail.fco.gov.uk (Passport Section)
Visa.Section@duesseldorf.mail.fco.gov.uk (Visa Section)
Commercial.Section@duesseldorf.mail.fco.gov.uk (Commercial Section)
Websites: www.britischebotschaft.de (for British nationals resident in Germany)
www.britischebotschaft.de (Visa enquiries)
www.uktradeinvest.de (trade promotion in Germany)
www.uktradeinvest.de (investment promotion in Germany)
Office Hours (GMT): Winter: Mon-Thurs 07 30 – 11 30 and 12 30 – 16 00. Fri 07 30 – 11 30 and 12 30 – 15 30
Summer: Mon-Thurs 06 30 – 10 30 and 11 30 – 15 00. Fri 06 30 – 10 30 and 11 30 – 14 30
Consul-General and Director of Trade and Investment in Germany (200): Mr Peter Tibber
Deputy Consul-General and Deputy Director of Trade and Investment in Germany (202):
Mr Tim Brownbill
Consul (Management) (231): Mr John K Hague
Consul (Investment) (207): Mr Peter Ivey
Consul (Commercial) (203): Mr Bill Kelly
Consul (Consular/Immigration) (260):
Mr David Pert
Vice-Consul (Commercial) (208): Mr Scott Melling
Vice-Consul (Immigration) (264):
Mrs Caroline Boyce
Vice-Consul (Consular/Passports) (234):
Mr Kevin McGlone
Vice-Consul (Consular) (255): Mr David Kelly
Commercial Officer (CCU) (219):
Mrs Sylvia A Tunmore
Commercial Officer (209): Mr Dirk Mokwinski
Commercial Officer (213): Mr Peter Foster
Investment Officer (205): Mr Christian Fehling
Investment Officer (182): Mr Georg H Rehberg
Press and Public Affairs (223): Mr Thomas Wittek
PR and Marketing (153): Ms Tanja Ziemus

Fiscal Liaison Office
Kaiser-Friedrich Strasse 19
53113 Bonn
Telephone: (00) (49) (228) 24 99 211/212
Facsimile: (00) (49) (228) 24 99 222
Office Hours (GMT): 08 00 – 12 00 and 1 3 00 – 16 30
Second Secretary (Fiscal Liaison Officer):
Mr Paul Taylor

Frankfurt
British Consulate-General – (Please note that Frankfurt is due to close on 31st December 2005)
Triton Haus
Bockenheimer Landstrasse 42
60323 Frankfurt-am-Main
Mail from United Kingdom only should be addressed:
British Consulate-General, Frankfurt
PO Box 2009, BFPO 10

FTN Code – 8345 + extn number
Telephone: (00) (49) (69) 17 000 20
Facsimile: (00) (49) (69) 72 95 53
Office Hours (GMT): Mon-Thurs: 07 30 – 12 00 and 13 00 – 16 00. Fri: 07 30 – 12 00 and 12 30 – 14 30
Consul-General (2250): Mr Neil C Paterson
Consul (Consular/Management) (2222): Mr Martin Scales
Vice-Consul (2225): Mrs Christine Townsend
Trade Officer (2237): Herr Rudolf Schneider
Trade Officer (2239): Frau Sabine Schnurbusch
Press and Public Affairs Officer (2235): Dr Wolfgang Dobler
Attaché (2236): Mr David Connelly
Attaché (2228): Mr David Hollingbery
Attaché (2257): Mr Robert Barber
Attaché (2240): Mr Roger Goodall
(Visa and Passport work is centralised in Dusseldorf.)

Hamburg
British Consulate-General
Harvestehuder Weg 8a, 20148 Hamburg
FTN Code – 8343 + extn number
Telephone: (00) (49) (40) 448 0320
Facsimile: (00) (49) (40) 410 7259
Airtech: (00) (49) (40) 448 032 31
Office Hours: (GMT): 07 30 – 11 30 and 12 30 – 16 00
Consul-General (2011): Mr Timothy Collard
Consul (Management/Consular) (2030): Mr Anthony J Hackett
Vice-Consul (Consular) (2036): Mrs Gwen Cochrane
Commercial Officer (2033): Herr Thomas Siems
Commercial Officer (2022): Mr John Holway
Commercial Officer (2023): Herr Bernd Klein
Press and Public Affairs Officer (2039): Ms Jo Dawes
(Visa and Passport work is centralised in Dusseldorf.)

Bremen
British Consulate
Herrlichkeiten 6, Postfach 10 38 60, 28199 Bremen
Telephone: (00) (49) (421) 590708
Facsimile: (00) (49) (421) 5907109
Office Hours (GMT): 07 30 – 11 30 and 13 30 – 14 30
Honorary Consul: Herr H-C Enge

Hanover
British Consulate
Hannover Ruchversicherungs AG
Karl-Wiechart-Allee 50
30625 Hannover
Telephone: (00) (511) 3883808
Facsimile: (00) (511) 5604690
Office Hours (GMT): 06 30 – 10 00 and 10 30 – 12 00
Honorary Consul: Herr W Zeller

Kiel
British Consulate
United Canal Agency GmbH
Schleuse, Maklerstrasse 11-14, 24159 Kiel
Telephone: (00) (49) 431 331971
Facsimile: (00) (49) 431 3053746
Telex: 299829 (a/b UBCK D)
Office (GMT): 06 30 – 11 00 and 12 00 – 15 00
Honorary Consul: Herr J Petersen

Munich
British Consulate-General
Bürkleinstrasse 10
D – 80538 München
(Mail from United Kingdom only should be addressed:
British Consulate-General, Munich
PO Box 2010, BFPO 105)
FTN Code – 8342 + extn number
Telephone: (00) (49) (89) 211090
Facsimile: 21109 166 Consul-General
21109 166 Press andPublic Affairs
21109 166 Science and Innovation Section
21109 155 Commercial Section
21109 155 Investment Section
21109 144 Management Section
21109 144 Consular Section
Office Hours (GMT): Mon-Thurs: 07 30 – 11 00 and 12 00 – 16 00. Fri: 07 30 – 11 00 and 12 00 – 15 00
Consul-General and Counsellor (Science and Innovation): Mr Steve Plater
Consul (Trade and Investment) and DHM: Mr Hugh Taylor
Consul (Consular/Management): Ms Julie Bell
Vice-Consul (Trade): Mr Charles Pattinson
Press and Public Affairs Officer: Mrs Birgit Dammert
Trade Officer: Dr Astrid Ritter-Heinrich
Investment Officer: Ms Heike Bieber
Vice-Consul (Consular): Mrs Christine Ruhstorfer
Science and Innovation Officer: Ms Muzinée Kistenfeger
(Visa and Passport work is centralised in Dusseldorf.)

Nuremburg
British Consulate
M Schmitt and Sohn GmbH and Co
Hadermuhle 9-15
D – 90402 Nuremburg
Telephone: (00) (49) (911) 2404-303
Facsimile: (00) (49) (911) 2404-111
Honorary Consul: Dr J Schmitt

Stuttgart
British Consulate-General
Breite Strasse 2, 70173
Stuttgart
Telephone: (00) (49) (711) 16 26 9-0
Facsimile: (00) (49) (711) 16 26 9-30
Office Hours (GMT): As Frankfurt
Consul-General: Mr Mark P Twigg
Commercial Officer: Frau A Seidler
Commercial Officer: Frau B Koch
Pro-Consul: Mrs M Braun

GHANA

Accra

British High Commission
Osu Link, off Gamel Abdul Nasser Avenue
(PO Box 296), Accra
FTN Code – 8541 + extn number
Telephone: (00) (233) (21) 7010650, 221665
(24 hours)
7010721 Immigration Section
Facsimile: (00) (233) (21) 7010655
221715 Immigration Section
Airtech: (00) (233) (21) 242936
e-mail: high.commission.accra@fco.gov.uk
Website: www.britishhighcommission.gov.uk/ghana
Office Hours (GMT): 07 45 – 15 45
Immigration Section Public Hours: 07 30 – 10 30 (Mon-Thurs)
Consular Section Public Hours: 07 30 – 13 30
High Commissioner: Mr Gordon Wetherell
Deputy High Commissioner: Mr Robin Gwynn
Defence Adviser:
Lieutenant Colonel Jonathan A F Howard
First Secretary (Senior Management Officer):
Mr David S Jones
First Secretary (Trade and Investment):
Ms Sarah Stevenson
First Secretary (Immigration): Mr Andy Holden
Second Secretary (Political, Press and Public Affairs): Mr Gary Nicholls
Second Secretary (Environment/Human Rights):
Ms Farida Shaikh
Second Secretary (Immigration/Consular):
Mrs Caroline Cross
Second Secretary (Immigration):
Mrs Margaret Brown
Second Secretary (Immigration): Mrs Gillian Elliot
Second Secretary (Immigration):
Ms Deborah Moore
Second Secretary (Immigration): (Vacant)
Second Secretary (Airline Liaison Officer):
Mr Julian Kennett
Second Secretary (Technical Management Officer):
Mr Jim Dunn
Third Secretary (Deputy Management Officer):
Mr Bernie Andrews
Third Secretary (Deputy Management Officer):
(Vacant)
Third Secretary (Technical Works): Mr John Neale
Third Secretary (Consular/Immigration):
Mrs Emma Mamet
Third Secretary (Immigration): Mr Matt Carter
Third Secretary (Immigration):
Mr Andrew Brimacombe
Third Secretary (Immigration): Ms Fiona Hayward
Third Secretary (Immigration): Mr Ian Abbott
Third Secretary (Immigration): Mr Steve Scott
Third Secretary (Immigration): Mr Rob Tait
Third Secretary (Immigration): Mr Murray Dalgety
Third Secretary (Immigration):
Ms Lorraine McColl
Third Secretary (Immigration): Mrs Fiona McPhail
Third Secretary (Immigration): Mr Rob Dixon
Third Secretary (Immigration): Mrs Julie Galvin
Third Secretary (Immigration): Mr Tim Galvin
Third Secretary (Immigration): Mrs Dawn Neale
Third Secretary (Immigration): Mr Danny Wells
Third Secretary (Immigration): Ms Jennifer Wong
Third Secretary (Immigration): Mr Jamie Russon
Third Secretary (Immigration): (Vacant)
Third Secretary (Immigration): (Vacant)

Department for International Development (DFID) Ghana
Masida House
Sankara Interchange
PO Box 296, Accra
FTN Code – 8774 + extn number
Telephone: (00) (233) (21) 253243
Facsimile: (00) (233) (21) 220172 or 253244
Acting Head of DFID Ghana: Ms Emma Spicer
Acting Deputy Head: Ms Catherine Martin
Office Manager: Mr Neil Mullin
Economic Adviser: Mr Paul Walters
Education Adviser: Dr Donald Taylor
Engineering Adviser: Ms Amanda Duff
Governance Adviser: Dr Daniel Arghiros
Private Sector Development Adviser:
Ms Catherine Martin
Rural Livelihoods Adviser: Mr Ben Davies
Social Development Adviser: Ms Kirsty Mason
Deputy Programme Manager: Ms Denise Hill
Deputy Programme Manager: Mr Will Guest

GREECE

Athens

British Embassy
1 Ploutarchou Street, 106 75 Athens
FTN Code – 8542 + extn number (switchboard: 8542 1000)
Telephone: (00) (30) 210 727 2600
Night (RSO): (00) (30) 210 723 7727
724 1331
Facsimile: (00) (30) 210 727 2734
Political and Commercial Section
2720 Consular Section
2876 Management Section
2723 Chancery/Political
2743 Press and Public Affairs
2725 Residence
2727 Fiscal and Drugs Liaison Section
Airtech: (00) (30) 210 722 7122
e-mail: information.athens@fco.gov.uk
Website: http://www.british-embassy.gr
Office Hours (GMT): 06 00 – 13 00
Ambassador: Mr Simon L Gass, CMG, CVO
Consul-General, Deputy Head of Mission:
Mr Ian Whitting
Counsellor: Mr Nicholas Langman
Defence and Naval Attaché:
Captain John R Wills, RN
Military and Air Attaché:
Colonel Mark Blatherwick, MBE, GM
Counsellor (Cultural) (British Council Director):
Mr Desmond Lauder
First Secretary (Head of Press and Political Section): Mrs Tracy Gallagher
First Secretary (Political/Information):
Mr Daniel Tarshish
First Secretary (Defence Supply): Mr John Bewley

First Secretary (Management):
Mr Keith McMahon, MBE
First Secretary (Commercial): Mr Frank Jones
First Secretary and Consul: Susan Mary Morrell
First Secretary (Cultural Affairs): (Vacant)
Drugs Liaison Officer: Mr Nick Jepson
Second Secretary and Vice-Consul:
Mr Andrew Self
Second Secretary (Political/Information):
Ms Lynda Burns
Second Secretary: Mr Nigel Willmer
Second Secretary (EU): Ms Beverley Darkin
Third Secretary (Management):
Ms Joanne Crabtree
Third Secretary and Vice-Consul:
Mrs Patsy McQuilton

Corfu
British Vice-Consulate
Menekratous 1, 491 00 Corfu
Telephone: (00) (30) 26610 30055
Facsimile: (00) (30) 26610 37995
e-mail: corfu@british-consulate.gr
Vice-Consul: Ms Lucy Steele, MBE

Heraklion (Crete)
British Vice-Consulate
16 Papa-Alexandrou Street
712 02 Heraklion
Telephone: (00) (30) 2810 224012
Facsimile: (00) (30) 2810 243935
e-mail: crete@british-consulate.gr
Vice-Consul: Mrs Claire Fragakis

Kos
British Vice-Consulate
8, Annetas Laoumtzi Street,
853 00 Kos
Telephone: (00) (30) 22420 21549
Facsimile: (00) (30) 22420 25948
e-mail: kos@british-consulate.gr
Honorary Vice-Consul: Mr Konstantinos Kourounis

Patras
British Vice-Consulate
Votsi 2
262 21 Patras
Telephone: (00) (30) 2610 277329
Facsimile: (00) (30) 2610 225334
Honorary Vice-Consul:
Mrs Marie Jeanne Morphy-Karatza, MBE

Rhodes
British Vice-Consulate
Pavlou Mela 3
PO Box 47
851 00 Rhodes
Telephone: (00) (30) 22410 27247 or 22005
Facsimile: (00) (30) 22410 22615
e-mail: rhodes@british-consulate.gr
Honorary Vice-Consul: Mr Peter John Spentzuris

Thessaloniki
British Consulate
21 Aristotelous Street
546 24 Thessaloniki
Telephone: (00) (30) 2310 278006
Facsimile: (00) (30) 2310 283868
e-mail: salonika@british-consulate.gr
Consul: Mrs Sarah Edwards-Economidi

Syros
British Vice-Consulate
8 Akti Petrou Ralli,
Hermoupolis
841 00 Syros
Telephone: (00) (30) 22810 82232 or 88922
Facsimile: (00) (30) 22810 83293
Honorary Vice-Consul:
Mrs Virginia Parissi-Thermou

Zakynthos
British Vice-Consulate
5 Foskolos Street
291 00 Zakynthos
Telephone: (00) (30) 26950 22906 or 48030
Facsimile: (00) (30) 26950 23769
e-mail: zakynthos@british-consulate.gr
Honorary Vice-Consul:
Mrs Evridiki (Vicky) Vitsou-Kotsoni

GRENADA

St George's (SP - see page 121)
British High Commission, Netherlands Building,
Grand Anse,
St George's, Grenada
Telephone: (00) (1) (473) 440 3536, 440 3222
Facsimile: (00) (1) (473) 440 4939
e-mail: bhcgrenada@caribsurf.com
Office Hours (GMT): Mon – Thurs: 12 00 – 17 00
and 17 30 – 20 00. Fri: 12 00 – 17 00
**High Commissioner:* Mr Duncan Taylor, CBE
Resident British Commissioner: Mr Vic Wallis
**Deputy High Commissioner:* Mr Alan Drury
**Defence Adviser:* Captain Steve G Wilson, RN
**First Secretary:* Mr Eamon Kearney
**First Secretary (Management):* Ms Ros Day, MBE
**Second Secretary (Chancery/Information):*
Mr Nick J Pyle, MBE
***Second Secretary (Technical Works):*
Mr David Holmes
**Second Secretary (Chancery):* Mr Rick Gomez
**Third Secretary:* Mr Philip Barker
**Third Secretary (Immigration):* Mr Mark Harrison
**Resides at Bridgetown*
***Resides at Mexico City*

GUATEMALA

Guatemala City (SP - see page 121)
British Embassy
16 Calle 00-55, Zona 10
Edificio Torre Internacional, Nivel 11
Guatemala City
FTN Code – 8459 + extn number
Telephone: (00) (502) 2367 5425-29
FTN Telephone: 8459 2000 (Receptionist)
8459 2011 (PA to HMA and DHM)
8459 2019 (Trade and Investment)
8459 2009 (PPA and Development)
8459 2020 (Management)
8459 2012 (Consular and Visa)
Facsimile: (00) (502) 2367 5430
e-mail: embassy@intelnett.com

Office Hours (GMT): Mon-Thurs 14 30 – 18 30 and 19 30 – 23 00. Fri 14 30 – 18 30
Ambassador (2032): Mr Richard D Lavers (Mr Ian Hughes w.e.f March 06)
First Secretary, Consul and Deputy Head of Mission (2031): Mr Kevin A Garvey
Defence Attaché (2016):
Colonel Ian Blair-Pilling, OBE
First Secretary (DLO) (resides at Panama City):
Mr Alan Pamplin
Second Secretary (Management/Consular) (2013):
Mr Colin Gracey
Second Secretary (Chancery) (2036):
Mrs Susie Kitchens
Assistant Defence Attaché (2015):
W.O. Eugene J McCran, RAF
Second Secretary (DLO) (resides at Panama City):
Mr Gary Foster
Third Secretary (2017): Mr Amar Shazad

GUINEA

Conakry
British Embassy
BP 6729 Conakry
Republic of Guinea
Telephone: (00) (224) 45 58 07 (Office)
(224) 45 29 59 (Home)
Facsimile: (00) (224) 45 60 20
Satellite Phone: 00 874 762 471260
Satellite Fax: 00 874 762 471262
e-mail: britcon.oury@biasy.net or ambroyu@yahoo.fr
Ambassador: Mr John McManus
Defence Attaché (Resident in Freetown):
Lieutenant Colonel Desmond J A Bergin, OBE
SMO (Resident in Freetown): Ms Kay Harris
Trade, Investment and Media Officer:
Mr Georges Gandhi Tounkara
Consular/Management Assistant: Mme Oury Barry

GUINEA-BISSAU

Bissau
British Embassy (all staff resident in Dakar)
Ambassador: Mr Peter Newall
Deputy Head of Mission and Consul:
Mr Derek Levoir
Vice-Consul/ECO: Ms Christine Johnson
Management Officer: Mr Nick Faulkner

Bissau
British Honorary Consulate
Mavegro Int., CP100, Bissau
Telephone: (00) (245) 20 12 24/20 12 16 (Office)
(00) (245) 20 16 07 (Home)
Facsimile: (00) (245) 20 12 65
e-mail: mavegro@gtelecom.gw
mavegro@hotmail.com
Honorary Consul: Mr Jan van Maanen

GUYANA

Georgetown (SP - see page 121)
British High Commission
44 Main Street, (PO Box 10849), Georgetown
FTN Code – 8543 + extn number
Telephone: (00) (592) (22) 65881/2/3/4
Facsimile: 53555 Management/Commercial/Development
50671 Immigration and Consular
37321 Chancery
68818 (Airtech)
6236340 (Duty Officer)
e-mail: firstname.surname@fco.gov.uk
Office Hours (GMT): 11 30 – 18 30
High Commissioner: Mr Steve J Hiscock
Deputy High Commissioner: Mr Malcolm Kirk
Defence Adviser (resides at Bridgetown):
Captain Steve G Wilson, RN
First Secretary (Development): Mr Jonathan Baxter
Second Secretary (Management/Entry Clearance Manager): Mr Graham Birse
Second Secretary (Development):
Mrs Lynn MacAulay
Second Secretary (Chancery) (resides in Port of Spain): Mr Noel Feeney
Third Secretary (Immigration/Consular):
Mr Neil Frape
Third Secretary (Technical Management) (resides at Bridgetown): Mr Phil Barker
Personal Assistant to High Commissioner:
Mr Matthew Nottingham

HAITI

Port-au-Prince
British Embassy
Ambassador (resides in Santo Domingo):
Mr Andrew R Ashcroft
Second Secretary and Consul (resides in Santo Domingo): Mr Kevin Shaughnessy

Port-au Prince
British Consulate
Hotel Montana (PO Box 1302), Port-au-Prince
Telephone: (00) (509) 257 3969
Facsimile: (00) (509) 257 4048
e-mail: britcon@transnethaiti.com
Office Hours (GMT): 13 00 – 18 00
Vice-Consul: Mrs Allison Insley-Madsen

HOLY SEE

British Embassy (SP - see page 121)
91 Via dei Condotti, I-00187, Rome
Telephone: (00) (39) (06) 699 23561
Facsimile: (00) (39) (06) 6994 0684
Office Hours (GMT): All Year: 08 00 – 12 00 and 13 00 – 16 00
Except:- Jul-Aug 07 00 – 13 00
Ambassador: Mr John Culver

HONDURAS

Tegucigalpa
British Embassy – (Closed)
(Please refer to Guatemala City)

British Consulate
Honorary Consul: (To be confirmed)

Department for International Development (DFID) Honduras
DFID Office
Colonia Palmira

Avenida Republica de Mexico #2402
Tegucigalpa MDC
Telephone: (00) (504) 221 2109, 2126, 2547, 2588
Facsimile: (00) (504) 221 1959
e-mail: v-heard@dfid.gov.uk
Office Hours: Mon-Fri 08 00 – 17 00
Head of British Development Office: Mr Vic Heard

San Pedro Sula
British Consulate
2° Calle, 18 y 19 Ave. N.O. Casa # 182
Colonia Moderna
Apartado Postal No. 63
San Pedro Sula, Cortés
Telephone: (00) (504) 550 2337
Facsimile: (00) (504) 550-2486
Office Hours (GMT): 08 00 – 11 30
14 00 – 16 00 (local time) – Monday to Friday inclusive
Honorary Consul: Mr Edgardo Dumas

HUNGARY

Budapest
British Embassy, Harmincad u. 6., Budapest 1051
FTN Code – 8478 + extn or 1000 for switchboard
Telephone: (00) (36) (1) 266 2888
Facsimile: (00) (36) (1) 266 0907 Management/PPA/Programmes (FTN – 8478 6221), 429 6360 Consular/Visa/Commercial (FTN – 8478 6360), 429 6301 Political (FTN – 8478 6301)
Airtech: (00) (36) (1) 429 6299
e-mail: info@britemb.hu
Website: http://www.britishembassy.hu
Office Hours (GMT): Summer 07 00 – 1500, Winter 08 00 – 16 00
Ambassador (6211): Mr John Nichols
Counsellor and Deputy Head of Mission (6212): Mr Michael Ward
Defence Attaché (6220): Colonel Anthony Patrick Burnside
Cultural Attaché: (British Council Director) (tel. 478 4700): Mr Jim McGrath
First Secretary (Commercial) (6250): Mrs Deirdre Brown
First Secretary (Political) (6203): Mr Robert Dear
First Secretary (Political) (6225): Mr Simon Wilson, OBE
First Secretary (Management/HM Consul) (6230): Mr Mike Goodwin
First Secretary (Political) (6205): (Vacant)
First Secretary (Technical Works Officer) (6327): Ms Sandra Agnew
First Secretary (Cultural) (tel. 478 4700): Mr Paul Clementson
First Secretary (Cultural) (tel. 478 4700): Mr Nigel Bellingham
Assistant Defence Attaché (6227): Squadron Leader Alan Fisher
Second Secretary (PPA and Political) (6350): Mr Jason Moore
Second Secretary (Commercial) (6287): Ms Jane Sanders
Second Secretary (Political) (6204): Mr Nick Catsaras
Second Secretary (Technical Management) (6215): Mr Paul Davies
Second Secretary (Technical Management) (6216): Mr Bob Bruton
Second Secretary (Airline Liaison Officer) (6249): Mr Steve Brown
Second Secretary (Organised Crime Liaison Officer) (6377): Mr Steve Bosanquet
Vice-Consul and Entry Clearance Officer (6240): Mr Mark Rush
Third Secretary (Management) (6231): Mr Michael Davies

ICELAND

Reykjavik (SP - see page 121)
British Embassy
Laufasvegur 31, 101 Reykjavik
Postal Address: PO Box 460, 121 Reykjavik
Telephone: (00) (354) 550 5100
Facsimile: (00) (354) 550 5105
Airtech: (00) (354) 550 5104
e-mail: britemb@centrum.is
Office Hours (GMT): Mon-Thurs 08 30 – 16 00, Fri 08 30 – 15 30
Ambassador and Consul-General: Mr Alp Mehmet, MVO
Deputy Head of Mission and Consul: Mr Simon Minshull
Trade and Investment Officer: Mrs Elsa Einarsdottir
First Secretary (Inward Investment) (resides in Stockholm): Mr Adrian Pinder

Akureyri
British Vice-Consulate
Central Hospital (Fjordungssjukrahusid a Akureyri)
v/Eyrarlandsveg PO Box 380
IS-602 Akureyri
Telephone: (00) (354) 463 0102
Facsimile: (00) (354) 462 4621
Office Hours (GMT): 09 00 – 12 00 and 13 00 – 17 00
Honorary Vice-Consul: Mr Halldor Jonsson

INDIA

New Delhi
British High Commission
Chanakyapuri, New Delhi 110021
FTN Code – 8414 + extn number
Telephone: (00) (91) (11) 2687 2161 2419 2100
Facsimile: (00) (91) (11) 2687 2882 Management Dept
2687 0068 Political Dept
2687 0062 Economic and Commercial Dept
2687 0065 Press and Communications Dept
2687 0060 Visa Dept
2611 4603 Defence Dept
2611 6094 Consular Dept
2467 0234 Estates
2410 5783 International Pension Service Officer

2687 9430 Supply Solutions
2412 1966 Representative of the DoH, UK
Airtech: (00) (91) (11) 2611 4601
e-mail: postmaster.NEDEL@fco.gov.uk
Office Hours (GMT): Mon – Fri 03 30 – 07 30 and 08 30 – 11 30
High Commissioner: Sir Michael A Arthur, KCMG
Minister and Deputy High Commissioner: Mr Mark Runacres
Defence and Military Adviser: Brigadier Ian D O Rees
Counsellor (Political): Mr Rob Macaire
Counsellor (Trade and Investment): Mr Stephen Lillie
Counsellor (Regional Affairs): Mr Christopher Burrows
Counsellor (Management): Mr Ian Kydd
Naval and Air Adviser: Group Captain Ian M Draper, RAF
First Secretary (Medical Officer): Dr John Llewellyn
First Secretary (Immigration): Ms Carol Doughty
First Secretary (Press and Communications): Mr Jeff Wilson
First Secretary (Trade and Investment): Mr Alan Attryde
First Secretary (Trade and Investment): Mr Tom Marchbanks (until Oct 05 – thereafter Ms Joanne Freeman)
First Secretary (Science and Technology): Ms Sarah Bamber
First Secretary (Environment and Trade Policy): Mr Daniel Shepherd
First Secretary (Political): Ms Sarah Lampert
First Secretary (Political – Internal): Ms Joanne Caley
First Secretary (Consular) and Director, Consular Affairs: Ms Lesley Beaton
First Secretary (Management): Mr John Greengrass, MBE
First Secretary (Estate Manager): Mr Alan McKerron
First Secretary (ALO Regional Manager): Ms Janet Battersby
First Secretary (Regional Aviation Security Liaison Officer): Mr Thomson Hunter
First Secretary (Defence Supply): Mr Lee Griffiths
First Secretary (Technical Management): Mr Richard Bellham
First Secretary (Technical Works): Mr Gavin Thomas
First Secretary (Consular): Mr Paul Baines
Assistant *Defence Adviser:* Lieutenant Commander Duncan Foster, RN
Second Secretary (Political): Ms Rachel Martinek
Second Secretary (Political): The Hon. R William Stonor
Second Secretary (Political): Mr Philip Reeves
Second Secretary (Political): Mr Jason Tierney
Second Secretary (Technical Management): Mr Phil Cullen
Second Secretary (Immigration): Mrs Margaret Partridge
Second Secretary (Immigration): Mr Mike Crozier
Second Secretary (Immigration): Mr Ed Bossley
Second Secretary (Immigration): Mr Peter Scott
Second Secretary (Trade and Investment): Vacant
Second Secretary (Science and Technology): Mr Thomas Mark Tomlinson
Second Secretary (Management): Mr Peter Carr (until Oct 05 – thereafter Mr Andy Partridge)
Second Secretary (Security Manager): Mr Robbie Robinson
Second Secretary (Airline Liaison Officer): Mr Jonathan Gray
Second Secretary (Airline Liaison Officer – Regional): Ms Sarah Williamson
Second Secretary (Programmes): Ms Nicola Murray
Third Secretary (Economic and Commercial): Mr Andy Partridge
Third Secretary (Trade and Investment): Mr Alistair Elder
Third Secretary (Political): Ms Caroline Wilson
Third Secretary (Consular): Mr Taranjit Jhita
Attaché (International Pension Service Officer): Mr Jim Torrance
Attaché and Private Secretary to the High Commissioner: Ms Lorraine Quinn
Attaché (Immigration): Mr Jon Mustafa
Attaché (Immigration): Ms Angela Parkes
Attaché (Immigration): Mr Stuart Gardner
Attaché (Immigration): Mr Martin Boylan
Attaché (Immigration): Mr Paul Michael
Attaché (Immigration): Ms Sarah Smith
Attaché (Immigration): Mrs Sarah Farmer
Attaché (Immigration): Mrs Stefany Bossley
Attaché (Immigration): Mr Ramesh Patel
Attaché (Immigration): Mr Steve Vosper
Attaché (Immigration): Mr George Farrell
Attaché (Immigration): Mrs Manisha Kotecha
Attaché (Immigration): Mrs Marie A Tomlinson
Attaché (Immigration): Ms Nicola Williams
Attaché and Personal Secretary to the High Commissioner: Ms Cheryl McGuinness
Attaché and Personal Assistant to the DHC: Ms Marie McCafferty
Attaché (Political): Ms Julie Gardner
Attaché (Political): Mrs Sue McAree
Attaché (Political): Ms Kate Hill
Attaché (Political): Ms Julie Richardson
Attaché (Political): Mr Chris Wright
Attaché (Political): Ms Helen Lloyd
Attaché (Defence Supply): Ms Sarah Poskitt
Attaché (Defence): Ms Gayle Blunt
Attaché (Defence): Mrs Christine Bennett

Department for International Development (DFID) India
B-28 Tara Crescent
Qutab Institutional Area
New Delhi 110 016
FTN Code – 8772 + extn number
Telephone: (00) (91) (11) 2652 9123
Facsimile: (00) (91) (11) 2652 9296
Minister (Development) and Head, DFIDI: Ms Susanne Moorehead
Counsellor (Development) and Deputy Head DFIDI: Mr Howard Taylor
First Secretary (Economic): Mr Andrew Kenningham

First Secretary (Infrastructure Urban Development): Mr Stephen W Young
First Secretary (Social Development): Ms Sushila Zetilyn
First Secretary (Development): Mr Mark Lewis
First Secretary (Governance): Ms Sylvia Bluck
First Secretary (Development): Ms Elizabeth Burgess
First Secretary (Economic): Mr Shantanu Mitra
First Secretary (Environment): Vacant
First Secretary (Human Development): Mr Michael Ward
First Secretary (Management): Mr Julian Hamilton-Peach
First Secretary (Contracts/Procurement): Mr William Starbuck
First Secretary (Human Development): Ms Joanna Reid
First Secretary (Rural Livelihoods): Mr David Radcliffe
First Secretary (Rural Livelihoods): Mr Ken Desouza
Second Secretary (Development): Ms Hester Norman
Second Secretary (Development): Mr Mihir Joshi
Second Secretary (Development): Ms Vina Malloo
Second Secretary (Economic): Vacant

British Council Division
17 Kasturba Gandhi Marg, New Delhi 110001
Telephone: (00) (91) (11) 2371 1401/2/3
Facsimile: (00) (91) (11) 2371 0717
e-mail: delhi.enquiry@in.britishcouncil.org
Minister (Cultural Affairs) and Regional Director India / Sri Lanka: Mr Rod Pryde
Counsellor (Cultural Affairs): Mr Les Dangerfield
First Secretary (Resource Management): Ms Rachel Hewitt
First Secretary (Education): Mr Tim Gore
First Secretary (Education Projects): (Vacant)
First Secretary (English Language Education): Ms Alison Sriparam
First Secretary (Education Services): Mr Mark Walker
First Secretary (Arts and Culture): Ms Alice Cicolini

Mumbai
Office of the British Deputy High Commissioner
Maker Chambers IV, 222 Jamnalal Bajaj Road, (PO Box 11714) Nariman Point, Mumbai 400 021
FTN Code – 8413 + extn number
Telephone: (00) (91) (22) 5650 2222
Facsimile: (00) (91) (22) 2202 7940
e-mail: postmaster@bombay.mail.fco.gov.uk
Office Hours (GMT): 02 30 – 07 30 and 08 30 – 10 30
Deputy High Commissioner (2240): Mr Ian Hughes
First Secretary (Commercial) (2232): Ms Helen Deas
First Secretary (British Council Acting Director): Ms Sue Beaumont (until end Jan 06)
First Secretary (Consular/Management) (2219): Ms Allison Marriott
First Secretary (Immigration) (2143): Mrs Mandy Ivemy
Second Secretary (Drug Liaison Officer) (2238): Mr Simon Sutcliffe
Second Secretary (Inward Investment) (2231): Mr Mark Dolan
Second Secretary (Commercial) (2250): Ms Claire Tuhey
Second Secretary (Immigration) (2145): Ms Marie-Louise Archer
Second Secretary (Immigration) (2111): Mr Rafi Husain
Second Secretary (Airline Liaison Officer) (2107): Mr Robert Smith
Third Secretary (Management) (2218): Mr Andy McFarlin
Attaché (Consular) (2149): Mr Glyn Bottrell

Ahmedabad
British Trade Office
4th Floor, 404 Kaivanna Building
Near Ambawadi Circle
Panchwati
Ahmedabad 380 006
Telephone: (00) (91) (79) 26467138
Facismile: (00) (91) (79) 26403537
e-mail: btoabad@iqara.net
Trade and Investment Adviser: Milind Godbole

Bhopal
British Information Centre
British Library
GTB Complex
Roshanpura Naka
Bhopal 462003
Telephone: (00) (91) (755) 527 3654
Facsimile: (00) (91) (755) 765 211
e-mail: bicbhopal@mantrafreenet.com
Commercial Officer: Mr Sunish Janhari

Pune
Business Information Centre
British Library
917/1 Fergusson College Road
Shivaji Nagar
Pune 411 004
Telephone: (00) (91) (20) 2567 1580 or 2567 9817
Facsimile: (00) (91) (20) 2567 1580
e-mail: bicpune@vsnl.com
Commercial Officer: Mr Arnish Malhotra

Goa
British Tourists' Assistance Office
S-13/14, Dempo Towers
Ground Floor, Patto Plaza
Panaji, Goa 403 001
Telephone: (00) (91) (832) 243 8897 or 8734
Facsimile: (00) (91) (832) 564 1297
e-mail: bcagoa@sancharnet.in
British Liaison Officer: Mrs Shilpa Caldeira

Kolkata
British Deputy High Commission
1A Ho Chi Minh Sarani, Kolkata, West Bengal 700071
FTN Code – 8212 + extn number

Telephone: (00) (91) (33) 22885172, 22885173, 22885174, 22885175, 22885176
22885909 Deputy High Commissioner
22886536 (after office hours)
Facsimile: (00) (91) (33) 22883435 General
22883683 Deputy High Commissioner
22883996 Visa Department
Airtech: 22885010
e-mail: Postmaster.CALCU@fco.gov.uk
Office Hours (GMT): 03 00 – 07 30 and 08 00 – 10 30
Deputy High Commissioner: Dr Andrew Hall
Second Secretary: Mr Paul Walsh
Third Secretary (Immigration and Consular): Mr Paul Dryden
Third Secretary (Immigration): Mr Gary Stilgoe

Chennai
Office of the British Deputy High Commissioner in Southern India
20 Anderson Road, Chennai 600 006
FTN Code – 8578 + 1000 for switchboard
Telephone: (00) (91) (44) 52192151
52192308/2310 Visa Office
52050600 British Council Division
Facsimile: (00) (91) (44) 52192321/28269004 Commercial
52192322/28203790 Management/PPA
52192320/28275130 Visa
52050688 British Council Division
e-mail: bdhcchen@vsnl.com
Office Hours (GMT): 03 00 – 07 30 and 08 00 – 10 30
Deputy High Commissioner: Mr Stuart H Innes
First Secretary (Cultural Affairs) (British Council Division): Ms Eunice Crook
First Secretary (Clerk of Works): Mr Patrick Sullivan
Second Secretary (Trade and Investment): Mr David Abbott
Second Secretary (Immigration): Mr Geoff Wood
Second Secretary (Airline Liason Officer) (Resides at Mumbai): Mr Robert Smith
Third Secretary (Management/Consular): Mrs Julia Campbell
Attaché (Immigration): Mr Simon Dadd
Attaché (Immigration): Mr Shashikant Patel
Attaché (Immigration): Ms Siu Lai-Ming
Attaché (Immigration): Ms Denise Engdahl
Attaché (Immigration): Mrs Susan Edghill
Attaché (Immigration): Mr Sean Hopkins

Bangalore
British Trade Office
Prestige Takt
23 Kasturba Road Cross
Bangalore 560 001
Telephone: (00) (91) (80) 22100200
Facsimile: (00) (91) (80) 22100400
e-mail: bto.bangalore@fco.gov.uk
First Secretary (Trade and Investment): Mr Andrew Dinsley
Hyderabad
British Trade Office
H-3-6-322, Chamber 104, 1st Floor
Mahavir House, Basheerbagh
Hyderabad 300 029
Telephone: (00) (91) (40) 55669147/48
Facsimile: (00) (91) (40) 55669149
e-mail: hyd_btohyd@sancharnet.in
Senior Trade Promotion Adviser: Mr M C Srinagesh

INDONESIA

Jakarta
British Embassy
Jalan M H Thamrin 75, Jakarta 10310
FTN Code – 8401 + extn number
Telephone: (00) (62) (21) 315 6264 (Switchboard)
Facsimile: (00) (62) (21) 314 1824 Development
315 4061 Commercial
390 7493 Management
392 6263 Chancery/Economic
390 2726 Defence
Office Hours (GMT): Mon – Thurs 00 45 – 09 00 and Fri 00 45 – 05 45

British Consulate-General
Deutsche Bank Building, (19th Floor)
J1 Imam Bonjol 80
Jakarta 10310
Telephone: (00) (62) (21) 390 7484 – 87 (Visa Section)
319 01314 (Consular Section)
Facsimile: (00) (62) (21) 316 0858
e-mail: Visa.Jakarta@fco.gov.uk (Visa Section)
Consulate.Jakarta@fco.gov.uk (Consular Section)
Office Hours (GMT): Mon – Thurs 00 45 – 09 00 and Fri 00 45 – 05 45
Visa public telephone enquiries: Mon – Thurs 08 30 – 09 30 (GMT 01 30 – 02 30)
Ambassador: Mr Charles Humfrey, CMG
Deputy Head of Mission: Mr Matthew Rous
Counsellor (Political): Mr Seamus Tucker
Defence Attaché: Colonel Stuart Jarvis
British Council Director: Mr Mike Hardy
First Secretary (Political/Economic): Miss Rochelle Cohen
First Secretary (Trade and Investment): Mr Jeremy Larner
First Secretary (Management): Mr Tim Fisher
First Secretary and *Consul-General:* Mr Jim Liddell
First Secretary (Development): Ms Sarah Richards
First Secretary (Development): Mr Martin Dawson
DFID – Governance Adviser: Mr Bill Baker
DFID – Social Development Adviser: Ms Shalini Bahuguna
DFID – Forestry Adviser: Mr Mike Harrison
DFID – Project Manager (Forestry): Mr Gus Mackay
Second Secretary (Development): Mr Liam Docherty
Second Secretary (Political): Ms Theresa O'Mahony
Second Secretary (Political/Economic): Mr Charles Morgan
Second Secretary (Political): Mr Simon Hall
Second Secretary (Counter Terrorism): Mr Duncan Brown

Second Secretary (Trade and Investment): Mr Robert Cawley
Third Secretary (Management): Ms Nicola James
Third Secretary and Vice-Consul: Mr Daryl Crooks
Third Secretary (Immigration): Mr Dave Lovell
Third Secretary (Immigration): Ms Lynn Averill

Bali
British Honorary Consulate
(Appointments by telephone)
Telephone: (00) (62) 361 270601
Facsimile: (00) (62) 361 287804
e-mail: bcbali@dps.centrin.net.id
Honorary Consul: Mr Mark Wilson MBE
Consular Assistant: Mrs Andi Meriem

Medan
British Honorary Consulate
(Appointments by telephone)
Telephone: (00) (62) (61) 661 3476
Facsimile: (00) (62) (61) 661 4390
e-mail: psbaskett@attglobal.net
Honorary Consul: Mr Patrick Baskett
Honorary Vice-Consul: Mrs Sue Baskett

Surabaya
British Honorary Consulate
(Appointments by e-mail)
e-mail: david.montgomery@tps.co.id
Honorary Consul: Mr David Montgomery

IRAN

Tehran
British Embassy
198 Ferdowsi Avenue, Tehran 11344
(PO Box No 11365-4474)
FTN Code – 8657 + extn number
Telephone: (00) (98) (21) 670 5011-19 (8 lines)
Facsimile: (00) (98) (21) 670 8021 Commercial
670 0720 Visa
671 0761 Management/Consular
e-mail: BritishEmbassyTehran@fco.gov.uk
visaenquiries.Tehran@fco.gov.uk
Consular.Tehran@fco.gov.uk
Commercial.Tehran@fco.gov.uk
Website: www.britishembassy.gov.uk/iran

British Council
Shariati Street, 200 metres below Sadr Bridge
Across from Elahieh Dead End Street
Tehran
Telephone: (00) (98) (21) 200 1222, 200 4060, 254 6099, 260 4905, 261 8664
Facsimile: (00) (98) (21) 200 7604
Office Hours (GMT): Sun – Thurs: (Sept-Mar) 04 00 – 11 00, (Apr-Aug) 03 00 – 10 00
Ambassador (2202): Sir Richard J Dalton, KCMG
Counsellor and Deputy Head of Mission (2205): Miss Kate Smith
First Secretary (Commercial) (2260): Mr Nick Coppin
First Secretary (British Council Director): Mr Michael Willson
First Secretary (Press and Public Affairs) (2210): Mr Andrew Dunn
First Secretary (Political) (2211): Miss Sarah Mannell
First Secretary (Management) and HM Consul (2280): Mrs Moira Stephens
Second Secretary (Political) (2298): Mr Gareth Wynn Owen
Second Secretary (Commercial) (2262): Mr Neil Wilson
Second Secretary (Technical Management) (2235): Mr Temu Bilimoria
Second Secretary (Immigration) (2300): Mr Andy McFarlin
Third Secretary (Political) (2220): Mr Rob Ellis
Third Secretary (Management) and Vice-Consul (2282): Mr Colin Glen
Third Secretary (Immigration) (2305): Mrs Olu Abayomi
Third Secretary (Immigration) (2306): Mr Paul Bellamy
Third Secretary (Immigration) (2304): Mr Tommy Sanmoogan
Third Secretary (Immigration) (2302): (Vacant)
Third Secretary (Immigration) (2307): (Vacant)
Third Secretary (Immigration) (2308): Mr Stuart Wright
Third Secretary (Security Manager) (2295): Mr Geoffrey McLaren-Oliver
Third Secretary (2223): Mr Alan Hale

IRAQ

Baghdad
British Embassy
International Zone
FTN Code – 8280 + extn number
Telephone: FTN 8280 1000 (Switchboard)
Facsimile: FTN 8280 2341
Office Hours (GMT): Sat – Wed: 05 00 – 13 00 and Thurs: 05 00 – 09 00
Ambassador (2201): Mr William Patey, CMG
Counsellor and Deputy Head of Mission (2204): Mr Tim Torlot (Mr Robert Gibson w.e.f Feb 06)
Defence and Military Adviser (2240): Colonel the Honourable Alastair Campbell
Counsellor (Political) (2207): Mr Peter Waterworth
Counsellor (Political) (2219): Mr Richard Thompson
First Secretary (Political) External (2209): Mr Martin Cronin
First Secretary (Political) Internal (2210): Ms Bridget Brind
First Secretary (Political/Military) (2213): Mr Kevin Cunningham
First Secretary (Political) (2211): Ms Julia Painting
First Secretary (Political) (2224): Mr Richard Etherington
First Secretary (Legal) (2208): Mr Douglas Wilson
First Secretary (Economic) (2214): Mr Les Hartley
First Secretary (Energy) (2212): Mr Keith Scott
First Secretary (Commercial) (2360): Mr Richard Hardiman
First Secretary (Management) and HM Consul (2300): Ms Eilidh Kennedy
First Secretary (Technical Management) (2301): Mr Fred Roissetter

Head of DFID Baghdad (2600):
Ms Lindy Cameron
First Secretary (Development):
Ms Helen Winterton
First Secretary (Culture) (2660):
Mr Zane Kanderian
Second Secretary (Economic/Energy) (2221):
Mr Patrick Tobin
Second Secretary (Press) (2350):
Ms Zeenat Khanche
Second Secretary (GCPP and Civil Society) (2216): Ms Abigail Boyle
Second Secretary (Political) (2215):
Mr Joshua Burch
Second Secretary (Political) (2218):
Mr Arthur Snell
Second Secretary (Management) (2303): (Vacant)
Second Secretary (Security) (2330):
Mr Peter Chamberlain
Deputy Head of DFID (2601):
Mr Scott MacArthur
Third Secretary (Security) (2331): Mr Tom Ring
Third Secretary (Visits) (2217): Ms Clare Bruce
Third Secretary (Political) (2218):
Mr Matthew Fairey
Third Secretary (Management) (2306):
Mr Barry Daniels
Third Secretary (Management) (2304):
Mr Mandeep Singh Gill
Third Secretary (Vice Consul/ECO) (2370):
Mr Colin Leeman
Third Secretary (Vice Consul/ECO) (2370):
Ms Trudi Kennedy
Development Officer: Ms Mary Lun
Third Secretary (Technical Works) (2302):
Mr Jason Fudgell
Third Secretary (Defence) (2244):
Flight Sergeant Dave Elder

Basra
Office of the British Embassy, Basra
Al Sarraji, Basra
FTN Code – 8357 + extn number
Telephone: (00) (964) 040 831000 (Switchboard)
(FTN 8357 6900)
Facsimile: (00) (964) 040 832344
(FTN 8357 2344)
Office Hours (GMT): Sat-Thurs: 04 30 – 13 00
Head of British Embassy Office, Basra and Consul-General (2202): Mr James Tansley
First Secretary and Deputy Consul-General (2204): Mr Fraser Wheeler
First Secretary and Head of Chancery (Political) (2212): (Vacant)
First Secretary (Management) (2210):
Mr Brian Cope, MVO
First Secretary (Development) (2208):
Mr Barry Kavnagh
First Secretary (Political) (2205): Mr Keith Green
First Secretary (Political) (2209): Mr Andrew Kent
Military Liaison Officer (2228):
Squadron Leader Tom Alford
Second Secretary (Political) (2216): Mr Alex Fox
Second Secretary (Commercial) (2213):
Mr Ross Hunter
Second Secretary (Press) (2211):
Ms Karen McLuskie
Second Secretary (Technical Management) (resides in Kuwait): Mr Tony White
Second Secretary (Development) (2216):
Ms Joanne Simpson
Third Secretary (Political) (2217):
Ms Yasmine Radi
Third Secretary (Political/Visits Officer) (2217):
Mr Jim Warren
Overseas Security Manager (2214):
Mr John Windham
Transport Manager (2223): Mr Peter Philpot
Deputy Security Manager (2215):
Miss Michelle Mackintosh
Assistant Transport Manager: Mr Tony Shaw

Kirkuk
Office of the British Embassy, Kirkuk
North Oil Compound
Arafa, Kirkuk
Contact details:
OP Telic
BFPO 684
Kirkuk (via Baghdad)
Telephone: (00) (1) (240) 553 0596 direct
(1) (240) 553 0590 extn 4131
Head of Post and Consul-General for Northern Iraq (Mobile +964 7701 309695):
Mr Colin Crorkin, MBE
Deputy Consul-General (Mobile +964 7701 309675): Miss Nicolette Smith

IRELAND

Dublin
British Embassy
29 Merrion Road, Ballsbridge, Dublin 4
FTN Code – 8302 + extn number
Telephone: (00 353) (1) 205 3700 (Main Switchboard)
205 3775 (Commercial)
205 3792 (Defence)
205 3700 (Passport/Visa)
205 3742 (Press and Public Affairs)
Facsimile: (00 353) (1) 205 3731 (Chancery)
205 3880 (Commercial)
205 3885 (Management)
205 3890 (Consular/Passport/Visa)
205 3893 (Press and Public Affairs)
205 3878 (Defence)
e-mail: chancery.dublx@fco.gov.uk (Chancery)
defence.dublx@fco.gov.uk (Defence)
trade.dublin@fco.gov.uk (Commercial)
publicaffairs.dubli@fco.gov.uk (Press and Public Affairs)
consular.dubli@fco.gov.uk (Consular)
visas.dubli@fco.gov.uk (Visas)
passports.dubli@fco.gov.uk (Passports)
management.dubli@fco.gov.uk (Management)
Website: www.britishembassy.ie
Office Hours (GMT): Mon-Thurs: 09 00 – 12 45 and 14 00 – 17 15. Fri: 09 00 – 12 45 and 14 00 – 17 00
Ambassador: Mr Stewart Eldon, CMG, OBE
Deputy Head of Mission: Mr Ted Hallett

Commercial Counsellor: Mr Andrew Heyn
Defence Attaché: Colonel John Steed
First Secretary (EU/Economic): Ms Anne Sherriff
First Secretary (Political): Mr Patrick Reilly
First Secretary (Management): Mr Ian Stevens, LVO
Second Secretary (Press and Public Affairs):
Ms Sharon Ewart
Second Secretary (Immigration/Consular):
Mr Randolph Jones
Second Secretary (Commercial):
Mr Matthew Donnelly
Second Secretary (EU/Economic):
Mr Jayd Davies, MBE
Third Secretary (Management): Mr Michael Lyall
Third Secretary (Management): Mrs Sarah Howard
Attaché: Ms Valerie Brimfield
Attaché (Defence): Mr Peter Hodgett

ISRAEL

Tel Aviv
British Embassy
192 Hayarkon Street, Tel Aviv 63405
FTN Code – 8447 + extn number
Direct Dial: (00) (972) (3) 7251 + last three digits of extn number (except where shown)
Telephone: (00) (972) (3) 725 1222 (switchboard)
Facsimile: (00) (972) (3) 524 3313 Trade and Investment
527 1572 Chancery
527 8574 Management
510 1167 Consular
Airtech: (00) (972) (3) 725 1283
e-mail: webmaster.telaviv@fco.gov.uk
Website: www.britemb.org.il
Office Hours (GMT): Mon – Thurs: 06 00 – 14 00
Fri: 06 00 – 11 30 (Aug/Sept-March/April)
Mon – Thurs: 05 00 – 13 00
Fri: 05 00 – 10 30 (March/April-Aug/Sept)
Ambassador (2245): Mr Simon McDonald, CMG
Counsellor,Consul-General and Deputy Head of Mission (2246): Mr Peter Carter
Counsellor (2261): Mr Andrew Gibbs
Defence and Military Attaché (2256):
Colonel Alan K M Miller, OBE
Naval and Air Attaché (2257):
Wing Commander Mike S Rafferty, RAF
Cultural Attaché (British Council Director) (direct 6113620): Mr Kevin Lewis, OBE
First Secretary (Director, Trade and Investment) (2231): Mr Peter Stephenson
First Secretary (Chancery) (2248): Mr Neil Wigan
First Secretary (Management) (2260): Mr Rick Lee
Second Secretary and Consul (3202 direct: 7251292): Mr Michael Hancock
Second Secretary (Chancery) (2266):
Mr Adam Sambrook
Second Secretary (Technical Management) (2265):
Mr John Walker
Assistant Cultural Attaché (British Council) (direct 6113625): Ms Ruth Ur
Third Secretary and Vice-Consul (3205 direct 7251295): Mr Paul Stokes
Third Secretary (Chancery) (2219): Mr Mark Bell
Assistant Defence Attaché (2259):
Staff Sergeant Brian Hogan

Tel Aviv
British Consulate-General
Migdalor Building (6 th Floor)
1 Ben Yehuda Street, Tel Aviv 63801
Telephone: (00) (972) (3) 7251222
Facsimile: (00) (972) (3) 5101167
Office Hours (GMT): Mon – Thur 05 30 – 13 00
Fri 05 30 – 11 30 (Aug/Sept-March/April)
Mon – Thur 04 30 – 12 30
Fri 04 30 – 10 00 (March/April-Aug/Sept)
Consul-General (2246): Mr Peter Carter
Consul (3202 or direct: 7251292):
Mr Michael Hancock
Vice-Consul (3205 or direct: 7251295):
Mr Paul Stokes

Eilat
British Consulate
c/o Aqua Sport
Coral Beach
P.O. Box 300
Eilat 88102
Telephone: (00) (972) (8) 6326287
Honorary Consul: Mrs Dafna Budden

ITALY

Rome
British Embassy
Via XX Settembre 80a, 00187 Rome
FTN Code – 8350 + extn number or 8350 1000 (switchboard)
Telephone: (00) (39) 06 4220 0001
06 478141 British Council
Facsimile: (00) (39) 06 4220 2347 Press and Public Affairs
06 4220 2333 Chancery
06 4220 2348, 4220 2363, 4220 2410 EandC Dept,
06 4220 2335 Management
06 4220 2334 Consular
06 4220 2283 Defence
Airtech: 06 4220 2257
e-mail: info@rome.mail.fco.gov.uk
cons@rome.mail.fco.gov.uk
RomeCommEnq@fco.gov.uk
Management.Rome@fco.gov.uk
Website: www.britain.it
Office Hours (GMT): Sept-July: Mon-Fri 08 00 – 16 00. Aug: Mon-Fri 08 00 – 14 00
Ambassador: Sir Ivor A Roberts, KCMG
Deputy Head of Mission and Minister:
Mr Alastair McPhail, OBE
Defence and Military Attaché:
Colonel Mike C D Montagu
Naval and Air Attaché:
Captain John H Hollidge, RN
Counsellor (Political): Mr Patrick J McGuinness
Counsellor (Economic and Commercial):
Mr Peter E Jones
Counsellor (British Council Director):
Mr Paul Docherty
Counsellor (Development): Mr S S Wyatt
First Secretary (Political, Press and Public Affairs): Mrs Imogen C Wiles
First Secretary (Political): Mr Anthony H Smith

First Secretary (Political): Mr Andrew J Whiteside
First Secretary (Political): Mrs Rebecca Fabrizi
First Secretary (Economic): Miss Nerys Jones
First Secretary (Management): Mrs Christine Dharwarkar
First Secretary (Agriculture and Environment): Mr Stephen Lowe
First Secretary (Social /Science andTechnology Affairs): Mr Ashley Prime
First Secretary (Consul): (Vacant)
Second Secretary (Management): Mrs Jillian FitzGerald
Second Secretary (Management): Mrs Michelle de Valencia
Second Secretary (Energy/Commercial): Mr Christopher Wigginton
Second Secretary: Mr Graham J Dempsey
Second Secretary: Mr Simon Grunwell
Second Secretary: Mr Mark C E Norman
Second Secretary: Mr Richard Osmond
Third Secretary: Mr Patrick Williams
Third Secretary (Political): Miss Claire Millington
Third Secretary (Political): Miss Frances O'Connor
Third Secretary (Vice-Consul): Mrs Sue Donegan
Vice-Consul: Mrs Angela T Sweeney, MBE

Rome United Kingdom Representation to the United Nations Food and Agriculture Agencies in Rome, see page 118

Florence
British Consulate
Lungarno Corsini 2,
50123 Florence
Telephone: (00) (39) 055 284133
(00) (39) 055 289556 (Commercial)
Facsimile: (00) (39) 055 219112
Airtech: (00) (39) 055 2654354
e-mail: Consular.Florence@fco.gov.uk
Commercial.Florence@fco.gov.uk
Office Hours (GMT): Apr-Oct 07 00 – 11 00 and 12 00 – 15 00. Nov-Mar 08 00 – 12 00 and 13 00 – 16 00
Consul (also Consul-General for the Republic of San Marino): Mrs Moira A Macfarlane
Vice-Consul: Ms Jane H de C Ireland, MBE
Pro-Consul: Ms Diane L Johnson

Milan (SP - see page 121)
British Consulate-General
Via San Paolo 7, 20121 Milan
FTN Code – 8353 1000 (switchboard)
Telephone: (00) (39) 02 723001
Facsimile: (00) (39) 02 72020153 Commercial
86465081 Consular, Management and PPA
(Visa and Passport work is centralized in Rome)
Office Hours (GMT): Apr – Oct 07 00 – 11 00 and 12 00 – 15 00. Nov – Mar 08 00 – 12 00 and 13 00 – 16 00
Director General for Trade and Investment and Consul-General: Mr Richard J Northern, MBE
Deputy Director General for Trade and Deputy Consul-General: Mr Laurence Bristow-Smith
Consul (Consular/Management): Mr Dave Wells
Consul (Press and Political Affairs): Ms Joanne Yeadon
Second Secretary (Investment): Ms Fiona Corby, LVO
Vice-Consul: Mrs Elizabeth Crosley, MBE
Pro-Consul: Mrs Julia Billingsley

Genoa
British Consulate
Piazza G Verdi 6/A
16121 Genoa
Telephone: (00) (39) 010 5740071
Facsimile: (00) (39) 010 5304096
Office Hours (GMT): Apr-Oct: Mon-Wed 07 30 – 10 30, Thurs 10 30 – 13 30. Nov Mar: Mon-Wed 08 30 – 11 30, Thurs 11 30 – 14 30
Honorary Consul: Mrs Denise Dardani

Turin
British Consulate
Via Madama Cristina, 99
10126 Turin
Telephone: (00) (39) 011 6509202
Facsimile: (00) (39) 011 6695982
e-mail: bcturin@yahoo.com
Office Hours (GMT): Apr – Oct Mon and Thurs: 07 00 – 10 00. Nov – Mar Mon and Thurs: 08 00 – 11 00
Honorary Consul: Mr Tim R Priesack

Venice
British Consulate
Piazzale Donatori di Sangue 2/5
30171 Venice-Mestre
Telephone: (00) (39) 041 5055990
Facsimile: (00) (39) 041 950254
e-mail: britconvenice@tin.it
Office Hours (GMT): Apr-Oct Mon – Fri 08 00 – 11 00. Nov-Mar Mon – Fri 09 00 – 12 00
Honorary Consul: Mr Ivor N Coward
Pro-Consul: Mrs Lita Santin, MBE

Trieste
British Consulate
Via Roma 15
34132 Trieste
Telephone/Facsimile: (00) (39) 040 3478303
e-mail: jododds@tin.it
Office Hours (GMT): Apr-Oct Tues: 08 00 – 10 00 Nov-Mar Tues: 09 00 – 11 00. Fri: 12 30 – 14 30 Fri: 13 30 – 15 30
Honorary Consul: Prof. John Dodds

Cagliari
British Consulate
Viale Colombo,160 Quartu S.E.
09045 Cagliari
Telephone: (00) (39) 070 828628 (Consular Enquiries)
813412 (Business Phone)
Facsimile: (00) (39) 070 862293
e-mail: agraham@iol.it
Honorary Consul: Mr Andrew Graham, MBE

Naples
British Consulate
Via dei Mille 40, 80121 Naples
UK Postal Address: Consulate, BFPO 8 London
Telephone: (00) (39) (081) 423 8911
Facsimile: (00) (39) (081) 422 434

422 419 (Commercial Section)
Airtech: (00) (39) (081) 423 8917
e-mail: info.naples@fco.gov.uk
Office Hours (GMT): August: 07 00 – 13 00
Winter: 08 00 – 12 00 and 13 00 – 16 00
Consul: Mr Michael Burgoyne, MBE
Commercial Officer: Mr Giuseppe Saraceno
Political and Public Diplomacy:
Mr Gerardo Kaiser
Vice-Consul: Mr Brian McKeever

Bari
British Consulate
David H Gavan and Sons Shipping SrL,
Via Dalmazia 127, 70121 Bari
Telephone: (00) (39) (080) 554 3668
Facsimile: (00) (39) (080) 554 2977
e-mail: gavan@tin.it
Honorary Consul: Mr David Gavan, MBE

Catania
British Consulate
Via G Verdi 53,
95129 Catania
Telephone: (00) (39) 095 715 1864
Facsimile: (00) (39) 095 715 1503
e-mail: consular@omnilog.com
Honorary Consul: Mr Richard Brown

Palermo
British Consulate
S Tagliavia and Co, Via Cavour 117
90133 Palermo
Telephone: (00) (39) 091 326412
Facsimile: (00) (39) 091 584240
e-mail: luigi@tagliavia.it
Honorary Consul: Mr Luigi Tagliavia

IVORY COAST (CÔTE D'IVOIRE)

Abidjan (SP - see page 121)
British Embassy
3rd Floor, Immeuble "Bank of Africa"
Angle Avenue Terrasson de Fougères, et Rue Gourgas
Plateau, Abidjan
Postal Address: 01 BP 2581, Abidjan 01
FTN Code – 8531 + extn number
Telephone: (00) (225) 20300800
Visa Section: (00) (225) 20300824
Facsimile: (00) (225) 20300834 Chancery
20300828 Visa Section
e-mail: britemb.a@aviso.ci
Website: www.britaincdi.com

JAMAICA

Kingston
British High Commission
PO Box 575, 28 Trafalgar Road, Kingston 10
FTN Code – 8282 + extn number or 1000 (switchboard)
Telephone: (00) (1) (876) 510 0700
960 9100 DFID
929 7049 British Council
Facsimile: (00) (1) (876) 510 0737 (Management)
511 5304 (Commercial)
511 5303 (Chancery)
510 0738 (Immigration)
511 5335 (Consular)
926 4246 (Development)
960 3030 British Council
Airtech: (00) (1) (876) 510 0711
e-mail: bhckingston@cwjamaica.com
bhckingston@mail.infochan.com
Office Hours (GMT): Mon – Thu: 13 00 – 18 00 and 19 00 – 21 30. Fri: 13 00 – 18 00
High Commissioner (3349/8):
Mr Jeremy Michael Cresswell, CVO
Deputy High Commissioner (3732/1):
Mr Phil Sinkinson
Defence Adviser (3743):
Colonel Charles G Le Brun
First Secretary (Management) (3727):
Mr Dennis Carter
First Secretary (Chancery) (3338): Mr Jim Day
First Secretary (Chancery) (3320):
Mr Laurence Lee
First Secretary (Development): Ms Tamsin Ayliffe
First Secretary (Development): Mr Mark James
Second Secretary (Chancery) (3730):
Miss Clara Quantrill
Second Secretary (Immigration) (3710):
Mr Adam Perks
Second Secretary (Chancery) (3339):
Mr Peter Walsh
Second Secretary (Chancery) (3302):
Mr Stewart Lister
Second Secretary (Chancery) (3832):
Mr Phil Powell
Second Secretary (Chancery) (3833):
Mr Ray Watters
Second Secretary (Chancery) (3334):
Mr Sean Cody
Second Secretary (Development) (3720):
Mr Gordon Saggers
Third Secretary (Consular) (3720): Mr Alex Curtis
Third Secretary (Chancery) (3330):
Ms Paula Jones
Third Secretary (Management) (3312):
Mr Alex McCann
Third Secretary (Chancery/Press and Public Affairs) (3746): Mr Mark Waller
Third Secretary: Mr Jim Smith
Third Secretary (Immigration) (3841/8):
Mr Andrew Fennell
Third Secretary (Immigration) (3841/8):
Miss Karen Chang
Third Secretary (Immigration) (3841/8):
Ms Jo Halliday
Third Secretary (Immigration) (3841/8):
Mr Chris Kellar
Third Secretary (Immigration) (3841/8):
Mr Raj Annis
Third Secretary (Immigration) (3841/8):
Ms Wendy McMinn
Attaché (International Pension Service Officer) (3712): Mr Neil Kirk
Attaché (3327): Mr Mark Ead
Attaché: Mr Paul Lane
Attaché: Mr Derek Hynd
Attaché: Mrs Louise Duncan-Smith
Attaché: Mr Colin Bowskill

British Council Manager: Ms Pauline Samuels

Montego Bay
Telephone/Facsimile: (00) (1) (876) 912 6859 (Home)
(1) (876) 954 6394/5 (Office Hours)
(00) (1) (876) 999 9693 (Cellular)
Honorary Consul: Mr John Terry

JAPAN

Tokyo
British Embassy
No 1 Ichiban-cho, Chiyoda-ku, Tokyo 102-8381
FTN Code – 8460 + extn number
Telephone: (00) (81) (3) 5211 1100
Facsimile: (00) (81) (3) 5275 3164 (All sections except those listed below)
5211 1111 (Ambassador's Office)
5211 1345 (Minister's Office)
5211 1270 (Energy and Environment Section)
3265 5580 (Commercial Section)
5275 0346 (Consular and Visa Section)
5211 1254 (Defence Section)
5211 1121 (Financial Section)
5211 1344 (Political Section)
3230 0624 (Press and Public Affairs)
3230 4800 (Science and Technology Section)
Airtech: 5211 1226
e-mail:
General Enquiries embassy.tokyo@fco.gov.uk
Consular Section consular.tokyo@fco.gov.uk
Visa Section visa.tokyo@fco.gov.uk
Commercial Section commercial-section.tokyo@fco.gov.uk
Defence Section defence.tokyo@fco.gov.uk
Energy and Environment Section energy.tokyo@fco.gov.uk
Inward Investment Section investukjapan.tokyo@fco.gov.uk
Management Section management.tokyo@fco.gov.uk
Political Section political.tokyo@fco.gov.uk
Press and Public Affairs Section ppas.tokyo@fco.gov.uk
Trade Policy Section trade-policy.tokyo@fco.gov.uk
Science and Technology Section science.tokyo@fco.gov.uk
Embassy Website: www.uknow.or.jp
Office Hours (GMT): 00.00 – 03.30 and 05.00 – 09.00
Ambassador: Mr Graham Fry
Minister: Mr Martin Hatfull
Defence Attaché: Captain Simon Chelton, RN
Counsellor (Political Affairs): Mrs Madeleine Alessandri
Counsellor (Management) and Consul-General: Mr Roger French
Counsellor (Cultural and Director, British Council): Mrs Joanna Burke
Counsellor (Science and Technology): Ms Philippa Rogers
Counsellor (Financial): Mr Harold Freeman
Counsellor (Commercial): Ms Jane Owen
Counsellor (Trade Policy)/Director, Inward Investment: Mr Alastair Morgan
First Secretary (Political): Mr Giles Lever
First Secretary (Press and Public Affairs): Ms Joanna Roper
First Secretary (Commercial): Mr Robin Ord-Smith, MVO
First Secretary (Inward Investment): Mr Simon Collier
First Secretary (Education and Deputy Director, British Council): Ms Lesley Hayman
First Secretary (Science and Technology): Mr Paul Johnson
First Secretary (Trade Policy): Mr Tom Goodwin
First Secretary (Science and Technology): Dr Edward Wright
First Secretary (Energy and Environment): Mr Chris Allan
First Secretary (Commercial): Ms Alison Scott
First Secretary and Consul: Mr Edward McEvoy
First Secretary (Management): Ms Gill Lever
First Secretary (Defence Supply): Mr John Palmer
Second Secretary (Political): Ms Jacqueline Kane
Second Secretary (Commercial): Dr Rhydian Phillips
Second Secretary (Political): Mr Dallas Windsor
Second Secretary (Financial): Mr Andrew King
Second Secretary (Political): Mr Tom Burn
Second Secretary (Commercial): Mr Tom Jackson
Second Secretary (Technical Management): Mr Robin South
Assistant Attaché (Political/Military): Mr Warren Daley
Third Secretary and Vice-Consul: Ms Louisa Noel
Third Secretary and Vice-Consul: Mr Matthew Matsumoto-Prouten, MBE
Third Secretary (Political): Mr Mark Montaldo
Third Secretary (Press and Public Affairs): Mr Clive Hughes
Third Secretary (Management): Mr Shaun Clarke
Third Secretary (Commercial): Mr Richard Koizumi

British Consulate-General
No 1 Ichibancho, Chiyoda-ku Tokyo 102-8381
Telephone: (00) (81) (3) 5211 1100
Facsimile: (00) (81) (3) 5275 0346
Office Hours (GMT): 00:00 – 03:30 and 05:00 – 09:00
Consul-General: Mr Roger French
Consul: Mr Edward McEvoy
Vice-Consul: Ms Louisa Noel
Vice-Consul: Mr Matthew Matsumoto-Prouten, MBE

British Council:
1-2 Kagurazaka Shinjyuku-ku Tokyo 162-0825
Telephone: (00) (81) (3) 3235 8031
Facsimile: (00) (81) (3) 3235 8040
e-mail: enquiries@britishcouncil.or.jp
Website: www.uknow.or.jp
Office Hours (GMT): Monday-Friday 00 00-08 00
Director: Ms Joanna Burke
Deputy Director: Ms Lesley Hayman

Osaka
British Consulate-General
Epson Osaka Building, 19F, 3-5-1 Bakuro-machi,

Chuo-ku, Osaka 541-0059
Telephone: (00) (81) (6) 6120 5600
Consular enquiries: (00) (81) (6) 6120 5601
Facsimile: (00) (81) (6) 6281 1731
e-mail: bcg.osaka@fco.gov.uk
bcgosaka@soleil.ocn.ne.jp
Consul-General: Mr Neil K Hook, MVO
Deputy Consul-General: Mr Chris Stuart
Consul (Commercial): Mr Paul Lynch
Consul (Science and Technology): (Vacant)
Consul (Consular and Management):
Mrs Wendy De Luca

Nagoya
British Consulate
Nishiki Park Building 15F
2-4-3 Nishiki, Naka-ku
Nagoya 460-0003, Japan
Telephone: (00) (81) (52) 223 5031
Facsimile: (00) (81) (52) 223 5035
e-mail: bcon.nagoya@fco.gov.uk
bc.nagoya@crux.ocn.ne.jp
Consul: Mr Julian Miller

Fukuoka
Honorary British Consulate
c/o The Nishi-Nippon Bank Ltd
1-3-6 Hakata-Ekimae
Hakata-ku, Fukuoka
Telephone: (00) (81) (92) 476 2155
Facsimile: (00) (81) (92) 476 2634
Office Hours (GMT): Mon – Fri 03 00 – 07 00
Honorary Consul: Mr S Koga

JERUSALEM

Jerusalem
British Consulate-General
19 Nashashibi Street, Sheikh Jarrah Quarter
PO Box 19690 East Jerusalem, 97200
FTN Code – 8446 + extn number
Telephone: (00) (972) (2) 541 4100 (24 hour switchboard)
(2) 532 8459/540 0451 (Development)
(2) 628 2545 (British Council)
Facsimile: (00) (972) (2) 532 5629 (Chancery)
(2) 532 2368 (Management and Commercial)
(2) 672 9820 (Consular)
(2) 628 3021 (British Council)
(2) 541 4157 (Visa)
Airtech (00) (972) (2) 541 4123
e-mail: britain.jerusalem@fco.gov.uk
Website: http://www.britishconsulate.org
Office Hours (GMT): Sept – Mar: Mon – Thurs 05 30 – 13 30 and Fri 05 30 – 11 30. Apr – Sept: Mon – Thurs 06 30 – 14 30 and Fri 06 30 – 12 30
Consul-General (2111): Dr John Jenkins, CMG, LVO
Deputy Consul-General (2108):
Mr Piers Cazalet, OBE
Consul (Political) (2103): Mr David Craig
Consul (Management and Public Services) (2188):
Mr Frank McGinley
Consul (Political) (2109): Mr Ross Allen
Consul (Development) (532 8462): Mr Jim Carpy
Vice-Consul (Management) (2130):
Mr Alasdair Hamilton
Vice-Consul (Consular/Immigration) (2129):
Mr Valentine Madojemu
Vice-Consul (Political) (2115): Mr John Murphy
Vice-Consul (Political) (2119): Mr John Kane
Vice-Consul (Political) (2133): Mrs Lucy Henry
Vice-Consul (2139): Mr Keith Squibb
Attaché (2112): Mrs Natalie Maguire
Attaché (2105): Mr Steve Haines
Attaché: Mr James Barton
Cultural Attaché (British Council Director) (628 2545): Ms Sarah Ewans, OBE
Assistant Cultural Attaché (British Council Deputy Director) (626 2545): Mr Martin Daltry

West Jerusalem (Temporarily closed)
British Consulate-General
Beit Ha'omot Building
1st Floor
101 Hebron Road
Jerusalem 93460
Telephone: (00) (972) (2) 671 7724
Facsimile: (00) (972) (2) 672 9820
e-mail: britain.jerusalem@fco.gov.uk
Office Hours (GMT): Sept – Mar: Mon – Fri 07 00 – 10 00. Apr – Sept: Mon – Fri 08 00 – 11 00

Gaza
British Information and Services Office
1st Floor, Al-Riyad Tower
Jerusalem Street
Al-Rimal South, Gaza
Telephone: (00) (972) (8) 283 7704
Facsimile: (00) (972) (8) 283 7734
e-mail: bisogaza@palnet.com
Office Hours (GMT) Sept – Mar: Sun – Wed 05 30 – 13 30, Thurs 05 30 – 11 30. Apr – Sept: Sun – Wed 06 30 – 14 30, Thurs 06 30 – 11 30

JORDAN

Amman
British Embassy
(PO Box 87) Abdoun, 11118 Amman
FTN Code – 8486 + extn number or 1000 (Switchboard)
Telephone: (00) (962) (6) 5909200
Direct: 5909 + (Last 3 digits of extension)
Facsimile: (00) (962) (6) 5909279
5909219 (Chancery)
5909352 (Visa)
5909319 (Defence)
e-mail: becommercial@nets.com.jo (Commercial)
Website: www.britain.org.jo (Information)
Office Hours (GMT): Winter: Sun – Mon 06 00 – 13 30; Tues – Thurs 06 00 – 13 00. Summer: Sun – Mon 05 00 – 12 30; Tues – Thurs 05 00 – 12 00
Ambassador (2203): Mr Christopher N R Prentice
Deputy Head of Mission (2204): Ms Pat Phillips
Counsellor (2227): Mr Richard Potter
Defence, Naval and Military Attaché (2210):
Colonel Richard W Currie
Air Attaché (2214):
Wing Commander C Jim Lawrence, RAF
British Council Manager: Mr Charlie Walker
First Secretary (Political) (2206):
Mr Charles Murdoch

Consul and First Secretary (Management) (2236): Mr Michael Snell, MVO
First Secretary (Commercial) (2251): Mr Bill Preston, LVO
Second Secretary (Political) (2326): Mr Allen Hodgson
Second Secretary (Political/Economic) (2313): Mr Richard Shaw
Second Secretary (Technical) (2225): Mr Pete Bishop
Second Secretary (ALO) (2312): Mr Bill Carmichael
Entry Clearance Manager (2283): Mr Gerry Grant
Security Manager (2244): Mr Graham Lindley
Third Secretary (Political) (2208): Mr Jon Goddard
Third Secretary (Management) (2237): Ms Alison Banks
Vice-Consul (2325): Mr Paul Hughes
Entry Clearance Officer (2290): Mr Leigh Culver
PA to Ambassador (2203): Ms Alison Balfour
Attaché (2226): Ms Rachel Cockayne
Attaché (2222): Mr Dan Mantini
Attaché (2212): Sergeant Chris Lake
Attaché (2211): Mrs Lindsay Daly

KAZAKHSTAN

Almaty (SP - see page 121)
British Embassy
U1 Furmanova 173, Almaty
FTN Code – 8721 + extn number
Telephone: (00) (73272) 506191, 506192, 506229
Facsimile: (00) (73272) 506260
e-mail: british-embassy@kaznet.kz
Opening Hours (GMT): Winter: Mon-Thurs 03 00 – 11 30; Fri 03 00 – 10 00. Summer: Mon-Thurs 02 00 – 10 30; Fri 02 00 – 09 00

Visa/Consular Section
158 Panfilova Street, Almaty
Telephone: (00) (73272) 508280
Facsimile: (00) (73272) 507432
e-mail: visa-british-embassy@nursat.kz
Opening Hours (GMT): Winter: Mon-Thurs 02.30 – 11.00; Fri 02 30 – 09 30. Summer: Mon-Thurs 01 30 – 10 00; Fri 01 30 – 08 30
Ambassador: Mr Paul Brummell
Defence Attaché: Lieutenant Colonel Graham J Sheeley, AFC
Cultural Attaché (British Council Director): Mr Chris Baxter
Deputy Head of Mission: Ms Catherine Inglehearn
Second Secretary (Management) and Consul: Mr George Scott
Second Secretary (Commercial): Mr Shozey Jafferi
Third Secretary and Vice-Consul: Mr Andrew Brand
Third Secretary (Political/Aid): Mr David Hinchon
Defence Assistant: Mr Kenny Macintosh

KENYA

Nairobi
British High Commission
Upper Hill Road, Nairobi PO Box 30465 – 00100 Nairobi
Commercial Department: PO Box 30133 – 00100 Nairobi
Consular Department: PO Box 48543 – 00100 Nairobi
FTN Code – 8300 + extn number
Telephone: (00) (254) (20) 284 4000 (15 Lines)
Facsimile: (00) (254) (20) 284 4033 (Chancery)
284 4088 (Management/Press and Public Affairs)
284 4077 (Commercial)
284 4239 (Consular)
284 4296 (UK Permanent Mission to UNEP and UNHSP)
284 4003 (Political Section)
284 4111 (Visa)
284 4102 (DFID)(K)
284 4325 (Defence)
284 4413 (DLO)
284 4069 ALO Fax
e-mail: Nairobi-Chancery@fco.gov.uk Chancery Section
CommercialSection.nairobi@fco.gov.uk Commercial Section
Comms.nairobi@fco.gov.uk Communications Section
ConsularSection.nairobi@fco.gov.uk Consular Section
ManagementSection.nairobi@fco.gov.uk Management Section
PressandPublicAffairsection.nairobi@fco.gov.uk Press and Public Affairs Section
UNSection.nairobi@fco.gov.uk UN Section
VisaSection.nairobi@fco.gov.uk Visa Section
Individual FirstName.Surname@fco.gov.uk
Office Hours: Mon – Thurs 07 00 – 17 00 and Fri 07 00 – 13 00 Local time. The office works Flexi-time within these hours.
High Commissioner: Mr Adam K C Wood
Deputy High Commissioner: Mr Ray W Kyles
Counsellor: Mr Nick Syrett
Defence Adviser: Colonel Alistair D K Inkster
First Secretary (Commercial): Mr Roger G Church
First Secretary (Political): Mr Alex Budden
First Secretary (Management): Mr J Barry Greenlee
First Secretary (United Nations): Mr John P Virgoe
First Secretary (Communications): Mr Adam Wootton
First Secretary: Mr Mark Harding
First Secretary: Mr John F Prior
First Secretary: Mr Clive P Wools
First Secretary (Regional Conflicts Adviser): Mr Mel W E McNulty
First Secretary (Human Rights Adviser): Ms M Garling
First Secretary (Somalia Unit): Mr Nick Pyle
Second Secretary (Consular): Mr Darren F Forbes-Batey
Second Secretary (Information/Press): Mr Mark R Norton
Second Secretary (Political/Economic): Mr Richard Cox
Second Secretary (Immigration/ECM-Regional): Ms Linda Smith
Second Secretary (Management): Mr Graham Hart

Second Secretary (Regional Affairs):
Mr Rowland P Barker
Second Secretary (Airline Liaison Officer):
Mr Dave Greenfield
Second Secretary (Communications):
Mr Tony Boyes
Second Secretary (Communications):
Mr Leigh Fennell
Third Secretary (Communications):
Mr Darren Rees
Third Secretary (Immigration):
Mrs Sharon B Shaw
Third Secretary (Immigration):
Ms Jane Farrar
Third Secretary (Immigration):
Mrs Laura R Powell
Third Secretary (Immigration): Mr Mike Stovold
Third Secretary (Political): Mr Darren P Lloyd
Third Secretary: Mr J Graham Fairweather
Attaché: Mr Peter K Bart-Plange
Attaché: Mrs Paulette E Hunter-Okulo
Attaché: Mr Mark A Bridgeman
Attaché: Mr John D Macleod
Attaché: Ms Katherine Short

Department for International Development (DFID) Kenya
c/o British High Commission
Upper Hill Road
P O Box 30465, 00100
Nairobi
Telephone: (00) (2542) 271 7609 (5 lines)
284 4000
Facsimile: (00) (2542) 284 4102
Office Hours (GMT): Mon – Thur 07 45 – 12 30 and 13 30 – 16 30. Fri 07 45 – 13 00
Head of DFID (Kenya): Mr Simon Bland
Education Adviser: Ms Louise Banham
Rural Livelihoods Adviser: Ms Rachel Lambert
Economic Adviser: Mr Tim Lamont
First Secretary (Somali Development):
Mr David Bell
First Secretary (Governance Adviser):
Ms Sue Lane
First Secretary (Health Adviser):
Ms Marilyn McDonagh
First Secretary (Sudan Programmes Co-ordinator):
Mr Ian Ruff
Regional/IT Manager: Mr Andy Friel

Nairobi United Nations Human Settlements Programme (Habitat), **See page 117**

Nairobi United Nations Environment Programme, **See page 117**

Mombasa
Honorary British Consular Representative
1st Floor, Cotts House, Moi Avenue
PO Box 85593, Mombasa
Telephone: (00) (254) (41) 313609/220023
Facsimile: (00) (254) (41) 312416
e-mail: jknight@africaonline.co.ke
Honorary British Consular Representative:
Mr James W L Knight

Watamu/Malindi
Watamu
PO Box 100
Watamu
Telephone: 042 32154 (H) 042 32132/32571(O)
Mobile: 0733 625646
Facsimile: 042 32132/32482
e-mail: Captandy@swiftmalindi.com
Honorary Correspondent: Mr A D Thomas

Malindi
PO Box 162
Malindi
Telephone: 042 21156 (H)
Honorary Correspondent: Mr I A D Robertson

KIRIBATI

Tarawa
British High Commission Office – (Closed)

KOREA (NORTH)

Pyongyang
British Embassy
Munsu Dong
Pyongyang
FTN Code – 8464 + extn number
Telephone (International): (00) (850) 2 381 7980-3 (4 lines)
Facsimile (International): (00) (850) 2 381 7985
Telephone (Within DPRK): 382 7980-2 (3 lines)
Facsimile (Within DPRK): 382 7983
FTN Facsimile: 8464 2285
Airtech: (00) (850) 2 381 7990
(FTN 8464 2223)
Office Hours (GMT): Mon-Fri: 00 01 – 08 30
Ambassador (2211): Mr John Everard
Deputy Head of Mission (2206):
Miss Lindsay Stent
Management Officer/Vice-Consul (2210):
Miss Sue Snowdon
AMO/Accountant/Archivist (2205):
Miss Kirsten Howell

KOREA (SOUTH)

Seoul
British Embassy
Taepyeongno 40
4 Jeong-dong, Jung-gu
Seoul 100-120
FTN Code – 8492 + extn number
Telephone: (00) (82) (2) 3210 5500 (General Enquiries)
Facsimile: (00) (82) (2) 725 1738 (Embassy General)
722 7270 (Airtech)
736 6241 (Commercial Section)
733 8368 (Defence Supplies)
738 2797 (Economic Section and Science/Technology/Environment Section)
735 7473 (Political Section)
720 4928 (Press and Public Affairs Section)
736 3174 (Residence)

FTN Telephone: 8492 5515 (HMA's Office)
FTN Facsimile: 8492 2285 (Consular Section)
8492 5528 (Defence Section)
e-mail: bembassy@or.kr
postmaster.seoul@fco.gov.uk
Website: www.uk.or.kr
Office Hours (GMT): Mon – Thurs: 00 00 – 08 15 and Fri: 00 00 – 08 00
Consular and Visa Section – public opening hours (GMT): Mon – Fri: 01 00 – 07 00
Ambassador (5510/5511): Mr Warwick Morris
Minister – Counsellor and Deputy Head of Mission (5517): Mr Guy Warrington
Counsellor and British Council Director (3702 0600 extn 0677): Mr Ian Simm
Counsellor (Political) (5530): Ms Judith Gough
Defence and Military Attaché (5524):
Brigadier J H Harry O'Hare, OBE
Naval and Air Attaché (5525):
Captain Tim Williams, RN
First Secretary (Defence) (5520):
Mr Jonathan Geddes
First Secretary (Science/Technology/Environment) (5590): Dr Jim Thomson
First Secretary (Commercial) (5620):
Mr Dai Billington
First Secretary (Management and Consul) (5655):
Mrs Diana Fitch
First Secretary (Education/British Council Deputy Director) (3702 0622): Mr Gavin Anderson
Second Secretary (Press and Public Affairs) (5560): Mr Tom Warwick
Second Secretary (Inward Investment) (5610):
Mr Matthew Smith
Second Secretary (Political) (5537):
Mr Mike Cowin
Second Secretary (Economic) (5600):
Mr David Wallace
Second Secretary (Commercial) (5621):
Ms Jacqueline Mullen
Assistant Cultural Attaché (British Council) (3702 0633): Mr Kevin McLaven
Second Secretary (Technical Works Office) (resides at Beijing): Mr Carl Gray
Second Secretary (Management/Consular) (5650):
Ms Angela Trott
Second Secretary (Technical Management Officer) (resides Tokyo): Mr Robin South
Entry Clearance Officer (5681): Mrs Helen Winder
Archivist/Post Security Officer (5532):
Mr Stephen Winder
Defence Staff Support Assistant (5526):
Staff Sergeant Catherine Munro
PA to HM Ambassador: Ms Christine Abrams
PA to Deputy Head of Mission: Ms Angela Leach

Pusan
Honorary Consul's Office
12th Floor
Yuchang Building, 25-2,
Chungang-Dong, 4-Ga
Chung-Gu,
Pusan, 600-014
PO Box No 75
Telephone: (00) (82) (051) 463 0041 and 463 4630
Facsimile: (00) (82) (051) 462 5933
Honorary Consul: Mr S E Wang, CBE
Honorary Vice-Consul: Mr H Guack

KUWAIT
British Embassy
Arabian Gulf Street
Postal Address: PO Box 2, Safat 13001, Kuwait
Commercial Section Address: PO Box 300, Safat 13003, Kuwait
FTN Code – 8607 + extn number
Telephone: (00) (965) 240 3335
Facsimile: 240 7395 Commercial
242 6799 Chancery/Defence
242 5778 Consular/Visa
240 7633 Management
e-mail: britemb@qualitynet.net
Office Hours (GMT): Sat – Wed: 04 30 – 11 30
Ambassador: Mr Stuart Laing
Counsellor and Deputy Head of Mission:
Mr James N G Bowden, OBE
Defence Attaché: Colonel Simon Tustin
First Secretary (Political): Mr Nick Watson
First Secretary (Commercial): Mr Steve Seaman
First Secretary (Defence Supply): Mr Keith Harper
First Secretary (British Council):
Mr Bob Steedman
First Secretary (Management) and Consul:
Mrs Cathy Cottrell
Second Secretary (Political/Press and Public Affairs): Miss Jaime Turner
Third Secretary (Management):
Miss Jo-Ann Sibbons
Third Secretary (Entry Clearance) and Vice-Consul: Mrs Tamsin Clayton
Third Secretary (Entry Clearance): Mr Phil Norris
Third Secretary (Iraq): Mr Ahmed Patel
Political Attaché: Mr Calvin Candy

KYRGYZSTAN

Bishkek
British Embassy
(All staff reside at Almaty)
Ambassador: Mr Paul Brummell
Defence Attaché:
Lieutenant Colonel Graham J Sheeley, AFC
Cultural Attaché: Mr James Kennedy
Deputy Head of Mission: Ms Catherine Inglehearn
Second Secretary and Consul: Mr George Scott
Second Secretary (Commercial): Mr Shozey Jafferi
Third Secretary (Political/Aid): Mr David Hinchon
Third Secretary and Vice-Consul:
Mr Andrew Brand

British Consulate
Osoo Fatboys
Prospekt Chyl 104
Bishkek, Kyrgyz Republic
Telephone: (00) (996 312) 584245
e-mail: fatboys@mail.kg
Honorary Consul: Mr Mike Atsoparthis

Department for International Development (DFID) Kyrgyzstan
215 Manaschy Sagynbaya (FM Kalinina) Street
Bishkek, Kyrgyz Republic 720010
Telephone: (00) (996 312) 690 231/3

Facsimile: (00) (996 312) 690 232
Head of Office: Mr J Lane

LAOS

Vientiane
British Embassy
(All staff reside at Bangkok)
PO Box 6626, Vientiane
Telephone: (00) (856) (21) 413606
Facsimile: (00) (856) (21) 413607
Ambassador: Mr David W Fall
Counsellor: Mr Andrew J Pearce
Counsellor (Commercial): Mr Martin Hill
First Secretary (Political): Mr Ian Proud
Consul and *First Secretary (Management):*
Mr Alan Mayland
First Secretary: Mr John Hector
Second Secretary (Immigration):
Mrs Jane F Lacey-Smith
Third Secretary: Mr Philip McKenzie

British Trade Office
Office Hours (GMT): Mon – Fri 01 00 – 05 00 and 06 00 – 09 30
Head of British Trade Office: Dr Robert Cooper

LATVIA

Riga (SP - see page 121)
British Embassy
5 J. Alunana Iela, Riga
LV 1010
Telephone: (00) (371) 777 4700
Facsimile: (00) (371) 777 4707
Chancery/Information/Management/Consular
777 4724 Commercial
Airtech: (00) (371) 777 4741
e-mail: british.embassy@apollo.lv
Website: www.britain.lv
Office Hours (GMT): 07 00 – 11 00 and 12 00 – 15 00
Ambassador: Mr Ian Bond
Deputy Head of Mission and Consul:
Ms Judith Gardiner
Defence Attaché:
Lieutenant Colonel Glen A B Grant
First Secretary (British Council Director):
Ms Agita Kalvina
Second Secretary (Commercial):
Ms Jeanette Stevens
Third Secretary: Ms Helen Teasdale
Third Secretary/Vice-Consul and Management Officer: Mrs Jackie White
Third Secretary (resides in Helsinki):
Mr Tim Goode
Attaché: Mr John Pond
Attaché: FS Joe Stansfield
Technical Works Supervisor: Mr Andrew Moore

LEBANON
Beirut
British Embassy
Serail Hill
Beirut Centre-Ville
PO Box 11-471 Beirut
FTN Code – 8490 + extn number
Telephone: (00) (961) (1) 990400 (24 hrs)
Facsimile: (00) (961) (1) 990420
e-mail: britemb@cyberia.net.lb
Website: www.britishembassy.org.lb
Office Hours (GMT): Mon-Thurs: 06 30 – 15 15 and Fri: 06 30 – 11 30
Ambassador: Mr James W Watt, CVO
Deputy Head of Mission: Mr Chris Poole, MBE
Defence Attaché:
Lieutenant Colonel Nigel R Forrestal
First Secretary (Education Culture) (British Council Director): Ms Amanda Burrell
First Secretary (Political): Mr James Baxendale
Second Secretary (Commercial):
Ms Karen Williams, MBE
Second Secretary (Management):
Mrs Karen Kavanagh
Third Secretary (Management):
Miss Doris Vir Singh
Third Secretary (Chancery):
Mr William Hopkinson
Vice-Consul: Mrs Trudy Curry
Entry Clearance Officer: Miss Michelle Callus
Overseas Security Manager: (Vacant)
Attaché: Ms Tsui-Ling Yu
Attaché: Miss Amanda Smillie

Mount Lebanon
Coolrite Building,
Beirut
Telephone: (00) (961) (4) 723 502
Honorary Consul: Mr William Zard, MBE

Tripoli
British Consulate
Daar Al Ain, Tripoli
Telephone: (00) (961) (6) 621320
Honorary Consul: Mr Anwar Arida, MBE

LESOTHO

Maseru (SP - see page 121)
British High Commission
PO Box 521, Maseru 100
FTN Code – 8294 + extn number
Telephone: (00) (266) 22313961
Facsimile: (00) (266) 22310120
(FTN extension 2226)
Airtech: (00) (266) 22310387
e-mail: Firstname.Surname@fco.gov.uk
Office Hours (GMT): Mon-Thurs 06 00 – 11 00 and 11 45 – 14 30 Fri 06 00 – 11 00
High Commissioner (ext. 2202): Mr Frank Martin
Deputy High Commissioner (ext. 2203):
Mr Mark Watchorn
Defence Adviser (Resides at Pretoria):
Brigadier David H Keenan, OBE
Please note that the Post will close at the end of 2005. Diplomatic and Consular relations will be handled by the British High Commission in Pretoria.

Department for International Development (DFID) Field Office
Address as for British High Commission
Telephone: (00) (266) 22321602
Facsimile: (00) (266) 22321600

Office Hours: as for British High Commission
Head of Field Office (ext 2209):
Miss Diana Webster
(email d-webster@dfid.gov.uk)

LIBERIA

Monrovia
British Embassy
(Staff accredited from Freetown unless otherwise stated)
Ambassador: Dr John E Mitchiner
Defence Attaché:
Lieutenant Colonel Desmond J A Bergin, OBE
First Secretary (Political) (UK based officer in Monrovia): Mr David Lelliott

British Honorary Consul
UMARCO,
Monrovia
Telephone: (00) (231) 226 056
Facsimile: (00) (231) 226 061
Mobile: (00) (231) 6 516 973
e-mail: chalkleyroy@aol.com
Office Hours: Mon-Thurs: 08 00 – 17 00;
Fri 08 00 – 13 30
Honorary Consul: Mr Roy Chalkley

LIBYA

Tripoli
British Embassy
PO Box 4206
Tripoli
FTN Codes – 8318 (Chancery) or 8609 (Consular/Visa/Management)+ extn number
Telephone: (00) (218) (21) 340 3644/5 (Chancery)
335 1084 (Consular/Visa/Management)
335 1419 (Consular)
Facsimile: (00) (218) (21) 340 3648 (Chancery)
335 1425 (Consular/Management)
335 1427 (Visa Section)
Office Hours (GMT): Sun – Thurs: 07 00 – 14 00
Ambassador (8318+2225): Mr Anthony M Layden
Deputy Head of Mission and Consul-General (8318+2227): Dr Robert Wilson
First Secretary (Political) (8318+2212):
Mr Justin Hustwitt
First Secretary (Management) (8609+2212):
Mr David Lusher
First Secretary (Commercial) (8609+2260):
Mr Trevor Hines
First Secretary (Education and British Council Director) (8609+3100): Mr Carl Reuter
Second Secretary (Political) (8318+2213):
Ms Helen Fazey
Second Secretary (Commercial) (8609+2262):
Mrs Joanne Finnamore-Crorkin
Second Secretary (Immigration) (8609+2242):
Mr Nicholas Bostin
Third Secretary (Management) and Vice-Consul (8609+2210): Mr Asif Choudhury
Third Secretary (Immigration) (8609+2252):
Mr John Valentine
Third Secretary (Immigration) (8609+2252):
Mr Rob Winstanley
Third Secretary (Immigration) (8609+2252):
Ms Su Sheppard
Attaché (8318+2226): Mrs Annette Moore
Attaché (8318+2215): Mr Simon Beglin

LIECHTENSTEIN

Vaduz
Ambassador (resides at Berne):
Mr Simon Featherstone
Consul-General (resides at Berne):
Mr D G Roberts

LITHUANIA

Vilnius (SP - see page 121)
British Embassy
Antakalnio 2
LT-10308 Vilnius
FTN Code – 8327 + extn number
Telephone: (00) (370) (5) 246 2900
Facsimile: (00) (370) (5) 246 2901
Airtech: (00) (370) (5) 246 2922
Website: www.britain.lt
Office Hours (GMT): Mon – Thur 06 30 – 10 00 and 11 00 – 15 00. Fridays 06 30 – 10 00 and 11 00 – 14 00
Ambassador (2904): Mr Colin Roberts
Deputy Head of Mission and HM Consul (2915):
Mr Keith Shannon
Defence Attaché:
Lieutenant Colonel Michael J Clements
Second Secretary (2914): (Vacant)
Third Secretary (Political) (2924):
Mr Andrew Calvert
Third Secretary (Management) Vice-Consul and Entry Clearance (2936): Mr Steve Price
Assistant Defence Attaché (2926):
CPO(W) Del Sharples
Attaché and Pro Consul (2902):
Miss Claire Staines
Head of Trade and Investment Section (2939):
Mrs Kate Shannon

LUXEMBOURG

Luxembourg (SP - see page 121)
British Embassy
14 Boulevard Roosevelt, L-2450 Luxembourg
FTN Code – 8305 + extn number
Telephone: (00) (352) 22 98 64/65/66
Facsimile: (00) (352) 22 98 67 (Office)
(352) 22 98 68 (Residence)
Airtech: (00) (352) 22 98 64 (extn. 2231)
e-mail: britemb@pt.lu
Website: webplaza.pt.lu/public/britemb
Office Hours (GMT): Summer 07 00 – 11 00 and 12 00 – 15 00. Winter 08 00 – 12 00 and 13 00 – 16 00
Ambassador and Consul-General: Mr James Clark
Counsellor (Commercial) (resides at Brussels):
Mr Matthew Rous
First Secretary, Consul and Deputy Head of Mission: Mr John Beyer
Defence Attaché (resides at The Hague):
Captain A Robin Davies, RN

Cultural Attaché (British Council Director) (resides at Brussels): Mr Stephen Kinnock
First Secretary (Commercial) (resides at Brussels): Mr Guy Harrison
Third Secretary (Management) and Vice-Consul: Mr Jason Lonsdale

MACEDONIA

Skopje (SP - see page 121)
British Embassy
Dimitrija Chupovski 4/26
Skopje 1000
FTN Code – 8386 +1000 for switchboard
Telephone: (00) (389) (2) 3299 299
Facsimile: (00) (389) (2) 3117 555
3117 566 (Consular/Visa)
Airtech: (00) (389) (2) 3299 226
e-mail: BritishEmbassySkopje@fco.gov.uk
Website: www.britishembassy.org.mk
Office Hours (GMT): Summer: Mon-Thurs: 06 00 – 14 30; Fri 06 00 – 11 00. Winter: Mon-Thurs: 07 00 – 15 30; Fri 07 00 – 12 00
Ambassador: Mr Robert Chatterton Dickson
Deputy Head of Mission: Mr Douglas Gray
First Secretary (Political): Mr Stuart Johnson
First Secretary (Cultural, Director British Council): Mr Andrew Hadley, MBE
Defence Attaché: Lieutenant Colonel D Steve English
HM Consul and Second Secretary *(Management/ECM):* Ms Christine Richardson
Second Secretary (Political): Ms Annabel Paterson
Second Secretary (ILO) (Resident in Sofia): Mr Adrian Barnard
Second Secretary (DLO) (Resident in Sofia): Mr Lee Williams
Third Secretary (Immigration): Mr Jon Ginsbury
Attaché: Ms Sarah Feetam
Assistant Defence Attaché: Sergeant Jerry Rushworth

Bitola
Honorary British Consulate
Marsal Tito 42
7000 Bitola
Telephone/Facsimile: (00) (389) (47) 22 87 65
e-mail: consulatebitola@britishembassy.org.mk
Honorary Consul: Mrs Lilijana Spirovska

MADAGASCAR

Antananarivo (SP - see page 121)
British Embassy
Lot II 164 Ter,
Alarobia – Amboniloha, BP 167
Antananarivo 101
FTN Code – 8726 + extn number
Telephone: (00) (261) (20) 22 49378/79/80
Facsimile: (00) (261) (20) 22 49381
e-mail: ukembant@simicro.mg
Office Hours (GMT): Mon-Wed: 04 30 – 09 00 and 09 30 – 13 00. Thur-Fri: 04 30 – 10 00
Ambassador (non-resident): Mr Anthony Godson
Deputy Head of Mission: Mrs Colin Glass, MBE
Defence Attaché (resides at London): Brigadier David H Keenan, OBE

Toamasina
British Consulate
Seal Tamatave
Telephone: (00) (261) (20) 5332548/5332569
Facsimile: (00) (261) (20) 5333937
e-mail: sealtmm@bow.dts.mg
Honorary Consul: Mr M Gonthier

MALAWI

Lilongwe
British High Commission
PO Box 30042, Lilongwe 3
FTN Code – 8610 + extn number
Telephone: (00) (265) 1 772 400
Facsimile: (00) (265) 1 772 657
Airtech: (00) (265) 1 772 153
e-mail: bhclilongwe@fco.gov.uk
Office Hours (GMT): Mon – Thurs: 05 30 – 10 00 and 1130 – 14 30. Fri: 05 30 – 10 30
High Commissioner: Mr David Pearey
Defence Adviser (resides at Harare): Colonel Bob J Griffiths, MBE
British Council Director: Mr Brendan Barker
First Secretary (Regional Medical Adviser): Dr Howard Friend
Second Secretary (Management/Consular): (Vacant)
Second Secretary (Political/Press and Public Affairs): Mr Chris Wraight
Third Secretary (Consular/Commercial): (Vacant)

Department for International Development (DFID) Malawi
Head of DFID (Malawi) and Deputy High Commissioner: Mr Roger Wilson
Deputy Head of DFID (Malawi): Ms Sharon Kinsley
Livelihoods Adviser: Ms Leigh Stubblefield
Health Adviser: Dr Julia Kemp
Education Adviser: Ms Sandra Barton
Governance Adviser: Ms Jackie Peace
Infrastructure Adviser: Mr Jim Craigie
Economics Adviser: Mr Alan Whitworth
Economics Adviser: Mr Bernabe Sanchez
Social Development Adviser: Mr Dennis Pain
Assistant Social Development Adviser: Ms Isabelle Cardinal
Human Resources Manager: Mr Tom Cushnan
HIV/AIDS Adviser: Ms Anna de Cleene
Private Sector Adviser: Mr Rob Rudy
Department Finance Officer: Mr Nick Duggin
Deputy Programme Manager (Pro-poor Governance): Ms Susan Pleri

MALAYSIA

Kuala Lumpur
British High Commission
185 Jalan Ampang, 50450 Kuala Lumpur
or PO Box 11030, 50732 Kuala Lumpur
FTN: 8402 2 + officer's three digit extension number
Telephone: (00) (60) (3) 2170 2200 – Switchboard
Direct Dial: (00) (60) (3) 2170 2 + officer's three digit extension number
Facsimile: (00) (60) (3) 2170 2370 Management

2170 2303 Political/Economic
2170 2325 Public Diplomacy
2170 2285 Trade and Investment
2170 2309 Defence/Defence Supply
2170 2360 Consular/Visa
Airtech: (00) (60) (3) 2170 2304
e-mail: political.kualalumpur@fco.gov.uk (Political/Economic)
press.kualalumpur@fco.gov.uk (Public Diplomacy)
scholarships.kl@fco.gov.uk (Scholarships)
trade.kualalumpur@fco.gov.uk (Trade and Investment)
defence.kualalumpur@fco.gov.uk (Defence/Defence Supply)
consular.kualalumpur@fco.gov.uk (Consular)
info@vfs.com.my (Visa)
Websites: www.britain.org.my and www.i-uk.com/malaysia
Office Hours (GMT): Mon – Fri 00 00 – 04 30 and 05 15 – 08 30
High Commissioner (PA: 224): Mr Bruce Cleghorn, CMG
Deputy High Commissioner (238; PA: 244): Mr Mark Canning
Counsellor (Commercial) and Director for Trade and Investment (PA: 307): Mr Gordon Reid
Counsellor (Political) (PA: 222): Mr Ian Anthony
Defence Adviser (226; PA: 206): Colonel Jamie Athill
First Secretary (Political, Economic and Public Diplomacy) (202): Mr Edward Hobart
First Secretary (Defence Supply) (242; PA: 206): Mr Dave Mew
First Secretary (Trade and Investment) (232): Mr Eamonn Staunton
First Secretary (Management) (258): Mr Mike Dunn
First Secretary (resides at Hong Kong): Mr Andy Lawson
Deputy Defence Adviser (228): Lieutenant Commander Martin Davis, RN
Second Secretary (Political) (306): Ms Katherine Rowe
Second Secretary (Political) (301): Mr Benjamin Conway
Second Secretary (Technical Management) (225): Mr Peter Haley
Second Secretary (Immigration Attaché) (207; Asst: 308): Ms Diane Drew
Second Secretary (Political/Public Diplomacy) (209): Mr Rob Noble
Second Secretary (Trade and Investment) (210): Mr Neil Floyd
Second Secretary (Consular) (204): Mrs Nicola Bowling
Third Secretary (Management) (254): Mrs Michelle Bond Howland

Johor Bahru
Office of the Honorary British Consul
4 Jalan Tudor Drive
80200 Johor Bahru, Johor
Telephone: (00) (60) (7) 224 9055
Facsimile: (00) (60) (7) 599 4301
e-mail: bradbury@tm.net.my
Honorary British Consul: Mr John Bradbury, MBE

Kota Kinabalu (Sabah)
Office of the Honorary British Consul
c/o Pekah Sdn Bhd
Suite 1-7-W5, CPS Tower, Centre Point Sabah
WDT 46
88000 Kota Kinabalu, Sabah
Telephone: (00) (60) (88) 253 333
Facsimile: (00) (60) (88) 267 666
e-mail: peter.mole@pekah.com
Honorary British Consul: Mr Peter Mole

Kuching (Sarawak)
Office of the Honorary British Consul
The English Language Centre
185C/D/E Fortune Land Business Centre
2 ? Miles, Jalan Rock
93250 Kuching, Sarawak
Tel/Fax: (00) (60) (82) 250 950
e-mail: efelc@pd.jaring.my
Honorary British Consul: Mrs Valerie Mashman

Miri (Sarawak)
Office of the Honorary British Consul
Sarawak Shell Berhad
Locked Bag No1
98009 Lutong, Miri
Sarawak
Telephone: (00) (60) (85) 453 612
Facsimile: (00) (60) (85) 453 617
e-mail: david.stenhouse@shell.com
Honorary British Consul: Mr David Stenhouse

Penang
Office of the Honorary British Consul
Suite 2, 15th Floor, Wing A
Northam Tower, No. 57
Jalan Sultan Ahmad
10050 Penang
Telephone: (00) (60) (4) 228 8368
Facsimile: (00) (60) (4) 228 9722
e-mail: robh@tm.net.my
Honorary British Consul: Mr Robert Henry Hawkins

MALDIVES

Malé
British High Commission
(All staff resident in Colombo except where otherwise stated)
High Commissioner: Mr Stephen N Evans, CMG, OBE
Deputy High Commissioner: Mr Peter J Hughes
Defence Adviser: Lieutenant Colonel Colin P G Martin
Cultural Attaché (British Council Director): Mr Tony O'Brien
First Secretary (Economic and Commercial): Mr Dave Waring
First Secretary (Management): Mr Mick Mitchell
First Secretary (Development): Miss Penny Thorpe
First Secretary (Development): Ms Anthea Mulakala
Second Secretary (Chancery): Miss Margaret Tongue

Second Secretary (Immigration/Consular):
Mr Haroon Suleman
Second Secretary (Immigration):
Mr Roger Goodall
Second Secretary (resides at Mumbai):
Mr Simon Sutcliffe
Deputy Cultural Attaché (British Council):
Ms Anna Searle
Third Secretary (Management): Mrs Rebecca Brett
Third Secretary (Chancery): Mr Colin Hicks
Attaché (Immigration): Miss Jo Ford
Attaché (Immigration): Mrs Yasmeen Rahman
Attaché (Immigration/Consular): Mr Ryan Griffin
Attaché (Immigration/Consular):
Mrs Sarah Downing
Attaché: Miss Julie Coleman
Attaché: Miss Jenny Jones
Attaché: Mr Mike Whyte
Attaché: Staff Sergeant Alistair Farrow
Attaché: Mr Tony Mason

MALI

Bamako
British Embassy Liaison Office (BELO)
(All staff resident in Dakar except where otherwise stated)
Enceinte Ambassade du Canada, sise à
L'hyppodrome sur la route de Koulikoro
BP. 2069 – Bamako
Telephone: (00) (223) 221 34 12 / 277 46 37
Facsimile: (00) (223) 221 34 12
e-mail: belo@afribone.net.ml
Office Hours (GMT): Mon-Thurs: 08 00 – 16 30, Fri 08 00 – 12 30
Ambassador: Mr Peter Newall
Deputy Head of Mission and Consul:
Mr Derek Levoir
Management Officer: Mr Nick Faulkner
Vice-Consul/ECO: Mrs Elizabeth Changai

BELO Staff:
Head of Office (mobile: 223 674 82 08):
Mr Mohamed Ba
Consular Assistant/Cashier (mobile: 223 674 90 77): Mr Benjamin Tessougue

MALTA

Valletta
British High Commission
Whitehall Mansions
Ta'Xbiex Seafront
Ta'Xbiex MSD 11
FTN Code – 8383 + extn number
Telephone: (00) (356) 2323 0000
Facsimile: (00) (356) 2323 2269 Management
2323 2226 Commercial
2323 2216 Chancery
2323 2234 Consular and Visa Section
e-mail: bhccomm@fco.gov.uk (Commercial Section)
Website: www.britishhighcommission.gov.uk/malta
Office Hours (GMT): Winter: Mon – Thur 07 00 – 15 45; Fri 07 00 – 12 15
Summer: Mon – Fri 05 30 – 11 30

High Commissioner: Mr Vincent Fean
(Mr Nicholas Archer, MVO w.e.f March 06)
Deputy High Commissioner and First Secretary (Commercial/Economic): Ms Janet Hancock
Defence Adviser (resides in Rome):
Captain John H Hollidge, RN
First Secretary (Political): Mr Jeremy Hart
British Council Director: Mr Ronnie Micallef
Second Secretary (Management/Consular):
Mr John Green
Second Secretary (EU/Economic):
Ms Sue Elliott, MBE
Third Secretary (Political/Information/Cultural):
Ms Ravinder Hans
Third Secretary (Consular/Immigration):
Ms Elaine Marsh
Registrar: Mr Rory O'Brien

MARSHALL ISLANDS

Majuro
British Embassy
Ambassador (resides at Suva): Mr Ian Powell

MAURITANIA

Nouakchott
British Embassy
(All staff resident in Rabat)
Ambassador: Mr Charles Gray
Deputy Head of Mission: Mr Kevin Lyne
Defence Attaché:
Lieutenant Colonel Simon J A Lloyd MBE
Second Secretary: Mr Steve Moore

Nouakchott
SOGECO
Route de l'Aeroport
B.P 351 Nouakchott
Telephone: (00) (222) 525 8331
(00) (222) 630 1217 (Mobile)
Facsimile: (00) (222) 525 3903
e-mail: sogeco@opt.mr or sab@opt.mr
Opening Hours: Sun-Thurs 08 00 – 16 00
Honorary Consul: Mr Sid' Ahmed Ould Abeidna

MAURITIUS

Port Louis
British High Commission
Les Cascades Building, Edith Cavell Street
Port Louis, PO Box 1063
FTN Code – 8612 + extn number or 1000 (switchboard)
Telephone: (00) (230) 202 9400
Facsimile: (00) (230) 202 9408
Airtech: (00) (230) 202 9448
Duty Officer: (00) (230) 252 8006 (Out of hours emergency)
e-mail: bhc@intnet.mu (All sections)

Commercial Section:
Les Cascades Building,
Edith Cavell Street, Port Louis, PO Box 1063
Telephone: (00) (230) 202 9400
Facsimile: (00) (230) 202 9408

Consular and Immigration Section:

Les Cascades Building
Edith Cavell Street
Port Louis, PO Box 1063
Telephone: (00) (230) 202 9400
Facsimile: (00) (230) 202 9407
Office Hours (GMT): Mon – Thur 03 45 – 11 45. Fri 03 45 – 09 30
High Commissioner (2420): Mr Anthony Godson
Deputy High Commissioner and First Secretary (Commercial) (2424): Mr Michael B G Plumb
Defence Adviser (resides at Pretoria): Commander Peter Lankester, RN
British Council Director: Mr Simon Ingram-Hill
Second Secretary (Chancery) (2422): Ms Ginny Silva
Third Secretary (Management) (2428): Mr Faruk Miah
Third Secretary (Immigration/Consular) (2411): Mrs Sandra Belfitt

Rodrigues
British Honorary Consulate
Craft Aid
Camp du Roi
Rodrigues, Mauritius
Telephone: (00) (230) 831 1766
Facsimile: (00) (230) 831 2276
e-mail: pdraper@intnet.mu
Opening Hours: (local time) Mon – Fri: 07 00 – 16 00. Sat: 08 00 – 12 00
Honorary Consul: Mrs Susan Auguste

MEXICO

Mexico City
British Embassy
Rio Lerma 71, Col. Cuauhtemoc
06500 Mexico City
FTN Code – 8457 + extn number
Telephone: (00) (52) (55) 5242 8500
Facsimile: (00) (52) (55) 5242 8517
e-mail: ukinmex@att.net.mx
Website: www.embajadabritannica.com.mx
Office Hours (GMT): Mon – Thurs 14 00 – 22 00 and Fri 14 00 – 19 30 (Winter)
Ambassador: Mr Giles Paxman, LVO
Counselor (Political/Economic/Internal Services): Dr Vijay Rangarajan
Counselor (Cultural) (British Council Director) (5263 1992): Mr Clive Bruton
Counselor (Public Services): Mr Richard Morris
Defence Attaché (resides in Guatemala City): Colonel Ian C D Blair-Pilling, OBE
First Secretary (Political): Dr Jeremy Hobbs
First Secretary (Cultural) (British Council) (5263 1962): Mr Eric Lawrie
First Secretary (Management/Internal Services): Mr Steve James
First Secretary (Technical Works): Mr David Holmes
First Secretary (Commercial): Ms Sarah Croft
Second Secretary (Technical Management): Mr Ian Taylor
Second Secretary (Global Issues GoF): Mr Gavin Tench
Second Secretary (Commercial) and Consul: Mr Andrew Morris
Second Secretary (Economic): Mr Thomas Barry
Third Secretary (Management/Internal Services): Ms Jane Atkinson
Attaché: Mrs Alison Diaz
Attaché: Mrs Kim Taylor
Attaché: Ms Katy Shrimpton

Mexico City
British Consulate
Embassy, Consular Section
Rio Usumacinta 30, Col Cuauhtémoc
06500, Mexico DF
Telephone: as for Embassy
Facsimile: (00) (52) (55) 5242 8523
e-mail: consular.section@fco.gov.uk
Consul: Mr Andrew Morris
Vice-Consul: Ms Julie Mayne

Acapulco
Honorary British Consulate
Centro Internacional Acapulco
Casa Consular
Costera M. Aleman
39851, Acapulco, Guerrero
Telephone: (00) (52) (744) 484 1735
Facsimile: (00) (52) (744) 481 2533 (ask for tone)
e-mail: gbconsul_aca@hotmail.com
Honorary Consul: Mrs Lorraine E Bajos

Cancun
Honorary British Consulate
The Royal Sands
Blvd Kulkukan, Km 13.5
Zona Hotelera
77500 Cancun, Quintana Roo
Telephone: (00) (52) (998) 881 0100
Facsimile: (00) (52) (998) 848 8229
e-mail: information@britishconsulatecancun.com
Honorary Consul: Mr Mark Carney, OBE

Ciudad Juárez
Honorary British Consulate
Calle Fresno 185, Campestre Juárez
32460 Ciudad Juárez, Chihuahua
Telephone: (00) (52) (656) 617 5791
Facsimile: (00) (52) (656) 617 5088
e-mail: rmaingot@juarez.chih.cablemas.comor rmaingot@jz.cablemas.com
Honorary Consul: Mr Rex Maingot

Guadalajara
Honorary British Consulate
Jesus de Rojas No. 20
Colonia Los Pinos
Zapopan
Jalisco CP 45120
Telephone/Facsimile: (00) (52) (33) 3343 2296
e-mail: simon@prodigy.net.mx
Honorary Consul: Mr Simon Cohen, MBE

Monterrey
British Consulate
Callejon de la Piedra 127
Colonia Las Lajas
C P 64638
Monterrey, Nuevo Leon

Telephone/Facsimile: (00) (52) (818) 315 2049
e-mail: hconsulate@terra.com.mx
Vice-Consul: Viveca Mortenson

Trade and Investment Office
Ave. Ricardo Margain Zozaya 240
Colonia Valle del Campestre
C P 66220
San Pedro Garza Garcia
Nuevo Leon
Telephone: (00) (52) (818) 356 5359
Facsimile: (00) (52) (818) 356 5379
Consul: Ms Bernadette Greene

Oaxaca
Hotel Xestal
Blvd. Chahue
Lote 37, Mza. 4 Sector R
70989 Bahias de Huatulco, Oaxaca
Telephone: (00) (52) (958) 587 2372 (leave a message)
Facsimile (00) (52) (958) 587 2773
e-mail: wolfgangww@hotmail.com
Consular Correspondent: Mr Wolfgang Wilczek

Tijuana
Honorary British Consulate
Blvd Salinas No 1500, Fracc Aviación Tijuana
22420 Tijuana, BCN
Telephone: (00) (52) (664) 686 5320/681 7323
Facsimile: (00) (52) (664) 681 8402
e-mail: consul@britishconsulatetijuana.com
Honorary Consul: Mr Erik M Baloyan

Veracruz
Honorary British Consulate
Independencia No 1349-1
Zona Centro (PO Box 724), 91700 Veracruz
Telephone: (00) (52) (229) 9311285 / 9310955
Facsimile: (00) (52) (229) 9311285, (ask for tone)
e-mail: lourdes.celis@lr.org
Honorary Consul: Mr Luis Carbajal

MICRONESIA

Pohnpei
British Embassy
Ambassador (resides at Suva): Mr Ian Powell

MOLDOVA

Chisinau
British Embassy
Str. Nicolae Iorga 18
Chisinau 2005
FTN Code – 8313 + extn number
Telephone: (00) (37322) 22 59 02 (Switchboard)
Facsimile: (00) (37322) 25 18 59 (Embassy)
25 18 69 (Visa Section)
Mobile (Duty Officers): (00) (373) 6910 4442 KB
6920 0321 LES
e-mail: enquiries.chisinau@fco.gov.uk
Website: www.britishembassy.md
Office Hours (GMT): Mon-Thurs: 07 00 – 15 30, Fri: 07 00 – 13 00
Ambassador and Consul-General (2201):
Mr Bernard G Whiteside, MBE
(Mr John C Beyer w.e.f Jan 06)
Deputy Head of Mission (2204): Mr Neil Martin
Defence Attaché (resides at Bucharest):
Colonel Anthony A A Beattie
Third Secretary (Management) (2250):
Mrs Nikki Mayhew
Third Secretary (Immigration/Consular) (2270):
Mr Arvinder Vohra

MONACO

British Consulate
33 Boulevard Princesse Charlotte,
BP 265, MC 98005 Monaco CEDEX
Telephone: (00) (377) 93 50 99 54
Facsimile: (00) (377) 97 70 72 00
Consul-General (resides at Marseille):
Mr Simon Lever
Honorary British Consul: Mr Eric Blair

MONGOLIA

Ulaanbaatar (SP - see page 121)
British Embassy
30 Enkh Taivny Gudamzh (PO Box 703)
Ulaanbaatar 13
FTN Code – 8728 + 1000 for switchboard
Telephone: (00) (976) (11) 458133
Facsimile: (00) (976) (11) 458036
FTN Facsimile: 8728 2034
e-mail: britemb@magicnet.mn
Office Hours (GMT): Winter: Mon-Thurs 00 30 – 05 00 and 06 00 – 09 00. Fri 00 30 – 05 30
Summer: Mon-Thurs 01 30 – 06 00 and 07 00 – 10 00. Fri 01 30 – 06 30
Ambassador: Mr Richard J Austen, MBE
Deputy Head of Mission: Mr Justin Tait
Vice-Consul and Management Officer:
Ms Lesley Beats, MBE
Defence Attaché (resides at Beijing):
Brigadier Archie J Miller-Bakewell

MOROCCO

Rabat
British Embassy
17 Boulevard de la Tour Hassan (BP 45), Rabat
FTN Code – 8387 + extn number
Telephone: (00) (212) (37) 72 96 96
Facsimile: (00) (212) (37) 70 45 31
(Management/Consular)
26 08 39 (Chancery)
Airtech: 72 99 62
e-mail: consular.rabat@fco.gov.uk
Website: www.britain.org.ma
www.fco.gov.uk
Office Hours (GMT): Winter: Mon – Thur 08 00 – 16 30; Fri 08 00 – 13 00.
Summer: Mon – Thur 08 00 – 14 00.
Fri 08 00 – 13 00
Ambassador: Mr Charles Gray
Deputy Head of Mission: Mr Kevin Lyne
Defence Attaché:
Lieutenant Colonel Simon J A Lloyd MBE
Cultural Attaché (British Council Director):
Mr Steve McNulty
First Secretary and Consul: Mr Steve Firstbrook

First Secretary (International Security):
Mr William Morgan
First Secretary (Technical Works):
Mr Robin Phillips
First Secretary (RASLO/Aviation Security):
Mr Sam Jenner
Second Secretary (Political/PPA):
Mr Adrian Chapman
Second Secretary (Commercial/Economic):
Mr Steve Moore
Second Secretary (Regional Affairs):
Ms Susannah Burns
Vice-Consul: Mrs Anne-Marie Teeuwissen
Attaché (Registry/Communications):
Ms Alexia Quail
Attaché (Chancery): Mrs Sue Kirk
Assistant Defence Attaché:
Staff Sergeant Paul Longman

Tangier
British Consulate
Trafalgar House
9 rue d'Amérique du Sud
BP 1203, 90000 Tangier
Telephone: (00) (212) (39) 93 69 39 or 93 69 40
Facsimile: (00) (212) (39) 93 69 14
e-mail: uktanger2@menara.ma
Office Hours (GMT): Winter: Monday to Thursday 08 00 – 16 30. Summer: Monday to Thursday 08 00 – 14 00; Friday 08 00 – 13 00
Consul: Miss Stephanie Sweet, MBE

Casablanca
British Consulate-General
Villa les Salurges
36 rue de la Loire
Polo, Casablanca
Telephone: (00) (212) 22 85 74 00
Facsimile: (00) (212) 22 83 46 25 (Commercial/Consular Section)
(00) (212) 22 83 46 26 (Visa Section)
e-mail: consular.casablanca@fco.gov.uk
commercial.casablanca@fco.gov.uk
visa.casablanca@fco.gov.uk
management.casablanca@fco.gov.uk
Office Hours (GMT) Winter: Mon – Thurs 08 00 – 16 30; Fri 08 00 – 13 00
Summer: Mon – Thurs 08 00 – 14 00;
Fri 08 00 – 13 00
Consul-General: Ms Biddy Brett-Rooks
Deputy Consul General: Mr Glyn Cartmell
Entry Clearance Officer: Mr Andrew Heseltine
Entry Clearance Officer: Miss Vanessa Thom

Agadir
British Consulate
Complet Tours
Immeuble Oumlil
No. 26, 3rd Floor
Avenue Hassan II
Agadir
Telephone: (00) (212) 48 823401, 823402
Facsimile: (00) (212) 48 823403
Honorary Consul: Ms Lesley Sanchez

Marrakech
British Consulate
55 Boulevard Zerktouni, Residence Taib,
Marrakech
Telephone: (00) (212) (44) 435095
Facsimile: (00) (212) (44) 439217
Honorary Consul: Mr Mohamed Zkhiri

MOZAMBIQUE

Maputo
British High Commission
Av Vladimir I Lenine 310, Caixa Postal 55
Maputo
FTN Code – 8614 + 1000 for switchboard
Telephone: (00) 258 21 356 000
Facsimile: (00) 258 21 356 060
Airtech: (00) 258 21 356 070
Office Hours (GMT): Mon – Thurs 06.00 10.30, 11.00 – 14.00; Fri 06.00 – 11.00
High Commissioner: Mr Howard Parkinson, CVO
Deputy High Commissioner and Consul:
Mrs Louise de Sousa
Defence Adviser (resides at Harare):
Colonel Bob J Griffiths, MBE
First Secretary (British Council Director):
Mr Peter Brown
Second Secretary (Management/Consular):
Mr Frances Gristock
Third Secretary (Commercial):
Miss Morven Williamson
Third Secretary (Vice-Consul/Press and Public Affairs): Mr Daniel Fieller

Department for International Development (DFID) Mozambique
37 Andar, Prédio JAT
Av 25 Setembro 420 , Caixa Postal 93
Maputo
Telephone: (00) 258 21 351400
Facsimile: (00) 258 21 351450
Head of Office: Mr Eamon Cassidy
Deputy Head of Office: Mr Sam Bickersteth
First Secretary, Senior Governance Adviser:
Ms Jane Rintoul
First Secretary, Economic Adviser:
Mr Simon Vanden Broeke
First Secretary, Health and Education Adviser:
Mr Paul Wafer
First Secretary, Adviser: Ms Elizabeth Jones
First Secretary, Social Development Adviser:
Ms Alicia Herbert
Second Secretary: Mr Phil Brown
Second Secretary, Head of Management Services:
Mr Tom Jamieson
Third Secretary, IS Manager: Mr Mike Hall
Third Secretary, Programme Officer:
Ms Sandra Grant
Second Secretary, Asst Governance Adviser:
Mr Andrew Preston
Third Secretary (Accountant): Ms Roma Nelson

Beira
British Honorary Consulate
Links Consulting Lda
Predio de AMI – 5th Floor
Av Poder Popular, Beira
Telephone: (00) 258 3 325997
e-mail: linksmoz@teledata.mz

Honorary Consul: Miss Carrie Davies

NAMIBIA

Windhoek (SP - see page 121)
British High Commission
116 Robert Mugabe Avenue
Windhoek
Postal Address: PO Box 22202, Windhoek
FTN Code – 8616 + extn number
Telephone: (00) (264) (61) 274800
Facsimile: (00) (264) (61) 228895
Airtech: (00) (264) (61) 239004
e-mail: bhc@mweb.com.na
Consular@fco.gov.uk
Visa@fco.gov.uk
Commercial@fco.gov.uk
Opening Hours: (April – September GMT+2)
Mon-Thurs 06 00 – 11 00; 12 00 – 15 00
Fri 06 00 – 10 00
(September – April GMT+1) Mon-Thurs 07 00 – 12 00; 13 00 – 16 00. Fri 07 00 – 11 00
High Commissioner: Mr Alasdair MacDermott
Deputy Head of Mission: Ms Sally Biskin
Defence Adviser (Resides at Pretoria):
Commander Peter Lankester, RN
Third Secretary (Management/Visa/Consular):
Mr Jim Couzens
Attaché: Ms Margaret Horsley

British Council
1-5 Peter Muller Street
Windhoek West
Windhoek
Postal Address: PO Box 13392
Telephone: (00) (264) (61) 226776
Facsimile: (00) (264) (61) 227530
e-mail: general.enquiries@bc-namibia.bcouncil.org
Website: www.britcoun.org/namibia
Opening Hours: same as British High Commission
Director: Ms P Mahlalela

NAURU

Nauru
British High Commission
(All staff resident at Suva)
High Commissioner: Mr Charles F Mochan
Deputy High Commissioner: Mr Ian Powell

NEPAL

Kathmandu
British Embassy
Lainchaur, Kathmandu (PO Box 106)
FTN Code – 8397 + extn number
Telephone: (00) (977) (1) 4410583, 4411281, 4414588, 4411590
Facsimile: (00) (977) (1) 4411789, 4416723
e-mail: britemb@wlink.com.np General
ukconsular@mos.com.np Consular
Office Hours (GMT) Mon-Thurs: 02 30 – 06 45 and 07 45 – 11 15; Fri 02 30 – 07 30
Ambassador: Mr Keith G Bloomfield
First Secretary and Deputy Head of Mission:
Mr Paul Bute
Defence Attaché: Colonel Jeremy Ellis
First Secretary (Cultural) (British Council Director): Ms Barbara Hewitt
First Secretary (Political): Mr Jamie Miller
First Secretary (Political): Mr Chris Jones
Assistant Defence Attaché: Major Peter Bullock
First Secretary (Resident in Mumbai):
Mr Simon Sutcliffe
Head of Management: Mr Paul Robbins
Second Secretary, HM Consul/ECM, (Head, Consular and Immigration Services):
Mr Richard Beeson
Third Secretary (Political): Mr Greg Gibson
Third Secretary (Immigration): Mr Chris Green
Vice-Consul: Ms Serena Brocklebank
Attaché: Ms Marcia Chadwick
Attaché: Ms Lesley Carlton
Attaché: Ms Susan Evans
Political Attaché and Information Officer:
Mr Mitra Pariyar

Department for International Development (DFID) Nepal
FTN Code – 8773 + extn number
Telephone: (00) (977) (1) 5542980/5542981
Facsimile: (00) (977) (1) 5542979
Head of DFID Nepal: Mr Mark Mallalieu
First Secretary (Head of Management):
Mr Alex Harper
First Secretary (Deputy Head of DFID Nepal):
Mr Bob Smith
First Secretary (Senior Governance Adviser):
Mr Alan Whaites
First Secretary (Economic Adviser):
Mr Andrew Hall
First Secretary (Senior Health and Population Adviser): Ms Susan Chapham
Second Secretary (Head of Finance):
Mr David Collingwood
Second Secretary (Head of HR and Office Services): Mr Jim Black
Conflict Adviser: Mr Mark Segal

British Council
Lainchaur, Kathmandu (PO Box 640)
Telephone: (00) (977) (1) 4410798, 4413003
Facsimile: (00) (977) (1) 4410545
Office Hours: Mon – Fri: 0245 – 0645 and 0745 – 1200
Regional Director Central and South East Asia (British Council and Cultural Attaché) (based in Nepal): Mrs Morna Nance
Assistant Director (British Council):
Mr John Linden
Country Manager (BC): Mr John Fry

NETHERLANDS

The Hague
British Embassy
Lange Voorhout 10, 2514 ED, The Hague
FTN Code – 8307 + extn number
Telephone: (00) (31) (70) 427 0427
Facsimile: (00) (31) (70) 427 0347 Ambassador's Office, DHM and Political Section
0346 Commercial Section
0345 General
Website: www.britain.nl

Office Hours (GMT): Mon – Fri 08 00 – 16 30
Ambassador (2202): Mr Lyn Parker
Deputy Head of Mission (2209): Ms Jane Darby
Counsellor (2216): Mr Tony Cowan
Defence Attaché (2330):
Captain A Robin Davies, RN
First Secretary and Head of Political Section (2205): Mr Andrew Price
First Secretary (Legal) (2474): Mr Dominic Raab
First Secretary (Chemical Weapons) (2242):
Mr Mark Matthews
First Secretary (Labour) (2413): Ms Gill Fraser
First Secretary (Management) (2250):
Ms Monique Foulcer
First Secretary (Trade and Investment) (2302):
Mr Neil Brigden
Second Secretary (Political) (2231):
Mr David Burton
Second Secretary (Chemical Weapons) (2241):
Ms Gabrielle Kruger
Second Secretary (Political) (2233):
Mr Russell Brett
Second Secretary (Economic) (2232):
Mr Chris Sims
Attaché (2350): Mr Paul Harris
Attaché (2351): Mr Keith Ditcham
Attaché (2353): Mr Andrew Dean
Attaché (2352): Mr Steve Cobbold
Attaché (2363): Mr Dave Waters
Attaché (2281): Mr Kevin Field

Amsterdam (SP)
British Consulate-General
Koningslaan 44, Amsterdam
(PO Box 75488, 1070 AL Amsterdam)
FTN Code – 8306 + extn number
Telephone: (00) (31) (20) 676 43 43 (6 lines) for extensions see individual officers
Facsimile: (00) (31) (20) 676 10 69
675 83 81 Consular Section
Airtech: (00) (31) (20) 676 4343
(Option 1, 2252#)
Telex: 15117 (a/b UKAMS NL)
e-mail: PassportEnquiries.amsterdam@fco.gov.uk
VisaEnquiries.amsterdam@fco.gov.uk
Office Hours (GMT): Mon-Fri 08 00 – 16 00
Consul-General (2209): Mr Bernhard Garside
British Council Director: Mr David Alderdice
Vice-Consul (Management) (2210): Ms Dawn Tok
Vice-Consul (Consular) (2222): (Vacant)
Vice-Consul (Immigration) (2216):
Mr Barry Wilde

Willemstad (Curacao)
British Consulate
Jan Sofat 38
(PO Box 3803)
Curacao
Netherlands Antilles
Telephone: (00) (599) (9) 747 3322
Facsimile: (00) (599) (9) 747 3330
e-mail: britconcur@attglobal.net (British Consulate)
owersa@curinfo.an (Honorary Consul)
Office Hours (GMT): 12 00 – 16 00
Honorary Consul (see address above):
Mr Antony W Owers

Philipsburg (St Maarten)
(Netherlands Antilles)
British Vice-Consulate (Closed)

NEW ZEALAND

Wellington
British High Commission
44 Hill Street, Wellington 1
Mailing Address: British High Commission
PO Box 1812, Wellington
FTN Code – 8480 + extn number
Telephone: (00) (64) (4) 924 2888
Facsimile: (00) (64) (4) 473 4982 Economic/Trade Policy Section
924 2810 Passports
924 2822 Immigration
924 2831 Chancery
924 2809 Management
Airtech: (00) (64) (4) 924 2836
e-mail: PPA.Mailbox@fco.gov.uk
bhc.wel@xtra.co.nz
Website: www.britain.org.nz
Office Hours (GMT): 20 45 – 05 00
High Commissioner (2874): Mr Richard T Fell, CVO
Deputy High Commissioner (2859):
Mr Martin Williamson
Defence Adviser (2875): Colonel Nigel Lloyd
First Secretary (Economic/Trade Policy) (2842):
Mr Paul D Noon
First Secretary (Political/Press/Public Affairs) (2861): Mr Matthew K Forbes
First Secretary (British Council Director) (2853):
Ms Paula Middleton
First Secretary (Political/External) (2881):
Ms A Ruth Walker
First Secretary (Senior Technical Management Officer) (resides at Canberra): Mr Larry King
Second Secretary (Management) (2871):
Mr Phil Hickson
Second Secretary (Political) (2862):
Ms Sarah M Weeks
Second Secretary (Consular) (2899):
Mr John D A Kenny
Third Secretary (Consular) (2891):
Mr Matthew R Simpson

Auckland
British Consulate-General
Level 17 IAG House
151 Queen Street
Auckland 1
Mailing Address: British Consulate-General
Private Bag 92014, Auckland 1
Telephone: (00) (64) (9) 303 2973
Facsimile: (00) (64) (9) 303 1836
Airtech: (00) (64) (9) 358 4538
e-mail: trade_enquiries.auckland@fco.gov.uk
Website: www.uktradeinvest.co.nz
Office Hours (GMT): 20 45 – 05 00
Consular, Visa and Passport work is centralised in Wellington
Director of Trade Development and Honorary *Consul-General:* (Vacant)

Trade Manager Development: Mrs Barbara Harris
Pro-Consul (Management): Miss Deborah Clay
Press and Public Affairs Officer:
Ms Katharine Fenton-Wells

Christchurch
British Trade Office and Consulate
PO Box 13292, Christchurch 8031
Telephone: (00) (64) (3) 337 9933
Facsimile: (00) (64) (3) 337 9938
Office Hours (GMT): 21 00 – 05 00
Trade Representative and Honorary Consul:
Mr Alister James

Cook Islands
Office of the Honorary British Consul
Muri Beach
PO Box 552
Rarotonga
Cook Islands
Telephone: (00) (682) 21080 (Office)
20444 (Home)
Facsimile: (00) (682) 21087
e-mail: mitchell@oyster.net.ck
Honorary British Consul: Mr Mike C Mitchell, MBE

NICARAGUA

Managua (SP - see page 121)
British Embassy – (Closed)
(Please refer to Costa Rica)
Department for International Development,
Managua (Central America)
PO Box C-194, Reparto Los Robles
#17-A Del Alke, 1 c. Oeste, 1½c. Sur
Managua
Telephone: (00) (505) (2) 702 985
Facsimile: (00) (505) (2) 702 988
Head of Office and First Secretary to the British Embassy: Ms Penny Davies
Private Sector Adviser: Ms Michelle Phillips
Violence Reduction and HIV/AIDS Adviser:
Ms Emilia Alduvin
Governance Adviser: Ms María José Jarquín
Social Development Adviser: Ms Matilde Neret

NIGER

Niamey
British Embassy
(All staff resident in Accra)
Ambassador: Mr Gordon Wetherell
Deputy Head of Mission: Mr Robin Gwynn
Defence Attaché:
Lieutenant Colonel Jonathan A F Howard
First Secretary (Management): Mr David S Jones
First Secretary (Trade and Investment):
Ms Sarah Stevenson
First Secretary (Immigration): Mr Andy Holden
Second Secretary (Political): Ms Farida Shaikh
Second Secretary (Political): Mr Gary Nicholls
Second Secretary (Consular): Ms Caroline Cross
British Honorary Consulate
BP 10151, Niamey
Telephone: (00) (227) 725046
Honorary Consul: Mrs Susan Jarrett

NIGERIA

Abuja
British High Commission
Shehu Shangari Way (North)
Maitama, Abuja
FTN Code – 8495 + extn number
Telephone: (00) (234) (9) 413 2010, 2011, 2796, 2880, 2883, 2887, 9817 (Chancery and Defence Sections)
Facsimile: (00) (234) (9) 413 3552 (Chancery and Defence Sections)
Airtech: (00) (234) (9) 413 2010
e-mail: Chancery.abuja@fco.gov.uk
Abujadefence@fco.gov.uk
Commercial.abuja@fco.gov.uk
Consular.abuja@fco.gov.uk
Management.abuja@fco.gov.uk
Visaenquiries.abuja@fco.gov.uk
Clinic.abuja@fco.gov.uk
Office Hours (GMT): 07 00 – 14 30

Trade Development, Management, Consular and Visa Sections:
Dangote House, Aguyi Ironsi Street,
Maitama, Abuja
FTN Code – 8495 + extn number
Telephone: (00) (234) (9) 413 4559-64, 0899, 0900, 3885-7, 3889
Facsimile: (00) (234) (9) 413 4565 (Visa Section)
(234) (9) 413 3888 (Management, Trade Development and Consular Sections)
Office Hours (GMT): 07 00 – 14 30

Department for International Development (DFID) Nigeria
Plot 607
Bobo Street
Maitama, Abuja
FTN Code – 8771 + extn number
Telephone: (00) (234) (9) 413 7710-19
Facsimile: (00) (234) (9) 413 7400, 7396
Office Hours (GMT): Mon-Thurs: 08 00 – 16 30.
Fri: 08 00 – 13 00

British Council
Plot 2935
IBB Way
Maitama, Abuja
Telephone: (00) (234) (9) 413 7870-7
Facsimile: (00) (234) (9) 413 7883, 0902
Office Hours (GMT): Mon-Thurs: 07 00 – 15 30
Fri: 07 00 – 12 00
High Commissioner (also Ambassador non-resident to the Republic of Benin):
Mr Richard Hugh Turton Gozney, CMG
Deputy High Commissioner:
Mr Martin Shearman, CVO
Defence Adviser: Colonel Neil J N Salisbury, OBE
Counsellor (Cultural): Dr John Richards
Counsellor (Political): Mr John Copleston
First Secretary (Political): Mr Michael Frost, OBE
First Secretary (Management): Mr Ken Clark
First Secretary (Cultural): Mr Rodney Bell
First Secretary (Medical): Mrs Karen Mitchell
Second Secretary (Political): Mr Alisdair Walker
Second Secretary (Political): Mr Neil Angell

Second Secretary (Political/Economic): Ms Claire Burges Watson
Second Secretary (Economic): Mr Tim Wyndham
Second Secretary (Immigration): Mr Timothy Bridges
Second Secretary (Immigration): Mr Ian Dinsdale
Second Secretary (Technical Management): Mr Nicholas Folker
Third Secretary (Political/Press and Public Affairs): Mr Graeme Bannatyne
Third Secretary (Management) and Vice-Consul: Mr Nicholas Snee
Third Secretary (Security and Transport): Mr Ian Bell
Third Secretary (Technical Works): Mr Steve Acott
Third Secretary (Immigration): Mrs Sharon Meeks-Williams
Third Secretary (Immigration): Mrs Jan Banks
Third Secretary (Immigration): Mrs Kamella Emmanuel
Third Secretary (Immigration): Mrs Laura Bell
Third Secretary (Immigration): Mr Gary McCall
Third Secretary (Immigration): Mrs Karen Higham
Attaché (Assistant Defence Adviser): Staff Sergeant Steve Noble

Lagos
British Deputy High Commission
11 Walter Carrington Crescent
Victoria Island, Lagos
(Private Mail Bag 12136)
FTN Code – 8326 + extn number
Telephone: (00) (234) (1) 2619531, 2619537, 2619541, 2619543, 2619566, 2619588, 2619592, 2619598
Facsimile: (00) (234) (1) 2614021
Office Hours (GMT): 0700 – 1400
Visa and Consular Sections
11 Walter Carrington Crescent
Victoria Island, Lagos
Telephone: (00) (234) (1) 2625930-7
Facsimile: (00) (234) (1) 2625940 Consular
(234) (1) 2625941 Visa
Office Hours (GMT): 0630 – 1330
Deputy High Commissioner: Mr David Wyatt
Director Visa Services (Immigration) and Deputy Head of Mission: Mr Chris Dix
Senior Management Officer: Mr Phil May
First Secretary (Immigration): Mr Charles Molloy
First Secretary (Commercial): Mr John Williams
First Secretary (Technical Management) (resides at Dakar): Mr Ian Willsher
Second Secretary (Commercial): Mrs Deborah Fern
Second Secretary (Consular): Mr Maurice Harper
Second Secretary (Immigration): Mr Stephen Brown
Second Secretary (Immigration): Mr John Mellor
Second Secretary (Immigration): Mr Stephen Hart
Second Secretary (Immigration): Mr Jason Ivory
Second Secretary (Immigration): Mrs Sue May
Second Secretary (Management): Mrs Carol Anne Ireland
Second Secretary (Political): Mr Jonathan King
Third Secretary (Consular): Mr Tony Ward
Third Secretary (Management): Mrs Sarah Morris
Third Secretary (Management): Mrs Josie Farrell

Kano
Tamandu Court
5 Tamandu Close
Nassarawa
Kano
Telephone: (00) (234) (64) 631 686
Facsimile: (00) (234) (64) 632 590
e-mail: bhckan@ecnx.net
Honorary Consul: Mr Harold A Blackburne, OBE

Warri
ABB Lummus Global
Unit 6, Jefia State
62 Enerhen Road
Delta State, Warri
Telephone/Facismile: (00) (234) (53) 245 523 or 255 929
Mobile: 080 3708 2048
e-mail: melhenthorn@hyperia.com
Honorary Consul: Mr Mel Henthorn

Kaduna
British High Commission Liaison Office
3 Independence Way, Kaduna
Telephone: (00) (234) (62) 243380/81
Facsimile: (00) (234) (62) 237267
e-mail: bhc@wwlkad.com
Liaison Officer: Mrs Tiffany Collings Hajaig

Port Harcourt
British Commercial/Liaison Office
Plot 300, Olu Obasanjo Road, Port Harcourt, Rivers State
Telephone: (00) (234) (84) 237173, 335104
Facsimile: (00) (234) (84) 237172
e-mail: bhcliaison@phca.linkserve.com

Ibadan
British Liaison Office
Rotimi Williams Avenue, Bodija, Ibadan
Telephone: (00) (234) (22) 810 4953
e-mail: blo.ibadan@skannet.com

Lagos
British Council Division
11 Alfred Rewane Road
Ikoyi, PO Box 3702
Lagos
Telephone: (00) (234) (1) 2692188-92, 261020, 2615047
Facsimile: (00) (234) (1) 2615047, 2622193
Office Hours (GMT): Mon-Thurs: 06 30 – 15 00. Fri: 06 30 – 11 30
First Secretary (Cultural): Mr Sam Harvey

British Council Division (Enugu, Ibadan and Kano)
Teachers House, Ogui Road, Enugu
Telephone: (00) (234) (42) 255577, 255677, 258456
Facsimile: (00) (234) (42) 250158

53 Magazine Road, PMB 5314, Jericho, Ibadan
Telephone: (00) (234) (22) 2410299, 2410678
Facsimile: (00) (234) (22) 2410796

10 Emir's Place Road, Kano
Telephone: (00) (234) (64) 646652, 643489
Director's Direct Line: (00) (234) (64) 643861
Facsimile: (00) (234) (64) 632500
First Secretary (Cultural and Aid, Kano):
Ms Sue Mace

NORWAY

Oslo
British Embassy
Thomas Heftyesgate 8, 0244 Oslo
FTN Code – 8324 + extn number
Telephone: (00) (47) 23 13 27 00
Facsimile: (00) (47) 23 13 27 41 Management
27 89 Chancery
27 38 Consular/Visa Section
27 05 Trade, Investment and Economic Department
27 27 Information Section
2797 Defence
Website: www.britain.no
Office Hours (GMT): Summer 06 30 – 14 00,
Winter 07 30 – 15 00
Ambassador (2701): Mrs Mariot Leslie, CMG
Counsellor (Head of Political Section) (2707):
Miss Anneli Conroy
Counsellor (2716): Mr Keith Beaven
Defence Attaché (2711):
Lieutenant Colonel Andy Canning, RM
First Secretary (Trade and Investment Dept) (2752): Mr Tom Salusbury
First Secretary (Management/Consul) (2751):
Mr Mark Forrester
Second Secretary (Trade, Investment and Economic Dept) (2759): Mr Duncan Hoyland
Second Secretary (Press and Public Affairs) (2718): Mr Peter Ruskin
Second Secretary (2708): Mr Rufus Drabble
Second Secretary (ALO) (resides at Copenhagen):
Ms Denise Broderick
Vice-Consul/DMO (2778): Mr Gerald Smith

Bergen
British Consulate
Postboks 273, 5804 Bergen
VISITING ADDRESS:
Øvre Ole Bulls plass 1
5804 Bergen
Telephone: (00) (47) 55 36 78 10
Telefax: (00) (47) 55 36 78 11
Honorary Consul: Mr R C Hestness (Norwegian)

Kristiansand
British Consulate
Post Box 479, 4664 Kristiansand
VISITING ADDRESS:
Tangen 10, 4610 Kristiansand
Telephone: (00) (47) 38 12 20 70
Facsimile: (00) (47) 38 12 30 71
Honorary Consul: Mr T Wiese-Hansen (Norwegian)

Stavanger
British Consulate
PO Box 28, 4001 Stavanger
VISITING ADDRESS:
Prinsensgate, 12 4008 Stavanger
Telephone: (00) (47) 51 52 97 13 / 51 53 83 00
Facsimile: (00) (47) 51 53 83 01
Honorary Consul: Mr T Falck, Jnr (Norwegian)

Tromsø
British Consulate
c/o Mack's Ølbryggeri, Postboks 6142
9291, Tromsø
VISITING ADDRESS:
c/o Mack's Ølbryggeri, Storgaten 5-13, 9008 Tromsø
Telephone: (00) (47) 77 62 45 00
Facsimile: (00) (47) 77 65 78 35
Honorary Consul: Mr H Bredrup (Norwegian)

Trondheim
British Consulate
VISITING and POSTAL ADDRESS:
c/o R Kjeldsberg AS
Beddingen 8, 7014, Trondheim
Telephone: (00) (47) 73 60 02 00
Facsimile: (00) (47) 73 60 02 50
Honorary Consul: Ms B Kjeldsberg (Norwegian)

Ålesund
British Consulate
Post Box 1301, 6001 Ålesund
VISITING ADDRESS:
Farstadgården, St Olav's Plass, 6001 Ålesund
Telephone: (00) (47) 70 11 75 00
Facsimile: (00) (47) 70 11 75 02
Honorary Consul: Mr S A Farstad (Norwegian)

Bodø
British Consulate
VISITING ADDRESS and POSTAL ADDRESS
Norconsult AS Bodø
Notveien 17
8013 Bodø
Telephone: (00) (47) 75 56 58 00
Facsimile: (00) (47) 75 56 58 01
e-mail: kan@norconsult.no
Opening Hours: 09 00 – 16 00
Honorary Consul: Mr Kjell Alf Nyvold (Norwegian)

OMAN

Muscat
British Embassy
PO Box 185, Mina Al Fahal, Postal Code 116
FTN Code – 8449 + extn number
Telephone: (00) (968) 24609000
24609001 (Consular/Visa)
24609002 (UK Trade and Investment)
24609224 (Defence)
Facsimile: (00) (968) 24609010 (General)
24609011 (Consular)
24609012 (UK Trade and Investment)
24609013 (Chancery)
24609014 (Defence)
e-mail: Enquiries.Muscat@fco.gov.uk (General)
UKTI.muscat@fco.gov.uk (UK Trade and Investment)
Muscat.Consular@fco.gov.uk (Visa and Consular)
Website: www.britishembassy.gov.uk/oman

Office Hours (GMT): Sat – Wed 03 30 – 10 30
Ambassador: Dr Noel Guckian, OBE
Counsellor and Deputy Head of Mission:
Mr Charles Hill
Defence and Military Attaché:
Brigadier Hugh C G Willing
Naval and Air Attaché:
Commander Bob P Thomas, RN
British Council Director: Mr Jim Scarth
First Secretary (Political): Mr Nicholas Diggle
First Secretary (Management) and Consul:
Mrs Clare Douglas
First Secretary (UK Trade and Investment):
Mr Malcolm Ives
First Secretary (Defence Equipment Co-operation):
Mr Jim Catchpole
Second Secretary (Chancery/Information):
Mr Richard Oppenheim
Second Secretary (Political): Mr William Stringer
British Vice-Consul: Mrs Susan Ives

PAKISTAN

Islamabad

British High Commission
Diplomatic Enclave, Ramna 5,
PO Box 1122, Islamabad.
FTN Code – 8405 + 1000 for switchboard
Telephone: (00) (92) (51) 201 2000
282 2131 – 5
220 6071 – 5
Direct Lines: (00) (92) (51) 2012101 High Commissioner
2012121 Counsellor (Political)
Facsimile: (00) (92) (51) 2012063 Chancery
2012066 Defence
2823439 Management
2012031 Commercial
2279355 Immigration
2824728 Immigration
2012019 Consular
2279351 Estates
2277159 Clinic
2012048 DFID
2012080 DLO
2012044 ALO
2012033 IPLO
Secure Facsimile: (00) (92) (51) 2012054 (Cryptek)
2012070 (Airtech)
Telegrams: Prodrome, Islamabad
e-mail: bhc-ukti@dsl.net.pk (Commercial Section)
bhcmedia@dsl.net.pk (Media and Public Affairs)
bhcdefence@isb.comsats.net.pk (Defence Section)
Office Hours (GMT): Mon – Thurs: 03 00 – 11 00 and Fri: 03 00 – 07 00 (High Commission)
Mon – Thurs: 02 30 – 09 30 and Fri: 02 30 – 08 30 (Immigration/Consular Sections)
High Commissioner: Mr Mark Lyall Grant, CMG
Deputy High Commissioner: Mr Simon Butt
Counsellor (Political): Mr Peter Waterworth
Counsellor (Political): (Vacant)
Counsellor (Regional Affairs):
Mr William Sandover
Counsellor (Head of DFID):
Dr Yusaf Samiullah, OBE
Defence and Military Adviser:
Brigadier Andrew J M Durcan
Naval and Air Adviser:
Colonel Mark W Bibbey, RM
Director UK Visas and Head of Consular:
Mrs Alex Pond
First Secretary (Political): Mr Martin Cronin
First Secretary (Political): Mr Richard Seddon
First Secretary (Immigration/Consular):
Mr Adrian Loxton
First Secretary (Management): Mr Peter Hardman
First Secretary (Estates): Mr Stuart Fenwick
First Secretary (Technical Manager):
Mr Hugh Smith
First Secretary (Deputy Head of DFID):
Mr Richard Martini
First Secretary (Health Adviser):
Ms Jane Edmondson
First Secretary (Governance Adviser):
Mr David Johnson
First Secretary (HRD-HW, Nursing Officer):
Ms Elizabeth McManus, MBE
Second Secretary (Political): Ms Emily Wilson
Second Secretary (Political): Mr William Gelling
Second Secretary (Political): Mr David Oakley
Second Secretary (Political/External):
Ms Alex Cole
Second Secretary (Political): Mr Andrew Priestley
Second Secretary (Political): Mr David Birrell
Second Secretary (DFID): Ms Julie Skone
Second Secretary (Technical Management):
Mr Alby Mills
Second Secretary (Technical Management):
Mr Paul Oliver (des)
Second Secretary (Commercial): Mr David Oswald
Second Secretary (Drugs): Mr Stuart O'Neil
Second Secretary (Drugs): Mr Eric Lane
Second Secretary (Estates): Mr Gary Holmes
Second Secretary (Estates): Mr Andrew Moore
Second Secretary (Immigration): Mr Lionel Chalke
Second Secretary (Immigration): Ms Doris Davis
Second Secretary (Immigration):
Mr Eric Humphries
Second Secretary (Immigration): Ms Kim Charman
Second Secretary (Immigration):
Ms Samantha Bethel
Second Secretary (Immigration):
Ms Caroline Edwards
Second Secretary (Immigration): Mr Jason Clarke
Second Secretary (Management): Mr David Denyer
Second Secretary (Consular): Ms Helen Feather
Second Secretary (Media and Public Affairs):
Mr Simon Smart
Second Secretary (ALO): Mr Simon Groves
Third Secretary (Political): Mr Michael Halpin
Third Secretary (Political): Mr Chris Dodgson
Third Secretary (Political): Mr Kevin Jones
Third Secretary (Political): Mr Jonathan Weeks
Third Secretary (Political): Ms Philippa Carnall
Third Secretary (Estates): Ms Caroline Gallagher
Third Secretary (Management): Ms Jean Tranter
Third Secretary (Management/Finance):
Mr Neil Scrambler
Third Secretary (Consular): Mr Jon Turner
Third Secretary (International Pensions):
Ms Helen Ibbott

Karachi
British Deputy High Commission
Shahrah-e-Iran, Clifton, Karachi 75600
FTN Code – 8405 + 1000 for switchboard
Telephone: (92) (21) 5827000
Facsimile: (92) (21) 5827005 General
5827008 Visa
5827012 Consular
Airtech (92) (21) 5827015
e-mail: tradeuk@cyber.net.pk
Office Hours (GMT): Mon – Thurs: 03 30 – 11 00
Fri: 03 30 – 07 30
Deputy High Commissioner:
Mr Hamish St. Clair Daniel, OBE
Deputy Head of Mission: Mr Ron Rimmer
British Council Director: Mr Marcus Gilbert
Second Secretary: Mr Allan Shearer
Second Secretary: (Vacant)
Second Secretary (Immigration): (Vacant)
Third Secretary (Management): Mr Steve Brown
Third Secretary (Consular/Immigration):
Ms Susan Farrent
Third Secretary (Immigration): Ms Sue Voak
Third Secretary (Immigration): Mr Esmail Ansari
Third Secretary (Immigration): (Vacant)
Third Secretary (Immigration): (Vacant)
Third Secretary (Immigration): (Vacant)
Third Secretary (Immigration): (Vacant)
Third Secretary (Immigration): (Vacant)
Security *Manager:* Mr David Wells
Attaché (Political): Mrs Jane Hicks

Lahore
British Trade Office
65 Mozang Road
PO Box 1679, Lahore
Telephone: (00) (92) (042) 6316589 – 90
Facsimile: (00) (92) (042) 6316591
Office Hours (GMT): Mon – Thurs 03 30 – 11 30,
Fri 03 30 – 07 30
Trade and Investment *Adviser:* Mr Waqar Ullah

PALAU

Koror
British Embassy
Ambassador (resides at Suva): Mr Ian Powell

PANAMA

Panama City (SP - see page 121)
British Embassy
Swiss Tower, Calle 53
P O Box 0816-07946 Panama City
FTN Code – 8458 + extn number
Telephone: (00) (507) 269 0866 (5 lines)
Facsimile: (00) (507) 223 0730
263 5138 (HMA's fax)
Airtech: (00) (507) 264 6846
e-mail: britemb@cwpanama.net
Office Hours (GMT): Mon – Thur 12 30 – 18 00
and 19 00 – 21 30. Fri 12 30 – 17 30
Ambassador and Consul-General:
Mr James I Malcolm, OBE
Deputy Head of Mission and First Secretary:
Ms Penny Walsh
First Secretary: Mr Alan Pamplin
Second Secretary: Mr Gary Foster
Defence Attaché (resides at Caracas):
Group Captain William G S Dobson, RAF
Second Secretary (Technical) (resides at Caracas):
Mr Colin Tully

PAPUA NEW GUINEA

Port Moresby (SP - see page 121)
British High Commission
Locked Mail Bag 212, Waigani NCD 131
Port Moresby
FTN Code – 8444 + extn number
Telephone: (00) (675) 3251643, 3251645,
3251659, 3251677
FTN Telephone: 8444 2201 (Switchboard)
8444 2209 (PA to HC)
8444 2215 (Consular/Visa)
8444 2202 (Management)
8444 2208/2210 (PPA)
8444 2206 (Chancery/Registry)
Facsimile: (00) (675) 3253547
Airtech: (00) (675) 3253953
e-mail: bhcpng@datec.net.pg
Office Hours: Mon-Thurs: 07 45 – 16 20 (Local)
Fri: 07 45 – 12 10 (Local)
The High Commission will continue to be open over lunch
High Commissioner (2207):
Mr David S Gordon-MacLeod
Deputy High Commissioner (2204):
Mr Alastair Dent
Defence Adviser (resides at Canberra):
Group Captain Steven Duffill, RAF

PARAGUAY

Asunción (SP - see page 121)
British Embassy – (Closed)
Please note that responsibility for Passport, Visa/Consular, Political and Commercial enquiries have been transferred to Buenos Aires.

PERU

Lima
British Embassy
Torre Parque Mar (Piso 22)
Avenida Jose Larco
1301 Miraflores
Lima
FTN Code – 8392 + extn number
Telephone: (00) (51) (1) 617 3000 Main
617 3030 Commercial
617 3050 Consular/Visa
617 3060 British Council
617 3070 DFID
Facsimile: (00) (51) (1) 617 3100 Main
617 3001 Chancery
617 3020 Management
617 3040 Commercial
617 3055 Consular/Visa
617 3065 British Council
617 3080 DFID
Airtech: (00) (51) (1) 617 3008
e-mail: belima@fco.gov.uk (General)
consvisa.lima@fco.gov.uk (Consular/Visa)

Office Hours (GMT): Mon – Thurs: 13 00 – 22 00; Fri 13 00 – 18 00
Ambassador (3002):
Mr Richard Peter Ralph, CMG, CVO
Deputy Head of Mission (3004): Mr Robert Webb
Defence Attaché (Resides at Bogotá) (3085):
Colonel Mike E Wilcox
Cultural Attaché (British Council Director) (3061):
Mr Frank Fitzpatrick
First Secretary (Management) and HM Consul (3016): Mr Ian Cormack
First Secretary (3013): Mr Steve Jones
Second Secretary (Commercial) (3031):
Ms Nicola Ware
Second Secretary (Works) (resides at Buenos Aires): Mr Ronnie Clark
Second Secretary: Mr Mark Williams
Second Secretary (Management) (resides at Bogotá): Mr Nick Moss-Norbury
Third Secretary (Chancery) (3005):
Mr Jonathan Clare
Third Secretary (Management/Immigration) and Vice-Consul (3051): Ms Abigail Boyle
Vice-Consul/Immigration (3054):
Mrs Nicola Standen

Arequipa
British Consulate
Tacna y Arica 156, Arequipa
Telephone: (00) (51) (54) 241 340
Facsimile: (00) (51) (54) 236 125
Office Hours (GMT): Mon – Fri 13 30 – 17 30 and 20 00 – 23 30
Honorary Consul: Mr Reynaldo Roberts, MBE

Cusco
British Consulate
Urbanizacion Magisterial G2 2da Etapa
PO Box 606, Cusco
Telephone: (00) (51) (84) 23-9974
Facsimile: (00) (51) (84) 23-6706
Office Hours (GMT): 16 00 – 17 00
Honorary Consul: Mr Barry Walker, MBE

Trujillo
British Consulate
Jiron Alfonso Ugarte 310, Trujillo
Telephone/ Facsimile: (00) (51) (44) 24 5935
Office Hours (GMT): 14 00 – 22 00
Honorary Consul: Mr Winston Barber

PHILIPPINES

Manila
British Embassy
15th – 17th Floors LV Locsin Building
6752 Ayala Avenue cor Makati Avenue
1226 Makati
(PO Box 2927 MCPO)
FTN Code – 8411 + extn number
Telephone: (00) (63) (2) 816 7116 – switchboard
816 7271/2, 816 7348/9 – Visa and Consular Sections
Facsimile: (00) (63) (2) 813 7755 – Chancery
819 7206 Management
815 4809 Information
810 2745 Visa
840 1361 Consular
815 6233 Commercial
Airtech: 894 3367
Telex: 63282 (a/b 63282 PRODME PN)
e-mail: uk@info.com.ph Information Section
uktrade@info.com.ph Commercial Section
Office Hours (GMT): Mon – Thurs: 00 00 – 08 30; Fri: 00 00 – 06 00
Consular/Visa Office Hours: 00 00 – 05 00
Ambassador: Mr Peter Beckingham
Deputy Head of Mission: Mr Robert Fitchett
Defence Attaché: Group Captain Rob Bailey
First Secretary (Commercial): Mr John Chick
First Secretary (Cultural) (British Council Director): Ms Gill Westaway (British Council)
HM Consul: Mr John Fielder
First Secretary (Management): Mr Clive McGill
Second Secretary (Commercial): Mr Rob Walker
Second Secretary (Political): Ms Sarah Parsons
Second Secretary (Immigration):
Mr Christopher Stacey
Second Secretary (Global and Economic Issues):
Ms Nicole Cadwallader
Third Secretary (Immigration): Mr Graham Sykes
Third Secretary (Immigration): Mr Nigel Greetham
Third Secretary (Immigration): Mr Mike Christie
Third Secretary (Immigration):
Mr Michael McKibben
Third Secretary (Immigration):
Mr Nuruddin Ahmad
Third Secretary (Immigration): Mr Kevin Jewula
Police Attaché: Mr Colin Warburton
Attaché: Mr Gary Postans
Attaché: Ms Louise Freegard
Attaché: Mrs Penny Garnham
Attaché: Mr Glen Garnham
Attaché: Staff Sergeant Stephen Walker

Manila UK representation at the Asian Development Bank, see page 117

Cebu
British Consulate
Villa Terrace, Greenhills Road
Casuntingan, Mandaue City, Cebu
Telephone: (00) (63) (32) 346 0525
Facsimile: (00) (63) (32) 346 0269
e-mail: moke@cebu.ph.inter.net
Honorary Consul: Mrs Moya Jackson

Angeles City
British Consulate
18-6 Concepcion Drive
Villa Teresa, Angeles City
Pampanga 2009
Tel/Fax: (00) (63) (45) 323 4187
Mobile: (00) (63) 917 817 1269
e-mail: dougalp@datelnet.net
Honorary Consul: Mr Douglas Paterson

Olongapo
British Consulate
Subic International Hotel
Subic Bay Freeport Zone
Olongapo, Zambales 2200
Telephone: (00) (63) (47) 252 2222
e-mail: sihgm@info.com.ph

Honorary Consul: Mr Michael Wilson

POLAND

Warsaw

British Embassy
Aleje Róz No 1, 00-556 Warsaw
FTN Code – 8298 + extn number
Telephone: (00) (48) (22) 311 0000
Facsimiles: (00) (48) (22) 311 0311
311 0313 (Management)
311 0315 (Chancery)
311 0316 (Defence)
Airtech: (00) (48) (22) 311 0317
e-mail: info@britishembassy.pl
Commercial, Visa and Consular Sections:
Warsaw Corporate Centre, 2nd Floor
Ul. Emilii Plater 28, 00-688 Warsaw
Telephone: (00) (48) (22) 311 0000
Facsimile: (00) (48) (22) 311 0250
e-mail: Commercial@britishembassy.pl (Commercial)
Consular@britishembassy.pl (Consular)
Visa@britishembassy.pl (Visa)
Website: www.britishembassy.pl
Office Hours (GMT + 1): 08 30 – 16 30
Ambassador (4110): Mr Charles Crawford, CMG
Counsellor and Deputy Head of Mission (4114): Mr Patrick Davies
Counsellor (4282): Mr Guy Spindler
Director of Trade Promotion/Consul-General (2201): Ms Julia Longbottom
Counsellor (Cultural) (695 5900 extn 20): Ms Susan Maingay OBE
Defence and Air Attaché (4146): Group Capain Tim J Williams, AFC, RAF
Naval and Military Attaché (4141): Lieutenant Colonel Stephen Croft
First Secretary (Political/Military) (4148): Mr Philip Barclay
First Secretary (Political) (4159): Mr Graham Horry
First Secretary (Management) (4127): Mr Roger Harmer
First Secretary (Commercial) (2203): Ms Geraldine McDermott
First Secretary (Education) (695 5900 extn 50): Ms Cherry Gough
Second Secretary (Political) (4140): Ms Sarah Riley
Second Secretary (Consul/Commercial) (2219): Ms Rosalind Corrigan
Second Secretary (Political) (4118): Mrs Emma Baines
Second Secretary (LELO) (4156): Mr Andy Sturgeon
Second Secretary (Commercial) (2243): Ms Emma Robinson
Second Secretary (Political) (4167): Mr James Lipsett
Second Secretary: Mr Thomas Cawdron
Second Secretary (Technical Management) (4103): Mr Simon Lochmuller
Third Secretary (Political) (4117): Mr Christopher Thompson
Third Secretary (Management) (4153): Ms Kathryn Lindsay
Attaché and Vice-Consul (2225): Ms Fiona Ogg
Attaché (4111): Ms Elizabeth Rowe
Attaché (4119): Ms Lorraine Findell
Attaché: Mr Marc Leslie
Attaché (4128): Mr Ara Tatoolian

Gdansk

British Consulate
ul Grunwaldzka 102, 80-244 Gdansk
Telephone: (00) (48) (58) 341 4365, 346 1558
Facsimile: (00) (48) (58) 344 1608
e-mail: consul@abcc.com.pl
Office Hours (GMT + 1): 09 00 – 15 00
Honorary Consul: Mr Andrzej Kanthak

Katowice

British Consulate
ul PCK 10, 40-057 Katowice
Telephone: (00) (48) (32) 206 9801
Facsimile: (00) (48) (32) 205 4646
e-mail: honcon@silesia.top.pl
Office Hours (GMT + 1): 09 00 – 15 00
Honorary Consul: Mr Alan Stretton

Kraków

British Consulate
ul. Sw.Anny 9
31-008 Kraków
Telephone: (00) (48) (12) 421 7030
Facsimile: (00) (48) (12) 422 4264
e-mail: ukconsul@bci.krakow.pl
Office Hours (GMT + 1): 09 00 – 15 00
Honorary Consul: Mr Kazimierz Karasinski

Lódz

ul. Piotrkowska 85
90-423 Lódz
Telephone: (00) (48) (42) 631 1818
Facsimile: (00) (48) (42) 631 1114
e-mail: brzezinska@signa or consulateUK@signa.pl
Office Hours (GMT + 1): 09 00 – 15 00
Honorary Consul: Mrs Malgorzata Brzezinska

Lublin

British Consulate
ul. Beskidzka 9
20-869 Lublin
Telephone: (00) (48) (81) 742 0101
Facsimile: (00) (48) (81) 742 9130
e-mail: ukconsul@uren.com.pl
Office Hours (GMT + 1): 09 00 – 15 00
Honorary Consul: Mr Jan Danilczuk

Poznan

British Consulate
ul Kochanowskiego 4/2, 60-844 Poznan
Telephone: (00) (48) (61) 665 8850 / 655 8851
Facsimile: (00) (48) (61) 853 29 19
e-mail: ukcons@protea.pl
info@protea.pl
Office Hours (GMT + 1): 09 00 – 15 00
Honorary Consul: Mr Wlodzimierz Walkowiak

Szczecin
British Consulate
ul. Starego Wiarusa 32
71-206 Szczecin
Telephone: (00) (48) (91) 487 0302
Facsimile: (00) (48) (91) 487 3697
e-mail: gacszz@fnet.pl
Office Hours (GMT + 1): 09 00 – 15 00
Honorary Consul: Mr Ryszard Karger

Wroclaw
British Consulate
ul. Olawska 2, 50-123 Wroclaw
Telephone/Facsimile: (00) (48) (71) 344 8961
e-mail: consulate@kmc.com.pl
Office Hours (GMT + 1): 09 00 – 15 00
Honorary Consul: Mr Marek Grzegorzewicz

PORTUGAL

Lisbon
British Embassy
Rua de São Bernardo 33, 1249-082 Lisbon
FTN Code – 8368 + extn number
Telephone: (00) (351) (21) 392 4000
Facsimile: 4178 Chancery
4184 Defence
4185 Information
4186 Commercial
4187 Management
4188 Consular
e-mail: Chancery@Lisbon.mail.fco.gov.uk
uktradeinvest@Lisbon.mail.fco.gov.uk
Consular@Lisbon.mail.fco.gov.uk
Management@Lisbon.mail.fco.gov.uk
Political2@Lisbon.mail.fco.gov.uk
ppalisbon@fco.gov.uk
Website: www.uk-embassy.pt
Office Hours (GMT): Summer 08 00 – 12 00 and 13 30 – 16 30
Winter 09 00 – 13 00 and 14 30 – 17 30
Ambassador: Mr John S Buck
Counsellor (Political): Mr Jamie Darke
Defence Attaché:
Commander Richard M Simmonds, OBE, RN
Counsellor (Cultural) (British Council Director):
Ms Rosemary Hilhorst, OBE
First Secretary (Head of Political Section):
Mr Ben Lyster-Binns
First Secretary (UK Trade and Investment):
Mr Richard Turner
First Secretary (Consul): Ms Elizabeth Dow, MBE
First Secretary (Management): Mr Henry Bradley
Second Secretary (Political/EU): Miss Julia Wright
Second Secretary (Political/Economic/Press and Public Affairs Officer): Mr Andrew Bowes
Second Secretary: Mr Glen Pounder
Second Secretary: Mrs Laura Leavy
Third Secretary (Vice-Consul): Mr Charlie Cosker
Third Secretary (Management):
Mrs Deborah Aliaga
Attaché (PA to Ambassador): Mrs Patricia Fletcher

Oporto
Honorary British Consulate
Travessa Barão de Forrester, 10
Apartado 26
4401-997 Vila Nova de Gaia
Telephone: (00) (351) (22) 618 4789
Facsimile: (00) (351) (22) 610 0438
e-mail: Britcon.oporto@sapo.pt
Honorary Consul: Mr John Symington

Portimão
British Consulate
Largo Francisco A Mauricio 7-1?
8500 Portimão
Telephone: (00) (351) (282) 490 750
Facsimile: (00) (351) (282) 490 758
e-mail: britcon.portimao@mail.telepac.pt
British Consul: Mr William Henderson
(e-mail: Bill.Henderson@mail.telepac.pt)
Pro-Consul: Mrs Angela Morado

Funchal, Madeira
Honorary British Consulate
Avenida de Zarco 2, CP 417
9000 – 956 Funchal, Madeira
Telephone: (00) (351) (291) 21 2860/61/62/63/64/65/66/67
Facsimile: (00) (351) (291) 21 2869
e-mail: brit.confunchal@mail.eunet.pt
Honorary Consul: Mrs Joy Menezes

Ponta Delgada, Azores
Honorary British Consulate
Rua Domingos Rebelo 43-A
9500-234 Ponta Delgada, Azores
Telephone: (00) (351) (296) 283 786
Facsimile: (00) (351) (296) 628 175
e-mail: amgm@net.sapo.pt
Honorary Consul: Mr Antonio Gomes de Menezes

QATAR

Doha
British Embassy
PO Box 3, Doha
FTN Code – 8630 + extn number (not Commercial or Visa Sections)
Telephone: (00) (974) 4421991
Facsimile: (00) (974) 4438692
e-mail: bembcomm@qatar.net.qa Commercial Section
consular_qatar@fco.gov.uk Consular Section
Office Hours (GMT): Sun – Thurs 04 30 – 11 30

Visa Section:
Ground Floor, AKC Building,
Al Saad Street
Telephone: (00) (974) 4364189
Facsimile: (00) (974) 4364139
Commercial Section:
8th Floor, Toyota Towers
Telephone: (00) (974) 4353543
Facsimile: (00) (974) 4356131
Ambassador (2000): Mr Simon P Collis
First Secretary (Commercial) and Deputy Head of Mission (2002): Mr Eric Mattey
Defence Attaché (2004):
Wing Commander Paul Cottell, RAF
Second Secretary (Commercial):
Mr Peter Harrington

Second Secretary (Defence Sales) (2005): Mr Alec Gribble
Second Secretary (Chancery/Information) (2008): Mr Mohammed Shokat
Second Secretary (Management) and Vice-Consul (2011): Mr Dale Harrison
Third Secretary (Immigration): Mr Danny Woodier
Third Secretary (Commercial): Mrs Dorothy Harris
Attaché (2010): Mrs Elizabeth McCormack
Military Assistant to Defence Attaché (2006): CPO Ian St. Paul, RN
Chaplain: The Rev. Ian Young

British Council
PO Box 2992, Doha
Telephone: (00) (974) 4426185
Facsimile: (00) (974) 4423315
Director: Mr Antony Jones

ROMANIA

Bucharest

British Embassy
24 Strada Jules Michelet, 70154 Bucharest
FTN Code – 8416 + extn number
Telephone: (00) (40) (21) 201 7200
Facsimile: (00) (40) (21) 201 7299 (Chancery)
7315 (Management)
7311 (Trade Development)
7317 (Consular)
Airtech: (00) (40) (21) 201 7225
Office Hours (GMT): Apr – Oct: Mon – Thurs: 05 30 – 14 00; Fri 05 30 – 10 30. Nov – Mar: Mon – Thurs: 06 30 – 15 00; Fri 06 30 – 11 30
Ambassador: Mr Quinton Quayle
Counsellor and Deputy Head of Mission: Mr Iain Lindsay
Defence Attaché: Colonel Anthony A A Beattie
Cultural Attaché (British Council Director): Ms Liliana Biglou
First Secretary (Head of Political/EU/Economic): Mr Michael Reilly
First Secretary (Political): Mr Gideon Beale
First Secretary (DFID): Mr Bob Napier
First Secretary (Trade Development): Mr Andy Garth
First Secretary (Defence Supply): Mr Christopher Comper
First Secretary (Airline Liaison Officer) (resides at Budapest): Mr Stephen Brown
Deputy Defence Attaché: Squadron Leader Mark Stanley, RAF
British Council Deputy Director: Mr Nicholas Butler
Second Secretary (Management): Mr Owen Richards
Second Secretary and Consul: Mr Iain Graham
Second Secretary (Political/Information): Mr Alex Brown
Second Secretary (Political/Projects): Mrs Lynne Smith
Second Secretary (Political): Mr Robert Fuller
Second Secretary (Immigration Liaison Officer): Mr Thomas Carter
Second Secretary (Works) (resides at Budapest): Mr Paul Davies
Second Secretary: Mr Emrys Tippett
Third Secretary: Mr Simon Thomas
Third Secretary: Mr Andy Davison
Vice-Consul: Mr Stuart Loughray
Vice-Consul: Ms Margaret Gallacher
Vice-Consul: Mrs Nita Humphreys
Assistant Defence Attaché: Mr Jim Osborne
Attaché (PA to Ambassador): Mrs Clare Docherty
Attaché (PA to Deputy Head of Mission): Miss Joan Johnson
Attaché (PA to First Secretary – Political): Mr Rob Ryan
Attaché (Registry): Miss Kate McNulty
Attaché (resides at Budapest): Mr Terry Wiltshire
Attaché (Works): Mr Brian Robinson
Chaplain: The Revd James Ramsey

RUSSIA

Moscow

British Embassy
Smolenskaya Naberezhnaya 10
Moscow 121099
FTN Code – 8375 + 1000 or extn number
Telephone: (00) (7) (095) 956 7200
(Main Switchboard)
Facsimile: (00) (7) (095) 956 7201 General
7480 Trade and Investment
7466 DFID
7328 Consular
7264 Defence
7442 Estates
7438 Fiscal, Drugs and Crime Liaison Office
7443 Management
7446 Medical Centre
7364 Political
7430 Press and Public Affairs
7480 Science
7444 TMS
7441 Visas
7394 Russian Resettlement Programme
7237 Registry/Comms
7201 Security
Airtech: (00) (7) (095) 956 7398
e-mail: moscow@britishembassy.ru Press and Public Affairs
consular.moscow@fco.gov.uk Consular
Cultural Department/The British Council
Library for Foreign Literature,
Nikoloyamskaya 1, Moscow 109189
Telephone: (00) (7) (095) 782 0200 (Switchboard)
Facsimile: (00) (7) (095) 782 0201
Office Hours (GMT): Winter: 06 00 – 10 00 and 11 00 – 14 00
Summer: 05 00 – 09 00 and 10 00 – 13 00
Ambassador (7234): Mr Anthony Brenton, CMG
Minister and Deputy Head of Mission (7206): Mr Stephen Wordsworth, LVO
Defence and Air Attaché (7231): Air Commodore Wilson Metcalfe
Counsellor (Political) (7212): Mrs Sian Macleod, OBE
Counsellor (Economic, Trade and Investment and Science) (7450): Ms Deborah Bronnert

Counsellor (Political Affairs) (7210):
Mr Robert Campbell
Counsellor (Management) and Consul-General (7385): Mrs Jessica Hand
Counsellor (Post Security) (7356):
Mr David Chitty
Counsellor (British Council Director) (Cultural Affairs): Mr James Kennedy
Military Attaché (7239): Colonel Pat Callan
Naval Attaché (7232): Captain Jon T Holloway, RN
First Secretary (Regional Medical Adviser) (7269):
Dr Iain McDonald
First Secretary (Development) (7473):
Mr Jim Butler
First Secretary (Political) (7280):
Mr Nigel Casey, MVO
First Secretary (Political) (7360): Mr Chris Bowers
First Secretary (Trade and Investment) (7452):
Mr David Goodwin
First Secretary (Science and Technology) (7491):
Mr David Vincent
First Secretary (Estate Management) (7258):
Mr John McLean
First Secretary (Technical Management) (7222):
Mr David Welsted
First Secretary (British Council Deputy Director/Info and Regions): Ms Ruth Addison
First Secretary (British Council Deputy Director/Operations): Mr Simon Kay
First Secretary (Press and Public Affairs) (7359):
Mr Alan Holmes
First Secretary (Consular/Immigration) (7240):
Mr Peter Smith
First Secretary (Management) (7257):
Mrs Carol Priestley
First Secretary (Fiscal, Drugs and Crime Liaison Officer) (7436): Mr Mark Bishop
First Secretary (Technical Management) (7223):
Mr Dai Pugh
First Secretary (Economic) (7338):
Mr Nigel Gould-Davies
First Secretary (British Council/ Asst Director):
(Vacant)
Assistant Naval Attaché (7233):
Lieutenant Commander Eamonn Grennan
Assistant Military Attaché (7238):
Major Alfonso C J Torrents
Assistant Air Attaché (7245):
Squadron Leader Gary Edwards
Second Secretary (Political) (7209):
Ms Esther McHugh
Second Secretary (Political) (7367):
Ms Faye O'Connor
Second Secretary (Political) (7355): Mr Marc Doe
Second Secretary (Political) (7215): Mr Paul Knott
Second Secretary (Economic) (7354):
Mr Anjoum Noorani
Second Secretary (Trade and Investment) (7453):
Mr Nick Latta
Second Secretary (Trade and Investment) (7476):
Ms Sayida Husain
Second Secretary (Immigration) (7267):
Mr Ian Underhill
Second Secretary (Immigration) (7433):
Mr Kevin Williams
Second Secretary (Airline Liaison Officer) (7410):
Mr Andrew Levi
Second Secretary (Technical Management) (7227):
Mr Christopher Broadbent
Second Secretary (Technical Management) (7225):
Mr Simon Edwards
Second Secretary (Technical Management) (7224):
Mr Sanjay Shah
Second Secretary (Development) (7467):
Mr Alan Reid
Attaché (Chief Security Officer) (7366):
Mr Rick Willams
Second Secretary (Russian Resettlement Programme) (7394): Squadron Leader Max Jardin
Third Secretary (Management) (7255):
Mrs Eram Qureshi-Hasan
Third Secretary (Visits) (7204): Mr Nik Duke
Third Secretary (Political Affairs) (7362):
Mr Paul Crompton
Attaché Vice-Consul (7321): Mr Neil Abbott
Attaché (Visas) (7336): Mr Sean Myers
Attaché (Visas) (7323): Mr Jim Simpson
Attaché (Visas) (7472): Mrs Melanie Morrison
Attaché (Visas) (7396): Mr Ian Marson
Attaché (Visas) (7236): Mr David Hall
Attaché (Visas) (7336): Ms Julie Stephenson
Attaché (Visas) (7236): Mr Christopher Ward
Attaché (Visas) (7312): Ms Mercedes Kelly

St Petersburg
British Consulate-General
PL Proletarskoy Diktatury 5, Smolninskiy Raion
191124 St Petersburg
FTN Code – 8376+ extn number
Telephone: (00) (7) (812) 320 32 00 Switchboard
320 32 39 Visa Reception
Facsimile: (00) (7) (812) 320 32 11 General
320 32 22 Commercial Section
320 32 33 Visa Section
320 32 44 Chancery (Airtech)
e-mail: bcgspb@peterlink.ru
dfid@peterlink.ru (DFID Russia)
management.stpetersburg@fco.gov.uk
commercial.stpetersburg@fco.gov.uk
consular.stpetersburg@fco.gov.uk
information.stpetersburg@fco.gov.uk
visa.stpetersburg@fco.gov.uk
Consul-General (3205): Mr C G Edgar
Deputy Head of Mission/Head of Trade and Investment (3220): Mr P Langham
Consul (Cultural) (British Council Director):
Ms A Coutts
Consul (Consular/Management) (3210):
Mr M J Woodham
Vice-Consul (Immigration) (3230): Mr S McColm
Vice-Consul (Immigration) (3231): Mrs K Cullen
Attaché (3214): Mr I Saunders

British Council
Fontanki Reki Nab 46
191025 St Petersburg
Telephone: (00) (7) (812) 118 5060
Facsimile: (00) (7) (812) 118 5061

Yekaterinburg
British Consulate-General
15a Gogol Street,

620075, Yekaterinburg
Telephone: (00) (7) (343) 379 4931
355 9201 Visa Section
Facsimile: (00) (7) (343) 359 2901
Airtech: (00) (7) (343) 777 068
e-mail: brit@sky.ru (General Enquiries)
ekatevisaenquiries@fco.gov.uk (Visa Enquiries)
Website: www.britain.sky.ru
Consul-General: Mr Clive Thompson
Vice-Consul: Ms Natalie Gowers

Novorossiysk
British Consulate
3a Fabrichnaya Street,
Novorossiysk, PO Box 85
Novorossiysk 353923
Telephone: (00) (7) (8617) 618100
Facsimile: (00) (7) (8617) 618291
e-mail: ecr@laroute.net
Honorary Consul: Mr E C Rumens

Vladivostok
British Consulate
5 Svetlanskaya Street, Vladivostok
Telephone: (00) (7) (4232) 411312
Facsimile: (00) (7) (4232) 410643
e-mail: tiger@ints.vtc.ru
Honorary Consul: Mr A M Fox

RWANDA

Kigali (SP - see page 121)
British Embassy
Parcelle No 1131
Boulevard de l'Umuganda
Kacyiru Sud
BP 576 Kigali
FTN Code – 8740 + extn number
Telephone: (00) (250) 585771, 585773, 584098, 586072
Facsimile: (00) (250) 582044, 511586
e-mail: ppao@rwanda1.com
Website: britishembassykigali.org.rw
Office Hours (GMT): Mon – Thurs 06 00 – 10.00 and 11 00 – 15 00. Fri 06 00 – 10.00
Ambassador: Mr J J Macadie
Deputy Head of Mission: Mr C W Frean
Defence Attaché (resides at Kampala):
Lieutenant Colonel C J A Wilton
Third Secretary (Political): Ms C Vaudrey

Department for International Development (DFID) Rwanda
BP 576 Kigali
Telephone: (same as Embassy)
Facsimlie: (00) (250) 510588
e-mail: @dfid.gov.uk
Office Hours (GMT): Mon-Thur 06 00 – 10 00 and 11 00 – 15 00. Fri 06 00 – 10 00
Head of Office: Mr Colin Kirk
Social Development Adviser: Ms Judy Walker
Economic Adviser: Mr Simon Stevens
Education Adviser: Ms Jo Bourne
Deputy Head – Programmes: Mr Matthew Maguire
Deputy Head – Administration: (Vacant)
Rural Livelihoods Adviser: Mr Rodney Dyer
Governance Adviser: Mr Arif Ghauri
Governance Officer: Mrs Doreen Muzirankoni
Deputy Programme Manager: Mr Cormac Quinn
Senior Management Officer – Finance and Procurement: Mr Liberal Seburikoko

ST KITTS AND NEVIS

Basseterre
British High Commission
PO Box 483, Price Waterhouse Coopers Centre
11 Old Parham Rd
St John's, Antigua
Telephone: (00) (1) (268) 462 0008/9, 463 0010
Facsimile: (00) (1) (268) 462 2806
e-mail: britishc@candw.ag
Office Hours (GMT): Mon – Thurs: 12 00 – 20 00
Fri: 12 00 – 17 00 (only)
Open to the Public: Mon – Fri: 12 00 – 16 30
**High Commissioner:* Mr Duncan Taylor, CBE
Resident British Commissioner:
Miss Jean Sharpe, OBE
Deputy Resident British Commissioner:
Mr Paul Lawrence
**Deputy High Commissioner:* Mr Alan Drury
**Defence Adviser:* Captain Steve G Wilson, RN
**First Secretary:* Mr Eamon Kearney
**Second Secretary (Chancery):* Mr Rick Gomez
**Second Secretary (Management):*
Ms Ros Day, MBE
**Second Secretary (Chancery/Information):*
Mr Nick J Pyle, MBE
**Third Secretary (Immigration):* Mr Mark Harrison
**Resides at Bridgetown*

British Consulate
Office of the Honorary British Consul
PO Box 559, Basseterre
Telephone: (00) (1 869) 466 5620
466 8888 Home
Facsimile: (00) (1 869) 466 8889
Honorary Consul: Mr Peter Allcorn

ST LUCIA

Castries (SP - see page 121)
British High Commission
Francis Compton Building
2nd Floor (P O Box 227), Waterfront
Castries
Telephone: (00) (1) (758) 45 22484/5
Facsimile: (00) (1) (758) 45 31543
Airtech: (00) (1) (758) 45 22486
e-mail: postmaster.castries@fco.gov.uk
britishhc@candw.lc
Office Hours (GMT): Mon- Thurs: 12 00 – 16 30 and 17 00 – 20 00. Fri: 12 00 – 17 00
Open to public: Mon-Fri: 12 00 – 16 30
**High Commissioner:* Mr Duncan Taylor, CBE
Resident British Commissioner: Mr Kelvin Green
**Deputy High Commissioner:* Mr Alan Drury
**Defence Adviser:* Captain Steve G Wilson, RN
**First Secretary:* Mr Eamon Kearney
**First Secretary (Management):* Ms Ros Day, MBE
**Second Secretary:* Mr Andy Danton
***Second Secretary (Technical Works):*
Mr David Holmes
**Third Secretary:* Mr Phil Barker

Third Secretary (Immigration): Mr Mark Harrison
**Resides at Bridgetown*
***Resides at Mexico City*

ST VINCENT

Kingstown (SP - see page 121)
British High Commission
Granby Street (PO Box 132)
Kingstown
Telephone: (00) (1) (784) 457 1701
Facsimile: (00) (1) (784) 456 2750
Office Hours (GMT): 12 30 – 20 00
High Commissioner: Mr Duncan Taylor, CBE
Resident Acting *High Commissioner:*
Mr Terry Knight
Deputy High Commissioner: Mr Alan Drury
Defence Adviser: Captain Steve G Wilson, RN
First Secretary: Mr Eamon Kearney
First Secretary (Management): Ms Ros Day, MBE
Second Secretary (Chancery/Information):
Mr Nick J Pyle, MBE
Second Secretary (Chancery): Mr Rick Gomez
Third Secretary: Mr Phil Barker
Third Secretary (Immigration): Mr Mark Harrison
Resides at Bridgetown

SAMOA

Apia
British High Commission (all staff resident in Wellington)
FTN Code – 8480 + extn number
Telephone: (00) (64) (4) 924 2888
Facsimile: (00) (64) (4) 473 4982
High Commissioner: Mr Richard T Fell, CVO
Deputy High Commissioner:
Mr Martin Williamson
First Secretary (External): Ms A Ruth Walker
First Secretary (Economic/Trade Policy):
Mr Paul D Noon
First Secretary (Political/Press and Public Affairs):
Mr Matthew K Forbes
Second Secretary (Political): Ms Sarah M Weeks
Second Secretary (Consular): Mr John D A Kenny
Third Secretary (Consular):
Mr Matthew R Simpson

Office of the Honorary British Consul
c/o Kruse Enari and Barlow
Barristers and Solicitors
PO Box 2029
2nd Floor, N.P.F. Building
Beach Rd, Central Apia
Telephone: (00) (685) 21895
Facsimile: (00) (685) 21407
e-mail: barlowlaw@keblegal.ws
Honorary British Consul:
Mr R M (Bob) Barlow, MBE

SAN MARINO

San Marino
British Embassy
Via XX Settembre 80/A
00187 Rome
Ambassador (resides at Rome):
Sir Ivor A Roberts, KCMG

British Consulate-General
Lungarno Corsini 2,
50123 Florence
Telephone: (00) (39) 055 284133
(00) (39) 055 289556 (Commercial)
Facsimile: (00) (39) 055 219112
Airtech: (00) (39) 055 2654354
e-mail: Consular.Florence@fco.gov.uk
Commercial.Florence@fco.gov.uk
Office Hours (GMT): Apr-Oct 07 00 – 11 00 and 12 00 – 15 00. Nov-Mar 08 00 – 12 00 and 13 00 – 16 00
Consul-General: (Resides at Florence):
Mrs Moira A Macfarlane

SÃO TOMÉ AND PRINCIPE

São Tomé
British Embassy
(All staff resident in Luanda)
Ambassador: Mr Ralph Publicover
Consul: Mr F J Martin
First Secretary: Mr D G Cox
Second Secretary (Aid): Mr E Rich

São Tomé
British Consulate
Residencial Avenida,
Avienda Da Independencia
CP 257, São Tomé
Telephone: (00) (239) (12) 21026/7, 22505 (Home)
Facsimile: (00) (239) (12) 21372
Honorary Consul: Mr J Gomes

SAUDI ARABIA

Riyadh
British Embassy
PO Box 94351, Riyadh 11693
FTN Code – 8418 + extn number
Telephone: (00) (966) (1) 488 0077
Facsimile: (00) (966) (1) 488 2373, 488 0623 Management
488 1209 Consular
488 3125 Chancery
Airtech: (00) (966) (1) 488 0674
Voicemail Numbers: see individual officers
e-mail: Officers firstname.surname followed by @fco.gov.uk
Office Hours (GMT): Sat – Wed 05 00 – 12 00
Ambassador (2201):
Sir Sherard Cowper-Coles, KCMG, LVO
Counsellor, Deputy Head of Mission and Consul-General (2204): Mr Barry Lowen
Counsellor (Political) (2215):
Mr Edmund Fitton-Brown
Deputy Director of Trade and Investment Promotion (2240): Mrs Sharon Wardle
Cultural Attaché (British Council Director):
Mr Alan Smart
Defence and Military Attaché (2230):
Brigadier Jim G Askew, OBE
Deputy Defence Attaché (2234):
Wing Commander Mike J Cole, RAF

First Secretary (Economic/PPA) (2242): Mrs Karen Bell
First Secretary (Political) (2208): Mr Sean Keeling
First Secretary (Head of Commercial Section) (2206): Mr Peter Millman
First Secretary and Consul (2271): Mr Ken Neill
First Secretary (Defence Supply) (2233): Mr Michael Salkeld
First Secretary (Political) (2367): Mr Mark Taylor
First Secretary (Technical) (2220): Mr J Malcolm Lawrie, MBE
First Secretary (Police Liaison): Mr Mark Cam
Second Secretary (Political) (2265): Mr Mark Syrett
Second Secretary (Management) (2261): Mr Stuart Sadler
Third Secretary (Political) (2212): Mr Barrie Peach, MBE
Third Secretary (Political) (2217): Mr Daniel Heard
Third Secretary and Vice-Consul (2277): Ms Kerenza C Holzman
Third Secretary and Vice-Consul (2272): Mr Sean McLean, MBE
Attaché (Management) (2264): Mr David Lawrie
Overseas Security Manager (2280): Mr Jim Neilson

Jeddah
British Consulate-General
PO Box 393, Jeddah 21411
FTN Code – 8417 + extn number
Telephone: (00) (966) (2) 622-5550, 5557, 5558
Facsimile: (00) (966) (2) 622-6249
Airtech: (00) (966) (2) 622-5551
e-mail: Officers first name . surname followed by fco.gov.uk
Office Hours (GMT): Sat-Wed 05 00 – 12 00
Consul-General (2209): Ms Carma Elliot
Consul (Commercial) and Deputy Head of Post (2212): Mrs Cecille El Beleidi
Senior Management Officer/HM Consul/Entry Clearance Manager (2237): Mr William John Neil
Vice-Consul (Immigration) (2232): Mr Ian F Hodges
Generalist/Deputy Management Officer (2201): Mr Dawood Mayet

Al Khobar
British Trade Office
PO Box 1868,
Al Khobar 31952
Telephone: (00) (966) (3) 882 5300
Facsimile: (00) (966) (3) 882 5384
e-mail: btokhobar@hotmail.com
officers firstname.surname followed by @ALKHOBAR.mail.fco.gov.uk
Office Hours (GMT): Sat –Wed: 05 00 – 12 00
Head of British Trade Office: Mr Mike Hurley
Second Secretary (Commercial): Mr Richard Wood
Vice-Consul/Commercial Officer: Mr Abdalla Abdalla
Pro-Consul/Commercial Assistant: Maha Fariz
(Visa and Passport work for Eastern Province is the responsibility of Riyadh)

SENEGAL

Dakar (SP - see page 121)
British Embassy
20 Rue du Docteur Guillet
(Boite Postale 6025), Dakar
FTN Code – 8636 + extn number
Telephone: (00) (221) 823 7392, 823 9971
Facsimile: (00) (221) 823 2766, 823 8415
e-mail: britemb@sentoo.sn
British Council e-mail: postmaster@britishcouncil.sn
Office Hours (GMT): Mon – Thurs 08 00 – 16 30, Fri 08 00 – 12 30
Ambassador: Mr Peter Newall
Deputy Head of Mission and Consul: Mr Derek Levoir
Defence Attaché (Resides at Rabat): Lieutenant Colonel Simon J A Lloyd, MBE
British Council Director: Mr Adrian Odell
Senior Technical Management Officer (West Africa): Mr Ian Willsher
Management Officer: Mr Nick Faulkner
Vice-Consul/ECO: Mrs Elizabeth Changai
Attaché: Mr Ivan Friday
Trade and Investment Assistant: Mme Christine Labelle

SERBIA AND MONTENEGRO

Belgrade
British Embassy
Resavska 46, 11000 Belgrade
FTN Code – 8372 followed by four digit extn number
Telephone: (00) (381) (11) 2645 055, 3060 900, 3615 660
Facsimile: (00) (381) (11) 659 651
3061 089 (Chancery)
3061 072 (Consular/Visa)
3061 059 (Commercial)
3061 077 (Information)
3060 930 (Management)
Airtech: (00) (381) (11) 3061 020
e-mail: britemb@eunet.yu
ukembcom@eunet.yu (Commercial)
ukembbg@eunet.yu (Information)
Website: www.britemb.org.yu
Office Hours (GMT): Mon–Thurs: 07 00 – 15 30 and Fri: 07 00 – 12 00
Ambassador: Mr David Gowan, CMG
Deputy Head of Mission: Mr David McIlroy
Counsellor: Mr John O'Callaghan
Defence Attaché: Colonel Simon Vandeleur
First Secretary (Management and HM Consul): Mr Stephen Weinrabe
First Secretary (Commercial): Mr David Webb
First Secretary (Development): Mr George McLaughlin
First Secretary (Culture/British Council Director): Mr Christopher Gibson
First Secretary (DLO) (resides in Sofia): Ms Gillian Potts
Second Secretary (Chancery): Mr Paul Edwards
Second Secretary (Chancery): Mr Piers Rennie

Second Secretary (Chancery):
Mr Andrew Kellaway
Second Secretary: Mr Roger Britton
Second Secretary (Technical Management Officer):
Mr Alexander Madisons
Second Secretary (Development):
Mrs Josephine McLaughlin
Third Secretary (Vice-Consul): Mrs Ruth Whelan
Third Secretary (Immigration): Mr Philip Jones
Third Secretary (Chancery):
Miss Katherine Lawrence
Third Secretary (Security): Mr Frederick Bennett
Third Secretary (Management):
Mrs Caroline de Ryckman de Betz
Attaché: Mr Kenneth Strachan
Chaplain: Rev Robin Fox

British Council
Terazije 8/I, 11000 Belgrade
Telephone: (00) (381) (11) 3023 800
Facsimile: (00) (381) (11) 3023 898
Office Hours (GMT): Mon – Fri: 08 00 – 15 15
Library Hours: Mon – Fri: 10 00 – 17 00;
Sat: 09 00 – 14 00
Director: Mr Christopher Gibson

Podgorica – Montenegro
British Office (see below for Honorary Consul)
(co-located with the British Council)
Bulevar Sv. Petra Cetinjskog b.b.
81000 Podgorica
Telephone: (00) (381) (81) 205 440
Facsimile: (00) (381) (81) 205 460
e-mail: britishoffice@cg.yu
Office Hours (GMT): Mon–Thurs: 07 30 – 15 30
and Fri: 07 30 – 11 30
Representative: Miss Irena Radović

Honorary Consul Office address:
Crnogorska Komercijalna Banka
Novaka Miloseva 6, 81000 Podgorica
Telephone: (00) (381) (81) 210 425
Facsimile: (00) (381) (81) 210 612
e-mail: dvugdelic@cg.yu
Honorary Consul: Mr Dragan Vugdelic

Pristina, Kosovo
British Office
Ismail Qemajli 6
Arberi, Dragodan
Pristina
FTN Code – 8425 + four digit extn number
Telephone: (00) (381) (38) 249 559
Facsimile: (00) (381) (38) 249 799
Airtech: (00) (381) (38) 548 971
Office Hours (GMT): Mon – Thurs: 07 30 – 16 00
and Fri: 07 30 – 12 30
Head of Office: Mr Mark Dickinson
Deputy Head of Office: (Vacant)
First Secretary (Political/Military): Ms Siân Jones
Second Secretary (Political): Mr Ruairí O'Connell
Third Secretary (Political): Mrs Joanna Genter
Management Officer/Vice-Consul: Mr David Mills
Assistant Management Officer/Visits Officer:
Mrs Annette Banas

Department for International Development (DFID) Kosovo
Ekrem Rexha Str No.8
Pristina
Telephone: (00) (381) (38) 249 724/5
Facsimile: (00) (381) (38) 249 723
Head of Office: Mr R Napier

SEYCHELLES

Victoria (SP - see page 121)
British High Commission
3rd Floor
Oliaji Trade Centre
PO Box 161, Victoria, Mahé
FTN Code – 8637 + extn number
Telephone: (00) (248) 283666
Facsimile: (00) (248) 283657
e-mail: bhcvictoria@fco.gov.uk
Office Hours (GMT): Mon – Thurs 04 00 – 12 00
Fri 04 00 – 10 00
High Commissioner: Ms Diana Skingle
Deputy High Commissioner:
Mrs Philippa Thompson
Defence Adviser (Resides in Nairobi):
Colonel Jock A D K Inkster
British Council Director (Resides in Port Louis):
Mrs Rosalind Burford

SIERRA LEONE

Freetown (SP - see page 121)
British High Commission
Spur Road, Freetown
FTN Code – 8380 + extn number
Telephone: (00) (232) (22) 232961, 232362, 232563-5
Facsimile: (00) (232) (22) 228169, 232070
Airtech: (00) (232) (22) 231824
e-mail: bhc@sierratel.sl
Office Hours (GMT): Mon-Thurs 08 00 – 16 30
Fri 08 00 – 13 00
High Commissioner: Dr John E Mitchiner
Deputy High Commissioner: Mr David Dunn
Defence Adviser:
Lieutenant Colonel Desmond J A Bergin, OBE
First Secretary (Political): Ms Alison Rogers
British Council Director: Mr Tom Walsh
First Secretary (British Council):
Ms Honor Flanaghan
Second Secretary (Political/PPA):
Mr James Roscoe
Second Secretary (Management/Immigration):
Miss Kay Harris
Third Secretary (Political): Mr Spencer Andy
Third Secretary (Overseas Security Manager):
Mr Dave Easton
Third Secretary (Immigration/Consular):
Mr Mark Gee
Third Secretary (Immigration): Mr Ian Bowring
Attaché: Miss Rachel Tanner
Assistant *Defence Adviser:*
Staff Sergeant Mark Armstrong

Department for International Development (DFID) Sierra Leone
4 Spur loop

Wilberforce
Freetown
Telephone: (00) (232) (22) 233620
e-mail: initial-surname@dfid.gov.uk
(e.g: r-hogg@dfid.gov.uk)
Counsellor Development (Head of DFID SL):
Mr Richard Hogg
First Secretary (Deputy Head of DFID SL):
(Vacant)
First Secretary (Infrastructure): Ms Morag Baird
First Secretary (Governance):
Ms Charlotte Duncan
First Secretary (Social Development):
Ms Frances Rubin
Second Secretary (Development): Mr Mark White
Second Secretary (Development): Ms Denise Hill
Second Secretary (Development):
Mr Desmond Woode
Third Secretary (Development): Mrs Nancy Stuart

SINGAPORE

Singapore
British High Commission
Tanglin Road, Singapore 247919
Commercial Section: Tanglin PO Box 19,
Singapore 247919
FTN Code – 8400 + extn number (For those direct dialling in over the PSTN: dial +65 6424 followed by the extension number)
Telephone: (00) (65) 6424 4200 (General)
Facsimile: (00) (65) 6424 4218 (Chancery)
6424 4250 (Management)
6424 4344 (Regional Training Centre)
6424 4356 (Trade and Investment)
6424 4264 (Consular)
6424 4230 (Defence)
6424 4263 (Pensions)
e-mail: Commercial.Singapore@fco.gov.uk
(Firecrest)
Website: www.britain.org.sg
Office Hours (GMT): Mon – Fri 01 30 – 06 00 and 07 00 – 10 00
High Commissioner (4202): Mr Alan Collins, CMG
Deputy High Commissioner and Counsellor (Economic/Trade and Investment) (4300):
Mr David Campbell
Defence Adviser (4227):
Group Captain Martin D Stringer
Head of Chancery (4204): Mr Philip Malone, MVO
First Secretary (4211): Mrs Juliette Wilcox
First Secretary (Management) (4256):
Mr Gavin Marshall
First Secretary (Trade and Investment) (4302):
Mr Ian Morrison
First Secretary (Science and Technology) (4343):
Mr Brian Ferrar
First Secretary (Technical) (4224):
Mr Richard M Hardy
First Secretary (Estate) (4254): Mr Andy Lelliott
First Secretary (DESO) (4225):
Mr Peter G Wythe, MBE
First Secretary (Aviation) (4284): Mr John Bartram
Assistant Defence Adviser (4229):
Commander Nigel Race
Second Secretary (Trade and Investment) (4310):
Miss Erica Ackerman
Second Secretary (Economic/Inward Investment) (4323): Mr Colin Dick
Second Secretary (Defence) (4209):
Mr Neil Deeley
Second Secretary (Technical) (4221):
Mr David Guy
Second Secretary (Consular/ECM) (4360):
Mr Peter McGregor
Second Secretary (Security) (4348):
Mr Mark Wardle
Third Secretary (Consular/Visa) (4274):
Mr Stephen Evans, MBE
Assistant Attaché (PA to High Commissioner) (4203): Mrs Fiona Mowbray
Assistant Attaché (4222): Mr Dale Heath
Assistant Attaché (4213): Ms Elizabeth Sprague
Assistant Attaché (PA Senior Management Team) (4205): Mrs Lynne Schulz
Administrative Officer (Defence) (4235):
Mrs Liz Brown
Pay and Pensions (Defence) (4262):
Warrant Officer Mick Saunders
Senior Trade and Investment Officer (4311):
Mrs Valsa Panicker
Senior Trade and Investment Officer (4309):
Mr Teo Chong Kee
Senior Trade and Investment Officer (4325):
Miss Elsie Yim
Regional Training Officer (4288):
Mr Brian Lawrence
Political Officer (4248): Mrs Carole Johnson
Director of Communications (4305):
Ms Elisabeth Brodthagen
Deputy Director Management Services (4242):
Mr Kevin Mowbray
Financial Controller (4261): Mr Alan Yeong, MBE
Manager IT Services (4308): Miss Serene Cheong
Interactive Media Manager (4320):
Miss Chloe Choong
Senior Inward Investment Officer (4420):
Ms Evelyn Gui
Senior Science and Technology Officer (4387):
Mr Christopher Tan
Security Manager (4243): Miss Karen Fulford

The British Council
30 Napier Road
Singapore 258509
Telephone: (00) (65) 6473 1111
Facsimile: (00) (65) 6472 1010
DID: (00) (65) 64707 followed by the three digit extension number
Regional Director East Asia (101):
Mr Andrew Fortheringham
Cultural and Educational Adviser (British Council Director) (104): Mr Martin Hope
Deputy Cultural and Education Adviser (Director, English Language Centre): Mr Roland Davies
Assistant Cultural and Educational Adviser (Education Director) (103): Miss Siobhan Wilson

SLOVAKIA

Bratislava (SP - see page 121)
British Embassy
Panska 16, 811 01 Bratislava
FTN Code – 8377 + extn number
Telephone: (00) (421) (2) 5998 2000
2258 Visa Section
UK Duty Officer: 0905 601 741
Facsimile: (00) (421) (2) 5998 2237 General
2225 Management/Consular
2241 Defence Section
2240 Commercial Section
2210 Visa Section
Airtech: 2204
e-mail: bebra@internet.sk
Website: www.britemb.sk
Office Hours (GMT): Mon-Fri: 07 30 – 16 00
Ambassador (2201): Mrs Judith Macgregor
Deputy Head of Mission (job share) (2203):
Mr Tom Carter / Ms Carolyn Davidson
Defence Attaché (2205):
Lieutenant Colonel Anthony W Sutherland
Second Secretary (Commercial) (2217):
Mr Richard Beams
Second Secretary (Political) (2230):
Mrs Wendy Roebuck
Second Secretary (EU) (2234): Mr Ian Fox
Second Secretary (Management/Consular) (2254):
Mr Spencer P O'Neil
Assistant Defence Attaché (2206):
Squadron Leader Lloyd F Barrett, RAF
Cultural Attaché (British Council Director) (5443, 1074 or 1793): Mr Huw Jones

SLOVENIA

Ljubljana (SP - see page 121)
British Embassy
4th Floor Trg Republike 3
1000 Ljubljana
FTN Code – 8639 + extn number
Telephone: (00) (386) (1) 200 3910 Main Reception
200 3940 Commercial Section
Facsimile: (00) (386) (1) 425 0174 Chancery
425 9080 Commercial Section
e-mail: info@british-embassy.si
postmaster.ljubljana@fco.gov.uk
Website: www.british-embassy.si
Ambassador (3921): Mr Timothy Simmons
Deputy Head of Mission (3922):
Mr James Setterfield
Defence Attaché (3950):
Lieutenant Colonel Lindsay R Wilson, MBE
Second Secretary and HM Consul (3914):
Mr David Blogg
Second Secretary (DLO): Mr Willie McColl
Third Secretary (Political) (3928):
Ms Hannah Cockburn
Cultural Attaché (Director, British Council):
Mr Stephen Green

SOLOMON ISLANDS

Honiara (SP - see page 121)
British High Commission
Telekom House, Mendana Avenue
Honiara
Postal Address: PO Box 676
Telephone: (00) (677) 21705, 21706
Facsimile: (00) (677) 21549
e-mail: bhc@welkam.solomon.com.sb
Office Hours (GMT): Mon – Fri 21 00 – 01 00 and 02 00 – 05 00
High Commissioner: Mr Richard J Lyne
Deputy High Commissioner: Mrs Caroline J Hall

SOMALIA

Mogadishu
British Embassy
Waddada Xasan Geedd Abtoow 7/8
(PO Box 1036), Mogadishu
Telephone: (00) (252) (1) 20288/9, 21472/3
Telex: 3617 (a/b PRODROME SM)
Staff withdrawn from post

SOUTH AFRICA

Pretoria
British High Commission
255 Hill Street, Arcadia 0002
FTN Code – 8303 + extn number
Telephone: (00) (27) (12) 421 7500
Facsimile: (00) (27) (12) 421 7555
e-mail: media.pretoria@fco.gov.uk
Website: http://www.britain.org.za
Office Hours (GMT): Mon-Thurs: 06 00 – 15 00
Fri: 06 00 – 10 30
High Commissioner: The Rt Hon. Paul Boateng
Counsellor and Deputy High Commissioner:
Mr Andrew Patrick
Counsellor (Political): Mr Phil Shott
Defence and Military Adviser:
Brigadier David Keenan, OBE
Air and Naval Adviser:
Commander Peter Lankester, RN
First Secretary: Ms Fiona Morrison
First Secretary: Mr Justin Shirodkar
First Secretary (Management): Mr Alan Bubbear
First Secretary (Technical Works): Mr Mark Jones
First Secretary: Mr Ade Onitolo
First Secretary (PPA): Mr Russ Dixon
First Secretary (Technical Management):
Mr Andrew McNair
Second Secretary: Mr Paul Anderson
Second Secretary (Management):
Mr Nicholas Collier
Second Secretary (Technical Management):
Mr Andrew Truelove
Second Secretary (Technical Management):
Mr Andy Norris
Second Secretary: Mr Tony Tenger
Second Secretary: Mr David McNaught
Third Secretary: Mrs Sally Forrester

Consular Section
Liberty Life Place, Block B
256 Glyn Street, Hatfield 0083
Postal Address: P O Box 13611
and P O Box 13612
Hatfield, 0028, Pretoria
Telephone: (00) (27) (12) 421 7802 Visas

421 7801 Passports
Facsimile: (00) (27) (12) 421 7888 Visas
421 7877 Passports
e-mail: PTA.PassportEnquiries@fco.gov.uk
PTA.VisaEnquiries@fco.gov.uk
Office Hours (GMT): Mon-Thurs: 05 45-14 00
Fri: 05 45-11 15
(*Based at High Commission, Pretoria*)
**Consul-General:* Mr Andrew Patrick
Consul: Mr Paul Seaby
Second Secretary (Immigration/ECM):
Mr Quintin Eyre-Wilson
Third Secretary (Consular): Mrs Yvonne Dimmock
Third Secretary (Immigration): Mr Peter Roberts
Third Secretary (Immigration): Mr Matthew Player
Third Secretary (Immigration): Miss Sarah Say
Third Secretary (Immigration):
Mr Martin Lawrence
Third Secretary (Immigration): Mr Alan Green

Department for International Development (DFID) Pretoria
Southern Africa
Sanlam Building
Cnr of Arcadia and Festival Street
Hatfield 0083, Pretoria, Gauteng
Telephone: (00) (27) (12) 431 2100
Facsimile: (00) (27) (12) 342 3429
Counsellor (Head of Office): Ms S Wardell
First Secretary (Rural Sustainable Livelihoods Adviser): Ms P Chalinder
First Secretary (Programme Manager and Deputy Head of Division): Mr J McAlpine
First Secretary (Economic Adviser): Mr D Pedley
First Secretary (Social Development Adviser):
Ms O Williams
First Secretary (Enterprise Development Adviser):
Mr H Scott
First Secretary (Regional Conflicts Adviser):
Brigadier S Gordon Hughes, CBE
First Secretary (HIV/AIDS and Health Adviser):
Mr T Martineau
First Secretary (Regional Humanitarian Adviser):
Mr T Kelly
First Secretary (Senior Regional Statistics Adviser): Mr M Dyble
Second Secretary (Regional Trade and Integration Adviser): Ms H McLeod
Second Secretary – Office Manager: Mr D Fidler
Second Secretary (IT Manager): (Vacant)
Second Secretary (Finance and Contracts Officer):
(Vacant)

Cape Town
British Consulate-General
15th Floor, Southern Life Building
8, Riebeeck Street
Cape Town, 8001
Postal address: PO Box 500, Cape Town, 8000
FTN Code – 8497 + extn number
Telephone: (00) (27) (21) 405 2400
Facsimile: (00) (27) (21) 405 2448
405 2477 Consular
405 2456 Chancery
405 2460 Trade and Investment
Airtech: (00) (27) (21) 405 2419
e-mail: firstname.surname@fco.gov.uk
consular.sectionCT@fco.gov.uk
capetrade@fco.gov.uk
Office Hours (GMT): Mon-Thurs: 06 00 – 10 30 and 11 15 – 14 30. Fri: 06 00 – 11 30
Consul-General (2428): Mr Mike Mayhew
Second Secretary (Political) (2467):
Mrs Caroline Scales, MBE
Vice-Consul (Trade and Investment) (2420):
Mr Colin Duncan
Vice-Consul (Management) (2421):
Mrs Chantal Francis
Vice-Consul (Consular) (2413): Mrs Lisa Woolley
Vice-Consul (Political) (2465):
Mrs Raziyah Johnston

Port Elizabeth
British Consulate
5th Floor 1st Bowring House
66 Ring Road, Greenacres
Port Elizabeth, 6045
Postal Address: PO Box 35098
Newton Park
Port Elizabeth, 6055
Telephone: (00) (27) (41) 363 8841
Facsimile: (00) (27) (41) 363 8842
e-mail: britconspe@pemail.co.za
Office Hours (GMT): 07 00 – 10 30
Honorary Consul: (Vacant)

Johannesburg
Trade and Investment
Callers – Dunkeld Corner, 275 Jan Smuts Avenue
Dunkeld West, 2196
Postal Address:
P O Box 1082, Parklands 2121, Johannesburg
Telephone: (00) (27) (11) 537 7000
Commercial Services
Facsimile: (00) (27) (11) 537 7257
Public Information Line:
Telephone: (00) (27) (11) 537 7206
Facsimile: (00) (27) (11) 537 7253
Management:
Telephone: (00) (27) (11) 537 7241
Facsimile: (00) (27) (11) 537 7253
Office Hours: Mon- Thurs 06 00 – 14.30
Fri 06 00 – 11.30
Director of Trade and Investment:
Mr Michael Mowlam
Deputy Director for Trade and Investment:
Ms Judith M Leon
Trade Investment Adviser: Mr Gareth Seaborne
Trade Investment Adviser: Mr Donal Ahern
Management Officer: Mr Yemi Odanye

British Council
Suite 1, Sanlam Gables
1209 Schoeman Street (cnr Duncan Street)
Hatfield, Pretoria 0083
PO Box 11759
Telephone: (00) (27) (12) 431 2400
Facsimile: (00) (27) (12) 431 2415
Cultural Attaché (British Council Regional Director South Africa): Ms Rosemary Arnott

Durban
UK Trade and Investment

Suite 1901, 19th Floor, The Marine
22 Gardiner Street, Durban 4001
Postal Address: P O Box 1404
Durban, 4000
Telephone: (00) (27) (31) 305 3041 extn 2213
Facsimile: (00) (27) (31) 307 4661
Office Hours (GMT): Mon-Thurs: 06 00 – 15 00
Fri: 06 00 – 11 30
Head of Trade and Investment – Durban:
Mr Clive Correa
Trade and Investment Adviser:
Mr Muhammed Ismail

SPAIN

Madrid
British Embassy
Calle de Fernando el Santo 16,
28010 Madrid
FTN Code – 8360 + extn number
Telephone: (00) (34) 91 700 82 00
Facsimile: (00) (34) 91 700 83 09 Chancery
83 07 Defence
83 29 EU/Economic
83 11 Commercial
82 72 Press and Public Affairs
82 10 Management
Website: www.ukinspain.com
Office Hours (GMT): Winter: Mon – Fri
07 00 – 15 30
Summer: Mon – Thurs 06 30 – 13 00 and
Fri 06 30 – 12 30
Ambassador: Mr Stephen John L Wright, CMG
Deputy Head of Mission: Mr Nicholas Kay
Counsellor (Commercial) and Director of Trade and Investment: Mr Dominic Jermey, OBE
Counsellor (Multilateral Affairs): Mr Peter Davies
Defence and Naval Attaché:
Captain Nigel J K Dedman, RN
Military and Air Attaché:
Colonel Mark J Rollo-Walker
Counsellor (Cultural Affairs) (British Council Director): Mr Chris Hickey
First Secretary (Head of Press and Public Affairs):
Ms Sarah Hill
First Secretary (Management): Mr Peter Hagart
First Secretary (Political): Mr Peter Spoor
First Secretary (Multilateral Affairs):
Mr Scott Livingstone
First Secretary (Multilateral Affairs):
Mr Matthew Wade
First Secretary (Social Affairs): Mr Bruce Bucknell
First Secretary (Justice and Home Affairs):
Ms Rachel James
First Secretary (Technical Management):
Mr Gary Peers
First Secretary (Cultural Affairs) (British Council Deputy Director): Ms Susan Barnes-Babic
Senior Economic Officer: Mr William Murray
Senior Officer (Agricultural and Environment):
Mr Matthew Desoutter
First Secretary: Mr Jon Hudson
First Secretary: Mr Geoff Chalder
First Secretary: Mr Neil Keeping
First Secretary: Mr William Browning
Second Secretary: Mr Roderick Mackenna
Second Secretary: Mr Matthew Clarke
Second Secretary: Mr Carl Vives
Second Secretary (Management):
Ms Karen Roskilly
Second Secretary (Trade and Investment):
Mr Anthony Bell
Second Secretary (Trade and Investment):
Mr Trevor Cayless
Second Secretary (Political/Economic):
Ms Elizabeth Green
Second Secretary (Technical Management):
Mr Paul Oliver
Third Secretary (EU and Protocol Issues):
Ms Rafia Choudhury
Third Secretary (Multilateral Affairs):
Ms Georgina Furr
Third Secretary: Mr Arron Jones
Director (Trade and Investment Andalucia) (resides in Seville): Mr J Cooper

Madrid
British Consulate-General
Paseo de Recoletos 7-9, 4ª
28004 Madrid
Telephone: (00) (34) 91 524 9700
Facsimile: (00) (34) 91 524 9730
Office Hours (GMT): Winter: 07 00 – 15 00
Summer: 06 00 – 12 30 (Mon-Thurs) and
06 00 – 12 00 (Friday)
Consul-General: Mr Michael John Holloway
Consul: Ms Julie Miller
Vice-Consul: Mrs Annie McGee
Vice-Consul: Mr Daniel Wickham, MBE

Alicante
British Consulate
Plaza Calvo Sotelo 1-2
Apartado De Correos 564
03001 Alicante
Telephone: (00) (34) 96 521 60 22
Facsimile: (00) (34) 96 514 05 28
e-mail: enquiries.alicante@fco.gov.uk
Office Hours (GMT): Winter: 06 00-13 30
Summer: 06 00-12 30
Consul: Mr Russell Thomson
Vice-Consul: Mr George Outhwaite, MBE
Vice-Consul: Miss Elizabeth Bell
Honorary Vice-Consul (resides at Benidorm):
Mr John A Seth-Smith (e-mail: jass@ctv.es)

Barcelona
British Consulate-General
Edificio Torre de Barcelona
Avenida Diagonal
477-13o, 08036 Barcelona
Telephone: (00) (34) 93 366 6200 (6 lines)
Facsimile: (00) (34) 93 366 6221
Airtech: (00) (34) 93 366 6222
e-mail: barcelonaconsulate@ukinspain.com
Website: www.ukinspain.com
Office Hours (GMT): 08 30 – 13 00
Consul-General (also Consul-General for Co-Principality of Andorra): Mr Geoff S Cowling
Deputy Consul-General/Consul (Trade and Investment Officer): Ms Yvonne E Cherrie
Director, British Council: Mr Cris Brandwood
British Consul (Consular): Ms Roser Clavell

Vice-Consul (Trade and Investment Officer): Mr John V Hankin
Trade and Investment Officer: Ms Eva Prada
Trade and Investment Officer: Mr Mike Thom
Management Officer/Accounts: Ms Raquel Salas
Pro-Consul: Ms Cecilia Bosch
Pro-Consul: Mr Adrian Cox

Bilbao
British Consulate-General
Alameda de Urquijo 2-8, 48008 Bilbao
Telephone: (00) (34) 94 415 76 00, 415 77 11, 415 77 22
Facsimile: (00) (34) 94 416 76 32
Airtech: (00) (34) 94 416 47 51
e-mail: bcgbilbo@readysoft.es
Office Hours (GMT): 07 00 – 16 00 (Apr – Jun, Sept and Oct) 08 00 – 17 00 (Nov – Mar) 06 30 – 12 30 (Jul – Aug)
Consul: Mr Derek Doyle, MBE
Pro-Consul: Mrs Flora Dorronsoro
Trade and Investment Officer: Mr Angel Beti

Ibiza
British Vice-Consulate
Avenida Isidoro Macabich
45-1, Apartado 307
07800 Ibiza
Telephone: (00) (34) 971 301818, 303816, 301058
Facsimile: (00) (34) 971 301972
e-mail: BritishConsulate.Ibiza@fco.gov.uk
Office Hours (GMT): Nov-March: 07 00 – 14 30
Apr-Jun and Sep-Oct: 06 00 – 13 30.
Jul-Aug: 06 00 – 12 30
Vice-Consul: Mrs Helen Watson, MBE
Pro-Consul: Miss Raquel de la Osa

Las Palmas, Canary Islands
British Consulate
Edificio Cataluña
Calle Luis Morote 6-3
35007 – Las Palmas de Gran Canaria
(Postal address: PO Box 2020, 35080 – Las Palmas de Gran Canaria)
Telephone: (00) (34) 928 262 508
Facsimile: (00) (34) 928 267 774
e-mail: LAPAL-Consular@fco.gov.uk (Consular)
LAPAL-Commercial@fco.gov.uk (Commercial)
Office Hours (local time = UK time): 08 00 – 15 30. (July and August) 08 00 – 14 30
Consul: Mr Peter J Nevitt
Vice-Consul: Mrs Anita J Pavillard
Trade and Investment Officer: Mrs Montse Clemente

Málaga
British Consulate
Edificio EUROCOM
C/Mauricio Moro Pareto, 2, 2
29006 Málaga
Telephone: (00) (34) (95) 235 2300
Facsimile: (00) (34) (95) 235 9211
e-mail: postmaster@malaga.mail.fco.gov.uk
Office Hours (GMT): Winter: 07 00-14 30
Summer: 06 00-12 30
Consul: Mr Bruce McIntyre, MBE
Vice-Consul: Mr Patrick Boyce
Vice-Consul: Ms Rosslyn D Crotty

Palma
British Consulate
Balearic Islands
Plaza Mayor 3D
07002 Palma de Mallorca
Balearic Islands
Telephone: (00) (34) 971 712445, 712085, 716048,718501,712696
Facsimile: (00) (34) 971 717520
e-mail: consulate@palma.mail.fco.gov.uk
Office Hours (GMT): Nov-March: 07 00 – 14 30
Apr-Jun and Sep-Oct: 06 00 – 13 30
Jul-Aug: 06 00 – 12 30
Consul: Mr Michael K Banham
Vice-Consul: Mr Esteban Mas Portell

Santa Cruz de Tenerife (Canary Islands)
British Consulate
Plaza Weyler 8-1
Santa Cruz de Tenerife 38003
Telephone: (00) (34) 922 28 68 63, 28 66 53
Facsimile: (00) (34) 922 28 99 03
e-mail: tenerife.enquiries@fco.gov.uk
Office Hours (GMT): 08 00-15 30
July and August: 08 00-14 30
Consul: Mr David G Ward
Vice-Consul: Mrs Helen Diaz de Arcaya Keating
Pro-Consul: Mrs Christine Trujillo

Andorra
Honorary Consulate (Superintending Post – Barcelona)
Tel/Fax: (00) (34) 376 83 98 40
e-mail: britconsul@andorra.ad
Honorary Consul: Mr Hugh Garner

Benidorm
Honorary Consulate (Superintending Post – Alicante)
Telephone: (00) (34) 966 86 00 33
e-mail: jass@ctv.es
Honorary Consul: Mr Jon Seth-Smith

Cadiz
Honorary Consulate (Superintending Post – Malaga)
Telephone: (00) (34) 956 26 44 79
e-mail: Cadiz@ukinspain.com
Honorary Consul: Mr Juan Castellvi, MBE

Denia
Honorary Consulate (Superintending Post – Alicante)
Telephone: (00) (34) 965 78 18 15
e-mail: petrie@teleline.es
Honorary Consul: Mr Mark Petrie

Menorca
Honorary Consulate (Superintending Post – Palma de Mallorca)
Telephone: (00) (34) 971 36 78 18
Facsimile: (00) (34) 971 35 46 90
e-mail: deborahhellyer@infotelecom.es
Honorary Vice-Consul: Mrs Deborah Hellyer, MBE

Seville
Honorary Consulate (Superintending Post – Malaga)
Tel/Fax: (00) (34) 954 15 50 18
e-mail: Sevilla@ukinspain.com
Honorary Consul: Mr Charles Formby, OBE

Valencia
Honorary Consulate (Superintending Post – Alicante)
Telephone: (00) (34) 963 52 07 10
Facsimile: (00) (34) 963 52 16 65
e-mail: garzaidiomas@telefonica.net
Honorary Consul: Mr Maximo Caletrio

Vigo
Honorary Consulate (Superintending Post – Madrid)
Telephone: (00) (34) 986 43 71 33
Facsimile: (00) (34) 986 43 71 33 / 11 26 78
e-mail: vigoconsulate@ukinspain.com
Office Hours (GMT): 08 00 – 12 00 (emergencies outside these hours via British Consulate-General, Madrid)
Honorary Consul: Mr James G Skinner

SRI LANKA

Colombo
British High Commission
190 Galle Road, Kollupitiya
(PO Box 1433)
Colombo 3
Telephone: (00) (94) (11) 2 437336/43
Facsimile: (00) (94) (11) 2 430308,
335803 Consular/Visa
e-mail: bhc@eureka.lk
Office Hours (GMT): Mon – Thurs: 02 00 – 11 00; Fri: 02 30 – 07 30
Visa Hours (GMT): Mon – Thurs: 02 00 – 05 30; Fri: 02 30 – 04 30
British Council: 49 Alfred House Gardens (PO Box 753), Colombo 3
Telephone: (00) (94) (11) 581171/2, 587078, 580301,502487, 582449
Facsimile: (00) (94) (11) 587079
e-mail: enquiries@britishcouncil.lk
High Commissioner (also High Commissioner to the Republic of Maldives):
Mr Stephen N Evans, OBE
Deputy High Commissioner: Ms Lesley Craig, MBE
Defence Adviser:
Lieutenant Colonel Colin P G Martin
Cultural Attaché (British Council Director):
Mr Tony O'Brien
First Secretary (Commercial): Mr Dave Waring
First Secretary (Management): Mr Ian Scantlebury
First Secretary (Development):
Ms Mandeep Kaur-Grewal
Second Secretary (Development):
Ms Kristen Ormston
Second Secretary (Chancery): Mr John Culley
Second Secretary (Immigration/Consular):
Mr Haroon Suleman
Second Secretary (Immigration): Mr Peter Talarico
Second Secretary (resides at Mumbai):
Mr Simon Sutcliffe
Deputy Cultural Attaché: (British Council):
Ms Anne Searle
Third Secretary (Chancery): Mr Colin Hicks
Attaché (Management): Mr Donald Spivey
Attaché (Consular): Mr Colin Coward
Attaché (Consular): Mrs Fouzia Suleman
Attaché (Consular): Mr Ryan Griffin
Attaché (Consular): Mrs Jane Elton
Attaché: Mrs Judith Griffin
Attaché: Miss Samantha Davies
Attaché (Security): Mr John Barclay
Assistant *Defence Adviser:*
Staff Sergeant Jack O'Regan
Attaché (Technical): Mr Tony Mason

SUDAN

Khartoum
British Embassy
Off Sharia Al Baladia, Khartoum East
(PO Box No 801)
FTN Code – 8381 + extn number
Telephone: (00) (249) (11) 777105
Facsimile: (00) (249) (11) 776457
775562 (Consular/Visa)
Airtech: 775492
e-mail: british@sudanmail.net
Office Hours (GMT): Sun – Thurs: 05 00 – 12 00
Visa Office Hours (GMT): Sun – Thurs: 05 00 – 12 00
Consular Section – public opening hours: Sun – Thurs: 09 00 – 12 00 (local time)
Ambassador: Mr Ian C Cliff, OBE
DHM/Consul-General: Mr Ric Girdlestone
Defence Attaché (Resident in Addis Ababa):
Colonel David S Charters
First Secretary (Aid): Mr Matthew Baugh
First Secretary (British Council):
Mr Bob Steedman
First Secretary (External Affairs):
Mr Rupert Gaskin
First Secretary (Head of Management and Public Services): Mrs Debbie Beynon
Second Secretary (Political/Information):
Mr Mark Bryson-Richardson, MBE
Third Secretary and Vice-Consul: Mr Doug Tunn
Third Secretary (Political): Mr Duncan Holtorp
Third Secretary Entry Clearance Officer:
Mr Jonathan Knight
Attaché (Security): Mr Roger Tomkins
Attaché (Technical Works): Mr Ted Stewart
Attaché: Mr Brian Mills
Attaché: Miss Natalie Gowers

SURINAM

Paramaribo
British Embassy
**Ambassador:* Mr Steve J Hiscock
**Consul and Deputy Head of Mission:*
Mr Malcolm Kirk
Defence Attaché (Resides at Bridgetown):
Captain Steve G Wilson, RN
**Second Secretary (Management/Entry Clearance Manager):* Mr Graham Birse

**Third Secretary (Immigration/Consular):*
Mr Neil Frape
**Resides at Georgetown*

Paramaribo
British Consulate
c/o VSH United Buildings, Van't Hogerhuysstraat, 9-11
PO Box 1860, Paramaribo
Telephone: (00) (597) 402558,402870
Facsimile: (00) (597) 403515,403824
e-mail: united@sr.net
Office Hours (GMT): 11 00 – 20 15
Honorary Consul: Mr James J Healy, Jnr

SWAZILAND

Mbabane (SP - see page 121)
British High Commission
Callers: 2nd Floor, Lilunga House
Somhlolo Street
Mbabane
Postal: Private Bag, Mbabane
FTN Code – 8289 + extn number
Telephone: (00) (268) 404 2581/2/3/4
Facsimile: (00) (268) 404 2585
Airtech: (00) (268) 404 2105
e-mail: enquiries.mbabane@fco.gov.uk
Office Hours (GMT): Mon – Thurs: 06 00 – 11 00 and 12 00 – 14 45. Fri: 06 00 – 11 00
Chargé d'Affaires (2130): Ms Liz Ripard
Defence Adviser (resides at Pretoria):
Brigadier David H Keenan, OBE

SWEDEN

Stockholm
British Embassy
Skarpögatan 6-8, Box 27819
115 93 Stockholm
FTN Code – 8312 + extn number
Telephone: (00) (46) (8) 671 3000 Direct Dial – use extensions below in brackets
Facsimile: (00) (46) (8) 662 9989 Management
671 3104 Chancery/Defence
671 3077 Commercial
661 9766 Consular/Visa
671 3100 Information
Airtech: 671 3137
Website: www.britishembassy.se
Office Hours (GMT): Winter: 08 00 -16 00
Summer 06 30 -14 30
Ambassador: (3102): Mr Anthony J Cary, CMG
Counsellor (Economic and Commercial) (3050):
Mr John Tucknott, MBE
Counsellor (3112): Mr John Macpherson, OBE
Defence Attaché (3105):
Wing Commander Nigel J Phillips, RAF
Cultural Attaché (British Council Director and Regional Director North / Central Europe) (3082):
Mr Peter Ellwood
First Secretary (Political) (3119):
Mr Kevin McGurgan
First Secretary (Inward Investment) (3067):
Mr Adrian Pinder
First Secretary (Management and Consul) (3070):
Mr David Broomfield
First Secretary (Commercial) (3053):
Ms Shirley Smith
Second Secretary (Political/Information) (3108):
Mrs Emma Sundblad
Second Secretary (Political/Economic) (3115):
Ms Gemma Sharp
Second Secretary (Media and Public Relations) (3006): Mr Damion Potter
Second Secretary (Science and Technology Affairs) (3117): Ms Alice Hague
Third Secretary (Political) (3191): (Vacant)
Airline Liaison Officer (resides at Copenhagen) (Tel: +45 352 62273): Ms Denise Broderick
Vice-Consul (3023): Ms Karen Farley
Entry Clearance Manager (3022):
Mr Henry Hodge
Honorary Chaplain: The V Rev. Bruce Evenson

Gothenburg
British Consulate-General
Södra Hamngatan 23
S 41114 Göthenburg
Telephone: (00) (46) (31) 339 3300
Facsimile: (00) (46) (31) 339 3302
Consul-General (resides in Stockholm):
Mr John Tucknott, MBE

Sundsvall
British Consulate
SCA Graphic
Sundsvall AB
Ostrand Pulp Mill
861 81 Timra
Telephone: (00) (46) (60) 16 40 00
Facsimile: (00) (46) (60) 57 49 90
Honorary Consul: (Vacant)

SWITZERLAND

Berne
British Embassy
Thunstrasse 50, 3005 Berne
FTN Code – 8370 + extn number
Telephone: (00) (41) (31) 359 7700
Facsimile: (00) (41) (31) 359 7701 General and Trade Section
359 7769 Political and Information Section
359 7765 Management and Consular Sections
359 7779 Airtech
Internet Address: http://www.britain-in-switzerland.ch
Office Hours (GMT): 07 30 – 11 30 and 12 30 – 16 00
Ambassador (also Ambassador to the Principality of Liechtenstein) (2713): Mr Simon Featherstone
Director of Trade and Investment (2721):
Mr Roy Osborne
Counsellor (2714): Mr William Jackson-Houlston
Head of Chancery (2716): Dr Simon Harkin
Defence Attaché (resides at Vienna) (2731):
Lieutenant Colonel Len Chapman
British Council Director: Ms Caroline Morrissey
First Secretary (Management) and Consul-General (also Consul for the Principality of Liechtenstein) (2739): Mr Tony Bates, MVO

First Secretary (Trade) (2723): Ms Susan Mortimer
First Secretary (Investment) (2751):
Mr Brian Hamill
Third Secretary (Political) (2717):
Mr Martin Webber
Third Secretary (Chancery) (2715):
Mrs Donna Very
Attaché (Trade) (2728): Mr Peter Mueller
Attaché (Science and Technology) (2752):
Mr Bernhard Sander
Pro-Consul (2741): Miss Wendy Page, MBE

Geneva
British Consulate-General
37-39 Rue de Vermont (6th Floor)
1211 Geneva 20
FTN Code – 8371 + extn number
Telephone: (00) (41) (22) 918 2400
Facsimile: (00) (41) (22) 918 2322
Telex: 414195 (a/b 414195 UKGV CH)
Office Hours (GMT): Summer: 06 30 – 10 30 and 12 00 – 15 00
Winter: 07 30 – 11 30 and 13 00 – 16 00
HM Consul-General (2458): Mrs Susan Gregory
HM Consul (2417): Mr Alistair Church
British Vice-Consul (Immigration/Consular) (2425): Ms Lynne Sowerby
Trade Attaché (2421): Mrs Eleanor Baha
Passport Officer (2308): Mrs Christine Kaczmarek
Pro-Consul (2480): Ms Julia Murray
Pro-Consul (2423): Mrs Elizabeth Long

Geneva
Joint Management Office
37-39 Rue de Vermont, 1211 Geneva 20
FTN Code – 8371 + extn number
Telephone: (00) (41) (22) 918 2300
Facsimile: (00) (41) (22) 918 2310
Telex: 414195 (a/b 414195 UKGV CH
Office Hours (GMT): Summer: 07 00 – 11 00 and 12 30 – 16 00
Winter: 08 00 – 12 00 and 13 30 – 17 00
First Secretary, Head of Joint Management Office (2458): Mrs Susan Gregory
Deputy Head of Joint Management Office (2452):
Mr Ian McKinlay
Technical Management Officer (2414):
Mr Matthew Smith
Assistant Management Officer (2425):
Ms Lynne Sowerby

Geneva United Kingdom Mission to United Nations, **see page 113**

Geneva United Kingdom Permanent Representation to the Conference on Disarmament, **see page 114**

Montreux/Vevey
British Vice-Consulate
13 chemin de l'Aubousset
1806 St Légier, Vaud
Telephone and Facsimile: (00) (41) (21) 943 3263
Honorary Consul: Mrs S Darra, MBE

Valais
British Vice-Consulate
Rue des Fontaines
CH 3974 Mollens – Valais
Telephone: (00) (41) (27) 480 3210
457 5111 (Radio Pager)
Facsimile: (00) (41) (27) 480 3211
Honorary Vice-Consul: Mr A Bushnell

Zurich
British Vice-Consulate
Hegibachstrasse 47
CH- 8032 Zurich
Telephone: (00) (41) (44) 383 6560
Facsimile: (00) (41) (44) 383 6561
Honorary Consul: Mr Antony McCammon

Lugano
British Vice-Consulate
Via Pretorio 22
PO Box 184
6900 Lugano
Telephone: (00) (41) (91) 950 0606
Facsimile: (00) (41) (91) 950 0609
Office Hours (GMT): 09 00 – 12 30
Honorary Consul: Mr Peter Steimle

Basel
British Vice-Consulate
Innovation Centre
Gewerbestrasse 14
CH4123
Allschwill
Tel/fax: (00) (41) (61) 483 0977
Mobile: (00) (41) 763 789 987
Honorary Consul: Dr Alan Chalmers

SYRIA

Damascus
British Embassy
Kotob Building
11 Mohammad Kurd Ali Street
Malki, PO Box 37, Damascus
FTN Code – 8489 + extn number or 1000 (Switchboard)
Telephone: (00) (963) (11) 373 9241/2/3/7
Facsimile: (00) (963) (11) 373 1600 Management
373 9236 Visa and Consular
373 9472 Commercial
Office Hours (GMT): Sun – Wed 06 00 – 13 30; Thurs 06 00 – 12 00
Ambassador: Mr Peter Ford
Counsellor and Deputy Head of Mission:
Mr Roddy Drummond, OBE
Defence Attaché: Colonel C Julian A Lyne-Pirkis
British Council Director: Mr Paul Doubleday
First Secretary (Political): Mr Anthony Ball
First Secretary (Management) and Consul:
Mr George Hodgson
Second Secretary (Commercial):
Mr Seifeldin Usher
Vice-Consul (Immigration/Consular):
Miss Kirsty Saunders
Third Secretary (Political/Information):
Miss Nicola Davies
Attaché: Mr Mark Harris
Attaché: Mrs Kathryn Richmond
Attaché: Miss Helen Ridley
Attaché: Mrs Janice Lytle

Attaché: Mr Simon Marshall
Attaché: Mr Jim Hall

Aleppo
British Consulate
PO Box 199
Aleppo
Telephone: (00) (963) (21) 267 2200, 266 1206 (Office)
267 5033 (Home)
Facsimile: (00) (963) (21)267 7640
Office Hours (GMT): Mon-Thurs and Sat: 07 30 – 11 30 and 15 00 – 18 30. Fri: 15 00 – 18 30
Honorary Consul: Mr Alexander Akhras

British Trade Office
P O Box 5547
Aleppo
Telephone: (00) (963) (21) 268 0502/3
Facsimile: (00) (963) (21) 268 0501
Senior Commercial Officer: Mr Zaher Abu Baker

Lattakia
British Consulate
13 Gabriel Saadeh Street
PO Box 828
Lattakia
Telephone: (00) (963) (41) 461 615
Facsimile: (00) (963) (41) 465 723
e-mail: albany@postmaster.co.uk
Opening Hours (GMT): 08 00 – 12 00 and 16 00 – 18 00
Honorary Consul: Mr Bassam Albany

TAIWAN

See Annex for details.

TAJIKISTAN

Dushanbe
British Embassy
65 Tursunzade Street
Dushanbe
FTN Code – 8311 + extn number
Telephone: (00) 992 372 51 01 85/86/87/92
Facsimile: (00) 992 372 27 16 38/27 17 26
e-mail: firstname.lastname@fco.gov.uk
Website: www.britishembassy.gov.uk/tajikistan
Staff resident in Dushanbe
Ambassador (2322): Mr Graeme Loten
Deputy Head of Mission (2319):
Ms Margaret Belof
Defence Attaché (resides at Almaty):
Lieutenant Colonel G J Sheeley, AFC
British Liaison Officer (2311): Mr Peter Cornell
British Council Director (resides in Tashkent):
Mr Neville McBain
Third Secretary/Vice-Consul (2328):
Mr Shanjeev Thiruchelvam

TANZANIA

Dar es Salaam
British High Commission
Umoja House
Garden Avenue, PO Box 9200
Dar es Salaam
FTN Code – 8499 + extn number
Telephone: (00) (255) (22) 211 0101
Facsimile: (00) (255) (22) 211 0102 Chancery
211 0112 Management
211 0296 Consular
211 0297 Visa
211 0080 Commercial
e-mail: bhc.dar@fco.gov.uk
Website:
www.britishhighcommission.gov.uk/tanzania
Office Hours (GMT): Mon-Thurs 07 30 – 15 30. Fri 07 30 – 13 00
High Commissioner: Dr Andrew Pocock
Deputy High Commissioner: Mr Mike Croll
Defence Adviser (resides at Nairobi):
Colonel Jock A D K Inkster
British Council Director: Ms Kate Ewart Biggs
Second Secretary (Commercial/Consular):
Mr Neal Hammond
Second Secretary (Management): Mrs Sally Oulmi
Second Secretary (Press and Public Affairs):
Mr Andrew Massey
Third Secretary (Political/Press and Public Affairs): Mr Ade Fehintola
Third Secretary (Consular/Immigration):
Mr Ian D Craig
Third Secretary (Immigration): (Vacant)
Third Secretary (Management):
Mrs Sarah Downing
Third Secretary (Security Manager):
Mr Norman Lingaya

Department for International Development (DFID) Eastern Africa (Tanzania)
5th Floor
Umoja House
Garden Avenue
PO Box 9200
Dar es Salaam
Telephone: (00) (255) (22) 2110141
Facsimile: (00) (255) (22) 2110130
Office Hours (GMT): Mon-Fri 04 30 – 13 00
Head of DFIDEA (T): Mr David Stanton
Deputy Head (Head of Human Resources):
Ms Patricia Barber
Deputy Head (Programmes): Mrs Liz Ditchburn
Programme Manager (Acc. Governance Group):
Mr Paul Whittingham
Deputy Programme Manager (Corporate Group):
Ms Fiona Lawless
Deputy Programme Manager (PRS Group):
Mr Andrew Felton
Economic Adviser: Mr John Piper
Assistant Economic Adviser: Mr Carl Kalapesi
Social Sector Adviser: Ms Pippa Bird
Governance *Adviser:* Ms Annabel Gerry
Poverty Policy Adviser: Mr Gerard Howe
Statistics Adviser: Mr Tim Harris
Growth Policy Adviser: Mr Kevin Quinlan
Governance Adviser: Ms Wamuyu Gatheru
Media and Communications Adviser:
Ms Eunice Urio
Head of Estate and Office Services:
Ms Deborah Affonso

Zanzibar
Office of the British Honorary Consul
PO Box 2113, Zanzibar
Telephone/Facsimile: (00) (255) (24) 223 3768 or 223 3670
Mobile: (00) (255) 748 750478
e-mail: carl@zanair.com
Honorary Consul: Mr Carl Salisbury

Arusha
Office of the British Honorary Consul
PO Box 2125, Arusha
Telephone/Facsimile: (00) (255) (27) 250 8625
Mobile: (00) (255) 748 700100
e-mail: beatty@africanenviroments.co.tz
Honorary Consul: Mr Richard Beatty

THAILAND

Bangkok
British Embassy
Wireless Road, Bangkok, 10330
FTN Code – 8419 + extn number
Telephone: (00) (66) (2) 305 8333
Facsimile: (00) (66) (2) 305 8372 or 8380 Chancery
305 8220 Defence
255 8619 Commercial/Press and Public Affairs
255 9278 Management
255 6051 Consular
254 9579 Immigration
Airtech: (00) (66) (2) 305 8342
Website: www.britishemb.or.th
Office Hours (GMT): Mon-Thurs: 01 00 – 05 00 and 05 45 – 09 30. Fri: 01 00 – 06 00 (Duty Staff until 09 30)
Ambassador (2301): Mr David W Fall
Counsellor and Deputy Head of Mission (2266): Mr Andrew J Pearce
Counsellor (Commercial) (2319): Mr Martin Hill
Defence Attaché (2222): Colonel Peter C Roberts, MBE
Counsellor (Political) (2288): Mr David Chambers
First Secretary (Political) (2224): Mr Ian Proud
Consul and First Secretary (Management) (2239): Mr Alan Mayland
British Council Director: Mr Peter Upton
First Secretary (2232): Mr John Hector
First Secretary (Technical) (2267): Ms Teresa Hyman
Second Secretary (Political) (2230): Mr Fergus Auld
Second Secretary (Commercial) (2294): Mr Trevor Adams
Second Secretary (Immigration) (2245): Mrs Jane Lacey-Smith
Second Secretary (Airline Liaison Officer) (2362): Mr Derek Swanson
Second Secretary (Management) (2317): Mr Malcolm Surman
Second Secretary and Vice-Consul (2253): (Vacant)
Second Secretary (Technical) (2369): Mr David Ellis
Third Secretary (Commercial) (2350): Mr Andrew Stephenson
Third Secretary (Economic/Development) (2291): Mr Philip McKenzie
Third Secretary and Vice-Consul (2229): Mrs Fiona Borisuth
Third Secretary (Immigration) (2363): Mr Stephen Taylor
Third Secretary (Immigration) (2352): Mr Kevin Newman
Third Secretary (Immigration) (2329): Ms Margaret Graham-Moses
Third Secretary (Immigration) (2338): Mrs Caroline Wright

Department for International Development (DFID) Thailand
c/o British Embassy
Wireless Road, Bangkok, 10330
Telephone: (00) (66) (2) 305 8333
Facsimile: (00) (66) (2) 253 7124
Head of Division (2250): Mr Marshall Elliott
Senior Governance Adviser (2335): Mr Chris Pycroft
Senior Rural Livelihoods Adviser (2261): Mr Simon Croxton
Senior Economic Adviser (2227): Mr Paul Walters
Social Development Adviser (2214): Mr Tom Beloe
Economic Adviser (2247): Mr Matt Butler
Senior Health and Population Adviser (2325): Mr Michael O'Dwyer
Programmes Manager (2202): Ms Claire Moran
Programmes Manager (2204): Mr Bob Leverington
Human Resources Development Officer (2383): Mrs Karen Parsons
Deputy Programme Manager (2215): Ms Paula Barrett
Programmes Officer (2280): Mr Alan Sach
Regional Management Officer (2227): Mrs Caroline Philips

Chiang Mai
British Consulate
198 Bumrungraj Rd
Muang, Chiang Mai, 50000
Telephone: (00) (66) (53) 263 015
Facsimile: (00) (66) (53) 263 016
e-mail: ukconsul@loxinfo.co.th
Office Hours (GMT): Mon – Thurs: 0100 – 0500 and 0545 – 0930. Fri: 0100 – 0600
Honorary Consul: Mr David Hopkinson

TOGO

Lomé
British Embassy
(All staff resident in Accra)
Ambassador: Mr Gordon Wetherell
Deputy Head of Mission: Mr Robin Gwynn
Defence Attaché: Lieutenant Colonel Jonathan A F Howard
First Secretary (Management): Mr David S Jones
First Secretary (Trade and Investment): Ms Sarah Stevenson
First Secretary (Immigration): Mr Andy Holden
Second Secretary (Political): Ms Farida Shaikh
Second Secretary (Political): Mr Gary Nicholls
Second Secretary (Consular): Ms Caroline Cross

Lomé
British Consulate – (Vacant)
British Commercial Office
Concession OTAM, Zone Portuaire,
Port de Peche, BP 9224, Lomé-Port, Lomé, Togo
Telephone: (00) (228) 2271141, 2275054
Mobile: (00) (228) 042180
Facsimile: (00) (228) 2274207
e-mail: tom@netcom.tg
Commercial Officer: Captain R A M Jones

TONGA

Nuku'alofa (SP - see page 121)
British High Commission
PO Box 56, Nuku'alofa, Tonga
Telephone: (00) (676) 24285/24395
Facsimile: (00) (676) 24109
Airtech: (00) (676) 23922
e-mail: britcomt@kalianet.to
Office Hours (GMT): Sun – Wed: 19 15 – 23 30 and 00 30 – 03 45. Thurs: 19 15 – 00 15
High Commissioner and Consul for American Samoa: Mr Paul Nessling
Management Officer: Mrs Kathryn Nessling
Defence Adviser (resides at Wellington): Colonel Nigel Lloyd

TRINIDAD AND TOBAGO

Port of Spain (SP - see page 121)
British High Commission
19 St Clair Avenue
St Clair, Trinidad
FTN Code – 8268 + extn number
Telephone: (00) (1) (868) 622 2748, 628 1234, 628 1068, 622 8985/86, 622 8960/61/62
Facsimile: (00) (1) (868) 622 4555 Management
622 9087 Commercial
628 3064 Consular/Immigration
628 8715 Chancery
Airtech: (00) (1) (868) 622 4533
e-mail: csbhc@opus.co.tt
Website: www.britain-in-trinidad.org
Office Hours (GMT): Mon – Thurs: 11 30 – 16 00 and 17 00 – 20 00. Fri: 11 30 – 16 30
High Commissioner: Mr Ronald Nash, CMG, LVO
Deputy High Commissioner: Mr Keith Allan
Defence Adviser (Resides at Bridgetown): Captain Steve G Wilson, RN
First Secretary (Regional Affairs): Mr Rob Kelly
British Council Manager: Ms Harriet Massingberd
Second Secretary (Management/Consular): Mr Bryan D Scarborough
Second Secretary (Chancery): Mr Tony Reader
Second Secretary (Commercial): Miss Helen Tanner
Second Secretary (Regional Affairs): (Vacant)
Third Secretary (Chancery/Information): Mr Philip Everest

TUNISIA

Tunis
British Embassy
Rue du Lac Windermere
Berges du Lac
Tunis 1053
FTN Code – 8328 + extn number
Telephone: (00) (216) 71 108 700 (switchboard)
71 108 777 Visa Enquiries
Facsimile: (00) (216) 71 108 703 Chancery
71 108 749 Management
71 108 769 Commercial
71 108 779 Visa
71 108 789 Consular
e-mail: TVI.tunis@fco.gov.uk (Visa)
TunisConsular@tunis.mail.fco.gov.uk (Consular)
Office Hours (GMT): Summer: Mon – Fri: 06 30 – 13 30. Winter: Mon – Thurs: 07 00 – 15 30; Fri: 07 00 – 13 00
Ambassador and Consul-General (2201): Mr Alan F Goulty, CMG
Deputy Head of Mission (2204): Mr Phil Batson
Defence Attaché (resides in London): Commander Matt P Briers, RN
British Council Director: Mr Peter Skelton
Second Secretary (Management) (2240): Mr Jim Buglass
Second Secretary (HMC/ECM/Pol/Econ) (2270 or 2206): Mr Gordon Stein
Second Secretary (Commercial) (2260): Mrs Marie-Claire Joyce
Third Secretary (Immigration) (2271): Mrs Rachel Mease
Third Secretary (Immigration) (2254): Mr David Burrows
Vice-Consul (2282): Mrs Sidsel Ghehioueche
Attaché (2220): Mr Peter Botham
Attaché (2202): Mrs Sharn Davison

Sfax
Honorary British Consulate
55 Rue Habib Maazoun, 3000,
Sfax 3000, Tunisia
Telephone: (00) (216) (74) 223 971
Facsimile: (00) (216) (74) 299 278
Honorary Consul: Mr Moneef Sellami

TURKEY

Ankara
British Embassy
Sehit Ersan Caddesi 46/A
Cankaya, Ankara
FTN Code – 8426 + extn number
Telephone: (00) (90) (312) 455 3344
455 + extension number
Facsimile: (00) (90) (312) 455 3351 UK Trade and Investment
455 3353 / 3344 Consular/Visa
455 3386 Clinic
455 3226 Defence
455 3259 Customs and Excise
455 3356 Press and Public Affairs
455 3352 Management
455 3350 Political
455 3320 HMA
Airtech: 455 3240
e-mail: britembank@fco.gov.uk (check Firecrest for individuals)
Website: www.britishembassy.org.tr

British Council
Karum Is Merkezi, Iran Cad No. 21 Kat 5
Room 437, Kavaklidere
Ankara, 06700
Telephone: (00) (90) (312) 455 3600
Facsimile: (00) (90) (312) 455 3636
Office Hours (GMT): Summer 05 45 – 10 00 and 11 15 – 14 30. July, August 05 45 – 10 00 and 11 15 – 14 30 (Mon – Thurs). 05 45 – 10 00 (Fri)
Winter 06 45 – 11 00 and 12 15 – 15 30
Ambassador (3201):
Sir Peter J Westmacott, KCMG, LVO
Counsellor and Deputy Head of Mission (3203):
Mr Michael Roberts
Defence and Military Attaché (3221):
Colonel Clive Hodges, MBE
Counsellor (British Council Director, Cultural Affairs): Mr Chris Brown, OBE
Naval and Air Attaché (3223):
Wing Commander Joe Gillan RAF
First Secretary (Head of UK Trade and Investment Department) (3241): Mr Steven Smith
First Secretary (Head of Political Section) (3210):
Ms Penny Miller
First Secretary (Political/Military) (3207):
Mr William Blanchard, OBE, MVO
First Secretary (Management) and Consul (3261):
Mr Dominic Clissold, OBE
First Secretary (British Council and Cultural Affairs): Mr Tony Lockhart
First Secretary (British Council and Cultural Affairs): Ms Gillian Cowell
First Secretary (Defence Equipment): (Vacant)
First Secretary (Technical Management) (3214):
Mr Paul Holmes
First Secretary (3325): Mr Roger Tate
Second Secretary (Economic) (3244):
Mr Stephen McCormick
Second Secretary (Political/Press and Public Affairs) (3209): Ms Chris Bradley
Second Secretary (Political) (3205):
Mr Geoff Collier
Second Secretary (Political) (3329):
Ms Paula Harrison
Second Secretary (3360): Mr Gary Brown
Second Secretary (3375): Mr Warren Spivey
Second Secretary (3380): Mr Gary Fennelly
Second Secretary (Technical Management) (3218):
Mr Bruce Hallybone
Second Secretary (Immigration) (3207):
Mr Rafi Husain
Third Secretary (Political) (3219): Mr Paul Ardley
Third Secretary (Management) (3262):
Ms Clarice Whiteside
Third Secretary (Immigration) (3277):
Mr Ciaran Hanley
Third Secretary (Immigration) (3277):
Mr Phil Dawber
Third Secretary (Immigration) (3235):
Ms Cynthia de Silva
British Vice-Consul (3257): Mrs Trudie Pak
Security Manager (3216): Mr Bob Lackenby

Antalya
British Vice-Consulate
Fevzi Çakmak Cad
1314 Sokak No.6/8
Antalya
Telephone: (00) (90) (242) 244 5313
Facsimile: (00) (90) (242) 243 2095
e-mail: britconant@turk.net
Vice-Consul: Mrs Jane Baz

Bodrum
British Consulate
Kibris Sehitleri Caddesi
Konacik Mevkii No 401/B
Bodrum
Telephone: (00) (90) (252) 319 0093-94
Facsimile: (00) (90) (252) 319 0095
e-mail: britconbod2@superonline.com
Honorary Consul: Mrs Fatma Nese Coskunsu

Izmir
British Consulate
1442 Sokak No 49
Alsancak
PK 300 Izmir
Telephone: (00) (90) (232) 463 5151
Facsimile: (00) (90) (232) 465 0858
e-mail: postmaster@izmir.mail.fco.gov.uk (check Firecrest for individuals)
Consul: Mr Willy Buttigieg

Marmaris
British Consulate
c/o Yesil Marmaris Tourism and Yacht Management Inc.
Barbaros Caddesi 13
P O Box 8, 48700 Marmaris
Telephone: (00) (90) (252) 412 6486
Facsimile: (00) (90) (252) 412 4565
e-mail: brithonmar@superonline.com
Honorary Consul: Mr Adnan Dogan Tugay

Istanbul
British Consulate-General
Mesrutiyet Caddesi No 34
Tepebasi, Beyoglu PK 33
34435 Istanbul
FTN Code – 8248 + extn number
Telephone: (00) (90) (212) 334 6400
Facsimile: (00) (90) (212) 334 6401

Visa Section:
Public Line: (00) (90) (212) 334 6525
Facsimile: (00) (90) (212) 334 6504
Consular Section:
Facsimile: (00) (90) (212) 334 6407
e-mail: bricons.istanbul@superonline.com
Website: www.britishembassy.org.tr
Office Hours (GMT): 06 30 – 11 00 and 11 45 – 14 45
Consul-General and Director of Trade and Investment Promotion (6411):
Ms Barbara L Hay, CMG, MBE
Deputy Consul-General (6440): Mr Peter Cook
Consul (British Council Director and Cultural Affairs) (355 5657): Mr Chris Edwards
Consul (Senior Management Officer and Consular Affairs) (6419): Mr Paul Ramsay
Consul (Political Affairs) (6415):
Mr Quentin Phillips

Consul (Technical Works) (6454):
Mr Mike Wood, OBE
Consul (Technical Works) (6428): Mr John Denoon
Consul (6463): Mr Steve Wren
Consul (Immigration) (6546): Mr Myron Reid
Consul (British Council Asst Director and Cultural Affairs) (355 5657): Mr Tim Hood
Consul (British Council Asst Director and Cultural Affairs (355 5657): Mr Peter Clack
Consul (6460): Mr Martin Lake
Consul (6461): Mr Alex Miller
Consul (6550): Mr Graeme Wiskar
Attaché (00 90 533 776 0392): Mr Alan Edwards
Consul (Immigration) (6511): Mr Tom Burke
Consul (Consular Affairs) (6414): Mr Joel Roden
Consul (Press and Public Affairs) (6435):
Mr Chris Kealey
Vice-Consul (Commercial) (6441):
Mr Colin Barratt
Vice-Consul (Management) (6421): Mr Les Jones
Vice-Consul (Consular Affairs and Immigration) (6420): Mr Simon Brown
Vice-Consul (Immigration) (6521/22):
Ms Ciara Palmer
Vice-Consul (Immigration) (6521/22):
Mr Gwyn Jones
Vice-Consul (Immigration) (6521/22):
Mr Steve Jackson
Vice-Consul (Immigration) (6521/22):
Ms Theresa Gecim
Vice-Consul (Immigration) (6521/22):
Mrs Julie Gorasia
Vice-Consul (6478): Mr Paul Carter
British Vice-Consul (6470):
Mr Shane Campbell, MBE
Chaplain: Canon Ian Sherwood

Bursa
British Honorary Consulate
Ressam Sefik Bursali Sokak
Basak Caddesi Zemin Kat
16010 Bursa
Telephone: (00) (90) (224) 220 25 34
Facsimile: (00) (90) (224) 220 88 01
Home Telephone: (00) (90) (224) 221 29 84
Honorary Consul: Mr E Kagitcibasi

TURKMENISTAN

Ashgabat (SP - see page 121)
British Embassy
3rd Floor, Office Building
Four Points Ak Altin Hotel
Ashgabat
FTN Code – 8752 + extn number
Telephone: (00) (993) (12) 363462, 363463, 363464, 363466, 363498
Facsimile: (00) (993) (12) 363465
Airtech: (00) (993) (12) 363463 x292
e-mail: beasb@online.tm (General)
beasbtrade@online.tm (Commercial)
beasbppa@online.tm (Press and Public Affairs)
Website: www.britishembassy.gov.uk/turkmenistan
Office Hours (GMT): Mon – Thurs: 04 00 – 08 00 and 09 00 – 12 30. Fri: 04 00 – 08 00 and 09 00 – 11 00
Ambassador (2201): Mr Peter Butcher
Deputy Head of Mission (2202): Mr Stephen Rapp
Defence Attaché (resides at Moscow):
Colonel Colin A Bulleid
Assistant Defence Attaché (resides at Moscow):
Major Alfonso C J Torrens
Cultural Attaché (resides at Tashkent):
Mr Neville McBain
Second Secretary (2270): Mr Stuart O'Neill
Third Secretary (Chancery) (2206):
Ms Rosie Tapper
Third Secretary (Management) and Vice-Consul (2210): Ms Jane Rowlands

TUVALU

Funafuti
British High Commission
(All staff resident at Suva)
High Commissioner: Mr Charles F Mochan
Deputy High Commissioner: Mr Ian Powell

UGANDA

Kampala
British High Commission
10/12 Parliament Avenue,
PO Box 7070, Kampala
FTN Code – 8656 + extn number
Telephone: (00) (256) (31) 312000
Facsimile: (00) (256) (41) 257304
(31) 312281 (Consular /Visa Section)
Airtech: (00) (256) (31) 312210
e-mail: bhcinfo@starcom.co.ug. (Press and Public Affairs Section)
bhccomm@starcom.co.ug (Commercial Section)
bhcimm@infocom.co.ug (Consular/Visa Section)
firstname.lastname@fco.gov.uk
Office Hours (GMT): Mon to Thurs: 05 30 – 10 00 and 11 00 – 14 00. Fri: 05 30 – 10 00
High Commissioner: Mr Francois Gordon, CMG
Deputy High Commissioner: Mr Jon Elliott
Defence Adviser:
Lieutenant Colonel Christopher J A Wilton
First Secretary (Regional Affairs):
Mr Robert Watson
First Secretary (British Council Director):
Mr Tom Cowin
First Secretary (Management): Mr John Heffer
First Secretary (British Council): (Vacant)
Second Secretary (Entry Clearance Manager):
Mr Stephen Powell
Second Secretary (Political External):
Mr Craig Fulton
Second Secretary (Consular/Commercial):
Ms Sarah Young
Second Secretary (Political/Press and Public Affairs): Ms Lynda St. Cooke
Second Secretary: Mr Andrew MacLean
Military Staff Assistant: Staff Sergeant Max Sexton
Third Secretary (Political): Mr Matt Caney
Third Secretary (Immigration):
Mr Orlando Ames-Lewis
Third Secretary (Immigration): Mr Clive Mead
Third Secretary (Security Manager):
Mr Andy Davis

Department for International Development (DFID) Uganda
3rd Floor Rwenzori Courts
Plot 2 Nakasero Road
P O Box 7306, Kampala
FTN Code – 8770 + extn number
Telephone: (00) (256) (41) 33100
Facsimile: (00) (256) (41) 348732
e-mail: initial-surname@dfid. gov.uk
Head of Office: Mr Eric Hawthorn
Deputy Head of Office: Mrs Janet Al-Utaibi
Deputy Programme Manager: Ms Charlotte Pierre
Livelihoods Adviser: Dr Alan Tollervey
Health Adviser: Dr Alastair Robb
Social Development Adviser: Mr Arthur Van Diesen
Assistant Governance Adviser: Mr Tom Wingfield
Economic Adviser: Mr Jonathan Beynon
Economist: Mr Andrew Keith
Enterprise Development Adviser: Mr Adrian Stone
Conflict and Humanitarian Adviser: Mr Graham Carrington

British Council
Ground Floor, Rwenzori Courts
Plot 2 Nakasero Road
PO Box 7306
Kampala
Telephone: (00) (256) (41) 234 730/7, 254 927, 031-206508/9
Facsimile: (00) (256) (41) 254 853
e-mail: firstname.lastname@britishcouncil.or.ug

UKRAINE

Kiev

British Embassy
01025 Kiev Desyatinna 9
FTN Code – 8658 3660 or extn number
Telephone: (00) (380) (44) 490 3660
Facsimile: (00) (380) (44) 490 3662
e-mail: ukembinf@sovamua.com
Consular/Visa Section/DFID Section:
4, Glybochytska Street,
Kiev 04050
Telephone: (00) (380) (44) 490 3400
(00) (380) (44) 490 2403 (DFID)
Facsimile: (00) (380) (44) 490 3480
(00) (380) (44) 490 2414 (Consular)
e-mail: britvisa.kiev@fco.gov.uk Consular and Visa Section
Office Hours (GMT): Mon – Thur 07 00 – 15 30. Fri 07 00 – 14 00

British Council:
040704 Kiev
4/12, Hryhoria Skovorody
Telephone: (00) (380) (44) 490 5600
Facsimile: (00) (380) (44) 490 5605
Ambassador: Mr Robert E Brinkley
Consul-General and Deputy Head of Mission: Mr Martin F Harris
Defence Attaché: Captain Rob E Drewett, MBE, RN
Counsellor (Political): Mr Lachlan Forbes
First Secretary (Economic): Ms Ruth Allen
First Secretary (Commercial): Mr David Moore
First Secretary (Management): Mrs Janice A Moore
First Secretary (British Council Director): Mr Terry Sandell
First Secretary (Development – DFID Ukraine): Mr John Stuppel
Deputy Defence Attaché: Major Stuart I Mehers
Defence Resettlement Officer: Major Donald Smith
Second Secretary (Chancery/Information): (Vacant)
Second Secretary (Immigration): Mr Chris Lain
Second Secretary (Immigration/Consul): Mr Jonathan Verney
Second Secretary (Assistant Director, British Council): Mr Colin Earley
Third Secretary (Political): Mr Stuart J Brown
Third Secretary (Management): Mr Barry Bobin-Martin
Third Secretary (Development): Mr Sam Adofo
Third Secretary (Immigration/Vice-Consul): Miss Karen Slater
Third Secretary (British Council): Mr Tony Hubbard
Third Secretary (Immigration): Mr David Haxton
Third Secretary (Immigration): Ms Anne Furey
Third Secretary (Immigration): Mr Andrew J Meighan
Defence Section Office Manager: Flight Sergeant Chris C Swain
Registrar: Ms Rebecca Smith

UNITED ARAB EMIRATES

Abu Dhabi

British Embassy
PO Box 248, Abu Dhabi
FTN Code – 8487 + extn number
Telephone: (00) (971) (2) 6101100
6101111 (Commercial)
Facsimile: (00) (971) (2) 6101518 (Chancery)
6101585 (Commercial)
6101586 (Consular/Management)
6101587 (Visa Section)
e-mail: chancery.abudhabi@fco.gov.uk
commercial.abudhabi@fco.gov.uk
consular.abudhabi@fco.gov.uk
defence.abudhabi@fco.gov.uk
management.abudhabi@fco.gov.uk
visa.abudhabi@fco.gov.uk
Website: www.britain-uae.org
Office Hours (GMT): Sat – Wed 03 30 – 10 30
Ambassador: Mr Richard Makepeace
Counsellor and Deputy Head of Mission: Mr Robert Deane
First Secretary (Political): Mr Alex Parsons
Defence Attaché: Colonel David Adams
First Secretary (Commercial): Mr Gordon Brown
First Secretary, Defence Supply: Mr Navin Patel, MBE
First Secretary (Airline Liaison Officer Regional Manager): Mr Robin Humphris
Second Secretary (Management and HM Consul): Mrs Christine Lufkin
Second Secretary (Chancery/Press and Public Affairs): Miss Alison Hall
Second Secretary (Commercial): Mr Steven Anderson

Second Secretary: Mr James Hall
Second Secretary (Airline Liaison Officer): Mr John Linehan
Third Secretary and Vice-Consul: Martin O'Neill
Third Secretary (Political/Consular): Mr James Robinson
Third Secretary (Immigration): Mrs Fiona O'Driscoll

Dubai
British Embassy
PO Box 65, Dubai
FTN Code – 8485 + extn number
Telephone: (00) (971) (4) 309 4444 Main Switchboard
309 4228 Chancery
309 4241 Management
309 4445 Commercial
309 4210 Consular
309 4333 Visa
309 4278 Communications
Facsimile: (00) (971) (4) 309 4301 Main
309 4225 Chancery
309 4302 Commercial
309 4303 Visa
Office Hours (GMT): Sat – Wed 03 30 – 10 30
Consul-General and Counsellor: Mr John Hawkins
First Secretary (Commercial) and Deputy Head of Mission: Ms Claire Evans
First Secretary (Political): Mr David Curran
Royal Navy Liaison Officer: Commander Steve Bateman, RN
First Secretary (Technical): Mr Gary Ward
Aviation Security Liaison Officer: Mr Rob Axworthy
Customs Liaison Officer: Mr Cameron Walker
Cultural Attaché (British Council Director): Ms Jo Maher
Second Secretary (Senior Management/Consul/ECM): Mrs Heather Reynolds
Airline Liaison Officer: Mr Steve Burns
Second Secretary (Commercial): Mr Mark Ellam
Second Secretary (Technical): Mr Steve Beard
Second Secretary (Press and Public Affairs): Mrs Vicky Lee-Gorton
Second Secretary (Economic): Mr Peter Whawell
Second Secretary (Political): Mrs Anne Marriott, MBE
Second Secretary (Regional Affairs): Ms Rachel Stewart
Third Secretary (Commercial): Mr Paul Smith
Third Secretary (Immigration): Mr Andy Palmer
Third Secretary (Immigration): Mr Noorel Haque
Vice-Consul: Mrs Suzanne Bastin

UNITED STATES

Washington
British Embassy
3100 Massachusetts Avenue, NW
Washington, DC 20008
FTN Code – 8430 + extn number
Telephone: (00) (1) (202) 588 6500 Embassy
7800 Consular
7830 British Council
Facsimile: (00) (1) (202) 588 7870 Foreign and Security Policy Group
7866 Management
7901 UKTI
7850 Consular
7667 Airtech
6511 Ambassador's Office
7887 Defence Attaché
Office Hours (GMT): Winter: 14 00 – 22 30
Summer: 13 00 – 21 30
Ambassador: Sir David Manning, KCMG
Deputy Head of Mission: Mr Alan Charlton, CMG
Minister (Economic): Mr Thomas Scholar
Defence Attaché and Head of British Defence Staff: Rear Admiral Anthony K Dymock, CB
Minister (Defence Material): Mr Jonathan Hoyle, CBE
Naval Attaché: Commodore C Joe Gass, RN
Military Attaché: Brigadier John Torrens-Spence, CBE
Air Attaché: Air Commodore Phil Goodman, RAF
Counsellor (Political and Public Affairs): Mr Dominic Martin
Counsellor (Foreign and Security Policy): Mr Frank Baker, OBE
Counsellor: Mr William Windle
Counsellor: Mr Michael Shipster, CMG, OBE
Counsellor (Change Management) and Consul-General: Mr Peter Hayes
Counsellor (Foreign and Security Policy): Mr Matthew Gould
Counsellor (Global Issues): Mr Julian Braithwaite
Counsellor: Dr Ruth Martin
Counsellor: Mr Robin Andrew
Counsellor and Director, Northern Ireland Bureau: Mr Tim Losty
Counsellor (Defence Science and Technology): Mr Adrian Baguley
Counsellor (Defence Equipment): Mr Andrew Radcliffe
Counsellor (Economic): Mr Alex Gibbs
Counsellor (Cultural) and Director, British Council: Mr Andrew Mackay
Counsellor (Defence Management): Ms Clare Tunbridge
First Secretary (Political): Mr Jonathan Sinclair
First Secretary (Foreign and Security Policy): Mr Colin Crooks
First Secretary (Foreign and Security Policy): Mr Matthew Taylor
First Secretary (Foreign and Security Policy): Ms Alison Blake
First Secretary (Foreign and Security Policy): Ms Clare Thomas
First Secretary (Foreign and Security Policy): Mr Marcus Winsley
First Secretary (Foreign and Security Policy): Ms Jo Adamson
First Secretary (Agriculture and Trade): Mr James Hughes
First Secretary (Energy and Environment): Dr Christian Turner
First Secretary (Economic): Ms Jenny Bates
First Secretary (Science, Technology and Innovation): Mr Philip Budden
First Secretary (Transport): Mr Clive Wright
First Secretary (Press and Public Affairs): Mr Paul "PJ" Johnston

First Secretary: Mr Paul Smith
First Secretary (Justice and Home Affairs): Miss Lizzy Gummer
First Secretary (Political): Mr Nigel Dakin
First Secretary (Change Management): Mr Colin Reynolds
First Secretary (Engineering Services): Mr Rod Baker
First Secretary (Engineering Services): Mr John Steers
First Secretary: Mr Peter Lewis
First Secretary (Scottish Affairs): Ms Susan Stewart
First Secretary (Estate Services): Mr John Miles
First Secretary (Consular): Mr Graeme Wise
First Secretary and Deputy Director Northern Ireland Bureau: Mr Michael Gould
First Secretary: Ms Julia MacGregor
Attaché (Defence Science and Technology – Sea/Air): Mr Paul Robinson
Attaché (Defence Science and Technology – Land): Mr Chris White-Horne
Attaché (Defence Science and Technology – Nuclear and Strategic Defence): Mr Robin Pitman
Attaché (Defence Equipment – Legal): Mr Graham Farnsworth
Attaché (Defence Equipment – Commercial): Mr Wilf Charlton
Attaché (Defence Equipment – Policy and Trade): Mr Chris Cook
Deputy Defence Attaché: Colonel S Tim Chicken, OBE, RM
Assistant Naval Attaché: Captain Henry Parker, RN
Head Defence Intelligence Liaison Staff North America: Colonel Michael K Hill
Assistant Military Attaché: Colonel Philip St. L Baxter
Assistant Air Attaché: Group Captain Davies-Howard
First Secretary (Defence Trade): Mr John Barton
First Secretary (Defence Equipment – Commercial): Mr Stephen Steel
First Secretary (Defence Finance and Resources): Mr Bernard Coughlin
First Secretary (Defence Governance): Mrs Alison Baldwin
First Secretary (Defence Human Resources): Lieutenant Colonel Steven Clifton
First Secretary (Defence Business Services): Mr Dean Churm
First Secretary: Mr Jim Fitzpatrick
First Secretary (Public Affairs): Mr Gerry McCrudden
Second Secretary (PS/HMA): Miss Susannah Payne
Second Secretary (Engineering Services): Mr Dave McDonald
Second Secretary (Management): Mr Tony Williams
Second Secretary (Chancery): Mrs Sarah Clarke
Second Secretary (Foreign and Security Policy): Ms Rachel Edis
Second Secretary (Foreign and Security Policy): Mr Jon Sharp
Second Secretary (Foreign and Security Policy): Mr Will Middleton
Second Secretary (Foreign and Security Policy): Mr Simon Mustard
Second Secretary (Economic): Miss Isabella McRae
Second Secretary (Security): Mr Colin Bowskill
Second Secretary (Consular): Mrs Marie Forsyth
Second Secretary (Scottish Affairs): Mr Stuart McLean
Third Secretary (Visits): Miss Paula Friston
Third Secretary: Ms Alison Tolfree
Third Secretary (Engineering Services): Mr Simon Antoine
Third Secretary (Engineering Services): Mr Chris Fox
Third Secretary (Engineering Services): Mr Barney Griffiths
Third Secretary (APS/HMA): Ms Erica Towsey, MBE
Third Secretary (PS/DHM): Ms Margaret Dunaway
Attaché: Mr Glyn Blows

Washington United Kingdom Delegation to the International Monetary Fund and International Bank for Reconstruction and Development, see page 117

Washington United Kingdom Representation at the Inter-American Development Bank, see page 117

Atlanta
British Consulate-General
Georgia Pacific Center, Suite 3400
133 Peachtree Street NE
Atlanta, GA 30303
FTN Code – 8438 + extn number
Telephone: (00) (1) (404) 954 7700
Facsimile: (00) (1) (404) 954 7702
Airtech: (00) (1) (404) 522 7739
Voicemail Numbers: see individual officers
Office Hours (GMT): 13.00 – 23.00
e-mail – {officers first name.surname} followed by @fco.gov.uk
Consul-General (7716): Mr Martin Rickerd
Deputy Consul-General (7720): Ms Helen Arbon
Consul (Trade and Investment) (7730): Mr Glen Whitley
Vice-Consul (Consular) (7710): Mrs Claire Newman
Vice-Consul (Press and Public Affairs) (7706): (Vacant)
Vice-Consul (Trade) (7737): Ms Marguerite Meyer
Vice-Consul (Trade) (7722): Ms Christina Lynton
Vice-Consul (Trade) (7725): Mr Mark Borst
Vice-Consul (Investment) (7731): Mr Ian Stewart
Vice-Consul (Science and Technology) (7738): Mr David Muller

Miami
British Consulate
Suite 2800, Brickell Bay Office Tower
1001, Brickell Bay Drive
Miami, FL 33131
FTN Code – 8437 + extn number
Telephone: (00) (1) (305) 374 1522
Facsimile: (00) (1) (305) 374 8196
Consul: Mr Simon J Davey, MBE

Head of Latin/American and Caribbean Co-ordination Unit: (Vacant)
Vice-Consul (Customs): Mr Barry Clarke
Vice-Consul (OTRCIS):
Mr Larry Covington, OBE, MA

Nashville
British Consulate
c/o Nashville Area Chamber of Commerce
211 Commerce Street
Nashville, TN 37201
Telephone: (00) (1) 615 743 3061
Facsimile: (00) (1) 615 256 6982
e-mail: jbutler@nashvillechamber.com
Honorary Consul: Mr J Butler

Orlando
British Consulate
Suite 2110, SunTrust Center,
200 South Orange Avenue,
Orlando, FL 32801
Telephone: (00) (1) 407 581 1540 Consular
Facsimile: (00) (1) 407 581 1550
Consul: Mr Dean Churm
Vice-Consul: Ms Rebecca Budgen

Charlotte
British Consulate
One Wachovia Center
301 South College St.
NC 0748, 9th Floor
Charlotte, NE 28288-0748
Telephone: (00) (1) 704 383 4359
Facsimile: (00) (1) 704 383 6545
e-mail: mdteden@bellsouth.net
Honorary Consul: Mr Michael Teden, OBE

Puerto Rico
British Consulate
Torre Chardón
Suite 1236
350 Chardon Avenue
San Juan, PR 00918
Telephone: (1) (787) 406 8777
Vice-Consul: Mrs Patricia Tully-Martinez

Boston
British Consulate-General
One Memorial Drive, 15th Floor
Suite 1500
Cambridge, MA 02142
FTN Code – 8434 + extn number
Telephone: (00) (1) (617) 245 4500
Facsimile: (00) (1) (617) 621 0220
Airtech: (00) (1) (617) 679 0054
e-mail: British.Consulate@fco.gov.uk
Postmaster@fco.gov.uk
Officers first name.last name followed by @fco.gov.uk
Office Hours (GMT): 14 00 – 22 00
Consul-General (4502): Mr John J Rankin
Deputy Consul-General (4515): Mr Geoff Plant
Consul (Science and Technology) (4547):
Mr Mark Sinclair
Vice-Consul (Science and Technology) (4549):
Dr Stefan Winkler
Vice-Consul (Trade) (4503): Ms Marguerite Meyer
Vice-Consul (Trade) (4510): Mr John Shipala
Vice-Consul (Press and Public Affairs) (4513):
Mrs Terri Evans
Vice-Consul (Management) (4520):
Mrs Kathy M Tunsley, MBE
Vice-Consul (Investment) (4507): Ms Alice Sloan
Vice-Consul (Life Sciences and Healthcare US-wide) (4530): Mrs Alice Pomponio

Chicago
British Consulate-General
The Wrigley Building,
400 N Michigan Avenue, Suite 1300
Chicago, IL 60611
FTN Code – 8453 + extn number
Telephone: (00) (1) (312) 970 3800
Facsimile: (00) (1) (312) 970 3852
970 3855 (Investment)
970 3858 (Trade)
970 3854 Consular and Visa Sections only
Airtech: (00) (1) (312) 970 3818
Office Hours (GMT): 14 30 – 23 00
HM Consul-General: Mr Andrew Seaton
Deputy Consul-General: Mr Jonathan Darby
Consul (Trade): Mr Jeff Taylor
Consul (Investment): Mr Rafe Courage
Head of Public Affairs: Ms Caroline Cracraft, MBE
Head of Management: Mr Chris Shaw
Trade Officer: Mr Ray Pimental
Trade Officer: Mrs Reet Robinson
Trade Officer: Mr Frank Phillips
Trade Officer: Mr Richard Knox
Trade Officer: Mr Brian Shapiro
Investment Officer: Ms Caroline Preece
Investment Officer: Mr Jonathan Wood
Entry Clearance Manager/British Vice-Consul:
Mrs Janet Bershers, MBE

Minneapolis
British Consulate
2600 U.S Bancorp Centre,
800 Nicollet Mall, suite 2600
Minneapolis, MN 55402-7035
Telephone: (00) (1) (612) 338 2525
Facsimile: (00) (1) (612) 339 2386
Office Hours (GMT): 14 30 – 23 00
Honorary Consul: Mr W R McGrann

Kansas City
British Consulate
12109 Aberdeen Road,
Shawnee Mission, Kansas City, KS 66209
Telephone: (00) (1) (913) 469 9786
Facsimile: (00) (1) (913) 469 8597
e-mail: britconkswmo@hotmail.com
Office Hours (GMT): 14 30 – 23 15
Honorary Consul: Mr J Scott Brown

St Louis
British Consulate
2323 Manor Grove Drive
#8, Chesterfield, MO 63017
Telephone: (00) (1) (636) 227 1334
Honorary Consul: (Vacant)

Houston
British Consulate-General
Suite 1900, Wells Fargo Plaza
1000 Louisiana Suite 1900, Houston, TX 77002

FTN Code – 8436 + extn number
Telephone: (00) (1) (713) 659 6270
659 6275 Commercial Department
Facsimile: (00) (1) (713) 659 7094
Airtech: (00) (1) (713) 659 5839
e-mail: bcg.houston@fco.gov.uk
Office Hours (GMT): 15 00 – 23 00
Consul-General (2116): Ms Judith Slater
Deputy Consul-General and Consul (Trade) (2114): Mr David Bull
Vice-Consul (Trade) (2113): Mr Kornel Rost
Vice-Consul (Trade, Oil and Gas) (713 425 6302): Mr Brian Foy
Vice-Consul (Information) (2117): Mr R Mitchell Jeffrey
Consul (Investment) (2140): Mr Matthew Hobbs
Vice-Consul (Investment) (2142): Miss Kim Fairweather
Vice-Consul (Science and Technology) (2134): Dr May Akrawi
Vice-Consul (Consular) (2120): Miss Linda Kelly
Management Officer (2126): Ms Anne Medlin

Denver
British Consulate
Suite 1030, World Trade Center
1675 Broadway
Denver, CO 80202
Telephone: (00) (1) (303) 592 5200 (General)
5205 (Consul – direct)
5212 (Trade Assistant – direct)
Facsimile: (00) (1) (303) 592 5209
e-mail: Mark.Stevens@britcondenver.com
info@britcondenver.com
Office Hours (GMT): 16 00 – 24 00
Consul (Trade): Mr Mark Stevens
Vice-Consul (Trade and Investment): Mr Barrett Stillings
Business Development Associate: Ms Vicky Lea
Business Development Associate: (Vacant)

Dallas
British Consulate – Closed

New Orleans
British Consulate
10th Floor, 321 St Charles Avenue
New Orleans, LA 70130
Telephone: (00) (1) (504) 524 4180
Office Hours (GMT): Sat and Wed 04 30 – 11 30
Honorary Consul: Mr James Coleman Jr
Consular Assistant: Ms Wendy Roberts

Los Angeles
British Consulate-General
11766 Wilshire Boulevard, Suite 1200
Los Angeles, CA 90025-6538
FTN Code – 8452 + extn number
Telephone: (00) (1) (310) 481 0031 (for officers direct lines see below)
481 2900 (Visa Enquiries)
Facsimile: (00) (1) (310) 481 2960
Airtech: (00) (1) (310) 481 2963
481-2961 (Visas only)
e-mail: trade.losangeles@fco.gov.uk
invest.losangeles@fco.gov.uk
pppa.losangeles@fco.gov.uk
visas.losangeles@fco.gov.uk
firstname.lastname@fco.gov.uk
Website: www.BritainUSA.com
Office Hours (GMT): 16 30 – 01 00
Consul-General (310 481 2950): Mr Peter Hunt, CMG
Deputy Consul-General/Consul Trade (310 996 3036): Mr Brian Conley
Consul Investment (310 996 3021): Mr David Slater
Consul (Consular/Entry Clearance) (310 481 2919): Mr Jeff Mee
Vice-Consul (Press, Political and Public Affairs) (310 996 3028): Mr Angus Mackay
Vice-Consul (Management) (310 996 3020): Mrs Nancy Bridi
Vice-Consul (Trade) (310 996 3030): Mr Mike Rosenfeld
Vice-Consul (Investment) (310 996 3024): Mr Andrew Lewis
Vice-Consul (Trade) (310 996 3031): Mr Carlo Cavagna
Vice-Consul (Consular/Entry Clearance) (310 481 2903): Ms Barbara Morgan
Vice-Consul (Entry Clearance) (310 481 2912): Ms Francesca Dooley
Vice-Consul (Entry Clearance) (310 481 2915): Mr Des Brewer
Consul (Defence) (310 481 2989): Mr Tim Johnson
Vice-Consul (Science and Technology) (310 996 3023): Dr Malcolm McLean

Phoenix
Honorary Consul: (Vacant)
British Trade and Investment Office
2375 East Camelback Road,
5th Floor, Phoenix, AZ 85016
Telephone: (00) (1) (602) 387 5092
Facsimile: (00) (1) (602) 387 5001
e-mail: Hank@btiophoenix.com
Office Hours (GMT): 15 00 – 23 30
Director: Mr Hank Marshall

Salt Lake City
British Consulate
c/o MK Gold Company
Eagle Gate Tower, Suite 2100
60 East South Temple
Salt Lake City, UT 84111
Telephone: (00) (1) (801) 297 6922
Facsimile: (00) (1) (801) 297 6940
e-mail: ijourney@mkgold.com
Office Hours (GMT): 16 00 – 01 00
Honorary Consul: Mr G Frank Joklik

San Diego
British Consulate
7825 Fay Ave, Suite 200
La Jolla, CA 92037
Telephone: (00) (1) (619) 459 8231
Facsimile: (00) (1) (619) 459 9250
e-mail: wblack@san.rr.com
Office Hours (GMT): 15.00-01 00
Honorary Consul: Mr William F Black

New York
British Consulate-General

845 Third Avenue
New York, NY 10022
FTN Code – 8450 + extn number
Telephone: (00) (1) (212) 745 0200 Consular
1 900 990 8472 Visa Enquiries Premium Rate
1 800 935 9993 Visa Enquiries Credit Card
1 900 285 7277 Visa Passport Enquiries Premium Rate
1 800 630 3332 Visa Passport Enquiries Credit Card
(00) (1) (212) 745 0495 Trade
745 0300 Investment
745 0258 / 745 0251 Press and Public Affairs
Facsimile: (00) (1) (212) 754 3062 Consular/Visa
745 0456 Trade and Investment
758 5395 Press and Public Affairs
758 4023 Management
Airtech: (00) (1) (212) 745 0296
e-mail: consular_visa@fco.gov.uk (Consular/Visa Enquiries)
enquiries@britainusa.com (General Enquiries)
info@uktradeinvestusa.com (Trade/Invest Enquiries)
Website: www.BritainUSA.com/ny
Consul-General and Director-General of Trade and Investment: Sir Philip Thomas, KCVO, CMG
Deputy Consul-General, Political, Press and Public Affairs and Deputy Head of Post: Mr Duncan J R Taylor, CBE
Deputy Consul-General, Director of Trade and Investment UKTI USA: Mr Alastair Newton
Consul (Deputy Director, Trade and Investment): Mrs Sarah Mooney
Consul (Trade and Investment) and Head of Marketing: Ms Shirar O'Connor-Mugler
Consul (Trade): (Vacant)
Vice-Consul (Trade): (Vacant)
Vice-Consul (Trade): Mr Michael Formosa
Vice-Consul (Trade): Ms Merrie Keller
Consul, Head of Trade and Investment – New York: Ms Kerry Appleton
Vice-Consul (Investment): Mr Steve Hawkins
Vice-Consul (National Market Research Co-ordinator): Mrs Francine J Conran
Vice-Consul (National Market Research Co-ordinator): Ms Charlotte Simcock
Vice-Consul (Fairs and Promotions): Ms Annie Wildey
Vice-Consul (Commercial Publicity): (Vacant)
Consul (Northern Ireland): Mr Andy Pike
Vice-Consul (Political): Dr Ray Raymond, MBE
Vice-Consul (Press and Public Affairs): Ms Leslie Slocum
Visits Officer: Ms Louise Redmond, MBE
Consul and Director of US Entry Clearance Issuing Posts: Mr Patrick Owens, OBE
Vice-Consul (Consular): Mrs Jacqueline Cerdan, MBE
Vice-Consul (Entry Clearance Manager): Mr Stephen Thompson
Vice-Consul (Entry Clearance Manager): Mr Martin Southey
Consul (Management): Mrs Christine Carr-Alloway
Head of Human Resources: Mrs Terri Lamon
Regional Training Officer: Ms Susan Skinner

British Information Services
Counsellor (Political and Public Affairs) and Head of BIS (resides at Washington): Mr Dominic Martin
Consul (Director, British Information Services): Mrs Judy Legg
Vice-Consul (Internet): Mr Mike Keen

New York United Kingdom Mission to United Nations, see page 113

Philadelphia
British Consulate
33rd Floor, 1818 Market St
Philadelphia, PA 19103
Telephone: (00) (1) (215) 557 7665
Facsimile: (00) (1) (215) 557 6608
Honorary Consul: Mr Oliver St C Franklin, OBE

Pittsburgh
University of Pittsburgh
Office of the Chancellor
107 Cathedral of Learning
Pittsburgh, PA 15260
Telephone: (00) (1) (412) 624 4200
Facsimile: (00) (1) (412) 624 7539
Honorary Consul: Mr Mark Nordenberg

San Francisco
British Consulate-General
Suite 850, 1 Sansome Street
San Francisco, CA 94104
FTN Code – 8435 + extn number
Telephone: (00) (1) (415) 617 1300
Facsimile: (00) (1) (415) 434 2018 Group 3
Website: www.britainusa.com/sf
Office Hours (GMT): 16 30 – 01 00
Consul-General: Mr Martin Uden
Deputy Consul-General and Consul (Commercial): Mr Peter Broom
Consul (Investment): Mrs Janet Coyle
Consul (Science and Technology): Dr Sharima Rasanayagam
Vice-Consul (Information): Ms Emma Stevenson
Vice-Consul (Commercial): Mr Dale Smith
Vice-Consul (Commercial): Ms Nicole Close
Vice-Consul (Investment): Ms Helen Moore
Vice-Consul (Management/Consular): Mrs Karen S Thomas
Vice-Consul (Commercial): Ms Carrie Ann Schiller
Vice-Consul (Commercial): Ms Shaan Libby
Vice-Consul (Science and Technology): Dr Stephen Lynn

Anchorage
British Consulate
College of Arts and Sciences
University of Alaska Anchorage
3211 Providence Drive
Anchorage, AK 99508
Telephone: (00) (1) (907) 786 4848
Facsimile: (00) (1) (907) 786 4647
e-mail: afdh1@uaa.alaska.edu
Honorary Consul: Dr Diddy R M Hitchins, MBE

Portland
British Consulate
Pacificorp
825 NE Multnomah
20th Floor
Portland, OR 97232
Telephone (Direct Line): (00) (1) (503) 227 5669
Facsimile: (00) (1) (503) 813 5378
e-mail: andy.macritchie@pacificorp.com
Honorary Consul: Mr Andy MacRitchie

San Jose
British Consulate
1139 Karlstad Drive
Sunnyvale
San Jose, CA 94089
Telephone: (00) (1) (408) 747 7140 x1200 or
x1400 (Assistant)
Facsimile: (00) (1) (408) 747 7198
e-mail: belder@genus.com
Honorary Consul: Dr W R Elder

Seattle
British Consulate
900 Fourth Avenue,
Suite 3001,Seattle, WA 98164
FTN Code – 8454 + extn number
Telephone: (00) (1) (206) 622 9255
Facsimile: (00) (1) (206) 622 4728
Airtech: (00) (1) (206) 336 4186
Office Hours (GMT): 16 30 – 01 30
Consul (Commercial) (4178): Mr Dennis Leith
Vice-Consul (Commercial) (4183): Ms Kim Chio
Vice-Consul (Commercial) (4184): Mr Dave Baron

URUGUAY

Montevideo (SP - see page 121)
British Embassy
Calle Marco Bruto 1073, 11300 Montevideo, PO Box 16024
FTN Code – 8659 + extn number
Telephone: (00) (598) (2) 622 3630, 622 3650
Facsimile: (00) (598) (2) 622 7815
e-mail: officer's
firstname.surname@mail.fco.gov.uk
Embassy e-mail address:
bemonte@internet.com.uy
Office Hours (GMT): Mid Mar – Mid Dec: 12 00 – 16 00 and 17 00 – 20 15. Mid Dec – Mid Mar: 11 00 – 17 00
For officers residing in Buenos Aires refer to e-mail addresses in Argentina.
Ambassador: Dr Hugh Salvesen
Deputy Head of Mission, First Secretary and Consul: Mr John Pearson
Defence Attaché (resides at Buenos Aires):
Group Captain Ian Capewell, RAF
First Secretary (resides at Buenos Aires):
Mr Michael Cavanagh
Second Secretary (Management) and Vice-Consul:
Mr Guy Parkinson
Second Secretary (TMO) (resides at Buenos Aires):
Mr Stuart Moss

UZBEKISTAN

Tashkent (SP - see page 121)
British Embassy
Ul. Gulyamova 67, Tashkent 700000
FTN Code – 8333 + extn number
Telephone: (00) (99871)
1206451,1206288,1207852,1207853,1207854
Facsimile: (00) (99871) 1206549 (General)
1206430 (Consular/Visa)
e-mail: brit@emb.uz
Office Hours (GMT)
Winter: 04 00-07 30 and 08 30-12 00 (GMT + 5 hours)
Summer: 05 00-08 30 and 09 30-13 00 (GMT + 4 hours)
Ambassador: Mr David Moran
Deputy Head of Mission: Mr Carl Garn
Defence Attaché: Lieutenant Colonel Nick J Ridout
British Council Director: Mr Neville McBain
British Liaison Officer (resides in Dushanbe):
Mr Peter Cornell
Third Secretary (Political/PPA):
Mr Daniel Grzenda
Third Secretary (Management): Mr Steve Brown
Third Secretary (ECO/VC): Mr Everol Wilson
British Council Deputy Director:
Mr Andrew Thomas
Attaché: Ms Angela Clark

VANUATU

Port-Vila (SP - see page 121)
British High Commission
Port Vila, Vanuatu
PO Box 567, Port Vila
Telephone: (00) (678) 23100 (3 lines)
Facsimile: (00) (678) 27153 (Airtech)
23651 (General)
e-mail: bhcvila@vanuatu.com.vu
firstname.surname@fco.gov.uk
Office Hours (GMT): Mon, Tue, Thu and Fri: 20 30 – 00.45 and 02 00 – 05 30. Wed: 20 30 – 00 45
The High Commission will close to the public on 21st October 2005 and the responsibilities transferred to BHC Suva on 15th December 2005.
High Commissioner:
Mr Michael T Hill (until 17th Aug 05)
Deputy High Commissioner:
Mr Joel Watson (until 15th Dec 05)

VENEZUELA

Caracas
Torre La Castellana, Piso 11
Avenida La Principal de la Castellana
La Castellana
Caracas 1061
FTN Code – 8660 + extn number
Telephone: (00) (58) (212) 263 8411
Facsimile: (00) (58) (212) 267 1275 (Main)
(00) (58) (212) 263 7604 (Chancery)
(00) (58) (212) 266 3232 (Commercial)
(00) (58) (212) 266 8279 (HMCandE)
Airtech: (00) (58) (212) 264 7983
e-mail: britishembassy@internet.ve
Website: www.britain.org.ve

Office Hours (GMT): Mon-Thurs: 12 00 – 20 30. Fri: 12 00 – 17 15
Consular Section Hours (GMT): Mon – Fri: 12 00 – 16 30. Wed (only): 17 30 – 20 00
Ambassador: Mr Donald A Lamont
Deputy Head of Mission: Mr Steven M Fisher
Defence Attaché:
Group Capitain William G S Dobson, RAF
British Council Director: Mrs Barbara Wickham
First Secretary: Mr Paul Roden
First Secretary (Commercial):
Mr Dominic McAllister
First Secretary (Management) and Consul:
Mrs Julie M Foster
First Secretary: Mr J Nicholas Cox
Second Secretary (Political): Mr Andrew Tate
Second Secretary: Mr Peter Nelson
Second Secretary: Mr James Phillips
Second Secretary (Technical): Mr Colin Tully
Second Secretary (Commercial): Mr John M Foster
Third Secretary (Management / Consular):
Miss Dawn Farr
Attaché: Mr Lee Farnsworth
Attaché: Mr Carl Dawber
Attaché: Mrs Valerie McGuinn

Maracaibo
British Consulate
Inspecciones C.A., Avenida 9B con Calle 77 (5 de Julio)
Edifcio Banco Industrial, Piso 4
Maracaibo, Estado Zulia
Telephone: (00) (58) (261) 797 7003 (Master)
(58) (261) 798 0245 / 8493 or 797 6743 / 5156
Facsimile: (00) (58) (261) 797 0025
e-mail: alexp@inspecciones.com
Opening Hours: Mon-Fri 09 00 – 17 30
Honorary Consul: Mr Alexander Kirk Podolecki

Margarita
British Consulate
Villa Bougainville, Avenida Las Gamboas
Santa Ana, Isla Margarita, Estado Nueva Esparta
Telephone: (00) (58) (295) 257 0518
Facsimile: (00) (58) (295) 253 0487
e-mail: barriedutton@hotmail.com
Opening Hours: Mon-Fri 09 00 – 17 00
Honorary Consul (Designate): Mr Barrie Dutton
Mérida

British Consulate
ULA, Post-Grado Ciencias Políticas
Facultad Ciencias Juridicas/Políticas
Avenida Las Americas, Mérida
Estado Mérida
Telephone: (00) (58) (274) 240 2030 or 240 2007
Facsimile: (00) (58) (274) 240 2007 / 2008
e-mail: robertkirby@hotmail.com
Honorary Consul: Dr Robert G Kirby

San Cristobal
British Consulate
AVECO, Edificio Britannia House
Avenida Rotaria, Esquina Parque Exposición
La Concordia, San Cristobal
Estado Tachira
Telephone: (00) (58) (276) 346 0434 / 347 1644
Facsimile: (00) (58) (276) 347 0544
e-mail: britcon-sc@cantv.net
Honorary Consul: Mr Roger Burnison

Valencia
British Consulate
Dalca. Urb., Industrial el Recreo
Calle B, Parcela 103, Valencia
Estado Carabobo
Telephone: (00) (58) (241) 878 3480 / 4823 / 3279
Facsimile: (00) (58) (241) 878 3603
e-mail: burguesdal@telcel.net.ve
Honorary Consul: Mr Ramón Burgues

VIETNAM

Hanoi
British Embassy
Central Building
Floors 4 and 5
31 Hai Ba Trung
FTN Code – 8493 + 1000 for switchboard
Telephone: (00) (84) (4) 936 0500
90340 4919 Duty Officer Mobile
Facsimile: (00) (84) (4) 936 0561
Chancery/Commercial
936 0562 Consular
936 0551 Management
e-mail: behanoi@fpt.vn
Website: www.uk-vietnam.org
Office Hours (GMT): Mon-Fri 01 30 – 05 30 and 06 30 – 09 30

British Council
40 Cat Linh Street
Hanoi
Telephone: (00) (84) (4) 843 6780
Facsimile: (00) (84) (4) 843 4962
e-mail: behanoi@britishcouncil.org.vn
Office Hours (GMT): Mon-Fri 01 30 – 05 00 and 06 30 – 10.00
Ambassador (2201): Mr Robert Gordon, CMG, OBE
Deputy Head of Mission (2204):
Mr Mac McLachlan
British Council Director and Cultural Attaché:
Mr Keith Davies
Defence Attaché (resides at Kuala Lumpur):
Colonel Jamie A Athill
British Council Deputy Director/Cultural Attaché:
Ms Soma Chakrabarti-Fezzardi
British Council Deputy Director/Cultural Attaché:
Mr Tim Hood
First Secretary (Defence Supply) (resides at Kuala Lumpur): Mr David Mew
Second Secretary (Political) (2205):
Mr Paul Gaskell
Second Secretary (Management) (2249):
Ms Sheila O'Connor
Second Secretary (Commercial) (2228):
Mr Kevin Ringham
Third Secretary – Vice-Consul/ECO (2244):
Mr Elliott Haynes
Third Secretary (Chancery) (2210):
Mr Richard Ridout
Attaché (2202): Mrs Molly Bicker
Attaché (2203): Mr Peter Digweed

Department for International Development (DFID) Vietnam
Central Building
7th Floor
Telephone: (00) (84) (4) 936 0555
Facsimile: (00) (84) (4) 936 0556
Office Hours (GMT): Mon-Thurs 01 00 – 05 00 and 06 00 – 09 30; Fri 01 00 – 06 30
Head of DFID Vietnam (2272): Ms Bella Bird
First Secretary (Development) (2269): Mr Donald Couper
First Secretary (Development) (2271): Mr Keith McGiggan
First Secretary (Development) (2273): Mr Steve Passingham
First Secretary (Development) (2268): Mr Simon Lucas
First Secretary (Development) (2270): Mr Alwyn Chilver

Ho Chi Minh City (SP)
British Consulate-General
25 Le Duan,
District 1, Ho Chi Minh City
FTN Code – 8424 + extn number or 1000 for switchboard
Telephone: (00) (84) (8) 8298433
(00) (84) 91392 0991 (Duty officer mobile)
Facsimile: (00) (84) (8) 8295257 (Visa/Consular)
8221971 (Commercial/Information)
e-mail: bcghcmc@hcm.vnn.vn
Website: www.uk-vietnam.org
Office Hours (GMT): Mon – Fri 01 30 – 05 00 and 06 00 – 09 30
HM Consul-General and Director, UK Trade and Investment (Vietnam) (2207): Mr Adrian Stephens
Consul (Trade and Investment) (2205): Mr Phil Wyithe
British Council Director (Tel: 825 6402): Mr Duncan Wilson

British Council:
25 Le Duan,
District 1, Ho Chi Minh City, Vietnam
Telephone: (00) (84) (8) 8232862/3 (Main Office)
8256403/4 (Teaching Centre)
Facsimile: (00) (84) (8) 8222105 (Main Office)
8232861 (Teaching Centre)
e-mail: bchcmc@britishcouncil.org.vn
Office Hours (GMT): Mon-Fri: 01 30 – 05 00; 06 30 – 10 00

YEMEN

Sana'a
British Embassy
129 Haddah Road, Sana'a
Postal address: PO Box 1287
Telephone: (00) (967) (1) 264081/82/83/84
Facsimile: (00) (967) (1) 263059
Office Hours (GMT): Sat – Wed: 04 30 – 11 30
Ambassador: Mr Michael Gifford
Deputy Head of Mission and Consul-General: Mr Andrew Goodwin
Defence Attaché (resides at Riyadh): Brigadier Jim G Askew, OBE
British Council Director: Ms Elizabeth White
First Secretary: Mr Dominic O'Neill
First Secretary: Mr Simon Walters
Second Secretary (Political): Mr Patrick Tobin
Second Secretary (Political): Mrs Emma Walters
Overseas Security Manager: Mr Darren Parnaby
Attaché: Miss Gemma Brady

Aden
British Consulate-General – (Closed)
Hodeidah
British Consulate
Sanaa Road, KM7
P O Box 3337, Hodeidah
Telephone: (00) (967) (3) 238130/131, 238958
Facsimile: (00) (967) (3) 211533, 238269
Office Hours (GMT): Mon – Wed: 08 00 – 13 00
Honorary Consul: Mr Abdul Gabbar Thabet

ZAMBIA

Lusaka
British High Commission
5210 Independence Avenue
P.O.Box 50050
15101 Ridgeway, Lusaka
FTN Code – 8395 + extn number
Telephone: (00) (260) (1) 251133
Facsimile: (00) (260) (1) 253798 (Management/Press and Public Affairs/ Development)
251923 (Consular)
252842 (Visa)
252848 (Chancery)
Airtech: (00) (260) (1) 253162
e-mail: BHC-Lusaka@fco.gov.uk
Office Hours (GMT): Mon – Thurs: 06 00 – 11 00 and 12 00 – 14 30. Fri: 06 00 – 11 00
High Commissioner: Mr Alistair Harrison, CVO
Deputy High Commissioner: Mr Fergus Cochrane-Dyet
Defence Adviser (Resides in Harare): Colonel Bob J Griffiths, MBE
Second Secretary (Management): Mr Richard Fielder
Second Secretary (resides in Harare): Mr Aidan Linnell
Second Secretary (Political/Press/Public Affairs): Ms Siân Price
Second Secretary (Consular/ECM): Mr Frank Drayton
Third Secretary (Immigration): Mr Steve Gordon
Overseas Security Manager: Mr Mark Wardle

Department for International Development (DFID) Zambia
(Address same as British High Commission)
FTN Code – 8555 + 4000 for DFID Switchboard
Telephone: (00) (260) (1) 251164
Facsimile: (00) (260) (1) 253580
e-mail: DFIDZambia@dfid.gov.uk
Individual e-mail addresses: initial-surname (e.g: c-murgatroyd@dfid.gov.uk)
Office Hours same as British High Commission
Head of DFID Zambia: Ms Beverley Warmington

Deputy Head of DFID Zambia:
Mr Richard Montgomery
Health and Population Adviser: Mr T Daly
Governance Adviser: Mr Chris Murgatroyd
Economics Adviser: Mr Alan Harding
Private Sector Adviser: Ms Susan Barton
Education Adviser: Mr Richard Arden
Social Development Adviser:
Mr Bruce Lawson-McDowall
Statistics Adviser (Resides in Pretoria):
Mr Martin Dyble
Environmental Adviser (Resides in Pretoria):
Ms Beth Arthy
Deputy Programme Manager: Mr Ricky Taylor
Health and Education Associate Professsional Officer: Ms Maria Skarphedinsdottir
Policy, Poverty and Performance Programme Officer: Mr Rajib Baisya
Management Support Officer: Ms Denise Avery
Vulnerable and Food Security Adviser:
Ms Kelley Toole
Trade Adviser (Resides in Pretoria):
Ms Helena Mcleod
Humanitarian and Food Security (Resides in Pretoria): Mr Tom Kelly
Senior Health Adviser (Resides in Pretoria):
Mr Tim Martineau

ZIMBABWE

Harare

British Embassy
Corner House, 7th Floor
Samora Machel Avenue/Leopold Takawira Street
(PO Box 4490), Harare
FTN Code – 8498 + extn number
Telephone: (00) (263) (4) 772990,774700
Facsimile: (00) (263) (4) 774617
Airtech: (00) (263) (4) 774703
Website: www.britainzw.org
Office Hours (GMT): Mon-Thurs: 06 00 – 10 30 and 11 30 – 14 30. Fri: 06 00 – 12 00
Ambassador (2201/2): Dr Rod Pullen
Deputy Head of Mission (2203/4):
Ms Alison Blackburne
Counsellor (2205): Mr Michael Regan
Counsellor (Regional Director, British Council):
Mr David Martin
Defence Attaché (2221):
Colonel Bob J Griffiths, MBE
First Secretary (Medical Officer) (resides in Lilongwe): Dr Howard Friend
First Secretary (Management) (2225):
Mr Roger Davies
First Secretary (Director Operations, British Council): Ms Louisa Waddingham
First Secretary (Political) (2207): Ms Gillian Dare
Second Secretary (Political) (2222):
Mr Rob Harrison
Second Secretary (Consular/Immigration) (2265):
Mr David Ashford
Second Secretary (Immigration) (2246):
Mr Alan Early
Second Secretary (Technical) (resides in Lusaka):
Mr Aidan Linnell
Second Secretary (Political/Projects) (2238):
Mr Jim Newman
Third Secretary (Management) (2226):
Mrs Tina Wicke
Third Secretary (Chancery) (2206):
Mr William Sims
Third Secretary (Consular/Immigration) (2332):
Mr Wayne N Pagett
Third Secretary (Immigration) (2334):
Mr John Collins
Third Secretary (Immigration) (2333):
Mr Ken Arundel
Third Secretary (Immigration) (2331):
Ms Catherine Ings
Third Secretary (Immigration) (2330):
Ms Sharon Thomas
Assistant to Defence Attaché (2223):
Warrant Officer Adam Moore

Department for International Development (DFID) Zimbabwe

Corner House, 6th Floor, Samora Machel Avenue/Leopold Takawira Street
PO Box 1030 Harare
FTN Code – 8777 + extn number
Telephone: (00) (263) (4) 774719-28
Facsimile: (00) (263) (4) 775695
e-mail addresses: Initial-Surname@dfid.gov.uk (eg: J-Barrett@dfid.gov.uk)
Office Hours (GMT): Mon-Fri: 06 00 – 14 30
Head of DFID Zimbabwe (3302): Dr John Barrett
Economic Adviser (3310): Mr Alex Ferrand
HIV and Health Adviser (3313):
Dr Desmond Whyms
Social Development Adviser (3228):
Dr Rachel Yates
Humanitarian Adviser (3375): Mr Shaun Hughes
Rural Livelihoods Adviser (3307): Mr Tom Barrett

PART II: MISSIONS AND DELEGATIONS

UNITED KINGDOM MISSION TO THE UNITED NATIONS

New York
One Dag Hammarskjold Plaza, 28th Floor
885 Second Avenue, New York, NY 10017
FTN Code – 8451 + 2 + extn number
Direct: (00) (1) (212) 745 9 + extn number
Telephone: (00) (1) (212) 745 9250
Facsimile: (00) (1) (212) 745 9316 (General)
745 9292 (Management)
Airtech: (00) (1) (212) 745 9272
Postal address: PO Box 5238 New York, NY 10150-5238
e-mail: UKUN@UN.INT
Website: http://wip.ukun.org/rmf.asp
Office Hours (GMT): Summer 13 00 – 22 00. Winter 14 00 – 23 00
United Kingdom Permanent Representative to the United Nations and United Kingdom Representative on the Security Council (with personal rank of Ambassador) (334):
Sir Emyr Jones Parry, KCMG
Deputy Permanent Representative to the United Nations (with personal rank of Ambassador) (337):
Mr Adam Thomson
Counsellor and Head of Political Section) (212):
Mr Paul Johnston
Counsellor (Economic, Social and Humanitarian Affairs) (319): Mr Michael O'Neill
Counsellor (Political) (343): Mr John Stephenson
Counsellor (Finance) (325): Ms Elizabeth Galvez
Counsellor (Legal Adviser) (339):
Mr Huw Llewellyn
Military Adviser to UK Permanent Representative (247): Colonel Jonathan Lloyd
First Secretary (Head of Management) (387):
Mr Michael Balmer
Deputy Military Adviser (340):
Lieutenant Colonel Ken Hume
Assistant Legal Adviser (225): Mr Gavin Watson
First Secretary (Political) (304):
Mr Nicholas Carrick
First Secretary (Political) (329):
Ms Rosemary Davis
First Secretary (Political) (357):
Miss Vanessa Howe-Jones
First Secretary (Economic) (275):
Mr James Kariuki
First Secretary (Finance) (351): Mr Bill Longhurst
First Secretary (Political) (214):
Mr Christophe McBride
First Secretary (Conflict Issues) (395):
Ms Joanna Moir
First Secretary (Political/Press) (394):
Mr Justin Mackenzie-Smith
First Secretary (Political) (311):
Ms Samantha Purdy
First Secretary (Senior Social Development Adviser) (255): Mr Michael Schultz
First Secretary (Environment) (215):
Ms Alice Walpole
First Secretary (Human Rights) (366):
Mr Richard Wood
Second Secretary (Political) (253):
Ms Catherine Brooker
Second Secretary (Political) (211): Mr Ian Collard
Second Secretary (Management) (371):
Mr Peter Collins
Second Secretary (Political) (342):
Mr Paddy Davie
Second Secretary (Technical Management) (321):
Mr Paul Deneiffe
Second Secretary (Finance) (264):
Mr Simon Horner
Second Secretary (Humanitarian Affairs) (244):
Mr Robin Lake
Second Secretary (Political) (370): Ms Anne Power
Second Secretary (Political) (398):
Mrs Clare Risman
Second Secretary (Political) (258):
Mr Simon Williams
Second Secretary (Social Affairs) (219):
Mr Tom Woodroffe
Third Secretary (Elections/ECOSOC) (270):
Ms Rachel Brazier
Third Secretary (Political) (309): Ms Ying Yee

UNITED KINGDOM MISSION TO THE OFFICE OF THE UNITED NATIONS AND OTHER INTERNATIONAL ORGANISATIONS AT GENEVA

Geneva
37-39 rue de Vermont, 1211 Geneva 20
FTN Code – 8371 + extn number
Telephone: (00) (41) (22) 918 23 00
Facsimile: (00) (41) (22) 918 23 33 Main No
24 35 Chancery
24 44 Spec Agencies
23 77 WTO/Economic
23 10 Joint Management Unit
Telex: 414195 (a/b 414195 UKGV CH)
Office Hours (GMT): Summer: 07 00 – 11 00 and 12 30 – 16 00.
Winter: 08 00 – 12 00 and 13 30 – 17 00
United Kingdom Permanent Representative (holds personal rank of Ambassador) (2358):
Mr N A Thorne, CMG
Minister and Deputy Permanent Representative (2434): Mr Julian Metcalfe
Counsellor (Development/Specialised Agencies) (2370): Dr Carole Presern
First Secretary (Human Rights) (2363):
Ms Caroline Rees
First Secretary (UN, Press Officer) (2371):
Mr Richard Bridge
First Secretary (Legal Adviser) (2323):
Mrs Helen Upton
First Secretary (Specialised Agencies and Humanitarian) (2376): Corinne Kitsell
First Secretary (Management) (2458):
Mrs Susan Gregory
First Secretary (WTO) (2378): Mr David Cairns

First Secretary (UNCTAD, ECE) (2359):
Mr Edward Brown
Second Secretary (WTO) (2379):
Mr Joseph McClintock
Second Secretary (WTO) (2369):
Miss Jo Lomas
Second Secretary (Specialised Agencies) (2353):
Mrs Pamela Tarif
Second Secretary (ECE, UNCTAD) (2368):
Mr Robert Fairweather
Second Secretary (Human Rights) (2360):
Mr Robert Dixon
Second Secretary (Management) (2452):
Mr Ian McKinlay
Second Secretary (Technical) (2414):
Mr Matthew Smith
Second Secretary (Humanitarian) (2338):
Mr John Webster

Geneva Joint Management Office, UK Government Offices, see page 97

UNITED KINGDOM DELEGATION TO THE UNITED NATIONS EDUCATIONAL, SCIENTIFIC AND CULTURAL ORGANISATION (UNESCO)

Paris
1 Rue Miollis
75732 Paris
Cedex 15
Telephone: (00) (33) 1 45 68 27 84
Facsimile: (00) (33) 1 47 83 27 77
United Kingdom Permanent Delegate (holds personal rank of Ambassador):
Mr Timothy Craddock
United Kingdom Deputy Permanent Delegate:
Ms Christine Atkinson
Third Secretary: Ms Hilary Izon

UNITED KINGDOM MISSION TO THE UNITED NATIONS IN VIENNA

Vienna
Jaurèsgasse 12, 1030 Vienna
FTN Code – 8310 + extn number
Telephone: (00) (43) (1) 716 130 or (43) (1) 71613 + extn number
Facsimile: (00) (43) (1) 71613 4900
e-mail: ukmis.vienna@fco.gov.uk
Office Hours (GMT): Winter: Mon – Fri 08 00 – 12 00 and 13 30 – 16 30
Summer: Mon – Fri 07 00 – 11 00 and 12 30 – 15 30
United Kingdom Permanent Representative (with personal rank of Ambassador) (4237):
Mr Peter Redmond Jenkins, CMG
Deputy Permanent Representative (4232):
Mr Tim Andrews
First Secretary (IAEA) (4240): Mr Gavin Newson
First Secretary (CTBTO) (4296): Ms Tracy Roberts (Mr Graham Styles w.e.f Jan 06)
First Secretary (UN) (4234): Mrs Alison Crocket
First Secretary (UN/UNIDO) (4297):
Mrs Creena Lavery
Second Secretary (CTBTO/UN/IAEA) (4298):
Mr Llywelyn Skidmore
Second Secretary (IAEA): Mrs Anna Love

Joint Management
First Secretary (Management) (2261):
Mr Eric Jones
Third Secretary (Management) (2260):
Miss Jan H Richardson

UNITED KINGDOM PERMANENT REPRESENTATION TO THE CONFERENCE ON DISARMAMENT

Geneva
37-39 rue de Vermont, 1211 Geneva 20
FTN Code – 8371 + extn number
Telephone: (00) (41) (22) 918 23 00
Facsimile: (00) (41) (22) 918 23 44
Telex: 414195 (a/b 414195 UKGV CH)
e-mail: ukdis.geneva2@fco.gov.uk
Office Hours (GMT): Summer: 07 00 – 11 00 and 12 30 – 16 00,
Winter: 08 00 – 12 00 and 13 30 – 17 00
United Kingdom Permanent Representative: (holds personal rank of Ambassador) (2321):
Dr John Freeman
Deputy Permanent Representative (2328):
Ms Fiona Paterson
First Secretary (Legal Adviser) (2323):
Mrs Helen Upton
First Secretary (2469): Mr Andrew Freeman
Second Secretary (2312): Mr Guy Pollard

Geneva Joint Management Office, UK Government Offices, see page 97

UNITED KINGDOM DELEGATION TO THE ORGANISATION FOR SECURITY AND COOPERATION IN EUROPE (OSCE) IN VIENNA

Vienna
Jaurèsgasse 12, 1030 Vienna
FTN Code – 8310 + extn number
Telephone: (00) (43) (1) 716130
71613 + extn number (for direct lines and voicemail)
Facsimile: (00) (43) (1) 71613 3900
Telegraphic address: UKDEL Vienna
e-mail: ukdel@netway.at
UKDEL@Britishembassy.at
Office Hours (GMT): Summer: Mon – Fri 07 30 – 17 00. Winter: Mon – Fri 07 30 – 17 00
Head of Delegation (Personal rank of Ambassador) (PA 3302): Mr Colin Munro, CMG
Counsellor and Deputy Head of Delegation (PA 3304): Ms Christine Ferguson
Counsellor (Arms Control) (PA 3318):
Mr Andrew Brentnall
Military Adviser (PA 3318):
Group Captain Peter Whitaker
First Secretary (Political) (3319):
Dr Amanda Tanfield
First Secretary (Political) (3318):
Mr Nicholas Chalmers
First Secretary (Arms Control) (PA 3336):
Mr Andrew Ford

Second Secretary (Political) (3306):
Mr Stuart Adam
First Secretary (Political) (3307):
Mr David Townsend
Third Secretary (3320): Mr Nicholas Robbins

Joint Management Office
First Secretary (Management) (2261):
Mr Eric Jones
Third Secretary (Management) (2260):
Miss Jan H Richardson

UNITED KINGDOM DELEGATION TO THE NORTH ATLANTIC TREATY ORGANISATION

Brussels
OTAN/NATO, Autoroute Bruxelles – Zaventem, Evere
1110 Brussels
Telephone: (00) (32) (2) 707 7211
Facsimile: (00) (32) (2) 707 7596
Airtech: (00) (32) (2) 707 7212
e-mail: ukdelnato@csi.com
Office Hours (GMT): 08 00 – 17 00
United Kingdom Permanent Representative on the North Atlantic Council (holds personal rank of Ambassador): Mr Peter F Ricketts, CMG
Minister, United Kingdom Deputy Permanent Representative: Mr John Kidd
United Kingdom Military Representative:
Air Marshal Rob A Wright, AFC, RAF
Deputy United Kingdom Military Representative/COS: Brigadier Nigel St. J Hall
Counsellor (Political): Mr Paul Arkwright
Counsellor (Defence): Mr Nigel Brind
Counsellor (Budget and Infrastructure):
Mr John Cunningham
First Secretary (Political): Mr Sam Selvadurai
First Secretary (European Defence):
Mr Paul V Devine
First Secretary (Defence Equipment):
Mr John Mattiussi
First Secretary (Nuclear Cooperation):
Ms Gill Atkinson
Staff Officer Plans and Policy:
Colonel Chris J Rose
First Secretary (Defence Plans and Policy):
Mr Graham Muir
Staff Officer (Operations):
Wing Commmander Bob D Jenkins, RAF
Staff Officer (Operations/Plans):
Lieutenant Colonel James Stuart
First Secretary (Infrastructure and Military Budget): Mr Richard Ladd-Jones
Staff Officer Intelligence:
Wing Commander Paul Edwards, RAF
Staff Officer (Resources and Arms Control):
Commander Nick Garland
First Secretary (Infrastructure and Military Budgets): Ms Helena Akiwumi
Second Secretary (Political): Mr Ernie Manley
Second Secretary (Political): Miss Susan Crombie
Second Secretary (Operations and Exercises):
Mrs Tanya Collingridge
Second Secretary (Management): Mrs Susan Pavis
Second Secretary: (Vacant)
Attaché (Defence): Mr Andrew Collingridge
Attaché (Defence): Mr Scott Gallacher
Attaché (Budget and Infrastructure):
Mr Nathaniel Wapshere
Staff Officer (CIS):
Wing Commander Rob Munday
Staff Officer (Cooperation):
Wing Commander Jim Squelch, RAF
Staff Officer (CEU Policy):
Wing Commander Tony Leggett

UNITED KINGDOM DELEGATION TO THE WESTERN EUROPEAN UNION

Brussels
c/o UK Permanent Representation to the EU, Avenue d'Auderghem 10
1040 Brussels
Telephone: (00) (32) (2) 287 8346
Facsimile: (00) (32) (2) 287 8396
United Kingdom Permanent Representative – (holds personal rank of Ambassador):
Mr Julian B King
Military Delegate:
Air Marshal R D Wright, AFC, RAF
Deputy UK Military Representative:
Commodore N J R Harland, RN
Deputy Permanent Representative – First Secretary (Pol/Mil Affairs): Ms Jennifer Anderson
First Secretary (Defence): Mr Sandy Johnston
Staff Officer EU (Ops/Plans):
Lieutenant Colonel Max Houghton
Staff Officer EU (Capabilities):
Commander Phil Stonor
Staff Officer EU (Policy):
Wing Commander Tony Leggett
Third Secretary (WEAG/WEAO):
Mr Scott Gallacher
Assistant Military Delegate:
Ms Alison MacLauchlan

Brussels Joint Management Office for the four Missions, see page 24

UNITED KINGDOM DELEGATION TO THE ORGANISATION FOR ECONOMIC CO-OPERATION AND DEVELOPMENT

Paris
140 avenue Victor Hugo, 75116 Paris
Telephone: (00) (33) 1 53 70 45 70
Facsimile: (00) (33) 1 53 70 45 86
e-mail: uk-del.oecd@wanadoo.fr
Website: www.fco.gov.uk/ukdeloecd
Office Hours (GMT): 08 30 – 17 00
United Kingdom Permanent Representative (holds personal rank of Ambassador):
Mr David E Lyscom
Deputy United Kingdom Permanent Representative and Counsellor (Institutional and Reform Issues):
Mr Richard Moon
Counsellor (Management), based in Embassy:
Mr Richard White
First Secretary (Energy, Environment and Budget):
Mr Craig Jones

First Secretary (Economic and Development): Mr David Bendor
First Secretary (Trade, Finance and Agriculture): Mr Jack McIver
First Secretary (Education, Employment, Social Affairs, Public Governance, Science, Technology and Industry, Regional Development): Mr Andrew McHallam

OFFICE OF THE UNITED KINGDOM PERMANENT REPRESENTATIVE TO THE EUROPEAN UNION

Brussels
Ave d'Auderghem 10, 1040 Brussels
Telephone: (00) (32) (2) 287 8211
Facsimile: (00) (32) (2) 287 8398 (2 lines)
Telex: 24312 (a/b 24312 UKEC BR B)
e-mail: ukrep@fco.gov.uk
Website: http://ukrep.fco.gov.uk
United Kingdom Permanent Representative: Sir John Grant, KCMG (holds personal rank of Ambassador)
Deputy UK Permanent Representative: Miss Anne Lambert
Political Security Committee Representative: Mr Julian B King
Counsellor (Political and Institutions): Mr Michael Aron
Counsellor (Agricultural): Mr David Barnes
Counsellor (External Relations): Dr Carolyn Browne
Counsellor (Justice and Home Affairs): Mr Jonathan Sweet
Counsellor (Industry): Mr Anthony Vinall
Counsellor (Economics and Finance): Mr Peter Curwen
Counsellor (Social Affairs, Environment, Regional Policy): Ms Shan Morgan
Counsellor (Legal Adviser): Mr Paul Berman
Counsellor (Development Policy): Mr Peter Landymore
First Secretary (External Relations): Mr Duncan Sparkes
First Secretary (External Relations): Mr Hamish Cowell
First Secretary (External Relations): Mr Geoff Cole
First Secretary (Development): Mr Phil Rose
First Secretary (Trade Policy): Mr Ian Vollbracht
First Secretary (External Relations): Miss Karen Betts
First Secretary (External Relations): (Vacant)
First Secretary (External Relations): Mr Sandy Johnston
First Secretary (External Relations): Mr Giles Portman
First Secretary (Agriculture and Food): Mr Roy Norton
First Secretary (Agriculture): Dr Katherine Riggs
First Secretary (Fisheries): Mr Gareth Baynham-Hughes
First Secretary (Commercial): Mrs Joyce Martin
First Secretary (Economic and Finance): Mr Edward Smith
First Secretary (Economic and Finance): Mr Gary Roberts
First Secretary (Budget): Mrs Fabia Jones
First Secretary (Taxation): Mr James Robertson
First Secretary (Transport): Mr Michael Rossell
First Secretary (Energy): Mr Ian Holt
First Secretary (Industry): Mr Chris Barton
First Secretary (Internal Markets): Mr Andrew van der Lem
First Secretary (Industry): Mr Benjamin Turner
First Secretary (Justice and Home Affairs): Mr Neil Bradley
First Secretary (Justice and Home Affairs): Miss Jane Ferrier
First Secretary (Justice and Home Affairs): Mr Paul McKell
First Secretary (Legal Section): Miss Hazel Cameron
First Secretary (Legal Section): Mr Michael Addison
First Secretary (Antici): Miss Caroline Wilson
First Secretary (European Parliament): Mrs Corin Robertson
First Secretary (Political): Mrs Fiona Bottomley
First Secretary (Political): Mr Matthew Taylor
First Secretary (Press): Mr Jonathan Allen
First Secretary (Environment): Mr Andrew Dalgleish
First Secretary (Environment): Mr Lindsay Croisdale-Appleby
First Secretary (Regional Policy): Mr Tim Figures
First Secretary (Social Affairs): Mr Marc Holland
First Secretary (Management): Mr Phil May
First Secretary (TMO): Mr Stephen Roseblade
Second Secretary (Agriculture and Fish): Mr Keith Morrison
Second Secretary (Agriculture): Ms Andrea Pearson
Second Secretary (Food and Veterinary): Mr Simon Stannard
Second Secretary (Commercial): Mr Paul Knott
Second Secretary (Budget): Ms Hannah Robinson
Second Secretary (Finance): Miss Rebecca Jones
Second Secretary (Customs): Miss Karen Parkes
Second Secretary (External Relations): Mr Stephen Hickey
Second Secretary (External Relations): Mr Damian Thwaites
Second Secretary (Trade Policy): Miss Harriet Rodger
Second Secretary (Pol/Mil): Ms Serra Tezisler
Second Secretary (Enlargement): Ms Sarah Cullum
Second Secretary (Transport): Ms Johanna Keech
Second Secretary (Industry): Mrs Lynne Vallance
Second Secretary (Industry): Miss Jennifer Young
Second Secretary (Consumer Affairs): Mr Nick Thompson
Second Secretary (Justice and Home Affairs): Mr Ben Llewellyn-Jones
Second Secretary (Justice and Home Affairs): Dr Rod McLean
Second Secretary (European Parliament): Mr Scott Furssedonn
Second Secretary (Political): Mr David Chitty
Second Secretary (Political): Ms Sarah Bell
Second Secretary (EU Staffing): Miss Hilary McFarland
Second Secretary (TMO): Mr Bob Bruton

Second Secretary (TMO): Mr Neil Sturgess
Second Secretary (Environment):
Mr Philip McMurray
Second Secretary (Health, Culture, Sport):
Mr Jonathan Orr
Second Secretary (Social Affairs): Mr Kevin Dench
Second Secretary (Youth, Education/Training):
Miss Jo Hawley

Strasbourg
(Office only open when the European Parliament is in session in Strasbourg)
Palais de l'Europe, Avenue de l'Europe
67000, Strasbourg
Telephone: (00) (333) 88 17 40 01
Facsimile: (00) (333) 88 35 41 30
First Secretary (European Parliament Team):
Miss Corin Robertson
Second Secretary (European Parliament Team):
Mr Scott Furssedonn

Brussels Joint Management Office for the four Missions, see page 24

UNITED KINGDOM DELEGATION TO THE COUNCIL OF EUROPE

Strasbourg
18 rue Gottfried, 67000-Strasbourg
FTN Code – 8337 + extn number
Telephone: (00) (333) (88) 35 00 78
Facsimile: (00) (333) (88) 61 83 25
United Kingdom Permanent Representative to Council of Europe (holds personal rank of Ambassador): Mr Stephen F Howarth
Deputy United Kingdom Permanent Representative: Ms Pamela Mitchison
Second Secretary: Miss Fern Horine
Third Secretary (Chancery/Management):
Mrs Louise Lassman

UNITED KINGDOM DELEGATION TO THE INTERNATIONAL MONETARY FUND AND INTERNATIONAL BANK FOR RECONSTRUCTION AND DEVELOPMENT

Washington
Room 11-120, International Monetary Fund,
700 19th Street, NW, Washington, DC 20431
Telephone: (00) (1) (202) 623 4562
Facsimile: (00) (1) (202) 623 4965
United Kingdom Executive Director of the International Monetary Fund and World Bank:–
e-mail: tscholar@imf.org: Mr T Scholar
Alternate Executive Director of the World Bank:–
e-mail: rstevenson@imf.org: Ms R Stevenson
Alternate Executive Director of the International Monetary Fund: –
e-mail: mbrooke@imf.org: Mr M Brooke
Assistant (IMF/IBRD): –
e-mail njoicey@imf.org: Mr N Joicey
Assistant (IMF/IBRD): –
e-mail: bkelmanson@imf.org: Mr B Kelmanson
Assistant (IMF/IBRD): –
e-mail: bmellor@imf.org: Mr B Mellor
Assistant (IMF/IBRD): –
e-mail: dmerotto@imf.org: Mr D Merotto
Assistant (IMF/IBRD): –
e-mail: astuart@imf.org: Ms A Stuart
Assistant (IMF/IBRD): –
e-mail: dtaylor@imf.org: Mr D Taylor

UNITED NATIONS HUMAN SETTLEMENTS PROGRAMME (HABITAT)

Nairobi
United Kingdom Permanent Representative:
Mr Adam Wood
Alternate Permanent Representative:
Mr Ray W Kyles
Deputy Permanent Representative: Mr John Virgoe

UNITED NATIONS ENVIRONMENT PROGRAMME

Nairobi
United Kingdom Permanent Representative:
Mr Adam Wood
Alternate Permanent Representative:
Mr Ray W Kyles
Deputy Permanent Representative: Mr John Virgoe

UNITED KINGDOM REPRESENTATION AT THE AFRICAN DEVELOPMENT BANK

Tunis
Office of the Executive Director
African Development Bank – EPI
B.P. 323, 1002 Tunis-Belvédère, Tunisia
Telephone: (00) (216) 71 10 28 18
Facsimile: (00) (216) 71 83 34 14
Executive Director: Mr Richard Dewdney
Alternate Executive Director: Mr Marc Verschuur
Adviser to the Executive Director:
Ms Birgit Gerhardus
Assistant to the Executive Director:
Mr Diogo Gomes de Araujo

UNITED KINGDOM REPRESENTATION AT THE ASIAN DEVELOPMENT BANK

Manila
6 ADB Avenue, Mandaluyong City, Manila
Postal address: PO Box 789, 0980 Manila
Telephone: (00) (632) 632 6079
Facsimile: (00) (632) 636 2056
Director's Adviser: Mr David Taylor

UNITED KINGDOM REPRESENTATION AT THE INTER-AMERICAN DEVELOPMENT BANK

Washington
1300 New York Avenue, N W Washington, DC 20577
Telephone: (00) (1) (202) 623 1059/1058/1773/1980
Facsimile: (00) (1) (202) 623 3610
Cable address: Intambanc, Washington, DC
Telex numbers: 64141, 44240
Executive Director: Mr Y Ueda (Japanese)
Alternate Executive Director: Mr Stewart Mills (British)
Senior Counsellor: Mr Kazuki Watanabe (Japanese)

Counsellor: Mr Nobuyuki Otsuka (Japanese)

UNITED KINGDOM PERMANENT REPRESENTATION TO THE UNITED NATIONS AGENCIES FOR FOOD AND AGRICULTURE IN ROME

Rome
Via di Monserrato, 48/1. 00186 Rome
Telephone: (00) (39) 06 6840 0901/2/3/4
Facsimile: (00) (39) 06 6840 0920
United Kingdom Permanent Representative (holds personal rank of Ambassador): Mr Matthew Wyatt
Deputy Permanent Representative to WFP: Mr Neil Briscoe
First Secretary: Mr Victor Heard
Information Manager: Ms Fiona Pryce
Office *Manager:* Ms Nicolette Ciorba

UNITED KINGDOM REPRESENTATIVE ON THE COUNCIL OF THE INTERNATIONAL CIVIL AVIATION ORGANISATION

Montreal
Suite 1415, 999 University Street
Montreal, Quebec
H3C 5J9
Telephone: (00) (514) 954 8302/3
Direct Line – see individual officers
Facsimile: (00) (514) 954 8001
Airtech: (00) (1) (514) 866 4867
(Located in British Consulate-General Offices)
e-mail: ndenton@icao.int
asayce@icao.int
Office Hours (GMT) 14 00 – 22 00
United Kingdom Representative (00) (1) (514) 954 8326: Mr Nicholas Denton
Deputy United Kingdom Representative (00) (1) (514) 954 8327: Mr Adrian G Sayce

ORGANISATION FOR THE PROHIBITION OF CHEMICAL WEAPONS

The Hague
United Kingdom Permanent Representative: Mr Lyn Parker
First Secretary: Mr D G Cole
First Secretary: Mr M E Rack

GOVERNORS & COMMANDERS-IN-CHIEF ETC. OF THE UK OVERSEAS TERRITORIES

Anguilla
Government House
Telephone: (00) (1) (264) 497 2621/2622 (Governor/EA)
497 3312/3313 (Deputy Governor)
497 3315 (Staff Officer)
Tel/Fax: 497 2292 (Residence)
Facsimile: (00) (1) (264) 497 3314 (Unclassified)
497 3151 (Airtech)
e-mail: governorsoffice@gov.ai
Office Hours (GMT): 12 00 – 16 00, 17 00 – 20 00
Governor: Mr Alan Huckle
Deputy Governor: Mr Mark Capes
Staff Officer: Mr Joe Legg
Defence Adviser (resides at Bridgetown): Captain Steve G Wilson, RN
Executive Assistant to the Governor: Ms Angela Finn

Immigration/Visas
Telephone: (00) (1) (264) 497 3994/2451
Facsimile: (00) (1) (264) 497 0310

Passport Office
Telephone: (00) (1) (264) 497 7394
Facsimile: (00) (1) (264) 497 2751

Police
Telephone: (00) (1) (264) 497 2333
Facsimile: (00) (1) (264) 497 3746

Bermuda
Government House, Hamilton
Telephone: (00) (1) (441) 292 3600
Deputy Governor's Office: (00) (1) (441) 292 2587
Facsimile: (00) (1) (441) 295 3823
e-mail Address: depgov@ibl.bm
Office Hours (GMT): Summer: 11 45 – 16 00 and 17 15 – 20 00
Winter: 12 45 – 17 00 and 18 15 – 21 00
Governor (e-mail: governor@gov.bm): Sir John Vereker, KCB
Deputy Governor (e-mail: deputygovernor@gov.bm): Mr Nick Carter
Executive Officer (e-mail: registrar@gov.bm): Mrs Charlotte Rickward

British Antarctic Territory
Foreign and Commonwealth Office
Overseas Territories Department
Telephone: 020 7008 2616
Commissioner: Mr Tony Crombie, OBE (non-resident)
Administrator: Dr M G Richardson (non-resident)

British Indian Ocean Territory
Foreign and Commonwealth Office
Overseas Territories Department
Telephone: 020 7008 2890
Commissioner: Mr Tony Crombie, OBE (non-resident)
Administrator: Mr Charles A Hamilton (non-resident)

Diego Garcia, c/o BFPO Ships
Facsimile: (00) 246 370 3943
Commissioner's Representative: Commander Chris Davies, RN

British Virgin Islands
Government House
Road Town, Tortola
Telephone: (00) (1) (284) 494 2345/70 Switchboard
468 3508 PA
3503 Head of Governor's Office
3507 Staff Officer
Facsimile: 4490
Airtech: (00) (1) (284) 494 5582
e-mail: bvigovernor@gov.vg
Website: http://www.bvi.gov.vg
Office Hours (GMT): 12 30 – 20 30
Governor: Mr Tom Macan
Head of Governor's Office: Mr Duncan Norman
Staff Officer: Mr Stuart Smith

Defence Adviser (resides at Bridgetown):
Captain Steve G Wilson, RN
Personal Assistant: Mrs Claire Means

Office of the Deputy Governor
Government Administration Building
Road Town, Tortola
Telephone: (00) (1) (284) 468 0346
Facsimile: (00) (1) (284) 494 6481
Acting Deputy Governor: Mrs Dancia Penn, OBE, QC

Royal Virgin Islands Police Force
Telephone: (00) (1) (284) 494 3822 (24 hrs)
Facsimile: (00) (1) (284) 494 6141

Immigration Department
Telephone: (00) (1) (284) 494 3471
Facsimile: (00) (1) (284) 494 4399

BVI Passport Office
Telephone: (00) (1) (284) 468 3701 extn 3035/3036
Facsimile: (00) (1) (284) 494 4435

Cayman Islands
4th Floor, Government Administration Building,
Elgin Avenue
George Town, Grand Cayman,
Telephone: (00) (1) (345) 949 7900 Switchboard
5776 PA direct
0980 Staff Officer
0479 Social Secretary
244 2431 AMO/Accountant/Archivist
Facsimile: (00) (1) (345) 945 4131 Governor's Office
Airtech: 949 6556
945 5537 Social Secretary
e-mail: staffoff@candw.ky
Office Hours (GMT): 13 30-18 00 and
19 00 – 22 00
Governor: Mr Stuart Jack, CVO
Chief Secretary: Mr George McCarthy
Deputy Chief Secretary: Mr Donnie Ebanks, MBE
Defence Adviser (Resides at Kingston):
Colonel Charles G Le Brun
Second Secretary and Staff Officer to the Governor: Ms Kate Joad
PA to the Governor: Mrs Alison Bach
AMO/Accountant/Archivist: Mrs Melenie Mylrea
Social Secretary: Mrs Jacqueline Hennings

Government Information Services
Telephone: (00) (1) (345) 949 8092
Facsimile: (00) (1) (345) 949 5936/946 0664
Immigration Department
Telephone: (00) (1) (345) 949 8344
Facsimile: 949 8486

Cayman Islands Passport Office
Telephone: (00) (1) (345) 244 2024
Facsimile: (00) (1) (345) 945 4355

Falkland Islands
Government House, Stanley,
Telephone: (00) (500) 27433 Office
22210 Residence
Facsimile: (00) (500) 27434
e-mail: gov.house@horizon.co.fk
firstname.lastname@fco.gov.uk
Office Hours (GMT): Winter: 11 00-15 15 and
16 30-19 30
Summer: 12 00-16 15 and 17 30-20 30
Governor: Mr Howard J S Pearce, CVO
(Mr Alan E Huckle w.e.f Spring 06)
First Secretary: Ms Harriet Hall
PA/Governor: Miss Annette G Moore
MO/Archivist: Mr Rob Kempsell

South Georgia and the South Sandwich Islands
Government House, Stanley
Falkland Islands
Telephone: (00) (500) 27433 Office
22210 Residence
Facsimile: (00) (500) 27434
e-mail: gov.house@horizon.co.fk
OfficeHours (GMT): Winter 11 00 – 15 15 and 16 30 – 19 30
Summer 12 00 – 16 15 and 17 30 – 20 30
Commissioner (Resides in Falkland Islands):
Mr Howard J S Pearce, CVO
(Mr Alan E Huckle w.e.f Spring 06)
Assistant Commissioner and Director of Fisheries (Resides in Falkland Islands): Ms Harriet Hall

Gibraltar
Office of the Governor
The Convent, Main Street
Telephone: (00) (350) 45440 (Switchboard)
47828 (PA to the Governor)
Facsimile: (00) (350) 47823 (Unclassified)
49487 (Management Section)
47830 (Airtech)
e-mail: enquiry.gibraltar@fco.gov.uk
Office Hours (GMT) 08 00 – 16 15 (Winter);
07 30 – 13 30 (Summer)
Governor and Commander-in-Chief:
Sir Francis N Richards, KCMG, CVO
Deputy Governor: Mr Philip Barton, OBE
Assistant *Deputy Governor:* Mr Chris Shute
Second Secretary (Management):
Mr David G Harries, OBE
Second Secretary (EU Affairs): Mr Martin Fenner
Third Secretary (Convent Liaison Officer):
Miss Jo Bowyer

Consular/Visa inquiries:
Civil Status and Registration Office
Telephone: (00) (350) 51727/59839/59840
Facsimile: (00) (350) 42706

Commercial inquiries:
Department of Trade and Industry:
Telephone: (00) (350) 52052
Facsimile: (00) (350) 71406

Montserrat
Farara Plaza
Brades
Telephone: (00) (1) (664) 491 2688/9 Office
6124 Governor's Residence
Facsimile: (00) (1) (664) 491 8867/9114
Airtech: 4553
e-mail: firstname.lastname@fco.gov.uk
Website: www.montserrat-newsletter.com
Office Hours (GMT): 12 00 – 16 00 and
17 00 – 20 00
Governor: Mrs Deborah E V Barnes-Jones

Head of Governor's Office: Mr Russ Jarvis
Personal Assistant to the Governor:
Mr Richard Mallion
Defence Adviser (resides at Bridgetown):
Captain Steve G Wilson, RN
Staff Officer: Mr David Sharp

Department for International Development (DFID) Montserrat
Telephone: (00) (1) (664) 491 5777, 5891, 6066
Facsimile: (00) (1) (664) 491 5885, 8777
e-mail: l-harmerl@dfid.gov.uk
i-young@dfid.gov.uk
Manager for DFID(M): Ms Liz Harmer
Engineering Sector Manager: Mr Ian Young

Pitcairn Henderson Ducie and Oeno Islands
British High Commission,
Wellington, New Zealand
Governor (non-resident): Mr Richard T Fell, CVO
Deputy Governor: Mr Matthew Forbes

Pitcairn Island
Telephone: (001) 413 0583 or (00872) 762 941 159
Facsimile: (001) 413 0584 0r (00872) 762 941 161
e-mail: govrep@memail.co.nz
Governor's Representative on Pitcairn:
Mr Richard Dewell

Pitcairn Logistics Team
Level 17 IAG House
151 Queen Street
Private Bag 92014, Auckland
Telephone: (00) (64) (9) 379 5933/5944
e-mail: pitcairnlogistics@xtra.co.nz
Office Hours (GMT): 20 45 – 05 00
Head of Team: Miss Jenny Lock
Deputy Head of Team: Mrs Rosemarie Bailey
Pitcairn Islands Administration, Private Box 105696
Auckland, New Zealand
Telephone: (00) (64) (9) 366 0186
e-mail: pitcairn@iconz.co.nz
Website: http://www.government.pn
Commissioner (non resident):
Mr Leslie Jaques, OBE

St Helena
Governor's Office
The Castle, Jamestown
Telephone: (00) (290) 2555 Office
4444 Residence
Facsimile: (00) (290) 2598 Office
4418 Residence
Airtech: 2476
e-mail: OCS@helanta.sh
joany@sainthelena.gov.sh
Office Hours (GMT): Mon-Fri: 08 30 – 12 30 and 13 00 – 16 00
Governor and Commander-in Chief:
Mr Michael Clancy
Staff Officer: Mr Amias Moores

Chief Secretary's Office
The Castle, Jamestown
Telephone: (00) (290) 4552 Residence
2525 Office
Facsimile: (00) (290) 2598 Office
e-mail: OCS@helanta.sh
sandrab@sainthelena.gov.sh
Office Hours (GMT): Mon-Fri: 08 30 – 12 30 and 13 00 – 16 00
Chief Secretary: Mr John Styles

Ascension
The Administrator's Office
Georgetown, ASCN IZZ
Telephone: (00) 247 6311 Office
4525 Home
Facsimile: (00) 247 6152
Airtech: (00) 247 6892
e-mail: administrator@atlantis.co.ac
Website: http://www.ascension-island.gov.ac
Office Hours (GMT): Mon-Fri: 08 30 – 12 30 and 13 30 – 16 30
Governor and Commander-in-Chief (Resides in St Helena): Mr Michael Clancy
Administrator: Mr Andrew Kettlewell

Tristan da Cunha
The Administrator's Office
Edinburgh of the Seven Seas
Telephone: (00) (871) 682 087 155
763 421 817
Facsimile: (00) (871) 682 087 158
600 245 563
e-mail: hmg@cunha.demon.co.uk
Office Hours (GMT): Mon-Fri: 08 30 – 12 30 and 13 00 – 16 30
Governor and Commander-in-Chief (Resides in St Helena): Mr Michael Clancy
Administrator: Mr Mike Hentley

Turks and Caicos Islands
Waterloo, Government House
Grand Turk
Telephone: (00) (1) (649) 946 2308/9
Facsimile: (00) (1) (649) 946 2903
Airtech: (00) (1) (649) 946 2766
e-mail: govhouse@tciway.tc
Governor: Richard D Tauwhare, MVO
First Secretary: Mr David L Brett
Staff Officer: Mr Ian Angus
Personal Assistant: Ms Michelle Ridley

Chief Secretary's Office
Government Secretariat, Grand Turk
Telephone: (00) (1) (649) 946 2910
Facsimile: (00) (1) (649) 946 2886
Chief Secretary: Mrs C Astwood, OBE
Defence Adviser (resides at Kingston):
Colonel C G Le Brun
Office Hours (GMT): Winter: Mon-Thu: 13 00 – 17 30 and 19 00 – 21 30. Fri: 13 00 – 17 30 and 19 00 – 21 00
Summer: Mon-Thu: 12 00 – 16 30 and 18 00 – 20 30. Fri: 12 00 – 16 30 and 18 00 – 20 00

SMALL POSTS

SOVEREIGN
Abidjan
Algiers
Almaty
Antananarivo
Ashgabat
Asunción
Baku
Banjul
Belmopan
Bratislava
Castries
Dakar
Dili
Freetown
Gaborone
Georgetown, Guyana
Guatemala City
Holy See
Honiara
Kigali
Kingstown, St Vincent
Kinshasa
La Paz
Luxembourg
Ljubljana
Maseru
Mbabane
Minsk
Montevideo
Nassau
Nuku'alofa
Panama City
Phnom Penh
Port Moresby
Port of Spain
Port-Vila
Quito
Rangoon
Reykjavik
Riga
St George's, Grenada
San José
Santo Domingo
Skopje
Strasbourg
Suva
Tallinn
Tashkent
Tbilisi
Tirana
Ulaanbaatar
Victoria
Vilnius
Windhoek
Yerevan

SUBORDINATE
Al Khobar
Alexandria
Amsterdam
Atlanta
Auckland
Barcelona
Bilbao
Bordeaux
Boston
Brisbane
Cape Town
Casablanca
Chiang Mai
Chicago
Dallas
Denver
Durban
Frankfurt
Hamburg
Ho Chi Minh City
Houston
Kolkata
Kuching
Lille
Los Angeles
Lyon
Marseille
Melbourne
Miami
Milan
Montreal
Munich
Oporto
Palma
Perth
San Francisco
Seattle
Stuttgart
Sydney
Tarawa
Toronto
Vancouver
Yekaterinburg
Zurich

OVERSEAS TERRITORY
Anguilla
Georgetown, Ascension
Gibraltar
Grand Cayman, Cayman Islands
Grand Turk, Turks and Caicos Islands
Hamilton, Bermuda
Plymouth, Montserrat
Stanley, Falkland Islands
Jamestown, St Helena
Tortola, British Virgin Islands
Tristan Da Cunha

ANNEX: NON GOVERNMENTAL TRADE OFFICES

TAIWAN

Her Majesty' s Government do not recognise Taiwan as a sovereign state and consequently have no diplomatic relations with it. However, there are non- governmental trade and cultural offices at the following addresses:

Taipei
British Trade and Cultural Office
8-10th Floor Fu Key Building
99 Jen Ai Road, Section 2,Taipei 100
FTN Code – 8308 + FTN extn number
Telephone: (00) (886) (2) 2192 7000
2192 + Tel extn number (Direct Line)
Facsimile: (00) (886) (2) 2394 8673 (Commercial)
2397 3559 (Inward Investment)
2393 1985 (Visa Handling Unit)
2397 3609 (Management)
Airtech: 2322 3265
e-mail: firstname.lastname@fco.gov.uk
Internet Website: www.btco.org.tw
Office Hours (GMT): 01 00 – 04 30 and 05 30 – 09 00
Director General (Tel extn 7009 FTN extn 2009): Mr Michael Reilly
Deputy Director General (Tel extn 7001 FTN extn 2001): Mr Charles Garrett
Head of Commercial Section (Tel extn 7006 FTN extn 2006): Mr Mark Robinson
Head of Inward Investment Section (Tel extn 7066 FTN extn 2066): Mr David Percival
Head of Political and Economic Section (Tel extn 7055 FTN extn 2055): Mr Den Moore
Head of Management Section (Tel extn 7002 FTN extn 2002): Mr David Walters, MVO
Head of Visa Handling Unit/BASS (Tel extn 7040 FTN extn 2040): Mr Stephen Taylor
Head of Science and Technology Section (Tel extn 7031 FTN extn 2031): Mr Chong-Loon Tai
Head of Press and Public Affairs Team (Tel extn 7015 FTN extn 2015): Ms Maggie Yeh

Education and Cultural Section
British Council
2nd Floor, No. 106 Hsin-yi Road
Section 5, Taipei 110
Telephone: (00) (886) (2) 8722 1000
Facsimile: (00) (886) (2) 8786 0985
e-mail: firstname.lastname@britishcouncil.org.tw
Website: www.britishcouncil.org.tw
British Council Director (1007): Mr Gordon Slaven

Kaohsiung
British Trade and Cultural Office (Kaohsiung Section)
Unit D, 7th Floor, Fu Bon Commercial Building
95 Ming-Tsu 2nd Road, Kaohsiung 800
Telephone: (00) (886) 7238 1034/5
Facsimile: (00) (886) 7238 1032
Director Kaohsiung Office: Ms Anne Lai

Education and Cultural Section
Unit D, 7th Floor, Fu Bon Commercial Building
95 Ming-Tsu 2nd Road, Kaohsiung 800
Telephone: (00) (886) 7235 1715
Facsimile: (00) (886) 7238 0411
Branch Manager: Ms Fay Chen

Guide to places and countries
Embassies, High Commissions, Deputy High Commissions and Consular Posts

Note: There is no HMG representation in Bhutan.
It is therefore omitted from the List.

A

Aabenraa, Denmark
Aalborg, Denmark
Aarhus, Denmark
Abidjan, Ivory Coast
Abuja, Nigeria
Abu Dhabi, United Arab Emirates
Acapulco, Mexico
Accra, Ghana
Addis Ababa, Ethiopia
Adelaide, Australia
Aden, Yemen
Agadir, Morocco
Ahmedabad, India
Akureyri, Iceland
Aland Island, Finland
Aleppo, Syria
Ålesund, Norway
Alexandria, Egypt
Algiers, Algeria
Alicante, Spain
Al Khobar, Saudi Arabia
Almaty, Kazakhstan
Amiens, France
Amman, Jordan
Amsterdam, Netherlands
Anchorage, AK, United States
Andorra, Principality of Andorra
Angeles City, Philippines
Anguilla, Anguilla, See Part III
Ankara, Turkey
Antalya, Turkey
Antananarivo, Madagascar
Antwerp, Belgium
Apia, Samoa
Arequipa, Peru
Arusha, Tanzania
Ascension, St Helena, See Part III
Ashgabat, Turkmenistan
Asmara, Eritrea
Asunción, Paraguay
Athens, Greece
Atlanta, GA, United States
Auckland, New Zealand
Azores, Portugal

B

Baghdad, Iraq
Bahrain, Bahrain
Baku, Azerbaijan
Bali, Indonesia
Bamako, Mali
Bandar Seri Begawan, Brunei
Bangalore, India
Bangkok, Thailand
Bangui, Central African Republic
Banja Luka, Bosnia and Herzegovina
Banjul, The Gambia
Barcelona, Spain
Bari, Italy
Basel, Switzerland
Basra, Iraq
Basseterre, St Kitts and Nevis
Beijing, China
Beira, Mozambique
Beirut, Lebanon
Belém, Brazil
Belgrade, Serbia and Montenegro
Belmopan, Belize
Belo Horizonte, Brazil
Benidorm, Spain
Bergen, Norway
Berlin, Germany
Berne, Switzerland
Biarritz, France
Bilbao, Spain
Bishkek, Kyrgyzstan
Bissau, Guinea Bissau
Bitola, Macedonia
Bodrum, Turkey
Bogotá, Colombia
Bordeaux, France
Boston, MA, United States
Boulogne-sur-Mer, France
Brasilia, Brazil
Bratislava, Slovakia
Brazzaville, Congo
Bregenz, Austria
Bremen, Germany
Bridgetown, Barbados
Brisbane, Australia
Brussels, Belgium
Bucharest, Romania
Budapest, Hungary
Buenos Aires, Argentina
Bujumbura, Burundi
Bursa, Turkey

C

Cadiz, Spain
Cagliari, Italy
Cahors, France
Cairo, Egypt
Calais, France
Calgary, Canada
Cali, Colombia
Canberra, Australia
Cancun, Mexico
Cape Town, South Africa
Caracas, Venezuela
Casablanca, Morocco
Castries, St Lucia
Catania, Italy
Cayenne, French Guiana, France
Cebu, Philippines
Charlotte, NC, United States
Chennai, India
Cherbourg, France
Chiang Mai, Thailand
Chicago, IL, United States
Chisinau, Moldova
Chongqing, China
Christchurch, New Zealand
Ciudad Juárez, Mexico
Clermont Ferrand, France
Colombo, Sri Lanka
Conakry, Guinea
Copenhagen, Denmark
Córdoba, Argentina
Corfu, Greece
Cotonou, Benin
Curitiba, Brazil
Cusco, Peru

D

Dakar, Senegal
Dallas, TX, United States
Damascus, Syria
Dar es Salaam, Tanzania
Denia, Spain
Denver, CO, United States
Dili, East Timor
Dhaka, Bangladesh
Djibouti, Djibouti
Doha, Qatar
Dubai, United Arab Emirates
Dublin, Ireland
Dubrovnik, Croatia
Dunkirk, France
Dushanbe, Tajikistan
Durban, South Africa
Düsseldorf, Germany

E

Edinburgh of the Seven Seas, Tristan da Cunha, St Helena, See Part III
Eilat, Israel
Esbjerg, Denmark

F

Faroe Islands, Denmark
Florence, Italy
Fort de France, Martinique, France
Fortaleza, Brazil
Frankfurt, Germany
Fredericia, Denmark
Freetown, Sierra Leone

French Guiana, France
Funafuti, Tuvalu
Funchal, Madeira

G

Gaborone, Botswana
Galápagos, Ecuador
Gaza (listed under Jerusalem)
Gdansk, Poland
Geneva, Switzerland
Genoa, Italy
Georgetown, Ascension
Georgetown, Guyana
Ghent, Belgium
Gibraltar, See Part III
Gothenburg, Sweden
Grand Canary, Spain
Grand Cayman, Cayman Islands, See Part III
Grand Turk, Turks and Caicos, See Part III
Graz, Austria
Guadalajara, Mexico
Guadeloupe, France
Guangzhou, China
Guatemala City, Guatemala
Guayaquil, Ecuador

H

Halifax, Canada
Hamburg, Germany
Hamilton, Bermuda, See Part III
Hanoi, Vietnam
Hanover, Germany
Harare, Zimbabwe
Havana, Cuba
Helsinki, Finland
Heraklion, Crete, Greece
Herning, Denmark
Ho Chi Minh City, Vietnam
Hobart, Tasmania, Australia
Hodeidah, Yemen
Holy See
Hong Kong, China
Honiara, Solomon Islands
Houston, TX, United States
Hyderabad, India

I

Ibadan, Nigeria
Ibiza, Spain
Innsbruck, Austria
Iquitos, Peru
Islamabad, Pakistan
Istanbul, Turkey
Izmir, Turkey

J

Jakarta, Indonesia
Jamestown, St Helena
Jeddah, Saudi Arabia
Jerusalem
Johannesburg, South Africa
Johor Bahru, Malaysia
Jyväskylä, Finland

K

Kabul, Afghanistan
Kaduna, Nigeria
Kampala, Uganda
Kano, Nigeria
Kansas City, KS, United States
Kaohsiung, Taiwan
Karachi, Pakistan
Kathmandu, Nepal
Katowice, Poland
Khartoum, Sudan
Kiel, Germany
Kiev, Ukraine
Kigali, Rwanda
Kingston, Jamaica
Kingstown, St Vincent and the Grenadines
Kinshasa, Congo (Democratic Republic)
Kirkuk, Iraq
Kolkata, India
Kos, Greece
Kosovo, Serbia and Montenegro
Kota Kinabalu, Malaysia
Kotka, Finland
Kraków, Poland
Kristiansand, Norway
Kuala Lumpur, Malaysia
Kuching, Malaysia
Kuopio, Finland
Kuwait, Kuwait

L

Lagos, Nigeria
Lahore, Pakistan
La Paz, Bolivia
La Réunion, France
La Rochelle, France
Las Palmas, Grand Canary, Spain
Lattakia, Syria
Le Havre, France
Leipzig, Germany
Libreville, Gabon
Liège, Belgium
Lille, France
Lilongwe, Malawi
Lima, Peru
Lisbon Portugal
Ljubljana, Slovenia
Lomé, Togo
Lorient, France
Los Angeles, CA, United States
Luanda, Angola
Lublin, Poland
Lugano, Switzerland
Lusaka, Zambia
Luxembourg, Luxembourg
Luxor, Egypt
Lyon, France

M

Macao, China
Madeira, Portugal
Madrid, Spain
Majuro, Marshall Islands
Malabo, Equatorial Guinea
Málaga, Spain
Malamo, Sweden
Malé, Maldives
Malindi, Kenya
Managua, Nicaragua
Manáus, Brazil
Manila, Philippines
Maputo, Mozambique
Maracaibo, Venezuela
Margarita, Venezuela
Mariehamn, Aland Islands, Finland
Marmaris, Turkey
Marrakech, Morocco
Marseille, France
Martinique, France
Maseru, Lesotho
Mbabane, Swaziland
Medan, Indonesia
Medellin, Colombia
Melbourne, Australia
Mendoza, Argentina
Menorca, Spain
Mérida, Mexico
Mérida, Venezuela
Minneapolis, MN, United States
Mexico City, Mexico
Miami, FL, United States
Milan, Italy
Minsk, Belarus
Miri, Malaysia
Mogadishu, Somalia
Mombasa, Kenya
Monaco, Monaco
Monrovia, Liberia
Montego Bay, Jamaica
Monterrey, Mexico
Montevideo, Uruguay
Montpellier, France
Montreal, Canada
Montreux, Switzerland
Moroni, Comoros
Moscow, Russia
Mount Lebanon, Lebanon
Mumbai, India
Munich, Germany
Muri Beach, Cook Islands
Muscat, Oman

N

Nagoya, Japan
Nairobi, Kenya
Nantes, France
Naples, Italy
Nashville, TN, United States
Nassau, The Bahamas
Nauru
Ndjamena, Chad
New Caledonia, France
New Delhi, India

New Orleans, LA, United States
New York, NY, United States
Niamey, Niger
Nice, France
Nicosia, Cyprus
Nouakchott, Mauritania
Novorossiysk, Russia
Nuku'alofa, Tonga
Nuremburg, Germany

O

Oaxaca, Mexico
Odense, Denmark
Olongapo, Philippines
Olveston, Monserrat, See Part III
Oporto, Portugal
Orlando, FL, United States
Osaka, Japan
Oslo, Norway
Ottawa, Canada
Ouagadougou, Burkina
Oulu, Finland

P

Palermo, Italy
Palma, Spain
Panama City, Panama
Papeete, French Polynesia, France
Paramaribo, Surinam
Paris, France
Patras, Greece
Penang, Malaysia
Périgueux, France
Perth, Australia
Philadelphia, PA, United States
Philipsburg, St Maarten, Netherlands Antilles
Phoenix, AZ, United States
Phnom Penh, Cambodia
Pittsburgh, PA, United States
Podgorica, Serbia and Montenegro
Pohnpei, Micronesia
Pointe-à-Pitre, Guadeloupe
Poitiers, France
Pori, Finland
Port-au-Prince, Haiti
Port Elizabeth, South Africa
Port Harcourt, Nigeria
Portimão, Portugal
Portland, OR, United States
Port Louis, Mauritius
Port Moresby, Papua New Guinea
Port of Spain, Trinidad and Tobago
Port Vila, Vanuatu
Porto Alegre, Brazil
Poznan, Poland
Prague, Czech Republic
Praia, Cape Verde
Pretoria, South Africa
Pristina, Kosovo, Serbia and Montenegro
Puerto Plata, Dominican Republic
Puerto Rico, United States
Punta Arenas, Chile
Pusan, Korea (South)
Pyongyang, Korea (North)

Q

Quebec City, Canada
Quito, Ecuador

R

Rabat, Morocco
Rangoon, Burma
Recife, Brazil
Reykjavik, Iceland
Rhodes, Greece
Ribeira Grande, Azores, Portugal
Riga, Latvia
Rio de Janeiro, Brazil
Rio Grande, Brazil
Riyadh, Saudi Arabia
Rodrigues, Mauritius
Rome, Italy
Roseau, Dominica
Rovaniemi, Finland

S

St George's, Grenada
St John's, Antigua and Barbuda
St John's, Canada
St Louis, MO, United States
St Malo-Dinard, France
St Petersburg, Russia
Salt Lake City, UT, United States
Salvador, Brazil
Salzburg, Austria
Sanaa, Yemen
San Cristobal, Venezuela
San Diego, CA, United States
San Francisco, CA, United States
San Jose, CA, United States
San José, Costa Rica
San Marino
San Pedro Sula, Honduras
San Salvador, El Salvador
Santa Cruz de Tenerife, Canary Islands, Spain
Santa Fe, Argentina
Santiago, Chile
Santo Domingo, Dominican Republic
Santos, Brazil
São Paulo, Brazil
São Tomé, São Tomé and Principe
Sao Vincente, Cape Verde
Sarajevo, Bosnia and Herzegovina
Saumur, France
Seattle, WA, United States
Seoul, Korea (South)
Seville, Spain
Sfax, Tunisia
Shanghai, China
Singapore
Skopje, Macedonia
Sofia, Bulgaria
Split, Croatia
Stanley, Falkland Islands, See Part III
Stavanger, Norway
Stockholm, Sweden
Stuttgart, Germany
Suez, Egypt
Sundsvall, Sweden
Surabaya, Indonesia
Suva, Fiji
Sydney, Australia
Syros, Greece
Szczecin, Poland

T

Taipei, Taiwan
Tallinn, Estonia
Tampere (Tammerfors), Finland
Tangier, Morocco
Tarawa, Kiribati
Tashkent, Uzbekistan
Tasmania, Australia
Tbilisi, Georgia
Tegucigalpa, Honduras
Tehran, Iran
Tel Aviv, Israel
The Hague, Netherlands
Thessaloniki, Greece
Tijuana, Mexico
Tirana, Albania
Toamasina, Madagascar
Tokyo, Japan
Toronto, Canada
Tórshavn, Faroe Islands, Denmark
Tortola, British Virgin Islands, See Part III
Toulouse, France
Tours, France
Trieste, Italy
Tripoli, Lebanon
Tripoli, Libya
Tromso, Norway
Trondheim, Norway
Trujillo, Peru
Tunis, Tunisia
Turin, Italy
Turku, Finland

U

Ulaanbaatar, Mongolia

V

Vaasa (Vasa), Finland
Varna, Bulgaria

Vaduz, Liechtenstein
Valais, Switzerland
Valencia, Spain
Valencia, Venezuela
Valletta, Malta
Valparaíso, Chile
Vancouver, Canada
Venice, Italy
Veracruz, Mexico
Victoria, Seychelles
Vienna, Austria
Vientiane, Laos
Vigo, Spain
Vilnius, Lithuania
Vladivostok, Russia

W

Warri, Nigeria
Warsaw, Poland
Washington, DC, United States
Watamu, Kenya
Wellington, New Zealand
Willemstad, Curacao Netherlands Antilles, Netherlands
Windhoek, Namibia
Winnipeg, Canada
Wroclaw, Poland

Y

Yaoundé, Cameroon
Yekaterinburg, Russia
Yerevan, Armenia

Z

Zagreb, Croatia
Zakynthos, Greece
Zanzibar, Tanzania
Zurich, Switzerland

Part III

Chronological Lists from 1985 onwards of Secretaries of State, Ministers of State, Permanent Under-Secretaries of State, British Ambassadors etc., High Commissioners, Permanent Representatives to International Organizations and Governors and Commanders-in-chief of Dependent territories

Reference should be made to the Foreign Office and Commonwealth Relations Office Lists of 1965, to the Colonial Office List of 1966 and to the Diplomatic Service List 2005 and earlier Lists for previous lists of officers holding these appointments.

Part III: Chronological Lists

The Foreign and Commonwealth Office was formed in October 1968 by the merger of the former Foreign Office and the Commonwealth Office

SECRETARIES OF STATE FOR FOREIGN AND COMMONWEALTH AFFAIRS 1985-2005/6

1989 July25 The Rt Hon. John Major, MP
1989 Oct26 The Rt Hon. Douglas Hurd, CBE, MP (later Baron Hurd of Westwell)
1995 July6 The Rt Hon. Malcolm Rifkind, QC, MP (later the Rt Hon. Sir Malcolm Rifkind)
1997 May2 The Rt Hon. Robin Cook, MP (Dec'd 6th Aug 2005)
2001 June8 The Rt Hon. Jack Straw, PC, MP

MINISTERS OF STATE FOR FOREIGN AND COMMONWEALTH AFFAIRS 1985-2005/6

1986 Jan13 Mrs Lynda Chalker, MP (later the Rt Hon. Baroness Chalker)
1986 Sept8 Christopher Patten, MP (later the Rt Hon. Christopher Patten)
1987 June16 The Lord Glenarthur
1987 June16 David Mellor, QC, MP (later the Rt Hon. David Mellor)
1988 July16 The Rt Hon. William Waldegrave, MP (later Baron Waldegrave)
1989 July25 The Hon. Francis Maude, MP (later the Rt Hon. Francis Maude MP)
1989 July25 The Lord Brabazon
1989 July25 The Hon. Timothy Sainsbury, MP (later the Rt.Hon Timothy Sainsbury)
1990 July23 Tristan Garel-Jones, MP (later the Rt Hon. Tristan Garel-Jones, MP)
1990 July23 The Rt Hon. The Earl of Caithness
1990 July23 The Hon. Mark Lennox-Boyd, MP (later the Hon. Sir Mark Lennox-Boyd)
1990 Nov1 The Hon. Douglas Hogg, QC, MP (later the Rt Hon. Douglas Hogg, QC, MP, later Viscount Hailsham)
1992 The Rt Hon. Alastair Goodlad, MP
1994 July20, David Davis MP (later the Rt Hon. David Davis MP)
1995 July5, The Rt Hon. Sir Nicholas Bonsor (Bt), MP
1995 July5, The Rt Hon. Jeremy Hanley, MP (later the Rt.Hon Sir Jeremy Hanley)
1997 May5, Derek Fatchett, MP (later the Rt Hon. Derek Fatchett, MP)
1997 May5, Tony Lloyd, MP
1997 May5, Doug Henderson, MP
1998 July28, Ms Joyce Quin, MP (later the Rt Hon. Joyce Quin, MP)
1999 May17, Geoff Hoon, MP (later the Rt Hon. Geoff Hoon, MP)
1999 July29, Peter Hain, MP (later the Rt Hon. Peter Hain, MP)
1999 July29, John Battle, MP (later the Rt Hon. John Battle, MP)
1999 July29, Baroness Scotland
1999 Oct12, Keith Vaz, MP
2001 Jan25, Brian Wilson, MP (later the Rt Hon. Brian Wilson, MP)
2001 June11, Peter Hain, MP (later the Rt Hon. Peter Hain, MP)
2001 June11, Baroness Symons
2001 June11, Ben Bradshaw, MP
2001 June11, Denis MacShane, MP
2001 June11, Baroness Amos
2002 May30, Mike O'Brien, MP
2002 Oct28, Bill Rammell, MP
2003 June13, Chris Mullin, MP
2004 Sept9, Douglas Alexander, MP
2005 May9, Dr Kim Howells, MP
2005 May9, Ian Pearson, MP
2005 May9, Lord Triesman

PERMANENT UNDER-SECRETARIES OF STATE FOR FOREIGN AND COMMONWEALTH AFFAIRS AND HEAD OF HM DIPLOMATIC SERVICE 1985-2005/6

1986 June23, Sir Patrick (Richard Henry) Wright, GCMG (later Baron Wright of Richmond)
1991 June28, Sir David (Howe) Gillmore, KCMG (later Baron Gillmore)(Dec'd 20th March 1999)
1994 Aug1, Sir (Arthur) John Coles, KCMG (later GCMG)
1997 Nov13, Sir John (Olav) Kerr, GCMG
2002 Jan14, Sir Michael (Hastings) Jay, KCMG

CHRONOLOGICAL LIST OF BRITISH REPRESENTATIVES ABROAD INCLUDING COMMONWEALTH COUNTRIES 1985-2005/6

Afghanistan
1987 Ian Warren Mackley, Chargé d'Affaires a.i. Jan8
Staff temporarily withdrawn from post February 1989
1994 Sir Nicholas Barrington, amb. ex. and plen. Feb22
2002 Ronald Peter Nash, amb. ex. and plen. May16
2004 Rosalind Mary Marsden, amb. ex. and plen. Jan

Albania
1992 Sir Patrick Stanislaus Fairweather, amb. ex. and plen. July20
1996 Harcourt Andrew Pretorius Tesoriere, amb.ex. and plen. Jan21
1998 Stephen Nash amb. ex. and plen. May15
1999 Dr Peter January amb. ex. and plen. March1
2001 Dr David Maurice Landsman OBE, amb. ex. and plen. July16
2003 Richard Hugh Francis Jones, amb. ex. and plen. Oct16

Algeria
1987 Patrick Howard Caines Eyers amb. ex. and plen. April12
1990 Christopher Charles Richard Battiscombe amb. ex. and plen. March6
1994 Christopher Donald Crabbie amb. ex. and plen Aug2
1996 Peter James Marshall, amb. ex. and plen Jan6
1997 (Jean) Francois Gordon, amb. ex. and plen. Nov4
1999 William Baldie Sinton OBE, amb. ex. and plen. July16
2001 Richard John Smale Edis, amb. ex. and plen. Sept15
2002 Graham Stewart Hand, amb. ex. and plen. July1
2004 Brian Edward Stewart, amb. ex. and plen. May
2005 Harcourt Andrew Pretorius Tesoriere, amb. ex. and plen. June

Andorra
1994 Anthony David Brighty amb. ex. and plen. Aug25
1998 Peter (later Sir P) James Torry amb. ex. and plen. Sep2
2003 Stephen John Leadbetter Wright, amb. ex. and plen. May

Angola
1985 Patrick Stanislaus Fairweather, amb. ex. and plen. Oct2
1987 Michael John Carlisle Glaze, amb. ex. and plen. Nov18
1990 John Gerrard Flynn, amb. ex. and plen. May9
1993 Anthony Richard Thomas, amb. ex. and plen. April8
1995 Roger Dudley Hart, amb. ex. and plen. July24
1998 Caroline Elmes, amb. ex. and plen. Sept14
2002 John Thompson, amb. ex. and plen. Feb21
2005 Ralph Martin Publicover, amb. ex. and plen. April

Antigua and Barbuda
HIGH COMMISSIONERS
1986 Kevin Francis Xavier Burns. Oct19
1991 Emrys Thomas Davies. Feb15
1994 Richard Thomas. Oct7
1998 Gordon Meldrum Baker Aug3
2001 (Charles) John Branford White. Aug11
2005 Duncan John Rushworth Taylor. Nov

Argentina
Diplomatic and Consular relations with the Argentine Republic were broken off with effect from 2 April 1982. Consular Relations were resumed on 19 October 1989 and Diplomatic Relations on 15th February 1990.
1989 Alan Charles Hunt, Consul General. Oct19
1989 Alan Charles Hunt, Chargé d'Affaires a.i. and Consul General. Feb15
1990 The Hon Humphrey John Hamilton Maud, amb. ex. and plen. July15
1993 Sir Peter Hall, amb. ex. and plen. Sept8
1997 William Marsden, amb. ex. and plen. July27
2000 Duncan Robin (later Sir R) Carmichael Christopher, amb. ex. and plen. Nov17
2004 Dr Edgar John Hughes, amb. ex. and plen. Nov

Armenia
1992 Sir Brian James Proetel Fall, amb. ex. and plen. July15
1995 David Ivimey Miller, amb. ex. and plen. July31
1997 John Edward Mitchiner, amb. ex. and plen. April1
1999 Timothy Aidan Jones, amb. ex. and plen. Nov13
2003 Thorhilda Mary Vivia Abbott-Watt, amb. ex. and plen. Jan
2006 Anthony John James Cantor, amb. ex. and plen. Jan

Australia
HIGH COMMISSIONERS
1988 (Arthur) John (later Sir J) Coles. March22
1991 Brian (later Sir B) Leon Barder. April11
1994 Roger (later Sir R) John Carrick. July27
1997 Alexander Claud Stuart Allan. Nov16
1999 Sir Alastair Goodlad KCMG. May25
2005 Helen Liddell. Aug

Austria
1986 Robert James O'Neill, amb. ex. and plen. Sept2
1989 Brian Lee Crowe, amb. ex. and plen. May31
1992 Terence Courtney Wood, amb. ex. and plen. April30
1996 Anthony (later Sir A) St John Howard Figgis, amb. ex. and plen. Sept29
2000 Antony Ford, amb. ex. and plen. Sept1

2003 John Malcolm Macgregor, amb. ex. and plen. May

Azerbaijan

1992 Sir Brian James Proetel Fall, amb. ex. and plen. July14
1993 Thomas Nesbitt Young, amb. ex. and plen. Sept1
1997 Roger Thomas, amb. ex. and plen. July1
2000 Andrew Victor Gunn Tucker, amb. ex. and plen. Nov1
2003 Dr Lawrence Stanley Charles Bristow, amb. ex. and plen. Dec2

Bahamas

HIGH COMMISSIONERS
1986 Colin Garth Mays. Oct16
1991 Michael John Gore. July16
1992 Brian Attewell. Sept16
1996 Peter Michael Heppell Young. May1
1999 Peter Richard Heigl. July15
2003 Roderick Gemmell. March21

Bahrain

1988 John Alan Shepherd, amb. ex. and plen. April4
1992 Hugh James Oliver Redvers Tunnell, amb. ex. and plen. Feb16
1996 David Ian Lewty, amb. ex. and plen. Jan13
1999 Peter Ford, amb. ex. and plen. April18
2003 Robin David Lamb, amb. ex. and plen. Aug25

Bangladesh

HIGH COMMISSIONERS
1989 Colin (later Sir C) Henry Imray. Oct21
1993 Peter James Fowler. Sept21
1996 David Critchlow Walker. Sept15
2000 David Carter. Jan19
2004 Anwar Choudhury. May

Barbados

HIGH COMMISSIONERS
1986 Kevin Francis Xavier Burns. Oct19
1991 Emrys Thomas Davies. Jan13
1994 Richard Thomas. Oct7
1998 Gordon Meldrum Baker. March8
2001 (Charles) John Branford White. Aug11
2005 Duncan John Rushworth Taylor. Nov

Belarus

1992 Sir Brian James Proetel Fall, amb. ex. and plen. July27
1993 John Vivian Everard, amb. ex. and plen. Oct12
1996 Jessica Mary Pearce, amb. ex. and plen. Jan22
1999 Iain Kelly, amb. ex. and plen. April6
2003 Brian Maurice Bennett, ex. and plen. March14

Belgium

1985 Peter (later Sir P) Charles Petrie, amb. ex. and plen. July7
1989 Robert James O'Neill, amb. ex. and plen. May10
1992 Sir John Walter David Gray, amb. ex. and plen. June18
1996 David Hugh Colvin, amb. ex. and plen. Oct6
2001 Gavin Wallace Hewitt, amb. ex. and plen. Feb2
2003 Richard Kinchen, amb. ex. and plen. Nov15

Belize

HIGH COMMISSIONERS
1987 Peter Alexander Bremner Thomson. Nov10
1991 David Patrick Robert Mackilligin. Feb13
1995 Gordon Meldrum Baker. March30
1998 Timothy James David. April15
2001 Philip John Priestley. July16
2004 David Alan Jones. Nov

Benin

1986 Martin (later Sir M) Kenneth Ewans, amb. ex. and plen. Aug8
1988 Brian (later Sir B) Leon Barder, amb. ex. and plen. Sept23
1991 (Alastair) Christopher (later Sir C) Donald Summerhayes MacRae, amb. ex. and plen. June17
1994 (John) Thorold Masefield, amb. ex. and plen. May14
1997 Graham (later Sir G) Stuart Burton, amb. ex. and plen. May2
2001 Philip (later Sir P) Lloyd Thomas, amb. ex. and plen. March5
2004 Richard Hugh Turton Gozney, amb. ex. and plen. June

Bolivia

1985 Alan White, amb. ex. and plen. March9
1987 Colum John Sharkey, amb. ex. and plen. Aug19
1989 Michael Francis Daly, amb. ex. and plen. June4
1991 Richard Michael Jackson, amb. ex. and plen. May15
1995 David Frederick Charles Ridgway, amb. ex. and plen. June1
1998 Graham Leslie Minter, amb. ex. and plen. Aug15
2001 William Baldie Sinton, amb. ex. and plen. Oct15
2005 Peter Bateman, amb. ex. and plen. June

Bosnia and Herzegovina

1994 Robert William Barnett, amb. ex. and plen. April26
1995 Bryan Hopkinson, amb. ex. and plen. March30

When Yugoslavia broke up "The Republic of Bosnia and Herzegovina" emerged as a new country. At Dayton in 1995 it was agreed that the country should be renamed "Bosnia and Herzegovina". This took effect in 1996

1996 Charles Graham Crawford, amb. ex. and plen. July2
1998 Graham Stewart Hand, amb. ex. and plen. July25
2001 Ian Cameron Cliff, amb. ex. and plen. Oct19
2005 Matthew Rycroft, amb. ex. and plen. March

Botswana

HIGH COMMISSIONERS

1986 Peter Albert Raftery. Feb21
1989 Brian Smith. Feb18
1991 John Coates Edwards. Nov19
1994 David Colin Baskcomb Beaumont. Dec19
1998 John Wilde. May17
2001 David Byron Merry. Aug18
2005 Francis James Martin. Oct

Brazil

1987 Michael John Newington, amb. ex. and plen. Dec15
1992 Peter William (later Sir P) Heap, amb. ex. and plen. Aug4
1995 Donald Keith Haskell, amb. ex. and plen. May15
1999 Roger (later Sir R) Bridgland Bone, amb. ex. and plen. May20
2004 Peter Salmon Collecott, amb. ex. and plen. July

Brunei

HIGH COMMISSIONERS

1986 Roger Westbrook. Sept8
1991 Adrian John Sindall. April9
1994 Ivan (later Sir I)Roy Callan. July7
1998 Stuart Laing. July27
2002 Andrew John Forbes Caie. Jan16
2005 John (Donald William) Saville. May

Bulgaria

1986 John Harold Fawcett, amb. ex. and plen. Aug30
1989 Richard Thomas, amb. ex. and plen. May5
1994 Roger Guy Short, amb. ex. and plen. Sept29
1998 Richard Stagg, amb. ex. and plen. July 8
2001 (Samuel) Ian Soutar, amb. ex. and plen. Dec3
2004 Peter Jeremy Oldham Hill, amb. ex. and plen. Jan

Burkina

(Country re-named on 3August 1984)

1988 Veronica (later Dame V) Evelyn Sutherland, amb. ex. and plen. Jan26
1990 Margaret Irene Rothwell, amb. ex. and plen. Dec17
1997 Haydon Boyd Warren-Gash, amb. ex. and plen. Oct7
2001 Jean Francois Gordon, amb. ex. and plen. June7
2004 David Coates, amb. ex. and plen. Aug
2005 Gordon Geoffrey Wetherell, amb. ex. and plen.

Burma

1986 Martin Robert Morland, amb. ex. and plen. Oct19
1990 Julian Dana Nimmo Hartland-Swann, amb. ex. and plen. May5
1995 Robert Anthony Eagleson Gordon, amb. ex. and plen. Sept6
1999 John Jenkins, amb. ex. and plen. April26
2002 Victoria Jane Bowman, amb. ex. and plen. Dec16

Burundi

1985 Patrick Howard Caines Eyers, amb. ex. and plen. Sept23
1987 Robert Linklater Burke Cormack, amb. ex. and plen. June11
1994 Edward Clay, amb. ex. and plen. Sept19
1995 Kaye Wight Oliver, amb. ex. and plen. Dec11
1998 Graeme Neil Loten, amb. ex. and plen. May11
2001 Susan Elizabeth Hogwood, amb. ex. and plen. July26
2004 Jeremy James Macadie, amb. ex. and plen. Oct

Cambodia

1994 Paul Reddicliffe, amb. ex. and plen. June24
1997 Christopher George Edgar, amb. ex. and plen. July29
2000 Stephen John Bridges, amb. ex. and plen. Dec17
2005 David George Reader, amb. ex. and plen. Jan

Cameroon

AMBASSADORS

1987 Martin Reith, amb. ex. and plen. Oct15
1991 William Ernest Quantrill, amb. ex. and plen. April16
1995 Nicholas Melvyn McCarthy, amb. ex. and plen. April11

In 1995 Cameroon joined the Commonwealth.

HIGH COMMISSIONERS

1998 George Peter Richard Boon. Feb8
2002 Richard James Wildash. July15
2006 David Sydney Maddicott. Feb

Canada

HIGH COMMISSIONERS

1987 Sir Alan Bedford Urwick. Dec4
1989 Brian (later Sir B) James Proetel Fall. Oct5
1992 Nicholas (later Sir N) Peter Bayne. April7
1996 Anthony (later Sir A) Michael Goodenough. March6
2000 Sir (Robert) Andrew Burns. July7
2003 David Norman Reddaway. Aug15

Cape Verde

1986 John Esmond Campbell Macrae, amb. ex. and plen. June17
1990 Roger Campbell Beetham, amb. ex. and plen. Oct18
1993 Alan Edwin Furness, amb. ex. and plen. Oct13
1997 David Raymond Snoxell, amb. ex. and plen. April 26
2000 Edward Alan Burner, amb. ex. and plen. Aug10
2004 Peter Newall, amb. ex. and plen. May

Central African Republic

1985 Michael John Carlisle Glaze, amb. ex. and plen. Feb9
1987 (vacant)
1988 Martin Reith, amb. ex. and plen. July2
1991 William Ernest Quantrill, amb. ex. and plen.

1998 George Peter Richard Boon, amb. ex. and plen. Feb8
2002 Richard James Wildash, amb. ex. and plen. July15
2006 David Sydney Maddicott, amb. ex. and plen. Feb

Chad
1985 Michael Francis Daly, amb. ex. and plen. March20
1987 Maeve Geraldine Fort, amb. ex. and plen. March7
1990 Charlotte Susanna Rycroft, amb. ex. and plen. March19
1991 William Ernest Quantrill, amb. ex. and plen. June
1994 John Thorold Masefield, amb. ex. and plen. May14
1995 Nicholas Melvyn McCarthy, amb. ex. and plen. April11
1998 George Peter Richard Boon, amb. ex. and plen. Feb8
2002 Richard James Wildash, amb. ex. and plen. July15
2006 David Sydney Maddicott, amb. ex. and plen. Feb

Chile
1987 Alan White, amb. ex. and plen. July31
1990 Richard Alvin Neilson, amb. ex. and plen. Aug31
1993 Frank Basil Wheeler, amb. ex. and plen. Oct27
1997 Madelaine (later Dame M) Glynne Dervel Evans, amb. ex. and plen. June8
2000 Leo Gregory Faulkner, amb. ex. and plen. April1
2003 Richard Denys Wilkinson, amb. ex. and plen. June16
2005 Howard Ronald Drake, amb. ex. and plen. Sept

China
1988 Alan (later Sir A) Ewen Donald, amb. ex. and plen. May14
1991 Sir Robin John Taylor McLaren, amb. ex. and plen. June5
1994 Sir Leonard Vincent Appleyard, amb. ex. and plen. Sept8
1997 Anthony (later Sir A) Charles Galsworthy, amb. ex. and plen. May21
2002 Christopher (later Sir C) Owen Hum, amb. ex. and plen. March19
2006 William Geoffrey Ehrman, amb. ex. and plen. Jan

Colombia
1987 Richard Alvin Neilson, amb. ex. and plen. Feb5
1990 Keith (later Sir K) Elliott Hedley Morris, amb. ex. and plen. Sept26
1994 (Arthur) Leycester (later Sir Leycester) Scott Coltman, amb. ex. and plen. Nov1
1998 Jeremy Walter Thorp, amb. ex. and plen. May,31
2001 Thomas (later Sir T) Joseph Duggin, amb. ex. and plen. Aug16
2005 Haydon Boyd Warren-Gash, amb. ex. and plen. Sept

Comoros
1986 Richard Borman Crowson, amb. ex. and plen. Aug29
1989 Michael Edward Howell, amb. ex. and plen. Sept27
1991 Dennis Oltrieve Amy, amb. ex. and plen. May14
1992 Peter John Smith, amb. ex. and plen. Oct20
1996 Robert Scott Dewar, amb. ex. and plen. April4
1999 Charlie Mochan, amb. ex. and plen. March30
2002 Brian Donaldson, amb. ex. and plen. Oct10
2005 Anthony Godson, amb. ex. and plen. Sept

Congo (Democratic Republic)
1985 Patrick Howard Caines Eyers, amb. ex. and plen. Feb24
1987 Robert Linklater Burke Cormack, amb. ex. and plen. June11
1991 Roger Westbrook, amb. ex. and plen. July30
1996 Marcus Laurence Hulbert Hope, amb. ex. and plen. Jan21
1998 Doug Scrafton CMG, amb. ex. and plen. June15
2000 James Oswald Atkinson, amb. ex. and plen. May3
2004 Andrew James Sparkes, amb. ex. and plen. July

Costa Rica
1986 Michael Francis Daly, amb. ex. and plen. June6
1989 William Marsden, amb. ex. and plen. April14
1992 Mary Louise Croll, amb. ex. and plen. July5
1995 Richard Michael Jackson, amb. ex. and plen. Sept1
1997 Alan Stanley Green, amb. ex. and plen. Sept10
1999 Peter Joseph Spiceley, amb. ex. and plen. Jan5
2002 Georgina Susan Butler, amb. ex. and plen. March8

Côte d'Ivoire - See Ivory Coast

Croatia
1992 Bryan Sparrow, amb. ex. and plen. July23
1994 Gavin Wallace Hewitt, amb. ex. and plen. June16
1997 Colin Andrew Munro, amb. ex. and plen. Aug8
2000 Nicholas Jarrold, amb. ex. and plen. Nov10
2004 Sir John (Charles Josslyn) Ramsden, amb. ex. and plen. April1

Cuba
1986 Andrew Eustace Palmer, amb. ex. and plen. July15
1989 (Anthony) David Brighty, amb. ex. and plen. Jan22
1991 (Arthur) Leycester (later Sir Leycester) Scott Coltman, amb. ex. and plen. March3

1994 Philip Alexander McLean, amb. ex. and plen. Nov25
1998 David Frederick Charles Ridgway, amb. ex. and plen. July27
2001 Paul Webster Hare, amb. ex. and plen. July11
2004 John Anthony Dew, amb. ex. and plen. Oct

Cyprus

HIGH COMMISSIONERS

1988 The Hon. Humphrey Maud. Sept7
1990 David (later Sir David) John Michael Dain. July4
1994 David Christopher Andrew Madden. May14
1999 Edward Clay. March12
2001 Lyn Parker. Sept16
2005 Peter Joseph Millett. June

Czech Republic

1985 Stephen Jeremy Barrett, amb. ex. and plen. March8
1988 (Peter) Laurence O'Keeffe, amb. ex. and plen. Nov1
1991 (Anthony) David Brighty, amb. ex. and plen. July21
1994 Sir Michael St Edmund Burton, amb. ex. and plen. Sept19
1997 David Stuart Broucher, amb. ex. and plen. Oct1
2001 Anne Fyfe Pringle, amb. ex. and plen. Nov8
2004 Linda Joy Duffield, amb. ex. and plen. Dec

Denmark

1986 Peter William Unwin, amb. ex. and plen. July9
1989 Nigel Christopher Ransome Williams, amb. ex. and plen. Jan4
1993 Hugh James Arbuthnott, amb. ex. and plen. June6
1996 Andrew Philip Foley Bache, amb. ex. and plen. Nov8
1999 Philip Astley, amb. ex. and plen. June4
2003 Sir Nicholas Walker Browne, amb. ex. and plen. Aug18

Djibouti

1985 David Everard Tatham, amb. ex. and plen. Jan14
1988 Mark Anthony Marshall, amb. ex. and plen. Jan18
1993 (Robert) Douglas Gordon, amb. ex. and plen. March20
1994 Duncan Robin Carmichael Christopher, amb. ex. and plen. April1
1997 Gordon Geoffrey Wetherell, amb. ex. and plen. Sept11
2000 Myles Antony Wickstead, amb. ex. and plen. Nov9
2004 Robert Scott Dewar, amb. ex. and plen. March

Dominica

HIGH COMMISSIONERS

1986 Kevin Francis Xavier Burns. Oct19
1991 Emrys Thomas Davies. Feb20
1994 Richard Thomas. Oct7
1998 Gordon Meldrum Baker. March8
2001 (Charles) John Branford White. Aug11
2005 Duncan John Rushworth Taylor. Nov

Dominican Republic

1985 Michael John Newington, amb. ex. and plen. July7
1988 Giles Eden FitzHerbert, amb. ex. and plen. May11
1993 John Gerrard Flynn, amb. ex. and plen. April4
1995 Dick Thomson, amb. ex. and plen. Sept.15
1998 David Gordon Ward, amb. ex. and plen. Sept18
2002 Andrew Richard Ashcroft, amb. ex. and plen. July30

East Timor

BRITISH REPRESENTATIVES

New British Mission (Dili) was formally opened in January 2000
2000 Dominic James Robert Jermey, Brit. Rep. Jan5
2000 Jane Elizabeth Mary Penfold, Brit. Rep. Nov21
On the 20th May 2002 East Timor became independent. The British Mission is now an Embassy.
2001 Hamish St Clair Daniel, amb. ex. and plen. May20
2003 Tina Susan Redshaw, amb. ex. and plen. Jan

Ecuador

1985 Michael William Atkinson, amb. ex. and plen. June28
1989 Frank Basil Wheeler, amb. ex. and plen. Aug18
1993 Richard Douglas Lavers, amb. ex. and plen.Nov18.
1997 John William Forbes-Meyler, amb. ex. and plen. June27
2000 Ian Gerken, amb. ex. and plen. Feb4.
2003 Richard George Lewington, amb. ex. and plen. June1

Egypt

1985 Sir Alan Bedford Urwick, amb. ex. and plen. Feb15
1987 (William) James (later Sir J) Adams, amb. ex. and plen. Dec14
1992 Christopher William Long, amb. ex. and plen. April26
1995 David Elliott Spiby Blatherwick, amb. ex. and plen. April25
1999 Graham (later Sir G) Boyce, amb. ex. and plen. Feb10
2001 (Robert) John Sawers, amb. ex. and plen. Sept19
2003 Sir Derek John Plumbly, amb. ex. and plen. Sept16

El Salvador

1987 David Joy, amb. ex. and plen. Sept8
1989 Peter John Streams, amb. ex. and plen. Sept13
1991 Michael Henry Connor, amb. ex. and plen. Nov25
1995 Ian Gerken, amb. ex. and plen. July1

1999 Patrick Morgan, amb. ex. and plen. July5
2003 Richard Douglas Lavers, amb. ex. and plen. (Accredited) Aug
2006 Ian Noel Hughes, amb. ex. and plen. March

Equatorial Guinea
1985 Michael John Carlisle Glaze, amb. ex. and plen. April25
1987 Martin Reith, amb. ex. and plen. Nov26
1991 William Ernest Quantrill, amb. ex. and plen.
1998 George Peter Richard Boon, amb. ex. and plen. Feb8
2002 Richard James Wildash, amb. ex. and plen. July15
2006 David Sydney Maddicott, amb. ex. and plen. Feb

Eritrea
1994 Duncan Robin Carmichael Christopher, amb. ex. and plen. April29
1997 Gordon Geoffrey Wetherell, amb. ex. and plen. Sept11
2000 Myles Antony Wickstead, amb. ex. and plen. Nov9
2002 Michael Thomas Murray, amb. ex. and plen. March17
2006 Nicholas Paul Astbury, amb. ex. and plen. Feb

Estonia
1991 Brian Buik Low, amb. ex. and plen. Oct8
1994 Charles Richard Lucien de Chassiron, amb ex. and plen. Oct15
1997 Timothy James Craddock, amb. ex. and plen. Sept20
2000 Sarah Squire, amb. ex. and plen. Sept6
2003 Nigel Robert Haywood, amb. ex. and plen. Nov22

Ethiopia
1986 Harold (later Sir H) Berners Walker, amb. ex. and plen. April29
1990 Michael John Carlisle Glaze, amb. ex. and plen. March21
1994 Duncan Robin Carmichael Christopher, amb. ex. and plen. April18
1997 Gordon Geoffrey Wetherell, amb. ex. and plen. Sept11
2000 Myles Antony Wickstead, amb. ex. and plen. Nov9
2004 Robert Scott Dewar, amb. ex. and plen. March

Fiji
AMBASSADORS
†From 1March 1988, the British High Commission became the British Embassy
†1988 Roger Arnold Rowlandson Barltrop, amb. ex. and plen. March1
1989 (Alexander Basil) Peter Smart, amb. ex. and plen. Aug19
1992 Timothy James David, amb. ex. and plen. March14
1995 Michael John Peart, amb. ex. and plen. April14.
1997 Michael Alan Charles Dibben, amb. ex. and plen. Dec3
2000 Michael Anthony Price, amb. ex. and plen. Oct16
2002 Charles Francis Mochan, amb. ex. and plen. Nov16

Finland
1986 (Hubert Anthony) Justin Staples, amb. ex. and plen. Feb25
1989 (George) Neil Smith. Nov21
1995 David Allan Burns, amb. ex. and plen. March9.
1997 Gavin Wallace Hewitt, amb. ex. and plen. Sept15
2001 Alyson Judith Kirtley Bailes, amb. ex. and plen. Jan5
2002 Matthew John Lushington Kirk, amb. ex. and plen. July24

France
1987 Sir Ewen Alastair John Fergusson, amb. ex. and plen. June22
1993 Sir Christopher Leslie George Mallaby, amb. ex. and plen. Jan29
1996 Sir Michael Hastings Jay, amb. ex. and plen. July10
2001 Sir John Eaton Holmes, amb. ex. and plen. Oct16

Gabon
1985 Ronald Henry Thomas Bates amb. ex. and plen. Feb18
1986 Mark Aubrey Goodfellow, amb. ex. and plen. Feb3
1990 Philip John Priestley, amb. ex. and plen. Nov22
1994 William Ernest Quantrill, amb. ex. and plen. Aug12
1995 Nicholas Melvyn McCarthy, amb. ex. and plen. April11
1998 George Peter Richard Boon, amb. ex. and plen. Feb8
2002 Richard James Wildash, amb. ex. and plen. July15
2006 David Sydney Maddicott, amb. ex. and plen. Feb

Gambia, The
HIGH COMMISSIONERS
1988 Alec Ibbott. Feb20
1990 Alan John Pover. Oct12
1994 Michael John Hardie. Jan7
1995 John Wilde. Feb13
1998 Tony Millson. March13
2000 John Gayford Perrott. April1
2002 Eric Jenkinson. Oct1

Georgia
1992 Sir Brian James Proetel Fall, amb. ex. and plen. June22
1995 Stephen Thomas Nash, amb. ex. and plen. Oct15
1998 Richard Thomas Jenkins, amb. ex. and plen. Jan27
2001 Deborah Elizabeth Vavasseur Barnes Jones, amb. ex. and plen. Apr6
2004 Donald MacLaren, amb. ex. and plen.

Germany

1988 Sir Christopher Leslie George Mallaby, amb. ex. and plen. March20
1993 Nigel Hugh Robert Allen Broomfield, amb. ex. and plen. Jan17
1997 Sir Christopher Meyer, amb. ex. and plen. March5
1997 Sir Paul Lever, amb. ex. and plen. Dec31
2003 Sir Peter James Torry, amb. ex. and plen. May1

German Democratic Republic

1988 Nigel Hugh Robert Allen Broomfield, amb. ex. and plen. May10
1990 Patrick Howard Eyers, amb. ex. and plen. Jan26
On 3 October 1990 the German Democratic Republic ceased to exist.

Ghana

HIGH COMMISSIONERS

1986 Arthur Hope Wyatt. Oct24
1989 Anthony Michael Goodenough. Oct16
1992 David Critchlow Walker. June14
1996 Ian Warren Mackley. July21
2000 Roderick Allen Pullen. Oct11
2004 Gordon Geoffrey Wetherell. March

Greece

1985 Sir Jeremy Cashel Thomas, amb. ex. and plen. June6
1989 Sir (Henry) David Alastair Capel Miers, amb. ex. and plen. May24
1993 (Richard) Oliver Miles, amb. ex. and plen. July19
1996 Michael (later Sir M) John Llewellyn Smith, amb. ex. and plen. April4
1998 David (later Sir D) Christopher Andrew Madden, amb. ex. and plen. Dec,8
2004 Simon Lawrence Gass, amb. ex. and plen. Dec

Grenada

HIGH COMMISSIONERS

1986 Kevin Francis Xavier Burns. Oct19
1991 Emrys Thomas Davies. Feb5
1994 Richard Thomas. Oct7
1998 Gordon Meldrum Baker. March8
2001 (Charles) John Branford White. Aug11
2005 Duncan John Rushworth Taylor. Nov

Guatemala

1987 Bernard Jonathan Everett, amb. ex. and plen. June25
1991 Justin Patrick Pearse Nason, amb. ex. and plen. March22
1995 Peter Marcus Newton, amb. ex. and plen. March28
1998 Andrew John Forbes Caie, amb. ex. and plen. July21
2001 Richard Douglas Lavers, amb. ex. and plen. Oct25
2006 Ian Noel Hughes, amb. ex. and plen. March

Guinea

1986 John Esmond Campbell Macrae, amb. ex. and plen. May6
1990 Roger Campbell Beetham, amb. ex. and plen. Nov29
1994 Alan Edwin Furness, amb. ex. and plen. April21
1997 David Raymond Snoxell, amb. ex. and plen. April4
2000 David Alan Jones, amb. ex. and plen. May4
2003 Helen Margaret Horn, amb. ex. and plen. Aug21
2004 John McManus, amb. ex. and plen. Dec

Guinea Bissau

1986 John Esmond Campbell Macrae, amb. ex. and plen. May30
1990 Roger Campbell Beetham, amb. ex. and plen. April12
1994 Alan Edwin Furness, amb. ex. and plen. Jan18
1997 David Raymond Snoxell, amb. ex. and plen. April4
2000 Edward Alan Burner, amb. ex. and plen. Aug10
2004 Peter Newall, amb. ex. and plen. May

Guyana

HIGH COMMISSIONERS

1985 John Dudley Massingham. April6
1987 David Purvis Small, July16
1990 (Robert) Douglas Gordon, Oct24
1993 David John Johnson, March22
1998 Edward Glover, Nov19
2002 Stephen John Hiscock, Aug29

Haiti

1987 Alan Jeffrey Payne, amb. ex. and plen. Oct15
1989 Derek Francis Milton, amb. ex. and plen. June29
1995 Anthony Richard Thomas, amb. ex and plen. Oct15
1998 David Gordon Ward, amb. ex. and plen. Sept18
2002 Andrew Richard Ashcroft, amb. ex. and plen. May2

Holy See

1985 David Neil Lane, amb. ex. and plen. May16
1988 John Kenneth Elliott Broadley, amb. ex. and plen. May18
1991 Andrew Eustace Palmer, amb. ex. and plen. Aug21
1995 Maureen Elizabeth MacGlashan, amb. ex. and plen. May27.
1998 Mark Edward Pellew, amb. ex. and plen. Jan1
2002 Kathryn Frances Colvin, amb. ex. and plen. July16

Honduras

1987 David Joy, amb. ex. and plen. July17
1989 Peter John Streams, amb. ex. and plen. July30
1992 Patrick Morgan, amb. ex. and plen. Jan30
1995 Peter Rodney Holmes, amb. ex. and plen. Aug3
1998 David Allan Osborne, amb. ex. and plen. July31

2002 Kay Coombs, amb. ex. and plen. Sept2

Hong Kong Special Administrative Region

CONSULS-GENERAL

1997 (Robert) Francis Cornish. July1
1997 Sir (Robert) Andrew Burns. Nov 26
2000 Sir James William Hodge. Aug26
2003 Stephen Edward Bradley. Dec1

Hungary

1986 Leonard Vincent Appleyard (later Sir L), amb. ex. and plen. July30
1989 John (later Sir J) Allan Birch, amb. ex. and plen. Aug21
1995 Christopher William Long, amb. ex. and plen. June2.
1998 Nigel James Thorpe, amb. ex. and plen. Apr17
2003 John Roland Nichols, amb. ex. and plen. Aug6

Iceland

1986 Mark Fenger Chapman, amb. ex. and plen. Oct8
1989 Richard (later Sir R) Radford Best, amb. ex. and plen. March15
1991 Patrick Francis Wogan, amb. ex. and plen. Sept16
1993 Michael Stuart Hone, amb. ex. and plen. June21
1996 James Rae McCulloch, amb. ex. and plen. May12
2001 John Howard Culver, amb. ex. and plen. Jan15
2004 Alper Mehmet, amb. ex. and plen. April16

India

HIGH COMMISSIONERS

1986 Sir (Arthur) David Saunders Goodall. April2
1991 Sir Nicholas Maxted Fenn. Nov13
1996 The Hon. David (later the Hon Sir D) Alwyn Gore-Booth. March9
1999 Sir (John) Rob(ertson) Young. Jan18
2003 Michael (later Sir M) Anthony Arthur. Oct16

Indonesia

1988 (William) Kelvin Kennedy White, amb. ex. and plen. March9
1990 Roger John Carrick, amb. ex. and plen. Aug3
1994 Graham Stuart Burton, amb. ex. and plen. Aug18
1997 (Duncan) Robin Carmichael Christopher, amb. ex. and plen. April13
2000 (Richard) Hugh Turton Gozney, amb. ex. and plen. Aug16
2004 Charles Thomas William Humfrey, amb. ex. and plen. March

Iran

1988 Gordon Andrew Pirie, Chargé d'Affaires a.i. Dec4
1989 Nicholas Walker Browne, Chargé d'Affaires a.i. Feb1
1990 David Norman Reddaway, Chargé d'Affaires a.i. Oct28
1993 Jeffrey Russell James, Chargé d'Affaires a.i. Aug16
1997 Nicholas Walker Browne, Chargé d'Affaires a.i. Nov13
1999 Nicholas Walker Browne, amb. ex. and plen. May
1999 Richard Anthony Neil Crompton, Chargé d'Affaires a.i. May24
2002 Richard (later Sir R) John Dalton, amb. ex.and plen. Nov

Iraq

1985 Terence Josph Clark, amb. ex. and plen. March18
1990 Harold (later Sir H) Berners Walker amb. ex. and plen. Feb9
1991 Embassy Staff Withdrawn.

Diplomatic relations with Iraq were broken off with effect from 6 February 1991.

An Iraqi Interim Government endorsed by the UN assumed authority for governing Iraq on 28 June 2004. Diplomatic relations were re-established on that date and the new British Embassy was opened in Baghdad.

2004 Edward Graham Mellish Chaplin, amb. ex. and plen. July1
2005 William Charles Patey, amb. ex. and plen. June

Ireland

1986 Nicholas (later Sir N) Maxted Fenn, amb. ex. and plen. Dec7
1991 David Elliott Spiby Blatherwick, amb. ex. and plen. Sept10
1995 Veronica (later Dame V) Evelyn Sutherland, amb. ex. and plen. March29
1999 Ivor (later Sir I) Anthony Roberts, amb. ex. and plen. Feb20
2003 Stewart Graham Eldon, amb. ex. and plen. Apr14

Israel

1988 Mark Elliott, amb. ex. and plen. June19
1992 Robert Andrew Burns, amb. ex. and plen. July12
1995 David Geoffrey Manning, amb. ex. and plen. Nov11
1998 Francis Cornish, amb. ex. and plen. Sept7
2001 Sherard (later Sir S) Louis Cowper-Coles, amb. ex. and plen. Sept16
2003 Simon Gerard McDonald, amb. ex. and plen. Aug14

Italy

1987 Sir Derek Morison David Thomas amb. ex. and plen. Dec3
1989 Sir Stephen Loftus Egerton, amb. ex. and plen. Nov14
1992 Sir Patrick Stanislaus Fairweather, amb. ex. and plen. July5
1996 Thomas (later Sir T) Legh Richardson, amb. ex. and plen. July10
2000 John (later Sir J) Alan Shepherd, amb. ex. and plen. July26
2003 Sir Ivor Anthony Roberts, amb. ex. and plen. May5

Ivory Coast (Côte d'Ivoire)

1987 Veronica (later Dame V) Evelyn Sutherland, amb. ex. and plen. June27
1990 Margaret Irene Rothwell, amb. ex. and plen. Dec17
1997 Haydon Boyd Warren-Gash, amb. ex. and plen. Oct7
2001 Jean Francois Gordon, amb. ex. and plen. June7
2004 David Coates, amb. ex. and plen. Aug

Jamaica

HIGH COMMISSIONERS
1987 Alan Jeffrey Payne. June23
1989 Derek Francis Milton. April13
1995 Anthony Richard Thomas. Oct1
1999 Anthony Smith. March29
2002 Peter James Mathers. July4
2005 Jeremy Michael Cresswell. July

Japan

1986 Sir John Stainton Whitehead, amb. ex. and plen. Nov12
1992 Sir John Dixon Ikl Boyd, amb. ex. and plen. July7
1995 David John Wright, amb. ex. and plen. Jan1
1999 Stephen (later Sir S) John Gomersall, amb. ex. and plen. May28
2004 Graham Holbrook Fry, amb. ex. and plen. July

Jordan

1988 Anthony Reeve, amb. ex. and plen. Feb3
1991 Patrick Howard Caines Eyers, amb. ex. and plen. April27
1993 Peter Robert Mossom Hinchcliffe, amb. ex. and plen. Oct19
1997 Christopher Charles Battiscombe, amb. ex. and plen. April14
2000 Edward Graham Mellish Chaplin, amb. ex. and plen. May16
2002 Christopher Norman Russell Prentice, amb. ex. and plen. June1

Kazakhstan

1992 Sir Brian James Proetel Fall, amb. ex. and plen. Sept14
1993 Noel Stephen Andrew Jones, amb. ex. and plen. Oct26
1996 Douglas Baxter McAdam, amb. ex. and plen. March7
1999 Richard George Lewington. Feb7
2002 James Lyall Sharp. Oct1
2005 Paul Brummell. Dec

Kenya

HIGH COMMISSIONERS
1986 John (later Sir J) Rodney Johnson, June15
1990 (William) Roger (later Sir R) Tomkys, Oct19
1992 Sir Kieran Prendergast, Oct19
1995 Simon Nicholas Peter Hemans. April14
1997 Jeffrey Russell James, July7
2001 Edward (later Sir E) Clay. Dec16
2005 Adam Kenneth Compton Wood. July

Kiribati

HIGH COMMISSIONERS
1990 Derek Leslie White. Jan17
1993 Frank McDermott. April14
1994 Timothy James David. Sept1
1995 Michael John Peart. April14
1997 Michael Alan Charles Dibben. Dec3
2000 Michael Anthony Price. Oct16
2002 Charles Francis Mochan. Nov16

Korea, North

New British Embassy (Pyongyang) was formally opened in July 2001
2001 Dr James Edward Hoare, Chargé d'Affaires Feb
2002 David Arthur Slinn, amb. ex. and plen. Oct16
2006 John Vivian Everard, amb. ex. and plen. Jan

Korea, South

1986 Lawrence John Middleton, amb. ex. and plen. Oct7
1990 David John Wright, amb. ex. and plen. April9
1994 Thomas George Harris, amb. ex. and plen. March19
1997 Sir Stephen David Reid Brown, amb. ex. and plen. April4
2000 Charles Thomas William Humfrey CMG, amb. ex. and plen. July1
2003 Warwick Morris, amb. ex. and plen. Nov1

Kuwait

1985 Sir Peter James Scott Moon, amb. ex. and plen. Feb17
1987 Peter Robert Mossom Hinchcliffe, amb. ex. and plen. May30
1990 Michael (later Sir M) Charles Swift Weston amb. ex. and plen. March18
1992 William Hugh Fullerton, amb. ex. and plen. Aug3
1996 Graham Hugh Boyce, amb. ex. and plen. March17
1998 Richard Muir CMG, amb. ex. and plen. Dec14
2002 Christopher Edward John Wilton, amb. ex. and plen. Aug16
2005 John Stuart Laing, amb. ex. and plen. Nov

Kyrgyzstan

1992 Sir Brian James Proetel Fall, amb. ex. and plen. Oct26
1994 Noel Stephen Andrew Jones, amb. ex. and plen. Feb2
1996 Douglas Baxter McAdam, amb. ex. and plen. March7
1999 Richard George Lewington. Feb7
2002 James Lyall Sharp. Oct1
2005 Paul Brummell. Dec

Laos

1985 (Hubert Anthony) Justin Staples, April25
1986 Derek Tonkin, amb. ex. and plen. June4
1990 (Michael) Ramsey Melhuish, amb. ex. and plen. Jan24
1992 (Charles) Christian Wilfrid Adams, amb. ex. and plen. March14
1997 Sir James William Hodge, amb. ex. and plen. Sept6

2000 Lloyd Barnaby Smith, amb. ex. and plen. March1
2003 David William Fall, amb. ex. and plen. July25

Latvia
1992 Richard Christopher Samuel, amb. ex. and plen. Feb2
1993 Richard Peter Ralph, amb. ex. and plen. Aug8
1996 Nicholas Robert Jarrold, amb. ex. and plen. Feb1
1999 Stephen Thomas Nash CMG, amb. ex. and plen. July16
2002 Harcourt Andrew Pretorius Tesoriere, amb. ex. and plen. March28
2005 Ian Andrew Minton Bond, amb. ex. and plen. April

Lebanon
1985 John (later Sir J)Walton David Gray, amb. ex. and plen. Nov28
1988 Allan John Ramsay, amb. ex. and plen. June16
1990 David Everard Tatham, amb. ex. and plen. April28
1992 Maeve (later Dame M) Geraldine Fort, amb. ex. and plen. July31
1996 David Ross MacLennan, amb. ex. and plen. Oct9
2000 Richard Kinchen, amb. ex. and plen. Dec16
2003 James Wilfrid Watt, amb. ex. and plen. Oct16

Lesotho
HIGH COMMISSIONERS
1988 John Coates Edwards. May31
1992 James Roy Cowling. Feb1
1996 Peter John Smith. April1
1998 Kaye Oliver. Dec15
2002 Francis James Martin. April19

Liberia
1985 Alec Ibbott, amb. ex. and plen. April19
1988 Michael Edward John Gore, amb. ex. and plen. Feb2
1990 Margaret Irene Rothwell, amb. ex. and plen. Dec17
1997 Haydon Boyd Warren-Gash, amb. ex. and plen. Oct7
2001 Jean Francois Gordon, amb. ex. and plen. June7
In 2003 accreditation was transferred from Abidjan to Freetown
2003 John Edward Mitchiner, amb. ex. and plen. (Accredited) Dec1

Libya
Diplomatic and Consular relations with Libya were broken off with effect from 30 April 1984
1999 Richard John Dalton CMG, amb. ex. and plen. Nov30
2002 Anthony Michael Layden, amb. ex. and plen. Oct31

Liechtenstein
1991 Christopher William Long, amb. ex. and plen. Dec12

1992 David Beattie, amb. ex. and plen. May21
1997 Christopher Hulse, amb. ex. and plen. April1
2001 Basil Stephen Talbot Eastwood, amb. ex. and plen. Aug15
2004 Simon Mark Featherstone, amb. ex. and plen. March20

Lithuania
1991 Michael John Peart, amb. ex. and plen. Oct8
1995 Thomas Townley Macan, amb. ex. and plen. Jan1
1995 Christopher William Robbins, amb. ex. and plen. July28
2001 Peter Jeremy Oldham Hill, amb. ex. and plen. Sept16
2004 Colin Roberts, amb. ex. and plen. March

Luxembourg
1985 (Richard) Oliver Miles, amb. ex. and plen. Feb26
1988 Juliet Jeanne d'Auvergne Campbell, amb. ex. and plen. Feb24
1991 The Hon. Michael Pakenham, amb. ex. and plen. Oct19
1994 John Nicholas Elam, amb. ex. and plen. May23
1998 William Ehrman, amb. ex. and plen. Sept13
2000 Gordon Geoffrey Wetherell, amb. ex. and plen. Sept5
2004 James Frame Clark, amb. ex. and plen. March

Macedonia
1993 Tony Millson, amb. ex. and plen. Dec23
1997 Woodman Mark Lowes Dickinson, amb. ex. and plen. April14
2001 Christopher George Edgar, amb. ex. and plen. Sept28
2004 Robert Maurice French Chatterton Dickson, amb. ex. and plen. July

Madagascar
1987 Anthony Victor Hayday, amb. ex. and plen. Dec28
1990 Dennis Oldrieve Amy, amb. ex. and plen. April26
1993 Peter John Smith, amb. ex. and plen. Jan2
1996 Robert Scott Dewar, amb. ex. and plen. April14
1999 Charles Francis Mochan, amb. ex. and plen. July2
2002 Brian Donaldson, amb. ex. and plen. Oct10
2005 Anthony Godson, amb. ex. and plen. Sept

Malawi
HIGH COMMISSIONERS
1987 Denis Gordon Osborne. Aug17
1990 (William) Nigel Wenban-Smith. Nov3
1993 John Francis Ryde Martin. Oct1
1998 George Finlayson. May15
2001 Norman Arthur Ling. Sept23
2004 David Dacre Pearey. Dec

Malaysia
HIGH COMMISSIONERS
1986 (John) Nicholas (later Sir N) Teague Spreckley Oct31

1992 Duncan Slater. March10
1994 David Joseph Moss. Aug15
1998 Graham Fry. June23
2001 Bruce Elliot Cleghorn. Nov17

†Maldives

†From 9July 1982 the British Embassy became a High Commission

HIGH COMMISSIONERS

1987 David Arthur Stewart Gladstone. June29
1991 Edward John Field. Dec30
1996 David Everard Tatham, March31
1999 Linda Joy Duffield. Jan18
2002 Stephen Nicholas Evans. July16

Mali

1986 John Esmond Campbell Macrae, amb. ex. and plen. March21
1990 Roger Campbell Beetham, amb. ex. and plen. Nov6
1993 Alan Edwin Furness, amb. ex. and plen. Sept3
1997 David Raymond Snoxell, amb. ex. and plen. April4
2000 Edward Alan Burner, amb. ex. and plen. Aug10
2001 Graeme Neil Loten, amb. ex. and plen. Oct1
2003 Edward Alan Burner, amb. ex. and plen. (Re-accredited) June
2004 Peter Newall, amb. ex. and plen. May

Malta

HIGH COMMISSIONERS

1985 Stanley Frederick St Clair Duncan. May3
1988 Brian Hitch. Jan10
1991 Peter (later Sir P) Gordon Wallis. Oct29
1995 Graham Robertson Archer. Jan3
1999 Howard John Pearce. June14
2002 Vincent Fean. Sept16
2006 Nicholas Stewart Archer. March

Marshall Islands

1992 Derek Leslie White, amb. ex. and plen. July22
1996 Vernon Marcus Scarborough, amb. ex. and plen. July23
2000 Christopher Haslam, amb. ex. and plen. Jan15
2003 Ian Francis Powell, amb. ex. and plen. March1

Mauritania

1986 John Esmond Campbell Macrae, amb. ex. and plen. April24
1993 Sir Allan John Ramsey, amb. ex. and plen. April26
1996 William Hugh Fullerton, amb. ex. and plen. April17
1999 Anthony Layden, amb. ex. and plen. March16
2002 Haydon Boyd Warren-Gash, amb. ex. and plen. July11
2005 (John) Charles (Rodger) Gray, amb. ex. and plen. July

Mauritius

HIGH COMMISSIONERS

1985 Richard Borman Crowson. Dec11
1989 Michael Edward Howell. Aug12
1993 John Clive Harrison. May5
1997 James Daly. May30
2000 David Snoxell. Sept21
2004 Anthony Godson. Nov

Mexico

1986 John (later Sir J) Albert Leigh Morgan, amb. ex. and plen. May21
1989 Michael (later Sir M) Keith Orlebar Simpson-Orlebar, amb. ex. and plen. July27
1992 Sir Roger Blaise Ramsay Hervey, amb. ex. and plen. March2
1994 Adrian John Beamish, amb. ex. and plen. Oct2
1998 Adrian Charles Thorpe CMG, amb. ex. and plen. Oct30
2002 Denise Mary Holt, amb. ex. and plen. June15
2005 (Timothy) Giles Paxman, amb. ex. and plen. Oct

Micronesia

1992 Derek Leslie White, amb. ex. and plen. July22
1996 Vernon Marcus Scarborough, amb. ex. and plen. July23
2000 Christopher Haslam, amb. ex. and plen. Jan15
2003 Ian Francis Powell, amb. ex. and plen. March1

Moldova

1992 Sir Brian James Proetel Fall, Aug28
1995 Sir Andrew Marley Wood. July12
1999 Richard Peter Ralph. Aug27
2002 Bernard Gerrard Whiteside. April16
2006 John Charles Beyer. Jan

Mongolia

1987 Guy William Pulbrook Hart, amb. ex. and plen. March19
1989 David Keith Sprague, amb. ex. and plen. April20
1991 Anthony Bernard Nicholas Morey, amb. ex. and plen. May29
1994 Ian Christopher Sloane, amb. ex. and plen. Jan18
1997 John Clive Durham, amb. ex. and plen. March1
1999 Kay Coombs, amb. ex. and plen. July30
2001 Philip Terence Rouse, amb. ex. and plen. Dec15
2004 Richard James Austen, amb. ex. and plen. Feb27

Morocco

1985 Ronald Archer Campbell Byatt, amb. ex. and plen. Jan28
1987 John William Richmond Shakespeare amb. ex. and plen. Nov15
1990 John Esmond Campbell Macrae, amb. ex. and plen. June12
1992 Sir Allan John Ramsey, amb. ex. and plen. Dec21
1996 William Hugh Fullerton, amb. ex. and plen. April17

1999 Anthony Layden, amb. ex. and plen. March16
2002 Haydon Boyd Warren-Gash, amb. ex. and plen. July11
2005 (John) Charles (Rodger) Gray, amb. ex. and plen. July

Mozambique
1986 James Nicholas Allan, amb. ex. and plen. Feb21
1989 Maeve (later Dame M) Geraldine Fort, amb. ex. and plen. Sept10
1992 Richard John Smale Edis, amb. ex. and plen. Aug10
1996 Bernard Jonathan Everett, amb. ex. and plen. Jan1
2000 Robert Scott Dewar, amb. ex. and plen. Aug4
2003 Howard Parkinson, amb. ex. and plen. Dec15

Namibia
HIGH COMMISSIONERS
1990 Francis Neville Richards. June4
1992 Henry George Hogger. Oct3
1996 Glyn Davies. Feb1
1999 Brian Donaldson. Jan17
2002 Alasdair Tormod MacDermott, April16

Nauru
HIGH COMMISSIONERS
1990 (Alexander Basil) Peter Smart. March15
1995 Michael John Peart. April14
1997 Michael Alan Charles Dibben. Dec3
2000 Michael Anthony Price. Oct16
2002 Charles Francis Mochan. Nov16

Nepal
1987 Richard Eagleson Gordon Burges Watson, amb. ex. and plen. March1
1990 Timothy John Burr George, amb. ex. and plen. Oct16
1995 Lloyd Barnay Smith, amb. ex. and plen. Dec9
1999 Ronald Nash, amb. ex. and plen. March26
2002 Keith George Bloomfield, amb. ex. and plen. June27

Netherlands
1988 Michael Romilly Heald Jenkins, amb. ex. and plen. Jan23
1993 Sir (Henry) David Alastair Miers, amb. ex. and plen. July1
1996 Dame Rosemary Jane Spencer, 1999, amb. ex. and plen. Nov15
2001 Colin (later Sir C) Richard Budd, amb. ex. and plen. Apr4
2005 Lyn Parker, amb. ex. and plen. Sept

New Zealand
HIGH COMMISSIONERS
1987 Ronald Archer Campbell Byatt. Dec15
1990 David Joseph Moss. Sept27
1994 Robert Alston. Aug1
1998 Martin Williams OBE. Apr15
2001 Richard Taylor Fell. Dec10

Nicaragua
1986 Michael Francis Daly, amb. ex. and plen. July14
1989 William Marsden, amb. ex. and plen. April19
1991 Roger Hugh Brown, amb. ex. and plen. Dec3
1992 John Howard Culver, amb. ex. and plen. Nov25
1997 Roy Paul Osborne, amb. ex. and plen. July15
2000 Harry Wiles, amb. ex. and plen. Sept
2002 Timothy Patrick Brownbill, amb. ex. and plen. Nov1

Niger
1987 Veronica (later Dame V) Evelyn Sutherland, amb. ex. and plen. Oct16
1990 Margaret Irene Rothwell, amb. ex. and plen. July10
1997 Haydon Boyd Warren-Gash, amb. ex. and plen. Oct7
2001 Jean Francois Gordon, amb. ex. and plen. June7
2004 David Coates, amb. ex. and plen. Aug
2005 Gordon Geoffrey Wetherell, amb. ex. and plen.

Nigeria
HIGH COMMISSIONERS
1986 Sir Martin Kenneth Ewans. Feb28
1988 Brian (later Sir B) Leon Barder. July27
1991 (Alastair) Christopher Donald Summerhayes MacRae. March7
1994 (John) Thorold Masefield. May14
1997 Graham (later Sir G) Stuart Burton. May2
2001 Philip (later Sir P) Lloyd Thomas. March5
2004 Richard Hugh Turton Gozney. June

Norway
1987 John Adam (later Sir J) Robson, amb. ex. and plen. March9
1990 David John Edward Ratford, amb. ex. and plen. May7
1994 Mark Elliott CMG, amb. ex. and plen. June4
1998 Richard (later Sir R) Dales CMG, amb. ex. and plen. July3
2002 Alison Mariot Leslie, amb. ex. and plen. Sept5

Oman
1986 Robert John Alston, amb. ex. and plen. June3
1990 Terence Joseph (later Sir T) Clark, amb. ex. and plen. Jan29
1994 Richard John Sutherland Muir, amb. ex. and plen. June5
1999 Sir Ivan Callan amb. ex. and plen. Feb15
2002 (John) Stuart Laing, amb. ex. and plen. April12
2005 Dr Noel Joseph Guckian, amb. ex. and plen. Dec

†Pakistan
AMBASSADORS
1987 Nicolas John (later Sir N) Barrington, amb. ex. and plen. July20

HIGH COMMISSIONERS
†1989 Nicholas (later Sir N) John Barrington. Oct1
1994 Sir (Alastair) Christopher Donald Summerhayes MacRae, May31
1997 David (later Sir D) John Michael Dain, May5
2000 Hilary Nicholas Hugh Synnott. Oct15
2003 Mark Justin Lyall Grant. May15
†From 30January 1972, the British High Commission became the British Embassy, then from 1October 1989 it reverted to the British High Commission

Palau
1996 Vernon Marcus Scarborough, amb. ex. and plen. July23
2000 Christopher Haslam, amb. ex. and plen. Jan15
2003 Ian Francis Powell, amb. ex. and plen. March1

Panama
1986 Margaret Bryan, amb. ex. and plen. April9
1990 John Grant MacDonald, amb. ex. and plen. Jan6
1992 Thomas Herbert Malcomson, amb. ex. and plen. Jan31
1996 William Baldie Sinton OBE, amb. ex. and plen. Jan19
1999 Robert Harold Davies, amb. ex. and plen. March15
2002 James Ian Malcolm, amb. ex. and plen. March16

Papua New Guinea
HIGH COMMISSIONERS
1986 Michael Edward Howell. Jan27
1989 (Edward) John Sharland. June11
1991 John Westgarth Guy. July12
1994 Brian Buik Low. Dec12
1997 Charles Drace-Francis. Dec16
2000 Simon Mansfield Scaddan. March1
2003 David Scott Gordon-Macleod. Nov1

Paraguay
1986 John Grant MacDonald, amb. ex. and plen. May3
1989 Terence Harry Steggle, amb. ex. and plen. May31
1991 Michael Alan Charles Dibben, amb. ex. and plen. March2
1995 Graham John Campbell Pirnie, amb. ex. and plen. Aug31
1998 Andrew Neil George, amb. ex. and plen. Oct15
2001 Anthony John James Cantor, amb. ex. and plen. Nov16

Peru
1987 Adrian John Beamish, amb. ex. and plen. Dec16
1990 (Donald) Keith Haskell, amb. ex. and plen. Feb11
1995 John Illman, amb. ex. and plen. May5
1999 Roger Hart, amb. ex. and plen. June4
2003 Richard Peter Ralph, amb. ex. and plen. May1

Philippines
1985 Robin John Taylor McLaren, amb. ex. and plen. May15
1987 Keith Gordon MacInnes, amb. ex. and plen. April27
1992 Alan Everard Montgomery, amb. ex. and plen. July11
1995 Adrian Charles Thorpe, amb. ex. and plen. July8
1998 Alan Stanley Collins CMG, amb. ex. and plen. Dec31
2002 Paul Stephen Dimond, amb. ex. and plen. April1
2005 Peter Beckingham, amb. ex. and plen. Feb16

Poland
1986 Brian (later Sir B)Leon Barder, amb. ex. and plen. May27
1988 Stephen (later Sir S) Jeremy Barrett, amb. ex. and plen. Aug20
1991 Michael John Llewellyn Smith, amb. ex. and plen. Sept20
1996 Christoper (later Sir C) Owen Hum, amb. ex. and plen. May6
1998 John Macgregor, amb. ex. and plen. Sept7
2001 The Hon Michael (later the Hon. Sir M) Aidan Pakenham, amb. ex. and plen. Jan5
2003 Charles Graham Crawford, amb. ex. and plen. Dec

Portugal
1986 Michael Keith Orlebar Simpson-Orlebar, amb. ex. and plen. March15
1989 Hugh James Arbuthnott, amb. ex. and plen. Aug23
1993 (John) Stephen (later Sir S) Wall, amb. ex. and plen. May31
1995 Roger Westbrook, amb. ex. and plen. July24
1999 John (later Sir John) Holmes, amb. ex. and plen. June14
2001 Dame (Madelaine) Glynne Dervel Evans, amb. ex. and plen. Sept16
2004 John Stephen Buck, amb. ex. and plen. Sept

Qatar
1987 Patrick Michael Nixon, amb. ex. and plen. June11
1990 Graham Hugh Boyce, amb. ex. and plen. Feb27
1993 Patrick Francis Michael Wogan, amb. ex. and plen. Oct23
1997 David Alan Wright OBE, amb. ex. and plen. June4
2002 David Ross MacLennan, amb. ex. and plen. June15
2005 Simon Paul Collis, amb.ex. and plen. Mar/Apr

Romania
1986 Hugh James Arbuthnott, amb. ex. and plen. Nov14
1989 Michael William Atkinson, amb. ex. and plen. Sept4
1992 Andrew Philip Foley Bache, amb. ex. and plen. April15

1996 Christopher Donald Crabbie, amb. ex. and plen. June30
1999 Richard Peter Ralph, amb. ex. and plen. Aug27
2002 Quinton Mark Quayle, amb. ex. and plen. Nov2

Russian Federation
1992 Sir Brian James Proetel Fall, amb. ex. and plen. June3
1995 Sir Andrew Marley Wood, amb. ex. and plen. July12
2000 Sir Roderic Michael Lyne, amb. ex. and plen. Jan14
2004 Anthony Russell Brenton, amb. ex. and plen. Sept

Rwanda
1985 Patrick Howard Caines Eyers, amb. ex. and plen. Aug20
1987 Robert Linklater Burke Cormack, amb. ex. and plen. June11
1991 Roger Westbrook, amb. ex. and plen. July30
1994 Edward Clay, amb. ex. and plen. Jan10
1995 Kaye Wight Oliver, amb. ex. and plen. Dec11
1998 Graeme Neil Loten, amb. ex. and plen. May11
2001 Susan Elizabeth Hogwood, amb. ex. and plen. July26
2004 Jeremy James Macadie, amb. ex. and plen. Oct

Saint Kitts and Nevis
HIGH COMMISSIONERS
1986 Kevin Francis Xavier Burns. Oct19
1991 Emrys Thomas Davies. Feb13
1994 Richard Thomas. Oct7
1998 Gordon Meldrum Baker. March8
2001 (Charles) John Branford White. Aug11
2005 Duncan John Rushworth Taylor. Nov

St Lucia
HIGH COMMISSIONERS
1986 Kevin Francis Xavier Burns. Oct19
1991 Emrys Thomas Davies. Feb13
1994 Richard Thomas. Oct7
1998 Gordon Meldrum Baker. March8
2001 (Charles) John Branford White. Aug11
2005 Duncan John Rushworth Taylor. Nov

St Vincent and the Grenadines
HIGH COMMISSIONERS
1986 Kevin Francis Xavier Burns. Oct19
1991 Emrys Thomas Davies. Feb11
1994 Richard Thomas. Oct7
1998 Gordon Meldrum Baker. March8
2001 (Charles) John Branford White. Aug11
2005 Duncan John Rushworth Taylor. Nov

Samoa
HIGH COMMISSIONERS
1987 Ronald Archer Campbell Byatt. Dec15
1991 David Joseph Moss. Aug6
1994 Robert Alston. Aug1
1998 Martin Williams. Apr15
2001 Richard Taylor Fell. Dec10

São Tomé and Principe
1986 Patrick Staislaus Fairweather, amb. ex. and plen. June9
1988 Michael John Carlisle Glaze, amb. ex. and plen. March25
1990 John Gerrard Flynn, amb. ex. and plen. May22
1993 Anthony Richard Thomas, amb. ex. and plen. April27
1996 Roger Dudley Hart, amb. ex. and plen. Sept18
1999 Caroline Elmes, amb. ex. and plen. Sept14
2002 John Thompson, amb. ex. and plen. Feb21
2005 Ralph Martin Publicover, amb. ex. and plen. April

Saudi Arabia
1986 Stephen (later Sir S) Loftus Egerton, amb. ex. and plen. April20
1989 Alan (later Sir A) Gordon Munro, amb. ex. and plen. Aug16
1993 The Hon. David Alwyn Gore-Booth, amb. ex. and plen. April4
1996 Andrew (later Sir A) Fleming Green, amb. ex. and plen. March27
2000 Derek (later Sir D) John Plumbly, amb. ex. and plen. June15
2003 Sherard (later Sir S) Louis Cowper-Coles, amb. ex. and plen. Sept

Senegal
1985 John Esmond Campbell Macrae, amb. ex. and plen. Dec18
1990 Roger Campbell Beetham, amb. ex. and plen. July7
1993 Alan Edwin Furness, amb. ex. and plen. Aug24
1997 David Raymond Snoxell, amb. ex. and plen. April4
2000 Edward Alan Burner, amb. ex. and plen. Aug10
2004 Peter Newall, amb. ex. and plen. May

Serbia and Montenegro (formerly Yugoslavia)
2001 Charles Graham Crawford, CMG, amb. ex. and plen. Jan12
2003 David John Gowan, amb. ex. and plen. Sept14

Seychelles
HIGH COMMISSIONERS
1986 (Alexander Basil) Peter Smart. Sept30
1989 Guy William Pulbrook Hart. June22
1992 Edward John Sharland. Jan24
1995 Peter Alexander Bremner Thomson. Feb17
1997 John William Yapp. Nov1
2002 Fraser Andrew Wilson. May7
2004 Diana Skingle. July

Sierra Leone
HIGH COMMISSIONERS
1986 Derek William Partridge. June6
1991 David Keith Sprague. May30
1993 Ian McCluney. Sept23
1997 Peter Alfred Penfold. March10
2000 David Alan Jones. May4
2003 Dr John Edward Mitchiner. Aug1

Singapore

HIGH COMMISSIONERS

1985 Sir (William Erskine) Hamilton Whyte. March16
1987 Michael (later Sir M) Edmund Pike. July13
1991 Gordon Aldridge Duggan. Jan12
1997 Alan Charles Hunt. Aug8
2001 Sir Stephen David Reid Brown. March1
2002 Alan Stanley Collins. Dec14

Slovakia

1993 David Brighty, amb. ex. and plen.
1994 Michael Charles Bates, amb. ex. and plen. July1
1995 Peter Gale Harborne, amb. ex. and plen. Feb20
1998 David Edward Lyscom, amb. ex. and plen. Oct15
2001 Damian Roderic Todd, amb. ex. and plen. Nov16
2004 Judith Anne Macgregor, amb. ex. and plen. June

Slovenia

1992 Gordon Mackenzie Johnston, amb. ex. and plen. Aug25
1997 David Andrew Lloyd, amb. ex. and plen. Feb21
2001 Hugh Roger Mortimer, amb. ex. and plen. Jan1
2005 Timothy Michael John Simmons, amb. ex. and plen. April

Solomon Islands

HIGH COMMISSIONERS

1986 John Bramble Noss. March17
1988 (David) Junor Young. Oct10
1991 Raymond Francis Jones. May12
1995 Brian Norman Connelly. Dec31
1998 Alan Waters. Sept1.
2001 Brian Paul Baldwin. May16
2004 Richard John Lyne. Dec

Somali Democratic Republic

1987 Jeremy Richard Lovering Grosvenor Varcoe, amb. ex. and plen. Feb15
1989 Ian McCluney, amb. ex. and plen. July9

South Africa

AMBASSADORS

†1987 Robin (later Sir R) William Renwick, amb. ex. and plen. July24
†1991 Anthony (later Sir A) Reeve, amb. ex. and plen. July1

†From 10 May 1961, the British High Commission became the British Embassy, then from 1June 1994 it reverted to the British High Commission.

HIGH COMMISSIONERS

1994 Sir Anthony Reeve. June1
1996 Maeve (later Dame Maeve) Geraldine Fort. Nov11
2000 Ann Grant. Oct1
2005 The Rt Hon. Paul Boateng. May31

Soviet Union now see Russian Federation

1985 Sir Bryan George Cartledge, amb. ex. and plen. July18
1988 Sir Rodric Quentin Braithwaite, amb. ex. and plen. Sept20

Spain

1989 (Patrick) Robin (later Sir R) Fearn, amb. ex. and plen. Nov23
1994 Anthony David Brighty, amb. ex. and plen. Sept1
1998 Peter (later Sir P) James Torry, amb. ex. and plen. Sept2
2003 Stephen John Leadbetter Wright, amb. ex. and plen. May

Sri Lanka

HIGH COMMISSIONERS

1987 David Arthur Stuart Gladstone. June29
1991 Edward John Field. Nov22
1996 David Everard Tatham. March21
1999 Linda Duffield. Jan18
2002 Stephen Nicholas Evans. July16

Sudan

1986 John Lewis Beaven, amb. ex. and plen. Dec3
1990 Allan John Ramsay, amb. ex. and plen. June23
1991 Peter John Streams, amb. ex. and plen. Nov29
1995 Alan Fletcher Goulty, amb. ex. and plen. March23
1999 Richard Edward Makepeace, amb. ex. and plen. July13
2002 William Charters Patey, amb. ex. and plen. Sept1
2005 Ian Cameron Cliff, amb. ex. and plen. May

Surinam

1985 John Dudley Massingham, amb. ex. and plen. July3
1987 David Purvis Small, amb. ex. and plen. July16
1991 (Robert) Douglas Gordon, amb. ex. and plen. April27
1993 David John Johnson, amb. ex. and plen. Feb19
1998 Edward Glover, Nov19
2002 Stephen John Hiscock, Aug29

Swaziland

HIGH COMMISSIONERS

1987 John Gerrard Flynn. May26
1990 Brian Watkins. May20
1993 Richard Hugh Turton Gozney. Aug8
1996 John Frederick Doble. Feb29
1999 Neil Kenneth Hook. Oct4
2001 David (George) Reader. Sept26
2004 George Thomas Squires. Nov3
2005 Elizabeth Anne Ripard, Chargé d'Affaires March5

Sweden

1987 Sir John Burns Ure, amb. ex. and plen. Dec7
1991 Robert Linklater Burke Cormack, amb. ex. and plen. June17
1995 Roger (later Sir R) Bridgland Bone, amb. ex. and plen. Sept1

1999 John Douglas Kelso Grant CMG, amb. ex. and plen. April6
2003 Anthony Joyce Cary, amb. ex. and plen. Oct2

Switzerland
1985 John Rowland Rich, amb. ex. and plen. May2
1988 Christopher William Long, amb. ex. and plen. July25
1992 David Beattie, amb. ex. and plen. May5
1997 Christopher Hulse, amb. ex. and plen. April
2001 Basil Stephen Talbot Eastwood, amb. ex. and plen. Aug15
2004 Simon Mark Featherstone, amb. ex. and plen. March20

Syria
The Syrian Republic severed Diplomatic and Consular Relations with the United Kingdom on 6June 1967 until 28May 1973
Diplomatic and Consular relations with the Syrian Arab Republic were broken off with effect from 31October 1986. They were resumed on 28November 1990
1991 Andrew (later Sir A)Fleming Green, amb. ex. and plen. Feb17
1994 Adrian John Sindall, amb. ex. and plen. May28
1996 Basil Stephen Talbot Eastwood, amb. ex. and plen. Sept30
2000 Henry George Hogger, amb. ex. and plen. June12
2003 Peter Ford, amb. ex. and plen. Sept5

Tajikistan
1994 Alexander Paul A'Court Bergne, amb. ex. and plen. Jan27
1995 Barbara Logan Hay, amb. ex. and plen. May15
1999 Christopher Ingham, amb. ex. and plen. Feb3
2002 Michael Forbes Smith, amb. ex. and plen. May26
2004 Graeme Neil Loten, amb. ex. and plen. June

Tanzania
HIGH COMMISSIONERS
Diplomatic Relations were broken off with Tanzania from 15December 1965 to 4July 1968
1986 Colin (later Sir C) Henry Imray. Jan6
1989 (John) Thorold Masefield. July22
1992 Roger Westbrook. Sept30
1995 Alan Everard Montgomery. July15
1998 Bruce Harry Dinwiddy. April22
2001 Richard Ian Clarke. Aug2
2003 Andrew John Pocock. Sept22

Thailand
1986 Derek Tonkin, amb. ex. and plen. Feb18
1989 (Michael) Ramsay Melhuish amb. ex. and plen. Nov7
1992 Charles Christian Wilfrid Adams, amb. ex. and plen. March14
1996 James (later Sir J) William Hodge, amb. ex. and plen. Sept6
2000 Lloyd Barnaby Smith, amb. ex. and plen. March1
2003 David William Fall, amb. ex. and plen. July25

Togo
1986 Arthur Hope Wyatt, amb. ex. and plen. Oct24
1989 Anthony Michael Goodenough, amb. ex. and plen. Dec5
1992 David Crithlow Walker, amb. ex. and plen. June16
1996 Ian Warren Mackley CMG, amb. ex. and plen. Jul7
2000 Roderick Allen Pullen, amb. ex. and plen. Oct 11
2004 Gordon Geoffrey Wetherell, amb. ex. and plen. March

Tonga
HIGH COMMISSIONERS
1987 Andrew Paul Fabian. March7
1990 William Lawson Cordiner. April3
1994 Andrew James Morris. Nov8
1998 Brian Connelly. Aug20
2002 Paul William Downs Nessling. Jan14

Trinidad and Tobago
HIGH COMMISSIONERS
1985 Martin (later Sir M) Seymour Berthoud. April11
1991 Brian Smith. Nov11
1996 Leo Gregory Faulkner. July3
1999 Peter Gale Harborne. July15
2004 Ronald Peter Nash. Jan16

Tunisia
1987 Stephen Peter Day, amb. ex. and plen. Dec17
1992 Michael Logan Tait, amb. ex. and plen. July9
1995 Richard John Smale Edis, amb. ex. and plen. Dec4
1999 Ivor Rawlinson, amb. ex. and plen. Feb15
2002 Robin Andrew Kealy, amb. ex. and plen. Jan15
2004 Alan Fletcher Goulty, amb. ex. and plen. Oct

Turkey
1986 Timothy (later Sir T) Lewis Achilles Daunt, amb. ex. and plen. Nov1
1992 Peter John Goulden, amb. ex. and plen. Oct23
1995 Sir (Walter) Kieran Prendergast, amb. ex. and plen. March23
1997 David Brian Carleton Logan, amb. ex. and plen. March28
2002 Peter (later Sir P) John Westmacott, amb. ex. and plen. Jan15

Turkmenistan
1993 Sir Brian James Proetel Fall, amb. ex. and plen. Jan31
1995 Neil Kenneth Hook, amb. ex. and plen. Sept15
1998 Fraser Wilson MBE, amb. ex. and plen. July6

2002 Paul Brummell, amb. ex. and plen. Feb16
2005 Peter Roderick Butcher, amb. ex. and plen. June

Tuvalu
HIGH COMMISSIONERS
1989 (Alexander Basil) Peter Smart. Nov29
1995 Michael John Peart. April14
1997 Michael Alan Charles Dibben. Dec3
2000 Michael Anthony Price. Oct16
2002 Charles Francis Mochan. Nov16

Uganda
HIGH COMMISSIONERS
Diplomatic Relations were broken off on 28July 1976 until 21April 1979
1986 Derek (later Sir D) Maxwell March. June29
1989 Charles Augustine Kaye Cullimore. Dec21
1993 Edward Clay. Oct1
1997 Michael Edgar Cook. April10
2000 Tom Richard Vaughan Phillips. May15
2002 Adam Wood. Oct14
2005 Jean Francois Gordon. July

Ukraine
1992 David Arthur Stewart Gladstone, Chargé d'Affaires. Jan17
1992 Simon Nicholas Peter Hemans, amb. ex. and plen. June4
1995 Roy Stephen Reeve, amb. ex. and plen. June5
1999 Roland Hedley Smith, amb. ex. and plen. May16
2002 Robert Edward Brinkley, amb. ex. and plen. Aug3

United Arab Emirates
1986 Michael Logan Tait, amb. ex. and plen. April27
1990 Graham Stuart Burton, amb. ex. and plen. Feb6
1994 Anthony Davis Harris, amb. ex. and plen. June25
1998 Patrick Michael Nixon, amb. ex. and plen. Nov1
2003 Richard Edward Makepeace, amb. ex. and plen. Feb21

United States
1986 Sir Antony Arthur Acland, amb. ex. and plen. Aug28
1991 Sir Robin William Renwick, amb. ex. and plen. Aug20
1995 Sir John Olav Kerr, amb. ex. and plen. Aug15
1997 Sir Christopher Meyer, amb. ex. and plen. Oct31
2003 Sir David Geoffrey Manning, amb. ex. and plen. Aug

Uruguay
1986 Eric Victor Vines, amb. ex. and plen. March14
1989 Colum John Sharkey, amb. ex. and plen. July14
1991 Donald Alexander Lamont, amb. ex. and plen. July14
1994 Robert Andrew Michie Hendrie, amb. ex. and plen. Sept1
1998 Andrew Murray, amb. ex. and plen. May23
2001 John Vivian Everard, amb. ex. and plen. Sept4
2005 Dr Charles Hugh Salvesen, amb. ex. and plen. May

Uzbekistan
1992 Sir Brian James Proetel Fall, amb. ex. and plen. Oct21
1993 Alexander Paul A'Court Bergne, amb. ex. and plen. Oct29
1995 Barbara Logan Hay, amb. ex. and plen. May15
1999 Christopher Ingham, amb. ex. and plen. Feb3
2002 Craig John Murray, amb. ex. and plen. Sept16
2005 David John Moran, amb. ex. and plen. March

Vanuatu
HIGH COMMISSIONERS
1985 Malcolm Lars Creek. Aug27
1988 John Thompson. March25
1992 Thomas Joseph Duggin. Jan15
1997 Malcolm Geoffrey Hilson.
2000 Michael Thomas Hill. Nov16

Vatican City (see Holy See)

Venezuela
1985 Michael John Newington, amb. ex. and plen. April28
1988 Giles Eden FitzHerbert, amb. ex. and plen. Jan18
1993 John Gerrard Flynn, amb. ex. and plen. April4
1997 Richard Denys Wilkinson, amb. ex. and plen. May2
2000 Dr Edgar John Hughes, amb. ex. and plen. July22
2003 Donald Alexander Lamont, amb. ex. and plen. July31

South Vietnam
(Vietnam was formally unified in July 1976)

Vietnam
1985 Richard Gilbert Tallboys, amb. ex. and plen. June12
1987 Emrys Thomas Davies, amb. ex. and plen. May27
1990 Peter Keegan Williams, amb. ex. and plen. Oct27
1997 David William Fall, amb. ex. and plen. Apr25
2000 Warwick Morris, amb. ex. and plen. June16
2003 Robert Anthony Eagleson Gordon, amb. ex. and plen. Sept16

Yemen
1987 Mark Anthony Marshall, amb. ex. and plen. Nov23
1993 (Robert) Douglas Gordon, amb. ex. and plen. March20

1995 Douglas Scrafton amb. ex. and plen. March4
1997 Victor Joseph Henderson CMG, amb. ex. and plen. Oct19
2001 Frances Mary Guy, amb. ex. and plen. March9
2004 Michael John Gifford, amb. ex. and plen. July

Yemen (People's Democratic Republic of)

1986 Arthur Stirling-Maxwell Marshall, amb. ex. and plen. Jan4
1989 (Robert) Douglas Gordon, amb. ex. and plen. Jan29

The People's Democratic Republic of Yemen and the Yemen Arab Republic merged on 22May 1990 to become the Republic of Yemen

Yugoslavia (Federal Republic of) (now see Serbia and Montenegro)

1996 Ivor (later Sir I) Antony Roberts, amb. ex. and plen. May6
1997 Joseph Brian Donnelly, amb. ex. and plen. Nov17

Diplomatic Relations with The Federal Republic of Yugoslavia were broken off with effect from 26 March 1999 and were restored on 17 November 2000.

2000 David Maurice Landsman, OBE, Chargé d'Affaires Nov17

Zambia

HIGH COMMISSIONERS

1988 John Michael Wilson. Jan21
1990 Peter Robert Mossom Hinchcliffe. May19
1994 Patrick Michael Nixon. Feb1
1998 Thomas Nesbitt Young. Jan3
2002 Timothy James David. May16
2005 William Alistair Harrison. Aug

Zimbabwe

HIGH COMMISSIONERS

1985 (Michael) Ramsay Melhuish. Feb20
1989 (Walter) Kieran (later Sir K) Prendergast. Aug10
1992 Richard Nigel Dales. Sept21
1995 Martin John Williams. Nov28
1998 Peter Longworth. Apr7
2001 Joseph Brian (later Sir B) Donnelly. June30

In December 2003 the British High Commission in Zimbabwe became the British Embassy.

AMBASSADORS

2004 Dr Roderick Allen Pullen, amb. ex. and plen. July

CHRONOLOGICAL LIST OF BRITISH REPRESENTATIVES TO INTERNATIONAL ORGANISATIONS 1985-2005/6

UNITED KINGDOM MISSION TO THE UNITED NATIONS

New York

1987 Sir Crispin Charles Cervantes Tickell, Perm. Rep. and Rep. on the Security Council with personal rank of amb. May29
1990 Sir David Hugh Alexander Hannay, Perm. Rep. and Rep. on the Security Council with personal rank of amb. Sept7
1995 Sir (Philip) John Weston, Perm. Rep. and Rep. on the Security Council with personal rank of amb. July15
1998 Sir Jeremy Quentin Greenstock, Perm. Rep. and Rep. on the Security Council with personal rank of amb. Aug8
2003 Sir Emyr Jones Parry, Perm. Rep. and Rep. on the Security Council with personal rank of amb. July1

UNITED KINGDOM MISSON TO THE OFFICE OF THE UNITED NATIONS AND OTHER INTERNATIONAL ORGANISATIONS AT GENEVA

1985 John Anthony Sankey, Perm. Rep. with personal rank of amb. Dec17
1990 Martin Robert Morland, Perm. Rep. with personal rank of amb. July13
1993 Nigel Christopher Ransome Williams, Perm. Rep. with personal rank of amb. Sept15
1997 Roderic Michael Lyne, Perm. Rep. with personal rank of amb. May1
2000 Simon William Fuller, Perm. Rep. with personal rank of amb. Jan16
2003 Nicholas Alan Thorne, Perm. Rep. with personal rank of amb. Nov30

UNITED KINGDOM DELEGATION TO THE CONFERENCE ON DISARMAMENT

(formerly the UK Delegation to the Conference of the 18-Nation Committee on Disarmament)

Geneva

1987 Tessa Audrey Hilda Solesby, Leader of Del. with personal rank of amb. Oct10
1992 Sir Michael Charles Swift Weston, Leader of Del. with personal rank of amb. April6
1997 (Samuel) Ian Soutar, Leader of Del. with personal rank of amb. Aug8
2001 David Stuart Broucher, Leader of Del. with personal rank of amb. Oct1
2004 Dr John PatrickGeorge Freeman, Leader of Del. with personal rank of amb. Sept

UNITED KINGDOM DELEGATION TO THE NORTH ATLANTIC TREATY ORGANISATION

Brussels

1986 Michael (later Sir M) O'Donel Bjarne Alexander, Perm. Rep. on the North Atlantic Council with personal rank of amb. Aug30
1992 Sir (Philip) John Weston, Perm. Rep. on the North Atlantic Council with personal rank of amb. Jan25
1995 Peter John Goulden, Perm. Rep. on the North Atlantic Council with personal rank of amb. April1
2000 David (later Sir D) Geoffrey Manning, Perm. Rep. on the North Atlantic Council with personal rank of amb. Dec
2001 Dr Emyr Jones Parry, Perm. Rep. on the North Atlantic Council with personal rank of amb. Sept16

2003 Peter Forbes Ricketts, Perm. Rep. on the North Atlantic Council with personal rank of amb. July1

UNITED KINGDOM DELEGATION TO THE WESTERN EUROPEAN COUNCIL

Brussels

1993 Sir (Philip) John Weston, Perm. Rep. on the Permanent Council of the Western European Union with personal rank of amb. Jan1

UNITED KINGDOM DELEGATION TO THE ORGANISATION FOR ECONOMIC CO-OPERATION AND DEVELOPMENT

Paris

1985 Nicholas Peter Bayne, Perm. Rep. with personal rank of amb. Oct1
1988 John Walton David Gray, Perm. Rep. with personal rank of amb. July11
1992 Keith Gordon MacInnes, Perm. Rep. with the personal rank of amb. July1
1995 Peter William Medlicott Vereker, Perm. Rep. with the personal rank of amb. Sept1
1999 Christopher Crabbie, Perm. Rep. with the personal rank of amb. June11
2004 David Edward Lyscom, Perm. Rep. with the personal rank of amb. Jan1

OFFICE OF THE UNITED KINGDOM PERMANENT REPRESENTATIVE TO THE EUROPEAN UNION (formerly UK Delegation to the European Communities)

Brussels

1985 David (later Sir D) Hugh Alexander Hannay, Perm. Rep. with personal rank of amb. Oct14
1990 John (later Sir J) Olav Kerr, Perm. Rep. with personal rank of amb. Sept2
1995 (John) Stephen (later Sir S) Wall, Perm. Rep. with personal rank of amb. Aug15
2000 Nigel (later Sir N) Elton Sheinwald, Perm. Rep. with personal rank of amb. Aug31
2003 John (later Sir J) Douglas Kelso Grant, Perm. Rep. with personal rank of amb. Aug1

UNITED KINGDOM DELEGATION TO THE COUNCIL OF EUROPE

Strasbourg

1986 Colin McLean, Perm. Rep. with personal rank of amb. Aug6
1990 Noel Hedley Marshall, Perm. Rep. with personal rank of amb. Sept6
1993 Roger Campbell Beetham, Perm. Rep. with personal rank of amb. Aug1
1997 Andrew Carter, Perm. Rep. with personal rank of amb. Aug1
2003 Stephen Frederick Howarth, Perm. Rep. with personal rank of amb. March1

UNITED KINGDOM MISSION TO THE INTERNATIONAL ATOMIC ENERGY AGENCY, THE UNITED NATIONS INDUSTRIAL DEVELOPMENT ORGANISATION AND THE UNITED NATIONS (VIENNA) (formerly UK Mission to the IAEA and to UN Organisations at Vienna)

Vienna

1987 Gerald Edmund Clark, Perm. Rep. with personal rank of amb. June3
1992 Christopher Hulse, Perm. Rep. with personal rank of amb. Nov26
1997 John Patrick George Freeman, Perm. Rep. with personal rank of amb. May2
2001 Peter Redmond Jenkins, Perm. Rep. with personal rank of amb. Aug9

UNITED KINGDOM DELEGATION TO THE CONFERENCE ON SECURITY AND COOPERATION IN EUROPE (OSCE)

Vienna

1989 (John) Michael Edes, Perm. Rep. with personal rank of amb. March6
1990 Paul Lever, Head of Del. with personal rank of amb. May7
1992 Terence Courtney Wood, Head of Del. with personal rank of amb. April4
1993 Simon William John Fuller, Head of Del. with personal rank of amb. Sept1
1999 John Robert de Fonblanque, Head of Del. with personal rank of amb. June16
2003 Colin Andrew Munro, Head of Del. with personal rank of amb. Dec21

CHRONOLOGICAL LIST OF GOVERNORS AND COMMANDERS-IN-CHIEF ETC. OF OVERSEAS TERRITORIES 1985-2005/6 (MEMBERS HM DIPLOMATIC SERVICE ONLY)

Anguilla

1985 Alistair Turner Baillie
1990 Brian George John Canty
1992 Alan William Shave
1995 Alan Norman Hoole
1997 Robert Malcolm Harris
2000 Peter Johnstone
2004 Alan Edden Huckle

Bermuda

1988 Major General Sir Desmond Langley
1992 The Rt Hon The Lord Waddington
1997 Thorold Masefield
2002 Sir John Vereker

British Indian Ocean Territory

1986 William Marsden
1988 Richard John Smale Edis
1991 Thomas George Harris
1994 David Ross MacLennan
1996 Bruce Dinwiddy
1999 John White
2001 Alan Edden Huckle
2004 Anthony Campbell Crombie

British Virgin Islands

1987 John Mark Ambrose Herdman

1992 Peter Alfred Penfold
1995 David Patrick Robert Mackilligin
1998 Francis Joseph Savage
2000 Thomas Townley Macan

Cayman Islands
1992 Michael Edward John Gore
1995 John Wynne Owen
1999 Peter Smith
2002 Bruce Harry Dinwiddy
2005 Stuart Duncan Macdonald Jack

Falkland Islands/British Antarctic Islands
1986 Gordon Wesley Jewkes
1989 William Hugh Fullerton
1993 David Edward Tatham
1996 Richard Peter Ralph
1999 Donald Lamont
2002 Howard John Stredder Pearce
2006 Alan Edden Huckle

Gibraltar
1992 Sir Hugo White
1997 The Rt Hon Sir Richard Luce (later Baron Luce)
2000 David (later Sir D) Robert Campbell Durie
2003 Sir Francis Neville Richards

Montserrat
1985 Arthur Christopher Watson
1987 Christopher John Turner
1990 David Pendleton Taylor
1993 Francis Joseph Savage
1997 Anthony John Abbott
2001 Anthony James Longrigg
2004 Deborah Elizabeth Vavasseur Barnes-Jones

Pitcairn, Henderson, Ducie and Oeno Islands
1985 Terrence Daniel O'Leary
1988 Robert Archer Campbell Byatt
1991 David Joseph Moss
1994 Robert John Alston
1998 Martin Williams
2001 Richard Taylor Fell

St Helena (incl. Ascension and Tristan da Cunha)
1989 Robert Frederick Stimson
1991 Alan Norman Hoole
1995 David Leslie Smallman
1999 David James Hollamby
2004 Michael Clancy

Turks and Caicos Islands
1987 Michael John Bradley
1993 Martin Bourke
1996 John Philip Kelly
2000 Mervyn Thomas Jones
2002 James Poston
2005 Richard David Tauwhare

CHRONOLOGICAL LIST OF NON GOVERNMENTAL TRADE OFFICES (ANNEX) 1992-2005/6

Taipei
1992 Philip Morrice
1995 Alan Stanley Collins, CMG
1999 David Coates
2000 Derek Richard Marsh, CVO
2005 Michael David Reilly

Part IV

Biographical Notes and List of Staff

ABBREVIATIONS

m	married
ptnr	partner
d	daughter
s	son
Diss	Dissolved
Dec'd	Deceased
AUSS	Assistant Under Secretary of State
BOTB	British Overseas Trade Board
CDA	Career Development Attachment
CDE	Conference on Confidence and Security- Building Measures and Disarmament in Europe
CENTO	Central Treaty Organisations
CFE	Negotiations on Conventional Armed Forces in Europe
CO	Cabinet Office
COI	Central Office of Information
CRO	Commonwealth Relations Office
CSBM	Negotiations on Confidence-and Security Building Measures
CSC	Civil Service Commission
CSCE	Conference on Security and Co-operation in Europe
CSD	Civil Service Department
CSO	Chief Security Officer
CSSB	Civil Service Selection Board
DoE	Department of Environment
DETR	Department for Environment, Transport and the Regions
DHC	Deputy High Commissioner
DoI	Department of Industry
DfID	Department for International Development
DS	Diplomatic Service
DSAO	Diplomatic Service Administration Office
DSS	Department of Social Security
DoT	Department of Trade
DTI	Department of Trade and Industry
DUSS	Deputy Under Secretary of State
ECGD	Export Credits Guarantee Department
ECSC	European Coal and Steel Community
ENA	Ecole Nationale d'Administration (Paris)
FCO	Foreign and Commonwealth Office
FO	Foreign Office
HCS	Home Civil Service
HMOCS	Her Majesty's Overseas Civil Service
HO	Home Office
IISS	International Institute for Strategic Studies
JSDC	Joint Services Defence College
MBFR	Mutual Reduction of Forces and Armaments (Vienna)
MECAS	Middle East Centre for Arab Studies
MoD	Ministry of Defence
MPBW	Ministry of Public Buildings and Works
MPNI	Ministry of Pensions and National Insurance
MPO	Management and Personnel Office
NATO	North Atlantic Treaty Organisation
OEEC	Organisation for European Economic Co-operation
OFTEL	Office of Telecommunications
OMCS	Office of the Minister for the Civil Service
POMEF	Political Office Middle East Forces
PRO	Principal Research Officer
RCDS	Royal College of Defence Studies
SEATO	South East Asia Treaty Organisation
SO	Security Officer
SOAS	School of Oriental and African Studies
SOWC	Senior Officers War Course
SRO	Senior Research Officer
SUPL	Special Unpaid Leave
UN	United Nations
UNHCR	United Nations High Commission for Refugees
WO	War Office

Part IV: Biographical List

Statement concerning the present appointments and some other particulars of the careers of established members of Her Majesty's Diplomatic Service.

A

Abayomi, Olufunke Adepeju; Third Secretary (Immigration) Tehran since June 2003; Born 09/04/65; FCO 1995; Transferred to the Diplomatic Service 2003; Band B3; m 1992 Olushola Abayomi (2d 1993, 2000).

Abbott, Belinda-Jayne (née Simmons); FCO since May 2001; Born 12/09/65; FCO 1988; Buenos Aires 1990; Phnom Penh 1996; Band B3; m 2000 Peter Douglas Abbott.

Abbott, David; Second Secretary (Commercial) Madras since September 2001; Born 06/06/64; FCO 1983; Singapore 1985; Africa/ME Floater 1989; Kaduna 1991; Abuja 1993; FCO 1994; Band C4; m 1990 Nor Hayati Binte Ibrahim (1d 1992; 1s 1993).

Abbott, Neil Middleton; Vice-Consul Moscow since August 2004; Born 21/06/65; FCO 1987; Riyadh 1990; FCO 1994; Third Secretary (Chancery/Consular) Abu Dhabi 1996; Third Secretary Ljubljana 1999; Band B3; m (1) 1990 Janet Probyn (diss 2003) (1s 1992; 1d 1995); (2) m 2005 Tina Gruden.

Abbott, Nicholas Robert John; First Secretary (Regional Expert, Arab World Projects) Cairo since January 2004; Born 25/04/63; FCO 1985; Language Training 1986; Third Secretary (Chancery/Information) Riyadh 1988; Brussels-Stagiare 1991; Third Secretary (Economic) Paris 1992; Second Secretary (Commercial) Doha 1995; FCO 1998; First Secretary (Economic) Riyadh 2000; m 1989 Marcelle Ghislaine Julienne Delvaux (2d 1995, 1996).

Abbott-Watt, Thorhilda Mary Vivia; HM Ambassador Yerevan since January 2003; FCO 1974; SUPL 1977; FCO 1978; Latin American Floater 1979; Paris 1981; Brussels (UKREP) 1984; Second Secretary FCO 1986; Second Secretary Bonn 1988; First Secretary FCO 1991; First Secretary(Commercial/Know How Fund) Kiev 1995; FCO/Home Office Joint Entry Clearance Unit 1999; ptnr, Reef Talbot Hogg.

Abel, Martin Jeremy; First Secretary Istanbul since December 2001; Born 30/04/51; MPBW 1969; FCO 1971; Paris 1974; Madras 1976; FCO 1978; Luxembourg 1979; Peking 1982; FCO 1984; Istanbul 1988; Wellington 1993; FCO 1997; Band C5; m (1) 1974 Lynne Diane Bailey (diss 1991) (1d 1978; 1s 1980); (2) 1992 Nilufer Fasiha Kantarci (1d 1984).

Abrahams, David William; Second Secretary FCO since August 1983; Born 14/07/53; FCO 1974; Geneva 1978; Brussels 1981; Band C4; m 1978 Susan Joy Denise Gibson (3d 1987, 1988, 1990).

Abrams, Christine Ann; Seoul since September 2004; Born 07/01/64; WRAC 1986-89; Derbyshire Police Force 1995-98; FCO 2000; World Wide Floater Duties 2002; Band A2.

Ackerman, Erica Alexandra (née Smith); Second Secretary (Commercial) Singapore since November 2001; Born 09/04/63; FCO 1983; Caracas 1985; SUPL 1989; FCO 1995; Third Secretary (Commercial/Aid) Manila 1998; SUPL 1998; Manila 1998; Band C4; m 1989 Robert Joseph Ackerman (dec'd 1992).

Adam, Stuart William; Second Secretary (Political) Vienna (UKDEL - OSCE) since May 2002; Born 20/03/71; FCO 1990; Bonn 1992; Peking 1995; Vienna (Embassy) 2000; Band C4; m 1996 Lesley Elizabeth Quate (1d 2000; 1s 2001).

Adams, Catherine Elizabeth; On loan to the Office of the Attorney General since July 2002; Born 29/11/65; Assistant Legal Adviser FCO 1994; First Secretary (Legal) Brussels (UKREP) 1997; Legal Counsellor FCO 2001.

Adams, Chloë Jayne; FCO since October 2004; Born 03/09/79; Band C4.

Adams, Geoffrey Doyne, CMG (2003); Private Secretary to the Secretary of State, FCO since July 2003; Born 11/06/57; FCO 1979; Language Training 1980; Third later Second Secretary Jedda 1982; First Secretary ENA Paris 1985; FCO 1986; Private Secretary to the PUS 1987; First Secretary (Head of Political Section) Pretoria/Cape Town 1991; FCO 1994; On loan to (European Secrerariat) Cabinet Office 1996; Counsellor and DHM Cairo 1998; Consul-General Jerusalem 2001; m 1999 Mary Emma Baxter (1d 2003).

Adams, Gillian; FCO since September 2001; Born 10/06/65; MOD 1982; FCO 1984; Nicosia 1986; Africa/Middle East Floater 1989; FCO 1993; Language Training 1997; Brussels (JMO) 1998; Band B3.

Adams, Trevor Malcolm; Deputy Director for Trade and Investment Bangkok since August 2002; Born 16/04/51; FCO 1971; Paris 1973; Middle East Floater 1976; Bucharest 1977; JAO New York 1979; FCO 1982; Vientiane 1984; Rangoon 1985; HM Consul Casablanca 1988; FCO 1993; First Secretary (Press and Public Affairs) Hong Kong 1998; Band C5; m 1979 Linda Jane Burgess (1d 1985).

Adamson, Donald Snaith; FCO since January 2000; Born 03/04/49; Ministry of Social Security 1967; FCO 1968; Khartoum 1971; Brussels (EC) 1972; Wellington 1975; Dacca 1978; On loan to ODA 1981; FCO 1983; Cape Town 1985; FCO 1988; Second Secretary (Consular) Islamabad 1992; Second Secretary FCO 1993; Abuja 1996; m 1970 June Alice Manson Hall (1s 1973; 1d 1977).

Adamson, Joanne; Washington since October 2002; Born 09/07/67; FCO 1989; Language Training Cairo 1991; Third later Second Secretary (Chancery/Comm) Jerusalem 1992; On secondment to UNWRA 1999.

Addiscott, Emily Margaret (née Dallas); Seconded to British Trade International later renamed UK Trade and Investment since August 2003; Born 27/05/72; FCO 1991; SUPL 1994; Kiev 1996; SUPL 1997; Band A2; m 1993 Fraser John Addiscott (2d 1997, 1999).

Addiscott, Fraser John; Seconded to British Trade International later renamed UK Trade and Investment since May 2002; Born FCO 1990; Vice Consul Helsinki 1994; Third Secretary (Management) Kiev 1996; Third Secretary (Political) Singapore 1997; SUPL 2001; Band C4; m 1993 Emily Margaret Dallas (2d 1997, 1999).

Ager, Keith; FCO since September 2002; Born 25/06/48; FO 1965; Bonn 1975; FCO 1977; Lilongwe 1979; FCO 1982; Montevideo 1982; FCO 1985; Rome 1988; FCO 1991; Madrid 1998; Band D6; m 1969 Ann Simmons (2d 1974, 1978).

Ager, Martyn Eric; FCO since August 1993; Born 17/06/55; FCO 1972; Moscow 1982; FCO 1985; Amman 1990; Band C4; m 1981 Kathryn Margaret Pierson (2s 1984, 1992; 1d 1986; twins, 1s, 1d 1994).

Ahmad, Asif Anwar; Head of Commonwealth Coordination Department FCO since April 2002; Born 21/01/56; DTI Business Link 1996; First Secretary FCO 1999; Deputy Head of Resource Budgeting Department FCO 2000; m (1) (diss 1991); m (2) 1993 Zubeda Khamboo (1d 1975; 3s 1980, 1982, 1984).

Al-Qaq, Stephanie Jane (née Powell); FCO since March 2003; Born 03/03/76; Band C4.

Alcock, Caroline; Second Secretary (Political) Cairo since November 2003; Born 08/12/70; FCO 1993; Full-Time Language Training 1993; Third Secretary Bahrain 1996; Third Secretary Cairo 1999; SUPL 2002; Band C4; m 1996 Amir Waguih.

Alcock, Michael Leslie, MBE (1986); FCO since April 1999; Born 07/08/50; Ministry of Labour 1967; DSAO (later FCO) 1968; Bangkok 1971; Port of Spain 1975; Tehran 1977; FCO 1979; Second Secretary (Chancery) and Vice-Consul Addis Ababa 1984; Second later First Secretary (Comm/Econ) New Delhi 1987; First Secretary FCO 1991; First Secretary (Aid/Commercial) Kathmandu 1994; m 1971 Barbara Ann Couch (2s 1972, 1976).

Alcock, Nicholas Harding; FCO since October 2004; Born 21/04/76; Band C4; m 2004 Ana Perowne.

Alderton, Clive; Consul-General Lille since January 2004; Born 09/05/67; FCO 1986; Vice-Consul Warsaw 1988; Third Secretary (External Relations) Brussels (UKREP) 1990; Second later First Secretary FCO 1993; Head of Chancery (DHM) Singapore 1998; m 1990 Catriona Mitchell Canning (1d 1998; 1s 2000).

Aldridge, Terence John; FCO since February 2000; Born 11/09/56; FCO 1980; Darwin 1982; FCO 1984; Tel Aviv 1987; FCO 1988; Rome 1997; Band C5; m 1988 Janet Lorna Shore (1d 1991; 1s 1994).

Alessandri, Madeleine Kay (née Hateley); Counsellor Tokyo since January 2004; Born 06/03/65; FCO 1988; Second Secretary (Chancery/Info) Vienna 1990; Second later First Secretary FCO 1993; Consul (Economic) Frankfurt 1996; Language Training 1999; FCO 2000; m 1990 Enrico Alessandri (1d 1993; 1s 1998).

Aliaga, Deborah Joy; Third Secretary (Press and Public Affairs) Lisbon since September 2002; Born 08/07/60; FCO 1979; Bonn 1980; La Paz 1983; Resigned 1986; Reinstated FCO 1987; Third Secretary (Man/VC/ECO) La Paz 1997; Band B3; m 1989 Kenny Aliaga (1d 1996; 1s 2000).

Allan, Duncan Brierton; T/D Kiev since September 2004; Born 22/11/61; FCO 1989; Moscow 1992; Principal Research Officer FCO 1996; m 1994 Joanne Clare Youde.

Allan, Jane Alison (née Higgs); Bahrain since December 2002; Born 09/03/63; HCS 1981; FCO 1981; Washington 1984; FCO 1987; SUPL 1989; Peking 1990; SUPL 1991; FCO 1996; SUPL 1998; Band B3; m 1987 Ian Allan.

Allan, Justine Rachael Anne; Second Secretary FCO since January 2000; Born 15/07/69; FCO 1990; Cape Town/Pretoria 1993; Jedda 1996; Floater Duties 1998; Band C4.

Allan, Keith Rennie; Deputy High Commissioner Port of Spain since July 2003; Born 25/08/68; MOD 1986; FCO 1988; Gaborone 1990; Floater Duties 1993; FCO 1996; Deputy Head of Mission Tashkent 1997; FCO 2000; British Trade

International 2002; Band D6; m 1996 Martha Harriette Medendorp (1s 2000; 2d 2001, 2004).

Allan, Lynne Fleming; SUPL since March 2002; Born 22/10/68; FCO 1989; Moscow 1993; FCO 1995; Ankara 1998; Band B3; m 1999 Marat Ucer (1s 2001).

Allan, Moira, MBE (2004); FCO since January 2005; Born 27/05/61; FCO 1983; Prague 1985; FCO 1987; Mexico City 1989; Santiago 1993; FCO 1996; Second Secretary Bogotá 2000; Band C4.

Allan, Nicholas Edward; First Secretary (Press and Public Affairs) Paris since September 2004; Born 03/08/65; FCO 1990; Brussels (UKREP) 1993; Africa/Middle East Floater Duties 1994; Language Training 1995; Third Secretary (Political) Brussels 1996; Third later Second Secretary FCO 1999; Assistant Private Secretary to Peter Hain later Brian Wilson and Baroness Symons 2001; First Secretary FCO 2002; Band D6; m 2001 Elizabeth Rosemary Waugh.

Allbless, Clare Brickley; SUPL since February 2005; Born 04/05/71; FCO 1997; Third Secretary (PPA) Tokyo 2000; Lilongwe 2004; Band B3; m Dan Lindfield.

Allen, Jonathan Guy; First Secretary (Information) Brussels (UKREP) since July 2003; Born 05/03/74; FCO 1997; Nicosia 1999; Band D6.

Allen, Keith; FCO since June 2003; Born 05/09/72; FCO 1992; New Delhi 1996; Full-Time Language Training 2000; Deputy Head of Mission San Salvador 2000; Band C4.

Allen, Ross Christopher Edward; Jerusalem since December 2003; Born 30/11/78; FCO 2001; Full-Time Language Training (Japanese) 2002; Band C4.

Allen, Ruth Alexandra; First Secretary Kiev since April 2004; Born 31/08/76; FCO 2000; Band C4.

Allen, Sylvia Ann; Port Stanley since February 2005; Born 08/08/60; FCO 1984; La Paz 1986; Tunis 1990; Floater Duties 1995; Hanoi 1999; T/D Abidjan 2003; SUPL 2004; Band A2.

Allman, Julie (née Lawrence); Doha since June 2005; Born 28/01/66; FCO 2000; Floater Duties 2002; Band A2; m 2004 Andy Allman.

Alloway, Terence Michael; FCO since October 1998; Born 18/05/59; FCO 1980; Budapest 1982; Tel Aviv 1983; FCO 1986; SE Asia Floater 1987; FCO 1988; Kuwait 1992; FCO 1994; Full-Time Language Training 1994; Third later Second Secretary (Chancery) Geneva (UKDIS) 1995; Band D6; m 1991 Christine Ann Carr.

Ambrose, Philip John; First Secretary seconded to the China Britain Business Council since 2003; Born 03/11/59; FCO 1978; Brussels (UKREP) 1980; Jedda 1983; Riyadh 1986; South-East Asia Floater 1987; Vice-Consul and AMO Buenos Aires 1990; Vice-Consul and MO Tehran 1991; FCO 1992; Deputy Head of Mission and Consul, Kinshasa - accredited non-resident Second Secretary and Consul, Brazzaville 1995; Second Secretary (Commercial) Beijing 1997; Deputy Consul-General and Consul (Commercial) Rio de Janeiro 2002; Band C5.

Amos, Rex; Kuala Lumpur since November 2004; Born 24/09/72; FCO 1999; Third Secretary (Political/PPA) Athens 2002; Band B3; m 1999 Jacqueline Palin (1s 2002).

Anderson, Annabel Mary; FCO since October 2000; Born 15/07/50; FCO 1995; Paris 1998; Band B3.

Anderson, Henry Ian; Counsellor (Political) Santiago since July 2004; Born 20/08/52; HO 1974; Dhaka 1983; Second Secretary FCO 1987; Vice-Consul Munich 1989; Second Secretary FCO 1994; First Secretary Budapest 1997; First Secretary FCO 2001; Band D6; m 1976 Janice Irene Leeman (1s 1984; 1d 1987).

Anderson, Jennifer Elizabeth; SUPL since March 2005; Born 16/11/68; Second later First Secretary FCO 1997; First Secretary (Political/Military) Brussels (UKREP) 2001; m 1997 Stephen Ashworth (1s 2003; 1d 2005).

Anderson, John; First Secretary (Commercial) Warsaw since January 2002; Born 25/08/49; FCO 1966; Abu Dhabi 1970; Peking 1974; Lagos 1975; FCO 1978; HM Consul Istanbul 1982; Second later First Secretary (Comm) Paris 1987; First Secretary FCO 1991; First Secretary (Management) Harare 1995; FCO 1998; m 1970 Jacqueline Thorburn (2d 1981, 1990; 1s 1983).

Anderson, Lorraine Michelle; FCO since May 1994; Born 29/12/63; FCO 1989; Damascus 1992; Band A2; m (1) 1988 Lawrence Malcolm Reginald Simpson (diss 1994); (2) 1999 Neil Barrowman (1s 2000).

Anderson, Paul James; Second Secretary (Political) Pretoria since August 2003; Born 25/09/78; FCO 2001; Band C4.

Anderson, Philip Brian; FCO since October 2001; Born 18/07/73; HCS 1993; FCO 1997; Nicosia 1999; Band A2; m 1997 Jennie Linda Willis (1s 1996).

Anderson, Steven Martin; Third Secretary (Commercial) Abu Dhabi since October 2004; Born 29/12/70; FCO Home Civil Service 1990; Dubai 1997; Moscow 1998; Third Secretary (Management/VC) Helsinki 2000; Band B3; m Eevamaija Sofia Laitinen (twins, 1s and 1d 2002) .

Andrews, Francesca Therese; FCO since July 1989; Born 23/02/54; FCO 1973; Cape Town/Pretoria 1975; Moscow 1978; FCO 1980; Brussels (UKDEL) 1982; Port of Spain 1986; Band A2.

Andrews, Moira Fraser, TD (1992); Legal Counsellor FCO since June 2000; Born 22/03/59; DTI 1995; Assistant Legal Adviser FCO 1998; m 1989 Ian Andrews (1s 1989; 1d 1992).

Andrews, Timothy John; First Secretary (IAEA) Vienna (UKMIS) since September 2001; Born

01/08/55; FCO 1976; Dacca 1979; Stuttgart 1982; Bonn 1984; FCO 1987; Second Secretary (Chancery/Info) Lusaka 1990; Deputy Head of Mission Port Louis 1994; First Secretary FCO 1997; m 1987 Carolyn Mary Moffat (1d 1989; 1s 1991).

Angell, Ben Thomas; FCO since February 2005; Born 27/12/76; FCO 2000; Second Secretary Ankara 2002; Band C4.

Ankerson, Dr Dudley Charles; Counsellor FCO since April 2002; Born 04/09/48; Second Secretary FCO 1976; Second Secretary Buenos Aires 1978; First Secretary FCO 1981; First Secretary Mexico City 1985; First Secretary FCO 1988; First Secretary FCO on secondment to the Private Sector 1991; FCO 1991; Counsellor Madrid 1993; FCO 1997; Counsellor Budapest 1998; m 1973 Silvia Ernestina Galicia (1d 1985; 1s 1986).

Anstead, Alan Roger Hugh; SUPL since April 2003; Born 06/02/62; FCO 1980; Moscow 1983; Monrovia 1985; Hamburg 1989; FCO 1991; On loan to the DTI 1993; Deputy Head of Mission Riga 1996; Bratislava 2000; Band C4; m 1986 Paula Marita Nikkanen (1s 1991).

Anthony, Ian Nicholas; Kuala Lumpur since June 2005; Born 18/01/60; FCO 1985; Second later First Secretary Lisbon 1988; First Secretary FCO 1990; First Secretary (Political) Brasilia 1993; First Secretary FCO 1997.

Anthony-Rigsby, Lisa; SUPL since September 2001; Born 01/04/65; FCO 1998; Full-Time Language Training 2000; Band A2.

Arbon, Helen Marie; Deputy Consul-General Atlanta since January 2004; Born 21/04/70; FCO 1988; Jakarta 1991; World-wide Floater 1995; SUPL 1998; T/D Montevideo 1998; SUPL 1999; FCO 1999; Second Secretary Chisinau 2001; SUPL 2003; Band C4; m 1998 Adolfo Pando Molina (diss); ptnr, Hugo Ellis (1d 2003).

Archer, Marie-Louise; Second Secretary (Immigration) Mumbai since July 2003; Born 27/10/61; FCO 1990; Third Secretary (Immigration) Karachi 1991; DHM Managua 1996; Seconded to London Chamber of Commerce and Industry 1999; SUPL 2001; Overseas Attachment Training Scheme Bangalore and New Delhi 2002; Band C4.

Archer, Nicholas Stewart, MVO (2001); British High Commissioner Valletta since March 2006; Born 24/12/60; FCO 1983; Third later Second Secretary (Chancery) Amman 1986; Second later First Secretary FCO 1989; PS/Minister of State 1992; Language Training 1995; First Secretary (Commercial) Oslo 1995; on loan to St James's Palace 1997; Head of Near East and North Africa Dept FCO 2002; m 1999 Erica Margaret Power.

Arkley, David Ballantine; Second Secretary FCO since August 2004; Born 10/10/66; FCO 1986; Moscow 1988; Floater Duties 1990; MO/Vice Consul São Paulo 1992; FCO 1995; Third Secretary (Press and Public Affairs) Washington 1997; Third Secretary (PPA) Moscow 2000; Band C4; m 1992 Melissa Lea Buchanan.

Arkwright, Paul Thomas; Counsellor (Political) Brussels (UKDEL NATO) since November 2001; Born 02/03/62; FCO 1986; Second Secretary (Chancery) BMG Berlin 1988; First Secretary FCO 1991; First Secretary (Chancery) New York (UKMIS) 1993; Attachement to Quai d'Orsay 1997; First Secretary (Chancery) Paris 1998; m 1997 Patricia Anne Holland (1d 1999; 1s 2001).

Armour, Nicholas Hilary Stuart; Head of North America Department FCO since November 2000; Born 12/06/51; Third Secretary FCO 1974; Language Training MECAS 1975; FCO 1976; Third later Second Secretary Beirut 1977; First Secretary FCO 1980; Head of Chancery Athens 1984; First Secretary FCO 1989; Counsellor and Deputy Head of Mission Muscat 1991; Counsellor on loan to the DTI 1994; Consul-General/Counsellor Dubai 1997; m 1982 Georgina Elizabeth Fortescue (2d 1985, 1987).

Armstrong, Catherine Fraser; FCO since January 2005; Born 16/07/53; FCO 1971; Paris 1974; Gaborone 1977; FCO 1980; Manila 1985; Athens 1989; FCO 1990; Full-Time Language Training 1994; Consul (Management) Caracas 1995; FCO 1997; HM Consul Brussels 2000; Band C4; m 1981 Clive Paul Ranson (diss 1986).

Armstrong, Mark Christopher; FCO since 2004; Born 04/05/72; FCO 1997; Geneva (UKDIS) 1998; Third Secretary (Political and Press) Tirana 2001; Band C4.

Arnold, Troy Zachary Moncur; Second Secretary (Economic) Nicosia since October 2000; Born 19/12/72; Second Secretary FCO 1997; Language Training 1999; Band C4.

Aron, Michael Douglas; Counsellor (Political) Brussels (UKREP) since September 2002; Born 22/03/59; FCO 1984; Conference Support Officer New York (UKMIS) 1985; on Secondment to European Commission 1986; Second later First Secretary FCO 1986; First Secretary Brasilia 1988; First Secretary FCO 1991; First Secretary (Political) New York (UKMIS) 1993; First Secretary later Counsellor FCO 1996; Deputy Head of Mission Amman 1999; m 1986 Rachel Ann Golding Barker (2d 1986, 1996; 2s 1990, 1994).

Aron, Dr Rachel Ann Golding (née Barker); SUPL since March 2004; Born 18/07/51; First Secretary FCO 1984; Head of Chancery Brasilia 1988; SUPL 1990; First Secretary FCO 1992; First Secretary (Political) New York (UKMIS) 1993; SUPL 1996; Counsellor on loan to RAS as CSSB Chairman 1997; SUPL (Amman) 1999; Counsellor (E-Guidance) remotely in Amman from 2000 and Brussels 2002; m 1986 Michael Douglas Aron (2d 1986, 1996; 2s 1990 1994).

Arroyo, James Jose-Maria, OBE (2003); First Secretary FCO since June 2002; Born 25/03/67; FCO 1990; Full-Time Language Training 1991; Full-Time Language Training Cairo 1992; Second

Secretary (Political) Amman 1993; Cairo 1996; Consul (Political) Jerusalem 1999; Band D6; m 1992 Kerry Ann Louise Ford (1d 2001).

Arthur, Hilary Jane; Sofia since September 2001; Born 28/01/61; FCO 1984; Karachi 1987; Vice Consul (Consular) Düsseldorf 1991; Frankfurt 1993; T/D Islamabad 1994; FCO 1995; Second Secretary (Development) Lusaka 1998; Band C4.

Arthur, Sir Michael Anthony, KCMG (2004), CMG (1992); High Commissioner New Delhi since October 2003; Born 28/08/50; FCO 1972; New York 1972; FCO 1973; Second Secretary Brussels (UKREP) 1974; Second Secretary Kinshasa 1976; Second later First Secretary FCO 1978; PS to Lord Privy Seal 1980; PS to Minister of State 1982; First Secretary (Chancery) Bonn 1984; Counsellor FCO 1988; Counsellor (Political) Paris 1993; Director (Resources) and Chief Inspector 1997; Minister Washington 1999; m 1974 Plaxy Gillian Beatrice Corke (2d 1978, 1980; 2s 1982, 1985).

Ash, Elizabeth; On secondment to Buckingham Palace since July 1996; Born 31/07/52; FCO 1975; New Delhi 1976; Geneva (UKMIS) 1978; Peking 1980; FCO 1982; Kingston 1983; FCO 1987; East Berlin 1988; FCO 1990; Band B3.

Ashcroft, Andrew Richard; HM Ambassador Santo Domingo since July 2002; Born 28/05/61; FCO 1980; Muscat 1982; Tel Aviv 1987; Second Secretary 1989; FCO 1991; First Secretary Harare 1996; FCO 1999; m 2001 Dr Amanda Sives.

Ashdown, Julie Anne; FCO since July 2001; Born 31/08/57; FCO 1976; Amman 1978; Asunción 1982; Brasilia 1983; FCO 1985; Belgrade 1990; Second Secretary FCO 1993; Second Secretary (Aid) Quito 1996; On loan to the Cabinet Office 1999.

Ashford, Leslie David; Second Secretary (Consular) Harare since January 2002; Born 07/09/50; Royal Air Force 1967-96; FCO 1996; T/D Khartoum 2000; T/D Abu Dhabi 2000; Band C4; m 1971 Francetta Xavier Marie (1d 1973; 1s 1979).

Ashley, David William; Second Secretary (Political) Belgrade since May 2002; Born 09/01/68; FCO 1999; Band C4; m 1994 Sophari Mao (1s 2002).

Ashton, John; SUPL since October 2002; Born 07/11/56; FCO 1978; Language Training Hong Kong 1980; Third later Second Secretary Peking 1981; FCO 1984; First Secretary on loan to the Cabinet Office 1986; Rome 1988; First Secretary later Counsellor Deputy Political Adviser Hong Kong 1993; On secondment as Visiting Fellow, Green College Oxford 1997; Counsellor FCO 1998; m 1983 Kao Fengning (1s 1986).

Ashworth, Patrick; Deputy Consul-General and Deputy Director of Trade Promotion São Paulo since January 2001; Born 02/11/50; FCO 1968; Dar es Salaam 1971; Castries 1975; Moscow 1978; FCO 1980; Valletta 1983; Vice-Consul (Commercial) São Paulo 1987; Second Secretary (UNCED) Brasilia 1992; Second Secretary FCO 1992; First Secretary (Press and Public Affairs) The Hague 1995; Band D6; m 1973 Pauline Mary Harrison (1d 1982; 1s 1986).

Aske, Antonia Jane; Brussels (UKDEL NATO) since January 2005; Born 01/08/72; FCO 1998; Floater Duties 2000; FCO 2003; Band C4.

Askham, Denise Ann (née Vaughan); SUPL since January 1999; Born 15/10/64; FCO 1983; Bonn 1985; Vienna (UKDEL) CSCE 1988; Washington 1988; Berne 1991; FCO 1995; SUPL 1995; FCO 1998; Band B3; m 1998 Stephen David Askham (1d 1997; 1s 2000).

Askham, Stephen David; Lisbon since October 2000; Born 20/05/60; RAF 1976-84; FCO 1984; Bonn 1991; FCO 1994; FCO 1994; Bahrain 1999; FTLT 2000; Band B3; m 1988 Denise Ann Vaughan (1d 1997; 1s 2000).

Aspden, Susan Elizabeth; Stockholm since September 2002; Born 20/01/57; FCO 1980; Rabat 1981; Jakarta 1983; Havana 1987; FCO 1989; On loan to DTI 1996; Band C4.

Aspery, Kevin; Dhaka since January 2004; Born 05/04/52; Army 1968-92; Havana 1993; Moscow (MNEB) 1997; Colombo 1998; Hong Kong 1999; m Penelope Jane (1d 1973; 2s 1975, 1977).

Asquith, Hon Dominic Anthony Gerard, CMG (2004); Director (Iraq), FCO since 2004; Born 07/02/57; FCO 1983; Second Secretary and Head of Interests Section Damascus 1986; First Secretary (Chancery) Muscat 1987; First Secretary FCO 1989; PS/Minister of State 1990; Washington 1992; Minister and Deputy Head of Mission Buenos Aires 1997; Deputy Head of Mission Riyadh 2001; m 1988 Louise Cotton (2d 1989, 1990; 2s 1992, 1994).

Astbury, Nicholas Paul; HM Ambassador Asmara since February 2006; Born 13/08/71; FCO 1994; Second Secretary (Chancery) Colombo 1995; First Secretary FCO 1999; First Secretary Kabul 2005; m 1995 Elayna Joanne Gutteridge (1s 1999).

Astill-Brown, Jeremy; First Secretary (Regional Conflict Adviser) Addis Ababa since May 2003; Born 14/03/67; FCO 1987; Kampala 1990; Addis Ababa 1993; FCO 1997; Second Secretary (Political/Development) Luanda 1999; Band D6; m 1991 Marie-Loiuse (Marisa) Alegria Gunner.

Astle, Marilia Silva; SUPL since April 2004; Born 14/04/68; FCO 1991; Vice-Consul later Press & Public Affairs Lisbon 1994; FCO 1998; Band D6; m 2000 Jonathan Jones (1s 2004).

Atkinson, Christine; Deputy Permanent Delegate Paris (UKDEL) UNESCO since June 2001; Born 05/07/57; British Museum 1979; COI 1986; FCO 1990; APS/Minister of State 1996; PS/PUSS DFID 1997.

Atkinson, Jane; Mexico City since June 2003; Born 20/07/60; MOD 1978-87; FCO 1987; Quito

1988; Floater Duties 1992; FCO 1996; Port Louis 1999; Band B3.

Atkinson, Kim Louise (née Kemp); FCO since May 2003; Born 04/04/74; FCO 1992; Islamabad 1996; Warsaw 1999; Band B3; m 1999 Simon Manington Atkinson.

Atkinson, Simon Manington; FCO since August 2003; Born 11/05/71; FCO 1989; Oslo 1992; FCO 1995; Pro-Consul Islamabad 1995; ECO/Vice Consul Warsaw 2000; Band B3; m 1999 Kim Kemp.

Attryde, Alan Robert James; First Secretary (Commercial) New Delhi since December 2003; Born 21/08/47; Ministry of Labour 1966; DSAO 1967; Middle East Floater 1970; Washington 1971; Jakarta 1974; FCO 1978; Cairo 1980; on loan to DTI 1985; Second Secretary 1985; FCO 1987; Consul (Commercial) Shanghai 1987; Second Secretary (Man/Cons) Caracas 1990; Full-time Language Training 1992; First Secretary (Commercial) Al Khobar 1993; FCO 1997; T/D as First Secretary (Management) Washington 1999; First Secretary (Commercial) Washington 2000; Band D6; m 1992 Ana Maria Diaz Molina.

Attwood, Ian; Kuala Lumpur since March 2000; Born 14/04/62; FCO 1983; Hong Kong 1991; FCO 1992; Bangkok 1993; FCO 1996; Band C4; m 1987 Tina Louise (1d 1989; 1s 1991).

Augustine-Aina, Felicity; Abuja since August 2002; Born 10/07/56; FCO 1989; Lagos 1991; FCO 1994; Dublin 1998; Islamabad 2000; Band A2; m 1992 Henry Aina (2d 1995, 1999).

Auld, Fergus Stephen; Second Secretary (Political/PPA) Bangkok since June 2002; Born 17/02/73; FCO 1999; Full-Time Language Training (Thai) 2000; Band C4; m 2001 Amy Louise Auld (1s 2003).

Auld, Steven James; Management Officer Yaoundé since March 2004; Born 09/07/71; FCO 1990; Moscow 1993; Nuku'alofa 1995; FCO 1996; Third Secretary (Management) and Vice Consul Tripoli 2001; Band B3; m 2001 Andrea Baity.

Austen, Richard James, MBE (1996); HM Ambassador Ulaanbaatar since February 2004; Born 25/05/55; Inland Revenue 1972-77; SUPL 1974-77; FCO 1981; Dar es Salaam 1983; Third Secretary (Consular) Ottawa 1987; Second Secretary FCO 1990; Deputy High Commissioner Banjul 1993; First Secretary FCO 1996; Deputy High Commissioner Port Louis 2001.

Austin, David John Robert, OBE (1999); SUPL since February 2003; Born 07/10/63; FCO 1986; Third later Second Secretary Dhaka 1989; FCO 1992; First Secretary (Political/Information) Belgrade 1993; On secondment as Political Adviser to Carl Bildt, ICFY/OHR 1995; FCO 1997; Deputy Head of Mission Zagreb 1999; m 1990 Emma Jane Carey (1d 1995; 1s 1997).

Austin, Vanessa Anne; FCO since October 2003; Born 04/08/71; FCO 1994; Cairo 1996; Nairobi 2000; Band A2.

Axworthy, Michael George Andrew; SUPL since July 2000; Born 26/09/62; FCO 1986; Third later Second Secretary Valletta 1988; Second Secretary FCO 1991; Second Secretary (Political/Military) Bonn 1993; Second Secretary (Economic) Bonn 1996; First Secretary FCO 1998; m 1996 Sally Hinds (1d 1999).

Axworthy, Sally Jane, MBE; On loan to the Home Office since July 2001; Born 01/09/64; FCO 1986; Language Training 1988; Third Secretary Moscow 1989; Second Secretary Kiev 1989; First Secretary FCO 1993; First Secretary Bonn 1994; FCO 1998; SUPL 2000; m 1996 Michael G A Axworthy (1d 1999).

Ayre, Andrew; Second Secretary Vienna since December 2001; Born 30/04/66; FCO 1986; Warsaw 1988; Rio de Janeiro 1990; FCO 1991; Nicosia 1994; SUPL 1997; Third later Second Secretary Tel Aviv 1998; Band C4; m 1990 Bettina Moosberger (1s 1997).

B

Bacarese-Hamilton, Michelle Jannine; FCO since May 2004; Born 25/02/78; Band A2.

Bach, Alison Helen (née Clews); Cayman Islands since May 2003; Born 04/11/65; ODA 1987; FCO 1990; Manila 1992; FCO 1994; T/D Sarajevo 1996; SUPL 1996; Bonn 1997; Reykjavik 2000; Brussels 2001; Band A2; m 1997 Anthony Gordon James Bach (1s 1998; 1d 2000).

Bagnall, Andrew William; FCO since June 2003; Born 28/02/48; GPO 1964-70; FCO 1970; Pretoria 1982; Second Secretary FCO 1985; Attaché Caracas 1987; Second Secretary Nairobi 1994; FCO 1997; Lagos 1999; m 1981 Margaret Christine Bromwich (1s 1981; 1d 1985).

Bah, Stephanie Marie (née Holmes); Geneva (UKDIS) since September 2002; Born 28/12/56; FCO 1997; Singapore 1999; Band A2; m 2004 Souleymane Bah.

Baharie, Ian Walter; FCO since May 2005; Born 03/05/61; FCO 1982; Language Training SOAS 1983; Third later Second Secretary (Chancery) Cairo 1985; Second later First Secretary FCO 1987; First Secretary Abu Dhabi 1991; First Secretary FCO 1994; Consul Jerusalem 1996; First Secretary (Political) Abuja 1999; Counsellor Riyadh 2003; m 1991 Bonaventura Agatha Jasperina Buhre (3d 1991, 1998, 2001).

Bailey, Ian Peter; FCO since December 1998; Born 21/08/57; DTI 1985; FCO 1987; Language Training 1988; Third Secretary (Political) Muscat 1990; Second Secretary (Commercial) Seoul 1995; Band D6; m 1990 Teresa Weronika Maria Frosztega (2s 1998, 2001).

Bailey, Rosemarie Anne (née Edwards); SUPL since March 1998; Born 20/04/59; FCO 1979; Tokyo 1983; FCO 1986; SUPL 1988; Vice-Consul Singapore 1992; SUPL 1996; FCO 1997; Band C4; m 1982 Mark Adrian Stephen Bailey (2s 1996, 1999).

Bailey, Stephen; FCO since October 2003; Born 13/04/53; FCO 1971; Mexico City 1975; Gaborone 1977; Sana'a 1981; FCO 1983; Wellington 1987; Budapest 1990; FCO 1995; Madras 2000; Band B3; m 1975 Carol Joan Sterritt (1d 1980).

Baird, Jamie Peter; Athens since January 2003; Born 25/08/72; FCO 1997; Band A2.

Baird, Nicholas Graham Faraday; On secondment to the Immigration Nationality Directorate of the Home Office as Senior Director (International) later (Policy) since April 2003; Born 15/05/62; FCO 1983; Third later Second Secretary Kuwait 1986; Second later First Secretary (Econ/Finance) Brussels (UKREP) 1989; Private Secretary to the Parliamentary Under Secretary of State FCO 1993; Counsellor and Deputy Head of Mission Muscat 1997; Counsellor (Justice/Home Affairs) Brussels (UKREP) 1998; Head of European Union Department (Internal) FCO 2002; m 1985 Caroline Jane Ivett (1s 1989; 2d 1990, 1992).

Baker, Catherine Margaret; FCO since January 1998; Born 11/09/68; FCO 1991; Third Secretary (Chancery/Information) Tel Aviv 1994; Band B3.

Baker, Denise; FCO since August 2003; Born 27/09/67; FCO 1987; Brussels 1991; Belgrade 1994; New York (UKMIS) 1997; Montserrat 1999; Band B3.

Baker, Francis Raymond, OBE (1997); Counsellor (Political/Military) Washington since July 2003; Born 27/01/61; FCO 1981; Panama City 1983; Third later Second Secretary Buenos Aires 1986; Second Secretary FCO 1991; First Secretary (Political/Military) Ankara 1993; First Secretary on secondment to State Department Washington 1996; First Secretary FCO 1997; Private Secretary to the Minister of State 1998; Head of Africa Department (Equatorial), 2000; m 1983 Maria Pilar Fernandez (1d 1989; 1s 1991).

Baker, Nigel Marcus, MVO (2003); Deputy Head of Mission Havana since October 2003; Born 09/09/66; Third Secretary FCO 1989; Third later Second Secretary (Econ) Prague 1992; Second Secretary later DHM Bratislava 1993; Resigned 1995; Reinstated 1998; First Secretary FCO 1998; on loan to St James's Palace 2000; m 1997 Alexandra Cechova.

Baker, Piers Howard Burton; Deputy Head of Mission Vienna since January 2001; Born 23/07/56; Second Secretary FCO 1983; First Secretary (Chancery) Brussels 1985; First Secretary FCO 1988; First Secretary Brussels (UKREP) 1993; First Secretary FCO 1996; m 1979 Maria Eugenia Vilaincour (1s 1984).

Baker, Rodney Kelvin Mornington; FCO since November 1996; Born 24/03/49; FO (later FCO) 1966; Warsaw 1974; FCO 1975; Athens 1977; Ankara 1978; FCO 1981; Third Secretary Tokyo 1984; FCO 1986; Third later Second Secretary Madrid 1989; FCO 1992; On loan to MOD Rheindahlen 1994; Band D6; m 1971 Christine Mary Holt (2d 1979, 1983).

Baker, Russell Nicholas John; First Secretary (Head of UK Trade Group) Paris since August 2004; Born 06/10/53; FCO 1977; Language Training 1979; Prague 1979; Private Secretary to HMA Bonn 1982; Second Secretary FCO 1986; APS to Minister of State 1987; Second Secretary (Political/Info /Comm) Lima 1990; First Secretary (Head of Scott Inquiry Unit) FCO 1994; First Secretary (Commercial) Dublin 1996; First Secretary FCO 2001; Band D6; m 1996 Silvia Chavez.

Baker-Mavin, Alison Bertha (née Baker), BEM (1991); SUPL since April 2003; Born 09/05/62; FCO 1989; Algiers 1991; Banjul 1995; Third Secretary (Management/Commercial) Freetown 1998; SUPL 2001; FCO 2002; Band B3; m 1997 Graham J Mavin (1s 2001; 1d 2004).

Baldwin, Peter Graham; FCO since April 1998; Born 28/08/43; Paymaster General's Office 1962; CRO 1963; Lusaka 1964; Calcutta 1967; Vienna (BE) 1971; Second Secretary Brussels (UKREP) 1973; FCO 1977; Algiers 1981; Second Secretary FCO 1983; Second Secretary (Immigration/Consular) Colombo 1987; Second Secretary (Consular) Jakarta 1991; Second Secretary (Immigration) Islamabad 1995; m 1968 Patricia Joyce Carter (2d 1970, 1972; 1s 1980).

Bale, Caroline Margaret; FCO since June 1991; Born 25/07/57; FCO 1980; Geneva (UKMIS) 1981; Moscow 1983; Port Stanley 1986; Sofia 1987; Gaborone 1989; Band A2.

Balfour, Alison Hannah; Amman since March 2002; Born 13/05/61; Scottish Office 1980-87; FCO 1987; Mexico City 1989; Nicosia 1992; Rome 1995; FCO 1999; Band B3.

Ball, Stephen; FCO since September 2003; Born 06/09/79; Band C4.

Ballett, Sarah Elizabeth; SUPL since October 2002; Born 31/10/71; FCO 1990; Washington 1994; SUPL 1997; Washington 1997; FCO 2000; Band B3.

Balmer, Michael Anthony; First Secretary, Head of Management New York (UKMIS) since July 2004; Born 21/07/51; MOD (Navy) 1969; FCO 1971; Geneva (UKMIS) 1973; Attaché Moscow 1975; LA Floater 1977; Third Secretary (Administration) Jedda 1979; Second Secretary (Commercial) Warsaw 1981; Second later First Secretary FCO 1984; Language Training 1987; First Secretary, Head of Commercial Section Athens 1988; First Secretary FCO 1992; Language Training 1995; Deputy Consul-General Düsseldorf and Deputy Director-General (Trade and Investment Promotion) Germany 1996; Deputy Head of Security Strategy Unit, FCO 2000; Band D7; m 1982 Helen Charmian Burgoine (2d 1984, 1987).

Bamber, Jonathan James; Third Secretary (Commercial) Maputo since August 2001; Born 24/09/65; FCO 1994; ECO later Vice-Consul Bangkok 1997; FTLT 2000; Band B3; m 2001 Sarah Louise Cooke.

Bamber, Sarah Ann; First Secretary New Delhi since May 2004; Born 06/01/74; FCO 1996; Second Secretary New York (UKMIS) 1998; Second Secretary FCO 2001; Band C4.

Bamford, Victoria Jane; SUPL since March 2004; Born 23/12/67; FCO 1989; Moscow 1992; FCO 1995; Nicosia 1996; FCO 1999; SUPL 2001; FCO 2002; Band B3; ptnr, Paul McLennan (1s 2001).

Banas, Annette Marie (née Lucey); Pristina since February 2004; Born 25/06/69; FCO 2002; Band A2; ptnr, Karl Banas.

Banham, Michael Kent; Consul Palma since September 2001; Born 20/09/44; FO 1963; Rawalpindi 1967; Quito 1970; FCO 1974; Tripoli 1976; Nairobi 1980; FCO 1983; Second Secretary (Commercial) Bombay 1987; Second Secretary (Management/Consular) Lima 1990; First Secretary (Management) Riyadh 1994; First Secretary (Management) Cairo 1998; m (1) 1965 Christine Scott (1s 1969; 1d 1971) (diss); (2) 1995 Marie Louise Smith.

Banks, Alison Elizabeth; Amman since April 2004; Born 10/01/70; FCO 1992; Canberra 1994; Peking 1998; FCO 2000; Band B3.

Banks, Jacinta Mary Catharine (née Cookson); FCO since August 2000; Born 25/11/57; FCO 1977; Paris 1980; Bombay 1983; FCO 1987; Nicosia 1990; Damascus 1994; Islamabad 1996; Band C4; m 1982 Jamie Paul Banks (1d 1992).

Banks, Jamie Paul; Consul (Investment) Sydney since February 2003; Born 09/06/57; FCO 1977; Paris (UKDEL OECD) 1980; Bombay 1983; FCO 1987; Nicosia 1990; Second Secretary (Commercial) Damascus 1994; Second Secretary (Development) Islamabad 1996; FCO 2000; Deputy Head, Asia Pacific, Invest UK 2001; Band C5; m 1982 Jacinta Mary Catharine Cookson (diss 2002) (1d 1992).

Banks, Janice Kathleen (née Robinson); Abuja since August 2004; Born 28/09/56; FCO 1995; Bonn 1997; Jerusalem 1999; Riyadh 2001; Band B3; m 2000 Fraser Banks.

Banks, Simon John; FCO since November 2002; Born 05/04/66; FCO 1988; Language Training 1990; Third later Second Secretary (Economic) Warsaw 1990; on secondment to DGIA EC Commission Brussels 1993; First Secretary FCO 1996; Deputy High Commissioner Dar es Salaam 1999; m 1989 The Hon Rowena Joynson-Hicks (3s 1994, 1996, 1999; 1d 2003).

Bannatyne, William Graeme; Abuja since February 2004; Born 05/03/67; FCO 1988; Canberra 1990; FCO 1993; Sofia 1993; FCO 1995; Full-Time Language Training 2000; Lima 2000; Band B3; m 1990 Caterina Prestigiacomo (1d 1995).

Banner, Nick; First Secretary (Information) Brussels since January 2002; Born 28/02/74; FCO 1999; First Secretary FCO 2000; Band D6; m 1999 Emma Reisz.

Bannerman, Alexander Campbell; T/D Sana'a since July 2002; Born 29/09/67; FCO 1988; Nicosia 1993; FCO 1995; Dubai 1998; Band B3; m 1998 Fiona Vari MacKillop.

Barclay, John Hamish; Colombo since March 2005; Born 11/09/64; Royal Air Force 1983-92; Department of Transport 1993-95; FCO 1995; Abu Dhabi 1997; Jedda 2000; FCO 2003; Band B3.

Barclay, Philip Jeremy; Warsaw since January 2003; Born 14/10/67; FCO 1999; Band D6; m 1996 Emma Robinson.

Barker, Caroline Susan; FCO since July 1999; Born 15/09/69; Language Training 1993; Second Secretary (KHF) Bratislava 1994; Second Secretary FCO 1995; SUPL 1997.

Barker, Philip John; Bridgetown since January 2004; Born 18/11/70; FCO 1989; Berlin 1998; FCO 2001; m 1998 Elizabeth Margaret Jean Hindle.

Barker, Rowland Gifford Palgrave; Second Secretary Nairobi since January 2004; Born 06/06/75; FCO 2000; Band C4.

Barklamb, Peter Richard; FCO since March 2003; Born 18/07/51; FCO 1970; Delhi 1973; Islamabad 1975; Geneva 1976; Brussels 1978; FCO 1981; Warsaw 1984; Second Secretary (Commercial/Aid) Bridgetown 1989; Second Secretary (Commercial) Riyadh 1991; FCO 1994; Consul (Head of Post) later Consul-General Amsterdam 1998; Band D6; m 1974 Jane Bosworth (2d 1979, 1981; 1s 1984).

Barlow, Andrew Watson; FCO since October 1987; Born 23/12/54; UKAEA 1977; FCO 1978; UKAEA 1981; Private Secretary to Chairman 1983-84; Band D7.

Barlow, Jacqueline; Anguilla since February 2002; Born 21/07/47; FCO 1969; Berne 1969; Baghdad 1971; Islamabad 1972; Moscow 1973; Phnom Penh and Hanoi 1975; FCO 1976; Moscow 1977; Floater Duties 1980; FCO 1984; Tokyo 1987; FCO 1990; Vice-Consul Shanghai 1994; Third Secretary (Commercial) Kuwait 1997.

Barlow, Richard David; Second Secretary (Chancery) Brasilia since December 2002; Born 17/01/75; FCO 2000; Band C4; m 2001 Silvia Claudia da Graça-Barlow (1s 2004).

Barnard, Michael Trevelyan; FCO since October 1995; Born 15/12/61; FCO 1986; Dar es Salaam 1989; Bratislava 1993; Band B3; m 1993 Tracy Dawn Clifford.

Barnes, Catherine Eleanor; FCO since May 2001; Born 12/06/68; FCO 1995; Human Rights Officer Jakarta 1998; Band C4.

Barnes, Nicholas John; FCO since May 2004; Born 25/11/72; FCO 2000; First Secretary (Political) Tirana 2002; Band D6.

Barnes Jones, Deborah Elizabeth Vavasseur (née Barnes); Governor Montserrat since April 2004; Born 06/10/56; FCO 1980; Moscow 1983; First

Secretary on loan to Cabinet Office 1985; Resigned 1986; Reinstated 1988; First Secretary (Chancery) Tel Aviv 1988; First Secretary FCO 1992; Deputy Head of Mission Montevideo 1996; HM Ambassador Tbilisi 2001; m 1986 Frederick Richard Jones (2d (twins) 1991).

Barnett, Robin Anthony; Head of Joint Entry Clearance Unit later Director (UKVisas) (FCO/HO) since January 2002; Born 08/03/58; FCO 1980; Third later Second Secretary Warsaw 1982; Second later First Secretary FCO 1985; First Secretary Vienna (UKDEL) 1990; First Secretary New York (UKMIS) 1991; First Secretary FCO 1996; Deputy Head of Mission Warsaw 1998; m (1) 1989 Debra Marianne Bunt (diss 1999) (1 step s 1987, 1s 1990), (2) Tesca Maria Osman (1 step d 1990; 1 step s 1990).

Barnsley, Pamela Margaret; FCO since September 2003; Born 02/06/57; FCO 1982; Second Secretary (Chancery) Brasilia 1983; First Secretary (Comm/Econ) Peking 1987; Trade Commissioner BTC Hong Kong 1989; SUPL 1990; First Secretary FCO 1995; SUPL 1999; Band D6; m 1986 Perry Neil Keller (1d 1999).

Barr, Christopher; Second Secretary FCO since September 1997; Born 23/07/57; FCO 1975; Dublin 1979; FCO 1983; Sana'a 1988; FCO 1992; Third later Second Secretary (Political) Kuwait 1995; Band C5; m 1982 Bronwyn Patricia Morrison (2s 1983, 1988; 1d 1984).

Barr, Richard Barclay; FCO since August 2001; Born 03/05/55; FCO 1975; Freetown 1977; FCO 1980; Prague 1981; Düsseldorf 1983; Accra 1988; FCO 1992; Second Secretary 1994; Full-Time Language Training 1997; Second Secretary (Press and Public Affairs) Buenos Aires 1997; m 1977 Jane Anne Greengrass (1s 1978).

Barras, Ian Alexander; Santo Domingo since May 2005; Born 27/04/50; FCO 1976; Geneva 1979; Peking 1981; Douala 1984; FCO 1986; Athens 1989; FCO 1990; Washington 1991; Third Secretary (Information/Visits) Islamabad 1994; FCO 1998; Band B3.

Barratt, Colin Ernest; Third Secretary (Commercial) Istanbul since June 2003; Born 02/03/62; FCO 1995; Third Secretary (Management/Vice-Consul) Banjul 1999; Band B3.

Barrett, Donna Alison; Floater Duties since June 2004; Born 14/01/63; FCO 1995; The Hague 1999; FCO 2002; Band B3; (1d 1981).

Barrett, Douglas Wilson; Second Secretary (Commercial) Shanghai since February 2001; Born 28/01/56; HCS 1976; FCO 1978; Brussels (UKREP) 1980; Havana 1983; Latin America Floater 1986; Islamabad 1988; T/D Manila 1992; T/D Geneva (UKDEL) 1993; FCO 1993; Second Secretary/Management Officer/HM Consul Bombay 1996; m 2000 Gayle Viegas.

Barrett, Janet Ceclyn; FCO since May 2000; Born 19/12/67; HCS 1988; FCO 1994; Geneva (UKMIS) 1997; Band A2.

Barrett, Jill Mary; Assistant Legal Adviser FCO since 1997; Born 06/07/58; Assistant Legal Adviser FCO 1989; First Secretary (Legal) New York (UKMIS) 1994.

Barrie, Patricia Ann (née Gallagher); FCO since October 1998; Born 17/04/65; FCO 1988; Athens 1991; Montevideo 1993; Band A2; m 1993 Alexander Barrie (1d 1995; 1s 1998).

Barros, Lesley Susan; Riyadh since August 2000; Born 02/05/60; FCO 1980; Brussels 1981; Havana 1982; Brasilia 1984; FCO 1987; Paris 1990; Tokyo 1993; Gibraltar 1996; Band B3; m 1989 José Barros Filho (2d 1991, 1994).

Barrow, Timothy Earle, LVO (1994), MBE (1993); Assistant Director of EU (External), FCO since April 2003; Born 15/02/64; FCO 1986; Language Training 1988; Second Secretary (Chancery) Moscow 1990; First Secretary FCO 1993; Private Secretary to the Minister of State, FCO 1994; First Secretary Brussels (UKREP) 1996; Private Secretary to the Secretary of State for Foreign and Commonwealth Affairs, FCO 1998; Head of Common Foreign and Security Policy Department FCO 2000.

Barry, Thomas John; First Secretary Mexico City since November 2003; Born 25/12/78; FCO 2002; Band C4.

Barson, Jacqueline Anne, MBE (1995); FCO since October 2002; Born 26/05/59; FCO 1979; Prague 1981; Belgrade 1982; Abu Dhabi 1982; Brunei 1985; Geneva (UKMIS) 1986; FCO 1990; Copenhagen 1992; Brussels 1992; Athens 1993; Ottawa 1994; Olympic Attaché Sydney 1999; Seconded to the Organising Committee for Manchester Commonwealth Games 2001; Band D6.

Barter, Craig Alan Roger; FCO since July 2001; Born 24/07/69; HCS 1990; FCO 1996; Tehran 1999; Band B3; m 2000 Lilis Purhaniah.

Barton, Helen Mary; SUPL since October 1999; Born 05/12/65; FCO 1991; Second Secretary (Political) The Hague 1996; m 1996 Alastair Matthew Wright.

Barton, Philip Robert, OBE (1997); Deputy Governor Gibraltar since February 2005; Born 18/08/63; FCO 1986; Third later Second Secretary Caracas 1987; First Secretary on loan to the Cabinet Office 1991; First Secretary FCO 1993; First Secretary (Political) New Delhi 1994; On loan as Private Secretary to the Prime Minister at No. 10 1997; Deputy High Commissioner Nicosia 2000; m (1) 1995 Sabine Friederike Schnittger (diss) (2) 1999 Amanda Joy Bowen (1d 2001; 1s 2003).

Bassnett, Stephen Andrew, MBE (1983); First Secretary FCO since July 1999; Born 24/01/49; Army 1967-86; FCO 1986; First Secretary (Chancery) Cairo 1991; First Secretary FCO 1993;

First Secretary (Political) Bahrain 1997; Band D6; m 1980 Judith Christine Anne Whitty.

Bastin, Suzanne Sarah (née Baxter); Dubai since September 2000; Born 03/07/69; Home Office 1989; Bombay 1994; Home Office 1994; Peking 1996; FCO 2000; Band B3; m 1998 David Richard Bastin.

Bateman, Peter; HM Ambassador La Paz since June 2005; Born 23/12/55; FCO 1984; Language Training Tokyo 1986; Second later First Secretary Tokyo 1987; First Secretary FCO 1991; First Secretary (Commercial) Berlin 1993; FCO 1997; Counsellor (Commercial) Tokyo 1998; FCO 2002; On secondment as Deputy Chief Executive to the International Financial Services London 2003; m 1985 Andrea Subercaseaux-Peters (2s 1987, 1990; 1d 1992).

Bates, Anthony Michael, MVO (1994); First Secretary (Management) and Consul Berne since August 2001; Born 12/11/58; FCO 1978; Islamabad 1980; Wellington 1982; FCO 1987; Language Training 1990; Private Secretary Bonn 1990; Cayman Islands 1993; Second Secretary FCO 1996; Band C5; m 1985 Colette Ann Stewart (2d 1988, 1992).

Bates, Michael Charles, OBE (1994); Consul-General Atlanta since June 2001; Born 09/04/48; DSAO later FCO 1966; Delhi 1971; Third Secretary Moscow 1974; Second Secretary FCO 1977; Second later First Secretary Singapore 1979; First Secretary (Inf/Chancery) Brussels 1983; On loan to No.10 Downing Street 1987; First Secretary FCO 1990; First Secretary Riga 1991; Chargé d'Affaires later HM Ambassador Bratislava 1993; First Secretary FCO 1995; Deputy High Commissioner Bombay 1996; m 1971 Janice Kwan Foh Yin (1d 1977; 1s 1978).

Bates, Vicki Louise; Floater Duties since July 2004; Born 07/12/71; FCO 2002; Band A2.

Batson, Philip David; Deputy Head of Mission Tunis since November 2004; Born 26/06/68; FCO 1987; Bombay 1991; Third Secretary Paris 1995; Second later First Secretary FCO 1997.

Battson, Andrew John; FCO since September 2001; Born 08/05/66; FCO 1984; Bombay 1991; Bonn 1995; Port of Spain 1997; SUPL 2000; Band C4; m 1993 Andrea Jaun.

Batty, Simon Robert; Second Secretary Athens since September 2000; Born 30/09/62; FCO 1982; New Delhi 1985; FCO 1989; Cairo 1990; Second Secretary FCO 1993; Second Secretary Bogotá 1997; Band C4; m 1991 Sharon Morris (1d 1996; 1s 1998).

Batty-Smith, Katharine Amelia Louise; FCO since April 2003; Born 19/08/64; FCO 1984; Budapest 1986; Brasilia 1988; Floater Duties 1992; On loan to DTI 1994; Vice-Consul Sana'a 1997; Prague 1999; Band C4.

Bavinton, Sharon Jayne (née Vince); FCO since January 1999; Born 17/12/58; FCO 1979; New York (UKMIS) 1981; FCO 1983; Canberra 1984; FCO 1987; Abu Dhabi 1989; FCO 1993; Overseas Inspectorate 1995; Band B3; m 1982 Russell Alexander Bavinton (diss 1992).

Baxendale, James Lloyd; First Secretary (Political) Beirut since February 2004; Born 23/02/67; FCO 1991; Language Training 1993; Language Training Cairo 1994; Second Secretary FCO 1995; First Secretary (Political) Amman 1997; First Secretary (Political) Brussels 1999; First Secretary FCO 2001; Band D6; m 1996 Valerie Nathalie Bouchet (1s 2001).

Baxter, Alison Jane; Beijing since February 2004; Born 15/05/67; FCO 1990; Islamabad 1992; Canberra 1993; SUPL 1996; FCO 1999; Full-Time Language Training 2002; Band C4.

Baxter Amade, Vicki Louise; Deputy Head of Mission San José since October 2004; Born 18/03/63; FCO 1982; T/D Luxembourg 1983; Lisbon 1984; Maputo 1987; FCO 1990; Khartoum 1993; Canberra 1996; FCO 2000; Band C4; m 1990 Amade Chababe Amade (diss 2000) (1s 1992).

Bayfield, Rachael (née Greenwood); SUPL since December 2003; Born 04/03/68; FCO 1993; Language Training 1994; Full-Time Language Training Tokyo 1995; Private Secretary Tokyo 1996; SUPL 2000; FCO 2003; Band C4.

Bayliss, Jill Elizabeth (née Hooper); Lagos since October 2002; Born 03/08/68; FCO 1989; Colombo 1995; Moscow 1998; Band B3; m 1994 (Buster) IHW Bayliss.

Beale, Gideon David; First Secretary Bucharest since August 2002; Born 09/07/62; FCO 1986; Third Secretary/ Vice-Consul Athens 1990; Second Secretary FCO 1994; First Secretary (Political) Lagos later Abuja 1995; First Secretary FCO 1999; Band D6.

Beats, Lesley, MBE (2004); Ulaanbaatar since November 2003; Born 01/04/65; Prague 1989; Brussels (UKREP) 1991; Phnom Penh 1994; Brussels (UKREP) 1996; FCO 1998; Band B3.

Beattie, Phoebe; Full-Time Language Training since November 2004; Born 25/11/59; FCO 1984; Bangkok 1985; Stanley 1988; Floater Duties 1989; FCO 1993; Jakarta 1994; Brussels 1998; FCO 2001; Band B3.

Beaven, Keith Andrew; Counsellor Oslo since February 2004; Born 07/01/61; FCO 1983; Third later Second Secretary (Chancery) Mexico City 1986; First Secretary FCO 1988; First Secretary (Political) Pretoria 1993; First Secretary FCO 1997; m 1986 Jane Marion Wells (1s 1996; 1d 1999).

Beckett, Alison Joan; SUPL since May 2004; Born 01/07/61; FCO 1989; Third Secretary (Management/Cons) Kiev 1992; Paris (UKDEL OECD) 1996; Second Secretary (Political) Bucharest 1999; FCO 2001; Band C4.

Beckford, Charles Francis Houghton; FCO since July 2003; Born 04/11/63; FCO 1991; First

Secretary (Political) Islamabad 1993; First Secretary FCO 1995; First Secretary (Political) Nicosia 1999; Band D6; m 1993 Clare Elizabeth Stourton (twin s 1997; 1d 1999).

Beckingham, Peter; HM Ambassador Manila since February 2005; Born 16/03/49; BOTB 1974; Director New York (BIS) 1979; First Secretary FCO 1983; First Secretary (Commercial) Stockholm 1988; First Secretary later Head of Political Section Canberra 1992; Director Joint Export Promotion Directorate (FCO/DTI) 1996; Consul-General Sydney 1999; m 1975 Jill Mary Trotman (2d 1980, 1982).

Bedford, Adrian Frederick; FCO since February 2004; Born 30/10/56; Land Registry 1975; FCO 1976; Islamabad 1978; Hanoi 1981; Johannesburg 1982; FCO 1985; Bogotá 1988; Second later First Secretary FCO 1992; Tehran 1996; First Secretary and Deputy Head of Mission Beirut 1999; Band D6; m (1) 1995 Alexandra Pamela Cole (diss 2001); (2) 2001 Sandra Eid (1d 2002; 1s 2003).

Bee, Stephanie Louise, MBE; T/D Kuala Lumpur since May 2005; Born 27/01/67; FCO 1986; Brussels (UKDEL) 1988; Warsaw 1988; Moscow 1992; FCO 1995; Hong Kong 1998; Third Secretary and Vice-Consul Yerevan 2001; T/D Osaka 2004; Band B3.

Beer, Nicola Geraldine (née Calvert); SUPL since January 2004; Born 21/06/67; FCO 1985; Nicosia 1988; Resigned 1990; Reinstated 1996; Second Secretary Dubai 2002; Band C4; m 1999 Andrew John Beer (1d 2000).

Beeson, Richard John; Second Secretary (Consular) Kathmandu since July 2004; Born 07/06/54; FCO 1973; East Berlin 1975; Damascus 1976; FCO 1977; Brussels (UKREP) 1978; Peking 1980; FCO 1983; Tripoli 1984; FCO 1986; Singapore 1988; Third Secretary (Management) and Vice Consul Hamburg 1991; Second Secretary FCO 1994; Full-time Language Training 1996; Taipei 1998; FCO 2001; m (1) 1978 Kim Margaret Cotter; (2) 1989 Elizabeth Ann Allin.

Begbie, James Alexander, OBE (2004); FCO since 2004; Born 10/12/53; FCO 1973; Bahrain 1975; Middle Eastern Floater 1979; FCO 1980; Tunis 1983; Shanghai 1986; Third later Second Secretary (Comm) Muscat 1989; FCO 1993; Deputy Consul-General Istanbul 1999; Band C5; m 1980 Janice Isobel Mills (1s 1984; 1d 1985).

Begbie, Janice Isobel (née Mills); FCO since October 2003; Born 18/04/51; FCO 1971; Lusaka 1973; FCO 1975; Middle East Floater 1977; FCO 1980; SUPL 1983; Muscat 1989; SUPL 1993; FCO 1994; Second Secretary 1996; SUPL 1999; Istanbul 1999; m 1980 James Alexander Begbie (1s 1984; 1d 1985).

Beggs, Katherine Elizabeth; Tbilisi since June 2005; Born 25/06/76; FCO 2002; Band B3.

Belcher, Patrick Fred; Havana since June 2004; Born 25/08/48; Royal Air Force 1965-90; LCD 1990-92; Prague 1992; Moscow 1994; World-wide Floater Duties 1996; Hong Kong 1998; Beijing 2002; Band B3; m 1971 Ann Carr (1s 1977).

Belfitt, Sandra Jane; FCO since August 2005; Born 14/03/65; HM Customs and Excise 1986-93; FCO 1996; Brasilia 1997; Port Louis 2002; Band C4; m 1984 Andrew Belfitt (1d 1990; 1s 1993).

Belgrove, David Raymond; FCO since October 2002; Born 18/01/62; FCO 1982; Prague 1984; Kuwait 1986; FCO 1991; Third Secretary (Consular/Economic) Calcutta 1994; Second later First Secretary (MPA) Ottawa 1998; Band C4; m 1985 Mette Ofstad (2d 1986, 1989).

Bell, Alan Douglas; Phnom Penh since March 2001; Born 26/05/72; FCO 1995; Madrid 1997; Band A2.

Bell, Jeremy Paul Turnbull; FCO since January 2003; Born 04/01/52; FCO 1974; The Hague 1976; Bahrain 1981; Hanoi 1982; FCO 1985; Tokyo 1988; Third Secretary (Management/Cons) Gaborone 1992; Second Secretary FCO 1996; First Secretary (UN) Nairobi 1998; Band C5; m (1) 1978 Jane Dorron Lee (diss 1981) (2) 1991 Setsuko Yamamoto (1d 1995).

Bell, Julie Dawn (née Raines); Munich since December 2004; Born 12/11/66; FCO 1989; Language Training 1990; Moscow 1991; Budapest 1994; Belgrade 1995; Second Secretary FCO 1997; Second Secretary (Management/Consular) Lilongwe 2001; m 1991 Andrew Michael Bell (2d 1993, 1997).

Bell, Karen Ann (née Norris); First Secretary (Economic) Riyadh since November 2003; Born 22/04/66; FCO 1983; Strasbourg 1986; New Delhi 1988; FCO 1991; Ottawa 1996; Second Secretary (Commercial) Abuja 1999; Band C5; m 1987 Adrian Bell (2s 1993, 1996).

Bell, Kay Beverley; Colombo since January 2002; Born 11/06/57; FCO 1984; Bonn 1986; Floater Duties 1989; New York (UKMIS) 1993; Band A2.

Bell, Laura (née Page); Abuja since December 2004; Born 06/09/69; FCO 1995; Algiers 1997; Bridgetown 1998; SUPL 1999; FCO 2000; SUPL 2002; Band B3; m 1999 Ian McDonald Bell.

Bell, Mark Robert; Third Secretary (Political) Tel Aviv since April 2004; Born 04/05/71; FCO 1997; Full-Time Language Training Cairo 1999; Third Secretary (Political/Press) Damascus 2000; Band B3.

Bell, Melvin, MBE (2002); New York (UKMIS) since November 1999; Born 14/05/65; FCO 1984; Madrid 1987; FCO 1990; Third Secretary Mexico City 1993; FCO 1997; Band C4; m 1997 Maria Louisa Toxtle de Bautista.

Bell, Samantha Jane; FCO since June 2002; Born 01/10/71; FCO 1997; Athens 1999; Band B3.

Bellas, David Livingston; FCO since September 2000; Born 06/11/74; Band C4.

Bellham, Richard Anthony; FCO since 1998; Born 26/01/50; HM Forces (Army) 1968 -74; FCO

1976; Bangkok 1986; FCO 1989; Tokyo 1995; Band C5; m 1987 Chidphan Jaiprasat (1d 1989).

Belof, Margaret Mary; Dushanbe since December 2003; Born 06/09/61; FCO 1990; Third Secretary Bucharest 1994; Third later Second Secretary (Economic/EU) Athens 1998; Band C4.

Bendor, David Ian; First Secretary (Financial & Economic) Paris since March 1999; Born 14/03/66; Economic Advisers FCO 1991-96; T/D Paris 1993; On secondment to IMF (European Division) 1996-98; Band D6.

Benham, Gary Edward; Phnom Penh since August 2003; Born 07/03/69; Royal Air Force 1987-96; FCO 1997; Santiago 1998; ECO Tunis 2000; Band C4; m 1998 Amanda Marsden (1s 1999; 1d 2002).

Benham, Nancy, MBE (2003); Dar es Salaam since March 2005; Born 02/08/60; FCO 2003; SUPL 2004; Band A2; m 1986 Colin (2d 1988, 1991).

Benjamin, Jon; Deputy Consul-General New York since July 2005; Born 19/01/63; ODA 1986; Third later Second Secretary Jakarta 1988; First Secretary FCO 1992; Private Secretary to Minister of State FCO 1993; Full-Time Language Training 1995; First Secretary and Head of Political Section Ankara 1996; SUPL 1999; Deputy Head of Drugs and International Crime Department FCO 2000; Head of Human Rights Policy Department FCO 2002.

Bennett, Alexander; Tehran since April 2003; Born 04/11/67; FCO 1987; Paris 1998; Band C4; m 1997 Deborah Karen Stirzaker (1d 2001).

Bennett, Brian Maurice; HM Ambassador Minsk since March 2003; Born 01/04/48; FCO 1971; Prague 1973; Helsinki 1977; Second Secretary FCO 1979; Second Secretary (Comm/Aid) Bridgetown 1983; Second later First Secretary Vienna (UKDEL) MBFR 1986; First Secretary (Chancery/Inf) The Hague 1988; First Secretary FCO 1992; Deputy Head of Mission Tunis 1997; m 1969 Lynne Skipsey (3s 1974, 1978, 1991).

Bennett, Frederick Michael; Belgrade since February 2002; Born 07/12/49; Royal Military Police 1967-92; Prague 1992; Floater Duties 1994; FCO 1997; Peking 1997; Band B3; m 1978 Lynne Louise Jane Russell (2d 1979, 1980).

Bennett, Marylyn; FCO (Hanslope Park) since August 2000; Born 16/12/48; New Delhi 1972; Monrovia 1974; FCO 1977; South America Floater 1979; FCO 1982; Floater Duties 1983; Panama City 1986; Third later Second Secretary FCO 1988; Deputy Head of Mission Asunción 1993; Second Secretary Lilongwe 1996.

Bennett, Stephen Paul; FCO since October 1997; Born 28/10/62; FCO 1982; Nairobi 1986; FCO 1990; SUPL 1993; FCO 1994; Moscow 1995; Band A2; m 1990 Stephanie Cattermole (1 step d 1986; 1s 1991).

Bennett-Dixon, Vanessa May (née Bennett); Paris since July 2001; Born 12/01/57; FCO 1975; Nairobi 1978; Havana 1981; Kuwait 1982; Montserrat 1988; Stanley 1992; Hanoi 1994; Luanda 1996; Band A2; m 1987 Ronald William Dixon.

Bensberg, Jacqueline Margaret (née Campbell); FCO since July 2000; Born 06/06/63; FCO 1983; Cape Town/Pretoria 1985; UKDEL CSCE 1987; Third Secretary UKDEL CFE 1989; FCO 1990; Accra 1994; FCO 1997; Third Secretary (Political) Brussels 1998; Band B3; m 1991 Mark Bensberg (1d 1999).

Bensberg, Mark; Deputy Head of Mission Kinshasa since June 2004; Born 19/07/62; FCO 1980; Paris 1982; Africa/ME Floater 1985; Vice-Consul Vienna 1988; FCO 1991; Accra 1994; Second Secretary (Political/Press & Public Affairs) Brussels 1997; FCO 2000; m 1991 Jacqueline Margaret Campbell (1d 1999).

Bentley, Sally (née Myers); Athens since October 1999; Born 13/08/68; FCO 1998; Band A2; m 2001 Paul Stephen Bentley.

Berg, Geoffrey, MVO (1976); Consul-General Toronto and Director Trade and Investment Canada since January 2002; Born 05/07/45; CRO 1963; DSA 1965; LA Floater Duties 1968; Bucharest 1970; Second Secretary 1970; FCO 1971; Second later First Secretary (Inf) Helsinki 1975; FCO 1979; First Secretary (Commercial) Madrid 1984; First Secretary FCO 1988; Counsellor on loan to the DTI 1990; Deputy Head of Mission Mexico City 1993; Deputy Consul General and Director of Trade New York 1997; m 1970 Sheila Maxine Brown (1s 1975).

Berman, Paul Richard; Legal Counsellor Brussels (UKREP) since August 2002; Born 23/11/64; Called to the Bar, Gray's Inn 1990; Assistant later Senior Assistant Legal Adviser FCO 1991; Seconded to the International Committee of the Red Cross, Geneva 1996; FCO 1998; Legal Counsellor on loan to the Attorney General's Chambers (LSLO) 2000.

Berry, Susanna Gisela; FCO since June 2001; Born 06/09/62; FCO 1986; Second Secretary Vienna (UKDEL) 1989; Second Secretary (Economic) Vienna 1990; Full-Time Language Training FCO 1992; Full-Time Language Training Cairo 1993; FCO 1994; SUPL 1997; Band D6; m 1996 Paul Adams (1s 1999).

Bertie, Julie Karina (née Finnigan); SUPL since October 1999; Born 08/06/71; FCO 1990; Nairobi 1996; Band A2; m 1995 Stewart Valentine Bertie (2d 1998, 2000).

Best, Eleanor Marion; Seconded to UK Trade & Investment since May 2003; Born 28/04/63; MOD 1986-89; FCO 1996; Brussels 1997; Copenhagen 2000; Band A2.

Bethel, Samantha Claire Risby; ECO Islamabad since November 2000; Born 25/02/70; FCO 1990; Jakarta 1993; Pro Consul Düsseldorf 1997; Band B3.

Betterton, Judith Anne; Ankara since September 2002; Born 02/08/57; FCO 1983; Warsaw 1984; Lilongwe 1987; Bogotá 1989; Canberra 1991; FCO 1994; Amman 1998; Band B3.

Bevan, Howard James; Brussels since July 2003; Born 19/11/54; Royal Signals 1970-92; FCO 1995; Brussels (UKREP) 1997; Pro Consul Düsseldorf 2000; Band A2; m 1973 Christine (1d 1975; 1s 1986).

Bevan, James David; FCO since July 1998; Born 13/07/59; FCO 1982; Kinshasa 1984; Second later First Secretary Brussels (UKDEL) 1986; First Secretary FCO 1990; First Secretary Paris 1993; First Secretary (Political) Washington 1994; m 1984 Alison Janet Purdie (3d 1986, 1989, 1998).

Bevan, Terence Richard; First Secretary FCO since May 1992; Born 10/04/54; FCO 1970; Bonn 1977; FCO 1980; Second later First Secretary Oslo 1988; Band C5; m 1978 Gillian Margaret Francis (2d 1981, 1984).

Bewley, Sarah Margaret; Second Secretary FCO since May 1999; Born 05/08/73; FCO 1995; Kuala Lumpur 1997; Band D6.

Beyer, John Charles; HM Ambassador Chisinau since January 2006; Born 29/04/50; Director, China-Britain Business Council 1991-98; First Secretary FCO 1999; Deputy Head of Mission Luxembourg 2002; Band D6; m 1972 Letty Marindin Minns (1d 1977, 1s 1988).

Beynon, Debra Jane; Management/Commercial Officer Khartoum since May 2003; Born 22/07/62; Department of Transport 1978; Department of Employment 1979; FCO 1983; Berlin BMG 1985; Kingstown 1988; Dhaka 1989; FCO 1993; Second Secretary (Immigration/Consular) Dhaka 1995; Second later First Secretary (Immigration) Islamabad 1998; FCO 2002; Band C4; m 1985 Paul Ogwyn Beynon.

Bicker, David Allen; St Helena since May 2002; Born 25/10/48; Army 1966-88; Brussels (UKDEL) 1989; Cairo 1991; FCO 1994; Tirana 1996; Anguilla 1998; Band B3; m 1974 Molly Patricia (1d 1976; 2s 1978, 1983).

Bickers, Esmé Lillian; FCO since June 2000; Born 18/12/54; FCO 1988; Ottawa 1989; FCO 1992; The Hague 1997; Band B3.

Bielby, Richard Stephen; FCO since 1997; Born 18/09/65; FCO (HCS) 1989; FCO 1991; Islamabad 1993; Band B3; ptnr, Loy Foo Cheong.

Biggerstaff, Sarah Jane; SUPL since September 2002; Born 04/11/70; FCO 1997; Budapest 1998; FCO 2000; Band A2.

Bilimoria, Tehemton Pirosha; Second Secretary Nairobi since August 2000; Born 21/01/46; HM Forces (Army) 1964-70; PO 1970-76; FCO 1979; Washington 1984; FCO 1987; Paris 1992; Band C5; m 1980 Tayariez Dastoor (1d 1984; 1s 1986).

Billing, Victoria Elizabeth; FCO since January 2003; Born 31/05/75; FCO 1997; SOAS University of London 1998; Rangoon 1999; Band D6.

Binfield, Marella Jane; FCO since May 2002; Born 12/01/69; FCO 1995; Warsaw 1996; Band B3.

Binnie, Serena Clare; FCO since October 1990; Born 04/09/63; FCO 1986; Montevideo 1989; Band C4.

Binnington, Mark; FCO since November 2004; Born 20/03/78; DFES 2003; Band C4; m 2005 Emma Greatorex.

Birch, Ann Elizabeth (née Ridge); FCO since January 2000; Born 23/10/62; FCO 1990; New Delhi 1992; FCO 1995; Hanoi 1997; Band B3; m 1996 Paul David Birch.

Bird, Charles Philip Glover; First Secretary (Political) Abuja since August 2001; Born 08/10/54; Second Secretary FCO 1986; Language Training 1987; Language Training Cairo 1988; Second Secretary (Chancery) Abu Dhabi 1989; Second Secretary Belgrade 1992; Second later First Secretary FCO 1993; First Secretary (Political) Athens 1995; m 1975 Clare St. John (2s 1978, 1980; 1d 1982).

Bird, Christabel Helen; Second later First Secretary FCO since May 1993; Born 18/11/53; Tehran 1978; FCO 1979; Caracas 1980; FCO 1982; Second Secretary Geneva (UKMIS) 1989; Consul Geneva 1990; Band C5.

Bird, Juliette Winsome; SUPL since September 2004; Born 04/10/63; FCO 1990; New Delhi 1992; Second later First Secretary FCO 1994; First Secretary (Political) Brussels 2001; FCO 2003; Band D6; m 2002 Donald Peter Scargill (1s 2002).

Birks, Ian Martin; FCO since 2004; Born 03/06/52; FCO 1971; Canberra 1973; Belgrade 1976; Georgetown 1978; New York 1981; FCO 1984; Islamabad 1988; Second Secretary (Aid) Lagos 1992; Second Secretary FCO 1994; Second Secretary (Commercial) New Delhi 1997; First Secretary (Commercial) Lagos 2000; m (1) 1976 Sheridan Elizabeth Grice (diss 1997) (2d 1987, 1991); (2) Anny Bhatti 1997 (1d 1999).

Bishop, Peter George; Amman since August 2004; Born 23/11/55; Home Civil Service 1984; Bonn 1998; FCO 2002; Band B3; m 1983 Fiona Christine Buchanan (2s 1988, 1992).

Biskin, Sally-Ann (née Peters); Deputy Head of Mission Windhoek since May 2003; Born 08/02/65; FCO 1983; Brussels 1985; Harare 1988; Maputo 1989; Lagos 1989; Istanbul 1990; FCO 1993; SUPL 1994; FCO 1994; SUPL 1997; FCO 1998; Second Secretary (Management) Islamabad 2001; Band C4; m 1991 Cneyt Cem Biskin (diss) (2d 1992, 1994).

Black, Janice Sarah; Second Secretary Canberra since June 2003; Born 11/08/66; FCO 1987; SUPL 1994; FCO 1995; Second Secretary (Immigration) Tehran 1998; FCO 2001; Tripoli 2002; Band C4.

Blackburne, Alison; Deputy High Commissioner Harare since June 2003; Born 20/06/64; FCO 1987; Third later First Secretary (Chancery) Warsaw 1989; First Secretary FCO 1992; First Secretary New York (UKMIS) 1996; First Secretary (Political) Stockholm 2000.

Blacker, Catherine Louise; FCO since June 2003; Born 15/09/68; FCO 1989; Brussels (UKDEL) 1991; FCO 1997; T/D Islamabad 2000; Kabul 2002; Band B3.

Blackwell, Christopher Robert; Second Secretary FCO since May 1984; Born 11/08/58; FCO 1975; Geneva (UKMIS) 1978; FCO 1981; Aden 1983; Band C4; m 1982 Catherine Rose Gallagher (1d 1987; 1s 1989).

Bladen, John; Second Secretary FCO since February 1987; Born 08/07/44; FCO 1971; Bangkok 1973; FCO 1975; Accra 1976; FCO 1979; Kingston 1980; FCO 1983; Second Secretary Harare 1984; m 1969 Nina Shaw (1d 1972).

Blake, Michael David; Head of Technical Group (Implementation) FCO Services since October 2001; Born 19/01/55; FCO 1971; HCS 1976; FCO 1978; Washington 1979; FCO 1981; Ottawa 1981; FCO 1984; FCO Services 1999; m 1978 Audrey Layfield (1s 1983).

Blake, Stanley Clement; Second Secretary (Consular) Canberra since November 2000; Born 14/07/44; FO 1964; UK delegation NATO Paris and Brussels 1966; Amman 1969; FCO 1970; Moscow 1974; Paris 1975; FCO 1978; Tunis 1981; Second Secretary 1984; Second Secretary (Admin) and Consul Muscat 1984; Second Secretary FCO 1988; Second Secretary (Management) Addis Ababa 1991; Second Secretary FCO 1992; Second Secretary (Consular/Immigration) Accra 1993; ECO Bangkok 1997; m (1) Marion Lesley Jelly (diss 1972) (1s 1968); (2) 1977 Lindsay Jane Townsend (1s 1981).

Blanchard, William Hume James, OBE (1997); MVO (1993); First Secretary (Political/Military) Ankara since August 2004; Born FCO 1988; Second Secretary (Information) Budapest 1992; Second Secretary FCO 1995; SUPL 1997; First Secretary (Chancery) Islamabad 1998; First Secretary FCO 2001; Band D6; m 1998 Meriel Beattie (1s 2000).

Blogg, David John; HM Consul and Management Officer Ljubljana since April 2002; Born 08/09/48; FCO 1971; East Berlin 1973; Khartoum 1974; Dacca 1977; FCO 1979; Calcutta 1981; Baghdad 1982; Jedda 1983; Athens 1986; Second Secretary Tripoli 1989; Second Secretary FCO 1991; Second Secretary (Management/Consular) Sana'a 1993; Second Secretary Ulaanbaatar 1994; Second Secretary FCO 1995; Second Secretary Lima 1996; Consul (Management) St Petersburg 1997; Second Secretary FCO 1998; m 1973 Susan Robinia Meloy.

Bloomfield, Clare Louise Bamford; FCO since April 2004; Born 23/05/71; Band C4; m 2001 Colin Bloomfield.

Bloomfield, Keith George; HM Ambassador Kathmandu since July 2002; Born 02/06/47; HCS 1969-80; Brussels (UKREP) 1980; First Secretary FCO 1985; Head of Chancery Cairo 1987; Counsellor, Consul-General and Deputy Head of Mission Algiers 1990; Counsellor (Political/Management) Rome 1994; Minister and Deputy Head of Mission Rome 1996; FCO 1998; m 1976 Geneviève Paule (3d 1979, 1982, 1985).

Blows, Glyn Christopher; Washington since March 2003; Born 27/08/70; FCO 1990; Nicosia 1995; FCO 1999; Band A2; ptnr, Jane Brewer (1d 2001).

Bloxham, Siân Landis; Bandar Seri Begawan since July 2000; Born 11/11/64; HCS 1990; FCO 1996; St Petersburg 1998; Band A2.

Blunt, David Graeme, LVO (1986); Deputy Governor Gibraltar since January 2002; Born 19/01/53; FCO 1978; Second later First Secretary Vienna 1979; First Secretary (External Affairs) Peking 1983; FCO 1987; First Secretary (Chancery) Canberra 1989; Counsellor FCO 1994; Deputy Head of Mission and Consul-General Oslo 1997; m 1975 Geirid Bakkeli (3s 1982, 1984, 1990).

Boam, Rachel Christine (née Wickens); SUPL since August 2003; Born 05/11/68; FCO 1988; New York (UKMIS) 1991; PA/Deputy Head of Mission Athens 1995; FCO 1998; SUPL 1999; Language Training 1999; PA/Ambassador Berlin 2000; Band A2; M 1993 Jason Daniel Boam (1s 1999).

Boardman, Clarence Ronald; FCO since August 1998; Born 11/12/48; DSAO/FCO 1965; Algiers 1970; Ottawa 1972; Warsaw 1974; FCO 1977; MECAS 1978; Aden 1979; Riyadh 1982; Second Secretary FCO 1986; Consul (Commercial) Vancouver 1989; Deputy High Commissioner and Head of Mission Bandar Seri Begawan 1995; m 1973 Marion Lynn Fraser (1s 1991).

Boath, Arlene; Tirana since September 2002; Born 09/06/71; FCO 1988; Geneva (UKMIS) 2000; Band A2.

Boddy, Ben; FCO since February 2004; Born 31/10/75; Band B3; ptnr, Caroline Sharman.

Boffa, Sandra Jean (née Isaac); Tokyo since February 2003; Born 22/08/67; Ministry of Agriculture 1984-90; FCO 1990; Tokyo 1995; FCO 1998; Vienna 1999; Band A2; m 1992 Anthony Paul Vincent Boffa (1d 1993; 2s 1994, 1998).

Bolgar, Andrew Ben; Third Secretary Freetown since August 2003; Born 03/07/75; FCO 1999; Band B3.

Bond, Clare Elizabeth; Second Secretary FCO since October 2001; Born 17/01/75; FCO 1997; Second Secretary (Political) Kuala Lumpur 1999; Band C4.

Bond, Ian Andrew Minton; HM Ambassador Riga since April 2005; Born 19/04/62; FCO 1984; Third later Second Secretary (Political) Brussels (UKDEL NATO) 1987; First Secretary FCO 1990; First Secretary (Political/Military) Moscow 1993; First Secretary FCO 1996; Deputy Head of Mission Vienna (UKDEL OSCE) 2000; m 1987 Kathryn Joan Ingamells (1d 1989; 2s 1993, 2000).

Bond, Simon; FCO since August 2003; Born 23/04/65; Home Office 1988-89; FCO 1989; Port of Spain 1993; Kampala 1997; FCO 1999; Dakar 2000; Band C4.

Bonnici, Gail Margaret; SUPL since December 1997; Born 11/12/60; FCO 1984; Madrid 1985; LA Floater 1988; Valetta 1989; FCO 1991; Riyadh 1992; Buenos Aires 1996; Band A2; m 1990 Martin Mario Bonnici (1s 1991).

Bonsey, Jennifer Elaine; FCO since April 2004; Born 23/12/46; MOD 1964; FCO 1981; Paris 1982; Tunis 1985; Brussels (UKREP) 1988; FCO 1989; Singapore 1997; Bucharest 2001; Band B3.

Booker, Jacqueline Alice; FCO since June 1997; Born 19/01/62; FCO 1982; Athens 1984; Hanoi 1987; LA Floater 1988; FCO 1992; Dar es Salaam 1995; Band D6.

Booth, Mark James; FCO since June 2002; Born 13/03/72; FCO 1991; Geneva (UKMIS) 1995; Hong Kong 1998; Band B3.

Booth, Susan Jane (née Corcoran); FCO since March 1996; Born 03/08/68; FCO 1986; New York (UNGA) (UKMIS) 1988; Cape Town/Pretoria 1989; Warsaw 1991; Rabat 1993; Band B3; m 1991 Rodney James Booth.

Borisuth, Fiona Jayne (née Lavender); Islamabad since January 2005; Born 12/06/70; FCO 1991; Tokyo 1992; La Paz 1996; Bangkok 2000; Band B3; m 2001 Wasan (Aek) Borisuth (1 step d 1995, 1d 2003; 1s 2001).

Borland, David; SUPL since June 2004; Born 20/06/60; on loan to DTI; second Secretary FCO 1991; T/D Second Secretary (Political) Maputo 1993; Second Secretary (Political) Caracas 1994; First Secretary (Political/Economic) Mexico City 1995; First Secretary Helsinki (EU) 2000; Band D6.

Borley, Salud Maria Victoria; On attachment to British Trade International since January 2003; Born 06/05/70; FCO 1989; Caracas 1992; Floater Duties 1996; FCO 1998; Band C4.

Bossley, Edward; New Delhi since January 2004; Born 22/09/71; FCO 1991; New York (UKMIS) 1994; Islamabad 1997; FCO 1999; Band C4; m 1994 Stefany Elizabeth Rocque (1d 1997).

Bossley, Stefany Elizabeth (née Rocque); FCO since April 1999; Born 28/07/66; FCO 1989; World-wide Floater Duties 1992; New York (UKMIS) 1994; Islamabad 1997; Band B3; m 1994 Edward Bossley (1d 1997).

Boswell, Clive Timothy; Washington since December 2001; Born 29/08/70; FCO 1996; Brussels (UKREP) 1998; Band A2.

Botha, Caroline Jane; SUPL since August 2003; Born 01/04/70; FCO 1996; Bratislava 1997; Attaché (Immig/Cons) Colombo 2000; Band B3; m 1993 Peter Botha (1d 1994; 1s 1998).

Botham, Peter; Tunis since June 2004; Born 10/08/78; FCO 2003; Band A2.

Bottomley, Patricia Fiona; First Secretary Brussels (UKREP) since January 2005; Born 29/03/59; FCO 1983; (Second Secretary) 1985; Second Secretary and Vice Consul Havana 1986; First Secretary (Chancery) Mexico City 1988; First Secretary FCO 1991; Brussels 1994; FCO 1998; First Secretary (Political) Rome 2000; FCO 2004; Band D6; m 1997 Arno Baecker (1s 1999).

Bouakaze-Khan, Najma (née Khan); Deputy High Commissioner Gaborone since November 2004; Born 11/06/67; FCO 1987; Addis Ababa 1989; Brussels (UKDEL)(NATO) 1993; FCO 1996; Full-Time Language Training 1999; Istanbul 1999; Band C4; m 1992 Didier Bouakaze-Khan. (2s 1996, 1999).

Bourke, Martin; Deputy High Commissioner Wellington since May 2000; Born 12/03/47; Third Secretary FCO 1970; Brussels 1971; Second Secretary Singapore 1974; Second later First Secretary FCO 1975; First Secretary Lagos 1978; FCO 1980; On loan to DOT 1980; Consul (Comms) Johannesburg 1984; First Secretary FCO 1988; Governor Turks and Caicos Islands 1993; Seconded to The Prince's Trust 1997; m 1973 Anne Marie Marguerite Hottelet (4s 1974, 1977, 1979, 1983).

Bowden, Christopher John, MBE (2004); Maputo since June 2001; Born 06/07/59; FCO 1977; Copenhagen 1979; Karachi 1982; Bucharest 1983; Paris 1985; FCO 1988; Calcutta 1991; Istanbul 1994; FCO 1998; Band C4; m 1983 Jane Susan Manville (1d 1986).

Bowden, James Nicholas Geoffrey, OBE (2002); Deputy Head of Mission Kuwait since May 2003; Born 27/05/60; Royal Green Jackets 1979-86; Second Secretary FCO 1986; Language Training 1988; Language Training Cairo 1989; Deputy, later Acting Consul-General Aden 1990; Second later First Secretary (Chancery) Khartoum 1991; First Secretary FCO 1994; First Secretary (Political) Washington 1996; First Secretary (Economic and Commercial) Riyadh 1999; First Secretary FCO 2000; m (1) 1985 Alison Hulme (diss) (1s 1993; 1d 1995); m (2) 1999 Sarah Peaslee (1d 2001; twin s 2003).

Bowe, Michael Henry; FCO since July 1999; Born 08/03/46; FCO 1971; Lagos 1974; New Delhi 1978; FCO 1981; Second Secretary (Commercial) Lilongwe 1982; Second Secretary (Comm) Gaborone 1986; Second Secretary FCO 1990; Second Secretary (Management) and Consul Maputo 1993; Second Secretary (Consular) Sarajevo 1997; m (1) 1970 Ann Frances Ballard (diss 1985) (1d 1976; 1s 1979); m (2) 1985 Sandra Jean Brown Lassale.

Bowes, Andrew Martin; Second Secretary (Political/Press & Public Affairs) Lisbon since July 2004; Born 10/08/74; FCO 1997; Third Secretary (Vice-Consul/Press & Public Affairs) Maputo 1999; Deputy Head of Mission Dili 2002; m 2001 Isabel Filipa Oliveira Goncalves.

Bowes, Jacqueline; FCO since October 1990; Born 28/02/60; Inland Revenue 1976-90; Band A2.

Bowie, Nigel John Graydon; Brussels since August 2004; Born 31/05/51; FCO 1975; Seoul 1977; Paris 1981; Athens 1983; Second Secretary FCO 1985; Second Secretary (Comm/Econ) Oslo 1988; First Secretary (Comm) Athens 1992; FCO 1997; First Secretary (Political) Abuja 1999; FCO 2002; m 1977 Mildred Alice Sansom (2s 1979, 1984; 1d 1982).

Bowling, Nicola Carron (née Jackson); SUPL since May 2005; Born 01/12/67; FCO 1991; Third Secretary (Aid/Commercial) Maputo 1994; Second Secretary Kuala Lumpur 1998; Band C4; m 1996 David John Robinson Bowling (1s 2000).

Bowman, Victoria Jane (née Robinson); HM Ambassador Rangoon since December 2002; Born 12/06/66; FCO 1988; Third later Second Secretary Rangoon 1990; First Secretary FCO 1993; First Secretary (Information/Press) Brussels (UKREP) 1996; SUPL 1999.

Bowskill, Robert Colin; Kingston since November 2002; Born 21/09/43; Army 1959-77; Police 1977-84; Prague 1984; Lusaka 1987; Warsaw 1989; New Delhi 1991; Bucharest 1995; Tel Aviv 1998; Band C4; m 1966 Jean Spencer (2s 1967, 1968).

Bowskill, Simon Colin, MBE (2005); Kampala since August 2005; Born 13/12/68; Army 1985; Police 1991; Istanbul 2001; Band B3; m 1993 Dawn Theresa Langdown (1s 1996; 2d 1998).

Bowyer, Aileen Jane (née Gemmell); SUPL since January 1994; Born 10/09/62; FCO 1983; Belgrade 1985; SUPL 1987; Kaduna 1990; FCO 1990; Band A2; m 1987 Anthony Harvey Bowyer (1d 1992).

Bowyer, Anthony Harvey; FCO since August 2001; Born 21/11/62; FCO 1982; Belgrade 1984; Kaduna 1987; FCO 1990; Harare 1994; Dublin 1997; Band C4; m 1987 Aileen Jane Gemmell (2d 1992, 1999).

Bowyer, Joanne Louise; Toronto since June 2001; Born 30/03/68; FCO 1989; Bogotá 1991; Abuja 1994; FCO 1998; Band B3.

Boxer, Peter John; Islamabad since January 2005; Born 24/07/71; FCO 1995; Second Secretary (Political) Nicosia 1997; On secondment 2001; FCO 2003; Band D6.

Boyden, Simon Denis; First Secretary FCO since July 2002; Born 24/02/68; FCO 1997; Second Secretary (Commercial) Moscow 1999; Band C4; m 1998 Geraldine Gallagher (1s 1999; 2d 2001, 2003).

Boyles, Elizabeth; SUPL since September 2003; Born 28/08/67; FCO 1990; Third Secretary (Political) Brussels 1994; New York (UKMIS) 1996; DHM San Salvador 1997; Second Secretary (Trade Policy) Brussels (UKREP) 2000; First Secretary (Economic and Social Affairs) Brussels 2003; Band D6; m 1997 Patrick Dens (1s 2003).

Bradbury, Jonathan Edward; FCO since 2004; Born 16/12/67; HCS 1989-95; Nairobi 1997; Dublin 2000; Band A2; m 1994 Rebecca Clare Sebborn (2s 1998, 2000; 1d 2003).

Bradley, Guy; FCO since March 1989; Born 03/02/62; FCO 1981; New Delhi 1983; FCO 1987; Havana 1988; Band C5; m 1987 Andrea Stannard. (1s 1993; 1d 1994).

Bradley, Henry Alexander Jarvie; Lisbon since November 2004; Born 23/07/52; HM Customs and Excise 1969; FCO 1971; Brussels (EC) 1975; Budapest 1978; Bahrain 1979; FCO 1982; Munich 1984; Third Secretary (AO/Vice-Consul) Maseru 1987; Second Secretary FCO 1992; Deputy High Commissioner Banjul 1996; First Secretary Vienna (UKDEL) OSCE 2000; Band C5; m 1979 Gabriella Maria Schwery.

Bradley, Joseph Maxwell; SUPL since October 2002; Born 14/02/60; FCO 1978; East Berlin 1981; Resigned 1983; Reinstated 1986; Lusaka 1987; Vienna (UKDEL) 1990; FCO 1993; Third Secretary (Information) Berlin 1995; Full-Time Language Training 1995; Second Secretary Geneva (UKMIS) 1998; m 1987 Melanie Rose (2d 1988, 1992; 1s 1990).

Bradley, Stephen Edward; Consul-General Hong Kong since December 2003; Born 04/04/58; FCO 1981; Language Training 1982; Second later First Secretary Tokyo 1983; SUPL (Guinness Peat Aviation) 1987; Deputy Political Adviser Hong Kong 1988; SUPL (Lloyd George Investment Management) 1993; FCO 1995; Head of West Indian Atlantic Department FCO 1997; Director of Trade and Investment Paris 1999; Minister Beijing 2002; m 1982 Elizabeth Gomersall (1s 1985; 1d 1988).

Bradley, Timothy Gawin, OBE (1991); First Secretary FCO since May 1999; Born 03/06/59; FCO 1983; Language Training 1984; Second later First Secretary (Chancery) Kuwait 1986; First Secretary FCO 1989; Belgrade 1996; Band D6; m 1990 Kathleen Scanlon (3s 1993, 1995, 1997; 1d 2002).

Bradney, Emily Theresa; FCO since October 2004; Born 28/09/79; Band C4.

Bradshaw, John Vincent; New Delhi since November 2000; Born 19/08/64; FCO 1999; Band C4; m 1994 Doris Jungling (2s 1994, 1996).

Braidford, Lindsey; FCO since February 1988; Born 20/04/47; Jedda 1975; Belize 1976; The Hague 1979; Rangoon 1982; Pretoria/Cape Town 1984; Band B3.

Braithwaite, Julian Nicholas; Washington since September 2004; Born 25/07/68; Second Secretary

FCO 1994; Seconded to ICFY, Zagreb 1995; Second Later First Secretary (Chancery) Belgrade 1996; On loan to No.10 Press Office 1998; Seconded to SHAPE 1999; Prime Minister's Speech Co-ordinator 2000; Sarajevo 2002; m 1999 Biljana Njagulj (1d 2000).

Bramley, Sheila Jane; Second Secretary FCO since February 2002; Born 25/10/63; FCO 1982; Tokyo 1984; Sofia 1987; SE Asia/FE Floater 1989; FCO 1991; Kuala Lumpur 1994; Canberra 1995; Islamabad 1998; Band C4.

Brammer, Geoffrey Ian; FCO since January 2002; Born 09/06/65; FCO 1985; Kaduna 1987; Nassau 1990; Tehran 1991; FCO 1992; Deputy Head of Mission Ashgabat 1995; Second Secretary (Management) Bridgetown 1998; Band C4; m 1991 Shelley Diane Chalmers.

Brandon, William Roland; FCO since January 2005; Born 07/06/64; FCO 1993; First Secretary (Economic) Vienna 1996; First Secretary FCO 1999; First Secretary (Political) Singapore 2001; Band D6; m 1991 Polly Jennifer Nyiri (3d (twins) 1996, 1998).

Brannigan, Virginia (née Reynolds); SUPL since July 1999; Born 16/01/62; FCO 1985; San José 1986; Madrid 1990; FCO 1998; Band A2; m 1992 Stuart Patrick Brannigan.

Brant, Andrew; FCO since March 2001; Born 13/02/74; Band B3.

Brant, Astrid Lorita Sophia; FCO since August 2002; Born 27/02/53; DHSS 1980-91; FCO 1991; Tunis 1992; Floater Duties 1997; Band B3.

Braun, David Alan; FCO since February 2000; Born 27/02/71; FCO 1991; Madrid 1998; Band C5; m 1998 Susan Jane Robottom.

Brazier, Colin Nigel; Consul (Commercial) New York since September 2000; Born 31/10/53; FCO 1973; Warsaw 1976; Singapore 1977; Accra 1980; FCO 1982; Dhaka 1985; Third Secretary (Comm)later Second Secretary (Development) Kingston 1989; Second Secretary FCO 1992; Deputy High Commissioner Georgetown 1997; m 1975 Jane Ann Pearson (1d 1979; 1s 1983).

Brear, Andrew James; FCO since July 2003; Born 28/01/60; Army 1979-90; Second later First Secretary FCO 1991; First Secretary (Inf) Santiago 1994; First Secretary FCO 1997; First Secretary (Political) Stockholm 2000; Band D6; m 1986 Jane Susan Matthews (1d 1991; 1s 1993).

Breeze, Christopher Mark; Cairo since June 2005; Born 13/08/63; FCO 1985; Second Secretary (Chancery) Nicosia 1988; Second later First Secretary FCO 1991; First Secretary (Trade Policy) New Delhi 1994; First Secretary (Political) Ankara 1997; First Secretary FCO 2001; m 1990 Janet Suzanne Champion (2d 1995, 1998).

Breeze, Christopher Mark; FCO since October 2002; Born 13/01/74; Band B3.

Breeze, Susan Jane (née Cockel); SUPL since April 2005; Born 09/03/66; FCO 1989; Language Training 1990; Full-Time Language Training Peking 1991; Third Secretary (Commercial) Peking 1992; On loan to China-Britain Trade Group 1995; T/D Moscow 1996; FCO 1996; m 2002 Paul Stothart Breeze.

Brennan, Anthony Bradford; FCO since December 2002; Born 06/02/66; FCO 1994; Second Secretary (Economic/KHF) later First Secretary (EU/Economic) Prague 1996; FCO 2000; Seconded to Czech Foreign Service 2002.

Brenton, Anthony Russell, CMG (2001); HM Ambassador Moscow since September 2004; Born 01/01/50; FCO 1975; MECAS 1977; First Secretary Cairo 1978; FCO 1981; Presidency Liaison Officer Brussels 1982; FCO 1982; First Secretary (Energy) Brussels (UKREP) 1985; On loan to the European Commission 1986; Counsellor FCO 1989; CDA Harvard University 1992; Full-Time Language Training 1993; Counsellor (Economic/Aid/Scientific) Moscow 1994; Director FCO 1998; Minister Washington 2001; m (1) 1971 Susan Mary Blacker (diss 1978); (2) 1982 Susan Mary Penrose (1s 1984; 2d 1987, 1988).

Brenton, Jonathan Andrew; First Secretary (Media) Berlin since April 2003; Born 24/12/65; FCO 1994; Second Secretary (Commercial) later First Secretary (Economic) Moscow 1996; FCO 2000; Band D6; m 2001 Sayana Yakovlena Virt (1d 1988).

Brett, David Lawrence; First Secretary Grand Turk since August 2004; Born 20/09/52; FCO 1978; Tehran 1980; Chicago 1983; FCO 1986; Second Secretary (Chancery) Kingston 1989; Consul-General Alexandria 1992; First Secretary FCO 1996; Consul-General Algiers 2001; SUPL 2003; m 1984 Carol Sue Lane (2s 1986, 1991; 1d 1988).

Brett, Rebecca Louise (née Fenwick); Colombo since September 2000; Born 27/11/64; FCO 1984; Washington 1987; The Hague 1990; SUPL 1992; FCO 1994; Abu Dhabi 1996; Band B3; m 1987 Paul Brett (2d 1992, 1996; 1s 1994).

Brett, Russell Michael; Second Secretary (Political) The Hague since June 2005; Born 14/09/69; FCO 1989; Athens 1995; FCO 1999; Band B3; m 1999 Simone Walsh (2d 2000, 2002).

Brett Rooks, Bedelia, LVO; Consul-General Casablanca since June 2005; Born 09/12/46; FCO 1969; On loan to SEATO Bangkok 1972; Copenhagen 1975; Rome 1976; Second Secretary FCO 1978; Second Secretary Accra 1983; Brussels (UKREP) 1986; First Secretary FCO 1987; First Secretary (Inf) Berlin (BMG) 1989; First Secretary FCO 1993; First Secretary Brussels 1996; FCO 2001.

Brettle-Cockman, Lynda Elizabeth; SUPL since March 2003; Born 02/10/62; FCO 1980; Tokyo 1983; SE Asia Floater 1987; Islamabad 1988; SUPL 1992; FCO 1993; Second Secretary (Management) and Consul Caracas 1997; First Secretary (Management) Mexico City 2000; Band

C5; m 1994 Michael Anthony Cockman (1d 1994; 1s 2001).

Brewer, Dr Jonathan Andrew; Counsellor FCO since January 2002; Born 20/03/55; FCO 1983; Second later First Secretary Luanda 1986; First Secretary FCO 1988; First Secretary (Chancery) Mexico City 1991; Counsellor FCO 1995; Counsellor (Political Affairs) Moscow 1998; m (1) 1978 Tessa Alexandra Swiney (diss 1990); (2) 1993 Angela Margarita Sosa Teran.

Brewer, Lesley Ann; FCO since July 2003; Born 29/07/57; FCO 1995; Prague 1997; Tripoli 2000; Band A2.

Brewer, Nicola Mary, CMG (2003); Director General (European Union), FCO since 2004; Born 14/11/57; FCO 1983; Second Secretary (Chancery) Mexico City 1984; First Secretary FCO 1987; First Secretary (Economic) Paris 1991; SUPL 1994; Counsellor FCO 1995; Counsellor New Delhi 1998; Director (Global Issues) FCO 2001; On loan as Director General (Regional Programmes) to DFID 2002; m 1991 Geoffrey Charles Gillham (1d 1993; 1s 1994).

Bridge, Heather Susan (née Brown); Second Secretary Kingston since November 2004; Born 19/04/62; FCO 1985; Second Secretary Skopje 2000; FCO 2002; Band C4; m 1986 Christopher Martin Gibbons Bridge (2d 1990, 1992).

Bridge, Karen Maria (née Chadbourne); Dhaka since July 2002; Born 03/09/70; FCO 1990; Brussels (UKREP) 1993; FCO 1995; Brussels (UKREP) 1996; FCO 1997; Riyadh 1999; Band A2; m 1992 Peter Charles Benson Bridge (2s 1998, 2000).

Bridge, Richard Philip; Counsellor Geneva since August 2004; Born 24/03/59; Second Secretary (Inf) Warsaw 1986; FCO 1988; First Secretary (Chancery) Moscow 1989; FCO 1993; Counsellor New Delhi 1998; Counsellor FCO 2001; m 1994 Philippa Anne Leslie-Jones (2s 1995, 1997).

Bridges, Stephen John; Dhaka since March 2005; Born 19/06/60; FCO 1980; Africa/ME Floater 1983; Luanda 1984; Third later Second Secretary (Comm) Seoul 1987; Second later First Secretary FCO 1992; First Secretary Kuala Lumpur 1996; HM Ambassador Phnom Penh 2000; m 1990 Yoon Kyung Mi.

Bridgwood, Alistair Charles Jeudwine; Second Secretary (Political) Sarajevo since February 2004; Born 12/05/73; FCO 2001; Language Training 2003; Band C4; m 2001 Rachel Beale.

Brier, Lucy Jane (née Richardson); FCO since October 2003; Born 18/03/69; FCO 1995; Kuala Lumpur 1997; SUPL 2000; Ulaanbaatar 2002; Band B3; m 1996 Simon Richard Brier.

Brier, Simon Richard; FCO since 2004; Born 15/09/67; FCO 1987; Prague 1989; SE Asia/Far East Floater Duties 1991; FCO 1994; Kuala Lumpur 1997; Deputy Head of Mission Ulaanbaatar 2001; m 1996 Lucy Jane Richardson.

Brierley, David Anthony; FCO since September 2002; Born 14/10/47; Royal Marines 1965; Budapest 1987; Madrid 1989; FCO 1991; Kuwait 1996; Tirana 1998; Band B3; (1s 1998).

Brigden, Neil Stephen; First Secretary (Commercial) The Hague since August 2004; Born 07/08/68; Colombo 1989; Bucharest 1992; Sana'a 1995; FCO 1996; Second Secretary (Commercial) New Delhi 2000; Band C5; m 1993 Joanne (1d 1996; 1s 1999).

Brigenshaw, David Victor; First Secretary FCO since April 1998; Born 01/06/56; FCO 1973; Nairobi 1976; FCO 1981; Kuala Lumpur 1983; Third Secretary (Commercial) Quito 1986; Second Secretary FCO 1990; m 1977 Yvonne Lesley Bush.

Briggs, Geoffrey; Second Secretary FCO since July 1997; Born 20/02/64; FCO 1988; Third Secretary (Econ/Aid) Cairo 1990; Second Secretary FCO 1992; Tirana 1995; Band C4.

Bright, Colin Charles; Consul-General Lyon since January 2004; Born 02/01/48; Second Secretary FCO 1975; First Secretary Bonn 1977; FCO 1979; On loan to the Cabinet Office 1983; Consul New York (BTDO) 1985; Counsellor and Head of Chancery Berne 1989; Consul-General Frankfurt 1993; FCO 1998; m (1) 1978 Helen-Ann Michie (diss 1990); (2) 1990 Jane Elizabeth Gurney Pease (1s 1992; 1d 1995).

Brimfield, Valerie; Dublin since August 2003; Born 27/07/49; FCO 1979; Tunis 1980; Tehran 1983; New Delhi 1985; Dhaka 1989; Ottawa 1992; FCO 1995; Tokyo 1996; Bucharest 1997; FCO 2001; Band B3.

Brind, Kevin James; Second Secretary (SMO/Consul) Santiago since February 2003; Born 05/10/59; FCO 1977; Bonn 1980; Khartoum 1982; Moscow 1986; FCO 1987; Canberra 1990; Third Secretary (Development) Kathmandu 1993; Second Secretary, Deputy Head of Mission Ulaanbaatar 1997; FCO 1998; m 1983 Jane Louise Burns.

Brinkley, Robert Edward; HM Ambassador Kiev since August 2002; Born 21/01/54; FCO 1977; Third Secretary UKDEL Comprehensive Test Ban, Geneva 1978; Language Training 1978; Second Secretary Moscow 1979; First Secretary FCO 1982; First Secretary (Political/Military) Bonn 1988; First Secretary later Counsellor FCO 1992; Counsellor (Political) Moscow 1996; Head of Joint Entry Clearance Unit (FCO/Home Office) 2000; m 1982 Frances Mary Webster (3s 1982, 1984, 1989).

Bristow, Dr Lawrence Stanley Charles; HM Ambassador Baku since January 2004; Born 23/11/63; FCO 1990; Full-Time Language Training 1991; Second Secretary (Chancery/Inf) Bucharest 1992; First Secretary FCO 1995; Private Secretary to Minister of State 1996; Full-Time Language Training 1998; Ankara 1999; CDA, NATO Defence College, Rome 2002; FCO 2003; m 1998 Fiona McCallum (1s 2000).

Bronnert, Deborah Jane; Counsellor (Commercial) Moscow since July 2002; Born 31/01/67; DOE 1989; Royal Commission on Environmantal Pollution 1990; Brussels (UKREP) 1991; DOE 1993; FCO 1994; On secondment to European Commission (Kinnock Cabinet) 1995; FCO 1999; Band D7.

Brook, John Edwin; FCO since November 1997; Born 21/03/45; FO 1964; Moscow 1967; Latin American Floater 1970; Calcutta 1972; Second Secretary FCO 1975; Second Secretary (Commercial) Moscow 1978; Second later First Secretary Berne 1981; First Secretary (Commercial) East Berlin 1984; First Secretary on attachment to JSDC 1988; First Secretary FCO 1989; Full-Time Language Training 1993; Consul-General Stuttgart 1993; m 1981 Moira Elizabeth Lands (1d 1983; 1s 1986).

Brookes, Carter, MBE (1990); On loan to the Cabinet Office since May 1997; Born 13/12/46; FCO 1971; Saigon 1973; FCO 1974; St Helena 1976; FCO 1978; Singapore 1980; FCO 1983; Moscow 1986; New Delhi 1989; Beirut 1991; FCO 1992; Band C4; m 1971 Margaret Jean Stewart (3s 1974, 1976, 1977).

Brookes, Diana Lorraine; SUPL since December 2003; Born 19/04/64; Solicitor 1989; Assistant Legal Adviser FCO 1989; First Secretary (Legal) Brussels (UKREP) 1995; FCO 1998; Legal Counsellor FCO 1999; m 1990 Gerald Blais (1d 1999).

Brooking, Karen (née Moore); Second Secretary (Political) Copenhagen since September 2002; Born 15/07/64; FCO 1987; Peking 1990; FCO 1992; SUPL 1994; FCO 1995; Band C4.

Brooking, Stephen John Allan, OBE (2002); FCO since June 2004; Born 13/03/64; FCO 1986; Second Secretary (Economic) Peking 1989; Second Secretary FCO 1992; First Secretary (Political) Sarajevo 1994; FCO 1995; First Secretary (ESCAP) Bangkok 1998; First Secretary FCO 2001; Counsellor (Political) Kabul 2002.

Brooks, Shelagh Margaret Jane; FCO since October 2002; FCO 1979; On loan to Hong Kong Government 1987; Legal Counsellor FCO 1991; Brussels (UKREP) 1998.

Broom, Peter David; Consul (Commercial) San Francisco since February 2003; Born 07/08/53; FCO 1970; Oslo 1974; Jedda 1977; Islamabad 1979; FCO 1981; Mbabane 1984; New Delhi 1987; Second Secretary FCO 1989; Consul (Commercial) Brisbane 1991; First Secretary (Commercial), Consul and DHM Yaounde 1997; Consul-General Cape Town 2000; Band C5; m 1976 Vivienne Louise Pyatt (5d 1979, 1981, 1985, 1988, 1994).

Broomfield, David Norman; SMO Stockholm since October 2002; Born 21/05/54; FCO 1973; Banjul 1975; LA Floater 1978; Prague 1980; FCO 1983; Tripoli 1986; Second Secretary (Chancery/Inf) Lusaka 1987; Vice-Consul Naples 1991; First Secretary FCO 1995; Consul (Commercial) Barcelona 1998.

Brosnan, Sheryl (née Landman); Kampala since August 2002; Born 05/12/71; FCO 1991; Bangkok 1993; Istanbul 1997; Abidjan 2000; m 1994 Mark Paul Brosnan (2s 1998, 2000).

Brough, Stuart Richard; FCO since May 2005; Born 24/06/65; FCO 1984; Second Secretary Bridgetown 2002; Second Secretary Port of Spain 2003; Band C4; m 1989 Delia Claire Hickman (1s 1992; 1d 1995).

Broughton, Sarah; FCO since 2004; Born 12/08/66; FCO 1984; Ottawa 1987; Lilongwe 1990; Floater 1992; FCO 1995; Second Secretary (Political) New York (UKMIS) 1999; Band C4.

Brown, Alexander Mark; FCO since May 2000; Born 21/07/64; DHSS 1986; FCO 1988; Lagos 1991; FCO 1992; Full-Time Language Training 1993; Hamburg 1994; Ashgabat 1997; Band C4; m 1997 A Gehrke.

Brown, Alexander Nicholas Seaton; Second Secretary (Political) Buenos Aires since March 2003; Born 31/07/72; FCO 2000; Band C4.

Brown, Andrew Paul; FCO since January 2002; Born 12/10/68; FCO 1987; New York (UKMIS) 1991; FCO 1994; Third Secretary Seoul 1998; Band B3; m 1998 Joanna Beresford.

Brown, Deirdre Rebecca (née Herdman), MBE (2002); First Secretary (Trade) Budapest since April 2005; Born 19/07/66; FCO 1986; Dhaka 1988; FCO 1992; Third Secretary (Political/Economic) Bangkok 1995; FCO 1998; SUPL 2002; Band C4; m 1991 Stephen William Brown (1d 1992; 1s 1994).

Brown, Edward James Murch, MBE (1991); Geneva (UKMIS) since May 2005; Born 27/08/59; FCO 1978; Bonn 1980; Prague 1983; Rabat 1985; FCO 1987; Düsseldorf 1992; FCO 1995; Second Secretary Geneva (UKMIS) 1996; On loan to DTI 2001; m 1980 Hannah Jane Gibbons.

Brown, Gordon Williams; FCO since April 2004; Born 17/10/54; Inland Revenue 1975; FCO 1976; Guatemala City 1979; The Hague 1981; SE Asia Floater 1983; Kampala 1985; FCO 1988; Second Secretary (Man and Consul) Havana 1991; Second Secretary (Management) and HM Consul Muscat 1995; British Trade International 1998; First Secretary and HM Consul Cairo 2001; m 1985 Rosalind Patricia Harwood (2s 1992, 1993).

Brown, Herbert George, MBE (1981); FCO since February 2001; Born 02/01/43; FO 1964; Rawalpindi 1966; Kuala Lumpur 1969; FCO 1973; Barcelona 1975; Maseru 1978; FCO 1981; Second Secretary and Vice-Consul Baghdad 1982; On loan to DTI 1985; First Secretary (Commercial) Rio de Janeiro 1988; First Secretary FCO 1990; HM Consul later HM Consul-General Cape Town 1996; m 1975 Susan Atkin (1d 1977).

Brown, John Mark; World Wide Floater Duties since May 2002; Born 15/05/43; RAF 1962-84;

Islamabad 1990; Belgrade 1993; Moscow 1996; Damascus 1999; Band B3; m 1965 Carole Elizabeth Thompson (2d 1966, 1970).

Brown, Kerry; FCO since April 2003; Born 13/06/67; FCO 1998; First Secretary Beijing 2000; Band D6; m 1995 Siqin Toya (1d 2000).

Brown, Linda; SUPL since October 2002; Born 24/12/55; FCO 1974; Bonn 1977; FCO 1980; Budapest 1980; Oslo 1982; FCO 1985; Rome 1992; Moscow 1996; FCO 2000; Band B3.

Brown, Richard Anthony; FCO since April 2005; Born 29/10/72; FCO 1996; Brussels 2002; Band B3.

Brown, Rosalind Patricia (née Harwood); SUPL since May 2004; Born 08/01/59; FCO 1981; Bangkok 1982; Rome 1984; Kampala 1985; FCO 1988; Resigned 1989; Reinstated, FCO 1990; Havana 1991; Muscat 1995; Resigned 1996; Reinstated, Cairo 2003; Band B3; m 1985 Gordon William Brown (3s 1992, 1993, 2002).

Brown, Sir Stephen (David Reid), KCVO (1999); Group Chief Executive (Permanent Secretary) British Trade International since October 2002; Born 26/12/45; HM Forces 1964-76; FCO 1976; First Secretary Nicosia 1977; First Secretary (Commercial) Paris 1980; FCO 1985; T/D DTI 1989; Consul-General Melbourne 1989; Counsellor (Commercial) Peking 1994; HM Ambassador Seoul 1997; Pre Post Training FCO 2000; High Commissioner Singapore 2001; m 1966 Pamela Gaunt (1s 1965; 1d 1969).

Brown, Stephen Leonard; T/D Baghdad since November 2003; Born 07/03/56; Army 1974-96; FCO 1998; Riyadh 1999; FCO 2001; Tehran 2001; Chisinau 2003; Band B3; m 1978 Gaynor Ruth (2d 1974, 1982).

Brown, Stephen Michael; Third Secretary (Management) Karachi since July 2005; Born 09/06/63; Household Cavalry 1980-95; FCO 1997; Mostar 1997; Amman 1998; Third Secretary (Management) Almaty 2000; Bahrain 2002; Third Secretary (Vice-Consul) Tashkent 2003; Band B3.

Brown, Stuart James; FCO since January 2005; Born 29/04/75; FCO 1994; Kiev 2001; Band B3; ptnr, Fiona Brougham.

Brown, Trevor Maurice; FCO since June 2003; Born 24/10/69; FCO 1996; Tirana 2000; m 2003 Laura Mooney.

Brownbill, Timothy Patrick; Deputy Consul-General Düsseldorf since November 2004; Born 06/02/60; FCO 1979; Lagos 1982; Madrid 1986; FCO 1989; Resigned 1990 (March), Reinstated 1990 (July); Language Training 1992; Deputy Head of Mission Vilnius 1992; Second Secretary 1994; Second Secretary (Commercial/Economic) Havana 1996; First Secretary FCO 1999; On loan to the DTI 2000; HM Ambassador Managua 2002; Full-Time Language Training (German) 2004.

Browne, Dr Carolyn; Counsellor (External) Brussels (UKREP) since June 2002; Born 19/10/58; FCO 1985; Language Training 1987; Second later First Secretary Moscow 1988; FCO 1991; First Secretary New York (UKMIS) 1993; FCO 1997; Counsellor FCO 1999; Full-Time Language Training FCO 2002.

Browne, Sir Nicholas Walker, KBE (2002), CMG (1999); HM Ambassador Copenhagen since August 2003; Born 17/12/47; Third Secretary FCO 1969; Tehran 1971; Second later First Secretary FCO 1975; On loan to the Cabinet Office 1976; First Secretary and Head of Chancery Salisbury 1980; First Secretary FCO 1981; First Secretary (Environment) Brussels (UKREP) 1984; Chargé d'Affaires Tehran 1989; Counsellor FCO 1989; Counsellor (Press and Public Affairs) Washington and Head of BIS New York 1990; Counsellor FCO 1994; Chargé d'Affaires Tehran 1997; HM Ambassador Tehran 1999; m 1969 Diana Marise Aldwinckle (2s 1970, 1980; 2d 1972, 1976).

Brownridge, Valerie (née Ewan), MVO; FCO since January 2003; Born 10/12/56; FCO 1979; Paris (ENA) 1980; Third Secretary Paris 1981; Third Secretary Rome 1985; Third Secretary Lagos 1986; Second Secretary FCO 1988; Second Secretary Berlin 1991; First Secretary FCO 1994; Deputy Consul-General Jerusalem 1999; Band D7; m 1999 John L. F. Brownridge.

Broyd, Laurence Paul; Deputy Head of Mission Sofia since July 2003; Born 12/11/60; FCO 1990; First Secretary (Economic) Moscow 1995; FCO 1999; Band PRO; m 1990 Catherine Mary Carslake (1s 1994; 1d 1998).

Brummell, Paul; HM Ambassador Almaty and HM Ambassador (non-resident) Bishkek since December 2005; Born 28/08/65; FCO 1987; Third later Second Secretary (Chancery) Islamabad 1989; First Secretary FCO 1993; Full-Time Language Training 1994; First Secretary (Political/Inf) Rome 1995; HM Ambassador Ashgabat 2002.

Bruton, Robert James; Brussels since August 1999; Born 01/01/57; FCO 1980; Band C4.

Bryant, John Edward; First Secretary FCO since 2000; Born 04/01/51; FCO 1970; Canberra 1972; Kingston 1975; FCO 1977; Bahrain 1978; Cairo 1979; FCO 1983; Nairobi 1986; FCO 1990; Dubai 1994; m 1972 Joyce Anne Barrie (1d 1975; 2s 1985, 1988).

Bryant, Richard John; Mumbai since November 2004; Born 22/09/53; DTI 1973; Department of Energy 1973; DOT 1975; DTI 1982; FCO 1984; Dhaka 1986; Brussels (UKREP) 1990; Brunei 1993; T/D Islamabad 1997; Floater Duties 1997; FCO 1998; Band B3; m 1986 Rosalyn Louise Morris (diss 1991) (1s 1991).

Bryce, Christopher James; FCO since January 2005; Born 29/12/69; HM Treasury 1992; Private Secretary to the Second Permanent Secretary for Overseas Finance 1995; Private Secretary to the Economic Secretary 1996; FCO 1998; Rome 2001; Baghdad 2004; Band D7.

Bryden, Lara-Jean; Floater Duties since November 2003; Born 15/10/71; Employment Service 1991-96; FCO 1996; Floater Duties 1997; Islamabad 2001; Band B3.

Bryson, Alan Robert; FCO since June 2002; Born 12/03/70; FCO 1991; Riyadh 1995; Bangkok 1998; Band B3.

Bryson-Richardson, Mark Edward, MBE (2005); Second Secretary (Chancery) Khartoum since January 2003; Born 30/10/76; FCO 1999; Full-Time Language Training 2000; Full-Time Language Training Cairo 2001; Band C4.

Bubbear, Alan Keith; First Secretary (Management) Pretoria since June 2004; Born 14/09/64; FCO 1983; Moscow 1985; SUPL 1988; Johannesburg 1990; FCO 1992; Second Secretary (Commercial) Helsinki 1996; First Secretary FCO 2000; m 1988 Theresa Bernice Allen (3d twins 1992, 1995).

Bubbear, Theresa Bernice (née Allen); FCO since September 2000; Born 14/12/62; FCO 1985; Moscow 1987; Johannesburg 1990; FCO 1992 (Second Secretary) FCO 1993; Second Secretary (Political) Helsinki 1996; Band D6; m 1998 Alan Keith Bubbear (3d twins 1992, 1995).

Buchanan, Sarah Louise (née Allen); FCO since March 2000; Born 31/07/69; FCO 1991; Full-Time Language Training 1994; Vice-Consul Stockholm 1994; Full-Time Language Training 1997; Third Secretary (Political/Press) Tel Aviv 1997; Band B3; m 1995 Hamish Malcolm Robert Buchanan (1s 1998).

Buck, Anthony Adrian; Copenhagen since July 2003; Born 26/08/71; FCO 2001; Band A2.

Buck, John Stephen; HM Ambassador Lisbon since September 2004; Born 10/10/53; FCO 1980; Second Secretary Sofia 1982; First Secretary FCO 1984; Head of Chancery Lisbon 1988; FCO 1992; Counsellor on loan to the Cabinet Office 1994; Counsellor and Deputy Head of Mission Nicosia 1996; Head of Public Diplomacy Department FCO 2000; Head, Communications and Information Centre, FCO/No. 10 Downing Street 2003; Director (Iraq) FCO 2003; m 1980 Jean Claire Webb (1d 1985; 1s 1989).

Buckle, Simon James; Deputy Head of Mission Kabul since April 2005; Born 29/02/60; Second Secretary FCO 1986; MOD 1988; First Secretary FCO 1991; First Secretary Dublin 1994; Counsellor (Political) and Consul-General Seoul 1997; Bank of England 1998; Counsellor FCO 2003; Consul-General Baghdad 2004; m 1990 Rajeshree Bhatt (1d 1997).

Buckley, Laura Margaret (née Clegg); FCO since September 2003; Born 29/03/65; FCO 1989; Vice-Consul Bucharest 1994; Deputy Head of Mission Antananarivo 1997; FCO 1999; SUPL 2002; Band C4.

Buckley, Stephen; First Secretary (Commercial) Peking since July 2000; Born 18/06/53; Export Credit Guarantee Department 1972; FCO 1972; Amman 1975; Canberra 1978; FCO 1980; Dakar 1983; Third later Second Secretary (Commercial) Seoul 1987; Second later First Secretary FCO 1992; First Secretary (Commercial) Kuala Lumpur 1996; m 1974 Barbara Frances Yelcich.

Bucknell, Bruce James; First Secretary Madrid since December 2003; Born 15/04/62; FCO 1985; Third Secretary Amman 1988; Secondment to EBRD 1992; FCO 1992; HM Consul Milan 1995; FCO 1999; Band D6; m 1993 Henrietta Dorrington-Ward (2s 1994, 1996).

Budd, Robin S; Dhaka since 2001; Born 19/03/68; FCO 1995; Abuja 1996; Maputo 1998; Band B3; m 1995 Grazyna Karwoska-Budd (2s 1996, 1999; 1d 2003).

Budden, Alexander James; FCO since September 2001; Born 18/04/68; FCO 1991; Third Secretary Kathmandu 1994; Third later Second Secretary Zagreb 1998; Band D6; m 1995 Diane Margaret Scott (1d 2000; 1s 2003).

Budden, Philip Marcus; First Secretary (Trade/Political) Washington since August 2002; Born 12/09/65; Second Secretary FCO 1993; First Secretary Vienna 1999; m 1992 Deborah Allen Tripp (1d 1997).

Buglass, Melvyn James; Management Officer Tunis since June 2002; Born 25/09/46; Army 1966-89; Rome 1989; Brussels (UKDEL/NATO) 1992; DSLC 1995; Vice-Consul Beirut 1998; Band B3; m 1973 Sandra Ann Whitehouse (1d 1974; 1s 1975).

Bull, David Thomas John; Deputy Consul-General and First Secretary (Trade) Houston since December 2002; Born 20/02/61; FCO 1982; Rio de Janeiro 1983; Lusaka 1986; FCO 1990; Third Secretary (consular /Passports) Kingston 1994; Second Secretary (Management) Kathmandu 1997; On loan to the DTI 2000; Band C5; m 1989 Aisling Maccobb (1d 1989).

Bulmer, Sandra Kay (née Ferguson); SUPL since September 2002; Born 11/11/67; FCO 1986; Vienna 1989; FCO 1991; Ottawa 1995; FCO 1998; Band A2; m 1995 Ian Bulmer (1s 1998).

Bundy, Rosalind (née Johnson); Moscow since July 1999; Born 25/01/45; FCO 1977; Paris 1977; Tripoli 1980; FCO 1983; Bonn 1985; FCO 1987; Algiers 1993; Ottawa 1995; Band B3; m 1984 David Alan Bundy.

Bunten, Roderick Alexander James; Deputy Director General Taipei since September 2002; Born 24/11/59; FCO 1984; SOAS 1985; Language Training 1986; Assistant Political Adviser Hong Kong 1987; SUPL 1990; First Secretary FCO 1991; First Secretary (Information) Canberra 1997; m 1990 Frances Jennifer Adamson (3d 1991, 1997, 2001; 1s 1995).

Burch, Andrew David; Second Secretary São Paulo since May 2002; Born 18/03/57; Department of the Environment 1972; FCO 1976; Nicosia 1980; New Delhi 1982; FCO 1986; Nairobi 1989; Budapest 1994; British Trade International 1998;

On loan to DTI 1999; Band C4; m 1982 Sarah Miranda Hodgson Clarke (2s 1989, 1991; 1d 1995).

Burch, Joshua; FCO since September 2003; Born 05/03/76; Band C4.

Burch, Stella Jane; Full-Time Language Training since April 2005; Born 30/05/76; FCO 2000; Second Secretary (Bilateral) Berlin 2002; Second Secretary (Economic) Vienna 2003; Band C4.

Burges Watson, Claire Rosamund; Abuja since January 2005; Born 26/04/71; FCO 2003; Band C4.

Burke, Alison Jane (née Wickham), MBE (2003); SUPL since May 2003; Born 25/07/65; FCO 1983; Prague 1988; Canberra 1990; SUPL 1991; Bucharest 1992; SUPL 1995; FCO 1998; SUPL 1998; New Delhi 1999; Band A2; m 1992 Thomas John Burke (1d 1995; 1s 1996).

Burke, Thomas John; Istanbul since August 2003; Born 12/12/50; Treasury 1968; FCO 1974; Brasilia 1976; FCO 1979; Harare 1979; Islamabad 1983; FCO 1984; Canberra 1987; Vice-Consul Düsseldorf 1991; Vice-Consul and later Second Secretary Bucharest 1992; Second Secretary (Immigration) New Delhi 1998; m 1991 Alison Jane Wickham (1d 1995; 1s 1996).

Burke-Wood, Alison Carmen (née Ferry); Muscat since March 2002; Born 07/06/66; FCO 1996; Canberra 1997; Band A2; m 1997 Joseph Burke-Wood.

Burlison, Sharon (née Clarke); Cape Town since May 1999; Born 22/07/70; FCO 1993; Harare 1996; Band A2; m 1998 Andrew Burlison.

Burn, Thomas Francis Southerden (known as Tom); Second Secretary Tokyo since November 2002; Born 12/11/75; FCO 1999; Full-Time Language Training 2000; Band C4.

Burn, Thomas Joseph; FCO since October 2003; Born 03/12/79; Band C4.

Burns, Lynda Edwards; Second Secretary (Political) Athens since April 2002; Born 19/07/75; FCO 1999; Full-Time Language Training FCO 2001; Band C4.

Burns, Nicholas John; FCO since October 2003; Born 20/03/62; FCO 1980; The Hague 1983; Kuala Lumpur 1984; Hanoi 1988; FCO 1989; Third Secretary (Management) Riyadh 1992; FCO 1995; Third Secretary and Vice-Consul Prague 2000; Band B3; m 2002 Ayten Ekiz .

Burns, Sean Gilbert Peter, MBE (2001); Second Secretary (Management) Nairobi since September 2000; Born 19/02/61; FCO 1978; Dar es Salaam 1983; Antigua 1987; FCO 1991; Dhaka 1993; Third Secretary (Management) and Vice Consul Dakar 1997; m 1983 Marina Higgins (1d 1989; 1s 1991).

Burran, John Eric; Washington since February 2001; Born 18/05/63; FCO 1982; Bucharest 1987; LA/Caribbean Floater 1989; Islamabad 1992; FCO 1995; On loan to DCMS 1998; Band C4; m 1999 Samantha Nash (twin d 2004).

Burrell, Demelza Fiona; New York (UKMIS) since September 2002; Born 09/12/70; FCO 1994; Madrid 1996; FCO 1999; World-wide Floater Duties 2000; Band A2.

Burrett, Louise Victoria; SUPL since May 2000; Born 16/08/61; FCO 1978; Bridgetown 1981; Dublin 1984; Bombay 1987; FCO 1990; SUPL 1993; On loan to the DTI 1995; Third later Second Secretary (Commercial/Management) Khartoum 1997; Second Secretary (Management) Tripoli 1999; Band C4; m 1996 William Anthony Frederick Ridout (1s 2000; 1d 2002).

Burrows, Christopher Parker; Counsellor New Delhi since March 2005; Born 12/09/58; FCO 1980; East Berlin 1982; Africa/Middle East Floater 1985; Second Secretary Bonn 1987; Second Secretary FCO 1989; First Secretary (Political/External) Athens 1993; First Secretary FCO 1996; First Secretary (Political) Brussels 1998; FCO 2001; m 1988 Betty Cordi (2d 1987, 1990; 1s 1992).

Burrows, Karl; Consul Monterrey since July 2000; Born 08/05/68; FCO 1988; Floater Duties 1990; Tegucigalpa 1992; FCO 1993; Panama City 1996; Band C4; m (1) 1991 Jane Marie O'Mahoney (diss 2001) (1d 1991); (2) 2001 Denise Victoria Vergara (1d 2002).

Burton, David Stewart; The Hague since February 2003; Born 12/08/77; FCO 2001; Band C4.

Burton, Simon David; Third Secretary (Vice-Consul) Guangzhou since November 2002; Born 11/04/73; FCO 1998; Floater Duties 1999; Band B3.

Busby, George Benedict Joseph Pascal, OBE (1996); FCO since April 2004; Born 18/04/60; FCO 1987; Second later First Secretary (Chancery) Bonn 1989; First Secretary FCO 1991; First Secretary Belgrade 1992; First Secretary FCO 1996; Counsellor Vienna 2000; m 1988 Frances Hurll (3d 1989, 1994, 2000; 1s 1991).

Busvine, Nicholas John Lewis, OBE (1995); Counsellor (Regional Affairs) Bogotá since January 2002; Born 13/05/60; FCO 1982; Third later Second Secretary Kuala Lumpur 1985; FCO 1988; First Secretary Maputo 1991; First Secretary FCO 1995; m (1) 1991 Sarah Ann Forgan (diss 1996) (2) 1997 Madeleine Ann Lewis (2d 1999, 2001).

Butcher, Peter Roderick; HM Ambassador Ashgabat since June 2005; Born 06/08/47; FCO 1974; Second Secretary Lima 1979; Second Secretary (Commercial) Bombay 1983; First Secretary FCO 1987; Deputy High Commissioner Maseru 1990; First Secretary FCO 1994; On secondment to DFID 1997; Deputy Head of Mission Maputo 2000; SUPL 2003.

Bute, Paul Kenrick; FCO since October 2002; Born 18/05/73; FCO 1994; Full-Time Language Training 1995; Third later Second Secretary

(Chancery) New Delhi 1996; First Secretary FCO 1999; MBA, Imperial College Business School 2001; Band D6.

Butler, Caroline Mary (née Whitehorn); Second Secretary FCO since 2002; Born 04/10/67; FCO 1990; Third Secretary Mexico City 1992; Second Secretary FCO 1996; Vice-Consul Buenos Aires 2001; Band C4; m 2003 Rupert James Butler.

Butler, Georgina Susan; HM Ambassador San José since February 2002; Born 30/11/45; FCO 1968; Paris 1969; Resigned on marriage 1970; Re-employed on contract FCO 1971; Reinstated in service 1972; SUPL (New York and Brussels UKREP) 1975; Seconded to European Commission, Brussels 1982; FCO 1985; Resigned (New Delhi/Brussels UKREP/Washington) 1987; Re-employed FCO 1999; m 1970 Stephen John Leadbetter Wright (diss 2000) (1d 1977; 1s 1979).

Butt, Simon John; Head of Eastern Department since April 2001; Born 05/04/58; FCO 1979; Third later Second Secretary Moscow 1982; Second Secretary Rangoon 1984; Second Secretary FCO 1986; First Secretary (External Relations) Brussels (UKREP) 1990; First Secretary FCO 1994; Deputy Head of Mission Kiev 1997.

Butt, Stephen; FCO since July 2003; Born 07/05/63; FCO 1981; Cairo 1986; Athens 1991; Third Secretary FCO 1992; Second Secretary (Chancery) Islamabad 1997; FCO 2000; First Secretary Athens 2001; Band C5.

Buttrey, Richard; FCO since September 2003; Born 15/01/75; Band C4.

Bye, Adam William; First Secretary (Chancery) New York (UKMIS) since June 2002; Born 06/11/72; Customs and Excise 1994; FCO 1996; Second Secretary on Attachment to the European Commission 1997; FCO 1998; First Secretary FCO 1999; On loan to Cabinet Office 2000.

Byford, Rebecca (née Mills); Washington since November 1999; Born 30/08/69; FCO 1991; Athens 1995; FCO 1996; Band A2; m 1999 David Byford.

Byrd, Margaret (née Allen); Yekaterinburg since September 2002; Born 19/06/61; FCO 1987; Nairobi 1990; SUPL 1993; Washington 1994; Lagos 1998; Band B3; m 1993 Roger Anthony Byrd.

Byrne, Declan Sean; Third Secretary (Management and Consular) Abuja since October 2001; Born 23/12/72; FCO 1995; Band B3.

C

Caie, Andrew John Forbes; High Commissioner Bandar Seri Begawan since January 2002; Born 25/07/47; FCO 1969; SRO (DS Gr.7) FCO 1972; Second Secretary Manila 1976; PRO (DS Gr.5) FCO 1980, First Secretary FCO 1983; First Secretary Head of Chancery and Consul Bogotá 1984; First Secretary later Counsellor FCO 1988; Deputy Head of Mission Islamabad 1993; On loan to CSSB 1996; FCO 1997; HM Ambassador Guatemala City 1998; m 1976 Kathie-Anne Williams (1s 1979; 1d 1987).

Cairns, Alison Marie; SUPL since June 2003; Born 03/12/72; FCO 1994; Tallinn 1996; Tehran 2000; FCO 2003; Band A2.

Cairns, David Seldon; First Secretary Geneva (UKMIS) since August 2002; Born 17/04/69; FCO 1993; Second Secretary Tokyo 1995; FCO 1999; Private Secretary to Baroness Scotland FCO 2000; m 1996 Sharon Anouk Aeberhard (1d 2000; 1s 2002).

Cairns, Gina Stephanie (née Tart), MVO (1992); FCO(S) since January 2001; Born 21/09/65; FCO 1984; Bridgetown 1986; Bonn 1990; FCO 1993; Vice-Consul Amsterdam 1997; SUPL 2000; Band C4; m 1987 William John Cairns (1s 1995; 1d 1998).

Calder, Stanley Shearer; Deputy Consul-General Toronto since May 2001; Born 07/02/44; Immigration Service 1965; Islamabad 1972; Second Secretary Lima 1975; FCO 1980; Deputy High Commissioner Belmopan 1982; First Secretary Peking 1986; First Secretary FCO 1990; First Secretary (Commercial) Caracas 1994; First Secretary (Commercial) Paris 1996; m 1967 Isobel Masson Leith (1s 1968; 1d 1970).

Caldwell, Christine Bernadette; SUPL since June 2005; Born 31/07/56; HCS 1973-77; FCO 1977; Warsaw 1979; Ankara 1979; Tripoli 1983; FCO 1984; SUPL 1986; Vice-Consul Johannesburg 1991; FCO 1993; SUPL 1995; Vice-Consul Vienna 1999; FCO 2000; Band C4; m 1982 Clive David Wright (2d 1986, 1989).

Caley, Joanne; First Secretary New Delhi since May 2004; Born 13/08/65; FCO 1991; Second Secretary Maputo 1993; FCO 1996; First Secretary (Chancery) Geneva (UKMIS) 1999; Full-Time Language Training 2003; m 1991 Peter David Morgan (3s 1996, 1998, 2001).

Callow, Judith Elizabeth; Athens since May 2001; Born 27/12/48; FCO 1970; Tananarive 1971; Geneva (UKMIS) 1973; Belgrade 1974; Abidjan 1975; Brussels (UKREP) 1977; Dakar 1979; Madrid 1983; Paris 1985; Brussels (UKDEL) 1987; Ottawa 1990; FCO 1993; Stockholm 1996; Band B3.

Callus, Michelle Anna Josephine; ECO Beirut since December 2003; Born 16/05/78; FCO 1999; Band B3.

Calvert, Andrew Paul; Third Secretary (Political) Vilnius since May 2002; Born 17/01/69; HCS Cadre FCO 1989; FCO 1992; Bonn 1994; Floater Duties 1999; Band B3; m 1994 Julie Louis (1d 1995).

Cambridge, Roger Alan, MVO (1985); Counsellor Brussels since January 2004; Born 12/09/52; FCO 1972; Africa Floater 1975; Stockholm 1977; Dar es Salaam 1979; Second Secretary (Chancery/Inf) Port of Spain 1983; Second later First Secretary FCO 1986; Consul (Commercial) New York (BTIO) 1990; First

Secretary New York (UKMIS) 1993; FCO 1996; Deputy Head of Mission Helsinki 1999.

Cameron, Hazel; First Secretary (Legal) Brussels since September 2003; Born 14/02/75; Solicitor; assistant Legal Adviser FCO 2000.

Cameron, James; Second Secretary and Consul Bucharest since January 2001; Born 21/04/50; Army 1966-90; FCO 1990; Peking 1990; Bucharest 1991; FCO 1993; Taipei 1994; Band C4; m 1977 Angela Jane Arnold (2d 1977, 1979).

Cameron, Lee; FCO since January 2003; Born 01/09/76; FCO 1999; Second Secretary Brussels (UKDEL NATO) 2000; Band D6.

Campbell, Amanda Joan; SUPL since July 2002; Born 24/01/69; FCO 1990; Full-Time Language Training 1999; Floater Duties 2000; Band B3.

Campbell, Christopher John; Brussels (UKDEL NATO) since August 2003; Born 12/04/63; FCO 1982; Khartoum 1985; Dhaka 1988; Jakarta 1992; FCO 1995; Second Secretary (Commercial) Caracas 1999; Band C4; m 1989 Sharon Isabel Hale.

Campbell, David Ian; Deputy High Commissioner and Counsellor (Commercial/Economic) Singapore since August 2003; Born FCO 1981; Budapest 1984; Third later Second Secretary Georgetown 1985; Second Secretary FCO 1988; First Secretary (Humanitarian) Geneva (UKMIS) 1989; First Secretary (Political) Belgrade 1994; First Secretary FCO 1994; Deputy Head of Mission Manila 2000.

Campbell, Julia Clare; Third Secretary (Management/Consular) Chennai since March 2003; Born 16/09/70; FCO 2001; Band B3; m 2002 John Campbell.

Campbell, Robert Pius; Moscow since October 2003; Born 19/10/57; FCO 1980; Second Secretary Nairobi 1984; FCO 1985; First Secretary (Economic) Belgrade 1986; First Secretary FCO 1990; First Secretary (Political) Helsinki 1992; First Secretary (Political) Skopje 1994; First Secretary FCO 1997; Counsellor (ESCAP) Bangkok 2001; m (1) 1985 Amanda Jane Guy (diss 1992) (1s 1989) (2) m 1992 Ailsa Irene Robinson (1s 1999).

Campbell, Sharon Isabel (née Hale); First Secretary (Management) Brussels since August 2003; Born 12/02/62; FCO 1983; Warsaw 1985; FCO 1986; Dhaka 1988; Jakarta 1992; FCO 1995 later Second Secretary FCO 1996; Caracas 1999; SUPL 1999; SMO/Consul Caracas 2000; m 1989 Christopher John Campbell.

Campbell, Susan Margaret; FCO since August 2004; Born 28/07/64; FCO 1984; Harare 1986; FCO 1990; Brasilia 1991; Floater Duties 1993; FCO 1995; Pretoria 2000; Band C4.

Canning, Mark; Deputy High Commissioner Kuala Lumpur since September 2001; Born 15/12/54; FCO 1974; Freetown 1976; FCO 1978; SUPL 1978; FCO 1981; Georgetown 1982; Chicago 1986; First Secretary FCO 1988; First Secretary (Commercial) Jakarta 1994; FCO 1998; m 1988 Leslie Marie Johnson (diss 2004); m 2004 Cecilia Kenny (1d 2004).

Cannon, Andrew Michael John; Brussels since September 2004; Born 03/02/73; Solicitor 1999; Assistant Legal Adviser FCO 2001.

Cannon, Nicholas, OBE (2002); on loan to No. 10 Downing Street since February 2003; Born 29/05/58; FCO 1988; Second Secretary Paris 1990; Second Secretary FCO 1992; Second Secretary (Political/Commercial) Nicosia 1994; Full-Time Language Training 2000; First Secretary (Chancery) Islamabad 2000; Band D6; m 1982 Alice Cheung (2s 1992, 1993).

Cantor, Anthony John James; HM Ambassador Yerevan since January 2006; Born 01/02/46; DSAO 1965; Rangoon 1968; Language Training Sheffield University 1971; Tokyo 1972; Second Secretary (Consular) Accra and Vice Consul Lomé 1977; Second Secretary FCO 1980; Consul (Commercial) Osaka 1983; Deputy Head of Mission Hanoi 1990; On loan to Invest in Britain Bureau DTI 1992; First Secretary (Commercial) Tokyo 1994; Consul (Commercial) later Deputy Consul-General Osaka 1995; T/D Hanover 2000; HM Ambassador Asunción 2001; m 1968 Patricia Elizabeth Naughton (2d 1969, 1972; 1s 1980).

Capelin, Melanie Jane; São Paulo since December 2004; Born 19/12/65; FCO 1998; PA/DHC Bridgetown 2000; Full-Time Language Training 2003; Band A2.

Capes, Mark Andrew; Deputy Governor Anguilla since August 2002; Born 19/02/54; FCO 1971; Brussels (UKREP) 1974; Lisbon 1975; Zagreb 1978; FCO 1980; Lagos 1982; Vienna 1986; Second Secretary FCO 1989; Deputy Chief Secretary Providenciales Turks and Caicos Islands 1991; First Secretary (Economic) Wellington 1994; First Secretary FCO 1999; m 1980 Tamara Rossmanith (2d 1985, 1988).

Carey, Colin Paul; FCO 1990 later Second Secretary FCO since 1994; Born 21/09/57; FCO 1974; Bonn 1988; m 1981 Janet Coleman (1d 1984; 2s 1986, 1990).

Carey, Joanne Claire; SUPL since November 2003; Born 06/02/72; FCO 1991; Islamabad 1995; T/D Peking 1999; Second Secretary (Commercial) Guangzhou 2000; Band C4.

Carlin, Neal Daniel; Second later First Secretary FCO since 2004; Born 22/03/71; FCO 1990; Geneva (UKMIS) 1994; Vice-Consul Khartoum 1996; T/D Cairo 1999; Full-Time Language Training 2000; Second Secretary and Deputy Head of Mission Tegucigalpa 2000; Band C5; m 1994 Tracey Alison Rae (2s 2002, 2004).

Carlin, Tricia Jane; FCO since February 2003; Born 08/10/78; Band A2.

Carnall, Philippa Jane, MBE (1986); Islamabad since November 2002; Born 31/07/57; FCO 1980; Beirut 1983; Damascus 1984; FCO 1986; Hanoi

1988; Washington 1991; FCO 1993; Cairo 1997; FCO 2000; Band B3.

Carney, Jonathan Patrick; FCO since December 2002; Born 23/02/68; DHSS 1986; FCO 1989; Islamabad 1992; Riyadh 1995; Bahrain 1999; Band C4; m 1996 Rhonda Ann Fitzgerald (2d 1997, 1999).

Carr, Corrinne Sharon (née Cannard); SUPL since May 2002; Born 28/02/70; FCO 1991; Berne 1994; FCO 1996; SUPL 1999; FCO 1999; Band B3; m 1996 Darren Andrew Carr (1s 1999; 1d 2002).

Carr, Peter Douglas; Deputy Management Officer New Delhi since July 2002; Born 02/05/47; DSAO (later FCO) 1967; Kaduna 1969; FCO 1970; Delhi 1971; Bogotá 1974; FCO 1978; Kuwait 1981; FCO 1984; New York (JAO) 1985; Second Secretary FCO 1988; Second Secretary (Consular) Jakarta 1997; m 1972 Cynthia Jane Begley (1s 1975; 2d 1977, 1983).

Carr-Alloway, Christine Anne (née Carr); Second Secretary (Management) New York since September 2004; Born 13/02/60; FCO 1978; Paris 1980; Brussels (UKREP) 1983; FCO 1986; Kuwait 1992; FCO 1994; Full-Time Language Training 1994; Third later Second Secretary Geneva (UKMIS) 1995; FCO 1998; Band C5; m 1991 Terry Alloway.

Carrick, Aileen Margaret; SUPL since March 2005; Born 21/02/69; FCO 1989; Rome 1992; Floater Duties 1995; Havana 1999; Brasilia 2003; Band B3.

Carrick, Nicholas John, OBE (2002); First Secretary (Chancery) New York since August 2004; Born 01/02/67; FCO 1990; Second Secretary (Political) Berlin 1993; Second later First Secretary FCO 1995; First Secretary Lagos 1999; First Secretary FCO 2002; Band D6.

Carrick, Robert Thomas; Jerusalem since March 2002; Born 05/05/64; FCO 1987; Damascus 1994; FCO 1997; SUPL 2000; Band B3; m 1997 Rachel Woodward (1d 2004).

Carroll, Heidi Amanda; FCO since September 2000; Born 09/05/68; FCO 1988; Brussels 1992; FCO 1995; Floater Duties 1998; Band B3.

Carroll, Jamie Russell; FCO since February 2003; Born 23/04/76; DETR 2000; DTI 2001; Band B3.

Carson, Christine; Riyadh since July 2004; Born 18/05/65; FCO 1990; Hong Kong (JLG) 1992; Lima 1995; Seoul 1998; Band B3.

Carter, Dennis Sidney; First Secretary and Senior Management Officer Kingston since October 2002; Born 12/06/47; Commonwealth Office 1964; DSAO (later FCO) 1966; Bogotá 1969; Moscow 1973; FCO 1974; Bonn 1978; Washington 1982; Harare 1984; Second Secretary FCO 1987; Second Secretary (Aid) Addis Ababa 1991; Second Secretary (Comm/Man/Vice Consul) Montevideo 1995; First Secretary (Management Officer) T/D Madrid 1998; First Secretary FCO 1999; m 1968 Catherine Rose (2s 1969, 1975).

Carter, Hannah Katharine; First Secretary (Political) Tehran since June 2003; Born 20/08/74; FCO 1998.

Carter, Kevin Robert; First Secretary FCO(S) since 2002; Born 26/08/55; OPCS 1972-76; Australian Government (AGRBO) 1977-78; Dar es Salaam (LE) 1979-82; FCO 1983; Warsaw 1984; Third Secretary (Consular) Valletta 1987; FCO 1989; Third Secretary Peking 1992; Full-Time Language Training 1994; Vice-Consul (Commercial) Düsseldorf 1995; Euro 2000 Football Attaché, T/D Amsterdam and Brussels 2000; FCO(S) 2000; Band D6; m 1976 Sandra Ann McHugh (2d 1985, 1986).

Carter, Nicholas Paul; Deputy Governor Bermuda since June 2003; Born 13/03/46; Commonwealth Office (later FCO) 1966; Belgrade 1970; Bombay 1972; Prague 1976; On loan to Midland Bank (International) 1980; FCO 1981; Second Secretary Bonn 1983; First Secretary (Commercial) Kuala Lumpur 1986; First Secretary FCO 1990; Consul-General Ho Chi Minh City 1994; Attached to the Department for International Development 1997; Deputy Head of Mission Riga 1999; Band D6; m (1) 1970 (2s 1971, 1978; 1d 1974); m (2) 1994 Andrea Helen Abrahams.

Carter, Peter Leslie; Counsellor, Consul-General and Deputy Head of Mission Tel Aviv since May 2001; Born 19/11/56; FCO 1984; Second later First Secretary (Chancery) New Delhi 1986; First Secretary FCO 1989; On Secondment as Principal Administrator CFSP Unit, EU Council Secretariat, Brussels 1994; Counsellor FCO 1998; m 1985 Rachelle Hays (1d 1991).

Carter, Thomas Henry; Full-Time Language Training since February 2003; Born 22/11/53; FCO 1976; Paris (ENA) 1978; Paris 1979; Vice-Consul later Second Secretary (Chancery) Bogotá 1983; Second Secretary FCO 1987; T/D Paris 1990; First Secretary (Environment) Bonn 1990; FCO 1995; Full-Time Language Training 1999; First Secretary (Head of Political Section) Bangkok 1999; m 1997 Carolyn Jayne Davidson (2s 1998, 1999).

Cartmell, Glyn Richard; Third Secretary Addis Ababa since December 2001; Born 23/02/69; British Army 1985-92 and 1996; FCO 1996; Royal Air Force 1997; Kiev 1997; FCO 1997; Kampala 1998; Band C4; ptnr, Vanessa Cathy Thom (1s 1992).

Cartwright, Peter John; Management Officer La Paz since December 2001; Born 23/03/55; FCO 1975; On loan to Masirah 1978; Athens 1979; Paris 1982; Kabul 1984; FCO 1986; UKDEL NATO 1990; Banjul 1992; FCO 1996; On secondment to Business Link , Shropshire, DTI 1999; Band B3; m 1984 Pamela Jane Edwards (2s 1988, 1992; 1d 1986).

Cartwright, Stephen Mark; Oslo since March 2000; Born 23/08/64; FCO 1985; East Berlin

1987; Bombay 1988; FCO 1993; Third Secretary (Aid) Gaborone 1996; Band C4; m 1988 Nicola Bjorg Joyce (1s 1991).

Carty, Helen Elizabeth (née Measures); SUPL since April 2004; Born 23/06/66; FCO 1992; Johannesburg 1994; Bonn 1998; Jedda 2000; Floater Duties 2001; Band B3.

Carver, Alice P H; FCO since November 2001; Born 16/09/76; Band B3.

Carwithen, Paul Ivor; First Secretary Berlin since February 2005; Born 18/02/64; FCO 1993; Copenhagen 1996; Second Secretary FCO 1999; Band C4; m 1992 Ann Davies (2s 1994, 1996).

Cary, Anthony Joyce, CMG (1997); HM Ambassador Stockholm since October 2003; Born 01/07/51; FCO 1973; Third Secretary Berlin (BMG) 1975; Second later First Secretary FCO 1978; Harkness Fellow at Stanford Business School 1980; FCO 1982; PS to Minister of State FCO 1984; First Secretary and Head of Chancery Kuala Lumpur 1986; Deputy Chef de Cabinet to Sir Leon Brittan, European Commission 1989; Counsellor FCO 1993; Counsellor Washington 1997; Chef de Cabinet to Chris Patten, European Commission 1999; m 1975 Clare Louise Katharine Elworthy (3s 1978, 1980, 1983; 1d 1985).

Casey, Claudia; FCO since July 2004; Born 05/10/67; FCO 1996; Third later Second Secretary Addis Ababa 1998; Full-Time Language Training 2002; Head of Investment Seoul 2003; Band C4.

Casey, Nigel Philip, MVO (1995); First Secretary (Political/Military) Moscow since December 2002; Born 29/05/69; FCO 1991; Vice-Consul (Political/Aid/Information) Johannesburg 1993; Second later First Secretary Washington 1996; FCO 1998; Full-Time Language Training (Russian) 2002; m 2002 Clare Maria Crocker (1s 2003).

Cassidy, Sarah Jayne (née Gardner); SUPL since July 2004; Born 27/12/68; FCO 1986; Bangkok 1989; Lilongwe 1992; SUPL 1996; FCO 1998; Maputo 2002; Band B3; m 1995 Eamon Martin Cassidy.

Cassim, Shezade; FCO since October 2004; Born 06/01/79; Band A2.

Cassy, Grace Aldren; FCO since December 2002; Born 04/08/76; FCO 1998; Second Secretary Islamabad 2000; Band D6.

Castillo, Oscar Luis; Kathmandu since December 2001; Born 05/08/69; FCO 1990; Islamabad 1993; FCO 1995; Floater Duties 1999; Band A2.

Caton, Dr Valerie; Head of Environment Policy Department, FCO since October 2002; Born 12/05/52; FCO 1980; Second later First Secretary (EC Affairs) Brussels 1982; First Secretary FCO 1984; First Secretary (Chancery) Paris 1988; Counsellor and Consul-General Stockholm 1993; Counsellor (Financial & Economic) Paris 1997; m 1987 David Mark Harrison (1d 1992; 1s 1994).

Catsaras, Zamir Nicholas; Second Secretary (Political) Budapest since September 2003; Born 19/02/73; Life Guards 1995-01; FCO 2001; Full-Time Language Training (Hungarian) 2002; Band C4; m 1999 Natasha Landell-Mills.

Caughey, Alan Marsh; SUPL since June 2004; Born 17/11/71; FCO 1990; Geneva (UKMIS) 1994; Bombay 1997; Third Secretary (Political/EU) Prague 2001; Band C4.

Caulfield, Tracy Ann; Düsseldorf since September 2001; Born 10/03/70; FCO 1988; Vienna (UKMIS) 1990; FCO 1993; Wellington 1994; FCO 1998; Band B3.

Cavagan, John Raymond; FCO since May 2001; Born 09/10/66; FCO 1990; Bogotá 1993; Madrid 1997; Band C4.

Cave, Dr Stephen James; Second later First Secretary FCO since January 2001; Born 30/01/73; FCO 2001; m 1993 Friederike Freiin von Tiesenhausen.

Cawdron, Thomas Andrew; Second Secretary Warsaw since January 2005; Born 27/05/78; FCO 2002; Band C4.

Cayless, Trevor Martin; Second Secretary (Commercial) Madrid since August 2001; Born 18/05/66; DHSS 1985; FCO 1986; Third Secretary (Aid) Lusaka 1990; Full-Time Language Training 1993; Frankfurt 1994; Second Secretary FCO 1997; m 1989 Rosemary Anne Whiting (1s 1996; 1d 1999).

Cazalet, Piers William Alexander, OBE (2003); Deputy Consul-General Jerusalem since December 2002; Born 20/10/66; FCO 1991; Language Training 1994; Second Secretary (Political/Information) Nicosia 1995; First Secretary FCO 1999; m 1994 Alyana Sharafutdinova (1s 1990; 1d 1995).

Cetti, Joanne Martine; FCO since June 2002; Born 18/01/72; Second Secretary FCO 1997; Second Secretary (Economic) Kampala 2000; Band C4.

Chadwick, Janine Linda (née Laurence); Kiev since January 2003; Born 09/04/54; FCO 1983; Brasilia 1987; Vienna (UKMIS) 1991; Reykjavik 1994; FCO 1997; Khartoum 1999; Band A2; m 1985 Peter Guy Chadwick.

Chadwick, Nigel Spencer; FCO since January 2003; Born 17/09/52; FCO 1971; Berne 1973; Buenos Aires 1977; Dacca 1980; Lima 1981; FCO 1984; Bombay 1988; FCO 1992; Banjul 1996; Athens 1999; Band B3; m 1991 Michelle Marina Dunne (1d 1996).

Chalmers, Nicholas John Pender; First Secretary FCO since May 2002; Born 04/05/71; FCO 1988; FCO 1993; Second Secretary (Political) Islamabad 1995; First Secretary Pristina 2000; Band D6.

Chamberlain, Valerie Ann (née Crocombe); SUPL since March 2005; Born 16/07/62; FCO 1980; Washington 1984; Gibraltar 1987; Prague 1989; FCO 1991; Bombay 1998; SUPL 2001;

Mumbai 2001; Kathmandu 2002; Band C4; m 1997 Martin Chamberlain (1s 2001).

Chambers, Dr David Ian; Counsellor (Political) Bangkok since August 2003; Born 04/12/47; Principal Research Officer FCO 1987; First Secretary and Consul Macao BTC Hong Kong 1994; FCO 1998; Band D6; m (1) 1978 Merilyn Figueroa (diss 1990); (2) 1991 Tharinee Plobyon.

Chandler, Julian; FCO since August 2003; Born 07/07/50; DSAO (later FCO) 1967; Istanbul 1971; Singapore 1976; Kuala Lumpur 1977; FCO 1979; Port Stanley 1982; Assistant Trade Commissioner Hong Kong 1984; First Secretary FCO 1989; Deputy High Commissioner Mbabane 1992; First Secretary (Commercial) Nairobi 1998; m 1998 Caroline Louise Parkinson (1d 1980; 3s 1982, 1992, 1994).

Chandler, Steven; Third Secretary (Chancery) Stockholm since March 2002; Born 27/01/71; FCO 1994; Ottawa 1994; SUPL 1999; T/D Belgrade 2000; Band B3; m 1996 Jenny Wieslander (1s 1997).

Chandler, Steven Clive; FCO since September 2003; Born 16/03/68; DHSS 1986; FCO 1987; Berlin (BMG) 1989; Dhaka 1992; Istanbul 1995; Sarajevo 1997; Third later Second Secretary FCO 1998; SUPL 2002; Band C4.

Chaplin, Edward Graham Mellish, CMG (2004), OBE (1998); HM Ambassador Baghdad since July 2004; Born 21/02/51; FCO 1973; MECAS 1974; Third Secretary Muscat 1975; Second Secretary Brussels 1977; Paris (ENA) 1978; Private Secretary to Lord President of the Council 1979; First Secretary FCO 1981; First Secretary and Head of Chancery Tehran 1985; First Secretary FCO 1987; Counsellor FCO on secondment to Price Waterhouse Management Consultants 1990; Deputy Permanent Representative and Head of Chancery Geneva (UKMIS) 1992; Counsellor FCO 1996; HM Ambassador Amman 2000; Director to Middle East Command FCO 2002; m 1983 Nicola Helen Fisher (2d 1984, 1989; 1s 1987).

Chapman, Adrian Paul; Rabat since February 2005; Born 14/08/69; FCO 1988; Brussels (UKREP) 1990; Islamabad 1993; FCO 1996; On loan to DTI 1998; Second Secretary (Political/Public Affairs) Seoul 2001; Band C4; m 1999 Fiona Witty (1d 2000; 1s 2003).

Chapman, Colin; FCO since September 2000; Born 12/01/58; Army 1974-79; FCO 1980; Bonn 1986; FCO 1988; Third Secretary Rome 1991; Second Secretary Ankara 1997; m 1983 Katherine Anne French (1d 1987).

Chapman, Yvonne Kay; Gibraltar since August 2003; Born 28/09/62; DETR 1987; FCO 1998; Geneva (UKMIS) 1999; Band A2; (1s 1991).

Chappell, Julie Louise Jo, OBE (2004); T/D Washington since January 2004; Born 02/04/78; FCO 1999; Full-Time Language Training 2000; Second Secretary (Political/Economic) Amman 2000; Band C4.

Charlton, Alan, CMG (1996); Deputy Head of Mission Washington since May 2004; Born 21/06/52; FCO 1978; Language Training 1979; Second later First Secretary Amman 1981; First Secretary FCO 1984; First Secretary (Deputy Political Adviser) Berlin (BMG) 1986; On loan to the Cabinet Office 1991; Counsellor FCO 1993; Counsellor (Political) and then Minister and Deputy Head of Mission Bonn 1996; Minister and Deputy Head of Mission Berlin 1999; Director South East Europe FCO 2001; Director Human Resources FCO 2002; m 1974 Judith Angela Carryer (2s 1979, 1985; 1d 1981).

Chassels, Avril (née Syme); Beijing since September 2002; Born 13/04/65; FCO 1987; Dublin 1989; Addis Ababa 1992; FCO 1993; Brussels 1994; FCO 1998; Ottawa 2000; FCO 2001; Band B3; m 2001 Mr Mirrlees Chassels.

Chatfield, Louise Mary; Floater Duties since December 2004; Born 28/04/71; FCO 1997; Mbabane 1999; FCO 2002; Band B3.

Chatt, Paul Anthony; FCO since October 2003; Born 07/04/56; FCO 1975; Ottawa 1977; East Berlin 1979; Khartoum 1981; FCO 1984; Third later Second Secretary (Aid/Comm) Banjul 1987; Second Secretary (Man/Cons) Berne 1990; Second later First Secretary FCO 1995; First Secretary (Management) Warsaw 2000; Band C5; m (1) 1979 Delyth Hudson (diss 1988); (2) 1990 Tracie Cavell Heatherington (2d 1992, 1993).

Chatterton-Dickson, Robert Maurice French; HM Ambassador Skopje since July 2004; Born 01/02/62; FCO 1990; Second Secretary (Chancery/Information) Manila 1991; First Secretary FCO 1994; First Secretary (Press, later PS/HMA) Washington 1997; First Secretary FCO 2000; m 1995 Teresa Bargielska Albor (2d 1996, 1997, 1 step d 1982; 1 step s 1984).

Cherrie, Yvonne Elizabeth; Deputy Consul-General and Consul (Commercial) Barcelona since July 2002; Born 31/03/62; FCO 1980; Brussels (UKREP) 1982; Sana'a 1985; Bahrain 1988; FCO 1989; On secondment to Birmingham Chamber of Commerce 1991; Third Secretary (Commercial) Berlin 1993; Second later First Secretary (Pol/PPA) Mexico City 1997; Band C5; m 1996 William Theodore von Minden.

Chick, John Charles, MBE (2003); First Secretary (Director, Trade & Investment) Manila since October 2004; Born 22/10/47; FCO 1971; Baghdad 1973; FCO 1975; Amman 1976; FCO 1979; Darwin 1980; FCO 1984; Hanoi 1985; FCO 1988; Third Secretary (Management) and Vice-Consul Quito 1990; Third Secretary (Comm/Chan/P&PA) Dhaka 1995; Second Secretary FCO 1999; Second Secretary (HM Consul/ECM) Kathmandu 2000; m (1) 1971 Denese Irene Smalley (diss); (2) 1989 Tran Thi Thuy Duong (1s 1989; 1d 1994).

Chilcott, Dominick John; Director EU (Bilateral, Mediterranean and Resources) FCO since September 2002; Born 17/11/59; Royal Navy 1978-79; FCO 1982; Language Training 1984; Third later Second Secretary Ankara 1984; First Secretary FCO 1988; First Secretary Lisbon 1993; First Secretary FCO 1996; Counsellor Brussels (UKREP) 1998; m 1983 Jane Elizabeth Bromage (1d 1986; 3s 1988, 1991, 1995).

Childs, Marie-Louise; SUPL since April 2002; Born 23/03/66; FCO 1989; Vice-Consul Bangkok 1991; Quito 1995; Band B3; m 1997 Mr S O'Sullivan.

Chown, Christopher James; FCO since August 1996; Born 05/03/67; FCO 1988; Paris 1993; Band C5; (1s 1994).

Chrimes, Neil Roy; Counsellor (Trade/Economic) Ottawa since July 2001; Born 10/06/54; MAFF 1975; Harkness Fellow MIT 1977; MAFF 1979; Economic Adviser FCO 1981; IMF Research Dept. 1987; Senior Economic Adviser FCO 1989; Deputy Permanent Representative Paris (UKDEL OECD) 1994; Jakarta 1998; Head of African Department (Southern) 1999; m 1982 Anne (Henny) Barnes (1s 1988; 1d 1990).

Christie, Iain Robert; SUPL since October 2000; Born 07/12/65; Called to the Bar (Inner Temple) 1989; Assistant Legal Adviser FCO 1992; Senior Assistant Legal Adviser FCO 1995; Bridgetown 1998; m Katherine Ann Gillam (2d 1996, 1997).

Christie, Katherine Ann (née Gillam); FCO since January 2003; Born 25/01/69; FCO 1992; SUPL 1997; Band B3; m 1995 Iain Robert Christie (2d 1996, 1998).

Chubbs, Sylvia Sharon; Geneva (UKMIS) since July 2004; Born 09/05/58; FCO 1984; Paris 1986; Colombo 1989; Moscow 1993; Brussels (UKREP) 1995; FCO 1998; Budapest 2001; Band A2.

Chugg, Daniel Patrick; FCO since January 2005; Born 26/01/73; FCO 1998; Language Training FCO 1999; Language Training Hong Kong 2000; Vice-Consul (Political) Hong Kong 2001; Band D6; m 1999 Alison Fiona Cubie (1s 2004).

Chun, David John; Deputy Consul-General Boston since August 2004; Born 04/04/64; FCO 1985; Lagos 1987; Moscow 1992; FCO 1996; Second Secretary (Commercial) Madrid 1999; Band C5; m 1987 Grace Fotheringham (1d 1994).

Chun, Grace (née Fotheringham); SUPL since August 1999; Born 24/07/66; FCO 1985; Lagos 1987; Moscow 1992; FCO 1996; Band B3; m 1987 David John Chun (1d 1994).

Church, Alistair John Bentley; Consul Geneva since August 2004; Born 23/08/63; FCO 1992; Kiev 1995; Second Secretary FCO 1998; SUPL 2000; FCO 2002; Band C4; m 1990 Michelina Patrizia Forgione (2d 1997, 2002).

Church, Roger Gilbert; First Secretary (Commercial) Nairobi since July 2003; Born 01/06/46; FO 1965; Abu Dhabi 1968; Bonn 1970; East Berlin 1973; Lusaka 1974; FCO 1976; Madras 1979; Colombo 1980; Quito 1982; Second Secretary (Commercial) Madras 1983; Second Secretary FCO 1988; Deputy High Commissioner Nassau 1990; Deputy Head of Mission Lima 1994; FCO 1998; Jedda 2000; Band C5; m 1972 Kathleen Wilson Dryburgh (2s 1974, 1977).

Clare, Debbie Marie; Algiers since August 2004; Born 21/03/69; FCO 1987; Resigned 1990; Reinstated (FCO) 1994; Berne 1996; Dar es Salaam 1997; Bonn 1998; Lusaka 1999; FCO 2000; Band C4.

Claridge, Susan Elisabeth; SUPL since January 2005; Born 10/05/60; FCO 1984; Brussels (UKREP) 1987; Geneva (UKDIS) 1990; FCO 1993; Bonn 1995; FCO 1998; On loan to the Cabinet Office 2000; Band B3.

Clark, Angela; Tashkent since February 2003; Born 22/11/67; FCO 1997; Kuala Lumpur 1998; Dubai 1999; SUPL 2000; Band A2; m 1998 Christopher Neil Walker (2s 1996, 1999).

Clark, Catherine Elizabeth (née Ferguson); SUPL since May 2000; Born 12/06/59; FCO 1979; Singapore 1981; Istanbul 1985; FE/SEA Floater 1988; Brussels (UKDEL NATO) 1991; Band C4; m 1990 Eldred Richard Wraighte Clark (2d 1994, 1996).

Clark, Christopher George; FCO since 2002; Born 15/04/70; FCO 1990; T/D Mostar 1994; Santiago 1995; Floater Duties 1999; Band B3.

Clark, Elizabeth; Lilongwe since December 2004; Born 18/03/61; FCO 2001; T/D Bucharest 2004; Band A2; m 1988 Roger Clark (dec'd).

Clark, James Frame; HM Ambassador Luxembourg since March 2004; Born 12/03/63; FCO 1988; Second Secretary 1989; Full-Time Language Training Cairo 1990; FCO 1990; Second Secretary (External Affairs) Brussels (UKREP) 1991; Second later First Secretary FCO 1993; On loan to German Foreign Ministry 1997; First Secretary (EU) Bonn 1998; Head of Conference and Visits Group, FCO(S) 1999; m 1990 Michele Taylor (diss 1998); ptnr, Anthony John Stewart.

Clark, Kenneth; Management Officer Abuja since January 2004; Born 18/08/49; Post Office Savings Department 1966; DSAO 1967; Kuwait 1971; Moscow 1974; Rio de Janeiro 1975; FCO 1978; New York 1981; Jedda 1983; Second Secretary FCO 1986; Second Secretary (Comm) Gaborone 1989; Second Secretary (Management) and Consul Lima 1994; FCO 1997; m 1970 Agnes Pearson Elder (3s 1971, 1974 1978).

Clark, Paul Nicholas; FCO since May 2001; Born 26/01/69; FCO 1988; Vienna 1992; Brussels (UKDEL NATO) 1993; Dhaka 1996; World Wide Floater Duties 2000; Band C4; m 1991 Katherine Walsh (diss 2002) (2s 1991, 1993).

Clark, Peter; SUPL since April 2002; Born 18/04/54; Principal Research Officer FCO 1982; First Secretary (Chancery) Peking 1988; First

Secretary FCO 1992; First Secretary Canberra 1996; FCO 2001; m 1977 Alison Padgett (1d 1982; 1s 1984).

Clarke, Pauline Joyce; FCO since August 2002; Born 08/10/67; FCO 1987; Dhaka 1989; Floater Duties 1993; FCO 1996; Zagreb 1999; Band C4.

Clarke, Roger Colin; Dublin since May 2003; Born 01/10/52; Armed Forces 1969-92; FCO 1992; Moscow 1993; New Delhi 1996; Cairo 2000; Band C4; m (1) 1971 Linda (2s 1973) (diss 1998); (2) Maria Louise Wesstrom.

Clarke, Rosemary Protase, MBE (1992); First Secretary (Commercial) Singapore since July 2000; Born 13/02/50; FCO 1977; Port Louis 1978; FCO 1982; Manila 1984; Bahrain 1988; Second Secretary FCO 1991; Second Secretary (Immigration) Dhaka 1992; Band C5; m 1982 Daniel Sinassamy (1s 1984; 1d 1987).

Clarke, Sarah (née Hutson); Second Secretary Washington since September 2004; Born 28/01/61; FCO 1983; Accra 1985; Ankara 1988; FCO 1991; Islamabad 1993; FCO 1996; Vice-Consul (Political) Jerusalem 1998; FCO 2002; Band C4; m 1993 Richard Henry Clarke.

Clarke, Shaun Jerome; Third Secretary (Management) Tokyo since July 2001; Born 07/11/67; Home Civil Service 1989-93; FCO 1993; Amman 1996; Valletta 1999; Band B3; m 1996 Karen Angela Evans.

Clarke Soper, Julie Linda; Vice-Consul Bogotá since April 2004; Born 13/01/64; FCO 1988; Moscow 1990; New York (UKMIS) 1993; Brasilia 1999; SUPL 2002; Band B3; m 2002 Gary Soper.

Clasen, Peter; FCO since March 2004; Born 02/12/74; FCO 1998; Vice-Consul Istanbul 2001; Band C4.

Clayden, Dr Timothy, OBE (2000); FCO since August 2004; Born 28/03/60; Second later First Secretary FCO 1989; First Secretary (Info) Warsaw 1991; FCO 1994; Lagos 1995; First Secretary FCO 1999; Counsellor (Political) Islamabad 2001; Band D6; m 1984 Katharine Susan Jackson.

Clayton, Mark Darrell; First Secretary Kabul since January 2003; Born 12/06/73; FCO 1997; Third Secretary (Political) Moscow 1998; Band D6.

Clayton, Tamsin Mary Clare; Third Secretary (Entry Clearance) & Vice-Consul Kuwait since September 2004; Born 25/05/69; FCO 2000; Third Secretary (Political Press and Public Affairs) Bahrain 2001; Band B3.

Cleary, Anthony Shaun; Basra since December 2004; Born 27/10/65; FCO 1988; Third later Second later First Secretary (Chancery) Pretoria/Cape Town 1990; First Secretary FCO 1994; First Secretary (Energy) Paris (OECD) 1998; FCO 2003.

Cleaver, Helen Louise; FCO since June 2001; Born 11/12/68; FCO 1989; Brussels 1996; FCO 1999; Stockholm 2000; Band A2.

Cleaver, Lucy Ann (née Humphreys); Washington since June 2005; Born 17/06/72; FCO 1993; New York (UKMIS) 1996; SUPL 1999; FCO 2000; Beijing 2001; Band A2; m 2003 Michael Anthony Cleaver (1s 2002).

Clegg, Leslie David, MVO (1985); Deputy Head of Consular Division since March 2000; Born 12/10/49; FO (later FCO) 1967; Banjul (formerly Bathurst) 1971; Wellington 1974; FCO 1977; New Delhi 1980; Second Secretary Lisbon 1984; First Secretary FCO 1988; First Secretary (Commercial) Madrid 1992; First Secretary (Management) Nairobi 1996; FCO 2000; m 1970 Louise Elizabeth Straughan (3d 1973, 1976, 1984).

Clegg, Sarah Jane; FCO since November 2003; Born 27/12/74; Band B3.

Cleghorn, Bruce Elliot; High Commissioner Kuala Lumpur since November 2001; Born 19/11/46; Second Secretary FCO 1974; Second Secretary Geneva (UKDEL CSCE) 1974; Second Secretary FCO 1975; First Secretary Brussels (NATO) 1976; First Secretary New Delhi 1980; First Secretary FCO 1983; Counsellor Vienna (UKDEL CSCE) 1987; Deputy Head of Delegation Vienna (UKDEL CFE) 1989; Counsellor and Deputy High Commissioner Kuala Lumpur 1992; Head of Non Proliferation Dept FCO 1995; Minister and Deputy Permanent Representative Brussels (UKDEL NATO) 1997; m 1976 Sally Ann Robinson (3s 1978, 1981, 1986).

Cleland, Deborah Julia (née Caldow); Second Secretary FCO since February 1999; Born 08/09/67; FCO 1987; Accra 1990; FCO 1992; Oslo 1994; Band C4; m 1993 James Cleland.

Clements, Martin Hugh, OBE (2002); Counsellor Kabul since June 2004; Born 26/07/61; FCO 1983; Second Secretary (Chancery) Tehran 1986; FCO 1987; First Secretary (IAEA) Vienna (UKMIS) 1990; First Secretary FCO 1994; First Secretary Bonn 1998; Counsellor Berlin 1999; Counsellor FCO 2003.

Clemitson, Lynne Dawn; SUPL since November 2002; Born 04/05/61; FCO 1979; Washington 1982; Dhaka 1985; Wellington 1988; FCO 1991; Band C4; m 1983 Malcolm John Clemitson.

Clephane, James Cavin Alexander, OBE (1996); SUPL since November 1999; Born 03/02/54; FCO 1973; Budapest 1976; Seoul 1977; Jakarta 1980; FCO 1983; Third later Second Secretary Muscat 1986; Second later First Secretary Bandar Seri Begawan 1991; First Secretary (Defence Co-operation) Bandar Seri Begawan 1995; On loan to MOD 1998; Band D6; m 1974 Mary Buchanan Dorman.

Cliff, Ian Cameron, OBE (1991); HM Ambassador Khartoum since May 2005; Born 11/09/52; FCO 1979; Language Training 1980; Second later First Secretary Khartoum 1982; First Secretary FCO

1985; First Secretary (Chancery) New York (UKMIS) 1990; Counsellor on loan to DTI 1993; Deputy Head of Mission Vienna 1996; HM Ambassador Sarajevo 2001; m 1988 Caroline Mary Redman (1s 1989; 1d 1993).

Clifton, Emma Jane; Warsaw since November 2004; Born 03/11/79; FCO 2002; Band C4.

Clissold, Sean Dominic, OBE (2004); First Secretary (Management) and Consul Ankara since November 2000; Born 06/04/58; FCO 1975; Geneva (UKMIS) 1978; Rabat 1981; Ankara 1983; Lagos 1987; FCO 1990; Third Secretary (Commercial) Istanbul 1993; Second Secretary (Consular) Warsaw 1997; Band C5; m 1986 Belgin Savaci (1d 1988).

Clough, Graham Ronald; Second Secretary Vienna (UKMIS) since March 2002; Born 13/05/55; FCO 1995; Second Secretary (Political) Dhaka 1998; Band B3; m 1995 Harvinder Kaur Sabharwal.

Cloughton, Stephen Paul; FCO since June 2000; Born 04/11/65; FCO 1986; Bangkok 1991; FCO 1994; Skopje 1996; Band B3; m 1997 Karen Dowen (1d 2005).

Clunes, Anna Louise, OBE (2003); First Secretary Brussels since January 2004; Born 12/03/73; FCO 1994; Full-Time Language Training 1996; Second Secretary Warsaw (KHF) 1996; First Secretary (Chancery) New York (UKMIS) 2000; Band D6.

Clyde, Dr Keane; SUPL since May 2004; Born 19/09/71; Senior Research Officer FCO 2002; Band C5; m 2000 Alistair Clyde.

Clydesdale, William Reginald; FCO since January 1997; Born 12/08/43; MOD 1960; FCO 1980; Lagos 1985; Third Secretary Sofia 1987; FCO 1990; Washington 1994; Band C5; m 1969 Noreen Foister (2s 1973, 1976).

Coates, David; HM Ambassador Abidjan and HM Ambassador non-resident to Niger and Burkina Faso since August 2004; Born 13/11/47; Second later First Secretary FCO 1974; Language Training Hong Kong 1977; First Secretary (Commercial) Peking 1978; FCO 1981; First Secretary Geneva (UKMIS) 1986; Counsellor Peking 1989; Counsellor FCO 1993; Director-General of Trade Taipei 1999; FCO 2002; m 1974 Joanna Kay Weil (2d 1976, 1978).

Coates, Sally Ann (née Mawby); FCO since March 2003; Born 29/07/60; FCO 1979; Washington 1984; FCO 1987; Tortola 1988; Georgetown 1992; FCO 1992; Mbabane 1993; Beirut 1996; Accra 1998; Band A2; m 1995 Alan Roger Coates.

Cobden, Alan; Consul-General Alexandria since July 2003; Born 15/07/54; FCO 1970; Canberra 1975; Tehran 1977; African Floater 1978; Bombay 1980; FCO 1983; Third later Second Secretary Sofia 1986; Second Secretary (Agriculture/Environment) Dublin 1989; Second Secretary FCO 1994; Deputy Consul-General and Consul (Commercial) Los Angeles 1998; m 1982 Karen Anne Fawn (1s 1985; 1d 1987).

Cochrane-Dyet, Fergus John; Deputy High Commissioner Lusaka since December 2004; Born 16/01/65; FCO 1987; Third later Second Secretary (Political) Lagos 1990; Second Secretary Abuja 1993; First Secretary FCO 1994; Head of BIS Tripoli 1996; First Secretary (Commercial) Jakarta 1998; Deputy Consul-General and Director of Trade and Investment Promotion Sydney 1998; Chargé d'Affaires Conakry 2001; T/D Kabul 2002; Deputy Head of Africa Department (Southern) FCO 2002; m 1987 Susan Emma Aram (3s 1990, 1991, 1996).

Codd, Steven; Seconded to the Welsh Development Agency since July 2004; Born 19/05/61; FCO 1981; Baghdad 1982; FCO 1985; Beirut 1986; FCO 1988; Hanoi 1990; Lusaka 1993; Second Secretary FCO 1996; First Secretary (Management) Kuala Lumpur 1997; Deputy Consul-General Shanghai 2000; Band D6; m 1993 Ruth Brown Mulligan (diss 2001); m 2005 Jacqueline Vanessa Codd (née Goodhew) (1s 2001).

Codrington, Richard John; Head of Afghanistan Group, FCO since February 2005; Born 18/12/53; MOD 1975; FCO 1978; Second later First Secretary Dar es Salaam 1980; FCO 1983; New Delhi 1985; First Secretary FCO 1989; On loan to SG Warburg & Co Ltd. 1992; Counsellor on loan to the Department of National Heritage 1994; Counsellor (Trade Promotion and Investment) Paris 1995; Deputy High Commissioner Ottawa 1999; Head of Online Communications Department, FCO 2003; m 1985 Julia Elizabeth Nolan (twin s 1991).

Cody, Anne Bridget; Brussels (UKDEL) since February 2003; Born 30/01/42; FCO 1995; Band A2; m 1964 Kevin Anthony Cody (1d 1968; 1s 1970).

Cogger, Darren Barry; Canberra since November 2001; Born 20/05/63; FCO 1984; Athens 1988; Belgrade 1991; New Delhi 1993; FCO 1996; Third Secretary (Management) Kiev 1997; Band B3; m 1986 Johanna Lesley Payne (1d 1989).

Coggles, Paul James; SUPL since March 2004; Born 24/06/66; FCO 1989; Third Secretary (Chancery) Sofia 1992; Third Secretary FCO 1995; Full-Time Language Training 1996; Second Secretary (Political) Prague 1997; First Secretary (Political) Prague 2000; Band D6.

Coglin, Gillian Joanna; First Secretary (Management) Tokyo since June 2002; Born 09/08/67; FCO 1989; Bucharest 1991; Bombay 1994; Second Secretary FCO 1997; SUPL 2000; SUPL (Japan) 2001; Band C4.

Colby, Sheila Joan, MBE (2001); Buenos Aires since January 2002; Born 07/05/56; FCO 1979; Lima 1980; FCO 1983; Floater Duties 1984; FCO 1988; Kuala Lumpur 1990; Madrid 1993; FCO 1996; Mexico City 1998; Band B3.

Cole, Alexandra Pamela; Second Secretary (Political) Sarajevo since July 2002; Born 02/06/70; FCO 1990; Tehran 1996; Full-Time

Language Training 2000; SUPL 2001; Band C4; m 1995 Adrian Frederick Bedford.

Coleman, Julie; Colombo since June 2001; Born 13/03/67; Department of Employment 1989-95; FCO 1995; Addis Ababa 1997; Band A2.

Coleman, Sandra Marie (née Duffy); The Hague since August 2001; Born 21/11/60; FCO 1984; Algiers 1985; Jerusalem 1987; Turks and Caicos Islands 1991; Dakar 1993; SUPL 1996; Washington 1997; Band B3; m 1995 Scott Stanley Coleman.

Coleman, Tracey; SUPL since April 2004; Born 23/01/71; FCO 1990; Ottawa 1992; World-wide Floater Duties 1995; Freetown 1999; Band A2.

Collard, Ian Frank; New York since December 2005; Born 13/04/76; FCO 2002; Band C4.

Collard, Timothy Michael; Consul-General Hamburg since May 2004; Born 21/03/60; FCO 1986; Language Training SOAS 1987; Language Training Hong Kong 1988; Second Secretary (Science and Technology) Peking 1989; First Secretary FCO 1993; First Secretary (Hong Kong) Peking 1995; FCO 2001; m 1985 Patricia Polzer (2s 1987, 1989).

Collecott, Dr Peter Salmon, CMG (2002); HM Ambassador Brasilia since July 2004; Born 08/10/50; Second Secretary FCO 1977; MECAS 1978; First Secretary 1979; First Secretary (Political) Khartoum 1980; First Secretary (Economic/Commercial/Agricultural) Canberra 1982; FCO 1986; Counsellor (Head of Political Section, later DHM) Jakarta 1989; Counsellor (EU and Economic) Bonn 1994; FCO 1998; Director Resources FCO 1999; Director General (Corporate Affairs, initially Chief Clerk) FCO 2001; m 1982 Judith Patricia Pead.

Collett, Robert James; FCO since October 2003; Born 22/05/80; Band C4.

Colley, Timothy John; Deputy Head of Mission Sofia since July 2000; Born 13/03/65; FCO 1989 (Second Secretary 1991); Full-Time Language Training 1991; Second Secretary (Political) Islamabad 1992; First Secretary FCO 1995; Full-Time Language Training 1999; Band D6; m 1993 Janet Mary Rodemark (1s 1997; 2d 1999, 2002).

Collier, Geoffrey Thomas Grey; Second Secretary (Political/PPA) Ankara since August 2002; Born 27/04/68; FCO 1990; Belgrade 1993; Dakar 1997; FCO 2000; Full-Time Language Training (Turkish) 2002; m 1999 Müge Elif Törüner.

Collier, Nicholas Gavin; Pretoria since January 2003; Born 10/02/69; FCO 1996; Third Secretary (Political/Economic) Vilnius 1998; Band C4; m 1999 Simona Gatti.

Collier, Stephen John, MVO (1991), RVM (1979); Deputy Head of Parliamentary Relations & Devolution Department FCO since February 2005; Born 11/01/52; DTI 1968; FCO 1969; Bonn 1972; Aden 1975; Lilongwe 1976; Lagos 1979; FCO 1983; Amman 1985; Second Secretary Windhoek 1989; Second Secretary FCO 1992; First Secretary (Commercial) Lima 1996; Deputy Consul-General and Consul (Commercial) Atlanta 1999; First Secretary (Management) Baghdad 2004; m 1987 Erica Mary Cholwill Wilson.

Collingridge, Andrew; Brussels (UKDEL NATO) since January 2002; Born 02/11/62; FCO 1985; Lagos 1990; FCO 1994; Bucharest 1998; FCO 2001; Band C4; m 1993 Tanya Suzanne Parsons (2d 1998, 2001).

Collingridge, Tanya Suzanne (née Parsons); Second Secretary Brussels (UKDEL NATO) since June 2002; Born 04/02/65; FCO 1984; Warsaw 1987; Vienna (UKDEL) 1989; Lagos 1991; FCO 1994; Full-Time Language Training 1997; Second Secretary (Political/Information) Bucharest 1998; FCO 2001; Band C4; m 1993 Andrew Collingridge (2d 1998, 2001).

Collings, Jane Lindsay; FCO since January 2003; Born 05/03/80; Band B3.

Collins, Alan Stanley, CMG; High Commissioner Singapore since December 2002; Born 01/04/48; Ministry of Defence 1970; Private Secretary to Vice Chief of the Air Staff 1973-75; FCO 1981; First Secretary and Head of Chancery Addis Ababa 1986; Counsellor (Commercial) and Deputy Head of Mission Manila 1990; Counsellor FCO 1993; Director of BTCO Taipei 1995; HM Ambassador Manila 1998; m 1971 Ann Dorothy Roberts (1d 1985; 2s 1988, 1995).

Collins, Helen Laura; FCO since January 2003; Born 15/11/70; FCO 1990; Washington 1994; Cairo 1998; Band B3.

Collins, James Robert; Bridgetown since November 2001; Born 09/11/63; FCO 1986; Strasbourg 1988; Moscow 1990; FCO 1993; Band B3; m 1987 Sheila Marie Barry.

Collinson, Martin; Dubai since January 2002; Born 07/09/66; FCO 1987; Band A2; m 1999 Sharon Particia Stillwell (2d 2000).

Collis, Simon Paul; HM Ambassador Doha since April 2005; Born 23/02/56; FCO 1978; Language Training 1979; Third later Second Secretary Bahrain 1981; First Secretary FCO 1984; New York (UKMIS) 1986; FCO 1987; First Secretary and Head of Chancery Tunis 1988; FCO 1990; First Secretary (Political) New Delhi 1991; First Secretary FCO 1994; Counsellor and Deputy Head of Mission Amman 1996; On secondment to the BP Amoco, 1999; Consul-General Dubai 2000; Consul-General Basra 2004.

Colloms, Catherine; On loan to OHR, Sarajevo since October 2004; Born 18/08/76; FCO 1998; On loan to Coalition Information Centre 2001; T/D (Public Diplomacy) Gibraltar 2002; FCO 2002; Band D6.

Collyer, Neil Patrick; FCO since 2002; Born 28/05/66; ODA 1985-89; FCO 1991; Pretoria 1996; Lagos 1999; Abuja 2000; Band B3; m 1997 Sara-Louise Hall.

Collyer, Nicholas Edwin; First Secretary (Management/Consular) Rabat since May 2003; Born 15/09/52; Forestry Commission 1969; FCO 1971; Moscow 1974; Colombo 1975; Budapest 1979; FCO 1981; Geneva (UKMIS) 1983; FCO 1986; New Delhi 1987; Second Secretary FCO 1989; Second Secretary (Commercial) Seoul 1992; Second Secretary (Commercial/Consular) Port of Spain 1995; First Secretary FCO 1999; m 1973 Kathryn Dobson (2s 1978, 1983).

Collyer, Sara-Louise (née Hall); FCO since 2002; Born 28/10/73; FCO 1992; SUPL 1996; Pretoria 1997; Lagos 1999; Abuja 2000; Band A2; m 1997 Neil Patrick Collyer.

Conley, Brian John; Consul (Commercial) Los Angeles since January 2003; Born 10/04/67; FCO 1986; Lusaka 1989; Third Secretary (Management) and Vice Consul Auckland 1993; FCO 1994; Second Secretary (Commercial/Information) Tunis 1999.

Conlon, Stephen Austin; Helsinki since November 2005; Born 01/11/75; FCO 1999; Band C4.

Connolly, Peter Terence; First Secretary FCO since September 2000; Born 02/05/65; FCO 1988; Third Secretary Managua 1990; Brussels (UKREP) 1993; Second Secretary FCO 1994; Second Secretary (Political) Lisbon 1996; Band D6.

Connolly, Sarah Ann; FCO since January 2004; Born 19/04/79; Band C4.

Connor, Michael Leslie; Chennai since May 2005; Born 15/11/49; FCO 1971; Vienna (UKDEL) 1975; Moscow 1975; Tehran 1977; FCO 1980, APS to Minister of State 1982; Second Secretary Bonn 1983; Second later First Secretary (Commercial) Abu Dhabi 1987; First Secretary FCO 1991; First Secretary (Commercial) Prague 1995; On loan to the DTI 2000; m 1973 Linda Helen Woolnough (1d 1984).

Conroy, Anne Elizabeth, MVO (1991); Full-Time Language Training since September 2004; Born 30/08/63; FCO 1985; Third later Second Secretary (Chancery) Manila 1988; Second later First Secretary FCO 1992; Full-Time Language Training 1995; First Secretary (Political) Budapest 1996; FCO 2001.

Contractor, Robert; Banja Luka since September 2003; Born 17/05/68; FCO 1989; Floater Duties 1992; FCO 1993; Warsaw 1995; FCO 1997; Second Secretary (Political) Skopje 2001; Full-Time Language Training (Serbian) 2003; Band C5.

Conway, Benjamin Simon; Singapore since November 2003; Born 19/09/78; FCO 2001; Band C4.

Conway, Nicholas Peter; Second Secretary Kabul since September 2004; Born 25/06/78; FCO 2001; Band C4.

Cook, Gavin Douglas; FCO since September 2002; Born 31/12/78; Band C4; m 2004 Elizabeth Carey.

Cook, Peter Duncan Gifford; First Secretary FCO since September 2001; Born 15/08/63; FCO 1982; Georgetown 1985; Doha 1989; Third later Second Secretary FCO 1992; Second Secretary (Political/Information) Bridgetown 1995; Second later First Secretary (Chancery) Copenhagen 1997; m 1993 Maureen Nanette Sharp (2s 1995, 1996).

Cooke, Ann; Hong Kong since March 2000; Born 26/02/66; DoT 1982; CCA 1989; FCO 1992; New York (UKMIS) 1996; Band A2; m 1986 Lloyd Norman Cooke (1d 1990).

Coombs, Nicholas Geoffrey; Counsellor FCO since July 2003; Born 14/12/61; FCO 1984; Language Training 1985; Second Secretary (Chancery) Riyadh 1987; Second later First Secretary FCO 1989; First Secretary Amman 1993; First Secretary FCO 1997; First Secretary later Counsellor Riyadh 2000; m 1990 Julie Elizabeth Hardman (2d 1996, 1998).

Cooper, Amanda Jane; Vice-Consul Dhaka since February 2003; Born 02/03/60; HSE 1987-95; FCO 1995; Vilnius 1996; Shanghai 1999; Tokyo 2002; Band B3.

Cooper, Andrew George Tyndale; Counsellor FCO since May 1999; Born 13/12/53; Royal Navy 1974-82; FCO 1983; First Secretary Canberra 1984; FCO 1987; First Secretary (UN/Press) Geneva (UKMIS) 1988; Counsellor FCO 1992; Stockholm 1995; m 1981 Donna Mary Elizabeth Milford (2s 1988, 1996).

Cooper, Derek John William, MBE (2005); Second Secretary (Political) Riyadh since July 2001; Born 07/01/68; FCO 1986; Islamabad 1989; FCO 1992; Zagreb 1994; FCO 1998; Band C4; m 1998 Sanja Vilus.

Cooper, Rachel Elizabeth; SUPL since February 2005; Born 03/11/65; FCO 1989; Vice-Consul Copenhagen 1992; Deputy Head of Mission Bratislava 1995; FCO 1999.

Cope, Brian Roger, MVO (2000); Basra since December 2004; Born 01/03/59; Inland Revenue 1975; FCO 1976; Paris 1979; Bucharest 1982; Islamabad 1984; FCO 1988; Third Secretary Colombo 1991; Second Secretary (Management) Accra 1995; Kampala 2000; FCO 2003; Band D6; m 1982 Heather Margaret Frensham (1d 1990; 1s 1993).

Cope, John Charles; FCO since October 1998; Born 10/08/46; FO 1964; Paris 1968; Moscow 1971; Delhi 1972; Karachi 1974; FCO 1976; Dakar 1978; Warsaw 1981; FCO 1982; Hanoi 1985; FCO 1987; Second Secretary (Admin/Consular) Kathmandu 1988; Second Secretary FCO 1991; Second Secretary (Management/Consular) Prague 1995.

Copland, Joanne Catherine; SUPL since August 2000; Born 02/09/71; FCO 1990; Washington 1993; Peking 1996; On loan to the Cabinet Office 1999; Band B3.

Copleston, John de Carteret; Abuja since June 2005; Born 26/01/52; FCO 1971; Paris 1975;

Third later Second Secretary FCO 1978; Second later First Secretary Islamabad 1980; First Secretary FCO 1983; First Secretary (Chancery) Jakarta 1987; First Secretary FCO 1990; Counsellor Abuja later Lagos 1993; Counsellor FCO 1995; Counsellor (Multilateral) Canberra 1997; Counsellor FCO 2000; m 1987 Jane Marie Francesca Wilcox (4d 1988, 1991, 1993, 1997).

Copley, Caroline Helen (née Hall); SUPL since June 2001; Born 19/01/65; FCO 1987; Third later Second Secretary (Chancery) Oslo 1990; Floater Duties 1991; FCO 1992 (First Secretary 1994); First Secretary (Political) Paris 1997; SUPL 1999; First Secretary (Political) Paris 2000; Band D6; m 1996 John Richard Copley (1d 1999).

Coppin, Nicholas James; Tehran since April 2005; Born 27/03/71; FCO 1992; Second Secretary (Pol/PPA) Bucharest 1995; First Secretary Skopje 1999; First Secretary FCO 1999; Seconded as Adviser, Bucharest 2004.

Corbett, Hannah Kathleen Taylor; On loan to DFID since July 2002; Born 04/08/74; FCO 1997; On loan to HM Treasury 1998; Second later First Secretary (External) Brussels (UKREP) 1999.

Cordery, Andrew David; Counsellor FCO since June 1999; Born 02/05/47; Second Secretary FCO 1974; Nairobi 1975; First Secretary New York (UKMIS) 1977; FCO 1981; First Secretary (Economic) Lusaka 1984; First Secretary Berlin (BM) 1988; First Secretary later Counsellor FCO 1991; Counsellor Oslo 1995; m 1970 Marilyn Jean Smith (2d 1975, 1977).

Cormack, Ian Ronald; First Secretary - SMO/Consul Lima since June 2004; Born 20/11/56; FCO 1975; Nairobi 1978; Havana 1980; Latin America and Caribbean Floater 1982; Africa/Middle East Floater 1984; FCO 1986; Shanghai 1989; Third Secretary Stockholm 1992; FCO 1995; First Secretary (Commercial) Stockholm 1998; T/D Victoria 2003.

Corner, Diane Louise; On loan to the Cabinet Office since October 2004; Born 29/09/59; FCO 1982; Second Secretary (Chancery) Kuala Lumpur 1985; Second Secretary FCO 1989; SUPL 1989; First Secretary FCO 1989; On loan to the Cabinet Office 1991; Deputy Head of Mission and First Secretary (Pol) Berlin 1994; FCO 1998; NATO College, Rome 2000; Deputy Head of Mission Harare 2001; FCO 2003; SUPL 2004; m 1986 Peter Timothy Stocker (4d 1989, 1991, 1994, 2004).

Cornwall, Finnbar Mac; FCO since October 2004; Born 06/12/81; Band C4.

Corrans, Paula Anne; Floater Duties since August 2001; Born 04/02/70; FCO 1995; Brussels (UKREP) 1997; São Paulo 1998; Band C4.

Correa, Clive Joel; Durban since August 2002; Born 05/11/64; FCO 1988; Transferred to Diplomatic Service 1989; Rangoon 1991; Full-Time Language Training 1995; Budapest 1996; FCO 1998; On loan to British Trade International 2000; Band C4; m 1990 Andrea Parker (2d 1993, 1996).

Corrigan, Rosalind Mary; Second Secretary (Consular) Warsaw since September 2004; Born 07/12/66; FCO 1991; New York (UKMIS) 1993; Third Secretary (Chancery) Buenos Aires 1994; Vice-Consul Toronto 1998; FCO 2001; Band C4.

Cotton, Susan Jayne; Tortola since May 2005; Born 03/05/65; FCO 1998; Geneva (UKMIS) 1999; FCO 2003; Band B3.

Cottrell, Cathy; First Secretary (Management) and Consul Kuwait since November 2003; Born 03/04/63; FCO 1991; Second Secretary (Commercial) Moscow 1999; Band C5; m 1984 Simon John (3d 1990, 1992, 2002).

Coulson, Graham; Istanbul since June 2004; Born 11/10/46; Army 1962-86; Vienna 1988; New Delhi 1989; Sofia 1992; Floater Duties 1996; Kingston 1999; FCO 2000; Moscow 2003; Band B3; m 1971 Maureen Joyce Howard (diss 1994) (1s 1971; 1d 1974).

Coulter, Anthony Julian; Counsellor Kiev since January 2004; Born 01/11/61; FCO 1984; Second Secretary (Chancery) Ankara 1987; Second Secretary FCO 1990; First Secretary (Political) Amman 1994; FCO 1998; First Secretary (Chancery) Baku 1999; Band D6; m 1997 Munire Gulay Kilic (1d 2000).

Courage, Rafe Philip Graham; Consul Chicago since August 2002; Born 20/10/63; FCO 1986; Third Secretary Brussels 1989; Third Secretary Islamabad 1991; Second Secretary FCO 1995; Full-Time Language Training 1997; Second Secretary (Economic/Commercial) Ankara 1998; m 1988 Theresa Jayne Pile (4d 1990, 1992, 1996, 1997).

Court, Robert Vernon; SUPL since January 2005; Born 28/01/58; FCO 1981; Concurrently Third Secretary and Vice-Consul Chad; Second Secretary Bangkok 1984; First Secretary FCO 1986; Private Secretary to the Minister of State FCO 1988; First Secretary (Political) Brussels (NATO) 1990; First Secretary (Press/Information) Brussels (UKREP) 1993; On loan to Rio Tinto Plc 1996; SUPL 1997; Deputy High Commissioner Canberra 2001; m 1983 Rebecca Ophelia Sholl (3s 1986, 1988, 1990; 1d 1993).

Courtney, Victoria Glynis; First Secretary (Political) Brussels (UKREP) since August 2004; Born 04/12/76; FCO 2000; On secondment to Quai d'Orsay 2001; Second Secretary (Political) Paris 2002; Band C4; ptnr, Marcus Dean.

Couzens, James McGeorge Dale; FCO since July 2004; Born 19/02/67; FCO 1990; Bridgetown 1995; Third Secretary Tunis 1997; Third Secretary Windhoek 2001; Band B3; m 1993 Susan Ann Phillips (1d 1994; 1s 1996).

Cowan, Anthony Evelyn Comrie; The Hague since November 2003; Born 28/03/53; Third Secretary FCO 1975; Language Training Cambridge 1977; Language Training Hong Kong 1978; Second later

First Secretary Peking 1980; First Secretary FCO 1982; First Secretary (Chancery) Brussels 1987; First Secretary FCO 1991; Consul (Political and Economic) Hong Kong 1996; Counsellor FCO 2000.

Cowell, (Andrew) (John) Hamish; First Secretary (External Relations) Brussels (UKREP) since July 2001; Born 31/01/65; FCO 1987; New York (UKMIS) 1988; Douala 1989; Third later Second Secretary Colombo 1989; First Secretary (Chancery) and Deputy Head of Mission Tehran 1992; First Secretary FCO 1994; Head of Political, Economic and Aid Sections Cairo 1996; FCO 1999; m 2000 Shadi Akhtar Khan Kasmai (2d 2000, 2002).

Cowell, Anita Ann; FCO since August 2003; Born 07/05/54; FCO 1993; Jakarta 2000; Band A2.

Cowin, Richard; FCO since November 2004; Born 28/03/72; Band B3; m 2002 Mi-Hyun Lee.

Cowling, Geoffrey Stanley; HM Consul General Barcelona since November 2002; Born 20/09/45; Board of Trade 1964; Colonial Office later Commonwealth Office (later FCO) 1966; Vice-Consul and Third Secretary Kabul 1970; Vice-Consul and Third Secretary Port Moresby 1974; Second Secretary (Tech Asst) Lima 1976; FCO 1979; First Secretary (Economic) Copenhagen 1982; First Secretary FCO 1982; Joint Service Defence College 1987; First Secretary FCO 1988; Deputy Consul-General São Paulo 1991; On loan to Rover International 1995; FCO 1996; Consul-General Rio de Janeiro 1999; m 1970 Irene Joyce Taylor (1s 1971; 2d 1975, 1980).

Cowper-Coles, Sir Sherard Louis, KCMG (2004), CMG (1997), LVO (1991); HM Ambassador Riyadh since September 2003; Born 08/01/55; FCO 1977; Language Training MECAS 1978; Third later Second Secretary Cairo 1980; First Secretary FCO 1983; Private Secretary to the Permanent Under-Secretary FCO 1985; First Secretary (Chancery) Washington 1987; First Secretary FCO 1991; On secondment to the International Institute for Strategic Studies 1993; Counsellor FCO 1994; Counsellor (Political) Paris 1997; Private Secretary to the Secretary of State FCO 1999; HM Ambassador Tel Aviv 2001; m 1982 Bridget Mary Elliot (4s 1982, 1984, 1987, 1990; 1d 1986).

Cox, David George; FCO since September 2004; Born 07/12/61; FCO 1984; Third later Second Secretary (Chancery) Canberra 1986; Second later First Secretary (Econ) Islamabad 1989; FCO 1992; First Secretary (Political) Luanda 1995; First Secretary FCO 2000; Counsellor (Political/Military) Islamabad 2002.

Cox, David Thomas; FCO since May 2001; Born 27/04/44; FO (FCO) 1967; Berlin 1970; FCO 1972; Prague 1974; Munich 1976; FCO 1979; Lusaka 1982; Second Secretary (Commercial) Budapest 1986; First Secretary FCO 1990; Copenhagen 1993; On loan to the DTI 1998; m 1975 Claudia Zeillinger (1s 1981; 1d 1989).

Cox, Deborah Maria; FCO since October 2004; Born 31/01/66; Band A2.

Cox, Jolyon Nicholas; Second Secretary Bogotá since July 2003; Born 21/09/61; FCO 1979; Bonn 1983; Sana'a 1985; FCO 1988; Second Secretary (Bilateral Relations) Bonn 1993; Second Secretary FCO 1998; Second Secretary (Political) Tehran 2000; Second Secretary FCO 2001; Band C4; m 1986 Francesca Ann Hindson (1s 1993).

Cox, Julie Ann, MVO (1996); Stockholm since August 2004; Born 10/07/62; FCO 1986; Peking 1988; Jerusalem 1990; Warsaw 1993; FCO 1996; New Delhi 2001; Band B3.

Cox, Laura; FCO since January 2003; Born 25/08/80; Band A2.

Cox, Nigel John; Director (Asia Pacific) FCO since May 2003; Born 23/04/54; FCO 1975; Language Training Cambridge 1976; Language Training Hong Kong 1977; Second Secretary Peking 1978; Second later First Secretary FCO 1981; Paris (ENA) 1984; First Secretary Paris 1985; First Secretary FCO 1990; Counsellor Peking 1992; Counsellor FCO 1996; Minister Peking 2000; m 1992 Olivia Jane Paget.

Cox, Olivia Jane (née Paget); First Secretary FCO since February 2003; Born 31/07/57; FCO 1978; Mexico City 1980; FCO 1982; Third Secretary (Chancery) Paris 1987; Third later Second Secretary FCO 1990; SUPL 1992; FCO 1996; SUPL 1999; Band C5; m 1992 Nigel John Cox.

Cox, Richard James; Second Secretary (Political/Economic) Nairobi since July 2005; Born 07/08/67; FCO 1991; ECO Addis Ababa 1993; Vice-Consul Hanoi 1997; FCO 2001; Second Secretary (Political/Commercial) Georgetown 2002; Band C4; m 1999 Thu Cox (1s 2001).

Coyle, Janet Clare (née Usher); SUPL since September 2004; Born 23/04/65; FCO 1983; Washington 1986; Prague 1989; Floater Duties 1991; FCO 1994; On loan to the DTI 1996; Cape Town 1999; San Francisco 2003; Band C5; m 2002 Damian Coyle.

Crabtree, Joanne Elizabeth; Athens since October 2002; Born 26/09/68; FCO 1988; Mexico City 1990; Dubai 1993; Sana'a 1999; Band B3.

Craddock, Timothy James; On loan to DFID since October 2000; Born 27/06/56; FCO 1979; Vice-Consul (Information) Istanbul 1981; Second Secretary Ankara 1982; First Secretary FCO 1985; First Secretary Paris (UKDEL) 1990; First Secretary FCO 1995; HM Ambassador Tallinn 1997.

Craig, David Hamilton; Consul Jerusalem since December 2004; Born 05/12/61; FCO 1989; Language Training 1990; Second Secretary (Chancery) Nicosia 1991; Second later First Secretary FCO 1993; Full-Time Language Training 1994; Full-Time Language Training Cairo 1995; Consul Jedda 1996; First Secretary FCO 1999; First Secretary (Political) Ankara 2001;

Band D6; m 1994 Hala el-Kara (2s 1995, 1997; 1d 1999).

Craig, Deborah Louise (née Tyson); SUPL since July 2002; Born 01/01/72; FCO 1990; Nicosia 1995; FCO 1998; Islamabad 2000; Band A2; m 1995 Ian Douglas Craig (1d 1999; 1s 2000).

Craig, John Jenkinson; Second Secretary FCO since September 1979; Born 08/01/49; FCO 1972; Third Secretary Rome 1978; Band C5; m 1965 Glenys Menai Edmunds (2d 1977, 1984; 2s 1979, 1981).

Craig, Lesley, MBE (1995); Deputy Head of Mission Colombo since March 2005; Born 13/05/67; FCO 1988; T/D Islamabad 1990; Vice-Consul Kathmandu 1991; Third Secretary (Chancery) Kampala 1994; FCO 1997; Tel Aviv 2000; FCO 2001; Band D7.

Craig, Robyn Jean; FCO since September 1997; Born 09/03/65; FCO 1984; Moscow 1986; Oslo 1987; Rabat 1990; FCO 1993; Addis Ababa 1996; Band B3.

Cramman, Ian Pallister; Third Secretary Yerevan since September 2004; Born 11/03/70; FCO 1989; Khartoum 1992; Full-Time Language Training 1994; Düsseldorf 1995; Addis Ababa 2000; Band B3; m 1997 Ding Yu.

Craven, Stella Susan; Wellington since July 2001; Born 24/03/50; WRAF 1967-71; FCO 1972; Suva 1973; FCO 1975; Khartoum 1976; FCO 1977; Resigned 1978; Reinstated, FCO 1979; Islamabad 1981; FCO 1984; Harare 1986; FCO 1989; Band B3.

Crawford, Charles Graham, CMG; HM Ambassador Warsaw since December 2003; Born 22/05/54; FCO 1979; Second later First Secretary (Information) Belgrade 1981; First Secretary FCO 1984; First Secretary Cape Town/Pretoria 1987; First Secretary FCO 1991; Counsellor Moscow 1993; HM Ambassador Sarajevo 1996; Harvard University 1998; Deputy Political Director then Director South East Europe 1999; HM Ambassador Belgrade 2001; m 1990 Helen Margaret Walsh (2s 1991, 1993; 1d 1999).

Crawford, Fabiola Magdalena; SUPL since May 2000; Born 01/04/66; FCO 1987; Vienna (UKDEL) 1988; Damascus 1991; FCO 1994; Riyadh 1996; Band B3.

Crawford, Marilyn Elisabeth; FCO since July 1995; Born 16/08/47; FCO 1975; Brussels (UKDEL NATO) 1977; Antigua 1980; FCO 1982; Brussels (UKDEL) 1988; FCO 1991; Paris 1994; Band A2.

Crawford, Michael James; Counsellor FCO since September 2001; Born 03/02/54; FCO 1981; Second later First Secretary Cairo 1983; First Secretary Sana'a 1985; First Secretary Riyadh 1986; First Secretary FCO 1990; First Secretary (Political) Warsaw 1992; FCO 1995; Counsellor Islamabad 1999; m 1984 Georgia Anne Moylan (twins, 1s 1d 1986; 1s 1989).

Crees, Ian Alec; FCO since January 2004; Born 31/01/43; Air Ministry 1960; Passport Office 1961; CRO 1963; Nairobi 1963; Nicosia 1966; FCO 1968; Rawalpindi (later Islamabad) 1971; Vice Consul Strasbourg 1975; FCO 1978; Second Secretary (Political/Aid) Kinshasa, also accredited to Congo-Brazzaville, Rwanda and Burundi 1980; Second later First Secretary (Commercial) Seoul 1984; First Secretary FCO 1989; First Secretary (Comm/DHM) Bombay 1993; Conference Department (European Council) FCO 1998; T/D Islamabad 1998; HM Consul General and Joint Management Officer Geneva 1999; m 1963 Betty Winifred Kelder (1d 1965; 1s 1967).

Cresswell, Jeremy Michael, CVO (1996); High Commissioner Kingston since July 2005; Born 01/10/49; FCO 1972; Third later Second Secretary Brussels 1973; Second Secretary Kuala Lumpur 1977; First Secretary FCO 1978; Private Secretary to Parliamentary Under-Secretary, then Minister of State FCO 1981-82; Deputy Political Adviser Berlin (BMG) 1982; First Secretary FCO 1986; Counsellor and Head of Chancery Brussels (UKDEL) 1990; Full-Time Language Training 1994; Deputy Head of Mission Prague 1995; Counsellor FCO 1998; Deputy Head of Mission and Head of Political and Public Affairs Berlin 2001; m 1974 Ursula Petra Forwick (1d 1978; 1s 1985).

Creswell, Alexander John Peter; First Secretary (Political) Kuwait since July 2001; Born 27/07/65; FCO 1993; Second Secretary (Political) Pretoria 1995; Second Secretary FCO 1998; Band D6; m 1995 Katharine Louise Reid.

Crockard, Gavin; Third Secretary (Political) Copenhagen since August 2004; Born 11/02/68; FCO 1989; Bombay 1991; Pretoria 1995; FCO 1996; Floater Duties 1998; Third Secretary Ottawa 2002; Band B3.

Crockett, Patricia Anne; FCO since January 1997; Born 19/11/48; Tokyo 1974; Copenhagen 1977; FCO 1980; Port Louis 1981; FCO 1983; Lusaka 1985; Peking 1989; FCO 1991; Nicosia 1993; Band C4.

Croisdale-Appleby, Lindsay; First Secretary (Environment) Brussels (UKREP) since August 2002; Born 12/05/73; FCO 1996; Second Secretary (Political/PPA/Aid) Caracas 1998; Band D6.

Crombie, Anthony Campbell, OBE (1997); FCO since August 2003; Born 18/10/56; COI 1980; FCO 1985; Second later First Secretary Havana 1987; First Secretary FCO 1990; Deputy Head of Mission Belgrade 1994; SUPL 1997; Counsellor (Political) Moscow 1999; m 1982 Jane Nicholls Talbot (diss 1987).

Crombie, Susan Elizabeth; Kabul since December 2004; Born 08/03/72; FCO 1998; Second Secretary Pristina 1999; Second Secretary Brussels (UKDEL NATO) 2001; Band D6.

Crompton, Angela Louise; Geneva (UKMIS) since January 2004; Born 04/05/64; FCO 1988;

Oslo 1991; T/D Islamabad 1994; Brasilia 1995; FCO 1998; Maputo 2001; Band A2.

Crompton, Richard Anthony Neil, CBE (2003); Head of Iraq Policy Unit, FCO since June 2003; Born 25/09/64; FCO 1995; Senior Research Officer, First Secretary FCO 1997; Full-Time Language Training 1998; Counsellor and Deputy Head of Mission Tehran 1999; m 1996 Rosa Zaragoza (1d 2000; 1s 2001).

Cronin, Martin Eugene; Consul-General Vancouver since August 2005; Born 22/01/65; DoE 1987; FCO 1988; Vice-Consul/AMO Sana'a 1990; FCO 1993; Second Secretary (Political/Economic) Amman 1994; FCO 1997; First Secretary Stockholm 1999; First Secretary (Political) Islamabad 2002; First Secretary (Political) Baghdad 2004; Band D6.

Crooks, Colin James, LVO (1999); Washington since June 2002; Born 18/02/69; FCO 1992; Full-Time Language Training (Korean) 1993; Full-Time Language Training (Korean) Seoul 1994; Seoul 1995; First Secretary FCO 1999; m 1996 Kim Young-Kee (1s 1997).

Crooks, Daryl; Third Secretary and Vice-Consul Jakarta since April 2003; Born 27/05/68; FCO 1991; ECO later Vice-Consul Dhaka 1998; Transferred to Diplomatic Service 1999; Band B3; m 1999 Dina R Napao (1d 2000).

Crorkin, Colin Wynn, MBE (1993); Consul-General Kirkuk since May 2005; Born 31/01/57; FCO 1975; Rome 1977; Beirut 1980; Brussels (UKREP) 1983; FCO 1984; Kinshasa 1987; Second Secretary BTIO New York 1992; Second later First Secretary FCO 1993; First Secretary (Management) later Deputy Head of Mission Lagos 1997; Deputy Head of Mission Tripoli 2002; m (1) 1978 Gillian Smith (diss 1991), (2) 1991 Joanne Lynn Finnamore (1s 1985; 1d 1998).

Cross, Caroline Janice, MBE (1991); Second Secretary (Immigration/Consular) Accra since June 2001; Born 30/09/64; FCO 1984; Warsaw 1986; Floater Duties 1989; Third Secretary (Chancery/Information) Kampala 1991; Third later Second Secretary FCO 1994; SUPL 1999; Band C4; m 1998 M Higgins.

Cross, Harriett Victoria Saltonstall; FCO since January 2002; Born 25/09/74; FCO 1997; Second Secretary (Political) Rabat 1998; Band C4; m 1999 Lieutenant Philip Saltonstall RN.

Cross, Linda Mary (née Guild), MBE (2004); Consul-General Yekaterinburg since February 2001; Born 15/03/56; FCO 1978; Rabat 1978; Prague 1981; Quito 1983; Paris 1985; FCO 1988; Vienna 1991; Third Secretary (Political) New York (UKMIS) 1994; T/D Tirana 1997; Deputy Head of Mission Baku 1998; Band C5; m 1989 Michael John Cross.

Crossland, Jennifer Patricia (née Brown); SUPL since August 2001; Born 28/08/64; FCO 1988; Brussels (UKREP) 1990; FCO 1993; SUPL 1995; New Delhi 1996; Bangkok 1998; Band A2; m 1993 Dudley Stewart Crossland (diss 2000).

Crossman, Steven Nigel; Deputy High Commissioner Yaoundé since September 2004; Born 16/11/55; FCO 1975; Muscat 1977; Washington 1978; Kuwait 1982; New Delhi 1984; FCO 1987; Third Secretary (Aid) Dar es Salaam 1990; Hanoi 1995; Deputy High Commissioner Freetown 1999; Deputy High Commissioner Georgetown 2001; m 1998 Le Hoang Lan (1s 2000).

Crowder, Richard Lawrence Robert; FCO since November 2002; Born 14/11/73; FCO 1996; Full-Time Language Training (Russian) 1998; Second Secretary (Economic) Moscow 1999; Band D6; m 2000 Hilary Jane Louise Scott.

Cruickshank, Diane (née Robinson); On loan to DFID since June 2002; Born 15/07/60; FCO 1981; Bogotá 1982; Jakarta 1985; FCO 1988; Lusaka 1990; SUPL 1992; Tehran 1994; New Delhi 1998; FCO 2001; Band B3; m 1994 Douglas Graham Cruickshank.

Cullen, Carol Dulceta (née Fisher); FCO since September 2002; Born 12/11/56; DOE 1975; FCO 1977; Paris 1979; Dublin 1982; FCO 1985; Nairobi 1988; SUPL 1992; FCO 1993; Bridgetown 1996; Lusaka 1999; Band C4; m 1979 Thomas Cullen (1d 1984; 1s 1988).

Cullens, Niall James David; Second Secretary Consul (Commercial) Warsaw since July 2000; Born 28/02/65; FCO 1986; Berlin (BMG) 1988; LA/Caribbean Floater 1990; FCO 1993; Rome 1996; Band C4; m 1998 Caroline Anne Stramik.

Culley, John Douglas; Second Secretary (Political) Colombo since May 2005; Born 26/05/71; MOD 1997; FCO 2001; Band C4; ptnr, Joanne Childs.

Culligan, Phillip David; First Secretary Brussels (UKDEL NATO) since September 2003; Born 27/02/61; FCO 1981; Tripoli 1982; Pretoria/Cape Town 1983; Düsseldorf 1986; FCO 1989; Full-Time Language Training 1992; Second Secretary (Commercial) Budapest 1993; Deputy High Commissioner Nassau 1997; on loan to the MOD 2001; m (1) (diss); (2) 1997 Elizabeth June Huggins (1d 1999).

Culshaw, Robert Nicholas, MVO (1979); Director (Americas and Overseas Territories) FCO since March 2003; Born 22/12/52; Third Secretary FCO 1974; Language Training MECAS 1975; Language Training 1976; Third Secretary Muscat 1977; Second Secretary Khartoum 1979; First Secretary Rome 1980; APS to the Secretary of State FCO 1984; First Secretary and Head of Chancery later Counsellor, Consul General and Deputy Head of Mission Athens 1989; Counsellor and Head of News FCO 1993; Minister-Counsellor (Trade and Transport) Washington 1995; Consul-General Chicago 1999; m 1977 Elaine Ritchie Clegg (1s 1992).

Culver, John Howard, LVO (2000); HM Ambassador Reykjavik since January 2001; Born

17/07/47; Board of Trade 1967; FO later FCO 1968; Latin American Floater 1971; FCO 1973; Third Secretary Moscow 1974; Second Secretary La Paz 1977; Second later First Secretary FCO 1980; First Secretary (Commercial) Rome 1983; Head of Chancery Dhaka 1987; First Secretary FCO 1990; HM Ambassador and Consul-General Managua 1992; Consul-General Naples 1997; T/D Rome 2000; Band D7; m 1973 Margaret Ann Davis (1d 1974; 2s 1978, 1981).

Cummins, John, CMG (2005), MBE (1983); Counsellor Moscow since September 2001; Born 07/09/46; FO later FCO 1964; Budapest 1969; Luxembourg 1971; Tunis 1973; FCO 1976; Second Secretary 1978; Consul and Second Secretary (Admin) Santiago 1980; First Secretary Libreville 1985; First Secretary FCO 1988; Full-Time Language Training 1991; First Secretary (Commercial) Prague 1992; First Secretary FCO 1995; m 1969 Gillian Anne Biss (2s 1970, 1972).

Cunningham, Duncan; FCO since September 2003; Born 11/05/78; Band C4.

Cunningham, Kevin Francis; First Secretary (Political/Military) Baghdad since March 2005; Born 08/03/63; Civil Aviation Authority/National Air Traffic Control Services 1982; Royal Navy 1987; FCO 1992; Gaborone 1995; Bangkok 1998; FCO 2002; Band D6; (2d 1995, 1999).

Cunningham, Raymond Peter, MBE (2001); Basra since June 2004; Born 21/01/45; Army 1963-89; FCO 1989; T/D Helsinki 1989; Warsaw 1990; Floater Duties 1992; FCO 1994; Floater Duties 1997; Islamabad 2000; FCO 2003; Band C4.

Cupac, Dawn (née Womersley); SUPL since July 2002; Born 02/02/64; FCO 1992; Belgrade 1995; Vienna 1999; SUPL 2000; Vienna 2000; Band A2; m 1997 Dkordje Cupac.

Curley, Eugene Gerard, OBE (1991); FCO since July 2004; Born 30/09/55; FCO 1981; Second later First Secretary Mexico City 1984; First Secretary FCO 1986; First Secretary later Counsellor Paris 1993; Counsellor FCO 1998; Counsellor New York (UKMIS) 2000; m 1982 Joanne England (diss 1991); (2) 1993 Jane Margaret Crosland (1d 1996; 1s 2000).

Curley, Jane Margaret (née Crosland); Second Secretary FCO since February 1998; Born 24/11/61; FCO 1989; Second Secretary (Political) Copenhagen 1992; SUPL 1993; Band C4; m 1993 Eugene Gerard Curley (1d 1996; 1s 2000).

Curotto, Francine Elene; FCO since November 1999; Born 29/08/63; FCO 1990; Copenhagen 1993; FCO 1995; Havana 1997; Band C4.

Curran, David; Dubai since June 2005; Born 08/06/60; FCO 1987; Second later First Secretary Manila 1989; First Secretary (Chancery) New York (UKMIS) 1992; First Secretary FCO 1994; First Secretary (Political) Lusaka 1997; First Secretary FCO 2000; Counsellor Tehran 2001; m 1989 Lesley Jane Thomas.

Currie, Jacqueline Ann; SUPL since March 2003; Born 08/02/67; FCO 1987; Baghdad 1989; FCO 1991; LA Floater 1992; Atlanta 1994; Kigali 1998; Deputy High Commissioner Victoria 2001; Band C4.

Curry, Trudy Gay (née Hibbs); Beirut since August 2004; Born 09/12/57; FCO 1975; SUPL 1980; Canberra 1981; Brussels 1984; SUPL 1987; FCO 1992; Accra 1994; Doha 1997; Third Secretary (Consular/Management) Berlin 2001; Band B3; m (1) 1980 Peter Ian Webb (diss 1983); (2) 1983 Peter Lester Curry (1d 1987; 1s 1990).

Curtis, Penelope Ann; Kabul since July 2003; Born 24/06/68; FCO 1990; Mexico City 1992; Madrid 1996; FCO 2000; Band B3.

Cushing, Martyn David; FCO since July 2003; Born 18/09/80; Band A2.

Cuthbertson, Deborah Ann; Islamabad since November 2000; Born 07/04/72; FCO 1991; Band C4.

Cutler, Charlotte Margaret; FCO since December 2003; Born 16/10/72; FCO 1998; Second Secretary (Chancery) New York (UKMIS) 2001; Band C4.

Cutler, Giles Peter; FCO since August 2003; Born 09/10/79; Band B3; ptnr, Victoria Chapman.

D

Dacey, Alan Treharne; Third Secretary (Commercial/Immigration) Havana since January 2003; Born 10/04/70; FCO 1988; Brussels (UKDEL NATO) 1991; Floater Duties 1994; FCO 1998; Full-Time Language Training 2002; Band B3; m 1999 Salomé Maritz (diss 2003).

Dakin, Nigel John; Washington since June 2005; Born 28/02/64; FCO 1996; First Secretary New Delhi 1999; FCO 2002; Band D6; m 1987 Amanda Louise Johnson (1d 1995).

Daley Goldsmith, Robyn Jean; SUPL since December 2003; Born 08/08/69; FCO 1990; World-wide Floater Duties 1993; Third Secretary Bombay 1995; Third later Second Secretary Belmopan 1998; FCO 2001; Band D6; m 1995 Simon Geoffrey Goldsmith (1s 2004).

Dallas, Andrew James; FCO since October 2002; Born 15/01/71; FCO 1990; Dublin 1995; Doha 1999; Band B3; m 2001 Sarah Gordon.

Dallas, Ian Michael; FCO since October 1999; Born 13/12/42; Board of Trade 1961; Commonwealth Office 1966; Peking 1969; Lagos 1971; Accra 1973; FCO 1975; Chicago 1978; Second Secretary FCO 1982; Second Secretary (Admin) Lusaka 1985; FCO 1988; Vice-Consul (Comm) Karachi 1989; First Secretary (Comm/Aid) Colombo 1993; First Secretary Dublin 1997; m 1968 Angela Margaret Moore (1s 1971; 1d 1976).

Dalton, Sir Richard John, KCMG (2005), CMG (1996); HM Ambassador Tehran since November 2002; Born 10/10/48; Third Secretary FCO 1970;

MECAS 1971; Second Secretary Amman 1973; Second later First Secretary New York (UKMIS) 1975; FCO 1979; First Secretary Head of Chancery and Consul Muscat 1983; First Secretary FCO 1987; Counsellor on loan to MAFF 1988; Counsellor on CDA at Chatham House 1991; Counsellor FCO 1992; Consul-General Jerusalem 1993; Counsellor FCO 1998; HM Ambassador Tripoli 1999; m 1972 Elisabeth Keays (2s 1978, 1982; 2d 1973, 1979).

Daltrey, Christopher; Third Secretary (Management) Paris since October 2002; Born 21/09/68; FCO 1988; Rome 1990; FCO 1992; Third Secretary Hong Kong (BTC) 1993; Secondment to China - British Trade Group 1997; Third Secretary Tunis 1999; m 1991 Kim Rowena Newson (1s 1992; 3d 1993, 1995, 2002).

Damper, Carol Ann; Brussels (UKDEL NATO) since September 2003; Born 17/12/44; FCO 1975; Mogadishu 1975; Bonn 1977; Belmopan 1979; FCO 1982; Vienna 1984; FCO 1987; Athens 1988; Bucharest 1991; FCO 1993; Sofia 1997; FCO 2000; Band B3.

Daniel, Hamish St Clair, OBE (2004), MBE (1992); Deputy High Commissioner Karachi since January 2004; Born 22/08/53; FCO 1973; Algiers 1975; Prague 1977; Lisbon 1978; Islamabad 1980; FCO 1982; San Francisco 1985; Second Secretary Khartoum 1989; Second Secretary FCO 1992; Deputy Head of Mission and HM Consul Sana'a 1994; First Secretary (Political/Economic) Jakarta 1997; British Representative Dili 2001; HM Ambassador Dili 2002; m (1) 1975 Susan Brent (diss) (1d 1981; 1s 1985); (2) 2002 Heather Ann Bull.

Daniels, Malcolm; FCO since September 1986; Born 04/09/48; FCO 1965; Singapore 1980; Helsinki 1984; Band D6; m 1976 Jeannette Susan (2s 1977, 1980).

Daniels, Suzanne Jane (née Woodworth); FCO since April 1989; Born 07/05/63; FCO 1983; New Delhi 1985; Band A2; m 1989 Mark Daniels (2s 1999, 2001).

Darby, Jane; Deputy Head of Mission The Hague since January 2002; Born 01/04/53; FCO 1984; Bonn 1990; HM Treasury 1994; Cabinet Office 1995; FCO 1996; Full-Time Language Training 2001; m 1984 Michael Reece (1s 1986; 1d 1988).

Darby, Jonathan; Deputy Consul-General Chicago since February 2002; Born 28/12/69; FCO 1999; Band D6.

Dare, Gillian Angela; First Secretary (Political) Harare since September 2004; Born 07/07/48; Local Government 1987-99; FCO 1999; First Secretary (Political) Abuja 2002; Band D6.

Darke, John Martin Jamie; Counsellor Lisbon since August 2003; Born 02/05/53; FCO 1975; MECAS 1977; FCO 1979; MBA London Business School 1981; Management Consultant HAY-MSL 1983; First Secretary FCO 1985; First Secretary (Chancery) Cairo 1988; First Secretary FCO 1991; First Secretary (Political) Dubai 1996; First Secretary FCO 1999; m 1980 Diana Taylor (1d 1989; 1s 1991).

Darker, Aidan; Dar es Salaam since July 2002; Born 08/10/62; Royal Air Force 1983-95; FCO 1995; Hong Kong 1996; Bahrain 1999; m 1989 Angela Darker (1s 1999).

Darker, Angela; SUPL since February 1999; Born 12/02/68; Royal Air Force 1986-90; FCO 1995; Hong Kong 1996; m 1989 Aidan Darker (1s 1999).

Darroch, Nigel Kim, CMG; On loan to the Cabinet Office since June 2004; Born 30/04/54; FCO 1976; Third later Second later First Secretary Tokyo 1980; FCO 1985; Private Secretary to the Minister of State 1987; First Secretary (Economic) Rome 1989; First Secretary later Counsellor Secretary FCO 1993; Counsellor (External Relations) Brussels (UKREP) 1997; Counsellor FCO 1998; Director (EU) FCO 2000; Director General (EU) FCO 2003; m 1978 Vanessa Claire Jackson (1s 1983; 1d 1986).

Dart, Jonathan, MVO; FCO since December 2003; Born 14/07/64; FCO 1988; Third Secretary (Science and Technology) Bonn 1991; Third Secretary Pretoria 1994; Full-Time Language Training 1998; Second Secretary (Inward Investment/Financial Services) Seoul 1999; Band D6; m 1990 Claire Emma Juffs (2s 1992, 1994; 1d 1998).

Dauris, James Edward; FCO since May 2002; Born 15/01/66; FCO 1995; First Secretary (Commercial) Moscow 1999; Band D6; m 1995 Helen Claire Parker (2d 2000, 2002).

Davda, Sheetal Arun (née Kotak); SUPL since January 2005; Born 27/08/69; FCO 1988; Madrid 1991; FCO 1993; Band C4; m 2001 Shailesh J Davda.

Davenport, Michael Hayward, MBE (1994); Deputy Head of Mission Cairo since April 2004; Born 25/09/61; FCO 1988; Warsaw 1990; FCO 1993; First Secretary (Political) Moscow 1996; Consul-General and Director of Trade Promotion Warsaw 2000; Full-Time Language Training 2003; m 1992 Lavinia Sophia Elisabeth Braun (1s 1994; 1d 1996).

Davey, Denise; Second Secretary (Management) Beirut since August 2001; Born 08/05/69; HCS 1987; FCO 1989; Dubai 1990; FCO 1994; Mexico City 1994; Guatemala City 1995; FCO 1996; Band B3.

Davey, Simon James, MBE (1985); Consul and Head of Post Miami since November 2001; Born 01/02/47; Army 1965-68; FCO 1969; Latin American Floater 1972; Havana 1973; Second Secretary (Development Aid) Kathmandu 1976; Second later First Secretary FCO 1980; Consul Durban 1983; First Secretary (Commercial) Prague 1988; First Secretary FCO 1992; First Secretary (Commercial) Bogotá 1995; First Secretary on loan to British Trade International 1999; m 1992 Marcela Eva Dzurikova.

David, Timothy James (known as Tim); High Commissioner Lusaka since May 2002; Born 03/06/47; FCO 1974; Second later First Secretary Dar es Salaam 1977; FCO 1980; On loan to the ODA 1983; First Secretary Geneva (UKMIS) 1985; First Secretary later Counsellor FCO 1988; HM Ambassador Suva, also non-resident High Commissioner to Kiribati, Nauru and Tuvalu 1992; Deputy High Commissioner Harare 1996; High Commissioner Belmopan 1998; m 1996 Rosemary Kunzel (1s 1998; 1d 2001).

Davidson, Barry Alexander; Montreal since January 2005; Born 01/08/64; HCS 1985; Geneva (UKMIS) 1988; Freetown 1990; FCO 1994; Kathmandu 1997; FCO 2001; On loan to British Trade International 2002; Band C4; m 1985 Elizabeth Helen Oxley (1s 1992; 2d 1994, 1999).

Davidson, Brian John; Seconded to International Financial Services London since April 2005; Born 28/04/64; FCO 1985; Language Training 1986; Third later Second Secretary (Chancery/Inf) Peking 1988; First Secretary on loan to the Cabinet Office 1992; First Secretary FCO 1994; First Secretary (Political) Canberra 1996; Full-Time Language Training 2001; Deputy Head of Mission Vilnius 2001.

Davidson, Carolyn Jayne; Deputy Head of Mission Bratislava since December 2003; Born 18/04/64; FCO 1986; Language Training 1987; Language Training Kamakura 1988; Tokyo 1989; European Commission 1993; Bonn 1993; Second later First Secretary FCO 1995; SUPL 2000; Full-Time Language Training 2003; Band D6; m 1997 Thomas Henry Carter (2s 1998, 1999).

Davidson, James Gerard; FCO since July 2003; Born 20/05/67; MOD 1985; FCO 1988; Budapest 1989; Lagos 1991; FCO 1994; Jerusalem 1997; Tripoli 2000; Band B3.

Davidson, Raymond John Bruce, MBE (1995); On loan to the DTI since August 2002; Born 24/12/62; FCO 1995; Paris 1997; Islamabad 1999; Band B3; m 1988 Shivaun Anne (2s 1991, 1994).

Davidson, Sarah Victoria (née Fox); Doha since January 2000; Born 08/10/65; FCO 1985; Warsaw 1987; Hamilton 1989; Budapest 1992; FCO 1994; SUPL 1999; Band C4; m 1997 Fraser Reid Davidson (1s 1999; 1d 2002).

Davidson, Susan; SUPL since August 2001; Born 13/12/57; FCO 1987; Tokyo 1990; FCO 1992; Bangkok 1996; FCO 1998; Band A2.

Davidson Harkins, Katherine Elizabeth (known as Kate); SUPL since April 2005; Born 27/04/74; FCO 2002; Belgrade 2003; Band A2.

Davies, Caroline Elizabeth; FCO since April 2002; Born 04/06/63; RAF 1983-88; FCO HCS 1991-99; Kuwait 1998; World-wide Floater Duties 2000; Band B3.

Davies, Elved Richard Malcolm; FCO since September 2004; Born 19/01/51; Army 1972-75; Third later Second Secretary FCO 1975; Language Training 1977; Second later First Secretary Jakarta 1977; FCO 1980; Athens 1984; FCO 1985; First Secretary (Chancery) Nairobi 1989; FCO 1991; First Secretary later Counsellor Oslo 1991; Counsellor FCO 1995; Deputy Consul-General Hong Kong 2000; m 1976 Elizabeth Angela Osborne (1d 1981; 1s 1984).

Davies, Gerald Howard; FCO since January 2001; Born 24/04/48; HCS 1965; FCO 1968; Paris 1971; Karachi 1973; Ibadan 1977; FCO 1978; Vice-Consul (Consular) Warsaw 1981; FCO 1984; Vice-Consul (Consular/Management) Melbourne 1986; FCO 1988; Consul and Second Secretary (Man) Muscat 1990; Consul Brussels 1995; m 1972 Yvonne Arnold (2d 1984, 1988).

Davies, Griselda Christian Macbeth (née Todd); SUPL since October 1999; Born 20/02/59; Budapest 1981; FCO 1982; Buenos Aires 1983; FCO 1985; Damascus 1987; FCO 1988; SUPL 1989; FCO 1990; Riga and Vilnius 1993; FCO 1997; Band A2; m 1989 John Howard Davies (1s 2001).

Davies, Ian; Deputy Head of Mission Lima since April 2002; Born 01/08/56; FCO 1976; Moscow 1978; SUPL 1980; FCO 1983; Paris 1985; Third later Second Secretary Moscow 1988; Second Secretary FCO 1990; Second Secretary (Com/Con) and Deputy Head of Mission La Paz 1993; Consul-General Marseille 1997; m 1979 Purificacion Bautista Hervias (2d 1985, 1988).

Davies, Jennifer Ann Tudor; Second Secretary FCO since February 1995; Born 02/03/50; FCO 1969; Khartoum 1972; Valletta 1974; Singapore 1977; FCO 1979; Buenos Aires 1980; FCO 1982; New Delhi 1984; FCO 1987; Hong Kong 1992; Band C4.

Davies, John Howard; FCO since July 2003; Born 31/01/57; FCO 1980; Riyadh 1983; Second later First Secretary FCO 1985; First Secretary and Head of Interests Section Damascus 1987; First Secretary FCO 1990; First Secretary (Political) Riga and Vilinius 1993; First Secretary FCO 1997; First Secretary (Political) Sofia 1999; Band D6; m 1989 Griselda Christian Macbeth Todd (1s 2001).

Davies, Jonathan Mark; Counsellor Madrid since November 2000; Born 01/12/67; FCO 1990; Language Training Cairo 1992; Second Secretary (Political/Information) Kuwait 1993; On loan to the Cabinet Office 1996.

Davies, Maureen Kerr Stewart (née Paisley); Brussels (UKREP) since August 1994; Born 12/06/53; FCO 1984; Washington 1987; Kathmandu 1990; Band A2; m 1988 Maxim Philip Davies.

Davies, Nicola Claire (née Dixon); SUPL since December 1998; Born 10/07/68; FCO 1990; Third Secretary (Political) Singapore 1993; Third Secretary FCO 1996; Band C4; m 1996 Jonathan Mark Davies.

Davies, Patrick James; Deputy Head of Mission Warsaw since January 2005; Born 08/05/68; FCO 1993; Full-Time Language Training 1994; Second

Secretary (Political/Press) Rabat 1995; First Secretary FCO 1999; Private Secretary FCO 2000; FCO 2003.

Davies, Paul Ronald; First Secretary FCO since May 2000; Born 30/03/53; FCO 1970; African Floater 1974; Dacca 1976; FCO 1979; Tripoli 1982; Kingston 1984; Third Secretary (Commercial) Peking 1988; Second Secretary FCO 1990; Second Secretary (Political/Commercial/Information) Lima 1993; Consul (Commercial/Economic/Press and Public Affairs) Shanghai 1996; Deputy Consul-General Shanghai 1997; m 1976 Fiona Avril Canning (1d 1979; 1s 1981).

Davies, Peter Brian; Counsellor Madrid since April 2003; Born 30/12/54; Third Secretary FCO 1977; Language Training Hong Kong 1980; Second Secretary FCO 1981; Second later First Secretary Rome 1983; First Secretary FCO 1987; First Secretary and Consul Peking 1988; First Secretary FCO 1992; Counsellor (Political) Jakarta 1996; Counsellor FCO 1999; m 1981 Charlotte Helena Allman Hall (1d 1984; 1s 1986).

Davies, Roger James; First Secretary (Management) Harare since October 2004; Born 23/09/47; HCS 1965; FO (later FCO) 1967; Moscow 1970; Kampala 1971; Islamabad 1973; Kathmandu 1974; FCO 1978; Baghdad 1981; Vice-Consul (Comm) Johannesburg 1985; Second Secretary FCO 1987; Second Secretary (Management/Consular) Doha 1991; Deputy Consul-General Melbourne 1994; FCO 1998; First Secretary (Management) Nicosia 2001; m (1) 1974 Catherine Yvonne Moorby (diss 1990) (1s 1982; 1d 1984); (2) 1990 Jean Thérésa Austin.

Davies, Samantha Jayne Elizabeth; Colombo since September 2004; Born 27/11/79; FCO 2002; Band A2.

Davis, Andrew Cornwall; Brussels (UKREP) since April 2003; Born 29/04/68; FCO 1995; ECMM Sarajevo 1997; Santiago 1999; Band A2.

Davis, Ashley James; FCO since July 1991; Born 23/02/59; FCO 1986; Islamabad 1987; Band B3; m 1988 Roberta Scott (1d 2000).

Davis, Doris; Second Secretary (Immigration) Islamabad since February 2003; Born 26/01/47; DSAO 1967; Baghdad 1968; Sofia 1970; FCO 1971; Kuala Lumpur 1972; Peking 1973; Washington 1975; FCO 1978; Cairo 1980; Cape Town/ Pretoria 1984; FCO 1988; Washington 1992; Third Secretary (Man) Rangoon 1995; Second Secretary (Commercial) Baku 1999; Band C4.

Davis, Kevin Roy; FCO since June 1998; Born 02/01/65; FCO 1981; Washington 1989; FCO 1991; SUPL 1997; Band C4; m 1991 Karen Roberts (1s 1994).

Davis, Rosemary; First Secretary (Chancery) New York (UKMIS) since July 2001; FCO 1987; Language Training 1988; Language Training Cairo 1989; FCO 1990; Brussels (UKREP) 1991; Third Secretary (Chancery) Damascus 1994; FCO 1998; Band D6.

Davis, Stephen Alexander James; Second Secretary (Management/Consul/ECM) Abu Dhabi since May 2001; Born 24/09/65; FCO 1983; Mexico City 1986; Warsaw 1990; FCO 1993; Third Secretary (Commercial) Accra 1997; m 1986 Maureen Patricia Oates.

Davison, Andrew James; Third Secretary (Commercial) Bucharest since February 2004; Born 11/08/70; FCO 1992; Kiev 1997; Third Secretary New Delhi 2000; FCO 2003; Band B3; m 1997 Lana Jane Sawa.

Davison, Brian William Edward; Mexico City since August 2005; Born 06/06/45; Royal Marines 1961; MOD Police 1985; HM Prison Service 1986; Lusaka 1988; Cairo 1992; Lagos 1995; Karachi 1999; Damascus 2002; Islamabad 2003; Band C4; m 1966 Sandra June Thompson (2s 1970, 1971).

Davison, Nicole April; Consul Beijing since November 2004; Born 06/08/68; FCO 1988; Pretoria/Cape Town 1990; Third Secretary Dhaka 1991; Third later Second Secretary FCO 1996; Second Secretary Kiev 2001; Full-Time Language Training (Mandarin) 2004; Band C5.

Dawbarn, John Nathaniel Yelverton; SUPL since November 2004; Born 03/05/65; FCO 1987; Language Training 1990; Third later Second Secretary (Chancery/ Information) Belgrade 1990; Second later First Secretary FCO 1993; First Secretary T/D (Political/Information) Belgrade 1995; FCO 1996; First Secretary (Political) Bonn later Berlin 1998; FCO 2002; m 1989 Katherine Sarah Urry.

Dawber, Mary Welsh (née Campbell); T/D New Delhi since June 2004; Born 04/04/56; FCO 1996; SUPL 1997; Moscow 1997; Ankara 2000; Band A2; m 1975 Philip Dawber (1d 1976).

Dawber, Philip; Ankara since March 2000; Born 01/04/54; Armed Forces 1971-94; FCO 1995; Band A2; m 1975 Mary Welsh Campbell (1d 1976).

Day, Mark Christopher; Belmopan since April 2003; Born 01/05/63; FCO 1994; Hong Kong 1996; Lusaka 1999; Band A2; m 2003 Carolyn Yetman.

Day, Martin Charles; First Secretary FCO since 2003; Born 04/11/65; FCO 1989; Language Training Cairo 1991; Second Secretary (Chancery) Cairo 1992; First Secretary FCO 1995; First Secretary (Commercial) Prague 2000; Band D6.

Day, Rosamund, MBE (2005); Bridgetown since September 2001; Born 27/06/64; FCO 1983; Bonn 1985; Suva 1987; Africa/ME Floater 1989; FCO 1991; Second Secretary (Management) Colombo 1996; SUPL 1999; Band C5; m 1993 Nicholas John Pyle (2s 1996, 2001; 1d 1999).

de Chassiron, Charles Richard Lucien, CVO (2000); Head of Protocol Division and Vice

Marshal of the Diplomatic Corps, FCO since May 2002; Born 27/04/48; FCO 1971; Third Secretary Stockholm 1972; First Secretary Maputo 1975; FCO 1978; First Secretary (Commercial) Brasilia 1982; First Secretary later Counsellor FCO 1985; Counsellor (Comm/Econ) Rome 1989; HM Ambassador Tallinn 1994; Consul-General Milan 1997; m 1974 Britt-Marie Sonja Medhammar (1d 1975; 1s 1976).

de Csillery, Patricia Katarina; Second Secretary FCO since April 1998; Born 30/04/69; FCO 1993; Second Secretary (Political) New York (UKMIS) 1996; Band D6; m 1993 Michael de Csillery (1d 2000; 1s 2002).

De Gier, Helen Majorie; Dhaka since June 2005; Born 19/02/59; HCS 1976-84; FCO 1984; Freetown 1986; FCO 1989; Peking 1998; FCO 2001; Band B3; m 1992 Joseph Eugene O'Carroll.

de Jeune d'Allegeershecque, Susan Jane (née Miller); Deputy Head of Mission Bogotá since October 2002; Born 29/04/63; FCO 1985; Brussels (UKREP) 1987 (Second Secretary 1989); FCO 1990; Second Secretary (Economic/Information) Singapore 1992; First Secretary FCO 1995; Deputy Head of Mission Caracas 1999; m 1991 Stephane Herv Marie le Jeune d'Allegeershecque (2s 1993, 1995).

De Luca, Wendy Alexandra (née Fleming); Second Secretary (Management/Consular) Osaka since April 2004; Born 11/05/70; FCO 1991; Jakarta 1995; Third Secretary (Commercial) Buenos Aires 1999; Full-Time Language Training (Japanese) 2003; Band C4; m 1995 Dino De Luca (1s 2004).

de Mink, Julie Maria (née Ingham); FCO since January 2003; Born 03/01/65; FCO 1984; Harare 1986; SUPL 1990; Dhaka 1991; SUPL 1994; FCO 1997; Cape Town 1997; Gaborone 1997; Pretoria 1999; SUPL 2002; Band B3; m 2002 Ian Paul de Mink (2s 1989, 1990; 1d 2003).

De Pauw, Amanda Jayne (née Rutter); SUPL since May 2002; Born 20/03/64; HM Land Registry 1984; FCO 1988; Brussels (UKREP) 1989; Yaoundé 1993; FCO 1996; Ottawa 1999; Band A2; m 1993 Luc Paul Solange Marie De Pauw (2d 1998, 2000).

De Ramos, Nicola Anne (née Smyth); SUPL since September 2002; Born 11/08/65; FCO 1988; Bucharest 1989; Quito 1992; Havana 1996; Mexico City 1999; Band A2; m 1994 Bryan Dubal Ramos Montero (2d 1995, 1997).

de Ridder, Kathryn Louise Carmel (née Peacock); FCO since September 2002; Born 16/07/60; FCO 1984; New Delhi 1985; Brussels (UKREP) 1988; FCO 1991; SUPL 1992; Lagos 1994; SUPL 1997; Tel Aviv 1998; Band B3; m 1992 Wouter de Ridder (1d 1993).

De Sousa, Louise Amanda (née Clark); Deputy High Commissioner Maputo since May 2003; Born 23/07/68; FCO 1991; Second Secretary (Political/Information/Aid) Brasilia 1993; First Secretary FCO 1997; SUPL 2000; FCO 2001; m 1994 Allan Rivail de Sousa (1s 1998; 1d 2001).

de Valencia, Michelle (née Lawler); Deputy Head of Mission Holy See since September 2001; Born 08/06/64; FCO 1987; Bogotá 1990; Third Secretary (Commercial later Chancery)) Stockholm 1993; Second Secretary FCO 1999; Band C4; m 1993 Jairo Alberto Valencia Diaz (1d 1996; 1s 1998).

de Waal, James Francis; Deputy Head of Mission Santiago since April 2003; Born 18/12/68; FCO 1990; New York (UKMIS) 1992; Full-Time Language Training 1994; Second Secretary (Political/ Information) Berlin 1994; FCO 1998; Washington 2002; Full-Time Language Training (Spanish) 2002.

Dean, Amy Charlotte; Full-Time Language Training Damascus since June 2005; Born 12/08/78; FCO 2003; Band C4.

Dean, Andrew John; FCO since January 2005; Born 06/02/55; FCO 1982; Second Secretary (UNIDO/UN) Vienna (UKMIS) 1984; Second later First Secretary FCO 1986; First Secretary (Chancery) Hanoi 1990; First Secretary FCO 1992; São Paulo 1997; First Secretary FCO 1999; Counsellor (Multilateral) Canberra 2000; m 1989 Nicola Moreton (1s 1993).

Dean, Robert John; FCO since December 2003; Born 21/05/59; MOD 1977; FCO 1978; Second Secretary Copenhagen 1987; Second later First Secretary FCO 1992; On secondment to MOD 1994; FCO 1995; First Secretary (External) Wellington 1999; Band C5; m 1981 Julie Margaret Scott (2d 1986, 1988).

Deane, Geoffrey; FCO since May 2005; Born 19/02/50; FCO 1976; Nairobi 1980; Second Secretary FCO 1984; First Secretary (Chancery) East Berlin 1988; FCO 1991; First Secretary FCO 1997; HM Consul Munich 2001; Band D6; m Karen Aileen Wallace (4d 1980, 1983, 1986, 1994).

Deane, Michael Boyd; FCO since March 2003; Born 01/08/72; Second Secretary FCO 1999; Second Secretary (Economic) Vienna 2001; Band C4; m 2001 Natalya Samantha Pilbeam.

Deane, Robert Edward; Full-Time Language Training (Arabic) since April 2004; Born 28/09/62; HM Treasury 1985; Bonn 1994; FCO 1998; Band D7; m 1993 Corinna Osmann (1s 1998; 2d 2000, 2003).

Deaney, Tina Marie; Floater Duties since June 2002; Born 18/04/72; FCO 1991; Islamabad 1995; Prague 1999; Band B3.

Dear, Robert Edward; First Secretary (Political/Economic) Budapest since October 2000; Born 19/02/55; FCO 1986; First Secretary 1987; First Secretary FCO 1992; Deputy Head of Mission Havana 1994; m 1982 Caroline Margaret Reuss.

Dearden, Christopher Robert; On loan to the DTI since April 2001; Born 07/12/59; FCO 1978; Wellington 1981; Ankara 1984; LA/Caribbean Floater 1987; FCO 1989; Athens 1993; Vice-Consul Warsaw 1997; FCO 2000.

Dearden, Janine Elaine (née Lawrence); SUPL since June 2001; Born 18/10/60; FCO 1982; Rome 1983; Nairobi 1985; SUPL 1988; FCO 1989; SUPL 1990; FCO 1998; Band A2; m 1985 Timothy John Dearden (2s 1987, 1989).

Dee, Pauline (née Thompson); SUPL since September 2000; Born 11/10/63; FCO 1987; Bridgetown 1989; FCO 1992; Peking 1993; Grand Turk 1996; Sarajevo 1998; Band A2; m 1998 Stewart Dee (1d 1999; 1s 2003).

Dee, Stewart; Third Secretary (Political) Gibraltar since November 2000; Born 12/08/69; FCO 1988; Bonn 1990; FCO 1993; SUPL 1996; Vice Consul Sarajevo 1998; Band B3; m (1) 1991 Claire Duggan (diss 1996); m (2) 1998 Pauline Thompson (1d 1999; 1s 2003).

Delaney, Michael; FCO since June 2002; Born 14/12/67; FCO 1988; Ankara 1989; Lagos 1990; Abuja 1992; Colombo 1995; Manila 1998; Band B3; m 1990 Zeliha Doganavsargil.

Deneiffe, Paul Michael; New York (UKMIS) since July 2004; Born 21/06/63; FCO 1982; Lagos 1984; Khartoum 1986; Cairo 1987; FCO 1989; Seconded to Belfast 1989; FCO 1993; Madrid 1995; FCO 1998; Band C4.

Dening-Smitherman, Major Peter Clemens Henri; Queen's Messenger since 1990; Born 12/07/47; HM Forces 1967-90.

Dennis, Catherine Teresa; SUPL since October 2005; Born 20/05/70; FCO 1998; Vienna (UKDEL) 1999; Beirut 2002; Band A2; m 2004 Zahi Talal Srour.

Dennis, John David; Minister, Consul General and Deputy Head of Mission Beijing since October 2003; Born 06/08/59; FCO 1981; Hong Kong 1983; Peking 1985; Second later First Secretary FCO 1987; First Secretary Kuala Lumpur 1992; On secondment to Standard Chartered Bank 1997; Counsellor on loan to the DTI 1998; Counsellor (Economic and Commercial) New Delhi 2001; m 1989 Jillian Margaret Kemp (2s 1994, 1999).

Dennison, Simon Becher; FCO since November 2003; Born 01/02/80; Band B3.

Denny, Ross Patrick; Deputy Head of Mission Luanda since April 2002; Born 13/09/55; RN 1972-79; FCO 1979; Santiago 1980; Doha 1983; Warsaw 1985; FCO 1988; Second Secretary (Political) The Hague 1992; FCO 1997; São Paulo 1998; m (1) 1977 Barbara Harvard (diss 1996) (1d 1979; 1s 1981); (2) 2000 Claudenise De Lima.

Dent, Alastair Ross Möller; Deputy High Commissioner Port Moresby since January 2004; Born 07/02/54; DHSS 1972; FCO 1974; Brussels (UKREP) 1976; Moscow 1979; FCO 1981; LA Floater 1984; Third Secretary (Management) Mexico City 1986; FCO 1989; Second Secretary (Commercial/Information) later Deputy High Commissioner Gaborone 1993; Second later First (Management) Manila 1997; Second Secretary FCO 2001; m (1) 1977 (diss 1983); m (2) 1985 (2s 1988, 1996).

Denwood, Judith Elizabeth; Second Secretary FCO since April 2000; Born 21/10/65; FCO 1986; Bridgetown 1988; FCO 1991; Third Secretary FCO 1993; T/D New Delhi, Accra, Damascus 1995; Third Secretary (Management) and Vice-Consul Bahrain 1997; Band C4.

Desloges, Christina Anne (née Sanders); Dhaka since December 2003; Born 30/11/63; FCO 1984; Lagos 1987; FCO 1991; Harare 1992; Bandar Seri Begawan 1996; Stanley 2000; Band A2; m 1989 Daniel Albert Joseph Desloges (1d 1990; 1s 1997).

Devine, John Joseph; Second Secretary FCO since November 2003; Born 03/07/70; FCO 1991; Floater Duties 1994; New Delhi 1996; Consul Tallinn 2000; Band C4.

Devine, Paul Graham; FCO since May 1995; Born 19/01/51; DHSS 1973; FCO 1981; Bonn 1983; Riyadh 1985; Suva 1988; Düsseldorf 1992; Band B3; m 1993 Losana Lewamoqe Di Lo Tuisawau.

Dew, John Anthony; HM Ambassador Havana since October 2004; Born 03/05/52; FCO 1973; Third Secretary Caracas 1975; Second later First Secretary FCO 1979; First Secretary Paris (OECD) 1983; First Secretary FCO 1987; Counsellor and Deputy Head of Mission Dublin 1992; Minister Madrid 1996; Head of Latin America and Caribbean Department FCO 2000; On secondment to Lehman Brothers 2003; m 1975 Marion Bewley Kirkwood (3d 1977, 1980, 1984).

Dewar, Robert Scott; HM Ambassador Addis Ababa since March 2004; Born 10/06/49; FCO 1973; Third later Second Secretary Colombo 1974; First Secretary FCO 1978; First Secretary (Comm) Head of Chancery and Consul Luanda 1981; First Secretary FCO 1984; First Secretary and Head of Chancery Dakar 1988; Deputy High Commissioner Harare 1992; HM Ambassador Antananarivo 1996; FCO 2000; High Commissioner Maputo 2000; m 1979 Jennifer Mary Ward (1d 1988; 1s 1995).

Dholakia, Nishi Rajendra; Second Secretary (EU/Political) Brussels (UKREP) since September 2004; Born 03/11/78; FCO 2002; Band C4.

Diaz, Alison Jean; Mexico City since March 2002; Born 24/02/68; FCO 1991; Belgrade 1993; Lima 1995; Vienna (OSCE) 1999; Band B3; m 1998 Juan Carlos Diaz (2s 1998, 2001).

Dibble, Hilary Anne (née Light); FCO since June 1998; Born 17/07/51; FCO 1973; Moscow 1974; FCO 1975; Rome 1976; Kingston 1980; Islamabad 1983; FCO 1987; Moscow 1990; Third later Second Secretary (Consular) Canberra 1993; m 1980 Geoffrey Walter Dibble.

Dick, Colin John; FCO since November 2005; Born 22/06/70; FCO 1990; World wide Floater

Duties 1994; Third later Second Secretary FCO 1996; Assistant Private Secretary to the Permanent Under Secretary FCO 1998; Second Secretary Singapore 2001; Band D6; m 2001 Elaine Hargreaves (1s 2003; 1d 2004).

Dickerson, Nigel Paul; On loan to the DTI since May 2002; Born 25/04/59; FCO 1978; Bonn 1981; Warsaw 1984; FCO 1987; Second Secretary 1990; Second Secretary (Management) and Consul Santiago 1992; Deputy High Commissioner and Second Secretary (Aid) Windhoek 1995; FCO 2000; m 1984 Marianne Gaye Tatchell (2d 1992, 1994; 1s 1995).

Dickins, Nicholas William; FCO since January 2001; Born 15/11/56; FCO 1985; Tel Aviv 1991; FCO 1994; New York (UKMIS) 1997; SUPL 2000; Band C5; m 1991 Marina Papaspyrou.

Dickinson, Woodman Mark Lowes, OBE (2000); Head of Office Pristina since August 2002; Born 16/01/55; FCO 1976; Second Secretary Ankara 1979; First Secretary FCO 1983; First Secretary (Pol/Inf) Dublin 1987; First Secretary FCO 1991; First Secretary on loan to the Bank of England 1994; Full-Time Language Training 1996; HM Ambassador Skopje 1997; SUPL 2001; m (1) 1986 Francesca Infanti (diss 1991); (2) 1995 Christina Houlder.

Dickson, Susan Jane; Legal Counsellor FCO since May 2003; Admitted as Solicitor (Scotland) 1989; Assistant later Senior Assistant Legal Adviser FCO 1990; First Secretary (Legal) New York (UKMIS) 1997; First Secretary (Overseas Territories Legal Adviser) Bridgetown 2000.

Dickson, William Andrew; FCO since August 1998; Born 17/12/50; FCO 1969; SUPL to attend University 1970; FCO 1974; Cairo 1976; Nairobi 1980; Second Secretary FCO 1982; Second Secretary (Commercial) Budapest 1982; Second later First Secretary FCO 1986; First Secretary (IAEA) Vienna 1989; First Secretary (Information) Hong Kong 1994; Band D6; m 1981 Gillian Ann Hague.

Digby, Simon; FCO since October 2003; Born 04/08/55; Crown Agents 1977; FCO 1980; Tehran 1982; LA Floater 1986; FCO 1987; Third Secretary (Admin/Cons) Mbabane 1989; FCO 1991; Luanda 1997; Consul and Second Secretary (Commercial) Bratislava 1999.

Diggle, Wadham Nicholas Neston; First Secretary (Political) Muscat since July 2004; Born 07/11/69; FCO 2002; Band D6.

Dillon, Alan Steven; Taipei since June 2002; Born 25/10/69; Royal Marines 1988-00; FCO 2000; Band B3; m 1994 Nichola Jane Clark (2d 1999; 2001).

Dimbleby, Andrew Timothy; Consul (Management) New York since April 2002; Born 20/05/59; FCO 1979; Accra 1981; FCO 1985; Pretoria 1986; Third Secretary (Commercial/Information/Chancery) Dubai 1989; Language Training 1989; Second Secretary FCO 1993; Second Secretary (Commercial) Manila 1996; First Secretary New York (UKMIS) 2000; Band C5; m 1981 Susan Margaret Joy Irvine (1s 1988; 2d 1991, 1996).

Dimond, Paul Stephen, CMG (2005); HM Ambassador Manila since March 2002; Born 30/12/44; FO 1963; DSA 1965; Language Training Tokyo 1966; Osaka 1968 (Consul - Comm 1970); Second Secretary Tokyo 1972; On loan to DTI 1973; Second Secretary FCO 1975; First Secretary (Economic) Stockholm 1977; First Secretary FCO 1980; First Secretary (Commercial) Tokyo 1981; First Secretary FCO 1986; on secondment to Smiths Industries Plc 1988; Counsellor (Commercial) Tokyo 1989; Deputy Head of Mission The Hague 1994; Consul-General Los Angeles 1997; m 1965 Carolyn Susan Davis-Mees (2s 1968, 1970).

Dinsdale, Ian McLean Taylor; Abuja since December 2003; Born 20/10/49; FCO 1969; Nairobi 1972; Colombo 1976; Second Secretary FCO 1979; Santo Domingo 1982; Maseru 1985; Riyadh 1986; FCO 1989; Islamabad 1993; Wellington 1996; FCO 1998; Second Secretary (Immigration) Lagos 2002; Band C4; m 1975 Elizabeth Ann Montaut.

Dinsley, Andrew; Bangalore since June 2004; Born 22/08/66; FCO 1990; Kiev 1992; FCO 1996; Deputy Head of Mission Almaty 2000; Band C4; m 2000 Larissa Kolomiyets (1s 1986; 1d 2002).

Dinwiddy, Bruce Harry, CMG (2003); Governor Cayman Islands since May 2002; Born 01/02/46; Second Secretary FCO 1973; First Secretary Vienna (UKDEL MBFR) 1975; FCO 1977; First Secretary and Head of Chancery Cairo 1981; First Secretary FCO 1983; Counsellor on loan to the Cabinet Office 1986; FCO 1988; Counsellor Bonn 1989; Deputy High Commissioner Ottawa 1992; High Commissioner Tanzania 1998; FCO 2001; m 1974 Emma Victoria Llewellyn (1d 1976; 1s 1979).

Dix, Christopher John, OBE (2003); Director Visa Services Nigeria and Deputy Head of Post Lagos since March 2004; Born 30/09/64; FCO 1983; Geneva (UKMIS) 1985; Dhaka 1988; Second Secretary FCO 1993; Language Training 1995; Second Secretary (Commercial) Madrid 1995; First Secretary (Immigration/Consular) New Delhi 1999; Band D7; m (1) 1988 Julia Milward (diss 2003) (1d 1991; 1s 1994); (2) 2003 Cristina Fernandez (1d 2004).

Dixon, Debra Audrey (née Churchill); First Secretary (Commercial) Amman since September 2000; Born 06/04/58; FCO 1978; Washington 1980; Sana'a 1983; FCO 1986; Düsseldorf 1989; SUPL 1992; Lusaka 1993; FCO 1998; Band C4; m 1978 Russell Kenneth Dixon (2d 1985, 1992; 1s 1990).

Dixon, Russell Kenneth; First Secretary (Management) Amman since July 2000; Born 24/01/58; MOD 1976; FCO 1978; Washington 1980; Sana'a 1983; FCO 1985; Düsseldorf 1989;

SUPL 1993; Second Secretary (Political/Information) Lusaka 1993; Band C5; m 1978 Debra Audrey Churchill (2d 1985, 1992; 1s 1990).

Dobson, Sharon Gail, MBE (2002); First Secretary FCO since 2003; Born 04/01/68; FCO 1991; Third Secretary (Chancery) Dakar 1995; Third Secretary Brussels (UKDEL NATO) 1997; Second Secretary FCO 1999; On loan to the BTI 2001; Band D7; m 2005 James Cybranet Lowen.

Docherty, Margaret Emily (née Taylor); On loan to the Cabinet Office since September 2003; Born 28/08/71; FCO 1994; Kathmandu 1995; FCO 1997; Band B3; m 2000 Stuart Docherty.

Docherty de Morell, Claire Elizabeth; Bucharest since March 2004; Born 30/07/68; FCO 1992; Santiago 1995; Havana 1999; Georgetown 2000; Band A2; m 2000 Raynol Morell Fernandez (1s 2000; 1d 2002).

Doe, Marc Gavin; Second Secretary (Political) Moscow since March 2004; Born 09/01/79; FCO 2001; Band C4.

Doherty, Emer Maria; SUPL since November 2002; Born 10/01/69; FCO 1990; Full-Time Language Training 1993; Geneva (UKMIS) 1993; Paris 1996; SUPL 2001; Paris 2001; Band C4.

Doidge, Mary Ellen; FCO since April 1995; Born 21/01/46; Bonn 1971; FCO 1974; Warsaw 1975; Tokyo 1977; FCO 1980; Floater Duties 1982; Moscow 1983; FCO 1985; Brussels (UKDEL NATO) 1988; On loan to the Home Office 1991; Band C4.

Doig, Michael David; FCO since April 2001; Born 28/05/54; FCO 1973; Tokyo 1975; Karachi 1979; Vienna 1982; Third Secretary (Consular/Visas) Kaduna 1983; FCO 1987; Third Secretary (Comm/Econ) Ottawa 1990; FCO 1993; Second Secretary (Press and Public Affairs) Cape Town 1998; m (1) 1983 Mary Walker McKinnie (diss 2000) (1d 1985); (2) 2002 Sarah Elizabeth Booker.

Domm, Lance Gavin; FCO since October 2004; Born 05/03/77; Band C4.

Donaldson, Brian; HM Ambassador Antananarivo since October 2002; Born 06/04/46; Ministry of Aviation 1963; DSAO (later FCO) 1965; Algiers 1968; La Paz 1971; FCO 1974; Lagos 1975; Luxembourg 1979; Second Secretary FCO 1982; APS to the Minister of State 1983; Second later First Secretary (Aid/Comm) Port Louis 1985; First Secretary (Comm) Head of Chancery and Consul Yaoundé 1989; First Secretary (Immigration/Consular) Dhaka 1992; FCO 1996; High Commissioner Windhoek 1999; m 1969 Elizabeth Claire Sumner (3s 1971, 1973, 1979).

Donaldson, Ian Martin; On loan to the Home Office since September 2003; Born 21/07/66; FCO 1988; Third later Second Secretary (Political) Jakarta 1991; FCO 1995; First Secretary Geneva (UKDEL) 1999; m 1990 Elspeth Jane Chovil Maguire (2d 1996, 1997).

Donegan, Susan Peta (née McAllister); Rome since June 2002; Born 28/05/67; FCO 1985; Paris 1987; LA Floater Duties 1990; Caracas 1992; SUPL 1993; Accra 1994; SUPL 1997; Band B3; m 1993 James Edward Donegan.

Donnelly, Sir Joseph Brian, KBE (2003), CMG (1997); FCO since April 2005; Born 24/04/45; Second Secretary FCO 1973; First Secretary (ECOSOC) New York (UKMIS) 1975; First Secretary and Head of Chancery Singapore 1979; First Secretary FCO 1982; Counsellor on loan to the Cabinet Office 1985; Counsellor and Consul-General Athens 1988; RCDS Course 1991; Counsellor FCO 1992; Minister and Deputy Permanent Representative Brussels (UKDEL NATO) 1995; HM Ambassador Belgrade 1997; Director and Special Representative for South East Europe FCO 1999; On secondment to BP/Amoco 2000; High Commissioner Harare 2001; m (1) 1966 Susanne Gibb (diss 1994) (1d 1970) (2) 1997 Julia Mary Newsome.

Donnelly, Marie Thérésa; SUPL since February 2003; Born 21/05/61; FCO 1996; Kathmandu 1997; Tehran 2001; Band A2.

Donnelly, Matthew; Second Secretary (Commercial) Dublin since October 2004; Born 21/11/61; FCO 1981; Algiers 1985; Nassau 1988; FCO 1990; Lagos 1992; Third Secretary (Commercial) Buenos Aires 1996; FCO 1999; Band C4; m 1988 Tracy May Basnett (2s 1989, 1993).

Donnelly, Tracy May (née Basnett); SUPL since May 1995; Born 26/03/62; FCO 1982; Berne 1983; Algiers 1985; SUPL 1988; T/D Lagos 1994; Band A2; m 1988 Matthew Donnelly (2s 1989, 1993).

Dorey, Gregory John; Deputy Head of Mission Hong Kong since July 2000; Born 01/05/56; MOD 1977; On loan at UKDEL NATO 1982; MOD 1984; First Secretary FCO 1986; First Secretary (Chancery) Budapest 1989; PS/Minister of State FCO 1992; Counsellor (Economic) and later Deputy High Commissioner Islamabad 1996; Seconded to Industry 2000; m 1981 Alison Patricia Taylor (1d 1990; 2s 1988, 1994).

Dorrian, Claire Hicks (née Jones); Nicosia since August 2003; Born 15/07/68; HCS 1987; DS 1989; Stanley 1992; Riyadh 1995; Kampala 1999; Band B3; m 1992 Stuart Forsyth Dorrian (1s 1996).

Douglas, Helen Clare; Consul/Management Officer Muscat since June 2004; Born 13/06/68; FCO 1987; Lagos 1990; FCO 1994; ECO/VC Bridgetown 1998; SUPL 2001; FCO 2002; Band C4; m (1) 1990 Michael Thomas Fallon (diss 1997) (2s 1991, 1992); (2) 1999 Paul Leslie Douglas (1d 2001, 1 step d 1983; 1 step s 1985).

Douglas, Janet Elizabeth; First Secretary FCO since June 2000; Born 06/01/60; FCO 1985; Language Training 1987; Second later First Secretary (Chancery/Inf) Ankara 1988; First Secretary FCO 1991; First Secretary on loan to the

ODA 1993; First Secretary (Political) Stockholm 1996.

Douglas, Paul Leslie; FCO since April 2002; Born 05/11/58; Army 1975-88; Hanoi 1998; SUPL 1999; Band A2; m 1993 Tina Marie Field.

Douglas-Hiley, Mark Charles Piers Quentin; Third Secretary (Consular/Management) Kinshasa since November 2001; Born 06/11/54; Department of Employment 1972; DHSS 1973; FCO 1974; Castries 1977; FCO 1979; Geneva (UKMIS) 1980; FCO 1983; Lagos 1987; New York (JMO) 1991; FCO 1994; FCO 1997; Sofia 1998; FCO 2000; Band B3.

Douse, Sarah Louise (née Ansell); FCO since March 1998; Born 08/04/70; FCO 1990; Rome 1992; Bonn 1995; Band B3; m 2001 Carl Anthony Douse.

Doust, Claire Heather (née Barlow); Lagos since October 2001; Born 07/03/72; FCO 1991; Brussels (UKDEL NATO) 1995; Third Secretary (Management) Islamabad 1998; Band B3; m 1998 Stephen Terence Doust.

Doust, Stephen Terence; Lagos since November 2001; Born 04/12/72; FCO 1992; Brussels (UKDEL NATO) 1995; Islamabad 1998; Band B3; m 1998 Claire Heather Barlow.

Dove, John Henry; FCO since October 1997; Born 10/03/65; HM Customs and Excise 1989; FCO 1990; Full-Time Language Training 1991; Deputy Head of Mission Tallinn 1992; Moscow 1993; Deputy Head of Mission Tashkent 1996; Band C5; ptnr, Deborah Williams.

Dow, Elizabeth Anne, MBE (2005); Consul Lisbon since July 2003; Born 09/03/58; FCO 1976; New Delhi 1978; Brasilia 1982; FCO 1984; New York (CG) 1988; Vice-Consul/MO Jerusalem 1991; FCO 1995; Consul Rabat 1999.

Downer, James Robert Stephen; FCO since September 1998; Born 09/07/68; FCO 1992; Full-Time Language Training 1993; Full-Time Language Training Cairo 1994; Sana'a 1995; Band D6; m 1998 Nicola Marguerite Neary (1d 2003).

Downing, Joanna Watson; FCO since September 2001; Born 17/12/71; FCO 1995; OHR - Bosnia 1997; Attaché Dakar 1998; Band B3.

Dowse, Timothy Michael; Counsellor FCO since 2001; Born 18/12/55; FCO 1978; Manila 1980; Second later First Secretary Tel Aviv 1982; First Secretary FCO 1986; Washington 1992; Counsellor, Cabinet Office 1997-98; On loan as Head of Defence, Diplomacy and Intelligence Spending to HM Treasury 1998-00; m 1989 Vivien Frances Life (2d 1991, 1994).

Drabble, Rufus John; Second Secretary Oslo since February 2002; Born 12/02/70; FCO 1995; Nairobi 1998; Band C4; m 1997 Stella Elizabeth Waldron (2d 2001, 2003).

Drake, David Allen; FCO since January 2001; Born 01/09/47; RAF 1967-75; FCO 1977; Lagos 1979; Kuwait 1982; Second Secretary 1984; Second later First Secretary FCO 1985; First Secretary (Civil Aviation) Bonn 1989; First Secretary (Commercial) Singapore 1991; Consul (Commercial) New York 1996; m 1972 Anne Veronica Paice.

Drake, Howard Ronald, OBE (2001); HM Ambassador Santiago since September 2005; Born 13/08/56; FCO 1975; LA Floater 1979; Los Angeles 1981; Second Secretary 1982; Second Secretary FCO 1983; Second Secretary (Chancery/Info) Santiago 1985; First Secretary FCO 1988; First Secretary and Head of Chancery Singapore 1992; First Secretary FCO 1995; Deputy Consul General and Director of Investment New York 1997; Assistant Director, Human Resources Directorate, FCO 2002; m 1988 Gill Summerfield (1s 1992; 1d 1994).

Drayton, Frank Anthony; FCO since December 2002; Born 10/12/54; FCO 1974; Islamabad 1976; Cape Town 1979; Munich 1982; FCO 1985; Prague 1989; Vice-Consul Doha 1990; FCO 1994; FCO British Trade International 1997; Second Secretary (Commercial) Riyadh 2000; Band C4; m 1988 Fidelma Bernadette Tuohy.

Drew, Simon Richard; Hong Kong since January 2004; Born 07/05/65; FCO 1981; Pretoria/Cape Town 1989; FCO 1992; Ankara 1993; FCO 1997; First Secretary Washington 1999; m 1991 Katharine Chappell (1d 1995).

Drew, Thomas; FCO since February 2002; Born 26/09/70; FCO 1995; Second Secretary Moscow 1998; First Secretary (Economic) Moscow 2000.

Drew, Timothy James; FCO since July 2003; Born 02/04/65; FCO 1994; Geneva (UKMIS) 1996; FCO 1999; Riyadh 2000; Band B3; m 1991 Claire Melanie (2d 1998, 2002).

Dring, Sarah Anne Maxwell; First Secretary FCO since March 2000; Born 23/11/48; FCO 1974; Sofia 1975; Nicosia 1977; FCO 1979; South East Asia Floater 1983; Algiers 1985; FCO 1987 (Second Secretary 1989); Johannesburg 1991; FCO 1995; First Secretary (Management) Kampala 1997; Band D6.

Drummond, Roderick Ian; Deputy Head of Mission Damascus since June 2004; Born 07/09/62; FCO 1985; Language Training SOAS 1986; University of Jordan 1987; Second Secretary (Political/ Economic) Algiers 1988; First Secretary FCO 1992; Deputy Consul-General (Trade/Investment) Johannesburg 1996; First Secretary (External) Brussels (UKREP) 1998; Deputy Head of Mission Amman 2002; m 1985 Carolyn Elizabeth Elliott (1s 1986; 2d 1988, 1990).

Drury, Alan Hyslop; Bridgetown since November 2004; Born 21/02/52; FCO 1970; Budapest 1973; Dacca 1975; LA Floater 1977; FCO 1980; Second Secretary (Comm) Muscat 1983; Second later First Secretary FCO 1987; Resident Representative St. Georges 1989; Consul (Commercial) Barcelona 1994; FCO 1998; m 1980 Joan Lamb (1d 1984; 1s 1986).

Dryden, Paul James; Kolkata since May 2005; Born 15/06/69; FCO 1990; Warsaw 1992; T/D Zagreb 1992; Ottawa 1993; Hamilton 1996; Ashgabat 1999; FCO 2002; T/D Maputo 2004; Band B3.

Drysdale, Craig Morrison; FCO since September 2004; Born 22/03/56; FCO 1981; Full-Time Language Training 1994; Full-Time Language Training Cairo 1995; First Secretary FCO 1996; First Secretary (Political) Muscat 2001; Band C5; m 1988 Clare Elizabeth (2d 1993, 1996).

Drysdale, Heather; FCO since August 2000; Born 02/06/56; Brussels (NATO) 1977; Tokyo 1980; FCO 1983; Reykjavik 1984; Floater Duties 1987; FCO 1988; Valletta 1993; Full-Time Language Training 1996; Warsaw 1997; Band C5.

Duckett, Keith Dyson; Washington since February 2005; Born 11/04/58; FCO 1977; Kuala Lumpur 1979; Maputo 1983; Brasilia 1985; FCO 1986; Jakarta 1989; Third Secretary (Man) Paris 1993; Second Secretary (Man) Damascus 1995; SUPL/Temporary Duties 1997; FCO 2002; SUPL 2004; Band C4; m 1989 Diane Puckridge (1d 1990; 1s 1991).

Dudgeon, Denise Ann (née Holland); FCO since October 2001; Born 13/04/63; FCO 1986; Washington 1989; JLG Hong Kong 1991; FCO 1994; British Trade International 1997; On loan to DTI 1999; Band C4; m 2000 Anthony James Dudgeon.

Duff, Janet Nancy; FCO since October 1997; Born 03/12/67; FCO 1990; Language Training 1991; Chiang Mai 1992; Vice-Consul Bangkok 1993; Addis Ababa 1996; Band D6.

Duff, Julie Anne; Helsinki since July 2002; Born 17/06/79; FCO 1999; Band A2.

Duffield, Linda Joy, CMG; HM Ambassador Prague since December 2004; Born 18/04/53; DHSS 1976; Paris (ENA) 1986; First Secretary FCO 1987; First Secretary (Comm) Moscow 1989; First Secretary later Counsellor FCO 1992; Deputy High Commissioner Ottawa 1995; High Commissioner Colombo 1999; Director (Wider Europe) FCO 2002.

Duffin, David Robert; FCO since 1996; Born 04/11/53; FCO 1972; New Delhi 1979; FCO 1981; Singapore 1987; FCO 1990; Berlin 1995; Band C5; m (1) 1980 Angela Thicke (diss 1984); (2) Carole Susan Matthews (diss 1996).

Duffy, Martin Patrick; First Secretary (Counter Narcotics) Kabul since March 2004; Born 11/01/70; British Army 1986 - 94; FCO 1999; On loan to No. 10 Downing Street 2000; Assistant Private Secretary to the Permanent Under Secretary, FCO 2002; Band D6; ptnr, Siân McLean.

Duffy, Peter John; First Secretary (Management) Paris since April 2001; Born 20/06/50; Ministry of Aviation (later Ministry of Technology) 1966; FCO 1967; Addis Ababa 1971; Maseru 1974; Khartoum 1977; FCO 1978; Yaoundé 1982; Johannesburg 1985; Attaché later Second Secretary Budapest 1989; Second Secretary FCO 1991; Second Secretary Amsterdam 1994; Second later First Secretary (Management) Kingston 1995; m 1971 Juliet Heather Woodward (1s 1972).

Duggin, Sir Thomas Joseph; HM Ambassador Bogotá since August 2001; Born 15/09/47; Commonwealth Office (later FCO) 1967; Oslo 1969; Bucharest 1973; Assistant Private Secretary to the PUSS, FCO 1977; Second Secretary Bangkok 1979; First Secretary FCO 1982; First Secretary (Commercial), Consul and Head of Chancery La Paz 1985; First Secretary and Head of Chancery Mexico City 1989; High Commissioner Vila 1992; Counsellor FCO 1995; m (1) 1968 (diss 1983) (2s 1973, 1975); (2) 1983 (diss 1996) (3) 1999 Janette Mortimer David.

Dun, Peter John; SUPL since November 2002; Born 06/07/47; FCO 1970; Third later Second Secretary Kuala Lumpur 1972; Second later First Secretary FCO 1976; First Secretary (External Relations) Brussels (UKREP) 1980; First Secretary New York (UKMIS) 1983; FCO 1987; Counsellor on secondment to RCDS 1989; Counsellor (Economic) Islamabad 1990; Foreign Policy Adviser to External Affairs Commissioner, EC Brussels 1993; Counsellor FCO 1996; On Commercial Secondment 2000; FCO 2001; m 1983 Cheng-Kiak Pang (2s 1987, 1989).

Duncan, Catherine Ellen; Assistant Legal Adviser FCO since October 2004; Born 06/02/79; Band D6.

Duncan, Colin; Second Secretary (Commercial) Cape Town since July 2003; Born 03/03/70; DSS 1988; FCO 1989; Brussels (UKREP) 1992; Sofia 1995; Floater Duties 1998; FCO 2000; Band C4; m 2003 Clare Donaghy.

Duncan, John Stewart, OBE (1993); Counsellor (Commercial) Paris since April 2002; Born 17/04/58; FCO 1980; Paris 1982; Khartoum 1985; Second Secretary FCO 1988; APS to Minister of State on loan to ODA 1991; NATO Defence College Rome 1992; Chargé d'Affaires Tirana 1992; Brussels (UKDEL WEU/NATO) 1993; First Secretary FCO 1996; On loan to SACEUR 1998; m 1984 Anne Marie Jacq (1d 1990; 1s 1994).

Duncan, Rachel Mignonne Bridget (née Blanche); SUPL since June 2002; Born 17/01/74; FCO 1997; Vice-Consul (Political) Jerusalem 2000; FCO 2002; Band B3; m 2000 Stuart Duncan.

Duncan, Reginald Arthur; Pyongyang since July 2002; Born 23/08/45; HM Forces 1963-93; FCO 1995; Ankara 1997; Stanley 2000; Band A2; m 1967 Cecily Coleman (2d 1971, 1974).

Duncan-Smith, Louise-Marie Veronica; Kingston since April 2003; Born 16/12/62; FCO 1984; Ottawa 1986; Banjul 1989; FCO 1989; Victoria 1992; Language Training 1996; Berne 1996; SUPL 2000; Sana'a 2000; Band A2; m 1986 Brian David Smith (2d 1996, 1999).

Dunlop, Alexander James Macfarlane; FCO since January 2001; Born 14/06/48; FCO 1968; Ottawa 1971; Vientiane 1974; FCO 1977; Sana'a 1980; Vienna 1983; FCO 1986; Second Secretary (Chancery/Info) Lilongwe 1989; First Secretary FCO 1994; First Secretary (Consular) Nairobi 1996; T/D Vienna (UKDEL OSCE) 2000; Band C5; m 1978 Ortrud Wittlinger.

Dunn, Andrew Patrick Rymer; Second Secretary (Press and Public Affairs) Tehran since October 2003; Born 14/09/69; FCO 2000; Band C4; m 1995 Caroline Nicola Cann (2s 1998, 2002).

Dunn, David Hedley; Deputy High Commissioner Freetown since November 2004; Born 21/09/68; FCO 1989; Oslo 1992; LA/Caribbean Floater Duties 1995; Second Secretary (Environment) seconded to UNEP Nairobi 1998; FCO 2001; Band D6.

Dunn, James Michael; Accra since March 2005; Born 07/01/59; FCO 1980; Washington 1984; FCO 1986; Paris 1990; Third Secretary Lagos 1993; Warsaw 1999; FCO 2003; Band C4; m 1993 B C Boyle.

Dunn, Jonathan Michael; FCO since September 2003; Born 07/03/75; FCO 1997; SOAS University of London 1998; Full-Time Language Training Hanoi 1999; Second Secretary (Chancery) Hanoi 2000; Band D6; m 2003 Karen Rex.

Dunn, Michael George; Kuala Lumpur since October 2003; Born 08/11/48; FO (later FCO) 1966; New York 1971; Lima 1974; FCO 1976; Copenhagen 1980; Harare 1983; Caracas 1986; FCO 1989; Quito 1992; Bogotá 1997; FCO 2000; m 1983 Mercedes Josefina Fuguet-Sanchez (3d 1987, 1990, 1998).

Dunnachie, Hugh, MBE (1987); Consul-General Perth since March 2000; Born 07/12/44; MOD (Navy) 1961-65; DSAO 1965; Singapore (Political Adviser's office) 1967; Warsaw 1972; Vice-Consul Cairo 1973; Second Secretary FCO 1976; Second Secretary (Commercial) The Hague 1980; Consul and Head of British Interests Tripoli 1984; First Secretary FCO 1989; Deputy Consul-General Melbourne 1992; First Secretary (Economic/Agriculture) Canberra 1994; Deputy Head of Post and HM Consul Dubai 1996; m (1) 1963 Elizabeth Mosman Baxter (diss 1986) (3d 1964, 1971, 1980; 1s 1965); (2) 1986 (Doreen) Carole Cleaver.

Dunne, John Richard; SUPL since December 2004; Born 04/10/67; FCO 1992; Third later Second Secretary New York (UKMIS) 1996; SUPL 2000; First Secretary FCO 2001; Deputy Head of Mission Pyongyang 2002; FCO 2004; Band C5; m 1997 Naomi Anita Scott.

Duranko, Elizabeth Jean (née Paris); SUPL since August 2000; Born 23/01/69; FCO 1993; Geneva 1996; SUPL 1998; Pretoria 1999; Band B3; m 1997 John Eric Duranko (1d 1998).

Durham, Anna Catherine; FCO since January 2004; Born 04/11/79; Band B3.

Duxbury, Julie Annette; SUPL since January 2004; Born 05/02/70; FCO 1988; Brussels (UKDEL NATO) 1990; FCO 1993; Full-Time Language Training 1995; Vice-Consul Athens 1996; Dubai 1998; Third Secretary (Immigration) Zagreb 2000; Band B3.

Dwyer, Michael John; FCO since October 2001; Born 29/12/55; DOE 1972-74; FCO 1974; Ottawa 1977; Belmopan 1979; FCO 1982; Warsaw 1982; Islamabad 1983; FCO 1986; Vice-Consul (Management/Commercial/Consular) Toronto 1990; Second Secretary (Commercial) Toronto 1991; Consul/ECM New York 1995; Consul and Director U.S Entry Clearance Issuing Posts, New York 1999; m 1982 Karen Leolin Meighan (2s 1983, 1985; 1d 1989).

Dyson, John Alva, MVO (1995); SMO Baghdad since August 2003; Born 15/04/49; DSAO (later FCO) 1966; Port of Spain 1970; Geneva 1973; Yaoundé 1976; FCO 1978; Nuku'alofa 1982; FCO 1985; Second Secretary (Commercial) Jedda 1987; Vice-Consul (Management Officer) Cape Town 1991; First Secretary FCO 1996; T/D Asmara 2001; Deputy High Commissioner T/D Suva 2002; Deputy High Commissioner T/D Bandar Seri Begawan 2003; m 1971 Deirdre Anne George (2s 1974, 1981).

E

Ead, Mark; Nicosia since March 2002; Born 20/04/76; FCO 1997; Band A2; m 2001 Victoria Swan (1s 2004).

Eager, Nigel Dominic; First Secretary FCO since August 2002; Born 09/05/62; FCO 1981; Dublin 1986; Third Secretary/Vice Consul Baghdad 1988; FCO 1990; First Secretary (Political) Valletta 1998; Band C5; m (1) 1987 Helen Christine Gillings (diss 1993); (2) 1998 Catherine Thomas.

Eakin, Christopher Howard; SUPL since July 2000; Born 01/12/64; FCO 1984; East Berlin 1985; Paris 1987; FCO 1990; Vienna 1993; Grand Cayman 1996; Band C4.

Earl, Jane Ann (née Kerr); SUPL since February 2001; Born 15/06/68; FCO 1989; Luanda 1991; Islamabad 1995; SUPL 1998; Brussels 2000; Band B3; m 1991 Shaun Earl (1d 1997).

Earl, Shaun; SUPL since May 2004; Born 04/01/70; FCO 1989; Luanda 1991; Third Secretary Brussels (UKDEL) 1998; Lilongwe 2001; Band B3; m 1991 Jane Ann Kerr (1d 1997).

Easson, Hilary; FCO since February 2004; Born 10/01/68; FCO 1987; Kuwait 1990; Algiers 1991; FCO 1994; Bogotá 1995; FCO 1999; Vienna 2000; Band A2.

Easter, Christine Marie; FCO since July 1994; Born 22/11/44; FCO 1975; Cape Town 1975; FCO 1979; Luxembourg 1982; Anguilla 1985; Rangoon 1987; Budapest 1989; Washington 1991; Band B3.

Eatwell, Jonathan David; SUPL since July 2001; Born 08/11/67; FCO 1986; Lusaka 1988; FCO 1992; Dhaka 1995; FCO 1998; Jakarta 1998; Band B3; m 1991 Lisa Ann Brecknell (1d 1997).

Ebeling, Adrian Stanley Arthur; FCO since November 2000; Born 20/01/48; FCO 1984; Paris 1989; FCO 1992; Pretoria 1998; Band C4; m 1979 Laura Phipps (1s 1987).

Edgar, Christopher George; Consul-General St Petersburg since August 2004; Born 21/04/60; FCO 1981; Moscow 1983; Lagos 1986; FCO 1988; Resigned 1992; Reinstated, First Secretary FCO 1995; HM Ambassador Phnom Penh 1997; Full-Time Language Training 2001; HM Ambassador Skopje 2001; m 1994 Yelena Nagornichnykh (2d 1994, 1998).

Edge, Christopher James; FCO since August 2003; Born 30/08/53; FCO 1972; Kabul 1975; East Berlin 1977; Rome 1980; Kaduna 1981; FCO 1984; Beirut 1985; Third Secretary (Commercial) Mexico City 1987; Deputy Head of Mission Tegucigalpa 1988; Second later First Secretary (Commercial) Madrid 1992; FCO 1996; First Secretary (Commercial), San José and Director of Trade Promotion in Central America 1999; Deputy High Commissioner Port of Spain 2001.

Edghill, Susan Christine (née Cranwell); Chennai since April 2002; Born 14/07/58; FCO 1990; Paris 1993; Port Louis 1996; Manila 1998; Band A2; m 1996 Samuel Carlisle Edghill.

Edis, Rachel Pauline; Second Secretary (Political/Military) Washington since December 2002; Born 24/11/76; FCO 2001; Band C4.

Edusei, Charmaine (née Howe); SUPL since July 2003; Born 17/09/59; FCO 1988; Brussels (UKDEL NATO) 1991; FCO 1993; Valletta 1994; FCO 1997; Band B3; m 1989 Isaac Edusei (1d 1993).

Edwards, Carole Lilian (née Hellier); Brasilia since April 2002; Born 07/07/45; FCO 1973; Freetown 1973; Washington 1975; Prague 1978; Belgrade 1978; FCO 1979; Beirut 1980; Ottawa 1982; Moscow 1985; FCO 1986; Washington 1989; FCO 1992; Band B3.

Edwards, David Vaughan; Tehran since May 2001; Born 27/09/43; RAF 1961-89; Budapest 1989; Islamabad 1990; Kingston 1994; Moscow 1996; Riyadh 1998; Band B3; m 1967 Patricia Ann (2d 1968, 1969; 1s 1972).

Edwards, Gillian Rose; FCO since November 2003; Born 07/02/64; FCO 1983; Resigned 1987; Reinstated FCO 1988; World wide Floater Duties 1991; St Petersburg 1993; FCO 1994; Vice-Consul New York 1996; Dublin 2000; Band B3; m 1995 David Jonathan Mead.

Edwards, Keith Nigel; Washington since March 2001; Born 09/05/53; FCO 1969; Warsaw 1977; Athens 1978; FCO 1981; Hong Kong 1985; FCO 1988; Second Secretary Madrid 1992; Second Secretary FCO 1995; m 1975 Wendy Ann Carrington (2d 1980, 1982).

Edwards, Lucy Anne; Vienna since January 2003; Born 05/05/71; FCO 1993; Brussels (UKREP) 1995; FCO 1997; SUPL 1999; Nairobi 2000; Band A2; m 1997 Jason Edward Lambert (diss 2003).

Edwards, Paul Martin; Second Secretary (Political) Belgrade since August 2004; Born 11/11/66; FCO 1996; Almaty 1998; Third Secretary (Political/PPA) Abuja 2002; Band C4; m 1990 Jane Baker (2d 1993; 2001; 1s 1999).

Edwards, Rose Catherine Amy; FCO since March 2004; Born 10/11/73; FCO 1998; Full-Time Language Training 1999; Second Secretary (Economic) Moscow 2001; Second later First Secretary (Economic) Kiev 2003; Band D6.

Eelbeck, Andrew; FCO since January 2002; Born 02/03/59; FCO 1979; Islamabad 1980; FCO 1982; Singapore 1982; FCO 1986; Third Secretary Prague 1988; Third Secretary Pretoria 1992; FCO 1995; Accra 1997; Band C5; m 1994 Miss F Botes (1s 1995).

Ehrman, William Geoffrey, CMG (1998); HM Ambassador Beijing since January 2006; Born 28/08/50; Third Secretary FCO 1973; Language Training Hong Kong 1975; Third later Second Secretary Peking 1976; First Secretary (ECOSOC) New York (UKMIS) 1979; First Secretary Peking 1983; FCO 1985; On secondment as Political Adviser to the Governor in Hong Kong 1989; Counsellor FCO 1993; Principal Private Secretary to the Secretary of State for Foreign and Commonwealth Affairs 1995; On secondment to Unilever 1997; HM Ambassador Luxembourg 1998; Director (International Security) FCO 2000; Director General (Defence & Intelligence) 2002; Chairman (JIC) 2004; m 1977 Penelope Anne Le Patourel (1s 1981; 3d 1977, 1979, 1986).

Eke, James Robert; FCO since June 2004; Born 28/06/78; Band B3.

El Beleidi, Cecille Maude (née Greaves); Consul (Commercial) Jedda since January 2003; Born 22/11/62; FCO 1982; Kuwait 1985; FCO 1986; Kathmandu 1989; Vice-Consul Casablanca 1992; APS/Baroness Symons FCO 1995; Second Secretary (Chancery) Riyadh 1999; SUPL 1999; Second Secretary (Chancery) Riyadh 2000; Full-Time Language Training 2002; Band C5; m 1987 Magdi El Beleidi (1d 1999).

El Ouassi, Sabine; FCO since 2003; Born 29/01/64; HCS 1990-93; FCO 1994; Riyadh 1995; Amman 1999; Band A2; m 1988 Mohamed El Ouassi (2s 1994, 2001).

El Roubi, Julie Anne (née Mooney); SUPL since August 2003; Born 21/04/71; Brussels (UKDEL NATO) 1991; Khartoum 1995; Lagos 1998; Abu Dhabi 2000; Band A2; m (1) 1992 Prince Felix Lewis (diss) (1d 1992); (2) 1999 Murtada Saad El Roubi (1s 2000).

Elder, Alistair Alexander; Third Secretary (Commercial) New Delhi since July 2001; Born 14/05/71; FCO 1989; Brussels (UKREP) 1992; FCO 1994; Vice-Consul Tel Aviv 1997; Band C4;

m 2001 Justine Elizabeth Pitts (2d 1992, 1995; 1s 2003).

Elder, Peter Edward; First Secretary Canberra since January 2005; Born 14/03/68; FCO 1989; Brussels 1992; FCO 1994; New Delhi 1994; FCO 1997; Band D6; m 1994 Rosalind Anita Hall (1d 1997; 1s 2002).

Elder, Rosalind Anita (née Hall); SUPL since March 2002; Born 19/07/65; FCO 1990; Brussels (UKREP) 1992; New Delhi 1994; FCO 1997; Band A2; m 1994 Peter Edward Elder (1d 1997).

Eldon, Stewart Graham, CMG (1999), OBE (1991); HM Ambassador Dublin since April 2003; Born 18/09/53; New York (UKMIS) 1976; FCO 1976; Third later Second Secretary Bonn 1978; First Secretary FCO 1982; Private Secretary to the Minister of State FCO 1983; First Secretary (Chancery) New York (UKMIS) 1986; First Secretary FCO 1990; Counsellor on loan to the Cabinet Office 1991; Fellow, Center for International Affairs, Harvard University 1993; Counsellor (Political) Brussels (UKDEL NATO/WEU) 1994; Director (Conferences) FCO 1997; Deputy Permanent Representative (with the personal rank of Ambassador) New York (UKMIS) 1998; Visiting Fellow, Yale University 2002; m 1978 Christine Mary Mason (1d 1982; 1s 1985).

Elliot, Caroline Margaret (Carma), OBE (2004); Consul-General Jeddah since October 2004; Born 24/08/64; FCO 1987; Peking 1989; Brussels 1991; EC Presidency Liaison Officer Bonn, Paris and Madrid 1994; Second later First Secretary FCO 1996; Consul-General Chongqing 2000; (1d adopted 2002).

Elliot, Christopher Lowther; Second Secretary FCO since March 1997; Born 26/12/54; DNS 1974; DOE 1975; FCO 1975; Cairo 1979; Bridgetown 1982; FCO 1986; Islamabad 1990; Muscat 1993; m 1975 Julie Lorraine Inman (1s adopted 1975; 1d 1982).

Elliot, Jacqueline Mary; Second Secretary FCO since September 2002; Born 25/01/64; FCO 1984; Lima 1986; LA Floater 1989; San José 1991; FCO 1996; Caracas 1998; Band C4; (1d 1991).

Elliott, Hugh Stephen Murray; Counsellor Paris since July 2002; Born 31/08/65; FCO 1989; Third later Second Secretary (Chancery) Madrid 1991; FCO 1996; Buenos Aires 1999; m 1989 Toni Martin-Elena (1s 1993; 1d 1995).

Elliott, Jonathan Andrew; Deputy High Commissioner Kampala since March 2003; Born 03/09/66; FCO 1991; Full-Time Language Training 1993; Tokyo 1995; Second Secretary FCO 1999; First Secretary FCO 2001; Band D6.

Elliott, Robert David, LVO (2003); FCO since June 2004; Born 25/11/60; FCO 1980; Prague 1981; Peking 1982; Language Training 1983; Abu Dhabi 1984; Port Louis 1988; FCO 1993; HM Consul Jerusalem 1997; First Secretary (Management) Abuja 2000; Band C5; m 1998 Victoria Louise Holloway (2s 1988, 2004; 1d 2000).

Elliott, Stuart; FCO since January 2003; Born 15/04/75; HCS 1994; FCO 1997; Athens 1999; Athens 1999; Band A2; m 1999 Margaret Redmond.

Elliott, Susan Jayne, MBE (1991); Valletta since December 2003; Born 13/06/61; FCO 1978; SUPL 1980; SUPL 1982; Rome 1982; Cairo 1984; FCO 1985; Beirut 1988; Bombay 1992; FCO 1992; Second Secretary (Chancery) Bandar Seri Begawan 1999; Second Secretary (Political) Bucharest 2003; Band C4; m 1980 John Anthony Tucknott (diss 1992).

Elliott, William, OBE (2002); Deputy Head of Mission Tallinn since September 2002; Born 16/03/68; Second Secretary FCO 1993; Language Training 1994; Second Secretary (Political) Warsaw 1995; First Secretary FCO 1998; First Secretary (Political) Kabul 2001; Band D6; m 2003 Daria Anna Chrin (1d 2003; 1s 2004).

Ellis, Alexander Wykeham; SUPL since January 2005; Born 05/06/67; FCO 1990; Third later Second Secretary (Political/Economic) Lisbon 1992; First Secretary (Economic) Brussels (UKREP) 1996; FCO 2001; Madrid 2003; m 1996 Maria Teresa Adegas.

Ellis, Amanda Jane; FCO since January 2003; Born 07/12/60; FCO 1987; Brussels 1989; FCO 1991; Jakarta 1995; Quito 1999; Band A2.

Ellis, David Edward; Second Secretary (Technical Management) Bangkok since June 2003; Born 07/03/67; FCO 1987; Lagos 1997; FCO 2001; Band C4; m 1996 Cherie Louise Wilson (1s 1997; 1d 2002).

Ellis, Hugo; SUPL since January 2004; Born 13/09/66; FCO 1988; Riyadh 1992; Strasbourg (UKDEL) 1995; FCO 1999; Band B3; ptnr, Helen Marie Arbon (1d 2003).

Ellis, John Arthur; First Secretary (Consul/MO) Sarajevo since July 2002; Born 27/03/52; DHSS 1969-71; FCO 1971; Wellington 1974; Khartoum 1976; Dar es Salaam 1979; FCO 1981; Islamabad 1982; Seoul 1986; Second Secretary FCO 1989; Second Secretary (Commercial/Aid) Cairo 1993; Second later First Secretary FCO 1996; m 1974 Law Kwai Chun (1s 1980; 1d 1983).

Ellis, Philip Donald; First Secretary FCO since October 1997; Born 09/05/57; FCO 1978; Brussels (NATO) 1981; Peking 1984; FCO 1987; New Delhi 1990; Vice-Consul São Paulo 1995; m 1981 Gail Teresa Drayton (1s 1997).

Ellis, Richard Anthony; Second Secretary (Political) Kabul since June 2005; Born 02/02/77; FCO 2000; Full-Time Language Training (Greek) 2002; Second Secretary (Economic) Nicosia 2002; Band C4.

Ellwood, Dr Sheelagh Margaret; FCO since October 1998; Born 21/02/49; FCO 1988;

Assistant Deputy Governor Gibraltar 1995; Senior Principal Research Officer 1998.

Elvins, Martyn Andrew; FCO since August 2003; Born 13/02/58; FCO 1984; Warsaw 1988; Pretoria 1999; Band C5; m 1988 Christine P Pettit.

Elvy, Simon David, OBE; FCO since February 2005; Born 08/12/61; FCO 1983; Baghdad 1985; Stockholm 1989; FCO 1992; Second Secretary (Political) Stockholm 1996; FCO 1997; On loan to the Cabinet Office 2001; FCO 2002; First Secretary Baghdad 2004; Band D6; m 1985 Lesley Jane (2s 1991, 1993).

Embleton, Robert Leitch; FCO since August 2003; Born 09/10/42; FO 1960; Leopoldville 1964; Bonn 1968; St Vincent 1969; FCO 1973; Stuttgart 1976; Prague 1979; Second Secretary FCO 1980; Second later First Secretary (Chancery) Washington 1984; Consul (Commercial) Düsseldorf 1989; First Secretary FCO 1993; First Secretary (Social/ Science) Rome 1998; m 1970 Ursula Biebricher (1d 1975).

Emery, Peter Michael; Lagos since October 2003; Born 25/11/72; FCO 1997; Helsinki 1999; Tokyo 2000; Band B3.

Empson, Jane Mary (née Silverwood); SUPL since March 2005; Born 05/08/60; FCO 1985; Mexico City 1987; FCO 1991; T/D Montevideo 1993; Muscat 1994; SUPL 1998; Rome 1999; Montevideo 2002; Band B3; m 1994 Richard Andrew Empson (1s 1996).

Enescott, Nicholas John; MO/VC Rangoon since March 2002; Born 06/12/51; FCO 1972; Cape Town 1975; Ankara 1977; Tripoli 1980; FCO 1983; Hanoi 1986; Third Secretary (Comm) and Vice-Consul Dakar 1989; Second Secretary (Management) Lilongwe 1991; Second Secretary FCO 1995; ECM Bombay 1998.

Engdahl, Denise Jean (née Sanders); Chennai since November 2004; Born 19/09/60; FCO 1982; Wellington 1983; Colombo 1986; Mbabane 1989; FCO 1993; SUPL 1995; Kingston 1996; Stockholm 2000; Band B3; m 1989 Geran Magnus Engdahl (1s 1991; 1d 1994).

Ennis, Alexandra Mary; FCO since September 2002; Born 18/05/79; Band A2.

Etherington, Richard David Ernest; FCO since 2002; Born 29/11/73; FCO 1999; T/D Dubai 2001; Band C4.

Etherton, Mark Roy; On loan to the House of Lords since September 2003; Born 17/03/58; FCO 1983; Second Secretary (Chancery) Paris 1988; First Secretary (Political/Economic) Warsaw 1991; First Secretary on loan to Cabinet Office 1994; FCO 1996; Deputy Permanent Representative Vienna (UKMIS) 1999; m 1991 Suzanne Margaret Miskin (2d 1994, 1996).

Evans, Alexander Ian Arthur; FCO since April 2003; Born 10/12/73; Band C5.

Evans, Carol Jeanette (née Kendall); FCO since January 2005; Born 10/04/59; FCO 1982; Vienna (UKDEL) 1984; Warsaw 1987; FCO 1988; SUPL 1997; Band B3; m 1991 Keith Dennis Evans (2d 1996, 1997).

Evans, Claire Elizabeth; Deputy Head of Mission and First Secretary (Commercial) Dubai since April 2003; Born 02/11/61; FCO 1987; Jakarta 1989; Third Secretary (Commercial) Islamabad 1992; Second Secretary FCO 1996; First Secretary FCO 2000; Band D6.

Evans, David Hugh; First Secretary (Political) Nairobi since May 2001; Born 27/03/59; FCO 1985; Islamabad 1988; FCO 1989; First Secretary (Political) on loan to the US State Department Washington 1995; On secondment as Senior Policy Adviser, CBI 1999; Band D6; m 1988 Nirmala Vinodhini Chrysostom (2d 1996, 2001).

Evans, Derek John; Paris since May 2005; Born 04/06/56; DOE 1978; FCO 1984; Second Secretary Dubai 1985; Second Secretary Pretoria 1989; FCO 1994; First Secretary Moscow 2000; m 1982 Dawn Marie Evans (1d 1984; 1s 1986).

Evans, Elizabeth Ann (née McNab); On loan to the MOD since October 2002; Born 26/07/61; FCO 1998; Third Secretary (Visits, Press and Public Affairs) Peking 1999; Band C4; m 1987 Laurance Bolton Evans (1s 1989).

Evans, Gayle Evelyn Louise (née Sperring); SUPL since April 1997; Born 01/09/62; FCO 1983; Accra 1984; Moscow 1986; FCO 1987; Floater Duties 1990; SUPL 1991; New York (UKMIS) 1992; FCO 1996; Band B3; m 1991 Julian Ascott Evans (2d 1997, 1999).

Evans, Gerald Stanley; FCO since October 2003; Born 26/10/51; FCO 1971; Havana 1973; Bonn 1974; Jedda 1977; FCO 1977; Third Secretary and Vice-Consul Dubai 1979; FCO 1983; Third Secretary (Commercial) Bogotá 1986; Third Secretary (Management) Athens 1990; Second Secretary FCO 1994; Deputy Head of Mission Asunción 1996; Second Secretary (Commercial) Montevideo 2000; m 1991 Graciela Elisa Casetta.

Evans, Gillian; Zagreb since June 2003; Born 01/09/59; FCO 1981; Berlin (BMG) 1982; Kinshasa 1984; Africa/Asia/ME Floater 1988; Zagreb 1992; Damascus 1996; Rabat 2000; Band A2.

Evans, Jennifer Louise; FCO since July 2001; Born 07/11/78; Band C4; ptnr, Nicholas Cole.

Evans, Julian Ascott; Deputy High Commissioner Ottawa since July 2003; Born 05/07/57; FCO 1978; Language Training 1980; Moscow 1982; Zurich 1985; Second Secretary FCO 1987; Second later First Secretary New York (UKMIS) 1991; First Secretary FCO 1996; Deputy High Commissioner Islamabad 2002; m 1991 Gayle Evelyn Louise Sperring (2d 1997, 1999).

Evans, Karen-Lane (née Williams); FCO since December 1999; Born 09/04/63; FCO 1989; Second Secretary (Chancery) The Hague 1992; Second Secretary FCO 1996; SUPL 1998; Band C4; m 1998 Paul Lawson Evans.

Evans, Kelly Jane (née Sage), MVO (1996); FCO since May 2002; Born 29/01/68; FCO 1989; The Hague 1992; Third Secretary (Visits/Information) Warsaw 1994; Third Secretary FCO 1996; SUPL 2000; Band C4; m 2000 David Evans.

Evans, Peter Dering; Deputy Head of Mission Quito since September 2003; Born 09/04/57; FCO 1976; Dhaka 1978; FCO 1980; Barcelona 1985; San Salvador 1988; Third Secretary (Management/Accounts) Caracas 1990; Third later Second Secretary FCO 1993; Deputy Head of Mission Reykjavik 1998; m 1985 Susan Elizabeth Parker (2s 1987, 1989).

Evans, Stephen Nicholas, CMG (2002), OBE (1994); High Commissioner Colombo since July 2002; Born 29/06/50; Third Secretary FCO 1974; Language Training SOAS 1975; Second Secretary FCO 1976; Head of Chancery and Consul Hanoi 1978; FCO 1980; Language Training Bangkok 1982; First Secretary Bangkok 1983; First Secretary FCO 1986; First Secretary (Political) Ankara 1990; Counsellor (Economic/Commercial/Aid) Islamabad 1993; Secondment to United Nations Special Mission to Afghanistan 1996; Counsellor FCO 1997; m 1975 Sharon Ann Holdcroft (2d 1981, 1984; 1s 1986).

Evans, Stephen Paul, MBE (2003); Third Secretary (Consular) Singapore since July 2002; Born 28/10/57; HM Forces (Army) 1975; Police Constable 1997; FCO 2000; Band B3; m 1986 Julie Spackman (1s 1988; 1d 1990).

Evans, Stephen Shane; FCO since July 2001; Born 07/12/54; FCO 1992; Second Secretary Zagreb 1998; Band C4; m 1995 Susan Jane (1d 1987).

Evans, Wayne; First Secretary (Political) The Hague since July 2000; Born 29/08/53; FCO 1971; Paris 1974; Maseru 1977; FCO 1979; Baghdad 1981; Vienna 1984; FCO 1987; Second Secretary (Aid) Dhaka 1989; Second later First Secretary FCO 1993; Deputy Head of Mission and Consul (Commercial) Jedda 1996; Band C5; m 1982 Jennifer Mary Lewis (3d 1985, 1988, 1994; 1s 1997).

Evans, William John Eldred; Counsellor (Political) Kabul since August 2004; Born 13/04/71; FCO 1994; Language Training 1996; On loan to OHR Sarajevo 1997; Second Secretary (Political/Military) Sarajevo 1998; Second Secretary FCO 1999; First Secretary (Political) Tallinn 2002; Band D6.

Everard, John Vivian; HM Ambassador Pyongyang since January 2006; Born 24/11/56; FCO 1979; Third later Second Secretary Peking 1981; Second Secretary Vienna 1983; Resigned 1984; Reinstated, Second later First Secretary FCO 1987; First Secretary (Commercial) Santiago 1990; HM Ambassador Minsk 1993; OSCE Mission to Bosnia-Herzegovina 1995; Counsellor FCO 1996; Counsellor Peking 1998; HM Ambassador Montevideo 2001; m 1990 Heather Ann Starkey.

Everard, Thomas James; Tehran since June 2001; Born 11/08/75; FCO 1998; Band A2.

Everest, Philip Ralph; Third Secretary (Political/PPA) Port of Spain since October 2002; Born 25/03/74; FCO 1999; Band B3.

Everett, Sara Gillian; First Secretary FCO since October 2002; Born 06/07/55; FCO 1979; Assistant Private Secretary to Minister of State 1980; Paris (ENA) 1981; Caracas 1983; Deputy Presidency Co-ordinator Brussels (UKREP) 1986; Second Secretary (Economic/Agriculture) Brussels 1987; First Secretary FCO 1991; Deputy later Director New York (BIS) 1996; m 1989 Christopher Ian Montague Jones (1s 1994).

Everitt, Oliver Hunter; FCO since January 2002; Born 28/12/71; FCO 1992; Vienna 1995; Third Secretary (Immigration) Lusaka 1999; Band B3.

Everson, Clare Elizabeth; SUPL since November 1999; Born 20/12/59; FCO 1981; Karachi 1983; SE Asia Floater 1988; FCO 1990; Deputy High Commissioner Vila 1994; Band D6.

Ewart, Sharon Linda (née Acheson); SUPL since September 2004; Born 15/02/73; FCO 1992; Kuala Lumpur 1995; Third Secretary (Consular) Kingston 1997; Third Secretary (Chancery) later Second Secretary (PPA) Dublin 2001; Band C4; m 2002 Andrew Robert Ewart (1s 2004).

F

Fabrizi, Rebecca Jane (née Chesman); First Secretary (Political) Rome since May 2005; Born 31/10/72; FCO 1994; Full-Time Language Training (Mandarin) 1995; Second Secretary (Economic/Commercial) later First Secretary (Political) Beijing 1997; SUPL 2002; First Secretary (Trade and Development) Geneva (UKMIS) 2003; Band D6; m 2001 Sem Fabrizi (2s 2002, 2004).

Fairweather, Maria Louise (née Latta); SUPL since November 2001; Born 25/05/67; MOD 1986; FCO 1988; Berne 1989; FCO 1992; Peking 1993; T/D Kiev 1995; FCO 1996; Band B3; m 1993 Robert John Fairweather.

Fairweather, Robert John; Second Secretary Geneva (UKMIS) since April 2002; Born 26/02/67; HMCE 1987-96; FCO 1996; Band C4; m 1993 Marie Louise.

Falconer, Lynne Marie; FCO since 2004; Born 27/09/67; HM Forces 1986-95; FCO 1995; Helsinki 1997; Lisbon 2000; Band A2.

Fall, David William; HM Ambassador Bangkok since July 2003; Born 10/03/48; Third Secretary FCO 1971; Language Training Bangkok 1973; First Secretary Bangkok 1976; On loan to Cabinet Office 1977; FCO 1979; First Secretary (Chancery) Pretoria/Cape Town 1981; First Secretary later Counsellor FCO 1985; Deputy Head of Mission and Counsellor (Commercial) Bangkok 1990; Deputy High Commissioner Canberra 1993; HM Ambassador Hanoi 1997; Estate Modernisation Manager, FCO 2000; m

1973 Margaret Gwendolyn Richards (3s 1976, 1977, 1980).

Falzarano, Assuntina; Second Secretary (Chancery) New York (UKMIS) since December 2000; Born 10/08/73; FCO 1998; Band C4.

Farish, Sandra Mary (née Olley); SUPL since December 2004; Born 07/06/71; FCO 1995; Copenhagen 1996; Beirut 2000; FCO 2002; Band B3; m 1996 Joseph Farish (1d 2001).

Farnham, Brian George; FCO since March 2005; Born 16/04/52; FCO 1968; Paris 1974; FCO 1977; Baghdad 1978; FCO 1980; Tokyo 1981; FCO 1984; Hong Kong 1988; Second Secretary FCO 1991; Singapore 1995; FCO 1998; Paris 2000; Band C5; m 1982 Emiko Ishida (2d 1985, 1990).

Farnsworth, Lee; Caracas since October 2002; Born 28/01/71; FCO 1998; La Paz 1999; Band A2; m 2001 Audrey Giovanna (née Vergara Rojas).

Farr, Charles Blanford, OBE (2003); First Secretary FCO since February 1995; Born 15/07/59; Second Secretary FCO 1985; Second Secretary Pretoria 1987; Second Secretary FCO 1990; First Secretary (Chancery) Amman 1992; Band D6.

Farr, Dawn Margaret; Caracas since October 2002; Born 05/07/70; FCO 1989; Nicosia 1992; Mostar 1995; Seoul 1996; Bogotá 1997; Band B3.

Farrand, John Percival Morey; First Secretary (Consul) Havana since July 2002; Born 04/06/54; HM Customs and Excise 1971; FCO 1972; Tokyo 1974; Mexico City 1977; Kuala Lumpur 1981; FCO 1985; San Francisco 1988; FCO 1990; Second Secretary FCO 1991; Deputy High Commissioner Nassau 1994; First Secretary (Management) Ottawa 1997; Band C5; m 1979 Sharon Anne Eddie (3d 1980, 1982, 1987).

Farrare, Jane; Jerusalem since September 2000; Born 05/02/72; FCO 1999; Band A2.

Farrell, Sarah Jane; SUPL since February 2003; Born 27/06/69; FCO 1991; Lisbon 1995; Istanbul Floater 1998; FCO 1999; Taipei 1999; SUPL 1999; Taipei 2000; Band A2.

Farrent, Susan Jennifer; Karachi since April 2004; Born 17/01/48; FCO 1986; Monrovia 1987; Port Moresby 1991; Port of Spain 1992; FCO 1995; Bangkok 1996; Dhaka 2000; Band B3.

Farrey, Sonia Louise; Full-Time Language Training Damascus since May 2005; Born 21/01/77; FCO 2001; Band C4.

Farrow, Stephen Alan; Islamabad since May 2003; Born 23/07/56; Armed Forces 1972-96; FCO 1996; Dar es Salaam 1997; FCO 2002; Band B3; m 1979 Linda Alexis Jeffrey (1s 1979; 1d 1981).

Faulkner, Nicholas Anthony; Dhaka since October 2003; Born 19/05/72; FCO 1991; Bonn 1994; Brussels 1997; Bangkok 2000; Band B3.

Fawcett, Christine Anne; T/D Freetown since January 2004; Born 17/08/50; FCO 1968; Dar es Salaam 1971; Lima 1973; Havana 1976; Freetown 1977; FCO 1979; SEA Floater 1982; Belgrade 1983; FCO 1986 (Second Secretary 1989); Second Secretary (Management/ Consular) Port of Spain 1991; Second Secretary FCO 1993.

Fay, Jacqueline Ann (née Builder); SUPL since August 2003; Born 22/09/61; FCO 1980; Dhaka 1983; Peking 1985; Vice-Consul New York 1987; SUPL 1991; FCO 1991; Third Secretary (Management/Consular) Bratislava 1995; Singapore 1998; Band B3; m 1987 Kevin Michael Fay (1s 1990; 1d 1994).

Fean, Vincent; British High Commissioner Valletta since September 2002; Born 20/11/52; FCO 1975; MECAS 1977; Third Secretary Baghdad 1978; Gaborone 1979; Second later First Secretary Damascus 1979; FCO 1982; First Secretary Brussels (UKREP) 1985; First Secretary FCO 1990; Counsellor Paris 1992; FCO 1996; Director Asia Pacific, International Group of Trade Partners UK 1999; m 1978 Anne Marie Stewart (2d 1979, 1981; 1s 1983).

Fear, Harriet; Second Secretary (PPA) Dublin since November 2002; Born 11/08/68; Department of Employment 1986; FCO 1987; Dakar 1989; World Wide Floater Duties 1992; T/D Phnom Penh 1994; FCO 1994; Prague 1997; Band C4.

Fearis, Timothy Rupert; FCO since July 1989; Born 05/02/58; FCO 1979; Accra 1982; FCO 1984; Attaché Islamabad 1987; Band B3.

Fearn, Thomas Daniel; Deputy Head of Mission Sarajevo since January 2001; Born 16/09/62; FCO 1991; Second Secretary (Political) Budapest 1992; First Secretary FCO 1996; Band D6.

Feasey, Susan Catherine; FCO since August 2000; Born 08/05/64; FCO 1983; Vienna (UKMIS) 1985; Dakar 1988; FCO 1990; Riga 1992; FCO 1993; Floater Duties 1998; Band C4.

Feather, Helen Mary; Islamabad since April 2004; Born 02/01/63; FCO 1982; Moscow 1985; Gaborone 1988; Latin American/Caribbean Floater 1990; Third Secretary Brussels (UKDEL WEU) 1993; Third Secretary FCO 1994; DTI 1996; Third Secretary (Immigration) Dar es Salaam 1999; Second Secretary (Management) Dar es Salaam 2000; Band C4; m 1999 L. Ross Field.

Featherstone, Simon Mark; HM Ambassador, Berne additionally HM Ambassador (non-resident) Liechtenstein since March 2004; Born 24/07/58; FCO 1980; Language Training Hong Kong 1982; Second Secretary (Chancery) Peking 1984; First Secretary FCO 1987; On loan to the Cabinet Office 1988; First Secretary (Environment) Brussels (UKREP) 1990; HM Consul-General Shanghai 1994; Counsellor (Political and Economic) Peking 1996; Counsellor FCO 1998; m 1981 Gail Teresa Salisbury (2d 1985, 1992; 1s 1988).

Fehintola, Adebowale Bamidele; Copenhagen since May 2000; Born 14/11/67; FCO 1987; Copenhagen 1989; Sana'a 1992; Gaborone 1993; Band B3.

Fell, Richard Taylor, CVO (1996); British High Commissioner Wellington, also British High Commissioner (Non resident) Samoa, Governor (Non resident) of the Pitcairn, Henderson, Ducie and Oeno Islands since December 2001; Born 11/11/48; FCO 1971; Third Secretary Ottawa 1972; Second Secretary Saigon 1974; Vientiane 1975; Second later First Secretary FCO 1975; Chargé d'Affaires a.i. Hanoi 1979; Brussels (NATO) 1979; First Secretary and Head of Chancery Kuala Lumpur 1983; First Secretary FCO 1986; On secondment to Industry 1988; Counsellor (Comm/Econ) Ottawa 1989; Counsellor and Deputy Head of Mission Bangkok 1993; Counsellor FCO 1997; Consul-General T/D Toronto 2000; m 1981 Claire Peta Gates (3s 1983, 1987, 1990).

Felton, Ian; FCO since September 2003; Born 16/05/66; FCO 1986; Brussels 1987; Floater Duties 1990; FCO 1993; New York (ECOSOC)-(UKMIS) 1995-99; Deputy Head of Mission Phnom Penh 2000; Band D6.

Fenn, Robert Dominic Russell; Nicosia since September 2004; Born 28/01/62; FCO 1983; Third Secretary (Chancery) The Hague 1985; Second Secretary (Chancery) Lagos 1988; First Secretary FCO 1990; First Secretary New York (UKMIS) 1992; First Secretary (EU/Economic) Rome 1997; Team Leader Emed, EU-Mediterranean, EUD FCO 2001; m 2002 Julia Lloyd Williams (1s 2003).

Fennell, Leigh; FCO since 2004; Born 13/12/60; FCO 1982; Darwin 1986; FCO 1988; Third Secretary Accra 1993; FCO 1997; Amman 2000; Band C4.

Fenning, Camilla Jane Vance (née Packman); SUPL since January 1998; Born 29/04/64; FCO 1985; Language Training 1986; Tokyo 1987; Second later First Secretary FCO 1990; SUPL 1992; FCO 1993; SUPL 1995; FCO 1995; m 1988 Richard John Fenning. (1s 1993; 1d 1995).

Fenton, Jennifer Muriel; Second Secretary (Consular) Muscat since June 2004; Born 30/12/57; Home Civil Service 1976; FCO 1977; Beirut 1980; Floater Duties 1982; Singapore 1984; SUPL 1986; FCO 1987; New Delhi 1989; Mbabane 1993; Second Secretary FCO 1996; Second Secretary (Management) Valletta 1999; (1d 1986).

Ferguson, Christine Julia; Deputy Head of Mission Vienna since July 2004; Born 05/10/57; FCO 1982; Language Training 1983; Second Secretary Cairo 1985; Second later First Secretary FCO 1987; First Secretary Geneva (UKDIS) 1990; FCO 1998; m 1990 Michael (later Sir Michael) Charles Swift Weston (1s 1993; 1d 1996).

Ferguson, Iain; FCO since July 2003; Born 18/02/70; FCO 1990; Lagos 1995; Vice-Consul Tokyo 1999; Band C4; m 1994 Helen Jane Lennie.

Ferguson, Jean McCauley; FCO since June 2002; Born 08/10/55; Department of Employment 1985; Inland Revenue 1988; FCO 1988; ECO/Vice-Consul Kathmandu 1999; Band C5; (1d 1975).

Fergusson, George Duncan; Cabinet Office since October 2003; Born 30/09/55; NIO 1978, Private Secretary to NIO Minister of State 1982-83; First Secretary Dublin 1988; Transferred to Diplomatic Service 1990; First Secretary FCO 1991; First Secretary (Political/Information)) Seoul 1993; First Secretary FCO 1996; Counsellor FCO 1997; Consul-General Boston 1999; m 1981 Margaret Wookey (3d 1982, 1986, 1991; 1s 1984).

Fern, Deborah Jeanne (née Keith); Lagos since March 2005; Born 01/07/68; FCO 1988; Tokyo 1990; Floater Duties 1993; SUPL 1995; FCO 1996; Full-Time Language Training 2000; Montreal 2000; Band C4; m 1999 Steven Rennie Fern.

Ferrand, Simon Piers; Private Secretary to the Ambassador Berlin since August 2004; Born 05/03/68; FCO 1989; Kinshasa 1991; Paris 1996; BTI 1999; FCO 2002; Band C4; m 1995 Bettina Barbara Paustian (2s 1998, 2002).

Fewster, Miles Nicholas, MBE (1991); Second Secretary FCO since August 1999; Born 26/08/62; FCO 1982; Khartoum 1985; Riyadh 1989; FCO 1992; Second Secretary (Political) Nairobi 1996; Band C4; m 1986 Alexandria Fusco (3d 1992, 1993, 1998).

Fidler, Martin Alfred; FCO since January 2003; Born 10/12/53; DHSS 1972; FCO 1974; Belmopan 1977; Africa/ME Floater 1980; Havana 1981; Third Secretary New York (UKMIS) 1984; FCO 1987; Nuku'alofa 1989; Gibraltar 1992; FCO 1996; Deputy High Commissioner Belmopan 1999; Band C5; m 1981 Nicky Williams (2s 1982, 1985).

Field, Robert; Second Secretary FCO since November 1995; Born 04/01/53; FCO 1971; Karachi 1975; Far East Floater 1979; Second Secretary (Commercial) Harare 1982; Second Secretary FCO 1987; Second Secretary (Management) Addis Ababa 1992.

Fielder, John; HM Consul/ECM Manila since July 2003; Born 27/06/47; CO (later Commonwealth Office) 1966; HM Forces 1967-73; FCO 1974; Accra 1976; Nassau 1977; Prague 1980; SE Asia/FE Floater 1982; FCO 1987; Second Secretary (Management/Consular) Maputo 1990; HM Consul Tel Aviv 1994; FCO 2002.

Fielder, Richard John; Second Secretary (Management) Lusaka since June 2002; Born 28/03/52; FCO 1971; Tokyo 1974; FCO 1975; Stockholm 1978; Khartoum 1981; FCO 1982; Dhaka 1985; Chicago 1988; Freetown 1990; FCO 1995; Second Secretary Ottawa 1997; m 1988

Samantha Louise Monton (3d 1988, 1993, 1996; 2s 1990, 2005).

Fieller, Daniel Richard Charles; FCO since September 2002; Born 14/07/78; Band B3; ptnr, Danielle Thomas.

Finch, Peter Leonard; FCO since November 1997; Born 01/01/58; FCO 1975; Geneva (UKMIS) 1978; Tel Aviv 1981; New Delhi 1983; FCO 1986; Tokyo 1991; Manila 1994; Band D6; m 1979 Mitsue Uchida (ld 1990).

Findlay, Matthew Ross; FCO since August 2002; Born 02/05/68; FCO 1996; Full-Time Language Training Bangkok 1998; Second Secretary (Political) Bangkok 1999; Band D6.

Fines, Barry John; FCO since April 2003; Born 13/09/69; FCO 1988; New Delhi 1991; FCO 1994; Lagos 1997; SUPL 2002; Band B3; m 1997 Monika Graf (2s 2002, 2004).

Finlay, Norah Ferguson Watson; Shanghai since January 2002; Born 13/04/70; FCO 1989; Singapore 1992; Islamabad 1995; Band A2.

Finlayson, Sharon Christine; FCO since June 2002; Born 04/05/58; Band A2; m 1976 Alexander Finlayson (dec'd 2004) (2d 1980, 1982).

Finley, Robert William; Sofia since December 2004; Born 21/08/68; FCO 2002; Band D6; m 1997 Claire Walker.

Finnamore Crorkin, Joanne Lynn; Second Secretary (Commercial) Tripoli since March 2002; Born 22/09/63; FCO 1982; Moscow 1984; Colombo 1985; Floater Duties 1989; SUPL 1992; Consulate-General New York 1992; FCO 1994; Second Secretary 1996; Lagos 1997; m 1991 Colin Wynn Crorkin (1d 1998).

Finnerty, Kevin John; FCO since February 2001; Born 01/02/49; FCO 1967; Kuwait 1970; Warsaw 1974; FCO 1976; Full-Time Language Training 1978; FCO 1979; Mogadishu 1983; Chicago 1985; Second Secretary FCO 1989; Full-Time Language Training 1992; Düsseldorf 1993; First Secretary and Consul Washington 1997; m (1) 1970 Sandra Tidy (diss 1982); (2) 1982 Norma Collins.

Firmstone, Imogen Joan; Santiago since January 2005; Born 21/06/74; FCO 1999; Havana 2002; FCO 2004; Band B3.

Firstbrook, Steven Paul; HM Consul Rabat since June 2005; Born 22/02/70; FCO 1989; Helsinki 1992; World-Wide Floater Duties 1994; FCO 1996; Second Secretary (Commercial) Mumbai 2000; Deputy High Commissioner Nassau 2004; Band C5; m 1997 Marie Joelle (née Nicole) (1d 2005).

Firth, Catherine Alison Jane (née Readdie); Deputy Head of Mission Rangoon since January 2005; Born 17/06/66; FCO 1990; Third Secretary (Chancery) Warsaw 1992; FCO 1994; Vice Consul Caracas 1995; FCO 1998; Full-Time Language Training 2001; First Secretary (Political) Mexico City 2001; Band C5; m 1994 Andrew Charleson Firth (1d 2002; 1s 2003).

Fisher, Deborah Joan; Deputy Head of Mission Addis Ababa since April 2004; Born 04/03/62; FCO 1985; Second Secretary (Chancery) Dar es Salaam 1988; First Secretary FCO 1991; SUPL 1996; FCO 1997; Paris 2002; m 1992 William James Lodge.

Fisher, Deryck John; FCO since September 2003; Born 26/07/46; Inland Revenue 1961; Department of Technical Co-operation, ODA 1964; FCO 1973; Kinshasa 1975; Islamabad 1978; Second Secretary FCO 1980; Second Secretary (Consular) Accra 1983; First Secretary (Admin/Consul) Copenhagen 1987; First Secretary FCO 1991; First Secretary (Management) Dhaka 1996; First Secretary (Management) Bangkok 2000; Band D6; m 1973 Lynda Elizabeth Robinson (2d 1974, 1975; 3s 1976, 1979, 1983).

Fisher, Emily Caroline Gay (née Shapland); SUPL since June 2005; Born 05/05/72; FCO 1997; Lusaka 1998; First Secretary (Political) Buenos Aires 2000; FCO 2004; Band D6; m 1998 Roland Barnabas Fisher.

Fisher, Gary John; Management Consultancy Reviewer FCO since August 2004; Born 27/12/69; FCO 1989; Peking 1992; Third Secretary Düsseldorf 1996; Second Secretary Bahrain 2000; Second Secretary (Euro 2004 Football Attaché) Lisbon 2003; Band C4; (1s 1998).

Fisher, John; Counsellor FCO since April 2003; Born 03/08/48; Third later Second Secretary FCO 1974; Language student SOAS 1975 and Bursar 1976; Second Secretary (Inf) Ankara 1976; First Secretary FCO 1979; Vienna (UKMIS) IAEA 1982; First Secretary FCO 1986; Counsellor Santiago 1993; Counsellor FCO 1997; Counsellor (Political) Jakarta 1999; m 1970 Lynette Joyce Corinne Growcott (1d 1978; 1s 1980).

Fisher, Miles Lyndon; SUPL since March 1999; Born 28/11/61; FCO 1981; Vienna 1995.

Fisher, Simon John; FCO since July 2005; Born 08/06/59; FCO 1983; Athens 1985; Language Training Kamakura 1989; Tokyo 1990; Osaka 1992; Second later First Secretary FCO 1996; Deputy Head of Mission Hanoi 1999 and 2001; On loan to the Population Council, Hanoi 2000; Director Trade Cairo 2002;Band D6.

Fisher, Steven Mark; Deputy Head of Mission Caracas since July 2002; Born 07/02/65; FCO 1993; Second Secretary (Economic/Commercial) Singapore 1995; FCO 1998; Band D6; m 1990 Linda Westwood (3s 1993, 1995, 1997).

Fisher, Timothy Dirk Colomb; First Secretary (Management) Jakarta since June 2003; Born 23/08/47; FCO 1975; Moscow 1976; FCO 1977; Port Moresby 1978; Nairobi 1981; FCO 1985; Colombo 1987; Third later Second Secretary (Aid) Jakarta 1991; FCO 1995; Second Secretary (Management) Hanoi 1998; m 1992 Patricia-Jane Van Der Vooren (1d 1993; 1s 1994).

Fisher, Timothy Sinnett; FCO since May 2004; Born 15/07/71; FCO 1998; Third Secretary

(Political) Kigali 2000; Band C4; m 2000 Joanna Dinnen.

Fishwick, Nicholas Bernard Frank; Counsellor FCO since July 2004; Born 23/02/58; FCO 1983; Language Training 1986; First Secretary (Inf) Lagos 1988; First Secretary FCO 1991; Consul (Political Affairs) Istanbul 1994; First Secretary FCO 1997; Seconded to HM Customs and Excise 2001; m 1987 Susan Thérésa Rouane Mendel (2s 1987, 1995; 1d 1989).

Fitch, Diana May (née Francis); Seoul since August 2002; Born 26/12/53; FCO 1975; Dar es Salaam 1976; Tortola 1977; FCO 1981; SE Asia Floater 1984; Singapore 1986; FCO 1988; Second Secretary Honiara 1995; FCO 1998; m Geoffrey William Fitch (1s 1988; 1d 1993).

Fitchett, Robert Duncan; Deputy Head of Mission Manila since August 2003; Born 10/06/61; FCO 1983; Dakar 1984; Second Secretary (Chancery) Bonn 1988; First Secretary FCO 1990; First Secretary on loan to the Cabinet Office 1993; Paris 1994; FCO 1998; m 1985 Adèle Thérèsa Hajjar (1s 1987; 2d 1988, 1993).

Fitton, David John, CMG (2004); Deputy Head of Mission Ankara since January 2001; Born 10/01/55; FCO 1980; Language Training Kamakura 1982; Second later First Secretary (Economics) Tokyo 1983; FCO 1986; First Secretary (Chancery) New Delhi 1990; First Secretary FCO 1994; Head of Chancery Tokyo 1996; m 1989 Hisae Iijima (1d 1996; 1s 1999).

Fitton-Brown, Edmund Walter; Counsellor Riyadh since April 2005; Born 05/10/62; FCO 1984; Third later Second Secretary Helsinki 1987; Second Secretary FCO 1989; First Secretary 1991; Language Training Cairo 1991; First Secretary FCO 1992; First Secretary (Political) Cairo 1993; First Secretary FCO 1996; First Secretary (Political) Kuwait 1998; FCO 2001; Counsellor Cairo 2003; m 1995 Julie Ann Herring (1d 1996; 1s 1998).

Fitton-Brown, Julie Ann (née Herring); SUPL since August 1994; Born 10/04/65; FCO 1984; Helsinki 1987; FCO 1989; SUPL 1993; Cairo 1994; Band B3; m 1995 Edmund Walter Fitton-Brown (1d 1996; 1s 1998).

FitzGerald, Jillian (née Lane); Second Secretary (Management) Rome since May 2002; Born 29/01/69; FCO 1989; Bonn 1992; Islamabad 1995; SUPL 1997; FCO 1998; Band B3; m 1998 Paul Edward FitzGerald (1s 1997; 1d 2000).

Fitzgerald-Prono, Antonia (née Fitzgerald); FCO since September 1999; Born 13/06/71; FCO 1990; Brasilia 1991; Brussels (UKDel WEU) 1995; Paris 1996; SUPL 1999; m 1999 Raphael Jacques Gerard Prono (1s 1999).

Flaherty, Shaun David; First Secretary (Management) Cairo since June 2001; Born 29/01/66; FCO 1984; Washington 1987; Ankara 1990; Lagos 1992; FCO 1996; Band C5.

Flear, Timothy Charles Fitzranulf, MVO (1989); FCO since May 2000; Born 22/01/58; FCO 1980; Third Secretary (Comm/Inf) Dubai 1982; Resigned and reinstated, FCO 1985; Third later Second Secretary Kuala Lumpur 1987; Second Secretary FCO 1991 (APS/Minister of State 1993); First Secretary (Economic) later First Secretary (Investment) subsequently First Secretary (Political) Seoul 1996; ptnr, Christopher Curtain.

Flessati, Francesca Josephine Giovanna, OBE (2003); First Secretary (Political) Athens since April 1999; Born 27/10/58; FCO 1990; Language Training 1991; Third Secretary (Aid) Moscow 1992; FCO 1996; m 1985 Nicholas John Foster.

Fletcher, Patricia Anne (née Jones); Lisbon since August 2002; Born 12/05/70; FCO 1989; Bonn 1991; FCO 1993; Brasilia 1994; SUPL 1999; FCO 2000; Band B3; m 1993 Richard Fletcher (1s 1996; 1d 1999).

Fletcher, Patricia May; FCO since January 2002; Born 08/09/42; FCO 1983; Berlin (BMG) 1984; Tortola 1986; FCO 1988; Brussels (UKDEL) 1990; FCO 1991; Munich 1994; Tel Aviv 1997; Second Secretary (Management) Beirut 2000; Band C4; m 1974 Herbert Fletcher (dec'd 1986) (1s 1978).

Fletcher, Thomas Stuart Francis; First Secretary (Political) Paris since September 2004; Born 27/03/75; FCO 1997; Nairobi 1998; Private Secretary to Baroness Amos later Chris Mullin FCO 2002; Band D6.

Fleurot, Tracey Marjorie (née Critoph); Gaborone since February 2002; Born 26/08/64; FCO 1988; Jakarta 1990; Port Louis 1994; FCO 1997; Bombay 1998; Band A2; m 1997 M J E Fleurot.

Flint, David Leonard; Liaison Officer Gibraltar since April 2001; Born 21/10/56; FCO 1975; Budapest 1979; Jedda 1980; FCO 1984; Athens 1986; Lagos 1990; Second Secretary FCO 1994; Deputy High Commissioner Gaborone 1997; m 1984 Mary Anne Elizabeth Goodale (3s twins 1986, 1988).

Flint, John David; Antigua since May 2001; Born 05/11/69; FCO 1996; Third Secretary (Political/PPA) Tallinn 1998; Band B3; m 1998 Sally Brazier.

Flisher, Nigel Frederick; FCO since December 1999; Born 20/04/53; FCO 1971; Singapore 1974; Vientiane 1978; Colombo 1979; FCO 1982; Islamabad 1984; Third Secretary (Passports/Visas) Dublin 1988; FCO 1991; Second Secretary 1994; Second Secretary (Immigration) Moscow 1996; m 1977 Valerie Tay Kim Heok (1d 1978; 1s 1980).

Floyd, Linda Vivienne (née Colvin); Kuala Lumpur since May 2002; Born 17/03/65; FCO 1987; New Delhi 1989; SUPL 1991; Georgetown 1994; SUPL 1997; FCO 1999; SUPL 2000; Band A2; m 1990 Neil Floyd (1d 1991; 2s 1993, 1995).

Floyd, Neil; Second Secretary (Commercial) Kuala Lumpur since September 2000; Born

20/05/67; FCO 1987; New Delhi 1989; Warsaw 1991; Georgetown 1993; FCO 1997; Band C4; m 1990 Linda Vivienne Colvin (1d 1991; 2s 1993, 1995).

Foakes, Joanne Sarah; SUPL since August 2001; Born 09/03/57; Called to the Bar, Inner Temple 1979; FCO 1984; Deputy Principal Crown Counsel Hong Kong 1991; Assistant Legal Adviser FCO 1994; SUPL 1995; Legal Counsellor 1997.

Foley, Victoria Beth Louise; FCO since December 1986; Born 23/06/60; FCO 1978; Budapest 1982; Paris 1984; Band B3.

Folker, Nicholas Mark; FCO since March 2005; Born 20/05/67; FCO 1989; Singapore 2000; Band C4; m 1998 Laura Elizabeth Samm (1d 2000).

Folland, Richard Dudley; Deputy Consul General Düsseldorf and Deputy Director of Trade and Investment in Germany since August 2000; Born 10/03/61; FCO 1981; Moscow 1983; Third Secretary (Consular/Management) Gaborone 1985; FCO 1988; Second Secretary (Political/Inf) Stockholm 1991; First Secretary FCO 1996; On secondment to British Aerospace 1998; m 1985 Gwen Alison Evans (2s 1989, 1993).

Folliss, Tarquin Simon Archer; Counsellor Copenhagen since September 2001; Born 23/10/57; HM Forces 1981-86; Second Secretary FCO 1986; Second later First Secretary (Chancery) Jakarta 1989; First Secretary FCO 1992; First Secretary Bucharest 1995; First Secretary FCO 1998; Band D6; m 1991 Anne Mary Segar (1d 1996; 2s 1998, 1999).

Fontaine-Harvey, Joan; SUPL since August 2003; Born 03/10/67; FCO 1990; Dubai 2000; Band B3; m 1999 Christopher Antonio Harvey.

Foote, Daniel Edward; Third Secretary (Deputy Management Officer) Freetown since August 2001; Born 11/02/46; Royal Navy 1965-90; Moscow 1991; Lagos 1992; Abuja 1994; FCO 1996; Pretoria 1997; Band B3; m 1967 Carol Elizabeth Combe (2d 1970, 1971).

Forbes, Lachlan Pelly Ferrar; First Secretary Baku since December 2002; Born 24/04/70; Second Secretary FCO 1996; Second Secretary (Political) Nairobi 1998; FCO 2001; Band D6; m 1999 Melanie Fiona Knights (1s 2000).

Forbes, Matthew Keith; First Secretary (Political) Wellington since October 2002; Born 19/04/66; FCO 1987; Peking 1989; Colombo 1990; FCO 1995; Deputy High Commissioner Maseru 1999; Band C5; m 1988 Lydia Mary Bagg (2s 1989, 1991; 1d 1994).

Forbes, Melanie Fiona (née Knights); FCO since May 2001; Born 03/03/64; FCO 1996; Second Secretary (Political) Nairobi 1999; Band C4; m 1999 Lachlan Pelly Ferrar Forbes (1s 2000).

Forbes Batey, Darren Francis; Second Secretary (Consular) Nairobi since June 2003; Born 09/01/66; FCO 1984; Rabat 1987; Kampala 1990; FCO 1993; Third Secretary (Management) Dublin 1996; Third Secretary (Commercial) Dubai 2000; Band C4; m 1993 Sarah Frances Trevelyan (1d 1995, 1s 1998).

Ford, Andrew James Ford, MVO (1995); First Secretary Vienna since September 2004; Born 21/06/64; FCO 1987; Third Secretary (Chancery/Information/Consular) Georgetown 1990; Third Secretary (Political) Pretoria/Cape Town 1993; Second Secretary FCO 1996; Second later First Secretary (Commercial) Mexico City 2000; m 1994 Claudeli Edna Dos Santos Silva (2 step d 1985, 1987).

Ford, Peter William; HM Ambassador Damascus since September 2003; Born 27/06/47; Third Secretary FCO 1970; MECAS 1971; Beirut 1973; Second later First Secretary Cairo 1974; First Secretary FCO 1977; ENA Paris 1980; First Secretary Paris 1981; First Secretary FCO 1985; Counsellor (Comm) Riyadh 1987; University of Harvard 1990; Counsellor Singapore 1991; Counsellor FCO 1994; HM Ambassador Bahrain 1999; m (1) 1975 Aurora Raquel Garcia Mingo (diss 1991), (2) 1992 Alganesh Haile Beyene.

Forman, Matthew; FCO since January 2004; Born 17/06/76; Band C5.

Forrester, Emma-Louise; Port Stanley since December 2004; Born 22/03/80; FCO 2002; Band A2.

Forrester, Mark Adrian; Second Secretary (Management) Oslo since October 2003; Born 29/06/59; FCO 1978; Geneva (UKMIS) 1980; Santiago 1983; Third Secretary FCO 1986; Dhaka 1989; Third Secretary (Management/Consular) Nuku'alofa 1992; Second Secretary FCO 1995; Second Secretary (Management) Hong Kong 1999; m 1982 Deborah Cannell (1d 1987; 1s 1990).

Forrester, Sally Joanne (née Watmough); Pretoria since April 2004; Born 22/05/64; FCO 1984; Belgrade 1987; FCO 1989; Buenos Aires 1990; FCO 1992; Vienna 1994; SUPL 1997; FCO 2000; Band A2; m 1993 Guy Hamilton Forrester (1d 1995; 1s 1998).

Forrester, Stuart Russell; FCO since January 2003; Born 10/02/62; FCO 1983; Washington 1990; FCO 1994; Moscow 2000; Band C4; m 1990 Deborah Channon.

Forryan, Anne May; SUPL since November 1999; Born 03/08/66; FCO 1990; Düsseldorf 1993; Vice-Consul Madrid 1996 (SUPL 1997); Madrid 1997; Band B3; m 1996 Joaquin Rodriguez-Toubes Muniz.

Forsyth, Brian Gilbert; FCO since November 2003; Born 27/02/65; FCO 1984; Bucharest 1987; Dhaka 1989; FCO 1992; Third Secretary Cairo 1996; Third later Second Secretary (Political) Doha 1999; Band C4; m 1987 Marie Boyle (1s 1989; 1d 1992).

Forsyth, Marie (née Boyle); FCO since November 2003; Born 26/04/66; FCO 1984; Mexico City 1986; SUPL 1987; Dhaka 1990; FCO 1993; Cairo

1996; Management Officer/Vice Consul Doha 1999; SUPL 2000; Third Secretary (Commercial) Doha 2000; Band C4; m 1987 Brian Gilbert Forsyth (1s 1989; 1d 1992).

Fortescue, Dominic James Lewis; Counsellor FCO since September 2004; Born 09/10/66; FCO 1991; Second Secretary (Political) Pretoria 1993; Cape Town 1995; Second later First Secretary FCO 1996; First Secretary New York (UKMIS) 2000; m 1990 Cathleen Rolls (2s 2001, 2003).

Fossaluzza, Lydia; T/D Madrid since October 2004; Born 12/03/64; FCO 1996; Buenos Aires 1999; Band A2.

Foster, Hazel; FCO since May 1998; Born 10/04/69; FCO 1989; Ankara 1991; World Wide Floater duties 1996; Band B3.

Foster, Joelene; FCO since October 2002; Born 27/11/73; Band B3; ptnr, Peter Josse.

Foster, John Michael; Second Secretary (Commercial) Caracas since March 2003; Born 07/05/55; FCO 1989; New Delhi 1991; Third Secretary Tel Aviv 1994; FCO 1997; Band C4; m 1986 Julie Bearfoot.

Foster, Julie Maria (née Bearfoot); Consul/Management Officer Caracas since February 2003; Born 19/12/59; FCO 1978; Brussels (UKDEL NATO) 1981; Doha 1983; FCO 1987; Third Secretary New Delhi 1991; Tel Aviv 1994; On loan to the DTI 1997; Second Secretary FCO 1998; Band C5; m 1986 John Michael Foster.

Foster, Sarah Louise; Madrid since June 2003; Born 04/11/73; FCO 1992; Assistant to Lord Owen (International Conference on Former Yugoslavia) 1993; UKMIS later UKDEL later Chancery Vienna 1995; Tokyo 2000; Band B3.

Foulcer, Monique Antoinette (née Twigg); First Secretary (Management) The Hague since January 2003; Born 22/07/64; DTI 1985; FCO 1987; Kinshasa 1989; Third Secretary (Chancery) Geneva (UKDIS) 1992; FCO 1995; SUPL 1997; Second Secretary (Political) Paris 1998; SUPL 1999; FCO 2000; Band C5; m 1995 Kevin Andrew Foulcer (1s 1998).

Foulds, Sarah Ann; SUPL since September 1998; Born 10/08/57; FCO 1979; PRO (Band D6) 1987; First Secretary FCO 1992; First Secretary Geneva (UKMIS) 1995; m(1) 1981 (diss 1995) (1d 1985; 1s 1988), m(2) 1999 Peter Van Wulfften Palthe (3 step d).

Fox, Alexander Norman Robson; Full-Time Language Training Cairo since September 2004; Born 20/09/77; FCO 2001; Band C4.

Fox, Christopher Roderick Henry; FCO since 2003; Born 19/09/70; FCO 1991; Ankara 2000; Band C4; m 2001 Leigh McCallum Forbes (2s 2001, 2003).

Fox, Ian David; Bratislava since November 2003; Born 02/06/66; FCO 1987; Peking 1988; Floater Duties 1991; FCO 1993; Secondment to London Chamber of Commerce 1995; Dubai 1997; Casablanca 2000; Band C4; m 1993 Alison Elizabeth Margaret Bain (1s 1998; 1d 2000).

Fox, John Frederick; First Secretary (Political) Beijing since September 2003; Born 09/04/75; FCO 1997; Brussels 1999; SUPL 1999; FCO 2000; Full-Time Language Training (Mandarin) 2002; Band C4.

Fox, Michael Roger; FCO since January 2005; Born 09/07/58; FCO 1988; Consul Geneva 1993; FCO 1997; First Secretary (Regional Affairs) Rabat 2003; Band C5; m 1993 Charlotte Jane Gray.

Fox, Paul Leonard; Head of Iraq Policy Unit FCO since May 2005; Born 24/07/62; FCO 1987; New Delhi 1990; Baku 1994; Bangkok 1996; FCO 1999 later Counsellor FCO 2005; m 1991 Vicki Ann Rathbun (3d 1997, 1998, 2002).

Foxwell, Rachael Louise; FCO since September 2001; Born 29/10/59; FCO 1982; Africa/Middle East Floater 1984; Harare 1985; Third later Second Secretary Hanoi 1988; Second Secretary FCO 1991; Tunis 1992; First Secretary (Economic/Commercial) Wellington 1999; (1d 1991).

Francis, John Alexander; Baghdad since July 2004; Born 14/12/42; FO 1962; Athens 1964; Beirut 1964; Stockholm 1965; Seoul 1968; Malta 1971; Paris 1972; FCO 1972; Dacca 1975; Prague 1979; Kaduna 1981; Second Secretary FCO 1983; Consul Bangkok 1988; First Secretary (Management) Ankara 1992; First Secretary (Management/Consular) Seoul 1996; HM Consul Kuwait 1999; m 1981 Grace Engelen.

Francis, Lindsay (née Harvey); Moscow since January 2005; Born 31/03/59; FCO 1984; Tehran 1986; Budapest 1987; Bridgetown 1988; FCO 1993; SUPL 1993; Grand Cayman 1997; Washington 2001; Band B3; m 2001 Paul Richard Francis.

Franklin, Joanna Mary Clare; SUPL since November 2000; Born 12/08/60; FCO 1978; Peking 1981; FCO 1982; Cairo 1986; Yaoundé 1989; FCO 1990; Beirut 1994; FCO 1997; Canberra 1998; Band C4; m 1988 Habib Elie Gouel.

Franklin-Brown, Alexander, MBE (2002); Second Secretary (Chancery) Muscat since November 2001; Born 30/03/72; FCO 1991; Full-Time Language Training 1996; Third Secretary (Chancery) Riyadh 1997; Third Secretary (Commercial) Al Khobar 1999; Band B3.

Fransella, Cortland Lucas; Counsellor FCO since September 1995; Born 09/09/48; Third Secretary FCO 1970; Language Training Hong Kong 1971; Assistant Trade Commissioner Hong Kong 1973; Second later First Secretary FCO 1975; Kuala Lumpur 1980; Santiago 1982; FCO 1986; Counsellor (Political) Rome 1991; m 1977 Laura Ruth Propper (2s 1979, 1981).

Frape, Neil Jeremy; ECO Georgetown since December 2004; Born 16/11/63; FCO 1984; Addis

Ababa 1986; Paris 1990; FCO 1992; Full-Time Language Training 1995; Vice-Consul (Press and Public Affairs) Istanbul 1996; Kuwait 2000; Band B3; m 1987 Christine Mary Allen (1d 1989; 1s 1992).

Frary, Helen Elizabeth; SUPL since January 1999; Born 23/02/69; FCO 1988; New Delhi 1991; Third later Second Secretary (United Nations) Geneva (UKMIS) 1995; Band C4.

Fraser, James Terence; First Secretary (Commercial) Zagreb since May 2002; Born 12/04/49; GPO 1966; FCO 1967; Nicosia 1971; Johannesburg 1972; Prague 1974; Africa Floater 1975; FCO 1978; Vice-Consul (Information) Düsseldorf 1981; Language Training 1983; Commercial Attaché Baghdad 1984; FCO 1988; Deputy Head of Political and Information Section later Head of Consular Section Ottawa 1993; First Secretary (Management) and HM Consul Copenhagen 1997; m 1988 Nada Babic (1s 1992; 1d 1995).

Fraser, Simon James; SUPL since December 2004; Born 03/06/58; FCO 1979; Third later Second Secretary Baghdad 1982; Second Secretary (Chancery) Damascus 1984; First Secretary FCO 1986 (Private Secretary to Minister of State) 1989; First Secretary (Economic) Paris 1994; Counsellor on secondment to the EU Commission 1996; Deputy Chef de Cabinet of the Vice President of the EU Commission 1997; Counsellor (Political) Paris 1999; Director for Strategy and Innovation FCO 2002; m 2003 Shireen Patel (1d 1993).

Frater, Charlene Adele; FCO since October 2002; Born 28/07/76; Band A2.

Frean, Christopher William; Deputy Head of Mission Kigali since November 2002; Born 31/07/64; HCS 1988; FCO 1990; Abidjan 1992; Third Secretary (Immigration) Karachi 1995; FCO 1997; Third later Second Secretary Abidjan 1999; Band B3; m 1994 Aya Esperance Gbakatchetche (2d 1995, 1996).

Freel, Philip John; FCO since December 1997; Born 24/12/55; FCO 1974; Paris 1976; Mogadishu 1979; Lisbon 1980; Addis Ababa 1983; FCO 1985; On loan to CAD, Hanslope Park 1986; Lagos 1987; Rome 1991; FCO 1992; Second Secretary (Management) Cape Town 1996; m 1977 Joan Winifred Hill (1d 1979; 1s 1986).

Freeman, Andrew John; First Secretary Geneva (UKDIS) since March 2004; Born 24/09/72; FCO 1995; Band D6.

Freeman, Judith Louise; FCO since 2004; Born 24/03/61; FCO 1984; Berne 1985; East Berlin 1989; Floater Duties 1991; FCO 1994; Luxembourg 1996; Geneva (UKMIS) 2000; Band B3.

Freeman, Timothy John; SUPL since July 2004; Born 24/04/65; FCO 1989; Paris 1992; Honiara 1996; Third Secretary (Aid/Chancery) Gibraltar 1997; Third Secretary (Passports/Visas) Dublin 2001; Band B3.

Freeman, Wendy Paula; FCO since 2002; Born 09/03/61; FCO 1980; Bonn 1982; Africa/ME Floater 1985; Abidjan 1988; FCO 1992; Kingston 1997; Beirut 2000; Band C4; ptnr, Richard Lethbridge (2d 2001, 2003).

French, Roger; Counsellor (Management) and Consul-General Tokyo since July 2003; Born 03/06/47; FCO 1965; Havana 1970; Vice-Consul Madrid 1971; San Juan 1973; FCO 1977; Second later First Secretary (Chancery) Washington 1980; First Secretary (Commercial) Muscat 1985; Deputy Head North America Dept FCO 1988; Deputy Consul-General Milan 1992; Counsellor (Management) and Consul General Washington 1997; Acting Deputy High Commissioner Abuja 2001; Head of Information Management Group FCO 2001; m 1969 Angela Joyce Cooper (1d 1974; 1s 1980).

Friel, Nicola; FCO since April 2002; Born 08/03/70; FCO 1989; Washington 1992; Moscow 1995; Floater Duties 1998; Band B3.

Friis, Andrew Stuart; FCO since March 2002; Born 04/04/60; Metropolitan Police 1981; FCO 1982; Kuwait 1986; FCO 1988; Hong Kong 1997; Band C5; m 1989 Maria Carina Lumatan Reyes (1s 1991; 1d 1994).

Friston, Paula Jane; Washington since September 2002; Born 27/01/69; FCO 1992; Washington 1996; Algiers 1999; FCO 2001; Band B3.

Frizzel, Squadron Leader John Stewart; Queen's Messenger since 1989; Born 12/07/46; HM Forces 1966-89.

Frost, David George Hamilton; Head of European Union (Internal), FCO since June 2003; Born 21/02/65; FCO 1987; Third Secretary Nicosia 1989; Resigned 1990, reinstated 1992; First Secretary Brussels (UKREP) 1993; First Secretary New York (UKMIS) 1996; FCO 1998; Counsellor (EU/Economic) Paris 2001; m 1993 Jacqueline Elizabeth Dias (1d 1998).

Frost, Michael Reginald, OBE (2001); First Secretary (Political) Abuja since July 2004; Born 02/12/52; FCO 1971; Prague 1974; Dar es Salaam 1976; Peking 1979; FCO 1982; Washington 1984; Consul (Political/Inf) Cape Town 1986; First Secretary (Aid/Comm) Kampala 1991; First Secretary FCO 1994; First Secretary (Political) Lagos 1996; First Secretary (Political) Pretoria 2000; Band D6; m 1973 Marie Thérésa McGlynn.

Frost, Simon Jaye; SUPL since February 2003; Born 24/05/70; FCO 1990; World-Wide Floater Duties 1993; T/D Mostar 1995; FCO 1996; Band B3.

Frost, Steven Alan; FCO since September 2002; Born 21/09/64; FCO 1987; Islamabad 1992; FCO 1996; Second Secretary Stockholm 1999; Band C4; m 1993 Angela Elaine Morrissey.

Fry, Graham Holbrook; HM Ambassador Tokyo since July 2004; Born 20/12/49; FCO 1972; Third later Second Secretary Tokyo 1974; First Secretary on loan to DOI 1979; FCO 1981; First Secretary Paris 1983; FCO 1987; Counsellor (Chancery) Tokyo 1989; Counsellor FCO 1993; AUSS (Northern Asia and the Pacific) 1995; High Commissioner Kuala Lumpur 1998; Director General (Economic) FCO 2001; m (1) 1977 Meiko Iida (diss), (2) 1994 Toyoko Ando.

Fulcher, Michael Adrian; Counsellor FCO since April 2003; Born 15/10/58; FCO 1982; Second later First Secretary Athens 1985; First Secretary FCO 1989; First Secretary (Political) Sofia 1993; First Secretary FCO 1996; Counsellor Rome 1999; m 1983 Helen Parkinson (1s 1987; 1d 1988).

Full, Ian Francis; FCO since December 1997; Born 16/08/54; FCO 1972; Paris 1975; San José 1978; Jedda 1981; FCO 1986; Islamabad 1989; Suva 1994; Band C4.

Fuller, Eleanor Mary (née Breedon); First Secretary Geneva (UKMIS) since January 2000; Born 31/12/53; FCO 1975; ENA Course, Paris 1977 and 1978; Resigned 1980, reinstated FCO 1981; On loan to the ODA 1983; SUPL 1986; Second later First Secretary FCO 1990; SUPL 1993; UNRWA Vienna 1994-96; First Secretary Vienna (UKDEL) 1998; m 1984 Simon William John Fuller (3s 1986, 1988, 1991).

Fuller, Robert; Second Secretary Bucharest since January 2005; Born 19/09/74; FCO 2001; Band C4; ptnr, Angela Richmond.

Fulton, Craig John; Second Secretary (Regional Affairs) Kampala since April 2002; Born 30/10/67; FCO 1987; Singapore 1990; Islamabad 1992; FCO 1996; Band C4.

Furssedonn, Scott; Second Secretary (Institutions) Brussels (UKREP) since October 2001; Born 13/02/78; FCO 2000; Band C4; ptnr, Elizabeth Wood.

Fussey, Lorraine Helen; FCO since February 2003; Born 30/01/67; FCO 1989; Bombay 1991; Tel Aviv 1995; FCO 1998; SUPL 2000; Band D6; m 1996 Alastair Walton Totty (2s 1997, 2001).

G

Gallacher, Ian Charles; Third Secretary (Consular) Paris since October 2001; Born 02/05/63; FCO 1983; Paris 1988; Peking 1990; FCO 1993; Band B3; m 1987 Diane Warren.

Gallacher, Margaret; Bucharest since January 2005; Born 05/12/63; MOD 1986-96; FCO 1996; Anguilla 1997; Kuala Lumpur 2001; Band B3.

Gallagher, Tracy Anne; First Secretary (Political) Athens since June 2003; Born 22/01/58; FCO 1981; Language Training 1982; Third later Second Secretary (Comm) later First Secretary (Econ), Moscow 1983; First Secretary FCO 1988; First Secretary (Chancery) Dublin 1991; SUPL 1994; First Secretary FCO 1998; m 1986 Ian Robert Whitting (2d 1990, 1994).

Galvez, Elizabeth Ann (née Sketchley); Counsellor New York (UKMIS) since June 2003; Born 24/12/51; FCO 1970; SUPL to attend University 1970; FCO 1973; Helsinki 1974; Geneva (UKMIS) 1977; FCO 1981; Second Secretary Tegucigalpa 1981; Second Secretary FCO 1985; SUPL 1987; FCO 1988; First Secretary Vienna (UKDEL) 1989; First Secretary FCO 1994; Language Training (FT) 1997; Deputy Head of Mission Bucharest 1997; On secondment 2001; m 1985 Roberto Arturo Galvez Montes (1d 1987).

Gamble, Adrian Mark; Counsellor Vienna since July 2004; Born 30/03/61; FCO 1991; Second Secretary (EC Affairs) Brussels 1993; First Secretary FCO 1995; First Secretary (Political) Rome 1998; First Secretary FCO 2001; Band D6; m 1990 Jane Brison (2s 1991, 1993; 1d 1995).

Ganderton, Jennifer Louise; SUPL since September 1999; Born 15/06/70; Inland Revenue 1988; MOD 1988; FCO 1989; Stockholm 1992; World-Wide Floater 1995; Band B3.

Ganney, Sharon Ann (née Feeney); FCO since 2005; Born 11/10/70; FCO 1989; Warsaw 1992; Hamilton 1994; FCO 1996; T/D Doha 1997; Vice-Consul St Petersburg 1998; Vice-Consul (Management) Rio de Janeiro 2002; Band C4; m 1998 Mark William Ganney.

Garden, Alyson Margaret; Hong Kong since February 2004; Born 21/03/69; FCO 1988; Canberra 1991; FCO 1994; Warsaw 1996; FCO 1999; Band B3.

Gardiner, Judith Margaret (née Farnworth); Deputy Head of Mission Riga since June 2005; Born 25/04/66; FCO 1991; Senior Research Officer 1992; Second Secretary (Chancery/Press and Public Affairs) Kiev 1996; First Secretary (Political) Prague 2000; SUPL 2004; m 1994 Christopher Gardiner.

Gardner, David Martin; SMO Kabul since August 2004; Born 11/11/60; FCO 1978; Mexico City 1981; Tegucigalpa 1984; FCO 1988; Third Secretary (Chancery) Warsaw 1991; Vice-Consul Paris 1993; Second Secretary (Commercial) Mexico City 1996; First Secretary (Management) Bogotá 2001; Band C5; m 1983 Ana Luisa Dominguez Ortiz (1s 1992; 1d 1994).

Gardner, John Ewart; First Secretary (Commercial) Abu Dhabi since November 2000; Born 28/02/53; FCO 1971; Abu Dhabi 1974; Kinshasa 1978; Wellington 1981; FCO 1984; Lagos 1986; Los Angeles 1989; FCO 1992; Second Secretary 1994; Deputy Head of Mission and Consul La Paz 1996; Band C5; m 1975 Alexandra Marie Donald.

Gardner, Julie Ann (née Taylor); SUPL since June 1999; Born 15/02/67; FCO 1988; Peking 1990; Buenos Aires 1993; Karachi 1997; Band A2; m 1997 Stuart William Gardner (1d 1999).

Gardner, Stuart William; Brussels since August 2001; Born 10/03/70; FCO 1989; Buenos Aires

1993; Karachi 1999; Band C4; m 1997 Julie Taylor.

Gare, Berenice Veronica (née Erry); FCO since June 1984; Born 27/04/56; FCO 1975; Accra 1977; Cairo 1979; New Delhi 1980; Kuala Lumpur 1981; Band C4; m 2002 Adam Robert Gare.

Garn, Carl Raymond; Deputy Head of Mission Tashkent since September 2003; Born 17/10/56; Cabinet Office 1977; CSD 1979; FCO 1981; Dacca 1982; SEA Floater 1985; Vice-Consul Istanbul 1986; FCO 1990; Deputy Head of Mission Tallinn 1993; Tortola 1996; FCO 2000; Band C5; m 1987 Lisa Elaine Walter (1d 1995; 1s 1997).

Garner-Winship, Stephen Peter; First Secretary FCO since September 1994; Born 26/10/56; FCO 1989; Consul Rio de Janeiro 1991; First Secretary (Political) Lisbon 1993; Band D6; m 1978 Mary Carmel (1s 1979; 1d 1982).

Garnham, Penelope Jane (née White); Manila since November 2004; Born 13/07/71; FCO 1989; Kingston 1992; Dubai 1996; Pretoria 2000; Band B3; m 1993 Glen Joseph Garnham (1d 1999; 1s 2002).

Garnham, Sandra Jayne (née Hibbert); Kiev since July 2001; Born 15/09/68; FCO 1989; Rome 1992; FCO 1996; Islamabad 1998; Band B3; m 1992 Clive Julian Marcus Westbrook Garnham (diss).

Garrett, Charles Edmund; FCO since November 2001; Born 16/04/63; FCO 1987; Language Training 1988; Language Training Hong Kong 1989; Second Secretary Nicosia 1990; Second Secretary Hong Kong (UKREP JLG) 1991; First Secretary FCO 1993; First Secretary Berne 1997; m 1991 Véronique Frances Edmonde Barnes (2d 1992, 1993; 3s 1995, 1999, 2000).

Garrett, Martin, MVO (1996); Deputy Head of Mission Rangoon since March 2002; Born 21/02/54; FCO 1974; Governor's Office Honiara 1976; Paris 1979; BERS Masirah 1981; Tripoli 1982; FCO 1984; Stockholm 1990; Second Secretary (Commercial/Aid) Hanoi 1994; Bangkok 1996; Second Secretary FCO 1997.

Garrity, Alison; Kathmandu since January 2001; Born 19/10/71; FCO 1999; Band A2.

Garside, Bernhard Herbert; Consul-General Amsterdam since February 2003; Born 21/01/62; FCO 1983; Masirah 1986; Dubai 1987; Lagos 1990; FCO 1994; Havana 1999; Band C5; m 1989 Jennifer Susan Yard (2d 1992, 1998; 1s 1996).

Garth, Andrew John; First Secretary (Trade Development) Bucharest since April 2004; Born 28/09/69; FCO 1988; Warsaw 1990; South/South East Asia Floater Duties 1992; FCO 1996; On loan to the DTI 1998; Taipei 1999; FCO 2002; Seconded to the South Yorkshire International Trade Centre 2003; Band C5; ptnr, Sarah Farrell (1d 2002).

Garvey, Kevin Andrew; First Secretary FCO since August 2005; Born 10/08/60; FCO 1978; Bangkok 1981; Hanoi 1985; Latin America Floater 1986; FCO 1988; Phnom Penh 1992; Second Secretary Turks and Caicos Islands 1993; FCO 1996; On loan to British Trade International 1999; First Secretary (Deputy Head of Mission) and HM Consul Guatemala City since December 2001, also accredited non-resident San Salvador and Tegucigalpa 2004.

Gaskill, Katriona; FCO since September 2003; Born 07/02/80; Band C4.

Gaskin, Rupert John Addison; First Secretary (Political) Khartoum since August 2003; Born 19/06/74; FCO 1997; Second Secretary (Political) Cairo 1999; Second Secretary FCO 2001; Band D6; m 2003 Jacqueline Gartland (1s 2005).

Gass, Simon Lawrance, CVO (1999), CMG (1998); HM Ambassador Athens since December 2004; Born 02/11/56; FCO 1977; Lagos 1979; Second later First Secretary Athens 1984; First Secretary FCO 1987; APS to the Secretary of State 1990; Rome 1993; FCO 1995; Deputy High Commissioner Pretoria 1998; Director (Finance) FCO 2001; m 1980 Marianne Enid Stott (2s 1986, 1989; 1d 1995).

Gates, Helen Deborah; Consul New York since August 2002; Born 31/01/67; FCO 1990; Third Secretary (Political) Berlin 1993; World-Wide Floater Duties 1996; FCO 1997; Second Secretary Geneva (UKDIS) 1999; T/D Johannesburg 2001.

Gatward, William Henry Richard; Second Secretary (Political) Vienna since June 2003; Born 01/03/73; FCO 1999; Full-Time Language Training (German) 2002; Band C4; m 2003 Lynne Morrice.

Gay, Andrew Michael; First Secretary Bogotá since September 2002; Born 04/03/70; First Secretary FCO 1998; Band D6.

Gebicka, Anna Maria Teresa; SUPL since October 2004; Born 27/01/64; FCO 1990; Tokyo 1992; Caracas 1995; T/D Stanley 1999; FCO 1999; Prague 2001; Band A2.

Gecim, Thérésa Ellen; Istanbul since August 2003; Born 05/06/60; FCO 1977; Geneva (UKMIS) 1982; Belgrade 1984; Manila 1987; FCO 1990; SUPL 1993; FCO 1994; SUPL 1994; FCO 1998; Band B3; m 1985 Ali Gecim (1d 1993; 1s 1995).

Geddes, Jonathan Paul; FCO since June 2001; Born 03/09/65; FCO 1985; Rome 1987; Madras 1990; FCO 1994; Dhaka 1998; Band D6; m 1996 Susan Jane Fleming (1s 2000).

Geddes, Leo Patrick Thomas; FCO since October 2004; Born 21/06/81; Band C4.

Geddes, Susan Jane (née Fleming); FCO since August 2002; Born 02/08/64; FCO 1984; Brussels (UKREP) 1985; Nassau 1988; FCO 1990; Dhaka 1998; SUPL 2001; Band C4; m 1996 Jonathan Paul Geddes (1s 2000).

Gedny, Philippa; SUPL since August 2000; Born 09/08/59; FCO 1977; Bonn 1979; Montevideo 1982; Antigua 1985; FCO 1987; APS to the PUS 1988; Lisbon 1992; Dubai 1995; FCO 1998; Band C4; (1d 1999; 1s 2000).

Gee, Mark Leonard; Freetown since May 2005; Born 27/06/70; FCO 1991; Moscow 1995; Pretoria 1999; Guangzhou 2002; Band B3; (1d 2000).

Gelling, William John; FCO since September 2001; Born 30/12/77; Band C4.

Gemmell, Roderick, OBE (2002); High Commissioner Nassau since March 2003; Born 19/08/50; POSB 1966; DSAO (later FCO) 1967; Bahrain 1971; Washington 1972; The Hague 1975; FCO 1979; Mbabane 1982; Stockholm 1984; Second Secretary (Comm/Econ) Ankara 1987; Second Secretary FCO 1991; First Secretary (Management) Kampala 1994; First Secretary (Consular/Immigration) later Director of Entry Clearance Lagos 1998; m 1975 Janet Bruce Mitchell (1d 1981).

George, Andrew Neil; Assistant Director (Medical and Welfare) FCO since June 2003; Born 09/10/52; Third Secretary FCO 1974; Language Training SOAS 1975; Third later Second Secretary Bangkok 1976; Second later First Secretary FCO 1980; First Secretary Canberra 1984; First Secretary and Head of Chancery Bangkok 1988; First Secretary FCO 1993; HM Ambassador Asunción 1998; Counsellor (Commercial) Jakarta 2002; m 1977 Watanalak Chaovieng (1d 1979; 1s 1982).

George, Christopher Stephen; FCO since July 2004; Born 08/05/62; Home Office 1982; FCO 1991; First Secretary (Commercial/Economic) Havana 2001; Band D6; m 1993 Susan Vince (1s 1999).

German, Robert Charles; First Secretary FCO since November 1999; Born 17/01/58; FCO 1978; Masirah 1985; FCO 1986; Third Secretary Kuala Lumpur 1990; Third Secretary FCO 1993; Second Secretary Tel Aviv 1997; m 1982 Penelope Jane Cooper (2s 1986, 1989; 1d 1996).

Gibbins, Ian Paul; First Secretary FCO since March 2001; Born 27/06/47; GPO 1963; FCO 1969; Washington 1975; later Third Secretary Brussels 1981; Third Secretary Prague 1984; Second Secretary FCO 1985; Second Secretary Bonn 1990; Second Secretary FCO 1992; Second Secretary Brussels 1995; Seconded to the Northern Ireland Office 1999; m 1975 Rose Elizabeth Devlin (2s 1978, 1980; 1d 1983).

Gibbs, Andrew Patrick Somerset, OBE (1992); Counsellor Tel Aviv since July 2002; Born 08/12/51; Third later Second Secretary FCO 1977; Vice-Consul later Consul (Econ) Rio de Janeiro 1979; First Secretary FCO 1981; Language Training 1983; First Secretary Moscow 1984; First Secretary FCO 1985; First Secretary (Inf) Pretoria 1987; First Secretary FCO 1989; SUPL 1991; First Secretary FCO 1993; Counsellor Lisbon 1994; Counsellor FCO 1998; m 1981 Roselind Cecilia Robey (2d 1982, 1986; 2s 1983, 1990).

Gibbs, Kristian Mark; FCO since August 2003; Born 12/05/74; FCO 1997; Caracas 2000; Band C4.

Gibbs, Timothy; FCO since September 1981; Born 20/10/48; FO (later FCO) 1967; Beirut 1974; FCO 1976; Paris 1978; Band C5; m 1978 Catherine MacDougall.

Gibson, John Stuart; FCO since November 2001; Born 15/03/48; Commonwealth Office 1967; FCO 1969; Moscow 1970; Bonn 1972; Berne 1974; Helsinki 1975; FCO 1977; Cairo 1979; Riyadh 1983; Düsseldorf 1984; Dhaka 1987; Second Secretary FCO 1991; Second Secretary (Consular/Management) Kathmandu 1994; Vice-Consul (Management) Maputo 1998; m 1972 Grete Sandberg (2d 1975, 1977).

Gibson, Pamela Ann (née O'Hanlon), MBE (2000); FCO since April 1996; Born 27/09/56; FCO 1975; Geneva (UKMIS) 1978; Kuwait 1981; FCO 1983; Copenhagen 1984; SUPL 1987; FCO 1990; Nairobi 1995; Band A2; m 1987 Graeme Robert Gibson (dec'd 1996).

Gibson, Robert Winnington; Deputy Head of Mission Baghdad since February 2006; Born 07/02/56; FCO 1978; Jedda 1981; Second Secretary UKREP Brussels 1984; Second Secretary (Chancery/Inf) Port of Spain 1986; Second later First Secretary FCO 1989; First Secretary (Political) UKDEL OECD Paris 1995; FCO 1999; Deputy Head of Mission Dhaka 2002.

Gifford, Michael John; HM Ambassador Sana'a since July 2004; Born 02/04/61; FCO 1981; Language Training 1982; Third Secretary (Commercial) Abu Dhabi 1983; Second Secretary (Chancery) Oslo 1988; On loan to European Commission Brussels 1990; Second later First Secretary FCO 1991; First Secretary (Economic) Riyadh 1993; First Secretary FCO 1996; Deputy Head of Mission Cairo 2001; m 1986 Patricia Anne Owen (1d 1989; 1s 1991).

Gilbert, Juliet; SUPL since December 2002; Born 20/02/69; FCO 1998; New York (UKMIS) 1999; Band A2.

Gilbert, Mary Jean; Auckland since April 2002; Born 17/01/52; New Zealand Army 1979-94; FCO 1995; Jakarta 1999; Band B3.

Giles, Alison Mary; First Secretary FCO since September 2002; Born 15/09/64; FCO 1988; Third later Second Secretary Pretoria 1990; Second Secretary FCO 1993; First Secretary (IAEA) Vienna (UKMIS) 1998; Band D6.

Gill, Anne Frances; Helsinki since November 2004; Born 06/07/63; FCO 1988; East Berlin 1989; FCO 1990; Brussels (UKREP) 1992; Rangoon 1995; Tehran 1999; FCO 2001; Band B3.

Gillett, Sarah, MVO (1986); Consul General Montreal since February 2002; Born 21/07/56; FCO 1976; SUPL 1978; FCO 1982; Washington

1984; Third later Second Secretary Paris 1987; Second Secretary on secondment to ODA 1990; Vice-Consul Los Angeles 1992; First Secretary FCO 1994; First Secretary (Economic), later Deputy Head of Mission Brasilia 1997.

Gillham, Geoffrey Charles; Assistant Director (EU-Mediterranean) FCO since April 2003; Born 01/06/54; FCO 1981; Second Secretary Caracas 1983; On loan to the Cabinet Office 1986; FCO 1988; First Secretary (Chancery) Madrid 1989; First Secretary (Economic) Paris (UKDEL OECD) 1991; First Secretary later Counsellor FCO 1995; Counsellor New Delhi 1998; Counsellor FCO 2001; m 1991 Dr Nicola Mary Brewer (1d 1993; 1s 1994).

Girdlestone, John Patrick; Deputy Head of Mission and Consul-General Khartoum since November 2002; Born 26/09/46; FO 1964; Khartoum 1968; Mexico City 1971; Cairo 1974; FCO 1976; MECAS 1978; Doha 1979; Madrid 1983; Second Secretary and Consul Al Khobar 1986; Second Secretary FCO 1991; Chairman, Diplomatic Service Trade Union Side 1991; First Secretary (Commercial) Abu Dhabi 1994; Deputy Head of Mission Lima 1998; m 1975 Djihan Labib Nakhla (1d 1976).

Glackin, Clare Siobhan; FCO since August 2004; Born 13/12/70; FCO 1999; Second Secretary (Chancery) Vienna 2002; Band C4.

Glass, Colin, MBE; Deputy Head of Mission Antananarivo since October 2004; Born 06/02/55; FCO 1973; Paris 1975; Luanda 1977; Warsaw 1978; Luanda 1981; Stockholm 1985; FCO 1988; Vice-Consul Bahrain 1991; Deputy High Commissioner Freetown 1995; FCO 1999; m 1981 Ruth Kathleen Elizabeth Pearce (1s 1986; 1d 1989).

Glen, Colin Ian; Third Secretary (Management) and Vice-Consul Tehran since April 2003; Born 11/03/60; FCO 1989; Beijing 1999; Band B3; m 2002 Luo Fan.

Glover, Esther Judith (née Hartless); FCO since February 2003; Born 17/10/76; Band A2; m 2004 Mark Glover.

Glover, Graham Dingwall; First Secretary (Commercial) Tripoli since December 2001; Born 14/08/68; FCO 1988; Peking 1989; FCO 1992; Warsaw 1993; Bangkok 1996; FCO 1996; Second Secretary (on loan to DfID), Kingston 1998; Band C5; m 1992 Joanne Ellen Whittle.

Glover, Joanne Ellen (née Whittle); Third later Second Secretary (Immigration) Tripoli since July 2002; Born 20/04/67; FCO 1987; Peking 1989; FCO 1992; Warsaw 1993; Bangkok 1996; FCO 1996; SUPL 1999; Kingston 2000; Band C4; m 1992 Graham Dingwall Glover.

Glynn, Christopher Barry; Deputy Consul-General Sydney since August 2001; Born 23/12/49; FO (later FCO) 1967; Bonn 1971; Abidjan 1973; FCO 1975; Alexandria 1978; FCO 1982; Canning House 1983; Vice-Consul (Commercial) São Paulo 1985; Second Secretary (Commercial) later First Secretary/Consul Lisbon 1988; First Secretary FCO 1992; First Secretary (Commercial) Manila 1994; Deputy Consul General and Deputy Director of Trade Promotion São Paulo 1997; m 1988 Dr Wilma Sarino Ballat.

Goddard, Colette (née Boyd); Lagos since July 2002; Born 09/05/65; FCO 1995; Singapore 1997; Karachi 2000; Band B3; m 1997 Paul Anthony Goddard (1s 1995).

Goddard, Jonathan; Full-Time Language Training Amman since April 2004; Born 21/12/66; Home Office 1994; FCO 1997; Third Secretary (Chancery) Kathmandu 2000; Full-Time Language Training (Arabic) 2003; Band B3; m 1996 Hayley Morgan (2s 1998, 2000).

Godfrey, Ian David; FCO since July 1997; Born 02/10/60; FCO 1980; Washington 1987; FCO 1989; Third Secretary Islamabad 1993; m 1994 C Hochreiter (1s 1994).

Godson, Anthony; High Commissioner Port Louis November 2004 and concurrently HM Ambassador (non-resident) Antananarivo and Moroni since September 2005; Born 01/02/48; FCO 1966; Bucharest 1970; Third Secretary Jakarta 1972; Private Secretary to the High Commissioner Canberra 1976; FCO 1979; Second Secretary 1980; Second later First Secretary New York (UKMIS) 1983; First Secretary FCO 1988; Deputy Head of Mission Bucharest 1990; First Secretary Geneva (UKMIS) 1991; FCO 1996; Counsellor later Deputy Head of Mission and Consul General Jakarta 1998; Counsellor FCO 2002; m 1977 Marian Jane Margaret Hurst.

Goksin, Jill Elaine (née Cooke); Belgrade since April 2005; Born 15/09/58; FCO 1982; Belgrade 1983; FCO 1986; Gaborone 1987; FCO 1989; Istanbul 1989; Colombo 1992; FCO 1996; Addis Ababa 1997; Vienna 2002; Band A2; m 1994 Cenk Bulent Goksin (2d 1996, 1997).

Gola, Elizabeth Ann; FCO since 2002; Born 04/07/61; FCO 1996; Havana 1998; Manila 2000; Band B3.

Golding, Terence Michael; Second later First Secretary FCO since October 2000; Born 26/07/49; FCO 1969; Washington 1973; Berne 1975; São Paulo 1978; FCO 1981; Budapest 1986; Kaduna 1988; FCO 1990; Second Secretary 1992; Second Secretary Singapore 1996; Band C5; m 1978 Irene Elizabeth Blackett.

Goldsmith, Simon Geoffrey; FCO since June 2001; Born 23/01/69; FCO 1990; Paris 1992; Bombay 1994; Third Secretary (On secondment to DFID) Belmopan 1998; Band B3; m 1995 Robyn Jean Daley (1s 2004).

Goldthorpe, Debra Kay, LVO (1999); First Secretary (Commercial) Budapest since November 2000; Born 30/01/58; FCO 1977; Africa Floater 1981; New York 1982; Second Secretary FCO 1985; Language Training 1989; Second Secretary Budapest 1989; First Secretary FCO 1993; HM

Consul Durban 1996; Band D6; m 1989 Roger William Lamping.

Golland, Roger James Adam, OBE (1993); Counsellor FCO since January 2001; Born 08/05/55; FCO 1978; Third later Second Secretary Ankara 1979; FCO 1982; Language Training 1983; First Secretary Budapest 1984; FCO 1986; First Secretary Buenos Aires 1989; First Secretary FCO 1992; Counsellor (Political) Brussels 1998; m 1978 Jane Lynnette Brandrick (2s 1985, 1987).

Gomersall, Sir Stephen John, KCMG (2000), CMG (1997); HM Ambassador Tokyo since July 1999; Born 17/01/48; FCO 1970; Language Student Sheffield and Tokyo 1971; Third later First Secretary Tokyo 1972; FCO 1977; Private Secretary to Lord Privy Seal 1979; First Secretary Washington 1982; Counsellor (Economic) Tokyo 1986; Counsellor FCO 1990; Minister New York (UKMIS) 1994; m 1975 Lydia Veronica Parry (2s 1978, 1980; 1d 1982).

Goodall, David Paul; FCO since June 2003; Born 16/04/57; FCO 1976; Wellington 1978; Seoul 1981; SEA Floater 1985; FCO 1987; Third Secretary (Commercial) Accra 1990 (Second Secretary 1994); Second Secretary FCO 1994; Second Secretary (Management) Rome 1998; Band C5; m 1996 Diane Bainbridge.

Goodall, Diane (née Bainbridge); SUPL since November 2003; Born 07/10/58; FCO 1985; Ankara 1987; Accra 1991; FCO 1995; Rome 1998; FCO 2002; Band B3; m 1996 David Paul Goodall.

Gooderham, Peter Olaf; Director (Middle East/North Africa) FCO since October 2004; Born 29/07/54; FCO 1983; Second later First Secretary (Chancery) Brussels (UKDEL NATO) 1985; First Secretary FCO 1987; First Secretary (Economic) Riyadh 1990; First Secretary FCO 1993; New York (UKMIS) 1996; Counsellor (Political) Washington 1999; Brussels (UKREP) 2003; m 1985 Carol Anne Ward.

Gooding, Mark; Second Secretary (Commercial) Shanghai since December 2002; Born 17/12/74; FCO 1999; SUPL 2000; Full-Time Language Training Peking 2001; Band C4.

Goodman, James Henry Adam; FCO since February 2004; Born 31/12/65; FCO 1993; Full-Time Language Training 1995; Full-Time Language Training Cairo 1996; Second Secretary (Political) Riyadh 1997; Second Secretary FCO 1999; First Secretary (Political) Amman 2002; Band D6; m 1992 Andrea Dawn Wells (3s 1994, 1996, 1998).

Goodrick, Clair Isabella; FCO since 2005; Born 16/09/71; FCO 1993; Pretoria 1996; Zagreb 1999; Brussels 2003; Band A2.

Goodrick, Sophie Louise; SUPL since November 2004; Born 28/02/70; FCO 1997; On secondment to the German Federal Ministry of Economics 2000; Second Secretary (EU/Economic) Berlin 2001; Band C4.

Goodwin, Andrew John; Deputy Head of Mission Sana'a since March 2004; Born 22/03/59; FCO 1978; Hong Kong 1980; Dhaka 1982; Africa/ME Floater 1984; Aden 1987; Lagos 1992; FCO 1993 (Second Secretary 1995); Deputy Head of Mission and Consul Ulaanbaatar 1998; Consul/Management Officer Tehran 2002; m 1997 (Carol) Louise Mottershead.

Goodwin, David Howard; First Secretary (Commercial) Moscow since April 2002; Born 16/08/46; FO (later FCO) 1964; Budapest 1969; Kinshasa 1970; Montevideo 1973; FCO 1975; Moscow 1978; San Francisco 1980; FCO 1983; Second Secretary (Immigration) New Delhi 1987; Second later First Secretary FCO 1990; First Secretary (Commercial) The Hague 1996; T/D Deputy Project Director Expo 2000 Hanover 2000; Band D6; m 1968 Dorothea Thompson (2d 1970, 1976).

Goodwin, Michael Roy; First Secretary (Management) Budapest since July 2004; Born 17/03/60; FCO 1981; Victoria 1983; FCO 1987; Dublin 1987; Third Secretary (Aid) Banjul 1990; FCO 1992; Ottawa 1995; Second Secretary (Immigration/Consular) Kingston 2001; Band C5; m 1983 Kerry Linda Graney (2d 1986, 1992).

Goodworth, Adrian Francis Norton; SUPL since January 2001; Born 06/07/53; FCO 1982; Third Secretary Seoul 1984; Third later Second Secretary Brussels (UKREP) 1988; FCO 1990; Second Secretary (Commercial) Jakarta 1992; First Secretary (Commercial) Caracas 1996; m (1) 1981 Caroline Ruth Steele (diss 1985), (2) 1987 Valerie Ann Chipcase (diss) (1s 1990; 1d 1992), (3) 1996 Susanti Djuhana (1s 1997).

Gordon, Alison Jill; Full-Time Language Training Damascus since May 2005; Born 02/02/72; FCO 2002; Band D6.

Gordon, Emma Louise; FCO since April 2002; Born 25/05/74; Band C4.

Gordon, Jean Francois, CMG (1999); High Commissioner Kampala since July 2005; Born 16/04/53; FCO 1979; Second later First Secretary Luanda 1981; First Secretary Geneva (UKDIS) 1983; First Secretary FCO 1988; First Secretary (Political) Nairobi 1990; First Secretary FCO 1992; HM Ambassador Algiers 1996; seconded to Royal College of Defence Studies 2000; HM Ambassador Abidjan and HM Ambassador non-resident to Liberia, Niger and Burkina Faso 2001; m Elaine Margaret Daniel (2d 1984, 1988).

Gordon, Pamela Jane (née Taylor); SUPL since July 2003; Born 03/09/51; FCO 1973; Havana 1975; Brussels 1977; SUPL 1978; FCO 2001; m 1978 Robert Anthony Eagleson (2d 1980, 1981; 2s 1985, 1988).

Gordon, Robert Anthony Eagleson, CMG (1999), OBE (1983); HM Ambassador Hanoi since September 2003; Born 09/02/52; FCO 1973; Language Student 1974; Third later Second Secretary Warsaw 1975; Second later First Secretary (Head of Chancery) Santiago 1978; First

Secretary FCO 1983; First Secretary (Economic) Paris (UKDEL OECD) 1987; Deputy Head of Mission Warsaw 1992; HM Ambassador Rangoon 1995; Counsellor FCO 1999; m 1978 Pamela Jane Taylor (2d 1980, 1981; 2s 1985, 1988).

Gordon-MacLeod, David Scott; High Commissioner Port Moresby since November 2003; Born 04/05/48; ODA 1973; Mbabane 1978; Second later First Secretary FCO 1983; First Secretary and Head of Chancery Maputo 1987; First Secretary FCO 1991; Full-Time Language Training 1994; Deputy Head of Mission Bogotá 1994; First Secretary (Economic) Athens 1998; m 1988 Adrienne Felicia Maria Atkins (2d 1989, 1992; 2s 1994, 1996).

Gotch, Chris; Second Secretary (Commercial/Energy) Baku since January 2003; Born 28/11/69; FCO 1996; Second Secretary (Political) later World Cup Liaison Officer Seoul 1997; m 2003 Ms Ran Her.

Gould, David Christopher; FCO then FCO Services since November 1990; Born 31/12/55; FCO 1976; Washington 1982; FCO 1985; On loan to Cabinet Office 1987; Band D7; m 1977 Susan Kensett (2d 1975, 1980).

Gould, John Richard William; Second Secretary FCO since April 2002; Born 28/11/73; FCO 1997; Second Secretary Sarajevo 2000; Band C4.

Gould, Matthew Steven, MBE (1998); Deputy Head of Mission Tehran since April 2003; Born 20/08/71; FCO 1993; Manila 1994; FCO 1997; T/D Islamabad 2002.

Gould, St. John Byrhtnoth; First Secretary (Political) Washington since July 2000; Born 12/08/68; FCO 1995; Band C5; m 1993 Siân Elizabeth Edwards.

Goulden, Katherine Lucy; FCO since May 2002; Born 20/06/67; FCO 1991; Third Secretary (Aid/Chancery) Port Louis 1994; Brasilia 1998; Band C4.

Goulty, Alan Fletcher, CMG (1998); HM Ambassador and Consul-General Tunis since October 2004; Born 02/07/47; Third Secretary FCO 1968; MECAS 1969; Third later Second Secretary Beirut 1971; Khartoum 1972; Second later First Secretary FCO 1975; On loan to Cabinet Office 1977; Washington 1981; First Secretary later Counsellor FCO 1985; Deputy Head of Mission Cairo 1990; HM Ambassador Khartoum 1995; Director Middle East 2000; UK Special Representative to Sudan 2002; m (1) 1968 Jennifer Wendy Ellison (1s 1970); (2) 1983 Lillian Craig Harris.

Gowan, David John, CMG (2005); HM Ambassador Belgrade since September 2003; Born 11/02/49; Ministry of Defence 1970; Home Civil Service 1973; Second Secretary FCO 1975; Second later First Secretary (Comm) Moscow 1977; First Secretary FCO 1981; Head of Chancery and Consul Brasilia 1985; On loan to the Cabinet Office 1988; FCO 1989; Counsellor on loan to the Cabinet Office 1990; Counsellor (Commercial and Know How Fund) Moscow 1992; Counsellor and Deputy Head of Mission Helsinki 1995; Counsellor FCO 1999; On loan at St Antony's College Oxford 1999; Full-Time Language Training 2000; Minister and Deputy Head of Mission Moscow 2000; m 1975 Marna Irene Williams (2s 1978, 1982).

Gowen-Smith, Stephen Donald; FCO since August 2000; Born 10/12/59; FCO 1984; Vice-Consul Geneva 1997; Band C4; m 1981 Janet Elizabeth (1s 1987; 1d 1991).

Gowers, Natalie Rachel; Yekaterinburg since April 2005; Born 30/01/80; FCO 2001; Khartoum 2002; Band B3.

Goya-Brown, Simon Nicholas; First Secretary (Financial) Beijing since February 2004; Born 19/07/73; FCO 1997; Full-Time Language Training 1998; Full-Time Language Training Kamakura 1999; Second Secretary Tokyo 2000; Band C4; m 2003 Yumiko.

Gozney, Richard Hugh Turton, CMG (1993); High Commissioner Nigeria, Ambassador (Non-resident) Benin since June 2004; Born 21/07/51; FCO 1973; Third Secretary Jakarta 1974; Second later First Secretary Buenos Aires 1978; First Secretary FCO 1981; Head of Chancery Madrid 1984; APS later PPS to Secretary of State FCO 1989; High Commissioner Mbabane 1993; Counsellor FCO 1996; On loan to the Cabinet Office (Chief of Assessment Staff) 1998; HM Ambassador Jakarta 2000; m 1982 Diana Edwina Baird (2s 1987, 1990).

Gracey, Colin; Guatemala City since June 2002; Born 25/03/47; FCO 1965; Anguilla 1969; Lima 1971; Bombay 1974; FCO 1976; La Paz 1979; FCO 1983; Geneva (UKMIS) 1986; Islamabad 1989; FCO 1992; Third later Second Secretary (Commercial) Caracas 1996; Consul (Commercial) Ho Chi Minh City 1999; Band C4; m 1972 Mercedes Ines Rosenthal (1d 1973; 1s 1977).

Graham, Alison Forbes; FCO since January 1994; Born 24/08/59; FCO 1980; East Berlin 1982; FCO 1984; Ottawa 1987; Paris 1990; Band C4.

Graham, David Frank; SUPL since October 2003; Born 27/06/59; FCO 1978; Vice-Consul (Commercial) Munich 1982; LA Floater 1985; Third later Second Secretary (Economic) Warsaw 1987; FCO 1991; Second Secretary (Commercial) Berlin 1992; First Secretary (Commercial) Seoul 1997; First Secretary (Head of Governor's Office) Montserrat 2000; m 1990 Anne Marie D'Souza.

Graham, Euan Somerled; FCO since January 2004; Born 21/06/68; Band C5.

Graham, Iain George; HM Consul Bucharest since September 2004; Born 01/03/70; FCO 1989; Cairo 1991; Anguilla 1995; Islamabad 1998; FCO 2001; Band C4; m 2003 Susanna Lickorish.

Graham, Steven; SUPL since October 2004; Born 08/07/68; FCO 1989; Islamabad 1993; Full-Time Language Training 1996; Vice-Consul

(Commercial) Rio de Janeiro 1996; Second Secretary (Commercial) Luanda 2001; Band B3; m (1) 1991 Pauline Lannie (diss 1995), (2) 2000 Luisa Maria Satiago.

Grahame, David Aonghas Rees; Second Secretary Brussels (UKREP) since January 2005; Born 21/02/79; FCO 2002; Band C4.

Grainger, David Quentin; FCO since April 2000; Born 02/02/69; FCO 1990; Lusaka 1992; Kampala 1996; Band B3.

Grainger, John Andrew, CMG (2005); Legal Counsellor later Deputy Legal Adviser, FCO since October 2001; Born 27/08/57; called to the Bar (Lincoln's Inn) 1981; Assistant Legal Adviser FCO 1984; First Secretary (Legal Adviser) BMG (later BM) Berlin 1989; Assistant Legal Adviser FCO 1991; Legal Counsellor FCO 1994; Legal Counsellor New York (UKMIS) 1997; m 1998 Katherine Veronica Bregou.

Grainger, Susan Carol; SUPL since January 2003; Born 17/06/67; FCO 1987; New York (UKMIS) 1989; Montserrat 1992; FCO 1996; Dublin 1997; FCO 2000; Band B3; m 1991 Angus Steele (diss 2001).

Grant, Sir John Douglas Kelso, KCMG (2005), CMG (1999); Permanent Representative Brussels (UKREP) since August 2003; Born 17/10/54; FCO 1976; Stockholm 1977; Language Training 1980; Moscow 1982; FCO 1984; Resigned 1985; Reinstated, First Secretary FCO 1986; First Secretary (Press) Brussels (UKREP) 1989; First Secretary on loan to the Cabinet Office 1993; Brussels (UKREP) 1994; Principal Private Secretary to the Secretary of State for Foreign and Commonwealth Affairs 1997; HM Ambassador Stockholm 1999; m 1983 Anna Lindvall (2d 1987, 1988; 1s 1993).

Gray, Douglas Macdonald; Second Secretary (Political) Skopje since April 2003; Born 13/03/54; FCO 1975; Far East Floater 1978; Istanbul 1980; Second Secretary Yaoundé 1983; Second Secretary FCO 1986; First Secretary (Commercial) Seoul 1989; Deputy Head of Mission and Consul Quito 1994; Counsellor FCO 1997; m 1980 Alison Ann Hunter (1d 1985).

Gray, John Charles Rodger; HM Ambassador Rabat since July 2005; Born 12/03/53; Third Secretary FCO 1974; Language Training 1975; Third later Second Secretary Warsaw 1976; FCO 1979; First Secretary FCO 1981; First Secretary Paris (UKDEL OECD) 1983; On loan to Cabinet Office 1987; First Secretary FCO 1989; Deputy Head of Mission Jakarta 1993; On secondment to Harvard University 1996; Washington 1997; FCO 2001; Head of Middle East Department FCO 2002; m 1988 Anne-Marie Lucienne Suzanne de Dax d'Axat (3s 1995, 1997, 2000).

Gray, Trudi Elisabeth Mary; Bogotá since July 2001; Born 19/07/47; FCO 1978; Buenos Aires 1979; Prague 1982; Port Stanley 1984; Nassau 1985; Lima 1988; Lisbon 1992; FCO 1995; Seoul 1997; Band A2.

Greatrex, Avril; Second Secretary FCO since February 1995; Born 17/04/47; DSAO (later FCO) 1967; Kuwait 1971; Lagos 1973; Latin America Floater 1976; FCO 1979; Second Secretary (Management) and Vice Consul Buenos Aires 1991.

Green, Andrew Philip; Third later Second Secretary FCO since August 1992; Born 12/05/58; FCO 1975; Moscow 1982; FCO 1984; Third Secretary Tokyo 1989; m 1982 Susan Mary Merry.

Green, Colin Harvey; SUPL since October 2004; Born 22/05/69; FCO 1989; New York (UKMIS) 1992; Abidjan 1995; Hong Kong 2001; Band B3; m 1997.

Green, Frances Moira; Moscow since February 2002; Born 29/04/48; Washington 1975; Georgetown 1977; The Hague 1981; FCO 1984; Maseru 1987; FCO 1991; Brussels (UKREP) 1993; Valletta 1997; Band A2.

Green, John Edward; Second Secretary (Management) Valletta since July 2004; Born 15/02/65; FCO 1983; Tehran 1991; World-Wide Floater Duties 1994; FCO 1996; Band C4; m 1994 Caroline Ann Hockings (1s, 1d (twins) 1999).

Green, Keith William; First Secretary later Counsellor FCO since August 2001; Born 14/02/64; FCO 1990; Second Secretary (Chancery) Buenos Aires 1992; Second Secretary FCO 1995; First Secretary Sarajevo 1998.

Green, Kelvin Edward; Resident British Commissioner Castries since September 2004; Born 19/01/63; Inland Revenue 1981; FCO 1982; Washington 1984; Kampala 1987; Lilongwe 1990; FCO 1993; Second Secretary (Commercial/Consular) Dar es Salaam 1997; Second Secretary Bangalore 2001; Band C5; m 1984 Gillian Mary Lewis (2d 1991, 1993).

Green, Muriel Ruth (née Bailey); FCO since October 2002; Born 13/06/49; WRAF 1971-75; FCO 1975; Mexico City 1976; Islamabad 1982; FCO 1984; SUPL 1992; FCO 1993; On loan to the Cabinet Office 1999; Band A2; m 1981 William Charles Green (2s 1984, 1988).

Green, Steven John; First Secretary (Commercial) Kuala Lumpur since August 2000; Born 17/05/55; HM Customs and Excise 1972-74; FCO 1974; Peking 1976; Stockholm 1978; SUPL (Exeter University) 1980; FCO 1983; Third Secretary Lilongwe 1985; Third Secretary Geneva (UKDIS) 1989; Second Secretary FCO 1992; Full-Time Language Training 1995; Second Secretary (Commercial) Paris 1996; m 1978 Ulla Marianne Nilsson (1s 1980; twin d 1986).

Greenall, Elaine Linda; SUPL since April 2004; Born 04/10/77; FCO 2003; Band A2; (1d 1997).

Greene, Bernadette Theresa; Consul (Commercial) Monterrey since July 2004; Born 17/04/66; FCO 1988; Geneva (UKDEL) 1991; Maseru 1994; T/D Bosnia 1996; FCO 1997; On loan to the DTI 2000; T/D Port of Spain 2001; On loan to British Trade

International later UK Trade & Investment 2002; Band C4.

Greengrass, John Kenneth, MBE (1999); New Delhi since January 2005; Born 19/07/53; Ministry of Housing and Local Government 1970; FCO 1971; Brussels (UKREP) 1975; Washington 1978; Islamabad 1981; FCO 1983; Lagos 1986; Second Secretary Kuala Lumpur 1989; Second Secretary FCO 1993; Second Secretary (Consular) New Delhi 1996; First Secretary (Commercial) Paris 2000; Band C5; m 1975 Marian Cecilia Williams (3d 1981, 1983, 1986).

Greenlee, James Barry; First Secretary (Management) Nairobi since November 2002; Born 21/12/45; FO (later FCO) 1963; Vienna 1969; Tokyo 1971; FCO 1974; Calcutta 1979; Second Secretary (Admin) and Consul Budapest 1983; Second Secretary (Commercial) Lagos 1986; Second Secretary FCO 1989; First Secretary (Management) and Consul Seoul 1993; First Secretary (Management) Warsaw 1996; First Secretary (Management) Dhaka 2000; Band D6; m 1971 Amanda Jane Todd (2d 1979, 1981).

Greenslade, Natalie Samantha Juliet; SUPL since October 2000; Born 28/06/72; FCO 1993; Tokyo 1994; Floater Duties 1998; FCO 2000; Band B3.

Greenstock, Andrew John; Second Secretary FCO since December 2003; Born 26/10/72; Second Secretary FCO 1998; Full-Time Language Training 2000; Second Secretary (DFID/Public Diplomacy) Tehran 2001; Band C4; m 1999 Katherine Emma Gardner (1s 2003).

Greenstock, Sir Jeremy (Quentin), GCMG (2003), KCMG (1998), CMG (1991); FCO since July 2003; Born 27/07/43; Second Secretary FCO 1969; MECAS 1970; Second later First Secretary Dubai 1972; First Secretary (Private Secretary to the Ambassador) Washington 1974; FCO 1978; Counsellor (Comm) Jedda (later Riyadh) 1983; Head of Chancery Paris 1987; Deputy Political Director and AUSS (Western and Southern Europe) FCO 1990; Minister (Political) Washington 1994; DUS (Middle East/Eastern Europe) 1995; DUS (Political Director) 1996; UK Permanent Representative to United Nations, New York and UK Permanent Representative on the Security Council 1998; m 1969 Anne Ashford Hodges (2d 1970, 1975; 1s 1973).

Greenwood, Christopher Paul; On loan to the DTI since June 2003; Born 22/04/53; FCO 1973; Islamabad 1975; Moscow 1977; Manila 1980; FCO 1982; APS to Secretary of State 1982; Los Angeles 1985; Third later Second Secretary Budapest 1988; Second Secretary 1989; Second Secretary FCO 1992; Full-Time Language Training 1994; Second later First Secretary (Comm) Berne 1995; Consul-General Göthenburg 1999; m 1976 Dorothy Gwendolyn Margaret Hughes (1s 1983; 1d 1988).

Gregg, Sophie Catherine; FCO since September 2002; Born 17/04/72; FCO 1998; Full-Time Language Training 1999; Consul (Political/Economic) Hong Kong 2000; Band D6.

Gregson, Stuart Willens; Consul-General Paris since April 2000; Born 26/04/50; FO (later FCO) 1966; Cairo 1971; Yaoundé 1973; Islamabad 1976; FCO 1978; Gaborone 1982; Vice-Consul Johannesburg 1983; Second later First Secretary and Parliamentary Clerk FCO 1987; First Secretary (Information) Rome 1991; First Secretary FCO 1996; Full-Time Language Training 2000; Band D6; m 1976 Anne-Christine Wasser (1d 1976; 1s 1979).

Grennan, Gemma Brigid Anne; FCO since September 1986; Born 04/07/43; FO 1962; Vientiane 1967; Singapore 1969; Brussels 1971; Special leave 1973; Addis Ababa 1974; FCO 1977; Islamabad 1981; FCO 1983; Ottawa 1984; Band C4; m 1973 Christopher Roy Heaven (1s 1981).

Grey, Catherine Alice Jane; FCO since January 2003; Born 07/11/79; Band B3.

Grice, Sheridan Elizabeth; Third Secretary (Commercial) Cairo since June 1999; Born 14/07/54; FCO 1973; Canberra 1974; SUPL 1976; Belgrade 1976; Georgetown 1978; New York (UKMIS) 1981; FCO 1984; SUPL 1987; Islamabad 1988; Lagos 1992; Third Secretary FCO 1994; SUPL 1997; (2d 1987).

Griffin, Joseph Francis; SUPL since September 2004; Born 14/03/73; FCO 1996; Second Secretary Paris 1999; On loan to the Cabinet Office 2002; Band D6.

Griffin, Judith Catherine (née Hitchings); Colombo since 2004; Born 16/06/71; FCO 1999; Vilnius 2000; Band A2; m 2005 Ryan John Griffin.

Griffin, Ryan John; Colombo since October 2003; Born 09/04/72; FCO 1991; Rome 1994; Vilnius 1999; Band B3; m 2005 Judith Catherine Hitchings.

Griffiths, Barney Mark; Washington since August 2001; Born 23/01/60; HM Forces 1977-00; FCO 2000; Band C4; m 1980 Beverley Jayne Morse (1d 1983).

Griffiths, Glyn Justyn; Hong Kong since March 2002; Born 11/07/61; FCO 1980; Darwin 1990; FCO 1993; Bonn 1996; FCO 1998; Band C4; m 1989 Susan Caroline Dover (1s 1995; 1d 1998).

Griffiths, Major David Allison; Islamabad since September 2004; Born 28/07/43; HM Forces 1966-90; Queen's Messenger 1990.

Griffiths, Nicholas Mark; FCO since January 2001; Born 20/11/58; FCO 1985; Second Secretary (Chancery) Moscow 1988; FCO 1990; First Secretary (Trade Policy) later Deputy Permanent Representative Paris (UKDEL OECD) 1996.

Griffiths, Trudy Maureen; FCO since May 2002; Born 10/09/70; FCO 1991; Warsaw 1993; Lusaka 1996; Brussels (UKDEL NATO) 1999; Band B3.

Griggs, Kenneth John; FCO since August 2002; Born 02/09/61; FCO 1984; Washington 1985; FCO 1988; Athens 1989; FCO 1992; BTC Hong Kong 1993; FCO 1996; Bangkok 1999; Band C5; m 1986 Leisa Jayne (3d 1988, 1991, 1992; 1s 1997).

Grime, Ann Kathleen (née Jenkins); Oslo since June 2003; Born 18/06/51; FCO 1975; Muscat 1976; FCO 1978; Moscow 1979; Brussels (UKREP) 1981; SUPL 1983; Bucharest 1988; Islamabad 1989; FCO 1990; Luxembourg 1990; Colombo 1993; FCO 1997; Budapest 1998; Band B3; m 1983 Stephen Howard Grime.

Grimes, Eleanor Claire; SUPL since January 2004; Born 22/08/63; First Secretary FCO 1997; Band D6; m 1998 Major Sean Robert Armstrong (1d 1999; 1s 2001).

Grimes, Susan (née Metcalfe); SUPL since March 2002; Born 02/10/65; DHSS 1984; FCO 1987; Copenhagen 1990; FCO 1993; Nairobi 1994; Colombo 1998; Band A2; m 1989 Jason Richard Grimes (1d 1993; twin s 1996).

Grinling, Scott MacKenzie; FCO since October 2001; Born 29/10/49; FCO 1991; Nairobi 1998; m 1974 Anita Fitzhugh.

Gristock, Frances Lorraine (née Alexander); Management Officer Maputo since October 2004; Born 21/07/59; FCO 1981; SE Asia Floater 1983; FCO 1985; Third Secretary Quito 1986; FCO 1990; SUPL 1991; Second Secretary (Commercial/Consular) Victoria 1992; SUPL 1998; m 1986 Keith Gristock (1s 1994).

Groocock, Vicki; FCO since September 2003; Born 23/10/66; FCO 1988; Washington 1990; FCO 1993; Tokyo 1996; New Delhi 2000; Band A2.

Grover-Minto, Helen Katherine (née Grover); FCO since September 2002; Born 18/04/65; FCO 1986; Addis Ababa 1988; FCO 1991; Lagos later Abuja later Lagos 1992; FCO 1995; Harare 1999; Band C4; m 1991 John Minto.

Groves, Eliot Sion; Management Officer Shanghai since July 2002; Born 17/07/69; FCO 1988; New York (UKMIS) 1994; Colombo 1997; New York 2000; Band B3; m 1996 Christine Ann Reynolds.

Growcott, Michael William; FCO since March 1998; Born 15/11/48; FCO 1968; Kampala 1972; Peking 1974; Pretoria 1975; FCO 1978; Assistant to Governor Port Stanley 1979; Second Secretary (Inf/Aid/Econ) Kuala Lumpur 1982; Second Secretary FCO 1986; Chairman Diplomatic Service Whitley Council Trade Union Side, FCO 1987; First Secretary (Management) Brussels 1990; Resident Acting High Commissioner Castries 1994; m 1971 Avril Heather Kemp (2d 1972, 1976; 1s 1974).

Guckian, Lorna Ruth (née Warren); SUPL since July 1994; Born 18/06/63; FCO 1983; Port Stanley 1986; Düsseldorf 1987; Africa/ME Floater 1989; FCO 1990; Kuwait 1991; FCO 1992; Band B3; m 1990 Dr Noël Joseph Guckian (3d 1992, 1994, 2001; 1s 1997).

Guckian, Dr Noël Joseph, OBE (2001); HM Ambassador Muscat since December 2005; Born 06/03/55; FCO 1980; Consul (Commercial) Jedda 1984; Second Secretary FCO 1987; Paris 1988; Second later First Secretary FCO 1988; Deputy Head of Mission Muscat 1994; FCO 1997; Head of British Interests Section later Chargé d'Affaires and then Deputy Head of Mission Tripoli 1998; Deputy Head of Mission Damascus 2002; Consul-General Kirkuk 2004; m 1990 Lorna Ruth Warren (3d 1992, 1994, 2001; 1s 1997).

Gudgeon, Jonathan Roy; FCO since May 1995; Born 09/05/64; GPO 1980-84; FCO 1984; Moscow 1988; Vienna 1992; Band C5; m 1988 Lisa Anne Forte (2s 1992, 1993).

Gudgeon, Simon Peter; FCO since August 2003; Born 08/02/66; FCO 1982; Lagos 1987; Moscow 1992; FCO 1996; On secondment to NIO, Belfast 1997; Second Secretary Tel Aviv 1999; Band C4; m 1994 Catherine Jane Stewart (2s 1999, 2003; 1d 2001).

Guha, Priya Victoria; FCO since September 2003; Born 21/09/73; FCO 1996; Second Secretary (EU) Madrid 1999; Band C4; m 2004 Luca Benedini.

Gunn, Janet Frederica (née Podolier), CMG (2005); FCO since June 1997; Born 04/10/48; Research Counsellor FCO 1970; SUPL 1976; FCO 1978; Moscow 1984; FCO 1985; Deputy Head of Mission Sofia 1994; (1s 1976).

Gunnett, Martin John; Islamabad since March 2005; Born 01/04/50; FO 1967; Darwin 1976; FCO 1978; Belgrade 1987; Second Secretary Prague 1990; Second Secretary FCO 1994; Second Secretary Peking 1995; FCO 1999; m 1973 Linda Leah (1d 1979; 1s 1981).

Gurney, Tim; Deputy Head of Mission Kabul since September 2003; Born 28/04/55; FCO 1973; Istanbul 1976; Karachi 1979; Montreal 1982; Second Secretary FCO 1985; Second Secretary (Chancery/Inf) Accra 1989; Deputy Director and Consul (Inf) New York (BIS) 1991; First Secretary FCO 1996; Deputy Governor Bermuda 1998; m 1976 Denise Elizabeth Harker (1d 1984; 1s 1986).

Guthrie, Marion (née Whalley); SUPL since August 2004; Born 04/03/69; FCO 1988; Paris 1990; Islamabad 1992; Belgrade 1994; FCO 1996; Yaoundé 1998; Kuala Lumpur 2001; Band B3; m 1998 Robin Guthrie.

Gutierrez-Jones, Llinos Dawn; SUPL since September 2001; Born 27/03/68; FCO 1988; Kuwait 1989; Warsaw 1990; New York (UKMIS) 1992; Bandar Seri Begawan 1993; Santiago 1997; Band A2.

Guy, Frances Mary; HM Ambassador Sana'a since March 2001; Born 01/02/59; FCO 1985; Language Training 1987; Second Secretary (Chancery) Khartoum 1988; First Secretary FCO 1991; First Secretary and Head of Political Section Bangkok 1995; Deputy Head of Mission Addis Ababa 1997;

m 1989 Guy Charles Maurice Raybaudo (2d 1991, 1996; 1s 1993).

Guymont, Sarah Jean (née Crouch); Full-Time Language Training (Spanish) since September 2004; Born 08/08/52; FCO 1975; Islamabad 1976; FCO 1977; Moscow 1978; Resigned 1980; Reinstated, FCO 1982; Africa/ME Floater 1983; FCO 1987; Dar es Salaam 1989; SUPL (Cairo) 1992; Cairo 1993; SUPL 1996; Washington 1997; SUPL 2001; Band B3; m 1991 Frederick James Guymont.

Gwynn, Diana Caroline (née Hamblyn); SUPL since February 1997; Born 15/08/64; DOE 1986 - 89; FCO 1989; Third Secretary (Political/Information) Nairobi 1992; SUPL 1995; Third later Second Secretary FCO 1996; m 1988 Robert Charles Patrick Gwynn (1d 1995; 2s 1997, 2003).

Gwynn, Robert Charles Patrick (known as Robin); Deputy High Commissioner Accra since January 2002; Born 17/03/63; Department of Employment 1986 - 88; FCO 1988; Second Secretary (Chancery/Information) Nairobi 1992; First Secretary FCO 1995; Private Secretary to the Minister of State 2000; m 1988 Diana Caroline Hamblyn (1d 1995; 2s 1997, 2003).

H

Hackett, Anthony John; HM Consul Hamburg since July 2001; Born 19/12/55; FCO 1975; Muscat 1977; FCO 1981; Karachi 1981; FCO 1985; Manila 1988; Oslo 1992; FCO 1996; On loan to the DTI 1999; m 1983 Nilofer Akbar (1d 1986).

Hackett, Nicholas Daniel; Third Secretary (Immigration) Banjul since July 2003; Born 18/08/80; FCO 1999; Bucharest 2001; Band B3; m 2003 Sarah Hackett (1d 2002; 1s 2004).

Haddock, Michael Kenneth; FCO since July 2001; Born 25/09/50; FCO 1973; Geneva (UKDEL) 1978; Moscow 1981; Kuwait 1983; Second Secretary Damascus 1986; Second Secretary (Commercial) Prague 1988; First Secretary (Commercial) Abu Dhabi 1991; First Secretary FCO 1995; First Secretary (Information) Moscow 1997; m 1972 Irene Doughty (1d 1979; 1s 1984).

Hafele, Alec Graham; T/D Prague since June 2004; Born 10/05/50; FCO 1995; Bucharest 1999; Istanbul 2003; Band B3; m 1976 Brigitte Ann.

Hagart, Peter Richard; First Secretary (Management) Madrid since September 2003; Born 11/07/48; Department of Agriculture and Fisheries for Scotland 1966; FCO 1969; Bucharest 1972; Quito 1974; Bonn 1975; FCO 1977; FE Floater 1980; Hanoi 1982; Second Secretary (Admin) and Vice-Consul Brasilia 1983; Second Secretary FCO 1986; Second later First Secretary (Commercial) Bombay 1990; Consul and Deputy Head of Mission Rangoon 1992; Consul (Commercial) Auckland 1994; FCO 1999; Full-Time Language Training (Spanish) 2003.

Hagger, Philip Paul; Consul Montreal since October 2001; Born 05/09/50; FCO 1970; Singapore 1973; FCO 1974; Washington 1975; Nicosia 1978; Casablanca 1981; Lagos 1982; Second Secretary FCO 1987; Second Secretary (Commercial) Riyadh 1989; Second Secretary (Consul) Caracas 1992; Second Secretary The Hague 1994; Second Secretary FCO 1995; Second Secretary (Commercial) Perth 1997; m (1) 1971 Janet Mary Milnes (dec'd 1975) (1s 1972); (2) 1976 Julie Elizabeth Eastaugh (diss 1988) (1d 1977); (3) 1990 Linda Mary Parmegiani (2s 1993, 1996).

Haggie, Paul; Counsellor FCO since October 2001; Born 30/08/49; Third Secretary FCO 1974; Second later First Secretary Bangkok 1976; FCO 1980; First Secretary (Economic) Islamabad 1982; First Secretary FCO 1986; First Secretary (Chancery) Pretoria 1989; First Secretary FCO 1993; Counsellor on loan to the Cabinet Office 1994; Counsellor FCO 1995; Counsellor Bangkok (ESCAP) 1998; m 1979 Deborah Frazer (1s 1984; 1d 1986).

Hague, John Keir; Consul (Management) Düsseldorf since June 2001; Born 26/03/47; CO (later FCO) 1966; Dakar 1970; Kuala Lumpur 1973; Munich 1975; Moscow 1977; FCO 1979; Houston 1983; Second Secretary Islamabad 1985; Second Secretary FCO 1989; Second Secretary (Commercial) Seoul 1992; First Secretary FCO 1995; m 1969 Julie Anne Knight (2d 1972, 1975).

Haigh, Trevor Denton; FCO since January 2000; Born 07/08/44; FCO 1982; Hong Kong 1985; FCO 1988; Moscow 1990; FCO 1993; Canberra 1997; m 1977 Freda Mary Porritt.

Hailey, Nicholas James; FCO since October 2003; Born 27/01/75; FCO 1997; Seconded to Ecole Nationale D'Administration, Paris 1999; Private Secretary to the Ambassador Berlin 2002; Band D6.

Haines, Dr David Michael; FCO since June 2005; Born 06/04/63; FCO 1989; Full-Time Language Training 1991; Full-Time Language Training Cairo 1992; First Secretary (Political) Tunis 1993; Consul (Political) Jerusalem 1994; First Secretary FCO 1996; First Secretary (Political) Damascus 2000; First Secretary (Political) Abuja 2003; Band D6; m 1993 Susan Caroline Goodman (1d 1994; 1s 1996).

Haines, Stephen Andrew; Jerusalem since January 2003; Born 12/06/64; FCO 1997; Minsk 1999; Band A2; m 2003 Tatiana Vladimirovna Pilipchyk.

Haley, Anthony Peter; Kuala Lumpur since September 2004; Born 14/03/59; RAF 1979; FCO 1988; New Delhi 1991; Third Secretary FCO 1994; Mexico City 1997; FCO 2001; m 1979 Elaine Cuthbertson (3s 1979, 1982, 1985).

Halksworth, Matthew Kenneth; T/D Kabul since September 2003; Born 21/02/75; FCO 2002; Band A2.

Hall, Alison Margaret; Full-Time Language Training Cairo since September 2004; Born 28/10/79; FCO 2002; Band C4.

Hall, Amy Lea; FCO since March 2003; Born 27/08/77; Band A2.

Hall, Dr Andrew Rotely, OBE (1994); Deputy High Commissioner Kolkata since February 2003; Born 03/05/50; FCO 1980; First Secretary New Delhi 1984; FCO 1987; Deputy Head of Mission and Consul Kathmandu 1991; FCO 1995; Research Counsellor 2000; m 1973 Kathie Wright (2d 1973, 1978).

Hall, Caroline Jane (née Oakley); Deputy Head of Mission Honiara since October 2002; Born 16/09/64; FCO 1984; Santiago 1987; Floater Duties 1990; SUPL 1992; Karachi 1993; FCO 1996; Second Secretary (Immigration) Moscow 1998; Band C4; m 1992 James William Hall.

Hall, Harriet; First Secretary (Political) Stanley since July 2003; Born 24/12/69; FCO 1992; Full-Time Language Training FCO 1994; Full-Time Language Training Peking 1995; Second Secretary (Political) Peking 1996; FCO 1999.

Hall, James William David; First Secretary FCO since May 2003; Born 01/03/65; FCO 1987; Third later Second Secretary (Economic) Lusaka 1989; Second Secretary (Commercial) New Delhi 1991; Second Secretary FCO 1994; First Secretary Vienna 1999; First Secretary Pristina 2002; Band D6; ptnr, Jacqueline Ann Loveridge.

Hall, Margaret Ann; FCO since December 1991; Born 01/04/48; FCO 1975; on CDA at SOAS 1991; Band PRO; m 1974 Govind Anant Walawalkar (dec'd 2001).

Hall, Rebecca; FCO since December 2001; Born 29/09/72; FCO 1994; FCO 1996; Brussels (UKREP) 1997; Second Secretary (Political) Vienna (EU) 1999; Band D6; m 2000 Robert Page.

Hall, Russell David; SUPL since October 2003; Born 12/03/64; FCO 1984; Sofia 1996; Santiago 2000; Band A2; m 1985 Karen Hipkiss (1s 1985; 2d 1988, 1993).

Hall, Simon David; Second Secretary Jakarta since November 2003; Born 20/03/76; FCO 2000; Second Secretary Kabul 2002; Band C4.

Hall, Simon Lee; Second later First Secretary FCO since May 2000; Born 29/04/63; FCO 1982; Rome 1984; Hanoi 1986; Africa/Middle East Floater 1987; FCO 1990; Seconded to the DTI 1991; Ottawa 1993; Kingston 1996; Band C5.

Hall, Thomas Mark; FCO since December 1985; Born 15/09/47; HM Inspector of Taxes 1964; Commonwealth Office (later FCO) 1967; Tokyo 1970; FCO 1973; Milan 1979; Algiers 1981; Athens 1984; Band B3.

Hall Hall, Alexandra Mary; Seconded to the Private Sector since July 2002; Born 01/02/64; FCO 1986; Full-Time Language Training Bangkok 1989; Second Secretary 1989; First Secretary FCO 1993; On loan to the Cabinet Office 1995; Washington 1999; SUPL 2001.

Hallett, Edward Charles; Deputy Head of Mission Dublin since July 2003; Born 15/07/47; FCO 1971; Bonn 1972; FCO 1975; PRO (Band D6) 1979; Dublin 1984; FCO 1985; On loan to NIO 1988; FCO 1990; Senior Principal Research Officer FCO 1995; T/D Dublin 1996, 1997, 1998; m 1972 Audrey Marie Tobin.

Hallsworth, Valerie; SUPL since March 2000; Born 09/11/48; FCO 1988; Band A2; m 1999 Yousif Rahhal.

Halperin, Claire Ruth; FCO since September 2002; Born 29/01/71; Band C4.

Halpin, Michael Christopher; Third Secretary (Political) Islamabad since March 2003; Born 04/09/75; FCO 1999; Floater Duties 2000; Band B3; ptnr, Adriana Auxtova.

Hamblett, Christine; New York (UKMIS) since January 2003; Born 08/12/60; FCO 1990; Rome 1992; Tel Aviv 1995; FCO 1998; Band B3.

Hamill, Brian William; Second Secretary (Investment) Berne since September 2001; Born 08/01/63; FCO 1981; Masirah 1983; Manila 1983; Budapest 1988; FCO 1989; Paris 1992; Third Secretary (Commercial) Berlin 1996; Second Secretary (Commercial) Düsseldorf 1998; Band C4; m 1987 Katrina Lacson Puentevella (1d 1991).

Hamilton, Alasdair Alexander; Jerusalem since August 2003; Born 13/04/71; FCO 1990; Kuala Lumpur 1993; Port Moresby 1997; Freetown 1998; Jakarta 1999; Band B3; m 1998 Erie Alu (1s 1999; 1d 2002).

Hamilton, Amanda Zoe; FCO since September 2002; Born 08/08/80; Band B3.

Hamilton, Charles Allan; Kampala since April 2005; Born 05/12/48; DSAO 1968; Vice-Consul Düsseldorf 1970; Third Secretary Prague 1973; Vice-Consul Phnom Penh 1974; Third later Second Secretary Cairo 1975; FCO 1979; Second Secretary Addis Ababa 1981; DHC and Head of Chancery Port Louis 1984; FCO 1988; Deputy Head of Mission Yaoundé 1992; Deputy Consul General Montreal 1997; FCO 2001; m Mary Indiana Lazare.

Hamilton, John; Kolkata since July 2002; Born 28/09/68; FCO 1988; Brussels (UKDEL NATO) 1990; Windhoek 1993; FCO 1996; Third Secretary (Political) Abuja 1998; Band C4; m 1998 Maxine Jones (1d 1999).

Hancock, Janet Catherine; Valletta since March 2005; Born 05/01/49; FCO 1970; SRO 1975; PRO 1983; First Secretary FCO 1995; Full-Time Language Training 2000; Deputy Head of Mission Tunis 2000; Band D7; m 1973 Roger A Hancock (diss 1980).

Hancock, Michael John; Second Secretary and Consul Tel Aviv since December 2002; Born 21/10/62; FCO 1982; Bonn 1984; Belgrade 1987; Islamabad 1989; FCO 1991; Vice-Consul Rome

1995; Deputy Head of Mission Tbilisi 1995; Second Secretary Chancery Brussels (UKREP) 1998; Band C4; m (1) 1983 Elizabeth Alison Ormrod (diss 1999) (2s 1989, 1991; 1d 1987); (2) 1999 Rusudan Gachechiladze (2s 1992, 2001).

Hancon, John Anthony; FCO since July 1991; Born 05/01/48; GPO 1965; FCO 1969; Kuala Lumpur 1971; FCO 1973; Paris 1976; FCO 1978; Sofia 1982; FCO 1984; Nicosia 1988; Band C5; m 1970 Anne Lesley Hawke (1d 1975; 1s 1980).

Hand, Graham Stewart; HM Ambassador Algiers since July 2002; Born 03/11/48; HM Forces 1967-80; FCO 1980; Second later First Secretary Dakar 1982; First Secretary FCO 1984; Language Training 1987; First Secretary and Head of Chancery Helsinki 1987; Counsellor FCO 1992; Deputy High Commissioner Lagos 1994; on loan to the Royal College of Defence Studies 1997; Ambassador Bosnia Herzegovina 1998; m 1973 Anne Mary Seton Campbell (1s 1979; 1d 1984).

Hand, Jessica Mary (née Pearce); Moscow since November 2004; Born 01/09/57; FCO 1985; Second Secretary (Chancery) Dakar 1987; First Secretary FCO 1990; Full-Time Language Training 1994; HM Ambassador Minsk 1996; First Secretary FCO 1999; SUPL 2001; On secondment as Counsellor 2002; m 1999 Robert Wayne Hand.

Handley, Timothy Sean; T/D Islamabad since July 2003; Born 08/02/51; HCS 1969; FCO 1971; Abu Dhabi 1973; Stockholm 1976; Warsaw 1979; FCO 1981; Georgetown 1985; FCO 1986; Düsseldorf 1988; Tel Aviv 1991; FCO 1994; Band C4; m 1985 Julie Anne Russell (1s 1986; 1d 1989).

Hannah, Craig John; FCO since November 1999; Born 02/06/63; Department of Employment 1980; FCO 1983; Accra 1984; Sofia 1987; FCO 1990; Kuala Lumpur 1994; Vienna 1998; Band B3.

Hans, Ravinder; Third Secretary (Political/PPA/Culture) Valletta since September 2002; Born 17/03/74; FCO 1996; Buenos Aires 1997; Band B3.

Hansen, Caroline (née Thearle); SUPL since October 1999; Born 17/02/66; FCO 1984; Copenhagen 1987; SUPL 1990; Bangkok 1992; SUPL 1995; Dhaka 1996; Band B3; m 1989 Jakob Hansen.

Hanshaw, Danielle May; Harare since August 2004; Born 11/02/71; MOD 1991-98; FCO 1998; Jakarta 2000; FCO 2001; Band A2.

Hanson, Timothy Myles; Hong Kong since January 2004; Born 27/06/65; FCO 1984; Third Secretary (Chancery) Muscat 1987; Third Secretary (Aid) New Delhi 1991; Second Secretary FCO 1994; Second Secretary (Commercial) Kuala Lumpur 1997; First Secretary (Commercial) Sarajevo 2001.

Harborne, Peter Gale; High Commissioner Port of Spain since July 1999; Born 29/06/45; DHSS 1966; FCO 1972; Ottawa 1974; Mexico City 1975; Resigned 1979; Reinstated, First Secretary FCO 1981; First Secretary and Head of Chancery Helsinki 1983; Counsellor and Head of Chancery Budapest 1988; FCO Overseas Inspectorate 1991-94; HM Ambassador Bratislava 1995-98; m 1976 Tessa Elizabeth Henri (2s 1980, 1981).

Hardman, Peter James William; SMO Islamabad since May 2003; Born 28/10/56; FCO 1974; SE Asia Floater 1978; Bombay 1979; Perth 1983; Bangkok 1986; Second Secretary on loan to the ODA 1988; Language Training 1990; Second Secretary Sofia 1991; First Secretary (Commercial) Bangkok 1996; Shanghai 2000; FCO 2001; Band D6; m 1983 Joelle Helene Schneider (1d 1984).

Hardy, Richard Martin; Singapore since July 2001; Born 07/10/50; FCO 1967; Brussels 1976; FCO 1978; Buenos Aires 1979; FCO 1982; Bridgetown 1986; Second Secretary FCO 1989; Paris 1993; FCO 1997; Band C5; m (1) 1975 Amanda Smith (diss 1981); (2) 1982 Astrid Posse (diss 1996); (3) 2001 Alison Jane Fossey.

Hare, Paul Webster, LVO (1985); Director, Shanghai World Expo 2010, UKTI, since August 2005; Born 20/07/51; FCO 1978; Second Secretary/PS to HMA Brussels (UKREP) 1979; First Secretary Lisbon 1981 (Head of Chancery 1983); FCO 1985; Consul (Investment) and Deputy Director Investment USA BTIO New York 1988; Deputy Head of Mission and later Counsellor (Commercial/Economic) Caracas 1994; Counsellor FCO 1997; HM Ambassador Havana 2001; Visiting Fellow at the Centre for International Affairs, Harvard University 2004; m 1978 Lynda Carol Henderson (3d 1979, 1982, 1994; 3s 1984, 1988, 1991).

Hargreaves, Roger John; First Secretary FCO since September 1999; Born 08/12/50; FCO 1968; Hong Kong 1973; FCO 1975; Sana'a 1976; FCO 1977; Second Secretary Hong Kong 1985; Second later First Secretary FCO 1990; First Secretary (Political) Wellington 1996; Band C5; m Andrea Margaret Kent (1s 1989; 1d 1992).

Harkin, Simon David; First Secretary (PPA) Berne since September 2001; Born 04/10/58; FCO 1989; New York (UKMIS) 1990; FCO 1991; Second Secretary (Political) Harare 1992; First Secretary FCO 1996; Full-Time Language Training 2000.

Harland, Amy Elizabeth; Second Secretary (Political) Buenos Aires since May 2005; Born 11/05/79; FCO 2003; Band C4.

Harland, Jeremy; FCO since September 2003; Born 08/04/63; FCO 1983; Moscow 1988; FCO 1992; Bridgetown 1992; FCO 1996; Washington 1999; Band C5.

Harle, Roger William; FCO since August 1988; Born 04/02/59; FCO 1982; Darwin 1986; Band C4.

Harmer, Roger William; First Secretary (Management) Warsaw since July 2003; Born 05/01/53; FCO 1972; Bucharest 1974; La Paz 1976; Maseru 1978; FCO 1980; Third Secretary

Muscat 1983; Ottawa 1986; FCO 1989; Riga 1992; Second Secretary FCO 1993; Geneva (Joint Management Office) 1998; m 1976 Cristobalina López Munoz (1d 1977).

Harper, Maurice Bertrand; Second Secretary (Consular) Lagos since December 2001; Born 03/12/46; FCO 1974; Bangkok 1976; East Berlin 1980; FCO 1981; Bombay 1984; Port Louis 1988; Second Secretary FCO 1993; HM Consul Bucharest 1996; FCO 2001; m (1) 1977 Susan Hayward (1s 1979); m (2) 1986 Veera Printer (1d 1987).

Harper, Monica Celia, CMG (2004); Consul-General Lille since September 1998; Born 18/08/44; FCO 1967; SEATO (Bangkok) 1969; ENA Paris 1972; BMG Berlin 1974; Second Secretary Bonn 1977; FCO 1979; Second Secretary Mexico City 1982; First Secretary Brussels (UKDEL NATO) 1984; First Secretary FCO 1989; Deputy Head of Mission Luxembourg 1994.

Harries, David George, OBE (1998), MBE (1990); Second Secretary (Management) Gibraltar since January 2003; Born 10/03/60; FCO 1980; BGWRS Darwin 1982; FCO 1984; Islamabad 1986; Beirut 1988; FCO 1991; Third Secretary (Consular/Management) Freetown 1993; Third Secretary (Commercial/Development) Maputo 1998; Second Secretary (Consular) BCG New York 2001; Band C4; m 1993 Carol Chammas (1d 2002; 1s 2004).

Harrington, Peter; Second Secretary (Commercial) Doha since August 2001; Born 29/09/62; FCO 1981; Baghdad 1984; Stockholm 1988; Georgetown 1990; FCO 1994; On loan to the DTI 1995; Madras 1997; Band C4; m (1) 1984 Angela Elizabeth Dent (diss); (2) 1993 Veronica Ann Clementson (1s 1993; 1d 1995).

Harris, Karina Lynn; FCO since September 2004; Born 28/02/62; FCO 1983; Cairo 1984; Tokyo 1988; FCO 1990; Vienna (UKMIS) 1993; Rabat 1997; T/D Jerusalem 2000; World Wide Floater Duties 2001; Band B3.

Harris, Kay; SMO Freetown since August 2004; Born 25/11/72; FCO 1992; Islamabad 1998; Pristina 2002; Band C4.

Harris, Martin Fergus; Deputy Head of Mission Kiev since December 2003; Born 17/05/69; FCO 1991; (CFE) UKDEL Vienna 1992; FCO 1997; Full-Time Language Training 1998; On loan to DFID as First Secretary (KHF), Moscow 1999; m 1993 Linda Margaret Maclachlan (2d 2001, 2003).

Harris, Peter Harold Charles; Counsellor FCO since September 2003; Born 25/01/50; FCO 1981; Second later First Secretary (Social and Agriculture) Lisbon 1981; FCO 1984; First Secretary Moscow 1985; FCO 1988; First Secretary Santiago 1990; FCO 1993; Counsellor Warsaw 1998; Counsellor Lisbon 2002; m 1976 Maria Judith Ocazionez (4s 1980, 1982, 1984, 1993).

Harrison, Caroline Margaret; First Secretary FCO since August 1999; Born 08/09/66; FCO 1989; First Secretary Helsinki 1997; Band C5.

Harrison, Charles Dale; Management Officer Doha since February 2003; Born 23/02/55; MOD 1971; FCO 1976; Accra 1978; Mbabane 1982; FCO 1985; Rome 1988; Islamabad 1991; FCO 1994; Second Secretary (Management) Brussels (UKREP) 1998; Band C4; m 1978 Lorraine Josie Richards (1d 1987; 1s 1990).

Harrison, Guy Andrew; First Secretary (Commercial) Brussels since June 2002; Born 30/05/64; FCO 1986; Language Training and later Third Secretary (Political) Seoul 1987; Munich 1992; Hanoi 1993; FCO 1995; Second Secretary (Economic) Seoul 1998; Band C5; m 1996 Ann Van Dyck (1d 1999).

Harrison, Paula Leslie; Second Secretary Ankara since January 2005; Born 05/09/78; FCO 2000; Band C4.

Harrison, Robert James; Second Secretary (Political) Harare since July 2005; Born 10/09/76; FCO 2002; Band C4; ptnr, Andrea Robinson.

Harrison, Stephen Thomas, MBE (2000); Deputy Head of Mission Bahrain since June 2005; Born 14/08/64; FCO 1986; Language Training SOAS 1987; Language Training Cairo 1988; Third Secretary (Chancery) Bahrain 1989; Full-Time Language Training (Russian) 1993; Moscow 1994; HM Consul-General Ekaterinburg 1998; FCO 2000; On attachment as Assistant Private Secretary to the Duke of York, Buckingham Palace 2001; Band D6; m 1995 Philippa Capper (1d 1993; 1s 1998).

Harrison, Victoria Jane; Second Secretary (Political) Helsinki since August 2000; Born 31/10/74; FCO 1997; Full-Time Language Training 1999; Band C4.

Harrison, William Alistair, CVO (1996); High Commissioner Lusaka since August 2005; Born 14/11/54; FCO 1977; Third later Second Secretary Warsaw 1979; Second later First Secretary FCO 1982; Private Secretary to the Parliamentary Under Secretary 1984; First Secretary New York (UKMIS) 1987; First Secretary FCO 1992; Deputy Head of Mission Warsaw 1995; On loan as Foreign Policy Adviser to the European Commission 1998; Counsellor and Head of Chancery New York (UKMIS) 2000; Head of United Nations Department, later International Organisations Department FCO 2003; m (1) 1981 Theresa Mary Morrison (diss 1991); (2) 1996 Sarah Judith Wood (1d 1999; twins, 1s and 1d 2003).

Harrocks, Nicholas James Laurent; SUPL since September 2002; Born 16/04/73; FCO 1996; Full-Time Language Training 1998; Second Secretary (Political) Riyadh 1999.

Harrod, Jean (née Geary); First Secretary (Political) Canberra since October 2000; Born 28/04/54; FCO 1972; Geneva (CSCE) 1973; East

Berlin 1975; Port Louis 1977; Peking 1980; SUPL 1983; FCO 1986; Third later Second Secretary (Chancery) Brussels (UKREP) 1992; Second Secretary and Consul Jakarta 1994; FCO 1997; m 1974 Jeffrey Harrod.

Harrod, Jeffrey; First Secretary (External Affairs) Canberra since October 2000; Born 01/04/54; FCO 1970; Geneva (CSCE) 1973; East Berlin 1975; Port Louis 1977; Vice-Consul (Commercial) and later Second Secretary Peking 1980; Consul (Commercial) Shanghai 1984; Second later First Secretary FCO 1986; First Secretary (Commercial) Brussels (UKREP) 1990; First Secretary (Political/Economic) Jakarta 1994; m 1974 Jean Geary.

Harrup, Christine Mary; FCO since August 2003; Born 18/04/49; FCO 1974; Baghdad 1974; Lagos 1977; FCO 1978; Dublin 1981; FCO 1985; Addis Ababa 1987; Colombo 1992; Budapest 1994; Kiev 1999; Kingston 2000; SUPL 2003; Band B3.

Harsent, Susan Elizabeth; FCO since November 2001; Born 16/06/49; FCO 1970; Bonn 1972; FCO 1975; Suva 1976; FCO 1978; Tel Aviv 1982; FCO 1984; Brussels (UKREP) 1989; Shanghai 1998; Band B3.

Harston, Stewart Ian; FCO since March 2000; Born 03/11/63; Singapore 1990; FCO 1994; Amman 1997; Band C5; m (1) 1990 Marianne Stallard (diss); (2) 1994 BG Carvello (2s 1995, 1998).

Hart, Graham Donald; FCO since January 2002; Born 25/10/46; FCO 1975; Tokyo 1977; Monrovia 1982; FCO 1985; JMO New York 1988; FCO 1992; New Delhi 1994; Canberra 1997; Band B3.

Hart, Jeremy Michael; First Secretary (Political) Valletta since September 2002; Born 24/02/57; FCO 1975; Paris 1978; FCO 1980; Second Secretary (Vice-Consul) Athens 1986; First Secretary FCO 1990; Band D6; m (1) 1979 Alison Jane Morrell (diss 1993) (1d 1984); (2) 1995 Penelope Helen Margaret Smyth (2d 1996, Hart, Simon Charles; FCO since September 2003; Born 13/12/57; FCO 1975; Brussels 1978; Tehran 1981; LA Floater 1983; Bogotá 1985; FCO 1989; Third Secretary Panama City 1993; Brasilia 1997; Bandar Seri Begawan 2000; Band C4; m 1987 Amparo Meza (2s 1993, 1995; 1d 1996).

Harte, Josephine Moira (née Campbell); SUPL since August 2003; Born 17/11/67; FCO 1988; Prague 1990; FCO 1992; Full-Time Language Training 1994; Vice-Consul Berlin 1995; SUPL 1999; Brussels (UKDEL NATO) 2000; Seconded to the North West Development Agency 2003; Band C4; m 1996 Derek Thomas Harte (1s 1999).

Hartley, James Leslie; FCO since November 2003; Born 18/08/49; St Helena 1975; FCO 1977; Lusaka 1978; FCO 1980; LA Floater 1983; Khartoum 1985; Second Secretary and Head of Chancery Ulaanbaatar 1989; Second Secretary FCO 1992; Deputy Head of Mission Phnom Penh 1994; First Secretary and Consul Kuwait 1997; Deputy Head of Mission Algiers 1999; Conakry 2002; Band D6; m 1984 Ann Lesley Oakley.

Harvey, Christopher Paul Duncan, CMG (2004); FCO since August 2003; Born 21/07/56; Second Secretary FCO 1986; Second Secretary Suva 1988; First Secretary (Chancery) Brussels 1990; First Secretary FCO 1995; UK Special Representative for Peace in Sierra Leone 1999; Deputy High Commissioner Nairobi 2000; m 1989 Anasaini Vesinawa Kamakorewa (1 step d 1987; 1 step s 1988).

Harvey, David; On loan to the DTI since July 2002; Born 10/11/57; FCO 1977; Dublin 1980; Kinshasa 1982; East Berlin 1986; FCO 1988; Guatemala City 1992; Second Secretary (WTO) Geneva (UKMIS) 1997; FCO 2001; m 1983 Bernadette Louise McMahon (1s 1987; 1d 1990).

Haslem, Michelle; FCO since November 2003; Born 18/02/74; FCO 1999; Second Secretary (Political) Kuala Lumpur 2001; Band C4.

Haslett, Matthew Frederick; Beijing since December 2001; Born 29/05/68; FCO 2000; Band A2.

Haswell, Charles Chetwynd Douglas; Director of Trade and Investment Promotion Beijing since November 2000; Born 18/02/56; FCO 1979; Language Training 1980; Beijing 1982; Second Secretary (Chancery) Ottawa 1986; First Secretary FCO 1989; First Secretary (Political) Vienna (UKDEL) 1994; First Secretary FCO 1996; Counsellor on loan to British Invisibles (now IFSL) 1998; m 1991 Sarah Caroline Folkes (1s 1994; 2d 1995, 1998).

Hatfield, Samuel Andrew Roland; FCO since November 2000; Born 15/01/63; FCO 1992; First Secretary (Political) Lagos 1995; First Secretary FCO 1996; SUPL 1999; Band D6; m 1995 Rachel Althea Rodney Pollaers (3d 1995, 1997, 2000).

Hatfull, Martin Alan; Deputy Head of Mission Tokyo since November 2003; Born 07/06/57; FCO 1980; Language Training 1982; Second later First Secretary Tokyo 1983; First Secretary FCO 1987; First Secretary Brussels (UKREP) 1991; First Secretary later Counsellor FCO 1995; Counsellor (Economic and Commercial) Rome 1998; Full-Time Language Training (Japanese) 2003; m 1980 Phyllis Morshead (2s 1984, 1987).

Haveron, Monica; Tel Aviv since November 2001; Born 29/06/67; FCO 1987; Nicosia 1990; FCO 1993; Valletta 1995; FCO 1998; World Wide Floater 2000; Band A2.

Hawkes, Julie Anne (née Carr); SUPL since November 1996; Born 05/07/64; FCO 1990; Budapest 1992; FCO 1996; Band A2; m 1996 Edward Clifford Hawkes.

Hawkins, Carl McArthur; FCO since August 2001; Born 25/09/50; FCO 1967; HCS 1974; FCO 1977; Third Secretary Bangkok 1989; Second Secretary FCO 1992; First Secretary Singapore 1998; m 1987 Yuko Shibuya (1d 1988).

Hawkins, John Mark; Consul-General Dubai since June 2004; Born 30/04/60; FCO 1982; Third later Second Secretary (Chancery) Pretoria/Cape Town 1984; First Secretary FCO 1989; First Secretary (Commercial) New Delhi 1993; First Secretary later Counsellor FCO 1997; Counsellor (Commercial) Madrid and Director of Trade and Investment Promotion for Spain 2000; m 1991 Rosemarie Anne Kleynhans (2s 1993, 1996).

Hay, Barbara Logan, CMG (1998), MBE (1991); Consul-General Istanbul since 2004; Born 20/01/53; FCO 1971; Language Training 1974; Moscow 1975; Johannesburg 1978; Second Secretary FCO 1980; Vice-Consul (Commercial) Montreal 1985; First Secretary (Information) Moscow 1988; HM Consul-General St Petersburg 1991; First Secretary FCO 1992; Language Training 1994; HM Ambassador Tashkent and non-resident Dushanbe 1995; Language Training 1999; Consul-General St Petersburg 2000.

Hay, Charles John, MVO (1996); FCO since September 2003; Born 22/09/65; HM Forces (Army) 1987-93; FCO 1993; Second Secretary (Political/Information) Prague 1995; First Secretary FCO 1998; First Secretary (Economic/Finance) Brussels (UKREP) 1999; m (1) 1992 Caroline Jane Windsor (diss 1997); (2) 2001 Pascale Sutherland.

Haydon, Joanna Mary; SUPL since February 2003; Born 14/03/69; FCO 1992; Full-Time Language Training Bangkok 1995; Vice-Consul Bangkok 1995; FCO 1999; On loan to the Cabinet Office 2001; Band C4; m 1998 Peter L Spoor.

Hayes, Julie Patricia; FCO since September 2002; Born 22/07/59; FCO 1988; Hanoi 1991; FCO 1993; Harare 1996; FCO 1999; SUPL 2001; Band B3.

Hayes, Kirsty Isobel (née Paton); First Secretary FCO since August 2005; Born 02/02/77; FCO 1999; Vice-Consul (Political and Economic) Hong Kong 2000; Private Secretary to the Ambassador Washington 2002; SUPL July 2004; Band C4; m 2002 Peter Richard Hayes (1d 2004).

Hayes, Oliver; FCO since October 2004; Born 10/06/78; Band C4.

Hayes, Peter Richard; Principal Private Secretary to the Secretary of State for Foreign and Commonwealth Affairs since July 2005; Born 11/04/63; DTI 1990; Cabinet Office 1994; FCO 1998; DTI 2000; Counsellor (Energy, Science and Environment) Washington 2001; Counsellor (Change Management) and Consul-General Washington 2004; m 2002 Kirsty Isobel Paton (1d 2004).

Haynes, Paul Elliott; Vice-Consul Hanoi since June 2005; Born 13/05/75; FCO 2001; Islamabad 2003; Band B3.

Haywood, Ian; FCO since January 2003; Born 02/10/59; FCO 1978; Kampala 1981; Düsseldorf 1985; FCO 1989; Peking 1994; Full-Time Language Training 1997; Lisbon 1998; m (1) 1984 Angela Jane Kennedy (diss 1988); (2) 1991 June Sandra Tyler.

Haywood, Nigel Robert; HM Ambassador Tallinn since November 2003; Born 17/03/55; HM Forces (Army) 1977-80; FCO 1983; Second later First Secretary Budapest 1985; First Secretary FCO 1989; Deputy Consul-General Johannesburg 1992; Counsellor and Deputy Head of Delegation UKDEL OSCE Vienna 1996; Assistant Director, Personnel FCO 2000; m 1979 Mary Louise Smith (3s 1984, 1985, 1991).

Hazlewood, Roger Derek; First Secretary (Management) Harare since January 2001; Born 10/01/50; FCO 1968; Georgetown 1971; Bonn 1975; Paris 1977; FCO 1980; Cairo 1983; Brussels (JMO) 1987; FCO 1990; Second Secretary 1991; Full-Time Language Training 1993; Second Secretary (Commercial) Warsaw 1994; Second Secretary (Management) Dhaka 1997; m 1971 Yvonne Helen Betty Johnston McPhee (3s 1973, 1976, 1978).

Head, Ian; FCO since April 1993; Born 21/10/46; Home Civil Service 1987; Bonn 1990; Band C4; m 1992 S. Bigonesse-Caron.

Healy, Claire Louise (née Roche); SUPL since March 2004; Born 17/03/72; FCO 1991; Warsaw 1995; Floater Duties 1998; Bucharest 2001; Band B3; m 2001 Gerard Peter Healy (1s 2003).

Healy, Denis Terence; Consul-General Casablanca since February 2002; Born 18/11/43; FO 1963; DSAO 1965; Belgrade 1967; FCO 1970; Port of Spain 1974; Second Secretary 1975; Vice-Consul Douala 1976; FCO 1979; Second Secretary (Chancery/Aid) Bridgetown 1983; First Secretary (Commercial) Brussels (UKREP) 1985; First Secretary FCO 1990; First Secretary (Commercial) Ankara 1991; First Secretary FCO 1996; First Secretary (Commercial) Tokyo 2000.

Healy, Dora Claire Sarah; FCO since August 1998; Born 30/08/52; Principal Research Officer; FCO 1982; Language Training 1986; Second later First Secretary (Chancery/Information) Addis Ababa 1987; FCO 1991; First Secretary (Political) Nairobi 1995; m 1983 Nicholas Guttmann (2d 1976, 1983; 1s 1985).

Healy, Martin Frederick; FCO since October 2000; Born 21/10/55; FCO 1972; Moscow 1978; FCO 1979; Third Secretary Pretoria 1984; FCO 1987; Hong Kong 1990; Second Secretary FCO 1993; Second Secretary Nairobi 1997; m 1977 Jane Catherine Stacey (2d 1981, 1983).

Hearn, Natalie Louise; FCO since March 2002; Born 13/07/72; FCO 1992; Peking 1995; ECO/VC Düsseldorf 1998; On loan to the DTI 2001; Band B3.

Heaslip, Lisanne Marie; FCO since October 2003; Born 16/01/69; FCO 1988; Belgrade 1998; FCO 1999; Tokyo 2000; Band B3.

Heath, Dale Anthony John; Singapore since July 2003; Born 26/03/63; HM Forces (RAF) 1983;

FCO 2000; Band A2; m 2005 Vanessa Vince (2 step s 1991, 1992).

Heath, David Jonathan; FCO since October 2004; Born 23/10/80; Band C4.

Heath, Gillian Carol; Suva since April 2001; Born 21/08/45; FCO 1969; Islamabad 1970; Kampala 1971; San Salvador 1973; Panama 1973; Kuala Lumpur 1975; Brunei 1976; FCO 1978; Havana 1980; Dar es Salaam 1981; Singapore 1984; Washington 1988; FCO 1989; Algiers 1990; FCO 1994; Cairo 1996; T/D Canberra 2000; Band B3.

Heatly, Charles Robert; Amman since January 2003; Born 07/08/70; FCO 1993; Full-Time Language Training Cairo 1995; Second Secretary (Political/Economic) Amman 1997; Second Secretary (Political/Economic) Sana'a 2000.

Hebden, Ian Mark; Washington since January 2001; Born 25/03/60; Royal Navy 1976-87; FCO 1987; Bonn 1990; Harare 1992; FCO 1996; Brussels (UKREP) 1997; Band A2; (1d 2002).

Hedges, Matthew James; Second Secretary (Political) Rabat since January 2002; Born 23/04/73; FCO 1999; T/D New York (UKMIS) 2000; Language Training 2001; Band C4.

Heffer, John William Charles; SMO Kampala since August 2003; Born 31/07/52; FCO 1971; Kampala 1973; FCO 1974; Victoria 1975; Bogotá 1977; Peking 1980; FCO 1981; Warsaw 1983; FCO 1984; Valletta 1988; Pretoria 1991; FCO 1994 (Second Secretary 1995); First Secretary (Management) Tripoli 2000; Band C5; m 1975 Lynne Ida Brown (2s 1977, 1980).

Heffield, Mandy Jane; Berlin since August 2003; Born 23/10/67; MOD 1986; FCO 2002; Band A2.

Hefford, Brian; Second Secretary (Consular) Bogotá since March 2003; Born 10/08/48; FCO 1969; Karachi 1972; Paris 1976; FCO 1979; Islamabad 1983; FCO 1986; Colombo 1989; Second Secretary Bangkok 1994; FCO 1997; m 1971 Susan Mary Gorman (1s 1975 (dec'd 1991)).

Helke, Jill Beynon (née Barker-Harland); SUPL since April 1999; Born 10/04/56; FCO 1978; Language Training Hong Kong 1981; Peking 1983; Second Secretary New York (UKMIS) 1986; First Secretary FCO 1990; SUPL 1990; New York (UKMIS) 1992; SUPL 1993; Geneva (UKMIS UN) 1993; m 1987 Heinz Michael Rudolf Juergen Helke (1s 1988; 1d 1990).

Hellen, Gary David; FCO since February 2003; Born 24/06/70; FCO 1990; Zagreb (ECMIS) 1992; FCO 1993; Dhaka 1995; Nicosia 1999; Band B3.

Helmer, Victoria Jane; Second Secretary FCO since July 2003; Born 19/10/75; FCO 1998; Full-Time Language Training 1999; Full-Time Language Training Cairo 2000; Second Secretary (Political) Amman 2001; Band C4.

Hemmings, Kathryn Louise; FCO since July 2003; Born 20/08/70; FCO 1991; New York (UKMIS) 1993; FCO 1996; Nairobi 1999; SUPL 1999; On loan to No.10 Downing Street 2002; Band B3.

Henderson, Andrew David Forbes; Consul-General São Paulo since September 2003; Born 12/07/52; FCO 1971; Latin America Floater 1975; Rio de Janeiro 1977; Second Secretary (Chancery) Oslo 1980; APS/Minister of State FCO 1985; Consul New York (CG) 1987; First Secretary Washington 1988; Consul and Deputy Head of Mission Luanda 1992; Cairo 1994; Head of Parliamentary Relations Department FCO 1998; Consul-General Jedda 2000; m 1987 Julia Margaret King (2d 1988, 1990).

Henderson, Christopher George; Vice-Consul (Commercial) Sydney since June 2004; Born 23/04/66; Metropolitan Police Office (Civil Staff) 1987; FCO 1990; Lilongwe 1993; FCO 1996; On T/D (Overseas) 1997 - 1999; Third later Second Secretary FCO 1999; Band C4.

Henderson, Matthew Magnus Murray; First Secretary FCO since March 1996; Born 19/07/60; Second Secretary FCO 1986; Second later First Secretary BTC Hong Kong 1988; First Secretary FCO 1990; First Secretary (External/Press) Peking 1992; Band D6.

Henderson, William Robert, LVO (1988); Director (Middle East/Africa), British Trade International since October 2001; Born 07/11/47; DSAO later FCO 1965; Moscow 1970; Sana'a 1971; Lima 1972; Rio de Janeiro 1973; FCO 1976; MECAS 1977; Dubai 1978; Second Secretary 1980; FCO 1983; First Secretary (Information) Madrid 1985; First Secretary FCO 1989; Deputy Head of Mission Abu Dhabi 1992; First Secretary FCO 1996; m 1969 Carol Mary Smith (1d 1973; 1s 1976).

Hendry, Ian Duncan, CMG (1996); Deputy Legal Adviser FCO since October 1999; Born 02/04/48; Assistant Legal Adviser FCO 1971; First Secretary (Legal Adviser) BMG Berlin 1982; Assistant Legal Adviser, later Legal Counsellor FCO 1986; Counsellor (Legal Adviser) Brussels (UKREP) 1991; Legal Counsellor FCO 1995; m (1) 1973 Elizabeth Anne Southall (1d 1975; 1s 1977); (2) 1991 Sally Annabel Hill.

Hennessy, Alexandra Mary (née Wintour); SUPL since September 2000; Born 25/03/66; Office of Fair Trading 1985; FCO 1987; New York (UKMIS) 1988; Vienna 1991; FCO 1995; SUPL 1996; T/D The Hague 2000; Band A2; m 1993 Anthony John Hennessy (1d 1996).

Hennessy, Anthony John; First Secretary (Commercial) The Hague since June 2000; Born 01/02/55; FCO 1980; Singapore 1981; FCO 1985; Second Secretary (Commercial) Riyadh 1987; Second Secretary (UN/UNIDO) Vienna (UKMIS) 1991; First Secretary FCO 1995; Band C5; m 1993 Alexandra Mary Wintour (1d 1996).

Henry, Elaine Monica; Hanoi since August 2001; Born 11/09/69; FCO 1989; New Delhi 1993; Maputo 1997; FCO 1999; T/D La Paz 2000; FCO 2001; Band B3; (1d 1991).

Henry, Mark; FCO since September 2003; Born 09/03/78; Band C4.

Hentley, Michael Joseph; Tristan da Cunha since April 2004; Born 13/07/46; CRO 1964; DSAO 1965; Benghazi 1969; Moscow 1972; Lagos 1973; Kaduna 1976; FCO 1978; Second Secretary (Commercial) Port of Spain 1982; Second Secretary FCO 1985; First Secretary (COCOM) Paris 1987; Deputy Head of Mission Dakar 1992; First Secretary FCO 1995; First Secretary and Consul Seoul 1999; First Secretary (Consular) Lagos 2002; m 1969 Janice Paterson (1s 1971; 2d 1973, 1979).

Herd, Theresa Ann; Second Secretary (Commercial) Brussels (UKREP) since August 2004; Born 24/10/54; FCO 1972; Resigned 1974; Reinstated 1980; Lilongwe 1981; FCO 1984; Pretoria 1986; Cape Town 1987; LA/Caribbean Floater 1989; FCO 1991; Full-Time Language Training 1994; Luanda 1995; Second Secretary FCO 1996; Full-Time Language Training 1999; Deputy Head of Mission Kinshasa 1999; FCO 2002; Band C4.

Heseltine, Lavinia Pauline; SUPL since July 2004; FCO 1974; Brussels 1975; Moscow 1979; Canberra 1981; Khartoum 1984; Lagos 1988; Dhaka 1992; SUPL 1995; FCO 1998; Peking 2000; Lagos 2002; Band B3; m 1990 Barry Heseltine.

Heseltine, Robert Andrew; ECO Casablanca since December 2002; Born 18/11/73; MAFF 1996-97; FCO 1997; St Petersburg 2000; Full-Time Language Training (French) 2002; Band B3.

Hetherington, Martin Duncan; FCO since July 2003; Born 22/02/74; DETR 1997; FCO 1998; T/D Second Secretary (Political) Islamabad 2002.

Hewer, Susan Jane; HM Consul Algiers since February 2005; Born 18/09/61; FCO 1980; Washington 1982; FCO 1985; New Delhi 1985; Strasbourg (UKDEL) 1989; Kuwait 1991; FCO 1995; New York (UKMIS) 1997; Floater Duties 2001; Band C4.

Hewitt, Norman; FCO since January 1989; Born 12/09/46; FCO 1981; Washington 1985; Band C4; m 1968 Catherine Georgina Sahadeo (1s 1975; 2d 1970, 1983).

Heyn, Andrew Richard; FCO since August 2000; Born 14/01/62; DTI 1985 - 89; Second Secretary FCO 1989; Second Secretary (Chancery) Caracas 1991; First Secretary FCO 1994; First Secretary (Political) Lisbon 1996; m 1988 Jane Carmel (1d 1994).

Hickey, Katherine (née Blair); Third Secretary (Political) Ottawa since December 2002; Born 11/02/69; FCO 1988; Tokyo 1989; Colombo 1992; Peking 1993; Full-Time Language Training FCO 1997; Third Secretary (Vice-Consul/ECO) Tokyo 1998; Band B3; m 2000 Sean Patrick Hickey.

Hickey, Patricia Helen; FCO since September 1997; FCO 1975; Bangkok 1977; FCO 1979; Canberra 1981; FCO 1984; New York 1986; Berlin 1988; FCO 1991; Hong Kong 1995; Band C5.

Hickey, Stephen Benedict; Brussels (UKREP) since November 2003; Born 07/06/79; FCO 2001; Band C4.

Hicking, Nicola Jane (née Boyles); SUPL since January 2005; Born 28/07/63; FCO 1983; Brasilia 1985; Lagos 1987; FCO 1988; Montevideo 1999; FCO 2002; Band A2; m 1992 Robert Hicking (2s 1994, 1996).

Hicks, Colin Michael, MBE (2002); Third Secretary (Chancery) Colombo since November 2002; Born 04/03/74; MAFF 1993-96; FCO 1996; Dublin 1997; Islamabad 2001; Band C4; m 1998 (1s 1999).

Hickson, Philip John; Wellington since November 2004; Born 21/03/65; FCO 1984; Kingston 1986; Floater Duties 1990; Tehran 1993; New Delhi 1996; FCO 1998; Band C4; m 1992 Amanda Ruth Woolham (2s 1993, 1995).

Higginbottom, Sandra Patricia (née Wright); SUPL since October 2003; Born 03/03/65; FCO 1984; Brussels 1986; Dhaka 1989; FCO 1992; Tunis 1997; Lagos 2000; Band B3; m (1) 1989 Robert Freeman Walker (diss); (2) 1997 Andrew Higginbottom (1s 1996).

Higgins, Gillian (née Newbury); SUPL since July 2002; Born 23/03/63; FCO 1987; Budapest 1989; FCO 1991; Grand Cayman 1995; SUPL 1997; Grand Cayman 1997; FCO 1999; New York (UKMIS) 2002; Band B3; m 1995 Russell Mark Higgins (2d 1997, 2002).

Higgins, Jean-Christophe; FCO since October 2004; Born 12/06/75; Band C4.

Higham, Andrew Bolton; Cairo since November 2002; Born 28/10/59; FCO 1982; Singapore 1986; FCO 1988; Government Secretary Hong Kong 1993; FCO 1997; Band C4; m 1989 Veronica Jane Nazareth (1d 1990; 1s 1993).

Hildersley, Sarah Jane; On loan to the DTI since November 2002; Born 30/05/68; FCO 1987; Brussels (UKDEL NATO) 1988; FCO 1989; Third Secretary (Management) JMO Brussels 1990; Floater Duties 1991; FCO 1994; Deputy Head of Mission Santo Domingo 1998; SUPL 2002; Band C4; (1s 1996).

Hill, Charles Edward; Deputy Head of Mission Muscat since December 2004; Born 31/03/63; FCO 1990; Third Secretary (Chancery) Doha 1993; Deputy Head of Mission Almaty 1997; First Secretary FCO 2000; Band D6; m 1996 Suzanne Victoria Stock (1s 2004, 1d 2004).

Hill, Duncan N; First Secretary (Trade & Investment) Santiago since October 2004; Born 08/12/68; FCO 1989; Berlin 1991; Full-Time Language Training 1994; Rio de Janeiro 1995; FCO 1997; Shanghai 2000; FCO 2002; T/D Basra 2004; Band C5; m 1992 Lisa Pegram (1d 2002; 1s 2005).

Hill, Jeremy John Leonard; FCO since September 2002; Born 03/05/57; FCO 1975; SOAS 1978; Tokyo 1979; Jakarta 1982; FCO 1986; Harare 1990; Second Secretary FCO 1994; Sana'a 1996; Second Secretary (Commercial) Seoul 1998; m 1985 Roosnadia (Nana) Roesno (1s 1990; 1d 1992).

Hill, Kristina Maria; Nicosia since October 2003; Born 10/04/72; FCO 1999; Third Secretary (External Relations) Brussels (UKREP) 2000; Second Secretary FCO 2003; Band C4.

Hill, Martin Henry Paul; Counsellor (Trade and Investmentl) Bangkok since February 2002; Born 17/05/61; Ministry of Agriculture, Fisheries and Food 1983; Privy Council Office 1985; MAFF 1986; First Secretary Bonn 1993; FCO 1996; Deputy High Commissioner Colombo 1998; m 1985 Kim Lydyard (3d 1992, 1993, 1996).

Hill, Michael Thomas; High Commissioner Vila since November 2000; Born 02/01/45; FO 1963; New York (UKMIS) 1966; Vientiane 1969; Kaduna 1970; FCO 1974; T/D Sana'a 1975; Second Secretary, DHM and Vice-Consul Ulaanbaatar 1978; Second Secretary (Cons/Immig/Aid) Port of Spain 1981; Second later First Secretary FCO 1985; Assistant to Deputy Governor Gibraltar 1988; First Secretary (Aid) Nairobi 1993; First Secretary FCO 1997; m 1977 Elizabeth Louise Carden (3s 1981, 1988, 1990; 1d 1983).

Hill, Peter Jeremy Oldham; HM Ambassador Sofia since January 2004; Born 17/04/54; FCO 1982; First Secretary (Legal Adviser) Bonn 1987; On loan to the Law Officers' Department 1991; Legal Counsellor Brussels (UKREP) 1995; Counsellor FCO 1999; HM Ambassador Vilnius 2001; m 1981 Katharine Hearn (1d 1987; 1s 1989).

Hill, Ruth; Copenhagen since April 2003; Born 30/06/71; FCO 2001; Band A2.

Hill, Sarah Margaret; Madrid since December 2004; Born 18/09/72; FCO 1995; Third Secretary (Aid) Belgrade 1996; Second Secretary (Political) Buenos Aires 1997; First Secretary FCO 2000; Band D6.

Hill, Simon Robert; SUPL since October 2000; Born 18/03/67; FCO 1994; Brussels 1996; FCO 1999; Band B3; m 1998 Carina Megia Abarca.

Hill, Steven John; FCO since May 2005; Born 07/04/62; FCO 1984; Second Secretary (UNIDO/UN) Vienna (UKMIS) 1988; Second later First Secretary FCO 1990; First Secretary New York (UKMIS) 1996; First Secretary FCO 1999; First Secretary (Political) Washington 2001; Band D6; m 1998 Geraldine Steele (2d 1995, 2001; 1s 1998).

Hill, Suzanne Victoria (née Stock), MBE (2003); SUPL since April 2005; Born 01/12/65; Home Office 1988-91; FCO 1991; T/D Accra 1993; Doha 1994; Third Secretary (Political/Aid) Almaty 1997; SUPL 1999; Second Secretary FCO 2000; Band C4; m 1996 Charles Edward Hill (1s 2004; 1d 2004).

Hillman, John; Deputy High Commissioner Valletta since July 2002; Born 30/05/48; FO (later FCO) 1967; Dhaka 1971; Budapest 1974; Calcutta 1975; Second Secretary (Commercial) Dublin 1979; Second Secretary FCO 1983; First Secretary and Consul Cairo 1988; Deputy Consul-General Sydney 1991; First Secretary FCO 1997; m 1978 Pushp Kanta Sahney (1d 1981).

Hilton, Christopher Charles Donald; FCO since November 2002; Born 07/11/69; FCO 1988; Budapest 1991; World Wide Floater Duties 1994; FCO 1997; Third Secretary (Chancery) Port of Spain 1999; Band C4.

Hilton, Margaret; FCO since September 1995; Born 09/08/53; FCO 1990; Strasbourg 1993; Band A2.

Hilton, Michael Anthony; FCO since October 1996; Born 07/03/50; Department of Employment 1973; FCO 1973; Manchester Business School 1975; Frankfurt 1977; FCO 1979; Second Secretary Ulaanbaatar 1981; Second later First Secretary FCO 1983; First Secretary (Dev/Comm) Kathmandu 1987; Hanoi 1990; First Secretary (Commercial) Tehran 1992; m 1976 Janet Elizabeth Tyler.

Himmer, Melanie (née Read-Ward); SUPL since December 1997; Born 16/05/68; FCO 1989; Warsaw 1991; Tashkent 1994; Band B3; m 1993 Alan Keith Himmer.

Hinchley, Carol Ruth; First Secretary (Commercial) Beijing since January 2005; Born 09/04/59; FCO 1981; Gaborone 1983; Stockholm 1987; Second Secretary FCO 1991; Second Secretary (Chancery) Wellington 1994; FCO 1999; Full-Time Language Training 2004.

Hinchon, David Alan; Third Secretary (Political) Almaty since September 2002; Born 15/04/67; FCO 2000; Band B3; m 2001 Anna Taylor (2s 1997, 1999).

Hines, Trevor John; First Secretary (Commercial) Tripoli since September 2004; Born 10/11/60; FCO 1979; Floater Duties 1982; Third Secretary (Consular) Jedda 1984; Riyadh 1985; FCO 1987; Third Secretary (Man/Cons) Belmopan 1990; Second Secretary (Commercial) Mexico 1995; Secondment to Fire Industry, 2000; On loan to British Trade International 2000; T/D First Secretary (Commercial) Bogotá 2002; On loan to Interchange-Partnership Sourcing Ltd. 2002; HLT 2004; Band C5; m 1985 Sandra Bradley (1s 1992; 1d 1994).

Hiorns, Sara Anya; FCO since September 2004; Born 26/09/72; Band A2; ptnr, Richard MacGregor Ashbridge (1d 2002).

Hiscock, Stephen John; High Commissioner Georgetown and Ambassador Paramaribo since August 2002; Born 16/06/46; Inland Revenue 1963; FO 1965; Kuala Lumpur 1968; Lusaka 1972; FCO 1976; Second Secretary 1977;

Islamabad 1978; First Secretary (Comm/Inf) Seoul 1982; First Secretary FCO 1986; Deputy High Commissioner Georgetown 1988; First Secretary FCO 1993; Consul-General Brisbane 1997; m (1) (diss 1982) (2s 1967, 1971); (2) 1983 Denise Mary Forster (1d 1986; 2s 1989, 1991).

Hitchens, Timothy Mark; Head of Africa Department (Equatorial), FCO since May 2003; Born 07/05/62; FCO 1983; Language Training Tokyo 1985; Second Secretary Tokyo 1986; Second later First Secretary FCO 1989; Private Secretary to the Minister of State 1991; First Secretary (Political/Info) Islamabad 1994; FCO 1997; On secondment to Buckingham Palace 1999; m 1985 Sara Kubra Husain (1d 1991; 1s 1993).

Ho, David Tat Lun; Stockholm since April 2003; Born 05/05/61; Home Civil Service 1989-1998; FCO 1998; Brussels (UKDEL NATO) 1999; Band A2.

Ho, Wai-Kit; FCO since November 2003; Born 25/11/75; Band B3.

Hoar, Gareth Keith; First Secretary (Commercial) Beijing since February 2002; Born 23/06/65; FCO 1984; Peking 1986; Santiago 1989; Washington 1991; FCO 1994; Language Training Guangzhou 1998; Consul (Economic) Guangzhou 1999; m 2000 Rebecca Xie.

Hoare, Michael John Antony; FCO since October 2003; Born 30/11/76; Band C4.

Hobart, Edward Andrew Beauchamp; Kuala Lumpur since May 2003; Born 30/11/71; FCO 1993; Third later Second Secretary Havana 1995; First Secretary FCO 1998; Band D7; m 1999 Suzanna Louise Massey (1s 2003; 1d 2004).

Hobbs, Jeremy Alexander; First Secretary (Chancery) Mexico City since May 2003; Born 08/02/61; Senior Research Officer FCO 1991; Second Secretary (Political/Technical Co-operation)) Bogotá 1995; Principal Research Officer FCO 1999; Band D6; m 1983 Ana Maria Erndira (1s 1990; 1d 1994).

Hodge, Christopher Martin; Brussels since June 2004; Born 29/08/73; MOD 1996; UK Delegation to NATO 1998; FCO 2000; Second Secretary (Political) Sana'a 2002; FCO 2003; Band D6; m 2000 Melanie Jean (1s 2002).

Hodges, Ian Foyle; Vice-Consul Jedda since April 2001; Born 30/10/67; FCO 1987; Budapest 1989; Paris 1990; FCO 1994; Third Secretary (Consular) Karachi 1994; Third Secretary FCO 1994; Third Secretary (Management) and Vice-Consul Tehran 1997; m 1991 Patricia Paule Andre Seguin (1s 1992; 1d 1993).

Hodges, Jeremy Andrew; FCO since April 2003; Born 16/07/67; FCO 1988; Floater Duties 1990; Peking 1992; Karachi 1994; Full-Time Language Training FCO 1998; Bucharest 1998; m 1992 Adele Bushnell.

Hodgson, Allen Richard; Second Secretary (Political) Amman since October 2003; Born 08/02/60; FCO 1977; Geneva (UKMIS) 1991; FCO 1995; Second Secretary (Regional Affairs) Cairo 1998; Second Secretary FCO 2001; Band C4; m 1989 Sally Maureen Cole-Hamilton (1d 1993; 1s 1997).

Hodgson, George Kenneth; SMO Damascus since September 2004; Born 15/02/49; FCO 1969; Lagos 1971; Belgrade 1974; Berlin CG 1975; Reykjavik 1976; Karachi 1977; FCO 1979; DHSS 1980-84; FCO 1984; Colombo 1985; Luxembourg 1989; Second Secretary FCO 1992; Second Secretary Ulaanbaatar 1995; Second later First Secretary (Management) Nicosia 1997; First Secretary (Management) Manila 2001; m 1971 Jill Taylor (1s 1975; 2d 1978, 1980).

Hogarth, Philip; Consul-General Bilbao since August 2003; Born 10/05/55; FCO 1976; Damascus 1978; Accra 1982; FCO 1984; Tokyo 1988; Paris 1991; Second Secretary FCO 1995; Deputy Head of Mission/Consul La Paz 2000; Band C4; m 1978 Monique Marie Therese Morand.

Hogg, Rachel Ann; Vienna since January 2002; Born 20/05/77; FCO 2000; Band A2.

Hoggard, Robin Richard; Head of Research Analysts, FCO since July 2004; Born 26/11/56; FCO 1982; Language Training SOAS 1983; Kamakura 1984; Second later First Secretary (Commercial) then (Economic) Tokyo 1985; First Secretary FCO 1989; On loan to DTI 1991; First Secretary (Political) Brussels (UKDEL NATO/UKDEL WEU) 1994; Counsellor (Management) & HMCG Tokyo 1998; Acting Deputy Head of Mission Ankara 2003; m 1988 Tonoko Komuro (1s 1995).

Hogwood, Jonathan Felix; SUPL since August 2004; Born 24/07/52; FCO 1971; Warsaw 1974; Islamabad 1975; Luanda 1978; FCO 1981; Dhaka 1986; Tokyo 1989; FCO 1992; SUPL 1995; Second Secretary (Commercial) Nairobi 1996; Second Secretary British Trade International 1998; m 1978 Susan Elizabeth Farmer.

Hogwood, Susan Elizabeth (née Farmer), OBE (2003), MBE (1981); T/D Nairobi since October 2004; Born 27/05/52; FCO 1971; Islamabad 1974; SUPL 1978; Second Secretary FCO 1982; Second Secretary (Aid) Dhaka 1986; Second later First Secretary (Consular) Tokyo 1989; First Secretary FCO 1992; First Secretary (Humanitarian) Nairobi 1994; FCO 1998; HM Ambassador Kigali 2001; m 1978 Jonathan Felix Hogwood.

Holbrook, Andy David; FCO since July 2003; Born 18/06/74; Band B3; ptnr, Donna Michelle Hart.

Holder, Donald John; HM Consul Athens since October 2000; Born 16/08/50; FCO 1976; Bonn 1978; Islamabad 1981; FCO 1984; Auckland 1985; BMG Berlin 1987; FCO 1988; Second Secretary (Commercial) Bahrain 1990; Language Training 1994; Second Secretary (Info/Visits)

Warsaw 1995; Consul (Immigration/Passports) Düsseldorf 1996.

Holdich, Patrick Godfrey Hungerford; FCO since September 1997; Born 19/09/56; Senior Research Officer; FCO 1985; Principal Research Officer 1990; First Secretary (Chancery) Ottawa 1992; m 1987 Ailsa Elizabeth Beaton (diss 1992).

Holland, Henry Robert Cumber; Deputy Head of Mission Bridgetown since October 2002; Born 25/11/57; FCO 1984; Second Secretary (Chancery) Nairobi 1986; First Secretary FCO 1989; First Secretary (Political/Information) Canberra 1993; First Secretary FCO 1997; m 1983 Anne Elizabeth Wardle (2s 1987, 1990; 1d 1988).

Holland, Neil R; Berlin since April 2005; Born 07/08/71; FCO 2001; Band D6; m 2000 (1d 2002).

Holland, Patricia Anne (Tricia); Counsellor on secondment to the European Commission since September 2002; Born 02/04/64; FCO 1986; Third Secretary (Chancery) Prague 1988; Second later First Secretary FCO 1989; First Secretary (Finance) New York (UKMIS) 1993; SUPL 1997; First Secretary (EU Affairs) Paris 1998; SUPL 2001; m 1997 Paul Thomas Arkwright (1d 1999; 1s 2001).

Holland, Stephen Peter; First Secretary (Internal) New Delhi since December 2000; Born 31/08/65; FCO 1999; Band D6; m Judith Kent.

Hollis, Ian Malcolm; Sofia since December 2003; Born 16/12/70; FCO 1989; Bonn 1994; Lisbon 1997; FCO 2000; Band B3; m 1997.

Holloway, Michael John; HM Consul-General Madrid since July 2005; Born 14/01/57; FCO 1976; Dubai 1978; Bucharest 1979; Africa/Middle East Floater 1981; Mexico City 1983; FCO 1984; Vice-Consul Barcelona 1988; FCO 1990; Second Secretary (Political/Information/Aid) Mexico City 1994; Deputy Consul-General Rio de Janeiro 1998; Director Immigration and Consul Dhaka 2002; First Secretary FCO 2003; Band D7; ptnr, Mauricio Rodrigues.

Hollywood, Jane Christina Emma; FCO since June 2002; Born 07/03/66; FCO 1991; Second Secretary (Political) The Hague 1998; Band C4.

Holmes, Alan Thomas; First Secretary (Press & Public Affairs) Moscow since September 2004; Born 25/09/53; FCO 1977; Brussels (UKDEL NATO) 1980; FCO 1982; Bridgetown 1986; Cairo 1989; FCO 1992; Full-Time Language Training 1996; Moscow 1997; FCO 1998; Second Secretary Sarajevo 2000; Full-Time Language Training 2003; Band C5; m 1980 Helen Hook.

Holmes, Helen (née Hook); Second Secretary FCO since December 1998; Born 26/05/51; Department of Employment and Productivity 1969; FCO 1969; Bangkok 1973; Lagos 1975; FCO 1976; SUPL 1980; FCO 1982; Bridgetown 1986; Cairo 1989; FCO 1992; Moscow 1998; m 1980 Alan Thomas Holmes.

Holmes, John Dominic; FCO since May 1994; Born 18/08/59; Inland Revenue 1977; FCO 1978; Paris 1984; FCO 1987; Warsaw 1989; The Hague 1991; Band C4.

Holmes, Sir John Eaton, GCVO (2004), KBE (1999), CVO (1998), CMG (1997); HM Ambassador Paris since October 2001; Born 29/04/51; Third Secretary FCO 1973; Language Training 1975; Third Secretary Moscow 1976; Second later First Secretary FCO 1978; First Secretary (Economic) Paris 1984; First Secretary FCO 1987; Counsellor 1989; On secondment to the De La Rue Company 1989; Counsellor and Head of Chancery (later Counsellor (Econ/Comm)) New Delhi 1991; Head of European Union Department (External) FCO 1995; Private Secretary to the Prime Minister for Overseas Affairs 1996; Principal Private Secretary to the Prime Minister 1997; HM Ambassador Lisbon 1999; m 1976 Margaret Penelope Morris (3d 1981, 1982, 1985).

Holmes, Michael, MVO (1991); First Secretary (Management) New Delhi since October 2001; Born 03/04/54; FCO 1973; Belmopan 1975; Rio de Janeiro 1978; Baghdad 1981; FCO 1985; Third Secretary Harare 1988; Second Secretary (Cons/Comm) Melbourne 1992; Second Secretary later Consul (Comm) Casablanca 1994; FCO 1998; m 1980 Jennifer Margaret Lesley Pike (1d 1982; 1s 1985).

Holmes, Paul Barry; FCO since 1997; Born 15/11/54; FCO 1972; Warsaw 1978; Bonn 1980; FCO 1982; Third Secretary Accra 1986; Addis Ababa 1990; FCO 1993; Hong Kong 1995; Band C5; m (1) 1975 Elaine Down (diss) (2s 1981, 1983); (2) 1988 Sarah Penelope Briggs (1d 1989; 1s 1991).

Holmes, Timothy Charles; Consul-General Sydney since April 2004; Born 26/04/51; Third Secretary FCO 1974; Language Training SOAS 1975; Language Training Tokyo 1976; Second later First Secretary Tokyo 1977; On loan to the DOT 1981; First Secretary FCO 1983; First Secretary (Chancery) Islamabad 1986; First Secretary FCO 1990; Deputy Head of Mission and Counsellor (Commercial/Economic) Seoul 1994; Deputy Head of Mission and Consul-General The Hague 1997; On loan to the DTI 2002; m 1973 Anna-Carin Magnusson (1s 1977; 1d 1988).

Holt, Denise Mary (née Mills), CMG (2002); HM Ambassador Mexico City since August 2002; Born 01/10/49; Research Analyst FCO 1970; First Secretary (Political) Dublin 1984; SUPL 1987; FCO 1988; SUPL 1990; First Secretary (Political) Brasilia 1991; Deputy Head of Eastern Department FCO 1993; SUPL 1994; Deputy Director Personnel Management FCO 1996; Counsellor and Deputy Head of Mission Dublin 1998; Director (Personnel Command) FCO 1999; m 1987 David Holt (1s 1987).

Holt, Sean Christopher Eric, OBE (1999); FCO since November 2004; Born 18/12/49; HM Armed Forces (Army) 1968-78; FCO 1978; Second

Secretary Havana 1979; First Secretary FCO 1980; Athens 1982; First Secretary FCO 1984; First Secretary (Chancery) Khartoum 1987; First Secretary FCO 1990; First Secretary (Political) Accra 1991; First Secretary FCO 1994; Counsellor Bogotá 1995; Counsellor Luanda 1999; Counsellor Freetown 2001; m (1) 1973 Jennifer Patricia Trevaskis (diss 1987) (1s 1974; 1d 1976); (2) 1987 Joyce Amanda Anderson (diss 1994); (3) 1999 Johanna Antonia Maria Rutten.

Homer, Richard David; Budapest since January 2001; Born 24/12/72; FCO 1992; Stockholm 1995; FCO 1997; Washington 1997; Band B3.

Honey, Sophie Margaret, MBE (2005); First Secretary Harare since October 2001; Born 18/11/72; FCO 1999; Cabinet Office 2000; Band D6.

Hook, Neil Kenneth, MVO (1983); Consul-General Osaka since October 2001; Born 24/04/45; FCO 1968; Moscow 1971; FCO 1972; Language Training Sheffield University 1974; Tokyo 1975; Second Secretary (Aid) Dhaka 1980; First Secretary FCO 1984; On loan to DTI 1986; First Secretary (Commercial) Tokyo 1987; First Secretary FCO 1992; HM Ambassador Ashgabat 1995; High Commissioner Mbabane 1999; m 1973 Pauline Ann Hamilton (1d 1975; 1s 1977).

Hopkins, Kathleen Elizabeth; Bratislava since March 2003; FCO 1994; Vienna 1996; Language Training 1999; Paris 1999; Band A2.

Hopkins, Melanie; Havana since December 2004; Born 09/08/73; FCO 2002; Band C4.

Hopkinson, Celia Lois; FCO since September 1995; Born 09/10/59; FCO 1979; New York (UKMIS) 1982; Sofia 1984; Paris 1986; FCO 1988; Lusaka 1992; Band B3.

Hopton, Nicholas Dunster; Counsellor (EU) Paris since July 2003; Born 08/10/65; FCO 1989; Second Secretary (Political/Information) Rabat 1991; First Secretary FCO 1995; First Secretary Rome 2000; m 1993 Maria Alejandra Echenique (2d 1998, 2000; 2s 2002, 2003).

Horder, Rebekah Elizabeth; FCO since September 2003; Born 28/09/79; Band B3.

Horine, Fern Marion; Strasbourg since September 2003; Born 28/07/69; FCO 1987; Vienna (UKDEL) 1990; FCO 1995; On loan to the DTI 1998; Second Secretary (Political) Baku 2000; Band C4.

Horne, Gordon; DMO Cairo since October 2002; Born 05/12/66; FCO 1986; Riyadh 1988; New York (UKMIS) 1992; FCO 1994; MO/VC/ECO Riga 1998; Band B3; m 1989 Susan Lisa Berry (2s 1991, 1993).

Horner, Katharine Sarah Julia; On loan to the Cabinet Office since May 2002; Born 15/08/52; FCO 1980; Moscow 1985; Senior Research Officer FCO 1987; PRO 1996; First Secretary (Political) (Internal) Moscow 1997; FCO 2000.

Horner, Simon; Second Secretary (Finance) New York (UKMIS) since June 2002; Born 10/12/69; DHSS 1987; FCO 1988; Nassau 1991; Floater Duties 1993; FCO 1995; Canberra 1998; Band C4; m 1995 Katharine Jean Gallager (1d1998; 1s 2000).

Horton-Jones, Sarah Caroline; Second Secretary FCO since July 1998; Born 13/10/68; Lord Chancellor's Department 1991-93; FCO 1993; Second Secretary (Political) The Hague 1996.

Hoskin, Thomas David; FCO since March 2003; Born 08/12/75; FCO 1998; Second later First Secretary Dublin 1999; Band D6.

Hosking, Simon Paul; FCO since June 2004; Born 15/06/71; FCO 1993; Second Secretary Santiago 1997; First Secretary FCO 1999; First Secretary (Science and Technology) New Delhi 2001; Band D6; m 1995 Allison Jane Christou (2d 1998, 1999; 1s 2001).

House, Greg Stewart; FCO since April 2001; Born 03/06/68; FCO 1988; Lilongwe 1991; Lagos 1995; Floater Duties 1999; Band B3.

Houston, Sharon (Sher) Linda; SUPL since September 2002; Born 14/06/68; FCO 1989; Bridgetown 1991; Brussels (UKREP) 1995; Islamabad 1998; Band B3; m 1993 Steve Giovanni Campbell (diss 1997) (1s 1996).

Howard, (Charles Andrew) Paul; Bangkok since December 2004; Born 23/09/60; FCO 1983; New Delhi 1985; Third Secretary Bridgetown 1989; FCO 1992; Third Secretary (Consular) Islamabad 1996; FCOS 1997; Second later First Secretary FCOS 1999; m 1984 Alayne Anne Whitehouse (2s 1987, 1988).

Howard, Alayne Anne (née Whitehouse); First Secretary FCOS since April 2000; Born 04/06/63; FCO 1982; New Delhi 1985; Third Secretary (Consular) Bridgetown 1989; SUPL 1992; Second Secretary FCO 1993; Second Secretary (Immigration) Islamabad 1996; FCOS 1997; Band C5; m 1984 Paul Howard (2s 1987, 1988).

Howard, Sarah Catherine (née Sullivan); Dublin since August 2003; Born 05/11/68; FCO 1987; Kingston 1989; Tehran 1993; FCO 1995; Harare 1998; Band B3; m 1989 Simon James Howard.

Howarth, Stephen Frederick; UK Representative with the Personal rank of Ambassador, to the Council of Europe at Strasbourg since March 2003; Born 25/02/47; FCO 1966; Vice-Consul Rabat 1971; Third later Second Secretary Washington 1975; Second later First Secretary FCO 1980; Seconded to ENA Paris 1982; First Secretary FCO 1984; Deputy Head of Mission Dakar 1984; First Secretary FCO 1988; Counsellor and Deputy Head of PUSD 1990; Head of Consular Department later Division 1992; Minister Paris 1997; m 1966 Jennifer Mary Chrissop (2d 1966, 1970; 1s 1974).

Howden, Yvonne Catherine Helen; Floater Duties since December 2003; Born 06/03/73; FCO 1997; Luanda 1998; FCO 1999; Prague 2000; Band B3.

Howe-Jones, Vanessa Jane; First Secretary (Political) New York (UKMIS) since September 2001; Born 23/06/65; FCO 1991; Full-Time Language Training 1992; Second Secretary Budapest (KHF) 1993; First Secretary FCO 1996; T/D Brussels (UKREP) 2000.

Howel, Iwan Gruffydd; SUPL since October 2002; Born 05/01/68; FCO 1988; Washington 1991; Brasilia 1994; Beijing 1999; Band B3.

Howells, Julie (née Satchell); SUPL since July 2001; Born 03/06/64; FCO 1982; Brussels (UKDEL NATO) 1986; Seoul 1991; Dar es Salaam 1996; Band B3; m 1991 David Howells.

Howitt, Derrick; Istanbul since May 1999; Born 14/02/43; Royal Navy 1958 - 83; Moscow 1983; Paris 1985; Singapore 1988; Colombo 1991; Floater Duties 1995; Band B3; m 1966 Averil E Rose (1d 1968; 1s 1972).

Howlett, David John; Senior Principal Research Officer FCO since June 1982; Born 17/01/55; m 1979 Bridget Mary de Boer.

Howlett, Keith Raymond; FCO since 1998; Born 29/03/50; FCO 1968; Moscow 1980; FCO 1982; Tokyo 1986; Second Secretary FCO 1989; Second Secretary Caracas 1994; Band D6; m (1) (diss 1998); (2) 1998 Natasha Mota Hurtado (1 step d 1996, 1d 2002; 1s 2001).

Huckle, Alan Edden; Governor Stanley and Commissioner for South Georgia and Sandwich Islands since 2006; Born 15/06/48; Civil Service Department 1971; On loan to Northern Ireland Office 1974; Civil Service Department 1975; On loan to Northern Ireland Office 1978; First Secretary FCO 1980; Executive Director British Information Services New York 1983; Head of Chancery Manila 1987; First Secretary FCO 1990; Counsellor and Deputy Head of Delegation Vienna (UKDEL CSCE) 1992; Head of Dependent Territories Regional Secretariat Bridgetown 1996; Head of OSCE/Council of Europe Department FCO 1998; Head of Overseas Territories Department FCO 2001; Governor Anguilla 2004; m 1973 Helen Myra Gibson (1s 1981; 1d 1985).

Huckle, Steven Allan; First Secretary Moscow since August 2000; Born 24/10/64; FCO 1981; Brussels (UKREP) 1989; FCO 1992; Sofia 1994; FCO 1997; Band C5; m 1987 Alison Elaine Porter (1s 1990; 1d 1991).

Hudman, Anne (née Lister); SUPL since December 2002; Born 01/09/62; FCO 1987; Helsinki 1989; FCO 1992; Bonn 1993; St Petersburg 1996; Third Secretary (Commercial) Vienna Embassy 1999; FCO 2002; Band B3; m 1991 Roger Grenville Hudman.

Hudson, James Alexander; Sarajevo since November 2003; Born 14/01/72; FCO 1994; Havana 1996; FCO 1998; Tirana 1999; T/D Budapest 2000; T/D Skopje 2000; St Petersburg 2000; Montserrat 2002; Band B3; m 1996 Sally Barrett (diss 1997) (1d 1995).

Huggins, Elaine Anne; Kuala Lumpur since July 2003; Born 04/05/59; WRAC 1978 - 82; MOD 1983 - 86; FCO 1997; Lisbon 1998; Band B3; m Michael James Huggins (1d 1988; 1s 1995).

Huggins, Elizabeth June; SUPL since July 2003; Born 25/06/70; DSS 1987; FCO 1989; Copenhagen 1992; FCO 1993; Budapest 1995; SUPL 1998; FCO 2001; Band B3; m 1997 Phillip David Culligan (1d 1999).

Hughes, Beverley Elizabeth (née Lewis); FCO since October 2002; Born 22/07/66; HCS 1985; FCO 1985; Karachi 1987; Africa/Middle East Floater 1991; FCO 1994; SUPL 1998; Band C4; m 1997 Peter John Hughes.

Hughes, Dr Edgar John; HM Ambassador Buenos Aires since November 2004; Born 27/07/47; FCO 1973; On secondment to Cabinet Office 1979; First Secretary CSCE Madrid 1981; FCO 1982; First Secretary and Head of Chancery Santiago 1983; First Secretary (Information) Washington 1985; First Secretary later Counsellor FCO 1989; Deputy Head of Mission Oslo 1993; Change Manager FCO 1997; On secondment to BAe Systems 1999; HM Ambassador Caracas 2000; Seconded to Shell as Vice President, International Relations 2003; m 1982 Lynne Evans (2s 1984, 1988).

Hughes, Geraldine Mary; FCO since November 2002; Born 24/03/76; Band A2.

Hughes, Ian Noel; Deputy High Commissioner Mumbai since October 2003; Born 05/12/51; FCO 1971; Latin America Floater 1974; Kabul 1976; Warsaw 1980; FCO 1982; Second Secretary and Vice-Consul Tegucigalpa 1985; First Secretary (Political) Berne 1988; First Secretary FCO 1993; First Secretary (Press/Information) New Delhi 1993; First Secretary FCO 1997; Deputy Head of Mission Mexico City 2000; m 1978 Teresa June Tinguely (2s 1979, 1981; 1d 1984).

Hughes, Peter John; Kabul since June 2005; Born 14/09/53; FCO 1976; Islamabad 1978; Rome 1980; Warsaw 1983; FCO 1985; Second Secretary 1987; Vice-Consul (Commercial) Sydney 1989; Second later First Secretary FCO 1994; Resident British Commissioner Castries 1998; Deputy Head of Mission Colombo 2001; m 1997 Beverley Elizabeth Lewis.

Hulands, Michael Robert; FCO since February 2000; Born 29/11/53; FCO 1970; Singapore 1976; Tel Aviv 1978; FCO 1981; Third Secretary Bangkok 1983; Addis Ababa 1986; FCO 1990; Second Secretary Bonn 1995; FCO 1998; North American IT Advisor Washington 1999; m 1979 Normah Binti Maznun (2d 1981, 1986).

Hulbert, Neil Peter; FCO since November 2004; Born 21/06/63; FCO 1995; Berlin 1997; Oslo 2001; Band A2; m 2004 Malgorzata Hulbert (née Gamanda).

Hum, Sir Christopher Owen, KCMG (2003), CMG (1996); HM Ambassador Beijing since March 2002; Born 27/01/46; FO 1967; Hong Kong

1968; Peking 1971; Second later First Secretary/Private Secretary to Permanent Representative Brussels (UKREP) 1973; FCO 1975; First Secretary Peking 1979; First Secretary (Chancery) Paris 1981; First Secretary FCO 1983; Counsellor and Deputy Head of Falkland Islands Department FCO 1985; Counsellor FCO 1986; Counsellor and Head of Chancery New York (UKMIS) 1989; AUSS (Northern Asia and the Pacific) FCO 1992; HM Ambassador Warsaw 1996; Chief Clerk 1998; m 1970 Julia Mary Park (1d 1974; 1s 1976).

Humfrey, Charles Thomas William, CMG (1999); HM Ambassador Jakarta since March 2004; Born 01/12/47; Third Secretary FCO 1969; Language Student Sheffield University 1970; Second Secretary Tokyo 1971; First Secretary FCO 1976; Private Secretary to Minister of State 1979; New York (UKMIS) 1981; First Secretary FCO 1985; Counsellor Ankara 1988; Tokyo 1990; Counsellor FCO 1994; Minister Tokyo 1995; HM Ambassador Seoul 2000; m 1971 Enid Wyn Thomas (2s 1975, 1983; 1d 1977).

Humphreys, Nita (née Saha); Bucharest since July 2004; Born 23/12/69; FCO 1990; SUPL 1998; FCO 1998; Amman 2001; SUPL 2003; Band B3; m 1997 Phillip David Humphreys (1d 1998).

Humphries, Eric Henri Edward; Islamabad since March 2003; Born 11/10/59; FCO 1978; Islamabad 1982; Nairobi 1984; Victoria 1987; FCO 1990; Zagreb 1992; FCO 1993; Dhaka 1995; Jakarta 1998; FCO 2001; Band B3; m 1982 Sara Dorothy Watts (1d 1984).

Hunt, Sara Jennifer; FCO since January 2003; Born 29/10/67; FCO 1987; Bonn 1990; Full-Time Language Training 1993; Latin America/Caribbean Floater 1993; FCO 1995; Third Secretary (Political) Warsaw 1999; Band C4.

Hunt, Stephen Anthony; FCO since June 2003; Born 03/09/57; MOD 1977; FCO 1978; Lisbon 1981; Prague 1984; Gaborone 1986; Moscow 1988; FCO 1990; La Paz 1994; Full-Time Language Training 1997; Second Secretary (Political) Vienna 1999; Band C5; m 1984 Eileen Crossan (2s 1994, 1s 1996).

Hunt, Stephen Paul; First Secretary FCO Services since 1998; Born 13/01/61; FCO 1993; Brussels 1994; FCO 1997.

Hunter, David Eric; FCO since September 2001; Born 08/12/71; FCO 1989; Third Secretary (Political) Kiev 1998; Band B3; m 2000 Peta Leigh Brennan.

Hunter, Gordon Robert Peter; Ljubljana since February 2004; Born 11/01/80; FCO 2002; Band A2.

Hunter, Robert; Zagreb since September 2003; Born 10/08/47; HM Forces 1964 - 70; Merchant Navy 1973 - 74; FCO 1974; Darwin 1975; Beirut 1976; Peking 1977; FCO 1979; Lilongwe 1980; Jedda 1981; FCO 1984; Pretoria 1985; FCO 1988; Vice-Consul (Consular/Management) Suva 1989; Full-Time Language Training 1994; Deputy Head of Mission Antananarivo 1995; Second Secretary FCO 1997; Full-Time Language Training 2000; Second Secretary (Management) and Consul Sana'a 2000; Band C4; m 1981 Carol Mary Chorley.

Hunter Okulo, Paulette Elaine; Nairobi since August 2001; Born 17/10/65; FCO 1985; Lagos 1987; Peking 1990; Bridgetown 1993; FCO 1997; T/D Islamabad 1997; FCO 1998; Band B3; m 2003 Anthony Akelo Okulo.

Huntington, Janet Elizabeth (née Bull); SUPL since February 2003; Born 22/09/63; FCO 1986; Third later Second Secretary (Chancery) Managua 1988; Second Secretary (Chancery) Lisbon 1990; Second later First Secretary FCO 1993; First Secretary (Political) Caracas 1995; First Secretary (Trade Policy) New Delhi 1997; First Secretary FCO 2001; Band D6; m 1995 Daniel Peter Huntington (2d 1997, 1999).

Hurd, Thomas Robert Benedict; FCO since December 2004; Born 22/09/64; FCO 1992; Language Training 1994; First Secretary (Political) Warsaw 1995; First Secretary Amman 1998; Consul (Political) Jerusalem 2002; Band D6; m 1994 Katherine Siân Aubrey (2s 1996, 1998; 1d 1997).

Hustwitt, Justin John; First Secretary Tripoli since April 2004; Born 08/09/67; FCO 1991; Full-Time Language Training 1992; Language Training Cairo 1993; Second Secretary (Political) Cairo 1994; Second Secretary (Commercial) Riyadh 1995; First Secretary FCO 1997; First Secretary (Regional Affairs) Kampala 2001; Band D6.

Hutchings, Nicholas Alexander; Second Secretary Kabul since July 2004; Born 29/02/80; FCO 2002; Band C4.

Hutchison, Jacqueline Margaret (née Wigzell); SUPL since August 2002; Born 12/05/65; FCO 1987; Third Secretary (Commercial) Berlin 1990; Third Secretary Port of Spain 1993; Third later Second Secretary FCO 1997; Band C4; m 1993 Ian James Hutchison (1s 1995; 2d 2000).

Hyde, Richard Damian; Deputy Head of Mission Yerevan since October 2004; Born 18/09/69; FCO 1989; Hamilton 1991; Vice-Consul Paris 1995; Second Secretary (Commercial) Jedda 2001; Band C4; m 1994 Jacqueline Pearl Sadio.

Hyland, Mark; SUPL since December 2003; Born 03/07/69; HCS 1986; FCO 1990; Brussels (UKDEL NATO) 1993; T/D New York (UKMIS) 1995; Belgrade 1996; SUPL 1999; Sarajevo 2000; Band A2; m 1992 Deborah Jane Tomlinson.

Hyland, Susan Margaret; T/D Paris since April 2005; Born 30/10/64; Second Secretary FCO 1990; Second Secretary (Political) Oslo 1992; New York (UKMIS) 1992; Second Secretary UKDEL OECD 1993; ENA Paris 1994; First Secretary FCO 1996; First Secretary (Political)

Moscow 2000; Private Secretary to the Permanent Under Secretary FCO 2001; Band D7.

Hyman, Teresa; First Secretary (Technical Management) Bangkok since July 2002; Born 11/09/65; FCO 1983; Band C5; (1d 1985; 1s 1994).

Hyne, Sarah Jean; New York (UKMIS) since August 2001; Born 20/04/74; FCO 1999; PA to Deputy Heads of Economic Policy 1999; Band A2.

I

Inglehearn, Catherine Mary; Deputy Head of Mission Almaty since October 2003; Born 15/05/65; FCO 1990; Rome 1992; Third Secretary Ljubljana 1996; FCO 2000; Full-Time Language Training (Russian) 2003; Band C5.

Ingold, Andrew Henrik; FCO since September 1994; Born 30/07/53; Customs and Excise 1972; FCO 1973; Valletta 1975; Monrovia 1978; Paris 1982; FCO 1984; Bombay 1987; Vice-Consul Abu Dhabi 1990; Band B3.

Ingram, Rachel Victoria; FCO since April 2001; Born 25/04/69; FCO 1994; Berne 1996; World Wide Floater Duties 1998; Band C4.

Inkster, Nigel Norman, CMG (2003); Counsellor FCO since January 1998; Born 11/04/52; Third Secretary FCO 1975; Language Student/Third Secretary Kuala Lumpur 1976; Third later Second Secretary FCO 1976; Second later First Secretary Bangkok 1979; FCO 1982; First Secretary and Consul Peking 1983; Buenos Aires 1985; First Secretary FCO 1989; Counsellor Athens 1992; Counsellor BTC Hong Kong 1994; m 1977 Leong Chui Fun (1d 1980; 1s 1981).

Innes, Stuart Harcourt; Deputy High Commissioner Chennai since June 2003; Born 30/10/55; FCO 1980; Doha 1983; Second Secretary Cairo 1986; First Secretary FCO 1989; Deputy Permanent Representative Vienna (UKMIS) 1993; Deputy Head of Mission Damascus 1999; m 1983 Susan Jane Wood (1s 1987; 2d 1989, 1992).

Innes-Hopkins, Christopher Randolph; Cairo since March 2005; Born 26/11/53; FCO 1976; Third Secretary Georgetown 1979; Commercial Attaché Paris 1982; Second Secretary FCO 1985; HM Consul and Second Secretary (Commercial) Tunis 1988; Deputy Consul-General Jerusalem 1993; First Secretary FCO 1996; On secondment as Political Adviser to EU Special Envoy for the Middle East 1997; First Secretary (Commercial/Economic) Ankara 2001; Counsellor and Deputy Head of Mission Kuwait 2004; m 1983 Soraya Dookie (1s 1986; 1d 1993).

Ireland, Carol Anne Walls (née Hendry); Second Secretary (Management) Lagos since March 2005; Born 07/12/66; FCO 1985; Brussels (UKREP) 1987; Tokyo 1990; World Wide Floater Duties 1993; FCO 1995; On loan to the DTI 1999; FCO 2001; SUPL 2002; FCO 2002; Band C4; m 2004 Roy Ireland (1s 2002).

Ireland, Jonathan Charles Wintour; Addis Ababa since September 2004; Born 02/07/72; FCO 2002; Band A2.

Irens, Jules Marie Nigel; First Secretary (Political) Brussels since June 2004; Born 11/08/68; FCO 2002; Band D6; m 2002 Nicola Clare Charlton (1d 2004).

Ives, Malcolm Albert; First Secretary (Commercial) Muscat since August 2001; Born 10/03/47; MPNI 1964; FO (later FCO) 1966; Dacca 1969; FCO 1971; Sana'a 1973; Addis Ababa 1974; Warsaw 1976; FCO 1978; São Paulo 1981; Jakarta 1985; Second Secretary (Development) Amman 1987; Second Secretary FCO 1991; On loan to the DTI 1992; Second Secretary (Commercial) Riyadh 1994; First Secretary (Commercial) Accra 1997; m 1973 Susan Robertson (3s 1969, 1974, 1976).

Ives, Susan; Muscat since August 2001; Born 08/02/44; FCO 1992; Riyadh 1994; FCO 1997; SUPL 1997; Accra 1999; Band B3; m 1973 Malcolm Albert Ives (3s 1969, 1974, 1976).

Ivey, Peter Robert; Düsseldorf since September 2001; Born 25/05/58; FCO 1982; Bahrain 1983; Language Training 1987; Second Secretary (Information/Chancery) Helsinki 1988; On loan to the London Chamber of Commerce 1992; On loan to the DTI 1993; Full-Time Language Training 1995; First Secretary (Commercial) Zagreb 1996; FCO 1999; Band D6; m 1998 Sally Helen Elizabeth Hill (2s 1998, 2000).

Ivey, Sally Helen Elizabeth (née Hill); SUPL since September 1998; Born 25/10/65; FCO 1987; New Delhi 1988; FCO 1990; World Wide Floater Duties 1992; Full-Time Language Training 1995; Zagreb 1996; Band A2; m 1998 Peter Robert Ivey (2s 1998, 2000).

Ivins, Suzanne Gillian (née Parker); Second Secretary (Immigration) Shanghai since December 2000; Born 05/02/65; FCO 1983; Tokyo 1985; FCO 1988; Third Secretary (Consular) Ottawa 1992; Third Secretary Ho Chi Minh City 1996; Band C4; m 1988 James Browell Ivins (1d 1994).

Ivory, Jason; Lagos since May 2004; Born 04/08/70; Madrid 1991; Bombay 1994; FCO 1998; New Delhi 2000; Band C4; m 1992 Susannah Ruth Knowles (1s 1994; 1d 1995).

Izzard, Richard Brian George; FCO since March 2002; Born 04/01/69; Metropolitan Police 1987; FCO 1988; Sofia 1990; Accra 1992; World Wide Floater Duties 1993; FCO 1997; Luanda 2000; Band C4; m 2003 Ceinwen Mary Reeves.

J

Jack, Stuart Duncan Macdonald, CVO (1994); Governor Cayman Islands since November 2005; Born 08/06/49; FCO 1972; Third later Second later First Secretary Tokyo 1974; FCO 1979; First Secretary and Press Attaché Moscow 1981; First Secretary FCO 1984; Bank of England 1984; First Secretary (Economic) Tokyo 1985; Counsellor FCO 1989; HM Consul-General St Petersburg

1992; FCO 1996; Minister Tokyo 1999; FCO 2003; m 1977 Mariko Nobechi (2d 1980, 1982; 1s 1986).

Jackson, Anna Elizabeth; Second Secretary (EU) Warsaw since May 2001; Born 08/06/78; FCO 1999; Band C4.

Jackson, Clare Charlotte Mabel; Hong Kong since May 2004; Born 04/09/77; FCO 2003; Band C4.

Jackson, Freya; FCO since October 2003; Born 10/04/74; FCO 1997; Support Officer New York (UKMIS) 1999; Full-Time Language Training 2000; Second Secretary Buenos Aires 2000; Band D6.

Jackson, Helen; SUPL since September 1999; Born 27/01/62; FCO 1981; Stockholm 1983; Port of Spain 1986; Moscow 1990; Bridgetown 1993; FCO 1998; Band A2; (1d 1998).

Jackson, Lee Barry Thomas; Deputy Head of Mission Dili since March 2004; Born 02/07/65; FCO 1996; Full-Time Language Training Hong Kong 1997; Vice-Consul (Consular) Hong Kong 2000; Band B3; m 1995 Vanda Morais-Jackson (diss 1999).

Jackson, Paul Michael, MBE (2000); FCO since August 2002; Born 05/04/63; FCO 1982; Islamabad 1985; FCO 1987; Washington 1991; FCO 1994; Belgrade 1997; Helsinki 1999; Band C5; m 1984 Cheryl Barrington (1d 1986; 1s 1988).

Jackson-Houlston, William Lester, OBE (1994); Berne since December 2003; Born 06/10/52; FCO 1979; Second Secretary Brussels (UKREP) 1980; Second later First Secretary FCO 1981; Buenos Aires (BIS) 1982; FCO 1986; First Secretary Belgrade 1990; First Secretary FCO 1993; Counsellor The Hague 1999; m 1985 Susana Olivia Fitzpatrick (twins, 1s and 1d 1989).

Jacobs, Lisa Claire; FCO since January 2000; Born 21/03/65; FCO 1986; Moscow 1988; Riyadh 1990; FCO 1993; Peking 1995; SUPL 1998; Band C4.

Jacobsen, Neil Marius; Counsellor FCO since August 2003; Born 16/06/57; Second Secretary FCO 1984; Second later First Secretary (Economics) Athens 1986; First Secretary FCO 1989; First Secretary (Political) Madrid 1992; First Secretary FCO 1996; First Secretary (Regional Affairs) Santiago 2000; Band D6; m 1982 Susan Clark (1d 1984; 2s 1988, 1990).

Jagoe, Neale David; FCO since January 2002; Born 11/06/68; Royal Hong Kong Police 1990 - 96; Second Secretary FCO 1996; Second Secretary (Political/Information) Manila 1997; Band D6; m 1992 Margarita Hanio (2d 1988, 1992).

Jagpal, Harjit Kaur; SUPL since March 2004; Born 08/10/68; FCO 1988; Lagos 1991; Abuja 1993; SUPL 1995; Moscow 1998; FCO 1999; Band B3; m 1996 Robin David Phillips (diss).

James, Darren Ian; FCO since January 2005; Born 18/04/72; FCO 1998; Full-Time Language Training 2000; Beirut 2001; Band C4; m 2002 Clare Mallett.

James, Harriet Lucy; Assistant Legal Adviser FCO since November 2004; Born 24/09/75; Band D6.

James, Neill; Bangkok since December 2003; Born 06/07/71; FCO 1991; Dhaka 1994; Manila 1998; Sana'a 2001; Full-Time Language Training (Thai) 2003; Band B3; m 1997 Rangsiya Promsrisuk (1 step s 1990, 1s 1999; 1d 2001).

James, Nicola Patricia; Jakarta since April 2002; Born 29/09/60; FCO 1980; Peking 1983; Kuala Lumpur 1985; Bandar Seri Begawan 1988; FCO 1993; Band B3.

James, Stephen Anthony; First Secretary (Management) Mexico City since July 2003; Born 01/09/51; Customs and Excise 1968; FCO 1971; Saigon 1973; Peking 1975; Warsaw 1976; Manila 1977; Berne 1981; FCO 1984; Islamabad 1987; Third Secretary (Aid/Commercial) Mbabane 1990; Second Secretary FCO 1994; Second later First Secretary Tokyo 1996; m 1979 Nikki Jean Smith (2d 1980, 1982; 1s 1984).

Jamieson, Rachel Janet; FCO since May 2003; FCO 1993; Full-Time Language Training 1995; Third Secretary (ECO/VC) Bucharest 1996; Third later Second Secretary (Press) Islamabad 1999; Band C4.

Janjua, Nadeem Hameed; FCO since October 2002; Born 14/07/71; FCO 1999; Yaoundé 2001; Band B3; ptnr, Kathryn Whale (1d 2003).

January, Dr Peter; Head of OSCE/CoE Department FCO since July 2001; Born 13/01/52; FCO 1983; First Secretary (Commercial) Budapest 1985; First Secretary FCO 1988; Consul and Deputy Head of Mission Maputo 1991; First Secretary later Counsellor FCO 1993; HM Ambassador Tirana 1999.

Jardine, Martine; FCO since March 1999; Born 27/09/70; FCO 1990; Madrid 1993; Floater Duties 1997; SUPL 1998; Band C4.

Jarrett, Anne; FCO since March 2001; Born 26/01/60; FCO 1978; Moscow 1981; Africa/Middle East Floater 1984; Brussels (UKDEL NATO) 1986; Second Secretary FCO 1989; Second Secretary (Political) Peking 1993; Full-Time Language Training 1997; First Secretary (Economic) Bucharest 1997; Band D6.

Jarrett, Caroline Julia Rachel; Full-Time Language Training since January 2005; Born 07/09/76; FCO 1999; Second Secretary (Political) Islamabad 2002; FCO 2004; Band C4.

Jarvie, Carole Marina; ECO/Vice-Consul Addis Ababa since January 2004; Born 26/09/54; FCO 1984; The Hague 1986; Canberra 1989; Brussels (UKDEL) 1992; FCO 1998; ECO Istanbul 2000; Band B3.

Jarvis, Russell Thomas; Deputy Head of Mission Plymouth since October 2003; Born 27/09/47; Commonwealth Office (later FCO) 1964; Sofia 1969; EC Brussels 1972; Sana'a 1972; Islamabad

1973; FCO 1975; Second Secretary Dar es Salaam 1978; Vice-Consul (Commercial) BTDO New York 1982; First Secretary FCO 1986; First Secretary (Management) BTC Hong Kong 1990; First Secretary FCO 1994; Deputy Head of Mission Stanley 1997; m 1969 Joan Ann Wyard (2s 1971, 1986; 1d 1973).

Jay, Sir Michael Hastings, KCMG (1997), CMG (1992); Permanent Under Secretary of State and Head of the Diplomatic Service FCO since January 2002; Born 19/06/46; ODM 1969; UKDEL IMF/IBRD Washington 1973; ODM 1975; First Secretary (Development) New Delhi 1978; First Secretary FCO 1981; Private Secretary to Permanent Under Secretary of State FCO 1982; Counsellor on loan to Cabinet Office 1985; Counsellor (Finance/Commercial) Paris 1987; AUSS (European Community) FCO 1990; DUS (European & Economic Affairs) FCO 1994; HM Ambassador Paris 1996; m 1975 Sylvia Mylroie.

Jeenes, Kelley Elizabeth; SUPL since May 2001; Born 23/02/71; FCO 1992; Nairobi 1995; FCO 1997; Band B3.

Jeffery, Claire Rachel; FCO since January 2005; Born 20/04/73; FCO 1997; Second Secretary (Political) Stockholm 2002; Band C4.

Jeffrey, John Peacock Reid; First Secretary FCO since September 2003; Born 04/04/53; FCO 1971; Jakarta 1974; Singapore 1975; Africa Floater 1977; FCO 1980; Mexico City 1982; Bucharest 1986; Second Secretary FCO 1988; Second Secretary (Commercial/Consular/Management) Montevideo 1992; Second Secretary FCO 1996; ECM/Consul Tunis 1998; Band C4; m 1980 Arlene Elizabeth Watson (1s 1991).

Jeffreys, Stella Ann; FCO since December 1999; Born 16/11/62; FCO 1990; Dar es Salaam 1992; Hanoi 1996; Band B3.

Jenkins, Dr John, CMG (2003), LVO (1989); Consul-General Jerusalem since July 2003; Born 26/01/55; Second Secretary FCO 1980; Second later First Secretary Abu Dhabi 1983; First Secretary FCO 1986; First Secretary and Head of Chancery Kuala Lumpur 1989; First Secretary FCO 1992; Deputy Head of Mission Kuwait 1995; SOAS, University of London 1998; HM Ambassador Rangoon 1999; m 1982 Nancy Caroline Pomfret.

Jenkins, Owen John; First Secretary (Political) Buenos Aires since June 2002; Born 21/08/69; FCO 1991; Full-Time Language Training 1993; Third later Second Secretary (Political/Information) Ankara 1994; FCO 1998; m 1998 Catherine Margaret Baker.

Jenkins, Paul David; On loan to the DTI since November 2000; Born 22/06/51; FCO 1968; Bonn 1972; FCO 1974; Prague 1974; Monrovia 1976; Kaduna 1978; FCO 1981; Nairobi 1984; Gaborone 1986; Second Secretary FCO 1990; Second Secretary (Commercial) Lagos 1992; First Secretary (Commercial) Islamabad 1996; Yaoundé 2000; m (1) 1972 Jennifer Whitmarsh (diss) (2s 1976, 1979); (2) 1987 Elaine Vera Walsh (née Avery).

Jenkins, Peter Redmond, CMG (2005); UK Permanent Representative with Personal rank of Ambassador Vienna (UKMIS) since August 2001; Born 02/03/50; FCO 1973; Third later Second Secretary UNIDO/IAEA Vienna 1975; First Secretary FCO 1978; First Secretary and PS to HM Ambassador Washington 1982; First Secretary FCO 1984; First Secretary (Economic) Paris 1987; Minister/Counsellor, Consul-General and Deputy Head of Mission Brasilia 1992; Minister and Deputy Permanent Representative Geneva (UKMIS) 1996; m 1990 Angelina Chee-Hong Yang (1d 1992; 1s 1994).

Jenkinson, Eric, OBE (2003); High Commissioner Banjul since October 2002; Born 13/03/50; FO 1967; EC Brussels 1971; Islamabad 1973; Second Secretary (Commercial) Jedda 1978; Second Secretary FCO 1982; First Secretary (Economic) Bonn 1986; Consul and Deputy Head of Mission Bahrain 1992; First Secretary FCO 1995; First Secretary Tehran 1999; m 1973 Kathleen Forster (2s 1980, 1981).

Jennings, Kay (née Henderson); FCO since April 2004; Born 27/02/72; FCO 1993; Nicosia 2001; Band A2; m 2000 Richard Llewellyn Jennings.

Jennison, Vanessa Sandford; SUPL since July 2003; Born 25/02/64; FCO 1988; Third Secretary Geneva (UKMIS) 1990; FCO 1993; Vice-Consul Paris 1995; SUPL 1998; Vice-Consul Amsterdam 2000; m 1989 Geoffrey John Peck (2s 1993, 1997).

Jermey, Dominic James Robert, OBE (2001); Counsellor (Commercial) Madrid since May 2004; Born 26/04/67; FCO 1993; Full-Time Language Training 1994; Second Secretary (Political/Information) Islamabad 1995; First Secretary Afghanistan 1998; T/D Skopje 1999; T/D Dili 2000; FCO 2000; m 2003 Clare Judith Roberts (1s 2004).

Joad, Kate Louise; Cayman Islands since July 2003; Born 18/03/69; FCO 1990; Tokyo 1992; Floater Duties 1996; T/D Pretoria 1999; Second Secretary FCO 1999; Band C4.

Johansen, Laura Suzanne; FCO since January 2003; Born 05/04/77; Band B3.

Johns, Allison Marie; Kuwait since October 2004; Born 20/11/66; FCO 1988; Washington 1991; Bonn 1993; FCO 1997; Damascus 2000; Band A2.

Johnsen, Emma Louise (née Williams); SUPL since September 1998; Born 23/02/66; FCO 1990; Geneva (UKMIS) 1993; FCO 1996; Band C4; m 1992 Per-Arne Johnsen.

Johnson, Alison Jane (née Sindon); SUPL since May 2001; Born 16/11/63; FCO 1983; Mexico City 1985; Asunción 1988; FCO 1991; Sofia 1995; SUPL 1997; FCO 1999; Band B3; m 1997 Clive Andrew Johnson.

Johnson, Christine; Dakar since August 2001; Born 12/04/73; FCO 1997; Budapest 1998; Full-Time Language Training 2001; Band B3.

Johnson, Gail Antoinette; Third Secretary (Vice-Consul) Beijing since January 2004; Born 06/04/65; FCO 1989; Canberra 1995; Dhaka 1999; Band B3; m 1995 Steve Johnson (1d 1997; 1s 1999).

Johnson, Helen (née Matthews); SUPL since September 2000; Born 27/03/62; FCO 1981; Dhaka 1984; Moscow 1985; Tunis 1985; Berne 1988; FCO 1991; Islamabad 1994; San José 1998; Band B3; m (1) 1987 R B L Marzouk (diss 1999) (1s 1994); (2) 2000 Ridha Ben Larbi.

Johnson, Julie Michelle; Second Secretary (Consular) Canberra since September 2004; Born 12/11/63; FCO 1983; Port Stanley 1985; FCO 1986; Vienna 1987; Hong Kong 1990; FCO 1991; Bombay 1993; FCO 1993; Third Secretary (Management) and Vice-Consul Guatemala City 1996; Second Secretary (Consular) Kuala Lumpur 2000; Band C4.

Johnson, Katrina; SUPL since July 2004; Born 10/03/66; FCO 1985; Paris 1987; FCO 1990; SUPL 1992; Third Secretary (Institutions) Brussels (UKREP) 1993; On loan to the ODA/DFID 1996; SUPL 1998; Second Secretary (Economic/Trade Policy) New Delhi 1999; FCO 2001; Band D6; m 1994 Richard Adam Noble (2s 1996, 1998).

Johnson, Matthew Alfred; FCO since October 2003; Born 11/06/70; FCO 1988; Cape Town/Pretoria 1990; FCO 1993; Osaka 1994; FCO 1996; Second Secretary 1998; On loan as Private Secretary to Head of Policy Unit, No 10 Downing Street 1999; Second Secretary (Social Policy Issues) New York (UKMIS) 2000; Band D6; m 1993 Heidi Suzanne Burton (1s 1997; 1d 1999).

Johnson, Simon William; FCO since December 1999; Born 26/05/64; FCO 1983; Budapest 1987; Istanbul 1989; FCO 1993; Third Secretary (Visits) Peking 1996.

Johnson, Stuart James; Second Secretary FCO since January 2002; Born 08/05/72; Second Secretary FCO 1998; Second Secretary (Pol/Mil) Banja Luka on secondment to MOD 2000; Band D6; ptnr, Sally Turnbull.

Johnston, Paul Charles; New York (UKMIS) since December 2004; Born 29/05/68; MOD 1990-93; FCO 1993; Private Secretary to Lord Owen (International Conference on Former Yugoslavia) 1994; Second Secretary (PS/HMA) Paris 1995; Second Secretary (Political) Paris 1997; FCO 1999; Deputy Head of European Union Department (External) FCO 2001; Counsellor FCO 2002.

Johnstone, James; Kuwait since May 2005; Born 16/03/44; Army 1962 - 88; New York 1988; Peking 1991; Geneva (UKMIS) 1992; T/D Moscow 1995; Moscow 1996; Hong Kong 1998; FCO 2002; Band C4; m (1) 1967 Patricia Anne Strong (1d 1968; 2s 1969, 1974) (diss 1983); (2) 1986 Rachel Baliti (1s 1991).

Johnstone, Lauren Clair (née Blagburn); SUPL since September 2002; Born 21/07/70; FCO 1989; SUPL 1992; Scottish Office 1992; FCO 1993; Gibraltar 1997; Band B3; m 1992 Andrew Johnstone (diss 1999).

Jones, Adrian Ellis; FCO since October 2002; Born 15/07/65; Home Office 1988; Brussels (UKREP) 1998; Band D6; ptnr, Stine Strømsnes (1s 2002).

Jones, Alison; Lagos since February 2003; Born 19/12/72; DSS 1995; FCO 1998; World Wide Floater Duties 1999; Band B3.

Jones, Amanda Louise; SUPL since June 2003; Born 16/03/69; FCO 1997; Kigali 1998; Baku 2001; Band A2.

Jones, Andrew; FCO since August 2000; Born 02/03/67; FCO 1988; Hong Kong 1997; Band C4; m 1989 Lisa Roberts (1d 1993; 2s 1997, 2000).

Jones, Andrew Martin; FCO since June 2003; Born 14/12/59; FCO 1980; Darwin 1981; FCO 1984; Singapore 1986; FCO 1989; Third Secretary Amman 1993; FCO 1997; Copenhagen 2000; Band C5; m 1985 Amanda Wainer (1s 1988; 1d 1990).

Jones, Dr Brian James; FCO since September 2003; Born 03/04/77; Band C4.

Jones, Caitlin Olga; FCO since December 2001; Born 03/06/67; FCO 1990; Nicosia 1993; Brussels (UKDEL) 1996; Guatemala City 1999; Band D6.

Jones, Catherine Helen Courtier, MBE (1999); SUPL since August 2000; Born 13/09/56; FCO 1976; Moscow 1979; Latin America Floater 1982; Bogotá 1984 (Second Secretary 1985); Second Secretary FCO 1989; Deputy Head of Mission Tirana 1997.

Jones, David Alan; High Commissioner Belmopan since November 2004; Born 26/10/53; Lord Chancellor's Department 1970; FCO 1971; Tehran 1975; Islamabad 1978; Second Secretary on loan to the MOD 1981; Second Secretary FCO 1983; First Secretary (Commercial) Cairo 1986; First Secretary FCO 1989; Full-Time Training 1993; Deputy Head of Mission/Consul Luanda 1993; Deputy High Commissioner Dar es Salaam 1996; High Commissioner Freetown and also non resident HM Ambassador to Republic of Guinea 2000; SUPL 2003; FCO 2004; m (1) 1975 Jennifer Anne Wright (diss 1992); (2) 1994 Daphne Patricia Foley (1d 2001).

Jones, David Stephen; First Secretary (Management) Accra since February 2003; Born 19/09/51; Public Record Office 1970-73; FCO 1976; Port of Spain 1978; Peking 1981; Africa/Middle East Floater 1982; FCO 1984; Brasilia 1988; Tripoli 1991; Second Secretary on loan to the DTI 1994; Second Secretary FCO 1995; Deputy High Commissioner Honiara 1998;

Band C5; m (1) 1973 Jane Martin (diss 1978) (2) 1997 Carole Banstead.

Jones, Eric Malcolm; First Secretary (Management) and Consul Vienna since November 2001; Born 07/10/45; Passport Office Liverpool 1963; DSAO 1966; Middle East Floater 1969; Düsseldorf 1970; Vice-Consul Peking 1973; FCO 1974; Third Secretary (Commercial) Kuwait 1976; Second Secretary FCO 1980; Second Secretary (Aid) later Second Secretary (Chancery) Dhaka 1982; Second Secretary (Commercial) later First Secretary (Development) Lilongwe 1985; First Secretary FCO 1990; First Secretary (Development) Jakarta 1994; First Secretary FCO 1998; m 1988 Sylvia Margaret Hayhurst (1s 1989).

Jones, Frank; First Secretary (Commercial) Athens since May 2001; Born 07/09/48; FO (later FCO) 1967; Kaduna 1970; Brussels (NATO) 1974; Sana'a 1977; FCO 1978; Ottawa 1982; FCO 1984; Second Secretary (Visa) Paris 1989; Second Secretary (Commercial) Kuala Lumpur 1994; FCO 1997; Band C5; m 1982 Elizabeth Mary Lendrum (1d 1985; 1s 1991).

Jones, Jennifer Annwen; FCO since October 2004; Born 07/03/75; Band A2.

Jones, Katherine; Second Secretary New Delhi since September 2002; Born 07/08/65; Home Office 1990-92; FCO 1992; SUPL 1998; FCO 2001; Band C4; m 1999 Richard Joseph David Perry (1d 1998).

Jones, Leslie Norman; Istanbul since October 2004; Born 26/05/48; Army 1964 - 88; Cairo 1988; Moscow 1991; Budapest 1993; FCO 1995; Language Training 1999; Berlin 2000; FCO 2003; Band B3; m 1972 Dorothy Alma Tanner (1s 1977; 1d 1978).

Jones, Mark Hampton; First Secretary (Tehnical Works Officer) Pretoria since July 2003; Born 10/12/64; HCS 1982; Mexico City 1999; Miami 2001; Band C5; m 1999 Jennifer Tracy Cliffe.

Jones, Neale Robert; Copenhagen since December 2003; Born 20/02/63; FCO 1986; Islamabad 1989; Istanbul 1992; Dubai 1999; Band B3; m (1) 1992 Catherine Ingham (diss 1999) (2s 1993, 1995); (2) 2000 Ebru Jones (1 step d 1996; 1d 2000).

Jones, Nerys Heledd; First Secretary (EU/Economic) Rome since January 2005; Born 25/01/73; FCO 1999; Band D6.

Jones, Peter; First Secretary Rome since April 2003; Born 23/07/57; FCO 1976; Port Stanley 1979; Madrid 1981; Kathmandu 1984; FCO 1986; Peking 1988; Luxembourg 1992; Third later Second Secretary FCO 1995; Second Secretary (Political) Washington 1997; m 1979 Elaine Frances Scott.

Jones, Peter Edward; Counsellor (EU/Economic/Commercial) Rome since October 2002; Born 28/08/61; FCO 1985; Second later First Secretary Vienna (UKDEL) 1989; First Secretary FCO 1992; First Secretary (Politico-Military) Bonn 1994; Assistant Director Personnel FCO 1998; m 1998 Sumita Biswas.

Jones, Phillip Roy; FCO since March 2000; Born 18/02/50; FO (later FCO) 1966; Washington 1976; FCO 1979; Attaché Muscat 1982; FCO 1985; Moscow 1996; Band C4; m (1) 1972 Lesley Pamela Goody (diss 1981) (2s 1973, 1978; 1d 1975); (2) 1982 Karen Patricia Lyle (2s 1985, 1995; 1d 1987).

Jones, Ralph Mahood; FCO since July 2002; Born 04/05/69; FCO 1989; Riyadh 1992; T/D New Delhi 1995; Karachi 1996; T/D Kuwait 1997; World Wide Floater Duties 1999; Band B3.

Jones, Randolph Thomas; Second Secretary (Consular) Dublin since April 2004; Born 12/09/56; FCO 1976; Islamabad 1978; Colombo 1982; FCO 1985; Peking 1989; Port of Spain 1989; Copenhagen 1993; Second Secretary FCO 1997; Second Secretary (Immigration) Pretoria 2000; Band C4; m 1980 Kathryn Rosemary Smith (2s 1984, 1987).

Jones, Rebecca Louise; Havana since September 2003; Born 18/10/74; FCO 1998; Cairo 2000; Band A2.

Jones, Richard Alexander Owen; Second Secretary Zagreb since September 2001; Born 19/04/71; FCO 1990; World Wide Floater Duties 1993; Third Secretary (Vice-Consul) Tashkent 1997; Band C4; m 2000 Madina H Sagindirova.

Jones, Richard Christopher Bentley; First Secretary FCO since March 2003; Born 22/03/53; Second Secretary FCO 1978; PS to HM Ambassador later Second Secretary Tokyo 1980; First Secretary FCO 1984; Deputy Head of Mission Suva 1988; First Secretary FCO 1992; First Secretary Tokyo 1998.

Jones, Richard Hugh Francis; HM Ambassador Tirana since October 2003; Born 28/09/62; FCO 1983; Third later Second Secretary Abu Dhabi 1986; Second later First Secretary FCO 1989; First Secretary (External Relations) Brussels (UKREP) 1994; First Secretary FCO 1998.

Jones, Robert Edward; First Secretary FCO since September 2002; Born 30/05/47; FCO 1966; Singapore 1973; FCO 1974; Belgrade 1978; FCO 1981; Attaché Prague 1985; FCO 1988; Second Secretary 1989; Second Secretary Budapest 1993; FCO 1994; Second later First Secretary Bonn 1998; First Secretary Berlin 2000; m 1972 Linda Joan Edith Watts (1d 1974; 1s 1977).

Jones, Siân; First Secretary (Political) Pristina since April 2005; Born 08/11/74; FCO 1999; Second Secretary (Pol/Mil) Nicosia 2000; FCO 2003; Band D6.

Jones, Timothy Aidan; FCO since February 2003; Born 05/09/62; FCO 1984; Language Training 1986; T/D Vienna (UKDEL CSCE) 1987; Second Secretary (Chancery) The Hague 1988; First Secretary FCO 1992; T/D Mostar (EUAM) 1994; Full-Time Language Training 1995; Deputy Head of Mission Tehran 1996; HM Ambassador Yerevan 1999; m 2001 Christin Marschall.

Jones Parry, Sir Emyr, KCMG, CMG (1992); United Kingdom Permanent Representative to the United Nations at New York and the United Kingdom Permanent Representative on the Security Council since July 2003; Born 21/09/47; FCO 1973; Second later First Secretary (Political) later First Secretary (Economic) Ottawa 1974; FCO 1979; First Secretary (Energy) later First Secretary (Institutions) Brussels (UKREP) 1982; Counsellor on SUPL Brussels (EC) 1987; Counsellor FCO 1989; Deputy Head of Mission Madrid 1993; Deputy Political Director 1996; Director EU 1997; Political Director 1998; Permanent Representative Brussels (UKDEL NATO) 2001; m 1971 Lynn Noble (2s 1977, 1979).

Jordan, Paul; ECO/Vice-Consul Tallinn since January 2004; Born 16/03/71; HM Customs and Excise 1989; FCO 1997; Berlin 2000; Band A2.

Joseph, Nicholas Eli; FCO since April 2004; Born 12/01/71; FCO 2000; Second Secretary Geneva (UKMIS) 2002; Band C4.

Joshi, Bharat Suresh; Private Secretary to the Parliamentary Under-Secretary of State, FCO since April 2004; Born 23/08/69; FCO 1995; Third Secretary later Deputy High Commissioner Banjul 1999; Second Secretary FCO 2001; Band C5; m 1997 Bhakti Oza (2d 2000, 2002).

Joy, Rupert Hamilton Neville; SUPL since June 2003; Born 05/09/63; FCO 1990; Full-Time Language Training 1991; Full-Time Language Training Cairo 1992; Second Secretary (Comm/Econ/Pol) Sana'a 1994; Second later First Secretary (Political) Riyadh 1995; First Secretary FCO 1996; Deputy Head of Mission Rabat 2000; Band D6; m 2004 Kirsteen Scarr Hall.

Joyce, Lucy Rebecca; Second Secretary (Political) Paris since July 2004; Born 11/12/69; FCO 1992; Third Secretary (Political) Sofia 1996; Second Secretary (Political/PPA) Brussels 2000; Band C4.

Joyce, Marie-Claire; SUPL since June 2004; Born 04/05/69; FCO 1995; Full-Time Language Training 1997; Third Secretary (Commercial) later Second Secretary (Political) Tokyo 1998; Second Secretary (Economic) Tunis 2004; Band C4; m Makoto Noguchi (1d 2001; 1s 2004).

Joynson-Squire, Richard James; Second Secretary FCO since April 2002; Born 11/09/74; FCO 1996; Full-Time Language Training 1998; Second Secretary (Political/External) Islamabad 1999; Band C4; m 1998 Rolla Khadduri.

Judd, Claire (née Rowswell); FCO since October 1988; Born 13/01/55; FCO 1979; Quito 1979; Brussels (UKREP) 1981; Moscow 1984; FCO 1985; Mexico City 1986; Band B3; m 1996 David Judd.

Judge, Christopher John; First Secretary FCO since September 2004; Born 19/05/64; FCO 1980; Second Secretary Moscow 1996; FCO 2000; First Secretary Washington 2001; Band C5; m 1995 Fiona Jane (2s 2000, 2002).

Juleff, Andrew John Gerent; Second Secretary (Commercial) Rio de Janeiro since May 2000; Born 03/05/60; FCO 1986; Third Secretary (Aid/Comm) Kampala 1989; Vice-Consul CG New York 1991; Second Secretary FCO 1994; Band C5.

Jupp, Sheridan Arlene; SUPL since January 2002; Born 02/01/57; FCO 1990; Stockholm 1993; Band A2.

K

Kadan, Nina; FCO since October 2004; Born 27/02/81; Band C4.

Kahlow, Bonita; SUPL since April 2004; Born 23/01/66; FCO 1989; Rome 1993; FCO 1996; Rome 1998; SUPL 2001; Rome 2002; Band A2; ptnr, Antonio Pennetti (2s 2004).

Kana-Rupal, Sadhana (née Rupal); SUPL since September 2002; Born 31/05/66; FCO 1995; Band A2; m 1996 Animesh Kana.

Kane, Jacqueline; SUPL since August 2002; Born 25/03/67; FCO 1987; Athens 1990; FCO 1993; New Delhi 1994; FCO 1998; Band B3.

Kane, John Michael; Vice-Consul (Political) Jerusalem since November 2002; Born 23/12/72; FCO 1994; World Wide Floater Duties 2000; Band B3; m 2002 Camelia Sterescu.

Kariuki, James; New York (UKMIS) since September 2002; Born 06/05/71; FCO 1993; On secondment to UN Special Commission (UNSCOM) Baghdad 1994; Second Secretary (Political/Economic) Caracas 1995.

Karmy, Peter John; Second Secretary (Consular) Bangkok since October 2004; Born 01/07/47; FO (later FCO) 1967; Benghazi 1969; San José 1970; Seoul 1973; Kuwait 1976; FCO 1977; Sofia 1980; FCO 1984; Second Secretary (Admin) and Consul Manila 1985; Second Secretary and Consul (later Second Secretary Commercial) Ankara 1989; Second Secretary FCO 1993; Bogotá 1998; Head of Management Section Taipei 2001; m 1977 Eui Jong Han (2d 1979, 1981).

Kavanagh, Karen Jane (née Williams); SMO Beirut since March 2004; Born 28/04/70; FCO 1991; Brussels (UKDEL NATO) 1994; Bombay 1997; FCO 2000; Band C4; m 1996 Neil Richard Kavanagh.

Kavanagh, Neil Richard; SUPL since April 2004; Born 28/03/72; FCO 1992; Brussels (UKDEL NATO) 1995; Bombay 1997; FCO 2000; Band C4; m 1996 Karen Jane Williams.

Kay, Anthony Paul; Deputy Head of Mission Chisinau since November 2002; Born 29/06/72; FCO 1992; Hong Kong 1995; Third Secretary (Vice-Consul) later Second Secretary (Political) Bucharest 1999; Band C4; m 2004 Michelle Htun.

Kay, Helen (née Crocker); Tortola since March 2005; Born 24/10/67; FCO 1999; Madrid 2000;

SUPL 2004; Band A2; m 2004 Richard John Kay (1d 2004).

Kay, Martin Paul; FCO since February 2003; Born 21/03/68; FCO 1987; New York (UKMIS) 1989; Suva 1991; FCO 1994; Pretoria 1999; Band C4; m 2000 Sue Bradley.

Kay, Nicholas Peter; Counsellor and Deputy Head of Mission Madrid since December 2002; Born 08/03/58; First Secretary FCO 1994; First Secretary and Deputy Head of Mission Havana 1997; First Secretary FCO 2000; Deputy Head of Policy Planning Staff, FCO 2001; m 1986 Susan Wallace (1s 1987; 2d 1988, 1991).

Kay, Susan Pauline (née Bradley); FCO since February 2003; Born 16/05/62; FCO 1987; Pretoria 1999; Band B3; m 2000 Martin Paul Kay.

Kealy, Robin Andrew, CMG (1991); HM Ambassador and Consul-General Tunis since February 2002; Born 07/10/44; Third Secretary FO 1967; MECAS 1968; Tripoli 1970; Second later First Secretary Kuwait 1972; First Secretary FCO 1975; Head of Chancery Port of Spain 1978; Political Advisor Belmopan 1978; First Secretary (Commercial) Prague 1982; First Secretary later Counsellor FCO 1986; Counsellor, Consul-General and Deputy Head of Mission Baghdad 1987; Counsellor, Director of Trade Promotion and Investment Paris 1990; Head of AMD FCO 1995; Consul-General Jerusalem 1997; m 1987 Annabel Jane Hood (2s 1989, 1992).

Keefe, Denis Edward Peter Paul; Head of Far Eastern Group, FCO since July 2004; Born 29/06/58; FCO 1982; Second Secretary (Chancery) Prague 1984; First Secretary FCO 1988; First Secretary (Political) Nairobi 1992; First Secretary FCO 1996; Counsellor and Head of ASEM Unit, FCO 1997; Deputy Head of Mission Prague 1998; On loan as Counter Terrorism Strategy Team Leader, Cabinet Office 2002; Head of China Hong Kong Department FCO 2003; m 1983 Catherine Ann Mary Wooding (3d 1985, 1993, 1996; 3s 1987, 1989, 1991).

Keegan, David Barclay; First Secretary FCO since May 2002; Born 04/04/63; FCO 1986; Vice-Consul (Economic) Rio de Janeiro 1989; Second Secretary FCO 1991; Washington 1995; First Secretary (Political) Accra 1999; Band D6; m 1987 Susan Amanda Line (1s 1994; 1d 1996).

Keeling, Alison Heather; Private Secretary to the Political Director FCO since January 2002; Born 29/08/72; FCO 1996; Geneva (UKMIS) 1997; Beirut 1998; Band C4; m 2002 Reuben Thorpe.

Keeling, Heather; Lilongwe since December 2001; Born 04/05/71; FCO 2000; Band B3; m 2005 Stuart Carney-Graham.

Keen, Gillian; Bangkok since September 2001; Born 18/02/61; Home Office 1979; Cabinet Office 1987; FCO 1992; Hanoi 1993; Tokyo 1997; Band A2; m 1987 Raymond Keen.

Keller, Ciaran Joseph; SUPL since August 2002; Born 02/02/77; FCO 1998; New York (UKMIS) 1999; Full-Time Language Training Lisbon 2000; Second Secretary (Political/EU) Lisbon 2000; Band C4.

Kelly, Iain Charles MacDonald; FCO since March 2003; Born 05/03/49; FCO 1974; Language Training 1975; Moscow 1976; Kuala Lumpur 1979; FCO 1982 (Second Secretary 1984); Istanbul 1986; FCO 1988; Los Angeles 1990; First Secretary (Commercial) Moscow 1992; Consul Amsterdam 1995; HM Ambassador Minsk 1999; m 1981 Linda Clare McGovern (2s 1984, 1988).

Kelly, Mark Terence; Brussels since August 2004; Born 17/09/71; GCO 1990; Amman 1994; World Wide Floater Duties 1996; Panama 1999; FCO 2000; Third Secretary (Chancery) Tel Aviv 2001; Band B3.

Kelly, Paul John, MBE (1984); First Secretary Beijing since March 1999; Born 11/03/64; FCO 1982; Pretoria 1987; FCO 1989; Nicosia 1994; FCO 1997; Band C5; m 1993 V L Stone (1d 1993, 1s 1997).

Kelly, Robert Anthony, OBE (2003); First Secretary (Regional Affairs) Port of Spain since February 2003; Born 10/12/59; FCO 1986; Third later Second Secretary Hong Kong 1990; Second Secretary FCO 1994; Second Secretary and Vice-Consul later First Secretary Athens 1996; First Secretary FCO 2000; Band D6; m 1986 Heather Erica Christina Smith (1s 1992; 1d 1993).

Kelly, William Charles; Consul (Commercial) Düsseldorf since March 2002; Born 05/01/61; FCO 1980; Jedda 1982; Lisbon 1985; Warsaw 1988; FCO 1990; Private Secretary to the Ambassador Bonn 1993; Third Secretary (Commercial) Paris 1996; FCO 1999; Band C4; m 1983 Carol Ann Villis (4s 1985, 1987, 1990, 1992; 1d 2000).

Kendall, Louise Margaret (née Wood); FCO since September 2002; Born 16/01/63; FCO 1981; Prague 1984; Tel Aviv 1986; FCO 1988; Language Training 1991; Third Secretary (Commercial) Budapest 1992; Vienna 1996; SUPL 2000; Band C4; m 1988 Philip Gary Kendall (1d 1992).

Kendall, Philip Gary; FCO since July 2002; Born 28/04/65; FCO 1984; Tel Aviv 1986; FCO 1988; Budapest 1992; SUPL 1996; Vienna 1998; Band B3; m 1988 Louise Margaret Kendall (née Wood) (1d 1992).

Keningale, Jacqueline; SUPL since October 1999; Born 18/02/66; FCO 1986; Moscow 1987; SUPL 1990; Jedda 1992; FCO 1994; Damascus 1996; Band B3; m 1990 Paul Bevan Downing.

Kennedy, Paul Vincent, OBE (2004); First Secretary FCO since August 2003; Born 18/04/57; FCO 1989; Second Secretary (Chancery) Riyadh 1991; FCO 1995; First Secretary (Political) Bahrain 1999; Band D6; m 1984 Najia Ben Salah (1d 1990).

Kennedy, Thomas John, LVO (2004); Consul-General Bordeaux since February 2002; Born 03/02/57; FCO 1992; Second Secretary

(Aid/Information) Buenos Aires 1994; First Secretary FCO 1997; m 1985 Clare Marie Ritchie (1s 2000).

Kennedy, Trudi Michelle; Baghdad since March 2005; Born 17/02/75; FCO 2003; Band B3.

Kenny, John David; Second Secretary (Consular) Wellington since September 2003; Born 07/06/55; FCO 1973; Vienna 1976; Georgetown 1978; East Berlin 1982; FCO 1984; Cairo 1987; Third Secretary Dublin 1991; FCO 1995; Colombo 1999; Band C4; m 1979 Pamela Bernadette Baptiste (1s 1981; 1d 1985).

Kent, Andrew Magnus; First Secretary FCO since January 2001; Born 30/11/65; FCO 1989; Second Secretary (Commercial) Tehran 1992; Second Secretary FCO 1995; Consul Jedda 1999; Band D6; m 1991 Sarah Louise Mills (1s 1994).

Kent, Mark Andrew Geoffrey; Counsellor FCO since July 2005; Born 14/01/66; FCO 1987; Third later Second Secretary (Chancery/Information) Brasilia 1989; Second later First Secretary Brussels (UKREP) 1993; First Secretary FCO 1998; First Secretary later Counsellor (Commercial) and Consul General Mexico City 2000; Special Adviser to SACEUR (on secondment to SHAPE, Mons) 2004; m 1991 Martine Delogne (1s 1992; 1d 1995).

Kent, Sarah Louise (née Mills); FCO since April 1996; Born 28/01/65; FCO 1983; Prague 1987; FCO 1989; SUPL 1992; Band B3; m 1991 Andrew Magnus Kent (1s 1994).

Kenwrick-Piercy, Theodore Maurice; Counsellor FCO since December 1998; Born 16/01/48; Third later Second Secretary FCO 1971; Second later First Secretary (Press) Brussels (UKREP) 1974; FCO 1977; Nicosia 1982; First Secretary FCO 1986; First Secretary (Chancery) The Hague 1988; First Secretary FCO 1992; Counsellor Athens 1994; m 1976 Elisabeth Kenwrick-Cox (1s 1981; 1d 1983).

Keogh, David John; On loan to the Cabinet Office since April 1998; Born 24/06/56; FCO 1979; Ankara 1980; Abu Dhabi 1981; FCO 1983; Islamabad 1984; FCO 1988; Khartoum 1988; FCO 1991; Band C4; m 1987 Carolyn Ann Connolly (diss 1990).

Kernohan, Neil Alexander, MBE (1997); Private Secretary to the Political Director, FCO since March 2003; Born 20/09/65; FCO 1989; Riyadh 1992; T/D Vice-Consul Sana'a 1994; Vice-Consul and Third Secretary (Management) BIS Tripoli 1995; Third Secretary (IAEA/UN) Vienna (UKMIS) 1997; FCO 2000; Band C4.

Kerr, Christine; Nicosia since July 2002; Born 07/04/60; FCO 1989; Cape Town/Pretoria 1991; Moscow 1994; FCO 1996; Lilongwe 1998; Band A2; m 1991 Andrew Tuck (diss 1996) (1d 1994).

Kerr, Douglas James; On secondment (Commercial) since January 2003; Born 04/11/58; FCO 1980; Bucharest 1982; Kampala 1984; Tel Aviv 1988; FCO 1991; First Secretary (Commercial) Lima 1999.

Kerr, Michael John; Deputy Head of Mission Sana'a since January 2003; Born 12/08/49; RAF 1969 - 73; FCO 1973; Islamabad 1975; FCO 1977; Dakar 1979; FCO 1983; Cairo 1985; Oslo 1989; Second Secretary FCO 1992; Jedda 1995; Second Secretary (Management) Prague 1998; FCO 2000; m 1975 Linda Ruth Campbell (2s 1982, 1984; 1d 1989).

Kerrison, Irene; FCO since November 2002; Born 09/02/65; FCO 1986; Peking 1988; FCO 1990; Nassau 1991; FCO 1995; Language Training 1998-99; Moscow 1999; Band B3.

Kerry, Catherine Anne; FCO since October 2001; Born 31/07/65; FCO 1988; Lagos 1991; Tortola 1998; Band B3.

Kettle, Mark Brian, MBE (2002); SUPL since October 2003; Born 22/10/66; FCO 1985; Vienna (UKMIS) 1990; FCO 1993; Muscat 1995; Third later Second Secretary (Consular) Islamabad 1999; Band B3; m 1995 Justine Carey (diss 2001); ptnr, Yvonne Dimmock (1d 2003).

Khan, Karim-ullah Akbar; Assistant Legal Adviser FCO since August 2003; Born 22/06/68; Band D7.

Khoo, Lionel John; FCO since February 2004; Born 30/04/68; Northern Ireland Office 1991; FCO 1994; Bandar Seri Begawan 1997; Tallinn 2000; Band B3; m 2003 Jun GE.

Khosla, Nick Mahindra; Consul (Science and Technology) Shanghai since February 2004; Born 10/09/50; m 1978 Harumi Ishiwata (2s 1981, 1984).

Kidd, Deborah Ann; FCO since October 2004; Born 23/09/70; FCO 1992; Islamabad 1996; FCO 1999; Seoul 2000; Band B3.

Kidd, John Christopher William; Deputy Permanent Representative Brussels (UKDEL NATO) since August 2004; Born 04/02/57; FCO 1978; Third later Second Secretary Nicosia 1980; Second Secretary and PS to HM Ambassador Paris 1984; First Secretary 1985; First Secretary FCO 1986; Deputy Head of Mission Addis Ababa 1990; First Secretary FCO 1993; Counsellor on secondment to European Commission 1996; Counsellor (Political) Bonn later Berlin 1998; Counsellor FCO 2001; m 1995 Carine Celia Ann Maitland (1 step d 1983; 1 step s 1986; twin d 1996).

Kidner, James Hippisley; On secondment as APS to HRH The Prince of Wales since April 2003; Born 26/02/61; FCO 1985; Second Secretary Kuala Lumpur 1987; First Secretary FCO 1990; On attachment to Privy Council Office as PS to Leader of the House of Commons 1992; First Secretary FCO 1993; First Secretary later Deputy Head of Mission Sofia 1996; FCO 2000; m 1987 Sally Baillie-Hamilton (3d 1996, 1998, 2002; 1s 2000).

Kilby, David James; First Secretary (Regional Affairs) Cairo since April 2003; Born 05/11/66; FCO 2000; First Secretary (Political) and Deputy Permanent Representative ESCAP Bangkok 2001; Band D6; m 1997 Alison Jean McKenna (2s 2002, 2004).

Kiloh, Eleanor Anne; Second Secretary (Political) Jakarta since March 2002; Born 20/04/77; FCO 1999; Band C4.

Kilvington, Sally Louise; SUPL since April 2005; Born 20/02/67; FCO 1989; Santiago 1991; FCO 1995; Band B3; m 2002 Harsharan Singh Nijjar.

Kinchen, Richard, MVO (1976); HM Ambassador Brussels since November 2003; Born 12/02/48; Third Secretary FCO 1970; Temporary secondment to British Commission on Rhodesian Opinion 1972; MECAS 1972; Kuwait 1973; Second Secretary FCO 1974; Second later First Secretary Luxembourg 1975; First Secretary (Economic) Paris 1977; FCO 1980; PS/Parliamentary Under-Secretary of State 1982; First Secretary and Head of Chancery Rabat 1984; Counsellor (Finance) New York (UKMIS) 1988; Head of Dependent Territories Secretariat Bridgetown 1993; HM Ambassador Beirut 2000; m 1972 Cheryl Vivienne Abayasekera (1s 1976; 3d 1973 (dec'd 1980), 1979, 1982).

King, Alison Jane; SUPL since December 2002; Born 11/06/66; FCO 1984; Brussels (UKREP) 1987; Mexico City 1989; FCO 1993; Floater Duties 1996; FCO 1998; Band C4.

King, Alyson Ruth Grace; FCO since October 2003; Born 02/01/76; Admitted Practice (New York and England/Wales) 2000; Band C4; m 1999 Ayman Jarjour (1d 2001; 1s 2003).

King, Julian Beresford; Brussels (UKREP) since November 2004; Born 22/08/64; FCO 1985; Third later Second Secretary Paris (including ENA) 1987; Luxembourg and The Hague 1991; Second later First Secretary FCO 1992; Private Secretary to Permanent Under-Secretary of State FCO 1995; First Secretary later Counsellor (Enlargement) Brussels (UKREP) 1998; Counsellor and Head of Chancery New York (UKMIS) 2003; m 1992 Lotte Knudsen.

King, Larry; First Secretary Canberra since July 2004; Born 01/07/62; FCO 1982; Amman 1985; FCO 1988; Pretoria 1995; FCO 1998; Band C5; m 1988 Elaine Margaret Neeve (2d 1992, 1996).

King-Smith, Alastair; on loan to DFID since January 2005; Born 27/09/74; FCO 1996; Full-Time Language Training (Arabic) 1997; Cairo 1998; Deputy Head of Interests Section later Acting Chargé d' Affaires Tripoli 1999; Head of Political/Information Sections Khartoum 1999; FCO 2003; Band C4.

Kingdom, David George, OBE (2004); Istanbul since November 2003; Born 19/08/46; FCO 1986; Third Secretary Brussels 1992; First Secretary FCO 1994; Ankara 2000; Band C5; m 1968 Janice (2s 1972, 1981).

Kingford, Paul; Third Secretary Beijing since September 2003; Born 05/04/56; MOD 1987-98; FCO 1998; Tehran 2000; Band B3.

Kingston, Iain Conger; Management Officer Bahrain since August 2003; Born 30/05/50; DOE (PSA) 1975; FCO 1976; Cairo 1979; Lilongwe 1983; FCO 1985; Houston 1988; Maseru 1991; Second Secretary FCO 1995; Band C4; m 1978 Georgia Georgiou (2s 1982, 1983).

Kinoshita, Susan Margaret (née Copnell), OBE (2003); FCO since October 2003; Born 28/07/61; FCO 1983; Language Training Tokyo 1985; Tokyo 1986; FCO 1989; SUPL 1991; FCO 1992; SUPL 1993; Osaka 1996; First Secretary (Press and Public Affairs) Tokyo 1999; Band D6; m 1989 Makoto Kinoshita (1d 1991; 1s 1993).

Kirby, Diane (née Tallon); SUPL since April 1995; Born 25/01/67; FCO 1986; Muscat 1988; Gibraltar 1993; Band A2; m 1988 Sean William Kirby (1s 1991).

Kirk, Andrew Philip; Second Secretary (Economic) The Hague since September 1999; Born 26/02/54; FCO 1972; Yaoundé 1975; Havana 1979; FCO 1981; Vice-Consul Lisbon 1985; Aid Attaché Nairobi 1987; Second Secretary FCO 1991; BTIO New York 1994; FCO 1997; Vice-Consul (Investment) San Francisco 1997; Band C4; m 1978 Cheryl Jeanne Nichols (2d 1983, 1987).

Kirk, Anna Theresa (née Macey); FCO since July 2002; Born 01/06/59; FCO 1982; Language Training 1984; Third later Second Secretary Oslo 1984; First Secretary FCO 1988; First Secretary (Political) Paris 1992; First Secretary FCO 1997; Counsellor on loan as Resident Chair to Civil Service Selection Board 1999; m 1989 Matthew John Lushington Kirk (2d 1995, 1998).

Kirk, Malcolm Braidwood; Deputy High Commissioner Georgetown since July 2004; Born 10/04/59; FCO 1978; Nassau 1980; Dakar 1981; FCO 1984; Havana 1985; FCO 1987; Paris 1990; Deputy Head of Mission Tegucigalpa 1993; FCO 1997; Staff Officer later First Secretary (Head of Governor's Office) Tortola 2000; Band C5; m 1982 Linda Patricia Greenwood (1 step s 1980; 1s 1983).

Kirk, Matthew John Lushington; HM Ambassador Helsinki since August 2002; Born 10/10/60; FCO 1982; Language Training 1984; Third later Second Secretary (Political/Information) Belgrade 1984; Second later First Secretary FCO 1988; ENA Paris 1992; First Secretary (Political/Military) Paris 1993; Counsellor FCO 1997; Counsellor on loan to the Cabinet Office 1998; Counsellor FCO 1999; m 1989 Anna Thérèse Macey (2d 1995, 1998).

Kirk, Susan Mary; Rabat since September 2002; Born 28/04/46; FCO 1994; Nairobi 1996; Floater Duties 2000; Band A2; m 1969 (1s 1975).

Kirkpatrick, Andrew John; Kiev since June 2005; Born 01/06/63; FCO 1988; Third Secretary (Chancery) Budapest 1990; Third Secretary FCO

1992; Third Secretary (Immigration) Islamabad 1995; Third Secretary FCO 1998; Second Secretary (Management) Lagos 1999; Second Secretary FCO 2002; Band C5; m 1992 Sara Elizabeth Pickering.

Kitsell, Corinne Angela; First Secretary Geneva (UKMIS) since January 2006; Born 18/10/69; FCO 1992; T/D New York (UKMIS) 1994; T/D Beijing 1995; Vice-Consul Beirut 1996; FCO 1998; Band D6; m 2004 Mark Lewis.

Knapp, Maria Grace; SUPL since February 2005; Born 03/04/70; FCO 1989; Madrid 1992; FCO 1995; On loan to HM Customs and Excise at Caracas 1996; FCO 1999; Santiago 2002; Band B3; m 2004 Connor Shields.

Knewstubb, Rosemary Anne (née Urch); SUPL since June 2004; Born 26/10/68; FCO 1992; Ottawa 1995; Bucharest 1999; Brussels (UKREP) 2002; Band A2; m 1996 Mark Andrew Knewstubb.

Knight, Terence Ronald; Resident British Commissioner Kingstown since August 2002; Born 03/09/51; FCO 1973; Rabat 1976; Lima 1978; Islamabad 1981; FCO 1983; Oslo 1986; Third later Second Secretary (Chancery) Port of Spain 1989; Second Secretary FCO 1993; First Secretary (Management) Washington 1997; m 1971 Jane Willcocks (2d 1975, 1980; 2s 1977, 1982).

Knott, Graeme Jonathan; First Secretary (Trade and Investment) Paris (UKDEL OECD) since September 2000; Born 02/11/66; FCO 1988; Third later Second Secretary (Chancery) Havana 1991; First Secretary FCO 1995; First Secretary Mexico City 1996; Full-Time Language Training 2000; Band D6.

Knott, Paul Robert; Second Secretary (Political) Moscow since October 2004; Born 30/06/70; FCO 1989; Bucharest 1992; Dubai 1993; Full-time Russian language training 1997; Third Secretary (Chancery) Tashkent 1997; Second Secretary (Political) Kiev 2000; Second Secretary (Commercial) Brussels (UKREP) 2001; Band C4; m 2002 Mwana Lugogo.

Knowlton, Richard Jonathan; Counsellor Helsinki since October 2003; Born 25/03/50; Third later Second Secretary FCO 1973; Language Student FCO and Finland 1977; Second later First Secretary Helsinki 1978; First Secretary FCO 1981; Harare 1984; FCO 1989; First Secretary (Chancery/Economic) Dubai 1991; First Secretary later Counsellor FCO 1995; Counsellor (Regional Affairs) Bridgetown 1997; Counsellor FCO 2000; Counsellor Caracas 2002; m 1995 Evelina Ravarino.

Koizumi, Richard Akio; Tokyo since January 2004; Born 25/08/77; FCO 2002; Band B3.

Korad, Mark David; Second Secretary (Political/PPAO) Islamabad since March 2003; Born 19/06/69; FCO 1991; Bucharest 1994; Paris 1998; Band C4; m 1996 Corina Ioana Mantu (diss 2003).

Kraus, John Arthur; First Secretary (Political Internal) Berlin since August 2003; Born 07/05/66; FCO 1993; Second Secretary (Political) Bonn 1995; FCO 1998; Band D6; m 1995 Judith Mary Smakman (1s 1996).

Kruger, Gabrielle Lisa; Second Secretary - BCW The Hague since September 2003; Born 22/02/76; FCO 2001; Band C4.

Kuenssberg, Joanna Kate; First Secretary (EU Economic) Paris since January 2001; Born 06/02/73; Second Secretary FCO 1997; Attachment to Foreign Ministry, Budapest 1999; Attachment to Quai d'Orsay, Paris 2000; m 1997 Finbarr O'Sullivan.

Kydd, Ian Douglas; SMO New Delhi since February 2003; Born 01/11/47; CO 1966; DSAO (later FCO) 1966; New Delhi 1970; Second Secretary (Radio/TV) BIS New York 1975; FCO 1979; First Secretary on loan to No 10 Downing Street 1981; Language Training 1983; First Secretary (Chancery) Lagos 1984; First Secretary (Economic/Commercial) Ottawa 1988; First Secretary FCO 1993; Counsellor (Management) Moscow 1995; Consul-General Vancouver 1998; m 1968 Elizabeth Louise Pontius (1s 1971; 1d 1973).

Kyle, Michael Anthony; Counsellor FCO since February 1998; Born 20/07/48; FCO 1970; Third later Second Secretary Saigon 1972; Second later First Secretary FCO 1975; Washington 1978; FCO 1981; First Secretary (Political/Economic) Accra 1984; First Secretary (Chancery) Dar es Salaam 1988; First Secretary later Counsellor FCO 1991; Counsellor Berlin 1995; m 1976 Wendy Suzanne Sloan (1d 1979; 1s 1981).

Kyles, Raymond William; Deputy High Commissioner Nairobi since July 2003; Born 10/03/56; FCO 1980; Geneva (UKMIS) 1982; Second Secretary Brussels (UKREP) 1985; First Secretary FCO 1987; First Secretary (Chancery) Pretoria 1991; First Secretary FCO 1996; Deputy Permanent Representative Paris (OECD) 1998; Deputy Head of News Department FCO 2000; On secondment to Unilever PLC 2001; ptnr, Katherine Ann Short (1s 2005).

L

Lacey-Smith, Jane Frances; Hong Kong since March 2005; Born 20/09/63; FCO 1984; East Berlin 1985; Dublin 1987; Algiers 1990; Vice-Consul/Management Frankfurt 1997; ECM Bangkok 2000; SUPL 2004; Band C4; m 1995 Martin Frederick Smith (1d 2001).

Lacourt, Alice Margaret (née Burnett); FCO since March 2005; Born 17/10/68; Senior Assistant Legal Adviser, called to the Bar, Middle Temple 1991; FCO 1994; First Secretary (Legal) New York (UKMIS) 2000; FCO 2003; SUPL 2004; Band D7; m 2002 Roberto Lacourt (2s 2002, 2004).

Ladd, Benjamin Dafydd Oswin; Second Secretary (Commercial) Beijing since November 2000; Born

18/02/76; FCO 1997; Full-Time Language Training 1998; Full-Time Language Training Beijing 1999; Band C4.

Ladd, Michael John; FCO since 1992; Born 23/10/54; FCO 1971; Washington 1980; FCO 1983; Baghdad 1986; Vienna 1990; Band D6; m 1979 Christine Jane Tate (1s 1983; 1d 1986).

Laffey, Susan; SUPL since August 2003; Born 09/10/61; FCO 1985; East Berlin 1987; Senior Research Officer (DS Band C4) 1987; Second Secretary (Chancery) Bucharest 1989; FCO 1992; UKDEL OSCE Budapest 1994; Principal Research Analyst FCO 1995; UKDEL OSCE Vienna 1996; FCO 1996; T/D Zagreb 1998; First Secretary (Political) Bucharest 2001; Band D6.

Laing, (John) Stuart; HM Ambassador Kuwait since November 2005; Born 22/07/48; Third Secretary FCO 1970; MECAS 1971; Third later Second Secretary Jedda 1973; Second later First Secretary Brussels (UKREP) 1975; FCO 1978; First Secretary and Head of Chancery Cairo 1983; First Secretary FCO 1987; Deputy Head of Mission Prague 1989; Counsellor and Deputy Head of Mission Riyadh 1992; Counsellor FCO 1995; DFID 1997; High Commissioner Brunei 1998; HM Ambassador Muscat 2002; m 1972 Sibella Dorman (1s 1974; 2d 1979, 1985).

Laing, Paul James; Counsellor FCO since 1993; HM Customs and Excise 1974; FCO 1980; Assistant Private Secretary to Parliamentary Under Secretary of State 1981; New Delhi 1983; FCO 1985; Seconded to the MOD 1987; Berlin 1990; m 1982 Dawn (3d 1986, 1988, 1990; 1s 1992).

Laird, Alison Margaret; FCO since May 2005; Born 05/12/75; FCO 2000; Second Secretary (Political) Buenos Aires 2003; Band C4.

Lake, Robin Duncan; Third Secretary New York (UKMIS) since January 2002; Born 15/12/70; FCO 1989; Berlin 1991; Ottawa 1994; FCO 1997; Third Secretary (Immigration) Tehran 1998; Band B3.

Lam, Steven Leslie; Brussels (UKDEL NATO) since June 2005; Born 08/05/75; FCO 2003; Band A2; ptnr, Sarah Nadia Slim (1s 2004).

Lamb, Robin David; HM Ambassador Bahrain since August 2003; Born 25/11/48; FCO 1971; Language Training MECAS 1974; FCO 1977 Research Officer (DS Band C4); Second Secretary Jedda 1979; Principal Research Officer FCO 1982; First Secretary (Economic) Riyadh 1985; FCO 1988 PRO (Band D6); First Secretary (Head of Political Section) Cairo 1993; FCO 1996; Counsellor, on loan to the DTI 1999; Counsellor and Deputy Head of Mission Kuwait 2001; m 1977 Susan Jane Moxon (1d 1982; 2s 1986, 1996).

Lambert, Jason Edward; Cairo since April 2003; Born 27/09/71; FCO 1990; Brussels 1994; FCO 1997; Nairobi 1999; Band B3; m 1997 Lucy Anne Edwards (diss 2003).

Lamont, Donald Alexander; HM Ambassador Caracas since July 2003; Born 13/01/47; Second later First Secretary FCO 1974; First Secretary (UNIDO/IAEA) Vienna 1977; First Secretary (Commercial) Moscow 1980; First Secretary FCO 1982; Counsellor on attachment to IISS 1988; Counsellor and Head of Chancery BMG (later BM) Berlin 1988; HM Ambassador Montevideo 1991; Head of Republic of Ireland Department 1994; Chief of Staff, OHR Sarajevo 1997; Governor Stanley and Commissioner for South Georgia and Sandwich Islands 1999; m 1981 Lynda Margaret Campbell (1d 1983; 1s 1986).

Lampert, Sarah Jane; First Secretary (Political) New Delhi since September 2003; Born 08/11/65; FCO 1988; Language Training 1990; Third later Second Secretary (Chancery) Sofia 1991; First Secretary FCO 1995; SUPL 1996; First Secretary FCO 1997; SUPL 1999; Full-Time Language Training 2003; Band D6; m 1993 Andrew William Kenningham (2d 1996, 1998).

Lamport, Martin Henry; First Secretary (Commercial) Lima since July 2002; Born 22/11/52; HM Forces 1972; FCO 1975; SUPL 1976; FCO 1979; Tripoli 1980; Caracas 1983; FCO 1987; Third Secretary (Institutions) Brussels (UKREP) 1990; Deputy High Commissioner Belmopan 1993; FCO 1996; Deputy Head of Mission Sana'a 1999; Band C5; m 1990 Catherine Priscilla Maxwell (3d 1992, 1994, 1996).

Lancaster, Ian Francis Millar; Counsellor Algiers since March 2005; Born 23/09/47; Second Secretary FCO 1974; Second later First Secretary and Consul Hanoi 1975; First Secretary FCO 1977; Prague 1978; First Secretary FCO 1981; First Secretary (Chancery) Brussels 1983; First Secretary FCO 1987; First Secretary (Chancery) later Counsellor Ankara 1991; Counsellor FCO 1995; m 1972 Simone Daniel (1d 1978; 1s 1981).

Landsman, Dr David Maurice, OBE (2000); FCO since October 2003; Born 23/08/63; FCO 1989; Second Secretary (Economic) Athens 1991; FCO 1994; Deputy Head of Mission Belgrade 1997; FCO 1999; Head of British Embassy Office Banja Luka and concurrently First Secretary (Regional Affairs) Budapest 1999; Chargé d'Affaires Belgrade 2000; HM Ambassador Tirana 2001; m 1990 Catherine Louise Holden (1s 1992).

Lane, Bari Albert; FCO since May 1997; Born 06/05/48; Ministry of Technology 1965; FO, DSAO and FCO 1966; Vice-Consul Aden 1970; Warsaw 1973; Bombay 1974; FCO 1975; Second Secretary (Admin) Peking 1978; Vice-Consul (Commercial) Sydney 1980; Second later First Secretary FCO 1985; First Secretary (Management) Paris 1992; m 1971 Jacqueline Mary Chatt.

Langham, Elizabeth Jane (née Webb); SUPL since July 2001; Born 04/08/61; FCO 1984; Moscow 1986; Washington 1988; FCO 1991; SUPL 1992; Bahrain 1995; SUPL 1996; Second Secretary Stockholm 1997; m 1989 Peter Andrew Langham (2d 1992, 1994).

Langham, Peter Andrew; Consul (Commercial) St Petersburg since January 2003; Born 26/09/64; FCO 1983; Moscow 1985; Hamilton 1988; Washington 1990; FCO 1991; Bahrain 1994; Second Secretary Stockholm 1998; m 1989 Elizabeth Jane Webb (2d 1992, 1994).

Langman, Nicholas John Andrew; Counsellor Athens since April 2003; Born 01/11/60; FCO 1983; Second Secretary Montevideo 1986; Second later First Secretary New York (UKMIS) 1988; First Secretary FCO 1991; Paris 1994; First Secretary FCO 1998; m 1992 Sarah Jane Pearcey (2d 1994, 1995).

Langridge, Pauline Anne; Bogotá since November 2004; Born 17/08/63; FCO 1988; Madrid 1990; Guatemala 1993; FCO 1995; Havana 2000; Full-Time Language Training 2004; Band A2.

Langrish, Sally (née Monk); SUPL since July 2003; Born 05/08/68; Called to the Bar Middle Temple 1991; Treasury Solicitors Department 1993; Assistant Legal Adviser FCO 1995; First Secretary (Legal) Brussels (UKREP) 2000; First Secretary (JHA) Brussels (UKREP) 2001; Band D7; m 1996 Richard Michael John Langrish.

Lapsley, Angus Charles William; First Secretary (Political/Internal) later (Political/Military) Paris since April 2001; Born 16/03/70; Second Secretary Department of Health 1991; Second Secretary Brussels (UKREP) 1994; Private Secretary Department of Health 1995; Private Secretary No 10 Downing Street 1996; First Secretary Head IGC Unit, EUD(I) FCO 1999; Band D6; m 1999 Georgina Maria Power (1s 2002).

Larden, Kendra Jane; FCO since May 2003; Born 07/03/71; FCO 1991; Paris 1993; Muscat 1996; Peking 2000; Band B3.

Larkins, Christopher Paul; FCO since March 2000; Born 02/10/63; FCO 1986; Warsaw 1991; FCO 1994; Hong Kong 1996; Band A2.

Larmouth, Helen Dorothy; Brussels (UKREP) since December 2002; Born 22/08/63; FCO 1989; Washington 1992; Lilongwe 1994; Rangoon 1998; Band A2.

Larner, Jeremy Francis; Jakarta since July 2005; Born 12/11/49; Inland Revenue 1967; FCO 1968; Cairo 1971; Benghazi 1972; Abu Dhabi 1972; Moscow 1975; Seoul 1975; Manila 1976; Monrovia 1977; FCO 1980; Third later Second Secretary (Commercial) Tunis 1983; Second Secretary (Commercial) Port Louis 1989; Second later First Secretary FCO 1992; Deputy Head of Mission and HM Consul Rangoon 1995; Deputy Director General BTCO Taipei 1999; FCO 2002; Band D6; m 1975 Sally Dewhurst (2s 1978, 1980).

Lassman, Louise (née Mason); Strasbourg since September 2003; Born 30/08/63; FCO 1986; Gibraltar 1993; Hong Kong 1996; FCO 2000; Band B3; m 1993 Nigel Abraham Lassman.

Latham, Sarah Jane; SUPL since September 2004; Born 24/06/70; FCO 1996; Ankara 1998; FCO 2002; Band B3; m 2002 Firat Ucer (1s 2004).

Latham-Green, Tracey Lynne; SUPL since October 2003; Born 06/09/76; FCO 2002; Band B3; m 2001 Duncan Aaron.

Latta, Nicholas Karim; Second Secretary (Commercial) Moscow since May 2002; Born 02/09/71; FCO 1995; Full-Time Language Training 1996; Full-Time Language Training Cairo 1997; Second Secretary Muscat 1998; Band C4; m 1997 Susanna Mary Davis (1d 2000; 1s 2002).

Lattin-Rawstrone, Howard; Deputy High Commissioner Belmopan since January 2003; Born 23/03/55; FCO 1975; Buenos Aires 1977; Maputo 1981; Brussels 1982; FCO 1984; Cairo 1988; Second Secretary (Commercial/Aid) Cairo 1991; Second Secretary Lilongwe 1993; FCO 1997; First Secretary (Commercial) Warsaw 1999; m 1987 Caroline Sarah Lattin (2 adopted d 1976, 1978; 1s 1987).

Lavers, Richard Douglas; HM Ambassador Guatemala City since October 2001, also accredited to San Salvador since August 2003 and Honduras since February 2004; Born 10/05/47; Third Secretary FCO 1969; Buenos Aires 1970; Second later First Secretary Wellington 1973; FCO 1976; First Secretary (Political/Economic) Brussels 1981; On secondment to Guinness Mahon 1985; First Secretary FCO 1987; NATO Defence College Rome 1989; Deputy Head of Mission and Consul-General Santiago 1993; HM Ambassador Quito 1993; Counsellor FCO 1997; Head of Research Analysts FCO 1999; m 1986 Brigitte Anne Julia Maria Moers (2s 1988, 1989).

Lavery, Creena Christina Maureen; Vienna (UKMIS) since March 2005; Born 17/05/62; FCO 1991; Brussels (UKDEL NATO) 1993; Presidency Liason Officer Luxembourg 1997; Bonn 1999; Consul (Consular/Immigration) Düsseldorf 2000; SUPL 2003; Band C4.

Lavery, Derek John; Baku since July 2002; Born 01/06/68; FCO 1987; Islamabad 1989; Bonn 1993; FCO 1996; Band B3; m 1992 Claire Ruth Haines.

Lavery, Sheena Anne; FCO since January 2003; Born 09/12/74; Band B3.

Lavocat, Amanda Joyce (née Thomas); SUPL since April 2003; Born 21/12/67; DHSS 1986; FCO 1987; Pretoria 1989; Algiers 1992; FCO 1994; Istanbul 1997; Dakar 2000; Band B3; m 1993 Frederic Paul Francis Lavocat (1s 1995).

Lawley-Woods, Claire Angela; HM Consul Guangzhou since July 2003; Born 14/06/62; FCO 1984; Rome 1985; SUPL 1988; Resigned 1989; Reinstated, FCO 1994; Ottawa 1996; Vice-Consul New Delhi 1999; FCO 2001; Band C4; m 2003 Roger Michael Woods (2s 1982, 1988; 1d 1985).

Lawrence, Joanne Louise (née Watson); SUPL since June 2005; Born 30/04/68; FCO 1986; Wellington 1988; SUPL 1992; Stanley 1995; Islamabad 1998; FCO 2001; T/D Kabul 2002;

FCO 2003; Band C4; m 1991 Martin Lawrence (2d 1993, 1999).

Lawrence, Paul David; T/D Bangkok since June 2005; Born 10/04/68; FCO 1989; New York (UKMIS) 1993; World Wide Floater Duties 1997; Kigali 2000; St John's 2002; Band B3.

Lawrie, James Malcolm, MBE (1985); Riyadh since June 2005; Born 01/06/44; FCO 1970; Jedda 1972; FCO 1973; Islamabad 1975; FCO 1977; Kuwait 1979; FCO 1983; Third Secretary Peking 1984; FCO 1986; Accra 1990; FCO 1993; Cairo 1995; FCO 1998; Second Secretary Lagos 2000; Band C5; m (1) 1971 Anne Margaret Martin (diss) (3s 1974, 1977, 1982); (2) 2000 Sheila Boxer.

Laxton, Rowan James; Deputy Head of Mission Kabul since September 2002; Born 19/02/61; FCO 1993; First Secretary (Chancery) Islamabad 1997; FCO 2000; Band D7; m 2000 Sonya L Laxton.

Layden, Anthony Michael; HM Ambassador Tripoli since October 2002; Born 27/07/46; Third Secretary FCO 1968; MECAS 1969; Second Secretary Jedda 1971; Second later First Secretary Rome 1973; FCO 1977; First Secretary and Head of Chancery Jedda 1982; First Secretary FCO 1982; Head of Chancery Muscat 1987; Counsellor (Commercial/Economic) Copenhagen 1991; Counsellor FCO 1995; HM Ambassador Rabat 1999; m 1969 Josephine Mary McGhee (3s 1973, 1974, 1977; 1d 1982).

Layden, Christopher; FCO since September 2004; Born 09/03/57; FCO 1981; Tehran 1983; Düsseldorf 1986; Resigned 1989; Reinstated, 2004; Band B3; m 2001 Zamira Alija.

Layfield, Jonathan Timothy Whitton; Second Secretary Basra since April 2004; Born 19/06/67; FCO 1997; Jedda 1999; Full-Time Language Training 2000; Amman 2001; m 1997 Rebecca Anne (2s 2001, 2003).

Leake, Nicholas Howard; On loan as Legal Adviser at HM Treasury since January 2003; Born 15/01/72; FCO 1994; Second Secretary (KHF) Budapest 1996; On loan to DFID 1998; First Secretary (Industry) Brussels (UKREP) 2000.

Lee, Adrian Jonathan; Second Secretary (Chancery) Luanda since February 2003; Born 24/10/68; FCO 1989; Full-Time Language Training Cairo 1991; Third Secretary (Commercial later Political) Riyadh 1992; British Vice-Consul and Management Officer São Paulo 1996; FCO 2000; Band C4.

Lee, Laurence John; First Secretary (Chancery) Kingston since July 2004; Born 03/08/69; Band D6; ptnr, Sarah Byrne (1s 1983).

Lee, Richard John Clifton; SMO Tel Aviv since September 2002; Born 26/09/51; FCO 1971; Copenhagen 1973; Addis Ababa 1976; Moscow 1979; FCO 1982; Accra 1984; Lusaka 1987; FCO 1989; Second Secretary (Commercial) Kuwait 1992; Jakarta 1994; Second Secretary FCO 1999; m 1973 Lesley Eleanor McConnell (1d 1980; 1s 1982).

Lee, Thomas David; Second Secretary FCO since May 2003; Born 09/05/63; FCO 1983; Nicosia 1987; Third later Second Secretary FCO 1990; SUPL 2002; Band C4.

Lee-Gorton, Victoria (née Lee); Second Secretary (Chancery/Information)Second Secretary (Chancery/Information) Dubai since February 2004; Born 05/03/70; FCO 1990; Full-Time Language Training 1992; Third Secretary Maputo 1993; Third Secretary EU Presidency Liason Officer Rome/Dublin/The Hague 1995; Third later Second Secretary FCO 1997; Full-Time Language Training FCO 2001; Second Secretary (Chancery/Information) Dubai 2002; SUPL 2003; Band C4; m 1992 Christopher John Gorton (2d 2001, 2003).

Lee-Smith, Richard James; FCO since July 2003; Born 17/07/79; Band B3.

Legg, Judy; SUPL since June 2005; Born 29/04/67; FCO 1991; Full-Time Language Training 1992; Second Secretary 1993; Moscow 1994; First Secretary FCO 1995; SUPL 2000; Director New York 2002; Band D6; m 1994 Graham Barry Stanley (1d 1998; 1s 2003).

Legg, Rufus Alexander; Second Secretary FCO since October 2000; Born 13/03/68; FCO 1990; Third Secretary Port Moresby 1993; Third later Second Secretary and Deputy Head of Mission Tegucigalpa 1997; Band C4.

Legge, Jeremy John; Counsellor on loan to the Cabinet Office since May 2005; Born 19/05/61; Second Secretary FCO 1985; Second Secretary Lusaka 1987; Second later First Secretary FCO 1989; First Secretary on loan to the Cabinet Office 1989; Vienna (UKMIS) 1994; First Secretary FCO 1998; First Secretary (Political) Paris 2001; Band D6; m 1990 Melanie King (3s 1991, 1992, 1994).

Leigh, David John; Second later First Secretary FCO since August 1987; Born 03/07/48; Post Office 1964; FCO 1969; Lagos 1974; FCO 1975; Third Secretary Tokyo 1978; FCO 1981; Third Secretary Sofia 1984.

Leinster, Norman Kennedy; FCO since November 2003; Born 04/06/65; Band B3.

Leister, Helen Grace (née McCarthy); SUPL since February 2003; Born 01/02/64; FCO 1983; Paris 1985; Luxembourg 1988; Paris 1991; Kiev 1994; FCO 1996; Ottawa 1999; SUPL 2000; Ottawa 2000; Band B3; m 1991 Alan Leister.

Leith, Dennis, RVM (1975); Seattle since April 2004; Born 10/12/48; FCO 1967; Moscow 1971; Mexico City 1972; Sofia 1975; FCO 1976; Guatemala City 1979; Vienna 1982; Second Secretary FCO 1984; Second Secretary (Commercial) Bahrain 1987; On secondment to the London Chamber of Commerce 1991; Consul-General Ho Chi Minh City 1992; Second Secretary FCO 1995; First Secretary (Commercial) Sofia 1998; FCO 2003; m 1971 Barbara Mary Hum (1s 1974; 1d 1979).

Lelliott, David Patrick; Monrovia since October 2003; Born 13/09/66; FCO 1993; Third Secretary Doha 1996; Second Secretary (Commercial) Mexico City 2000; Band D6.

Lennard, Sarah Jill; First Secretary FCO since November 1998; Born 19/04/56; FCO 1981; Third Secretary Montevideo 1982; Second Secretary FCO 1983; Brussels (UKREP) 1983; First Secretary FCO 1985; Budapest 1994; Band D6; m 1987 Mark Kilroy (1s 1989; 1d 1992).

Leon, Judith Mary; Deputy Consul-General Johannesburg since June 2001; Born 17/07/63; Home Office 1984; FCO 1987; New York 1989; Bangkok 1992; FCO 1994; Second Secretary 1995; Second Secretary (Commercial) Bombay 1997.

Leslie, Alison Mariot (née Sanderson), CMG (2005); HM Ambassador Oslo since August 2002; Born 25/06/54; FCO 1977; Singapore 1978; Bonn 1982; FCO 1986; Quai d'Orsay Paris 1990; Head of ESED 1992; Scottish Office 1993 - 95; Head of Policy Planning Staff FCO 1996; Deputy Head of Mission Rome 1998; m 1978 Andrew David Leslie (2d 1987, 1990).

Leslie, Thomas Gary; FCO since April 2003; Born 27/04/69; FCO 1989; Karachi 1991; FCO 1993; Tokyo 1994; Kamakura 1998; Tokyo 1999; Band C4; m 2001 Angela Burns.

Leslie-Jones, Philippa Anne; SUPL since July 2004; Born 19/07/59; FCO 1984; Second Secretary Warsaw 1986; First Secretary FCO 1989; First Secretary (Chancery) Moscow 1991; On loan to No. 10 Downing Street 1994; SUPL 1995; FCO 1995; SUPL 1996; On secondment Cabinet Office 2002; m 1994 Richard Philip Bridge (2s 1995, 1997).

Less, Timothy Garnham; FCO since January 2004; Born 26/07/73; Band C5.

Lever, Giles; SUPL since May 2004; Born 20/03/68; FCO 1990; Third later Second Secretary (Political) Hanoi 1993; First Secretary FCO 1997; Full-Time Language Training 2000; Tokyo 2001.

Lever, Simon Jeffrey; Consul-General Marseilles since September 2001; Born 04/01/63; FCO 1983; Doha 1985; SE Asia/FE Floater 1988; Full-Time Language Training FCO 1989; Language Training Hong Kong 1990; Third later Second Secretary Beijing 1991; On loan to the DTI 1996; FCO 1997; HM Consul Chiang Mai 1998; Peking 2000; Band C5; m 1993 Krisana Khumnuan (1d 2000; 1s 2002).

Levey, Joanna Claire (née Brewis); SUPL since November 2002; Born 22/09/60; FCO 1981; Kuwait 1983; Luanda 1986; FCO 1989; Copenhagen 1990; FCO 1992; Band A2; m 1997 Robert Edward Levey (1d 2000).

Levi, Andrew Peter Robert; Head of Aviation, Maritime and Energy Department, FCO since April 2003; Born 04/03/63; FCO 1987; Second Secretary 1989; Second Secretary (Chancery, subsequently Economic/EC) Bonn 1990; First Secretary FCO 1993; On secondment to the European Commission (EU enlargement) 1996; On secondment to OECD Secretariat (eastern European administrative reform) 1998; First Secretary (Political) Bonn 1998; Seconded to the EU Presidency CFSP Team at the German Foreign Office 1999; Seconded to Special Co-ordinator of the Stability Pact for South Eastern Europe (Deputy Chief of Staff) 1999; Deputy Head of Eastern Adriatic Department, FCO 2001; m 2002 Roswitha Elisabeth von Studnitz.

Levoir, Derek Charles; Deputy Head of Mission Dakar since June 2003; Born 08/08/46; DSAO 1965; Latin America Floater 1969; Rome 1971; FCO 1974; Second Secretary 1976; Asunción 1978; Lisbon 1982; Vice-Consul Naples 1986; FCO 1991; First Secretary (Consular) Nairobi 1999; m 1973 Liana Annita Ugo (2d 1975, 1976).

Lewington, Richard George; HM Ambassador Quito since June 2003; Born 13/04/48; DSAO (later FCO) 1968; Attached to Army School of Languages 1971; Ulaanbaatar 1972; Second Secretary (Chancery/Information) Lima 1976; FCO 1980; Second Secretary (Commercial) Moscow 1982; Second later First Secretary FCO 1983; First Secretary (Commercial) Tel Aviv 1986; First Secretary FCO 1990; EU Monitoring Mission Yugoslavia 1991; Deputy High Commissioner Valletta 1995; HM Ambassador Almaty and HM Ambassador (non-resident) Bishkek 1999; m 1972 Sylviane Paulette Marie Cholet (1s 1982; 1d 1984).

Lewis, Claire Samantha; SUPL since December 2002; Born 03/06/66; FCO 1990; Madras 1993; New Delhi 1998; FCO 2001; Band C4; m 2000 Ian David Booth (1s 2003).

Lewis, Harriet Catherine; FCO since October 2002; Born 13/06/79; Band B3.

Lewis, Dr John Ewart Thomas; Counsellor (Regional Affairs) Buenos Aires since October 2002; Born 05/11/55; FCO 1987; First Secretary (Chancery) Bonn 1991; Consul (Economic) Frankfurt 1993; First Secretary FCO 1996; Band D6.

Lewis, Joy Suzanne (née Spalding); SUPL since September 2002; Born 01/08/60; FCO 1980; Rio de Janeiro 1983; Buenos Aires 1986; FCO 1988; SUPL 1991; FCO 1998; Band C4.

Lewis, Marion Rachel (née Douche); SUPL since March 1999; Born 19/03/69; FCO 1991; SUPL 1996; Berlin 1997; Band B3; m 1994 Peter Robert Lewis (2s 1997, 1999; 1d 2001).

Lewis, Matthew Dafydd; FCO since October 2002; Born 04/10/78; Band C4.

Lewis, Peter Robert; First Secretary Washington since June 2003; Born 16/08/68; Second Secretary FCO 1994; Second Secretary Berlin 1997; First Secretary FCO 1999; Band D6; m 1994 Marion Rachel Douche (2s 1997, 1999; 1d 2001).

Lewis, Trevor James; FCO since October 2003; Born 08/10/60; FCO 1979; Brussels (UKREP)

1982; Accra 1984; FCO 1988; Washington 1991; Third Secretary (Commercial/Information) Dubai 1994; FCO 1997; Second Secretary (Commercial) Shanghai 2000; Band D6; m 1993 Claire Louise Hawthorne.

Ley, Graham John; First Secretary FCO since September 2003; Born 31/05/61; FCO 1984; Second Secretary Cairo 1987; Second later First Secretary FCO 1989; First Secretary (Chancery) Nicosia 1994; First Secretary FCO 1998; First Secretary (Regional Affairs) Cairo 1999; Band D6; m 1988 Carol Anne Buchan (1d 1991; 1s 1995).

Leyland, Amy Jane; FCO since October 2004; Born 18/12/79; Band C4.

Liddell, James; First Secretary and Consul-General Jakarta since July 2003; Born 20/06/45; FCO 1970; Buenos Aires 1973; Blantyre 1975; FCO 1977; Seoul 1980; Suva 1984; FCO 1988; Consul (Commercial) Perth 1992; Bridgetown 1997; Consul Harare 1999; m 1978 Jillian Stella Coventry (1d 1981; 1s 1985).

Liddle, Aidan Thomas; Second Secretary Brussels (UKREP) since August 2004; Born 06/07/79; DTI 2001; FCO 2003; Band C4.

Liddle, Johanna Mary; Second Secretary Nicosia since April 2005; Born 13/09/71; FCO 2002; Band C4.

Life, Vivien Frances; Counsellor FCO since April 1999; Born 30/05/57; Civil Service Dept. 1979; HM Treasury 1981; FCO 1988; First Secretary Washington 1992; First Secretary FCO 1996; m 1989 Timothy Michael Dowse (2d 1991, 1994).

Lilley, George Arthur, MBE (1997); First Secretary (Works) Cairo since April 2003; Born 21/01/51; Tokyo 1987; Kuwait 1989; Wellington 1990; Dublin 1993; Canberra 1995; Lagos 1997; FCO 1999; Dar es Salaam 2001; Band D6; m 1996 Marjorie.

Lillie, Stephen; Counsellor (Economic/Commercial) New Delhi since August 2003; Born 04/02/66; FCO 1988; Full-Time Language Training 1989; Full-Time Language Training Hong Kong 1990; Second later First Secretary (Economic/Political) Peking 1992; FCO 1996; Consul-General Guangzhou 1999; m 1991 Denise Chit Lo (2s 1997, 1999).

Lillington, Leisa; FCO since November 2002; Born 23/01/65; Home Office 1985; FCO 1991; Vienna (UKDEL) 1992; FCO 1995; SUPL 2000; Band A2.

Lindfield, John Richard, MBE (1999); Consul (Investment) San Francisco since July 1999; Born 12/05/59; DHSS 1978; FCO 1978; Cairo 1981; Floater Duties 1984; Karachi 1985; FCO 1989; Second Secretary 1994; Vice-Consul (Commercial) Cape Town 1995; m 1985 Judith Christine Brown (2s 1988, 1990).

Lindley, Graham; Amman since April 2004; Born 18/03/46; Royal Navy 1964; HOPD 1982; Bucharest 1988; Prague 1990; Brussels 1992; Hong Kong 1996; Kampala 2000; FCO 2003; Band B3; m 1967 Anita Wood (1s 1969; 1d 1976).

Lindsay, Bridget Clare (née O'Riordan); SUPL since June 2003; Born 13/08/59; FCO 1980; Warsaw 1982; Tokyo 1984; SUPL 1986; Canberra 1987; FCO 1989; SUPL 1991; FCO 1992; SUPL 1994; Tokyo 1995; SUPL 1995; Second Secretary British Trade International 2001; m 1983 Iain Ferrier Lindsay (1s 1991).

Lindsay, Iain Ferrier, OBE (2002); Deputy Head of Mission Bucharest since August 2003; Born 09/03/59; FCO 1980; Warsaw 1982; Tokyo 1983; Third later Second Secretary (Political) Canberra 1986; Second Secretary FCO 1989; First Secretary (Political) Tokyo 1994; FCO 1999; m 1983 Bridget Clare O'Riordan (1s 1991).

Lindsay, Kathryn Hilary (née Buchanan); Warsaw since April 2005; Born 07/07/70; FCO 1989; T/D Moscow 1991; Brussels (UKREP) 1992; Dakar 1995; SUPL 1998; Belgrade 2002; Band B3; m 1994 Douglas Tennant Lindsay (1d 1998; 1s 2000.

Lindsay, Richard Stephen; FCO since October 2001; Born 18/02/69; Second Secretary FCO 1996; Second Secretary Harare 1998; m 1997 Xanthe Critchett (2s 1998, 2003; 1d 2000).

Ling, Norman Arthur; High Commissioner Lilongwe since September 2001; Born 12/08/52; Second Secretary FCO 1978; Second Secretary Tripoli 1980; Second later First Secretary Tehran 1981; First Secretary FCO 1984; Deputy Consul-General Johannesburg 1988; Full-Time Language Training 1992; Deputy Head of Mission Ankara 1993; Counsellor FCO 1997; m 1979 Selma Osman.

Lingwood, David Michael; Second Secretary (Management) Lisbon since October 2002; Born 10/05/68; FCO 1989; Cairo 1991; Bonn 1994; FCO 1997; Yerevan 2000; Band C4; m 2003 Deborah Berns.

Link, Joan Irene (née Wilmot), LVO (1992); Counsellor FCO since August 1996; Born 03/03/53; FCO 1974; Third Secretary Bonn 1975; Third later Second Secretary FCO 1977; Second later First Secretary Geneva (UKDIS) 1980; First Secretary FCO 1983; First Secretary (Information) Bonn 1990; First Secretary FCO 1994; (2s 1977, 1985).

Linnell, Aidan John; FCO since March 2002; Born 13/04/60; FCO 1982; Canberra 1987; FCO 1989; Third Secretary Bonn 1993; FCO 1996; Second Secretary Caracas 1998; Band C4; m 2000 Zenaida Degadillo.

Lion, Stephanie Ann (née Smith); SUPL since August 2000; Born 16/02/65; FCO 1986; Madrid 1988; SUPL 1989; FCO 1992; Berne 1994; FCO 1997; Band A2; m 1997 Dominique Lion (1d 1999).

Lisbey, Lisa Marie (née Harrison); FCO since September 2003; Born 23/02/69; Customs and Excise 1992-95; FCO 1995; Belmopan 1996; New

Delhi 2000; Band B3; m 1999 Nestor Lisbey (1s 2001).

Lister, Kirsten Fiona; Islamabad since December 2004; Born 04/05/68; FCO 2001; Floater Duties 2002; Band B3.

Litman, Lee; FCO since September 2003; Born 11/09/72; Band D6.

Little, Alison Jane; FCO since September 2001; Born 03/04/68; FCO (HCS) 1986; FCO (DS) 1988; Lusaka 1990; FCO 1992; Maseru 1993; Tunis 1994; FCO 1997; On loan to the DTI 1999; Band C4.

Livesey, Timothy Peter Nicholas; SUPL since February 2002; Born 29/06/59; FCO 1987; Rabat 1988; FCO 1988; Second later First Secretary (Aid) Lagos 1989; FCO 1993; Head of Press and Public Affairs Section Paris Embassy 1996; On secondment to No. 10 Downing Street (Press Office) 2000; m 1986 Catherine Eaglestone (3d 1990, 1996, 1999; 2s 1992, 1997).

Livingston, Catherine Mary (née Bramley); Hong Kong since April 2002; Born 22/06/56; FCO 1975 Cairo 1977; (Resigned 1980); Reinstated, FCO 1982; Rome 1984; Muscat 1986; SUPL 1990; FCO 1991; SUPL 1991; FCO 1995; Hong Kong 1996; SUPL 2001; Band B3; m 1985 Richard Ian Livingston (1s 1990; 1d 1992).

Livingstone, Carolyn B; Management Officer Windhoek since June 2004; Born 04/11/48; FCO 1997; Abidjan 1999; Wellington 2000; Band B3; (1d 1974).

Livingstone, Scott, OBE (2002), MBE (Mil) (1995); First Secretary Madrid since September 2003; Born 28/11/65; First Secretary FCO 1996; First Secretary (Political) Islamabad 1998; First Secretary FCO 2000; Band D6; m 1996 Lorna Jane Pettipher (2d 1998, 2000).

Llewellyn, Huw; New York (UKMIS) since August 2004; Born 21/05/59; Assistant Legal Adviser FCO 1988; Legal Counsellor, FCO 1999; m 1990 Fiona Jane Boote (2d 1994, 1995).

Lloyd, Andrew, MBE (1995); Head of African Department (Southern), FCO since September 2003; Born 22/10/64; FCO 1982; Washington 1984; Kaduna 1987; FCO 1990; Second Secretary 1992; Second Secretary (Economic) Seoul 1993; Second later First Secretary (Political/Press) New York (UKMIS) 1995; Head of Post Pristina 2000; m (1) 1987 Sandra Leigh Craven (diss 1996) (1s 1990); (2) 1997 Tania Mechlenborg (1s 2003).

Lloyd, Diane Elizabeth; SUPL since September 2004; Born 27/02/68; FCO 1987; Warsaw 1989; Full-Time Language Training FCO 1989; Full-Time Language Training Tokyo 1990; Vice-Consul Tokyo 1991; Rabat 1995; T/D Japan 1999; Osaka 2000; Band C4; m (1) 1994 Souichiroh Saito (dec'd); (2) 2003 Takeshi Watanabe (1s 2004).

Lochmuller, Simon; Warsaw since January 2003; Born 26/07/70; FCO 1986; Bonn 1993; FCO 1996; Cairo 1998; Band C4; m 1998 Verena Mackenzie (1d 1995).

Lock, Jennifer Hazel; Auckland since May 2004; Born 09/07/59; FCO 1978; Jakarta 1982; Stockholm 1985; FCO 1988; Tunis 1991; Third Secretary (Management/Consular) Almaty 1994; Second Secretary (Immigration) Islamabad 1998; FCO 2001; Pitcairn 2003; Band C4.

Lockwood, Emma Constance, MVO (2000); Second Secretary (Press and Public Affairs) Brussels since April 2004; Born 01/01/71; FCO 1996; Language Training 1999; Third Secretary (Political) Rome 1999; FCO 2003; Band C4.

Lodge, Katherine Rosemary; SUPL since March 2003; Born 03/08/59; FCO 1984; Language Training Tokyo 1985; Third Secretary Tokyo 1986; FCO 1990; Second Secretary 1992; SUPL 1994; FCO 1998.

Lodge, Matthew James; Private Secretary to the PUS FCO since August 2004; Born 03/06/68; FCO 1996; Second Secretary (Political) Athens 1998; Second Secretary (PPS) Paris 2001; Second Secretary (Political/Military) Brussels (UKREP) 2001; First Secretary FCO 2003; m 2001 Alexia Ipirotis (2s 2002).

Logan, Marilla Joy Fiona (née Tandy); First Secretary FCO since April 1998; Born 12/09/53; FCO 1974; Moscow 1977; FCO 1978; Düsseldorf 1980; FCO 1983; Second Secretary Kuala Lumpur 1992; FCO 1996; m 1986 Allan Robert Logan (1s 1994).

Lomas, Joanne; Second Secretary (WTO) Geneva (UKMIS) since July 2001; Born 07/09/70; FCO 1993; Full-Time Language Training 1995; Secondment to UNSCOM Baghdad 1997; Third Secretary (Political/Information) Damascus 1997; Band C4.

Lomax, Christopher Thomas; FCO since June 2004; Born 02/05/80; Band B3.

Long, Alastair Douglas; FCO since 2002; Born 06/08/77; Band C4.

Longbottom, Julia Margaret; Counsellor Warsaw since June 2003; Born 13/07/63; FCO 1986; Attachment to European Commission 1988; Language Training 1988; Second Secretary (Chancery) Tokyo 1990; First Secretary FCO 1994; First Secretary (Political) The Hague 1998; m 1990 Richard James Sciver (2d 1992, 1993; 1s 1995).

Longdon, Catherine Mary; SUPL since August 2000; Born 15/12/64; FCO 1990; Islamabad 1993; FCO 1997; SUPL 1997; FCO 1998; Band C4.

Longhurst, William Jesse; First Secretary (Finance) New York (UKMIS) since June 2001; Born 07/02/67; FCO 1990; Seoul 1992; Second Secretary 1992; First Secretary (Commercial) Tokyo 1995; On loan to the DTI 1998; m 1991 Eriko Niimi (diss 2005) (2d 1991, 1993).

Lonsdale, Charles John; First Secretary FCO since February 2003; Born 05/07/65; FCO 1987; Vienna

CSCE 1988; FCO 1989; Third later Second Secretary Budapest 1990; On loan to the Cabinet Office 1993; First Secretary FCO 1995; First Secretary (Political) Moscow 1998.

Lonsdale, Jason Peter; Third Secretary (Management/Consular) Luxembourg since August 2002; Born 27/11/67; HM Forces (Royal Navy) 1988 - 94; FCO 2000; Band B3; m 1999 Emma Sarah Vero.

Lorimer, Eamonn Barrington; Secondment (Commercial) since April 2003; Born 11/12/64; Home Civil Service 1985 - 88; Washington 1989; FCO 1993; Valletta 1994; FCO 1997; On loan to the DTI 2002; Band B3.

Loten, Graeme Neil; HM Ambassador Dushanbe since June 2004; Born 10/03/59; FCO 1981; Brussels (UKDEL NATO) 1983; Khartoum 1986; Second Secretary (Economic/Agriculture) The Hague 1988; Full-Time Language Training 1993; Second Secretary Almaty 1993; FCO 1997; HM Ambassador Bamako 2001.

Lott, Ann Veronica (née Lewis); Second Secretary FCO since November 1996; Born 22/11/55; FCO 1978; Algiers 1979; Montevideo 1982; FCO 1984; Latin America Floater 1987; FCO 1988; Canberra 1989; SUPL 1992; m 1989 Justin Karl Lott (1d 1993).

Louizos, Alexandra Emma; Full-Time Language Training Beijing since January 2004; Born 09/10/78; FCO 2001; Full-Time Language Training (Mandarin) 2003; Band C4.

Louth, Michael; FCO since July 1999; Born 21/05/63; FCO 1981; Lagos 1984; East Berlin 1988; FCO 1989; Third Secretary (Management/Commercial) Ljubljana 1992; Vienna 1994; Port of Spain 1996; m 1992 Carmen Elena Fuentes (1s 1994; 1d 1998).

Love, Darren Mark; Floater Duties since February 2001; Born 26/02/68; FCO 1988; Warsaw 1989; Accra 1991; FCO 1993; Colombo 1997; Band B3.

Love, Stephanie Cynthia; FCO since January 1993; Born 24/07/45; Bogotá 1969; Rio de Janeiro 1969; Cairo 1971; Antigua 1971; Manila 1973; New York (UKMIS) 1975; FCO 1978; Bahrain 1979; FCO 1984; Budapest 1986; Islamabad 1988; FCO 1990; Lisbon 1991; Band B3.

Loveday-Baugh, Christine; FCO since August 2001; Born 15/08/59; FCO 1984; Muscat 1986; Kingston 1989; FCO 1991; Rome 1994; New York (UKMIS) 1999; Band B3; m 1992 C. Anthony Baugh.

Lovett, Elizabeth Ann; Dar es Salaam since February 2004; Born 16/04/77; FCO 2002; Band A2.

Low, Nicholas David; Deputy Head of Mission Algiers since June 2004; Born 14/12/57; Metropolitan Police 1982 - 92; FCO 1993; T/D Rabat 1994; Santiago 1995; Full-Time Language Training 1999; Brasilia 1999; FCO 2003; Band D6.

Lowen, Barry Robert; Counsellor (Commercial) Riyadh since August 2003; Born 09/01/64; FCO 1986; Language Training Cairo 1987; Third later Second Secretary (Chancery) Kuwait 1989; First Secretary FCO 1993; First Secretary (Economic) New York (UKMIS) 1997; FCO 2001; m 1989 Karin Rhiannon Blizard.

Loweth, Alan Robert; First Secretary later Counsellor FCO since May 1995; Born 12/12/52; FCO 1973; Language Training 1977; Copenhagen 1978; FCO 1981; Language Training 1984; Second Secretary Moscow 1985; First Secretary FCO 1988; First Secretary Warsaw 1991; m 1986 Linda Susan Parr.

Lownds, Matthew John; Brasilia since August 2003; Born 06/08/65; FCO 1987; Dublin 1989; Düsseldorf 1990; Luanda 1992; Second Secretary FCO 1995; Second Secretary (Political) UKDEL OSCE Vienna 1996; First Secretary FCO 2000; Band D6; m 1996 Rebecca Louise Allen (1s 1997; 2d 1999, 2002).

Lowson, Gillian (née Murray); FCO since October 2002; Born 18/09/69; FCO 1990; Language Training 1991; Paris 1992; Language Training 1994; Vienna 1995; Third Secretary Beijing 1999; Band B3; m 1999 Paul James Lowson (1s 2002).

Lucas, Stephen John; FCO since July 2000; Born 30/06/62; DTI 1986 - 90; FCO 1990; Third Secretary (Press/Information) Paris 1992; HM Consul Mexico City 1996; m 1994 Claudia Bautista Alfonso (1s 1998).

Lucey, Janette Margaret (née Mansley); SUPL since July 2003; Born 14/07/64; FCO 1983; New Delhi 1985; Luanda 1989; Suva 1992; Canberra 1997; FCO 2001; Band A2; m 1994 James Courtney Lucey.

Lucien, Valerie Linda; FCO since October 2003; Born 12/08/47; FCO 1977; Lagos 1978; Brussels (UKREP) 1981; Africa/Middle East Floater 1984; FCO 1987; Third Secretary Kingston 1990; Third Secretary (Cultural/Information) Valletta 1993; Second Secretary FCO 1996; Consul-General Mexico City 2000; Band C5.

Luckock, Ben; Third Secretary (Visa) Islamabad since June 2003; Born 03/11/77; FCO 2001; Band B3.

Luff, Jonathan James; First Secretary (Political) Paris since June 2005; Born 19/04/73; FCO 1998; Full-Time Language Training 1999; Full-Time Language Training Cairo 2000; Second Secretary (Political) Riyadh 2001; FCO 2003; Band C4; m 2004 Stephanie Kay (née Harris).

Lufkin, Christine Anne (née Wilson), MVO; SUPL since August 2004; Born 05/01/66; FCO 1988; Washington 1990; Kuwait 1994; Second Secretary FCO 1997; SUPL 2000; Second Secretary (Economic) The Hague 2000; m 1996 David Jonathan Peter Lufkin (1d 1999).

Luke, Robert Haydon Vernon; Second Secretary Brasilia since August 2002; Born 09/09/74; FCO 2000; Band C4.

Lungley, Gareth Geoffrey; First Secretary Zagreb since October 2002; Born 08/01/71; FCO 1994; Full-Time Language Training 1996; Second Secretary (Commercial) Tehran 1997; Second Secretary FCO 1999; Band D6; m 1997 Suzanne Clare Smith (1s 2001).

Lunt, Iain Andrew; Second Secretary (Political) Tbilisi since September 2005; Born 11/05/77; FCO 2001; Band C4; m 2004 Clare Louise Titcomb.

Lusher, David; First Secretary (Management) Tripoli since September 2002; Born 27/12/55; DOE 1973; FCO 1975; Belgrade 1977; Seoul 1978; Accra 1982; FCO 1984; Islamabad 1987; Vice-Consul Milan 1991; Second Secretary FCO 1994; Second Secretary (UN/UNIDO) UKMIS Vienna 1998; m 1978 Soon-Ja Chung (1s 1983).

Lusty, Gregor Malcolm; FCO since October 2001; Born 12/03/69; FCO 1991; Full-Time Language Training Cairo 1993; Third Secretary (Chancery) Amman 1994; Kinshasa 1998; Second Secretary on loan to the DTI 1999.

Luttrell, David Charles; FCO since August 2003; Born 03/06/72; FCO 1999; Freetown 2001; Band B3.

Lyall, Michael David; Riyadh since November 2003; Born 09/09/43; Royal Navy 1961-89; Moscow 1991; Warsaw 1992; Geneva (UKMIS) 1993; Moscow 1996; Peking 1998; Moscow 2002; Band B3; m 1967 Janet Haugh (1s 1969).

Lyall Grant, Mark Justin, CMG (2003); High Commissioner Islamabad since May 2003; Born 29/05/56; FCO 1980; Second Secretary Islamabad 1982; First Secretary FCO 1985; First Secretary (Chancery) Paris 1990; First Secretary FCO 1993; Counsellor on loan to the Cabinet Office 1994; Deputy High Commissioner Pretoria 1996; FCO 1998; Director (Africa) FCO 2000; m 1986 Sheila Jean Tresise (1s 1989; 1d 1991).

Lyall Grant, Sheila Jean (née Tresise); FCO since 1999; Born 16/12/60; FCO 1980; Islamabad 1982; FCO 1985; Vice-Consul Paris 1990; FCO 1993; SUPL 1997; Band C4; m 1986 Mark Justin Lyall Grant (1s 1989; 1d 1991).

Lycett, Nadine Claire; FCO since July 2000; Born 19/04/65; FCO 1984; Brussels (UKDEL NATO) 1986; FCO 1988; Washington 1992; Ankara 1997; Band A2.

Lynch, Paul Francis; Consul (Commercial) Osaka since May 2002; Born 18/08/63; Home Office 1991; Cabinet Office 1994; First Secretary (Science and Technology) Tokyo 1996; Full-Time Language Training 2000; Band D6; m 1992 Yoko Hirayama (1s 1997).

Lyne, Kevin Douglas; Deputy Head of Mission Rabat since April 2003; Born 06/11/61; Research Officer FCO 1988; Senior Research Officer FCO 1989; Second Secretary (Chancery) Santiago 1991; Principal Research Officer FCO 1995; First Secretary FCO 1996; First Secretary (Human Rights) Geneva (UKMIS) 1998; m 1988 Anne Francoise Dabbadie (2d 1989, 1995).

Lyne, Richard John; High Commissioner Honiara since December 2004; Born 20/11/48; FCO 1970; Belgrade 1972; Algiers 1974; Damascus 1977; FCO 1980; On loan to DTI 1981; Second Secretary (Commercial) New Delhi 1984; Second later First Secretary (Chancery/Information) Stockholm 1988; First Secretary FCO 1992; Deputy High Commissioner Port of Spain 1996; FCO 2000; m 1977 Jennifer Anne Whitworth (1d 1982; 1s 1985).

Lyon, Jamie; FCO since October 2004; Born 24/06/74; Band D6.

Lyon, Julian Edmund; Belgrade since August 2001; Born 20/10/65; FCO 1990; Transferred to Diplomatic Service 1999; Third Secretary and Vice-Consul Yerevan 1999; Band B3; (1d 2000).

Lyons, Benedict David; FCO since January 2005; Born 15/02/72; FCO 1997; Third Secretary Madrid 2000; Second Secretary Algiers 2003; m Amanda Louise Crowhurst (2d 1996, 2000).

Lysaght, Stephen Peter; FCO since 1999; Born 17/05/70; FCO 1989; Washington 1992; Moscow 1995; Band D6.

Lyscom, David Edward; UK Representative for the Organisation for Economic Co-operation and Development, Paris since January 2004; Born 08/08/51; FCO 1972; Third later Second Secretary Vienna 1973; Second Secretary Ottawa 1977; Second later First Secretary FCO 1979; First Secretary 1980; First Secretary Bonn 1984; First Secretary (Economic) Riyadh 1988; First Secretary FCO 1990; Counsellor (Science and Technology) Bonn 1991; Counsellor FCO 1996; HM Ambassador Bratislava 1998; FCO 2002; m 1973 Nicole Jane Ward (2d 1983, 1987; 1s 1985).

Lyster-Binns, Benjamin Edward Noël; First Secretary (Political) Lisbon since September 2003; Born 19/10/65; FCO 1989; Third Secretary (Development) Lilongwe 1991; Third Secretary (Chancery/Information) Muscat 1995; Second later First Secretary FCO 1998; m 1995 Belinda Hunter Blair (2d 1999, 2000; 1s 2002).

Lytle, Janice; SUPL since October 2004; Born 17/06/62; FCO 2002; Damascus 2003; Band A2; m 2004 Ali Al-Shatti.

M

Macadie, Jeremy James; HM Ambassador Kigali since October 2004; Born 10/07/52; FCO 1972; Dakar 1975; Addis Ababa 1980; FCO 1981; Sana'a 1984; Antananarivo 1986; FCO 1991; Assistant Private Secretary to Minister of State for Europe 1995; Deputy Head of Mission Algiers 1997; FCO 2000; On loan to French MFA, Paris 2003; Band D6; m 1975 Chantal Andrea Jacqueline Copiatti (1d 1978).

Macaire, Robert Nigel Paul; Counsellor (Political) New Delhi since July 2004; Born 19/02/66; MOD 1987 - 90; FCO 1990; Second Secretary (Know

How Fund) Bucharest 1992; FCO 1995; First Secretary Washington 1998; Head of Counter-Terrorism Policy Dept FCO 2002; m 1996 Alice MacKenzie (2d 1997, 1999).

Macan, Thomas Townley; Governor British Virgin Islands since October 2002; Born 14/11/46; FCO 1969; Third later Second Secretary Bonn 1971; Second later First Secretary Brasilia 1974; FCO 1978; First Secretary (Press and Information) Bonn 1981; First Secretary later Counsellor FCO 1986; Counsellor and Deputy Head of Mission Lisbon 1990; HM Ambassador Vilnius 1995; On loan to the BOC Group 1998; Minister New Delhi 1999; m 1976 Janet Ellen Martin (1s 1981; 1d 1984).

MacCallum, Fiona, MBE (1997); First Secretary (Political) Tallinn since July 2004; Born 25/06/62; FCO 1986; Moscow 1989; FCO 1992; Second Secretary Riga 1995; First Secretary (Political) Kiev 2000; First Secretary FCO 2003; Band D6.

MacDermott, Alastair Tormod; High Commissioner Windhoek since April 2002; Born 17/09/45; FO (later FCO) 1966; Kabul 1971; FCO 1973; Accra 1973; FCO 1977; Language Training Tokyo 1978; Second Secretary Tokyo 1979; Colombo 1983; First Secretary (Information) Tokyo 1986; First Secretary FCO 1991; Full-Time Language Training 1995; First Secretary (Commercial) Ankara 1995; m (1) 1968 Helen Gordon (diss 1992) (2d 1969, 1971); (2) 1994 Gudrun Geiling.

MacDonald, Catriona MacLeod; FCO since November 2000; Born 18/04/64; FCO 1988; Belgrade 1990; FCO 1992; Berlin 1993; FCO 1996; Vienna 1997; Band C4.

MacDonald, Michelle; SUPL since February 2002; Born 18/09/78; FCO 2000; Band A2.

MacDougall, David; SUPL since May 2004; Born 07/07/73; FCO 1991; Helsinki 1995; Tel Aviv 1997; T/D Kinshasa 1999; Guatemala City 1999; SUPL 2002; T/D Basra 2003; Band C4.

Mace, Andrew Stephen; FCO since January 2003; Born 31/12/73; FCO 1995; Brussels (UKREP) 1997; FCO 1999; Copenhagen 1999; Band D6.

Macgregor, John Malcolm, CVO (1992); HM Ambassador Vienna since May 2003; Born 03/10/46; FCO 1973; Second later First Secretary New Delhi 1975; First Secretary FCO 1979; Private Secretary to Minister of State 1981; Counsellor and Head of Chancery Prague 1986; Counsellor and Head of Chancery Paris 1990; Counsellor FCO 1993; Consul-General Düsseldorf 1995; HM Ambassador Warsaw 1998; Director Wider Europe FCO 2000; m 1982 Judith Anne Brown (1d 1984; 3s 1986, 1987, 1990).

Macgregor, Judith Anne (née Brown), LVO (1992); HM Ambassador Bratislava since June 2004; Born 17/06/52; FCO 1976; First Secretary (Chancery/Information) Belgrade 1978; FCO 1981; SUPL 1986; First Secretary (Political/Information) Prague 1989; SUPL 1990; First Secretary (Chancery) Paris 1992; First Secretary FCO 1993; SUPL 1995; Counsellor (Head of Security Strategy Unit) FCO 2001; SUPL 2003; m 1982 John Malcolm Macgregor (1d 1984; 3s 1986, 1987, 1990).

Macintosh, Anne; SUPL since October 1997; Born 15/04/61; FCO 1980; Rome 1982; Havana 1985; FCO 1988; Third later Second Secretary (Commercial) Buenos Aires 1991; m 1993 Gustavo Javier Barreiro (1d 1996).

MacIntosh, Sarah; SUPL since November 2005; Born 07/08/69; FCO 1991; Third Secretary (IAEA/UN) Vienna (UKMIS) 1994; Second Secretary (Economic/EU) Madrid 1996; First Secretary FCO 1997; First Secretary (Political/Development/Economic) New York (UKMIS) 2000; FCO 2002.

Maciver, Graham; Assistant Legal Adviser FCO since October 2001; Born 26/07/76.

Mackay, Gavin Anderson, MBE (1994); On loan to the Cabinet Office since September 2001; Born 01/11/49; FCO 1973; Wellington 1975; Suva 1978; Dhaka 1981; FCO 1983; Dubai 1986 (Second Secretary 1988); Second Secretary Nicosia 1989; FCO 1994; m 1975 Glenys Pickup (1d 1977; 2s 1980, 1984).

MacKenna, Roderic Hamish; Second Secretary (Political) Madrid since February 2005; Born 15/08/58; FCO 2000; Third Secretary (Political) later Second Secretary and Deputy Head of Mission Tbilisi 2002; m 1991 Ayoma Indrani Nethsingha (2d 1992, 1993).

MacKenzie, Angela Susan (née Wright); SUPL since September 2003; Born 17/01/67; FCO 1985; Lilongwe 1989; SUPL 1993; FCO 1995; SUPL 1997; Jerusalem 2001; Band B3; m (1) 1988 Mohammed Ouassine (diss 1992); (2) 1997 Graham John MacKenzie.

MacKenzie, Catherine Louise Hay; SUPL since June 2004; Born 09/08/66; FCO 1989; Language Training FCO 1991; Language Training Tokyo 1992; Second Secretary 1992; Second Secretary (Chancery) Tokyo 1993; New York (UKMIS) 2000; Band D6; m 1992 John Page.

Mackenzie, Dorothy (née Byers); FCO since September 2001; Born 01/03/56; FCO 1974; The Hague 1976; Lusaka 1979; FCO 1982; Ottawa 1985; SUPL 1990; Singapore 1991; FCO 1993; SUPL 1999; Muscat 2000; Band C4; m 1978 Robert Mackenzie (1d 1987).

MacKenzie, Kenneth John Alexander; First Secretary FCO since July 2001; Born 09/09/49; FCO 1973; Brussels 1975; Second later First Secretary FCO 1978; Buenos Aires 1981; First Secretary FCO 1982; First Secretary (Economic) Bucharest 1985; First Secretary FCO 1988; First Secretary Vienna 1992; First Secretary FCO 1995; Consul Munich 1997; Band D6; m 1980 Alison Mary Linda Sandford (1d 1983; 1s 1987).

MacKenzie, Nina Ruth (née McBratney); Third Secretary (Political) Canberra since June 2003;

Born 08/06/73; FCO 1999; Third Secretary (Political) Abidjan 2001; Band C4; m 2002 Scott MacKenzie.

MacKenzie, Robert (known as Rab); FCO since December 2001; Born 05/03/54; Dept of National Savings 1973; FCO 1974; The Hague 1976; Lusaka 1979; FCO 1982; Ottawa 1985; Second Secretary FCO 1988; Second Secretary (Commercial) Mexico City 1988; Second Secretary (Commercial) Singapore 1990; Second Secretary FCO 1993; First Secretary (Commercial) Muscat 1998; m 1978 Dorothy Byers (1d 1987).

MacKerras, Carl Anthony; Second Secretary (Consular/Management) Belmopan since April 2001; Born 13/11/69; Land Registry 1988 - 90; FCO 1990; St Petersburg 1995; Vice-Consul Copenhagen 1997; m 1997 Vera Ermolova (2d 1997, 2000).

Macklin, Diane Elaine (née Crowther); FCO since October 2002; Born 05/09/64; FCO 1981; SUPL 1995; FCO 1995; SUPL 1996; Band A2.

Maclean, Andrew Mark; Second Secretary Kampala since May 2004; Born 25/11/72; FCO 2002; Band D6.

MacLean, Gillian Anne; FCO since October 2004; Born 22/03/72; Band D6.

MacLennan, David Ross; HM Ambassador Doha since June 2002; Born 12/02/45; FO 1963; DSAO 1965; MECAS 1966; Aden 1969; Civil Service College 1972; Second later First Secretary FCO 1972; First Secretary UKDEL OECD Paris 1975; First Secretary, Head of Chancery and Consul Abu Dhabi 1979; First Secretary FCO 1982; On secondment to European Commission 1984; Counsellor (Commercial) Kuwait 1985; Counsellor and Head of Chancery Nicosia 1989; HM Consul-General Jerusalem 1990; Counsellor FCO 1994; HM Ambassador Beirut 1996; m 1964 Margaret Lytollis (2d 1964, 1966).

MacLeod, Gordon Stewart; Nicosia since February 2002; Born 15/02/52; FCO 1971; Ankara 1973; Washington 1977; Dacca 1979; FCO 1982; Valletta 1985; Third later Second Secretary New Delhi 1988; Second Secretary FCO 1992; Consul (Commercial and Information) Casablanca 1998; m 1978 Susan Raggatt (2d 1981, 1984).

MacLeod, Iain; Counsellor (Legal Adviser) New York (UKMIS) since August 2001; Born 15/03/62; Assistant Legal Adviser FCO 1987; First Secretary (Assistant Legal Adviser) Brussels (UKREP) 1991; FCO 1995; Legal Secretariat to the Law Officers 1997; m 1988 Dr Alison Mary Murchison (2d 1991, 1995; 2s 1993, 1997).

MacLeod, Siân Christina, OBE (2002); On loan to the Cabinet Office since January 2002; Born 31/05/62; FCO 1986; Language Training 1987; Second Secretary (Chancery) Moscow 1988; Second later First Secretary FCO 1992; First Secretary (Political) The Hague 1996; FCO 2000; m 1987 Richard Anthony Robinson (2d 1991, 1994; 1s 1998).

MacMillan, Alison Flora; SUPL since February 2004; Born 22/08/61; FCO 1982; Mexico City 1983; Washington 1987; SUPL 1989; FCO 1990; Third Secretary Vice-Consul and Deputy Head of Mission Managua 1993; Second Secretary (EU) Gibraltar 1996; FCO 2001; m 1997 Julian Thomas Lee (1s 1997; 1d 1999).

Macpherson, John Bannerman, OBE (2004); Counsellor Stockholm since June 2003; Born 23/06/51; Third later Second Secretary FCO 1975; Language Training MECAS 1977; Second Secretary Khartoum 1979; Second later First Secretary Sana'a 1980; FCO 1983; Language Training 1985; First Secretary Sofia 1987; First Secretary FCO 1990; Counsellor Cairo 1993; Counsellor FCO 1996; m 1985 Monica Jane Lancashire (2s 1986, 1988; 1d 1992).

Macpherson, Kara Isobel; Second Secretary FCO since September 1998; Born 03/08/60; FCO 1981; Islamabad 1983; Prague 1986; Africa/Middle East Floater 1988; FCO 1992; T/D Khartoum 1994; FCO 1994; T/D New York (UKMIS) 1996; FCO 1997; Band C4.

MacQueen, Christine Ann; Counsellor Brussels since July 2002; Born 24/05/59; FCO 1982; Second Secretary (Economic) Brasilia 1984; Second later First Secretary FCO 1987; New York 1989; First Secretary and UNESCO Observer Paris 1990; First Secretary later Counsellor FCO 1995; m 1992 Bruno Pascal Castola (1d 1992; 1s 1994).

Madden, Kevin Peter; Transferred to the Diplomatic Service since May 2002; Born 27/06/82; FCO (HCS) 2000; Band B3.

Madden, Paul Damian; Counsellor FCO since September 2003; Born 25/04/59; DTI 1980; PS/PUSS 1984; Language Training FCO/Kamakura 1987; First Secretary Tokyo 1988; First Secretary FCO 1992; First Secretary Washington 1996; Deputy High Commissioner and Counsellor (Commercial/Economic) Singapore 2000; m 1989 Sarah Pauline Thomas (2s 1991, 1992; 1d 1996).

Maddicott, David Sydney; British High Commissioner Yaoundé since February 2006; Born 27/03/53; First Secretary FCO 1994; Full-Time Language Training 1996; On attachment to the Canadian Government 1996; First Secretary (Head of Pol/Info Section) Ottawa 1997; First Secretary FCO 2000; m 1980 Elizabeth Wynne (4s 1980, 1984, 1990, 1993; 1d 1982).

Maddinson, Paul Francis; FCO since July 2004; Born 16/05/72; FCO 1995; Second Secretary (Political) Nairobi 1996; Second Secretary FCO 1998; Full-Time Language Training 2000; First Secretary (Political) Moscow 2001; Band D6; m 1996 Rebecca Anne Jackson (1s 2000; 1d 2002).

Madisons, Alexander Emil; Second Secretary (Technical Management Officer) Belgrade since June 2004; Born 09/11/62; FCO 1983; Peking 1990; Belgrade 1994; FCO 1997; Third Secretary Rome 1999; Band C4.

Madojemu, Valentine Isi; Jerusalem since February 2003; Born 27/03/58; FCO 1998; Karachi 2000; Band B3; m 1989 Rita (1s 1992; 1d 1997).

Maguire, John; HM Consul Denver since January 2000; Born 04/06/49; FCO 1968; Moscow 1971; Belmopan 1972; New Delhi 1974; Tokyo 1978; FCO 1982; Alexandria 1985; Consul (Commercial) Perth 1988; FCO 1992; Deputy Head of Mission, Consul and First Secretary (Commercial) Doha 1995; FCO 1999; Band C5; m 1978 Mette Lucie Konow Monsen.

Maguire, Natalie (née Rule); Jerusalem since June 2004; Born 22/05/62; MOD 1985-2000; FCO 2000; Bahrain 2001; Band A2; m 1981 Robin Maguire.

Maher, Heather Kirsten Maria; FCO since April 2003; Born 12/01/70; FCO 1988; Bangkok 1990; FCO 1993; Athens 1994; Kuwait 1995; Harare 1999; FCO 1999; Abidjan 2000; Kiev 2000; Band A2.

Major, Pamela Ann; Berlin since October 2002; Born 04/03/59; FCO 1982; Language Training SOAS 1983; Second Secretary (Chancery) Peking 1986; First Secretary FCO 1988; First Secretary Moscow 1993; First Secretary later Counsellor FCO 1996; SUPL 1998; On secondment 2001; m 1992 Robert Leigh Turner (1s 1992; 1d 1994).

Makepeace, Richard Edward; HM Ambassador Abu Dhabi since February 2003; Born 24/06/53; FCO 1976; Language Training MECAS 1977; Third later Second Secretary Muscat 1979; Second later First Secretary (Chancery) Prague 1981; FCO 1985; Private Secretary to the Parliamentary Under-Secretary of State 1986; First Secretary Brussels (UKREP) 1989; Counsellor FCO 1993; Cairo 1995; HM Ambassador Khartoum 1999; m 1980 Rupmani Catherine Pradhan.

Makin, John; Second Secretary (Commercial) Perth since March 2001; Born 13/01/64; DHSS 1984; FCO 1985; Kaduna 1987; Düsseldorf 1990; Floater Duties 1992; FCO 1996; Jakarta 1999; Band C4.

Makriyiannis, Lorraine Elizabeth (née Colhoun); SUPL since May 1999; Born 10/06/69; FCO 1991; Sofia 1993; Nicosia 1995; Band A2; m 1995 Michael Makriyiannis.

Malcolm, James Ian, OBE (1995); HM Ambassador Panama City since March 2002; Born 29/03/46; MPBW 1964; FO 1966; Brussels (UKDEL NATO) 1969; Rangoon 1972; FCO 1974; Nairobi 1977; Damascus 1980; Second Secretary (Commercial) Luanda 1983; Second Secretary FCO 1985; First Secretary (Political/Economic) Jakarta 1987; First Secretary FCO 1994; Deputy High Commissioner Kingston 1997; m 1967 Sheila Nicholson Moore (1s 1976; 1d 1980).

Malin, Carl Spencer; FCO since August 2002; Born 07/07/69; FCO 1987; Ottawa 1989; FCO 1992; Floater Duties 1993; FCO 1995; Vice-Consul Lagos 1996; SUPL 1998; Lilongwe 1999; Kathmandu 2000; Lusaka 2002; Band C4; m 1995 Kerstin Ruge (1d 2001).

Malin, Keith Ian; Counsellor FCO since November 1999; Born 11/12/53; FCO 1976; Third Secretary (Developing Countries) Brussels (UKREP) 1978; Second later First Secretary FCO 1979; First Secretary on secondment to HCS 1983; First Secretary (UN/Press) Geneva (UKMIS) 1984; FCO 1986; First Secretary (Chancery/Economic) Sofia 1990; First Secretary later Counsellor FCO 1993; Counsellor Peking 1996; m 1977 Gaynor Dudley Jones (2s 1985, 1992).

Mallion, Richard Julian; Montserrat since December 2004; Born 23/12/68; FCO 1999; Addis Ababa 2001; Band A2.

Malone, Philip, MVO; Head of Chancery Singapore since April 2003; Born 03/12/61; FCO 1981; Buenos Aires 1983; Guatemala City 1986; FCO 1989; Third Secretary (Commercial/Information) Luxembourg 1992; Second Secretary (Chancery) Bandar Seri Begawan 1995; First Secretary FCO 1999; Full-Time Language Training (Mandarin) 2002; m 1999 Sarah Tan Yee Whey (1d 2001).

Mamet, Emma Kate (née Miller); SUPL since March 2005; Born 06/08/70; FCO 1991; Third Secretary (Chancery) Geneva (UKMIS) 1994; Port Louis 1995; Third Secretary (Economic) Ottawa 1999; FCO 2002; ECO/Vice-Consul Abidjan 2003; Band B3; m 2000 Anthony Roger Mamet.

Man, Kam Lon; FCO since April 2003; Born 16/06/72; FCO 1996; Islamabad 2000; Band A2.

Manley, Ernest George; Brussels (UKDEL NATO) since June 1999; Born 15/02/51; FCO 1970; Aden 1973; Milan 1975; East Berlin 1978; FCO 1980; Kuala Lumpur 1983; Consul Milan 1986; FCO 1990; Band C4; m 1973 Mary Catherine Whelan (1s 1975).

Manley, Simon John; Deputy Head of European Union Department (Internal) later Head of the EU Economic Team, FCO since September 2002; Born 18/09/67; FCO 1990; On secondment to the European Commission 1993; Second later First Secretary (Political) New York (UKMIS) 1993; On secondment to the EU Council Secretariat Brussels 1998; m 1996 Maria Isabel Fernandez-Utges (2d 2000, 2001).

Manley, Suzanne Marie Theresa; Quito since October 2004; Born 12/12/64; FCO 1987; La Paz 1990; T/D Havana 1993; Santiago 1994; T/D Buenos Aires 1998; FCO 1998; Moscow 2001; Band B3.

Manning, Sir David Geoffrey, KCMG (2001), CMG (1992); HM Ambassador Washington since August 2003; Born 05/12/49; Third Secretary FCO 1972; Language Training 1973; Third later Second Secretary Warsaw 1974; Second later First Secretary New Delhi 1977; FCO 1980; First Secretary Paris 1984; Counsellor on loan to the

Cabinet Office 1988; Political Counsellor Moscow 1990; Head of Eastern Department FCO 1993; UK Member of ICFY Contact Group for Bosnia 1994; Head of Policy Planning FCO 1994; HM Ambassador Tel Aviv 1995; Deputy Under-Secretary FCO 1998; Permanent Representative Brussels (UKDEL NATO) 2000; Foreign Policy Adviser to the Prime Minister 2001; m 1973 Dr Catherine Parkinson.

Manuel, Francesca Jane (née Lintner); Paris since August 2002; Born 05/04/72; FCO 1995; Washington 1997; FCO 2001; Band A2; m 1997 (1s 1998).

March, Shirley Elizabeth; SUPL since October 2004; Born 04/02/61; FCO 1984; Second Secretary (EC Affairs) Brussels 1988; First Secretary FCO 1990; First Secretary (UNPR) Geneva (UKMIS) 2000; Band D6; m 1984 Paul Louis March (2s 1990, 1992).

Marden, Nicholas; FCO since September 2002; Born 02/05/50; Army 1971-74; Third later Second Secretary FCO 1974; Second Secretary Nicosia 1977; First Secretary FCO 1980; Warsaw 1982; FCO 1985; First Secretary Paris 1988; First Secretary FCO 1993; Counsellor Tel Aviv 1998; m 1977 Melanie Gaye Glover (2d 1980, 1982).

Markey, Donna Maria; FCO since July 2004; Born 03/11/80; Band A2.

Marmion, Elisabeth Claire (née Terry); Dhaka since August 2004; Born 09/07/72; FCO 1995; Hong Kong 1999; Band A2; m 1999 Nicholas Paul Marmion.

Marren, Marrena Ruby; Muscat since September 2002; Born 15/01/68; FCO 1987; Paris 1989; Prague 1992; Geneva 1994; FCO 1994; Brussels (UKREP) 1998; Band B3.

Marriott, Allison Mary, MBE (1997); SUPL since October 2004; Born 31/03/66; FCO 1987; Vice-Consul Amman 1990; Third Secretary Brussels (UKDEL) 1993; Copenhagen 1996; Second Secretary FCO 1997; First Secretary (Management) Addis Ababa 2000; Mumbai 2004; Band C5.

Marriott, Anne Stewart Murray (née Corbett), MBE (2002); Second Secretary Dubai since June 2003; Born 29/10/57; FCO 1979; Brasilia 1982; FCO 1984; Abu Dhabi 1985; Bangkok 1988; FCO 1992; Amman 1997; FCO 2001; Band C4; m 1988 Paul James Marriott.

Marsden, Ian Thomas; SUPL since February 2004; Born 05/10/69; Department of Social Security 1989; FCO 1990; Colombo 1993; FCO 1996; Sarajevo 1997; On loan to the DTI 1998; T/D Pristina 1999; Third Secretary (Commercial) Bucharest 2002; Band B3.

Marsden, Rosalind Mary, CMG (2003); HM Ambassador Kabul since January 2004; Born 27/10/50; Third Secretary FCO 1974; Language Training SOAS 1975; Third, Second and later First Secretary Tokyo 1976; First Secretary FCO 1980; First Secretary (Economic) Bonn 1985; First Secretary FCO 1989; Counsellor on secondment to the National Westminster Bank 1991; Head of Chancery Tokyo 1993; Counsellor FCO 1996; Director (Asia Pacific) FCO 1999.

Marsh, Derek Richard, CVO (1999); Director-General of British Trade and Cultural Office Taipei since July 2002; Born 17/09/46; MOD 1968; DTI 1988; Seconded to the FCO 1997; Deputy Head of Mission and Consul-General Seoul 1997; m 1969 Frances Anne Roberts (1s 1972; 1d 1975).

Marsh, Elaine (née Skinner); Third Secretary Valletta since August 2002; Born 06/01/57; FCO 1976; Port of Spain 1978; Bucharest 1982; Valletta 1984; FCO 1987; New Delhi 1989; Third Secretary (Consular) Dar es Salaam 1992; Third Secretary FCO 1994; Washington 1998; Band B3; m 1985 Andrew Peter Marsh (diss 1989) (1s 1988).

Marshall, Alan John; Management Officer Bogotá since May 2004; Born 11/09/52; FCO 1971; Cairo 1973; Lilongwe 1975; Salisbury 1978; Sana'a 1980; FCO 1981; Islamabad 1983; Lisbon 1987; Luanda 1990; Second Secretary FCO 1993; Lisbon 1996; Consul Lisbon 1998; Second Secretary (Consular) Jakarta 2001; Band C5; (1s 1979; 1d 1986).

Marshall, Angela Rosemary; Brussels (UKREP) since July 2002; Born 22/08/60; FCO 1988; Maseru 1991; Kiev 1994; FCO 1997; Lisbon 2000; Band B3.

Marshall, Aurea Jane; Cairo since July 2003; Born 12/01/74; FCO 1999; Sofia 2000; Band A2.

Marshall, Bernard Alan; First Secretary FCO since January 2002; Born 23/03/48; FCO 1968; Bombay 1971; Islamabad 1971; Moscow 1973; Anguilla 1974; Bonn 1976; FCO 1978 (Second Secretary 1979); Vice-Consul (Commercial) Melbourne 1982; Second Secretary FCO 1986; First Secretary (Commercial) Bucharest 1989; First Secretary FCO 1993; Full-Time Language Training 1995; Consul Munich 1995; Sarajevo 1997; First Secretary FCO 1998; T/D Tehran 1999; Second Secretary (Commercial) T/D Tripoli 2001; Band C5.

Marshall, Brian; Second Secretary FCO since April 1985; Born 13/12/51; FCO 1971; On loan to HCS 1974; FCO 1977; Second Secretary Muscat 1984; Band C4; m 1973 Susan Joyce Bishop (2d 1976, 1980).

Marshall, Francis James; Deputy High Commissioner Freetown since November 2002; Born 10/08/46; CRO 1963; Commonwealth Office (later FCO) 1965; Mogadishu 1969; Singapore 1971; FCO 1974; Port Louis 1977; Tripoli 1981; Addis Ababa 1983; FCO 1984; Vice-Consul Toronto 1987; Second Secretary (Management) JMO Brussels 1991; SUPL 1994; Deputy Head of Mission Rangoon 1999; m 1971 Clare Wray (1s 1972; 1d 1976).

Marshall, Jonathan Neil; On secondment since September 2003; Born 26/08/70; FCO 1992; Full-

Time Language Training 1993; Athens 1994; SUPL 1999; FCO 2000; Band D6; m 1997 Maria Kontou (1s 1998; 1d 2001).

Marshall, Michael Gavin; First Secretary (Management) Singapore since June 2002; Born 13/09/60; FCO 1980; Moscow 1982; Baghdad 1983; Floater Duties 1988; FCO 1990; Second Secretary (Consul) St Petersburg 1992; Seoul 1995; Second later First Secretary FCO 1998; m 1993 Amanda Louise O'Connor (1d 1997; 1s 1999).

Marshall, Robert John; FCO since July 2003; Born 19/06/65; FCO 1988; Second Secretary Tokyo 1992; First Secretary FCO 1995; First Secretary Kuala Lumpur 2000; Band D7.

Marshall, Simon; Damascus since December 2003; Born 31/05/68; FCO 1999; Band A2; m 2003 Sarah Jane Biggerstaff.

Martens, Alexandra Mary; SUPL since March 2005; Born 20/10/57; FCO 1978; Johannesburg 1980; FCO 1981; Paris 1987; FCO 1987; Vienna 1989; FCO 1991; Second Secretary Paris 2000; FCO 2004; Band C4.

Martin, Alexander Benedict Lowry; First Secretary Prague since March 2004; Born 16/09/70; FCO 1996; Second Secretary (Economic) Jakarta 1999; Second Secretary FCO 2001; Band C4; m 1999 Nicola Barbara Hill.

Martin, Angus Charles Trench; FCO since June 2003; Born 27/12/71; FCO 1991; World Wide Floater Duties 1995; T/D Geneva (UKMIS) 1998; FCO 1999; World Wide Floater Duties 2001; Band B3.

Martin, Craig Keith; FCO since September 2001; Born 16/11/69; FCO 1988; Washington 1998; Band C4; m 1998 Natalie Jayne Wren.

Martin, Dominic David William; Washington since August 2004; Born 25/11/64; FCO 1987; Third later Second Secretary (Chancery) New Delhi 1989; First Secretary FCO 1992; First Secretary (Head of Political and Economic Section) Buenos Aires 1996; FCO 2000; Counsellor (Political) New Delhi 2001; m 1996 Emily Rose Walter (3d 1996, 1998, 2001).

Martin, Frances Edith Josephine; First Secretary (Commercial) Brussels (UKREP) since March 2001; Born 20/02/48; MOD 1965; FCO 1973; Montevideo 1973; Peking 1976; Tehran 1977; Moscow 1979; FCO 1981; Washington 1987; Athens 1990; FCO 1993; Second Secretary Montreal 1996.

Martin, Francis James (known as Frank); High Commissioner Gaborone since October 2005; Born 03/05/49; DSAO later FCO 1968; Reykjavik 1971; Stuttgart 1973; FCO 1976; Second Secretary 1978; Vice-Consul (Political/Information) Cape Town 1979; Second later First Secretary (Institutions) Brussels (UKREP) 1983; FCO 1988; Deputy High Commissioner Freetown 1988; First Secretary FCO 1991; On loan to the DTI 1992; Full-Time Language Training 1995; Deputy Head of Mission Luanda 1995; First Secretary (Commercial) Copenhagen 1998; High Commissioner Maseru 2002; m 1970 Aileen Margaret Shovlin (2s 1973, 1975; 2d 1976, 1978).

Martin, Neil Richard; Deputy Head of Mission Chisinau since November 2004; Born 14/03/67; FCO 1987; Tunis 1989; Sofia 1991; Ho Chi Minh City 1994; On secondment to China Britain Trade Group 1996; FCO 1997; First Secretary and Deputy Head of Mission Asunción 2000; T/D Managua 2003; Band C4.

Martin, Nicholas Jonathan Leigh; FCO since March 2003; Born 29/01/48; First Secretary FCO 1979; First Secretary (Chancery) Nairobi 1981; First Secretary FCO 1984; First Secretary (Chancery) Rome 1987; First Secretary FCO 1991; Counsellor Jakarta 1993; Counsellor FCO 1996; Counsellor Regional Affairs Bridgetown 2000; m 1980 Anna Louise Reekie (1s 1983; 2d 1985, 1987).

Martin, Siân Kurstin; Attaché Phnom Penh since July 2004; Born 05/01/76; FCO 2002; Band A2.

Martin, Simon Charles; Deputy Head of Mission Prague since May 2005; Born 15/05/63; FCO 1984; Language Training 1986; Third later Second Secretary and Vice-Consul Rangoon 1987; Second later First Secretary FCO 1990; Full-Time Language Training 1995; First Secretary (Commercial) Budapest 1996; FCO 2001; Secondment (Commercial) 2003; m 1988 Sharon Margaret Joel (1s 1996; 1d 1998).

Martinek, Rachel Anne Emily; Second Secretary (Political) New Delhi since June 2005; Born 24/04/79; FCO 2002; Band C4.

Martinez, Paul Lawrence; Consul Dallas since September 1999; Born 06/11/53; FCO 1972; Dublin 1975; Paris 1975; Kingston 1977; Chicago 1981; FCO 1984; Second Secretary (Chancery/Information) Lima 1986; Second Secretary FCO 1990; Assistant Private Secretary to Minister of State 1990; Second Secretary and HM Consul Mexico City 1993; First Secretary FCO 1996; m 1978 Ann Elizabeth Stokes (2d 1982, 1985).

Maryan-Green, Kerri-Lyn (née Miller); FCO since February 2000; Born 11/11/64; FCO 1987; Shanghai 1989; Port Louis 1990; SUPL 1994; FCO 1996; SUPL 1998; Band B3; m 1992 James Richard Maryan-Green (2d 1993, 1998).

Mason, Colette Hazel, MBE (1999); SUPL since September 2001; Born 15/07/65; FCO 1987; Mogadishu 1989; Port of Spain 1991; FCO 1994; Peking 1996; Vice-Consul Maseru 1998; Band B3.

Mason, Edward Charles; Deputy Head of Mission Zagreb since August 2002; Born 11/05/68; FCO 1990; Third later Second Secretary Oslo 1992; Second later First Secretary FCO 1995; m 2002 Fiona Isabel Macleod.

Mason, Fiona Isabel (née MacLeod); SUPL since December 2003; Born 19/10/70; FCO 1992; Seoul

1994; T/D Belmopan 1996; FCO 1997; Zagreb 2002; Band B3; m 2002 Edward Charles Mason.

Mason, Ian David; Second Secretary Chennai since December 2004; Born 26/10/67; FCO 1987; Mogadishu 1989; Floater Duties 1991; Phnom Penh 1993; FCO 1994; Third Secretary (Chancery) Buenos Aires 1997; Second Secretary (Political/Press/Public Affairs) Lusaka 2001; Band C4; m 1992 Judith Caroline Elizabeth Owens (1s 1994; 3d 1996, 1998, 2000).

Mason, Judith Caroline Elizabeth (née Owens); SUPL since July 1994; Born 11/08/64; FCO 1984; Washington 1986; Warsaw 1988; Floater Duties 1990; Phnom Penh 1993; Band A2; m 1992 Ian David Mason (1s 1994; 3d 1996, 1998, 2000).

Massam, David Robert; FCO since July 2000; Born 02/10/70; Second Secretary FCO 1996; Second Secretary (IAIE) Vienna (UKMIS) 1998; Band C4; m 1996 Elisabeth Katharine Jenkinson (1d 1999).

Massey, Andrew Fraser; Second Secretary (Political) Dar es Salaam since January 2003; Born 24/07/63; FCO 1984; Bangkok 1987; Jedda 1989; FCO 1994; Bonn 1998; Band C4; m 1996 Patricia Elizabeth Parsons (1d 1997; 2s 2000, 2002).

Massingham, Andrea Sharron; Floater Duties since November 2002; Born 10/03/71; FCO 1990; SUPL 1992; Brussels (UKDEL NATO) 1992; FCO 1995; Kathmandu 1995; BTCO Taipei 1999; Band B3.

Mastin-Lee, Christopher Ernest; Legal Counsellor FCO since April 1995; Born 11/08/56; Assistant Legal Counsellor FCO 1990; m 1988 Katherine Louise Heron (2s 1994, 1996; 1d 1998).

Mathers, Peter James, LVO (1995); High Commissioner Kingston since July 2002; Born 02/04/46; HM Forces 1968-71; FCO 1971; SOAS 1972-73; Tehran (Commercial) 1973; Bonn (Chancery) 1976; FCO 1978; Copenhagen (Chancery and Information) 1981; Tehran (Commercial) 1986; FCO 1987; On secondment to UN Offices Vienna 1988; FCO 1991; Deputy High Commissioner Bridgetown 1995; Counsellor (Commercial and Economic) Stockholm 1998; m 1983 Elisabeth Hoeller (1s 1984; 1d 1986).

Mathews, Harriet Lucy, OBE (2005); FCO since January 2003; Born 22/12/73; FCO 1997; On secondment Brazilian Diplomatic Academy (Instituto Rio Branco) 1999; Second Secretary Brasilia 1999; Band D6.

Mathewson, Iain Arthur Gray, CMG (2004); Counsellor FCO since August 1996; Born 16/03/52; HM Customs and Excise 1974-77; DHSS 1977-80; FCO 1980; First Secretary New York (UKMIS) 1981; FCO 1985; Warsaw 1985; First Secretary FCO 1989; Counsellor Prague 1993; m 1983 Jennifer Bloch (1s 1984; 1d 1986).

Mathison, Beverley; Islamabad since January 2003; Born 28/09/69; Bonn 1999; Band A2.

Matsumoto-Prouten, Matthew David, MBE (1996); Vice-Consul Tokyo since November 2002; Born 10/03/69; FCO 1988; Tokyo 1992; FCO 1996; Third Secretary (Political) Vilnius 1997; FCO 2000; Full-Time Language Training FCO 2000; Band C4; m 1994 Akino Matsumoto (2s 1997, 2004; 1d 2000).

Mattey, Eric; Deputy Head of Mission and Consul Doha since December 2003; Born 26/03/49; FCO 1968; Bucharest 1971; Rabat 1973; Moscow 1975; FCO 1977; Vienna 1980; Port Louis 1983; Second Secretary FCO 1985; Second later First Secretary (Commercial) Kuala Lumpur 1990; Consul Oporto 1995; FCO 2000; Band D6; m 1970 Janet Walker (1s 1971; 1d 1974).

Matthews, Andrew John; FCO since May 2001; Born 28/04/55; FCO 1974; Bonn 1976; Singapore 1979; FCO 1982; Dublin 1982; FCO 1985; Colombo 1988; Paris 1992; FCO 1995; Berlin 1998; Band B3; m (1) 1976 Carole Susan Thomson (diss 1986) (1d 1976; 1s 1978); (2) 1988 Denise Ann Mary Carroll (1d 1992).

Matthews, David Alan; FCO since October 2002; Born 09/10/72; Band B3; m 2002 Sara Blackall.

Matthews, Mark Julian; First Secretary (Chemical Weapons) The Hague since July 2003; Born 24/08/68; FCO 1990; Third Secretary (Defence) Brussels (UKDEL NATO) 1992; Full-Time Language Training (Arabic) 1996; Second Secretary (Political/Press and Public Affairs) Abu Dhabi 1997; Foreign Office Spokesman for the Middle East, 2000; m 1997 Shauna Rudge (1s 1998; 1d 2001).

Maxton, Fiona; FCO since November 2003; Born 19/12/67; FCO 1985; Bonn 1988; Third Secretary (Management) Rabat 1989; Third Secretary FCO 1993; Vice-Consul Kiev 1997; Zagreb 2000; Band C4.

May, Philip; Lagos since December 2004; Born 12/11/60; Ottawa 1982; Moscow 1985; Islamabad 1986; FCO 1988; Resigned later reinstated 1990; Tehran 1992; BTC Hong Kong 1994; Second Secretary FCO 1997; DSTUS Chairman 1998; First Secretary (Management) Brussels (UKREP) 2001; Band D6; m 1985 Susan Ann Checketts (2d 1989, 1990).

May, Susan Ann (née Checketts); SUPL since June 2001; Born 18/08/56; FCO 1978; Peking 1980; Ottawa 1982; Moscow 1985; Islamabad 1986; SUPL 1989; FCO 1997; Band B3; m 1985 Philip May (2d 1989, 1990).

Mayhew, Michael John Ernest; HM Consul General Cape Town since December 2002; Born 06/11/46; DSAO (later FCO) 1966; Mexico City 1969; Algiers 1972; Tokyo 1974; FCO 1975; Prague 1978; Second Secretary (Information) Oslo 1981; Second Secretary FCO 1985; First Secretary (Commercial/Development) Bangkok 1987; First Secretary (Commercial) The Hague 1990; First Secretary FCO 1993; Deputy High Commissioner Bridgetown 1998; m 1976 Elizabeth Carol Owen (1d 1987).

Mayhew, Nicola Ann; Third Secretary (Management) Chisinau since July 2003; Born 14/08/66; WRAC 1985-88; Employment Services 1992; FCO 1998; Jakarta 2000; Band B3; m 1988 David Mayhew.

Mayland, Alan John; First Secretary (Management) Bangkok since July 2003; Born 05/11/46; FO 1965; Warsaw 1968; Cairo 1970; Brussels 1971; Calcutta 1974; Budapest 1975; FCO 1976; Paris 1981; Ottawa 1982; Second Secretary FCO 1986; Second Secretary (Admin) Colombo 1989; Bucharest 1993; Consul Rome 1999.

Mayne, Julie Ann; Mexico City since October 2003; Born 03/04/58; FCO 1989; Caracas 1992; Quito 1996; World Wide Floater Duties 1999; FCO 2002; Band B3.

McAllister, Andrew Thornton; Second Secretary (Commercial) Dhaka since June 2001; Born 30/11/67; FCO 1988; Karachi 1990; Seoul 1993; FCO 1998; Band C4; m 1995 Han Boon AE.

McAllister, Dominic James; First Secretary Caracas since June 2004; Born 12/02/64; FCO 1990; Full-Time Language Training 1992; Full-Time Language Training Cairo 1993; Third Secretary (Information) Riyadh 1995; Second Secretary (Management) Taipei 1998; FCO 2001; m 1993 (Nelly) Hei Yee Chan-McAllister (2d 1996, 1997; 2s 1999, 2002).

McAllister, Lesley (née Dorris); SUPL since July 2004; Born 04/04/72; FCO 1999; Peking 2001; Band A2; m 2000 Gordon McAllister (1s 2002).

McAree, Kevin Thomas; SUPL since December 2001; Born 27/06/52; FCO 1971; Caracas 1974; FCO 1974; Honiara 1974; Moscow 1977; Georgetown 1979; FCO 1983; Munich 1988; FCO 1989; Istanbul 1993; Brussels (UKDEL) 1997; FCO 1999; Band B3; m 1975 Susan Margaret Humphrey (2s 1980, 1984).

McAree, Susan Margaret (née Humphrey); New Delhi since December 2004; Born 26/06/55; FCO 2000; Bangkok 2001; Band A2; m 1975 Kevin Thomas McAree (2s 1980, 1984).

McBride, Christophe Charles Rene; First Secretary New York (UKMIS) since September 2003; Born 20/03/75; FCO 1997; Second Secretary (Political) Abuja 1998; Second later First Secretary FCO 2001; Band D6; m 2001 Caroline Jane Davies.

McCafferty, Marie Claire; SUPL since May 2004; Born 17/05/65; FCO 1988; Bonn 1990; Nairobi 1993; FCO 1996; Wellington 1998; New Delhi 2003; Band A2; m 2001 (1d 2002).

McCall, Gary; Abuja since March 2004; Born 08/02/69; FCO 1987; Bridgetown 1989; Dhaka 1993; Karachi 1997; ECO Sofia 2000; Band B3; m (1) 1990 Patricia Ann Chin (diss 1993); (2) 1993 Sharon Anne Thomas (diss) (1s 1994); ptnr, Puticha NaNongkai (1d 1998).

McCallum, Robert Campbell; Havana since April 2004; Born 04/11/45; Moscow 1989; New York (UKMIS) 1991; Kiev 1993; Moscow 1997; T/D Tripoli 2000; T/D Moscow 2001; Cairo 2001; Band C4.

McCallum, Ruth Elizabeth (née Thomson); FCO since April 1995; Born 12/11/63; FCO 1985; Moscow 1988; FCO 1989; Ankara 1991; Band C4; m 1997 Martin Douglas McCallum.

McCann, Alec; Kingston since May 2003; Born 04/11/70; FCO 1988; Rome 1991; Lisbon 1994; Lagos 1997; Band B3.

McCarthy, Susan Margaret (née Hutton); FCO since September 2003; Born 01/04/59; FCO 1984; Khartoum 1985; Georgetown 1989; Tortola 1994; SUPL 1998; Band B3; m 1990 Jonathan Paul McCarthy (1d 1992; 1s 1996).

McCarthy, Tina Ann; FCO since December 1998; Born 25/01/66; FCO 1984; Peking 1987; FCO 1988; Dar es Salaam 1990; FCO 1993; Budapest 1995; Band B3.

McCleary, William Boyd; Director Trade and Investment in Germany and Consul- General Düsseldorf since November 2000; Born 30/03/49; HCS 1972; First Secretary (Agriculture later Chancery) Bonn 1975; First Secretary FCO 1981; First Secretary, Head of Chancery and Consul Seoul 1985; First Secretary FCO 1988; Counsellor, Deputy Head of Mission and Director of Trade Promotion Ankara 1990; Counsellor (Economic) Ottawa 1993; Head of Overseas Estate Department, later Estate Strategy Unit FCO 1997; m (1) 1977 Susan Elizabeth Williams (diss 1999) (2d 1983, 1985); (2) 2000 Jenny Collier (1d 2001).

McCleery, Katherine Louise (known as Kate); Assistant Legal Adviser, FCO since September 2002; Born 25/04/74; Band D6.

McCluskie, Matthew William; FCO since January 2001; Born 06/05/65; FCO 1984; Bonn 1986; Prague 1988; Tunis 1990; FCO 1992; Warsaw 1997; Band B3.

McCole, Kevin John; Second Secretary (Management) Bucharest since April 2002; Born 06/05/69; FCO 1989; The Hague 1992; Valletta 1995; FCO 1998; Band C4; m 2001 Margaret Rose Howie.

McCole, Margaret Rose (née Howie); SUPL since May 2005; Born 07/03/66; FCO 1985; Tokyo 1988; Stockholm 1990; FCO 1993; Rome 1994; Third Secretary FCO 1997; Second Secretary (Political/PPA) Bucharest 2002; m 2001 Kevin John McCole.

McColl, Lorraine Helen, RVM (1992); Accra since September 2004; Born 20/08/57; FCO 1989; Bonn 1990; Ottawa 1993; Berlin 1996; Tunis 2000; Band B3; m 1992 Alan McElroy (1d 1996).

McColm, Sean; St Petersburg since October 2002; Born 10/07/72; FCO 1990; Copenhagen 1994; Dhaka 1997; FCO 1998; Band B3.

McCooey, Geraldine Mary; First Secretary (Political) Sarajevo since October 2004; Born 25/05/73; FCO 1996; Second Secretary (Economic) Nicosia 1998; Full-Time Language Training 2000; Second Secretary FCO 2001; Band D6.

McCormick, Stephen; Second Secretary (Economic/Commercial) Ankara since June 2002; Born 05/09/67; FCO 1990; Bangkok 1993; Istanbul 1993; Tbilisi 1997; Tokyo 1997; Full-Time Language Training FCO 2001; Band C4; m 1996 Sevda Unalan (1d 1999).

McCosh, Andrew David; First Secretary (Political) Kathmandu since March 2003; Born 06/01/72; FCO 1994; Vice-Consul (Political) Istanbul 1997; FCO 1999; Kabul 2002; Band D6; m 2002 Malika Geraldine Browne.

McCoy, Peter Owen David; Deputy Head of Mission Lagos since January 2002; Born 28/04/52; FCO 1971; New Delhi 1974; Kaduna 1977; FCO 1981; Maseru 1984; AO/Vice-Consul/Comm Montreal 1987 (later Second Secretary); Second Secretary FCO 1990; Vice-Consul (Commercial) Los Angeles 1992; Assistant Trade Commissioner (China Trade) BTC Hong Kong 1993; First Secretary (Commercial) Bombay 1996; m 1975 Sally Ann Lord (2d 1976, 1978; 1s 1982).

McCreadie, Katrina; Beijing since July 2003; Born 10/05/73; FCO 2001; Band A2.

McCrory, Mark Frank; On loan to HM Treasury since November 2004; Born 28/01/74; FCO 2003; Band C4.

McCrory, Susan Margaret Therese; SUPL since January 2005; Born 17/12/64; Solicitor; legal Adviser MAFF 1992; Assistant Legal Adviser FCO 1996; Legal Adviser Geneva (UKMIS) 2001; m 1990 Ignacio de Castro (1s 1998).

McCrudden, Patrick Gerald, MBE (1993); First Secretary (Public Affairs) Washington since July 2005; Born 22/04/50; FCO 1969; Saigon 1971; Mexico City 1974; Bahrain 1976; FCO 1977; Tristan da Cunha 1980; Brussels 1981; Pretoria 1982; Second Secretary FCO 1985; Second Secretary (Chancery) Bridgetown 1988; First Secretary (Somalia/Humanitarian) and Deputy Permanent Representative UNEP/UNCHS Nairobi 1991; First Secretary FCO 1995; Director BIS and Deputy Consul General New York 1997; First Secretary (Press and Public Affairs) New Delhi 2000; First Secretary FCO 2003; Band D7; m 1973 (diss 1989) (1s 1974; 2d 1974, 1976).

McCurrie, Marianne Linzi Claire; FCO since November 2003; Born 19/03/79; Band B3.

McDonald, David Christopher; Washington since September 2003; Born 12/05/64; FCO 1984; Washington 1990; FCO 1993; Band C4.

McDonald, Simon Gerard, CMG (2004); HM Ambassador Tel Aviv since August 2003; Born 09/03/61; FCO 1982; Language Training SOAS 1983; Third later Second Secretary Jedda (later Riyadh) 1985; Second Secretary (Economic) Bonn 1988; First Secretary FCO 1990; Private Secretary to Permanent Under-Secretary 1993; First Secretary (Chancery) Washington 1995; Counsellor and Deputy Head of Mission and Consul-General Riyadh 1998; Private Secretary to the Secretary of State for Foreign and Commonwealth Affairs 2001; m 1989 The Hon. Olivia Mary Wright (2s 1990, 1994; 2d 1992, 1996).

McDuff, Nicholas Frederic; Second Secretary FCO since March 1995; Born 22/07/50; MOD (Navy) 1967; FCO 1970; Muscat 1972; Brussels (UKDEL NATO) 1972; BMG Berlin 1975; Karachi 1978; Islamabad 1980; FCO 1982; Athens 1983; Brussels (UKDEL NATO) 1984; Bandar Seri Begawan 1987; On loan to the DTI 1990; Second Secretary Casablanca 1992; m 1978 Jennifer Mary Cain (3s 1981, 1985, 1986).

McEvoy, Edward James; Consul Tokyo since July 2004; Born 06/02/46; CRO (later FO) 1962; Belgrade 1968; Mbabane 1970; FCO 1972; Aden 1975; Luxembourg 1977; Addis Ababa 1979; On loan to Home Office 1982; Second Secretary (Immigration) Dhaka 1985; Second Secretary (Commercial) Manila 1989; Vice-Consul (Commercial) Cape Town 1990; FCO 1995; First Secretary Manila 1997; First Secretary FCO 2001; m 1967 Patricia Gibbs (diss 1991) (1s 1972).

McEwen, Christine Elizabeth; HM Consul and First Secretary (Management) Buenos Aires since April 2001; Born 04/10/58; FCO 1978; BMG Berlin 1981; Peking 1984; Bombay 1987; FCO 1990; Rome 1994; Deputy Head of Mission Guatemala City 1997; FCO 2000; Band C5.

McFarlane, David Andrew; First Secretary (Political) Beijing since November 2003; Born 20/10/77; FCO 1999; T/D Beijing 2002; Band D6.

McFarlane, Jacqueline (née Stewart); SUPL since May 2005; Born 01/11/67; FCO 1986; Manila 1988; FCO 1992; Damascus 1994; Islamabad 1997; Mumbai 2001; Band B3; m 1988 Neil Ross McFarlane (1s 2001).

McFarlane, Neil Ross; Dubai since May 2005; Born 26/03/69; FCO 1991; Damascus 1994; Islamabad 1997; Mumbai 2001; Band C4; m 1988 Jacqueline Stewart (1s 2001).

McFarlin, Andrew John; Mumbai since February 2002; Born 30/08/70; FCO 1990; Vienna 1993; Floater Duties 1996; Georgetown 1998; Band B3; m 1999 Juanita Adrian.

McGee, Annie (née Brown); SUPL since October 2004; Born 14/10/68; HCS FCO 1987; FCO 1994; Tunis 1996; FCO 1999; Full-Time Language Training (Spanish) 2002; Vice-Consul Madrid 2003; Band C4; m 1996 W M V McGee (2s 1999; 2004).

McGill, Clive John; Manila since April 2005; Born 09/10/58; FCO 1978; Belmopan 1982; Stockholm 1985; FCO 1988; Karachi 1991; Baku 1995; Deputy Head of Mission Ashgabat 1999;

FCO 2003; Band C5; m (1) 1983 Thelma Garcia; (2) 1988 Angela Raw.

McGinley, Francis John; Jerusalem since November 2004; Born 12/01/49; FCO 1971; Brussels (NATO) 1974; Nairobi 1977; FCO 1980; Banjul 1982; Second Secretary (Information) Oslo 1984; Second Secretary FCO 1989; Second Secretary (Commercial) Zagreb 1992; First Secretary (Management/Consular/Immigration) Kiev 1995; Full-Time Language Training 2001; First Secretary (Management) Damascus 2001; m 1994 Neriman Kreso.

McGlone, Andrea Lynne (née Webb); New Delhi since June 2005; Born 27/03/66; FCO 1985; The Hague 1987; FCO 1990; Harare 1995; Riyadh 1999; Assistant Private Secretary to the Permanent Under Secretary, FCO 2002; Band C5; m 1993 Kevin McGlone (2d 1994, 1997).

McGrath, Dominic James; FCO since November 2003; Born 25/03/75; Band A2.

McGregor, Julie; FCO since February 2005; Born 23/06/80; FCO 1999; Jerusalem 2001; Islamabad 2004; Band B3.

McGregor, Peter; Singapore since January 2003; Born 30/05/50; FCO 1970; Jedda 1972; Lusaka 1976; FCO 1979; Damascus 1982; Port of Spain 1986; New Delhi 1989; Second Secretary FCO 1992; Second Secretary Peking 1994; HM Consul Tel Aviv 1998; m (1) 1972 Vanessa Avril Utteridge (dec'd 1989) (1s 1980); (2) 1991 Alexandra Davenport Gillies (1d 1991).

McGregor-Bell, Sharon Ann (née McGregor); SUPL since January 2005; Born 23/06/71; FCO 1990; Brussels 1993; FCO 1996; SUPL 1998; Tel Aviv 1999; FCO 2001; Band C4; m 1995 Kevan Watson Bell.

McGuinness, Cheryl Vinetta (née Lynch); New Delhi since August 2003; Born 04/11/66; FCO 1988; Peking 1991; Abidjan 1994; SUPL 1997; Band A2; m 1996 Mark John McGuinness.

McGuinness, Mark Andrew, MBE (2004); FCO since August 2003; Born 25/08/67; FCO 1988; Islamabad 1990; FCO 1992; Doha 1996; Abidjan 1999; Band B3; m 2001 Elizabeth Krauk (1d 2003).

McGuinness, Patrick Joseph, OBE (1997); Counsellor Rome since September 2003; Born 27/04/63; FCO 1985; Language Training 1986; Second Secretary (Chancery) Sana'a 1988; Second Secretary FCO 1991; First Secretary (Political) Abu Dhabi 1994; First Secretary Cairo 1996; First Secretary FCO 1999; m 1994 Susannah Imogen Mills (1d 2001; twins, 1s, 1d 2005).

McGurgan, Kevin; First Secretary (Political) Stockholm since October 2003; Born 31/05/71; FCO 1990; Floater Duties 1992; Brussels (UKREP) 1994; Sarajevo 1996; Third later Second Secretary (Chancery) New York (UKMIS) 1997; FCO 2000; Band D7; m 1997 Victoria Ann Harrison.

McGurgan, Victoria Ann (née Harrison); SUPL since August 2003; Born 13/08/71; FCO 1994; New York (UKMIS) 1997; FCO 2000; SUPL 2002; FCO 2002; Band A2; m 1997 Kevin McGurgan (1s 2002).

McGurk, Gerard, MBE (2000); Second Secretary (Chancery) New York (UKMIS) since August 2000; Born 22/12/70; FCO 1988; Athens 1991; Floater Duties 1994; Deputy Head of Mission and Vice-Consul Skopje 1996; Band C4; m 1998 Sonja Kurcieva (2d 2002, 2004).

McHallam, Andrew James; First Secretary Paris (UKDEL OECD) since July 2004; Born 03/04/57; Association of Chief Police Officers 1999; FCO 2001; Band D6.

McHugh, Esther Phoebe; Second Secretary (Political) Moscow since December 2002; Born 08/09/75; FCO 2000; Band C4.

McHugh, Susan Mary; Second later First Secretary FCO since November 1994; Born 12/02/44; FCO 1971; On loan to SEATO Bangkok 1974; New Delhi 1977; SUPL 1980; Victoria (Seychelles) 1981; Second Secretary FCO 1983; Second Secretary Nicosia 1994; Band C5.

McIlroy, David Thomas; Deputy Head of Mission Belgrade since February 2004; Born 03/03/68; FCO 2000; Band D7; m 2000 Victoria Stone (1d 2004; 1s 2005).

McIntosh, Margaret Claire; FCO since August 2001; Born 31/05/63; FCO 1995; Brussels (UKREP) 1997; World Wide Floater Duties 1999; Band C4.

McIntosh, Martin Howard, OBE (1994); Counsellor (Commercial) later Director of Trade and Investment Dublin since April 2001; Born 26/12/47; FO (later FCO) 1966; Jakarta 1970; Tokyo 1970; Moscow 1972; Beirut 1973; FCO 1976; Madrid 1979; Second Secretary Bogotá 1982; Second later First Secretary (Commercial) Nairobi 1984; First Secretary FCO 1989; First Secretary (Commercial) Buenos Aires 1990; First Secretary (Commercial) Mexico City 1994; On loan to the DTI 1997; m 1970 Erika Wagner (2d 1983, 1985).

McIver, Damian John; Paris since December 2004; Born 02/11/61; HM Customs and Excise 1986; FCO 1986; Third Secretary (Political) Belgrade 1987; Second Secretary FCO 1991; Political Adviser ECMIS Zagreb 1992; FCO 1993; Second Secretary (KHF) Bucharest 1995; First Secretary (Political) Belgrade 1998; First Secretary FCO 1999; Band D6; m 1998 Raluca Vasiliu.

McKee, Tracey Anne; World Wide Floater Duties since March 2004; Born 03/06/77; FCO 2000; Kigali 2000; Band B3.

McKell, Paul Leo; Brussels (UKREP) since September 2001; Born 01/09/66; Assistant Legal Adviser FCO 1997; m 2001 Elizabeth C Hanlon.

McKelvey, Diane Elizabeth; FCO since July 2001; Born 06/07/67; FCO 1989; Third Secretary (Political) Copenhagen 1992; FCO 1994; Second Secretary (Political/Press and Public Affairs) Lusaka 1998.

McKen, Dawn; First Secretary FCO since January 2000; Born 23/07/66; FCO 1995; Second Secretary (Political) Moscow 1996; m Matthew Edward Sparrowhawk (1d 2003).

McKendrick, Ian; Full-Time Language Training Beijing since January 2004; Born 04/10/70; FCO 1991; BTC Hong Kong 1995; Floater Duties 1998; FCO 2000; Full-Time Language Training (Mandarin) 2003; Band C4.

McKenzie, Hilary (née Grace); Second Secretary (Commercial) Johannesburg since August 1999; Born 01/03/59; FCO 1980; Islamabad 1982; Oslo 1984; Bombay 1987; Amsterdam 1989; FCO 1992; Vice-Consul Helsinki 1996; Band C4; m 1989 Ian James McKenzie (1d 1999).

McKenzie, Philip; Third Secretary (Political/Economic) Bangkok since September 2001; Born 26/04/65; FCO 1986; Lusaka 1987; San José 1991; FCO 1993; BTC Hong Kong 1996; Band B3.

McKenzie Smith, Justin James; First Secretary New York since February 2004; Born 04/02/69; FCO 1994; Full-Time Language Training 1995; Second Secretary (Political) Moscow 1996; First Secretary FCO 1999.

McKeogh, Fiona (née Sutherland), MBE (1993); Paris since February 2003; Born 17/09/59; FCO 1983; Bonn 1984; Cape Town 1987; Brussels (UKREP) 1989; FCO 1993; SUPL 1993; FCO 1995; Moscow 1997; New York (UKMIS) 1999; Band B3; m 1992 Paul Nicolas McKeogh.

McKerron, Alan; New Delhi since August 2004; Born 20/03/65; Scottish Office 1981-99; FCO 1999; Islamabad 2003; Band C5; m 2002 Susan Road-Night.

McKerron, Susan Catherine (née Road-Night); SUPL since July 2004; Born 13/03/67; FCO 1991; Kiev 1992; Full-Time Language Training 1995; Mexico City 1995; FCO 1999; Islamabad 2003; Band B3; m 2002 Alan McKerron.

McKerrow, Elizabeth Mary (née Foot); SUPL since February 2001; Born 18/01/67; FCO 1986; Buenos Aires 1990; FCO 1991; Band B3; m 1991 Ian Bernard Harry McKerrow (1s 1998; 1d 2000).

McKie, Margaret Stevenson; Brussels (UKREP) since May 2001; Born 07/08/62; FCO 1988; Prague 1991; Cairo 1993; FCO 1996; Floater Duties 1998; Full-Time Language Training 2001; Band A2.

McKinlay, Ian Leonard; Second Secretary (Management) Geneva since August 2002; Born 17/09/58; FCO 1978; Geneva (UKMIS) 1980; Tehran 1983; FCO 1986; Addis Ababa 1989; Dakar 1992; FCO 1997; m 1984 Ann Hugoline Cameron (1s 1989; 2d 1991, 1993).

McLachlan, Malcolm Orde; Deputy Head of Mission Hanoi since September 2001; Born 10/09/63; FCO 1981; Karachi 1984; Guatemala City 1988; FCO 1993; Second later First Secretary (Political) Nairobi 1998; m 1989 Maricruz Mendia Moynes (1d 1995).

McLaren, Marilynn, MBE (1993); SUPL since January 1998; Born 20/07/47; Scottish Office 1963; FCO 1981; Dacca 1981; Tehran 1985; Lisbon 1987; FCO 1989; Tehran 1990; Washington 1994; Band B3.

McLaren-Oliver, Geoffrey Harold; Tehran since November 2003; Born 11/06/48; HM Forces 1965-88; Moscow 1989; Madrid 1991; World Wide Floater Duties 1993; Moscow 1998; Khartoum 2000; Band B3.

McLean, Sean Nicholas, MBE (2005); Vice-Consul Riyadh since August 2002; Born 07/10/70; FCO 2000; Band B3; m 1999 Parimala Chandramohanadas (1s 2004).

McLean, Siân Alexis; FCO since November 2003; Born 12/09/69; FCO 1993; Full-Time Language Training Peking 1996; Consul (Economic) Hong Kong 1997; First Secretary (Economic) Peking 2001; Band D6.

McLuskie, Karen-Louise; Basra since October 2004; Born 21/06/78; FCO 2003; Band C4.

McMahon, Brian Patrick; FCO since December 2002; Born 26/03/46; CRO and DSAO 1963; Prague 1968; Bonn 1969; Kabul 1972; FCO 1975; Islamabad 1978; Geneva (UKMIS) 1981; Second Secretary FCO 1984; Second Secretary (Immigration/Consular) Colombo 1990; HM Consul Rome 1994; FCO 1999; British Trade International 1999; m 1967 Eileen Conroy (1d 1970; 1s 1975).

McMahon, Dr David John Hugh; SUPL since August 2004; Born 04/05/65; FCO 1991; Second Secretary (Political/Information) Dhaka 1993; FCO 1997; First Secretary (Environment and Trade Policy) New Delhi 2001; Band D6; m 1994 Kay Taylor Lacey.

McMahon, Keith David, MBE (1998); First Secretary (Management) Athens since April 2003; Born 10/03/68; FCO 1988; Lusaka 1990; SE Asia/Middle East Floater Duties 1993; Deputy Head of Mission Yerevan 1995; FCO 1998; Band C5; m 2000 Melissa Schwartz.

McManus, John Andrew; HM Ambassador Conakry since December 2004; Born 20/05/55; FCO 1977; Paris 1980; Algiers 1983; FCO 1985; Language Training FCO 1987 (Second Secretary 1987); Second Secretary Moscow 1988; Second Secretary Brussels (UKREP) 1992; Second later First Secretary (Information) Berne 1993; FCO 1997; First Secretary (Political) Brussels 2001; Band D6.

McMinn, Wendy Lily Alexandra; SUPL since March 2005; Born 07/07/71; MOD 1991; FCO 1999; Canberra 2001; Kingston 2003; Band B3.

McMurrie, Jane Patricia (née Hannah); FCO since June 1997; Born 23/09/70; FCO 1989; Athens 1991; Floater Duties 1995; Band B3.

McNair, Richard Andrew; First Secretary Pretoria since June 2003; Born 18/02/59; FCO 1979; Lagos 1980; FCO 1982; Ankara 1984; FCO 1987; Cairo 1991; FCO 1995; Band C5; m 1978 Julie Elaine Stephen (1d 1981; 1s 1983).

McNaught, David Douglas; Second Secretary (Political) Pretoria since March 2005; Born 10/02/72; FCO 1994; World Wide Floater Duties 1999; FCO 2000; Amman 2004; Baghdad/Kirkuk 2004; Band C4.

McNeill, Alasdair Morrell; FCO since February 1999; Born 13/11/67; FCO 1988; Istanbul 1992; FCO 1995; Moscow 1997; Band B3; m 1994 Elizabeth Hall (1s 2000; 1d 2003).

McNeill, Christine Mary; First Secretary (Commercial) Sofia since December 2002; Born 12/03/62; FCO 1979; Cairo 1983; Suva 1987; Second Secretary FCO 1991; Madras 1995; Deputy High Commissioner Mbabane 1999; m 1982 Scott Robertson McNeill (1d 1994; 1s 1998).

McPhail, Dr Alastair David, OBE (2005); Deputy Head of Mission & Minister Rome since January 2006; Born 02/03/61; FCO 1994; Language Training 1995; second later First Secretary (Political/Military) Ankara 1996; FCO 2000; m 1989 Pamela Joanne Davies (2s 1992, 1994).

McPhail, Pamela Joanne (née Davies); First Secretary FCO since August 2000; Born 03/12/62; FCO 1990; Third Secretary (Press and Public Affairs) Moscow 1992; FCO 1995; SUPL 1996; Band C5; m 1989 Alastair David McPhail (2s 1992, 1994).

McQuibban, Peter James, OBE (2003); Counsellor Paris since July 2004; Born 07/11/55; Third later Second Secretary FCO 1981; Second Secretary (Economic) Brasilia 1982; First Secretary FCO 1985; First Secretary (Political) Warsaw 1988; First Secretary on loan to the Cabinet Office 1992; Counsellor FCO 1995; Counsellor on sabbatical at Copenhagen University 1996; SUPL at the Danish School of Public Administration 1997; Counsellor FCO 2002; Counsellor on loan to the Cabinet Office (Civil Contingencies Secretariat) 2002; m (1) 1982 Susan Jennifer Magdalen Hitch (diss 1996); (2) 1996 Annegrethe Felter Rasmussen (1d 1996; 3s 1998, 2002, 2005).

McQuilton, Patricia Bernadette (née Edwards); Athens since March 2002; Born 15/03/69; Home Civil Service 1988; FCO 1996; Nicosia 1998; Band B3; m 1999 Craig McQuilton.

McVey-Dobson, Andrea; SUPL since August 1997; Born 28/01/64; FCO 1988; Paris 1991; Luxembourg 1993; FCO 1996; Band A2.

Meacock-Bashir, Danaë Miranda; FCO since September 2002; Born 22/07/74; Band C4.

Means, Claire Stewart (née Hunter); SUPL since April 2005; Born 02/03/69; FCO 1990; Kuala Lumpur 1993; SUPL 1994; T/D Suva 1997; New York (UKMIS) 1997; Tortola 2001; Band A2; m 1994 Thomas E Means.

Mearns, Stuart; FCO since June 2003; Born 21/11/58; FCO 1982; Khartoum 1985; FCO 1989; Paris 1995; FCO 1998; Addis Ababa 2000; Band C4; m 1983 Andrea Chapman (2s 1993, 1996).

Mease, Rachel Elizabeth (née Tunn); Tunis since October 2003; Born 28/05/68; FCO 1989; Bucharest 1991; Hanoi 1993; New York (UKMIS) 1995; T/D Croatia 1996; FCO 1997; Dublin 1999; Band B3; m 1994 Paul Mease.

Meath Baker, William John Clovis, OBE (2002); Counsellor FCO since October 2002; Born 11/05/59; FCO 1985; Second later First Secretary (Chancery and Information) and Consul Kabul 1988; FCO 1989; First Secretary and Consul Prague 1989; First Secretary FCO 1993; Consul (Political) Istanbul 1997; First Secretary FCO 2000; Counsellor Kabul 2002; m 1985 Elizabeth Diana Woodham-Smith (4d 1988, 1990, 1992, 1995).

Meconi, Anne-Marie; Brussels (UKREP) since February 2003; Born 14/01/61; Transferred from the Scottish Office 1997; FCO 1997; Hanoi 1999; Band A2.

Mee, Jeffery Bryan; Second Secretary (Consular) Los Angeles since July 2003; Born 08/07/56; Passport Office 1975; FCO 1976; Kathmandu 1978; FCO 1980; Khartoum 1982; Peking 1985; Vancouver 1987; FCO 1987; Vice-Consul Vienna 1991; Lisbon 1994; Second Secretary FCO 1997; (1s 1990; 1d 1993).

Meehan, Sean Patrick; Lisbon since November 2003; Born 15/07/73; FCO 1995; Sarajevo 1998; SUPL (Sarajevo) 1999; Budapest 2000; Band A2; m 2000 Mirela Krajnc (1s 2003).

Mehmet, Alper, MVO (1990); Ambassador and Consul-General Reykjavik since April 2004; Born 28/08/48; Immigration Service 1970; Lagos 1979; FCO 1983; Second Secretary 1986; Bucharest 1986; Second Secretary (Head of Chancery) Reykjavik 1989; FCO 1993; First Secretary (Information) Bonn 1999; m 1968 Elaine Susan Tarrant (2d 1969, 1971).

Mehta, Nikesh A; Second Secretary (Regional-Multilateral) Kampala since May 2004; Born 07/04/77; FCO 2002; Band C4.

Meiklejohn, Dominic Francis; FCO since April 2003; Born 14/11/67; HM Customs and Excise 1989 - 90; FCO 1990; Full-Time Language Training 1993; Second later First Secretary (EU/Public Affairs) Warsaw 1993; Band D7; m 1997 Anna Iwona Reichel.

Melbourne, Sean; Baku since September 2002; Born 09/12/68; FCO 1988; Maputo 1990; Tashkent 1994; FCO 1998; Band C4; m 1997 Elmira Vakkasova.

Melling, Scott Richard; Third Secretary (Commercial) Düsseldorf since April 2004; Born 10/05/72; FCO 1990; Madrid 1994; FCO 1997; World Wide Floater Duties 1998; FCO 1999; Third Secretary (Management) Warsaw 2000; Band B3; (1d 2002).

Mellor, John; Lagos since October 2003; Born 09/02/52; Department of National Savings 1968; FCO 1971; Belgrade 1973; Middle East Floater 1975; Dar es Salaam 1977; FCO 1979; Strasbourg 1980; FCO 1982; Washington 1987; Ankara 1990; FCO 1993; Jakarta 1997; Sana'a 2002; Band C4; m 1987 Mary Bridget Ann McGettigan.

Meredith, Richard Evan; Counsellor FCO since July 1998; Born 31/01/61; FCO 1983; Third Secretary Bridgetown 1985; Second Secretary Managua 1987; Second later First Secretary FCO 1989; First Secretary later Counsellor Bonn 1995; Band D6; m (1) 1986 Louisa Jane Oriel (dec'd 2000) (2d 1992, 1995); (2) Penelope Jane Lee (1s 1992; 1d 1994).

Merritt, Christopher; FCO since October 2003; Born 25/02/81; Band C4.

Merry, David Byron, CMG (2000); High Commissioner Gaborone since August 2001; Born 16/09/45; Ministry of Aviation 1961; CRO (later Commonwealth Office, later FCO) 1965; Bangkok 1969; Second Secretary (Information) Budapest 1974; Second later First Secretary FCO 1977; First Secretary (Civil Air Attaché) Bonn 1981; Head of Chancery East Berlin 1985; First Secretary FCO 1989; Deputy Head of Mission Manila 1993; Deputy High Commissioner Karachi 1997; FCO 2000; m 1967 Patricia Ann Ellis (2d 1969, 1972; 1s 1971).

Mesarowicz, Anthony David; Algiers since June 2003; Born 28/07/70; FCO 1991; Paris 1995; Guatemala City 1999; Band B3.

Metcalfe, Julian Ross; Geneva since January 2005; Born 24/02/56; Economic Adviser FCO 1983; First Secretary Cairo 1987; First Secretary FCO 1991; Full-Time Language Training 1994; Deputy Head of Mission Zagreb 1995; First Secretary FCO 1997; Head of Estate Strategy Unit, FCO 2000; m 1985 Rachel Mai Jones (1d 1997).

Metreweli, Blaise Florence; FCO since March 2003; Born 30/07/77; FCO 1999; Second Secretary (Economic) Dubai 2000; Band C4.

Miah, Faruk; Third Secretary (Management) Port Louis since February 2002; Born 18/12/70; FCO 1990; Singapore 1994; Dar es Salaam 1997; FCO 1998; Band B3; m 1993 Nilufa Yasmin (3d 1996, 2001, 2004).

Micallef, Janice Pauline (née Roughley); Caracas since May 2000; Born 15/01/66; FCO 1993; New Delhi 1996; SUPL 1999; Band A2; m 1996 Mark Antoine Micallef (2d 1999, 2002).

Michael, Alan Rhys; FCO since July 2002; Born 02/01/48; FCO 1971; MECAS 1973; Jedda 1975; Jedda/Riyadh 1976; FCO 1978; Second Secretary Geneva (UKMIS) 1982; First Secretary (Commercial) Kuwait 1986; First Secretary FCO 1988; Brussels (UKREP) 1994; Consul-General Casablanca 1999; m 1973 Anita Ruth Ford (1s 1973; 1d 1977).

Middel, Julie; SUPL since May 2003; Born 26/04/58; DHSS 1976; FCO 1979; Copenhagen 1982; Floater Duties 1985; Sofia 1986; Brussels 1987; FCO 1990; SUPL 1990; Karachi 1994; FCO 1994; On loan to the DTI 1996; FCO 1999; Band B3; m 1988 Wolfgang Middel.

Middlemiss, Matthew, MBE (1991); First Secretary FCO since January 2004; Born 11/01/62; First Secretary FCO 1998; First Secretary (Humanitarian) Geneva (UKMIS) 2001; Band D6; m 2001 Phyllida Alison Cheyne (1d 2000).

Middleton, David Farquharson; Counsellor FCO since August 2001; Born 21/11/53; FCO 1982; Language Training Kamakura 1984; First Secretary Tokyo 1985; First Secretary FCO 1988; First Secretary Lusaka 1991; First Secretary FCO 1994; Counsellor Amman 1998; m 1984 Georgina Mary Housman (1s 1987; 2d 1989, 1992).

Middleton, William Alexander; Washington since January 2005; Born 03/01/78; FCO 2002; Band C4.

Miles, Joanne Denise, MBE (1993); SUPL since January 2003; Born 10/06/57; FCO 1980; Prague 1982; FCO 1984; Bandar Seri Begawan 1986; Guatemala City 1988; San José 1991; FCO 1992; Caracas 1994; FCO 1997; Second Secretary (Political) Nairobi 1999; Band C4.

Miles, John; First Secretary Washington since October 2000; Born 30/10/46; Nepal 1972; Germany 1974; Home Civil Service 1978; Hong Kong 1980; New Delhi 1984; FCO 1988; Moscow 1995; Band D6; m 1968 Lynda Patricia Frances McNair (1d 1972; 1s 1974).

Millar, Andrew James; First Secretary (Economic/Political) Pretoria since September 2000; Born 13/07/65; Office of Gas Supply 1994; FCO E/Advs 1996; FCO 1999; Band D6; m 1996 Catherine Jo Russell Davis.

Millar, Lindsey; SUPL since December 2000; Born 18/06/67; Scottish Office 1984 - 90; FCO 1991; Berlin 1993; The Hague 1997; Band A2.

Miller, Andrew John; FCO since December 2003; Born 29/05/66; FCO 1985; Munich 1991; FCO 1995; Abu Dhabi 1998; Second Secretary Muscat 2002; Band C4; m 1991 Coral Annabel (1d 1997; 1s 1999).

Miller, David; FCO since July 2004; Born 19/05/66; Second Secretary FCO 1997; First Secretary (Chancery) Bogotá 2000; Band D6; m 1993 Carmen Delgado.

Miller, David Roland; First Secretary FCO since February 2003; Born 01/11/52; FCO 1972; Bucharest 1975; Tripoli 1976; Rome 1979; FCO 1982; Kuala Lumpur 1985; Second Secretary FCO

1989; Deputy High Commissioner Vila 1990; Second later First Secretary FCO 1994; Resident Acting High Commissioner Grenada 1998; Band D6; m 1976 Gillian Mary Cornthwaite (2s 1980, 1983).

Miller, Helen; FCO since November 2004; Born 15/07/82; Band C4; ptnr, Sean Coyne.

Miller, Jamie Jonathan, MBE (1999); FCO since March 2002; Born 01/05/72; FCO 1996; Second Secretary (Chancery) Islamabad 1998; First Secretary (Political) Freetown 2000; Band D6.

Miller, Julian Peter; HM Consul Nagoya since October 2002; FCO 1987; Language Training 1989; Language Training Kamakura 1989; Tokyo 1990; San José 1994; FCO 1998; m 1993 Yasuko Yanai (2s 1995, 1998).

Miller, Julie; Second Secretary (Consul) Madrid since September 2004; Born 21/11/70; FCO 1988; Jakarta 1991; FCO 1994; Buenos Aires 1995; FCO 1998; Band C4.

Miller, Nicholas Michael; Bogotá since June 2005; Born 10/10/62; FCO 1982; Bangkok 1984; Peking 1987; FCO 1990; Tehran 1993; Full-Time Language Training 1996; Hamburg 1997; FCO 2001; m 1995 Raquel Evangelina Varela (2d 1994, 1999).

Miller, Pablo; FCO since August 2002; Born 27/02/60; FCO 1990; First Secretary (Political) Abuja later Lagos 1992; First Secretary FCO 1995; First Secretary Tallinn 1997; Band D6; m 1989 Elke Schmidt (3d 1991, 1994, 1996).

Miller, Penelope Helen; First Secretary (Political) Ankara since October 2004; Born 18/03/70; FCO 1995; Language Training Kamakura 1997; Second Secretary (Commercial) Tokyo 1998; FCO 2001; Band D6.

Miller, Shirley; Vienna since June 2002; Born 06/12/56; FCO 1976; Reykjavik 1981; Geneva (UKDIS) 1984; Port Stanley 1987; FCO 1988; Brussels (UKREP) 1992; Helsinki 1995; FCO 1998; Band A2; m 1997 Martin Corcoran.

Millett, Peter Joseph; High Commissioner Nicosia since June 2005; Born 23/01/55; FCO 1974; LA Floater 1976; Caracas 1978; Doha 1981; Second Secretary FCO 1985; First Secretary (Energy) Brussels (UKREP) 1989; Counsellor FCO 1993; Deputy Head of Mission Athens 1997; FCO 2001; Head of Security Strategy Unit, FCO 2002; m 1981 June Harnett (3d 1984, 1987, 1991).

Millington, Claire; Third Secretary (Political) Rome since January 2003; FCO 1999; Band B3.

Mills, Anwen Eluned (née Rees); SUPL since April 1999; Born 22/07/64; FCO 1991; T/D New York (UKMIS) 1992; Resigned 1993; Reinstated 1994; Cape Town 1995; Band A2; m 1993 (William) Gary Mills (1s 1997).

Mills, Beverley; FCO since March 2003; Born 09/05/69; FCO 1990; Brussels 1995; FCO 1997; Washington 1999; Band A2.

Mills, David Paul; Pristina since February 2004; Born 02/10/67; FCO 1987; Cairo 1989; FCO 1992; Addis Ababa 1993; HO 1999; Dar es Salaam 2000; Band B3.

Mills, Emma, MBE (2001); SUPL since September 2003; Born 27/02/69; FCO 1988; Baghdad 1990; Peking 1991; Bogotá 1994; FCO 1997; Pristina 1999; Second Secretary (Political/Information) Athens 2001; FCO 2002; Band C4.

Milne, Carole Lesley; SUPL since August 2001; Born 01/10/66; FCO HCS 1989; FCO 1994; Executive Assistant Lusaka 1996; Staff Officer Montserrat 1998; FCO 1999; Band B3.

Milne, Hilary Taylor; SUPL since August 2001; Born 07/06/65; FCO 1984; Rome 1985; Freetown 1988; FCO 1990; FCO 1991; Windhoek 1994; Moscow 1998; Band B3; m 2001 John Burton.

Milton, Kirstie Jane (née Levitt); FCO since July 1997; Born 04/07/69; FCO 1988; Cairo 1991; FCO 1992; The Hague 1995; Band A2; m 2000 Jonathan Milton.

Minshall, Heidi Jane; First Secretary FCO since May 1997; Born 02/03/67; FCO 1990; Full-Time Language Training Cairo 1993; Second Secretary (Political/Information) Abu Dhabi 1995.

Minshull, Simon Peter; Deputy Head of Mission Reykjavik since April 2003; Born 21/11/68; DHSS 1987; FCO 1988; Moscow 1990; Islamabad 1992; FCO 1996; Vice-Consul Bridgetown 1999; Band C4; m 1992 Hrefna Dis Luthersdottir (2d 1991, 1994; 1s 2002).

Minter, Graham Leslie, LVO (1983); Deputy Head of Economic Policy Department, FCO since June 2002; Born 04/01/50; FCO 1968; Anguilla 1971; Latin America Floater 1973; Asunción 1975; FCO 1978; First Secretary (Economic/Political) Mexico City 1979; First Secretary FCO 1984; First Secretary (Economic/Trade Policy) Canberra 1990; First Secretary later Counsellor FCO 1994; HM Ambassador La Paz 1998; m 1975 P Anne Scott (1s 1978).

Mir, Wasim Ullah; First Secretary Brussels (UKREP) since April 2005; Born 11/08/71; Department of Education 1994; European Commission 1997; Second Secretary (EU/Economic) Brussels 1998; First Secretary (Political) Brussels (UKREP) 2000; First Secretary FCO 2001.

Mistry, Hemlata; FCO since September 2001; Born 07/06/62; FCO Home Civil Service 1988; FCO 1990; Floater Duties 1992; FCO 1994; Mumbai 1998; Band B3.

Mitchell, Andrew Jonathan; Counsellor FCO since September 2002; Born 07/03/67; FCO 1991; Second Secretary (Political) Bonn 1993; First Secretary FCO 1996; Deputy Head of Mission Kathmandu 1999; m 1996 Helen Sarah Anne Magee (2s 1998, 2000; 1d 2001).

Mitchell, Carole, RVM (1990); Budapest since December 2002; Born 07/06/57; Scottish Office 1975; FCO 1987; Reykjavik 1988; The Hague 1991; Geneva (UKDIS) 1994; FCO 1999; Sarajevo 2000; Band A2.

Mitchell, Helen Sarah Anne (née Magee); SUPL (c/o Kathmandu) since May 1999; Born 18/10/67; FCO 1990; Second Secretary (EU) Bonn 1993; First Secretary FCO 1997; m 1996 Andrew Jonathan Mitchell (2s 1998, 2000).

Mitchell, John Steven; Second Secretary (Management) Beijing since April 2003; Born 28/11/67; FCO 1985; Tokyo 1988; Stockholm 1990; T/D Riga 1991; FCO 1992; Dhaka 1995; Riyadh 1999.

Mitchell, Jonathan Kenneth Milton; First Secretary Bucharest since June 1998; Born 18/12/59; Second Secretary FCO 1987; Second later First Secretary (Information) Amman 1989; First Secretary FCO 1990; First Secretary (Chancery) Harare 1991; First Secretary FCO 1994; Band D6; m 1986 Joyce Ann Henderson (2d 1990, 1993).

Mitchell, Marcia Julia; Santiago since October 2004; Born 22/11/77; FCO 1999; Brussels (UKREP) 2000; Full-Time Language Training 2004; Band A2.

Mitchell, Michael James, MVO (1989); First Secretary (Management) Colombo since October 2002; Born 07/08/54; HM Customs & Excise 1980; FCO 1985; Third Secretary (Aid) Kampala 1986; Third Secretary (Chancery) Singapore 1989; Full-Time Language Training 1993; Deputy Head of Mission Guatemala City 1993; Second Secretary FCO 1997; First Secretary (Management) Karachi 1999; Band C5; m 1982 Dominique Steggle (1d 1994).

Mitchell, Sheilah Dawn (née Bramley); Second Secretary (Management) Abidjan since October 2003; Born 15/04/59; FCO 1979; Brussels (UKDEL NATO) 1980; Maputo 1982; Floater Duties 1987; FCO 1990; Third Secretary (Management)/Vice-Consul Jerusalem 1994; SUPL 1998; Seconded to Bacon & Woodrow, Cardiff 2000; Islamabad 2002; Band C4; m 1994 Alan Stuart Mitchell.

Mitchell, Simon Andrew; Islamabad since July 2004; Born 27/11/64; PSA DoE 1987; The Court Service 1995; FCO 1999; Dhaka 2001; Band A2.

Mitchiner, Dr John Edward; High Commissioner Freetown since August 2003 and HM Ambassador non-resident to Liberia since December 2003; Born 12/09/51; FCO 1980; Language Training 1981; Third later Second Secretary Istanbul 1982; Second Secretary FCO 1985; Second Secretary (Development) New Delhi 1987; Second later First Secretary (Political) Berne 1991; First Secretary FCO 1995; HM Ambassador Yerevan 1997; Deputy High Commissioner Calcutta 2000; m 1983 Elizabeth Mary Ford.

Mitchison, Pamela Denise; Deputy Head of Mission Strasbourg since September 2003; Born 28/12/58; FCO 1978; Far East Floater 1981; Moscow 1982; Paris 1985; Second Secretary FCO 1988; APS Minister of State 1989; First Secretary (Chancery) Washington 1991; First Secretary FCO 1995; SUPL 1996; First Secretary FCO 1997; SUPL 1997; m 1996 Ian Richard Whitehead (1d 1996).

Mititelu, Alexandra Marie; FCO since April 2004; Born 15/09/76; FCO 1999; Full-Time Language Training 2001; Second Secretary (Political) New Delhi 2002; Band C4.

Mochan, Charles Francis; High Commissioner Suva since November 2002; Born 06/08/48; MOD (Navy) 1966; FCO 1967; Port Elizabeth 1970; Kingston 1972; FCO 1974; Second Secretary 1975; Seoul 1977; FCO 1980; Second later First Secretary (Commercial) Helsinki 1981; First Secretary FCO 1984; Deputy High Commissioner and Head of Chancery Port Louis 1988; First Secretary FCO 1991; Consul-General Casablanca 1995; HM Ambassador Antananarivo 1999; m 1970 Ilse Sybilla Carleon Cruttwell (1d 1971; 1s 1974).

Mohipp, Sarah Nadia; Bangkok since August 2005; Born 24/03/78; FCO 1999; Baghdad 2004; Band A2; ptnr, Shannon Michael Wade.

Monck, Anthony; FCO since October 2003; Born 14/04/79; Band C4.

Monckton, The Honourable Anthony Leopold Colyer; FCO since September 2004; Born 25/09/60; HM Forces 1979-87; Second Secretary FCO 1987; Second later First Secretary Geneva (UKDEL) 1990; First Secretary FCO 1992; First Secretary (Political) Zagreb 1996; British Embassy Banja Luka Office 1998; First Secretary FCO 1999; Counsellor Belgrade 2001; Band D6; m 1985 Philippa Susan Wingfield (1s 1988; 1d 1989).

Monk, Rachel; British Trade International since April 2002; Born 12/09/69; FCO 1994; Chennai 2000; Band B3.

Montagnon, Giles; Full-Time Language Training Beijing since January 2004; Born 08/12/77; FCO 2001; Full-Time Language Training (Mandarin) 2003; Band C4.

Moody, Patrick Thomas Robert; FCO since December 2002; Born 17/03/66; FCO 1988; Third later Second Secretary (Political/Information) Mexico City 1990; First Secretary FCO 1994; First Secretary (Political) Brussels (UKDEL NATO) 1998; m 1996 Atalanta Sturdy (1s 1998; 1d 2000).

Moon, Dorian Lawrence; FCO since March 1993; Born 02/01/59; HCS 1985; BEMRS Cyprus 1986; HCS 1989; FCO 1990; Moscow 1992; Band C4; m 1989 Joanne Ashley (1d 1989; 1s 1991).

Moon, Michael Yelland; Consul (Inward Investment) Toronto since July 2003; Born 19/08/59; FCO 1977; Brussels (UKREP) 1979; Khartoum 1982; Africa/Middle East Floater 1986;

FCO 1990; Third Secretary (Aid/Information) Mbabane 1993; Consul Brussels 1995; Second Secretary Bandar Seri Begawan 1996; British Trade International 1999; On loan to the DTI 2001; Band C5; m 1997 Christine Jo-Anne Florendo.

Moon, Nancy Patricia (née Handyside); SUPL since March 2003; Born 27/08/51; Islamabad 1984; Kampala 1988; Khartoum 1991; Sana'a 1995; Bucharest 1998; Brussels (UKREP) 1999; Band A2.

Moon, Dr Richard John; New York (UKMIS) since March 1999; Born 03/01/59; FCO 1983; Second Secretary Jakarta 1985; First Secretary FCO 1988; First Secretary (Political) Rome 1993; FCO 1997; m 1987 Sandra Sheila Francis Eddis (1s 1990; 1d 1993).

Moon, Sandra Sheila Francis (née Eddis), MVO (1984); SUPL since January 1994; Born 11/03/56; FCO 1980; Washington 1982; Jakarta 1984; FCO 1988; Band C4; m 1987 Richard John Moon (1s 1990; 1d 1993).

Mooney, Laura; FCO since June 2003; Born 30/04/73; MOD 1989 - 96; FCO 1996; Wellington 1997; World Wide Floater Duties 2001; Band B3.

Moore, Charles Jonathan Rupert; SUPL since May 2005; Born 14/04/63; FCO 1982; Harare 1984; Masirah 1987; Gaborone 1987; FCO 1991; Third Secretary (Commercial) Jakarta 1995; Second Secretary (UN/UNIDO) Geneva (UKMIS) 1998; FCO 2002; Band C5; m 1988 Deborah Mary Ford (1s 1989; 1d 1992).

Moore, Cristina Silvia Gibson; FCO since October 2004; Born 10/04/80; Band C4.

Moore, David; First Secretary (Commercial) Kiev since April 2002; Born 18/06/59; HO 1977; FCO 1978; Moscow 1980; Wellington 1982; FCO 1986; Vice-Consul Osaka 1990; FCO 1992; Second Secretary 1994; Full-Time Language Training 1996; Second Secretary (Commercial) Madrid 1996; Full-Time Language Training 2001; m (1) 1981 Annette May Gardner (diss) (1d 1982; 1s 1985); (2) 1996 Janice Ann Bell.

Moore, Deborah Mary (née Ford); Accra since April 2005; Born 15/04/63; FCO 1982; Muscat 1985; SUPL 1988; FCO 1991; SUPL 1993; Jakarta 1995; SUPL 1998; Band B3; m 1988 Charles Jonathan Rupert Moore (1s 1989; 1d 1992).

Moore, Janice Ann (née Bell); Kiev since March 2002; Born 06/10/64; FCO 1984; Accountant Nairobi 1986; Vice-Consul Budapest 1989; Resigned 1991; Reinstated, FCO 1992; Second Secretary 1994; Second Secretary Madrid 1996; Band C5; m 1996 David Moore.

Moore, Jason Richard Alexander; Second Secretary (Press and Public Affairs/Programmes) Budapest since September 2000; Born 06/04/73; FCO 1998; Full-Time Language Training 1999; m 2000 Rebecca Marie Letts.

Moore, Richard Peter; Counsellor (Political) Kuala Lumpur since November 2001; Born 09/05/63; Second Secretary FCO 1987; Second Secretary Ankara 1990; Consul (Information) Istanbul 1991; First Secretary FCO 1992; Islamabad 1995; First Secretary FCO 1999; m 1985 Margaret Martin (1s 1989; 1d 1992).

Moore, Sarah Jane; SUPL since January 2005; Born 20/09/66; Assistant Legal Adviser FCO 1995; Band D7.

Moore, Stephen Lawrence; Rabat since March 2002; Born 22/07/68; Paris 1991; FCO 1993; Islamabad 1994; FCO 1997; On loan to DTI 1999; Band C4; m 1992 Carolyn Andrea (1d 1998; 1s 2001).

Moore, Trevor Charles; FCO since June 2001; Born 19/01/58; FCO 1980; Belgrade 1982; Vice-Consul New York 1986; Second Secretary Washington 1987; Second later First Secretary FCO 1989; First Secretary (CTBT) Vienna (UKMIS) 1997; m 1991 Diane Elizabeth Burns (3s 1994, 1997, 1999).

Moores, Amias Steven; St Helena since August 2004; Born 31/03/71; FCO 1990; Geneva (UKMIS) 1994; Abu Dhabi 1997; FCO 1997; Third Secretary and Vice-Consul Abu Dhabi 2001; Band C4; m 2000 Lindsey Cave (1s 2002).

Moorhead, Michelle Anne; Tel Aviv since August 2002; Born 02/02/70; FCO 1988; Washington 1991; Accra 1995; FCO 1998; SUPL 2000; FCO 2001; Band B3; m 1990 Ian William Moorhead (1s 2000; 1d 2002).

Moran, David John; HM Ambassador Tashkent since March 2005; Born 22/08/59; DTI 1985; ODA 1985; Second Secretary (Programmes Adviser) British Development Division in Eastern Africa Nairobi 1988; First Secretary ODA/FCO 1991; First Secretary (Know How Fund) Moscow 1993; First Secretary FCO 1996; Deputy Permanent Representative UKDEL OECD Paris 2001; m 1993 Carol Ann Marquis.

Moran, Karen (née Pinkney); FCO since September 2003; Born 02/03/65; National Savings Department 1984; FCO 1984; Washington 1986; Seoul 1989; FCO 1993; Third Secretary (Management) Hong Kong 1996; Deputy Head of Mission Tashkent 2000; Band C4; m 1986 Sean Moran (diss 1995).

Moran, Lindy Jane (née Preston); SUPL since July 2000; Born 09/10/58; FCO 1981; Caracas 1982; Grand Turk 1986; FCO 1989; Warsaw 1990; Nairobi 1992; Band B3; m 1995 Eamon Andrew Moran.

Moran, Sean; Second Secretary FCO since March 2001; Born 06/03/64; Inland Revenue 1984; FCO 1984; Washington 1986; Seoul 1989; FCO 1993; On secondment to DTI 1996; World Wide Floater Duties 1998; Band C4; m 1986 Karen Pinkney (diss 1995).

Morgan, Angela Merril; Consul Shanghai since July 2004; Born 14/03/68; FCO 1989; Warsaw

1991; FCO 1992; Riga 1993; FCO 1994; New Delhi/Karachi 1995; FCO 1996; Third Secretary (Political) Suva 1997; SUPL 2000; Suva 2000; Second Secretary (Consular) Bangkok 2001; Band C4; m 2001 Sainivalati Tokalau (diss 2003) (1d 2000).

Morgan, Charles Edward William; Second Secretary Jakarta since March 2004; Born 24/08/73; FCO 2001; Band C4.

Morgan, John Philip Arwyn; World Wide Floater Duties since June 2001; Born 17/12/71; FCO 1999; Band B3.

Morgan, Karen; Lisbon since August 2002; Born 11/08/71; FCO 2000; Band A2.

Morgan, Linda; SUPL since June 2003; Born 09/07/72; FCO 2002; Band A2; ptnr, Stephen Watson.

Morgan, Mark Scott Thomas, MBE (1997); FCO since April 2005; Born 26/04/58; FCO 1976; Geneva 1984; FCO 1986; Second Secretary and Vice-Consul Aden 1988; Second Secretary FCO 1990; Second later First Secretary Valletta 1994; First Secretary FCO 1998; First Secretary Budapest 2001; Band C5; m 1998 Samantha Thompson.

Morgan, Richard de Riemer; First Secretary (PPA) Paris since September 2000; Born 09/05/61; FCO 1984; Language Training Tokyo 1986; Second Secretary (Commercial) Tokyo 1987; First Secretary FCO 1991; First Secretary (Political/Aid) Pretoria 1995; m 1987 Susan Carolyn McGaw (1s 1992; 1d 1994).

Morgan, Steven Leonard; Second Secretary (Political) Bogotá since August 2002; Born 14/01/65; Department of Employment 1983; FCO 1984; Budapest 1986; FCO 1987; Paris 1988; Guatemala City 1990; Mexico City 1993; FCO 1994; Madrid 1999; Band C4; m 1995 Maria del Carmen Toledo Municio.

Morgan, Stuart John; FCO since December 1990; Born 02/12/63; FCO 1983; Khartoum 1988; Band B3; m 1993 Milla Heidi Susan Chapman (1s 2000).

Morgan, William Donovan; First Secretary Rabat since November 2004; Born 02/06/71; Second Secretary FCO 1996; Full-Time Language Training 1998; Full-Time Language Training Peking 1999; Second later First Secretary (Political) Peking 2000; Band D6; m 1992 Lucy Bullock (2s 1992, 1995).

Morley, David John; First Secretary FCO since September 2001; Born 23/10/54; MAFF 1972; FCO 1973; Geneva (UKMIS) 1975; Port Stanley 1978; Kuala Lumpur 1980; FCO 1981; Kaduna 1984; FCO 1988; Second Secretary (Management) Moscow 1991; Second Secretary FCO 1994; Deputy High Commissioner Mbabane 1995; First Secretary (Information) Brussels (UKDEL NATO) 1999; Band C5; m 1978 Jacqueline Ann Wells.

Morley, Ian Robert; Zagreb since October 2000; Born 24/07/71; FCO 1992; New York (UKMIS) 1996; Luanda 1999; Band A2.

Morley, Jacqueline Ann (née Wells), MBE (1991); FCO since November 2001; Born 20/07/55; FCO 1973; New York (UKMIS) 1974; FCO 1975; Geneva (UKMIS) 1975; Port Stanley 1978; SUPL (Kuala Lumpur) 1980; Kuala Lumpur 1981; FCO 1981; SUPL (Kaduna) 1984; Kaduna 1987; FCO 1988; Moscow 1991; FCO 1994; SUPL (Mbabane) 1995; FCO 1999; SUPL (Brussels) 1999; Brussels (UKDEL NATO) 2000; Band B3; m 1978 David John Morley.

Morley, Michael Donald; HM Consul Dallas since February 2004; Born 18/02/53; FCO 1973; Moscow 1975; Kuala Lumpur 1977; Latin America Floater 1981; Beirut 1983; FCO 1984; Third later Second Secretary La Paz 1987; Second Secretary (Commercial) Santiago 1991; FCO 1995; First Secretary (Management) Athens 1999; m 1983 Carmen Gloria Del Prado (2s 1987, 1989).

Morley, Stuart Richard, OBE (2002); First Secretary FCO since April 1999; Born 26/01/59; Second Secretary FCO 1988; Second later First Secretary (Chancery/Information) San José 1989; First Secretary (Chancery) Bridgetown 1990; First Secretary FCO 1992; First Secretary (Chemical Weapons) The Hague 1996; m 1987 Janet Henry (3d 1990, 1993, 1998; 1s 1996).

Morrell, Susan Mary; HM Consul Athens since January 2005; Born 07/11/50; FCO 1977; New York (UKMIS) 1978; Budapest 1981; Khartoum 1982; Islamabad 1985; Moscow 1988; Brussels (UKREP) 1989; FCO 1992; Sofia 1996; First Secretary and Consul Peking 2001; Band C5.

Morris, Jill; Brussels (UKREP) since January 2005; Born 14/08/67; FCO 1999; Second Secretary (Political) Nicosia 2001; Band D6.

Morris, Neil Andrew; FCO since November 2003; Born 05/11/64; Home Office 1988.

Morris, Richard Charles; Counsellor Mexico City since December 2004; Born 01/11/67; New York (UKMIS) 1993; Third Secretary (Political) Ottawa 1993; Second Secretary (Political) Bridgetown 1996; First Secretary later Counsellor FCO 2000; m 1992 Alison Jane Waring (1d 1996; 2s 1998, 2003).

Morris, Richard Peter; First Secretary (Management) Brussels since August 2004; Born 08/09/64; FCO 1983; Dhaka 1985; Bucharest 1988; FCO 1991; Full-Time Language Training 1995; Vice-Consul Rome 1995; Second Secretary (Management) Colombo 1999; FCO 2002; m 1990 Diane Jacqueline Harvey.

Morris, Sara Joanne; FCO since May 1995; Born 19/10/62; FCO 1983; Mexico City 1987; FCO 1991; Floater Duties 1993; Band A2.

Morris, Timothy Colin; Deputy Head of Mission Lisbon since January 2003; Born 17/09/58; FCO 1981; SOAS 1982; Language Training Tokyo 1983; Second Secretary (Commercial) Tokyo

1984; First Secretary FCO 1987; On loan to the DTI 1989; First Secretary (Head of Political Section) Madrid 1991; First Secretary FCO 1996; Counsellor (Trade and Investment) Tokyo 1998; m 1996 Patricia Tena Garcia (3s 1998, 1999, 2001).

Morris, Warwick; HM Ambassador Seoul since November 2003; Born 10/08/48; FCO 1969; Paris 1972; Language Training Seoul 1975 (Second Secretary 1977); FCO 1979 (PS to Deputy PUS 1979 - 80); First Secretary 1982; First Secretary (Commercial) Mexico City 1984; First Secretary and Head of Chancery Seoul 1988; First Secretary later Counsellor FCO 1991; Counsellor (Commercial/Economic) New Delhi 1995; Career Development Attachment Royal College of Defence Studies 1999; HM Ambassador Hanoi 2000; m 1972 Pamela Jean Mitchell (1s 1976; 2d 1978, 1982).

Morrison, Alan; Hong Kong since December 2002; Born 04/01/70; FCO 1989; Islamabad 1992; FCO 1995; Ottawa 1997; Band B3; m 1997 Lynne Jean Gregory.

Morrison, Fiona Margaret; First Secretary (Political) Pretoria since September 2004; Born 23/01/67; FCO 1989; Third Secretary (Chancery) Brussels (UKDEL) 1991; FCO 1994; Third Secretary (Commercial) Oslo 1995; Third Secretary (Chancery/PPA) Kingston 1996; Second Secretary FCO 2000; First Secretary (Political) Kabul 2002; Band D6.

Morrison, Ian Kenneth; Singapore since November 2004; Born 27/12/54; Inland Revenue 1974; FCO 1977; Budapest 1979; Islamabad 1981; Madrid 1983; FCO 1986; Third Secretary Accra 1988; Vice-Consul (Political/Information) Cape Town 1991; FCO 1996; First Secretary (Commercial) Tel Aviv 1999; Band D6; m (1) 1978 Gillian Winifred Turk (diss) (1d 1982); (2) 1994 Jean MacAlpine Kerr (2s 1995, 1998).

Morrison, Jonathan James Howard; Counsellor FCO since 2002; Born 31/12/67; Home Office 1989 - 91; Third later Second later First Secretary Brussels (UKREP) 1994; FCO 1999; Private Secretary to Minister for Europe 2000; m 1994 Helen Louisa Pope (3d 1996, 1998, 2002).

Morrison, Melanie Kathryn (née Girling); Moscow since January 2002; Born 18/03/62; FCO 1995; Wellington 1997; Band B3; m 1997 John Morrison.

Morrissey, Gillian Lesley (née Worrall); FCO since February 1990; Born 02/02/60; FCO 1979; Helsinki 1981; Doha 1984; Bonn 1988; Band C4; m 1984 Patrick John Morrissey (1d 1993).

Mortimer, Hugh Roger, LVO (1992); Deputy Head of Mission Berlin since June 2005; Born 19/09/49; FCO 1973; Rome 1975; Singapore 1978; FCO 1981; Second later First Secretary New York (UKMIS) 1983; First Secretary FCO 1987; On attachment to the Auswärtiges Amt 1990; First Secretary (Chancery) Berlin 1991; Counsellor FCO 1994; Royal College of Defence Studies (RCDS) 1996; Deputy Head of Mission Ankara 1997; HM Ambassador Ljubljana 2001; m 1974 Zosia Cecylia Rzepecka (2d 1976 (dec'd 1993), 1980).

Morton, David Stanley Thomas; First Secretary (Management) Copenhagen since January 2002; Born 06/12/45; FO 1963; Kinshasa 1967; Cairo 1967; Wellington 1969; Brussels (UKREP) 1972; FCO 1975; Beirut 1977; Washington 1979; Dacca 1982; Second Secretary FCO 1985; Second Secretary (Commercial) Baghdad 1990; Second Secretary (Commercial) Nairobi 1991; Second Secretary FCO 1995; Consul (Management) Istanbul 1998; m (1) 1972 Judith Anne Amies (diss 1983) (1s 1973); (2) 1987 Beverley Anne Sheppard (2s 1988, 1991).

Morton, Ralph Christopher; SUPL since September 2004; Born 13/12/55; FCO 1979; Khartoum 1982; Brussels (UKDEL NATO) 1984; Third later Second Secretary (Chancery) East Berlin 1987; Second Secretary FCO 1991; Second Secretary (Commercial/Consular) Kampala 1992; Second Secretary (Commercial) Johannesburg 1995; Second Secretary FCO 1996; Second Secretary (Political) Vienna Embassy 1998; Consul (Commercial/CCU) Düsseldorf 2001.

Moseley, Simon Arthur; Peking since July 2002; Born 11/02/72; FCO 1989; Band C4; m 1999 Aleesha (1s 2004).

Moser-Andon, Barbara; Grand Turk since December 2002; Born 04/08/47; FCO 1991; Damascus 1993; FCO 1996; Kathmandu 1997; Tehran 2000; Band B3.

Moss, Alexander (Sandy) Robert Fraser; Second Secretary Brussels (UKDEL NATO) since April 2005; Born 21/09/72; FCO 2001; Band C4; m 2005 Valerie Sandra Belloli.

Moss, Kerry May (née Ford); Buenos Aires since April 2002; Born 04/05/67; Home Office 1990-93; FCO 1994; Hanoi (T/D) 1996; The Hague (T/D) 1996; Hong Kong 1997; FCO 2000; SUPL 2001; Full-Time Language Training (Spanish) 2001; Band A2; m 2001 Stuart Moss.

Moss, Stuart; Second Secretary (Technical) Buenos Aires since March 2001; Born 14/06/67; FCO 1987; Washington 1994; FCO 1996; Band C4; m 2001 Kerry May Ford.

Moss-Norbury, Nicholas Adam; Second Secretary Bogotá since May 2003; Born 12/05/72; FCO 1991; Third Secretary Peking 1997; FCO 2000; Band C4.

Mott, Alan Lawrence; FCO since November 1999; Born 05/10/65; FCO 1984; Washington 1989; FCO 1991; Bridgetown 1996; Band C5; m 1988 Tina Michaela.

Mowbray, Fiona (née Roberts); Singapore since October 2003; Born 08/11/63; FCO 1983; Washington 1984; Addis Ababa 1986; Nassau 1990; Ankara 1991; SUPL 1994; FCO 1996; Grand Cayman 1999; Band B3; m 1986 Kevin Lewis Mowbray (1s 1993).

Mowbray, Kevin Lewis; SUPL since August 2003; Born 05/04/59; FCO 1977; Brussels (UKREP) 1979; Africa/Middle East Floater 1982; FCO 1984; Addis Ababa 1986; Nassau 1990; Second Secretary (Chancery/Consular) Ankara 1991; FCO 1996; SUPL 1999; Grand Cayman 2000; m 1986 Fiona Roberts (1s 1993).

Muir, David John; FCO since March 2003; Born 22/05/58; FCO 1995; Floater Duties 1996; Attaché Tashkent 1999; Third Secretary (Vice-Consul) Tashkent 2000; Band B3; m 1999 Deborah Okey.

Mulheirn, Gregory; FCO since October 2003; Born 16/11/75; Band C4.

Mullee, Patrick; First Secretary FCO since December 2003; Born 08/10/54; FCO 1974; Prague 1976; Caracas 1977; Africa Floater 1980; Latin America Floater 1983; FCO 1985; Third later Second Secretary San José 1988; Second Secretary (Chancery/Information) Bridgetown 1991; Second later First Secretary FCO 1995; Deputy Head of Mission Quito 2000; Band D6; m 1987 Joanna Louise Johnson (2d 1989, 1994).

Mullender, Andrea; Moscow since March 2004; Born 16/08/73; FCO 1999; Dar es Salaam 2001; Band A2.

Mulvaney, Isabella Maria; SUPL since November 2004; Born 18/03/68; FCO 1986; Brussels (UKDEL) 1988; Karachi 1991; FCO 1994; Lusaka 1998; Bahrain 2001; Band C4; m 2000 Dean Ashley Horton.

Mulvein, Helen Jane, OBE (2004); Assistant Legal Adviser FCO since April 2000; Born 04/12/70.

Muncie, Heather; SUPL since March 2001; Born 19/08/67; FCO 1992; Jakarta 1994; Paris 1998; Band A2.

Munks, Robert John; FCO since January 1997; Born 14/02/72; Band C4.

Munro, Colin Andrew, CMG (2002); Head of UK Delegation to OSCE Vienna since December 2003; Born 24/10/46; Inland Revenue 1968; Third Secretary FCO 1969; Bonn 1971; Second later First Secretary Kuala Lumpur 1973; FCO 1977; Private Secretary to Minister of State 1979; First Secretary and Head of Chancery Bucharest 1981; First Secretary FCO 1983; Counsellor East Berlin 1987; HM Consul-General Frankfurt 1990; Counsellor FCO 1993; HM Ambassador Zagreb 1997; Deputy High Representative Mostar (Bosnia ang Herzegovina) 2001; On secondment to the Royal College of Defence Studies 2002; m 1967 Ehrengard Maria Heinrich (2s 1967, 1978).

Murdoch, Charles Edward; First Secretary Amman since April 2004; Born 02/11/66; FCO 2002; Band D6; m 2001 Jocelyn Drew.

Murduck, Ann Victoria; Third Secretary (Political) Basra since May 2004; Born 11/08/77; FCO 2003; Band B3.

Muronen, Victoria Evelyn (née Foster); SUPL since September 2003; Born 28/12/72; FCO 1990; Geneva (UKMIS) 1994; FCO 1997; Band C4.

Murphy, John Matthew; FCO since January 2004; Born 10/03/70; HCS 1990 - 93; Moscow 1995; Vice-Consul Beijing 1999; Band B3.

Murphy, Jonathan Philip; FCO since October 2003; Born 20/01/77; FCO 1999; Second Secretary (Chemical Weapons) The Hague 2001; Band C4.

Murray, June; FCO since March 2003; Born 09/06/50; FCO 1986; Tegucigalpa 1988; Johannesburg 1990; Moscow 1992; FCO 1995; Ankara 1998; Band B3.

Murray, Michael Thomas; HM Ambassador Asmara since March 2002; Born 13/10/45; FO DSAO 1964; Prague 1967; Vienna 1971; Vice-Consul (Commercial) Frankfurt 1973; Second Secretary (Development) Khartoum 1977; FCO 1980; First Secretary and Head of Chancery Banjul 1983; First Secretary FCO 1987; First Secretary (Development/Economic) Lusaka 1995; On loan to DFID at Lusaka 1998; Deputy Consul-General Chicago 1999; Band D6; m 1968 Else Birgitta Margareta Paues (1s 1974; 1d 1981).

Murray, William Richard; FCO since March 2003; Born 09/04/72; Band C4.

Murray, Winston Anthony; FCO since April 1999; Born 04/07/64; OFT 1985; FCO 1985; Bonn 1991; Bahrain 1994; Band B3; m 1990 Judith Muponda (1s 1992).

Murtagh, Michael Louis; Chennai since October 2001; Born 12/02/53; RAF Flt Lt 1981-97; Defence Attaché's Office, Moscow 1995-97; Moscow, New Embassy Project 1997-00; FCO 2000; Band B3; m 1988 Diana Morford (2s 1980, 1983).

Murton, John Evan; SUPL since January 2004; Born 18/03/72; FCO 1997; Full-Time Language Training Tokyo 1998; Second Secretary (Global Issues) later First Secretary (Energy and Environment) Tokyo 2000; Band D6; m 1998 Sarah Elizabeth Harvey (1s 2002).

Murton, Sarah Elizabeth; Brussels since April 2005; Born 06/04/76; FCO 2001; Third Secretary (PS/HMA) Tokyo 2001; SUPL 2002; Band B3; m 1998 John Murton (1s 2002).

Musgrave, David William; Deputy Head of Mission and Consul Riga since November 2002; Born 12/05/53; FCO 1983; Second later First Secretary Copenhagen 1985; First Secretary FCO 1989; First Secretary (Political/Information) Lagos 1994; First Secretary (Political) Abuja 1995; First Secretary FCO 1998; m 1978 Madeleine Nnomo Assembe (2d 1979, 1991; 1s 1981).

Mustafa, Jon; Third Secretary (Immigration) New Delhi since May 2003; Born 22/12/61; FCO 1988; Band B3; m 1995 Marilyn Melanie Mongal (1s 1999; 1d 2001).

Mustard, Simon; Washington since January 2005; Born 03/08/71; FCO 2000; Third Secretary (Chancery) Belmopan 2002; Band C4; m 2003 Mary Roberton.

Myers, Sharon Theresa; Gibraltar since August 2004; Born 19/04/65; FCO 1987; Moscow 1988; Bogotá 1991; FCO 1995; Copenhagen 2001; Band A2; m 1993 Manuel Bolano (diss 2003) (2s 1996, 2002).

N

Nailard, Allison Mary (née Abbott); Abu Dhabi since February 2004; Born 03/07/73; FCO 1999; Moscow 2000; Band A2; m 1999 Michael Nailard.

Nalden, Philip Nigel; Floater Duties since September 2002; Born 30/03/45; Army (CRMP) 1963-88; Moscow 1988; Lagos 1989; Peking 1993; Dhaka 1994; FCO 1997; Belgrade 1998; Colombo 1999; Band B3; m 1982 Heather McIntosh.

Nandi, Mark Debal; FCO since December 2003; Born 02/02/72; Band C5.

Nash, Ronald Peter, CMG (2004), LVO (1984), MVO (1983); High Commissioner Port of Spain since January 2004; Born 18/09/46; FCO 1970; Second later First Secretary Moscow 1974; First Secretary Vienna (UKDEL) 1976; FCO 1979; New Delhi 1983; First Secretary FCO 1986; Counsellor and Head of Chancery Vienna 1988; Deputy High Commissioner Colombo 1992; Counsellor FCO 1996; HM Ambassador Kathmandu 1999; HM Ambassador Kabul 2002; m 1976 Annie Olsen (3s 1979, 1981, 1983).

Naughton, Dawn Karen; Kuala Lumpur since June 2005; Born 22/08/69; FCO 1988; Brussels (UKDEL) 1990; Maputo 1993; Lagos 1997; Jerusalem 2000; HM Consul Mexico City 2003; Band C4; m 1993 Steven John Horsup.

Neale, Dawn Teresa; SUPL since May 2004; Born 13/08/60; FCO 1996; Abuja 1998; Band B3; m 1995 John Harry Albert Neale, MBE (2s 2001, 2004).

Needham, David Brent; Pretoria since September 2005; Born 22/02/51; Royal Marines 1968-91; Moscow 1992; Kingston 1996; Brussels (UKDEL NATO) 1999; Floater Duties 2002; Jakarta 2003; Band B3; m 1992 Karen Dawn Ackers (2s 1993, 1995).

Neely, Maxine Lorna (née Hunter); SUPL since September 2001; Born 09/12/64; FCO 1988; Washington 1989; Bangkok 1992; FCO 1995; Tokyo 1997; British Trade International 1999; Band B3; m 2000 Peter Gordon Neely.

Neil, Andrew Alasdair; FCO since August 2004; Born 11/06/68; FCO 1991; Second Secretary (Political) Nairobi 1994; Second Secretary FCO 1996; First Secretary (Political) Abu Dhabi 2001; Band D6; m 1998 Amanda Lewis (2s twins 2000).

Neil, William John; Jedda since January 2002; Born 23/05/67; FCO 1988; T/D Sofia (CSCE Conference) and East Berlin 1989; Brussels (UKDEL NATO) 1990; Brussels (UKREP) 1990; Baku 1993; Bombay 1995; Vice-Consul (Visas) Shanghai 1999; Band C4.

Neill, Kenneth Andrew; HM Consul Riyadh since July 2001; Born 06/11/44; FO 1961; Tripoli 1967; Moscow 1970; Vientiane 1970; FCO 1974; Hanoi 1977; Karachi 1979; Second Secretary (Chancery/Information) Lilongwe 1982; Second Secretary FCO 1986; Second later First Secretary Honiara 1988; First Secretary (Commercial/Consular) Lusaka 1992; First Secretary FCO 1996; Deputy Head of Mission T/D Yaoundé 2000; m 1977 Julie C Brown (2s 1981, 1991; 2d 1987, 1993).

Neilson, James George Lovie; Riyadh since June 2005; Born 27/07/44; Army 1965-88; Geneva 1988; Moscow 1991; Budapest 1992; Pretoria 1994; Peking 1997; Ankara 2000; Floater Duties 2004; Band C4; m 1967 Lorraine (1d 1968; 1s 1971).

Nellthorp, Helen Rosemary, OBE (2002); First Secretary (Specialised Agencies) Geneva (UKMIS) since September 2001; Born 10/05/62; FCO 1980; Athens 1984; Floater Duties 1987; Third Secretary (Commercial) Washington 1989; Second Secretary (Commercial) Prague 1991; Second later First Secretary FCO 1994; Band D6.

Nelson, Diana June (née Gordon); FCO since September 1997; Born 17/06/58; FCO 1981; Paris 1984; Algiers 1987; Second Secretary FCO 1989; SUPL 1991; FCO 1992; SUPL 1995; m 1985 Miles Christopher Nelson (diss 2002) (2d 1991, 1993).

Nelson, Matthew Charles; FCO since March 2004; Born 19/06/74; FCO 2000; Full-Time Language Training FCO 2002; Full-Time Language Training, Amman 2003; Band C4.

Nessling, Paul William Downs; High Commissioner Nuku'alofa since January 2002; Born 26/09/45; Chicago (From BOT) 1971; Bahrain (From DOI) 1975; Second Secretary FCO 1979; Lisbon 1981; Warsaw 1982; First Secretary (Aid) Nairobi 1984; T/D Aden 1984; FCO 1987; First Secretary (Commercial) Harare 1989; First Secretary (Commercial) Muscat 1993; First Secretary Sarajevo 1996; FCO 1997; Deputy High Commissioner Lusaka 1998; m 1975 Kathryn Freeman.

Nethersole, Jonathan Sebastian; FCO since 2001; Born 07/11/69; FCO 1988; Pretoria/Cape Town 1990; Sana'a 1993; FCO 1995; EU Presidency Liaison Officer Bonn, Helsinki, Lisbon, Paris 1999-00; Band C4.

Nettleton, Catherine Elizabeth, OBE (1999); Counsellor (Political/Economic) Peking since October 2000; Born 13/03/60; FCO 1983; Language Training 1984; Peking 1987; Second Secretary 1988; Second Secretary FCO 1989; First Secretary (Political/Economic) Mexico City 1991; First Secretary FCO 1995; Counsellor FCO 1999.

Nevin, Michael Patrick; FCO since August 2003; Born 13/01/69; FCO 1993; Osaka 1996; Second Secretary (Chancery) Lilongwe 1999; Band C4; m 1997 Sawako (1 step d 1989; 1s 1998).

Newall, Peter; HM Ambassador Dakar since May 2004; Born 20/03/47; DSAO (later FCO) 1966; Tehran 1970; Delhi 1972; FCO 1976; Second Secretary (Commercial) Belgrade 1979; First Secretary (Commercial) Kuwait 1982; FCO 1986; HM Consul Marseilles 1989; First Secretary (Management) Geneva (UKMIS) 1990; FCO 1995; Counsellor, Head of Joint Management Office Brussels 1999; m 1969 Marina Joy McHugh (2d 1972, 1973; 1s 1976).

Newell, Clive Dare; Ottawa since December 2003; Born 22/12/53; FCO 1976; Third Secretary (Commercial) later Second Secretary Tehran 1979; FCO 1980; Second later First Secretary Kabul 1982; FCO 1984; First Secretary Addis Ababa 1986; FCO 1990; First Secretary on secondment to the Ministry of Defence 1992; FCO 1993; First Secretary on loan to the Cabinet Office 1993; Counsellor (Political) Ankara 1994; Counsellor FCO 1998; Counsellor Moscow 2001; m 1997 Gamze Ozen (1s 1999; 1d 2002).

Newlands, Andrew; Deputy Consul-General Vancouver since August 2003; Born 10/02/68; DHSS 1984; FCO 1988; Bonn 1990; FCO 1992; Manila 1993; T/D Hong Kong 1996; FCO 1997; Deputy Head of Mission Panama City 2000; Band C4; m 1989 Eileen Mitchell (1s 1993; 1d 1996).

Newman, James Michael; Third Secretary (Political) Harare since September 2002; Born 31/03/70; Metropolitan Police 1989; FCO 1990; Cairo 1992; Cape Town 1996; FCO 1999; Band C4; m 2000 Sarah Louise.

Newman, Kevin Paul; Bangkok since September 2002; Born 31/07/73; Home Office 1994; FCO 1995; Abuja 1998; T/D Harare 2001-02; Band B3.

Newns, Carl Edwin Francis; First Secretary (Chancery) Washington since March 2000; Born 30/06/68; FCO 1989; Third later Second Secretary (Political) The Hague 1992; First Secretary FCO 1996; Private Secretary to the Parliamentary Under-Secretary of State 1997; Band D6; m 1999 Christina Klaassen.

Newson, Gavin Erskine Walter; First Secretary Vienna (UKMIS) since August 2005; Born 20/07/71; FCO 1996; Second Secretary (Financial/Economic) Tokyo 1998; Second Secretary FCO 2001; Band D6.

Newsum, Wendy Elizabeth; FCO since June 2004; Born 11/05/78; Band B3.

Newton, Alastair Dan Barr; Head of IUK USA New York since July 2002; Born 08/01/54; FCO 1985; Second later First Secretary Kinshasa 1986; First Secretary FCO 1989; First Secretary Paris (UKDEL) 1992; On secondment as Economic Adviser to Lehman Bros 2000; m 1988 Vivienne Jane Ivanich (2d 1979, 1980).

Nicholas, Barry Stewart; FCO since March 2003; Born 01/11/62; FCO 1981; East Berlin 1984; Dubai 1986; Warsaw 1988; FCO 1991; Cairo 1995; Second Secretary (Commercial) Port of Spain 1999; m 1989 Susan Jane Parker (1s 1992; 1d 2002).

Nicholas, Susan Jane (née Parker); SUPL since May 2003; Born 17/09/62; FCO 1981; Warsaw 1984; Bonn 1987; Düsseldorf 1988; Warsaw 1989 (Second Secretary 1991); FCO 1993; SUPL 1995; Cairo 1996; SUPL 1999; Port of Spain 2000; m 1989 Barry Stuart Nicholas (1s 1992; 1d 2002).

Nicholas, Suzanne Elizabeth; FCO since March 2000; Born 14/08/70; FCO 1995; Second Secretary (Political) Warsaw 1999; Band C4.

Nicholls, Gary Patrick; Second Secretary (Chancery) Accra since October 2003; Born 04/10/68; FCO 1988; Tokyo 1990; Islamabad 1993; FCO 1998; HM Consul Guangzhou 2000; Band C4; m 1993 Helen Marie Glanfield (diss 1998) (1s 1994; 1d 1997).

Nichols, John Roland; HM Ambassador Budapest since August 2003; Born 13/11/51; Third later Second Secretary FCO 1977; Second later First Secretary Budapest 1979; FCO 1982; First Secretary (Commercial) Brasilia 1985; First Secretary FCO 1989; Counsellor and Deputy High Commissioner Dhaka 1993; Consul-General Geneva 1995; Deputy Head of Mission and Director of Trade Promotion Berne 1997; On secondment to British Invisibles 2000; m 1983 Angela Suzanne Davies (1s 1987; 1d 1989).

Nichols, Martin Christopher; On loan to the Cabinet Office since May 1998; Born 04/05/62; FCO 1981; Tel Aviv 1984; FCO 1987; Darwin 1988; FCO 1990; New Delhi 1991; FCO 1994; Band C4; m 1983 Julie Marie Wilkins (2s 1983, 1988; 1d 1992).

Nicholson, Emma Jane (née Woodward); SUPL since June 2005; Born 06/06/70; FCO 1996; BTCO Taipei 1997; BCG Jerusalem 2000; Attaché Shanghai 2001; Band A2.

Nicholson, Karen Jayne (née Baudains); FCO since June 2003; Born 29/09/55; FCO 1977; Mexico City 1979; South East Asia Floater Duties 1983; Second Secretary FCO 1985; First Secretary (Commercial) Lisbon 1992; FCO 1994; On loan to British Trade International 1998; Seconded to the Private sector 2002; m 1994 David J Nicholson.

Nickels, Tina; Bandar Seri Begawan since August 2004; Born 15/06/78; British Trade International 2002; FCO 2002; Band A2.

Nicolopulo, Evangelo Paul; First Secretary FCO since January 2000; Born 14/01/50; FCO 1969; Lourenço Marques 1972; Saigon 1973; FCO 1974; Kingston 1977; Madrid (CSCE) 1980; Alexandria 1982; Second Secretary FCO 1985; Vice-Consul (Commercial) Montreal 1988; First Secretary FCO 1993; First Secretary (Political) Copenhagen 1995; m 1981 Kareen Elizabeth Sun.

Nithavrianakis, Elizabeth Rosemary (née Hingston-Jones); FCO since April 2002; Born 27/06/63; FCO 1983; Peking 1985; Kuala Lumpur 1986; FCO 1990; Moscow 1990; FCO 1992; T/D Riyadh 2001; Band B3; m 1992 Michael Stephen Nithavrianakis (1s 1996; 1d 2000).

Nithavrianakis, Michael Stephen, MVO (2000); FCO since January 2002; Born 30/04/67; FCO 1984; Kuala Lumpur 1987; Moscow 1990; FCO 1992; Second Secretary (Chancery) Accra 1997; First Secretary (Commercial) Riyadh 2000; Band D6; m 1992 Elizabeth Rosemary Hingston-Jones (1s 1996; 1d 2000).

Noakes, Stephen Martin, OBE (1993); First Secretary FCO since August 2000; Born 06/02/57; Home Civil Service 1979-88; Second Secretary FCO 1988; First Secretary (Chancery) Luanda 1990; First Secretary FCO 1993; First Secretary New York (UKMIS) 1996; Band D6; m 1989 Hazel Clarke.

Nobes, Paula Louise; First Secretary (Commercial) Brussels (UKREP) since June 2005; Born 01/08/69; FCO 1988; Language Training 1990; Third Secretary (Chancery) Belgrade 1991; APS Lord Owen, Peace Conference on Former Yugoslavia, Geneva 1993; Kiev 1994; Zagreb 1995; Second Secretary FCO 1998; Deputy Head of Mission Baku 2002; Band C5; m 2005 Andy Page.

Noble, Andrew James, LVO (1995); Deputy Head of Mission Athens since August 2001; Born 22/04/60; FCO 1982; Third Secretary (Chancery/Information) Bucharest 1983; On attachment to Auswärtiges Amt, Bonn 1986; Second Secretary (Chancery) Bonn 1987; First Secretary FCO 1989; First Secretary (Political) and Head of Political Section Pretoria/Cape Town 1994; FCO 1998; m 1992 Helen Natalie Pugh (2s 1995, 1996; 2d 2000, 2003).

Noble, Helen Natalie (née Pugh); SUPL since May 1994; Born 17/07/66; FCO 1988; On secondment to Auswärtiges Amt 1989; Third later Second Secretary Bonn 1990; Second Secretary FCO 1992; Second Secretary on loan to the ODA 1993; m 1992 Andrew James Noble (2s 1995, 1996; 2d 2000, 2003).

Noble, Richard Adam; Deputy Head of Mission Hong Kong since December 2004; Born 09/06/62; FCO 1987; Third later Second Secretary (Chancery) Moscow 1987; Second later First Secretary FCO 1989; First Secretary The Hague 1993; FCO 1995; First Secretary (Political) New Delhi 1998; Head of Research Analysts FCO 2001; m 1994 Katrina Johnson (2s 1996, 1998).

Noël, Louisa Veronica; Tokyo since June 2003; Born 24/04/62; FCO 1988; Kuala Lumpur 1989; Amman 1993; FCO 1996; Bangkok 1999; Band B3.

Nolan, Julia Elizabeth; FCO since September 2003; Born 02/01/59; FCO 1983; Bangkok 1984; SUPL 1986; New Delhi 1987; Second Secretary FCO 1989; First Secretary FCO 1993; SUPL 1994; First Secretary (Political) Paris 1995; SUPL 1997; m 1985 Richard John Codrington (twin s 1991).

Noon, Paul David; First Secretary (Trade) Wellington since September 2001; Born 01/06/68; FCO 1989; Damascus 1991; Bonn 1995; FCO 1998; Band C5; m 1990 Karren Lesley Robson (1d 1993; 1s 1998).

Noorani, Anjoum Aziz; Second Secretary (Economic) Moscow since December 2002; Born 06/04/79; FCO 2000; Band C4.

Norburn, Jonathan Edward; Second Secretary FCO since March 2002; Born 16/08/76; FCO 1999; Second Secretary (Chancery) Bridgetown 2001; Band C4.

Norman, Duncan Charles, MBE (2000); Tortola since March 2004; Born 12/10/71; FCO 1990; Riyadh 1994; Yerevan 1998; FCO 2000; m 1997 Kerry Jones (1d 2000).

Norman, Paul Stephen Raymond; First Secretary (Political) Brussels since July 2002; Born 04/05/56; FCO 1992; Consul Hong Kong 1995; First Secretary FCO 2000; Band D6; m 1989 Felicity Shan Abram (1s 1991; 2d 1993, 1998).

Norman, Sarah Caroline; SUPL since October 2000; Born 16/12/70; FCO 1990; New Delhi 1991; FCO 1992; SUPL 1994; FCO 1998; Band C4.

Norris, George E P; Second Secretary (Economic) Ottawa since August 2004; Born 24/02/76; FCO 2002; Band C4; m 2003 Ching-Yi Yang.

Norris, Peter James; FCO since September 2000; Born 22/12/55; FCO 1982; First Secretary Lagos 1985; FCO 1988; Deputy Head of Mission and Consul Guatemala City 1990; First Secretary FCO 1993; First Secretary (Political) Jakarta 1997; Band D6; m 1982 Dilvinder Kaur Dhaliwal (2d 1986, 1990; 2s (twins) 1993).

Norsworthy, Sean Francis; FCO since April 2003; Born 18/04/68; FCO 1987; Islamabad 1989; Tunis 1992; FCO 1996; Brussels (UKREP) 2001; Paris 2001; Band A2.

Northern, Richard James, MBE (1982); Consul-General Milan since September 2001; Born 02/11/54; FCO 1976; MECAS 1978; Language Training FCO 1978; Riyadh 1980; Second later First Secretary (Chancery) Rome 1983; First Secretary FCO 1987; First Secretary (Economic/Commercial) Ottawa 1992; Deputy Consul-General and Deputy Director Trade/Investment Toronto 1994; Counsellor (Commercial/Economic) Riyadh 1997; Counsellor FCO 2000; m 1981 Linda Denise Gadd (2s 1983, 1986; 1d 1992).

Norton, Mark Rolffe; Head/Press and Public Affairs Nairobi since September 2001; Born 03/01/55; Customs and Excise 1974; Immigration Service 1983; On secondment to Kaduna 1987; FCO 1992; On secondment to ICFY/Observer Mission to Serbia and Montenegro 1994; Addis Ababa 1995; Copenhagen 1996; Ottawa 1996;

Georgetown 2000; m 1995 Gelila Assefa Wedajo (2d 1996, 1998).

Norton, Redmond; FCO since October 2002; Born 30/04/46; Board of Trade 1962; FCO 1969; Rio de Janeiro 1972; Caracas 1975; Dacca 1977; FCO 1980; Second Secretary (Admin) Tripoli 1984; Second Secretary Quito 1985; Second later First Secretary (Commercial) Helsinki 1988; First Secretary FCO 1992; Consul (Commercial) Houston 1994; Deputy Head of Mission Montevideo 1999; Band D6; m 1969 Jean McGarrigle (1d 1974; 1s 1979).

Nye, Alison Claire (née Edwards); SUPL since March 2001; Born 18/12/64; FCO 1983; SUPL 1985; Vienna 1986; Algiers 1987; Third Secretary Karachi 1990; FCO 1993; Third later Second Secretary (Development) Lilongwe 1997; Band C4; m 1985 Richard Paul Nye (1s 1999).

Nye, Richard Paul; On loan to British Trade International, later UK Trade & Investment since October 2002; Born 29/02/64; FCO 1982; Vienna 1984; Algiers 1987; Third Secretary Karachi 1990; FCO 1994; Second Secretary 1996; Second Secretary Lilongwe 1997; SUPL (Private Sector) 2001; Band C4; m 1985 Alison Claire Edwards (1s 1999).

O

O'Brien, Gareth David; seconded to the Corporation of London since February 2005; Born 27/07/65; FCO 1982; Copenhagen 1985; Warsaw 1988; Africa/Middle East Floater 1990; FCO 1991; Belmopan 1995; Consul (Commercial) Jedda 1998; First Secretary (Commercial) Riyadh 2001; Band C5; m 1991 Lisa Margaret Donagher (2s 1997, 1999).

O'Brien, Julie Ann Valentine; Beijing since May 2005; Born 20/03/61; FCO 1994; Moscow 1996; Kuwait 1999; FCO 2001; Band A2.

O'Brien, Lisa Margaret (née Donagher); SUPL since June 1997; Born 30/10/66; FCO 1984; BMG Berlin 1986; Floater Duties 1989; FCO 1991; Belmopan 1995; Band B3; m 1991 Gareth David O'Brien (2s 1997, 1999).

O'Callaghan, Dominic Paul Hutton; Islamabad since May 2004; Born 26/01/46; FCO 1998; Third Secretary (Immigration) Abuja 2001; Band B3.

O'Callaghan, John Matthew; Counsellor Belgrade since July 2004; Born 27/04/66; FCO 1990; Second Secretary (Information) Santiago 1992; Second Secretary FCO 1994; First Secretary (Political) Moscow 1998; First Secretary FCO 2001; First Secretary Stockholm 2003; m 1996 Sophie Dauchez (2d 1998, 2001).

O'Connell, Charles; Second Secretary Islamabad since March 2005; Born 02/11/77; FCO 2003; Band C4.

O'Connell, Ruairí; Second Secretary (Political) Pristina since August 2003; Born 22/02/77; FCO 2001; Band C4.

O'Connell, Terence; SMO Algiers since June 2004; Born 19/09/58; MOD 1976; FCO 1978; Stockholm 1980; Tripoli 1983; FCO 1984; Santiago 1984; Bombay 1987; FCO 1990; Full-Time Language Training 1995; Mexico City 1996; Full-Time Language Training 2000; Peking 2000; Band C4; m 1991 Valerie Anna-Maria Gonsalves.

O'Connor, Christopher Paul; FCO since December 2003; Born 18/12/68; Third later Second Secretary FCO 1993; Full-Time Language Training Cairo 1995; Riyadh 1996; First Secretary Brussels (UKDEL NATO) 1999; On secondment to the Canadian Government 1999-00; Head of Political Section Ottawa 2000; m 2001 Martha Nelems (2d 2002, 2005).

O'Connor, Faye Emily; Second Secretary (External) Moscow since November 2002; Born 04/04/74; FCO 2001; Band C4.

O'Connor, Paul Vincent; Berlin since May 2003; Born 29/06/56; FCO 1975; Jedda 1977; Washington 1980; Floater Duties 1983; FCO 1985; Istanbul 1987; Second Secretary (Aid/Commercial) Maseru 1991; On loan to the DTI 1995; Language Training 1998; Deputy Head of Mission and Consul (Commercial) St Petersburg 1999; m 1985 Georgina Louise Jayne (2s 1987, 1989; 1d 1991).

O'Connor, Sheila Mary; SMO Hanoi since January 2003; Born 28/12/60; FCO 1982; Brussels (UKREP) 1983; Yaoundé 1986; Rangoon 1989; Prague 1991; FCO 1993; OSCE Sarajevo 1996; Third Secretary (Chancery/Development) Kathmandu 1997; FCO 2000; Band C4.

O'Donnell, Sara Jane (née Sharp); SUPL since September 2001; Born 24/12/67; FCO 1991; Third Secretary Brussels (UKDEL WEU) 1994; Yaoundé 1996; m 1996 Francis Joseph O'Donnell.

O'Flaherty, Kenneth James; First Secretary (Global Issues) Paris since August 2004; Born 04/03/72; FCO 1996; Secondment to French Foreign Ministry 1998; Second Secretary (Political) Paris 1999; First Secretary (External Relations) Brussels (UKREP) 2000; m 1997 Maria de los Reyes Lopez Garcia (diss 2000) (1d 1998).

O'Hagan, Mark; Second Secretary Bogotá since July 2002; Born 25/10/67; FCO 1996; Band C4.

O'Henley, Andrew Alexander; FCO since October 2001; Born 07/08/76; FCO 1998; Cape Town 1999; Freetown 2001; Band C4.

O'Keeffe, Deanna Maureen; FCO since October 1991; Born 24/09/61; FCO 1980; Vienna 1989; Band C4.

O'Mahony, Angela Millar (née Lindsay); SUPL since June 2000; Born 17/08/66; FCO 1989; Paris 1991; Kampala 1994; Stockholm 1996; FCO 1996; Band B3; m 1994 Daniel Lawrence O'Mahony.

O'Neill, Martin Gerard Francis; Third Secretary and Vice-Consul Abu Dhabi since June 2004; Born 10/06/71; FCO 2001; Third Secretary (Press and

Public Affairs) Tokyo 2002; Band B3; m 2002 Sachiko Suzuki.

O'Neill, Michael Angus; Counsellor (Economic) New York (UKMIS) since July 2002; Born 25/05/65; MOD 1988; Second Secretary UKDEL NATO/WEU 1991; FCO 1994; First Secretary (Political) Washington 1998; m 1991 Claire Bannerman (1d 1994; 3s 1996, 1998, 2001).

O'Reilly, Mark Carne; Third Secretary (Political) Brussels since May 2001; Born 08/06/73; FCO 1999; Band B3.

O'Rourke, Peter Vincent; FCO since April 2000; Born 26/09/60; FCO 1980; Maputo 1981; Lisbon 1984; Rabat 1987; FCO 1990; Yaoundé 1993; Third later Second Secretary (Management) Beirut 1997; Band C4; m 1999 Louise Karen (1s 2004).

O'Shaughnessy, Jonathan Edward; ECO/Vice-Consul Vienna since August 2002; Born 07/10/71; FCO 1991; Bonn 1995; Gibraltar 1998; ECO Islamabad 2000; Band B3; m 1997 Lisa Diane.

Oakden, Edward Anthony; Director (International Security) later (Defence & Strategic Threats) FCO since November 2002; Born 03/11/59; FCO 1981; Third later Second Secretary (Chancery) Baghdad 1984; Second Secretary (Chancery) Khartoum 1985; First Secretary and Private Secretary to HM Ambassador Washington 1988; First Secretary FCO 1992; Private Secretary to Prime Minister (Overseas/Defence) 1995; Counsellor FCO 1997; Counsellor Madrid 1998; Deputy Head of Mission and Minister Madrid 2000; Head of Security Policy Department, FCO 2002; m (1) 1999 (diss) (1d 1995); m (2) Ana Romero.

Oakley, Matthew Edward, MVO (1999), MBE (2003); SUPL since December 2004; Born 19/07/65; FCO 1983; Athens 1985; Pro-Consul Jedda 1988; Vice-Consul Riyadh 1990; Third Secretary FCO 1992; Third Secretary (Political) Cape Town 1996; Second Secretary (Commercial) Singapore 2000; Band C4.

Oertle-Hurt, Jane Michelle; SUPL since February 1995; Born 13/09/65; HCS 1987-89; Rome 1990; Africa/Middle East Floater 1994; Band B3; m 1995 Horst Dietrich Oertle.

Ogg, Fiona; Warsaw since April 2003; Born 25/07/70; FCO 1989; Warsaw 1992; Paris 1994; FCO 1996; Lagos 1999; Band B3.

Oliphant, Jeremy Craig; Principal Research Officer FCO since April 1999; Born 04/04/56; MOD 1989-99; NATO 1992-94; OSCE 1996-99; Band D6; m 1983 Eithne Grant (2d 1985; 1989).

Oliver, Matthew Keith; Second Secretary FCO since June 2003; Born 16/08/51; Blantyre 1973; Washington 1975; Belgrade 1978; FCO 1979; Tehran 1980; Bombay 1980; Warsaw 1983; FCO 1984; Auckland 1986; Istanbul 1989; Second Secretary FCO 1993; Baku 1996; Second Secretary (Management) The Hague 1999; m 1993 Hatice lker Urgen (dec'd 1999).

Oliver, Paul John; Madrid since July 2000; Born 11/02/74; FCO (Hanslope Park) 1996; Band C4.

Olley, John (Brian); First Secretary (Political and Public Affairs) Helsinki since May 2004; Born 14/02/57; FCO 2001; Band D6; m 1989 Pascale Eliane (2s 1996, 1999; 1d 2004).

Oman, Magnus Paul; On loan to the DTI since November 1999; Born 05/08/68; FCO 1989; Valletta 1991; Doha 1994; FCO 1998; Band B3; m 1998 Ms S Broderick.

Ord-Smith, Robin Jeremy, MVO (1998); First Secretary (Commercial) Tokyo since July 2003; Born 08/10/65; FCO 1989; Vice-Consul Bucharest 1991; Third Secretary (Political/Information) Kuala Lumpur 1994; Second Secretary (State Visit) Kuala Lumpur 1998; Seconded to Auswärtiges Amt 1999; Second Secretary FCO 1999; Full-Time Language Training 2000; Seconded to Bae Systems Japan 2001; Full-Time Language Training 2002; Band D6; m 1995 Tania Jane Vallis (2s 1996, 1998).

Ormiston, Ewan Kenneth; On secondment to TPUK, British Trade International since November 2002; Born 27/08/68; FCO 1989; Brussels 1992; Luanda 1995; Third Secretary Lima 1996; Third later Second Secretary Kampala 1999; Band C4; m 1994 Gillian Keating (1s 1997; 1d 2000).

Ormiston, Gillian (née Keating); on secondment to TPUK, British Trade International since 2003; Born 01/06/66; FCO 1988; Brussels (UKREP) 1991; Luanda 1995; Lima 1996; Kampala (SUPL) 1999; later ECO Kampala 2001; Band A2; m 1994 Ewan Kenneth Ormiston (1s 1997; 1d 2000).

Ormond, Matthew John; Washington since January 2001; Born 23/04/73; FCO 1991; Band C4.

Osborn, Andrew Robert; Third Secretary (Management/Consular/Immigration) Suva since February 2004; Born 13/02/64; FCO 1982; Lagos 1987; Budapest 1990; Moscow 1992; FCO 1994; Vice-Consul Dar-es-Salaam 1997; Third Secretary (Consular/Management) Maseru 2001; Band B3; m 1988 Karyn Lindsay Heraty (2d 1993, 1997).

Osborn, Karyn Lindsay (née Heraty); SUPL since July 1997; Born 12/02/66; FCO 1986; Lagos 1988; Budapest 1990; Moscow 1992; FCO 1994; Band B3; m 1988 Andrew Robert Osborn (2d 1993, 1997).

Osborne, Christopher Wyndham; Deputy Head of Protocol Division and Assistant Marshal of the Diplomatic Corps, FCO since November 2001; Born 18/06/46; Commonwealth Office (later FCO) 1966; Lusaka 1968; Kampala 1970; Bridgetown 1973; FCO 1976; Second Secretary Dacca 1979; Second Secretary (Commercial) Caracas 1982; First Secretary FCO 1986; First Secretary (Information) BTC Hong Kong 1989; First Secretary FCO 1994; First Secretary T/D BTC Hong Kong 1996; Deputy Head of Mission Luanda 1998; m 1967 Gillian Mary (3s 1967, 1974, 1979).

Osborne, Roy Paul; Berne since January 2005; Born 13/07/51; FCO 1970; Oslo 1972; Islamabad 1974; Vice-Consul Rome 1978; Second Secretary FCO 1981; Second Secretary (Commercial/Development), later First Secretary, Head of Chancery and Consul Yaoundé 1985; First Secretary (Chancery/Information) Madrid 1989; First Secretary FCO 1993; HM Ambassador Managua 1997; Deputy Head of Overseas Territories Department, FCO 2001; m 1977 Vivienne Claire Gentry (2d 1983, 1984).

Ostler, Malcolm Thomas; FCO since November 2003; Born 20/09/66; FCO 1988; Bonn 1997; Berlin 1999; Hamilton 2002; Band A2.

Oswald, David; Chennai since April 2005; Born 15/06/46; FO 1965; Amman 1968; Zomba 1970; Blantyre 1971; Tokyo 1973; FCO 1976; Gaborone 1978; FCO 1982; Jedda 1986; Second Secretary FCO 1990; Second Secretary (Management) Dhaka 1993; Consul (Commercial/Economic) Shanghai 1997; Second Secretary (Commercial) Islamabad 2001; m 1972 Jane Avril Bennett Edmunds (2d 1974, 1977).

Oughton, Carolyn Ann; FCO since September 2003; Born 23/06/81; Band A2.

Oulmi, Sally Teresa (née Cashman); Consul (Management) Dar es Salaam since January 2004; Born 04/10/52; FCO 1974; Brussels (UKREP) 1975; Abidjan 1979; Strasbourg 1983; FCO 1986; Ottawa 1987; Stockholm 1990; FCO 1993; Second Secretary (Management) Dhaka 1996; Band C4; m 1976 Hocine (Frank) Oulmi (dec'd) (2s 1993, 1994).

Owen, Amy Grace; FCO since October 2004; Born 29/08/75; FCO 1999; Full-Time Language Training 2000; Full-Time Language Training Peking 2001; Vice-Consul Hong Kong 2002; Band C4.

Owen, Caroline Jane; Jakarta since October 2001; Born 29/10/66; FCO 1986; Washington 1990; FCO 1992; Bombay 1994; Dhaka 1998; Band A2.

Owen, Gareth Wynn; Second Secretary Tehran since January 2005; Born 24/11/69; FCO 1989; Prague 1992; FCO 1993; Warsaw 1994; Lusaka 1996; Baku 1999; FCO 2001; SUPL 2002; Band B3.

Owen, Helen Patricia; FCO since August 1987; Born 09/04/49; FCO 1974; Sana'a 1974; FCO 1976; Bandar Seri Begawan 1981; Manila 1982; Madrid 1984; Band B3.

Owen, Jane Caroline; Counsellor (Commercial) Tokyo since May 2002; Born 15/04/63; FCO 1987; Language Training (Japanese) 1988; Second Secretary (Commercial) Tokyo 1989; First Secretary DTI Exports to Japan Unit 1993; FCO 1996; Deputy Head of Mission Hanoi 1998; SUPL 1999; Deputy High Commissioner Hanoi 2000; m 1998 David Donnelly.

Owen, Kara Justine (née Palmer); Private Secretary to the Foreign Secretary since February 2003; Born 27/05/71; FCO 1993; Vice-Consul later Vice-Consul (Political) Hong Kong 1996; Second Secretary FCO 2000; Assistant Private Secretary to Minister of State 2001; First Secretary FCO 2002; Band D6; m 1995 Craig Sterling Owen.

Owen, Philip Haydn, MBE; Second Secretary (Political) Berlin since May 2003; Born 03/03/66; FCO 1997; Islamabad 1998; Band C4; m 1996 Elizabeth Jane Knight (1s 2003).

Owen, Richard Lloyd; Counsellor FCO since January 1998; Born 21/04/48; Second Secretary FCO 1975; Language Training 1976; Language Training MECAS 1977; First Secretary Abu Dhabi 1978; Beirut 1980; FCO 1981; San José 1983; BMG Berlin 1986; First Secretary FCO 1988; Counsellor Copenhagen 1993; m 1985 Eva Maria Steller (2d 1986, 1988).

Owens, Patrick Eldred, OBE (2002), MBE (1998); HM Consul and Director of US Visa Issuing Posts New York since July 2001; Born 20/04/53; FCO 1972; Muscat 1974; Bucharest 1977; Algiers 1979; FCO 1981; Jakarta 1984; Third later Second Secretary Riyadh 1988; Second Secretary FCO 1994; First Secretary (Information) Madrid 1997; Band D6; m 1978 Merle de Ceuninck van Capelle (1d 1980; 2s 1982, 1985).

Owens, Ruth Mary; FCO since August 2002; Born 28/03/67; FCO 1987; Nairobi 1989; FCO 1992; Moscow 1995; Antananarivo 1999; Band B3.

P

Packer, Deborah (née Wilde); SUPL since November 2003; Born 10/05/66; FCO 1985; NEDO 1986; Tokyo 1994; Bridgetown 1997; Tokyo 2000; Band A2; m 1990 Philip Anthony Packer (2s 1995; 2001; 1d 2003).

Page, Alexander Simon; FCO since July 2003; Born 20/10/64; FCO 1987; Dhaka 1989; Warsaw 1989; FCO 1993; Valletta 1996; Third Secretary (Management) Mexico City 1999; Band C4; m 1989 Isabella Lynn Marshall (1s 1996; 1d 2004).

Page, Andrew John Walter; First Secretary (Chancery) Paris since September 2000; Born 17/09/65; FCO 1990; Full-Time Language Training 1991; Second Secretary Kiev 1992; Second Secretary FCO 1996.

Page, Derek Alan; On loan to the DTI since August 2002; Born 29/09/50; FCO 1975; Pretoria 1977; Bombay 1979; FCO 1981; Frankfurt 1984; Montevideo 1987; FCO 1990 (Second Secretary 1992); Second Secretary Taipei 1994; Second Secretary (Commercial) Abu Dhabi 1998; FCO 2001; m 1972 Inger Merete Ebbesvik (2s 1977, 1981).

Page, Isabella Lynn (née Marshall); FCO since July 2003; Born 06/01/64; FCO 1981; Kuala Lumpur 1984; Prague 1987; SUPL 1989; Warsaw 1989; Dhaka 1990; FCO 1993; Third Secretary (Political/Information) Valletta 1996; Second Secretary (Economic/Political) Mexico City 1999; Band C4; m 1989 Alexander Simon Page (1s 1996; 1d 2004).

Page, Simon Graham; First Secretary (Political) Bahrain since June 2005; Born 22/11/61; FCO 1979; Kuala Lumpur 1983; Floater Duties 1987; Dublin 1988; FCO 1990; Third Secretary (Chancery) New Delhi 1992; FCO 1996; Second Secretary (Political) Riyadh 1998; Second Secretary FCO 2001; Band C4; m 1985 Sharon Ann Murphy (2s 1990, 1995; 1d 2000).

Pagett, Christopher Robert Geoffrey, OBE (1990); Counsellor FCO since September 2000; Born 13/06/52; Third Secretary FCO 1975; Second Secretary Havana 1978; Second later First Secretary (Economic) Lusaka 1979; First Secretary FCO 1984; First Secretary (Chancery) Maputo 1988; First Secretary FCO 1991; Counsellor New York (UKMIS) 1997; m (1) 1974 Anne-Marie Roberts; (2) 1988 Diane Brown (1s 1993).

Pagett, Ian William; FCO since February 1995; Born 19/09/69; FCO 1988; Khartoum 1989; FCO 1992; Warsaw 1993; Band B3.

Pagett, Wayne Norman; Third Secretary (Consular/Immigration) Harare since March 2001; Born 26/03/67; FCO 1988; New Delhi 1990; Tel Aviv 1994; FCO 1997; Band B3; m 1990 Kay Louise Clements (1d 1994).

Paginton, David Alan; Management Officer São Paulo since December 2000; Born 01/04/51; Board of Inland Revenue 1968; FCO 1971; Istanbul 1973; Brussels (UKREP) 1976; Sofia 1979; FCO 1981; São Paulo 1984; Islamabad 1988; FCO 1991; Second Secretary (Commercial) Dar es Salaam 1994; HM Consul Buenos Aires 1998; m 1986 Marcia Rosana Antonio (1s 1986; 1d 1987).

Pain, Warren David; Vice-Consul (Political/Economic) Hong Kong since February 2000; Born 17/05/71; FCO 1992; Peking 1995; World Wide All-Rounder 1998; m 2000 Armine Ghevondyan.

Painter, Anthony Clifford; FCO since December 2002; Born 20/03/59; FCO 1994; Paris 1996; Hanoi 1999; Band A2; m 1984 Lisa Nelson (1d 1984).

Painting, Julia, MBE (1993); Baghdad since January 2005; Born 24/04/60; FCO 1981; Prague 1983; Africa/Middle East Floater 1985; South East Asia Floater 1987; FCO 1989; Tallinn 1991; FCO 1992; Milan 1994; HM Consul Naples 1995; Second Secretary FCO 1997; First Secretary FCO 1998; Deputy Head of Mission Lusaka 2001.

Pakes, Stuart Murray; FCO since June 2002; Born 08/05/49; FO 1967; FCO 1968; Aden 1970; Anguilla 1973; Reykjavik 1973; East Berlin 1976; FCO 1977; Madrid 1981; Cairo 1984; FCO 1987; Second Secretary 1989; Accra 1990; Abu Dhabi 1994; First Secretary 1998; Islamabad 1998; Band C5; m 1972 Linda Anne Rawlings (2d 1977, 1981; 1s 1984).

Palmer, Andrew David; ECO Dubai since July 2003; Born 21/01/76; FCO (HCS) 1994; Transferred to Diplomatic Service 2000; World Wide Floater Duties 2000; Band B3.

Palmer, John Benjamin Oswald; FCO since October 2004; Born 26/08/74; Band C4.

Pankhurst, Andrea Jane; FCO since November 2004; Born 27/05/65; OGD 1995; FCO 2001; Kuala Lumpur 2003; Band B3; m 2003 Jeff Relf.

Pankhurst, Donia Lee; Floater Duties since July 2002; Born 27/05/65; House of Commons 1991-97; FCO 1997; Geneva (UKMIS) 1998; Band B3.

Parfitt, Alan Frank, MBE (1997); SUPL since October 1998; Born 06/08/66; Senior Research Officer FCO 1989; Vienna (UKDEL) 1994.

Parham, Philip John; FCO since September 2003; Born 14/08/60; FCO 1993; Private Secretary to the Parliamentary Under-Secretary of State 1995; First Secretary (Chancery) Washington 1996; Director Trade and Investment Promotion, Riyadh 2000; m 1985 Kasia Giedroyc (2d 1986, 1994; 5s 1988, 1989, 1990, 1992, 1996).

Parish, Colin; Pristina since September 2002; Born 27/11/43; Royal Navy 1961-70; FCO 1970; Phnom Penh 1973; Accra 1974; SUPL 1978; FCO 1982; Belgrade 1986; Consul (Commercial) Jedda 1990; Second Secretary FCO 1995; Budapest 1997; m (1) 1966 Carole Grace (diss 1978); (2) 1978 Fairroligh Janet Lee Syme (2s 1985, 1989).

Parish, Paul Edward; FCO since March 2002; Born 10/08/63; FCO 1983; Vienna 1986; FCO 1989; SUPL 1992; Second Secretary FCO 1995; Second Secretary (Bilateral) Bonn 1998; Second Secretary Berlin 1999; Band C4.

Parker, Cindy; Third Secretary (Consular) Islamabad since March 2003; Born 01/02/72; FCO 1997; T/D Third Secretary Tashkent 2000; Vice-Consul Bogotá 2000; Band C4.

Parker, Katherine Clare (known as Katy); Management Officer Rangoon since May 2005; Born 14/07/70; FCO 1988; Manila 2001; Band C4; ptnr, Steve Dolan.

Parker, Lyn; HM Ambassador The Hague since September 2005; Born 25/11/52; FCO 1978; Second later First Secretary Athens 1980; FCO 1984; Counsellor on loan to the Cabinet Office 1989; Counsellor and Head of Chancery New Delhi 1992; Counsellor (Political) Brussels (UKREP) 1995; Counsellor FCO 1999; British High Commissioner Nicosia 2001; m 1991 Jane Elizabeth Walker (2d 1993, 1996).

Parker, Nigel Denis; Legal Counsellor FCO since February 2001; Born 25/08/61; Called to the Bar, Middle Temple 1985; Assistant Legal Adviser FCO 1988; Legal Adviser Bridgetown 1995; Assistant Legal Adviser FCO 1998.

Parker, Nigel Graham; Geneva (UKMIS) since April 2000; Born 13/09/56; FCO 1982; Kingston 1985; FCO 1988; Budapest 1990; Band C4; m 1983 Paula Northwood (1s 1987; 1d 1991).

Parker, Rod; Second Secretary Vienna since August 2004; Born 14/11/60; FCO 1996; Peking 2000; Baghdad 2003; Band C4; m 1981 Bernadette Corr (2d 1987, 1991).

Parker, Susan Caroline; FCO since June 1993; Born 01/07/63; FCO 1985; Brussels (UKREP) 1987; FCO 1988; Vienna 1990; Band A2.

Parker-Brennan, Michael; Abuja since March 2004; Born 30/05/52; Royal Corps of Transport 1967-92; FCO 1992; Helsinki 1992; Bucharest 1993; Pretoria 1996; Moscow 1997; FCO 1999; Band B3; m (1) 1982 Catherine Mary Parker (diss); (2) 1988 Carmen Dorina.

Parkins, David Alan; FCO since August 1997; Born 07/05/64; GPO 1980 - 84; FCO 1984; Third Secretary Nairobi 1989; FCO 1993; Third Secretary Bucharest 1994; Band D6; m 1991 Diane Reed (2s 1992, 1994).

Parkinson, Guy Paul; Second Secretary (Commercial) Montevideo since April 2002; Born 05/06/70; FCO 1989; Budapest 1992; Moscow 1995; Floater Duties 2000; Band B3; m 2002 Romina Rodriguez del Puerto.

Parkinson, Howard, CVO (1998); High Commissioner Maputo since December 2003; Born 29/03/48; BOT 1967; FCO 1969; LA Floater 1972; Tegucigalpa 1974; Buenos Aires 1975; Second Secretary 1977; Maputo 1978; Second later First Secretary FCO 1981; First Secretary (Commercial) Lisbon 1985; First Secretary on loan to British Gas 1989; First Secretary FCO 1991; Consul-General and Counsellor (Management) Washington 1994; Counsellor (Commercial) Kuala Lumpur 1997; Deputy High Commissioner Mumbai 2001; m 1974 Linda Wood (1d 1979; 1s 1982).

Parsons, Alexander Colin; Abu Dhabi since September 2004; Born 26/03/73; FCO 1997; Second Secretary (Political) Santiago 1999; Second Secretary FCO 2001; First Secretary (Political) Nicosia 2003; Band D6.

Parsons, Sarah Anne Pascale; FCO since November 2002; Born 22/10/74; Band C4.

Parton, Charles William, OBE (1995); Counsellor (Political) Nicosia since December 2003; Born 23/03/56; FCO 1979; Language Training Hong Kong 1982; Second Secretary FCO 1983; First Secretary (Economic) Peking 1985; First Secretary FCO 1987; First Secretary Joint Liaison Group Hong Kong 1990; Counsellor FCO 1994; Counsellor Kabul 2002; m 1983 Charmian Constance Denman (1d 1987; 1s 1990).

Partridge, Andrew Warren; Third Secretary (Economic/Commercial) New Delhi since August 2003; Born 26/04/68; FCO 1986; Islamabad 1989; Moscow 1992; FCO 1995; SUPL 1997; Third Secretary Vienna 2000; SUPL 2003; Band B3; m 1988 Margaret Robertson (1s 1996; 1d 1998).

Partridge, Diane Freda; Deputy Head of Mission Antananarivo since June 2002; Born 29/11/44; OECD Paris 1966; Yaoundé 1969; Lagos 1970; Rio de Janeiro 1971; FCO 1972; Antananarivo 1974; FCO 1976; Buenos Aires 1977; FCO 1979; Brasilia 1981; FCO 1985; Third Secretary (Aid) Belmopan 1989; Third Secretary ATTC Taipei 1993; FCO 1995; Second Secretary (Commercial) Luanda 1999; T/D Durban 2001; Band C4.

Partridge, Margaret (née Robertson), MBE (1995); Second Secretary (Immigration) New Delhi since February 2003; Born 03/03/66; FCO 1986; Islamabad 1989; Vice-Consul Moscow 1992; FCO 1995; Vice-Consul Muscat 1997; SUPL 2000; Band C4; m 1988 Andrew Warren Partridge (1s 1996; 1d 1998).

Pasquill, Derek James; FCO since November 2001; Born 11/01/59; HCS 1984; FCO 1986; Kampala 1988; Maseru 1990; FCO 1993; Vice-Consul Abu Dhabi 1997; m 2002 Nony Verioti.

Patel, Shofiya; FCO since January 2004; Born 03/02/69; DSS 1988; FCO 1990; Canberra 1992; FCO 1995; Riga 1996; Floater Duties 2000; Dushanbe 2002; Band B3.

Patel, Vaishali; FCO since March 2003; Born 28/03/74; Home Office 2000; Band B3; ptnr, Bruce McMahon.

Paterson, Annabel Christina Mary; Second Secretary Skopje since March 2005; Born 19/05/79; FCO 2003; Band C4.

Paterson, Fiona; Geneva (UKDIS) since November 2004; Born 06/04/51; FCO 1977; Bogotá 1979; Ottawa 1983; Second Secretary FCO 1987; Second Secretary (Chancery/Information) Bangkok 1989; Second Secretary (Information) later First Secretary (Science and Technology) Paris 1990; First Secretary FCO 1994; First Secretary (Political) Lisbon 1999; Band D7.

Paterson, Ian Robert; Second Secretary (Political/Economic) Nairobi since April 2002; Born 22/09/62; FCO Communications 1986; FCO 1996; Third Secretary (Political) Berne 1998; Band C4; m Diane (2d 1992, 1997).

Paterson, Lynne Kathryn; Wellington since September 2001; Born 22/05/63; FCO 1999; Band A2.

Paterson, Robert Ralston; FCO since January 2005; Born 31/01/74; FCO 2000; Second Secretary (Political/Economic) Abuja 2002; Band C4.

Paterson, William Neil Carlton; Consul-General Frankfurt since April 2001; Born 19/10/50; FCO 1978; Sofia 1980; FCO 1981; Düsseldorf 1983; Second Secretary (Commercial/Aid) Yaoundé 1986; Second Secretary FCO 1989; Consul (Commercial) Montreal 1992; Consul-General Stuttgart 1997; m 1975 Margaret Christine Schmidt-Feuerheerd (1s 1976; 3d 1978, 1981, 1983).

Patey, William Charters, CMG (2005); HM Ambassador Baghdad since June 2005; Born 11/07/53; FCO 1975; MECAS 1977; Abu Dhabi 1978; Second Secretary (Commercial) Tripoli

1981; First Secretary FCO 1984; First Secretary (Chancery) Canberra 1988; First Secretary later Counsellor FCO 1992; Deputy Head of Mission Riyadh 1995; Head of Middle East Department, FCO 1999; HM Ambassador Khartoum 2002; m 1978 Vanessa Carol Morrell (2s 1987, 1991).

Patrick, Andrew Silas; Deputy Head of Mission Pretoria since February 2004; Born 28/02/66; FCO 1988; Third later Second Secretary (Chancery) Nicosia 1991; First Secretary T/D Brussels (UKDEL) 1995; FCO 1996; Assistant Private Secretary to Secretary of State FCO 1998; FCO 2000.

Patrick, Claire Mary Angela; FCO since March 2003; Born 17/11/78; Band C4.

Patterson, Ernest Mark; Plymouth since November 2003; Born 22/02/69; FCO 1989; Vienna 1989; Addis Ababa 1996; Floater Duties 1998; Sarajevo 2000; Band B3.

Patterson, Hugh William Grant; FCO since August 2004; Born 17/10/50; FCO 1979; First Secretary BMG Berlin 1980; First Secretary FCO 1984; First Secretary (Head of Chancery) and Consul Guatemala City 1987; First Secretary FCO 1990; First Secretary later Counsellor Caracas 1992; Counsellor FCO 1995; Counsellor Berne 2000; m 1981 Philippa Anne Colbatch Clark (1d 1986; 1s 1997).

Pattison, Stephen Dexter; Director (International Security), FCO since 2004; Born 24/12/53; FCO 1981; Nicosia 1983; FCO 1986; First Secretary (Chancery) Washington 1989; FCO 1994; Director of Trade Promotion and Consul-General Warsaw 1997; Head of United Nations Department, FCO 2000; On secondment to Harvard 2003; m 1987 Helen Andrea Chaoushis 1987 (1d 1993).

Patton, Geoffrey Joseph Laurence; FCO since January 2003; Born 26/04/62; MOD 1985 - 86; FCO 1986; Warsaw 1989; Floater Training 1991; Floater Duties 1991; Colombo 1994; FCO 1998; T/D Bombay 2000; Plymouth, Montserrat 2000; Band C4.

Paver, James Edward Luke, MVO (1994); First Secretary FCO since September 2001; Born 02/10/63; FCO 1991; Third Secretary (Press and Public Affairs) Moscow 1994; Second Secretary FCO 1997; Second Secretary (Political) Brussels (UKDEL) 1998; m 1992 Rebecca Jane Ash (3d 1993, 1995, 1997; 1s 2005).

Pavey, Emma; Nicosia since August 2004; Born 30/01/79; FCO 1997; Abuja 2002; Band B3; (1s 1998).

Pavis, Susan Mary (née Hartland); Brussels (UKDEL NATO) since August 1999; Born 16/04/64; FCO 1983; Washington 1986; Riyadh 1988; FCO 1991; Vice-Consul Singapore 1995; Band C4; m (1) 1985 Neil Cronin (diss 1994) (1s 1993); (2) 2002 Christopher Pavis (1d 2003).

Paxman, Timothy Giles, LVO (1989); HM Ambassador Mexico City since October 2005; Born 15/11/51; Department of Environment/Transport 1974; First Secretary Brussels (UKREP) 1980; FCO 1985; First Secretary and Head of Chancery Singapore 1989; Counsellor on loan to the Cabinet Office 1992; Full-Time Language Training 1994; Counsellor (Commercial/Economic) Rome 1994; Counsellor (Political) Brussels (UKREP) 1999; Minister Paris 2002; m 1980 Segolene Claude Marie (3d 1982, 1984, 1988).

Peacock, Paula Geraldine (née Hackett); SUPL since May 2004; Born 01/01/65; FCO 1990; Third Secretary Nairobi 1993; Full-Time Language Training 1996; Vice-Consul Prague 1997; FCO 2000; SUPL 2002; Second Secretary (Immigration) Colombo 2003; Band C4; m 1997 David Laurance Peacock (1d 2002).

Peake, Philippa Jane; SUPL since December 2000; Born 30/03/64; FCO 1990; Moscow 1993; UKDEL NATO 1996; FCO 1999; Band A2; m 1997 Dominic Alister Stephens.

Pearce, Andrew John; Counsellor and Deputy Head of Mission Bangkok since December 2003; Born 07/10/60; FCO 1983; Third later Second Secretary Bangkok 1985; First Secretary FCO 1988; First Secretary (Chancery) Tel Aviv 1992; First Secretary (Economic) Pretoria 1996; Counsellor and Deputy Head of Mission Bucharest 2000; m 1986 Pornpun Pathumvivatana (1s 1989; 1d 1994).

Pearce, David Avery; FCO since April 2003; Born 17/02/52; FCO 1971; New York (UKMIS) 1973; Rome 1976; FCO 1979; Dhaka 1982; FCO 1986; Second Secretary Paris 1987; Second Secretary and Deputy Head of Mission Libreville 1990; Consul Douala 1991; Deputy Head of Mission and Consul-General Sana'a and Aden 1996; HM Consul-General Durban 2000; m (1) 1973 Anne Matthews (dec'd 1986) (1d 1980; 1s 1984); (2) 1988 Virginia Martin (diss 2001) (2d 1991, 1995; 1s 1993); (3) 2001 Randa Al Harazi (1d 2001).

Pearce, Howard John Stredder, CVO (1993); Governor Stanley and Commissioner for South Georgia and Sandwich Islands since December 2002; Born 13/04/49; FCO 1972; Buenos Aires 1975; First Secretary FCO 1978; First Secretary and Head of Chancery Nairobi 1983; First Secretary later Counsellor FCO 1987; Language Training 1990; Deputy Head of Mission Budapest 1991; On loan at Harvard University 1994; Head of Central European Department 1996; British High Commissioner Valletta 1999; m 2004 Caroline Dorothée Thomée.

Pearey, (Dorothy) Jane, MBE (1980); FCO since September 1999; Born 31/05/45; OECD Paris 1969; Moscow 1972; FCO 1973; Belgrade 1977; FCO 1980; New York (UKMIS) 1983; Seconded to NATO 1984; Seconded to 21st Century Trust 1988; FCO 1989 (Second Secretary 1991); Second Secretary (Aid) Harare 1995; On secondment to DFID (Harare) 1998.

Pearey, David Dacre; High Commissioner Lilongwe since December 2004; Born 15/07/48;

On secondment from MOD to Ankara 1979; First Secretary FCO 1983; First Secretary and Head of Chancery Kampala 1987; First Secretary later Counsellor FCO 1990; Counsellor (Commercial/Economic) Lagos 1995; Deputy High Commissioner Karachi 2000; m 1996 Susan Anne Knowles (1d 2000).

Pearson, Frances; Prague since October 2002; Born 17/07/54; FCO 1987; Washington 1988; Brussels (UKREP) 1991; Moscow 1994; FCO 1996; Buenos Aires 1998; Band B3.

Pearson, John Anthony; Deputy Head of Mission Montevideo since October 2005; Born 28/04/68; FCO 1990; Madrid 1992; FCO 1994; Brasilia 1996; FCO 2000; SUPL 2001; FCO 2002; Band D6; m 2002 Leyla-Claude Werleigh.

Pearson, Julian Christopher; Tirana since December 2001; Born 08/07/69; FCO 1990; Third Secretary Prague 1992; Third Secretary Kinshasa 1995; FCO 1998; Minsk 1998.

Pearson, Ruth Alexandra (née Stephens); SUPL since February 2002; Born 30/01/71; FCO 1993; Full-Time Language Training 1995; Budapest 1996; Second Secretary (Political) Brussels (UKREP) 1999; Band C4; m 1996 Simon Mark Pearson (1s 2000; 1d 2002).

Peart, Christopher John Stuttle; Moscow since January 2002; Born 23/08/75; FCO 1998; Band A2.

Pease, Simon Robert Hellier; Assistant Director, Personnel Management FCO since September 2001; Born 20/02/52; FCO 1972; Ibadan 1975; SUPL 1978; FCO 1981 (Second Secretary 1982); Second later First Secretary UKDEL CDE Stockholm 1984; First Secretary FCO 1986; First Secretary and Head of Chancery Rabat 1988; First Secretary later Counsellor FCO 1992; Deputy Head of Mission and Consul-General Tel Aviv 1997; m 1975 Catherine Elizabeth Bayley (1d 1981; 1s 1983).

Peate, David James, OBE (1989); First Secretary Turks and Caicos Islands since July 2001; Born 02/07/44; FO 1964; DSAO 1965; Delhi 1967; Warsaw 1971; Second Secretary Lomé 1972; FCO 1975; Melbourne 1978; FCO 1983; First Secretary Brussels 1984; First Secretary (Commercial) East Berlin 1989; First Secretary FCO 1993; Deputy Consul-General Milan 1996; m 1971 Siri Jean Jessica Elizabeth Zetter (2d 1973, 1990; 2s 1975, 1986).

Peers, Gary Clive; Madrid since July 2002; Born 06/12/58; FCO 1985; Third Secretary Bonn 1990; Third Secretary Pretoria 1995; FCO 1997; Band C5; m 1979 Pamela Jane Tailby (1d 1981; 2s 1983, 1985).

Peers, Tracy Ann (née Rose); Taipei since September 2002; Born 29/11/63; FCO 2000; Band A2; m 2004 David Peers.

Peirce, Robert Nigel; On secondment to Financial Dynamics Ltd, Washington since September 2004; Born 18/03/55; FCO 1977; Language Training Cambridge 1978; Language Training Hong Kong 1979; Second later First Secretary (Chancery) Peking 1980; First Secretary FCO 1983; On loan to the Cabinet Office 1985; On secondment as Deputy Political Adviser to Hong Kong Government 1986; Assistant Private Secretary to the Secretary of State 1988; First Secretary (Chancery) New York (UKMIS) 1990; Political Adviser Hong Kong 1993; On secondment to the Royal College of Defence Studies 1998; Secretary to the Independent Commission on Policing for Northern Ireland 1998; Counsellor Washington 1999; m (1) 1978 Christina Anne Skipworth Davis (1s 1986; 1d 1988); (2) 2000 Robin Lynn Raphel (2 step d 1986, 1990).

Pendered, Jo; FCO since October 2002; Born 02/11/65; FCO 1984; Bombay 1987; Santiago 1990; FCO 1992; Athens 1996; Cape Town 1999; Dili 2001; Band C4.

Penfold, Jane Elizabeth Mary (née Govier); FCO since June 2002; Born 21/03/62; FCO 1984; Language Training 1986; Third Secretary (Commercial) Peking 1987; Vice-Consul (Management) Istanbul 1990; Presidency Liaison Officer Luxembourg 1990 (Second Secretary 1991); T/D Bangkok 1991; Second Secretary FCO 1992; Full-Time Language Training 1994; Second Secretary (Political) Sofia 1995; FCO 1998; First Secretary Dili 2000; m 1997 Nigel John Penfold.

Pengelly, Rachel Jane (née Laycock); FCO since October 2004; Born 20/05/71; FCO 1994; Second Secretary (Chancery/External) Washington 2000; Band C4; m 2000 Owen Pengelly.

Penrith, Alan Paul; FCO since 2001; Born 24/05/58; Inland Revenue 1977; FCO 1978; Mexico City 1980; Yaoundé 1983; FCO 1985; Third later Second Secretary (Political/Information) Ottawa 1988; Assistant to Governor British Virgin Islands 1993; Second later First Secretary FCO 1996; On loan to the DTI 1999; m 1982 Karen Cooper (2s 1987, 1991).

Penton-Voak, Martin Eric; First Secretary Vienna (UKDEL) since May 2001; Born 09/11/65; Third later Second Secretary FCO 1991; Moscow 1995; First Secretary FCO 1998; Band D6; m 1994 Lucy Katrina Howarth.

Percy, Michael Vivian; First Secretary FCO since July 2002; Born 09/08/50; DSAO (later FCO) 1968; Paris 1972; Brasilia 1975; Vice-Consul Budapest 1977; FCO 1980; Third Secretary (Commercial) Quito 1983; Third Secretary (Management) Warsaw 1987; FCO 1989; Second Secretary 1991; Deputy Head of Mission Riga 1993; Second Secretary FCO 1994; Second Secretary British Trade International 1998; Band C5; m 1972 Susan Roslyn Penrose (2d 1974, 1981; 1s 1977).

Perkins, Jacqueline Louise (née Gage); Bahrain since October 2003; Born 03/10/64; FCO 1989; Second Secretary 1990; Language Training Cairo 1991; Second Secretary (Chancery/Information) Abu Dhabi 1992; First Secretary FCO 1995; SUPL

1996; First Secretary Cairo 1999; SUPL 2001; First Secretary Cairo 2001; m 1991 Stuart Blair Perkins (1s 1996; 1d 2001).

Perks, Adam Cecil; Kingston since October 2004; Born 03/05/66; FCO (HCS) 1984; Kuwait 1988; FCO 1991; Third Secretary (Consular) Ottawa 1991; Third Secretary FCO 1994; Vice-Consul Luxembourg 1998; Second Secretary (Immigration) Moscow 2002; Band C4; m 1990 Nicola Rose Wardle (2s 1992, 1996; 1d 1998).

Perry, Christopher Ian; Lagos since June 2002; Born 27/05/70; FCO 1990; Brussels (UKREP) 1993; Paris 1995; New Delhi 1999; Band B3; m (1) 1992 Charlotte Dawson (diss 1995) (1d 1992); (2) 1995 Lesa Jayne Elliot (3d 1996, 1997, 1998).

Perry, Thomas Ian; Consul/Management Officer Bratislava since August 2004; Born 29/03/55; MOD 1972; FCO 1974; New York (UKMIS) 1976; Africa/Middle East Floater 1979; T/D Dubai 1979; Jakarta 1981; FCO 1983; The Hague 1986; FCO 1988; T/D Warsaw 1990; T/D Dar es Salaam 1990; Islamabad 1991; FCO 1995; Jerusalem 1998; T/D Kabul 2001; FCO 2001; Band C4; m 1982 Jeannie Bell (2s 1992, 1995).

Persighetti, Stephen Victor; FCO since March 2002; Born 31/03/56; FCO 1975; Moscow 1977; Beirut 1978; Tokyo 1981; Floater Duties 1983; On loan to the ODA 1985; Third Secretary (Aid) Jakarta 1988; Second Secretary FCO 1991; Second Secretary (Political/Aid) Cape Town 1996; SUPL 1998; Band C5; m 1992 Rozany Deen.

Pert, David John; Consul Düsseldorf since November 2004; Born 21/01/68; Royal Navy 1987-94; FCO 1994; Third Secretary (Political) Sofia 1996; Kiev 2001; m 1990 Christine Walsh (2s 1991, 1994).

Petch, Eleanor; Prague since August 2001; Born 26/01/77; FCO 1998; Full-Time Language Training 2000; Band C4.

Peters, Mark Crispin; FCO since November 2000; Born 07/06/64; Royal Engineers 1987-94; FCO 1994; Second Secretary (Chancery) Oslo 1996.

Peters, Siobhan; SUPL since April 2004; Born 27/06/70; FCO 1996; Full-Time Language Training 1998; Second Secretary (Economic) later First Secretary (Environment) Beijing 1999; FCO 2003; Band D6; m Mark Davies (1d 1999; 1s 2001).

Petherbridge, Richard Sydney; FCO since January 1996; Born 23/08/55; DHSS 1975; FCO 1980; Nicosia 1982; Seoul 1985; FCO 1987; Prague 1990; Riyadh 1992; Band A2; m 1982 Pauline Joan Mulvey (1s 1984; 1d 1986).

Pethick, Mark Julian; FCO since January 2001; Born 03/04/68; FCO 1990; Karachi 1993; Deputy Head of Mission Minsk 1997; Band C5.

Pettigrew, Marina, MVO (2004); Third Secretary (Visits) Paris since April 2001; Born 17/01/64; FCO 1984; Berne 1986; Budapest 1989; Tel Aviv 1991; Floater Duties 1997; Band B3; m 1999 Mark Pettigrew (1d 2000).

Phillips, Alison Jane (née Francis), OBE (1991); SUPL since January 2001; Born 18/04/56; FCO 1974; New York (UKMIS) 1981; Second Secretary FCO 1982; First Secretary Paris 1986; First Secretary FCO 1990; Band D6; m 1978 Richard Charles Jonathan Phillips, QC.

Phillips, Linda Ann; SUPL since August 2003; Born 17/01/56; FCO 1995; Accra 1997; Washington 2000; Band A2.

Phillips, Patricia Ruth; Deputy Head of Mission Amman since June 2004; Born 11/03/62; MAFF 1984; First Secretary (Trade Policy/Agriculture) Washington 1992; First Secretary FCO 1997; Counsellor (Economic/Trade/Investment) The Hague 2002.

Phillips, Quentin James Kitson; Consul (Political Affairs) Istanbul since January 2004; Born 20/10/63; FCO 1986; Second Secretary (Information) Budapest 1989; Second later First Secretary FCO 1992; First Secretary (Political) Moscow 1995; First Secretary FCO 1996; First Secretary (Political) Kiev 1997; First Secretary FCO 2000; Band D6; m 1989 Gillian Lynne Murray (2d 1993, 1996; 1s 1999).

Phillips, Russell James; Deputy Head of Mission Luanda since June 2005; Born 24/02/64; FCO 1983; Georgetown 1985; Khartoum 1988; FCO 1991; Bombay 1995; Abuja 1998; FCO 2001; Band C5.

Phillips, Tom Richard Vaughan, CMG; UK Special Representative for Afghanistan, August 2002 and Director (South Asia and Afghanistan) since January 2003; Born 21/06/50; DHSS 1977; FCO 1983; First Secretary Harare 1985; First Secretary FCO 1988; Counsellor, Consul-General and Deputy Head of Mission Tel Aviv 1990; Counsellor (External) Washington 1993; Counsellor FCO 1997; High Commissioner Kampala 2000; m 1986 Anne Renee Marie de la Motte (2s 1987, 1989).

Phillpotts, Claire Louise; FCO since September 2003; Born 15/07/81; Band C4.

Philpott, Hugh Stanley; Deputy Head of Mission Muscat since October 2001; Born 24/01/61; FCO 1980; Oslo 1982; Budapest 1985; Language Training 1987; Third Secretary (Commercial) Baghdad 1988; FCO 1990 (Second Secretary 1992); Second Secretary (Political/Military) Washington 1993; On loan to DFID 1997; First Secretary FCO 1999; Band D6; m 1984 Janine Frederica Rule (1d 1998).

Philpott, Janine Frederica; FCO since September 2004; Born 30/01/60; FCO 1980; Brussels (UKDEL NATO) 1982; Budapest 1985; FCO 1986; Baghdad 1988; FCO 1990; Third Secretary (Press) Washington 1993; FCO 1998; Third Secretary (Commercial) Muscat 2001; Band C5; m 1984 Hugh Stanley Philpott (1d 1998).

Pickering, Helen Mary; FCO since January 2004; Born 10/07/64; FCO 1986; Moscow 1988; Algiers 1989; Geneva 1990; FCO 1993; Second Secretary (EU) Warsaw 1997; FCO 2001; SUPL 2003; Band D6; m 1996 James Owen (1d 2003).

Pickering, Sara Elizabeth; FCO since January 2002; Born 22/04/67; FCO 1988; Vice-Consul Budapest 1991; FCO 1992; Islamabad 1995; Second Secretary (Commercial) Lagos 1998; Band C5; m 1992 Andrew John Kirkpatrick.

Pickett, Jane Louise (née Houghton), MBE (1994); SUPL since August 2003; Born 05/12/64; FCO 1984; Santiago 1987; FCO 1991; Bogotá 1993; FCO 1995; Band C5; m 1998 Peter Derek Pickett.

Pickup, Lawrence; FCO since October 2003; Born 10/09/52; FCO 1976; Dar es Salaam 1980; Dubai 1982; Floater Duties 1986; On loan to the DTI 1989; FCO/DTI 1991; Consul Warsaw 1993; Deputy Head of Mission Phnom Penh 1997; Deputy Head of Mission Khartoum 2000; T/D Amman 2003; Band C5.

Pierce, Karen Elizabeth; Head of Eastern Adriatic Department, FCO since November 2002; Born 23/09/59; FCO 1981; Language Training 1984; Tokyo 1985; FCO 1987; Private Secretary to the Ambassador Washington 1991 (First Secretary 1994); FCO 1996; Counsellor FCO 2001; m 1987 Charles Fergusson Roxburgh (2s 1991, 1997).

Pigott, Carsten Orthöfer; Consul-General Jedda since June 2003; Born 31/05/53; FCO 1972; Lagos 1975; Language Training MECAS 1977; Language Training FCO 1978; Third Secretary (Commercial) Khartoum 1979; Second Secretary (Commercial) Tripoli 1982; Second Secretary FCO 1984; First Secretary (Chancery) Peking 1987; First Secretary FCO 1991; Deputy Head of Mission Addis Ababa 1993; First Secretary (Chancery) New Delhi 1997; Counsellor FCO 1998; Full-Time Language Training 2002; m 1976 Susan Kathlyn Pugh (1d 1981; 1s 1983).

Pike, Andrew Kerry; Consul New York since December 2003; Born 06/06/64; Dept of Transport 1982; FCO 1984; Sana'a 1985; Warsaw 1990; FCO 1993; Second Secretary (Chancery and Information) Dublin 1998; SUPL 2002; Band D6.

Pike, Richard Mark; FCO since September 2004; Born 28/08/80; Band B3.

Pilling, Jonathan James; First Secretary (Technical Works) Nairobi since November 2004; Born 25/08/75; FCO 2002; Band C5.

Pilmore-Bedford, Jeremy Patrick; FCO since July 2004; Born 22/08/67; FCO 1990; Singapore 1993; Full-Time Language Training 1995; Third Secretary (Aid) Moscow 1995; FCO 1998; Second Secretary (Economic) Kuala Lumpur 2001; Band D6; m Amanda Joanne West (1d 1997; 1s 1999).

Pinsent, Guy Hume; FCO since March 2005; Born 07/03/76; FCO 2000; Full-Time Language Training 2002; Second Secretary Warsaw 2003; Band C4.

Pinson, David Richard; FCO since October 2004; Born 07/05/77; FCO 2000; Full-Time Language Training FCO 2002; Second Secretary Kabul 2003; Band C4.

Pinto, Alison Louise (née Johnson); SUPL since January 2005; FCO 1989; Vice-Consul Tokyo 1992; Third Secretary (Chancery) Berlin 1995; FCO 1997; SUPL 2002; FCO 2004; Band D6; m 2001 Andrew Pinto (1d 2003).

Pisa, Adrian; FCO since February 2005; Born 13/03/72; FCO 2001; Second Secretary New York (UKMIS) 2002; Band C4.

Pitchford, Wendy (née Tivey); Tirana since November 2003; Born 20/07/61; FCO 1995; Copenhagen 1997; Accra 2000; Band A2; m 1999 Colin Pitchford.

Pitts, Barbara Anne, MVO (1989); Copenhagen since October 2000; Born 26/01/54; FCO 1975; Lagos 1975; Moscow 1977; FCO 1979; Nairobi 1981; FCO 1984; Kuala Lumpur 1987; FCO 1990; New Delhi 1997; Band B3.

Plank, John; FCO since January 2003; Born 03/10/64; FCO 1986; Second Secretary (Political) Pretoria 2000; Band C4; m 1997 Corinne Lambshead (1s 2001).

Plant, Michael Geoffrey; Deputy Consul-General Boston since May 2000; Born 12/10/46; Post Office 1964; DSAO 1966; Moscow 1969; Rabat 1970; Peking 1973; Brussels (JAO) 1975; FCO 1978; Banjul 1980; Los Angeles 1984; Second Secretary FCO 1987; Second Secretary (Commercial/Consular) Al Khobar 1990; First Secretary (Management) Yerevan, Tbilisi and Ashgabat 1995; FCO 1998; Band C5; m 1971 Hayfa Theodora Massouh (2d 1972, 1975).

Plater, Stephen James; Consul-General Munich since December 2003; Born 23/01/54; FCO 1976; Second Secretary Tokyo 1978; Second later First Secretary FCO 1982; First Secretary and Head of Chancery Vienna (UKDEL MBFR) 1987; First Secretary Vienna (UKDEL CACN) 1989; First Secretary (Commercial) Tokyo 1990; First Secretary FCO 1995; m 1980 Keiko Kurata (1d 1990).

Platt, David Watson; New Delhi since October 2001; Born 09/04/54; Inland Revenue 1972; FCO 1973; Beirut 1977; Brasilia 1980; Sofia 1981; FCO 1983; Dhaka 1985; Bridgetown 1988; FCO 1992; Dubai 1997; Band B3.

Platt, Janet Elizabeth (née Howells); SUPL since July 2001; Born 26/03/61; Brussels (NATO) 1982; Washington 1985; FCO 1987; Anguilla 1988; FCO 1991; Brussels (UKREP) 1992; Band A2; m 1988 Philip Charles Platt (2s 1987, 1990; 1d 1997).

Plumb, Michael Barry George; Deputy High Commissioner Port Louis since January 2003; Born 16/05/45; DSAO 1965; Kampala 1968; Lahore 1971; FCO 1975; Washington 1977; Canberra 1979; Baghdad 1982; FCO 1986; Jakarta 1990; FCO 1995; Deputy High Commissioner Port Moresby 1997; T/D Jakarta 2001; Management

Officer Kuala Lumpur 2002; m 1968 Linda Wills Gledhill (1s 1972; 1d 1975).

Plumbly, Sir Derek John, KCMG (2001), CMG (1991); HM Ambassador Cairo since September 2003; Born 15/05/48; FCO 1972; Reporting Officer New York 1972; FCO 1973; MECAS 1973; Second later First Secretary Jedda 1975; First Secretary Cairo 1977; FCO 1980; First Secretary (Commercial) Washington 1984; Counsellor and Head of Chancery Riyadh 1988; Counsellor and Head of Chancery New York (UKMIS) 1992; AUS FCO 1996; HM Ambassador Riyadh 2000; m 1979 Nadia Youssef Gohar (1d 1983; 2s 1985, 1987).

Pocock, Dr Andrew John; High Commissioner Dar es Salaam since September 2003; Born 23/08/55; FCO 1981; Second later First Secretary (Commercial) Lagos 1983; First Secretary FCO 1986; First Secretary (Chancery) Washington 1988; First Secretary FCO 1992; Counsellor on loan to the Royal College of Defence Studies 1996; Deputy High Commissioner Canberra 1997; Head of African Department (Southern) FCO 2001; m (1) 1976 Dayalini Pathmanathan (diss); (2) 1995 Julie Eyre-Wilson.

Polatajko, Mark Alexander; FCO since June 2002; Born 16/10/70; FCO 1991; Cairo 1995; New Delhi 1998; Band C4; m 1998 Chloe Robson (1d 2000; 1s 2003).

Poll, Gillian Anne (née Smith); FCO since September 2002; Born 30/04/58; HCS 1976; FCO 1985; Brussels 1987; Brussels (UKREP) 1990; FCO 1991; SUPL 1994; Band A2; m 1988 Christopher John Poll (dec'd 2005) (1d 1994; 1s 1998).

Pollard, Guy Sephton; SUPL since June 2003; Born 03/06/71; FCO 1991; Islamabad 1995; Third later Second Secretary (Political) Bratislava 1998; Band C4; ptnr, Catherine Louise Nicol (1d 2000; 1s 2002).

Pond, John; Riga since January 2003; Born 22/05/52; Armed Forces 1969-92; FCO 1995; Brussels (UKDEL NATO) 1997; Band A2; m 1973 Catherine Herbert (1s 1971).

Ponsonby, Gareth James; Kabul since April 2005; Born 25/05/70; FCO 1991; Islamabad 1996; FCO 2000; Band B3; m 1995 Natalie Lalanie Beverley Yeo (1d 2000).

Poole, Christopher George Robert; Deputy Head of Mission and Consul La Paz since June 2003; Born 19/04/52; FCO 1970; Algiers 1973; Brasilia 1974; Rio de Janeiro 1976; Freetown 1978; Paris 1981; Kinshasa 1984; FCO 1988; Third later Second Secretary Antananarivo 1991; Vice-Consul (Commercial/Information) São Paulo 1995; FCO 1998; T/D Second Secretary (Political) Freetown 2000; FCO 2000; Band C5; m 1977 Maria Madalena Gomes Ferreira.

Poole, Christopher James, MBE (1987); Deputy Head of Mission Beirut since July 2003; Born 24/12/46; CRO 1964; FCO 1968; Georgetown 1969; Africa Floater 1969; St Lucia 1971; Bridgetown 1973; FCO 1976; Munich 1979; FCO 1982; Second Secretary Beirut 1985; Second Secretary Luxembourg 1987; EC Monitor Mission Former Yugoslavia 1992; Deputy Head of Mission Zagreb 1993; Deputy Head of Mission Jerusalem 1995; First Secretary FCO 1996; First Secretary (Commercial) Sarajevo 1998; SUPL (OSCE Albania) 2001; T/D Deputy Head of Mission Tirana 2002; m (1) 1973 Lillian Hodgson (diss) (2d 1979, 1980); (2) 1987 Marilyn Kathleen Povey (diss 1996); (3) 1996 Lynne Diana Merrin.

Pooley, Nigel Arthur, CMG; FCO since August 2001; Born 12/11/61; FCO 1991; Third later Second Secretary (Chancery) Vienna 1994; First Secretary FCO 1998; On secondment to Oxfam 2000; m 1985 Helena Falle (3s 1986, 1991, 1994; 1d 1988).

Porter, Gillian Sarah; FCO since August 2003; Born 07/04/66; FCO 1988; Moscow 1991; Manila 1993; New York (UKMIS) 2000; SUPL 2002; Band A2; m 2004 Steve Knight (1d 2002).

Porter, Neil David; FCO since February 2003; Born 14/04/63; FCO 1982; Riyadh 1985; Budapest 1989; FCO 1992; Third Secretary Johannesburg 1996; Valletta 1999; Band B3; m 1986 Gajetana Dominica Maria de Wit (3s 1988, 1992, 1997; 1d 1989).

Portman, Giles Matthew; First Secretary (External) Brussels (UKREP) since March 2003; Born 25/05/71; Department of Transport 1994; FCO 1995; Second Secretary (Political/Information) Prague 1998; FCO 2002; Band D6.

Potter, Richard William; Counsellor Amman since July 2004; Born 22/05/60; FCO 1983; Third later Second Secretary Riyadh 1985; Second Secretary FCO 1988; First Secretary (Information) Nicosia 1990; First Secretary FCO 1994; First Secretary Sarajevo 1995; FCO 1998; First Secretary Skopje 1999; First Secretary FCO 2002.

Potter, Rupert James; SUPL since October 2004; Born 14/11/68; FCO 1992; Amman 1995; Third Secretary (Political) Stockholm 1999; On loan to the Cabinet Office 2002; Band C4; m 1995 Juliette Wilcox (1s 1998).

Powell, David Herbert; Assistant Director (Personnel Services) FCO since September 2002; Born 29/04/52; MOD 1974; FCO 1984; First Secretary Tokyo 1988; First Secretary FCO 1992; Counsellor on loan to the Cabinet Office 1995; Political Counsellor UKDEL NATO/WEU Brussels 1997; m 1984 Gillian Mary Croft (1d 1994).

Powell, Hugh Eric; FCO since 2003 October; Born 16/02/67; FCO 1991; Second Secretary Paris 1993; First Secretary FCO 1998; Full-Time Language Training 2000; First Secretary Political (Internal) Berlin 2000; Band D6; m 1993 Catherine Claire Young (2s 1996, 1997).

Powell, Ian Francis, OBE (1995); Deputy High Commissioner Suva and HM Ambassador (non-resident) to Federal States of Micronesia, Palau and Marshall Islands since March 2003; Born 30/12/47; Commonwealth Office (later FCO) 1966; Freetown 1970; Havana 1973; FCO 1975; Stockholm 1978; Dublin 1981; Second Secretary 1983; Second Secretary FCO 1986; First Secretary 1988; First Secretary (Management/HM Consul) Kingston 1989; Deputy Head of Mission Sana'a 1994; First Secretary FCO 1995; Assistant Deputy Governor Gibraltar 1998; m 1969 Priscilla Ann Fenton (2d 1974, 1980).

Powell, Martin; FCO since April 1998; Born 21/10/46; FCO 1969; Warsaw 1973; FCO 1974; Brussels 1982; FCO 1985; Second Secretary Singapore 1988; FCO 1991; Dubai 1994; m (1) 1972 Susan Kay Bower (diss); (2) 1982 Patricia Helen Scruby (1d 1985; 1s 1987).

Powell, Nicola Julie; FCO since September 2004; Born 24/06/73; Band B3.

Powell, Richard Stephen; Deputy Head of Mission Helsinki since June 2003; Born 19/10/59; FCO 1981; Third later Second Secretary Helsinki 1983; First Secretary FCO 1988; First Secretary (Science) Tokyo 1992; CDA Imperial College London 1996; FCO 1997.

Power, Anne Maria; New York since March 2002; Born 14/08/65; FCO 1989; Strasbourg UKDEL 1992; Consulate-General Geneva 1993; Strasbourg UKDEL 1993; SUPL 1996; FCO 1999; Band C4.

Power, Carmel Angela; Copenhagen since September 2001; Born 30/10/63; FCO 1990; Third Secretary (Political) Vienna (UKDEL) 1992; Vice-Consul (Commercial) Damascus 1995; FCO 1997; Band D6.

Prentice, Christopher Norman Russell; HM Ambassador Amman since June 2002; Born 05/09/54; FCO 1977; Language Training MECAS 1978; Third later Second Secretary Kuwait 1980; First Secretary on loan to the Cabinet Office 1983; First Secretary Washington 1985; First Secretary FCO 1989; Deputy Head of Mission Budapest 1994; Counsellor FCO 1998; m 1978 Marie-Josephine (Nina) King (2s 1981, 1988; 2d 1982, 1985).

Preston, James David; Copenhagen since May 2003; Born 21/04/68; FCO 1987; Helsinki 1994; FCO 1997; Band C4; m 1992 Kim Dickinson (2s 1995, 1997).

Preston, Joseph Raymond; Deputy Head of Mission Tirana since March 2003; Born 01/06/61; FCO 1980; Dhaka 1983; Kathmandu 1985; Nicosia 1989; FCO 1993; Third Secretary (Commercial) Islamabad 1995; FCO 1999; On loan to BTI (Institute of Export) 1999; Band C5; m 1993 Sandra Elizabeth Cook.

Preston, Olivia Denise; FCO since September 2003; Born 13/07/72; Band C4.

Preston, Sandra Elizabeth (née Cook); Tirana since June 2003; Born 12/06/64; FCO 1987; Nicosia 1990; FCO 1992; Islamabad 1996; FCO 1999; Full-Time Language Training (Albanian) 2002; Band B3; m 1993 Joseph Raymond Preston.

Preston, William Edward Johnston, LVO (2004); First Secretary (Commercial) Amman since July 2004; Born 07/07/47; FCO 1965; Ankara 1969; Kinshasa 1972; FCO 1974; Rabat 1976; Oslo 1979; Second Secretary (Admin) Moscow 1983; Second Secretary FCO 1985; Second Secretary (Commercial) Port of Spain 1988; First Secretary (Commercial) Bucharest 1992; First Secretary Nicosia 1996; First Secretary FCO 2000; Head of Royal Household Secretariat FCO 2001; m 1969 Anne Kathleen Smith (1s 1974).

Price, Adrian James; Port of Spain since August 2003; Born 25/04/65; Ekaterinburg 1999; FCO 2001; Band A2; m 2000 Tatyana Arkhipova (1d 2002; 1s 2005).

Price, Andrew Haydn; First Secretary (Political) The Hague since July 2002; Born 09/11/63; MAFF 1985; FCO 1997; On attachment to Netherlands Foreign Ministry 2002; Band D6; m 1993 Amanda Kirby (2s 1995, 1998; 1d 2000).

Price, Denis Charles; Berlin since January 2002; Born 20/04/52; Royal Electrical and Mechanical Engineers 1973-95; FCO 2000; Band C4; m 1977 Jane Ann (1s 1978).

Price, Kenneth George; FCO since August 2002; Born 12/04/65; FCO 1983; Bonn 1985; Accra 1988; FCO 1991; Third Secretary (Political/Aid) Almaty 1994; World Wide Floater Duties 1997; Second Secretary FCO 1998; Deputy Head of Mission Kinshasa 2001; Band C4.

Price, Sarah Helena; FCO since April 2004; Born 04/06/66; FCO 1990; Second Secretary Helsinki (UKDEL CSCE) 1992; Second Secretary (Economic/KHF) Prague 1993; First Secretary FCO 1996; Secondment to the EU Secretariat of the Finnish Ministry for Foreign Affairs 1999; Full-Time Language Training 2000; Deputy Head of Mission Belgrade 2000.

Price, Siân Rhyannon; Second Secretary (Political) Lusaka since August 2004; Born 17/02/76; FCO 2000; Assistant Private Secretary to Minister of State FCO 2001; Band C4.

Price, Tristan Robert Julian; Head of Resource Budgeting Department, FCO since April 2003; Born 24/11/66; Economic Assistant 1993; Economic Adviser 1995; SUPL 1999; m 1988 Judith Ann Torrance (1d 1996; 1s 1998).

Priest, Timothy Ian; Counsellor FCO since October 2003; Born 27/10/47; FCO 1972; Vienna 1975; First Secretary (Chancery) Helsinki 1981; FCO 1985; First Secretary (Chancery/Information) Athens 1989; Counsellor FCO 1993; Counsellor (Political) Helsinki 1999; m Teresa Jean Bagnall (2d 1975, 1980; 2s 1978, 1987).

Priestley, Andrew Howard James; Second Secretary Islamabad since December 2004; Born 10/12/76; FCO 2003; Band C4.

Priestley, Carol Ann (née Edwards); First Secretary (Management) Moscow since July 2003; Born 11/11/53; FCO 1974; Paris 1976; Düsseldorf 1979; Kathmandu 1980; FCO 1982; Dhaka 1985; Auckland 1989; Second Secretary FCO 1993; Second Secretary (Management) later HM Consul Washington 1997; m 1976 Lawrence Minton Priestley.

Priestley, Philip John, CBE (1996); High Commissioner Belmopan since July 2001; Born 29/08/46; FCO 1969; Third Secretary Sofia 1971; Third later Second Secretary Kinshasa 1973; First Secretary FCO 1976; Head of Chancery Wellington 1979; First Secretary FCO 1984; Counsellor (Commercial) Manila 1987; HM Ambassador Libreville 1990; CDA Harvard University 1991; Consul-General Geneva 1992; Head, North America Department FCO 1996; m 1972 Christine Rainforth (1d 1976; 1s 1978).

Prime, Ashley Walter John; First Secretary Rome since March 2003; Born 06/08/59; FCO 1978; Bonn 1980; Kingston 1983; Peking 1986; FCO 1989; Full-Time Language Training 1993; Milan 1993; Rome 1995; Full-Time Language Training 1996; Deputy Consul-General Guangzhou 1996; On loan to Invest UK 1999; FCO 2001; Band D6; m 1997 Silvia Ardizzone (1s 1999).

Pring, Alison June; First Secretary (Science & Technology) Berlin since August 2004; Born 18/06/61; FCO 1983; SUPL 1983; FCO 1984; Third Secretary Brussels 1986; Third later Second Secretary Caracas 1989; Second Secretary FCO 1991; Full-Time Language Training 1995; Second Secretary (Commercial) and Deputy Head of Mission St Petersburg 1996; First Secretary (Commercial) Berne 1999; Band D6.

Pring, Mary; FCO since January 1999; Born 29/06/60; FCO 1991; Full-Time Language Training 1993; Language Training Cairo 1994; Jerusalem 1995; Band B3.

Pringle, Anne Fyfe, CMG (2004); Director for Strategy and Information FCO since September 2004; Born 13/01/55; FCO 1977; Moscow 1980; San Francisco 1983; Second Secretary Brussels (UKREP) 1986; Second later First Secretary FCO 1987; First Secretary on secondment to European Political Cooperation Secretariat 1991; First Secretary later Counsellor FCO 1994; Full-Time Language Training 2001; HM Ambassador Prague 2001; m 1987 Bleddyn Glynne Leyshon Phillips.

Pringle, Julia Margaret Georgina (née Wright); Luxembourg since June 2004; Born 28/03/48; FCO 1966-71; Metropolitan Police 1971; FCO 1991; SUPL 1993-98; Bogotá 1998; Band A2; m 1971 Raymond Elliot Pringle (diss 2003) (1d 1981).

Pringle, Raymond Elliott; SUPL since July 2004; Born 28/11/51; Department of Employment 1968-69; FCO 1970; Brussels (UKREP) 1972; Quito 1975; FCO 1978; Bilbao 1981; Barcelona 1983; Second Secretary (Chancery/Information) Lilongwe 1986; Second later First Secretary FCO 1989; Deputy Consul-General and Consul (Commercial) San Francisco 1993; SUPL 1999; First Secretary (Management) Washington 1999; First Secretary (Trade & Investment) Copenhagen 2001; m (1) 1971 Julia Margaret Georgina Wright (diss 2003) (1d 1981); (2) 2003 Mary Ellen Sullivan Murphy.

Pritchard, Grant; Pitcairn since March 2004; Born 02/06/70; FCO 1990; Peking 1994; Third Secretary (Management) and Vice-Consul Kuwait 1997; Third Secretary Vienna (OSCE) 2000; m 1996 Rebecca Louise Williams (diss 2001).

Proctor, Jacqueline (née Jones); FCO since April 2002; Born 03/10/71; FCO 1991; Athens 1993; SUPL 1996; Geneva (UKDis) 1996; Kampala 1999; Band B3; m 1996 Matthew Joel Proctor (1d 2003).

Proctor, Matthew Joel; FCO since May 2002; Born 16/07/71; FCO 1991; SUPL 1993; Geneva (UKMIS) 1996; Kampala 1999; Band B3; m 1996 Jaqueline Jones.

Prodger, David Wilce; First Secretary (Commercial) Buenos Aires since March 2002; Born 28/09/66; FCO 1999; Band D6; m 1993 Tiffany Darwent (2s 1997, 2000).

Proudfoot, David Owen; Baku since August 2002; Born 15/04/71; HCS 1991; FCO 1995; Sarajevo 1998; FCO 2001; Band B3.

Pruce, Daniel Robert; On loan to No. 10 Downing Street since January 2002; Born 24/07/66; FCO 1990; Brussels (UKREP) 1993; FCO 1996; First Secretary (Information) Brussels (UKREP) 1999; Band D6.

Pryce, Andrew William; Second Secretary (Political) Helsinki since November 2003; Born 09/02/70; FCO 1988; Washington 1991; FCO 1993; Karachi 1994; FCO 1997; Band C4; m 1993 Corienne Marie Madden (1d 2002).

Publicover, Ralph Martin; HM Ambassador Luanda since April 2005; Born 02/05/52; FCO 1976; Language Training MECAS 1977; Second later First Secretary Dubai 1979; First Secretary (Economic) Ottawa 1981; First Secretary on loan to the Cabinet Office 1985; FCO 1987; First Secretary (Chancery) Washington 1989; First Secretary FCO 1992; Full-Time Language Training 1994; Bucharest 1994; Deputy Head of Mission Lisbon 1999; FCO 2003; m 1973 Rosemary Sheward (2d 1979, 1988; 1s 1983).

Pugh, David Evan; FCO since July 2000; Born 26/04/51; FCO 1982; Pretoria 1983; FCO 1985; Cairo 1988; FCO 1991; Tokyo 1992; FCO 1995; Vienna 1997; Band C5; m (1) 1976 Bethan Jones (diss 1989) (4d 1980, 1982, 1984, 1986); (2) 1992 Sally Anne Jones.

Pullen, Richard David; FCO since October 2004; Born 07/09/78; Band C4.

Pullen, Roderick Allen; HM Ambassador Harare since July 2004; Born 11/04/49; MOD 1975; Second Secretary Brussels (UKDEL NATO) 1978;

MOD 1980; First Secretary Madrid (UKDEL CSCE) 1981; FCO 1982; DHC Suva 1984; First Secretary FCO 1988; Counsellor (Technology) Paris 1990; Deputy High Commissioner Nairobi 1994; Deputy High Commissioner Lagos 1997; FCO 2000; High Commissioner Accra 2000; m 1971 Karen Lesley Sketchley (1d 1975; 4s 1978, 1989, twins 1994).

Purdon, Michael; FCO since October 2003; Born 01/05/80; Band C4.

Purdy, Samantha Louise, MVO (1996); First Secretary (Political) New York (UKMIS) since August 2004; Born 22/08/71; FCO 1992; Full-Time Language Training FCO 1994; Full-Time Language Training Bangkok 1995; Second Secretary (Political/Information) Bangkok 1996; First Secretary FCO 1999.

Purves, Michael; First Secretary (Management) Berlin since March 2004; Born 03/11/57; FCO 1975; New Delhi 1978; ME Floater 1982; Mogadishu 1983; FCO 1986; Third later Second Secretary (Economic/Aid) Kuala Lumpur 1989; Second Secretary (Management) Colombo 1992; First Secretary FCO 1996; First Secretary (Commercial) and Deputy Head of Mission Doha 2000; m 1985 Ruth Joan Goodwin (1d 1986; 1s 1990).

Puryer, Stuart John; Consul Copenhagen since May 2004; Born 03/06/67; FCO 1987; Copenhagen 1990; Ljubljana 1993; FCO 1996; DFID 1997; FCO 1998; Band D6.

Pye, Catherine Ann; FCO since September 2004; Born 29/01/75; Band B3.

Pykett, Alexander Richard John; FCO since 2004; Born 27/07/76; Band C4.

Pyle, Nicholas John, MBE (1999); Nairobi since April 2005; Born 09/12/60; FCO 1981; Geneva (UKMIS) 1984; Kabul 1986; Jedda 1990; FCO 1992 (Second Secretary 1995); Second Secretary (Immigration) Colombo 1996; Second Secretary Bridgetown 2000; SUPL 2004; Band D6; m 1993 Rosamund Day (2s 1995, 2001; 1d 1999).

Pyper, Alan; Cairo since September 2004; Born 13/06/62; DSS 1990-97; FCO 1999; Berlin 2001; Band A2; m 1995 Patrocinia Haban.

Q

Quantrill, Clara Jane; Second Secretary (Political/Economic) Kingston since December 2002; Born 06/08/68; FCO 1999; Band C4.

Quarrey, David; FCO since October 2003; Born 06/01/66; FCO 1994; Second Secretary (Political) Harare 1995; First Secretary (Political) New Delhi 2000.

Quayle, Quinton Mark; HM Ambassador Bucharest since November 2002; Born 05/06/55; FCO 1977; Language Training 1978; Third Secretary (Chancery) Bangkok 1979 (Second Secretary 1981); FCO 1983 (First Secretary 1984); ENA Paris 1986; First Secretary Paris 1987; First Secretary FCO 1991; First Secretary seconded to Price Waterhouse 1993; Counsellor FCO 1994; Deputy Head of Mission Jakarta 1996; Director British Time International 1999; International Group Director Trade Partners UK 1999; m 1979 Alison Marshall (2s 1982, 1985).

Quinn, James Gregory; Deputy Head of Mission Minsk since February 2004; Born 16/06/71; Second Secretary FCO 1999; Language Training 1999; Second Secretary (Political/PPA) Accra 2000; Band C4; m 1995 Wendy Ann Dackombe.

Quinn, Jean Margaret (née Leiper); FCO since May 2003; Born 21/03/53; FCO 1975; Abidjan 1978; Brasilia 1982; Second Secretary FCO 1984; SUPL 1990; FCO 1994; Second Secretary (Commercial/ECM) Tunis 1996; Second Secretary (Commercial/Management) Riga 2000; Band C4; m 1985 Peter Nugent Quinn (1d 1987; 1s 1989).

Quinn, Lorraine; New Delhi since April 2004; Born 25/06/66; FCO 1991; Bonn 1993; Gibraltar 1997; Helsinki 2000; FCO 2002; Band B3; m (1) 1986 Martin Quinn (diss 2000) (1s 1988); (2) 2000 Stephen Andrew Pettigrew.

Qureshi-Hasan, Eram (née Qureshi); Moscow since October 2003; Born 18/07/68; FCO 1989; Islamabad 1999; Band B3; m 2003 Ali Hasan (1s 2003).

R

Raab, Dominic; First Secretary (Legal) The Hague since March 2003; Born 25/02/74; Assistant Legal Adviser FCO 2000.

Raby, Charlotte Jane; FCO since May 2002; Born 05/05/72; HCS FCO 1992; FCO 1996; Peking 1998; Band A2.

Rack, Martin Elliott; First Secretary Islamabad since November 2004; Born 30/12/73; FCO 1997; Second Secretary (Political) The Hague 1999; Second Secretary FCO 2001; Band C4.

Radcliffe, Adam, MBE (2002); Third Secretary (Consular) Washington since June 2002; Born 10/06/67; FCO 1988; Geneva (UKMIS) 1990; Istanbul 1993; FCO 1996; Band B3; m 1992 Julie Anne Nichols (1s 1994; 2d 1995, 1996).

Rae, Karen (née Hooper); FCO since August 2002; Born 28/05/60; FCO 1980; Port Stanley 1983; Berne 1984; Cairo 1987; FCO 1990; Third Secretary (Consular) Islamabad 1993; Language Training 1997; Second Secretary (Commercial) Prague 1997; Band C5; m 1984 Thomas Park Rae (1d 1993).

Raine, John Andrew, OBE (2003); Counsellor FCO since April 2004; Born 12/07/62; FCO 1984; Language Training 1986; Second Secretary (Information) Kuwait 1988; First Secretary FCO 1991; First Secretary (Political) Damascus 1994; First Secretary Riyadh 1997; FCO 2000; Counsellor Baghdad 2003; Band D6.

Raine, Sarah Emily; FCO since March 2004; Born 16/07/76; FCO 1999; Full-Time Language Training 2001; Second Secretary (Political) Sarajevo 2002; Band C4.

Rajguru, Harish L; FCO since April 2003; Born 23/04/61; HCS cadre of the FCO 1989; FCO 1990; Sofia 1992; Kiev 1994; FCO 1996; Floater Duties 1999; Yekaterinburg 2001; SUPL 2002; Band B3.

Rakestraw, Mark Andrew; Consul Cairo since April 2004; Born 30/11/67; FCO 1988; Athens 1990; FCO 1993; Full-Time Language Training 1996; Vice-Consul Lisbon 1997; Second later First Secretary FCO 2001; Band C5; ptnr, Lorna Wood.

Ralph, Richard Peter, CMG (1997), CVO (1991); HM Ambassador Lima since May 2003; Born 27/04/46; Third Secretary FCO 1969; Third later Second Secretary Vientiane 1970; Second later First Secretary (Information) Lisbon 1974; First Secretary FCO 1977; First Secretary and Head of Chancery Harare 1981; First Secretary later Counsellor FCO 1985; Counsellor Washington 1989; HM Ambassador Riga 1993; HM Governor Stanley 1996; HM Ambassador Bucharest 1999; m (1) 1970 (diss 2001) (1s 1970; 1d 1974); (2) 2002 Jemma Victoria Elizabeth Marlor.

Ram, Sutnam; ECO New Delhi since December 2001; Born 12/02/61; FCO 1999; Band B3; m 1987 Reeta Vaish (2d 1987, 1998).

Rampling, Christopher Maxwell, MBE (2005); Second Secretary (Political/PPA) Tripoli since May 2002; Born 08/10/73; FCO 1999; Full-Time Language Training (Arabic) 2000; Band C4.

Ramsay, Paul Andrew, MBE (1988); First Secretary FCO since April 2000; Born 10/10/55; FCO 1975; East Berlin 1977; Istanbul 1979; Brussels (UKDEL NATO) 1981; Tehran 1984; FCO 1987 (Second Secretary 1990); Second Secretary Madrid 1992; First Secretary (Management) Singapore 1997; m 1980 Carey-Jane Lambert (1d 1987; 2s 1989, 1993).

Ramscar, Michael Charles; Counsellor FCO since December 2000; Born 26/02/48; Second Secretary FCO 1975; Second Secretary (Economic) Lagos 1977; First Secretary (Economic) Brasilia 1979; First Secretary FCO 1982; Madrid 1986; San José 1989; First Secretary FCO 1991; Counsellor Madrid 1997; m 1970 Janis Lemon (2s 1976, 1981).

Ramsden, Sir John (Charles Josslyn), Bt; HM Ambassador Zagreb since April 2004; Born 19/08/50; FCO 1975; Third later Second Secretary Dakar 1976; First Secretary Vienna (UKDEL MBFR) 1979; First Secretary, Head of Chancery and Consul Hanoi 1980; First Secretary FCO 1982; On loan to HM Treasury 1988; First Secretary FCO 1988; Counsellor and Deputy Head of Mission East Berlin later British Embassy Berlin Office 1990; Counsellor FCO 1993; Deputy Head of Mission Geneva (UKMIS) 1996; Head of Central and North West European Department FCO 1999; FCO 2003; m 1985 Jane Bevan (2d 1987, 1989).

Ramsey, Patricia Anne; FCO since February 2004; Born 09/01/48; FO 1967; Brussels (UKDEL EEC) 1969; Rio de Janeiro 1972; FCO 1974; Athens 1980; Geneva (UKMIS) 1983; FCO 1986; Paris 1987; SUPL 1991; FCO 1992; SUPL 1997; Second later First Secretary (Political) Berlin 1998; SUPL 2003; Band D6; m 1990 Paul Lever.

Randall, John Mark; Beijing since June 2005; Born 01/11/76; FCO 2001; Band A2; m 2003 Melissa Rix.

Rangarajan, Francis Vijay Narasimhan; Deputy Head of Mission Mexico City since September 2003; Born 22/09/69; FCO IGC Unit, EUD(I) 1995; Second later First Secretary (Trade Policy and Antici) Brussels (UKREP) 1997; Private Secretary to Permanent Under-Secretary of State 1999; FCO 1999; m 2000 Rosie Francis Cox.

Rankin, John James; Consul-General Boston since November 2003; Born 12/03/57; Assistant, later Senior Legal Adviser FCO 1988; Legal Adviser Geneva (UKMIS & UKDIS) 1991; Legal Counsellor FCO 1995; First Secretary FCO 1996; First Secretary Dublin 1998; Counsellor and Deputy Head of Mission Dublin 1999; m 1987 Lesley Marshall (2d 1989, 1991; 1s 1993).

Rapp, Stephen Robert; Deputy Head of Mission Ashgabat since December 2002; Born 09/03/52; Home Office 1986; FCO 1986; Accra 1988; Hanoi 1992; FCO 1994; Vice-Consul Jedda 1996; Ekaterinburg 1999; Vice-Consul Lahore 2001; Band C4; m 1978 Judy Elizabeth Flewett.

Ratcliffe, Deborah; FCO since September 2001; Born 06/04/62; FCO 1980; Geneva (UKMIS) 1982; Harare 1985; ECO Manila 1988; Third Secretary - VC/ECM Hanoi 1995; Third Secretary (Management) Kingston 1997; Second Secretary (Management) T/D Islamabad 2001; Band C4.

Ratcliffe, Yvonne; FCO since December 2003; Born 18/06/62; FCO 1988; Athens 1989; Peking 1992; FCO 1994; Prague 1996; T/D Khartoum 1999; Singapore 2000; Band B3.

Raven, Martin Clark; On loan to the DTI since May 2001; Born 10/03/54; FCO 1976; Third Secretary Lagos 1978; FCO 1979; Third later Second Secretary New Delhi 1979; Second later First Secretary FCO 1983; First Secretary New York (UKMIS) 1988; First Secretary FCO 1993; Counsellor FCO 1996; Counsellor Stockholm 1998; m 1978 Philippa Michaela Morrice Ruddick (2s 1982, 1984).

Rawbone, Jane Lynn; FCO (Wilton Park) since January 2003; Born 21/03/53; FCO 1976; Vienna (UKDEL MBFR) 1977; Helsinki 1980; FCO 1982; Mexico City 1984; New York (UKMIS) 1988; Madrid 1991; FCO 1993; Kuala Lumpur 1996; Canberra 2000; Band B3.

Rawlings, Menna Frances; Accra since May 2005; Born 16/09/67; FCO 1989; Third later Second Secretary (Institutions) Brussels (UKREP) 1991; Second Secretary (Economic/Environment) Nairobi 1993; FCO 1997; SUPL 1998; First Secretary Tel Aviv 1998; Private Secretary to the Permanent Under Secretary, FCO 2002; m 2000 Mark John Rawlings (2d 1998, 2000).

Rawlins, Helen Catherine; FCO since July 2002; Born 31/07/64; FCO 1986; Bonn 1988; Manila 1991; Second Secretary FCO 1994; Second Secretary (Consular) Kampala 1998.

Rawlins, Isabel May; FCO since September 2003; Born 24/07/79; Band B3.

Rawlinson, Colin James; Consul-General Vancouver since November 2002; Born 21/02/46; FCO 1967; Reykjavik 1968; Nicosia 1971; Hamburg 1973; Second Secretary FCO 1976; Copenhagen 1979; Second Secretary (Commercial) New Delhi 1981; First Secretary FCO 1984; New York (UKMIS) 1993; FCO 1994; Consul-General Bordeaux 1998; m 1966 The Hon Catharine Julia Trend (2d 1967, 1969).

Rawlinson, Ivor Jon, OBE (1988); FCO since March 2002; Born 24/01/42; FO 1964; Warsaw 1966; Bridgetown 1969; Second Secretary FCO 1971; Assistant Private Secretary to Minister of State FCO 1973; Second Secretary (Economic) Paris 1974; First Secretary FCO 1978; First Secretary (Commercial) Mexico City 1980; Consul Florence 1984; First Secretary later Counsellor FCO 1988; Royal College of Defence Studies 1993; Consul-General Montreal 1993; HM Ambassador Tunis 1999 - 2002; m 1976 Catherine Paule Caudal (1s 1980; 2d 1977, 1983).

Rawlinson, Timothy Simeon; First Secretary FCO since May 2000; Born 12/01/62; Second Secretary FCO 1988; Second later First Secretary (Information) Lagos 1991; First Secretary FCO 1993; First Secretary (Political) Stockholm 1996; Band D6; m 1998 Janet Mary Cooper.

Ray, Steven; FCO since July 2004; Born 09/07/75; Band A2.

Rayner, Robert Alan; Deputy Consul-General and Director (Trade and Investment) Hong Kong since October 2003; Born 14/12/50; FCO 1968; Islamabad 1972; Language Training 1974; Tokyo 1975; DOT 1979; FCO 1981; Second Secretary (Chancery/Information) and Vice-Consul Lima 1984; FCO 1987; Consul (Commercial) Osaka 1989; First Secretary (Press and Public Affairs) Tokyo 1995; First Secretary FCO 1999; Counsellor (Atomic Energy) Tokyo 2000; m 1984 Dawn Carol Richards (1d 1991).

Rea, Elizabeth Rose, MBE (1993); FCO since May 1996; Born 31/10/54; FCO 1976; Luxembourg 1978; Lima 1981; Washington 1984; FCO 1987; Brussels (UKREP) 1992; Band C4.

Read, Rachel Frances; Pretoria since January 2003; Born 23/10/65; FCO 1989; Cairo 1991; Sofia 1995; Grand Turk 1998; Band B3.

Reader, David George; HM Ambassador Phnom Penh since January 2005; Born 01/10/47; CRO, DSAO and FCO 1964; Warsaw 1969; Paris 1972; Bucharest 1974; FCO 1976; Kinshasa 1979; Kathmandu 1982; Second Secretary FCO 1984; Vice-Consul (Commercial) Brisbane 1987; First Secretary (Management) and Consul Belgrade 1992; First Secretary FCO 1996; First Secretary Cairo 1998; High Commissioner Mbabane 2001; m 1969 Elaine McKnight (1s 1975; 1d 1980).

Rebecchi, Silvano Marco Raffaele; Second Secretary (Commercial) Helsinki since August 2000; Born 14/08/52; Department of Education and Science 1972; FCO 1975; Baghdad 1977; Valletta 1981; Dhaka 1984; FCO 1986; Paris 1990; Amman 1992; Cairo 1992; Second Secretary FCO 1996; Full-Time Language Training 2000; m 1984 Eileen Zammit (2s 1985, 1987).

Reddaway, David Norman, CMG (1993), MBE (1980); High Commissioner Ottawa since August 2003; Born 26/04/53; FCO 1975; Language Training SOAS 1976; Language Training Iran 1977; Third later Second Secretary (Commercial) Tehran 1977; Second later First Secretary (Chancery) Tehran 1978; First Secretary (Chancery) Madrid 1980; First Secretary FCO 1985; Private Secretary to Minister of State 1986; First Secretary (Chancery) New Delhi 1988; Chargé d'Affaires a.i. Tehran 1990 (Counsellor 1991); Minister and Deputy Head of Mission Buenos Aires 1993; FCO 1997; Director, Public Services 1999; UK Special Representative for Afghanistan, with personal rank of Ambassador and Visiting Fellow at Harvard University 2002; m 1981 Roshan Taliyeh Firouz (2s 1983, 1996; 1d 1987).

Redden, Michael James; Management Office Gaborone since January 2002; Born 22/02/70; DHSS 1987; FCO 1990; Khartoum 1994; FCO 1997; Colombo 1998; Band B3; m 1995 Nicola Jane Elizabeth Sharp (1d 1997).

Reddicliffe, Paul, OBE; Senior Principal Research Officer FCO since August 1997; Born 17/03/45; FCO 1977; First Secretary Canberra 1985; First Secretary FCO 1989; HM Ambassador Phnom Penh 1994; Band D7; m 1974 Wee Siok Boi (2s 1977, 1979).

Redshaw, Tina Susan; HM Ambassador Dili since January 2004; Born 25/01/61; FCO 1999; First Secretary (Political) Beijing 2000; Band D6; (1d 2001).

Reed, Pamela Karen (née Williams); FCO since August 1999; Born 10/05/70; HCS 1989; FCO 1994; Brasilia later São Paulo 1997; Band A2; m 1997 Antony Jason Reed.

Reeve, Charles Michael Campbell; First Secretary Skopje since September 2002; Born 12/07/71; Second Secretary FCO 1997; Second Secretary (Political/Military) Banja Luka 1999; Full-Time Language Training 2001; First Secretary (Political) Zagreb 2001; Band D6.

Reeve, Richard Robert; Counsellor FCO since June 2000; Born 28/07/48; FCO 1971; Third later Second Secretary Singapore 1973; Language Training Cambridge University 1975; Language Training Hong Kong 1976; Trade Commissioner Hong Kong 1977; First Secretary FCO 1981; First Secretary Hong Kong 1983; First Secretary FCO 1987; Counsellor Berne 1996; m 1971 Monique Marie-Louise Moggio (2s 1974, 1977).

Reeves, Ceinwen Mary; FCO since September 2001; Born 09/06/57; FCO 1976; SUPL 1976; FCO 1979; Bonn 1982; Lilongwe 1984; Paris 1987; FCO 1989; Vice-Consul Sofia 1993; Second Secretary (Commercial) Beijing 1995; FCO 1998; SUPL 2000; m 2003 Richard Brian George Izzard.

Regan, Michael John; Counsellor Harare since September 2004; Born 17/08/55; FCO 1983; Second later First Secretary Kabul 1986; FCO 1988; First Secretary (Chancery/Economic) Dubai 1989; First Secretary FCO 1991; Bangkok 1995; Counsellor FCO 1998; m 1986 Carolyn Gaye Black (2s 1987, 1989).

Rehal, Opinder Kumar; FCO since February 1995; Born 15/09/48; FCO 1979; Bonn 1982; FCO 1985; Islamabad 1989; FCO 1990; Canberra 1992; Band C5; m 1974 Jagdeep Nandra (1s 1975 (dec'd 1990); 1d 1978).

Reid, Gordon Bryden; Counsellor (Commercial) Kuala Lumpur since May 2003; Born 09/05/56; FCO 1980; Second Secretary Budapest 1982; First Secretary FCO 1985; First Secretary (Chancery) Santiago 1988; First Secretary (Chancery) Islamabad 1990; First Secretary FCO 1994; Deputy Head of Mission Budapest 1998; m 1979 Marinella Ferro (2s 1982, 1988; 1d 1984).

Reid, Norma Fraser; FCO since December 2000; Born 19/08/43; Saigon 1968; Rome 1970; Bucharest 1971; FCO 1973; HCS 1975; Latin America Floater 1977; Peking 1979; FCO 1980; Moscow 1983; FCO 1984; Rome 1986; FCO 1988; Bucharest 1993; Third Secretary (Consular) Nicosia 1997.

Reid, Robert Lloyd; Washington since December 2002; Born 12/06/59; FCO (HCS) 1995; Kingston 1999; Band A2; m 1997 Janet Manning (1s 1989; 1d 1996).

Reid, Thomas Samuel; Vice-Consul Istanbul since June 2003; Born 28/12/76; FCO 2000; T/D Second Secretary Harare 2002; Band C4.

Reidy, Andrea Jane, OBE (2004); First Secretary (International Liaison) Baghdad since July 2004; Born 24/11/58; FCO 1995; Second Secretary (KHF) Bratislava 1997; Deputy High Commissioner Freetown 2000; FCO 2003; (1d 1981).

Reilly, Julian; FCO since June 2000; Born 03/02/71; FCO 1993; Full-Time Language Training 1994; Full-Time Language Training Cairo 1995; Second Secretary (Chancery) Khartoum 1996; Nairobi (Khartoum Unit) 1998; Deputy Head of Mission Khartoum 1999; Band D6.

Reilly, Michael David; Head of South East Asia Department since February 2003; Born 01/03/55; FCO 1978; Language Training Seoul 1979; First Secretary FCO 1984; First Secretary Paris (UKDEL OECD) 1988; First Secretary (Political) and Consul Seoul 1991; First Secretary FCO 1994; Deputy Head of Mission Manila 1996; Head of Cultural Relations Department FCO 2000; m 1981 Won-Kyong Kang (1d 1987; 1s 1992).

Reilly, Michael Patrick; First Secretary (Political/Economic) Bucharest since March 2003; Born 30/07/66; FCO 1984; Bonn 1987; Bombay 1990; FCO 1991; Third Secretary (Development) Lilongwe 1994; FCO 1997; Band D6; m 1991 Andrea Louise Bradley.

Reilly, Patrick; First Secretary (Political) Dublin since January 2002; Born 03/11/70; FCO 1995; Second Secretary (Political) Cape Town 1997; FCO 2000; Band C4.

Reilly, Thomas Saul Anthony; FCO since September 2003; Born 17/11/70; Second Secretary FCO 1998; Second Secretary (Political) Buenos Aires 2001; Band C4.

Remmington, Gillian Elizabeth; FCO since January 2004; Born 26/02/56; FCO 1984; Quito 1985; Berne 1988; World Wide Floater Duties 1991; FCO 1993; Nicosia 1997; Hong Kong 2000; Band B3.

Rennie, Alexander Thomson Inglis; Brasilia since February 2004; Born 03/03/53; FCO 1998; Bangkok 2000; Full-Time Language Training 2003; Band A2.

Rennie, Nadia Jane; FCO since October 2002; Born 30/09/71; FCO 1990; Brussels (UKDEL NATO) 1994; Kiev 2000; Band C4.

Rennie, Paul Joseph Gordon; Second Secretary (Economic/Political) Brasilia since August 2003; Born 10/02/78; FCO 2001; Band C4.

Rennie, Piers Damian Lee; Full-Time Language Training since November 2004; Born 20/04/74; FCO 2003; Band C4.

Reuter, Alan; Consul Milan since February 2000; Born 05/07/51; FCO 1970; Bucharest 1972; Kaduna 1974; Frankfurt 1978; Gaborone 1980; FCO 1982; Tel Aviv 1986; Third Secretary (Commercial) Kuala Lumpur 1988; Second Secretary FCO 1992; Second Secretary (Consular/Immigration) Lagos 1995; Nairobi 1998; FCO 1999; Band C4; m (1) 1973 Christine Caton; (2) 1982 Brenda Yvonne Mary Neumann (1s 1983; 1d 1985).

Revell, James Austen; FCO since October 2004; Born 24/09/73; Band C4; m 2004 Sally Poole.

Reynolds, Colin; Washington since August 2004; Born 03/07/71; FCO 1990; Nicosia 1992; Africa/Middle East Floater 1995; Assistant Private Secretary to Minister of State, FCO 1999; First Secretary 2000; Board Chair and Head of Professional Development Operations Team, FCO 2003.

Reynolds, Gillian Marjorie; FCO since October 1993; Born 16/10/50; FCO 1976; New Delhi 1977; Budapest 1979; Mbabane 1981; FCO 1984; Singapore 1987; Peking 1991; Band C4.

Reynolds, Heather (née Turnbull); Dubai since March 2003; Born 30/05/54; FCO 1973; Moscow 1975; FCO 1976; Brasilia 1977; Bridgetown 1980; SUPL 1983; Kuala Lumpur 1984; FCO 1986; Prague 1988; SUPL 1990; FCO 1991; New Delhi

1993; FCO 1997; Moscow 1999; Band C4; m 1982 Keith James Reynolds (1s 1990).

Reynolds, Leslie Roy; FCO since January 2003; Born 22/09/59; DTI 1978; Passport Office 1979; HO 1984; FCO 1984; Wellington 1986; Islamabad 1988; FCO 1992; Dublin 1997; FCO 2000; Bucharest 2002; Band B3; m 1982 Tracey Sapsford (3s 1986, 1989, 1991).

Reynolds, Martin Alexander Baillie; FCO since January 2002; Born 05/06/69; FCO 1997; Second Secretary (Economic/Commercial) Singapore 1998; Band D6.

Rhodes, Ian Peter; Second Secretary FCO since September 1998; Born 12/04/60; Second Secretary FCO 1986; Nicosia 1995; Band C4.

Richards, Sir Francis Neville, KCMG (2002), CMG (1994), CVO (1991); Governor Gibraltar since May 2003; Born 18/11/45; Army 1967-69; Third Secretary FCO 1969; Moscow 1971; Second later First Secretary Vienna (UKDEL MBFR) 1973; First Secretary FCO 1976; Counsellor (Commercial/Economic) New Delhi 1985; Counsellor FCO 1988; High Commissioner Windhoek 1990; Minister Moscow 1992; AUS (Central and Eastern Europe) FCO 1995; Director (Europe) 1996; DUSS (Defence and Intelligence) 1998; Head of GCHQ Cheltenham 1998; m 1971 Gillian Bruce Nevill (1s 1975; 1d 1977).

Richards, Ian; SUPL since June 2005; Born 07/10/62; FCO 1993; Full-Time Language Training 1994; Consul (Commercial) Shanghai 1996; First Secretary (Political) Beijing 2000; FCO 2002; On loan to DFID 2004; Band D6.

Richards, Owen Jeremy; SMO Bucharest since June 2005; Born 28/06/66; FCO 1988; Bombay 1991; Third Secretary (ECE/UNCTAD) Geneva (UKMIS) 1995; On loan to the DTI 2000; Second Secretary (Political) Addis Ababa 2001; Band C4.

Richards, Steven Thomas; FCO since December 2004; Born 29/01/58; FCO 1978; New Delhi 1980; Beirut 1982; Floater Duties 1985; FCO 1987; Warsaw 1988; FCO 1988; Vice-Consul Moscow 1990; FCO 1993 (Second Secretary 1994); Second Secretary (Management/Consular) Valletta 1996; Second Secretary (Commercial) Dublin 2000; Band C5; m 1989 Tracey Lee Barnett (1d 1995).

Richardson, Christine Lynn; Skopje since August 2003; Born 04/10/67; FCO 1987; Brussels (UKREP) 1989; Africa/Middle East Floater 1992; On loan to DTI 1997; Baku 1998; Band C4.

Richardson, Michael John; FCO since July 2004; Born 16/05/66; FCO 1985; Warsaw 1988; FCO 1991; Attaché Cairo 1993; FCO 1996; Second Secretary (Regional Affairs) Seoul 2001; Band C4; m 1989 Audrey Zena Fairall (1s 1994).

Richmond, Alan Thomas; Second Secretary (Economic) Ottawa since July 1999; Born 22/04/55; Department of Education 1973; FCO 1975; Maputo 1977; Lima 1981; FCO 1983; Islamabad 1985; Singapore 1988; FCO 1991; Full-Time Language Training 1994; Abidjan 1995; Band C4; m 1976 Iseabal MacLean Graham (1d 1986).

Richmond, David Frank, CMG (2004); FCO since August 2003; Born 09/07/54; FCO 1976; Language Training MECAS 1977; Third later Second Secretary Baghdad 1979; Second later First Secretary FCO 1982; First Secretary (External Trade) Brussels (UKREP) 1987; Deputy Head of NENAD FCO 1991; Head of Economic Relations Department 1994; Head of Chancery New York (UKMIS) 1996; Political and Security Committee Representative and Permanent Representative to the Council of the WEU Brussels (UKREP) 2000; m 1990 Caroline Florence Pascale Matagne (1s 1992; 1d 1994).

Rickerd, Martin John Kilburn, OBE (2004), MVO (1985); Team Leader for North America, Americas Directorate FCO since August 2003; Born 17/08/54; FCO 1972; Brussels (UKDEL NATO) 1975; Wellington 1978; Assistant Private Secretary to Parliamentary Under Secretary of State 1980; Bridgetown 1982; Consul (Information) Milan 1986; First Secretary FCO 1991; Head of Chancery Singapore 1995; On secondment to the Standard Chartered Bank 1998; FCO 2000; Deputy Head of Mission Abidjan 2000; Band D7; m 1976 Charmain Gwendoline Napier (2s 1986, 1988).

Ricketts, Peter Forbes, CMG (1999); Permanent Representative Brussels (UKDEL NATO) since July 2003; Born 30/09/52; FCO 1974; New York 1974; FCO 1975; Third Secretary Singapore 1975; Second Secretary Brussels (UKDEL NATO) 1978; First Secretary FCO 1982; APS to Secretary of State 1983; First Secretary (Chancery) Washington 1986; First Secretary later Counsellor FCO 1989; Counsellor (EC/Finance) Paris 1994; Deputy Political Director FCO 1997; Director International Security FCO 1999; On loan as Chairman of the Joint Intelligence Committee to the Cabinet Office 2000; Political Director and Deputy Under-Secretary FCO 2001; m 1980 Suzanne Julia Horlington (1s 1982; 1d 1987).

Rickward, Charlotte Lucy; Hamilton since November 2003; Born 12/05/72; FCO 1997; Manila 2000; Band B3; m 1994 Jarlath Ambrose.

Ridley, Michelle; Grand Turk since August 2002; Born 22/01/63; DHSS 1986-87; FCO 1987; Kaduna 1990; Peking 1993; New York (UKMIS) 1997; Band A2.

Ridout, Anthony Robert; FCO since July 2004; Born 31/03/66; FCO 1986; New Delhi 1989; Paris 1992; FCO 1995; Second Secretary Cairo 1996; Second Secretary FCO 1998; Second Secretary (Political) Kingston 2001; Band C4; m 1989 Karen Marie Hendy (1d 1991).

Ridout, Richard William; Third Secretary (Political) Hanoi since July 2002; Born 19/11/67; FCO 1986; Moscow 1990; FCO 1993; Third Secretary Riyadh 1994; FCO 1998; Band B3; m 1992 Sarah Beth Evans (1d 1996).

Ridout, William Anthony Frederick; HM Consul Hong Kong since July 2001; Born 27/04/50; MOD 1970; FCO 1974; Islamabad 1976; Stuttgart 1979; Bridgetown 1982; FCO 1982; Bombay 1984; Second Secretary (Commercial) East Berlin 1988; Consul Milan 1990; FCO 1995; Deputy Head of Mission Khartoum 1997; Head of Khartoum Unit, Nairobi 1998; First Secretary (Commercial) Tripoli 1999; m 1996 Louise Victoria Burrett (2s 1986, 2000; 1d 2002).

Riley, John Lawrence; FCO since September 2003; Born 13/08/61; FCO 1982; Cairo 1984; FCO 1986; Ankara 1986; Hanoi 1991; FCO 1992; New Delhi 1995; Third Secretary (Aid) Gaborone 1999; m (1) 1982 Caroline Peacock (diss); m (2) 1990 Ayce Birergin.

Rimmer, Ronald Stanley; Karachi since April 2005; Born 24/02/54; Royal Air Force 1972-95; FCO 1995; Lagos 1998; Deputy High Commissioner Banjul 2001; Band C5.

Ringham, Christine Mary; SUPL since October 2002; Born 11/12/61; FCO 1988; Brussels (UKDEL) 1991; Prague 1995; FCO 1998; SUPL 2000; FCO 2001; Band B3; m 1998 Kevin P Ringham (2d 2000, 2002).

Ripard, Elizabeth Anne (née Auld); Deputy High Commissioner Mbabane since March 2002; Born 27/06/57; FCO 1976; Madrid 1979; SE Asia Floater 1982; San José 1984; FCO 1988; Third Secretary Valletta 1991; Third later Second Secretary FCO 1994; Language Training 1998; Second Secretary Abidjan 1998; m 1992 Nicholas Charles Ripard (diss).

Ritchie, Joseph Battle; Lilongwe since April 2004; Born 13/07/44; RAF 1961-91; FCO 1998; New York 1999; Band A2; m Paula May (1d 1975; 1s 1980).

Ritchie, Paul John, OBE (1994); Counsellor FCO since December 2003; Born 26/03/62; FCO 1983; Second Secretary (Chancery) Nicosia 1986; Second later First Secretary FCO 1988; First Secretary New York (UKMIS) 1991; First Secretary FCO 1996; Counsellor Nicosia 1999; m 1991 Jane Risely (1d 1997; 1s 2002).

Rixon, Margaret Carol; FCO since August 2003; Born 16/02/57; FCO 1976; Castries 1978; Washington 1980; Peking 1982; FCO 1983; Vienna (UKMIS) 1984; East Berlin 1987; Kingston 1988; FCO 1991; Dublin 1999; Band B3.

Robbins, Nicholas Martin; Third later Second Secretary (Political) Vienna (UKDEL OSCE) since September 2003; Born 17/07/67; FCO 1998; Mumbai 2000; Band B3; m 1998 Beverly Dawn Goodhew.

Roberts, Amanda Claire; FCO since May 2000; Born 06/09/67; FCO 1989; Santiago 1996 (Second Secretary 1997); Band C4.

Roberts, Camilla Frances Mary (née Blair); SUPL since May 2004; Born 23/11/66; FCO 1988; Full-Time Language Training 1990; Third later Second Secretary Prague 1991; First Secretary FCO 1994; m 2000 Colin Roberts (1s 2002).

Roberts, Catherine Mary; SUPL since July 2002; Born 05/10/68; FCO 1995; Washington 1997; Band A2.

Roberts, Colin; HM Ambassador Vilnius since March 2004; Born 31/07/59; Called to the Bar 1986; FCO 1989; Second Secretary (Economic) later First Secretary (Political) Tokyo 1990; First Secretary FCO 1995; First Secretary (Political/Military) Paris 1997; Counsellor FCO 1998; Counsellor (Political) Tokyo 2001; m 2000 Camilla Frances Mary Blair (1s 2002).

Roberts, David Eric; FCO since September 2003; Born 15/08/54; Customs and Excise 1971; FCO 1973; Lagos 1977; Doha 1979; FCO 1983; Washington 1986; Helsinki 1989; On loan to London Chamber of Commerce 1993; HM Consul Jedda 1995; Vancouver 1999; m 1979 Kim Louise Fyleman (3d 1990, 1992, 1993).

Roberts, David George; Deputy Head of Mission, Director of Trade and Investment and Consul-General for Switzerland and Liechtenstein at the British Embassy in Berne since August 2000; Born 11/04/55; FCO 1976; Third later Second Secretary (Chancery) Jakarta 1977; Second Secretary (Chancery) Havana 1981; First Secretary FCO 1984; First Secretary (Economic) Madrid 1988; First Secretary (Financial/EC) Paris 1991; FCO 1994; First Secretary FCO 1994; Deputy Head of Mission Santiago 1996; m 1985 Rosemarie Rita Kunz (1d 1990; 1s 1992).

Roberts, Gareth Daniel; FCO since September 2003; Born 07/09/77; Band C4.

Roberts, Gillian (née Phenna); Moscow since June 2002; Born 03/12/68; FCO 1986; Cape Town/Pretoria 1988; Buenos Aires 1992; FCO 1995; Third Secretary (Passports) Paris Embassy 1998; Band B3; m 1993 Michael John Roberts.

Roberts, Sir Ivor Anthony, KCMG (2000), CMG (1995); HM Ambassador Rome since May 2003; Born 24/09/46; Third Secretary FCO 1968; MECAS 1969; FCO 1970; Paris 1970; Second Secretary 1971; Second later First Secretary FCO 1973; First Secretary (Chancery) later First Secretary (Economic/Commercial/Agriculture) Canberra 1978; First Secretary FCO 1982; Counsellor FCO 1986; Minister Madrid 1989; Chargé d'Affaires and HM Consul-General later HM Ambassador Belgrade 1994; On loan to St Antony's College, Oxford 1997; HM Ambassador Dublin 1999; m 1974 Elizabeth Bray Bernard Smith (2s 1976, 1979; 1d 1982).

Roberts, Michael John Wyn; Deputy Head of Mission Ankara since July 2004; Born 04/07/60; Second Secretary FCO 1984; Second later First Secretary (Chancery) Athens 1987; First Secretary FCO 1991; First Secretary (Institutions) Brussels (UKREP) 1995; Head of Division Cabinet Office (European Secretariat) 1999; FCO 2003; m 1985 Margaret Anne Ozanne (2d 1989, 1991; 1s 1993).

Roberts, Peter Raymond; FCO since June 2002; Born 09/02/62; Band B3; m 1992 Diane Margaret.

Roberts, Philip John Barclay; Counsellor FCO since June 1999; Born 04/12/49; FCO 1973; Third later Second Secretary Islamabad 1977; First Secretary FCO 1980; Head of Chancery and Consul Hanoi 1982; First Secretary Tokyo 1984; First Secretary FCO 1987; First Secretary (Chancery) later Counsellor Lisbon 1991; Counsellor Bogotá 1994; Counsellor FCO 1995; Counsellor Vienna 1997; m 1996 Amparo Jimenez Avilan (1d 1997).

Roberts, Tracy Melissa Renata Juliet (née Dodge); First Secretary Vienna (UKMIS) since May 2001; Born 31/01/62; HM Customs and Excise 1985; FCO 1998; On loan to CSSB 2000; Band D6; m 1993 David William (1s 1999).

Roberts-Gurr, Anne Catherine; SUPL since January 2005; Born 07/05/63; FCO 1985; Bucharest 1988; FCO 1990; Floater Duties 1991; FCO 1993; Athens 1995; FCO 1997; Band B3; m 2001 Andrew William George Gurr.

Robertson, Corin Jean Stella (née Leatherbarrow); First Secretary (Institutions) Brussels (UKREP) since December 2002; Born 15/01/72; FCO 1994; Full-Time Language Training 1995; Second Secretary (Trade Policy) Tokyo 1997; First Secretary FCO 2001; Band D6; m 1996 James Francis Robertson.

Robertson, Emma Jane; FCO since September 2002; Born 25/12/71; FCO 1997; Third Secretary (Economic) Damascus 2000; Band C4.

Robertson, William Smellie; FCO since March 2004; Born 05/03/66; FCO 1984; Dublin 1986; Riyadh 1989; On loan to the ODA 1992; Third Secretary (Aid/Information) Harare 1996; Second Secretary (Consular) Wellington 2001; Band C4; m 1986 Catherine Elizabeth McGregor (1d 1992; 2s 1995, 2002).

Robins, Terence Frederick; FCO since September 2003; Born 15/10/66; FCO 1989; Vice-Consul Algiers 1991; Victoria 1995; Second Secretary (Chancery) Strasbourg 1999; Band C5; m 1994 Wassila Kerri (1s 1998).

Robinson, Carole May (née Davis); SUPL since August 1999; Born 26/03/59; FCO 1994; Washington 1996; Band A2; m 1995 Miles Gordon Robinson.

Robinson, Julie Anne (née Whitehead); FCO since September 1995; Born 02/08/63; FCO 1984; Washington 1985; Bahrain 1988; FCO 1991; SUPL 1993; Band B3.

Robinson, Kathleen Julia Anne (known as Julia); T/D Cairo since March 2005; Born 24/09/50; FCO 1995; The Hague 1996; New York (UKMIS) 2000; SUPL 2003; FCO 2004; Band A2.

Robinson, Philip Andrew; First Secretary (Management) Beijing since July 2001; Born 18/09/51; FCO 1970; Warsaw 1973; Jedda 1974; FCO 1977; Wellington 1978; Islamabad 1980; FCO 1982; Johannesburg 1985; Moscow 1987 (Second Secretary 1988); Second Secretary FCO 1991; HM Consul Hong Kong 1996; Band D6; m 1972 Elizabeth Andrina Mathieson Riding (2d 1976, 1980).

Robinson, Tanya Mari; Beijing since June 2004; Born 07/04/81; FCO 2000; Transferred to DS 2001; Band A2; ptnr, Mickel Braithwaite (1d 2002).

Robinson, William; New Delhi since August 2003; Born 26/11/44; RAF Regiment 1962; Islamabad 1987; Moscow 1991; Pretoria 1992; Amman 1996; Dublin 2000; Band C4; m 1966 Cynthia Margaret Pugh (2s 1966, 1969).

Roche, Shaun Martin; FCO since August 2004; Born 23/01/68; FCO 1992; Nairobi 2001; Band C4; m 2001 Rebecca Louise York.

Rocks, Lynne; FCO since September 2003; Born 28/10/79; Band A2.

Rodemark, Janet Mary; SUPL since January 2002; Born 28/05/65; FCO 1988; Islamabad 1992; Second Secretary FCO 1995; SUPL 1997; FCO 1998; SUPL 1999; Sofia 2001; Band C4; m 1993 Timothy John Colley (1s 1997; 2d 1999, 2002).

Roden, Joel Charles; Vice-Consul Istanbul since June 2005; Born 24/02/77; FCO 2002; Band C4; m 2000 Camila Miranda.

Rogan, Janet Elizabeth; FCO since April 2001; Born 19/12/62; FCO 1986; Language Training 1988; Language Training Hong Kong 1989; Second later First Secretary (Chancery) Peking 1991; On loan to the Cabinet Office 1994; First Secretary FCO 1995; Deputy Head of Mission Sarajevo 1998.

Rogers, David Alan, OBE (2004); Counsellor FCO since December 1996; Born 16/05/49; FCO 1971; Copenhagen 1974; Second later First Secretary FCO 1978; Jakarta 1981; First Secretary Brunei 1983; First Secretary FCO 1985; First Secretary (Chancery) Islamabad 1988; First Secretary FCO 1991; First Secretary (Political) Muscat 1993; First Secretary (Chancery/Economic) Dubai 1995; m 1989 Julie Anne Gardiner (1d 1990; 2s 1992, 1994).

Rogers, Diana Caroline; SUPL since November 2001; Born 30/07/74; FCO 1998; World Wide Floater Duties 2000; Band B3.

Rogers, Jonathan Mark; FCO since September 2004; Born 04/04/74; MOD 1999; FCO 1999; World Wide Floater Duties 2002; Band B3.

Rogers, Michael Roy; SUPL since August 2000; Born 14/12/48; FCO 1967; Tunis 1973; Bridgetown 1975; Pretoria/Cape Town 1976; FCO 1978; Bahrain 1981; Wellington 1984; Resigned 1989; Reinstated, Second Secretary FCO 1990; Second Secretary (Management) JMO New York 1995; m 1970 Elaine Anne Stewart (2s 1980, 1986).

Röhsler, Caron Amanda; FCO since January 2000; Born 28/08/72; Band C4; ptnr, David Mingay.

Roissetter, Frederick Charles; First Secretary (Technical Management) Baghdad since August 2004; Born 09/10/50; Army 1966-77; FCO 1978; Cabinet Office 1979-81; Paris 1982; FCO 1984; Third later Second Secretary Tel Aviv 1989; FCO 1992; Athens 1995; Second later First Secretary FCO 1998; Band C5; m 1979 Kay Jacqueline (2d 1981, 1984; 1s 1986).

Rolt, Colette; FCO since February 2001; Born 10/08/71; FCO 1989; Washington 1997; Band C4.

Rooney, Kay (née Smith); FCO since July 2003; Born 01/07/68; FCO 1990; Vienna 1993; FCO 1996; Vice-Consul Frankfurt 1996; SUPL 1998; Band B3; m 2000 Sean Michael Rooney.

Rooney, Sean Michael; FCO since June 2003; Born 17/02/72; FCO 1991; Vienna (UKDEL) 1995; Dhaka 1996; Düsseldorf 2000; Band C4; m 2000 Kay Smith.

Roper, Martyn Keith; FCO since October 2003; Born 08/06/65; FCO 1984; Tehran 1986; Maputo 1988; Vice-Consul Kuwait 1990; Third Secretary (Political/Aid) Karachi 1991; FCO 1994; First Secretary 1996; First Secretary (Development/Economic) Paris (UKDEL OECD) 1999; Band D7; m 1989 Elisabeth Melanie Harman Watson (1s 1992; 1d 1995).

Roper, Neil Gregson; Second Secretary (Technical Management) Pretoria since August 2000; Born 27/11/65; FCO 1987; Madrid 1993; FCO 1995; Band C4.

Roscoe, James Paul; Second Secretary (Political/PPA) Freetown since July 2004; Born 29/06/76; FCO 2001; Basra 2003; Band C4.

Roskilly, Karen Elizabeth; Second Secretary (Management) Madrid since September 2001; Born 18/10/65; FCO 1990; Amsterdam 1991; Gibraltar 1994; SUPL 1998; Band C4; m 1995 Antonio Gonzalez Saugar (1d 1997; 1s 2000).

Ross, William Lawson; First Secretary (Consular) Dhaka since July 2003; Born 13/09/53; FCO 1973; New York (UKMIS) 1975; CG New York 1977; Tunis 1978; Kinshasa 1981; FCO 1984; Nassau 1985; Warsaw 1988; FCO 1991 (Second Secretary 1993); HM Consul and Second Secretary (Commercial) Al Khobar 1995; Full-Time Language Training 2000; First Secretary (Commercial) Nicosia 2000; Band C5; m 1978 Mary Margaret Delaney (1d 1980; 1s 1982).

Ross McDowell, Amanda (née Ross); Vice-Consul (Commercial) Sydney since June 1999; Born 25/11/62; FCO 1981; 10 Downing St 1985; Cape Town 1988; Zurich 1991; Second Secretary FCO 1994; Second Secretary (Commercial) Addis Ababa 1997; m 1987 Christopher McDowell (1d 1990; 1s 1992).

Rossiter, Lynne; Copenhagen since July 2002; Born 10/08/50; FCO 1990; Tel Aviv 1992; Floater Duties 1995; Band B3.

Rothery, James Peter; FCO since September 1985 (Second Secretary 1993); Born 15/04/51; FCO 1975; Masirah 1977; Washington 1982; Band D6; m 1996 Agnes Maria Smith.

Rous, Matthew James; Deputy Head of Mission and Consul-General Brussels Embassy since February 2002; Born 29/06/64; FCO 1991; Full-Time Language Training SOAS 1992; Full-Time Language Training Peking 1993; Second later First Secretary (Chancery) Peking 1994; First Secretary (Commercial) Tokyo 1998; m 1989 Beryl Ann Scott (2d 1992, 1998; 1s 1994).

Rowbottom, Major Kenneth John; Queen's Messenger since 1988; Born 04/03/47; HM Forces 1966-86.

Rowe, David Ian; FCO since July 2000; Born 16/06/66; FCO 1985; Addis Ababa 1987; Bucharest 1991; FCO 1992; Manila 1996; Band C4; m 1993 Nancy Elizabeth Vince.

Rowe, Elizabeth Jane; Warsaw since January 2003; Born 19/01/71; FCO 1997; Sarajevo 1998; Floater Duties 2001; Band B3.

Rowe, Jane Victoria; SUPL since June 2004; Born 20/05/73; FCO 2001; Paris 2003; Band B3.

Rowe, Katherine Jane; Second Secretary Kuala Lumpur since May 2004; Born 30/01/78; FCO 2002; Band C4; ptnr, Robert Long.

Rowe, Victoria Helen (née Goodwin); FCO since August 2004; FCO 1995; Vice-Consul Geneva 2000; Band C4; m 1996 Richard David Rowe.

Rowett, Caroline Sarah; FCO since September 1999; Born 16/09/58; FCO 1990; Jakarta 1992; Paris 1996; Band C4; m 1992 Joseph Spurgeon (1d 1998).

Rowland, Keith Irving, MVO (2004); Kabul since February 2004; Born 09/11/46; Royal Navy 1963-88; Islamabad 1988; Moscow 1992; New York 1993; FCO 1996; Attaché (Management) Abuja 2001; Band A2; m 1971 Helena Sloan (1s 1972).

Rowlands, Jane Ellen; Third Secretary (Management) and Vice-Consul Ashgabat since August 2001; Born 16/03/67; FCO 1987; Mexico City 1989; Seoul 1993; Third Secretary FCO 1997.

Rowlandson, Peter Roderick Saxby; FCO since January 1997; Born 22/09/49; FCO 1970; Georgetown 1972; FCO 1976; Brussels 1978; Moscow 1981; FCO 1982; Brussels 1984; Madrid 1985; New Delhi 1988; FCO 1991; Dhaka 1995; Band B3; m (1) 1973 Nancy Lee Townsend (1d 1974); (2) 1989 Jillian Roberts (1s 1990; 1d 1992).

Rowney, Michael Ernest, MBE (1991); FCO since January 2001; Born 23/06/53; FCO 1972; Warsaw 1975; Kinshasa 1976; Hamilton 1979; Bahrain 1982; FCO 1985; Vice-Consul Monrovia 1988;

Lisbon 1991; FCO 1994; First Secretary Security Officer Moscow 1998.

Rowton, Alastair Clifford; FCO since January 1998; Born 28/11/46; FCO 1979; Gaborone 1981; FCO 1982; Darwin (BGWRS) 1984; FCO 1986; Second Secretary Budapest 1994; Band C5; m 1976 Jean Margaret Cowie (2d 1982, 1986).

Royal, Caroline Patricia; New York (UKMIS) since February 2001; Born 22/01/57; MOD 1973; FCO 1990; Lisbon 1992; FCO 1995; Sana'a 1998; Band A2.

Royle, Catherine Jane; Deputy Head of Mission Buenos Aires since September 2003; Born 17/08/63; FCO 1986; Third later Second Secretary (Chancery) Santiago 1988; First Secretary FCO 1991; First Secretary (EU/Economic) Dublin 1997; FCO 2001; m 1991 Marcelo Enrique Camprubi Valledor (1s 2000).

Rudge, Peter Alan; FCO since November 2003; Born 05/09/73; Second Secretary FCO 1999; Second Secretary (Political) Rome 2001; Band C4.

Runacres, Mark Alastair; Minister New Delhi since July 2002; Born 19/05/59; FCO 1981; Third later Second Secretary New Delhi 1983; Second later First Secretary FCO 1986; First Secretary (Chancery) Paris 1991; First Secretary FCO 1995; On loan to the DTI 1998; Counsellor (Economic) New York (UKMIS) 1999; m 1989 Shawn Reid (1s 1994; twins 1s/1d 2000).

Ruse, Lynne Elaine (née Gerrish); SUPL since December 1997; Born 15/05/58; FCO 1988; Paris 1991; FCO 1995; Band A2; m 1996 Howard Michael Ruse (1d 1998; 1s 1999).

Ruskin, Peter Jonathan; Second Secretary (Press & Public Affairs) Oslo since August 2004; Born 29/11/76; FCO 2002; Full-Time Language Training (Norwegian) 2003; Band C4.

Russell, Gerard Simon Joseph, MBE (2002); Baghdad since May 2005; Born 11/07/73; FCO 1995; Full-Time Language Training (Arabic) 1996; Cairo 1997; Consul (Political) Jerusalem 1998; FCO 2001; Band D7.

Russell, Malcolm Arthur; FCO since May 2001; Born 27/02/54; FCO 1973; Kuala Lumpur 1976; FCO 1980; Frankfurt 1983; Tehran 1985; Third Secretary Nuku'alofa 1988; Peking 1989; FCO 1992; Suva 1999; Band C4; m 1982 Jean Frances Matthews (1d 1987; 1s 1992).

Russell, Neil; SUPL since April 2001; Born 18/02/69; FCO 1989; Abu Dhabi 1992; Brasilia 1994; Full-Time Language Training 1998; Third Secretary (Information) Warsaw 1998; Band B3; m 1993 Trudie Helen Denby (1d 1995).

Russell, Roger; Accra since November 2001; Born 14/05/54; FCO 1970; Brussels 1983; FCO 1986; Canberra 1989; FCO 1999; Band C4; m 1983 Teresa Mary McGeough.

Rutherford, John, OBE (2003); SUPL since December 2002; Born 02/01/59; FCO 1978; Nairobi 1980; Jedda (later Riyadh) 1983; Second Secretary Warsaw 1990 (Second Secretary 1988); Los Angeles 1994; Regional Director, Invest in Britain Bureau Hong Kong 1998; m 1989 Karen Chapman (1s 1991).

Rutherford, Karen (née Chapman); FCO since November 2002; Born 19/02/59; FCO 1977; Rome 1979; Floater Duties 1982; FCO 1986; Warsaw 1990; SUPL 1992; Band B3; m 1989 John Rutherford (1s 1991).

Ryan, Elizabeth Jane Karen; Zagreb since August 2003; Born 02/02/61; FCO 1998; Bratislava 1999; Band B3; m 1993 Chaeil Ok-soon (1d 1994).

Ryan, Robert Christopher; Bucharest since January 2002; Born 21/02/72; HCS 1991; FCO 1994; New Delhi 1997; FCO 2001; Band A2.

Rycroft, Matthew John, CBE; HM Ambassador Sarajevo since March 2005; Born 16/06/68; FCO 1989; Third Secretary Geneva (UKDIS) 1990; Third later Second Secretary (Chancery) Paris 1991; First Secretary FCO 1995; First Secretary (Political) Washington 1998; Private Secretary to the Prime Minister for Foreign Affairs, No.10 Downing Street 2002; m 1997 (2d 1998, 2000).

Ryder, Michael; FCO since July 2003; Born 13/11/53; FCO 1984; Second later First Secretary BMG Berlin 1986; First Secretary FCO 1988; First Secretary Brussels (UKREP) 1993; First Secretary FCO 1996; Counsellor (Head of Security Policy Department) FCO 1997; Special Representative for International Drugs Issues and Head of Drugs and International Crime Department FCO 1998.

S

Sadler, Stuart Roger; Second Secretary (Management) Riyadh since October 2002; Born 22/12/70; FCO 1990; Pretoria 1994; Moscow 1998; Karachi 2001; Band C4; m 1995 Wendy Jane Hoole (1d 1997; 2s 2000, 2003).

Sadler, Tiffany Alexandra (née White); FCO since August 2003; Born 10/06/71; FCO 1994; Language Training 1995; Third later Second Secretary (Political and Economic) Rangoon 1996; FCO 1999; Economics Training 2001; m 2002 Stephen Paul Sadler (1d 2003).

Sagar, Rebecca Ann; Kabul since December 2003; Born 09/09/76; FCO 1999; Second Secretary (Political) Islamabad 2001; Band D6.

Sainty, Christopher James; First Secretary (Political/EU) Madrid since March 2000; Born 29/03/67; FCO 1989; Language Training FCO 1991; Third later Second Secretary (Chancery) New Delhi 1992; First Secretary FCO 1996; Language Training FCO 1999; m 1993 Sarah Helen Norris (1s 1996; 2d 1998, 2000).

Salt, Richard André; First Secretary (Commercial) Sarajevo since August 2003; Born 30/07/62; FCO 1980; Brussels (UKREP) 1983; Algiers 1985; Banjul 1988; FCO 1990; New Delhi 1993; Second Secretary (Commercial) Damascus 1996; On secondment to Petrofac UK Ltd 2000; Band C5; m 1992 Karen Baden Davies (1s 1995).

Salter, Leigh Audra; SUPL since June 2002; Born 16/03/69; FCO 1988; Wellington 1991; Windhoek 1994; Floater Duties 1998; Band B3.

Salvesen, Charles Hugh; HM Ambassador Montevideo since May 2005; Born 10/09/55; Second Secretary FCO 1982; First Secretary BMG Berlin 1984; First Secretary Bonn 1985; FCO 1988; Head of Political Section Buenos Aires 1993; Counsellor and Deputy High Commissioner Wellington 1996; FCO 2000; m 1983 Emilie Maria Ingenhousz (2s twins 1987; 1d 1990 (dec'd 1995)).

Samarasinghe, Cheryl; FCO since July 2004; Born 04/11/80; Band A2.

Sambrook, Adam John; Second Secretary (Political) Jerusalem since October 2004; Born 01/02/78; FCO 2001; Full-Time Language Training (Hebrew) 2003; Full-Time Language Training Jerusalem 2004; Band C4; m 2004 Cristina.

Sampson, Jerome; Rangoon since January 2005; Born 11/11/74; FCO 2002; Band A2.

Sampson, William; FCO since October 2003; Born 17/02/80; Band C4.

Samuel, Edwin Douglas Lincoln; Private Secretary to the Ambassador, Berlin since December 2003; Born 08/08/72; FCO 2001; Band C4.

Sancar, Kim (née Neilson); SUPL since July 2002; Born 30/09/71; FCO 1991; Islamabad 1995; Third Secretary (Immigration) Tehran 1998; Third Secretary (Commercial) and Vice-Consul Al Khobar 2001; Band B3; m 1997 Rizkul Oktay Sancar.

Sanderson, Michael John; First Secretary FCO since July 1995; Born 21/01/48; FO 1967; Cairo 1972; FCO 1976; New York (UKMIS) 1979; Second Secretary (Chancery) Oslo 1984; Second Secretary FCO 1988; First Secretary Hong Kong 1993; Band C5; (1d 1979; 1s 1985).

Sandover, William Geoffrey; Counsellor Islamabad since August 2004; Born 07/04/55; FCO 1979; Third later Second Secretary Vienna (UKMIS) 1981; First Secretary FCO 1984; First Secretary (Chancery) Dublin 1986; First Secretary FCO 1987; First Secretary (Chancery) Buenos Aires 1992; First Secretary FCO 1996; Counsellor Paris 2002; Band D6; m (1) 1981 Sharman Winsome Knight (diss 1985); (2) 1992 Beatrice Martin.

Sargeant, Ian Charles; Consul Shanghai since July 2004; Born 24/04/52; FCO 1971; Language Training SOAS 1974; Bangkok 1975; LA Floater 1979; FCO 1982; Manila 1986; Deputy Economic Adviser Berlin 1990; Vice-Consul (Commercial) Düsseldorf 1991; FCO 1995; First Secretary and HM Consul Manila 1998; FCO 2003; m 1988 Mari Grace Eddun (diss 1999) (1d 1989).

Satheesan, Sujeevan; Paris since June 2003; Born 25/03/77; FCO 2001; Band C4.

Sattaur, Christopher; Assistant Secretary Diplomatic Service Trade Union Side, FCO since April 2004; Born 25/04/71; FCO 1991; Athens 1996; Amman 2000; FCO 2003; Band A2.

Saunders, Caroline Ann; Deputy Consul-General Brisbane since October 2000; Born 28/09/60; FCO 1983; New Delhi 1986; FCO 1988; Third Secretary (Chancery) Kuala Lumpur 1991; Second Secretary FCO 1995; Second Secretary British Trade International 1998; m 1989 Rhodri Christopher Kevin Meredith (1s 1993; 1d 1996).

Saunders, Ian David; St Petersburg since April 2002; Born 20/01/67; COI 1989-99; FCO 2000; Band A2.

Saunders, Kirsten Mary Margaret; Vice-Consul Damascus since November 2003; Born 08/10/68; FCO 1995; Bangkok 1997; Third Secretary (Immigration) Dhaka 2000; Band B3.

Saunders, Liane, OBE (2004); On attachment to the Coalition Provisional Authority, Northern Iraq since April 2003; Born 24/10/68; FCO 1993; Full-Time Language Training FCO 1994; Full-Time Language Training Cairo 1995; Second Secretary Kuwait 1996; First Secretary (Chancery) Ankara 2000; Band D6; m 1994 Andrew Stewart Smith (1d 1998).

Saunderson, Lesley Margaret; SUPL since February 2003; Born 18/11/69; FCO 1991; New Delhi 1993; St Petersburg 1994; Dar es Salaam 1997; On loan to DFID 1998.

Savill, Margaret Ann; First Secretary FCO since April 1995; Born 06/04/46; FCO 1968; Third Secretary Georgetown 1972; Geneva 1975; Second Secretary Rio de Janeiro 1975; FCO 1980; Second later First Secretary (Information) Berne 1984; First Secretary FCO 1989; First Secretary (Information/Management) Brussels (UKDEL NATO) 1993.

Saville, John Donald William; High Commissioner Bandar Seri Begawan since May 2005; Born 29/06/60; FCO 1981; Third later Second Secretary Jakarta 1983; FCO 1985; Second later First Secretary (Information) Warsaw 1988; First Secretary FCO 1991; First Secretary (Political) Vienna 1995; FCO 1998; Deputy Head of Mission Havana 2000; Counsellor FCO 2004; m 1992 Fabiola Moreno de Alboran (1d 1993).

Sawers, Robert John, CMG (1996); DUS (Political), FCO since July 2003; Born 26/07/55; FCO 1977; Sana'a 1980; SUPL 1980; Language Training 1981; Second Secretary Damascus 1982; First Secretary FCO 1984 (PS to Minister of State 1986); First Secretary Pretoria/Cape Town 1988; Head of European Union Department (Presidency) 1991; Principal Private Secretary to the Secretary of State for Foreign and Commonwealth Affairs 1993; Career Development Attachment Harvard University 1995; Counsellor (Political/Military) Washington 1996; Foreign Affairs Private

Secretary to the Prime Minister 1999; HM Ambassador Cairo 2001; m 1981 Avril Helen Shelley Lamb (2s 1983, 1985; 1d 1987).

Say, Sarah Gillian; Pretoria since July 2003; Born 02/04/59; FCO 1986; Paris 1988; Washington 1991; Havana 1993; FCO 1994; Mexico City 1996; T/D Helsinki 1999; Brussels (UKREP) 2000; Band B3.

Sayle, Lorraine Mary; SUPL since August 2003; Born 22/09/72; FCO 1990; Brussels (UKDEL NATO) 1994; Lilongwe 1996; SUPL 1998; Lilongwe 1998; Luanda 2001; Band B3; (1s 1998).

Scales, Caroline Ann (née Smyth), MBE (1999); Cape Town since April 2002; Born 02/06/61; FCO 1980; Moscow 1982; Strasbourg 1983; Peking 1987; FCO 1989; Washington 1993; Tripoli 1997; FCO 1998; Band C4; m 2001 Michael Scales.

Scales, Martin Milner; HM Consul Frankfurt since January 2005; Born 31/01/65; FCO 1997; Vice-Consul Oslo 2001; Band C4; m 2001 Caroline Smyth.

Scanlon, Edward Joseph; FCO since February 2003; Born 18/05/70; HCS 1990-93; FCO 1993; Peking 1995; Istanbul 1999; Band B3; m 2002 Jenni Williams.

Scanlon, Jenni (née Williams); FCO since March 2003; Born 21/12/70; FCO 1990; Peking 1995; FCO 1999; Istanbul 1999; Band B3; m 2002 Edward Scanlon.

Scantlebury, Ian Patrick; FCO since July 2003; Born 12/09/60; FCO 1978; Georgetown 1981; SE Asia Floater 1985; Calcutta 1987; FCO 1991; Third Secretary (Commercial) Accra 1994; Second Secretary Lima 1997; FCO 2001; On secondment (Commercial) 2002.

Scarborough, Bryan David; Consul (Management) Port of Spain since January 2003; Born 19/01/45; FCO 1973; Warsaw 1975; Douala 1976; Delhi 1979; Freetown 1983; FCO 1985; Lilongwe 1988; Third Secretary (Commercial) Jakarta 1991; FCO 1995; Consul (Commercial) Shanghai 1999; m 1969 Kathleen Mary Johnston (1s 1980).

Scarratt, Claire Rebecca; Hong Kong since May 2003; Born 07/02/75; HCS 1997; FCO 1999; Stockholm 2000; Band A2.

Schofield, Nigel; FCO since 2001; Born 17/04/70; FCO 1990; Bonn 1993; FCO 1993; Lagos 1994; On loan to the DTI 1999; Floater Duties 2000; Band C4; m 1994 Rebecca Imogen.

Scholes, Elizabeth Marian; SUPL since September 1998; Born 28/04/66; FCO 1987; Third later Second Secretary (Chancery) Buenos Aires 1990; Second later First Secretary FCO 1993; First Secretary (Chancery) Tel Aviv 1996; m 1998 Richard Wrigley.

Schroeder, Dominic Sebastian; FCO since October 2001; Born 13/11/65; FCO 1988; Third later Second Secretary Kinshasa 1989; Second Secretary FCO 1992; Second Secretary New York (UKMIS) 1993; Second later First Secretary FCO 1994; First Secretary (Commercial) Berlin 1997; m 1997 Susan Caroline Kerr (1s 2001).

Schroeder, Susan Caroline (née Kerr); SUPL since September 1999; Born 09/04/69; FCO 1988; Prague 1990; Rabat 1992; FCO 1994; On loan to the DTI 1996; Third Secretary (Political) Berlin 1998; Band B3; m 1997 Dominic Sebastian Schroeder (1s 2001).

Schulz, Lynne; Pretoria since April 2002; Born 16/11/66; HCS 1997; SUPL 1998; FCO 2000; SUPL 2001; Band A2; m 1994 Sven Schulz (1s 1998; 1d 2001).

Schumann, Carol Ann (née Hill); Buenos Aires since April 2005; Born 18/07/46; FCO 1976; Paris 1977; FCO 1980; Washington 1981; FCO 1987; The Hague 1988; Bonn 1991; FCO 1995; SUPL 1996; Third Secretary (Finance) Bonn 1997; Consul/MO Frankfurt 2000; Band C4; m 1980 Jürgen Klaus Dieter Schumann (2s 1981, 1983).

Scott, Gavin David; First Secretary (Management) Prague since September 2004; Born 26/06/60; FCO 1978; Paris 1981; Beirut 1983; Washington 1985; FCO 1988; Third Secretary (Commercial) Bogotá 1991; Third Secretary FCO 1995; Bridgetown 1995; Private Secretary to the Group Chief Executive British Trade International 2002; Band C5; m 1992 Julie Ann Owen (1s 2003).

Scott, George; Almaty since July 2002; Born 11/10/56; FCO 1981; East Berlin 1982; Luxembourg 1984; Lagos 1986; FCO 1991; Kigali 1995; Tirana 1999; Band C4.

Scott, Julie Ann (née Owen); SUPL since August 2004; Born 18/07/68; DSS 1986; FCO 1989; World Wide Floater Duties 1990; SUPL 1992; Bridgetown 1997; FCO 1999; Band C4; m 1992 Gavin David Scott (1s 2003).

Scott, Keith John; First Secretary (Political) Kabul since August 2005; Born 19/02/69; FCO 1991; Abuja 1994; Second Secretary FCO 1995; SUPL 1998; On loan to the DTI 1999; FCO 2002; First Secretary (Energy) Baghdad 2004; Band D6.

Scott, Victoria; FCO since October 2003; Born 04/03/81; Band C4.

Scott-Dunne, Naomi Anita; SUPL since April 2002; Born 25/09/68; FCO 1990; Geneva (UKMIS) 1995; SUPL 1997; FCO 2001; Band A2; m 1997 John Richard Dunne.

Scroby, Gary Vance; Second Secretary (Commercial) Kuala Lumpur since March 2005; Born 15/07/69; FCO 1988; Brussels (UKREP) 1989; Floater Duties 1992; FCO 1994; Deputy Head of Mission Managua 1999; Counsellor (Commercial) Auckland 2003; Band C4; m 1999 Lisa Marie Dowell (1d 2000; 1s 2003).

Seaby, Paul Robert; HM Consul Pretoria since August 2002; Born 24/05/56; FCO 1975; Warsaw 1978; Masirah 1978; Ottawa 1979; Floater Duties 1982; Port Moresby 1984; Third Secretary

(Commercial) Muscat 1991; Second Secretary (Management) Lusaka 1994; First Secretary (Management) and Consul Tehran 1999; Band C5; m 1984 Lynette Margaret Heffernan (1d 1995).

Sealy, Amanda Sarah (née Franklin); Gaborone since September 2003; Born 03/01/59; FCO 1980; Peking 1982; Pretoria/Cape Town 1984; Warsaw 1986; FCO 1988; Windhoek 1991; Jakarta 1995; FCO 1999; Band C4; m 1989 Dominic John Sealy (1s 1992; 1d 1995).

Seaman, Michael William; First Secretary (Political) Tbilisi since May 2002; Born 01/11/55; FCO 1975; Jakarta 1977; Bombay 1981; FCO 1984; Second Secretary (Chancery) The Hague 1988; Second Secretary FCO 1992; On loan to the MOD 1992; First Secretary FCO 1994; Athens 1999; Full-Time Language Training 2001; Band C5; m 1978 Jane Lesley Stockwell (2d 1984, 1987).

Seaman, Stephen James, MBE (1991); First Secretary (Commercial) Kuwait since July 2004; Born 04/12/55; DOT 1975; Copenhagen 1979; Salisbury 1980; DOT 1980; FCO 1982; Vice-Consul Bucharest 1983; FCO 1986; Second Secretary and Deputy Head of Mission Monrovia 1988; Second Secretary (Commercial) Lilongwe 1991; Second Secretary (Management) Nicosia 1993; First Secretary FCO 1997; First Secretary (Commercial) Caracas 2000; m (1) 1980 Katherine Ann Barker (dec'd 1996); (2) 2001 Magda Guillermina.

Searight, Pauline Mabel; SUPL since August 1999; Born 27/06/55; FCO 1988; Banjul 1990; Karachi 1993; Kuala Lumpur 1996; Band A2; m 1991 Graham Kenneth Denham (1d 1997).

Searl, Alan; FCO since January 2002; Born 06/05/71; Band C4.

Seaton, Andrew James; Consul-General Chicago since August 2003; Born 20/04/54; FCO 1977; Third later Second Secretary Dakar 1979; Trade Commissioner (China) BTC Hong Kong 1981; First Secretary FCO 1987; Trade Counsellor BTC later Deputy Consul-General and Trade Counsellor Hong Kong 1995; Head of China Hong Kong Department FCO 2000; m 1983 Helen Elizabeth Pott (3s 1989, 1992, 1995).

Seddon, Christine; Mexico City since June 2005; FCO 1988; Brasilia 1990; Wellington 1994; FCO 1998; Floater Duties 2001; Band A2.

Seddon, David William; Deputy Consul-General Melbourne since February 2003; Born 30/05/48; FO (later FCO) 1966; Bonn 1970; FCO 1971; Port of Spain 1973; Vila 1977; FCO 1981; Milan 1983; Vice-Consul later Consul Douala 1987; Second Secretary FCO 1991; Kampala 1995; First Secretary (Commercial) Harare 1999; m 1972 Monica Elisabeth Josefina van Loon (1s 1976).

Seddon, Richard Charles Leslie; First Secretary (Political) Islamabad since June 2003; Born 25/09/68; FCO 1992; Second Secretary (Political) New Delhi 1994; First Secretary FCO 1997; First Secretary Washington 1999; Band D6; m 1999 Alice Kim Fugate.

Sedwill, Mark Philip; Counsellor and Deputy High Commissioner Islamabad since February 2003; Born 21/10/64; FCO 1989; Language Training 1990; Second Secretary Language Training Cairo 1991; Second Secretary (Political/External) Cairo 1992; First Secretary FCO 1994; First Secretary (Political) Nicosia 1998; First Secretary FCO 1999; Private Secretary to the Foreign Secretary, 2000; m 1999 Sarah-Jane Lakeman.

Seedhouse, Richard; FCO since September 2003; Born 23/08/79; Band A2.

Self, Andrew Paul; Second Secretary FCO since December 1998; Born 02/04/64; FCO 1982; Hong Kong 1986; FCO 1988; Third Secretary (Information) Sana'a 1992; Third Secretary FCO 1993; Tehran 1996; Band C4; m (1) 1987 Michele Carmichael Crouch (diss 1995); (2) 1997 Andrea Louise Carter (2s 1998, 2001).

Selvadurai, Louise Mary (née McCallum); SUPL since September 2002; Born 26/04/69; FCO 1990; Vienna (UKDEL) 1992; Full-Time Language Training 1995; Third Secretary Moscow 1996; FCO 1999; Band C4; m 2000 Samuel Selvadurai (1s 2002).

Selvadurai, Samuel Dayalan; First Secretary Brussels (UKDEL NATO) since January 2003; Born 01/10/70; FCO 1993; Full-Time Language Training 1994; Second Secretary (KHF) Moscow 1995; First Secretary FCO 1998; Band D6; m 2000 Louise Mary McCallum (1s 2002).

Sen-Gupta, Millie Sharmila; Second Secretary (Press and Public Affairs) Dhaka since July 2003; Born 13/06/76; FCO 2001; Band C4; ptnr, David McDevitt.

Senior, Major Michael Roger; Queen's Messenger since 1987; Born 15/11/45; HM Forces 1964-87.

Setterfield, (James) Robert; Deputy Head of Mission Ljubljana since February 2004; Born 06/05/47; DSAO (later FCO) 1967; Bombay 1969; New Delhi 1971; FCO 1973; Second Secretary (Aid/Information) Rangoon 1976; Assistant Secretary (Political) Vila 1980; Vice-Consul Stuttgart 1980; Vice-Consul (Commercial) Düsseldorf 1982; First Secretary FCO 1985; First Secretary (Chancery) Wellington 1987; FCO 1992; First Secretary Helsinki 1995; Full-Time Language Training 2000; Deputy Head of Mission Bratislava 2000; Band D6; m 1980 Margaret Jean McMahon (1s 1983; 1d 1985).

Seymour, Irene Frances (née McDonagh); SUPL since September 1995; Born 02/12/64; FCO 1984; San José 1987; FCO 1990; Band A2; m 1991 Peter James Seymour.

Seymour, Peter James; First Secretary FCO since March 2001; Born 10/02/62; FCO 1984; Second Secretary (Chancery/Information) and Vice-Consul San José 1987; Second Secretary FCO 1989; SUPL 1990; First Secretary FCO 1991; Berlin

1995; First Secretary Vienna 1999; Band D6; m 1991 Irene Frances McDonagh.

Shackell, Robin John; SUPL since March 2004; Born 04/02/63; HCS 1983; FCO 1985; Vienna 1987; T/D Munich 1989; Doha 1990; Management Officer/Vice-Consul La Paz 1991; FCO 1995; Quito 1999; Band C4; m 2002 Lezlie Lynae Van Hiel (1s 1991; 1d 2003).

Shackleton, Richard David; Second Secretary (Economic) Sofia since January 2004; Born 26/05/68; FCO 1990; Third Secretary (Political) New York (UKMIS) 1992; Third Secretary (Commercial) Bogotá 1995; SUPL 1998; Band C4.

Shaikh, Farida; Second Secretary (Environment/Human Rights) Accra since June 2002; Born 16/10/65; FCO 1990; Third Secretary (Chancery/Information) Harare 1992; Third Secretary (Chancery) Singapore 1996; SUPL 1997; FCO 1998; University College London 2001; m 1997 Emil Levendoglu.

Shand, Ian, LVO (2000); FCO since September 2003; Born 17/01/54; FCO 1973; Accra 1975; Munich 1979; FCO 1982; Bonn 1985; Islamabad 1988; FCO 1991; Language Training 1994; Santiago 1995; Second Secretary (Press and Public Affairs) Milan 1999; m 1975 Lyndsey Elizabeth Hall (2d 1983, 1985).

Shanks, Karen; Pretoria since July 2005; Born 04/05/64; FCO 2003; Band A2.

Shanmuganathan, Krishna; First Secretary FCO since August 2003; Born 14/02/74; FCO 1995; Second Secretary (Political) Pretoria 1998; Athens 2000; Band D6.

Shannon, Keith; Deputy Head of Mission and HM Consul Vilnius since November 2004; Born 17/09/66; FCO 1988; Third Secretary (Aid/Commercial) Maputo 1991; Second Secretary (Technology) Paris 1995; FCO 1999; m 2002 Kate Levesley.

Shapland, Anthony Gregory; FCO since July 1992; Born 17/12/49; PRO (Band D6) ; FCO 1979; On loan to the Cabinet Office 1990; m (1) 1973 Margaret Elizabeth Moriarty (diss); (2) 1982 Leonora Alexandra Hebden (1s 1983).

Sharma, Ajay; Deputy Head of Security Policy Group, FCO since January 2005; Born 05/07/70; FCO 1995; Full-Time Language Training 1996; Second Secretary (Political/Information) Ankara 1997; Seconded to HM Treasury 2000; Full-Time Language Training 2001; First Secretary (Economic) Moscow 2002; Head of Political Section Ankara 2003; m 2000 Evren Birdal.

Sharman, Edwin; Berlin since September 2004; Born 03/10/80; Lord Chancellors Office 2000; FCO 2002; Full-Time Language Training (German) 2004; Band B3; ptnr, Derek Cox.

Sharp, David Stewart; Floater Duties since March 2003; Born 19/01/71; FCO 1989; New York (UKMIS) 1992; Gibraltar 1995; FCO 1999; Band B3.

Sharp, Gemma Goulding; Second Secretary Stockholm since January 2005; Born 07/08/72; Second Secretary FCO 1995; Second Secretary (Political) Copenhagen 1998; FCO 2002; Band C4.

Sharp, James Frederick Bailey; FCO since December 2003; Born 01/04/72; FCO 1994; SUPL 1998; New Delhi 2000; Band A2.

Sharp, James Lyall; HM Ambassador Almaty and HM Ambassador (non-resident) Bishkek since October 2002; Born 12/04/60; Second Secretary FCO 1987; Language Training Cairo 1988; Second Secretary Cairo 1989; First Secretary FCO 1992; First Secretary Vienna (UKDEL) 1996; FCO 1998; m 1992 Sara Essam el-Gammal (2s 1998, 2002).

Sharp, Jonathan Dinsdale; Second Secretary (Political) Lagos since August 2000; Born 31/03/67; FCO 1988; Karachi 1990; Paris 1991; LA/Caribbean Floater 1994; FCO 1997; Third Secretary (Political) Tunis 1997; m 1995 Tracey Ennis.

Sharp, Paul John Gibson; Second later First Secretary FCO since April 1993; Born 24/09/48; FCO 1967; New Delhi 1975; FCO 1976; Rome 1978; FCO 1981; Attaché Ankara 1981; FCO 1985; Attaché Moscow 1987; Second Secretary FCO 1989; Second Secretary Pretoria 1990; Band D6; m (1) 1969 Anita Tsang (2s 1972, 1976) (diss 1986); (2) 1996 J Tuckey.

Sharp, Richard; First Secretary (Management) Ottawa since February 2002; Born 08/03/49; FO (later FCO) 1967; Karachi 1971; Canberra 1972; Port Moresby 1974; Santiago 1975; Jakarta 1977; FCO 1980; Cairo 1984; Second Secretary (Admin) Moscow 1987; Second Secretary FCO 1990; Second Secretary and Vice-Consul Luanda 1993; First Secretary (Management) New Delhi 1997; m 1974 Patricia Anne Whitby (1s 1979; 1d 1983).

Sharpe, Jean Cynthia, OBE (1994); Resident British Commissioner St John's since November 2002; Born 18/10/47; CO 1964; DSAO 1965; The Hague 1970; Kingston 1973; FCO 1974; Dubai 1974; FCO 1975; Freetown 1978; JAO Brussels 1981; Second Secretary FCO 1984; On loan to the DTI 1986; Second Secretary (Commercial) Nairobi 1988; First Secretary and Consul Bangkok 1991; First Secretary FCO 1996; Trade Commissioner Hong Kong 1998.

Sharpe, Rosemary Helen; Counsellor FCO since April 2003; Born 11/03/56; Second Secretary FCO 1982; Second Secretary (Information) New Delhi 1985; First Secretary Brussels (UKREP) 1987; First Secretary FCO 1988; First Secretary (Economic) Berlin 1991; First Secretary FCO 1996; Counsellor Madrid 2000.

Sharpless, Fiona Ure (née McGowan); FCO since April 2005; Born 23/02/65; FCO 1988; Brussels (UKREP) 1989; SUPL 1992; Kathmandu 1993;

1995; First Secretary Vienna 1999; Band D6; m 1991 Irene Frances McDonagh.

Shackell, Robin John; SUPL since March 2004; Born 04/02/63; HCS 1983; FCO 1985; Vienna 1987; T/D Munich 1989; Doha 1990; Management Officer/Vice-Consul La Paz 1991; FCO 1995; Quito 1999; Band C4; m 2002 Lezlie Lynae Van Hiel (1s 1991; 1d 2003).

Shackleton, Richard David; Second Secretary (Economic) Sofia since January 2004; Born 26/05/68; FCO 1990; Third Secretary (Political) New York (UKMIS) 1992; Third Secretary (Commercial) Bogotá 1995; SUPL 1998; Band C4.

Shaikh, Farida; Second Secretary (Environment/Human Rights) Accra since June 2002; Born 16/10/65; FCO 1990; Third Secretary (Chancery/Information) Harare 1992; Third Secretary (Chancery) Singapore 1996; SUPL 1997; FCO 1998; University College London 2001; m 1997 Emil Levendoglu.

Shand, Ian, LVO (2000); FCO since September 2003; Born 17/01/54; FCO 1973; Accra 1975; Munich 1979; FCO 1982; Bonn 1985; Islamabad 1988; FCO 1991; Language Training 1994; Santiago 1995; Second Secretary (Press and Public Affairs) Milan 1999; m 1975 Lyndsey Elizabeth Hall (2d 1983, 1985).

Shanks, Karen; Pretoria since July 2005; Born 04/05/64; FCO 2003; Band A2.

Shanmuganathan, Krishna; First Secretary FCO since August 2003; Born 14/02/74; FCO 1995; Second Secretary (Political) Pretoria 1998; Athens 2000; Band D6.

Shannon, Keith; Deputy Head of Mission and HM Consul Vilnius since November 2004; Born 17/09/66; FCO 1988; Third Secretary (Aid/Commercial) Maputo 1991; Second Secretary (Technology) Paris 1995; FCO 1999; m 2002 Kate Levesley.

Shapland, Anthony Gregory; FCO since July 1992; Born 17/12/49; PRO (Band D6) ; FCO 1979; On loan to the Cabinet Office 1990; m (1) 1973 Margaret Elizabeth Moriarty (diss); (2) 1982 Leonora Alexandra Hebden (1s 1983).

Sharma, Ajay; Deputy Head of Security Policy Group, FCO since January 2005; Born 05/07/70; FCO 1995; Full-Time Language Training 1996; Second Secretary (Political/Information) Ankara 1997; Seconded to HM Treasury 2000; Full-Time Language Training 2001; First Secretary (Economic) Moscow 2002; Head of Political Section Ankara 2003; m 2000 Evren Birdal.

Sharman, Edwin; Berlin since September 2004; Born 03/10/80; Lord Chancellors Office 2000; FCO 2002; Full-Time Language Training (German) 2004; Band B3; ptnr, Derek Cox.

Sharp, David Stewart; Floater Duties since March 2003; Born 19/01/71; FCO 1989; New York (UKMIS) 1992; Gibraltar 1995; FCO 1999; Band B3.

Sharp, Gemma Goulding; Second Secretary Stockholm since January 2005; Born 07/08/72; Second Secretary FCO 1995; Second Secretary (Political) Copenhagen 1998; FCO 2002; Band C4.

Sharp, James Frederick Bailey; FCO since December 2003; Born 01/04/72; FCO 1994; SUPL 1998; New Delhi 2000; Band A2.

Sharp, James Lyall; HM Ambassador Almaty and HM Ambassador (non-resident) Bishkek since October 2002; Born 12/04/60; Second Secretary FCO 1987; Language Training Cairo 1988; Second Secretary Cairo 1989; First Secretary FCO 1992; First Secretary Vienna (UKDEL) 1996; FCO 1998; m 1992 Sara Essam el-Gammal (2s 1998, 2002).

Sharp, Jonathan Dinsdale; Second Secretary (Political) Lagos since August 2000; Born 31/03/67; FCO 1988; Karachi 1990; Paris 1991; LA/Caribbean Floater 1994; FCO 1997; Third Secretary (Political) Tunis 1997; m 1995 Tracey Ennis.

Sharp, Paul John Gibson; Second later First Secretary FCO since April 1993; Born 24/09/48; FCO 1967; New Delhi 1975; FCO 1976; Rome 1978; FCO 1981; Attaché Ankara 1981; FCO 1985; Attaché Moscow 1987; Second Secretary FCO 1989; Second Secretary Pretoria 1990; Band D6; m (1) 1969 Anita Tsang (2s 1972, 1976) (diss 1986); (2) 1996 J Tuckey.

Sharp, Richard; First Secretary (Management) Ottawa since February 2002; Born 08/03/49; FO (later FCO) 1967; Karachi 1971; Canberra 1972; Port Moresby 1974; Santiago 1975; Jakarta 1977; FCO 1980; Cairo 1984; Second Secretary (Admin) Moscow 1987; Second Secretary FCO 1990; Second Secretary and Vice-Consul Luanda 1993; First Secretary (Management) New Delhi 1997; m 1974 Patricia Anne Whitby (1s 1979; 1d 1983).

Sharpe, Jean Cynthia, OBE (1994); Resident British Commissioner St John's since November 2002; Born 18/10/47; CO 1964; DSAO 1965; The Hague 1970; Kingston 1973; FCO 1974; Dubai 1974; FCO 1975; Freetown 1978; JAO Brussels 1981; Second Secretary FCO 1984; On loan to the DTI 1986; Second Secretary (Commercial) Nairobi 1988; First Secretary and Consul Bangkok 1991; First Secretary FCO 1996; Trade Commissioner Hong Kong 1998.

Sharpe, Rosemary Helen; Counsellor FCO since April 2003; Born 11/03/56; Second Secretary FCO 1982; Second Secretary (Information) New Delhi 1985; First Secretary Brussels (UKREP) 1987; First Secretary FCO 1988; First Secretary (Economic) Berlin 1991; First Secretary FCO 1996; Counsellor Madrid 2000.

Sharpless, Fiona Ure (née McGowan); FCO since April 2005; Born 23/02/65; FCO 1988; Brussels (UKREP) 1989; SUPL 1992; Kathmandu 1993;

SUPL 1994; Lagos 1998; SUPL 1999; Dhaka 2001; SUPL 2002; Band B3; m 1990 Kristian Sharpless (1d 1993; 1s 1995).

Sharpless, Kristian; FCO since April 2003; Born 17/06/67; Dept of Employment 1985; FCO 1987; Brussels 1989; Kathmandu 1992; FCO 1995; Lagos 1996; FCO 1999; Dhaka 2001; Band D6; m 1990 Fiona Ure McGowan (1d 1993; 1s 1995).

Shaughnessy, Kevin John; Deputy Head of Mission Santo Domingo since January 2002; Born 10/11/64; FCO 1983; Tehran 1986; Kingston 1988; Bonn 1991; Second Secretary FCO 1994; Second Secretary (Commercial) Bahrain 1998; m 1997 Elizabeth Ann Churchill (2d 1998, 2001).

Shaw, Alan John; Second Secretary (Political/Information) Dhaka since January 2002; Born 09/06/66; FCO 1987; Washington 1989; Peking 1992; FCO 1995; Bangkok 1998; Prague 1999; Band C4; m 1989 Claire Louise Morgan.

Shaw, Andrew John; FCO since November 2003; Born 03/03/70; FCO 1989; Bonn 1991; Tehran 1994; FCO 1996; Prague 2000; Band C4; m 1995 Sarah Gosling (2s 1996, 1999).

Shaw, Andrew William; Harare since June 2002; Born 31/03/50; FCO 1997; Band A2; m 1981 Ruth Heeps (s 1984, 1989; 1d 1990).

Shaw, Claire Louise (née Morgan); Second Secretary (Immigration/Consular) Dhaka since November 2001; Born 18/06/68; FCO 1987; Washington 1989; FCO 1992; Peking 1993; FCO 1995; Bangkok 1998; Band C4; m 1989 Alan John Shaw.

Shaw, Samantha; Nicosia since October 2001; Born 31/03/67; FCO 1999; Band A2.

Shaw, Sarah Elaine (née Gosling); FCO since April 2001; Born 29/07/69; FCO 1990; Bonn 1992; FCO 1994; Tehran 1994; FCO 1996; SUPL 1997; Band B3; m 1995 Andrew John Shaw (2s 1996, 1999).

Shaw, Sharon Beverley (née Dolan); Nairobi since October 2002; Born 28/11/66; MAFF 1991; FCO 1993; Peking 1994; MO/VC Guangzhou 1998; ECO Pretoria 1999; Band B3; m 2001 Andrew Shaw.

Shead, Robert John; Second Secretary (Commercial) Shanghai since July 2002; Born 14/04/50; FCO 1969; Bonn 1973; Seoul 1976; FCO 1977; Paris 1978; Damascus 1982; FCO 1985; Damascus 1986; FCO 1987; Nairobi 1988; Second Secretary Manila 1992; FCO 1997; Second Secretary Guangzhou 1998; m (1) 1981 Carol Ann Bostock (diss 1987); (2) 1987 Fayha Sultan (1s 1987).

Shearing, Sally Louise; SUPL since February 2004; Born 20/04/66; FCO 1985; Budapest 1988; FCO 1990; Sofia 1992; FCO 1995; Band A2.

Shearman, Martin James, CVO (2004); Deputy High Commissioner Abuja since July 2003; Born 07/02/65; FCO 1989; Language Training (Japanese) 1991; Second later First Secretary Tokyo 1993; On loan to DTI later Cabinet Office 1996; NATO Secretariat 1999; First Secretary later Counsellor FCO 1999; m 1996 Miriam Elizabeth Pyburn (2s 2001, 2004).

Shearman, Miriam Elizabeth (née Pyburn); SUPL since 2004; Born 11/06/65; FCO 1990; Language Training (Japanese) 1990; PS/HMA Tokyo 1992; APS/PUS 1996; T/D Brussels (UKREP) 2000; First Secretary FCO 2000; m 1996 Martin James Shearman (2s 2001, 2004).

Sheikh, Soraya Zia; SUPL since June 2003; Born 03/07/72; FCO 1998; Brussels 2000; Band A2.

Sheinwald, Sir Nigel Elton, KCMG (2001), CMG (1999); Foreign Policy Adviser to the Prime Minister, No. 10 Downing Street since August 2003; Born 26/06/53; FCO 1976; Moscow 1978; Second later First Secretary FCO 1979; First Secretary (Chancery) Washington 1983; First Secretary later Counsellor FCO 1987; Counsellor and Head of Chancery Brussels (UKREP) 1993; Head of News Department FCO 1995; Director FCO (European Union) 1998; Permanent Representative Brussels (UKREP) 2000; m 1980 Julia Dunne (3s 1984, 1985, 1987).

Shelly, Simon Richard; Full-Time Language Training (French) since November 2003; Born 05/07/60; HM Customs & Excise 1981-83; FCO 1983; Kabul 1986; Paris 1988; FCO 1991; Ankara 1995; FCO 1998; m 1991 Monique Marie Renée Le Roux (1d 1995; 1s 1996).

Shepherd, Daniel James Owen; First Secretary New Delhi since August 2004; Born 05/11/71; FCO 1994; Full-Time Language Training 1995; Third later Second Secretary (Political/PPA) Hanoi 1996; New York (UKMIS) 2000; First Secretary FCO 2001; Band D6; m 2001 Marina Naomi Yanai (1 step s 1991, 1s 2003).

Shepherd, Wendy Elizabeth; Shanghai since May 2005; Born 03/07/71; OFFER 1993; FCO 1996; Port of Spain 1997; Peking 2000; Band B3.

Sheppard, David Anthony; Second later First Secretary FCO since November 1995; Born 06/07/51; HCS 1968; Hong Kong 1977; FCO 1980; Baghdad 1983; Tel Aviv 1986; FCO 1989 (Second Secretary 1992); Second Secretary Brussels 1993; Band D6; m 1988 Bonita Dorsman (dec'd).

Sheppard, Jane Louise (née McMullin); Tel Aviv since April 2001; Born 19/07/70; FCO 1997; Ottawa 1998; SUPL 2000; Band A2; m 1998 William John Crean Sheppard (1d 2000).

Sheppard, Nicholas Ugo; First Secretary (Media and Public Affairs) Pretoria since June 2001; Born 02/06/56; DTI 1973; FCO 1974; Paris (UKDEL OECD) 1977; Islamabad 1980; FCO 1982; Aden 1983; Canberra 1986; Second Secretary FCO 1989; Second Secretary (Commercial) New Delhi 1992; First Secretary (Commercial) Bucharest 1995; First Secretary FCO 1998; Band C5.

Sherar, Paul Desmond; Beijing since May 2005; Born 24/02/53; FCO 1970; Brussels 1973; Africa

Floater 1976; Georgetown 1978; FCO 1981; Vice-Consul (Commercial) New York (BTDO) 1986; Second Secretary (Commercial/Aid) Luanda 1991; Second later First Secretary FCO 1995.

Shercliff, Simon, OBE (2004); FCO since May 2004; Born 23/12/72; FCO 1998; Full-Time Language Training 1999; Second Secretary Tehran 2000; First Secretary FCO 2003; Private Secretary, PM's Special Representative for Iraq, Baghdad 2003; Band D6; m 2002 Emma Louise.

Sheriff, Philip Mark; First Secretary Bogotá since June 2004; Born 30/11/71; FCO 2002; Band D6.

Sherman, Sheila Ann (née Baker); FCO since April 1993; Born 06/06/60; FCO 1984; Peking 1985; FCO 1988; Nicosia 1990; Band A2; m 1995 Christopher Sherman.

Sherrin, Barrie Robert; FCO since May 2001; Born 20/07/44; Royal Marines 1961-84; Baghdad 1989; Moscow 1991; Lisbon 1992; Dublin 1996; New Delhi 2000; Band B3; m 1967 Kathleen Mary.

Sherrington, Simon Richard; SUPL since June 2000; Born 27/05/55; FCO 1980; Language Training Kamakura 1982; Tokyo 1983; Second Secretary FCO 1987; Second Secretary (Chancery/Admin) Johannesburg 1987; Second Secretary FCO 1989; First Secretary on loan to the DTI 1994; Deputy Consul-General Boston 1996; Band D6.

Sherry, Daniel Thomas; FCO since March 2002; Born 01/02/72; Cabinet Office 1999; Band B3.

Shield, William George Rupert; FCO since March 2003; Born 18/12/78; Band C4.

Shingler, Michael John; First Secretary FCO since April 2003; Born 31/01/47; Post Office 1963; DSAO 1965; Manila 1969; Prague 1973; Dacca 1975; FCO 1979; Dar es Salaam 1981; Consul (Commercial) Casablanca 1984; FCO 1988; Consul (Management) Istanbul 1991; Deputy Consul-General Atlanta 1995; First Secretary FCO 1999; On loan to No. 10 Downing Street 2002; m 1969 Katina Janet Wall (1d 1972; 1s 1975).

Shipster, Michael David, OBE (1990); Counsellor Washington since July 2004; Born 17/03/51; Second later First Secretary FCO 1977; First Secretary (Chancery) Moscow 1981; First Secretary FCO 1983; New Delhi 1986; First Secretary (Chancery) Lusaka 1990; Consul Johannesburg 1991; First Secretary later Counsellor FCO 1994; m 1974 Jacquelynne Mann (2d 1981, 1982; 1s 1987).

Shirodkar, Dr Justin; First Secretary Pretoria since August 2005; Born 30/10/73; FCO 2003; Band D6; m 2004 Vasanti Samant.

Shivers, Marie Louise (née Stone); SUPL since September 2004; Born 27/08/74; FCO 1992; Singapore 1996; FCO 1999; New York (UKMIS) 2002; Band A2; m 1999 Gavin John Shivers (1d 2004).

Shokat, Mohammed; Amman since September 2003; Born 07/11/75; FCO 2001; Full-Time Language Training 2002; Band C4.

Short, James Walter; Bangkok since November 2004; Born 19/10/66; FCO 1986; Calcutta 1989; Shanghai 1991; Third Secretary Tehran 1994; FCO 1997; Dhaka 1999; Band B3; m 1990 Stephanie Sanjukta Ghosh (1s 1998).

Short, Katherine Anne; SUPL since January 2005; Born 19/02/70; FCO 1992; Berne 1994; FCO 1996; SUPL 1998; FCO 2003; Baghdad 2004; Band B3; ptnr, Raymond William Kyles (1s 2005).

Shorter, Hugo Benedict; Deputy Head of Mission Brasilia since October 2004; Born 11/08/66; FCO 1990; Second Secretary on attachment to ENA Paris 1992; Second later First Secretary Brussels (UKDEL NATO) 1994; FCO 1998; Private Secretary to Minister of State 2000; FCO 2001; m 2001 Laura Mercedes Lindon (1d 2002; 1s 2004).

Shott, Philip Nicholas; Counsellor Pretoria since November 2001; Born 27/11/54; Second Secretary FCO 1980; First Secretary Lagos 1983; First Secretary FCO 1986; First Secretary (Chancery) Nicosia 1987; First Secretary FCO 1991; First Secretary (Political) Lusaka 1994; First Secretary FCO 1997; m 1981 Lesley Ann Marsh (1s 1986; 1d 1987).

Shrimpton, Katy Emma; Mexico City since October 2004; Born 27/07/78; FCO 2002; Band A2.

Shute, Christopher David; Gibraltar since December 2002; Born 08/10/49; HMIT 1968; FCO 1969; Middle East Floater 1972; Lagos 1974; Cairo 1975; FCO 1979; Rome 1983; Second Secretary FCO 1986; Second Secretary (Commercial) Warsaw 1987; Second Secretary FCO 1990; First Secretary (Chancery) Wellington 1995; FCO 1999; First Secretary FCO 2000; Band D6; m 1975 Peta Ann Dewhurst (2s 1987, 1990).

Siddiq, Irfan; Private Secretary to the Foreign Secretary FCO since February 2005; Born 27/01/77; FCO 1998; Second Secretary (Economic/Commercial) New Delhi 1999; Full-Time Language Training FCO 2000; Full-Time Language Training Cairo 2001; Second Secretary (Political/Press) Cairo 2002; Seconded to the Coalition Provisional Authority, Baghdad 2003; Seconded to the US Department of State, Washington 2004; Band D6.

Sidebottom, Jane Louise; FCO since September 2003; Born 12/11/79; Band B3.

Sidnell, Gail Marilyn, MBE; FCO since 2002; Born 09/04/53; FCO 1974; Addis Ababa 1975; Monrovia 1977; Gibraltar 1981; FCO 1982; Prague 1983; FCO 1985; Nairobi 1989; FCO 1993 (Second Secretary 1994); Second Secretary (Commercial) Jakarta 1996; FCO 1999; SUPL 2001.

Silva, Ginny Anne (née Kesterton); Port Louis since July 2004; Born 09/07/63; Immigration Service 1985; FCO 1987; Seoul 1989;

Luxembourg 1994; FCO 1998; Port Louis 2002; SUPL 2004; Band C4; ptnr, Mel Ferson (1d 1993, 1s 2004).

Simcox, Paul Alan; FCO since March 2003; Born 19/06/65; Band C4.

Simmons, Ian Paul; Counsellor Dhaka since September 2004; Born 05/09/55; FCO 1983; Second Secretary (Information) New Delhi 1987; First Secretary FCO 1989; Full-Time Language Training Point Cook, Melbourne 1992; First Secretary (Political) Hanoi 1992; First Secretary (Regional Affairs) Bangkok 1993; FCO 1996; Counsellor Nairobi 1999; Counsellor FCO 2003; m 1999 Elisabeth Jozina van de Ree (1d 2002).

Simmons, Timothy Michael John; HM Ambassador Ljubljana since April 2005; Born 08/04/60; FCO 1982; Third later Second Secretary Warsaw 1985; First Secretary FCO 1987; First Secretary Geneva (UKMIS) 1993; Seconded to Price Waterhouse Coopers MCS 1997; Assistant Director FCO 1999; Deputy Head of Mission Warsaw 2001; m 1989 Caroline Mary Radcliffe (2s 1990, 1993).

Simon, Susannah Kate; On loan to the Home Office since September 2003; Born 07/06/64; FCO 1988; Third later Second Secretary Bonn 1989; Second Secretary Almaty 1992; FCO 1994; First Secretary (Political) Bonn 1999; m 1994 Mikhail Mnaidarovich Kubekov (1s 1996).

Simpson, Brian; Third Secretary (Visits) Hong Kong since May 2003; Born 08/05/67; FCO 1986; Warsaw 1988; Lagos 1991; FCO 1995; Vice-Consul Budapest 1999; Band B3.

Simpson, Faye Marie; Paris since June 2004; Born 03/06/78; FCO 2003; Band A2.

Simpson, Georgina Felicity (née Little); FCO since September 1999; Born 23/02/64; FCO 1986; Language Training 1987; Second Secretary Amman 1989; SUPL 1991; Second Secretary (Commercial/Economic/Political) Sana'a 1991; FCO 1994; SUPL 1999; m 1991 Dominic Mark Simpson (1d 1996).

Simpson, Gordon Grant; HM Consul Oporto since June 2003; Born 25/08/46; FO 1964; Peking 1968; Lisbon 1970; Ibadan 1972; FCO 1975; Bucharest 1978; Nairobi 1979; Lisbon 1982; Second Secretary FCO 1985; Second Secretary (Commercial) Luanda 1987; Second Secretary (Immigration) Islamabad 1990; First Secretary FCO 1992; Deputy Consul-General Rio de Janeiro 1994; Deputy Consul-General and HM Consul (Commercial) San Francisco 1998; m 1970 Jenny Frances Parker (1d 1974; 2s 1975, 1982).

Simpson, Louise Jane; FCO since 2002; Born 24/06/66; FCO 1986; Lima 1988; SUPL 1990; FCO 1992; Moscow 1993; FCO 1996; Kampala 1998; Band C4.

Simpson, Matthew Richard; Third Secretary (Consular) Wellington since February 2004; Born 04/05/72; FCO 1999; Floater Duties 2001; Band B3; m 2003 Anita Angela Krishna.

Simpson, Scott, MBE (2005); FCO since May 2003; Born 28/03/70; FCO 1991; Bangkok 1995; Lima 1999; Band B3.

Simpson, Timothy John; FCO since September 1998; Born 14/09/60; FCO 1988; Third Secretary (Political) Budapest 1994; Band B3; m 1985 Lise Margaret Finlay (3d 1986, 1992, 1995).

Sims, Christopher Julien Bouyer; Second Secretary The Hague since December 2004; Born 08/05/78; FCO 1999; Full-Time Language Training 2000; Second Secretary (Political) Seoul 2001; Band C4.

Sinclair, Fiona Louise; FCO since October 2003; Born 13/01/71; FCO 1993; Full-Time Language Training 1995; Third Secretary (Political) Strasbourg 1996; Third Secretary (Political) Zagreb 1999; Band C4.

Sinclair, Robert Nelson Gurney; Paris since December 2004; Born 10/12/52; FCO 1972; Dacca 1975; Algiers 1978; East Berlin 1980; CG Berlin 1981; FCO 1984; Third later Second Secretary Jakarta 1987; FCO 1991; Second Secretary (KHF) Sofia 1996; On loan to the DTI 1999; Band C5; m 1975 Diana Sawyer (1s 1986; 1d 1988).

Singh, Mala; SUPL since August 2003; Born 01/01/73; FCO 1996; Buenos Aires 2000; Band A2.

Singh, Tracey Michelle (née Chapman); SUPL since April 2004; Born 30/10/68; FCO 1988; New Delhi 1990; FCO 1994; Dubai 1996; SUPL 1999; FCO 2000; Third Secretary (Immigration) Accra 2001; Band B3; m 1995 Jasminder Singh (2d 1999, 2002).

Sinkinson, Philip Andrew; Deputy Head of Mission Kingston since September 2001; Born 07/10/50; Inland Revenue 1967; FCO 1970; Warsaw 1973; FCO 1974; East Berlin 1974; Rome 1975; FCO 1976; Rio de Janeiro 1978; Quito 1978; Prague 1979; FCO 1981; Blantyre 1982; Lilongwe 1985; FCO 1986; Second Secretary (Commercial) São Paulo 1991; Olympic Attaché Atlanta 1995; First Secretary (Commercial) Lisbon 1996; m 1971 Clare Maria Catherine Jarvis (1s 1974).

Sisum, Thomas George; FCO since March 2005; Born 16/10/73; FCO 1999; Second Secretary (Political) Islamabad 2001; Second Secretary Dubai 2002; Band D6; m 2002 Sophie Katherine Devonshire.

Sizeland, Paul Raymond; Director (Consular Services), FCO since July 2003; Born 19/02/52; FCO 1980; Brussels (UKDEL NATO) 1981; Doha 1985; Second Secretary FCO 1986; First Secretary (Chancery/Aid) Lagos 1988; Private Secretary to the Chairman of EC Conference on Yugoslavia 1991; First Secretary later Counsellor FCO 1991; Deputy Head of Mission Bangkok 1996; Consul-General Shanghai 2000; m 1976 Vasantha Jesudasan (2d 1981, 1982).

Skidmore, Jonathan Richard Llywelyn; Second Secretary Vienna (UKMIS) since October 2001; Born 06/01/70; FCO 1998; Band C4.

Skilton, Christopher Paul; FCO since June 2003; Born 07/04/54; Bonn 1974; Santiago 1976; FCO 1980; Buenos Aires 1983; Madrid 1986; Resigned 1991; Reinstated, FCO 1993; Madrid 1996; FCO 1998; Deputy High Commissioner Kampala 2001; m 1978 Kathleen Jane (1d 1982; 1s 1980).

Skingle, Diana; High Commissioner Victoria since July 2004; Born 03/05/47; Commonwealth Office (later FCO) 1966; Kampala 1970; FCO 1972; Abidjan 1974; Vila 1975; Prague 1977; Casablanca 1979; Second Secretary FCO 1982; Second Secretary (Aid/Commercial) Georgetown 1985; Second Secretary (Development) Bridgetown 1986; First Secretary (Information) Brussels (UKDEL NATO) 1988; First Secretary FCO 1993; Deputy Head of Mission Addis Ababa 2001; ptnr, Christopher John Marshall Carrington.

Skinner, Dawn Emma; Bucharest since June 2002; Born 18/05/65; FCO 1985; Prague 1987; Brussels (UKREP) 1989; Anguilla 1991; FCO 1993; World Wide Floater Duties 1995; SUPL 1996; Sarajevo 1997; FCO 1998; Band B3.

Skinner, Gillian (née Smith); SUPL since August 2002; Born 09/01/57; FCO 1976; SUPL 1978; Beirut 1980; SUPL 1980; Beirut 1982; FCO 1982; Brussels 1983; FCO 1984; Kinshasa 1987; FCO 1988; Second Secretary 1992; Band C4; m (1) 1978 Colin Wynn Crorkin (diss 1991) (2s 1985, 1992); (2) 1996 Graeme John Skinner.

Skoll, Lindsay Samantha (née Stent); Deputy Head of Mission Pyongyang since October 2004; Born 26/9/70; FCO 1996; First Secretary 2000; Full Time Language Training 2002; On loan to Cabinet Office 2003; Band D6; m 2005 Richard Skoll.

Skyring, Andrea; SUPL since July 2002; Born 01/08/66; FCO 1998; Dar es Salaam 1999; Band A2.

Slater, Angela (née Caldwell); SUPL since July 2002; Born 09/03/67; FCO 1986; Washington 1988; Floater Duties 1992; Third later Second Secretary FCO 1994; SUPL 1999; Second Secretary (Consular) New Delhi 2000; Band C4; m 1998 David John Slater (1d 1999; 1s 2001).

Slater, David John; HM Consul (Investment) Los Angeles since August 2002; Born 02/03/68; FCO 1987; Abu Dhabi 1989; Third Secretary Accra 1991; Third later Second Secretary FCO 1995; Second Secretary (Commercial) New Delhi 1999; Band C5; m 1998 Angela Caldwell (1d 1999; 1s 2001).

Slater, Gina Michelle (née Lambert); Second later First Secretary FCO since March 1996; Born 29/07/54; FCO 1974; Port Stanley 1976; SUPL 1978; Lisbon 1982; FCO 1986; Dhaka 1988; Harare 1992; m 1976 Gordon Slater (diss) (1d 1981).

Slater, Jacqueline (née Brewitt); SUPL since January 2002; Born 02/08/65; FCO 1985; Dublin 1989; FCO 1989; Beirut 1992; Bonn 1996; Band B3; m 1997 Steven Haigh Slater.

Slater, Judith Mary; Consul-General Houston since August 2004; Born 26/06/64; FCO 1988; Third later Second Secretary (Political) Canberra 1989; New York (UKMIS) 1992; First Secretary FCO 1993; Private Secretary to Minister of State 1994; First Secretary (Press and Public Affairs) New Delhi 1997; Assistant Director, Personnel Policy FCO 2001; SUPL 2003; Full-Time Language Training 2004; m 1998 Philip Frederick de Waal (1d 2000; 1s 2003).

Slater, Karen Elizabeth Sunley; Kiev since August 2002; Born 07/03/70; FCO 1988; Lagos 1991; Anguilla 1995; Tunis 1999; Band C4.

Slinn, David Arthur, OBE (2000); HM Ambassador Pyongyang since October 2002; Born 16/04/59; FCO 1981; Geneva (UKDIS) 1983; Language Training 1986; Second Secretary and Head of Chancery Ulaanbaatar 1987; Second Secretary (Information/Aid) Pretoria/Cape Town 1990; Second Secretary FCO 1993; Chargé d'Affaires T/D Tirana 1995; First Secretary (Commercial) later (Chancery) Belgrade 1996; Head of British Government Office Pristina 1999; On loan to MOD 2001; T/D Belgrade 2001; T/D Skopje 2001; m 1982 Melody Sarah Hesford.

Sloan, Kevin Joseph Carnegie; Counsellor FCO since October 2002; Born 31/08/58; HM Forces 1976-84; FCO 1984; Second later First Secretary (Chancery) Islamabad 1987; First Secretary FCO 1990; First Secretary Phnom Penh 1992; First Secretary (Economic) Kuala Lumpur 1993; First Secretary FCO 1997; Counsellor New Delhi 2001; m 1991 Christine Ruth Lowson (2d 1993, 1994).

Smart, Christopher David Russell; Second Secretary (Consular) Ottawa since December 2001; Born 22/05/52; FCO 1971; Paris (UKDEL OECD) 1974; Bridgetown 1977; Lilongwe 1980; Third Secretary FCO 1983; Port Moresby 1987; Kingston 1991; Second Secretary FCO 1995; Second Secretary (Commercial) Nairobi 1998; m 1980 Patricia Margaret King (2 adopted d 1993, 1998).

Smart, Melanie Jane; Sofia since August 2002; Born 12/04/67; MOD 1986 - 2000; FCO 2000; Band A2; m 1989 David Michael Smart (4d 1991, 1993, 2001, 2002).

Smart, Simon James; Islamabad since July 2003; Born 29/04/71; FCO 2002; Band B3.

Smart, Timothy Spencer; First Secretary (Political) Basra since July 2004; Born 17/09/74; FCO 1999; Second Secretary (Political) Tel Aviv 2001; Band D6.

Smith, Andrew Dominic Charles; FCO since January 2002; Born 01/06/67; FCO 1990; Bangkok 1992; Full-Time Language Training 1992; Third Secretary (Economic) Warsaw 1993;

Third Secretary (Political) Bonn 1996; SUPL 2001; Band D6.

Smith, Carol Ann; On secondment to Greater Merseyside Enterprise since January 2003; Born 11/11/63; FCO 1987; Pretoria/Cape Town 1989; Budapest 1992; Moscow 1995; FCO 1997; Khartoum 1999; SUPL 2000; Band B3.

Smith, Claire Helen (née Stubbs); FCO since July 2004; Born 23/12/56; FCO 1979; Language Training Hong Kong 1981; Second Secretary Peking 1983; First Secretary FCO 1985; SUPL 1990; On secondment to German MFA Bonn 1994; Bonn 1997; Counsellor (Political/Aid) Islamabad 1999; On loan to the Cabinet Office 2001; m 1986 Michael Forbes Smith (1d 1989; 1s 1992).

Smith, Colin Anthony; SUPL since September 2004; Born 19/09/69; FCO 1995; Secondment to European Commission Brussels 1997; Second Secretary FCO 1998; Second Secretary (Political) Sofia 1998; On loan to DFID Sofia 1999; FCO 2001; Band D6; m 2000 Suzanne Hunnewell (1s 2002).

Smith, David Joseph; HM Consul Osaka since February 1998; Born 12/01/51; FCO 1969; Tokyo 1972; Kuwait 1977; Warsaw 1979; FCO 1981; Osaka 1984; Second later First Secretary (Assistant Trade Commissioner) BTC Hong Kong 1989; First Secretary to T/D Taiwan 1994; First Secretary FCO 1994; First Secretary (Commercial) Tokyo 1996; m 1975 Hitomi Takahashi (2d 1978, 1982).

Smith, Deborah Ann (née Connor); FCO (working remotely from Dhaka) since 2005; Born 10/02/64; FCO 1992; New Delhi 1994; Amman 1997; SUPL 1999; FCO (working remotely from Bangkok) 2004; Band B3; m 1997 (2d 1987, 1999).

Smith, Derek Moir; Second Secretary Freetown since February 2001; Born 12/09/67; Department of Employment 1986; FCO 1987; Riyadh 1989; Latin America/Caribbean Floater 1993; SUPL 1995; FCO 1996; Band C4.

Smith, Gerald Dominic; Oslo since June 2004; Born 04/04/70; FCO 1988; Islamabad 1992; Luanda 1996; FCO 1998; Bratislava 2002; Band B3; m 1992 Penelope Jane Clifford (1d 1996; 1s 1999).

Smith, Hugh Maxwell Spencer; FCO since April 2005; Born 04/04/59; FCO 1981; Brussels 1985; FCO 1988; New York 1992; FCO 1995; Tokyo 1998; FCO 2002; Islamabad 2003; Band C5.

Smith, Jason R; Second Secretary (Political) Abu Dhabi since December 2000; Born 20/11/70; FCO 1989; Sofia 1991; Dar es Salaam 1993; FCO 1998; Band C4; m 1994 Andreana Vlaeva (1s 1994).

Smith, John Lawrence; Deputy High Commissioner Gaborone since November 2000; Born 15/10/65; FCO 1988; Vice-Consul Chicago 1990; Third Secretary Nairobi 1993; Second Secretary FCO 1997; m 1990 Gillian Monsen (2s 1993, 1997).

Smith, Justine Mary (née Bunn); SUPL since June 2003; Born 02/10/64; FCO 1983; Budapest 1986; Doha 1987; FCO 1991; Bangkok 1995; Durban 1999; SUPL 2001; Durban 2002; FCO 2002; Band C4; m 2000 Stephen Thomas Smith (1d 2001).

Smith, Katherine Jane; SUPL since April 1999; Born 21/05/67; FCO 1990; Third Secretary (Information) Istanbul 1993; T/D Suva 1997; Band B3.

Smith, Katherine Lucy; Deputy Head of Mission Tehran since June 2005; Born 10/01/64; FCO 1987; Full-Time Language Training 1990; Second Secretary (Chancery/Inf) Athens 1991; First Secretary FCO 1994; New York (UKMIS) 1997; FCO 2001.

Smith, Lynne Marie; Bucharest since September 2003; Born 17/02/63; FCO 1982; Peking 1984; Ankara 1987; FCO 1990; SUPL 1994; Istanbul 1999; Band C4; m 1989 Ahmet Kalaycio Fglu.

Smith, Mairi (née Dyer); Helsinki since March 2001; Born 03/03/71; FCO 1991; SUPL 1995; FCO 1996; Canberra 1997; Band A2; m 1997 Daniel Beaton Smith (1d 2001; 1s 2003).

Smith, Nicolette Jane; Baghdad since December 2004; Born 30/04/70; FCO 1989; Kuala Lumpur 1992; SUPL 1995; FCO 1997; Beirut 2001; Band B3.

Smith, Peter; First Secretary (Consular/Immigration) Moscow since November 2001; Born 06/08/51; FCO 1971; Canberra 1974; East Berlin 1976; Khartoum 1978; FCO 1982; Dhaka 1983; Manila 1988; Washington 1989; FCO 1991 (Second Secretary 1994); New Delhi 1994; Muscat 1996; m 1974 Cynthia Angela Shearn (1d 1975).

Smith, Shirley Kathleen (née Sandford); First Secretary (Trade Development) Stockholm since December 2002; Born 05/01/56; FCO 1974; Bonn 1977; Karachi 1979; FCO 1981; Nicosia 1984; Manila 1987; FCO 1991; Dublin 1994; m 1978 Roland Berkeley Smith (diss 1993) (1s 1988).

Smith, Simon John Meredith; Head of Eastern Dept since July 2004; Born 14/01/58; Department of Employment 1981; Second Secretary FCO 1986; Language Training FCO/Kamakura 1987; Second later First Secretary (Economic) Tokyo 1989; FCO 1992; Counsellor (Commercial/Economic/S&T) Moscow 1998; Head of North East Asia and Pacific Dept FCO 2002; m 1984 Siân Rosemary Stickings (2d 1989, 1993).

Smith, Stephen Jeremy, OBE (2004); First Secretary FCO since November 2004; Born 25/10/44; FO later DSAO 1964; Baghdad 1968; Sofia 1973; FCO 1974; Vice-Consul Sydney 1977; Assistant Parliamentary Clerk FCO 1982; Second Secretary (Admin) and HM Consul Algiers 1983; FCO 1986; On secondment to the Birmingham Chamber of Industry and Commerce 1989; Second Secretary (Commercial) Dar es Salaam 1991; First Secretary, Deputy Consul-General and Consul

(Commercial) Shanghai 1994; First Secretary FCO 1998; First Secretary (Management) and HM Consul Kabul 2002; m 1969 Delyth Morris (dec'd 2002) (2d 1973, 1977; 2s 1975, 1978).

Smith, Stuart Harris; Beijing since January 2005; Born 24/04/48; Nicosia 1989; Belgrade 1991; World Wide Floater Duties 1993; Moscow 1996; Kiev 1998; Floater Duties 2004; Band B3; m 1969 Carol Ann (1s 1971; 1d 1974).

Smith, Stuart Vaughan; Tortola since June 2002; Born 05/07/72; FCO 1991; New Delhi 1995; Rio de Janeiro 1999; Band B3.

Smith, Susan Lesley; FCO since January 2000; Born 29/12/63; FCO 1983; New Delhi 1985; T/D Belgrade 1988; Kathmandu 1989; FCO 1992; Pretoria 1996; T/D Casablanca 1999; Band C4.

Smith, William John; Karachi since April 2002; Born 20/02/48; Royal Marines 1964-88; Bonn 1988; Floater Duties 1993; Sofia 1994; Peking 1998; Band B3; m 1971 Doreen (1s 1973; 2d 1971, 1976).

Snee, Nicholas James Michael; Management Officer Abuja since January 2005; Born 10/07/65; HM Forces Army 1982-94; FCO 1996; Windhoek 1998; Vice-Consul Moscow 2001; Band B3; m 2000 Valerie Johr.

Snell, Arthur Gordon; FCO since January 2005; Born 30/10/75; FCO 1998; Second Secretary (Political/Economic) Harare 2000; Second Secretary (Political/Economic) Abuja 2001; Full-Time Language Training (Arabic) 2003; Second Secretary (Political) Sana'a 2003; Band C4.

Snell, Michael George, MVO (1980); Consul & First Secretary (Management) Amman since July 2004; Born 09/06/47; FCO 1972; Darwin 1973; FCO 1975; Rome 1978; Banjul 1981; FCO 1982; Sofia 1983; Second Secretary FCO 1985; Second Secretary (Chancery) Washington 1988; First Secretary (Management) Jakarta 1994; First Secretary FCO 1998; Consul & First Secretary (Management) Muscat 2001; m (1) 1973 Diana Mary Powell-Williams (diss) (2d 1977, 1979; 1s 1982); (2) Victoria Blagden Curry (2s 1996, 1999; 1d 2005).

Snook, Andrew John; FCO since August 2002; Born 18/07/72; FCO 1992; World Wide Floater Duties 1995; Full-Time Language Training 1997; Rio de Janeiro 1998; Band C4; m 1999 Priscila de Medeiros Ivo Santos (1d 2000).

Snowdon, Susan Carol (known as Sue); FCO since 2000; Born 12/07/65; MOD 1983; FCO 1985; Brussels 1987; Manila 1989; FCO 1993; Accra 1997; Band B3.

Snoxell, David Raymond; High Commissioner Port Louis since September 2000; Born 18/11/44; FCO 1969; Islamabad 1972; Geneva (UKMIS) 1976; Second later First Secretary FCO 1984; Executive Director and Consul (Information) New York (BIS) 1986; First Secretary FCO 1991; HM Ambassador Cape Verde, Dakar, Guinea, Guinea Bissau and Mali 1997; m 1971 Anne Carter (2s 1972, 1977; 1d 1973).

Sommerlad, Alistair Martin; FCO since October 2004; Born 15/10/65; FCO 1996; Lagos 1996; First Secretary FCO 1999; First Secretary (Political) Sarajevo 2001; Band D6.

Soper, Andrew Keith; Deputy Head of Mission Brasilia since June 2001; Born 06/07/60; FCO 1985; Second later First Secretary (Chancery) Mexico City 1987; First Secretary FCO 1990; First Secretary Washington 1995; FCO 1999; m 1987 Kathryn Garrett Stevens (1s 1991; 1d 1993).

Southern, Thomas Andrew Oliver; FCO since January 2005; Born 15/01/75; FCO 2000; Second Secretary (Political) Skopje 2002; Band C4.

Sowerby, Karen Dorothy Howell; Rangoon since November 2002; Born 14/06/46; FCO 1991; La Paz 1993; Yaoundé 1997; Luanda 2000; Band A2.

Sowerby, Lynne; Geneva since June 2002; Born 17/09/67; FCO 1988; East Berlin 1990; Ankara 1993; FCO 1997; Band B3.

Sparkes, Andrew James; HM Ambassador Kinshasa since July 2004; Born 04/07/59; FCO 1982; Second Secretary (Chancery) Ankara 1985; First Secretary FCO 1988; First Secretary (Political) Bangkok 1992; First Secretary later Counsellor FCO 1995; On loan to the DTI 1997; Deputy Head of Mission Jakarta 1999; Deputy High Commissioner Pretoria 2001; m 1985 Jean Mary Meakin (1s 1988; 1d 1992).

Sparrow, Rosalyn Louise (née Morris), MVO (1999); SUPL since June 2001; Born 15/05/61; FCO 1983; Dhaka 1986; Brussels (UKDEL) 1989; Second Secretary (Economic) Brussels 1991; Second Secretary (Commercial) Singapore 1993; Second Secretary Seoul 1998; m (1) 1986 Richard John Bryant (diss) (1s 1991); (2) David John Sparrow.

Spearman, Richard David, OBE (2005); First Secretary FCO since August 2001; Born 30/08/60; FCO 1989; Consul Istanbul 1992; First Secretary FCO 1994; First Secretary (Political) Paris 1997; Band D6; m 1987 Caroline Jill Scoones (1s 1992; 2d 1995, 1998).

Speller, Paul Anthony; Deputy Head of Mission Jakarta since January 2002; Born 21/01/54; FCO 1983; Second later First Secretary Bonn 1986; First Secretary FCO 1989; Private Secretary to the Parliamentary Under Secretary of State 1991; First Secretary (External Relations) Brussels (UKREP) 1993; FCO 1996; Deputy Governor Gibraltar 1998; m 1998 Jane Hennessey.

Speller, Susan Barbara (née Arnold); FCO since October 2001; Born 22/10/56; FCO 1984; Vice-Consul (Commercial) Munich 1987; Vice-Consul (Information) Düsseldorf 1988; FCO 1990; Second Secretary FCO 1992; On loan to the ODA 1994; Second later First Secretary (PPA/Management) Bonn 1996; First Secretary (Public Relations) Berlin 1999.

Spellman, Antoinette Marie (née Mills); FCO since June 2002; Born 24/05/65; FCO 1988; Brussels (UKDEL NATO) 1991; Abuja 1993; Kuwait 1996; Islamabad 1999; Band A2; m 1990 Garry James Spellman (2s 1993, 1998).

Spencer, David Paul, MBE (1988); First Secretary FCO since July 2002; Born 04/04/59; FCO 1978; Kuala Lumpur 1981; FCO 1983; Aden 1985; First Secretary FCO 1988; First Secretary (Political) Stockholm 1992; FCO 1996; First Secretary (Political) Dubai 1999; Band D6; m 1988 Patricia Anne McCullock (2s 1990, 1993).

Spencer, Sarah; FCO since June 2003; Born 31/05/68; FCO 1988; Kathmandu 1990; FCO 1993; Bucharest 1995; Cairo 1999; Band C4; m 1997 Mark Anthony James Hamilton (1s 2000; 1d 2003).

Spicer, Haden Richard; Consul (Commercial) Guangzhou since February 2002; Born 18/06/62; FCO 1985; Abu Dhabi 1989; Moscow 1992; FCO 1995; Second Secretary (Commercial) Bandar Seri Begawan 1999; Band C4; m 1988 Carole E Pymble.

Spindler, Guy David St. John Kelso; Counsellor (Political) Warsaw since August 2002; Born 09/06/62; Second Secretary FCO 1987; Second later First Secretary (Commercial) Moscow 1989; First Secretary FCO 1992; First Secretary (Political) Pretoria 1997; First Secretary FCO 2000; Band D6; m 1999 Laura Jane Brady (1d 2000; 1s 2001).

Spires, David Mark, MVO (1992); Deputy High Commissioner Belmopan since February 2005; Born 18/11/61; FCO 1980; Warsaw 1982; Lima 1985; FCO 1986; Islamabad 1987; Paris 1991; Full-Time Language Training 1993; San Salvador 1993; Belgrade 1997; Second Secretary (Management) Dublin 1999; Second Secretary (Commercial) Beijing 2001; Band C5; m 1987 (2s 1986, 1996; 1d 1990).

Spivey, Donald; Colombo since June 2004; Born 12/04/68; FCO 1989; Tokyo 1992; FCO 1995; Kamakura 1998; Tokyo 1999; Band B3.

Spoor, Peter Logan; Full-Time Language Training (Spanish) since November 2003; Born 04/11/68; FCO 1992; Full-Time Language Training 1994-96; Third Secretary (Commercial) Bangkok 1996; Second later First Secretary FCO 1999; Band D6; m 1998 Joanna M Haydon (1s 2002).

Sprod, Caroline; FCO since June 2002; Born 02/03/71; FCO 1993; T/D Kiev 1995; Full-Time Language Training 1995; Third Secretary Hong Kong 1996; Full-Time Language Training 2000; Madrid 2000; Band C4.

Sprunt, Patrick William; Counsellor FCO since January 2004; Born 13/04/52; Third Secretary FCO 1975; Language Training SOAS 1976; Second later First Secretary Tokyo 1978; FCO 1982; Brussels (UKREP) 1982; First Secretary Bonn 1983; First Secretary FCO 1986; First Secretary Tokyo 1987; First Secretary (ECOSOC) New York (UKMIS) 1992; First Secretary FCO 1996; Counsellor (Political Affairs) Tokyo 1999; m 1979 Haang Ai-Yuan Wong (1s 1985; 1d 1989).

Squibb, Keith Norman; Jerusalem since November 2002; Born 02/09/49; Prague 1989; Tel Aviv 1991; Warsaw 1993; Moscow 1995; Lagos 1998; Cairo 1999; Band B3; m 1974 Brigitte Pronier (3s 1974, 1978, 1984).

Squire, Richard James; FCO since June 2004; Born 11/09/74; FCO 1996; Full-Time Language Training 1998; Kabul 2002; First Secretary Pristina 2003; Band D6.

Squires, George Thomas; High Commissioner Mbabane since November 2004; Born 20/10/48; FCO 1968; Dacca 1971; Antigua 1973; Warsaw 1975; Jakarta 1976; FCO 1979 (Second Secretary 1983); Vice-Consul later Consul and Administration Officer Sydney 1985; First Secretary (Commercial/Development) Bangkok 1990; First Secretary FCO 1993; First Secretary (Management) Peking 1997; On loan to the DTI 2000; m 1979 Helen Mary Thomas (2s 1983, 1985).

Squires, Helen (née Thomas); SUPL since October 2004; Born 18/10/51; FCO 1973; Third Secretary (Commercial) Jakarta 1976; Third Secretary FCO 1979; SUPL 1983; Vice-Consul Bangkok 1990; FCO 1993; Second Secretary (Management) Peking 1997; FCO 2000; m 1979 George Thomas Squires (2s 1983, 1985).

Stacey, Christopher Robin; ECM Manila since September 2002; Born 09/12/47; RAF 1965-74; FCO 1974; Islamabad 1976; Budapest 1980; Singapore 1983; FCO 1984; Manila 1988; Nicosia 1992; FCO 1995; New Delhi 1999; Band C4; m 1977 Coral Jane Chargé (2s 1981, 1987).

Stafford, Andrew Jeremy; Counsellor FCO since June 2003; Born 01/02/53; Third Secretary FCO 1975; Stockholm 1977; FCO 1979; Second Secretary Accra 1979; Second later First Secretary FCO 1981; First Secretary and Consul Prague 1984; First Secretary FCO 1987; First Secretary (Chancery) Brussels 1991; FCO 1994; Counsellor (Political) Stockholm 1999; m (1) 1977 Felicity Joanna Maria Kelly; (2) 1983 Elizabeth Rosemary Kempston (2d 1985, 1992; 1s 1988).

Stafford, Rosemary Anne Jane (née Fish); SUPL since June 2002; Born 28/08/49; Ankara 1974; Honiara 1976; Bogotá 1978; FCO 1979; Far East Floater 1980; FCO 1982; On loan to DTI 1984; Second Secretary (Commercial) Rio de Janeiro 1986; FCO 1988; SUPL 1992; Second Secretary (Commercial) Singapore 1994; On loan to the DTI 1999; m 1987 Anthony John Stafford (1s 1991; 1d 1993).

Stagg, Charles Richard Vernon, CMG (2001); Director General (Corporate Affairs) FCO since December 2003; Born 27/09/55; FCO 1977; Third later Second Secretary Sofia 1979; The Hague 1982; First Secretary FCO 1985; Brussels (UKREP) 1987; First Secretary FCO 1988; First Secretary (Information) Brussels (UKREP) 1991;

First Secretary FCO 1993; HM Ambassador Republic of Bulgaria 1998; Director (Information) FCO 2001; m 1982 Arabella Clare Faber (3s 1984, 1985, 1990; 2d 1992, 1997).

Standbrook, Timothy William; Second Secretary (Commercial) Shanghai since May 2003; Born 08/06/63; FCO 1988; Language Training Seoul 1990; Third Secretary (Political) Seoul 1992; FCO 1994; Peking (ECO) 1995; Karachi 1997; FCO 1997; On loan to British Trade International 2000; m 1997 Jia Lei (1d 2000).

Stanton, Emma Jane Elizabeth; FCO since June 2005; Born 21/04/78; FCO 2000; Second Secretary (Political) New Delhi 2002; Band C5.

Stanton, Karen Jane (née Owen); First Secretary (Commercial) Prague since August 2003; Born 25/01/62; FCO 1984; Language Training Kamakura 1986; Vice-Consul Tokyo 1987; Third Secretary (Chancery) Rome 1991; Second Secretary FCO 1994; First Secretary FCO 1996; First Secretary (Commercial) Tokyo 1999; m 1990 Graham Stanton.

Stanton, Louise Jane; FCO since April 1999; Born 14/08/68; FCO 1990; Language Training (Japanese) SOAS 1991; Full-Time Language Training Kamakura 1993; Third Secretary (Commercial) Tokyo 1993; World Wide Floater Duties 1997; Band C4.

Stanyer, Julie Grace (née Robins); FCO since February 2000; Born 15/03/48; FCO 1984; Bridgetown 1985; Brussels (UKDEL NATO) 1989; FCO 1992; Oslo 1994; Brussels (UKDEL NATO) 1997; Band B3; m 1988 Patrick Julian Serville (diss 1995).

Staples, Graham Raymond; FCO since March 2001; Born 24/01/69; FCO 1988; Dublin 1989; Warsaw 1992; FCO 1994; Vice-Consul and Third Secretary Windhoek 1997; Band B3; m 1994 Sarah Kathleen Paterson (1d 1998).

Starkey, Nicholas Andrew; FCO since January 2003; Born 20/12/52; FCO 1972; SE Asia Floater 1975; Warsaw 1977; Bridgetown 1979; FCO 1981; Kuwait 1985; Second Secretary (Consular) Lagos 1989; Second Secretary FCO 1992; Second Secretary (Management) Bucharest 1995; Senior Management Officer Islamabad 1999; Band C5; m 1981 Rhodora Corrales Maroto (2s 1983, 1999; 1d 1985).

Staunton, Andrew James; Head of Political Section, Ottawa since September 2003; Born 07/08/67; FCO 1987; Peking 1989; Third Secretary (Chancery/Management) Strasbourg 1991; Third Secretary (Economic) Bucharest 1994; Second later First Secretary FCO 1997; Seconded to the Canadian Department for Foreign Affairs and International Trade, Ottawa 2002; Band D6; m 1990 Rebecca Anne Nixon (1s 1991; 1d 1993).

Stead, Michael; FCO since April 2002; Born 19/01/58; British Library 1976; FCO 1979; Jedda 1981; Riyadh 1982; LA Floater 1985; Rio de Janeiro 1988; FCO 1991; Second Secretary (Political) Addis Ababa 1994; Second Secretary (Commercial) Lisbon 1997; Band C5.

Steele, Christopher David; First Secretary FCO since September 2002; Born 24/06/64; FCO 1987; Second Secretary (Chancery) Moscow 1990; Second later First Secretary FCO 1993; First Secretary (Financial) Paris 1998; Band D6; m 1990 Laura Katharine Hunt (2s 1996, 1998; 1d 2000).

Steen, Barry John; Commercial Attaché Damascus since June 2005; Born 10/12/75; Benefits Agency 1997; Inland Revenue 1998-02; FCO 2002; UK Trade & Investment 2004; Band B3.

Steers, John Leonard; First Secretary (Technical Management) Washington since December 2003; Born 20/10/58; FCO 1988; Third Secretary (Technical Management) Washington 1996; FCO 1999; Band C5; m 1995 Claire Margaret Bullock (1s 1999; 1d 2000).

Stein, Gordon; ECM Tunis since July 2002; Born 20/02/69; FCO 1989; Geneva (UKMIS) 1991; Rabat 1994; Third Secretary Peking 1998; Band C4; m 1994 Deborah Anne Hooper.

Stephen, Ann (née Barbour); Tripoli since April 2002; Born 02/04/66; FCO 1988; Paris 1991; Freetown 1993; Banjul 1998; Brussels (UKDEL NATO) 1999; Band A2; m 1992 Robert Stephen (1s 1995).

Stephens, Adrian Charles; Consul-General Ho Chi Minh City since January 2001; Born 19/03/46; DSAO (later FCO) 1964; Karachi 1968; Colombo 1970; Budapest 1972; FCO 1974; Islamabad 1976; FCO 1978 (Second Secretary 1979); Bangkok 1982; Consul Berlin 1986; First Secretary FCO 1990; Seoul 1993; First Secretary (Commercial) Mexico City 1997; m 1968 Susan Jane Everitt (1d 1971; 1s 1973).

Stephens, Moira Elizabeth (née Hopkinson); SMO Tehran since June 2004; Born 28/08/59; FCO 1980; Copenhagen 1982; Peking 1985; Islamabad 1986; FCO 1990; Beirut 1992; FCO 1994; SUPL 1997; On loan to the DTI 2002; Band C4.

Stephenson, John Edmund; Counsellor New York since July 2004; Born 19/12/60; FCO 1986; Second later First Secretary (Information) Santiago 1989; First Secretary FCO 1992; First Secretary Havana 1994; First Secretary FCO 1998; Band D7; m 1986 Jacqueline Denise Clayton (3s 1990, 1992, 1993).

Sterling, Janice Aeyesha Odanna; FCO since August 2002; Born 08/08/69; FCO 1997; New York (UKMIS) 2000; Band A2; m 1994 Dwight Sterling.

Steven, John Young; Third Secretary (Political) New York (UKMIS) since December 2002; Born 21/05/68; FCO 1988; Moscow 1989; Washington 1992; FCO 1995; Floater Duties 2000; Band B3.

Stevens, Ian James; First Secretary (Management) Dublin since June 2002; Born 15/05/66; FCO 1985; Brussels (UKDEL NATO) 1989; New Delhi

1992; FCO 1996; First Secretary (Management/Consul) Oslo 1998; Band C5; m 1987 Adele Oliver (1d 1989; 1s 1991).

Stevens, Jill Frances; FCO since December 1992 (Second Secretary 1996); Born 10/03/57; FCO 1977; Damascus 1979; Bridgetown 1982; FCO 1984; Dar es Salaam 1987; FCO 1989; Moscow 1990; Band C4.

Stevens, Mark; First Secretary & Consul Denver since May 2004; Born 05/07/49; DSAO 1966; FCO 1968; Georgetown 1970; Madrid 1973; East Berlin 1976; FCO 1978; Kingston 1982; New Delhi 1985; Second Secretary FCO 1988; Second Secretary (Management) and Vice-Consul Tunis 1992; FCO 1995; Consul-General Alexandria 1999; m 1970 Pauline Elaine Graber (2d 1973, 1976).

Stevens, Paul David; FCO since September 2003; Born 08/09/59; MOD 1977; FCO 1981; Geneva (UKMIS) 1983; Kampala 1985; Washington 1988; FCO 1991; Full-Time Language Training 1994; Second Secretary Los Angeles 1999; Band C4; m 1985 Faye Jaqueline Brand (1s 1992; 1d 1995).

Stevenson, William Michael; First Secretary (Management) Dhaka since October 2002; Born 04/09/51; FCO 1971; Brussels (UKDEL NATO) 1973; Luxembourg 1977; Addis Ababa 1979; Moscow 1983; FCO 1985; Khartoum 1988; Second Secretary Ankara 1993; FCO 1997; Band C5; m 1982 Laura Birse Stirton (2s 1986, 1987).

Stew, Timothy David, MBE (1996); First Secretary (Political/Economic) Cairo since August 2003; Born 08/10/66; FCO 1988; Language Training 1989; Language Training Cairo 1990; Third Secretary (Chancery) Riyadh 1991; Sarajevo 1995; Deputy High Commissioner Belmopan 1996; FCO 2000; Band D6; m 1991 Michelle Louise Mealor (1d 1996; 1s 1998).

Stewart, Iain Jamieson; Sofia since June 2003; Born 03/12/71; Geneva (UKDIS) 1994; World Wide Floater Duties 1999; Full-Time Language Training (Bulgarian) 2002; Band C4.

Stewart, Rachel Lovett; Second Secretary Dubai since June 2004; Born 09/02/79; FCO 2002; Band C4.

Stewart, Roderick James Nugent; SUPL since July 2000; Born 03/01/73; FCO 1995; Second Secretary (Economic) Jakarta 1997; Second Secretary British Embassy Office Banja Luka 1999; Band C4.

Stimpson, Chris; FCO since October 2004; Born 27/03/80; Band C4.

Stitt, (Thomas) Clive Somerville; British Trade International since May 1999; Born 01/01/48; Third Secretary FCO 1970; Language Training Tehran 1972; Kabul 1972; Third later Second Secretary New Delhi 1974; First Secretary FCO 1977; Geneva (UKMIS) 1982; First Secretary later Counsellor FCO 1986; Counsellor New York (UKMIS) 1992; m 1977 Margaret Ann Milward (2d 1982, 1984).

Stokes, Antony, LVO (1996); First Secretary (Political) Seoul since April 2000; Born 21/01/65; FCO 1994; First Secretary and Head of Political Section Bangkok 1996; Full-Time Language Training 1999; Band D6.

Stokes, Karen Ann (née Chambers); FCO since February 2003; Born 18/12/67; FCO 1987; Bonn 1989; FCO 1991; Vienna 1993; FCO 1996; Tel Aviv 1999; m 1998 Paul Terence Stokes.

Stokey, Tracey Joanne Tudor; Brussels (UKDEL) since September 2002; Born 10/03/65; FCO 1988; Bonn 1990; Luxembourg 1993; Band A2; m 1988 Brendan Stokey (2s 1996, 1998).

Stokoe, Kay; FCO since 1997; Born 23/06/69; FCO 1989; Madrid 1992; Floater Duties 1995; Band B3.

Stone, Jemma Catherine; Riyadh since March 2002; Born 08/01/70; FCO 1991; Bonn 1994; Moscow 1998; Band A2.

Stones, Adrian; FCO since September 2004; Born 16/10/60; FCO 1986; Second later First Secretary (Information) New Delhi 1989; First Secretary FCO 1991; First Secretary (Chancery) Washington 1992; First Secretary FCO 1995; First Secretary later Counsellor Harare 2000; m 1990 Gillian Ruth Millman (2s 1992, 1994; 1d 1998).

Stonor, Ralph William Robert Thomas; Second Secretary New Delhi since April 2004; Born 10/09/74; FCO 2002; Band C4.

Storey, Neil William; First Secretary (Management) Brasilia since June 2004; Born 10/09/61; FCO 1982; Third Secretary Brasilia 1994; FCO 1998; First Secretary (Management) and HM Consul Lima 2000; Band C5; m 1992 Oyami Azevedo (2d 1992, 1996; 1s 1999).

Stott, Adam Paul; FCO since June 2003; Born 26/03/71; FCO 1993; Geneva (UKMIS) 2000; Band A2.

Strain, Scott Robert; Second Secretary FCO since June 2003; Born 04/10/70; FCO 1989; Attaché Pretoria/Cape Town 1991; Attaché later Third Secretary Vice-Consul Peking 1995; Consul-General Chongqing 2000; Band C4; m (1) 1995 Caroline Joanne Ewing (diss 2000); (2) 2001 Liu Xiao Meng.

Stringer, Roger Marshall; FCO since October 2004; Born 11/11/75; Band C4.

Stubbings, Graham James; Port of Spain since October 2004; Born 17/09/57; DHSS 1974; FCO 1976; New York (UKMIS) 1979; Kingston 1982; FCO 1986; New Delhi 1989; Johannesburg 1996; Pretoria 1996; FCO 1999; Band B3; m 1989 Kirsty Alexander (2s 1987, 1994).

Sturgeon, Christopher Charles Alexander; FCO since October 2001; Born 15/03/68; FCO 1988; Floater Duties 1990; Colombo 1993; Sana'a 1996; Islamabad 1998.

Sturgeon, Mary Nicol, MBE (2004); Amman since May 2005; Born 27/05/48; FCO 1973;

Bangkok 1974; Kuwait 1976; Suva 1978; Khartoum 1980; FCO 1982; Resigned 1985; Reinstated 1988; Nicosia 1991; Amman 1994; FCO 1998; Brussels (UKDEL NATO) 2001; Basra 2003; Band B3.

Sturgess, Neil Christopher; Brussels since July 2003; Born 13/05/62; FCO 1980; Helsinki 1991; FCO 1994; Band C4; m 1988 Wendy Alison (1d 1995).

Styles, Graham Charles Trayton; FCO since August 1998; Born 16/04/58; FCO 1977; SUPL 1978; FCO 1981; Port Louis 1985; Paris 1989; FCO 1992; Vienna (UKDEL) 1995; Band D6; m 1984 Rachael Jane Hopkins (2d 1989, 1991).

Styles, Rachael Jane (née Hopkins); FCO since February 2000; Born 14/05/62; FCO 1980; Port Louis 1985; SUPL 1988; Paris 1989; SUPL 1990; Band B3; m 1984 Graham Charles Trayton Styles (2d 1989, 1991).

Sullivan, Janet Ann; Havana since July 2004; Born 15/02/58; FCO 1977; Kuala Lumpur 1980; Montevideo 1984; Tel Aviv 1988; Floater Duties 1992; FCO 1996; Floater Duties 1999; On loan as Director to the DTI 2002; Band C4.

Summers, David; FCO since May 2003; Born 13/11/64; FCO 1983; Islamabad 1985; Lisbon 1988; FCO 1991; Lagos 1994; Third Secretary (Management) Ankara 1997; Abidjan 2001; Band C4; m 1987 Anita Cecilia Marsh (2d 1991, 1999).

Summers, Timothy Andrew; Chongqing since July 2004; Born 17/02/72; FCO 1994; Full-Time Language Training 1995; Consul Hong Kong 1997; On loan to the Cabinet Office 2001; Full-Time Language Training (Mandarin) 2003; Band D7.

Sundblad, Emma Louise; Second Secretary (Political/PPA) Stockholm since August 2001; Born 28/10/75; FCO 1999; Band C4; m 1998 Morgan Sundblad (3s 1994, 1997, 2004).

Surman, Derek Malcolm; Canberra since December 2004; Born 20/06/47; Commonwealth Office/DSAO 1967; Kinshasa 1969; FCO 1970; Madrid 1971; Dacca 1974; Stuttgart 1976; Beirut 1977; Durban 1978; Salisbury 1980; Khartoum 1982; FCO 1985; Canberra 1990; Second Secretary (Immigration) Bombay 1994; Prague 1999; FCO 1999; Bangkok 2001; m 1982 Frances Louise Stapelberg.

Sutcliffe, Nicholas Derek; First Secretary FCO since September 2001; Born 09/12/57; FCO 1985; Second Secretary (Economic) Brasilia 1990; Second Secretary FCO 1993; First Secretary (Commercial) Havana 1998; Band D6; m 1985 Carole Ann Hunter (4s 1990, 1992, 1994 (twins)).

Sutherland, Julia Marie Ludmila (née Haworth); FCO since January 2002; Born 09/09/73; FCO 1995; Language Training 1996; Beijing 1998; Band D6; m 2003 Dr Duncan Sutherland.

Sutton, Janet (née Christie); FCO since February 1996; Born 25/03/64; Department of Employment 1983; FCO 1984; Abidjan 1987; Paris 1990; FCO 1991; SUPL 1994; Band C4; m 1986 Andrew Richard Sutton (2s 1987, 1995).

Sutton, Rebecca Claire; FCO since August 2004; Born 25/09/73; FCO 1999; Full-Time Language Training 2001; Second Secretary (Political) Pristina 2002; Band C4.

Swainson, Emma Mary Dillwyn; FCO since September 2004; Born 28/12/75; FCO 2000; Full-Time Language Training 2002; Band C4.

Sweeney, Carole Mary (née Crofts); First Secretary later Counsellor FCO since August 1999; Born 24/06/59; MOD 1985; FCO 1987; Second Secretary Bonn 1989; Second Secretary East Berlin 1990; Second later First Secretary FCO 1991; First Secretary (Economic) Oslo 1997; m 1988 Paul Martin Sweeney (1d 1990; 1s 1992).

Sweeney, Ian John; First Secretary Vienna since July 2001; Born 01/07/49; Second Secretary Bangkok 1984; Second later First Secretary Lagos 1989; FCO 1993; First Secretary Washington 1996; FCO 2000; m 1975 Mairead Aine Condron (2d 1977, 1988; 2s 1978, 1988).

Sweet, Kay (née Rose); Brussels (UKREP) since January 1997; Born 11/11/63; FCO 1984; Budapest 1985; Paris 1987; Floater Duties 1991; Brussels (UKREP) 1993; Paris 1995; SUPL 1996; Band B3; m 1996 Jonathan Charles Sweet (1d 2002).

Sweid, Janice Ann Townsend (née Oldfield); FCO since January 2004; Born 13/06/50; FCO 1970; On loan to the Cabinet Office 1973; FCO 1974; Accra 1977; FCO 1979; Washington 1984; Second Secretary (Management) Tel Aviv 1987; FCO 1992; First Secretary (Management) JMO Brussels 1998; m 1980 Youda Yomtob Sweid.

Swift, Hans Eric; Counsellor FCO since April 2001; Born 14/05/58; FCO 1980; New Delhi 1982; Second Secretary FCO 1986; Second later First Secretary (Chancery) Stockholm 1988; FCO 1991; First Secretary (Political) Washington 1998; m (1) 1981 Susan Mary Brown (diss 1995) (1d 1988; 1s 1991); (2) 1999 Elined Clare Evans.

Sykes, Christopher Rowland Charlesworth; Counsellor and Deputy Consul-General Hong Kong since September 2004; Born FCO 1986; Second later First Secretary Hong Kong 1987; SUPL 1990; Resigned 1991; Reinstated, FCO 2003; First Secretary FCO 2004; m 1981 Sandra Ross (1d 1983; 1s 1985).

Sykes, Graham Leslie; Manila since July 2003; Born 20/09/60; FCO 1987; New Delhi 1992; FCO 1995; Pretoria 1995; Sana'a 1999; Band B3; m 1995 Wei Li Ming.

Sykes, Roger Michael Spencer, OBE (2002); Deputy Head of Mission Karachi since February 2002; Born 22/10/50; FCO 1968; Caracas 1971; Freetown 1972; Karachi 1976; Valletta 1978; Lagos 1982; Port Vila 1986; Second Secretary FCO 1990; Amman 1993; First Secretary and Head of British Trade Office Al Khobar 1997-01;

Band D6; m 1976 Anne Lesley Groves-Gidney (3s 1977, 1980, 1988).

Syposz, Shelley Liann (née Mayman); SUPL since May 2001; Born 02/05/70; FCO 1991; New Delhi 1993; FCO 1995; Prague 1998; Band A2; m 1996 Julian Jeremy Syposz.

Syrett, Mark Robert; Second Secretary (Political) Riyadh since November 2004; Born 09/04/69; FCO 1993; Second Secretary (Political) Oslo 1998; Second Secretary FCO 2002; Band C4.

Syrett, Nicholas Simon; Counsellor Nairobi since February 2003; Born 07/12/60; FCO 1989; First Secretary (Political) Luanda 1993; First Secretary FCO 1996; First Secretary (Political) Bogotá 1998; First Secretary FCO 2000; m 1993 Elena Fircks (1s, 1d 1997 (twins)).

T

Tandy, Arthur David; Second later First Secretary FCO since May 1989; Born 16/08/49; HO 1974-85; FCO 1985; Second Secretary Riyadh 1987; Band C5; m 1973 Hilary Denise Watson (1s 1978; 1d 1982).

Tansley, Anthony James Nicholas; Consul-General Basra since September 2005; Born 19/07/62; FCO 1984; Language Training 1986; Second Secretary (Chancery) Riyadh 1988; Second Secretary (Chancery) Baghdad 1989; First Secretary FCO 1991; Dublin 1994; Counsellor and Deputy Head of Mission Muscat 1998; m 1998 Blaithin Mary Curran (1s 2002).

Tarif, Pamela (née Neave); Second Secretary Geneva (UKMIS) since January 2003; Born 03/06/65; FCO 1985; Lagos 1988; Ottawa 1992; FCO 1994; Quito 1997; Second Secretary Yaoundé 2000; m 1988 Nacer Tarif (1d 1992; 1s 1995).

Tarry, Stephen Norman; Second Secretary (Political) Suva since July 2001; Born 21/01/54; FCO 1971; Washington 1974; Damascus 1977; Brussels 1981; FCO 1983; Islamabad 1983; FCO 1988; Warsaw 1991; Dublin 1993; Vilnius 1997; Band C5; m (1) 1981 Julie Christine Lawrence (dec'd 1985) (1d (adopted) 1984); (2) 1992 Elzbieta Jaskaczek (1s 1997).

Tarshish, Daniel Morton; First Secretary (Political) Athens since August 2003; Born 14/10/69; FCO 1994; Second Secretary New York (UKMIS) 1998; Second Secretary FCO 2000; Band D6; m 1999 Pamela Goddard (1d 1999).

Tatham, Michael Harry; SUPL since June 2005; Born 02/07/65; FCO 1987; Third later Second Secretary (Chancery) Prague 1990; First Secretary FCO 1993; Deputy Head of Mission and HM Consul Sofia 1997; On loan to 10 Downing Street 1999; Deputy Head of Mission Prague 2002.

Tauwhare, Richard David, MVO (1983); Governor Turks and Caicos Islands since June/July 2005; Born 01/11/59; FCO 1980; Third later Second Secretary (Chancery/Information) Nairobi 1982; Second later First Secretary Paris (UKDEL OECD) 1986; First Secretary FCO 1989; First Secretary Geneva (UKDIS) 1994; FCO 1999; Assistant Director (Training) FCO 2002; m 1985 Amanda Jane Grey (2d 1991, 1998; 1s 1994) .

Taylor, Andrea Lynn (née Reid); Asmara since April 2002; Born 06/02/70; FCO 1989; Lagos 1992; Banjul 1995; Abuja 1999; Band B3; m 1996 Charles Richard Taylor.

Taylor, Duncan John Rushworth, CBE (2002); High Commissioner Bridgetown since November 2005; Born 17/10/58; FCO 1982; Third later Second Secretary Havana 1983; First Secretary FCO 1987; Language Training 1991; First Secretary (Commercial) Budapest 1992; On loan to Rolls Royce Plc 1996; Counsellor FCO 1997; Deputy Consul General (Political, Press and Public Affairs) New York 2000; m 1981 Marie-Béatrice (Bébé) Terpougoff (3 step d 1972 (twins), 1973; 2s 1984, 1986).

Taylor, Emma Louise; FCO since November 2004; Born 02/01/82; FCO 2000; Abu Dhabi 2002; SUPL 2004; Band B3; ptnr, John Galbraith (1s 2004).

Taylor, Eric Raymond; Second Secretary FCO since August 2004; Born 09/01/69; FCO 1994; Vice-Consul & Deputy Head of BIS Tripoli 1999; Vice-Consul BE Tripoli 1999; Third Secretary (Political) New Delhi 2001; Band C4; m 1998 Lynn Dudley (2s 2001, 2005).

Taylor, Hugh Mackay; Consul (Commercial) Munich since November 1999; Born 15/05/54; FCO 1972; Brussels (UKREP) 1975; Brunei 1978; FCO 1981; Munich 1985; Second Secretary (Chancery/Information) Lisbon 1988; Second Secretary FCO 1993; Warsaw 1996; m 1977 Christine Caggie.

Taylor, Ian Stewart; Mexico City since August 2001; Born 27/01/70; FCO 1986; Cairo 1994; FCO 1998; Band C4; m 1998 Kim Catherine Higgins (2s 2001, 2003).

Taylor, Jeffrey; First Secretary (Commercial) Chicago since January 2002; Born 15/08/57; FCO 1976; BMG Berlin 1979; Lusaka 1982; Moscow 1984; FCO 1985; Melbourne 1988; Canberra 1990; Second Secretary (Commercial) Helsinki 1992; Second Secretary FCO 1997; Second Secretary British Trade International 1999; m 1981 Janette Anne Hunt (diss) (2s 1987, 1990).

Taylor, Karen Ruth (née Nelms); FCO since July 2000; Born 23/06/57; FCO 1978; New Delhi 1978; Peking 1982; Washington 1983; FCO 1985; Port Louis 1992; SUPL 1996; Band B3; m 1991 Nigel David Muir Taylor (1d 1993; 1s 1995).

Taylor, Kenneth James; FCO since November 2003; Born 06/09/79; Band B3.

Taylor, Kim Catherine (née Higgins); Mexico City since July 2002; Born 14/10/66; FCO 1987; Lagos 1989; FCO 1993; Cairo 1994; FCO 1998; SUPL 2001; Band B3; m 1998 Ian Stewart Taylor (2s 2001, 2003).

Taylor, Louise Elizabeth; Third Secretary (Pol/PPA) Tirana since March 2004; Born 30/11/75; FCO 2000; Third Secretary (Management) Dar es Salaam 2002; Band B3.

Taylor, Mark Christopher; First Secretary (Political/Military) Riyadh since January 2005; Born 04/06/76; FCO 2000; Second Secretary (Political) Damascus 2002; FCO 2004; Band C4.

Taylor, Matthew John; First Secretary (Chancery) Washington since December 2004; Born 27/08/72; FCO 1995; Second later First Secretary New York (UKMIS) 1997; Private Secretary to the Minister of State FCO 2001; First Secretary Brussels (UKREP) 2002; Band D6.

Taylor, Nigel David Muir; On loan to the DTI since July 2002; Born 21/04/61; FCO 1981; Kaduna 1982; Africa/Middle East Floater 1986; FCO 1989; Port Louis 1992; Second Secretary Grand Turk 1996; Second Secretary FCO 1999; Band C4; m 1991 Karen Ruth Nelms (1d 1993; 1s 1995).

Taylor, Robert James; SUPL since October 2000; Born 07/04/57; HCS 1987; FCO 1989; Prague 1990; Havana 1992; FCO 1993; Buenos Aires 1996; Band A2.

Taylor, Stephen Andrew; Bangkok since January 2002; Born 15/09/66; FCO 2000; Band B3.

Teale, Ian Robert McKinnon; Islamabad since May 2003; Born 28/02/71; FCO 1991; The Hague 1995; Kingston 1996; Sana'a 1999; T/D Antigua 2000; FCO 2000; Band B3.

Tebbit, Sir Kevin Reginald, KCMG (2002), CMG (1997); On secondment to the Ministry of Defence since July 1998; Born 18/10/46; MOD 1969-79; UKDEL NATO 1979; First Secretary FCO 1982; First Secretary and Head of Chancery Ankara 1984; On secondment as Directeur du Cabinet, Cabinet of the Secretary-General of NATO, Brussels 1987; Counsellor (Political/Military) Washington 1988; Counsellor FCO 1992; m 1966 Alison Tinley (1d 1972; 1s 1975).

Telford, Sarah Elizabeth; FCO since January 2003; Born 15/06/75; Band A2.

Templar, Mark Stuart; Assistant Private Secretary to the Minister for Europe since June 2004; Born 07/03/76; FCO 2000; Band C4.

Temple, Tracey Joy; FCO since September 2000; Born 09/08/65; FCO 1993; Buenos Aires 1995; Helsinki 1998; Band A2.

Tench, Gavin Andrew; Mexico City since May 2003; Born 29/08/68; FCO 1995; Second Secretary (Commercial) Kingston 1999; Band B3.

Terrett, Nicola; FCO since May 2003; Born 02/09/66; HCS 1985; FCO 1994; Havana 1999; Band B3.

Tesoriere, Harcourt Andrew Pretorius; HM Ambassador Algiers since July 2005; Born 02/11/50; Royal Navy 1969-73; FCO 1974; Language Training SOAS and Iran 1975; Oriental Secretary Kabul 1976; Nairobi 1979; Second Secretary Abidjan 1981; FCO 1985; First Secretary and Head of Chancery, later Chargé d'Affaires a.i. BIS Damascus 1987; First Secretary FCO 1991; SUPL on secondment as UNOCHA Head of Field Operations (Afghanistan) 1994; HM Ambassador Tirana 1996; Head of UN Special Mission Afghanistan 1998; Full-Time Language Training 2001; Chargé d'Affaires a.i. Kabul 2001; HM Ambassador Riga 2002; Seconded to OSCE, Electoral Support Team, Kabul 2004 and 2005; m 1987 Dr Alma Gloria Vasquez.

Tett, Tracey Joanne (née Holland); FCO since September 2000; Born 16/07/66; FCO 1990; Language Training 1991; Full-Time Language Training Tokyo 1992; FCO 1993; SUPL 1996; Band C4.

Thain, Robert; First Secretary FCO since December 2002; Born 09/09/52; FCO 1975; Warsaw 1977; Rabat 1979; Zagreb 1982; FCO 1984; Canberra 1986; FCO 1990; Vice-Consul Helsinki 1992; Second Secretary FCO 1994; HM Consul Pretoria 1997; m 1977 Susan Mary Nice (1s 1989; 1d 1992).

Thakrar, Paresh; FCO since October 2003; Born 31/01/75; Band C4.

The MacLaren of MacLaren, Donald; HM Ambassador Tbilisi since 2004; Born 22/08/54; FCO 1978; Third later Second later First Secretary BMG Berlin 1980; Language Training 1983; First Secretary and Press Attaché Moscow 1984; First Secretary FCO 1987; Deputy Head of Mission Havana 1991; First Secretary FCO 1994; Consul-General and Deputy Head of Mission Kiev 2000; m 1978 Maida-Jane Aitchison (3s 1980, 1981, 1984; 2d 1987, 1994).

Thiel, Ann Bernadette; Second Secretary FCO since May 1997; Born 02/08/52; FCO 1971; Moscow 1973; Kuwait 1975; Düsseldorf 1978; FCO 1981; Floater Duties 1984; Moscow 1986; FCO 1988; Second Secretary FCO 1991; HM Consul Johannesburg (later Pretoria) 1995.

Thom, Dr Gordon; SUPL since September 1998; Born 18/05/53; DOE 1978; FCO 1979; Second later First Secretary Tokyo 1981; FCO 1985; First Secretary (Commercial) New Delhi 1989; Counsellor (Economic) Tokyo 1994; m 1977 Margaret Pringle (1s 1982; 1d 1986).

Thomas, Dr Catherine Clare Mitchell; First Secretary (Chancery) Washington since August 2004; Born 03/02/58; FCO 1987; Senior Research Officer (DS Band C4) later Principal Research Officer (Band D6) ; m 1989 Martin Brian Howe (2d 1990, 1994).

Thomas, Colin Ronald; Third Secretary FCO since October 1987; Born 27/03/49; Board of Trade 1967; FCO 1969; Dacca 1971; Havana 1974; Maputo 1975; FCO 1979; Geneva 1984; Rio de Janeiro 1987.

Thomas, David Lloyd; FCO since July 2003; Born 04/08/70; FCO 1996; Lagos 1997; Pretoria

2000; Band D6; m 2003 Lauren Sarah Hill (1d 2004).

Thomas, Graeme Gordon; First Secretary (Commercial/Economic) Tehran since November 2002; Born 26/09/48; FCO 1968; Africa Floater 1971; Sana'a 1975; Jedda 1976; Far East/South East Floater 1977; FCO 1980; Victoria 1982; FCO 1986; Consul Warsaw 1987; Second Secretary FCO 1988; Riyadh 1992; Full-Time Language Training 1996; First Secretary (Commercial) Athens 1997; FCO 2001; m 1981 Penelope Ann Richmond.

Thomas, Jeffrey, MBE (1995); Consul-General Paris since May 2004; Born 13/07/47; CO 1964; FO (later FCO) 1966; Manila 1969; Berlin 1973; FCO 1975; Ibadan 1978; Kaduna 1980; Second Secretary FCO 1984; Second Secretary (Admin/Consular) Muscat 1987; Consul Oporto 1991; First Secretary FCO 1996; HM Consul-General Madrid Embassy 1999; m 1969 Lesley Anne Wishart (3s 1973, twins 1975).

Thomas, Katherine Louise; World Wide Floater Duties since December 2004; Born 17/06/76; FCO 2002; Band A2.

Thomas, Lauren Sarah (née Hill); SUPL since January 2004; Born 14/02/73; FCO 1992; Conference Officer Brussels (UKREP) 1995; World Wide Floater Duties 1997; Johannesburg 1999; FCO 2003; Band C4; m 2003 David Lloyd Thomas (1d 2004).

Thomas, Mark; Prague since June 2003; Born 13/03/72; FCO 2001; Band A2; ptnr, Nicky Luff.

Thomas, Penelope Ann (née Richmond); Tehran since November 2002; Born 17/02/50; FCO 1973; Brussels (UKREP) 1974; Caracas 1977; FCO 1979; Victoria 1982; SUPL 1987; FCO 1988; Riyadh 1992; FCO 1996; SUPL 1997; Athens 1997; FCO 2001; Band B3; m 1981 Graeme Gordon Thomas.

Thomas, Peter; Third Secretary (Consular/Immigration) Harare since July 2005; Born 05/10/71; FCO 2002; Band B3; m 2000 Sarah Louise (1s 2002; 1d 2004).

Thomas, Peter James; FCO since January 2002; Born 04/05/74; Band B3.

Thomas, Sir Philip Lloyd, KCVO (2004), CMG (2001); Consul-General New York since August 2004; Born 10/06/48; FCO 1972; Second Secretary Belgrade 1974; Second later First Secretary FCO 1977; First Secretary (Commercial) Madrid 1981; FCO 1984; First Secretary (Press) Brussels (UKREP) 1987; Counsellor on loan to the Cabinet Office 1989; Counsellor (Political/Military) Washington 1991; FCO 1996; Consul-General Düsseldorf 1999; High Commissioner Nigeria, Ambassador (Non-resident) Benin 2001.

Thomas, Ryder Hugh; FCO since June 2002; Born 24/05/73; Band C4.

Thomas, Simon D; Full-Time Language Training since December 2005; Born 24/05/75; FCO 1997; Second Secretary (Political) Warsaw 1998; First Secretary on loan to the Cabinet Office 2002; First Secretary FCO 2003; Band D6.

Thompson, Christopher Colin; Third Secretary (Political) Warsaw since December 2002; Born 18/05/69; FCO 1989; Floater Duties 1992; Tokyo 1995; On loan to the Football Association 1999; Port Moresby 2000; Full-Time Language Training 2002; Band B3.

Thompson, Clive Vincent; First Secretary (Commercial) Yekaterinburg since October 2004; Born 03/04/47; FCO 1973; MECAS 1975; Islamabad 1976; Tunis 1978; Stuttgart 1981; Second Secretary FCO 1983; Second Secretary (Consul) Moscow 1987; Second Secretary FCO 1990; Consul later First Secretary (Commercial) Munich 1990; First Secretary FCO 1996; Acting Deputy Head of Mission T/D Zagreb 1999; First Secretary (Commercial) and Deputy Director of Trade New York 1999; m 1969 Carol Knight (2d 1973, 1974).

Thompson, Jan, OBE (2005); First Secretary later Counsellor FCO since March 2000; Born 25/08/65; FCO 1990 (Second Secretary 1991); Second Secretary Bonn 1991; First Secretary FCO 1994; First Secretary New York (UKMIS) 1997.

Thompson, Lindsy; Third Secretary Brussels (UKREP) since September 2004; Born 06/12/75; FCO 2003; Band B3.

Thompson, Lynne Diana; Floater Duties since January 2003; Born 20/08/59; FCO 1981; Warsaw 1982; Bandar Seri Begawan 1983; FCO 1986; Vienna 1987; FCO 1988; Istanbul 1996; FCO 2000; Band B3.

Thompson, Philippa Ann (née Hadley); Deputy High Commissioner Victoria since March 2004; Born 03/08/62; FCO 1980; Brussels 1983; Bridgetown 1985; FCO 1989; Ottawa 1991; Second Secretary Brussels (UKREP) 1994; FCO 1995; ENA Paris 1998; Second Secretary (PPA) Paris 1999; SUPL 2003; m 2000 Alphaeus Randolph Thompson (2s 2001, 2003).

Thompson, Richard Paul Reynier, OBE (2001); First Secretary FCO since January 2001; Born 17/08/60; FCO 1989; Second later First Secretary Stockholm 1991; First Secretary FCO 1993; First Secretary Geneva (UKMIS) 1996; Band D6; m 1991 Louisa Halliday-Yates (1d 1992).

Thomson, Adam McClure; New York (UKMIS) since August 2002; Born 01/07/55; FCO 1978; Third later Second Secretary Moscow 1981; Second later First Secretary Brussels (UKDEL NATO) 1983; FCO 1986; On loan to the Cabinet Office 1989; First Secretary (Chancery) Washington 1991; Counsellor (Head of Chancery) New Delhi 1995; Counsellor FCO 1998; m 1984 Fariba Shirazi (2d 1991, 1993; 1s 1996).

Thomson, Andrew Robert Hay; Second Secretary FCO since September 2002; Born 23/06/75; FCO

1998; Second Secretary (Political) Pristina 2000; Band C4.

Thomson, Jonathan Hiroshi Stewart; FCO since June 2001; Born 13/05/72; FCO 1996; Full-Time Language Training 1997; Second Secretary Tokyo 1998.

Thorne, Nicholas Alan, CMG (2002); Permanent Representative Geneva (UKMIS) since November 2003; Born 31/03/48; FO (later FCO) 1965; Yaoundé 1971; Brussels (UKREP) 1974; Second Secretary FCO 1977; Central London Polytechnic 1977; FCO 1978; Second later First Secretary New York (UKMIS) 1980; First Secretary and Head of Chancery Manila 1983; First Secretary FCO 1987; On secondment to Thorn EMI 1989; Counsellor (Commercial) and Deputy Head of Mission Helsinki 1991; Counsellor (Financial) New York (UKMIS) 1995; m 1974 Ann Margaret Boorman (1s 1978; 1d 1980).

Thornton, Claire Veronique Alison; FCO since October 2004; Born 23/01/80; Band C4.

Thornton, James Sebastian; Deputy Head of Sudan Unit FCO since April 2005; Born 02/11/64; UKAEA 1986-89; FCO 1989; Second Secretary (Commercial/Information) Algiers 1992; Second later First Secretary FCO 1994; First Secretary (Chancery) Mexico City 2000; Deputy Head of Mission Abidjan 2003; Band D6; m 1999 Anne Fiona Scrase (1d 2002).

Thornton, John Norris; First Secretary (Technical) Beijing since January 2003; Born 06/07/59; FCO 1978; BGWRS Darwin 1980; FCO 1982; Beirut 1983; FCO 1984; Third Secretary Tehran 1986; FCO 1987; Third Secretary Geneva 1991; FCO 1993; Third Secretary Berlin 1996; FCO 1999; Band C5; m 1980 Angela Dawn Clarke (1d 1989; 1s 1994).

Thornton, Sarah; New Delhi since May 2004; Born 05/06/72; FCO 1992; Rome 1995; SUPL 1999; FCO 2000; Band B3.

Thurlow, John Robert; FCO since December 2003; Born 28/08/67; HCS 1984; FCO 1988; Algiers 1990; Bridgetown 1992; FCO 1995; On loan to the DTI 1998; Second Secretary (Commercial/Industrial Relations) Rome 2000; Band C4; m 1992 Joanna Welch (1d 1988).

Thursfield, Martin Robert; FCO since September 2004; Born 08/06/67; FCO 1989; Full-Time Language Training Peking 1991; Second Secretary (Information) BTC Hong Kong 1993; First Secretary FCO 1995; First Secretary (Political) Vilnius 2000; Band D6; m 1996 Ingrid Katharina Corbyn Hale (1s 1997; 1d 2000).

Thurston, Brenda Pauline; Yaoundé since June 2002; Born 09/11/49; DHSS 1980; FCO 1984; Damascus 1986; Port Louis 1987; Karachi 1990; Pretoria 1994; Abuja 1998; Band A2; m 1974 John Anthony Thurston.

Tibber, Dr Peter Harris; Full-Time Language Training since October 2004; Born 07/09/56; Second Secretary FCO 1984; Second later First Secretary Paris 1986; First Secretary FCO 1989; PS to the Minister of State 1990; Full-Time Language Training 1992; First Secretary (Political) Ankara 1993; Deputy Head of Mission Mexico City 1996; On loan to British Trade International 2000 (Director of Business Group 2002); m 1983 Eve Levy-Huet (3s 1986, 1988, 1992).

Tiffin, Sarah Anne; SUPL since April 2004; Born 05/11/65; FCO 1988; ENA Paris 1989; Third later Second Secretary Paris 1990; Second later First Secretary 1993; First Secretary (Political) New Delhi 1997; On secondment to the Irish Department of Foreign Affairs 2000; Dublin 2001; m 2000 Pádraig Francis (2s 2002, 2004).

Tillson, Clare Nicola (née Studham); SUPL since February 2003; Born 29/06/58; FCO 1977; Washington 1979; FCO 1982; Floater Duties 1983; Brasilia 1984; FCO 1988; Second Secretary (ECOSOC) New York (UKMIS) 1994; Consul Tokyo 1996; FCO 2000.

Timsit, Milli (née Abbott); Luxembourg since November 2004; Born 11/06/56; FCO 1975; Washington 1977; Africa/Middle East Floater 1981; FCO 1982; Islamabad 1984; Tokyo 1986; FCO 1988; Tel Aviv 1991; Casablanca 1995; Consul/MO Munich 2000; Band C4; m 1992 Uzi Timsit (1s 1995; 1d 1997).

Tindell, Derek Graham; Second Secretary The Hague since April 2002; Born 11/08/69; FCO 1987; Oslo 1989; Moscow 1992; FCO 1995; Band C4; m 1993 Gail Joyce Brodie (1s 1999).

Tiney, Michael Charles; Floater Duties since March 2002; Born 12/09/66; HCS 1989-92; Bucharest 1993; Kampala 1996; Kathmandu 1998; Band B3.

Tinline, Robert John; First Secretary FCO since January 2003; Born 13/08/76; FCO 1997; Second Secretary Bogotá 1999.

Tissot, Philip Marius Arthur; Trade Commissioner Hong Kong since September 2002; Born 10/02/60; FCO 1978; Africa Floater 1981; Lagos 1983; FCO 1986; Vice-Consul Toronto 1988; Second Secretary 1989; Second Secretary (Chancery) New York (UKMIS) 1990; FCO 1994; Deputy High Commissioner Valletta 1999; m (1) 1985 Julie Anne Grant (diss 1999) (1s 1989; 1d 1990); (2) 2001 Caroline Victoria Agius (1d 2002).

Tobin, Patrick Michael; Second Secretary (Economic/Energy) Baghdad since June 2005; Born 21/04/71; FCO 2000; Full-Time Language Training 2001; Full-Time Language Training (Amman) 2002; Third Secretary (Political) Cairo 2002; Second Secretary (Political/Press/Aid) Sana'a 2003; Band C4.

Todd, Damian Roderic; Finance Director, FCO since 2004; Born 29/08/59; FCO 1980; Third later Second Secretary Pretoria/Cape Town 1981; Second Secretary FCO 1984; First Secretary and Consul Prague 1987; First Secretary FCO 1989; First Secretary (Economic) Bonn 1991; HM Treasury 1995; FCO 1997; On secondment as

Head of EU Co-ordination and Strategy Team at HM Treasury 1998; HM Ambassador Bratislava 2001; m 1987 Alison Mary Digby (1s 1989; 2d 1992, 1999).

Tolfree, Alison (née Oxenford); Washington since December 2003; Born 17/02/66; FCO 1985; Belgrade 1992; FCO 1995; Lusaka 1999; FCO 2002; Band B3; m 1991 Mark Tolfree (1d 1997; 1s 2000).

Tollyfield, Caroline Leslie (née Brewer); Second Secretary FCO since September 1998; Born 20/06/61; FCO 1994; Second Secretary (Political) Vienna 1995; Band C4; m 1995 Andrew John Tollyfield (1s 2000).

Tomkins, Michael Paul; FCO since October 2003; Born 23/12/50; FCO 1970; Honiara 1972; Aden 1976; Kingston 1977; Wellington 1980; Warsaw 1982; FCO 1983; Dhaka 1986; Geneva (UKMIS) 1989; FCO 1992 (Second Secretary 1994); Second Secretary (Commercial) Dubai 1996; First Secretary (Management) Jakarta 2000; m 1979 Eleanor Michelle Ritch (1d 1986; 1s 1989).

Tomkins, Roger James; Khartoum since May 2003; Born 30/06/48; Royal Navy 1966-88; Prison Service 1988-90; Budapest 1990; Islamabad 1992; Lagos 1994; Moscow 1998; Band B3; m 1971 Pauline Bennett (1s 1974; 1d 1976).

Tomlinson, Deborah Jane, MVO (1996); Deputy Head of Mission Kinshasa since January 2003; Born 16/02/63; FCO 1981; Islamabad 1984; Jakarta 1986; FCO 1990; Third Secretary (Visits) Brussels (UKREP) 1993; Third Secretary Belgrade 1996; Second Secretary (KHF) Sarajevo 1998; SUPL 2000; Band C5; m 1992 Mark Hyland.

Tomlinson, Thomas Mark; Second Secretary (Science and Technology) New Delhi since August 2002; Born 02/02/63; Third Secretary (Management) and Vice Consul Maputo 1995; Jedda 1998; Second Secretary (Chancery) Belgrade 2001; Band C4.

Tonge, Simon David; FCO since June 2002; Born 18/09/69; FCO 1996; New York (UKMIS) 1997; Jakarta 1998; Band D6.

Tongue, Margaret Lee; Second Secretary (Political) Colombo since April 2002; Born 19/09/74; FCO 2000; Band C4; ptnr, Paul Thomas Griffiths.

Tonkin, Ramsey Harris; First Secretary (Management) Berlin since May 2001; Born 17/04/44; FO 1964; Ankara 1966; Bonn 1969; FCO 1972; Tehran 1975; Second Secretary (Commercial) Port of Spain 1978; Second Secretary FCO 1982; Second later First Secretary (Admin/Consul) Bombay 1987; First Secretary (Management) Oslo 1989; First Secretary FCO 1995; First Secretary Bangkok 1997; Full-Time Language Training 2000; m 1966 Valerie Anne Duff (2d 1967, 1969).

Toothe, Adrian Gerald; Counsellor FCO since August 2004; Born 07/01/52; FCO 1972; Jedda 1976; Second Secretary FCO 1980; Geneva (UKMIS) 1985; First Secretary later Counsellor FCO 1989; Seconded to the Home Office 2001; m 1976 Diane Whitehead (2s 1982, 1985).

Toovey, Rebecca; Dublin since November 2003; Born 28/05/81; FCO 2001; Band A2.

Topping, Dr Patrick Gilmer; Counsellor Canberra since January 2005; Born 05/09/59; FCO 1986; Second later First Secretary (Chancery) Kuala Lumpur 1990; First Secretary FCO 1991; Washington 1994; First Secretary FCO 1998; m 1985 Indira Annick Coomaraswamy (1s 1992; 1d 1993).

Torlot, Timothy Achille; On loan to DTI since January 2002; Born 17/09/57; FCO 1981; Muscat 1984; Second Secretary (Chancery) Wellington 1987; Second later First Secretary FCO 1992; First Secretary (Commercial) Santiago 1997; m 1986 Bridie Morton (1d 1990).

Torrance, David John Baillie; Seoul since December 2001; Born 29/02/56; FCO 1975; Bangkok 1978; LA Floater 1982; Doha 1984; FCO 1987; Third Secretary and Vice-Consul San Salvador 1990; Third later Second Secretary FCO 1994; Second Secretary (Commercial) Muscat 1998; Band C4.

Torry, Sir Peter James, GCVO (2004), KCMG (2003); HM Ambassador Berlin since May 2003; Born 02/08/48; FCO 1970; Third Secretary Havana 1971; Second Secretary (Economic/Commercial) Jakarta 1974; First Secretary FCO 1977; First Secretary (Chancery) Bonn 1981; First Secretary later Counsellor FCO 1985; Counsellor Washington 1989; Counsellor later AUSS (Personel and Security) FCO 1993; HM Ambassador Madrid 1998; m 1979 Angela Wakeling Wood (3d 1980, 1982, 1985).

Totty, Alastair Walton; FCO since January 2003; Born 24/07/69; FCO 1988; Abu Dhabi 1991; Jerusalem 1994; SUPL 1997; FCO 1998; Rangoon 2000; Band C4; m 1996 Lorraine Helen Fussey (2s 1997, 2001).

Towe, Sheila; Sofia since November 2004; Born 26/07/62; FCO 1981; East Berlin 1983; FCO 1985; Baghdad 1987; FCO 1990; On loan to the DTI 1992; Vice-Consul Jedda 1994; On loan to the DTI 1996; Second Secretary (Commercial) Toronto 1999; Band C4.

Towner-Evans, Louise; Floater Duties since June 2001; Born 12/08/71; FCO 1994; Jakarta 1996; FCO 2000; Band A2.

Townsend, David John; Second Secretary (Political) Vienna (UKDEL) since June 2001; Born 31/05/57; ECGD 1984-89; FCO 1989; Vienna 1991; Language Training 1994; Vice-Consul Prague 1995; FCO 1997; Band C4; m 1993 Sarah Ann Garry (2s 1994, 1997).

Townsend, Stephen Thomas; Second Secretary (Commercial) Cairo since March 2002; Born 10/07/61; FCO 1980; Caracas 1982; Kinshasa 1986; FCO 1990; Full-Time Language Training

1992; Madrid 1993; FCO 1997; Band C4; m 1996 Fiona Maria Kilpatrick.

Townson, Jennifer Caroline; FCO since June 2002; Born 22/02/68; FCO 1989; On loan to the ODA 1991; Third Secretary (Chancery) Paris 1992; Vice-Consul Port Louis 1995; FCO 1999; On secondment (Commercial) 2001; Band C4.

Towsey, Erica Pamela (née Filder), MBE (2003); Washington since November 2003; Born 05/06/53; FCO 1974; Rabat 1975; Dhaka 1976; Resigned 1978; Reinstated, FCO 1992; T/D Lagos 1992; Abuja 1993; FCO 1994; On loan to the Prime Minister's Office 2001; Band B3; m 1976 Malcolm John Towsey (diss 2003) (1s 1979; 1d 1981).

Towsey, Malcolm John; First Secretary FCO since August 2003; Born 06/05/47; MOD 1963; FO (later FCO) 1965; Baghdad 1969; Warsaw 1972; Rabat 1973; Dhaka 1976; FCO 1979; Maseru 1982; Second Secretary FCO 1984; Second Secretary (Commercial) Dublin 1986; Second Secretary FCO 1990; First Secretary (Management) Lagos 1991; First Secretary (Management/Consular) Abuja 1993; First Secretary FCO 1994; First Secretary (Commercial) Helsinki 1999; m 1976 Erica Pamela Filder (diss 2003) (1s 1979; 1d 1981).

Trail, Amanda Ann; First Secretary (Technical Works) Nairobi since November 2004; Born 10/12/74; FCO 2002; Band C5.

Traylor, Owen John; FCO since January 2004; Born 26/09/55; FCO 1977; Language Training Tokyo 1980; Second Secretary (Economic) Tokyo 1981; First Secretary FCO 1985; First Secretary (Chancery) Berlin 1990; First Secretary FCO 1994; Consul Istanbul 2000; Band D6; m (1) 1981 Angela Carmel Webb (1d 1985) (diss 1989); (2) 1991 Carola Wangerin.

Treadell, Alan; SUPL since March 2003; Born 08/11/51; FCO 1971; Stockholm 1973; Sana'a 1976; FCO 1977; Islamabad 1979; FCO 1983; Kuala Lumpur 1985; FCO 1990; British Trade International 1999; Band C4; m 1985 Victoria Marguerite Jansz.

Treadell, Victoria Marguerite (née Jansz), MVO (1989); First Secretary British Trade International since March 1998; Born 04/11/59; FCO 1978; Islamabad 1981; FCO 1983; Kuala Lumpur 1985; FCO 1990 (First Secretary 1998); Band D6; m 1985 Alan Treadell.

Treherne, Susan Elizabeth (née Morton); SUPL since April 1998; Born 25/02/62; FCO 1986; First Secretary (Chancery) Peking 1992; First Secretary FCO 1995; m 1996 Simon Grant Treherne.

Trevelyan, Sarah Frances; SUPL since December 1995; Born 06/02/65; FCO 1983; Lisbon 1987; Kampala 1990; FCO 1993; Band A2; m 1993 Darren Francis Forbes-Batey (1d 1995, 1s 1998).

Trott, Angela Christine; Seoul since March 2005; Born 23/06/66; FCO 1990; Manila 1999; FCO 2002; Band C4.

Trott, Christopher John; FCO since April 2003; Born 14/02/66; FCO 1991; Second Secretary 1992; Consul and Deputy Head of Mission Rangoon 1993; First Secretary (Commercial) later First Secretary (Political) Tokyo 1996; Band D7; m 1992 Sunna Park.

Truelove, Andrew John; FCO since April 2001; Born 03/04/64; FCO 1991; New Delhi 1997; Band C4; m 2003 Helen Todd.

Truman, Gary Douglas; FCO since March 1994; Born 15/10/63; Home Civil Service 1981; FCO 1990; Bonn 1993; Band A2.

Tucker, Andrew Victor Gunn; Counsellor FCO since January 2004; Born 20/12/55; Joint Technical Language Service 1978-81; FCO 1981; Second Secretary Dar es Salaam 1982; First Secretary on loan to the Cabinet Office 1985; First Secretary Moscow 1987; FCO 1991; First Secretary on loan to the German Ministry of Foreign Affairs 1993; First Secretary Bonn 1994; Deputy High Commissioner Nairobi and concurrently Alternate Permanent Representative to UNEP and UNHCS (Habitat) 1997; HM Ambassador Baku 2000; m 1986 Judith Anne Gibson.

Tucker, Ernest; Harare since May 2004; Born 16/03/45; Army 1963-91; Warsaw 1991; Moscow 1993; Lagos 1996; Amman 1999; Band B3; m 1965 Ute Elli Wilkelmine (1s 1978).

Tucker, James Philip, OBE; Counsellor (Political) Jakarta since April 2003; Born 10/01/66; FCO 1990; Second Secretary (Political) Prague 1993; Second Secretary (Political) Bratislava 1994; Second Secretary FCO 1996; First Secretary (Political) Islamabad 2001; First Secretary FCO 2002; m 1991 Susie Elizabeth Betts (2d 1994, 1995).

Tucknott, John Anthony, MBE (1990); Director Trade and Investment Development Stockholm since May 2002; Born 02/01/58; DOE 1975; FCO 1977; Rome 1980; Cairo 1982; FCO 1985; Second Secretary (Admin) later Deputy Head of Mission Beirut 1988; FCO 1993; First Secretary 1994; New York (UKMIS) 1995; FCO 1998; Counsellor 2000; m 2000 Riitta-Leena Irmeli Lehtinen (1s 2001).

Tuhey, Claire Elizabeth; Second Secretary (Commercial) Mumbai since May 2002; Born 07/02/57; FCO 1976; SUPL 1976; FCO 1979; Paris 1982; Africa/Middle East Floater 1985; Vice-Consul New York 1987; FCO 1991; Dublin 1994; On temporary duty secondment to the Glencree Centre 1997; FCO 1998; T/D Suva 2000; Band C4.

Tully, Colin Nigel; Caracas since March 2002; Born 15/07/58; FCO 1980; Amman 1982; FCO 1985; New Delhi 1987; FCO 1991; Buenos Aires 1995; FCO 1997; Band C4; m 1983 Wendy Joyce Ogden (1s 1985; 1d 1989).

Tunn, Douglas Charles; Khartoum since May 2003; Born 18/02/68; FCO 1987; New York

(UKMIS) 1989; Port Moresby 1992; Jakarta 1998; Tehran 2000; Band B3; m 1996 Cecilia Rosemary Tokilala.

Tunney, Davina; Brussels since January 2004; Born 31/07/67; Home Civil Service 1987-89; FCO 1998; Washington 1999; FCO 2003; Band A2.

Turnbull, David Robert; On secondment to British Trade International since July 2002; Born 25/08/55; MOD 1976; Ankara 1980; FCO 1983; Maputo 1984; The Hague 1988; Third later Second Secretary FCO 1991; Second Secretary (Commercial) Beirut 1995; Second Secretary (Finance) New York (UKMIS) 1997; Band D6; m 1987 Eva Marianne Persson.

Turnbull, Jane; FCO since February 2004; Born 25/05/76; Band A2; ptnr, Nathan Dorrington.

Turnbull, Nicholas Piers, MBE (1999); First Secretary Tirana since May 2004; Born 23/09/62; FCO 2002; Band D6.

Turner, Alan Roger; FCO since October 1995; Born 09/04/48; Royal Air Force 1965-68; Caracas 1992; Band C5; m 1974 Caroline Grace.

Turner, Andrew Williams; FCO since August 2001; Born 08/12/63; FCO 1986; Language Training 1987; Third later Second Secretary (Chancery) Muscat 1989; Second Secretary (Chancery) Damascus 1992; Second later First Secretary FCO 1994; First Secretary (Political) Pretoria 1998; m 1992 Angeline Marie Biegler (1d 2001).

Turner, Mark Robin; First Secretary (Commercial) Lisbon since April 2001; Born 23/08/55; FCO 1975; Budapest 1977; Maseru 1979; Islamabad 1982; FCO 1984; Los Angeles 1988; Second Secretary FCO 1991; Consul and Second Secretary (Management) Buenos Aires 1994; First Secretary FCO 1998; m 1981 Patricia Louise Brown (2d 1984, 1987).

Turner, Richard Patrick; Lisbon since June 2004; Born 19/01/63; FCO 1981; Brussels (UKREP) 1984; Dar es Salaam 1986; Third Secretary (Admin) Strasbourg (UKDEL) 1988; FCO 1991 (Second Secretary 1993); São Paulo 1996; Full-Time Language Training 2000; First Secretary (Press and Public Affairs) Moscow 2001; Band D6.

Turner, Robert Leigh; SUPL since October 2002; Born 13/03/58; Department of Transport 1979; PSA 1980; DOE 1981; HM Treasury 1982; FCO 1983; Second Secretary (Chancery) Vienna 1984; First Secretary FCO 1987; Language Training 1991; First Secretary (Economic) Moscow 1992; First Secretary FCO 1995; Counsellor FCO 1997; Counsellor (EU/Economic) Bonn (later Berlin) 1998; m 1992 Pamela Ann Major (1s 1992; 1d 1994).

Turney, Nicholas; FCO since September 1984; Born 31/03/53; FCO 1971; Washington 1981; Band C4.

Turunc, Susan Kay (née Powell); Canberra since April 2003; Born 27/03/49; FCO 1968; Peking 1970; FCO 1971 (Resigned 1972); Home Civil Service 1975-79; Reinstated, FCO 1989; Istanbul 1990; Seoul 1994; FCO 1997; Cairo 1999; Band B3; m 1991 Gokhan Turunc (1 step d 1984).

Turvill, Carol May (née Massingham); SUPL since June 2004; Born 17/06/66; FCO 1985; Pretoria/Cape Town 1988; Havana 1990; FCO 1992; SUPL 1995; Islamabad 1995; FCO 1998; Accra 2000; FCO 2003; Band B3; m 1994 Stuart Graham Turvill.

Turvill, Stuart Graham; FCO since October 2003; Born 18/02/71; FCO 1991; Islamabad 1995; FCO 1998; Accra 2000; Band B3; m 1994 Carol May Massingham.

Twigg, Mark Paul; Consul-General Stuttgart since October 2001; Born 01/03/56; FCO 1975; Beirut 1979; FCO 1980; Harare 1981; Düsseldorf 1983; Tripoli 1987; FCO 1989 (Second Secretary 1991); Full-Time Language Training 1994; Second Secretary (Commercial) Prague 1994; First Secretary British Trade International 1999.

Twyman, Robin Edward; Second Secretary Geneva (UKMIS) since March 2001; Born 27/08/68; FCO 1987; Harare 1989; Africa/Middle East Floater 1993; FCO 1996; Band C4; m 2005 Laura Frances Hanslik.

Tylor, Paul Andrew; FCO since December 2005; Born 22/09/64; RAF 1985-95; FCO 1995; Peking 1997; Third later Second Secretary Karachi 2002; Band C4; m 1988 Yvonne Margaret Wilson.

U

Uden, Martin David; Consul-General San Francisco since September 2003; Born 28/02/55; FCO 1977; Seoul 1978; Second later First Secretary FCO 1982; First Secretary Bonn 1986; First Secretary FCO 1990; Counsellor (Political) and Consul-General Seoul 1994; Counsellor (Trade/Economic) Ottawa 1997; Director International Invest UK 2001; m 1982 Fiona Jane Smith (2s 1986, 1990).

Underwood, Sheila Bridget; SUPL since January 2004; Born 26/11/70; HCS 1995; FCO 1995; World Wide Floater Duties 1999; Band B3; m 2001 Neil Francis McConnell.

Upton, Helen Margaret; First Secretary (Legal) Geneva (UKMIS) since September 2004; Born 05/10/74; Called to the Bar, Lincoln's Inn 1998; Assistant Legal Adviser FCO 2000; m 2001 John Dominic Upton.

Upton, Michael John; Deputy Consul-General Toronto since February 2004; Born 28/10/51; RAF 1970-76; FCO 1976; Havana 1978; Aden 1982; FCO 1982; Bogotá 1984; Second Secretary New York (UKMIS) 1986; Vice-Consul (Inward Investment) Los Angeles 1990; First Secretary FCO 1992; HM Consul (Commercial) Seattle 1995; FCO 2000; m 1978 Susan Marshall (1s 1981; 1d 1983).

Usher, Judith; FCO since June 1999; Born 14/10/69; FCO 1988; Peking 1991; Zagreb 1993; Lagos 1995; Band B3.

Usher, Seifeldin; Second Secretary (Commercial) Damascus since May 2003; Born 27/06/69; FCO 1987; Vienna (UKMIS) 1989; New Delhi 1991; Khartoum 1994; FCO 1997; Accra 1999; Band C4; m 1995 Nihad Elnujumi (3s 1997, 1999, 2002).

V

Vallat, Joanna Clare; SUPL since January 2005; Born 17/06/74; FCO 2003; Band D6; m 2002 Jurgen Lootens.

Van Der Plank, Ian Derrick; FCO since October 1999; Born 21/08/56; Royal Navy 1972-77; FCO 1981; Paris 1987; Third Secretary Lagos 1990; Third Secretary FCO 1992; Second Secretary Islamabad 1997.

van-de-Cappelle, Clair Louise; FCO since November 2002; Born 24/05/77; Band C4.

Vargas, Emlyn Barry; First Secretary (Technical Management) New Delhi since January 2000; Born 02/02/46; HM Forces 1964-86; FCO 1986; Caracas 1989; Helsinki 1992; FCO 1997; Band C5; m 1991 Carmen Rafaela Velazquez.

Vaygelt, Robin (née Maitland); FCO since June 2000; Born 14/06/61; FCO 1984; Rio de Janeiro 1986; FCO 1988; Johannesburg 1993; Paris 1996; Band A2; m 1992 Marek Stephen Fernyhough Vaygelt.

Venn, Robert Lawrence; First Secretary FCO since August 2001; Born 15/04/65; FCO 1992; Second Secretary (Economic) Jakarta 1994; First Secretary (Political) Peking 1997; Band D6; m 1990 Wendy Ann Wightman (1s 1994; 1d 1996).

Vereker, Sir John, KCB (1999), CB (1992); Governor Hamilton since April 2002; Born 09/08/44; ODM 1967; World Bank 1970; ODA/ODM 1972; Prime Minister's Office 1980; ODA 1983; DES 1988; Permanent Secretary ODA/DFID 1994-02; m 1971 Judy Rowen (1d 1973; 1s 1975).

Very, Donna (née Grant); Berne since October 2003; Born 27/07/69; FCO 1988; SUPL 1992; FCO 1994; Tehran 1996; FCO 1999; Band A2; m 1994 Steve Jason Very (1s 1997; 1d 1999).

Vickers, David Victor Edwin; First Secretary FCO since March 2003; Born 01/05/53; FCO 1973; Lusaka 1975; Kathmandu 1979; Sofia 1983; FCO 1984; Islamabad 1985; Ankara 1989; FCO 1992; Deputy Head of Mission Tallinn 1996; Grand Turk 1999; Band C5; m 1983 Pamela Barron (née Scott).

Villamizar, Bernadette Teresa (née Edwards); Ottawa since February 2003; Born 02/03/63; FCO 1983; Brussels (UKREP) 1985; Shanghai 1987; Rio de Janeiro 1988; FCO 1992; Madrid 1993; Caracas 1996; FCO 2000; Band B3; m 1999 Igor Antonio Villamizar Rivas (1d 2000; 1s 2001).

Vineall, Katherine Patricia (née Jenkins); SUPL since January 1999; Born 07/11/63; FCO 1987; Second Secretary 1989; Second Secretary (Chancery) Madrid 1991; Second Secretary FCO 1992; SUPL 1995; First Secretary FCO 1995; m 1992 Nicholas Edward John Vineall (1s 1995).

Vir Singh, Doris Nefertiti; Paris since November 2005; Born 03/02/64; FCO 1993; Geneva (UKMIS) 1996; Paris 2000; FCO 2002; Beirut 2003; Band B3.

Virgoe, John; Deputy Permanent Representative to UNEP and UN-HABITAT and First Secretary (Environment) Nairobi since November 2002; Born 01/09/69; FCO 1991; Full-Time Language Training 1994; Jakarta 1995; FCO 1999; m 1999 Tuti Suwidjiningsih (1d 2004).

Voak, Susan; Karachi since June 2004; Born 02/06/69; FCO 1999; Lilongwe 2001; Band B3.

Vosper, Alistair John; FCO since January 2000; Born 09/04/70; FCO 1989; Islamabad 1992; Manila 1996; Band C5; m 1995 Lucy Jane Medforth (2s 2001, 2004).

Vowles, John Philip, MBE (1994); Hong Kong since September 2003; Born 13/08/47; Royal Marines 1962-87; Moscow 1987; Pretoria/Cape Town 1989; Tehran 1991; Kampala 1995; Havana 1999; Band C4; m 1968 Maureen Cann.

Vowles, Richard; FCO since October 2003; Born 16/11/76; Band C4; m 2003 Kelly Susanne.

W

Waddington, Jane Caroline; Tripoli since July 2004; Born 12/10/64; HO 1988; FCO 1998; Stockholm 2000; FCO 2001; Abu Dhabi 2003; Band A2.

Wade, Emma Lesley; FCO since January 2002; Born 15/09/73; FCO 1995; Second Secretary (Political) Santiago 1998; Band D6.

Wadvani, Sanjay Mark; Deputy Consul-General and Head of Commercial Section Guangzhou since May 2002; Born 06/12/66; FCO 1987; Peking 1989; Damascus 1991; FCO 1995; Santiago 1998; Band C5.

Wahab, Mohammed Toafiq (Toff); Head of Consular Section (Consul) Dhaka since April 2005; Born 02/04/75; HM Customs & Excise 1993-94; FCO 1997; Islamabad 1998; Lagos 2001; Band C4; m 1996 Rozmina Muhammad Anwar (2s 1998, 2000).

Wain, Geoffrey William; British Trade International since August 2003; Born 10/05/65; FCO 1983; Islamabad 1986; Istanbul 1989; FCO 1992 (Second Secretary 1994); Maseru 1995; Second Secretary (Commercial) Manila 2000; Band C5; m 1985 Kathleen Anne Lowe (1d 1992).

Wain, Kathleen Anne (née Lowe); FCO since August 2003; Born 11/02/63; FCO 1982; Addis Ababa 1984; FCO 1985; Islamabad 1986; Istanbul 1989; FCO 1992; SUPL 1995; Third Secretary

(Immigration) Manila 2000; Band C4; m 1985 Geoffrey William Wain (1d 1992).

Waite, Timothy Matthew; FCO since August 2003; Born 21/07/62; PSA 1988-91; FCO 1991; Jedda 1994; MO/Consul/ECM St Petersburg 1999; Band C5.

Wales, Lee Anne; New York (UKMIS) since June 2005; Born 07/01/67; FCO 1996; Canberra 1998; Brussels 2002; Band A2.

Walker, Alisdair James; Second Secretary (Political) Abuja since August 2004; Born 14/09/65; FCO 1989; Third Secretary (Chancery) Islamabad 1991; FCO 1995; Assistant Management Officer Moscow 1995; FCO 1999; Band C4; m 1992 Susan Mary Ireland (2s 1996, 2000; 1d 1998).

Walker, Angela Ruth; First Secretary Wellington since October 2003; Born 07/05/54; FCO 1980; The Hague 1983; Vice-Consul Rio de Janeiro 1986; FCO 1989; On secondment to the MOD 1997; Band C4.

Walker, Helen Mary; First Secretary Brussels (UKDEL NATO) since November 2003; Born 23/07/69; FCO 1991; Full-Time Language Training 1993; Athens 1994; First Secretary FCO 1999.

Walker, Ian Michael; Third Secretary (Immigration) Tehran since May 2002; Born 06/03/71; FCO (HCS) 1990; Transferred to the DS 2002; Band B3; m 1996 Nargis (2d 1999, 2001).

Walker, John Frank; Tel Aviv since August 2003; Born 10/02/64; Royal Engineers 1980-85; FCO 1987; Buenos Aires 1991; Budapest 1998; On loan to the Northern Ireland Office 2002; Band C4; m 1990 Caroline Jane Masters (2s 1985, 1991).

Walker, John Ronald; Senior Research Officer FCO since March 1985; Born 04/05/60; Band D6.

Walker, John Stanley; Baghdad since June 2004; Born 20/10/66; FCO/HCS 1984; FCO 1988; Bucharest 1989; Doha 1991; FCO 1994; Hong Kong 1997; T/D Bombay 1999; Vice-Consul Damascus 1999; Band B3.

Walker, June (née Erwin); FCO since June 1997; Born 01/06/59; FCO 1992; Dar es Salaam 1996; Band A2; m 1996 Vincent Charles Walker (1s 1997).

Walker, Neil; On loan to the DTI since January 2003; Born 29/04/63; Royal Navy 1979-89; FCO 1997; Washington 1998; Band B3; m 1992 Angela Seatter (2d 1995, 1997).

Walker, Patricia Arlow; SUPL since May 1997; Born 29/09/63; FCO 1988; Berlin 1990; Ankara 1993; Band A2; m 1998 Paul A Bertrand.

Wall, Eric Simon Charles; Counsellor FCO since September 2001; Born 04/09/57; Royal Navy 1976-86; Second Secretary FCO 1986; Second later First Secretary Geneva (UKMIS) 1988; First Secretary FCO 1991; First Secretary (Political) Kampala 1994; First Secretary FCO 1995; Counsellor Harare 1998; m 1983 Elizabeth Anne Gibson (2s 1988, 1990; 1d 1994).

Wallace, David Malcolm; Second Secretary (Chancery) Seoul since August 2004; Born 09/10/80; FCO 2002; Band C4.

Wallace, Euan; Second Secretary FCO since June 1999; Born 15/06/63; FCO 1981; Paris 1984; Moscow 1986; Resigned 1988; Reinstated, FCO 1990; New York (UKMIS) 1993; Vice-Consul New York 1994; Brussels (UKDEL) 1996; m 1987 Gillian Whittaker (1d 1996; 1s 2000).

Wallace, Gillian (née Whittaker); SUPL since November 1996; Born 14/11/63; FCO 1983; Paris 1985; Moscow 1987; FCO 1988; New York (UKMIS) 1993; Band B3; m 1987 Euan Wallace (1d 1996; 1s 2000).

Waller, Mark; Kingston since July 2003; Born 29/09/67; FCO 1987; Kingston 1989; FCO 1992; Abuja 1995; Third Secretary (Political) Almaty 1999; Band B3.

Walley, Martin; Deputy High Commissioner Bandar Seri Begawan since July 2003; Born 11/06/58; HMIT 1977; FCO 1978; Ankara 1980; Mexico City 1984; FCO 1984; Budapest 1985; Dhaka 1987; FCO 1990; Third Secretary (Commercial) Manila 1992; Bangkok 1995; Second Secretary FCO 1996; On loan to DFID 1997; Second later First Secretary (Management) Moscow 1999; m 1981 Dilek Sule (2s 1991, 1995).

Wallis, Victor Charles; Resident British Commissioner Grenada since October 2002; Born 06/02/47; CO 1963; Commonwealth Office (later FCO) 1966; Bermuda 1969; Accra 1972; FCO 1975; Second Secretary Helsinki 1979; Vice-Consul (Commercial) Sydney 1985; First Secretary FCO 1989; Deputy Consul-General Los Angeles 1994; First Secretary FCO 1999; m 1971 Jacqueline Wadhams (1s 1979).

Walmsley, Alan; FCO since July 1998; Born 06/09/61; FCO 1981; Abu Dhabi 1984; FCO 1988; Washington 1996; Band C5; m 1992 C Richardson (1d 1999).

Walmsley, Mark Ronan; First Secretary (Commercial) Jakarta since October 2001; Born 17/06/58; FCO (HCS) 1978; FCO 1980; Bucharest 1981; Africa/Middle East Floater 1983; FCO 1984; Nicosia 1987; Second Secretary (Consular) Bombay 1990; Second Secretary FCO 1994; Head of Inward Investment Section Taipei 1997; m 1986 Andrea Elizabeth (1s 1995; 1d 1997).

Walpole, The Hon Alice Louise; New York (UKMIS) since August 2001; Born 01/09/63; FCO 1985; Third later Second Secretary (Developing Countries) Brussels (UKREP) 1987; Language Training 1990; Second Secretary Dar es Salaam 1991; First Secretary FCO 1994; First Secretary UKDEL NATO 1998; SUPL 1999; Brussels (UKREP) 2000; m 1990 Angel Carro Castrillo (diss 2002) (3d 1990 (twins), 1993; 3s 1996, 1999 (twins)).

Walsh, Nicola Jane; FCO since July 1996; Born 24/01/61; FCO 1980; Bahrain 1982; Bridgetown 1985; Kingston 1986; LA/Caribbean Floater 1988; Bridgetown 1993; Band C4.

Walsh, Paul Richard; Consul (Management) Calcutta since April 2002; Born 15/03/69; DHSS 1987; FCO 1988; Berlin 1990; FCO 1990; Islamabad 1991; Third Secretary (Commercial) Warsaw 1995.

Walsh, Paula Ellen; First Secretary FCO since June 2003; Born 21/12/66; FCO 1998; Second Secretary (Commercial) Buenos Aires 1999; Band D6; m 1995 Nicholas Gibson.

Walsh, Penelope Ruth (known as Penny); Deputy Head of Mission Panama since July 2003; Born 19/12/66; FCO 1990; Third Secretary (UN) Geneva (UKMIS) 1991; Third Secretary Tirana 1994; T/D Rome (UKMIS) 1996; Consul Naples 1996; Consul and Second later First Secretary (Management) Sana'a 1998; FCO 2000; Band C4; m 1998 Primo Grilli.

Walter, Emily Rose; SUPL since August 2001; Born 18/05/67; FCO 1992; Second Secretary (Political) Buenos Aires 1995; First Secretary FCO 2000; Band D6; m 1996 Dominic William Martin (3d 1996, 1998, 2001).

Walters, Alison Jane (née Lund); SUPL since February 1996; Born 28/08/57; FCO 1976; Yaoundé 1978; FCO 1982; Sofia 1985; Paris 1987; SUPL 1988; Third later Second Secretary (Information/Chancery) Islamabad 1989; SUPL 1991; FCO 1995; m 1978 Robert Leslie Walters (2s 1987, 1994).

Walters, David Anthony, MVO (1985); Second Secretary (Management) Taipei since August 2004; Born 03/01/57; NSB 1975; FCO 1977; Tehran 1979; Bonn 1980; Port of Spain 1982; FCO 1986; Dhaka 1988; Vice-Consul Atlanta 1991; FCO 1994; T/D Abuja 1998; T/D Bogotá 1998; T/D Tirana 1999; Islamabad 2000; Band C4; m 1980 Janis Anne McPhail (3s 1982, 1984, 1991).

Walters, Helen Elizabeth; Second Secretary (Economic) Berlin since August 2004; Born 27/03/80; FCO 2001; Band C4.

Walters, Robert Leslie; SUPL since October 2000; Born 23/01/50; FCO 1970; Havana 1972; Kaduna 1973; Valletta 1976; Masirah 1977; FCO 1977; Yaoundé 1978; FCO 1982; Sofia 1985; Paris 1987; Third Secretary (Commercial) Islamabad 1989; Second Secretary FCO 1993; T/D Shanghai 1993; Second Secretary FCO 1994; Vice-Consul (Commercial) Brisbane 1996; Band C4; m (1) 1973 Mary Elaine Lee (diss 1978); (2) 1978 Alison Jane Lund (2s 1987, 1994).

Walters, Simon Christopher; First Secretary Sana'a since February 2005; Born 03/07/71; FCO 1995; Full-Time Language Training 1997; Full-Time Language Training 1998; Second Secretary Riyadh 1999; Second Secretary FCO 2001; Band D6.

Walton, Derek Antony Ruffel; Senior Assistant Legal Adviser later Legal Counsellor FCO since October 2001; Born 21/07/66; Called to the Bar (Lincoln's Inn) 1989; Assistant Legal Adviser FCO 1991; First Secretary (Legal) Geneva (UKMIS) 1997; m 1994 Claire Margaret Hughes (2s 1996, 2004; 1d 2000).

Walton, Gillian Mary (née Booth); First Secretary FCO since November 1994; Born 16/08/54; FCO 1975; Second Secretary Moscow 1987; Second Secretary FCO 1989; First Secretary Oslo 1992; Band C5; m 1979 (diss 1986).

Walwyn, David Scott; SUPL since June 2001; Born 14/04/59; FCO 1985; Second later First Secretary (Chancery) Bangkok 1987; First Secretary FCO 1990; Paris (UKDEL OECD) 1995; FCO 1999; m 1988 Fiona Cassels-Brown (1s 1997).

Ward, Anthony John; Lagos since July 2004; Born 08/05/47; Royal Marines 1964-88; Brussels (UKREP) 1988; Moscow 1991; Paris 1992; FCO 1995; Port Louis 1998; Washington 2002; Band B3; m 1996 Penelope Joan Walter (3s 1974, 1975, 1977).

Ward, Christine (née Gray); SUPL since May 1997; Born 25/12/59; FCO 1978; Budapest 1980; Istanbul 1982; SUPL 1986; Paris 1988; Manila 1992; Band B3; m 1986 Michael John Ward.

Ward, Christopher Edwin; Attaché (Visa) Moscow since April 2003; Born 11/05/75; FCO 1995; Dhaka 2000; Band B3; m 2001 Donna Michelle Perry (2s 2002, 2004).

Ward, Christopher James; FCO since May 2001; Born 04/01/78; FCO 1997; Gibraltar 1999; Band A2.

Ward, David; Deputy Head of Mission Kathmandu since April 2002; Born 11/06/68; FCO 1992; Tokyo 1994; FCO 1998; Band D6.

Ward, Gareth Edward; FCO since January 2003; Born 17/01/74; FCO 1996; Second Secretary (KHF) Moscow 1998.

Ward, Katherine Georgina Louise (Cathy), LVO (2004); SUPL since May 2005; Born 07/04/65; Research Officer FCO 1994; Senior Research Officer 1995; Second Secretary Havana 1998; First Secretary FCO 2001; On secondment to Quai d'Orsay 2002; First Secretary (Political/Internal) Paris 2002; Band D6.

Ward, Michael David; FCO since July 1989; Born 01/06/63; FCO 1983; New Delhi 1986; Band C4.

Ward, Michael John; Deputy Head of Mission Budapest since August 2002; Born 25/12/58; FCO 1982; Istanbul 1985; Third Secretary (Commercial) later Second Secretary (Science and Technology) Paris 1988; Second later First Secretary FCO 1993; First Secretary Brussels (UKREP) 1997; Seconded to the European Commission 2000; m 1986 Christine Gray (2d 1990, 1995; 1s 1991).

Ward, Rebecca; FCO since October 2004; Born 09/09/76; Band C4.

Wardle, Mark Thomas; Lusaka since October 2003; Born 22/11/62; Royal Navy 1979-89; Police 1990-95; FCO 1995; Kuala Lumpur 1997; Pretoria 2000; Band B3; m 1994 Julie Anne Russell (1d 1999; 2s 2001, 2002).

Wardle, Mark William; FCO since April 2004; Born 25/02/75; FCO 1997; Second Secretary (Chancery) Vienna 2000; Full-Time Language Training 2002; Band D6; ptnr, Sarah Kenny.

Wardle, Sharon Anne; Riyadh since January 2005; Born 02/03/65; FCO 1985; Moscow 1987; FCO 1989; Ex-Floater Duties 1990; Vice-Consul Beirut 1991; On loan to British Trade International 1996; Secondment to Private Sector 2000; On loan to British Trade International 2003; Band D7; m 2002 Peter Nicholas Millman.

Ware, Jillian Angela; SUPL since February 1999; Born 17/12/62; FCO 1982; New York (UKMIS) 1984; Africa/Middle East Floater 1988; FCO 1990; Amman 1994; Band B3; m 1990 David Edward Ware (2d 1991, 1995).

Waring, Lynn Elizabeth (née Cuthbert); Reinstated FCO since January 2003; Born 16/01/53; FCO 1973; Bonn 1978; Kuwait 1981; Resigned 1985; Band B3; m 1974 David Waring (1s 1987, 1d 1990).

Warr, Martyn John, OBE (2005); FCO since December 1997; Born 01/05/59; FCO 1981; Language Training 1983; Jedda 1984; FCO 1988 (Second Secretary 1989); Second Secretary (Commercial) Lisbon 1993; Band D7; m 1992 Sarah Jane Thompson Warr (2d 1993, 1996; 1s 2001).

Warren, David Alexander; Director, Business Group, Trade Partners UK since April 2000; Born 11/08/52; Third Secretary FCO 1975; Language Training (Japanese) 1976-78; Second Secretary and Private Secretary to the Ambassador Tokyo 1978; Second later First Secretary (Economic) Tokyo 1979; First Secretary FCO 1981; Head of Chancery Nairobi 1987; FCO 1990; Counsellor on loan to the Science and Technology Secretariat, later Office of Science and Technology at the Cabinet Office 1991; Counsellor (Commercial) Tokyo 1993; Head of Hong Kong Department, later China Hong Kong Department 1998; FCO 1998; m 1992 Pamela Pritchard.

Warren-Gash, Haydon Boyd; HM Ambassador Bogotá since September 2005; Born 08/08/49; FCO 1971; Language Training London University 1972; Third Secretary Ankara 1973; Second later First Secretary (Chancery) Madrid 1977; First Secretary FCO 1981; First Secretary (Commercial) Paris 1985; First Secretary FCO 1989; Deputy High Commissioner Nairobi 1991; Counsellor FCO 1994; HM Ambassador Abidjan and HM Ambassador non-resident to Liberia, Niger and Burkina Faso 1997; FCO 2001; HM Ambassador Rabat and (non-resident) to Mauritania 2002; m 1973 Caroline Emma Bowring Leather (1s 1975; 1d 1977).

Warrington, Guy Murray; Deputy Head of Mission Seoul since February 2005; Born 23/09/63; FCO 1986; Third later Second Secretary (Economic/Information) Singapore 1988; Second Secretary New York (UKMIS) 1992; First Secretary FCO 1993; Geneva (UKMIS) 1997; FCO 2001; m 2000 Karen Malia.

Warwick, Sharon Joy; SUPL since April 2002; Born 31/01/57; FCO 1979; Rangoon 1980; Kuala Lumpur 1982; FCO 1983; Band B3; m 1983 Aiden Eustace Warwick.

Watchorn, Kenneth Graham; First Secretary FCO since April 2000; Born 20/09/54; FCO 1971; Washington 1979; FCO 1982; Vienna 1984; FCO 1987; Riyadh 1987; Second Secretary FCO 1992; Paris 1997; Band D6; m 1980 Rossalyn Keen (2s 1983, 1985).

Watchorn, Mark; Deputy High Commissioner Maseru since July 2002; Born 28/07/65; FCO 1984; Cape Town/Pretoria 1987; Africa/Middle East Floater 1990; FCO 1992; On loan to DTI 1996; Band C4; m 1996 Christine Jacqueline Holding (1s 1998; 1d 2001).

Waterhouse, Christine; FCO since November 2002; Born 15/09/67; FCO 1987; Nairobi 1991; FCO 1994; Athens 1998; Band B3.

Waterhouse, Peter Laurance; Addis Ababa since June 2003; Born 03/02/58; FCO 1975; Bonn 1987; FCO 1990; Nicosia 1991; FCO 1994; Warsaw 1996; NIO 1999; Band C4; m 1985 Clare Rachel Dewar (2d 1993, 1999).

Waterton, James, LVO (1995); Deputy Head of Mission Montevideo since May 2002; Born 25/04/49; FCO 1968; Havana 1970; Valletta 1972; Bonn 1974; FCO 1977; Wellington 1981; Second Secretary and Vice-Consul Montevideo 1984; Second Secretary FCO 1987; HM Consul later First Secretary Durban 1991; Deputy Consul-General Istanbul 1996; First Secretary FCO 1999; m 1994 Judith Kerwin.

Waterworth, Peter Andrew; Counsellor (Political) Islamabad since March 2003; Born 15/04/57; Assistant later Senior Legal Adviser FCO 1987; First Secretary (Legal Adviser) Bonn 1990; First Secretary FCO 1994; First Secretary (Political/External) Rome 1996; Head of Political Affairs Division NIO (Belfast) 2000; m 1994 Catherine Finnigan.

Watkinson, Barry; FCO since April 2000; Born 22/08/44; FCO 1984; Brussels 1988; FCO 1991; Moscow 1996; Band C4; m 1988 Patricia Rose.

Watson, David James; First Secretary FCO since August 1999; Born 04/03/57; FCO 1988; Second later First Secretary Harare 1989; First Secretary FCO 1992; First Secretary (Political) Madrid 1996; Band D6; m 1989 Sheelah McKeown (2d 1989, 1991).

Watson, Gavin Christopher; First Secretary (Legal) New York (UKMIS) since July 2003; Born 21/07/70; Solicitor; legal Assistant Home Office 1995; Assistant Legal Adviser FCO 2000.

Watson, James Spencer Kennedy; First Secretary FCO since October 2000; Born 30/11/64; FCO 1988; Second Secretary (Economic) Kuwait 1991; Second Secretary FCO 1994; First Secretary (Political) Damascus 1997; Band D6.

Watson, Joel Aaron; Deputy High Commissioner Vila since February 2002; Born 14/09/69; FCO 1989; Belmopan 1991; Islamabad 1994; FCO 1998; Band C4; m 1990 Victoria Jane Baxter (1s 1999; 1d 2004).

Watson, Nicholas Henry Lewis; First Secretary (Political) Kuwait since October 2003; Born 12/06/71; FCO 1995; Full-Time Language Training 1997; Full-Time Language Training Cairo 1998; Second Secretary (Political) Amman 1999; Second Secretary FCO 2001; Band D6; m 1997 Catriona Ann (1s 2000; 1d 2004).

Watson, Robert Emmerson; First Secretary (Regional Affairs) Kampala since March 2004; Born 10/08/70; FCO 1996; Second Secretary Tel Aviv 1998; FCO 2001; Band C4; m 2002 Cerys Anwen Evans (1d 2004).

Watson, Stephen; Chairman DSTUS FCO since July 2001; Born 18/06/57; HO 1975; FCO 1976; Jedda 1979; Hong Kong 1982; Brasilia 1986; FCO 1988; Band C5.

Watson, Terence Paul; Second Secretary (Technical Management) New Delhi since April 2001; Born 07/12/48; HM Forces 1964-76; FCO 1988; Band C4; m 1969 Jennifer Margaret (2s 1970, 1972).

Watt, James Wilfrid, CVO; HM Ambassador Beirut since October 2003; Born 05/11/51; FCO 1977; MECAS 1978; Second later First Secretary Abu Dhabi 1980; FCO 1983; First Secretary (Chancery) New York (UKMIS) 1985; First Secretary FCO 1989; Deputy Head of Mission Amman 1992; Deputy Head of Mission Islamabad 1996; SOAS 1999; Head of Consular Division 2000; m 1980 Elizabeth Ghislaine Villeneuvre (dec'd) (1s 1981; 1d 1986).

Wattam, John; First Secretary FCO since November 2004; Born 11/05/63; FCO 1982; Bonn 1984; Karachi 1987; FCO 1991; Third Secretary (Commercial) Lagos 1994; Third Secretary (Political/Information) Lagos 1995; Full-Time Language Training 1998; Second Secretary (Political) Geneva (UKDIS) 1998; m 1991 Anne Michelle Watson (2d 1993, 1998; 1s 1995).

Watts, Elizabeth Helen; FCO since June 2004; Born 22/03/79; OFTEL 1997; FCO 1999; Bucharest 2000; SUPL 2003; Band A2; (2s 2002).

Waugh, Linda Alison; FCO since May 2005; Born 20/03/65; MOD 1984; FCO 1992; Athens 1996; FCO 1999; Ottawa 2004; Band A2.

Waugh, Lisa Helen (née Maley); FCO since August 2000; Born 28/08/67; FCO 1988; Brussels 1990; FCO 1992; Hong Kong 1993; Istanbul 1996; FCO 1999; SUPL 2000; Band C5; m 1995 Graeme Stewart Waugh (1d 1998; 1s 2000).

Webb, Robert, OBE (2000); FCO since July 2000; Born 06/06/50; Montserrat; DSAO (later FCO) 1966; Singapore 1971; Guatemala City 1974; FCO 1978; Floater Duties 1982; Hanoi 1984; Second Secretary and Consul Mexico City 1985; Second Secretary FCO 1989; Deputy Head of Mission Georgetown 1993; First Secretary Plymouth 1997; m 1989 Maria Del Carmen Colin Irieta (1s 1994).

Webb, Sarah Jane; FCO since July 2002; Born 02/12/66; FCO 1987; Budapest 1990; FCO 1992; Kuala Lumpur 1994; FCO 1997; Floater Duties 2000; Band A2.

Webber, Barbara Ann (née Leatherbarrow); FCO since July 1995; Born 06/03/66; FCO 1987; Peking 1992; Band B3; m 1996 Martin George Webber (1s 1998; 1d 2001).

Webber, Martin George; Third Secretary (Political) Berne since March 2002; Born 19/10/60; HO 1979-81; FCO 1989; Geneva (UKMIS) 1990; FCO 1992; Peking 1993; FCO 1995; Third Secretary (Management) Quito 1998; Band B3; m 1996 Barbara Ann Leatherbarrow (1s 1998; 1d 2001).

Webster, John Auld; Geneva (UKMIS) since July 2003; Born 06/09/68; FCO 1988; Nicosia 1990; FCO 1992; Port Louis 1996; Strasbourg 1999; Band C4.

Weeks, Sarah Marguerite; Second Secretary (Chancery) Wellington since July 2002; Born 15/10/68; FCO 1987; Abidjan 1990; Floater Duties 1993; Paris 1995; FCO 1998; Band C4.

Weinrabe, Stephen Michael; Management Officer/Consul Belgrade since November 2004; Born 13/06/50; FO (later FCO) 1967; Bucharest 1971; Paris 1972; Dublin 1973; Tehran 1975; FCO 1977; Nicosia 1981; Bangkok 1984; Second Secretary (Admin) Lagos 1988; Second Secretary FCO 1991; Second Secretary (Commercial) Canberra 1994; Second Secretary (Commercial) Sydney 1994; Assistant Personal Secretary to the Minister of State 1999; Full-Time Language Training 2000; First Secretary (Management) Brasilia 2001; Band C5; m 1973 Eugenia Del Transito Poppescov Lazo (2s 1975, 1995).

Welch, David Thomas; FCO since October 2004; Born 04/04/77; Band C4.

Weldin, Jonathan Michael; First Secretary FCO since December 2001; Born 23/02/59; FCO 1982; Second later First Secretary (Chancery) Sana'a 1986; First Secretary FCO 1988; First Secretary (Chancery) Tunis 1990; First Secretary FCO 1993; First Secretary (External) Athens 1996; Band D6; m 1984 Fiona Jean Nesbitt (1s 1987; 1d 1989).

Weldon, Lawrence John, MVO (1980); First Secretary FCO since June 2005; Born 06/03/50; FCO 1972; Attaché (Development) Bangkok 1975;

Attaché (Commercial) Tunis 1978; FCO 1981; British Vice-Consul Johannesburg 1983; Second Secretary FCO 1986; Second Secretary (Commercial) Caracas 1989; SUPL 1992; Second Secretary FCO 1995; Convent Liaison Officer Gibraltar 1997; Second Secretary Moscow 2002; m 1984 Sarah Helen Burn (1d 1989; 2s 1991, 1999).

Weldon, Paul; Athens since August 2000; Born 03/04/59; FCO 1975; Pretoria 1987; FCO 1989; Band C4; m 1986 Karen Louise Ritchie (2s 1988, 1992).

Wells, Andrew Justin; Second Secretary (Commercial) Prague since June 2002; Born 08/03/68; FCO 1988; Floater Duties 1991; Zagreb 1993; FCO 1995; Language Training Cairo 1997; Third Secretary Amman 1998; Band C4; m 1994 Juliette Swain (2s 1996, 1999; 1d 2001).

Wells, Colin Neil; Deputy Head of Mission Baku since December 2004; Born 29/09/67; FCO HCS 1987; DS 1990; Bridgetown 1992; Geneva (UKMIS) 1996 (Second Secretary 1997); FCO 1999; Second Secretary (Political) Abuja 2001; Band C5; m 1997 Rebekah Wells (2d 1993, 1995; 1s 1997).

Wells, Daniel; Accra since April 2004; Born 21/07/70; FCO 1989; Bucharest 1992; FCO 1994; Lagos 1995; FCO 1998; New Delhi 2000; Band B3.

Wells, David John; HM Consul Milan since May 2004; Born 29/06/63; FCO 1982; New Delhi 1988; FCO 1990; Vice-Consul Moscow 1995; FCO 1998; Deputy High Commissioner Nassau 2000; Band C5; m 1994 Helen Paula McCarron (1d 1996; 1s 1999).

Wells, Helen Paula (née McCarron); FCO since July 2005; Born 29/06/68; FCO 1986; New Delhi 1989; Geneva (UKMIS) 1992; Moscow 1995; FCO 1998; SUPL 2000; FCO 2004; SUPL 2004; Band C4; m 1994 David John Wells (1d 1996; 1s 1999).

Welsh, Jolyon Rimmer; FCO since August 2002; Born 22/12/67; FCO 1990; Second Secretary (Chancery/Information) Colombo 1992; First Secretary FCO 1995; New York (UKMIS) 1998; m 1999 Susan Lynley Welsh (1d 2002).

Welsh, Patricia Angela (née Sherry); SUPL since July 2003; Born 23/08/64; FCO 1985; Madrid 1989; FCO 1992; Brasilia 1994; SUPL 1997; FCO 1999; Oslo 2000; Band A2; m 1993 James Ormsby Welsh (2d 1996, 1998).

Welsh, Paul Anthony; Second Secretary (Commercial) Lisbon since March 2002; Born 12/10/67; FCO 1986; Harare 1988; Floater Duties 1992; FCO 1994; Deputy Head of Mission Tbilisi 1998; Band C4; m (1) 1988 Ann McCoy (diss 1993); (2) 1994 Emel Elif Icbilen.

Welsted, David Curtis; Moscow since May 2003; Born 17/10/52; FCO 1969; Attaché Warsaw 1975; FCO 1976; Tehran 1978; FCO 1978; Nairobi 1980; FCO 1983; Attaché Amman 1984; FCO 1987; Washington 1992; First Secretary FCO 1995; m 1974 Gillian Mary Harris (1s 1978; 1d 1982).

Wenban, Mark; Lima since July 2001; Born 29/05/67; FCO 2000; Band A2.

West, Brian William; HM Consul Paris since January 2002; Born 04/01/48; FCO 1968; Moscow 1971; Kampala 1972; Strasbourg 1975; FCO 1977; Port Louis 1980; Second Secretary (Commercial) Abidjan 1984; Second Secretary FCO 1988; T/D Athens 1990; Second Secretary (Commercial) Paris 1991; T/D New Delhi 1996; T/D Guangzhou 1997; Second Secretary (Commercial) Beirut 1997; m 1976 Marie-Odile Gilbert (2s 1977, 1980).

West, Peter Bernard; Consul-General Melbourne since July 2004; Born 29/06/58; FCO 1977; Ankara 1978; Buenos Aires 1980; Auckland 1984; Second later First Secretary FCO 1986; First Secretary (Political/EU) Copenhagen 1992; First Secretary FCO 1997; Deputy Head of Mission Bangkok 2000; m 1980 Julia Anne Chandler (1d 1993; 2s twins 1995).

Westcott, Nicholas James, CMG (1998); Head of IT Strategy Unit, FCO since June 2002; Born 20/07/56; Second Secretary FCO 1982; Seconded to European Commission, Brussels 1984; First Secretary (Agriculture/Finance) Brussels (UKREP) 1985; First Secretary FCO 1989; Deputy Head of Mission Dar es Salaam 1993; Counsellor FCO 1996; Minister-Counsellor for Trade and Transport Policy Washington 1999; m 1989 Miriam Pearson (1d 1996; 1s 2000).

Westgarth, Nicholas Philip; On loan to the Cabinet Office since December 2002; Born 25/11/56; FCO 1980; Third Secretary (Economic) Athens 1981; Second Secretary FCO 1984; Language Training 1985; First Secretary Hong Kong 1986; First Secretary FCO 1989; First Secretary (Chancery) Nicosia 1991; First Secretary FCO 1995; Counsellor Peking 1999; RCDS 2002; m 1988 Kate Judith Sykes (2s 1989, 1992).

Westmacott, Sir Peter John, KCMG (2003), LVO; HM Ambassador Ankara since January 2002; Born 23/12/50; FCO 1972; Third later Second Secretary Tehran 1974; FCO 1978; Seconded to EC Commission Brussels 1978; First Secretary Paris 1980; FCO 1984; PS to Minister of State 1984; Head of Chancery Ankara 1987; Counsellor on secondment as Assistant Private Secretary to TRH the Prince and Princess of Wales at Buckingham Palace 1990; Head of Chancery Washington 1993; Director (Americas) 1997; DUS (Wider World) 2000; m (1) 1972 Angela Margaret Lugg (diss 1999) (2s 1975, 1979; 1d 1977); m (2) 2001 Susie Nemazee.

Wetherell, Gordon Geoffrey; High Commissioner Accra since March 2004; Born 11/11/48; FCO, concurrently Third Secretary Vice-Consul British Embassy, Chad 1973; Third later Second Secretary East Berlin 1974; First Secretary FCO, concurrently First Secretary UKDEL CTB at

Geneva 1977; First Secretary UKDEL CTB Geneva 1979; New Delhi 1980; First Secretary FCO 1983; On loan to HM Treasury 1986; FCO 1987; Counsellor and Deputy Head of Mission Warsaw 1988; Counsellor (Political/Military) Bonn 1992; Counsellor FCO 1994; HM Ambassador Addis Ababa and (non-resident) Djibouti and Asmara 1997; HM Ambassador and Consul-General Luxembourg 2000; m 1981 Rosemary Anne Myles (4d 1982, 1985, 1987, 1989).

Whaanga-Jacques, Lorna (née Jacques); Santiago since April 2003; Born 15/09/59; FCO 1985; Vienna (UKDEL CSCE) 1988; Rangoon 1988; Phnom Penh 1992; SUPL 1993; FCO 1997; Muscat 1999; Band A2; m 1994 Dean Tamaku Whaanga.

Whale, Geoffrey; FCO since March 2001; Born 03/07/52; FCO 1983; Peking 1988; FCO 1990; Berlin 1998; Band C5; m 1985 Ingrid Moore (1s 1987).

Whanstall, Lisa Caroline Rachel; FCO since March 2003; Born 20/09/69; FCO 1995; Brasilia 1999; Band C4.

Whatley, Malcolm George; Beijing since October 2003; Born 05/09/52; FCO 1973; Washington 1975; Kuwait 1978; Budapest 1982; Dhaka 1984; FCO 1985; Muscat 1986; FCO 1989; Rio de Janeiro 1992 (Second Secretary 1995); Second Secretary (Commercial) Hong Kong 1999; Band C4; m 1975 Mary Elizabeth Niven (2s 1979, 1985; 1d 1983).

Whawell, Peter Gerald Maber; Second Secretary Dubai since February 2005; Born 19/01/69; FCO 2003; Band C4.

Wheeler, Fraser William; Basra since January 2005; Born 23/03/57; FCO 1980; Accra 1982; FCO 1984; Geneva (UKMIS) 1985; FCO 1988; Language Training 1990 (Second Secretary 1991); Second Secretary (Commercial) Moscow 1991; Deputy Consul-General Vancouver 1994; SUPL 1999; FCO 2000; Band D6; m 1988 Sarah Humphreys (1d 1990; 1s 1993).

Whitaker, Giles David Humphrey; FCO since September 2000; Born 05/03/62; HM Forces 1980-88; Second Secretary FCO 1988; Second Secretary (Chancery) Brussels (UKDEL NATO) 1990; First Secretary FCO 1994; Deputy Head of Mission Berlin 1998; First Secretary (Political) Berlin (on attachment to Auswärtiges Amt) 1999; m 1990 Lucy Phyllida Whately Anderson (2s 1992, 1998; 2d 1994, 1996).

Whitby, John Benjamin; First Secretary Vienna since August 2002; Born 21/02/67; FCO 1990; Language Training 1993; Second Secretary (Political) Tokyo 1994; First Secretary FCO 1997; Band D6; m 1992 Ruth Alexander (1s 1995; 1d 1997).

White, (Charles) John (Branford); High Commissioner Bridgetown since August 2001; Born 24/09/46; Government of Botswana 1968; ODM 1971; Economic Advisers 1977; ODM 1982; CDA at UCL (London) 1983; FCO 1986; First Secretary Lagos 1990; Counsellor, Consul-General and Deputy Head of Mission Tel Aviv 1993; Commissioner for the British Antarctic Territory, Commissioner for the British Indian Ocean Territory and Counsellor FCO 1997; m 1975 Judy Margaret Lewis.

White, Anthony William; Bridgetown since October 1999; Born 29/12/54; FCO 1973; Peking 1980; FCO 1982; Lilongwe 1985; FCO 1988; Third Secretary Kuala Lumpur 1993; FCO 1996; Band C4; m 1996 Rahani Mat Tahir.

White, Benjamin Matthew; Second Secretary Kabul since January 2004; Born 02/01/79; FCO 2001; Band C4.

White, Jacqueline Denise (née Hill); Riga since October 2002; Born 24/05/64; FCO 1987; Dar es Salaam 1989; FCO 1993; New York (UKMIS) 1993; SUPL 1996; New York (UKMIS) 1996; SUPL 1997; FCO 2000; Grand Turk 2000; Band B3; m 1990 Jerry Lee White (3s 1996, 1998, 2002).

White, Kate Georgina; FCO since September 2003; Born 24/01/73; FCO 1995; Full-Time Language Training 1996; Full-Time Language Training, Beijing 1997; Hong Kong 1998; Taipei 2000; Band C4.

White, Richard Michael, MBE (1983); Counsellor (Management) Paris since June 2003; Born 12/07/50; FCO 1969; UKDEL (later UKREP) EC Brussels 1971; Language Training SOAS and Yazd 1974; Tehran 1975; Second Secretary 1978; APS to the Minister of State 1978; APS to the Lord Privy Seal 1979; FCO 1979; Second Secretary (Commercial/Admin) and Consul Dakar 1980; First Secretary (Technology) Paris 1984; First Secretary FCO 1988; Deputy High Commissioner Valletta 1992; First Secretary FCO 1996; Counsellor, Head of Migration and Visa Division 1997; Assistant Director, Personnel Services 2000; m 1979 Deborah Anne Lewis (1s 1984; 1d 1986).

Whitecross, Andrew Ronald; First Secretary FCO since July 2001; Born 14/04/49; Army 1964-76; FCO 1976; Private Industry 1978; FCO 1980; Sana'a 1981; Baghdad 1985; Second Secretary FCO 1989; First Secretary (Political) Muscat 1998; Band C5; m 1980 Nancy-Jane Evans (dec'd 1994).

Whiteford, Kathryn Elizabeth; Pretoria since May 2004; Born 05/08/78; FCO 2002; Band A2.

Whitehead, Laurence Jeremy; First Secretary FCO since June 2002; Born 17/04/61; FCO 1984; Second Secretary Jakarta 1987; Second later First Secretary FCO 1990; First Secretary (Political) Vienna 1995; First Secretary (Political) Tirana 1999; Band D6; m 1995 Marjella Djorghi.

Whitehead, Roger; First Secretary FCO since January 2002; Born 22/05/54; FCO 1976; Lagos 1979; Kathmandu 1982; FCO 1984; Third Secretary (Management/Consular) Rangoon 1988;

Third Secretary (Management/Consular/Commercial) Toronto 1991; Second Secretary FCO 1994; Second Secretary (Commercial) Singapore 1997; Band D6; m 1979 Diane Mann (1s 1987; 1d 1989).

Whiteley, Richard John Clive; Kiev since December 2004; Born 29/07/67; MOD 1984; FCO 1994; Third Secretary (Management) Ankara 2001; Band B3; m 2001 Louise Carol (1s 1989; 1d 2003).

Whiten, Peter Frank, MBE (1991); FCO since August 1998; Born 05/12/51; FCO 1974; SE Asia Floater 1976; Brussels (UKDEL NATO) 1978; Port of Spain 1981; Second Secretary FCO 1986; Second Secretary (Commercial) Madras 1991; Consul Chiang Mai 1995; m 1987 Antonia Ramsaroop (3s 1989, 1991, 1993; 1d 1994).

Whiteside, Andrew John; First Secretary (Political) Rome since February 2002; Born 21/09/68; FCO 1991; Language Training 1994; Second Secretary (Political) Budapest 1995; First Secretary FCO 1997; Band D6; m 1994 Fiona Elizabeth Bradley (1d 1999; 1s 2001).

Whiteside, Bernard Gerrard, MBE (1994); HM Ambassador Chisinau since April 2002; Born 03/10/54; FCO 1979; Moscow 1983; Geneva (UKDIS) 1986 (Second Secretary 1988); Second Secretary FCO 1989; Second Secretary (Chancery/Aid) Bogotá 1991; First Secretary FCO 1995; First Secretary on loan to DFID 1999.

Whiteway, Paul Robin; Director (International) Invest UK since July 2003; Born 01/12/54; FCO 1977; Third later Second Secretary Dublin 1980; First Secretary FCO 1984; First Secretary Stanley 1986; First Secretary FCO 1987; Seconded to MOD (Navy) 1988; Deputy High Commissioner Kampala 1990; First Secretary FCO 1993; Counsellor and Deputy Head of Mission Damascus 1996; Counsellor and Deputy Head of Mission Santiago 2000; m 1996 Maha Georges Yannieh (1s 1998).

Whitford, Victoria, OBE (2005); Washington since May 2005; Born 06/06/74; FCO 1999; Second Secretary (Political) Pristina 2001; First Secretary (Press and Public Affairs) Baghdad 2003; Band D6.

Whittaker, Andrew Mark; Consul (Political) Jerusalem since October 2001; Born 22/06/76; FCO 1998; Full-Time Language Training (Arabic) 1999; Cairo 2000; Band C4.

Whitting, Ian Robert; First Secretary (Economic) Athens since July 2003; Born 02/04/53; FCO 1972; Moscow 1975; Tunis 1976; Athens 1980; Second Secretary 1981; FCO 1983; Second Secretary (Chancery) Moscow 1985; Second Secretary FCO 1988; Second Secretary (Chancery) Dublin 1990; First Secretary (Economic) FCO 1997; m 1986 Tracy Anne Gallagher (2d 1990, 1994).

Whittingham, Nick; Beijing since January 2004; Born 06/04/64; FCO 1995; Language Training 2000; Consul (Economic) Guangzhou 2001; Band C4; m 1999 Yuehping Yen.

Whittingham, Stephen Arthur; FCO since September 1990; Born 29/01/56; FCO 1972; Brussels 1981; FCO 1983; Hong Kong 1988; Band C5; m 1977 Christine Mary Ruth Hodgson (1d 1978).

Whittle, Lesley Elizabeth; SUPL since July 1999; Born 04/07/58; FCO 1980; Amman 1981; Cairo 1984; FCO 1987; Paris 1990; Islamabad 1994; Band B3; m 1986 Simon F D Mallett (1s 1995).

Whomersley, Christopher Adrian; Legal Counsellor FCO since 1997; Born 18/04/53; Assistant Legal Adviser FCO 1977; Legal Counsellor FCO 1991; Legal Secretariat to the Law Officers 1994; m 1977 Jeanette Diana Szostak (1s 1991; 2d 1993, 1998).

Whyte, Michael James; Colombo since October 2002; Born 24/03/42; Royal Navy 1958-89; Bucharest 1992; Peking 1994; Cairo 1998; Band B3; m 1979 Karen Nina Renée Walters.

Wicke, Tina (née Thackstone); Third Secretary (Political/Information) later (Management) Harare since August 1999; Born 05/02/61; HM Treasury 1980; FCO 1982; Stanley 1983; Kingston 1984; Peking 1986; FCO 1989; Harare 1993; SUPL 1997; Band B3; m 1996 Jürgen Manfred Wicke (1s 2003).

Wickenden, Peter James; Second Secretary (Political/Press) Prague since October 2003; Born 04/09/63; Second Secretary (Political/Economic) Taipei 1999; FCO 2000; Full-Time Language Training 2002; m 1989 Wendy Wang (2s 1991, 2000; 1d 1993).

Wicks, Genevieve Harriot-Jane; Brussels (UKREP) since March 2003; Born 29/06/54; FCO 1973; Geneva (UKMIS) 1974; Islamabad 1977; Peking 1979; Karachi 1981; FCO 1983; Victoria 1986; SUPL 1988; Band A2; m 1978 Graham Wicks (2s 1988, 1989).

Wicks, Graham; Second Secretary (Russia/Partnership) Brussels (UKDEL) since July 2003; Born 02/07/55; FCO 1974; Luxembourg 1976; Islamabad 1976; Peking 1979; Karachi 1981; FCO 1983; Victoria 1986; Vice-Consul Sofia 1990; Third later Second Secretary FCO 1992; Second Secretary (Commercial) Bombay 1995; FCO 1997; Second Secretary (Aid) Khartoum 2000; m 1978 Genevieve Harriot-Jane McCrossan (2s 1988, 1989).

Wickstead, Myles Antony; HM Ambassador Addis Ababa, also HM Ambassador (non-resident) Djibouti since November 2000; Born 07/02/51; Ministry of Overseas Development 1976; APS to Lord Privy Seal FCO 1979; Assistant to UK Executive Director IMF/IBRD 1980; Principal ODA 1984; Private Secretary to Minister for Overseas Development 1988; Head of ODA European Community and Food Aid Development 1990; Head of British Development Division in East Africa (BDDEA) 1993; UK Alternate

Executive Director World Bank and Counsellor (Development) Washington 1997; m 1990 Shelagh Paterson (1s 1996; 1d 1999).

Wigginton, Christopher James; Second Secretary (Immigration/Consular) Bogotá since November 2000; Born 23/05/60; FCO 1982; Language Training 1984; Tehran 1984; Stockholm 1988; FCO 1991 (Second Secretary 1992); Islamabad 1994; FCO 1997; Full-Time Language Training 2000; Band C4.

Wightman, Andrew Norman Scott; Deputy Head of Mission Rome since January 2002; Born 17/07/61; FCO 1983; Full-Time Language Training 1984; Second Secretary Peking 1986; First Secretary FCO 1989; On loan to the Cabinet Office 1989; First Secretary FCO 1991; On secondment to Quai d'Orsay 1994; First Secretary Paris 1995; Assistant Director Personnel Policy 1998; m 1988 Anne Margaret Roberts (2d 1993, 1997).

Wigley, Christopher Martin; FCO since October 2004; Born 21/06/77; Band C4.

Wilbourn, Lillian; Kuwait since August 2002; Born 27/07/47; FCO 1985; Madrid 1987; Brasilia 1990; Maputo 1994; Buenos Aires 1998; Band A2.

Wilcox, Juliette Sarah (née Hannah); Counsellor Singapore since March 2005; Born 29/06/66; FCO 1988; Full-Time Language Training Taiwan 1991; Second Secretary (Chancery) Peking 1992; First Secretary FCO 1995; First Secretary later British Representative, (JLG) Hong Kong 1996; FCO 2000; On loan to the Cabinet Office 2003; Band D6; m 1996 Wayne Philip Wilcox (1 step s 1984; 2s 1999, 2002).

Wildash, Elizabeth Jane (née Walmsley), MVO (1997); SUPL since September 2001; Born 17/10/58; FCO 1978; East Berlin 1980; FCO 1981; Abidjan 1983; FCO 1984; SUPL 1987; FCO 1988; Harare 1989; FCO 1992; Third Secretary (Chancery) New Delhi 1994; SUPL 1998; Second Secretary (Economic) Kuala Lumpur 1999; m 1981 Richard James Wildash (2d 1987, 1996).

Wildash, Richard James, LVO (1997); High Commissioner Yaoundé since July 2002; Born 24/12/55; FCO 1977; East Berlin 1979; Abidjan 1981; FCO 1984; Language Training 1986; FCO 1986; Harare 1988; FCO 1992; New Delhi 1994; Deputy High Commissioner Kuala Lumpur 1998; m 1981 Elizabeth Jane Walmsley (2d 1987, 1996).

Wildman, Richard Hugh; FCO since January 2002; Born 18/08/54; FCO 1983; Bridgetown 1989; FCO 1992; Brasilia 1999; Band C4; m (1) 1989 Fay Dawn Reid (1d 1983); (2) 1994 S E Odle.

Wiles, Celia Imogen; First Secretary Rome since February 2004; Born 23/04/63; FCO 1986; Language Training Kamakura 1988; Third Secretary (Commercial) Tokyo 1989; SUPL 1993; FCO 1995; On loan to the European Commission 1998; FCO 1999; SUPL 2000; FCO 2001; First Secretary (Economic and Public Affairs) Canberra 2001; Band D6; (1s 2000).

Wilkes, Jennifer Siobhan; FCO since February 2003; Born 06/09/75; Band A2.

Wilkinson, Richard Denys, CVO (1992); HM Ambassador Santiago since June 2003; Born 11/05/46; FCO 1972; Second later First Secretary Madrid 1973; FCO 1977; First Secretary (Economic/Commercial) Ankara 1983; Counsellor and Head of Chancery Mexico City 1985; Counsellor (Info) Paris 1988; Counsellor FCO 1993; HM Ambassador Caracas 1997; Director (Americas) FCO 2000; m 1982 Maria Angela Morris (2s 1983, 1986; 1d 1991).

Wilks, Jonathan Paul; Deputy Head of Mission Baghdad since April 2003; Born 30/09/67; FCO 1989; Full-Time Language Training Cairo 1992; Second Secretary (Political/Information) Khartoum 1993; First Secretary (Economic) Riyadh 1996; SUPL 1999; Band D7.

Willasey-Wilsey, Timothy Andrew; Counsellor FCO since April 2002; Born 12/09/53; Second Secretary FCO 1981; First Secretary (Chancery) Luanda 1983; First Secretary, Head of Chancery (later Deputy Head of Mission) and Consul San José 1986; First Secretary FCO 1989; Counsellor Islamabad 1993; Counsellor FCO 1996; Counsellor (UN Affairs) Geneva (UKMIS) 1999; m 1983 Alison Middleton Mackie (3s 1986, 1988, 1989).

Williams, Alexander Patrick; Rome since January 2004; Born 13/02/69; FCO 1986; Bangkok 1996; FCO 2000; Band C4.

Williams, Curtis; Brasilia since December 2004; Born 07/01/77; FCO 2002; Band A2.

Williams, David John; FCO since October 2004; Born 06/06/67; FCO 1986; Geneva (UKMIS) 1988; Bombay 1990; Second Secretary FCO 1995; Deputy High Commissioner Yaoundé 2001; m 1990 Denise Nowak (1d 1991; 1s 1995).

Williams, Douglas James; FCO since September 2001; Born 09/02/55; FCO 1978; Suva 1981; Brussels (UKREP) 1984; New Delhi 1987; FCO 1991; Bridgetown 1994; Second Secretary (Commercial) Madras 1998; Band C5; m 1981 Susan Anwen Jones (1s 1984; 1d 1986).

Williams, George (aka Rick), BEM (1975); Moscow since July 2003; Born 06/02/43; HM Forces 1962-84; Prague 1984; Singapore 1985; Moscow 1987; Washington 1988; Dhaka 1991; Colombo 1995; Lagos 1998; New Delhi 2001; Band C4 (CSO); m 1965 Eileen (2s 1965, 1968).

Williams, John; Deputy Director (Trade & Investment) Lagos since January 2004; Born 17/06/59; FCO 1978; Moscow 1981; Rabat 1982; FCO 1985; Masirah 1985; LA Floater 1986; FCO 1988; Vice-Consul Johannesburg 1992; Second Secretary (Political) Gibraltar 1996; On loan to the DTI 1997; Consul (Inward Investment) Toronto 1999; m 1994 Cheryl Ann Sim.

Williams, Karen Lesley, MBE (2001); Second Secretary (Commercial) Beirut since August 2002; Born 28/06/63; FCO 1987; Riyadh 1988; New York (UKMIS) 1991; World Wide Floater Duties 1993; FCO 1995; Rangoon 1999; Band C4.

Williams, Laura Kate Elizabeth; Second Secretary (Political/Information) Addis Ababa since April 2001; Born 03/04/74; FCO 1998; First Secretary Paris Embassy 1999; First Secretary Brussels (UKREP) 2000; Full-Time Language Training 2000; T/D Second Secretary (Political) Brussels (UKREP) 2000; Band C4.

Williams, Paul; First Secretary (Political) Berlin since October 2001; Born 25/11/48; Immigration Service 1969; Islamabad 1977; Dhaka 1982; Lagos 1987; Second later First Secretary Muscat 1996; First Secretary Houston 1998; m 1969 Barbara Jane Briggs (2s 1975, 1979).

Williams, Philip George; FCO since July 1988; Born 26/07/54; FCO 1972; Nairobi 1985; Band D6; m 1987 Susan Traise McAlden.

Williams, Prue, RVM; SUPL since November 2001; Bonn 1978; Moscow 1980; FCO 1981; Port of Spain 1983; FCO 1985; Bangkok 1996 (State Visit); The Hague/Luxembourg (Presidency) 1997; FCO 1998; Band B3.

Williams, Rebecca Louise; SUPL since July 2004; Born 17/08/71; FCO 1989; Geneva (UKMIS) 1991; Peking 1994; PA/HMA Kuwait 1997; Berne 2000; Band A2; m 1996 Grant Pritchard (diss 2001).

Williams, Dr Rhodri Huw; FCO since July 2004; Born 14/05/59; FCO 1990; First Secretary (Economic) Vienna 1992; First Secretary FCO 1996; Counsellor Amman 2001; m 1986 Hilary Clair Wakeham (1s, 1d (twins) 1991; 1s 1994).

Williams, Roger Gordon; Cairo since March 2004; Born 28/07/48; Army 1963-89; Prague 1989; Washington 1991; Cairo 1993; T/D Cairo 1997; Belgrade 1997; Lagos 1997; Jakarta 1999; Kabul 2003; Band C4; m 1974 Anne Elizabeth (1d 1974; 2s 1978, 1980).

Williams, Simon John; Casablanca since January 2002; Born 22/08/60; FCO 1979; Manila 1981; Mbabane 1984; Kaduna 1986; FCO 1992; Full-Time Language Training 1995; Third Secretary (Commercial) Riyadh 1995; Second Secretary (Commercial) Doha 1998; Band C5; m 1987 Rosemarie Caguntas Williams (1s 1989).

Williams, Stephen Michael; Head of Latin America and Caribbean Department FCO since September 2003; Born 20/07/59; FCO 1981; Third later Second Secretary Sofia 1984; Second later First Secretary FCO 1987; On loan to Barclays Bank 1990; First Secretary (Commercial/Economic) Oslo 1991; First Secretary (External Relations) Brussels (UKREP) 1995; Counsellor FCO 1998; Full-Time Language Training 2001; Counsellor and Deputy Head of Mission Buenos Aires 2001; m 1983 Fiona Michele Hume (2d 1986, 1989; 1s 1991).

Williams, Steven; First Secretary FCO since July 2003; Born 30/04/69; FCO 1987; Brussels 2000; Band C5; m 2000 Leah Victoria Cox.

Williams, Tony Scott; Second Secretary Washington since November 2004; Born 12/09/62; FCO 1981; Brussels (UKDEL NATO) 1984; Prague 1986; Dhaka 1988; FCO 1989; Athens 1993; Third Secretary (Commercial) New Delhi 1996; Second Secretary (Management) Sofia 2000; m 1985 Denise Tilbrook (1s 1992).

Williamson, George Moray; Full-Time Language Training Damascus since September 2004; Born 25/02/74; FCO 2001; Band C4.

Williamson, Martin Charles; Deputy High Commissioner Wellington since November 2004; Born 28/01/53; FCO (HCS) 1977; Economic Adviser FCO 1981; IMF Research Department 1984; Economic Adviser FCO 1987; Cabinet Office 1989; OECD Secretariat, Paris 1991; Senior Economic Adviser and Joint Head of Economic Advisers FCO 1994; Deputy Head of Economic Policy Department 1999; Head of Resource Budgeting Department 1999; Prism Team 2003; m 1978 Elizabeth Michelle Darvill (2s 1984, 1987).

Williamson, Morven Jane; Maputo since April 2004; Born 16/04/71; FCO 1991; Hanoi 1994; Jedda 1999; Band B3.

Willis, Iain Edward; FCO since January 2003; Born 25/05/71; FCO 1991; T/D Karachi 1995; Vice-Consul Tokyo 1996; Third Secretary (Political) Valletta 1999; Band B3.

Willis, Ruth Valerie (née Coward); FCO since June 2002; Born 18/09/60; FCO 1985; New Delhi 1988; Mexico City 1991; The Hague 1996; FCO 1999; SUPL 2001; Band C4; m 2000 Barry Willis.

Willmer, Nigel Stuart; Athens since January 2005; Born 03/07/65; FCO 1983; Madrid 1990; FCO 1993; Lusaka 1997; FCO 2000; m 1985 Jackie Mann (diss 2001) (1d 1986).

Willmott, Emily Margaret; Assistant Legal Adviser FCO since October 2001; Born 02/11/72; Solicitor 1998; m 1999 Simon Nathan Willmott.

Willock, Oriel; T/D Bandar Seri Begawan since November 2004; Born 23/04/68; FCO 1988; Amman 1990; Floater Duties 1994; FCO 1997; T/D Islamabad 1999; T/D Ekaterinburg 2000; San José 2001; Band B3.

Wills, Jane Stirling; First Secretary FCO since January 2001; Born 12/12/46; Commonwealth Office (later FCO) 1964; Prague 1969; Copenhagen 1971; Vienna (UKDEL MBFR) 1973; Bombay 1976; FCO 1980; Prague 1983; Ankara 1986; Second Secretary FCO 1989; Deputy Head of Mission Reykjavik 1995; Deputy Head of Mission Bratislava 1999.

Wills, Ruth Margaret; Second later First Secretary FCO since December 1991; Born 07/11/54; FCO 1977; Rio de Janeiro 1980; Paris 1984; Second Secretary (Press/Information) Bonn 1989.

Willsher, Ian Robert; Dakar since February 2005; Born 14/04/47; Washington 1974; Vienna 1977; FCO 1979; Accra 1982; Geneva 1985; FCO 1988; Nairobi 1990; FCO 1994; British Forces Germany 1996; Brussels 1998; Lagos 2003; m 1976 Amanda Jane (2s 1978, 1979; 1d 1985).

Wilson, Allan Richard James; Mexico City since August 2001; Born 11/05/77; FCO 1999; Band A2; m 2003 Yessica Reyes Guisa.

Wilson, Caroline Melanie Cherry (née Meath); SUPL since July 2003; Born 16/09/69; FCO 1990; Canberra 1992; Moscow 1995; SUPL 1998; FCO 1999; Band B3; m 1993 James Jeffrey Wilson.

Wilson, Douglas Ian; Baghdad since February 2005; Born 26/12/77; Assistant Legal Adviser FCO 2001; Band D6.

Wilson, Fraser Andrew, MBE (1980); High Commissioner Victoria (Seychelles) since May 2002; Born 06/05/49; Commonwealth Office (later FCO) 1967; Havana 1970; SE Asia Floater 1971; Seoul 1973; Salisbury 1977; Second Secretary FCO 1980; Language Training 1983; Second Secretary (Commercial) Moscow 1984; Second Secretary (Commercial) and Vice-Consul (later First Secretary (Commercial)) Rangoon 1986; First Secretary FCO 1990; Deputy Consul-General São Paulo 1994; Full-Time Language Training 1998; HM Ambassador Turkmenistan 1998; m 1981 Janet Phillips (2s 1982, 1985).

Wilson, Gillian Grace; SUPL since October 2002; Born 19/04/65; ODA 1981; FCO 1989; T/D Dhaka 1991; Accra 1991; Third Secretary (Chancery) Nairobi 1995; FCO 1998; Band C4.

Wilson, Harry Kenneth, BEM (1991); Buenos Aires since January 2003; Born 07/05/52; RAF 1971-97; FCO 1998; Madrid 1999; Band A2; m 1979 Elaine Carrick (1s 1981; 1d 1983).

Wilson, Ian Laurence; FCO since July 2002; Born 19/06/44; FO 1962; Moscow 1966; Colombo 1967; FCO 1971; Brussels (UKDEL NATO) 1974; Banjul 1977; FCO 1981; Canberra 1983; FCO 1987; Second Secretary (Consular/Admin) Calcutta 1987; Second Secretary (Management) Bucharest 1992; First Secretary FCO 1995; Consul and First Secretary (Management) Tehran 1997; HM Consul Riyadh 2000; HM Consul Beijing 2001; Band C5; m (1) 1970 (1d 1974; 1s 1976) (diss 1999); (2) 1999 Monica Dorri (1s 2000).

Wilson, James Jeffrey (Jeff); First Secretary New Delhi since July 2003; Born 07/08/67; FCO 1988; Canberra 1992; Moscow 1995; Ekaterinburg 1997; FCO 1999; Band D6; m 1993 Caroline Melanie Meath.

Wilson, Michael George; FCO since January 2002; Born 10/12/70; FCO 1989; Dhaka 1991; World Wide Floater Duties 1995; ECO Delhi 1998; Band B3.

Wilson, Peter Michael Alexander; FCO since January 2003; Born 31/03/68; FCO 1992; Full-Time Language Training 1993; Full-Time Language Training Peking 1994; Second Secretary (Commercial) Peking 1995; SUPL 1999; First Secretary (Institutions) Brussels (UKREP) 1999; Band D7; m 2001 Mónica Roma (1d 2002; 1s 2004).

Wilson, Dr Robert Thomas Osborne, OBE (2004); Deputy Head of Mission Tripoli since October 2004; Born 28/01/52; Senior Research Officer; FCO 1982; First Secretary and Head of Chancery Abu Dhabi 1989; Principal Research Officer FCO 1993; Deputy Head of Mission, HM Consul Bahrain 1998; FCO 2002; m 1979 Susan Ann Watson (2d 1985, 1988).

Wilson, Roy Andrew; Tbilisi since October 2004; Born 03/12/59; HCS 1978; FCO 1979; Karachi 1982; Seoul 1985; FCO 1987; Bombay 1990; Zurich 1994; First Secretary Banja Luka 2000; Deputy Head of Mission Yerevan 2002; Band C5.

Wilson, Sarah Elizabeth; Ankara since July 2002; Born 08/03/70; FCO 2000; Band A2.

Wilson, Simon Charles Hartley; Deputy Head of Mission and Head of Political Section Bahrain since November 2001; Born 09/08/57; FCO 1975; Johannesburg 1978; Helsinki 1981; FCO 1984; Tehran 1987; Riyadh 1987; Second Secretary (Chancery/Information) Lisbon 1992; Second later First Secretary FCO 1997; m 1984 Heather Graine Richardson (2s 1990, 1994).

Wilson, Simon Jules, OBE (1996); First Secretary Budapest since February 2002; Born 13/03/66; FCO 1988; Third later Second Secretary (Economic) Athens 1991; Second later First Secretary (Political) Zagreb 1993; First Secretary FCO 1996; First Secretary New York (UKMIS) 1999; FCO 2000; Band D6.

Wilson, Susan Jean; Vice-Consul New Delhi since January 2002; Born 01/02/70; FCO 1989; Bangkok 1994; Istanbul 1997; Band B3; m 2001 Ahmet Cikit.

Wilton, Christopher Edward John, CMG; HM Ambassador Kuwait since September 2002; Born 16/12/51; FCO 1977; MECAS 1978; Second later First Secretary Bahrain 1979; FCO 1981; First Secretary (Chancery) Tokyo 1984; On loan to the Cabinet Office 1988; Counsellor (Commercial) Riyadh 1990; Consul-General Dubai 1994; Counsellor FCO 1998; m 1975 Dianne Hodgkinson (1d 1981; 1s 1984).

Wiltshire, Terence Keith; Buenos Aires since April 2005; Born 24/12/57; FCO 1981; New Delhi 1983; FCO 1987; Lagos 1994; FCO 1997; Second Secretary (Technical Management) Budapest 2001; Band C4.

Windle, William James; Counsellor Washington since August 2002; Born 03/07/52; FCO 1972; On loan to the MOD 1975; FCO 1977; Second Secretary (Commercial) Muscat 1980; Second later First Secretary FCO 1984; First Secretary (Chancery) Washington 1989; First Secretary later Counsellor FCO 1992; Band C5; m 1974 June Constance Grimmond (3s 1980, 1982, 1985).

Windsor, Dallas Frederick; Tokyo since October 2003; Born 24/04/74; FCO 2001; Language Training 2003; Band C4; m 2001 Kiyoe Higashi.

Winnington-Ingram, Charles Pepys; FCO since 2000; Born 06/10/55; Barrister 1977; Export Credits Guarantee Department 1979; FCO 1980; Third Secretary (Commercial) Tokyo 1981; Second Secretary FCO 1985; Second Secretary (Chancery/Information) Oslo 1989; HM Consul (Commercial) and Deputy Head of Mission St Petersburg 1995; HM Consul and Deputy Head of Mission Jerusalem 1996.

Winsley, Marcus Justin; First Secretary (Political) Washington since June 2002; Born 01/09/67; ODA 1993; First Secretary Moscow 1996; FCO 2000; Band D6; m 1996 Claire Underwood.

Winter, Douglas; First Secretary (Management) Addis Ababa since March 2004; Born 21/01/51; FCO 1969; Mogadishu 1972; Antigua 1974; FCO 1978; Bangkok 1981; Zagreb 1984; Warsaw 1985; Second Secretary FCO 1987; Second Secretary (Commercial) Abu Dhabi 1990; FCO 1994; Second Secretary (Consular/Management) Sarajevo 1999; m 1972 Linda Margaret Harmer (1s 1975; 1d 1978).

Winter, Simon; UK Trade & Investment since July 2004; Born 10/04/68; FCO 1990; Tokyo 1995; Budapest 1999; ECO Accra 2000; Band B3; m 1993 Alyson Barnett (1s 1994; 2d 1997, 2001).

Winterburn, Christine Catherine (née Lowrie); Deputy Head of Mission Asunción since July 2003; Born 20/04/67; FCO 1986; Copenhagen 1987; FCO 1989; Kaduna/Abuja 1992; Lima 1996; Sofia 1999; Band C4; m 1989 (diss 2002) (2s 1995, 2000).

Wise, Graeme Michael; HM Consul Washington since June 2002; Born 17/06/64; FCO 1984; Addis Ababa 1985; Lagos 1988; Floater Duties 1991; FCO 1992; Second Secretary (Commercial) Buenos Aires 1997; SUPL 1999; FCO 2001; First Secretary (Management) Dublin 2001; Band C5.

Wise, Patricia (née Donnelly); Nicosia since March 2000; Born 24/02/58; FCO 1982; Port Stanley 1983; Lusaka 1983; Rome 1987; Cape Town/Pretoria 1990; FCO 1993; SUPL 1994; Helsinki 1994; SUPL 1996; FCO 1997; Band B3; m (1) 1985 Edward Meredith Leighton (diss 1991); (2) 1992 David Wise (dec'd 1999) (1d 1994).

Wisker, Rita; Berlin since February 2003; Born 15/09/51; FCO 1972; Tokyo 1973; FCO 1975; Washington 1977; Brussels (UKREP) 1980; BMG Berlin 1983; New York (UKMIS) 1984; FCO 1985; Brussels (UKDEL) 1992; FCO 1996; Band B3.

Withers, John Walter Charles; FCO since August 1994; Born 24/11/47; FCO 1975; Moscow 1979; FCO 1982; Lagos 1982; FCO 1985; Ottawa 1986; New York 1987; FCO 1989; Third later Second Secretary Bucharest 1991; m 1970 Vivienne Chater (1d 1976; 1s 1986).

Withers, Matthew Robert; Third Secretary (Political) Buenos Aires since January 2001; Born 14/10/67; FCO 1987; Kuala Lumpur 1988; Kathmandu 1992; Lagos 1994; FCO 1998; Band B3; m 1992 Leigh Cooper (2d 1994, 1996).

Witting, Lisa Marie; Vienna (UKMIS) since January 2000; Born 22/02/69; FCO 1988; Dublin 1989; FCO 1993; Berlin 1995; Band A2.

Wolstenholme, Jonathan David; FCO since December 2002; Born 15/01/60; FCO 1980; Baghdad 1982; Moscow 1984; Harare 1986; FCO 1990 (Second Secretary 1992); Second Secretary (Management) Brussels (UKREP) 1994; Second Secretary (Chancery) Wellington 1998; Band C5; m 1986 Karen Suzanne Vivian (2d 1989, 1994; 1s 1992).

Wolstenholme, Karen Suzanne (née Vivian); FCO since March 2003; Born 16/10/62; FCO 1980; Language Training 1983; Moscow 1984; FCO 1985; Harare 1986; Second Secretary FCO 1990; SUPL 1992; Second Secretary FCO 1993; Brussels (UKREP) 1994; Second later First Secretary Wellington 1998; Band D6; m 1986 Jonathan David Wolstenholme (2d 1989, 1994; 1s 1992).

Wong, Josephine; First Secretary Vienna since July 2004; Born 17/12/72; FCO 2001; Band D6.

Wong, Lillian Paterson (née Walker); FCO since February 1976; Born 16/02/44; Senior Principal Research Officer; FCO 1970; Second Secretary (Information/Aid) Yaoundé 1973; Band D7; m 1979 Robert Puck Keong Wong.

Wood, Adam Kenneth Compton; High Commissioner Nairobi since July 2005; Born 13/03/55; ODA 1977; Assistant Private Secretary to the Lord Privy Seal 1980; Assistant to UK Executive Director, World Bank Washington 1983; ODA 1986; Programme Manager ODA Nairobi 1988; Adviser to Director General EC Brussels 1993; Head, DFID South East Asia, Bangkok 1996; Counsellor (Development) UKREP Brussels 2000; High Commissioner Kampala 2002; m 1993 Catherine Richardson (1d 1999).

Wood, Christopher Terence; Consul-General Guangzhou since July 2003; Born 19/01/59; FCO 1981; Hong Kong 1983; Seconded to the Hong Kong Government as Assistant Political Adviser 1984; FCO 1987; Department of Environment later Department of Environment, Transport & the Regions 1992; Private Secretary to the Minister of State 1995; Cabinet Office 1998; Counsellor 2000; Office of the Deputy Prime Minister 2002.

Wood, Ian David; SUPL since August 2001; Born 14/09/69; FCO 1992; Third later Second Secretary UKDEL OECD 1994; Second Secretary (Political) New Delhi 1996; UKDEL NATO 1996; FCO 1998.

Wood, James Sebastian Lamin, CMG (2002); FCO since 2005; Born 06/04/61; FCO 1983; Language Training 1984; Second Secretary Bangkok 1986; Second later First Secretary FCO

1989; Full-Time Language Training Taiwan 1991; First Secretary and Consul for Macau BTC Hong Kong 1992; First Secretary UKREP JLG Hong Kong 1994; FCO 1996; On loan to the Cabinet Office 1998; Seconded to Harvard 2000; Counsellor Washington 2001; m 1990 Sirinat Penguam (3d 1992, 1993, 1995; 1s 1996).

Wood, Sir Michael Charles, KCMG (2004), CMG (1995); Legal Adviser FCO since December 1999; Born 05/02/47; Called to the Bar, Grays Inn 1968; Assistant Legal Adviser FCO 1970; Legal Adviser Bonn 1981; Legal Adviser later Legal Counsellor FCO 1984; Counsellor (Legal) New York (UKMIS) 1991; Legal Counsellor FCO 1994; Deputy Legal Adviser 1996.

Wood, Michael John Hemsley; FCO since August 2003; Born 16/09/48; FCO 1972; Third later Second Secretary Athens 1974; FCO 1976; First Secretary Harare 1980; Language Training 1983; First Secretary and Head of Chancery and Consul Hanoi 1984; First Secretary FCO 1987; Counsellor (Political) Helsinki 1993; Counsellor FCO 1997; Counsellor Lusaka 2000; Counsellor (Regional Affairs) Accra 2002; m (1) 1975 Susan Christine Langford; (2) 1983 Wendy Mary Smith.

Wood, Dr Peter Gilruth; Counsellor Peking since September 2002; Born 02/11/53; FCO 1982; Language Training 1983; Taiwan 1984; First Secretary (Economic) Peking 1986; First Secretary FCO 1989; Counsellor 1994; Kuala Lumpur 1995; Counsellor FCO 1998; m 1998 Pamela Sue Shookman.

Wood, Richard John; First Secretary (Economic) New York (UKMIS) since August 2002; Born 27/08/67; FCO 1991; Cape Town/Pretoria 1993; First Secretary FCO 1998.

Wood, Richard Lewis; Second Secretary (Consular) Al Khobar since February 2004; Born 07/06/61; FCO 1982; Sofia 1984; Bandar Seri Begawan 1986; FCO 1989; Vice-Consul Riyadh 1992; Third Secretary (Commercial) Johannesburg 1996; FCO 1999; m 1994 Frances Anne Curley (2s 1995, 1998).

Wood, Simon Andrew; FCO since November 2004; Born 25/02/73; FCO 1998; Language Training (Japanese) 2000; Second Secretary (Commercial) Tokyo 2001; Band C4; m 1998 Philippa Hargrave (2s 2003, 2004).

Woodcock, Andrew; SUPL since August 2004; Born 18/09/65; FCO 1988; Vice-Consul Baghdad 1990; AMO/Vice-Consul Brasilia 1991; Third Secretary (Science and Technology) Bonn 1995; Third Secretary (Economic/Political) Mexico City 1996; Second Secretary FCO 2000; Band C4.

Woodham, Mark John; Consul St Petersburg since July 2003; Born 18/11/67; FCO 1988; Helsinki 1991; Islamabad 1994; Bangkok 1998; Band C4; m 1993 Sari Hannele Hakkarainen.

Woodier, Daniel Robert; Third Secretary (Immigration) Doha since February 2004; Born 02/09/65; FCO 1996; Third Secretary (External Affairs) Canberra 2000; Band B3; m 1989 Sarah Harmer (2s 2000, 2001).

Woodrow, John Peter Gayford; FCO since February 2002; Born 21/11/47; FCO 1972; Barcelona 1975; Quito 1976; FCO 1979; La Paz 1983; Consul Istanbul 1988; FCO 1992; Consul Oslo 1995; Second Secretary (Consular) Helsinki 1997; m 1977 Yvonne Leffmann.

Woodruffe, John Michael; Second Secretary (Political) Gibraltar since August 2001; Born 26/06/57; FCO 1986; Dublin 1989; Amman 1992; FCO 1995; Shanghai 1998; Band C4; m 1989 Marian Barrett.

Woods, David John; Counsellor (Political) Berlin since August 2002; Born 04/08/51; Third later Second Secretary FCO 1976; Second later First Secretary (UNIDO & IAEA) Vienna 1978; FCO 1981; First Secretary (Economic) Bucharest 1981; First Secretary FCO 1985; Counsellor Harare 1992; Counsellor FCO 1995; Counsellor (Political) Pretoria 1997; m 1972 Rachel Haydon White (1s 1977; 1d 1979).

Woods, Harvey John; FCO since July 2004; Born 29/10/70; FCO 1999; Full-Time Language Training 2001; First Secretary Islamabad 2002; Band D6.

Woods, Ian Alexander; Counsellor Sofia since July 2003; Born 10/06/51; Third Secretary FCO 1976; Second Secretary New York (UKMIS) 1977; First Secretary FCO 1980; BMG Berlin 1984; Bonn 1986; First Secretary later Counsellor FCO 1989; Warsaw 1995; Counsellor FCO 1998; m 1978 Stephanie Flett (2s 1982, 1986).

Woodward, Amanda Jane; Rome since June 2002; Born 29/04/56; FCO 1978; Brasilia 1979; New Delhi 1982; Moscow 1985; FCO 1988; Lisbon 1989; FCO 1991; Kuala Lumpur 1993; Muscat 1997; Band B3.

Woodward, Barbara Janet, OBE; Counsellor (Political) Beijing since December 2003; Born 29/05/61; FCO 1991; Second Secretary Moscow 1994; FCO 1998.

Woodward, Gillian Yvonne (née Aplin); SUPL since November 1996; Born 20/12/46; DSAO (later FCO) 1966; Paris (UKDEL OECD) 1969; Yaoundé 1972; FCO 1974; Lagos 1979; SUPL 1981; Helsinki 1984; FCO 1987; Mexico City 1990; FCO 1993; Band B3; m 1977 Roger Charles Woodward.

Woodward, Roger Charles; First Secretary (Management) and HM Consul Helsinki since October 2001; Born 15/03/48; Commonwealth Office (later FCO) 1967; Dacca 1970; Caribbean Floater 1972; Doha 1973; FCO 1976; Lagos 1979; Helsinki 1982 (Second Secretary 1984); FCO 1987; Second Secretary (Commercial) Mexico City 1990; Second Secretary FCO 1993; First Secretary (Management) Paris 1997; m 1977 Gillian Yvonne Aplin.

Wooten, Sarah Elisabeth; FCO since October 2002; Born 04/02/68; FCO 1989; Third Secretary

(Consular) Valletta 1992; Full-Time Language Training 1994; Full-Time Language Training Tokyo 1995; Osaka 1996; Consul (Commercial and Investment) Nagoya 1999; Band C4.

Wootton, Adam Nicholas; FCO since September 1996; Born 19/05/60; FCO 1983; Baghdad 1985; FCO 1988; Nairobi 1993; Band C5; m 1984 Adele Wright (2s 1989, 1991; 1d 1993).

Wordsworth, Stephen John, LVO (1992); Minister and Deputy Head of Mission Moscow since May 2003; Born 17/05/55; FCO 1977; Third later Second Secretary Moscow 1979; FCO 1981; First Secretary (Economic/Commercial) Lagos 1983; On loan to the Cabinet Office 1986; First Secretary FCO 1988; First Secretary (Political) Bonn 1990; Counsellor (Deputy International Affairs Adviser) SHAPE Mons 1994; Head of Eastern Adriatic Dept FCO 1999; m 1981 Ellyse Nichole Mingins (1s 1987).

Worham, Paul Andrew; FCO since 2002; Born 15/12/66; HCS 1988; FCO 1997; Moscow 1999; Band A2; m 1999 Elizabeth Mary Smith.

Workman, Daniel John; Second Secretary (Chancery) Belgrade since August 2003; Born 11/09/78; FCO 2000; Band C4.

Worster, Paul Anthony; FCO since September 2002; Born 14/05/62; FCO 1983; Warsaw 1985; Washington 1986; Helsinki 1989; FCO 1992; Tehran 1996; Third Secretary (Consular) Singapore 1999; Band B3.

Worthington, Ian Alan, OBE (1999); First Secretary (Commercial) Berlin since October 2001; Born 09/08/58; FCO 1977; Language Training 1978; Moscow 1980; Lusaka 1982; Second Secretary FCO 1985; Second Secretary (Commercial) Seoul 1988; Second Secretary (Chancery) Kingston 1992; Head BETO later Consul-General Ekaterinburg 1995; FCO 1998; Band D6.

Wotton, Rosaleen Mary (née McManus); FCO since September 2003; Born 15/01/62; FCO 1987; Oslo 1988; Brussels 1991; FCO 1992; T/D Geneva 1993; Berne 1993; FCO 1996; SUPL 1998; ECO Nicosia 2000; Band B3; m 1997 Alan Leslie Wotton (1s 1998).

Wragg, Ann Desson (née Traill); FCO since August 1992; Born 20/03/65; FCO 1983; Paris 1985; FCO 1988; New York (UKMIS) 1989; Band C5; m 1988 John Wragg.

Wraight, Dr Christopher David; Second Secretary (Chancery) Lilongwe since July 2003; Born 19/11/75; FCO 2001; Band C4.

Wright, Carol; FCO since October 2003; Born 27/06/62; FCO 1988; Pretoria 1992; Johannesburg 1993; FCO 1996; Third Secretary (Management) Baku 2001; Band C4; m 2004 Jeyhun Javadov.

Wright, Christopher David; FCO since September 2003; Born 25/10/74; Band C4.

Wright, Clive David, MBE; First Secretary (Transport) Washington since November 2004; Born 14/01/58; Royal Marines 1976; FCO 1977; Ankara 1980; Tripoli 1983; FCO 1984; Doha 1986 (Second Secretary 1989); Vice-Consul (Political/Admin) Johannesburg 1989; Second later First Secretary FCO 1993; First Secretary Vienna (UKDEL OSCE) 1996; FCO 2000; m 1982 Christine Bernadette Caldwell (2d 1986, 1989).

Wright, David Alan, OBE (1984); FCO since August 2002; Born 27/05/42; FO 1965; APS to Minister of State FO 1966; MECAS 1968; Baghdad 1971; Second Secretary (Commercial) and Vice-Consul Doha 1973; On loan to the DHSS 1976; Second later First Secretary FCO 1978; Consul and Head of Post Durban 1980; First Secretary (Commercial) Baghdad 1984; First Secretary later Counsellor FCO 1987; HM Consul-General Atlanta 1992; HM Ambassador Doha 1997; m 1966 Gail Karol Mesling (4s 1966, 1968, 1971, 1983; 1d 1978).

Wright, David Stephen; FCO since January 2003; Born 04/02/63; FCO 1989; Second Secretary (Chancery) Mexico City 1991; First Secretary FCO 1993; First Secretary (Political) Bogotá 2000; Band D6; m 1992 Tania Victoria Gessinger (2d 1999, 2001).

Wright, Julia Helen; Second Secretary (Political) Lisbon since May 2002; Born 06/02/65; FCO 1991; Amsterdam 1994; Oslo 1997; Band C4.

Wright, Nicola (née Daubney); Dubai since January 2005; Born 31/01/70; FCO 1989; Peking 1992; FCO 1993; Zagreb 1996; FCO 1999; Singapore 2001; Band B3; m 1998 Alan David Wright (1s 2003).

Wright, Stephen John Leadbetter, CMG (1997); HM Ambassador Madrid since May 2003; Born 07/12/46; Third Secretary FCO 1968; Havana 1969; Second later First Secretary FCO 1972; Director of Policy and Reference Division and Consul (Information) New York (BIS) 1975; Brussels (UKREP) 1980; First Secretary FCO 1984; Counsellor 1985; On loan to the Cabinet Office 1985; Counsellor and Head of Chancery New Delhi 1988; Counsellor (External Relations) Brussels (UKREP) 1991; Director (EU Affairs) FCO 1994; Minister Washington 1997; Director (Wider Europe) FCO 1999; Deputy Under-Secretary FCO 2000; m (1) 1970 Georgina Susan Butler (diss 2000) (1d 1977; 1s 1979); (2) 2002 Abbey Rosemont.

Wurr, Adam; Second Secretary FCO since January 2002; Born 14/12/71; Second Secretary FCO 1995; Second Secretary Geneva (UKMIS) 2000; Band C4.

Wyatt, David; Deputy High Commissioner Lagos since October 2001; Born 18/04/46; DSAO 1965; Lusaka 1968; SOAS 1971; Bangkok 1972 (Second Secretary 1975); Second Secretary Yaoundé 1976; Second later First Secretary FCO 1977 (First Secretary 1979); National Defence Course Latimer 1980; First Secretary (Commercial) Athens 1981; First Secretary and Head of Chancery Bangkok 1984; First Secretary FCO 1988; Deputy High

Commissioner Accra 1994; FCO 1998; Counsellor (Commercial) Bangkok 1999; m 1969 Rosemary Elizabeth Clarke (1s 1972; 1d 1974).

Wye, Roderick Francis; FCO since 1999; Born 13/09/50; Research Officer FCO 1973; PRO 1983; Peking 1985; First Secretary FCO 1988; First Secretary (Chancery) Peking 1995; m 1989 Katelin Rebecca Teller (1s 1994).

Wyithe, Philip Leslie; Second Secretary (Commercial) Ho Chi Minh City since March 2002; Born 30/12/64; FCO 1983; Moscow 1987; Floater Duties 1990; Third Secretary (Consular) Sana'a 1992; Third Secretary (Immigration) Valletta 1994; FCO 1995; Second Secretary (Management/Consular) Seoul 1997; Band B3; m 1992 Gina Olofernes Daniel (1d 1994).

Wylde, Richard Norman Gordon; First Secretary Kabul since June 2003; Born 18/10/58; FCO 1985; Second later First Secretary (Chancery) and Deputy Permanent Representative ESCAP Bangkok 1989; First Secretary FCO 1992; First Secretary (Political) Rome 1996; First Secretary FCO 2000; Band D6; m 1987 Lesley Tennison (1d 1991; 1s 1995).

Wyver, Wendy Anne; Copenhagen since August 2004; Born 26/10/64; FCO 1993; Full-Time Language Training 1995; Second Secretary (Political) Tokyo 1996; First Secretary FCO 1999; m 1995 Jakob Windfeld Lund (1s 2001).

Y

Yaghmourian, Paul Barkef; Consul-General Rio de Janeiro since March 2002; Born 14/02/58; FCO 1984; Second later First Secretary Lisbon 1986; First Secretary FCO 1989; First Secretary (Political) Brasilia 1993; Secondment to British Aerospace 1997; Counsellor and Deputy Head of Mission Copenhagen 1997.

Yamauchi, Mara Rosalind (née Myers); First Secretary FCO since December 2002; Born 13/08/73; FCO 1996; Language Training FCO 1997; Language Training Kamakura 1998; Second Secretary (Political) Tokyo 1999; Band D6; m 2002 Shigetoshi Yamauchi.

Yapp, John William; FCO since October 2002; Born 14/01/51; FCO 1971; Islamabad 1973; Kuala Lumpur (Consular) 1975; APS to Minister of State FCO 1978; Dubai (Commercial) 1980; Second Secretary (Economic/Commercial) The Hague 1984; First Secretary FCO 1988; First Secretary (Information/Political) Wellington 1991; Deputy Head of North America Department FCO 1995; High Commissioner Victoria (Seychelles) 1998; m (1) 1973 (1d 1975); (2) 1979 (1s 1981; 2d 1983, 1987); (3) 1997 Petra Jodelis (1d 1998).

Yarrow, Jon William; Second Secretary Dubai since August 2003; Born 29/01/69; FCO 1987; Washington 1989; Berne 1992; FCO 1995; Third later Second Secretary (Political/Information) Dubai 1998; Second Secretary (Economic) Tunis 2002; m (1) 1989 Helen Mugridge (1d 1992; 1s 1995) (diss 1995); (2) 1999 Katherine Anne Short (diss 2004).

Yarunina, Maggie; SUPL since June 2004; Born 08/07/72; FCO 2000; Prague 2003; Band B3; m 1999 Alexandre (Sasha) V Yarounine.

Yeadon, Joanne Mary; Second Secretary (Press and Public Affairs) Milan since May 2003; Born 01/08/65; FCO 1983; Washington 1986; Gibraltar 1989; FCO 1992; Budapest 1996; FCO 1999; Band C4.

Yearsley, Sara Elizabeth; Kigali since January 2004; Born 16/02/76; FCO 2002; Band A2.

York, Jennifer Ann; FCO since April 2000; Born 01/11/60; FCO 1980; BMG Berlin 1982; Africa/Middle East Floater 1985; Mogadishu 1988; FCO 1989; Vice-Consul Durban 1992; Second Secretary (Management) Nairobi 1996; Band C5; m 1988 Murray Rex Clarkin (diss 1996).

Young, Amanda Elizabeth (née Mitchell); SUPL since December 2002; Born 03/06/59; FCO 1977; Paris 1979; Cayman Islands 1982; FCO 1986; Riyadh 1987; Muscat 1989; FCO 1994; SUPL 1995; Dubai 1999; Band B3; m 2000 Murray Andrew James Young.

Young, Andrew John; SUPL since February 2000; Born 02/04/60; Assistant Legal Adviser FCO 1990; Solicitor 1988 (Northern Ireland) and 1990 (England and Wales); Seconded as Deputy Principal Crown Counsel to Hong Kong Government 1994; Assistant Legal Adviser FCO 1997; Legal Counsellor FCO 1999; m (1) 1991 Lucy Stojak (diss 1996); (2) 1997 Annette Lee (1d 1997).

Young, Helena; FCO since September 1982 (First Secretary 1989); Born 08/10/60; Band D6.

Young, Marianne; SUPL since May 2005; Born 08/08/71; FCO 2001; Band D6; m 2002 Barry Young (1d 2003).

Young, Sarah Louise (née Boxall); Second Secretary (Consular) Kampala since June 2002; Born 16/09/63; FCO 1984; Lisbon 1987; FCO 1989; Cape Town 1997; Band B3; m 1990 Alan Young (2d 1991, 1992) (diss 1995).

Young, Thomas Richard; Second Secretary (Economic) Vienna since June 2005; Born 26/04/77; FCO 2001; Second Secretary (Political) Kabul 2003; FCO 2004; Band C4.

Younger, Alexander William; FCO since May 2005; Born 04/07/63; Second Secretary FCO 1991; First Secretary (IAEA) Vienna (UKMIS) 1995; First Secretary FCO 1998; First Secretary (Political) Dubai 2002; Band D6; m 1993 Sarah Hopkins (1d 1994; 2s 1996, 1998).

Younis, Fouzia; SUPL since April 2004; Born 08/07/78; FCO 2000; Islamabad 2001; Band B3; m 2001 Haroon Suleman.

Yu, Tsui-Ling; Attaché Beirut since August 2005; Born 20/07/79; FCO 2003; Band A2.

Yvon, Christopher John Robin; FCO since September 2002; Born 11/11/69; FCO 1989; Prague 1991; FCO 1993; Full-Time Language Training 1994; FCO 1995; Riyadh 1995; Second Secretary (Chancery) Port Louis 1999; Band D6; m (1) 1991 Veronica Mary Walters (1d 1989; 1s 1992) (diss 1995); (2) 1996 Zara Louise Chapman (diss 2004); (3) 2004 Joanne Margaret Yvon.

Z

Ziaullah, Suman Rafique; FCO since March 2003; Born 27/10/76; FCO 1999; Second Secretary (Political/Economic) Jakarta 2001; Band C4.

Printed in the United Kingdom by The Stationery Office
182034 c22 12/05 321415